OPERATING SYSTEMS

Third Edition

…is so much more than a textbook!

Continuing in the tradition set by the previous editions of OPERATING SYSTEMS, Gary Nutt has developed a comprehensive online supplements package* with everything students need to master the material in the course as well as everything instructors need to assist them in their teaching.

For the Student:

- Additional Linux, UNIX, and Windows lab projects
- Self-assessment quizzes to test your knowledge of the concepts in the textbook
- Chapter notes that elaborate on selected topics from the book
- C and UNIX reference materials

For the Instructor:

- Complete instructors' supplements package including PowerPoint slides, lab project solutions, exercise solutions manual, and syllabi

*Purchasers of a new copy of **Operating Systems**, Third Edition are entitled to six months of access to the online supplements at no additional charge.

To log on simply locate the access card in the front of the book and follow the instructions.

Congratulations!

As a student purchasing a new copy of **OPERATING SYSTEMS,** **_Third Edition_** you are entitled to six months of prepaid access to the book's Companion Website. This prepaid subscription gives you full access to all student support areas of this Website, including:

- self-assessment quizzes to test your knowledge of the concepts in each chapter
- chapter-by-chapter review notes and content summaries that revisit the key ideas of each chapter
- online lab projects for Windows, Linux, and UNIX
- UNIX and C reference material

To Access the OPERATING SYSTEMS Companion Website for the First Time:

You will need to register online using a computer with an Internet connection and a Web browser. The process takes just a couple of minutes and only needs to be completed once.

1. Go to **http://www.aw.com/nutt**.
2. Click **Student Resources**.
3. Click the **Register** button.
4. Use a coin to scratch off the gray coating below and reveal your student access code.* Do not use a knife or other sharp object, which can damage the code.

5. On the registration page, enter your student access code. Do not type the dashes. You can use lowercase or uppercase characters.
6. Follow the on-screen instructions. If you need help at any time during the online registration process, simply click the **Need Help?** icon.
7. Once your personal Login Name and Password are confirmed, you can begin using the *Operating Systems* Companion Website!

To Log on to the OPERATING SYSTEMS Companion Website After You Register:

You only need to register for this Companion Website once. After that, you can access the site by going to **http://www.aw.com/nutt**, clicking Student Resources, and providing your Login Name and Password when prompted.

*****Important:** The access code on this page can only be used once to establish a subscription to the *Operating Systems,* Companion Website. This subscription is valid for six months upon activation, and is not transferable. If this access code has already been scratched off, it may no longer be valid. If this is the case, you can purchase a subscription by going to **http://www.aw.com/nutt** and clicking Student Resources.

OPERATING SYSTEMS

Third Edition

GARY NUTT

University of Colorado, Boulder

PEARSON

Addison
Wesley

Boston San Francisco New York
London Toronto Sydney Tokyo Singapore Madrid
Mexico City Munich Paris Cape Town Hong Kong Montreal

Sponsoring Editor: Maite Suarez-Rivas

Editorial Assistant: Maria Campo

Senior Production Supervisor: Juliet Silveri

Production Services: Kathy Smith

Composition and Art Rendering: Gillian Hall, The Aardvark Group

Cover and Text Design: Regina Hagen Kolenda

Marketing Manager: Nathan Schultz

Senior Marketing Coordinator: Lesly Hershman

Print Buyer: Caroline Fell

Cover Image: ©2003 Creatas

Access the latest information about Addison-Wesley titles from our World Wide Web site:
http://www.aw.com/cs

Many of the designations used by manufacturers and sellers to distinguish their products are claimed as trademarks. Where those designations appear in this book, and Addison-Wesley was aware of a trademark claim, the designations have been printed in initial caps or all caps.

The programs and applications presented in this book have been included for their instructional value. They have been tested with care, but are not guaranteed for any particular purpose. The publisher does not offer any warranties or representations, nor does it accept any liabilities with respect to the programs or applications.

Library of Congress Cataloging-in-Publication Data

Nutt, Gary J.
   Operating systems / Gary Nutt.—3rd ed.
     p. cm.
   Includes bibliographical references and index.
   ISBN 0-201-77344-9 (alk. paper)
     1. Operating systems (Computers) I. Title

QA76.76.O63N89 2003
005.4'3--dc21

For information on obtaining permission for the use of material from this work, please submit a written request to Pearson Education, Inc., Rights and Contracts Department, 75 Arlington St., Suite 300, Boston, MA 02116 or fax your request to 617-848-7047.

3 4 5 6 7 8 9 10—CRW—060504

To my wife and best friend, Mary,
and my grandson and best buddy, Scott.

Preface

• TO THE STUDENT

Operating systems is an exciting software area because the design of an operating system (OS) exerts a major influence on the overall function and performance of the entire computer. When studying operating systems for the first time, I think that it is important to understand the *principles* behind the designs of all operating systems, and also to see how those principles are put into *practice* in real operating systems.

• FEATURES

This mainstream of the book is a comprehensive description of all relevant OS issues and principles. Supplementary material provides background information, real-world examples, and programming practice:

- *Comprehensive examples* show how the principles are applied in practice in the UNIX and Windows families of operating systems.
- *Lab exercises* enable you to gain hands-on experience with the details using Windows and Linux/UNIX.
- An extensive *companion web site* includes a chapter-by-chapter study guide as well as reference material that provides background information on C programming and helps you use UNIX and Linux.

The goal of this book is to provide a complete discussion of OS principles, supplemented with code, algorithms, implementation issues, and Lab Exercises to provide you with an understanding of contemporary OS practice, particularly in UNIX and Windows operating systems. I have attempted to differentiate the conceptual material from the applied material by discussing the principles in the main flow of the text and placing most of the practice material in supplemental discussions and Lab Exercises.

The heart of the matter is the conceptual material. Many OS principles can be described either in formal (mathematical) terms or in informal discussion. Informal descriptions are relatively easy to read, but formal descriptions are more precise. For example, an informal discussion of a dictionary might explain that it is "a list of terms with their definitions," whereas a formal description might indicate that a dictionary is "a mechanism, f, to map a term, x, to its definition, $f(x)$." The first explanation is intuitive, the second focuses on the logical intent of the dictionary. The first description suggests a list or table implementation; the second admits implementations ranging from tables to lists, to associative memories, to databases, to web servers, and so on. The informal definition suggests word dictionaries, but the formal definition applies just as well to compiler symbol tables. My goal is to explain general OS principles so you will have a deep understanding of how an OS is designed. You can understand the principles best using formal descriptions because they focus on the logical intent of the concept rather than on an example of how the concept is implemented. To ease into the formalism, concepts are introduced using informal or specific descriptions. Discussions in the early chapters have little or no formal descriptions, but as you progress through the book, you will see increasing amounts of formal description. The formal discussion of concepts is always accompanied by informal discussion and examples.

Operating systems are designed around performance issues. If the OS is too slow, it will be considered a failure. Sometimes detailed discussions of performance tend to obscure the concepts. Since the concepts are the most important part of learning about operating systems, I decided to forego extensive coverage of analysis and performance theory. I will try to remind you periodically of performance considerations, and provide informal explanations of performance issues. This will encourage you to develop your intuition on performance issues so that you can study them formally later. If the comments about performance fit naturally into the description of the concept, I have included them with the discussion of the concept.

As I mentioned earlier, experimentation with real code provides you with an understanding of how OS concepts are implemented in real systems. I have provided two types of material especially to help you learn about current OS practice: boxed examples and Lab Exercises.

■ *Boxed examples* explain how concepts are used or implemented in UNIX, Linux, Windows, or other operating systems. Many of the boxes contain code examples so you can see how an OS can implement the theory you have learned. Most of the examples are C *code fragments* from completed programs. In these cases, the completed programs have been compiled and executed. Other examples contain descriptions of algorithms or techniques using the C programming language. These abbreviated descriptions deliberately omit a lot of detail that would be necessary in an actual implementation, but that does not contribute to the understanding of the algorithm. The context in which the code appears will make clear when the code is an actual implementation. Otherwise, you should assume that the code fragment is a description of an algorithm or technique. I have experimented with using pseudocode languages for these descriptions, but students and reviewers have consistently preferred the use of C. Be careful not to interpret the descriptions in C as complete implementations.

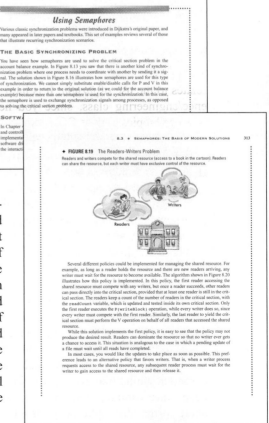

■ This book also includes several *Lab Exercises.* Each exercise poses a problem and then provides you with comprehensive background information that you will need to solve the problem and a section to help you plan your solution. These Lab Exercises will give you valuable practice with various UNIX and/or Windows operating systems.

■ UNIX or Windows? Instructors can come to blows while debating which of these families of operating systems is the best example OS. When I teach an OS course sometimes I use UNIX and other times I use Windows. I have included enough examples and Lab Exercises for you to learn operating systems with either approach. Your instructor will probably choose one or the other of these systems and expect you to read

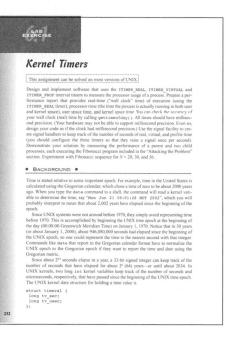

the examples and solve the Lab Exercises for that OS. Don't be afraid to skim the materials for the "other OS," since this will give you a broad view that will be invaluable in your future programming career.

There are only a couple of more points that I want to mention to you. The first one relates to the use of *jargon.* It is hard to avoid the use of jargon in an upper division science/engineering class, since you need to know at least some terminology to learn advanced topics such as OS. By the time you begin this study, you will have built up a collection of terms (such as "algorithm," "RAM," "gigabytes," and "linked list") that you use to talk to other programmers. None of us know or remember *all* of these technical terms. In an effort to address this problem, there is a glossary at the end of the book. Whenever a term is first used (or used again after it has not been mentioned for a couple of chapters), I have used a **bold font** to identify it and included it in the glossary. Obviously, I will miss some terms. If you encounter one that I did not define, take a look at a software jargon dictionary such as the one at http://inf.astrian.net/jargon/.

There are many complex ideas in operating systems. Sometimes when we encounter such systems, we have to "learn about them in layers." For example, when you learn how to ride a bicycle, you need to learn turning, stopping, balancing, and motion. If you were going to write a paper to explain how to ride a bike, you would probably mention all these things before describing any of them in detail. This "first pass" description identifies all the parts without telling your reader much about them. Your second pass then provides the details of turning (for example, you need to turn the handlebar while leaning slightly in the direction of the turn to maintain your balance, while also maintaining forward motion, … or something like that). Operating systems are also hard to learn in "one pass." If you start to learn about processes, then you wonder about memory and files. In the "two pass" strategy, you learn what the parts are and what they are supposed to do in the first pass. In the second pass, you learn the details. Sometimes there is a "third pass," especially if you want to see how this fits into a particular OS. This multi-pass strategy is used recursively. In the book, Chapters 1–3 are the first pass for all of the OS. Chapters 4–14 are the second pass on the main parts of the OS. Chapters 15–18 are the second pass on topics that are closely related to the core materials. Chapter 19 is the second pass on design, and Chapters 20–21 are a "third pass" on Linux and Windows NT. Most chapters use the multi-pass strategy within the topic: The first section of the chapter is the first pass, and the remaining sections are the second pass. The Lab Exercises are the third pass for UNIX and/or Windows.

The study of operating systems has traditionally been one of the most challenging and exciting software disciplines in computer science. I hope this book makes complex aspects of operating systems easy to understand and avoids making simple aspects boring. Good luck in your study of operating systems; I hope you enjoy it as much as I do!

● TO THE INSTRUCTOR

THE VISION   I was originally motivated to write this book because I sought a book that had more content on principles than the existing ones. At the same time, I felt that my students needed to be exposed to extensive OS practice; otherwise, the principles would be difficult to absorb. This continues to be the vision in this third edition: The discussion of principles is comprehensive (in both depth and breadth), and I have added substantial, new supplementary information about OS design and programming.

● IN BRIEF: THIRD EDITION CHANGES

In all three editions we have used *boxed information* to provide examples and other topics that could be separated from the main flow of the book. The feedback about these boxes has been very positive, although there was sometimes confusion between the performance and example boxes. In this edition we have gone to a single box type—with a new design—that primarily contains examples. We have also added many more UNIX and Windows code examples (in the boxes).

The text has been rewritten to include new material, and also to present the ideas in a more relaxed style that is easier to read and learn from.

Almost every chapter has been reorganized and revised to reflect the contemporary

CHANGES FOR THE THIRD EDITION   This third edition is based on the constructive criticism I have received from people who used and/or reviewed the first two editions as well as drafts of the third edition. Our goals are to:

■ Revise the presentation so that it spends more time explaining the general concepts, using more analogies and real-world examples.

■ Provide the most comprehensive content that is appropriate for an undergraduate OS book.

■ Expand the pedagogy with more examples and programming projects, as well as a student and instructor supplements package unlike any other on the market.

Many instructors who used the second edition of the book (particularly the use of *threads*. We have also added new coverage in various chapters to discuss mobile computing, embedded operating systems, multiprocessors, and new devices. Additionally, we have increased our coverage of other important topics: the chapter on *security* has been rewritten to unify the discussion and to provide more coverage of contemporary security mechanisms (particularly cryptography). A new chapter has been added on *distributed programming runtime systems*; this is where we see how topics such as Java and Microsoft .NET fit into the OS course. Finally, we have completely reorganized the material so that there is now a chapter on *general OS design methodologies*, followed by a chapter for Linux and another for the Windows NT/2000/XP kernel.

In the second edition, we introduced a set of comprehensive lab exercises. We have added new lab exercises so that there are now 15 of them. Some of these lab exercises apply only to UNIX systems, some only to Windows systems, but 4 of them apply to both Windows and UNIX systems.

Finally, we have introduced a *companion web site* that includes comprehensive materials for both students (a study guide, reference material on Unix and C, more lab exercises) and instructors (solutions, suggested syllabi, test bank, and lecture presentations).

lab update edition) recommended that the process description be updated to reflect multithreaded processes. Interestingly, a few reviewers of the third edition drafts objected to the inclusion of threads. (It's not easy writing a book to please everyone!) Today, there are few operating systems that do *not* provide support for kernel threads. (In Linux and other UNIX systems, the support is exported via the POSIX thread interface, so it "looks" the same as user space implementation.) I would be remiss if I did not recast the discussion of the process model without talking about threads. I have described *classic processes* in the usual way and then provided an explanation of how *modern processes* with multiple *threads* evolved from that model. Thereafter, I have tried to use "process" or "process/thread" to mean a single-threaded classic process, or a modern process with a single thread.

The descriptions of concepts and issues have been completely rewritten so that they are easier to understand. Professional development editors have worked on this edition to ensure that this happens. We have also added more figures and many more examples. People who used earlier editions asked for more code, so we have greatly increased the amount of code in the book, but we have put most of it in boxes so that it can be skipped if desired.

In terms of providing comprehensive coverage of the materials, we intended to include all topics recommended by the ACM/IEEE curriculum recommendations. Next, we have asked previous students and instructors to tell us what was missing. This has led us to include coverage of threads, mobile and wireless computing, embedded OS technology, new devices work, and more about multiprocessors. We have also updated the chapter on security so that it presents the important concepts in a more regular manner, and also provides much more discussion of cryptography. This edition reflects the general evolution in operating systems since the time the second edition was written. Besides changes such as updating from the process view to the thread/process view, every chapter has been revised to reflect contemporary OS technology. Some of the changes are only minor (for example, the chapters on scheduling and deadlock), but others are major updates to reflect contemporary technology (for example, Chapters 1, 5, 6, 14, 17, and 18). Chapter 18 on distributed programming runtime systems is an entirely new chapter that reflects the relationship of system software technologies such as Java Virtual Machine and the Microsoft Common Language Runtime to mainstream OS technology.

Finally, we are building up considerable supplementary student materials on the web. There is now a companion web site at www.aw.com/nutt with a wealth of student study materials and instructor resources. For more on this see the "Supplements" description below.

SUPPLEMENTS One of the top goals of the third edition was to provide the most extensive supplements package on the market both for students and professors. In preparation for this edition, Addison-Wesley surveyed hundreds of OS professors. In terms of student support we learned that:

- Many professors want to get students involved in programming projects.
- More than half of the professors require or recommend a second book for the course—specifically, a book on UNIX or Linux.
- Many professors were struggling with students who needed help with basic C programming concepts and with reviewing the principles of the course.

The student companion web site to this book (http://www.aw.com/nutt) addresses all these items. There is a chapter-by-chapter study guide that I wrote as I taught my students at UC-Boulder. It includes a review of fundamental concepts from each chapter and over 300 study questions. Addison-Wesley has provided a reference section that includes material on UNIX commands and basic C programming. And for those of you who want further (or more in-depth) programming practice, we have included lab exercises from the two previously published lab manuals [Nutt, 1999; Nutt, 2001].

The instructor's companion web site has also been expanded so that it now contains:

- A new set of comprehensive lecture presentation materials,
- A suggested syllabus
- A bank of example test questions
- An updated solutions manual

These materials have been prepared exclusively for professors using the book in a course. Please contact your local Addison-Wesley sales representative, or send e-mail to aw.cse@aw.com, for information about how to access them.

LABORATORY ENVIRONMENT There are only a few widely used commercial operating systems. While studying these systems is valuable, there are practical barriers to experimenting with any of them in the classroom. First, commercial operating systems are very complex since they must offer full support to commercial applications. It is impractical to experiment with such complex software because it is sometimes difficult to see how specific issues are addressed within the software. Small changes to the code may have unpredictable effects on the behavior of the overall OS. Second, the OS software sometimes has distinct proprietary value to the company that implemented it. As a consequence, the company may be reluctant to provide OS source code to anyone wishing to study and learn how the implementation was done.

I have experimented with two approaches to this problem in the classroom:

- Base the course on an *external view* of real operating systems; this is essentially the approach in the ACM/IEEE 2001 curriculum recommendation.
- Base the course on an *internal view* of some "manageable" OS.

I have also discussed this problem with numerous OS instructors (including participants at a Birds of a Feather session at the Operating Systems Design and Implementation (OSDI) meeting in New Orleans in February 1999). There is general confusion about choosing the right laboratory component for the undergraduate OS course. However, those in attendance at the OSDI session *unanimously* agreed that the external view of an OS should be used in the first OS course. All of our Lab Exercises ask students to write user space code for either UNIX or Windows; the exercises are designed to allow students to get specific insight into the way the kernel works by using the mechanisms (rather than modifying them). The approach has the added benefit on not requiring you to have "crashable" lab facilities just for your OS course.

While there is general consensus that teaching OS internals in the first course is too difficult for most students, there is also a strong desire to offer a course on OS internals as early as possible in the curriculum. If you decide to teach an internals course—as the first or second course—your choices are a little limited: probably Linux or FreeBSD if you want to study a real OS, or one of the pedagogical systems otherwise. The material on the supplementary web site provides more than enough Linux 2.2.12 kernel internals for a semester course.

LAB EXERCISES   In each edition of this book I have attempted to provide strong, current conceptual material, accompanied by extensive programming exercises. In the first edition, the programming practice appeared as conventional exercises with little background explanation. In the second edition, I added a few lab exercises that introduced a problem, provided comprehensive background remarks, and then presented a solution plan. (I had learned to write these lab exercises in a Windows NT projects manual [Nutt, 1999] and a Linux internals book [Nutt, 2001].) The lab exercises provide teaching assistants with the material that they need to teach students to solve the programming exercises during recitation meetings. This, in turn, allows you to spend more time talking about principles during lectures. You also have the assurance that your students have OS-specific examples to read on their own.

I began to teach a "Windows version" of my OS course in Fall, 1998, and a "UNIX version" in the spring term. This meant that I needed lab exercises and examples for the external view of each version of the OS. In short, I either needed two books, or a book that focused on OS principles but had extensive examples and exercises for UNIX and another similar book for Windows. This book contains enough lab exercises to enable you to concentrate on either UNIX or Windows. There are 15 Lab Exercises—10 that can be solved in a UNIX environment, and 9 that can be solved in a Windows environment. When you choose to focus on either one of the systems, your students can concentrate on the boxed examples and Lab Exercises for the target OS, while skipping the ones relating to the other OS. Your most curious students will get the bonus of learning about both operating systems. Finally, by incorporating the Lab Exercises into the book, you have the added benefit of providing your students with a consistent description of principles in the textbook and the practice in the Lab Exercise.

TOPIC ORGANIZATION The order of presentation is based on the response to the first and second editions of the book, my experience teaching OS, and the input from many other instructors. This organization reflects the combined knowledge and practice of many different teachers and I believe the result is logical, conducive to learning, and generally accepted by most OS instructors.

Chapters 1 through 4 consist of important introductory material that provides a solid foundation for the study of operating systems. You may decide to go over this material rather quickly, perhaps assigning it as outside reading material, especially if this was covered in prerequisite courses. However, understanding this material is critical before you dive into the further study of the meat of operating systems, starting in Chapter 5. My experience shows that it is really worth the time to talk about the material in Chapter 2, since only a few students have written concurrent programs before they take an OS course. The Lab Exercises in Chapter 2 allow students to study with basic concurrency concepts (although they cannot really address synchronization yet). If you like the classic shell exercise, you will see that the framework now first appears as an extended example in Chapter 2; then it is fleshed out with Lab Exercises in Chapters 2 and 9.

I start the detailed discussion of operating systems with device management. At first, you may find this approach unusual, although it follows the traditional evolution of operating systems. A natural segue exists from the discussion of interrupts in Chapter 4 to the discussion of device management in Chapter 5. This approach provides a sound foundation for introducing independent threads of execution (in the hardware and the software), concurrency, and synchronization. After you have finished the device material, it is natural to generalize these ideas into process and resource management, scheduling, synchronization, and deadlock.

Memory management is also an important topic instructors usually want to address as soon as possible. I chose to phase it in after process management and then move to file management. Then I finish the essential material with a discussion of protection and security, which is deferred until the student has had a chance to absorb the notions of process and various kinds of resources (generic resources, memory, and files).

Any contemporary OS must be built to operate in (or be evolved to) distributed systems. All current research on operating systems is deeply influenced by distributed operating systems. Chapters 15 through 17 introduce distributed operating systems after all the discussion of traditional topics has been covered. Because of the nature of commercial systems and networks, many instructors wish to at least introduce this material. In a one-semester course, I am only able to spend a couple of weeks on this material.

The new material on distributed programming runtime systems was motivated by the success of Java (and the specter of .NET and the CLR). OS teachers often want to talk about Java-like technology or to describe the OS as if it were written in Java. Unfortunately (at least at the time of this writing, 2001–2003), these technologies are not used to build OS kernels, nor are they built into commercial kernels. Sun still implements the JVM on top of Solaris, and Microsoft implements the CLR on top of Windows. I decided that this book should attempt to reflect that reality: OS kernel technology is still described as a C-based technology. Nevertheless, Java-like technology is an important consideration and there should be an explanation of what it is and how it fits into the scheme of things. This is the rationale for adding a new chapter on runtime systems, particularly the part of these new runtime systems that supports concurrent (distributed) programming. Over time, some of the functionality that exists in these runtime systems will pop up in the kernel.

■ **Chapter 1** shows how operating systems fit into evolving computer products (from mainframes to workstations, to mobile computers) and into other software technology. In the first drafts of this book, a historical perspective was included. Instructors tend to like a little history and context, but many students think it is boring, so I have dispensed with a separate discussion of history. Instead, remarks about the history of individual aspects of operating systems are included when these aspects are discussed.

■ **Chapter 2** is unique among conceptual operating system books in that it focuses on how to use an operating system, particularly how to write programs that use multiple threads or processes. This chapter was added because my experience with computer science juniors and seniors is that they may have written considerable single-threaded code, but they are far less likely to have written or studied multithreaded software. If students have learned concurrent programming with Java or another modern thread-based language, the material in this chapter is still worthwhile because of the examples and discussion of concurrent C programming. The UNIX shell and the Windows Lab Exercise are great programming and practice components for the material in the chapter.

■ **Chapter 3** describes the fundamental organization of operating systems, including implementation strategies. The Lab Exercise provides a first glimpse into UNIX OS internal operation.

■ **Chapter 4** finishes the preliminaries for studying operating systems—computer organization. For students who have already taken a computer organization class, the first half of Chapter 4 is review. The second half describes interrupts, emphasizing the aspects that are critical to multiprogramming operating systems.

■ **Chapter 5** describes device management—specifically general techniques, buffering, and device drivers. It is tempting to become completely immersed in Linux device drivers. However, in the main part of the chapter, I have resisted this temptation to focus instead on a macro level view of the purpose and general organization of interrupt-driven I/O. Extensive discussions of device drivers are included, but they stop short of providing an actual Linux driver. The Lab Exercise provides a nice user space example of a device driver. I have used this exercise with both UNIX and Windows. Students like the idea that they can write code that directly manipulates the floppy disk (even though it is through the file interface). The chapter examines devices before considering processes because devices provide an elementary case in which physical concurrency exists in the computer and the software must be carefully designed to control that concurrency. This provides a natural introduction to process management.

■ **Chapters 6–10** focus on process management. They start from the basic tasks and organization of process and resource managers (Chapter 6) and move to scheduling (Chapter 7), synchronization (Chapters 8 and 9), and deadlock (Chapter 10). The Lab Exercises in these chapters expand on the topics in the text.

■ **Chapter 11** deals with traditional issues in memory management, and **Chapter 12** covers the contemporary approach to memory managers using virtual memory. Because of the popularity of paging, most of the discussion is directed at this technology. However, with the current trends in memory technology, it would be a mistake to ignore segmentation. Thus part of this discussion deals with segmentation. Unfortunately, the best example of a robust segmentation system is still the (now obsolete) Multics system. The Lab Exercise for Chapter 11 addresses the UNIX shared memory mechanism, and in Chapter 12, the Lab Exercise addresses Windows memory mapped files.

■ **Chapter 13** describes file management. Less space is devoted to file management than is customary in OS books because it is not as difficult to understand as process management and memory management. The Lab Exercise provides a means for taking a closer look at the details of file management. This discussion is augmented in Chapter 16, which talks about remote files. The Lab Exercise can be solved in either UNIX or Windows. It is a challenging exercise because of the amount of work (rather than the complexity of file systems).

■ **Chapter 14** provides a general discussion of protection mechanisms and security policies. It might be argued that this section belongs in the process management discussion, although much of the technology is just as closely related to files, memory, and other resources. It is much easier for students to appreciate the need for protection and security after they have seen the process, memory, and file managers.

■ **Chapters 15–17** introduce distributed systems technology. Distributed computing is a dominant aspect of modern operating systems and I feel strongly that coverage of this important issue belongs in all introductory texts on operating systems, even if you are unable to get to it in your course. There are Lab Exercises to learn about TCP/IP and remote procedure call.

■ **Chapter 18** is a new chapter in this edition that describes how modern distributed programming runtime systems are built to augment kernel services. This is currently a very exciting area that intersects operating systems, programming languages and compilers, and distributed programming.

■ **Chapter 19** is a big picture chapter that reconsiders all the OS technology in terms of software design and implementation. This chapter is intended to describe high-level design choices that OS designers must make and to direct the student to successful operating systems that have used each of these approaches. I have also included a detailed discussion of Mach in this chapter.

■ **Chapters 20–21** are case studies of Linux and Windows NT/2000/XP, respectively. Many examples from these two operating systems are provided throughout the book. This chapter provides a unified picture of each OS.

Finally, in spite of all good intentions, it is impossible to organize this material so that it meets every instructor's desires. The organization I use in my course is reflected in the book. However, there is no particular harm caused by shuffling the material to suit individual desires.

HAPPY SAILING! Today, there is a wealth of information on operating systems available on the World Wide Web; I encourage you to point your students toward the web. In this edition, I have included a few URLs to materials that I think will persist, for example, to standards organizations.

Finally, thank you for considering adopting this book for your course. I welcome your questions, comments, suggestions, and advice (and I will even try to accept your criticism in good humor ☺). You can contact me at Gary.Nutt@colorado.edu.

● ACKNOWLEDGEMENTS

Many people have helped to edit and refine this book. First, there are the students at the University of Colorado: Jason Casmira, Don Lindsay, Ann Root, and Sam Siewert were great teaching assistants who created lab exercises and solutions, and generally helped make the book better. Scott Brandt provided comments and insight into how the material should be presented. Adam Griff spent many hours helping me with my Linux system. Scott Morris set up my Windows NT machine, and offered insider tips about how it worked.

Addison-Wesley arranged to have additional students from other institutions look at the manuscript: Eric F. Stuckey, Shawn Lauzon, Dan Dartman, and Nick Tkach at Montana State University, and Jeffrey Ramin now at Berbee Information Networks Corporation. There were many people who spent hours looking at drafts or otherwise suggesting ways to organize and improve it: Divy Agrawal (University of California at Santa Barbara), Vladamir Akis (California State University at Los Angeles), Kasi Anantha (San Diego State University), Charles J. Antonelli (University of Michigan), Lewis Barnett (University of Richmond), Lubomir F. Bic (University of California, Irvine), Paosheng Chang (Lucent Technologies), Randy Chow (University of Florida), Wesley J. Chun, Carolyn J. Crouch (University of Minnesota, Duluth), Peter G. Drexel (Plymouth State College), Joseph Faletti, Gary Harkin (Montana State University), Dr. Sallie Henry (Virginia Tech), Mark A. Holliday (Western Carolina University), Marty Humphrey (University of Virginia), Kevin Jeffay (University of North Carolina at Chapel Hill), Phil Kearns (The College of William and Mary), Qiang Li (University of Santa Clara), Darrell Long (University of California at Santa Cruz), Junsheng Long, Michael Lutz (Rochester Institute of Technology), Carol McNamee (Sacramento State University), Donald Miller (Arizona State University), Jim Mooney (West Virginia University), Ethan V. Munson (University of Wisconsin—Milwaukee), Deborah O'Neill, Douglas Salane (John Jay College), Henning Schulzrinne (Columbia University), C.S. (James) Wong (San Francisco State University), and Salih Yurttas (Texas A&M University).

The second edition was reviewed by Toby Berk (Florida International University), David Binger (Centre College), Richard Guy (UCLA), Sami Khouri (San Jose State University), Zhiyuan Li (Purdue University), John Noll (University of Colorado, Denver), Kenneth A. Reek (Rochester Institute of Technology), Joseph J. Pfeiffer, Jr. (New Mexico State University), and Irene Tseng (Galludet University).

The third edition was reviewed by Dan Andresen (Kansas State University), Remzi Arpaci-Dusseau (University of Wisconsin), Gojko Babic (The Ohio State University), Anthony Q. Baxter (University of Kentucky), Roy Campbell (University of Illinois at Champaign-Urbana), Stephen Cooper (Saint Joseph's University), Ajoy K. Datta (University of Nevada Las Vegas), Eduardo B. Fernandez (Florida Atalantic University), Richard Guy (University of California, Los Angeles), Sami Khuri (San Jose State

University), Gopal Lakhani (Texas Tech University), Hsun K. Liu (California State Polytechnic University, Pomona), Xiuwen Liu (Florida State University), Dennis Mumaugh (Depaul University), N. Park (Oklahoma State University), William Sakas (Hunter College, City University of New York), Chien-Chung Shen (University of Delaware), Prashant Shenoy (University of Massachusetts, Amherst), Emin G. Sirer (Cornell University), Justin R. Smith (Drexel University), Quinn Snell (Brigham Young University), Thomas B. Sprague (Cornerstone University), and D. Zhang (California State University, Sacramento). Thank you all for sharing your experience, insight, and suggestions.

The editorial staff at Addison-Wesley and several freelance consultants have been invaluable in helping me produce this book. In the first edition, Christine Kulke, Angela Buenning, Rebecca Johnson, Dusty Bernard, Laura Michaels, Pat Unubun, Dan Joraanstad, and Nate McFadden provided invaluable help and direction. Carter Shanklin (Acquistion Editor for the first edition) had a vision for how the book should be written, and I am indebted to him for his considerable effort in getting the correct organization and content for the first edition.

Maité Suarez-Rivas has been the Acquisition Editor for the second and subsequent editions. Maité has provided the marketing insight for the book and pushed for the inclusion of critical components to make it better address the needs of OS instructors and students everywhere. Over the years, Maité and her assistants Maria Campo, Lisa Hogue, Molly Taylor, and Jason Miranda have continued to work tirelessly to keep a finger on the pulse of the marketplace, and then to refine the book into what people want and need. Maité has been a true partner in setting the tone and style of the book, and I am immensely indebted to her for her contribution. The second edition production staff made the book much easier to read. This team included Karen Wernholm, Amy Rose, and Tracy Treeful. Helen Reebenacker handled the detailed production for the second edition lab update.

For the third edition, Rebecca Ferris and Maxine ("Max") E. Chuck worked on improving the text with development editing on several of the chapters. Juliet Silveri managed the overall production coordination, including the new art styling. Kathy Smith handled the day-to-day production and copy editing, a job that was made particularly difficult by the incorporation of a new design and new figures. Holly McLean-Aldis was the proofreader, Regina Hagen Kalinda designed the cover and interior, and Gillian Hall did the text and art composition. Besides assisting Maité, Maria Campo also worked on production with Juliet's team. Thanks to these people for their long hours of work to put the book into production.

The book has benefited immensely by these collective efforts, but of course the remaining errors are solely my responsibility.

Gary Nutt
Boulder, Colorado

Contents

Chapter 11   MEMORY MANAGEMENT   414

CHAPTER 1

Introduction

As suggested by Figure 1.1, the **operating system**, or **OS**[1] is like a conductor: It is responsible for coordinating all of the computer's individual components so that they work together according to a single plan. When an orchestra is warming up, the collective instruments produce a cacophony of unrelated sounds. But when the conductor takes charge, the collection of instruments act together to produce a coordinated set of (hopefully) pleasing sounds. The conductor sets the tempo for the music, signals different instruments when they should play, controls the volume of the individual sections of the orchestra, and so on. Similarly, the OS allocates the computer's components to different programs, synchronizes their individual activities, and generally provides the mechanisms that are needed so that the programs execute in perfect harmony.

Efficiency and functionality are key to an operating system's usefulness. The efficiency sets the stage for the performance of all software on a computer. One of the most important reasons to study operating systems is to learn how to extract the most efficient performance from them. The OS also provides a wide range of functions that assist in program execution. A high-performance OS that provides little functionality forces more work onto its application programs. This book will teach you how to use the system's functionality most effectively. Specifically, you will learn how an OS is designed so that you will be able to exploit that design during program execution.

---

[1] It is popular in conversation and in the technical literature to refer to an operating system by its abbreviation, "OS." In this book, we use both the term and the abbreviation interchangeably. However, there is no good abbreviation for the plural, so we always use "operating systems" for the plural.

✦ **FIGURE 1.1**   The OS as a Symphony Conductor

Operating systems have earned a reputation for being the most critical software in a computer system. Only the most skilled and experienced programmers are allowed to design and modify a computer's operating system.

You will explore the issues that arise during the OS design process, as well as the different approaches used to analyze and resolve those issues. All operating systems are designed under various constraints and circumstances. Design decisions are often reflected in the OS interface that is exported for use by application programs. The design may seem to have discontinuities, anomalies, or other logical inconsistencies. As you learn about OS design, many of these inconsistencies will disappear because you will understand the rationale behind design decisions. You will have refined your mental model of how an OS operates. As you learn more about operating systems you will see that they still have design flaws. This book will enable you to learn how to work around those flaws. By gaining an understanding of the design issues and decisions, as well as the tradeoffs involved, you will better be able to write software that takes advantage of the OS design.

This chapter explains what an operating system is and how it evolved into its current state of development. First, you will learn about the overall software environment so that you can see how an OS fits in. Next, you will become familiar with the demands on modern operating systems—abstraction and sharing—and how they came about. Finally, the chapter examines the popular OS strategies and how they have influenced the services provided by modern operating systems.

1.1 • COMPUTERS AND SOFTWARE

Computer systems consist of *software* and *hardware* that are combined to provide a tool to solve specific problems. Software is differentiated according to its purpose. **Application software**[2] is intended to solve a specific problem, or to provide generic tools for end users. For example, inventory control application software uses the computer to track and report a company's inventory, electronic mail software allows people to communicate with one another, document editor programs provide a tool for composing and editing text documents, and spreadsheet programs allow users to store and manipulate information for decision support. Ultimately, the cost of any computer is justified by the value of its application software. That is, a person or a company buys a computer to solve information processing problems specific to their needs. As suggested by Figure 1.2(a), the end user's view of the computer is of the application software. Any other software or hardware is just part of the overhead cost required to execute the application software that solves the problem.

✦ FIGURE 1.2 Perspectives of the Computer

End users, application programmers, and OS programmers use different aspects of a computer. The end user employs the application programs, the application programmer uses the system software to produce application programs, and the OS programmer uses the hardware to implement system software.

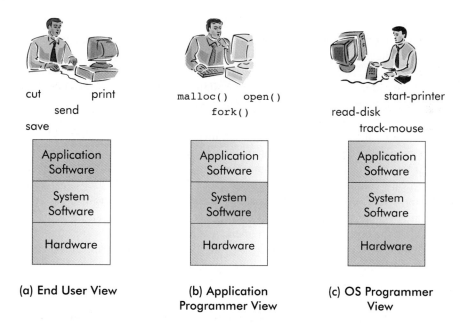

| (a) End User View | (b) Application Programmer View | (c) OS Programmer View |

---

[2]Terms are defined at the point where they appear in **boldface** type. They are also defined in the Glossary at the end of the book.

System software provides a general programming environment in which programmers can create specific applications to suit their customers' needs. This environment is made up of programming tools (such as editors and compilers) and abstractions (such as files and objects). The application programmer uses the system software, which includes the OS, to provide a set of applications for end users (see Figure 1.2(b)). From the application programmer's perspective, the system software is important because it defines the environment in which programs can be implemented for eventual deployment to end users. However, from the end user's perspective, the system software may be no more important than, say, the power supply in the hardware. *System software and hardware exist to support the creation and effective use of application software.* Because of this role, system software should provide as much *functionality* as possible to application programmers, yet be as unobtrusive as possible to the end user. Part of being unobtrusive is being *efficient*: The system software should try to minimize its use of the machine's resources (such as processor time and memory), in order to maximize the time that those resources are available to application programs.

We could minimize the system software use of the resources by eliminating all system software. But then each program would have to provide the functionality that is implemented by that system software. Imagine if you had to implement an entire file system just so you could read and write a disk device! We know now that we want system software: The question is how much and what functionality? This question is the basis of competing software models: Macintosh system software provides one set of programming tools, Microsoft environments provide a different set of tools, Java has its own set of system software functions, and UNIX systems offer yet another distinct set of programming tools.

The original motivation for system software was to provide functions that a programmer could use to implement application software. Over time, another important purpose of system software (*particularly operating systems*) evolved: Enabling application software to *share* the hardware in an orderly fashion. For example, one program may be reading information from a disk drive while another program is computing the square root of a number. This sharing increases overall system performance by allowing different programs to use different parts of the computer hardware simultaneously, thereby decreasing the time needed to execute a collection of programs and increasing the system's performance. To ensure that this sharing is done safely and efficiently, the system software controls the use of the hardware components by the various executing application programs. Generally speaking, the **operating system** is the part of the system software that manages the use of the hardware by other system software and all application software. Because of this, we say that the OS is the software that is implemented "closest to the hardware." The OS programmer writes software that controls the hardware (to implement sharing and abstraction), providing a software environment used by the application programmer (see Figure 1.2(c)).

GENERAL SYSTEM SOFTWARE

System software creates two kinds of environments: One that allows human users to interact with the computer, and a second that provides tools and subassemblies used with application programs. The human–computer interface supports both end users and programmers by providing them with tools such as electronic desktops and text editors for managing information. End users manage their mail, documents, and numerical information, while programmers manage their software.

✦ **FIGURE 1.3** Using the System Software

The system software provides a wide variety of services, ranging from compilers to database management systems. Application programs invoke system services by calling functions on the system software's application programming interface (API). The OS is part of the system software, so like the other parts of the system software, it exports a set of functions used to invoke its services.

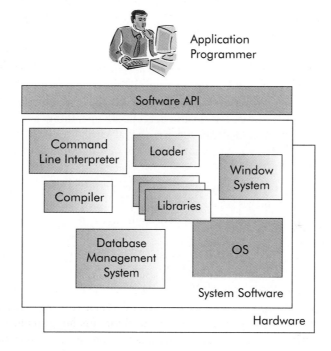

In your previous programming classes you learned to write programs that use the software **application programming interface (API)** to the system software (see Figure 1.3): A compiler to translate the program into a form suitable for execution, a loader to copy the program into memory for execution, and libraries to perform functions such as formatting input/output or creating an object. For example, in the C and C++ programming environments, important tools are implemented in the C **runtime libraries** system software (accessed using various `.h` files), including:

■ The standard input/output (I/O) library provides procedures to perform buffered input/output, such as `printf()` and `scanf()`, on a stream of data.

■ The math library provides functions, such as `sqrt()`, to compute mathematical functions.

■ Graphics libraries provide functions such as `drawCircle()` to render images on a bitmapped display.

Other system software implements logical components of the system. Whereas libraries provide collections of functions that can be called from application programs, these components are essential elements of the computing environment. Here are some examples of these kinds of components:

■ A **command line interpreter** (often just called a **shell**) is a text-based program that the user invokes to interact with the system software. The user sends commands, such as `dir` to Windows and `ls` to UNIX, to the command line interpreter that cause the system software to perform desired actions, such as listing the entries in a directory. The UNIX `sh` and `csh` programs, the Linux `bash` program, and the Windows `cmd.exe` program are examples of command line interpreters.

■ A **window system** is system software that provides a virtual terminal to an application program. The window is termed "virtual" because the programmer constructs the application software using functions to read and write the window as if it were a terminal device, even though there is no physical terminal uniquely associated with the window. The system software maps these virtual terminal operations so that they apply to a specific physical region on a screen. It then translates the software's operations on the virtual terminal to appropriate operations on the physical terminal. One physical terminal can support several virtual terminals. For example, the Macintosh desktop, the Microsoft Windows desktop, and the Gnome desktop in Linux are window systems.

■ A **database management system** (**DBMS**) can be used to store information on the computer's permanent storage devices. The database system provides abstract data types (called *schema*) and creates new application-specific software optimized for efficient queries/updates on the data according to the schema definition. The more instances of complex data structures that an application uses, the greater the benefit from using a database management system. Examples of database management systems include the Oracle or MySQL relational database systems.

People and organizations buy computers to solve their information processing problems. For example, a business buys some computers to handle accounting information; a military organization may buy a computer to compute ballistic trajectories; and an individual may buy a computer to play games and surf the Internet. Each of the reasons for buying a computer defines an **application domain**, or collection of problems that can be addressed by the computer. In the accounting application domain, the programs of interest can create invoices, keep track of account balances, and so on. In the ballistics trajectory domain, the programs are expected to solve problems related to aiming a missile. In the personal computing domain, the programs should be able to support graphics-intensive game programs, on-screen text editing, and a web browser.

Some system software, such as a graphics library, may be quite useful in one application domain but not be used at all in others. Other system software, like a relational database, is intended to be reasonably general. It can support programs written for many different application domains. As an additional level of complexity, in the case of databases, different kinds of DBMSs can be customized for different domains. For example, the database system may be specialized to support a subdomain such as image processing or an artificial intelligence expert system. And even within the image processing database system software, further specialization of the system software may be appropriate so that it supports specific applications. For example, the image database may be designed to support only monochrome topographic images.

How is an OS distinguished from other system software? Here are some essential differences. You will continue to learn about others as you learn more about operating systems.

■ An OS interacts directly with the hardware to provide an interface used by other system software and application software.

■ A general purpose OS is domain-independent. This means that the same OS can be used to support a broad range of application domains, such as inventory management software as well as software for computing fluid flow over an airplane wing.

■ The application program uses resource abstractions provided by the OS to determine its detailed interaction with the hardware components.

■ The OS allows different applications to share the hardware resources through its resource management policies.

Resource abstraction and sharing are two key aspects of the operating system. Let's now look at these two aspects in more detail.

RESOURCE ABSTRACTION

System software hides (from the user) the details of how the underlying machinery operates. This means that a user can operate a computer without knowing very much about how the hardware operates. This idea extends to the application programmer by providing operational models that are relatively easy to use compared to directly interacting with the hardware. The technique is for the system software to provide an abstract model of the operation of hardware components. We encounter these kinds of abstractions frequently in our everyday life: For example, to drive a modern automobile, it is not necessary for you to understand the details of motors, brakes, and steering mechanisms. In fact, in an automobile with an automatic transmission, you do not even have to know how to shift gears (or even if there *are* gears). This is possible because of abstraction of the "programming interface." For the first half century of their existence, automobiles only used manual transmissions. This meant that anyone who wanted to drive a car would have to learn about a clutch and different gears—low gears for low speeds and high gears for high speeds. With the automatic transmission abstraction, a driver only has to know about "P," "D," and "R," whether they are selected with a pushbutton or lever. The other gears (neutral and low range) never need to be used. Today, drivers can concentrate on higher-level functions of driving, instead of shifting, braking, and steering—things like route selection, speed, cutting off other drivers, cell phone conversations, and so on (hmmm, maybe this abstraction thing has gotten out of hand with automobiles).

In a computer system, abstractions are used to eliminate tedious detail that a programmer otherwise would have to handle. Without a suitable abstraction for writing characters to a screen (such as a print function), imagine how much you would have to learn to set a screen bitmap so that it would print "Hello, world" in 12 point Arial font on a video display. Rather than learning all those details, the C programmer just learns about `printf()` and the `stdio` library. The time that a programmer would have spent writing code to form characters on a screen can now be spent writing code to solve the problem at hand.

The dark side of abstraction is that while it simplifies the way the application programmer controls the hardware, it can also limit the flexibility by which specific hardware can be manipulated. Generality has its price in specificity. That is, while certain operations become easy to perform, other operations may be impossible to achieve using the abstraction. You can see how this might happen by thinking about an automatic bank teller machine. Teller machines allow people to withdraw variable amounts of money from their accounts using a series of button pushes that specify the exact amount of money to be withdrawn. Some teller machines provide an abstract operation that allows a user to withdraw $40 from a checking account by pushing a *single* button. Suppose the teller machine *only* allowed abstract operations to withdraw $20, $40, $100, or $200 from your account. Then it would no longer be possible for you to withdraw exactly $30. The machine would be easier to operate, but less flexible.

Computers are composed of many different kinds of hardware components—part of the system's **resources**—that an application program may use. Any particular resource, such as a disk drive, has an interface that defines how the programmer can make the resource perform a desired operation. An abstraction, however, can be made much simpler than the actual resource interface. For example, writing information to a file (an abstraction of a disk device) is much less complicated than generating the commands required to write it directly to a disk storage device. Abstractions are implemented within the system software. The lowest level abstractions—the ones that deal directly with the hardware—are implemented in the OS, while higher-level abstractions such as a window system are implemented in non-OS system software. Like the automobile transmission and teller machine abstractions, the programmer doesn't have to learn each specific resource's interface in order to use the resource. Instead, the abstract interface (which ignores the fine detail of how the device is operated) can be used. Then the programmer can focus on higher-level issues.

In many cases, similar resources can be abstracted to a *common* abstract resource interface. For example, the system software can abstract floppy disk and hard disk operation into a single abstract disk interface. While an application programmer must be aware of the general behavior of drives, learning the details of disk input/output is not necessary or even desirable. The programmer needs to know about and use only the disk abstraction. In the case of driving an automobile, abstractions are so common that you can rent a car that you have never seen before and immediately get in it and drive it. The abstractions used in the rental car are the same as those used in your own car. Imagine the disaster if automobile driving abstractions were not common: Suppose some cars turned left when the steering wheel was rotated in a clockwise direction, but other cars turned right in this case.

In designing system software, you must first define a set of abstractions that will be general across resources, yet intuitive for a programmer and suited to one or more application domains. The file abstraction for disk device operation is such an example. Good abstractions will be easy for the programmer to understand and use and will allow the programmer to easily perform every kind of operation on the resources used in the domain.

Object-oriented programmers use abstraction at multiple levels when they work with class hierarchies. A base class defines the most abstract operations for objects, and subclasses refine the operations for more specific members of the family. The disk driver abstraction example in the accompanying box[3] shows how abstraction can be used at more than one level. Once a hardware component has been simplified with an interface, higher-

---

[3]Throughout this book, there are many large examples and other comments that appear in boxed sections of the text. This information is put in a box so that you can follow the discussion of the content that appears in the main flow of the text, and then consider an example or other side discussion when it best fits your reading style. Some of the boxed discussions apply only to UNIX or only to Windows. You will find it helpful to read the example boxes that relate to the OS used with your class.

level system software may then be defined to abstract that resource into an even higher-level interface. The raw disk block model of operation is abstracted to provide a track-sector write operation, which is generalized again to use integer block addresses. Next the integer-addressed blocks are abstracted into a list of related blocks that contain a logical stream of bytes. Now you can see that a significant reason for referring to hardware components as "resources" is to allow the resource abstraction to apply to computer components—physical resources—and to software artifacts implemented in the system software—*abstract resources*.

An Abstraction of a Disk Drive

The idea behind resource abstraction can be examined more closely by considering how disk output operations can be represented at different levels of abstraction. The device is controlled with software operations for copying a block of information from the computer's main memory into the device's buffer memory (see Figure 1.4(a)):

```
load(block, length, device);
```

for moving the read/write head to specified areas on the disk surface:

```
seek(device, track);
```

and other operations such as writing a block of data from the buffer to the device:

```
out(device, sector);
```

Thus a series of commands is required to write information from a primary memory block onto a disk, such as

```
load(block, length, device);
seek(device, 236);
out(device, 9);
```

A simple abstraction (see Figure 1.4(b)) would be to package these commands, with any other necessary supplementary commands, into a `write()` procedure such as

```
void write(char *block, int len, int device, int track,
int sector)
{
...
load(block, len, device);
seek(device, 236);
out(device, 9);
...
}
```

Data block addresses on a disk are specified by a track number, such as 236 in the `load` instruction, and sector number, such as 9 in the `out` instruction. A higher-level abstraction might translate every block specification so that a nonnegative integer address is used instead of a disk-specific address such as track 236 in the `seek()` function and sector 9

◆ FIGURE 1.4 Disk Abstractions

Here are three different ways of writing information to a disk device. In (a), the software directly manipulates the hardware to select the block address, then writes the information with the `out()` call. In (b), the machine instructions are packaged into the abstract `write()` function. It also writes a block of information to the device, but is easier to use than (a). In (c), the `write()` function is abstracted into a C runtime library function, `fprintf()`, that performs buffered, formatted I/O.

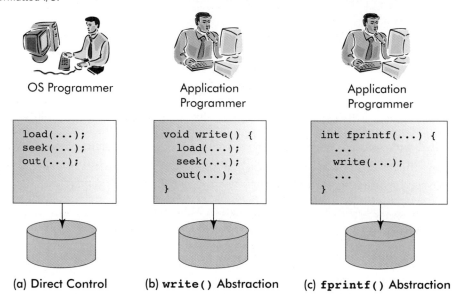

OS Programmer   Application   Application
                                 Programmer   Programmer

```
load(...);        void write() {        int fprintf(...) {
seek(...);           load(...);            ...
out(...);            seek(...);            write(...);
                     out(...);             ...
                  }                     }
```

(a) Direct Control   (b) `write()` Abstraction   (c) `fprintf()` Abstraction

in the `out()` function. This allows the programmer to ignore physical addresses defined by disk drive technology in favor of logical addresses that apply to any kind of storage device. Now an output operation such as

```
write(block, 100, device, 236, 9);
```

can be written as

```
write(block, 100, device, 3788);
```

An even higher-level abstraction provides software with a way to treat the disk as file storage. Suppose the system software provides a file identification, `fileID`, as the abstraction of the disk. Then a library, such as the C `stdio` library, can provide a function to write an integer variable, `datum` (stored in a small memory block), onto the device at an implicit offset from the beginning of the file. The programmer then uses operations such as

```
fprintf(fileID,"%d", datum);
```

to write information to the disk (see Figure 1.4(c)). Such an abstraction also could be used for tape device input/output operations by having a different part of the system software implement the same abstraction for the tape device. Such abstractions will be considered in detail throughout the book.

RESOURCE SHARING

Computers are known for their computational speed. A computer can evaluate in microseconds a numerical expression that would take a human several minutes to solve. This speed difference allows a computer to fool humans so that it looks like the computer is executing multiple programs simultaneously, even though they are really being executed sequentially. The OS accomplishes this illusion by switching the hardware among programs at a very high rate. This is similar to a scenario in which a chess master is able to "simultaneously" play several opponents at the same time: In reality, the chess master plays the opponents sequentially by playing one opponent for a moment, then switching to another opponent while the first is contemplating the current game state.

Computers can sometimes support *true* simultaneous operation. For example, if one program wants to do numerical computation at the same time as another wants to read a disk device, then the OS schedules the hardware use so that both programs execute at the same time. This is possible because the computer's processing unit and disk device are physically distinct components that can be used at the same time.

In the study of operating systems, we blur the distinction between the *appearance* and the *true occurrence* of simultaneous operations. We say that a system supports **concurrent execution** (or exhibits **concurrency**) when either it *appears* that two or more programs are being executed simultaneously, or they *really are* executing at the same time. If there are true simultaneous operations, we say that there is **parallel** (or simultaneous) **execution** between the two programs.

Concurrent and parallel execution are related to the notion of resource **sharing**: For executing programs to be concurrent or parallel, they must share the computer. An OS manages some of the resources by **transparently sharing** among the abstract machines. That is, users and application programmers are unaware that resources are being shared. An OS also allows **explicit sharing** among executing programs by providing mechanisms by which the application programmers manage the way the machine's resources are to be shared. First, we will describe transparent sharing and then discuss explicit sharing.

ABSTRACT MACHINES AND TRANSPARENT RESOURCE SHARING

Concurrency is pervasive in both the OS design and the model of operation used by the application programmer. This is most apparent when you think about the program execution environment that is presented to the application programmer and end user: Multiple program executions each *appear to have their own private computer* on which to execute. This is accomplished by designing the OS so that it carefully manages the computer's processor, memory, devices, and all other abstract resources so that they are shared among the executing programs, then by presenting an abstraction of the machine itself—called an **abstract machine**—to the programmer (see Figure 1.5). Each abstract machine is a "simulation" of a real computer: Each program is given its own abstract machine on which to execute. The OS will implement these abstractions by sharing the underlying hardware in a manner that, ideally, is invisible to the application programmer. A program that is being executed by an abstract machine is classically called a **process** (we will refine this process idea in Chapters 2 and 6).

✦ FIGURE 1.5 Abstract Machines

An OS can provide an abstract machine for the use of an application programmer by creating a simulation of a computer. By simulating the abstract machine, the OS can direct the physical machine to simulate several abstract machines at the same time.

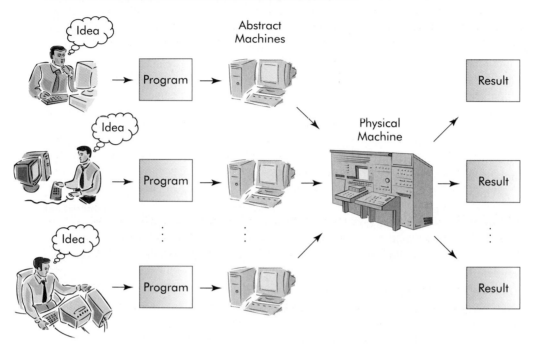

Two kinds of sharing are used to create the abstract machines: space-multiplexed sharing and time-multiplexed sharing. In **space-multiplexed sharing**, a resource is divided into two or more distinct units, and then the individual parts are allocated to processes. For example, a complex of condominiums is space-multiplexed by dividing the building into a collection of condos, then allocating each condo to a different occupant. A city bus is another example of space-multiplexed sharing, because many people share the bus by each occupying one seat. In computers, abstract machines (processes) can space-multiplex a resource when the OS allocates exclusive control of different units of a resource at the same time. The main memory and disks are examples of space-multiplexed resource sharing.

In **time-multiplexed sharing**, a resource is not divided into units, but instead, one process can use the entire resource for a period of time, and then another process uses it at a later time. For example, a metered automobile parking space is shared using the time-multiplexing technique: One car at a time can have exclusive control of the entire parking space, but after a certain amount of time has passed, the first car leaves and a second car takes up the parking space. (Just to complicate things, an automobile parking *lot* uses space-multiplexing to divide the lot into individual parking spaces, but time-multiplexing for sharing each individual parking space.) In the city transportation scenario, a taxi cab is an example of time-multiplexed sharing, since one occupant uses the cab exclusively, and then another occupant uses it after the first person leaves. In computer systems, a process can have exclusive control of an entire resource for a period of time. After that time has elapsed, the resource is deallocated from the process and allocated to another. Time-multiplexing is used with the computer's processor resource.

Different processes use their abstract machines concurrently provided the OS is able to ensure *each* underlying physical machine component is shared using either space- or time-multiplexing. For example, three processes' abstract machines might be time-multiplexed sharing the processor, while another process's abstract machine is reading one disk, and another process is reading another disk. The three process types are using three different space-multiplexed parts of the hardware.

Time-multiplexed sharing of the machine's processor is such a crucial aspect of the abstract machine implementation that it is usually studied as a special case of resource sharing. The abstract machine for one process used the physical processor for a fraction of a second (called a **timeslice**), and then the OS time-multiplexes the processor to a different abstract machine. Meanwhile, the computer's memory is shared using space-multiplexing. This technique for sharing the processor is so important (and widely used) that it is identified by a name: **multiprogramming**. We will study multiprogramming throughout the book, but for now we can develop our intuition with an informal description (see Figure 1.6). In this figure, there are N different abstract machines (named P_i, P_j, ... P_k). The OS divides the physical memory into N different blocks, and then allocates a block to each abstract machine. When the program for P_i is loaded into its block of memory, it can then share the processor using time-multiplexed sharing. Over a time period

✦ **FIGURE 1.6** Multiprogramming

Multiprogramming is the key OS technology that implements multiple abstract machines. It is accomplished by space-multiplex sharing the memory among the abstract machines, and time-multiplex sharing the physical processor. The OS coordinates these sharing tasks.

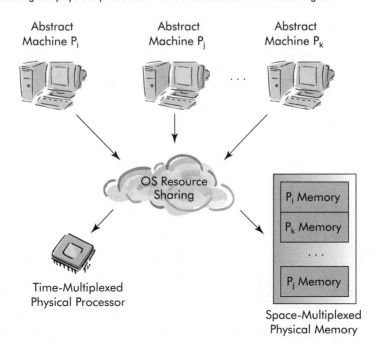

equal to N timeslices, each P_i uses the processor for only one timeslice, but it occupies its block of memory for the entire time.

Does multiprogramming improve the performance of a computer? *It cannot improve any single process's performance, but it can improve the overall system performance.* Here is how the idea might work in a car wash: There are three cars to be cleaned. The complete operation requires that the car be washed, dried, and the inside vacuumed (see Figure 1.7(a)). The car wash coordinator schedules the work so that car 1 is being washed at the same time as car 2 is being vacuumed, while car 3 is waiting (see Figure 1.7 (b)). Now, when car 1 has been washed, it is then dried. At the same time, car 2 will be washed and car 3 vacuumed. When car 1 has been dried, it is vacuumed at the same time that car 2 is dried and car 3 is washed. As soon as car 1 has been vacuumed, and car 2 has been dried, they are both finished. The only remaining work is to dry car 3 (while the vacuum and wash stations are idle). Notice that cars 1 and 2 both required the same amount of time to complete as they would have in a "sequential" car wash, although both will think that they were the first to receive service. Car 3 will require a little more time, but less time than if it had to wait for both cars 1 and 2 to be vacuumed before it began to be cleaned. The car wash system required only 4 time stages to wash 3 cars. If it had cleaned the 3 cars with the same vacuum-wash-dry sequence, then it would have taken 5 time stages.

✦ FIGURE 1.7 Speeding up the Car Wash

In (a), cars pass through each stage of the procedure in the same order. The third car has to wait for the first two cars to be cleaned inside before it can begin to be cleaned. In (b), the third car is cleaned inside at the same time the second car is being washed. The third car now only has to wait for the second car to be cleaned inside before it begins to be washed.

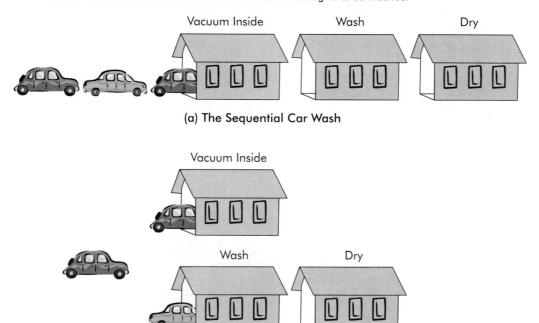

Vacuum Inside   Wash   Dry

(a) The Sequential Car Wash

Vacuum Inside

Wash   Dry

(b) The Parallel Car Wash

The same basic idea can be applied to processes. Here are some characteristics of process execution that we can exploit in order to speed up the system using parallelism:

- In modern computers, I/O operations take much more time to complete than do processor operations.

- The process, P_i, does not need the processor while it is doing I/O (such as when the user enters information, debugs programs, and so on).

- Each P_i spends most of its time using the I/O devices in the hardware (see Figure 1.8(a)).

- In a conventional computer, there are multiple devices but only one processor.

✦ FIGURE 1.8 Multiprogramming Performance

In (a), we see how P_i only uses the processor for three short time bursts, with intervening I/O operations. When we consider the processor and I/O activity of all *N* processes in (b), we see that it might be possible to coordinate their execution so that each uses the processor when all other processes are involved in I/O operations.

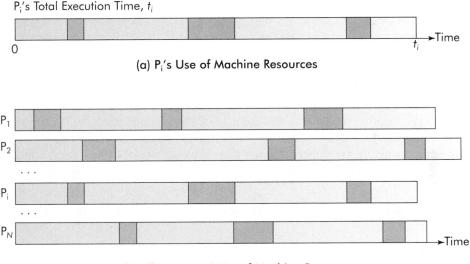

P_i's Total Execution Time, t_i

(a) P_i's Use of Machine Resources

(b) All Processes' Use of Machine Resources

Suppose the OS controls the processor usage so that whenever P_i is involved in I/O, some other process, P_j, uses the processor (Figure 1.8(b)). Then we will achieve true parallelism by having processes simultaneously using different parts of the computer.

In a system without multiprogramming (like the sequential car wash), if *N* processes have execution times of t_1, t_2, ..., t_N, then the total time to service all *N* users would be

$$t_1 + t_2 + ... + t_N$$

We know that the *minimum* amount of time to execute any P_i is t_i, since the process has to do computation and I/O according to its program. That means that if we were able to schedule the execution of all the processes so that each was always able to use a different component of the computer at the same time, then the amount of time that the system would require to execute all N processes would be equal to the length of time to execute the longest-running process, which is

$$\text{maximum}(t_1, t_2, ..., t_N)$$

We could only achieve this maximum increase of speed if conditions were "just right." However, we can see that the time to execute the N processes, T, using a multiprogrammed system should be

$$\text{maximum}(t_1, t_2, ..., t_N) \leq T$$

Usually (but not always!) we also have

$$T \leq t_1 + t_2 + ... + t_N$$

There are many things that can cause the situation to not be "just right." For example, the programs for the processes must have the right balance between processing and device I/O; there must be the right amount of OS time to determine the schedule; there must be $N-1$ devices in the system; processes must use all $N-1$ devices, and so on. That is why we have to express the performance increase as an inequality rather than as an exact statement. We will study these issues throughout the rest of the book.

EXPLICIT RESOURCE SHARING

Explicit resource sharing mechanisms allow processes to use common resources through their own coordination strategy (as opposed to the OS's coordination strategy). For example, two processes may be cooperatively computing the monthly payroll, so they need to share a file containing the number of hours each employee worked. There are two important aspects to explicit resource sharing, independent of whether it is time or space-multiplexed:

- The system must be able to *isolate* resource access according to an allocation policy.
- The system must be able to allow processes to *cooperatively share* resources when that is desired.

Resource isolation refers to the OS's obligation to prevent unauthorized access of resources by one abstract machine when they are currently allocated to another abstract machine. For example, a memory isolation mechanism allows two processes to be loaded in different parts of memory at the same time, but neither abstract machine has access to the memory block used by the other abstract machine. Similarly, the processor isolation mechanism forces the abstract machines to sequentially share the system's processor. Neither process will be able to change or reference the memory contents being used by the other process.

Resource isolation is mandatory for the correct operation of most abstract machines. However, in cases where two or more processes are intended to work cooperatively on a common problem, the OS must explicitly enable the corresponding abstract machines to *share resource access* when that is desired. Authorized sharing is desirable when, for example, one process wants to share a result that it has computed with another process; the two processes need to share a common block of memory in which shared information can be stored.

By providing an OS mechanism to isolate resources, we typically introduce a new problem. Suppose the programmer intends for two executing programs to share a resource such as a file. The OS must also include facilities to allow the two processes to authorize sharing despite the presence of the isolation mechanism. This can be tricky, since there is always the possibility that a malicious process might attempt to gain access to a resource that has been allocated to another process. If the malicious process were allowed to gain unauthorized access to memory, for example, then the second process would be unable to prevent the malicious process from copying or overwriting the information it had stored in its memory.

The requirement for resource isolation suggests another important property of systems software and operating systems. If a process relies on resource isolation, then the system software must be able to provide that functionality. Your previous experience with software has taught you that software does not always do exactly what you intended. Suppose the part of the system software that is responsible for isolating resources did not do what it was intended to do? Then resource isolation might fail. In the real world, this would be like a situation in which you relied on police to enforce laws: The intent is clear, but if the police were to fail to enforce the laws—it would not matter whether it was because of incompetence or corruption—then the law enforcement mechanism would not be very useful. The system software is expected to enforce the resource isolation requirement. If it fails because of program bugs or inadequate algorithms, then it is not very useful. Contemporary operating systems (in contrast to general system software) are constructed as **trusted software**, meaning that they are required to perform exactly as intended in order for the overall system to behave correctly. The crucial parts of the resource isolation software are in the operating system in order to provide the most assurance that they are correct.

Summarizing what you have learned about shared resources, Figure 1.9 shows that the OS manages the computer's physical hardware resources (using the software-hardware interface). The OS is designed as trusted software that is responsible for correct sharing and isolation of the hardware resources. The OS abstractions can be manipulated using the OS interface (usually called the **system call interface** or a similar name). Non-OS system software also implements its own abstract resources and sharing mechanisms (like databases and windows). This system software is not implemented as trusted software. Its correctness depends on the trusted operation of the OS. All of the system software abstractions are accessible through an API. Application programs use the system software API to export the human–computer interface, which is used by the end user. In general, programmers refer to any software interface as an API, although "system call interface" always refers to the OS interface. Microsoft has named its Windows system call interface the "Win32 API" instead of the Windows system call interface.

✦ FIGURE 1.9   Application Software, System Software, and the OS

There is a hierarchy among application software, system software, and the OS. The OS uses the functionality at the software–hardware interface to implement the OS interface. The system software uses the OS interface to export the API. Application programs use the API to create software that implements the human–computer interface.

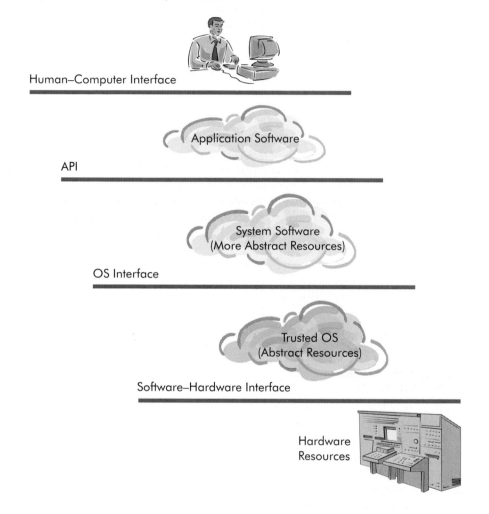

Human–Computer Interface

Application Software

API

System Software
(More Abstract Resources)

OS Interface

Trusted OS
(Abstract Resources)

Software–Hardware Interface

Hardware
Resources

1.2 ● OPERATING SYSTEM STRATEGIES

During the short, happy history of operating systems (the last 45 or so years), several different strategies have been used to provide OS services. In this case, the strategy refers to the general characteristics of the programmer's abstract machine. For example, there may be a fixed number of abstract machines in the system, or abstract machines may be especially designed to allow end users to interact with the software.

The preferred strategy for any given computer depends on business and engineering criteria such as how will the computer be used? Is human interaction more important than the rate at which processes are completed? Will there ever be more than one person (perhaps controlling multiple processes) using the computer at a time? Is it possible to implement a strategy without unduly affecting the overall performance? Since the first operating systems, there have only been about half a dozen general strategies. All of them use some variant of the abstract machine idea to address resource abstraction and resource sharing. Let's briefly consider the most significant OS strategies.

The earliest computers were dedicated to a single program-in-execution at a time (no multiprogramming, and essentially no OS). Then, as now, applications justified the cost of the entire system. Since computers were so expensive, they were used only in critical tasks such as national defense applications. A programmer was given exclusive access to an entire machine in order to develop and debug his or her program. When the program was ready for production use, the machine was allocated to the end user to execute the program. Since there was only one program in execution, there was no need for resource sharing. The only purpose of the system software was to simplify device programming through abstraction.

By 1960, economic pressures and software technology evolved to a point where users expected concurrent execution of multiple programs on a single computer—a new OS strategy was required where resources could be shared. This led to the ideas of abstract machines and multiprogramming that you have learned about so far. The rest of this chapter describes six different classes of operating systems and computers that have identifiable baseline strategies.

- **Batch systems** handle collections, or **batches**, of jobs. A **job** is a predefined sequence of commands (such as "compile a program" or "execute a program"), programs, and data. The job is self-sufficient in the sense that it contains *all* of the programs and data required for execution *without human intervention*. For this reason, batch systems are also referred to as *noninteractive* systems. Batch processing systems were the first to use multiprogramming. This allowed the OS to execute a few jobs (but usually *not* the entire batch) concurrently.

- **Timesharing systems** support multiple *interactive* users. Rather than the user preparing a job for execution ahead of time, the user establishes an interactive session with the computer and then provides commands, programs, and data as they are needed during the session. These systems stimulated development of more sophisticated multiprogramming mechanisms than were used in batch systems. For example, the OS needed to support multiple processes under the control of a single user. Timesharing also drove the need for the OS to provide timely response for users and sharpened the focus on resource management and protection mechanisms.

- **Personal computers and workstations** established a trend away from sharing a single computer among multiple users and toward an environment in which an entire machine is devoted to a single human user. In timesharing systems, the interactive response times depend on the number of people sharing the machine, but in these dedicated machines, program execution times are very predictable because all processes belong to a single user. This approach represents a substantial change in

OS strategy because it is based on the idea that it is more important to minimize wait time for the person instead of trying to maximize the utilization of the hardware. Even so, single-user machines are usually multiprogrammed so that the computer can be performing several different tasks (using several different processes) concurrently.

■ **Embedded systems** were originally used to control "autonomous systems" such as hydroelectric dams, satellites, and robots. In these kinds of applications, the OS is usually required to guarantee response times for particular computing tasks. If the system cannot provide the desired service prior to a deadline, the application is deemed to have failed. Today, the technology is rapidly elevating in importance because of the desire to support multimedia computing (with more flexible deadline strategies than in traditional real-time systems).

■ **Small, Communicating Computers** (including **mobile**, **wireless computers**) are the representatives of the newest class of machines. Examples of this kind of system include Internet appliances, tablet computers, set-top boxes, cell phones, and personal digital assistants (PDAs). These machines are built as a small, portable, communicating computer, yet they should support many of the same kind of applications as desktop or notebook computers. This has stimulated development of a new class of operating systems with new resource management policies, power management strategies, limited device storage, and so on.

■ **Network technology** has evolved rapidly since 1980. Modern computer configurations use high-speed networks (including the public Internet) to interconnect groups of personal computers, workstations, batch systems, timesharing systems, real-time systems, and small computers. This has an influence on OS strategy because of the need for strategies to handle resource and information sharing across the machines interconnected with a network.

BATCH SYSTEMS

A batch processing system services individual jobs from a predefined collection of jobs. Each batch job is specified by a predefined list of OS commands (such as "copy a file" or "print a file") called a **job control specification**. Once an OS begins to execute a job, it executes all commands in the list in sequence. Users have no opportunity to interact with an executing job.

In the 1960s, batch jobs were entered into the machine as a deck of keypunched cards. Today, batch execution specifications use files (such as shell scripts in UNIX or Windows `autoexec.bat` files) to specify the command list. The OS reads the entire job description and then stages it for execution. When the resources required by the job become available, the OS executes it. After the job has completed, results are printed and returned to the user.

THE USER'S PERSPECTIVE

From the user's perspective, the job control specification defines all the requests necessary for the OS to perform an information processing task. For example, if the job is to produce a corporation's monthly invoices, the OS may have to execute a suite of program executions to produce the invoices: one process to accumulate sales in each division, another process to determine the invoice amounts, a third process to update the company's accounts payable information, and so on. These programs operate on information contained in files rather than information supplied by an interactive user so there is no need for human interaction with the job while it is running. Each user prepares a job, and then the jobs are collected into a batch and submitted to the computer (see Figure 1.10). After the computer has finished executing the batch, it produces a batch of output listings (one for each job). The output listing is given to the user to reflect the result of running their job.

✦ FIGURE 1.10   Batch Processing System

A batch processing system handles jobs a batch-at-a-time. An input spooler groups jobs into a batch, then sends the batch to the computer. As the computer completes jobs, it writes each job's output to the output spool. The output spool is printed and the job results are returned to the end user.

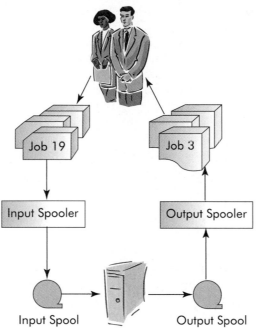

Modern operating systems do not use the pure batch OS strategy in which jobs are copied from an input device into a system queue for processing. Nevertheless, the idea of a noninteractive job is still useful. In this case, the user prepares a job control specification as a list of OS commands (stored in a file). The user then directs the OS to execute the commands in the file, causing the "job" to be executed without user interaction. Many contemporary applications are well suited to this style of batch processing, since they do not require any human interaction as they are executed. For example, monthly invoices are still prepared this way. Other batch applications include printing payroll checks, updating telephone directories, or collecting and analyzing seismic data.

BATCH PROCESSING TECHNOLOGY

In a batch system, an input **spooling** component reads each job and saves it in the current batch of jobs (again see Figure 1.10). The earliest systems used punched card input and a separate spooling computer for creating the batch. The jobs were saved onto a magnetic tape, and then the tape was mounted on the main computer. The main computer then read jobs from the input batch tape, executed them, and wrote the results to an output spool tape. After the job had executed on the main computer, the output spool tape was printed by another spooling computer. As systems got faster, the input and output spooling operations could be performed by I/O subsystems on the main computer, and the batch could be saved on a disk instead of magnetic tape.

The OS uses scheduling **policies** to determine the order to execute the jobs. Once the OS selects a job from the batch, it allocates a block of the computer's main memory to the job (called **medium-term scheduling**). After the job is allocated memory, it can begin to compete for the processor. When the processor becomes available, the processor scheduler (also called the **short-term scheduler**) selects a job currently loaded in the memory and allocates the processor to it.

A job can use the process only while it is loaded in the memory. When a job completes execution, its memory is released and the output for the job is copied to an output spool for later printing. In some batch systems, the OS preemptively releases the memory allocated to a job; this means that the job can no longer compete for the processor. Such systems are called **swapping systems** (swapping is also used in timesharing systems). The swapping policy might be to release the job's memory and move the contents to a disk device if the job has been a particularly heavy or particularly light user of the processor. In one strategy, a heavy processor user is penalized by swapping it out so that other programs can have more access to the processor. A light processor user might be swapped out because it is not using the processor very much. The rationale is that it should not tie up the memory resource while it is idle.

When batch processing was the dominant OS strategy, computers were primarily used to manage bulk information. Business data processing became a viable computer application domain, encouraging the development of file technology. Files are a natural abstraction of disk storage for batch processing systems because they provide a way to control collections of similar information (such as files of timecard records, trajectory data records, or personnel records). By creating and refining the file abstraction, programmers not only had a collection of information, they were also released from the obligation of knowing the details of disk I/O (see the example in Section 1.1).

Batch systems provided a major step forward in allowing multiple users to share a machine. However, multiprogrammed batch systems discouraged real-time interaction between the user and the computer—the user's intent was represented by the job control specification. In the systems predating batch systems, the user was able to sit at the system console and debug a program. In batch systems, programs could be debugged only by preparing a job, submitting it to the spooler, and then waiting for the job to be executed and returned. To aggravate the problem, batch system users were typically not allowed to enter their own jobs into the system or to remove the output from the line printer. In fact, the batch system might be located at some geographically distant point. It was not unusual for a professional programmer to have only two opportunities a day to enter a job into the batch stream. Contrast that mode of software development with today's environment in which you can recompile and execute a program in seconds!

Batch Files

Contemporary operating systems such as UNIX and Windows support batch file processing. Even though the operating systems are interactive timesharing systems, a user can prepare a batch file with a set of commands that the OS will execute without user intervention. The simplest examples of batch files in DOS are the `config.sys` and `autoexec.bat` files. These files provide a list of commands to be executed when the computer begins operation.

Figure 1.11 shows a batch file (shell script) for a UNIX system. The batch file can be executed by a shell, causing each line in the file to be treated as a command to the OS. In the example, the first step is to compile a file named `menu.c`, producing a relocatable file named `menu.o`. The second line in the command file compiles a file named `driver.c` and links its relocatable object file with `menu.o` and the C library. The third line executes the file `driver` produced by the link edit execution by reading the input file named `test_data` and writing the output file named `test_out`. The fourth line prints the `test_out` file to a printer named `thePrinter`. The fifth line produces a tar file named `driver_test.tar` that contains the source code and test output. The last line in the command file encodes the tar file and writes the result into a file named `driver_test.encode`.

◆ **FIGURE 1.11** A Shell Script Batch File for a UNIX System

A UNIX shell script is a batch file. It contains a series of commands (6 commands in this example) that can be read and then executed by the shell without human intervention.

```
cc -g -c menu.c
cc -g -o driver driver.c menu.o
driver < test_data > test_out
lpr -PthePrinter test_out
tar cvf driver_test.tar menu.c driver.c test_data test_out
uuencode driver_test.tar driver_test.tar >driver_test.encode
```

TIMESHARING SYSTEMS

Timesharing systems began to become popular in the 1970s. Their goal was to enable many users to interact with the computer system at the same time, each using his or her own terminal keyboard and display device. This strategy was the first step in making the computer available to many people who were involved in many different types of information processing tasks. Before this time, computers were used by a very small number of computer specialists.

There were four early systems that defined the timesharing OS strategy:

■ **CTSS, the Compatible Time Sharing System.** CTSS was developed in the mid-1960s at MIT [Corbato, et al., 1962]. It was the vehicle that supported the first research on radical multiprogramming scheduling algorithms (radical when compared to those in existence at that time) and modern memory-management techniques.

- **Multics** [Organick, 1972]. Multics replaced CTSS soon after it became operational. Prior to the deployment of Multics, operating systems were usually unreliable, sporadically crashing for no apparent reason. Multics was explicitly designed to be highly reliable. It was also the leading edge system (of its time) in experimentation with virtual memory, protection, and security.

- **Cal.** The Cal timesharing system was designed and implemented about the same time as CTSS and Multics [Sturgis, 1973]. This system focused on generic time-sharing technology, protection, and security.

- **UNIX.** AT&T Bell Labs designers had been associated with Multics, but wished to have a simpler OS to manage a small laboratory computer, so they developed UNIX in 1970. The early contribution of UNIX was in the "small is beautiful" OS design philosophy. UNIX demonstrated the idea of creating a tiny OS **kernel** with minimum functionality, but capable of supporting a very broad class of OS services executing as application programs. While CTSS, Multics, and Cal disappeared years ago, UNIX is still a leading operating system technology (with much updating over the years).

THE USER'S PERSPECTIVE

Batch systems forced the user to carefully plan how a job was to be executed before the job was ever submitted to the computer. Timesharing systems follow a philosophy whereby the user can establish a session with the system—called "logging onto/into" the system—and then decide which command to process immediately before it is executed. During execution, the user interacts directly with the OS and the process, supplying information in response to the program's read statements and seeing the direct result of the program's write statements. This encouraged users to experiment with information, for example, to attack decision support problems by testing different "what if" scenarios. The computer could be harnessed for a whole new kind of information processing work that was not cost-effective in the earlier noninteractive systems.

The description of the multiprogrammed abstract machines in Figure 1.5 also describes the user's perspective of a timeshared OS. A timesharing system uses multiprogramming, but it *also* allows its users to interact with executing programs (see Figure 1.12). As in multiprogramming, each abstract machine is a simulation of real hardware, but a user interacts with the computer by typing a command to the abstract machine on an abstract system console and receiving results back from the machine as soon as the command is executed.

Timesharing systems focus on policies to implement equitable processor sharing. This allows users to treat the machine as if they have exclusive control of a comparatively slow computer—the abstract machine. As long as the timesharing system does not become overloaded, the relative response time is usually so small that no user ever perceives any comparative slowness in the computer's performance.

TIMESHARING TECHNOLOGY

A timesharing OS uses multiprogramming to support multiple abstract machines. However, the scheduling and memory allocation strategies of timesharing systems differ significantly from those used for batch systems. Whereas batch systems attempted to optimize the number of jobs that could be processed in an hour, a timesharing system attempts to provide

✦ FIGURE 1.12 Timesharing Systems

Timesharing systems are multiprogramming systems that allow the end user to interact with the computer between any two OS commands. Timesharing systems are interactive computers.

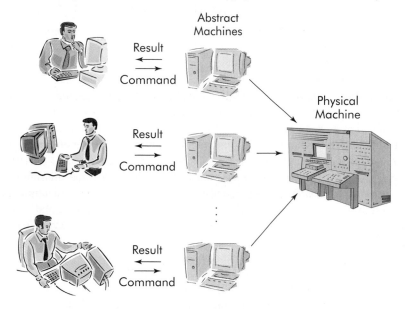

equitable amounts of processor and memory resources to each abstract machine. A timesharing system uses different resource allocation policies than does a batch system.

As timesharing environments evolved, they caused designers to distinguish between the notion of a job and that of a program in execution, since a timesharing user might implicitly or explicitly execute two different programs at the same time. This thinking led directly to the notion of a process as any "program in execution." A timesharing user might run two or more processes at any given time, while a batch job would execute only one program at a time on behalf of the job. For example, in timesharing environments, one process might be translating a document from one format to another, at the same time another process is reading a mail file. As timesharing evolved, processes were sometimes called **tasks**. A timesharing multiprogramming system that supports multiple processes per user is sometimes called a **multitasking** system.

While all multiprogrammed machines support multiple users, timesharing systems highlight the importance of establishing barriers and safeguards among the users and their processes. This is partly due to the fact that timesharing systems allow many processes to exist at once, while only a few exist at a time in a batch system. Without barriers between processes, one process might inadvertently damage the memory image of another process. The barriers put into place to ensure memory protection also make information sharing between two jobs more difficult to support, since the two jobs must override the memory protection scheme. The protection barriers also extend into the file system shared by the users. In many cases, it is desirable for a user to create files that are not to be written to by other users and sometimes not even to be read by other users. Protection and security became major issues in the early days of timesharing, even though these issues apply equally to batch systems.

The UNIX Timesharing System

The UNIX operating system was introduced to the public in a research paper in 1974 [Ritchie and Thompson, 1974]. UNIX was developed by two researchers at AT&T Bell Laboratories who were dissatisfied with the OS on their research computers. UNIX established two new trends in OS design: Previous operating systems were huge software packages—typically the largest software package that ran on the computer—and they were designed for a specific hardware platform—the OS was provided by the computer manufacturer. *By contrast, UNIX was intended to be a small, no-frills OS that could be ported to any small computer.* Also, the UNIX philosophy was that the OS, called the kernel, should provide the minimum essential functionality, and that new functionality should be added (as user programs) only as needed. UNIX was revolutionary, and by 1980, it had become the preferred OS by programmers in multivendor hardware environments (universities, research laboratories, and system software development organizations).

Even though the UNIX kernel could be ported onto a new hardware platform without redeveloping the entire OS, there was a different barrier to the wide use of the OS. The source code was owned by AT&T Bell Laboratories, and could only be used by acquiring a license. Other organizations could obtain a license (for example, to port UNIX onto their preferred computer hardware) by paying a fee to AT&T. By 1980, many universities and research labs had obtained the source code and were busily modifying it to meet their own needs, the most prominent work being done at the University of California at Berkeley under a Defense Advanced Research Projects Agency (DARPA) research contract. Commercial computer vendors had also begun to use the UNIX source code to derive their own version of the UNIX operating system.

By 1985, there were two primary versions of UNIX (running on many different hardware platforms): the main line version from AT&T Bell Labs (called System V UNIX) and an alternative version from the University of California at Berkeley (called BSD UNIX). The DEC VAX version of BSD UNIX was referred to as Version 4 BSD UNIX, or simply 4.x BSD UNIX. Both versions implemented system call interfaces that were recognizable as UNIX, although they differed from one another in several details. There were, however, substantial differences in the way the two OS kernels were implemented. The competition between System V and BSD UNIX systems was very active, with programmers swearing by one version or the other. Ultimately, the leading commercial proponent of 4.x BSD UNIX (Sun Microcomputers) and AT&T reached a business agreement by which these two leading versions would be merged into a common version of UNIX (the Sun Solaris operating system).

Meanwhile, other computer makers pushed for an alternative implementation of the UNIX system call interface. An important event was the formation of a committee to develop a standardized UNIX system call interface—**POSIX.1.** (This system call interface is often simply called "POSIX," although that can be misleading since the POSIX committee also developed several other APIs and only one of these standards addresses the kernel system call interface. In this book we consider only POSIX.1, so we generally use the more popular, but less accurate, designation of "POSIX" to refer to the POSIX.1 system call interface.) Once POSIX had been established, developers were free to design and build their own kernels that provided the functionality specified by this API. For example, at Carnegie Mellon University, a group of OS researchers led by Richard Rashid developed the Mach operating system with a POSIX/UNIX system call interface (see Section 19.4). Mach was an alternative to the 4.x BSD and System V UNIX kernel implementations. A version of Mach was used as the basis of the Open Systems Foundation OSF-1 kernel, which is the basis of the Macintosh OS X system. The trend had been set whereby various open source implementations of UNIX (such as Linux and FreeBSD) subsequently appeared. Eventually, software developers began to use these open source implementations, and the licensed UNIX source code barrier began to disappear.

The UNIX command line interpreter—the Bourne shell—also established an important trend in the way users could interact with the OS. The fundamental ideas that were developed and implemented in the Bourne shell are almost universal in text-based human-computer interfaces (see the first Laboratory Example in Chapter 2).

UNIX was created after CTSS, Multics, and Cal research systems, so it benefited considerably from the exploration done in these pioneering systems. It was built on a notion of supporting many processes and the need for a high degree of interaction with the end user. UNIX was a testbed for refining the fundamental OS concepts of reconfigurable devices, abstract machines, security, and virtual memory.

By the mid-1980s, UNIX was established as the dominant timesharing OS, as well as an important OS for workstations.

PERSONAL COMPUTERS AND WORKSTATIONS

The Apple II was launched in April 1977, and the IBM Personal Computer was released in August 1981. For the next decade, personal computer system software was generally designed to allow one user to execute one program at a time—no multiprogramming. Because there was no multiprogramming, there was no requirement for resource isolation or sharing. The primary requirement for system software was to provide hardware abstraction. Apple provided a set of functions (that later became the Toolbox), and the IBM Personal Computer provided its own device abstraction software (the IBM Basic Input/Output System, **BIOS**). Both Apple and IBM stored their abstraction software in a **read-only memory** (**ROM**) so that it would always be present when the machine was powered up. That is, a ROM is an internal memory device that has the property that information can be stored in it, and the information will persist even when the computer is powered down. These early personal computers disappeared by 1990, although the idea of the IBM BIOS abstraction software is still used in today's Intel-based microprocessors.

In 1982, Sun announced its first small computer. Various other manufacturers (such as HP, Apollo, and Three Rivers) also began delivering these "workstation" computers at about that time. A **workstation** was distinctly different from a personal computer (such as an IBM Personal Computer or an Apple II). Workstations were configured with enough resources that it made sense to use timesharing OS technology, especially multiprogramming, for their OS. Almost all workstations eventually used some form of UNIX.

By 1990, there were three distinct small computer camps: Apple personal computers (the Macintosh was announced 1984), IBM Personal Computers, and UNIX workstations. The competition was ferocious between the two personal computer camps, although the workstations were generally considered to be a different breed of cat. By 1995, personal computer hardware had become so sophisticated that these machines began to compete with workstations. Meanwhile, Microsoft upgraded its OS offerings with Windows NT and Windows 95. The new competition was between IBM-compatible personal computers (IBM had turned its attention to other types of computers) and workstations. Today, there is no real distinction between a personal computer and a workstation. Most of the principles and concepts described in this book exist in operating systems for contemporary personal computers and workstations.

THE USER'S PERSPECTIVE

Personal computers and workstations gave users new freedom in computing, which changed the way people perceived the computer. Rather than viewing it as an ominous corporate resource, people began to think of it as a tool for accomplishing everyday work, similar to a telephone, typewriter, or photocopier. As personal productivity tools such as word processors, desktop publishing systems, spreadsheets, and personal databases evolved, the single-user computer became deeply entrenched in corporations.

OS TECHNOLOGY

The trend toward single-user computers began with the development of personal computers that could be placed directly in the office rather than in a special computer room. Minicomputers, which first began to appear in the 1970s, were the first instance of such a technology. The first minicomputers, such as the Digital Equipment PDP 8 and the Data General Nova, were very inexpensive and easy to install in any location (compared with conventional computers of the day, which required air conditioning and special power). Minicomputers were very popular in the 1980s, since they could be used as both personal computers (usually for software development), and small timesharing machines. The Digital Equipment PDP-11 minicomputer was a favorite hardware platform for UNIX— both as a personal software development machine and as a small timesharing machine. Ultimately, the PDP-11 evolved into the highly popular Digital Equipment VAX timesharing computer [Levy and Eckhouse, 1989], probably the most widely used timesharing computer in the 1980s.

At the same time that minicomputers were becoming larger, smaller machines— **microcomputers**—began to evolve from minicomputer technology. The fundamental element of a microcomputer is a single integrated-circuit implementation of a processor. Early microcomputers such as the Intel 8008 were built with 8-bit processor chips with clock rates of around 1 million cycles per second (1 MHz). By comparison, contemporary microcomputers employ 32-bit (or even 64-bit) microprocessors with clock rates exceeding 2,500 MHz (2.5 GHz). Personal computers and workstations both use microcomputers as their processors.

The first personal computers incorporated the barest essentials of an operating system (such as the IBM BIOS). These ROM-based "operating systems" provided a few routines to control the personal computer's devices. Soon, ROM-based systems were enhanced by additional OS software, usually to manage files, that could be loaded from a disk into the computer's readable/writable **random access memory (RAM)**. The most popular of the early personal computer operating systems was CP/M, which was ultimately displaced by Microsoft MS-DOS (or the IBM version, PC-DOS). These operating systems extended the device abstraction software by providing a file system.

Personal computers with MS-DOS eventually dominated other operating system products in the commercial marketplace. Today, many personal computers use Microsoft's follow-on operating systems, Windows 95/98/Me and Windows NT/2000/XP. The major contribution of MS-DOS (to OS technology) was that it popularized computing and offered flexibility in configuring parts of the OS when the machine was initialized.

Workstation hardware was originally more flexible and faster than personal computer hardware. Workstations used hardware that was quite similar to minicomputers of the day (such as the PDP-11). They typically incorporated more resources than a personal computer. For example, they had more memory, a faster, more powerful processor, larger disk storage, and higher-resolution graphics monitors for the console. Because of the resource configurations, workstations required a more complex OS than MS-DOS to manage those resources.

Although UNIX was designed as a timesharing system, its multiprogramming support as well as the extensibility of function fit naturally into the workstation environment, particularly when the workstation was used for software development. UNIX grew with the workstation (and minicomputer) market. As the market called for graphics support, UNIX incorporated means to support high-resolution graphics. Similarly, as network protocols became important to workstation technology, UNIX began to accommodate network protocols. Now that personal computer and workstation hardware are indistinguishable, either the evolved personal computer operating systems or UNIX can be used as the machine's OS.

CONTRIBUTIONS TO MODERN OS TECHNOLOGY

Personal computers and workstations stimulated tremendous growth in system software to support personal computing tools. This demand in turn caused the interests of OS developers and human-computer interface developers to converge, for example, in creating effective point-and-select interfaces. The Sun OpenWindows/NeWS window systems and the X/Motif window systems are deeply rooted in system software technology (and implementation). Interest in this class of machines also stimulated new OS developments to support multiple sessions and virtual terminals.

The Microsoft Windows OS Family

The first Microsoft OS was MS-DOS. Its purpose was primarily device abstraction, as the first personal computers were not envisioned to be multiprogrammed computers. Today, the BIOS used with Intel processor computers still reflects the remnants of the MS-DOS device abstraction. MS-DOS was the dominant OS for personal computers until the mid 1990s, when it was gradually replaced by more modern operating systems—usually a newer Microsoft OS.

Contemporary Microsoft operating systems—called the family of *Windows operating systems*—export their own subset of a single system call interface, the *Win32 API* (see Figure 1.13). This API is large and dynamic. In the year 2000, the Win32 API contained about 2,000 different functions ranging from ones to create a process to others that query a performance counter. Different members of the Windows OS family implement different subsets of the Win32 API. Windows NT/2000/XP implements all functions on the API,

Windows 95/98/Me implemented about three-quarters of the functions on the API, and Windows CE (also known as Pocket PC) implements about a quarter of the functions.

The rationale for basing all OS APIs on a single API relates to application portability among the family members: If all Microsoft operating systems implement different nested subsets of the same API, then an application writer would be able to produce application software that would work without change on several OS versions. By having different Windows family members implement nested subsets of the API, the family implements upward compatibility. For example, an application written for Windows CE would work without modification on Windows Me and Windows XP, and an application written for Windows Me would work on Windows XP. In addition, enhancements to any of the OS products can still provide the same services (presumably of a better quality) via the same, fixed interface. The cost of adopting this strategy is the necessity of establishing and maintaining a concrete definition of the API. The implementations of Win32 API functions by Windows 98/Me differ little from Windows NT/2000/XP implementations of the same functions. However, since Windows CE is aimed at hardware such as palmtop computers and television set-top boxes, its variant of the Win32 API does have some significant differences from the "mainstream" API.

✦ FIGURE 1.13 The Microsoft OS Family

There are three different members of the Microsoft OS family: Windows CE is the smallest member, and exports the smallest part of the full Win32 API. Windows 95/98/Me is a larger system, exporting about 75% of the total Win32 API functions. Windows NT/2000/XP is the largest family member, which implements the full Win32 API.

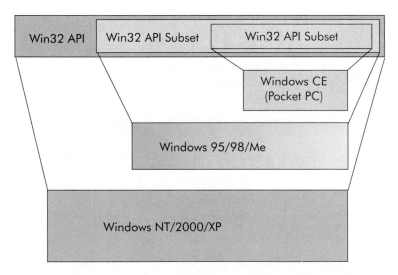

WINDOWS XP, 2000, AND WINDOWS NT

Windows NT development began in the late 1980s and the OS was first released for public use (as Version 3.1) in July 1993 [Solomon and Russinovich, 2000]. Version 4.0 was released in July 1996. Version 5.0 was renamed Windows 2000 and released in 2000.

Windows XP uses the same Windows NT code base, along with code from Windows 98; it was released in October 2001. In this book, "Windows NT" refers to any version of the operating systems built from the Windows NT code base, including Windows 2000 and XP. If a discussion refers to a particular version, that will be noted.

Windows NT is the flagship Windows OS family. Its Windows NT Executive (the OS) and the Win32 Subsystems (complementary system software) implement all functions on the Win32 API. It is the most complex member of the OS family.

WINDOWS 95/98/ME

Windows 98 is an updated release of Windows 95, and Windows Me is an updated release of Windows 98. Windows 95/98/Me was the workhorse OS until 2001. Since that time, many personal computers have begun to use Windows NT/2000/XP.

Windows 95/98/Me differs from Windows NT in that it implements fewer Win32 API functions. Windows NT supports a comprehensive security model that is not part of Windows 95/98/Me. Many of the extra functions are references to parts of the kernel security system. The network support in Windows 95/98/Me is also a subset of the Windows NT functionality. The other major difference is in the virtual memory implementation. Windows NT allows application programs to manipulate various parameters that influence the behavior of the virtual memory manager, while that is not possible using Windows 95/98/Me.

WINDOWS CE

Windows CE (Consumer Electronics) is the smallest member of the family. It was developed to address the emerging small computer market, and is introduced later in this section.

EMBEDDED SYSTEMS

An embedded system is a computer that is a component in some more complex system. It is dedicated to the support of its host system. Examples of embedded systems include computers that control the floodgates of a dam, control the cooling process of a nuclear reactor, guide a missile, control a point-of-sale terminal, and even regulate a residential sprinkler system. Embedded systems have been commercially successful for many years, but they reached new levels of popularity with the introduction of large-scale integrated circuits in the 1970s and 1980s. Today, they are an important aspect of computer technology.

THE USER'S PERSPECTIVE

Embedded systems do not have a human user. Instead, the system's "user" is a set of sensors and actuators. The original motivation for embedded systems was an economic argument based on implementation costs: It was less expensive to design an electronic subassembly so that it used a computer and software, than to implement the subassembly using only hardware. Disk controllers are a good example of this approach. A disk controller can be implemented completely in hardware logic, or it can be implemented as a combination of some hardware logic controlled by a tiny computer. Today, almost all disk controllers use an embedded system. One benefit of this approach is that the same controller hardware can be used to implement various controller strategies (such as SCSI and IDE). It also allows the disk manufacturer to change the behavior of the controller by just providing a new program for the embedded computer!

OS TECHNOLOGY

Embedded system OS requirements differ dramatically from one application of the technology to another because the computer the system controls is really just a component in some larger system. However, commercial embedded system OS developers focus on processor scheduling (especially real-time scheduling), minimizing the amount of memory and processor cycles used by the OS, and designing the OS so that all the software running on it uses as little electrical power as possible.

Real-time computing is based on the idea that the "user" (a collection of hardware sensors and actuators) is required to receive a guaranteed response time for any request to perform work. For example, a sensor detects an increase in a reactor's core temperature, so the embedded system must send a signal to an actuator to enable the reactor cooler within a small, fixed amount of time. This real-time constraint poses two challenging problems:

- How to guarantee that the response time will not exceed some maximum value.
- How to achieve a minimum response time.

Real-time systems technology is driven by such response-time guarantees. Many real-time applications specify a "soft" deadline rather than a hard one. Soft deadlines are like late homework policies: If the deadline is a hard deadline, there is no point on working on a homework assignment after its due date. But if the deadline is soft so that you can get partial credit for late homework, then you might decide that it is worth completing an assignment even though it is late. In the soft real-time world, we say that the OS should make its *best effort* to meet the deadline, but if it fails to meet the deadline, the system should continue to provide service rather than abandoning the service request due to failure.

Sometimes an embedded system has only a single purpose: to run a single application program. If there is often only one application in the embedded system, it may not be necessary to implement resource isolation and sharing among concurrent processes. Instead, the main purpose of the OS will then be to provide hardware resource abstractions. In this case, the designer may decide to implement the resource management as part of the application. This would be done to avoid performance penalties associated with interactions between the application program and the OS. As a result, it reduces the amount of machine resource used by the OS, leaving more for the application.

Contemporary embedded systems are often concerned with the amount of power the processor is consuming at any given moment. For example, if the embedded system is part of a battery-operated unit, the less power the embedded system uses, the more power available to the rest of the overall system. Contemporary embedded systems are built to operate properly when various devices are spontaneously powered down during "normal" operation. This might mean that disks, displays, sensors, or actuators are temporarily powered down, although the embedded system should continue to operate.

CONTRIBUTIONS TO MODERN OS TECHNOLOGY

Embedded system techniques tend to trade off generality of operation for efficiency in order to ensure that real-time processing constraints are met. Designers of other classes of operating systems commonly use techniques employed in embedded systems when raw performance or some form of real-time processing is the goal.

Core real-time technology is also used to address quality of service (QoS) issues in other operating systems. For example, application processes may require that information be delivered over a network in a prescribed amount of time or with a minimized deviation in its delivery rate (minimized "jitter"). The solutions to these requirements are difficult, and they are the subject of considerable effort in contemporary real-time operating system designs.

VxWorks

The Wind Rivers VxWorks runtime environment and operating system earned a strong reputation as an OS for embedded systems (see http://www.windriver.com/). The OS component of the product is the *wind microkernel* with a complementary, configurable core OS (see Figure 1.14). An embedded system designer decides which parts of an OS are desired for the particular system, and then configures the core OS so that it includes only the OS functions that are needed.

✦ FIGURE 1.14 VxWorks Organization

VxWorks is a modular OS, based on the wind microkernel. The Configurable Core OS Extension provides software that uses the microkernel to implement an operational OS. The runtime system and applications run on top of the OS extensions.

Applications
VxWorks Runtime System
VxWorks Configurable Core OS Extension
Wind Microkernel

The microkernel handles multiprogramming, interrupts, and scheduling. This part of the OS is able to implement the real-time support that is required at the application layer. The core OS augments the microkernel functionality by providing optional facilities for message passing, shared memory, network support, graphics support, Java support, synchronization, and so on. This extreme flexibility enables the OS to be configured so that it uses very little memory (Wind Rivers says the OS can be configured to run on a "few kilobytes of memory") although such a minimal system would provide little functionality to applications.

SMALL, COMMUNICATING COMPUTERS

Advances in chip technology and the ubiquity of the Internet have been the catalyst for a revolution in computing devices. The demand for consumer electronics has provided the incentive for the rapid commercial development of a whole new class of **small, communicating computers** (**SCC**s). Many of these devices are used for specific tasks—from portable MP3 players, to Internet-capable mobile phones, to TV set-top boxes that digitize and store television programming. Mobile computers—small computers with a wireless network connection—are an important subclass of SCCs. Even though the devices differ widely, many of the underlying OS concepts are the same. Perhaps surprisingly, many fundamental OS concepts are the same for SCCs as for desktop and server machines. However, there are marked differences in implementation philosophy because of the scarcity of certain resources (for example, memory, network bandwidth, and/or power) in an SCC.

THE USER'S PERSEPECTIVE

An SCC OS is responsible for the same requirements as any other OS (provide hardware abstractions and manage sharing). The differences between an SCC OS and an OS for a larger machine are:

■ SCC devices are different from conventional machine devices, so the hardware abstractions for an SCC need to be different from those used in conventional machines.

■ The SCC's implementation of the different hardware abstractions differs from conventional OS implementations due to the relatively constrained resources in an SCC.

■ A family of similar SCCs will use the same basic OS, but the resource constraint may require that different members of the family use different abstract machine policies, depending on the specifics of the physical SCC. For example, VxWorks can be used as the OS for an SCC. The OS should support flexible configuration and policies.

■ SCCs may appear as some form of embedded system. In the simplest case, the SCC is a player for streaming media being delivered over the network connection. Traditional operating systems generally do not use real-time techniques for resource management, whereas it is often necessary in an SCC.

■ Since SCCs are the foundation of new computing environments such as Internet appliances, it is likely that the OS will need to adapt to different computing paradigms such as rapid evolution toward web browsers as OS and interpreted execution.

OS TECHNOLOGY

SCC requirements encourage the evolution of OS technology. There has been a steady move toward thread-based computing in modern operating systems. Thread-based computing changes several basic assumptions about the OS design: The barriers between executing threads are different than the barriers between processes. Because thread-based computing uses fewer system resources than does process-based computing, SCCs are designed around thread computation rather than process computation.

Streaming media support is important in all modern computer systems. Its support is nearly mandatory in an SCC. This is because SCCs contain little or limited amounts of device storage. A technology challenge for the SCC OS is to adjust the abstract machine philosophy so that the OS can provide adequate support for soft real-time data delivery.

Conventional operating systems are designed with the understanding that when the applications jointly request more resources than are available in the computer, the OS has a fixed, best effort policy for allocating the resources. The policy is determined at the time that the OS is designed, and is independent of the environment in which the computer is being used. In SCC operating systems, the system will frequently be oversubscribed. However, it will be unacceptable for the OS to use a best effort resource allocation policy, as it will create a situation in which the OS is working at odds with the purpose of the computer. Future SCC operating systems will need to be designed to make use of application knowledge in using a particular resource allocation policy.

SCCs operate in situations where resource management is more challenging than in conventional systems. For example, an SCC in a mobile computer is required to conserve as much battery power as possible, since the amount of time the battery can sustain system operation is a limiting factor on the overall utility of the computer. The resource management strategy should be able to cope with devices that spontaneously power down, and perhaps even include strategies to determine that devices should be powered down (or configured to run using less power).

In a mobile computing environment, a network connection may not be available at certain times during the machine's operation. Alternatively, the characteristics of the network may vary with time—sometimes a wireless signal is strong and the bandwidth is high, while at other times, the signal is weak and the bandwidth is correspondingly lower. SCC resource management strategies need to be able to adapt to dynamic resource availability.

Finally, SCCs will not be used in an isolated environment. Modern computing is at the convergence of many traditional businesses: telecommunications, entertainment broadcasting, real-time command and control, Internet information delivery, and others. This is a result of the change in the business climate in the real world, and the wide use of information for a person's everyday life. Any computer that will operate in this confluence of businesses will have to deal with a broad range of network protocols, network server information delivery paradigms, content caching, and so on. An OS for an SCC that will be used in the emerging commercial world will be required to deal with this wide variety of protocols and behaviors.

SCC OS technology is in its early stages—but not too early to begin studying it. There are a number of proprietary operating systems that have been designed to be used with SCCs:

- VxWorks can be used for an SCC.

- Microsoft Windows Embedded and Windows CE (also known as Pocket PC) are especially designed for SCCs—see http://www.microsoft.com/windows/embedded/.

- The Palm Pilot OS was designed especially for PDAs, including the Palm Pilot, Handspring Visor, Sony CLIE, and others (see http://www.palmos.com). There is a large commercial following for this OS, including a substantial number of applications that use the abstract machine interface, and several different development systems.

- The Java Virtual Machine (JVM) can be considered to be an SCC OS. Generally, the JVM is implemented as an application on top of a host OS. However, there is nothing in its specification that prevents it from being implemented as a native OS.

Windows CE (Pocket PC)

Windows CE—also called Pocket PC when it is used with PDAs—grew out of two Microsoft development projects that did not culminate in products: Microsoft-at-Work and Pulsar. Both projects had their own OS effort even though their operating systems had similar requirements, and a corporate decision was made to design a new OS that could meet the requirements of both projects. The original Windows CE OS was an object-oriented (OO) OS, but as the OO system was being developed, a small group of CE designers created an alternative OS kernel that implemented a subset of Win32 API—the "new kernel" or simply "nk" [Murray, 1998]. The nk kernel ultimately became the Windows CE OS.

Windows CE goals differ considerably from those that drove Windows NT. For example, Windows NT was required to support legacy OS interfaces; thus, it had to execute MS-DOS, Win16, and even OS/2 applications on Windows NT. Windows CE is not required to support any legacy software since it is directed at an application domain that is distinct from all previous Microsoft operating systems. However, Windows CE was designed to be implemented on a spectrum of different hardware platforms. As a result, it employs a hardware abstraction layer called the OEM abstraction layer (OAL).

Version 1.0 Windows CE was implemented to work on a handheld PC. Version 2 and later are modular systems that can be configured (like VxWorks) using a Platform Builder tool. That is, rather than recompile the OS for different hardware configurations, different sets of OS components can be combined to create different versions of the OS that are tailored for use with handheld PCs, automotive computers, game computers, cable set-top boxes, and so on.

An OS for a consumer electronic device is not normally expected to provide the same level of graphics and network support as is required in a desktop system. Windows CE

✦ FIGURE 1.15 Windows CE Organization

Windows CE is built on top of an OEM Abstraction Layer so that it will be easy to port the OS from one hardware platform to another. The OS is composed of a kernel, device drivers, an object store, and network and communication services. The graphics, window manager, and event manager are logically distinct from the rest of the OS, but are considered to be part of the Windows CE OS.

Shells and Applications			
Win32 API (& Network Extensions)			
Kernel	Object Store	Network and Communication Services	Graphics, Window Manager, and Event Manager
	Device Drivers		
OEM Abstraction Layer			

does not support the full set of graphics, window management, and network functions that are defined in Win32 API (that is, that are implemented in Windows NT). This greatly simplifies the design of Windows CE.

Windows CE is designed to be used as an embedded system [Murray, 1998]. Embedded system applications often require that the OS guarantee that it can provide certain types of service before a given deadline. This influences the design of Windows CE's interrupt handling, device driver and thread scheduling designs so that they differ considerably from the approach taken in Windows NT.

NETWORKS

The popularity of personal computers and workstations led to a high demand for systems that can perform nontrivial local computing and also use information stored at another computer accessible via a high-speed network. Today, system software is highly focused on supporting the use of individual computers interconnected via local area networks and wide area networks. Resource isolation, sharing, and abstraction for local and remote resources provide a new challenge for system software designers and essentially define the leading edge of contemporary research in the area.

Until 1980, computers were generally interconnected with point-to-point, bit-serial communication media that operated at speeds of less than 10 kilobits per second (Kbps). If an operator needed to interconnect more than two machines, then either a fully connected network of point-to-point connections was used or machines were interconnected with a routing network. (In a routing network, a logical "path" exists between any pair of machines. Each machine must be able to forward information to other machines so that all machines collectively implement a logical network that behaves as if it were fully connected.)

Local area networks (LANs) became a cost-effective communication technology at about the same time personal computers and workstations began to evolve. In 1980, both Ethernet and Token Ring LAN technology provided a fully connected network capable of transmitting 10 to 16 megabits per second (Mbps)—three orders of magnitude faster than point-to-point forwarding networks. These LANs enabled small machines to be interconnected, both among themselves and to large machines, at relatively high-speed connections and at reasonably low costs. The result was a revolution in the way computing was accomplished in all organizations.

Since 2000, wireless network technology has emerged as an important communication technology. Wireless technology depends on the availability of a range of broadcast spectrum that is not being used by other broadcast technologies (such as radio, television, satellite, and so on). There is a public band that can be used by anyone (2–5 GHz band). Draft communication standards exist for two popular wireless LANs in this band: the IEEE 802.11b ("WiFi") and IEEE 802.15 ("Bluetooth"). These wireless networks are intended to operate in a small physical area (a sphere with a radius less than 100 feet), and to transmit packets of information at 11 Mbps. Since their introduction, they have had an enormous impact on the nature of computing devices, particularly SCCs. Newer, faster, more secure wireless networks continue to be introduced. For example, the IEEE 802.11a network is similar to the IEEE 802.11b, but it is orders of magnitude faster. The next generation of computers and operating systems will be influenced by wireless network technology.

Software technology has been stimulated by the presence of inexpensive computer hardware and network bandwidth. This is leading to a new, rapidly evolving, approach to large-grained, loosely coupled distributed computation. Today, network disk servers, file servers, print servers, database servers, communications servers, and others are commonplace in 10–100Mbps LAN installations. There are even higher-speed networks (1,000Mbps) that are used to connect high-speed computers and subnetworks. The evolution of network computing has driven operating systems to evolve from timesharing and multiprogramming systems to ones that support network communication, distributed resource management strategies, new interprocess communication strategies, and new memory management strategies.

In the last several years, a new "killer application" has evolved for networks: web browsers that operate over the public Internet. The first wave of this new computing model enabled people to use a personal computer to search and access information on computers located all over the world. This was made possible because of network protocols, specifically the Internet Protocol (IP), the Transmission Control Protocol (TCP), and a protocol specially created for web browsing (HTTP). The dominance of web browsers and Internet content delivery is influencing OS technology, although it is too early to predict exactly what the long-term effect will be.

THE GENESIS OF MODERN OPERATING SYSTEMS

Modern operating systems evolved from all of the systems discussed in the previous sections: batch, timesharing, personal computer and workstation software, embedded systems, small computers, and operating systems for networks of computers (see Figure 1.16). They inherited multiprogramming technology from batch and timesharing systems. While protection and security first appeared in batch systems, both developed rapidly in timesharing environments. Human–computer interaction technology became an issue with timesharing systems, and continues to grow in importance with SCCs. The trend was accelerated with the dedicated memory and processors offered with personal computers and workstations. Users began to demand windows and other visually oriented technologies. The client-server network programming model (file servers, print servers, database servers, and so on) evolved from systems that supported network communications. Embedded systems have influenced real-time management, synchronization approaches, scheduling, and data movement in modern operating systems.

1.3 ● SUMMARY

Computer purchases are justified by the functionality provided by application software. If the application software is not effective, the entire computer system is not effective. The system software and hardware are transparent to the end user—the person using the application software to process information—so they provide no direct value to that end user. Rather, they are intended to support the programmer.

System software abstracts the interface to resources so that they are easy for application programmers to use. In particular, the OS allows applications to time-multiplex the processor (and space-multiplex the memory) to create an illusion of parallel execution called *multiprogramming*. The existence of multiprogramming encourages us to think about a program application as a process. It also causes us to consider properties of

✦ FIGURE 1.16 The Evolution of Modern Operating Systems

Modern operating systems have evolved from batch systems, timesharing systems, personal computer and workstation software, embedded systems, and networks of computers.

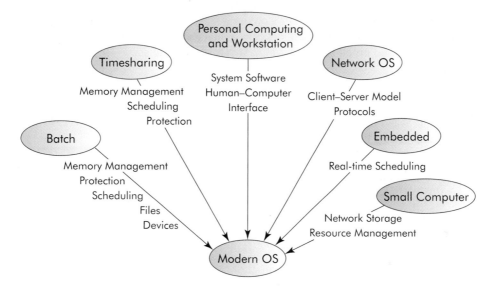

abstract parallel process execution, called *concurrent execution*. Specifically, the OS manages resources so that they can be used exclusively by a process or shared among a community of cooperating processes.

Operating systems have evolved from single-user computers to batch multiprogramming systems, to timesharing systems, to personal computers and workstations interconnected with networks, to embedded systems and SCCs. Batch multiprogramming systems introduced technology to support concurrency among jobs. Timesharing operating systems extended multiprogramming so that each job could have multiple processes executing on behalf of the user at any one time. Because of the proliferation of processes in timesharing systems, protection and security among processes and users became critical. Today, protection and security have continued to grow in importance due to the ubiquity of computers.

As a continuation of the introduction to operating systems, the next chapter considers the programmer's model of the abstract resources provided by system software in general, and the OS in particular.

1.4 • EXERCISES

1. Differentiate between an abstract resource and a physical resource. Give two examples of each.

2. What abstractions do the IBM PC BIOS routines provide to the Intel 8088 abstract machine that are not available by using the hardware directly? (*Hint*: In general terms, what is the difference between the commands you would have to execute to write a character to the display if you did not have BIOS?)

3. Suppose that you had a collection of "widgets," stored in a rectangular grid (like a table). You could reference the widget stored in the ith row, j^{th} column by using the ordered pair of numbers, (i, j). Describe how you could create a new set of widget addresses where each address is a single number. For example, instead of referring to the widget in row 12, column 30 using (12, 30), you might say that its address is 1230. (*Hint*: Think about how hotels number their rooms.) Notice that this is the same problem as abstracting a disk's track and sector into a single address.

4. In an object-oriented programming language like Java or C++, how can a program cause a value to be stored into a private variable inside of a different object? Another way to think about this is that if a class provides an abstraction for reading and writing its private variables, what is that abstraction?

5. Identify which of the following are examples of space-multiplexed sharing, and which are time-multiplexed sharing. If there is a sense that it could be either strategy, explain.

   a. The land in a residential subdivision

   b. A personal computer

   c. A whiteboard in a classroom

   d. A bench seat on a bus

   e. A single-user file in UNIX

   f. A printer on a timesharing system

   g. The heap in the C/C++ runtime system

6. Discuss some factors that must be considered in determining the maximum number of multiprogrammed processes for a particular system. You may assume a batch system with the same number of processes as jobs. (Several of these factors will be discussed in detail in later chapters.)

7. Suppose that a multiprogrammed system has a load of N processes with individual total execution times of $t_1, t_2, ..., t_N$. How would it be possible that the execution time could be as small as

   maximum($t_1, t_2, ..., t_N$)?

8. Suppose that a multiprogrammed system has a load of N processes with individual total execution times of $t_1, t_2, ..., t_N$. How would it be possible that

   $T > t_1 + t_2 + ... + t_N$?

   That is, what could cause the total execution time to exceed the sum of the individual process execution times?

9. When is batch processing the preferred strategy for work to be done by the computer? When is timesharing the preferred strategy?

10. How might a timesharing processor scheduler's policy differ from a policy used in a batch system?

11. What are some distinctions among Windows NT, Windows 2000, and Windows XP?

12. What are some distinctions between AT&T (System V) UNIX and BSD UNIX?

13. What is the relationship of POSIX.1 and Linux?

14. What is the purpose of the hardware abstraction layer in a Windows operating system?

15. How is a UNIX `makefile` similar to a batch file? How is it different from the control file described in the chapter?

16. What is the contribution of timesharing technology to contemporary operating systems?

17. What is the contribution of embedded systems technology to contemporary operating systems?

CHAPTER 2

Using the Operating System

This chapter describes an OS from the application programmer's perspective. You will learn the concepts underlying an OS system call interface, which act as a loose set of requirements for the design of the OS. If you are an experienced programmer, you will already know the nature of one or more OS interfaces. If you are still learning about programming, this chapter will provide a unifying view of the OS interface concepts you will need to know before you can make the most effective use of the computer. The discussion is organized as a conceptual description of how to use OS abstract machines, accompanied by practical examples for the UNIX and Windows abstract machines. It is important that you understand this conceptual model before proceeding, since the remainder of the book presumes this knowledge as it considers the internal OS design from the system designer/programmer's point of view.

2.1 • THE PROGRAMMER'S ABSTRACT MACHINE

Everything should be made as simple as possible, but not simpler.

Albert Einstein

A programmer's job is to create software that directs the computer hardware to perform specific information processing tasks for end users. Each end user's specific needs may vary considerably from those of other end users: The computer may be used for keeping personal records, performing corporate accounting, solving numerical computations, guiding spaceships, and so on. Application programmers create software that uses a general purpose computer to solve each of these specific information processing tasks in its specific application domain. The programmer must know enough about the application domain to be able to create effective solutions for the end user, and enough about how the computer works to be able to make efficient use of its features to construct the application program.

The OS defines a logical software environment on top of the hardware: the abstract machine idea introduced in Chapter 1. Like the abstractions Einstein had in mind, this one must be as simple as possible, yet still be powerful enough to allow the programmer to exploit the features of the underlying hardware. For example, an airplane pilot uses a complex abstract model for flying a jet airplane (see Figure 2.1). Although it would be nice if the pilot just had to know about steering, speed, and braking (like driving a car), the automobile driving model is too simple because it ignores altitude, the dynamics of flight when turning, and so on. The pilot's model is simplified, but still more complex than the automobile driver's model because it is harder to fly an airplane than to drive a car.

✦ FIGURE 2.1   The Airplane Pilot's Abstract Machine

A pilot has a complex instrument panel and set of controls for flying the airplane. The instruments tell the pilot things like the air speed, altitude, attitude (is the airplane level?), angle of climb/descent, angle of left/right bank, and so on. There are controls for each engine, thrust reversers, ailerons, flaps, landing gear, and many other parts.

Programmers rely on the conceptual tools in this environment to reduce the amount of detailed knowledge they must know in order to create application software. Further, since all modern computers use multiprogramming, the abstract machine environment must be sophisticated enough to support the idea of concurrent execution in a way that is easy for the programmer to understand and use. The reason for the concurrency abstraction is to provide an environment in which concurrent processes have exclusive access to system components—resource isolation—while being able to control the way that these resources are shared.

SEQUENTIAL COMPUTATION

Since the earliest days of application software, we have used the idea of **sequential computation**; algorithms are the basis of this approach to computation. An **algorithm** is a collection of instructions along with the sequential order in which they should be executed. For example, a sorting algorithm describes the steps to order an array of integers according to their respective values (smallest first, or largest first). Algorithms may be expressed in mathematical notation, pseudocode (code that "looks like" a programming language, but is used for human-human communication), and natural language (such as English). An algorithm has a single entry point where execution is to commence. Once the execution begins at the entry point, it continues sequentially according to the flow of control definition specified in the program. Statements are executed one after the other, with control flow altering the sequence using conditional branching (analogous to C `if-then-else` statements) and loop (analogous to `while` and `for` statements) constructs.

Algorithm languages are good for designing a solution, but usually omit detail or contain ambiguity. A programming language is used to encode an algorithm so that it is a complete, unambiguous expression of the algorithm. The resulting algorithm encoding is called a **source program**. There are many programming languages that can represent sequential algorithms (such as Java, C, and C++). Programming involves the creation of an algorithm and the encoding of that algorithm into a source programming language (see Figure 2.2).

✦ FIGURE 2.2 Algorithms, Programs, and Processes

Programmers create solutions by thinking of algorithms that will solve a problem. They then encode the algorithm into a source program. The source program is translated into a binary program that can be loaded and executed. In a multiprogramming environment, the binary program is loaded into a process abstract machine. The process abstraction collects the resources that the executing program will need and includes an execution engine to keep track of the progress of the process.

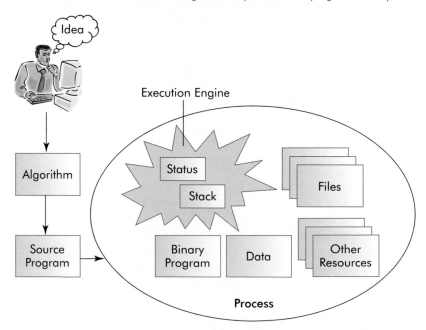

A development computer's system software includes translation tools that can convert a source program into a **binary program** (sometimes called the *object program*, *binary object program*, or *executable program*) representation. The binary program is another alternative representation of the original algorithm, a representation that can be directly executed by the computer hardware. The binary program uses a form of procedure call to invoke OS features. For example, to halt the algorithm, the process calls an OS procedure such as `exit()`; to read information from a file, the process calls an OS procedure such as `read()`; and so on. That is, the binary program contains only machine instructions, specifically including an instruction to call OS procedures.

The normal machine instructions such as add and multiply cause the hardware to perform a direct action. The OS procedure calls are used to abstract some of the operations of the hardware. For example, the `exit()` call enables the algorithm to terminate execution without affecting the actual operation of the computer hardware; we only want to halt the algorithm/program execution, not the computer. Similarly, the `read()` function enables an application program to perform an input operation from a hardware device, passing the resulting information back to the calling program as a result or parameter from the function call. The programmer should not have to know the details for reading a disk. The set of function calls implemented by any given software package is called its *application programming interface* (API); in most operating systems, the API to its software is referred to as the *system call interface*.

The other part of Figure 2.2 illustrates the idea of packaging sequential computation within the context of multiprogramming. Programmers write software with the explicit understanding that the statements in the program will be executed in a sequential fashion according to the semantics of the language used to write the program, even though the OS may time-multiplex the processor so that instructions from different programs may be interleaved in their execution. The OS ensures that the effect will be that multiple programs are in execution at one time (using time-multiplexed processor sharing).

Once a program has been constructed, the programmer knows that it can be run by:

1. Invoking a language-specific translation system
2. Providing data for the program
3. Directing the OS to begin executing at the main entry point
4. Continuing to execute the program statements according to the control specification

Sequential statement execution continues until the program halts, either implicitly by having the program control flow to the last statement in the program or explicitly by having the program call `exit()`.

The OS supports this programmer's view of program execution by defining processes: A program in execution is a classic **process**. In this refinement of the term (as it was introduced in Chapter 1), the process is the computational environment that includes the program, data, files, and other resources. It also includes an OS abstraction that we call an *execution engine* in the figure. The execution engine represents the part of the process that the OS uses to implement multiprogramming. This includes the OS's internal data structures to represent the current status of the process abstract machine execution and a copy of the process's runtime stack. (The stack contains C-style automatic variables, procedure return addresses, and so on—see your introductory programming book for more information.)

MULTITHREADED COMPUTATION

Sequential computation can be extended to allow multiple threads to execute a single program concurrently. The idea is a software version of teamwork: Suppose that an accountant in an office is supposed to organize all the company's invoices, check them against purchase orders, and then issue checks to pay the invoices. The accountant has a fixed procedure (analogous to a program) for doing this work. There is also specific data (the invoices and purchase orders) that the accountant must handle. The single accountant working in the accounting office is analogous to traditional sequential process execution. If we wanted to process invoices faster, we could hire another accountant. We might provide the new accountant with his or her own office, and then assign half the invoices to each accountant (see Figure 2.3(a)). However, both accountants will use the same procedure (program) and will reference the same purchase order file.

✦ FIGURE 2.3 Multithreaded Accountant

A thread in a process is like an accountant in an office. There is one executing entity in an environment. In (a) there are two accountants in two offices. They cannot easily share purchase orders. In (b) there is an accountant and his clone in one office—two executing entities in one environment.

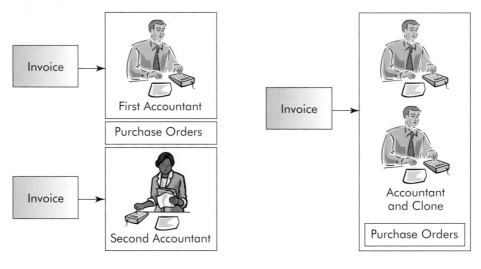

(a) Separate Processes   (b) One Process with Two Threads

Here is an alternative approach (very useful in software, but perhaps a little awkward in the accountant's office). Suppose we cloned the accountant and placed the clone in the same office as the original accountant (see Figure 2.3(b)). Now both accountants use the same procedure, the same pool of invoices, and the same purchase order file, but there are two accountants processing the invoices. In the software world, this would be like having a process define a program and data, but having two different executions of the program in progress at the same time (the original execution and a clone execution). This approach is called **multithreaded** computation. Each execution (analogous to an accountant) is called a **thread**. The two threads use the same program and global data, but they execute the program at their own rate. Since they may be calling different procedures at different times, each thread will have its own stack.

Java supports multithreaded computation with its `Thread` base class. A programmer can define a subclass, `MyThread`, of the `Thread` base class. When an instance of `MyThread` is created, it defines a new, independent thread that executes on the global data in the process. This means that a single Java computation can be executing with multiple threads.

Multithreading means that if the program were to be executed on a multiprogramming system, two or more threads could be time-multiplexing the processor with one another, even though they are using the same program and data. Also, if such a multithreaded computation were to be executed on a computer that had more than one processor, it would even be possible for two threads to be executing in parallel.

Multithreaded processes are a relatively recent innovation in computing. Some operating systems only support the classic idea of a process for a sequential computation. In these systems, multithreaded processing models are possible, although they are implemented in libraries instead of the OS. For example, Java threads are implemented in the Java Virtual Machine rather than in the OS.

2.2 • RESOURCES

When a process (or a thread in a process) executes, it requires some of the computer's resources, at least the processor and memory. It also needs to be able to store and retrieve information to/from the computer's input/output devices. In the programmer's view of the computer, all components (physical and logical) of the abstract machine that are needed to execute a program are called **resources**. The OS is responsible for managing its resources, no matter how diverse they may be. With regard to resources:

- When a process/thread is executing, it must *request* a resource from the OS before using it.
- Once a thread requests a resource, it *suspends* its operation until the resource is allocated to it.

Beyond these basic aspects, the way the OS abstracts processor and memory resource management is traditionally distinguished from the way it manages all the other resources. A process/thread implicitly requests the processor whenever it is ready to run; this is part of the multiprogramming abstraction. Memory is also implicitly requested: When a user logs into a computer, a login thread/process is allocated memory so that it can interact with the user to authenticate the login. Once the authentication is complete, the login process/thread requests enough memory to run a shell through which the user can run other programs. Whenever the user directs the OS to load and execute a program, the loader automatically requests enough memory to run the program.

Most other resources are explicitly requested by action of the program. The most common resource is a file. A process/thread must request a file before it can read it or write it. This is done using an `open()` system call. Further, if the file is unavailable, the process must wait until it becomes available, that is until the `open()` system call returns. An interesting property of processes, threads and resources is that once one thread obtains a resource, then all the other threads that execute in that process can also use the resource. We say that the process *owns* the resource, and all its related threads *share access* to the process's resources. When all threads in a process have completed their use of a resource, then one of the threads must release the resource back to the OS; in the case of a file resource, this is done with a `close()` call.

USING FILES

A **file** is a named, linear stream of bytes of information that are kept on a device. You can store information by opening a file and writing a block of bytes into the file. Similarly, you can access information stored in a file by opening the file and reading the block of bytes stored in the file. The OS is responsible for implementing the basic file abstraction on top of storage devices such as magnetic/optical disks, CD-ROMs, or tapes. Files are distinguished from other resources for two reasons:

- They are the prevalent form by which information is stored in a computer.
- Operating systems often take the file as a primitive and then model other resource abstractions after it.

POSIX Files

A POSIX file is a named sequential collection of bytes, also called a **byte stream file**. There is a **file pointer** associated with each instance of an open file. When a file is opened, the file pointer is set to zero. When an I/O operation reads or writes K bytes, then the file pointer is advanced by K. The POSIX interface specifies basic operations for manipulating a file (see Table 2.1). Any POSIX compliant OS (like Linux) provides OS functions to implement each function on the API. The details of each file function are best left to online documentation (since they change from time to time and from system to system). On a Linux system, you can learn more about exactly how to use these system calls by reading the online documentation. This is done using the man command. For example, to read the documentation on the `open()` command, type "man open" to the shell. It will display the documentation on the screen. (The man man command describes the online documentation for the man command itself. ☺)

TABLE 2.1 POSIX File Operations

Command	Description
open()	The `open()` call specifies the path name of a target file to be prepared for reading or writing. Parameters to the call enable a programmer to lock the file, thus providing exclusive reading or writing as long as the file is open. When the file is opened, a system pointer addresses the first byte in the stream (or, if the file is empty, the location where the first byte will be written). The call returns an unsigned integer file reference when it is successful; this value is used to identify the open file.
close()	The `close()` call closes the file, thereby releasing locks and system resources used to represent the status of the open file.

TABLE 2.1 POSIX File Operations *(continued)*

read()	The read() call specifies a file descriptor (returned by open), a buffer address, and a buffer length. Normally, this call causes the process to block until the read has completed. However, the semantics can be changed with an appropriate call to the fcntl() command, explained shortly.
write()	The write() call is similar to read(), except it transmits information to the file.
lseek()	The lseek() call explicitly moves the read/write pointer in the byte stream, since the file is construed as a linear byte stream. This movement affects subsequent read and write commands.
fcntl()	The fcntl() call (it stands for "file control") provides a means for sending arbitrary control requests to the operating system. For example, normal file read operations block the calling process if it performs a read on an empty file; using fcntl(), it is possible to have the read operation return to the caller if an attempt to read the file would block the calling process.

Suppose you wanted to write a C program that would read all the bytes in one file, and then write them into a second file. The complete C program shown in Figure 2.4 illustrates how this can be done using the POSIX interface. The program copies the contents of the file named in_test, character-by-character, to another file named out_test. This program opens an input file for reading and an output file for writing. Then it copies each byte from the input file to the output file.

✦ FIGURE 2.4 A Linux File Manipulation Program

This Linux program opens two files, and then copies the entire contents of one file into the other, one byte at a time.

```
#include <stdio.h>
#include <fcntl.h>
int main() {
  int inFile, outFile;
  char *inFileName = "in_test";
  char *outFileName = "out_test";
  int len;
  char c;

  inFile = open(inFileName, O_RDONLY);
  outFile = open(outFileName, O_WRONLY);
/* Loop through the input file */
  while((len = read(inFile, &c, 1)) > 0)
  write(outFile, &c, 1);
/* close files and quit */
  close(inFile);
  close(outFile);
}
```

Windows Files

The Win32 API also defines a file as a named byte stream. There is a 64-bit file pointer associated with each instance of an open file. When a file is opened, the file pointer is set to zero. When an I/O operation reads or writes K bytes, then the file pointer is advanced by K.

When a program opens the file, the OS creates an internal data structure to keep track of the operations on the file (like the current file pointer location). The OS call returns a typed HANDLE (reference) to this OS data structure so that it can be used to identify the file for other system calls. There are many file commands in Windows, but Table 2.2 describes the basic commands (similar to the POSIX set shown in Table 2.1). Figure 2.5 is a complete Windows C program to copy a file (block-by-block instead of byte-by-byte) from a file named in_test to one called out_test.

TABLE 2.2 Windows Basic File Commands

Command	Description
CreateFile()	The CreateFile() (or OpenFile()) call is used to create an open file object in the OS, to prepare the file for reading or writing, and to initialize the OS data structure. When the file is opened, a system pointer addresses the first byte in the stream (or, if the file is empty, the location where the first byte will be written).
CloseHandle()	The CloseHandle() call closes the file, thereby closing the system resources used to represent the status of the open file.
ReadFile()	The ReadFile() call reads a block of information from the file and advances the file pointer.
WriteFile()	The WriteFile() call writes a block of information to the file and advances the file pointer.
SetFilePointer()	The SetFilePointer() call moves the file pointer to a new position.

✦ FIGURE 2.5 A Windows File Manipulation Program

This Windows program copies the contents of one file to another, a block at a time.

```
#include <windows.h>
#include <stdio.h>
#define BUFFER_LEN ... // # of bytes to read/write
/* The producer process reads information from the file name
   in_test then writes it to the file named out_test.
*/
```

(continued)

```
int main(int argc, char *argv[]) {
// Local variables
   char buffer[BUFFER_LEN+1];
// CreateFile parameters
   DWORD dwShareMode = 0; // share mode
   LPSECURITY_ATTRIBUTES lpFileSecurityAttributes = NULL;
                  // pointer to security attributes
   HANDLE hTemplateFile = NULL;
                  // handle to file with attributes to copy
// ReadFile parameters
   HANDLE sourceFile; // Source of pipeline
   DWORD numberOfBytesRead; // number of bytes read
   LPOVERLAPPED lpOverlapped = NULL; // Not used here
// WriteFile parameters
   HANDLE sinkFile; // Source of pipeline
   DWORD numberOfBytesWritten; // # bytes written
// Open the source file
   sourceFile = CreateFile (
      "in_test",
      GENERIC_READ,
      dwShareMode,
      lpFileSecurityAttributes,
      OPEN_ALWAYS,
      FILE_ATTRIBUTE_READONLY,
      hTemplateFile
   );
   if(sourceFile == INVALID_HANDLE_VALUE) {
      fprintf(stderr, "File open operation failed\n");
      ExitProcess(1);
   }
// Open the sink file
   sinkFile = CreateFile (
      "out_test",
      GENERIC_WRITE,
      dwShareMode,
      lpSecurityAttributes,
      CREATE_ALWAYS,
      FILE_ATTRIBUTE_NORMAL,
      hTemplateFile
   );
   if(sinkFile == INVALID_HANDLE_VALUE) {
      fprintf(stderr, "File open operation failed\n");
      ExitProcess(1);
   }
// Main loop to copy the file
   while
   (
      ReadFile(
         sourceFile, buffer,
         BUFFER_LEN, &numberOfBytesRead,
```

(continued)

```
        lpOverlapped
      )
      &&
        numberOfBytesRead > 0
    ) {
      WriteFile(sinkFile, buffer, BUFFER_LEN,
        &numberOfBytesWritten, lpOverlapped);
    }
// Terminating. Close the sink and source files
    CloseHandle(sourceFile);
    CloseHandle(sinkFile);
    ExitProcess(0);
  }
```

USING OTHER RESOURCES

A resource is any abstract machine component, including a file, that a process must have explicitly allocated before it can execute the program. If a process/thread requests a resource that is unavailable, the thread normally discontinues execution and remains suspended until the resource becomes available.

Every operating system provides access to a number of resources in addition to files, including the processor, memory, keyboards, and displays. If the interface to all resources is the same, then it is easier for the programmer to know how to use all of these resources than if the interface differs from resource type to resource type.

In UNIX, the file abstraction is used for pipes and devices. Devices, such as keyboards and displays, are described in more detail in Chapter 5. For now, it suffices to say that a device has `open()`, `close()`, `read()`, `write()`, `seek()`, and `fcntl()` commands implemented in the driver, similar to the file interface. The `read()` and `write()` operations work with byte streams, so a device `read()` operation appears much like a file `read()` operation. Pipes are an abstract resource used to enable two different processes to communicate with one another. They are described in Chapter 9.

2.3 ● PROCESSES AND THREADS

A computation is a combination of a process, at least one (implicit or explicit) thread, and a collection of resources. The process component is made up of (see Figure 2.2):

- **A binary program** (or **object code**) to be executed.
- **Data** on which the program will execute (obtained either from a file or interactively from the user of the process).
- **Resources** required for execution, including **files**, that contain data on which the executing program will work.

Notice that the process is an abstract machine *framework* in which computation can take place, and that the active element of the execution is provided by the execution engine. In the single-threaded computation shown in Figure 2.2, there is only one execution engine in the process. Traditionally, operating systems (such as classic UNIX systems) only allow one execution engine in each process, so we call this type of process/thread combination a **classic process**. In modern operating systems such as Windows, the process component is able to contain multiple execution engines as suggested by Figure 2.6. Each execution engine component is called a **thread** (or **lightweight process**), and we call this approach the **modern process** and thread approach. In either case, the thread part is made up of:

- Thread data that is private to the thread. This data is usually allocated on a thread-specific **stack**. Each thread may also have its own, private data workspace.

- The thread **status**, which is an OS data structure that holds all of the properties that are unique to the thread. For example, the status includes the address of the next instruction to be executed by the thread, data about whether or not the thread is blocked waiting for a resource, information about which resource it is waiting for if the thread is blocked, and so on.

Figure 2.6 represents a multithreaded computation in which 3 different threads are executing within a process. The three threads use the same program, global process data, files, and other resources, but they each have their own local data and status.

✦ **FIGURE 2.6** A Process with Multiple Threads

A process defines an execution environment for threads. The environment provides a common binary program, data, and resources (including files). Each thread executes the program with its own stack and status, so different threads are normally executing different parts of the binary program concurrently.

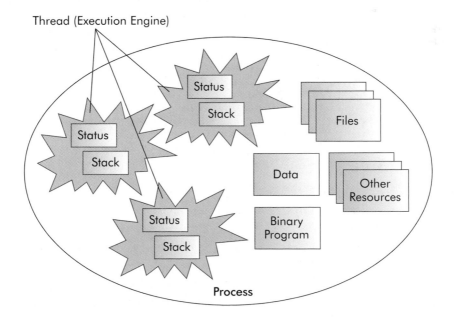

Although there is a clear trend toward the multithreaded computation model, some operating systems still support only the classic process model. In these cases, there is no separate notion of thread—the execution engine is a built-in part of the process. Even though it sounds as though classic processes are an ancient concept, it is worth noting that Version 2.0 of Linux used classic processes (Version 2.2 provides kernel support for threads). Even if a UNIX system provides kernel thread support, it exports the classic process model on the conventional system call interface and the thread model with the POSIX threads extension.

The classic process model was used for over a quarter of a century before it began to be replaced by the modern model in the late 1990s. The motivation for evolving the classic process model to the newer process and thread model was to create a simple OS abstraction where there could be multiple entries that execute the same program, using the same files and devices. During the 1990s, programmers began to want different units of computation that shared facilities (for example, see [Bershad, et al., 1988; Hauser, et al., 1993]). A common motivating example for threads was for a server that managed shared file systems, but that needed to have an individual thread to service each client that used the server. Another example was a window system that used the thread paradigm for managing virtual terminal sessions in the context of a physical terminal. Suppose a window system is built with a physical screen manager, with several related virtual screen threads (see Figure 2.7). All threads run the same code, and all share the physical screen, yet each thread manages just one window in the collection of windows.

✦ FIGURE 2.7 Using Threads

The process provides a program that handles window operations such as writing to the display, moving the window, and changing its size. The process's resources include the physical display. Each thread uses the common program to write information to part of the physical display. Each thread's execution is independent of the other threads, but they cooperate to implement overlapping windows.

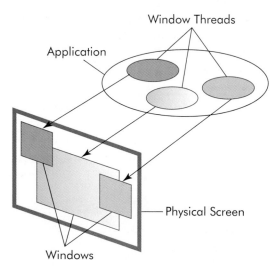

During the early 1990s, there were a few thread libraries, such as the Mach C thread package [Walmer and Thompson, 1989]. These libraries were a collection of functions with an API that allowed a programmer to create and control threads. Thread libraries use a single classic process to execute the threads: Calls to the thread library provide the illusion of multithreaded applications (including thread multiplexing). Programmers made heavy use of these libraries, even though there are several flaws in this approach (for example, if one thread that is implemented in a classic process becomes blocked, then all threads in the process are blocked).

Today, threads are an important tool in the repertoire of the concurrent programmer. Threads executing in a common process share that process's program, data, and resources. However, each thread is an independent unit of computation: The OS can control the progress of each thread in a community of threads. If one thread in a process blocks, the others can still execute.

CREATING PROCESSES AND THREADS

When a computer is started, it must begin executing instructions stored in memory. Conceptually, there is an **initial process** that will perform the bootstrap loading task described in detail in Section 4.2. This initial process/thread loads the OS into memory. Then the computer will begin to execute the OS. How do subsequent processes and threads come into existence? Before considering modern processes and threads, let's consider how this is done with classic processes. The conventional tool for creating a classic process is to execute a process creation system call. The semantics of the classic process creation are derived directly from early work on designing process abstractions.

FORK(), JOIN(), AND QUIT(): THE HISTORICAL PERSPECTIVE

In 1963, Conway introduced three OS functions named FORK(), JOIN(), and QUIT() [Conway, 1963]. Dennis and Van Horne described a variant of them in 1966 [Dennis and Van Horne, 1966]. These primitives are used to create and execute a family of single-threaded processes. Unlike classic UNIX processes (but very much like threads), the process created with the FORK() command executes on the same copy of a program and information that is used by the "parent" process (the process that created the new one). The behavior of the functions is defined as follows:

■ FORK(label) results in the creation of a second, "child" process. The child process begins executing the same program as the original process, but at the statement with the specified label. The process executing FORK() continues execution at the next instruction. Once the new process has been created, the original process and the new process coexist and proceed concurrently.

■ QUIT() is used by the process to terminate itself. The command destroys the calling process.

■ JOIN(count) is used to logically merge two or more processes into a single process. When a process executes this statement, it executes code equivalent to

```
/* Decrement a shared variable */
  count = count - 1;
  /* QUIT unless this the last process */
if (count!= 0) QUIT();
```

count is a shared variable, used by all processes. Only one process can execute the JOIN() statement at any given time. Once a process begins to execute the JOIN() system call, no other process can get control of the processor until the process finishes executing it.

FORK(), JOIN(), and QUIT() can be used to describe computations made up of cooperating sequential processes executing on common data, using a common program.

Using FORK(), JOIN(), and QUIT()

Consider the program segments shown in Figure 2.8. Process A is executing procA that will compute some value (in the code segment designated by <compute section A1>) and then update the information into a shared variable, x. Concurrently, a process B begins to execute procB, although it should not be allowed to execute the retrieve(x) statement until after process A has performed its update(x) operation. Similarly, process A should not perform the retrieve(y) operation on the shared variable, y, until after process B has completed the update(y) instruction. This particular code segment is complex because the two processes execute loops and one process may be able to iterate through its loop much faster than the other. This implies that the values passed back and forth via x and y may be lost because the faster process overwrites a value before the slower one can read it.

✦ FIGURE 2.8 Cooperating Processes

Processes A and B share the variables x and y. Process A writes x and reads y, while process B writes y and reads x. The two processes need to cooperate so that B does not read x until after A has written it, and so that A does not read y until after B has written a new value to y.

```
procA() {                      procB() {
  while(TRUE) {                  while(TRUE) {
    <compute section A1>;          retrieve(x);
    update(x);                     <compute section B1>;
    <compute section A2>;          update(y);
    retrieve(y);                   <compute section B2>;
  }                              }
}                              }
```

The process create/destroy primitives allow two logical processes, A and B, to execute concurrently and to coordinate their execution to prevent shared values from being overwritten before they are read. To force an ordering throughout the execution of some of the statement, we rewrite the procedures as shown in Figure 2.9. The two procedures are encoded as a single body of code that is shared by A and B. Blocks of work are executed by creating a process, and then coordination is accomplished by destroying all but one process. This may be the first piece of high-level code you have seen that uses goto and labels. A statement such as goto L0; causes the control to flow to the statement with the L0: label.

✦ FIGURE 2.9 FORK( ), JOIN( ), QUIT( ) Example

This code fragment accomplishes the concurrent processing task shown in Figure 2.8. The idea in this code is that the two "count" variables are used to count the number of JOIN( ) operations for two different groups of code. The first process begins executing at L0, executes the A1 computation, updates the x variable, creates a new process to begin executing at L2, then performs the A2 computation. It then executes the L1: JOIN(count1); statement. If it is the first to encounter this statement, it will quit. If it is second, it will continue executing by reading the y value, and so on.

```
L0:  count1 = 2;
     count2 = 2;
     <compute A1>;
     update(x);
     FORK(L2);
     <compute A2>;
L1:  JOIN(count1);
     retrieve(y);
     JOIN(count2);
     goto L0;
L2:  retrieve(x);
     <compute B1>;
     update(y);
     FORK(L3);
     goto L1;
L3:  <compute B2>;
     JOIN(count2);
     goto L0;
```

CLASSIC PROCESS CREATION

Today's classic process model evolved from the Conway/Dennis and Van Horne work. The early work actually resembled threads more than it did classic processes, since all processes shared the same program and data. By 1970, the process idea had been refined so that a process captured the ideas pictured in Figure 2.2. Besides the process having allocated resources, they were assigned their own, private **address space**, or set of machine components (mainly memory addresses) that could be referenced by the execution engine. Elements of the stack, status, data, and program blocks were referenced using addresses from the address space. Address spaces were motivated by the need for a memory protection mechanism: By giving a process a set of addresses that it could use to read or write a predefined object, it is possible to determine whether a process is reading/writing the memory assigned to it. This enables the OS to prevent one process from reading or writing another process's allocated memory.

When a classic process creates a child process, a new address space is created for the child process. In the simplest mechanism (the POSIX/UNIX `fork()` system call), the child process's address space is an exact copy of the original process's address space. That means that when a parent process creates a child process, the child process begins execution with an exact replica of the parent's address space. The child and the parent execute copies of the same code with the same variable names, although they refer to address locations in different address spaces (the parent process's addresses refer to the parent's address space, and the child process's addresses refer to the child's copy of the address space).

CREATING MODERN PROCESSES AND THREADS

In systems with modern processes, there are separate system calls to create processes and to create threads. A process creation system call defines a new modern process, but not necessarily any threads. The child process will have its own address space, program, data, files, and other resources. The parent will define how those components are to be configured when it creates the child process. Of course, this child process has no dynamic element—no thread (execution engine). Before the process's program can be executed, at least one thread must be created to execute in the process. For this reason, a modern OS system call to create a process also usually creates a **base thread** to execute the process. For example, the Windows `CreateProcess()` system call first creates a modern process, and then it creates a base thread for the process.

A thread that is executing in a process can create another modern process with its own address space and thread(s). It can also create child threads to execute within the same process—coinciding with the example shown in Figure 2.6. This is accomplished with a mechanism similar to that used in the old Conway `FORK()` system call: The child thread is created to run in the process's address space, using the process's program and resources. However, it will have its own thread data and status. For example, the Windows `CreateThread()` system call creates another thread in the process containing the thread that made the call.

2.4 • WRITING CONCURRENT PROGRAMS

This section provides C program examples for using processes and threads. The classic process model is still heavily used (and generally supported in all operating systems, even if they also support modern processes and threads). Our classic process example comes from UNIX. The code in this example can be compiled and executed on most contemporary UNIX systems, including thread-based Linux systems.

MULTIPLE SINGLE-THREADED PROCESSES: THE UNIX MODEL

The behavior of a UNIX process is defined by its text segment, data segment, and stack segment. The **text segment** contains the compiled binary instructions, the **data segment** contains static variables, and the **stack segment** holds the runtime stack used to store temporary variables. A set of source files is translated—compiled and linked—into an executable form, and then is stored in a file with the default name of `a.out` (of course, the file can be given any explicit name by the programmer). This executable file defines the three segments of the executable program (see Figure 2.10). In the text segment, program branch and procedure call addresses refer to locations within the text segment. If the program references statically defined data, such as C static variables, the addresses refer to the data segment. The data segment will be created and initialized to contain values and space for variables when the executable file is loaded and executed. Variable references to C automatic variables point to the stack segment where the compiler allocates storage for dynamic elements of the program. As in most block-structured programming languages, variables are created when they come into scope and are destroyed when they pass out of scope. In the figure we have tried to emphasize that the idea of a thread is absorbed by the process definition. The execution engine for the single thread is part of the process definition.

✦ FIGURE 2.10 UNIX Processes

A UNIX classic process is described by its text, data, and stack segments. As the process begins to run, it can acquire various resources, including files. The execution engine is built into the process definition, so there is no explicit notion of a thread.

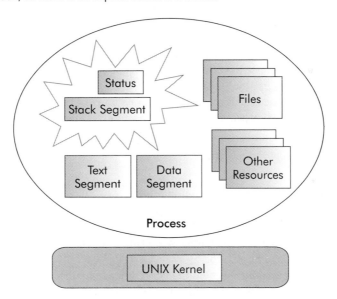

When a process is created, the OS creates an instance of a data structure called a **process descriptor** to keep all the details required to manage the process. A process has a unique **process identifier**, a **PID**, that is a reference to the OS process descriptor data structure. In UNIX, the PID is actually an integer index into an OS table of process descriptors. Whenever one process references another process in a system call, it provides the PID of the target process. For example, the UNIX ps shell command lists each process associated with the user executing the command. The PID of each process appears as a field in the descriptor of each process. The next time you are using UNIX, try the ps -aux command to observe the PID value identifying each process in the system.

The UNIX command for creating a new process is the fork() system call.

```
int fork ();
```

Whenever a (parent) process calls `fork()`, a new child process is created with its own *copies* of the parent's program text, data, and stack segments, and access to all open file descriptors (in the kernel). When the OS creates the new process, it also creates new instances of the process descriptor and others of internal data structures that are referenced by the child's PID value. The `fork()` function returns the PID of the child function to the parent, but it returns a value of zero to the child. The parent then uses the PID as the reference to the child process (in subsequent interactions with the OS).

The child and parent processes execute concurrently, but in their own separate address spaces. This means that even though they have access to the same information, when the child is created, the child and its parent each reference their own copies of the information. No part of the address space of either process is shared. In particular, the parent and child cannot communicate by referencing variables stored at the same address in their respective address spaces. In UNIX, the only thing the two processes can reference in common is open files (UNIX processes exploit this mechanism for interprocess communication, as explained in Chapter 9).

After the child has been created, both the parent and child processes are ready to use the processor; that is, they each have their own abstract machine. In a computer with only one physical processor, only one process can ever use the processor at a time. The programmer cannot assume that either the parent or child process will be the next process to actually use the processor once the `fork()` call has completed. The OS may choose either, or some other process, to use the processor next.

In UNIX, the child process begins to execute in its copy of the program in exactly the same location as the parent process. That is, in the code fragment

```
theChild = fork();
printf("My PID is %d\n", theChild);
...;
```

the parent executes the `fork()` call, then the `printf()` statement. The first statement that the new child process executes is also the `printf()` statement. As mentioned above, in the parent process, the value of `theChild` is the PID of the new process, but in the child process the value is zero. The parent will print a nonzero value that is the PID for the child, but the child will print zero.

Suppose that the programmer wanted the child to execute different code than the parent's code. This can be accomplished using a conditional test:

```
childPID = fork();
if(theChild == 0) {
/* The child will execute here */
  codeForTheChild(...);
  exit(0);
}
/* The parent will execute here */
...
```

In this code fragment, the parent and child both test the value of the `childPID` variable: The parent's copy of the variable will contain a nonzero reference to the PID, while the child's copy of the variable will contain zero. The child will call the `codeForTheChild()` procedure, while the parent will continue with different code that, in this case, is never executed by the child.

There is another system call that can dynamically call the loader to redefine a process's text, data, and stack areas: execve(). UNIX systems provide several forms of the execve() system call. Here is one of them:

```
int execve(char *path, char *argv[], char *envp[]);
```

This call causes the binary program stored in the file at path to replace the text, data, and stack currently being executed by the process. After execve() has completed executing, the program that called it is no longer loaded. Hence, the OS does not return from the execve() call. After the new program has been loaded, the stack is cleared, variables are initialized, then the process begins to execute at the new program's main entry point. The new process is passed the argument list, argv, and the process uses a new set of environment variables, envp.

UNIX also provides a system call, wait() (and a frequently used variant, waitpid()), to enable a parent process to detect when one of its child processes terminates. Details of the terminating child's status may be either returned to the parent via a value parameter passed to wait() or ignored by the parent. The waitpid() variant allows the parent to wait for a particular child process (based on its PID) to terminate, while the wait() command does not discriminate among child processes. When a process exits, its resources, including the OS process descriptor, are released. The OS signals the parent that the child has terminated, but it will not deallocate the OS data structures that contain the child process's complete status until the parent has received the signal. The parent executes the wait() call to acknowledge the termination of a child process, causing the OS to release the relevant data structures.

Executing Commands in UNIX

The fork(), execve(), and wait() system calls are used in UNIX shell programs (also called **command line interpreters**) to execute commands. A shell program allows each interactive user to issue commands to the OS and the OS to respond directly to the user.

A shell program should be able to execute *any* command given to it, even if the program that implements the command is buggy. Operating systems are built so that if a process is executing a program that contains a fatal error, then the process is terminated. If the shell process were to call the command code directly, and the command code contained a fatal error, then the shell process would terminate. At the user interface, you would call the bad command, and the shell would suddenly terminate! This can be avoided by designing the shell so that it creates a *child* process to execute each command. Then if the command execution fails, the OS will terminate the child process but the shell process will continue to execute. Now, if you call a bad command, the shell process can simply report the command failure and be ready to accept a new command.

Next we will design a program, called launch, that behaves like a shell program. You can use this code as part of your solution to the UNIX shell Laboratory Exercise at the end of the chapter. This program reads a list of commands from a file, then executes each command just as a shell would execute it. Each command line in the file will be the same as a line you would type to the shell, such as

```
ls
```

to list all the files in the current directory. If you wanted to list the files with the "long" listing that shows the permissions, owner, and the time that the file was last accessed, you would type

```
ls -l
```

The syntax for a command line is simple: When our launch program sees a command line such as

```
a.out foo 100
```

it will parse it, placing each "word" in the line into a string that will be kept in an array of strings, char *argv[]. This command line would be parsed so that

```
argv[0] = "a.out"
argv[1] = "foo"
argv[2] = "100"
```

You probably recognize the argv name from writing C programs in your previous programming classes. For example, when you write a C program and you want the shell to pass parameters (from the command line) to your program, you declare the function prototype for your main program with a line like

```
int main(int argc, char *argv[]);
```

In the shell case, when a user enters a command line of the form

```
a.out foo 100
```

it is intended to mean that a main program with a standard main header is to be executed with argc set to 3 (since there are three words on the command line), with the argv[] array initialized as shown above. The a.out main program will then interpret the first parameter (argv[1]) as, say, a file name, and the second parameter (argv[2]) as, say, an integer record count. When the shell passes these arguments to the a.out main program, it will treat argv[1] and argv[2] as strings.

Our command launch program is required to read command lines from the file, and then to parse them so that it has a value for int argc, and for char *argv[]. Here is a C data structure that we can use to save these arguments:

```
struct command_t {
  char *name;
  int argc;
  char *argv[MAX_ARGS];
};
```

We added the char *name field to the struct, since we are going to use it to keep the name of the file that contains the binary program for the command. Of course this char *name is redundant, since it is the same string as argv[0] (the first word on the command line). Here is a function that parses a command line, returning the result in the struct command_t *cmd argument:

```
#include    <string.h>

/* Determine command name and construct the parameter list.
 * This function will build argv[] and set the argc value.
```

```
 * argc is the number of "tokens" or words on the command line
 * argv[] is an array of strings (pointers to char *). The last
 * element in argv[] must be NULL. As we scan the command line
 * from the left, the first token goes in argv[0], the second in
 * argv[1], and so on. Each time we add a token to argv[],
 * we increment argc.
 */
int parseCommand(char *cLine, struct command_t *cmd) {
  int argc;
  char **clPtr;
/* Initialization */
  clPtr = &cLine;   /* cLine is the command line */
  argc = 0;
  cmd->argv[argc] = (char *) malloc(MAX_ARG_LEN);
/* Fill argv[] */
  while((cmd->argv[argc] = strsep(clPtr, WHITESPACE)) != NULL) {
    cmd->argv[++argc] = (char *) malloc(MAX_ARG_LEN);
  }


/* Set the command name and argc */
  cmd->argc = argc-1;
  cmd->name = (char *) malloc(sizeof(cmd->argv[0]));
  strcpy(cmd->name, cmd->argv[0]);
  return 1;
}
```

Next, we will write the main program that executes the binary object program in the file identified by argv[0]. To do this, our (parent) shell process will create a child process, then use a form of the execve() system call to load and execute the named file. The parent process will "launch" the executable file in a child process so that even if the executable file contains a fatal error (which destroys the process executing it), the parent process can continue executing other commands.

Our program needs to know the name of a file, say launch_set that contains a list of command lines. For example, the launch_set file might contain the following lines:

```
date
gcc main.c
mv a.out foobar
cd
ls -l
```

If the name of the launch_set file was passed to our program, it should execute the 5 commands using 5 different child processes. Suppose we pass the file name to our launch program as a shell argument, meaning that our launch program is executed with a shell command such as

```
launch launch_set
```

Here is a plan for our program to solve the problem:

1. Read the command line parameter (launch_set in the example).
2. Open the file that contains the set of commands.

3. For every command:
   a. Read a command from the file.
   b. Parse the command so we know the name of the program and its arguments.
   c. Create a new process to execute the command.

4. Terminate after all commands have finished.

Here is a solution that uses the parseCommand() function above. In this solution, we use a variant of execve() called int execvp(char *file, char **argv) (see the man page for execvp() for details).

```c
#include <stdio.h>
#include <unistd.h>

#define MAX_ARGS     64
#define MAX_ARG_LEN 16
#define MAX_LINE_LEN       80
#define WHITESPACE  " .,\t\n"

struct command_t {
  char *name;
  int argc;
  char *argv[MAX_ARGS];
};

/* Function prototypes */
int parseCommand(char *, struct command_t *);

int main(int argc, char *argv[]) {
  int i;
  int pid, numChildren;
  int status;
  FILE *fid;
  char cmdLine[MAX_LINE_LEN];
  struct command_t command;

/* Read the command line parameters */
  if(argc != 2) {
    fprintf(stderr, "Usage: launch <launch_set_filename>\n");
    exit(0);
  }

/* Open a file that contains a set of commands */
  fid = fopen(argv[1], "r");

/* Process each command in the launch file */
  numChildren = 0;
  while (fgets(cmdLine, MAX_LINE_LEN, fid) != NULL) {
    parseCommand(cmdLine, &command);
    command.argv[command.argc] = NULL;
  /* Create a child process to execute the command */
    if((pid = fork()) == 0) {
```

```
        /* Child executing command */
          execvp(command.name, command.argv);
        }
        /* Parent continuing to the next command in the file */
        numChildren++;
    }
    printf("\n\nlaunch: Launched %d commands\n", numChildren);

/* Terminate after all children have terminated */
    for(i = 0; i < numChildren; i++) {
        wait(&status);
    /* Should free dynamic storage in command data structure */
    }
    printf("\n\nlaunch: Terminating successfully\n");
    return 0;
}
```

Notice that the first few lines of the main program check to be sure that the launch_set file name was passed to the program by the shell (using argv[1]). Then it opens the named file so that the main loop can process each command line in the file.

The while loop is executed once for each command in the file. It gets a command line (using a stdio library function, fgets()). Next it parses the command line to define the argv[] array and the name of the file containing the code for the command. The execvp() command requires that the argv[] array be terminated with a NULL pointer, so we do that next. The next couple of lines create the child process with fork(), and then direct the new child to use execvp() to execute the command. While the child is executing the command line, the parent increments the number of children it created, and then *concurrently* goes to the top of the while loop to launch the next command. If this launch program were executed with a launch_set containing 5 commands, then there could be 5 child processes and the parent process all executing concurrently.

MULTIPLE PROCESSES AND MULTIPLE THREADS PER PROCESS: THE WINDOWS MODEL

In Windows, one process creates another process using the Win32 API with the CreateProcess() function. Whenever a process is created, the calling process is telling the OS to perform a large amount of work—to create a new address space and allocate resources to the process, and to create a new base thread. Like UNIX, once the new process has been created, the old process will continue using its old address space, but unlike UNIX, the new child process operates in a newly defined address space with a new base thread. This means that there can be many different options for creating the process, so the CreateProcess() function has many parameters, and some of these parameters can be quite complex. Contrast this with the UNIX fork() call, where there are *no* parameters—the child's behavior is completely defined by parent's profile and default behavior. After the Windows OS has created the new process, it will return a handle for the child process and a handle for the base thread in the process.

Below is a copy of the function prototype for CreateProcess() (taken from the Win32 API reference manual). The function prototype does not use any standard C types.

Instead, it uses a set of types defined in the `windows.h` file, many of which are just aliases for standard C types. This level of indirection in name types creates an abstract interface that OS implementers can use as they wish.

```
BOOL CreateProcess(
  LPCTSTR lpApplicationName,
     // pointer to name of executable module
  LPTSTR lpCommandLine,
     // pointer to command line string
  LPSECURITY_ATTRIBUTES lpProcessAttributes,
     // pointer to process security attributes
  LPSECURITY_ATTRIBUTES lpThreadAttributes,
     // pointer to thread security attributes
  BOOL bInheritHandles, // handle inheritance flag
  DWORD dwCreationFlags, // creation flags
  LPVOID lpEnvironment,
     // pointer to new environment block
  LPCTSTR lpCurrentDirectory,
     // pointer to current directory name
  LPSTARTUPINFO lpStartupInfo,
     // pointer to STARTUPINFO
  LPPROCESS_INFORMATION lpProcessInformation
     // pointer to PROCESS_INFORMATION
);
```

The ten parameters in `CreateProcess()` provide great flexibility to the programmer, but for the simple case, a default value can be used for many of them. For example, the following code shows how to create a child process with a single thread using the Win32 API to Windows NT/2000/XP:

```
#include <windows.h>
#include <stdio.h>
#include <string.h>
...
STARTUPINFO startInfo;
PROCESS_INFORMATION processInfo;
...
strcpy(lpCommandLine,
  "C:\\WINNT\\SYSTEM32\\NOTEPAD.EXE temp.txt");
ZeroMemory(&startInfo, sizeof(startInfo));
startInfo.cb = sizeof(startInfo);
if(!CreateProcess(NULL, lpCommandLine, NULL, NULL, FALSE,
     HIGH_PRIORITY_CLASS CREATE_NEW_CONSOLE,
     NULL, NULL, &startInfo, &processInfo)) {
  fprintf(stderr, "CreateProcess failed on error %d\n",
    GetLastError());
  ExitProcess(1);
};
...
```

```
CloseHandle(&processInfo.hThread);
CloseHandle(&processInfo.hProcess);
```

You can also create additional threads in the current process using the Win32 CreateThread() Win32 API function. Since each thread represents an independent computation of a shared program on shared data, all within the context of a single process's address space, creating a thread requires that the programmer supply information relating to the execution environment for this thread while presuming all the process-specific information.

The best way to discuss the procedure for creating a thread is to first look at the function prototype (additional discussion of thread creation, particularly in a C environment, is included in the thread Laboratory Exercise at the end of this chapter):

```
HANDLE CreateThread(
   LPSECURITY_ATTRIBUTES lpThreadAttributes,
      // pointer to thread security attributes
   DWORD dwStackSize,
      // initial thread stack size, in bytes
   LPTHREAD_START_ROUTINE lpStartAddress,
      // pointer to thread function
   LPVOID lpParameter, // argument for new thread
   DWORD dwCreationFlags, // creation flags
   LPDWORD lpThreadId
      // pointer to returned thread identifier
);
```

As is the case with CreateProcess(), this system call is intended to be very flexible. The lpThreadAttributes are used to control the resource access that the new thread will have; the dwStackSize is used to allocate space for the thread's stack—a value of zero causes the child thread to have the same stack size as the parent thread; the lpStartAddress is an entry point in the encompassing process's address space—entry points are defined as function prototypes such as

```
DWORD WINAPI childFunc(LPVOID lpParam);
```

The lpParam is the void * pointer that is passed to the thread when it is started. The dwCreationFlags default value causes the thread to immediately become ready for execution (rather than being suspended); and the lpThreadId is a variable that will have the child thread identifier returned to the calling thread. One thread can create a sibling thread, executing in the same process with a call such as

```
CreateThread(NULL, 0, childFunc, (LPVOID) NULL, o, &childID);
```

Warning: Before you try to use CreateThread() with C libraries, you will need to read the background information for the Windows Laboratory Exercise at the end of this chapter.

Launching Windows Processes

A command line interpreter (such as Windows' `cmd.exe` or UNIX's shell) is a program that provides a text-based interface for a user to direct the OS. A user runs a program from a command line interpreter by typing the name of a file that contains an executable program, followed by a set of parameters used by the program. This is the same information provided as the `lpCommandLine` parameter that is passed to `CreateProcess()`. The command line interpreter parses the line to get the name of the file and then causes another thread or process to execute the command. In `cmd.exe`, the command line process actually creates a new process that will load and execute the program from the file. The command line interpreter waits for the command to be executed and its host thread to terminate before returning a command line prompt to the user.

A command line interpreter should be able to execute any command given to it, even if the program that implements the command is buggy. Operating systems are built so that if a process is executing a program that contains a fatal error, then the process is terminated. If the command line interpreter process were to call the command code directly, and the command code contained a fatal error, then the shell process would terminate. At the user interface, you would call the bad command, and the command line interpreter would suddenly terminate! This can be avoided by designing the command line interpreter so that it creates a *child* thread to execute each command. Then if the command execution fails, the OS will terminate the child thread but the command line interpreter process will continue to execute. Now, if you call a bad command, the command line interpreter process can simply report the command failure and be ready to accept a new command.

Next we will design a program, called `launch`, that behaves like a command line interpreter program. This program reads a list of commands from a file, then executes each command just as a command line interpreter would execute it. Each command line in the file will be the same as a line you would type to the shell, such as

```
dir
```

to list all the files in the current directory. If you wanted to list the files with the "long" listing that shows the permissions, owner, and the time that the file was last accessed, you would type

```
dir /l
```

The syntax for a command line is simple: When our launch program sees a command line such as

```
a.exe foo 100
```

it will parse it, placing each "word" in the line into a string that will be kept in an array of strings, `char *argv[]`. This command line would be parsed so that

```
argv[0] = "a.exe"
argv[1] = "foo"
argv[2] = "100"
```

You probably recognize the `argv` name from writing C programs in your previous programming classes. For example, when you write a C program and you want the command line interpreter to pass parameters (from the command line) to your program, you declare the function prototype for your main program with a line like

```
int main(int argc, char *argv[]);
```

In the command line interpreter case, when a user enters a command line of the form

```
a.out foo 100
```

it is intended to mean that a main program with a standard "main" header is to be executed with `argc` set to 3 (since there are three words on the command line), with the `argv[]` array initialized as shown above. The `a.out` main program will then interpret the first parameter (`argv[1]`) as, say, a file name, and the second parameter (`argv[2]`) as, say, an integer record count. When the shell passes these arguments to the `a.out` main program, it will treat `argv[1]` and `argv[2]` as strings..

Since the goal of the example is to illustrate how to create multiple processes, we need some way to provide multiple command lines to the program. We can use a text editor (such as `notepad`) to prepare a file with command lines such as a user might type to `cmd.exe`. Each line should be an exact replica of a command that one would type to `cmd.exe`. Store the series of command lines in a file, which you could name `launchset.txt`. Here is a short example `launch_set` file:

```
C:\WINNT\SYSTEM32\NOTEPAD.EXE jnk.txt
C:\WINNT\SYSTEM32\CALC.EXE
C:\WINNT\SYSTEM32\CHARMAP.EXE
```

Next, we will implement a program named `launch.exe` to create a new process to execute each command line in the file. So if the launch set file has 20 command lines, the program will "launch" 20 processes to execute the 20 command lines. The program must also read the name of the launch set file from its own command line. Then, if a user types

```
launch launchset.txt
```

the program will execute on the `launchset.txt` file. The `launch` program must open the `launchset.txt` file, read each command line from the file, and launch a process to execute the command.

There are two things in the lab environment that you might need to know about before preparing your solution on a Windows system. The first is a simple matter of ensuring that the compiler and link editor know that you are writing code to be executed from the `cmd.exe` command line, not to operate in the graphics window environment. The second is related to the compiler and link editor environment for using the C runtime library with a multithreaded program.

WIN32 CONSOLE APPLICATIONS

When your code is compiled, the compiler needs to know if it should generate code that makes your program use the Windows graphics facilities or if it should treat your program like an "ordinary old C program." Because the focus of this textbook is on OS issues, this example is an ordinary old C program that uses `cmd.exe`.

The first difference between a Windows graphics program and a conventional C program is the prototype for the main program. A standard prototype has the form

```
int main(int argc, char *argv[]);
```

A Windows graphics program has a prototype of the following form.

```
int WINAPI WinMain(
    HINSTANCE hInstance,       // handle to current instance
    HINSTANCE hPrevInstance,   // handle to previous instance
    LPSTR lpCmdLine,           // pointer to command line
    Int nCmdShow               // show state of window
);
```

We will use the standard prototype (called a *console application* in Windows land) for our solution.

If you are using Visual C++ to create your software, you will be preparing your software in a robust environment that has workspaces and projects (see the Visual C++ documentation). When you open the Visual C++ environment, it might try to use a workspace and/or project that was used earlier. Close that workspace, and open a new project using the "File" menu. Visual C++ will want you to tell it where the new project should be placed in your directory hierarchy and the type of project. You *must* select the new project option that says "Win32 Console Application" so that the compiler and link editor will be working with the right libraries and header files.

MULTITHREADED PROGRAMS USING THE C RUNTIME LIBRARY

The Microsoft C library has versions that work with ordinary old C programs, and others that work with the graphics environment. To compile the code in this example, you will have to change some compiler and loader options: First, in the Visual C++ "Project/Settings" dialog, there is a tab for setting C/C++ parameters. The default command line has a setting of /MLd that must be changed to /MTd to tell the compiler that the code is multithreaded.

Second, in the "Link" tab, the list of libraries must include /libcmt.lib or /libcmtd.lib. (The first version is for production-level linking, and the second is compatible with the debugger, so it is used if you are compiling and linking a debug version—which you should be doing for these exercises.) Add /libcmtd.lib to the list of libraries to be used by the link editor.

SOLVING THE PROBLEM

The problem requires that we write a program to perform the following steps:

1. Read the command line parameters.
2. Open a file that contains a set of commands.
3. For every command:
   a. Read a command from the file.
   b. Create a new process to execute the command.
4. Terminate after all commands have finished.

Here is a code skeleton, based on these steps:

```c
#include <windows.h>
#include <stdio.h>
#include <string.h>

#define MAX_LINE_LEN        80

int main(int argc, char *argv[]) {

// Function prototypes

// Local variables
  FILE *fid;
  char cmdLine[MAX_LINE_LEN];

// CreateProcess parameters
  LPSECURITY_ATTRIBUTES processSA = NULL;    // Default
  LPSECURITY_ATTRIBUTES threadSA = NULL;     // Default
  BOOL shareRights = TRUE;                   // Default
  DWORD creationMask = CREATE_NEW_CONSOLE;   // Window per process
  LPVOID environment = NULL;                 // Default
  LPTSTR curDir = NULL;                      // Default
  STARTUPINFO startInfo;                     // Result
  PROCESS_INFORMATION procInfo;              // Result

// 1. Read the command line parameters
  if(argc != 2) {
    fprintf(stderr, "Usage: launch <launch_set_filename>\n");
    exit(0);
  }
// 2. Open a file that contains a set of commands
  fid = fopen(argv[1], "r");

// 3. For every command in the launch file:
  while (fgets(cmdLine, MAX_LINE_LEN, fid) != NULL) {
  // a. Read a command from the file
    if(cmdLine[strlen(cmdLine)-1] == '\n')
      cmdLine[strlen(cmdLine)-1] = '\0';    // Remove NEWLINE

  // b. Create a new process to execute the command
    ZeroMemory(&startInfo, sizeof(startInfo));
    startInfo.cb = sizeof(startInfo);
    if   (!CreateProcess(
            NULL,              // File name of executable
            cmdLine,           // Command line
            processSA,         // Process inherited security
            threadSA,          // Thread inherited security
            shareRights,       // Rights propagation
            creationMask,      // Various creation flags
            environment,       // Environment variabkesr
```

```
                    curDir,              // Child's current directory
                    &startInfo,
                    &procInfo
                )
            )
    {
        fprintf(stderr, "CreateProcess failed on error %d\n",
            GetLastError());
        ExitProcess(0);
    }
}

// 4. Terminate after all commands have finished
    return 0;
}
```

One aspect of this program that is difficult to solve is how to determine when all of the processes have finished. Unfortunately, we have not yet learned enough about Windows to know how to do this gracefully! However, each of the child processes can be started in its own console window (or detached using the DETACHED_PROCESS flag for the dwCreationFlags parameter to CreateProcess()) and then left to terminate on its own; that is, the parent process launches each of the children and then terminates. This is normally considered to be questionable style, but it is the best you can do with the tools currently at your disposal.

2.5 ● OBJECTS

Objects were originally derived in simulation languages. An object was a model of an autonomous entity to represent the operation of those units in the simulated system. A simulation program can be thought of as a program that manages a large number of individual units of computation, each of which performs small amounts of computation at a time and each of which is closely correlated with sibling units of computation. The Simula 67 simulation language created the idea of *classes* to define the behavior of a simulation unit of computation, just as a program defines the behavior of a process and thread. The definition of the class includes facilities that allow an object to declare its own data that are private to the class computation. Thus a class is similar to an abstract data type that maintains its own state in its private variables and can be executed as an autonomous unit of computation. Notice that is also similar to a tiny process, since it defines an address space with data and functions that can be applied to that data. The simulation then is defined by specifying a set of class instances—objects—that interact with one another only by passing messages.

Contemporary object-oriented systems still use this class model to define the behavior of a unit of computation. Thus a "model of a process" is used to define objects as an alternative unit of computation. Objects react only to messages. Once an object is created, other objects send it messages. It responds by performing computation on its internal data and by sending other messages either back to the original sender or to other objects. Since an object's behavior is defined by its class definition, the object-oriented programmer designs a system by defining a set of classes and describing when objects should be instantiated from the class definitions.

Objects were first widely used in user interface systems. The InterViews systems [Linton, Vlissides, and Calder, 1989] is representative of many of these systems; every item that appears on a screen—even a character in a document editor—is represented by an object. When objects interact with one another, such as when they are formatted for display, they do so exclusively by sending messages back and forth, rather than by sharing common variables. InterViews and related systems have clearly illustrated the power of object-oriented programming in building document editors, graphics editors, and other visually oriented interfaces. Today, the object approach is also used in almost all application domains.

Object-oriented programming has had a profound effect on the way people write programs. In 1990, most UNIX and Windows programs were written in C, and then later in C++. Today, Java is an important application programming language. Programmers are now comfortable writing their software within the object context. When object-oriented designs are implemented in Java, the OS calls are typically into the JVM abstract machine API rather than into the underlying OS system call interface. That is, languages such as Java are object-oriented languages that place an abstract machine between the application program and the OS; a Java programmer perceives the OS as JVM.

Only a few operating systems have ever been built using objects internally. The Sun Spring OS was an ambitious experiment to make a commercial object-oriented OS [Hamilton and Kougiouris, 1993; Khalidi and Nelson, 1993], although it was eventually abandoned as not being sufficiently cost-effective (high performance) to be commercially viable. Choices was a research OS that was built using object-oriented technology (see Chapter 19). The essential argument that the Choices designers always had to make about their OS was that its performance was nearly on par with operating systems written in C.

The Windows NT/2000/XP kernel has an interesting twist on object-oriented programming. The Windows NT Kernel creates primitive OS components as specialized objects—objects implemented as ordinary C functions. The NT Executive uses the NT Kernel objects whenever it creates an internal data structure. Although there is no language inheritance, the NT Executive code effectively inherits the NT kernel objects, and then adds functionality as required. For example, the NT Kernel defines a "class" called a dispatcher object: Whenever a thread is created by the NT Executive, it instantiates a dispatcher object, and then adds additional fields to the object to capture the status of a thread. The NT Kernel code manipulates the dispatcher object fields in the thread object, but the NT Executive manipulates the fields that it added. The power of this approach is the same as in any object-oriented system: The NT Kernel functionality can be uniformly applied to a broad class of NT Executive abstract data types.

Objects are significant in the context of operating systems because they define another mechanism for specifying the behavior of a distributed system of computational units. This is done by specifying the behavior of individual units of serial computation and the model by which they are coordinated when they execute. The operating system may use this approach for its implementation, as well as being required to provide efficient support for objects.

2.6 ● SUMMARY

With modern operating systems, application programmers use an abstract machine made up of processes, threads, files, and other resources. Processes define the computational infrastructure used by an execution engine. Threads (execution engines) are the fundamental unit of computation representing the execution of a program. Files are persistent information containers used to save information from one session to the next. All operating systems provide support for files. Other resources include the processor, memory, devices, and anything else that a thread can request from the operating system. Resources, such as files, are system-controlled items a thread needs before it can execute. The threads in a process share a common program to define their behavior, resources that are used to carry out the execution, and data on which to operate. In UNIX, the fundamental unit of computation managed by the operating system is the process, and the fundamental unit of secondary memory is the file. In Windows, every computation is organized in terms of threads and processes.

With an understanding of how operating systems are used, you are now ready to begin studying the operating system design. In the next chapter, the discussion begins by considering the overall OS organization.

2.7 ● EXERCISES

1. Write a program to merge two sorted files into a single file using Linux/UNIX.

2. Write a program to merge two sorted files into a single file using any version of Windows.

3. Write a UNIX program that creates a child process that prints a greeting, sleeps for 20 seconds, then exits. The parent process should print a greeting before creating the child, and another after the child has terminated. It should then terminate.

4. Write a Windows program that creates a child process that prints a greeting, sleeps for 20 seconds, then exits. The parent process should print a greeting before creating the child, and then terminate.

5. Suppose that a UNIX kernel supports threads. Would you expect the thread system call to take about the same amount of time to execute as `fork()`? Why or why not?

6. Provide a C code fragment to show how you could implement the Windows

```
CreateFile( LPCTSTR lpFileName,
   DWORD dwDesiredAccess,
   DWORD 0,
   LPSECURITY_ATTRIBUTES NULL,
   DWORD dwCreationDisposition,
   DWORD FILE_ATTRIBUTE_NORMAL,
   HANDLE NULL
)
```

function on top of the POSIX.1 (or your local UNIX) system call interface. For the dwCreationDisposition parameter, ignore the TRUNCATE_EXISTING argument. You can read the precise description of the function and its parameters in the MSDN library.

7. Describe how a shell script (or any other file containing a reference to a program) could "automatically" be executed once every hour in a UNIX system. (*Hint*: See the UNIX cron facility.)

8. POSIX defines a standard thread package in the context of the C programming language. Several manufacturers provide a POSIX thread package as a user library along with their C programming facilities. If you have a system available to you that supports threads, then design and implement a thread program so that one thread reads a file, while a second thread writes the data to another file.

9. Consider the program shown in Figure 2.4. The C stdio library provides a similar set of file operations using the FILE data structure for a file description. Rewrite the simple file copy example in the figure using the C stdio library routines rather than the UNIX kernel routines.

10. Write a shell script to interrogate the operating system to determine the number of processes considered by the short-term scheduler for processor allocation (processes currently "ready to run") at any given time. Then append the result, along with a time-stamp, on a log file. Be sure to say which operating system and shell version you are using. (*Hint*: See the Linux/UNIX man pages for the ps and wc commands. Consider all processes that are in the machine.)

11. Write a C/C++/UNIX procedure, getTime(), that returns the execution time of code segments by calling it before the code segment is executed and again after the code segment is executed; for example:

```
double getTime(int);
start = getTime(-3);
<code segment>;
stop = getTime(-3);
elapsedTime = stop - start; // in milliseconds
```

Use the UNIX kernel gettimeofday() call to read the clock on your host system. The parameter specifies the resolution of the time. If the parameter is i, then the length of time for one time unit is 10^i. (i = 2^{-3} means return the time in milliseconds and i = 2^{-6} means return the time in microseconds.) State the smallest clock resolution for which your routine operates properly on your host machine.

A Simple Shell

This exercise can be solved on any UNIX system.

Starting with the code in Section 2.4, design and implement a simple, interactive shell program that prompts the user for a command, parses the command, and then executes it with a child process. In your solution you are required to use `execv()` instead of `execvp()`, which means that you will have to read the `PATH` environment variable, then search each directory in the `PATH` for the command file name that appears on the command line.

● **BACKGROUND** ●

The OS exports its functionality as the system call interface. All non-OS software uses OS services by making function calls such as `read()` and `fork()` on the system call interface. Human users such as a batch computer operator or an interactive user also need to interact with the OS so they can run programs, inspect the collection of files, and so on. Should the OS provide a specialized human–computer interface just for this purpose? In modern computer systems, the OS does *not* include such an interface. Instead, there are one or more command line interpreter programs that use the conventional system call interface to invoke OS services, and which export an "operator's console" to a user (see Figure 2.11). Since a command line interpreter is just an application program, programmers can create their own if they don't like the ones delivered with the OS.

✦ **FIGURE 2.11** The Shell Command Line Interpreter

The shell command line interpreter is an application program that uses the system call interface to implement an operator's console. It exports a character-oriented human-computer interface, and uses the system call interface to invoke OS functions.

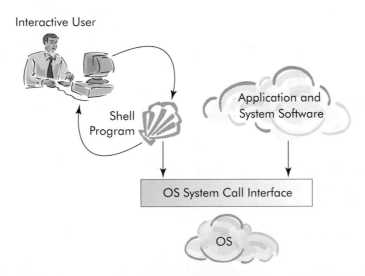

The original UNIX developers were the first to adopt this technique for constructing a command line interpreter [Ritchie and Thompson, 1974]. They called their command line interpreter the shell program, a name that has stuck (and is now used to refer to any program that provides a human–OS interface). The inspiration for the name is that the shell program provides a protective cover over the OS, much like a shell protects an oyster.

The simplest shell programs are text-based programs (more complex shell programs use graphics with point-and-select interfaces). A text-based shell assumes a screen display with a fixed number of lines (usually 25) and a fixed number of characters (usually 80) per line. The user interacts with the OS by typing a string of characters (terminated with the "enter" or "return" key) to the shell, and the OS responds by printing lines of characters back to the shell display.

When a user logs onto a system, a shell program is started to handle the interaction. Once the shell has initialized its data structures and is ready to start work, it clears the 25-line display, and then prints a prompt in the first few character positions on the first line. Sometimes the shell is configured to include the machine name as part of the prompt. My Linux development machine is named `kiowa.cs.colorado.edu` and I use the `bash` shell, so my shell prints

```
kiowa$
```

as its prompt string. (My BSD workstation uses the C shell, so its prompt is `pawnee%`.) The shell then waits for the user to type a command line in response to the prompt. The command line could be a string such as

```
kiowa$ ls -al
```

terminated by an `enter` or `return` character (in UNIX, the character is represented internally by the `NEWLINE` character, '\n'). When the user enters a command line, the shell program makes the appropriate system calls to execute the command that appears on the command line.

Every shell has its own language syntax and semantics. In conventional UNIX shells a command line has the form

```
command argument_1 argument_2 ...
```

where the command to be executed is the first word in the command line and the remaining words are arguments expected by that command. As discussed in Section 2.4, the number of arguments depends on which command is being executed. For example, the directory listing command can be used with no arguments—by typing "ls," or it may have arguments prefaced by the "-" character, as in "ls -al" where "a" and "l" are arguments. *Each command uses its own syntax for interpreting an argument.* For example, a C compiler command might look like

```
kiowa$ cc -g -o deviation -S main.c inout.c -lmath
```

where the arguments "g", "o", "deviation," "S," "main.c," "inout.c," and "lmath" are all being passed as parameters to the C compiler, "cc." That is, the specific command determines which of the arguments may be grouped (like the "a" and "l" in the ls command), which arguments must be preceded by a "-" symbol, whether the position of the argument is important, and so on.

The shell relies on an important convention to accomplish its task: The command is usually the name of a file that contains an executable program. For example, `ls` and `cc` are the names of files (stored in `/bin` on most UNIX-style machines). In a few cases, the command is not a file name, but is actually a command that is implemented within the shell; for example `cd` ("change directory") is usually implemented within the shell rather than in a file. Since the vast majority of the commands are implemented in files, think of the command as actually being a file name in some directory on the machine. This means that the shell's job is to find the file, prepare the list of parameters for the command, and then cause the command to be executed using the parameters.

There is a long line of shell programs used with UNIX variants, including the original Bourne shell (`sh`), the C shell (`csh`) with its additional features over `sh`, the Korn shell, and so on, to the standard Linux shell (`bash`—meaning Bourne-Again shell). All of these shells follow a similar set of rules for command line syntax, although each has its own special features. The `cmd.exe` shell for Windows uses its own similar, but distinct, command language.

BASIC UNIX-STYLE SHELL DESIGN

A shell could use many different strategies to execute the user's computation. The basic approach used in modern shells is the one described in Section 2.4—to create a new process (or thread) to execute any new computation. For example, if a user decides to compile a program, the process interacting with the user creates a new child process. The first process then directs the new child process to execute the compiler program.

This idea of creating a new process to execute a computation may seem like overkill, but it has a very important characteristic. When the original process decides to execute a new computation, it protects itself from any fatal errors that might arise during that execution. If it did not use a child process to execute the command, a chain of fatal errors could cause the initial process to fail, thus crashing the entire machine.

The UNIX paradigm for executing commands is illustrated in Figure 2.12. Here, the shell has prompted the user with the `%` character and the user has typed "`grep first f3.`" This command means the shell should create a child process and cause it to execute the `grep` string search program with parameters `first` and `f3`. (The semantics of `grep` are that the first string is to be interpreted as a search pattern and the second string is a filename.)

The Bourne shell is described in Ritchie and Thompson's original UNIX paper [Ritchie and Thompson, 1973]. The Bourne shell and others accept a command line from the user, parse the command line, and then invoke the OS to run the specified command with the specified arguments. When a user passes a command line to the shell, it is interpreted as a request to execute a program in the specified file—even if the file contains a program that the user wrote. That is, a programmer can write an ordinary C program, compile it, and then have the shell execute it just like it was a normal UNIX command. For example, you could write a C program in a file named `main.c`, then compile and execute it with shell commands like

```
kiowa$ cc main.c
kiowa$ a.out
```

The shell finds the `cc` command (the C compiler) in the `/bin` directory, and then passes it the string "`main.c`" when it creates a child process to execute the `cc` program. The C

✦ FIGURE 2.12 The Shell Strategy

The shell isolates itself from program failures by creating a child process to execute each command specified by the human user. The grep command is executed by a child of the process executing the shell.

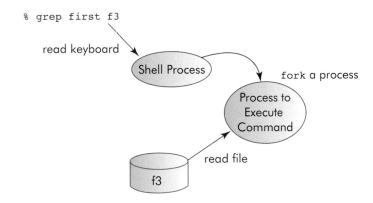

compiler, by default, translates the C program that is stored in main.c, then writes the resulting executable program into a file named a.out in the current directory. In the second command, the command line is just the name of the file to be executed, a.out (without any parameters). The shell finds the a.out file in the current directory, and then loads it and executes it.

Consider the detailed steps that a shell must take to accomplish its job:

■ **Printing a prompt.** There is a default prompt string, sometimes hardcoded into the shell, e.g., the single character string "%," "#," ">" or other. When the shell is started, it can look up the name of the machine on which it is running, and prepend this string name to the standard prompt character, for example, giving a prompt string such as "kiowa$." The shell can also be designed to print the current directory as part of the prompt, meaning that each time the user employs cd to change to a different directory, the prompt string is redefined. Once the prompt string is determined, the shell prints it to stdout whenever it is ready to accept a command line. For example, this function prints a prompt:

```
void printPrompt() {
/* Build the prompt strting to have the machine name,
 * current directory, or other desired information
 */
  promptString = ...;
  printf("%s ", promptString);
}
```

■ **Getting the command line.** To get a command line, the shell performs a blocking read operation so that the process that executes the shell will be blocked until the user types a command line in response to the prompt. When the command has been provided by the user (and terminated with a NEWLINE character), the command line string is returned to the shell.

```
void readCommand(char *buffer) {
/* This code uses any set of I/O functions, such as those in
 * the stdio library to read the entire command line into
 * the buffer. This implementation is greatly simplified,
 * but it does the job.
 */
  gets(buffer);
}
```

■ **Parsing the command.** This is described in the example in Section 2.4.

■ **Finding the file.** The shell provides a set of *environment variables* for each user—this variable is first defined in the user's `.login` file, although it can be modified at any time with the set command. The PATH environment variable is an ordered list of absolute pathnames that specifies where the shell should search for command files. If the `.login` file has a line such as

```
set path=(.:/bin:/usr/bin)
```

the shell will first look in the current directory (since the first pathname is "`.`" for the current directory), then in `/bin`, and finally in `/usr/bin`. If there is no file with the same name as the command (from the command line) in any of the specified directories, the shell responds to the user that it is unable to find the command. The solution needs to parse the PATH variable before it begins reading command lines. This is done with

```
int parsePath(char *dirs[]) {
/* This function reads the PATH variable for this
 * environment, then builds an array, dirs[], of the
 * directories in PATH
 */
  char *pathEnvVar;
  char *thePath;

  for(i=0; i<MAX_ARGS; i++)
    dirs[i] = NULL;
  pathEnvVar = (char *) getenv("PATH");
  thePath = (char *) malloc(strlen(pathEnvVar) + 1);
  strcpy(thePath, pathEnvVar);

/* Loop to parse thePath. Look for a ':'
 * delimiter between each path name.
 */
  ...
}
```

The user may have provided a full pathname as the command name word, or only have provided a relative pathname that is to be bound according to the value of the PATH environment variable. If the name begins with a "/", then it is an absolute pathname that can be used to launch the execution. Otherwise, you will have to search each directory in the list specified by the PATH environment variable to find the relative pathname. Each time you read a command, you will need to see if there is an executable file in one of the directories specified by the PATH variable. The `lookup()` function is intended to serve that purpose:

```
char *lookupPath(char **argv, char **dir) {
/* This function searches the directories identified by the dir
 * argument to see if argv[0] (the file name) appears there.
 * Allocate a new string, place the full path name in it, then
 * return the string.
 */
  char *result;
  char pName[MAX_PATH_LEN];

// Check to see if file name is already an absolute path name
  if(*argv[0] == '/') {
    ...
  }

// Look in PATH directories.
// Use access() to see if the file is in a dir.
  for(i = 0; i < MAX_PATHS; i++) {
    ...
  }

// File name not found in any path variable
  fprintf(stderr, "%s: command not found\n", argv[0]);
  return NULL;
}
```

● **ATTACKING THE PROBLEM** ●

Begin your solution by reading the UNIX example in Section 2.4. You will have to rewrite that code to support user interaction. Here is a header file, `minishell.h`, for your mini-shell:

```
...
#define LINE_LEN     80
#define MAX_ARGS     64
#define MAX_ARG_LEN 16
#define MAX_PATHS    64
#define MAX_PATH_LEN       96
#define WHITESPACE   " .,\t\n"

#ifndef NULL
#define NULL ...
#endif

struct command_t {
  char *name;
  int argc;
  char *argv[MAX_ARGS];
};
```

Here is the skeleton of a solution:

```
/*
 * This is a very minimal shell. It finds an executable in the
 * PATH, then loads it and executes it (using execv). Since
 * it uses "." (dot) as a separator, it cannot handle file
 * names like "minishell.h"
 *
 * The focus on this exercise is to use fork, PATH variables,
 * and execv. This code can be extended by doing the exercise at
 * the end of Chapter 9.
 */
#include ...
#include "minishell.h"

char *lookupPath(char **, char **);
int parseCommand(char *, struct command_t *);
int parsePath(char **);
void printPrompt();
void readCommand(char *);
...
int main() {
  ...
/* Shell initialization */
  ...
  parsePath(pathv); /* Get directory paths from PATH */

  while(TRUE) {
    printPrompt();

  /* Read the command line and parse it */
    readCommand(commandLine);
    ...
    parseCommand(commandLine, &command);
    ...

  /* Get the full pathname for the file */
    command.name = lookupPath(command.argv, pathv);
    if(command.name == NULL) {
      /* Report error */
      continue;
    }

  /* Create child and execute the command */
    ...

  /* Wait for the child to terminate */
    ...
  }

/* Shell termination */
  ...
}
```

A Multithreaded Application

This exercise can be solved on any current Windows OS.

Write a single-process, multithreaded program—one that will create multiple threads to execute within a single process. Your program (call it `mthread.exe`) will take a single integer parameter to specify the number of supplementary threads to be created and executed in the process's address space. Thus, the command line to run your program is:

```
mthread N
```

where `N` is an unsigned integer parameter that tells `mthread.exe` to create and execute `N` additional threads. Optionally, you may add other parameters to the command line; for example, to provide input parameters to control the execution of each thread.

● **BACKGROUND** ●

Each Windows process is created with a base thread. As described in Section 2.4, you can also create additional threads in the current process using the `CreateThread()` Win32 API function:

```
HANDLE CreateThread(
  LPSECURITY_ATTRIBUTES lpThreadAttributes,
    // pointer to thread security attributes
  DWORD dwStackSize,
    // initial thread stack size, in bytes
  LPTHREAD_START_ROUTINE lpStartAddress,
    // pointer to thread function
  LPVOID lpParameter, // argument for new thread
  DWORD dwCreationFlags, // creation flags
  LPDWORD lpThreadId
    // pointer to returned thread identifier
);
```

The function prototype uses six parameters to describe the characteristics of the new thread. When the function executes, the OS creates kernel objects to hold data structures that describe the new object. By convention, whenever the OS creates a new entity like a thread, it returns a reference (pointer), called a HANDLE, to the user space program. The HANDLE returned by `CreateThread()` identifies the thread for all subsequent OS system calls. Since a system object—a resource—is allocated on a successful call to `CreateThread()`, the programmer is obliged to explicitly release the handle (by closing it) when it is no longer being used.

To understand how `CreateThread()` is called, consider the parameters used to create a thread to run in the current process.

■ **lpThreadAttributes.** Windows NT/2000/XP uses this security attribute parameter to control how the handle may be propagated to other processes and threads. (The parameter must be set to NULL in other versions of Windows.) For this problem, and for all other simple cases, it should be set to NULL. The example CreateThread call looks like this:

```
CreateThread(NULL, ...);
```

■ **dwStackSize.** Each thread has its own stack, since it executes independently of the other threads in the process. This parameter gives the programmer a chance to set the size of the stack, although usually you would just use the default—signified by setting the value of the parameter to zero:

```
CreateThread(NULL, 0, ...);
```

■ **lpStartAddress and lpParameter.** To create a thread, it is necessary to provide the OS with an address in the current address space where the new thread should begin to execute. The lpStartAddress parameter is such an address. In conventional programming languages (such as C), it is generally not possible for a computation to simply start off in the middle of some procedure; a branch to a new logical context is handled by bundling the new code in a procedure, and then calling the procedure at its entry point. The lpStartAddress is the address of an entry point for a function that has a prototype of the form

```
DWORD WINAPI ThreadFunc(LPVOID);
```

That is, in a language that checks the type of a called entry point compared to the function call (as is done in ANSI C and C++), there must be a function prototype before an entry point address can be used as a parameter. Of course, this means that there must also be a function to implement the prototype—the function that the new thread will begin executing after it is created.

One other complication in this scenario relates to passing parameters to the function that will be executed by the new thread. Since there is a function call and prototype, if a parameter is to be passed, then its type must either be known and declared, or a void * type must be used (to tell the compiler that the type of the parameter to the thread's function is unknown at compile time). CreateThread uses the latter approach, which is why the function prototype uses LPVOID (which is defined as a void *). The lpParameter value will be passed to the function when the new thread starts to execute it.

For the example call, assume that there is a function with the prototype

```
DWORD WINAPI myFunc(LPVOID);
```

that the new thread is to begin executing. Further, assume that the "parent thread" intends to pass an integer argument, theArg, to the new "child thread." Now the example call will take the form

```
int theArg;
...
CreateThread(NULL, 0, myFunc, &theArg, ...);
```

■ **dwCreationFlags.** The dwCreationFlags parameter is used to control the way the new thread is created. Currently there is only one possible flag value, CRE-ATE_SUSPENDED, that can be passed for this parameter. This will cause the new thread to be created, but suspended until another thread executes

```
ResumeThread(targetThreadHandle);
```

on the new thread (`targetThreadHandle` is the handle of the new thread). The default value is zero, which causes the thread to be active when it is created. Adding this parameter, the example call becomes

```
CreateThread(NULL, 0, myFunc, &theArg, 0, ...);
```

■ **lpThreadId.** The last parameter is a pointer to a system-wide thread identification DWORD:

```
DWORD targetThreadID;
...
CreateThread(NULL, 0, myFunc, &theArg, 0, &targetThreadID);
```

COMPLICATION IN USING `CreateThread()`

The previous section explains how to create a thread, *unless you happen to be using the C runtime library* (which you are, for the exercises in this book). The C library was derived in a UNIX context where there is no distinction between processes and threads. In the Windows OS context, many threads can be executing in a single address space. The threads all have access to all the information in the address space—after all, that is the very meaning of "executing in an address space." On the positive side, it means that it is easy for threads to share information with one another by writing into the process's variables (ones that are not allocated in some thread's stack). On the negative side, it means that every variable that is not in a stack can be read or written by every thread—even if the variable might have only information that is relevant to one of the threads.

[Richter 1997] provides an excellent example of such a variable, `errno`. If you have never used `errno`, think of it as being a global variable that is set by a runtime function if there happened to be an error on the call. In the UNIX context, the process-thread simply reads `errno` to determine the type of an error that might have occurred on a C library call.

As long as there is only one thread executing the process, this works fine. But in Windows a race condition can arise: Suppose there are two threads, R and S, executing in a process and both decide to call C runtime functions concurrently. This means that on a single processor system either R or S, say R, will call the function and return. For the example suppose that R's call resulted in an error, and that `errno` got set to reflect the nature of the error (that is, R should check `errno` as soon as it has detected that its call failed). Now suppose that the thread scheduler interrupts R just after it returns but before it checks `errno`. The scheduler then dispatches S and it calls its runtime routine. The call that S made also fails, so the runtime package sets `errno` to let S know the nature of the error, *overwriting the previous value that R would have read had it not been interrupted.* S detects the call error and reads `errno` without a problem. Eventually R is given the processor and resumes execution; the first thing it does is check `errno`—*seeing the result from S's call rather than from its own call.*

This situation will happen only under certain situations, so the error it produces will be sporadic and extremely difficult to find. How can this problem be avoided? Microsoft has provided an alternative function to `CreateThread()` called `_beginthreadex()`, to be used with programs that use multiple threads at the same time they use the C runtime library. The problem occurs with any globally accessible variable used by the runtime library (there are others). The Microsoft solution is to have the Windows C runtime library provide a *copy* of each of these variables for each thread. Then, when a thread interacts with the runtime library, variables are shared only between the runtime code and the thread, not among all threads. The `_beginthreadex` function creates the copy for a thread in conjunction with an embedded call to `CreateThread()`.

The details of `_beginthreadex()` follow, beginning with its function prototype:

```
unsigned long _beginthreadex(
   void *security,
   unsigned stack_size,
   unsigned ( __stdcall *start_address )( void * ),
   void *arglist,
   unsigned initflag,
   unsigned *thrdaddr
);
```

Despite the apparent differences between the types of the parameters to `_beginthreadex` and those for `CreateThread()`, you can declare the parameters described for `CreateThread()`, then pass them to `_beginthreadex()`. This means we can translate the example `CreateThread()` call we just described and program it as

```
DWORD WINAPI myFunc(LPVOID);
...
LPSECURITY_ATTRIBUTES lpThreadAttributes = NULL;
DWORD stackSize = 0;
int theArg;
DWORD dwCreationFlags = 0,
DWORD targetThreadID;
...
_beginthreadex(
   (void *) lpThreadAttributes,
   (unsigned) stackSize,
   (unsigned (_stdcall *)(void *)) myFunc,
   (void *) &theArg,
   (unsigned) dwCreationFlags,
   (unsigned *) &targetThreadID
);
```

It is ugly, but it works; you can make it look better with judicious use of macros. Before you code this up and try to compile it, be sure to see additional related remarks in the Windows example in Section 2.4.

● ATTACKING THE PROBLEM ●

This exercise requires that you write a program to perform the following steps:

- ■ Read the command line argument, N.
- ■ For 1 to N, create a new thread to execute simulated work.
- ■ Terminate after all threads have finished.

Here is a skeleton for a solution:

```
#include <windows.h>
#include <math.h>
#include <stdio.h>
#include <stdlib.h>

static int runFlag = TRUE;

void main(int argc, char *argv[]) {
  unsigned int runTime;

  SYSTEMTIME now;
  WORD stopTimeMinute, stopTimeSecond;

// Get command line argument, N
// Get the time the threads should run, runtime
// Calculate time to halt (learn better ways to do this later)
  GetSystemTime(&now);
  printf("mthread: Suite starting at system time
    %d:%d:%d\n", now.wHour, now.wMinute, now.wSecond);
  stopTimeSecond = (now.wSecond + (WORD) runTime) % 60;
  stopTimeMinute = now.wMinute + (now.wSecond +
    (WORD) runTime) / 60;

// For 1 to N
  for (i = 0; i < N; i++) {
// Create a new thread to execute simulated work
    Sleep(100);              // Let newly created thread run
  }

// Cycle while children work ...
  while (runFlag) {
    GetSystemTime(&now);
    if ((now.wMinute >= stopTimeMinute)
        &&
        (now.wSecond >= stopTimeSecond)
      )
      runFlag = FALSE;
    Sleep(1000);
  }
  Sleep(5000);
}
```

Notice the Sleep(K) call; this is a Win32 API function that causes the current thread to yield the processor and block itself until K milliseconds have elapsed. The thread will then awaken and enter its appropriate scheduling queue. This call is placed just after the call that creates a new thread so that the creating thread will block for 100 milliseconds (0.1 seconds), giving the newly created thread a chance to run. It is a standard technique in multithread programming.

This code skeleton uses system time to determine how long a child thread should run. The code reads the amount of time the process and thread community should exist, figures out the current time, then computes the time at which the community should halt. After the worker threads have been created to do the simulated work, the coordinator thread checks the current time to see if it is time to halt; if it is not time to halt, the coordinator thread goes to sleep for 1,000 milliseconds (a second), and then awakens and checks the time again. When enough time has elapsed, the coordinator thread sets a global flag, runFlag, FALSE, waits for five seconds, and then terminates. Before you can really understand this strange protocol, take a look at the code skeleton used by the worker threads:

```
// The code executed by each worker thread (simulated work)
DWORD WINAPI threadWork(LPVOID threadNo) {
// Local variables
   double y;
   const double x = 3.14159;
   const double e = 2.7183;
int i;
   const int napTime = 1000;              // in milliseconds
   const int busyTime = 40000;
   DWORD result = 0;

// Create load
   while(runFlag) {
   // Parameterized processor burst phase
     for(i = 0;  i < busyTime;  i++)
        y = pow(x, e);
   // Parameterized sleep phase
     Sleep(napTime);
   // Write message to stdout
   }
// Terminating
   return result;
}
```

Each worker thread goes through phases of using as many processor cycles as it can get to compute a power function, and then it goes to sleep for a while. Each worker does this until it sees the runFlag go FALSE, and then it terminates. Notice that this solution relies on the use of a shared variable within the thread community to decide when to quit—an approach that would be impossible in a community of processes! Think carefully about why threads can do this but processes cannot.

CHAPTER 3

Operating System Organization

This chapter is the first to focus on OS concepts and internal designs. The OS creates a myriad of abstract components used by application programmers. It also provides a means for coordinating the operation of those components, much like a conductor coordinates musicians in an orchestra. We begin by introducing the basic functions required of any OS: device management, process and resource management, memory management, file management, and functional organization. Next, we will address general implementation methodologies: performance and trusted software. Software modularization issues are introduced in this chapter, and are discussed in more detail in Chapter 19. This chapter concludes with a description of the general organization of UNIX kernels and the Windows NT kernel.

3.1 • BASIC FUNCTIONS

There are two basic responsibilities of the OS (see Figure 3.1):

- *Create* an abstract machine environment with multiple, autonomous abstract components. Many of the components can be in use concurrently. For example, the OS uses multiprogramming to create an abstract machine for each process.
- *Coordinate* the use of the components according to the policies of the machine's administrator. For example, the scheduler decides when and which different processes should be allocated the processor.

The creation part of the OS provides the spectrum of abstractions (such as processes, threads, and resources) that programmers use, and the coordination part manages their concurrent use so that the community of processes works in harmony.

✦ FIGURE 3.1 Purpose of an OS

Part of an OS creates a set of abstractions that will be used by application programmers. These abstractions include processes, threads, and files. In a multiprogramming OS, multiple processes compete for the use of the abstract resources, so the OS coordinates the way that these processes use the abstract resources.

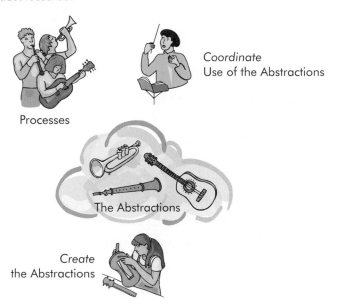

There is no complete agreement about the exact set of functions required for an OS. Instead, each OS provides a set determined by engineering and marketing choices. Our goal is to learn the general principles behind OS functions, and then to put those principles to work in OS-specific Laboratory Exercises. Over the years, OS functions have been characterized as satisfying one of the following basic requirements:

- Device management
- Process, thread, and resource management
- Memory management
- File management

We will use these general characterizations as a framework for considering detailed requirements, design issues, architectures, and implementation. Let's first consider a general description of each of these components of an OS.

DEVICE MANAGEMENT

The OS manages the allocation, isolation, and sharing of the devices according to policies chosen by the designer or system administrator. Even operating systems that do not support multiprogramming incorporate device management. Most operating systems treat all devices such as disks, tapes, terminals, and printers in the same general manner, but they provide special management approaches for the processor and memory. Device management refers to the way the generic devices are handled.

There are device-dependent and device-independent parts of a device manager (see Figure 3.2). The dependent parts, called **device drivers**, implement the aspects of device management that are unique to each device type. For example, a device driver for a keyboard is constructed explicitly to sense keystrokes from a keyboard device as the corresponding keys are pressed. A device manager for a display screen is constructed to write characters or graphics to a video display.

✦ FIGURE 3.2 Device Management

The device manager is composed of a device-independent part and a collection of device-dependent parts, one for each type of device. The device-dependent parts export services to the device-independent part, which provides a unified interface for all the different device types.

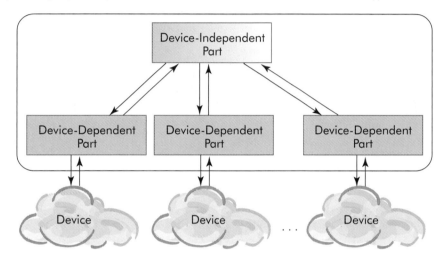

The independent part of the device manager defines a general software environment in which a device-dependent driver can execute. For example, the independent part includes the system call interface and a mechanism to forward the calls to the correct device driver. The independent part of the device management system is a relatively small part of the device manager. Most of the functionality is implemented in the collection of device drivers.

By partitioning the design into dependent and independent components, the task of adding a device to a computer is greatly simplified. First, the OS designer decides which aspects of device management are device-dependent and which parts can be independent of all devices. The independent parts are then implemented in the base operating system (they will work with all devices). The dependent parts are implemented in the driver for each device type. This means that the independent part of the device manager has system calls to read and/or write any device. A printer device driver contains all the software that is specific to a particular type of printer (such as a Postscript printer). Since the independent parts are generic for all devices and are built into the OS, the designer can add device drivers to the OS whenever a device is added to the computer.

Device management is an important but relatively simple part of the overall OS design. Chapter 4 introduces device behavior (from a system programmer's perspective) as part of the computer organization discussion. Chapter 5 addresses device management in detail.

PROCESS, THREAD, AND RESOURCE MANAGEMENT

Processes and threads are the basic units of computation defined by programmers, and (abstract) resources are the elements of the computing environment needed by a process so that its threads can execute. This part of the OS implements all parts of the abstract machine that create the abstractions of processes, threads, and resources (see Figure 3.3). This part of the OS is completely responsible for managing the hardware processor resource and various abstract resources such as messages. It shares the responsibility of managing the hardware primary memory with the memory manager.

✦ **FIGURE 3.3** Process, Thread, and Resource Management

The process, thread, and resource manager is responsible for the administration of the processor and various abstract resources. It cooperates with the memory manager to administer the primary memory.

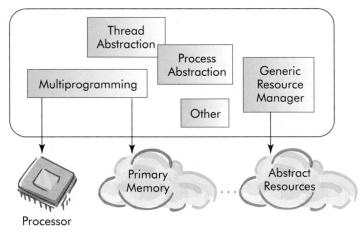

Process management, thread management, and resource management could be separated into their own logical units, but most operating systems combine them into a single module, since together they define the essential parts of the abstract machine environment. In this book, this part of the OS is simply referred to as the "process manager" rather than the more proper (and longer) name "process, thread, and resource manager."

In Chapter 2, the UNIX process model was described as one example of how an OS can define a computational environment. A UNIX-style OS provides a set of process management facilities for creating, destroying, blocking, and running a process. Chapter 2 also described the more modern thread-based approach in which the computational element is divided into a static process part and a dynamic thread part. The process manager for thread-based systems is more complex than one for process-based systems since it must manage processes and threads as separate entities.

The resource manager allocates resources to processes when they are requested by a thread, and keeps track of resources when a thread finishes using them. Logically, a designer could separate resource management functionality from process/thread management. However, changes in status to a resource are usually related to a change in status of a process, so OS designers tend to talk about resource management as if it were a part of process management.

The process manager allows multiple users (or processes and threads) to share the machine by providing multiple execution contexts and scheduling the processor so that each thread receives an equitable fraction of the available time. Primary considerations of the process manager are how it will enforce isolation of resource access among the processes (according to some policy) and how it will allow the processes to circumvent the isolation mechanism when the policy calls for the processes to share a resource. Chapters 6 through 10 describe the issues related to designing a process manager.

MEMORY MANAGEMENT

The memory manager cooperates with the process manager to administer the allocation and use of the **primary** (also called the executable or main) **memory** resource—see Figure 3.4. Every process requests and uses memory according to its program definition. The memory manager allocates memory to competing processes according to a specified policy and enforces resource isolation. A strategy that allows sharing is more complex to manage than one with no sharing. Hence, the memory manager incorporates mechanisms to allow blocks to be shared in the presence of the isolation mechanism.

✦ FIGURE 3.4 Memory Management

The memory manager cooperates with the process manager to administer the primary memory. If the OS supports virtual memory, then that part of the memory manager cooperates with the device and/or the file managers to manage the memory and paging devices.

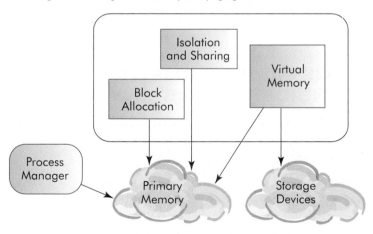

Modern memory managers provide **virtual memory** extensions so that the abstract machine's primary memory appears to be larger than the physical machine's memory. This is accomplished by integrating the computer's primary memory and the memory from its storage devices, allowing processes to reference information stored on a storage device as if it were stored in the primary memory. Virtual memory requirements differ from conventional memory management requirements. This is because the system is managing an abstract resource—the virtual memory space—which must be managed by controlling the way the primary memory and the storage devices are used together. Chapters 11 and 12 discuss memory management approaches, issues, and designs.

Modern memory managers also provide a means for a thread on one machine to access and share physical memory on another machine. They do this by using an interconnecting network to transmit and receive messages in order to provide a distributed shared memory abstraction. In this case, the memory manager is combining its "native" functionality with network device functionality. Chapter 17 explains how this distributed shared memory works.

FILE MANAGEMENT

Files are an abstraction of storage devices. Information stored in the main memory will be overwritten as soon as the memory is deallocated from a process. Information that is to be saved must be copied to a persistent storage device, such as a CD-ROM or magnetic disk. The file manager implements this abstraction by interacting with the device manager and the memory manager. As pointed out in Chapter 2, the need to produce abstractions of the details of I/O operations for storage devices was one of the first pushes toward operating systems, and files are the classic abstract resource in operating systems.

Different file managers provide different abstractions of storage devices, with the requirements ranging from those that model the storage system as a byte stream to those that treat it as a logical repository for indexed records. Chapter 13 explains how local file systems are defined and implemented.

In modern operating systems, the file system can be distributed across a network of machines so that a process on one machine can read and write files stored on its local system, as well as those stored in the storage devices of other machines accessible using a network. Chapter 16 generalizes the discussion of Chapter 13 to cover remote file systems implemented in a network environment.

3.2 ● GENERAL IMPLEMENTATION CONSIDERATIONS

The OS is a collection of algorithms and data structures. In achieving the functional requirements related to abstraction and resource sharing, there are two recurring issues in the software design:

- ■ **Performance.** The OS must be implemented so that it is as efficient as possible in its use of machine resources (especially processor time and memory space), maximizing the availability of the resources for the use by applications.

- ■ **Exclusive use of resources.** The OS must provide resource isolation, allowing a process's resources to save information without fear that the information will be altered or copied. Failure to ensure isolation is a critical failure of the OS.

Three basic implementation mechanisms are used in every contemporary operating system design to address these issues:

- ■ **Processor modes.** A processor hardware mode bit is used to distinguish between instruction execution on behalf of an OS and execution on behalf of a user.

- ■ **Kernels.** The most critical part of the OS is implemented in a kernel. The kernel is designed as a *trusted* software module that supports the correct operation of all other software.

■ **Method of invoking system service.** This issue is concerned with the way user processes request services from the operating system: This is accomplished either by calling a system function or by sending a message to a system process.

In the remainder of this section we'll take a closer look at these requirements and mechanisms.

PERFORMANCE

People use computers because the potential for very rapid information processing is vastly greater than what can be accomplished using manual techniques. With computers, people can attack problems they would never consider if the related computation were to be carried out manually. For basic number crunching, the benefit of automatic electronic computation is obvious. For character and image processing, the computer has become a consumer appliance; people use the high performance of computers for web browsing, document search, and presentation in ways that were nearly inconceivable in 1990.

At the basic requirements level, operating systems are justified by their ability to provide simplified programming interfaces and a mechanism to manage resource sharing. Both of these tasks are overhead in the sense that they do not contribute directly to problem solutions but, rather, provide an abstract machine environment in which solutions can be produced by application programmers in a cost-effective manner. Even though every programmer and end user accepts that this management function is justified by the overall effectiveness of the computer, there remains the issue of the overhead cost of the service to individual processes. Even if some specific abstraction in the overall machine makes it easier to write a program to solve a particular problem, how much does the use of the abstraction slow down the execution of the program? For example, what is the performance cost of using files rather than commands that directly manipulate storage devices?

Every design issue in an OS must be evaluated with respect to its contribution to the functionality of the system *and* its impact on the computer's performance. Such performance considerations have often prevented an otherwise excellent function from being incorporated into an OS. In many of these cases, increases in performance at the hardware level eventually led designers to use the functionality in spite of its inefficiencies. Traditional examples of this are high-level programming languages, objects, graphics, and network functions.

There is no clear way to determine when a costly function should be implemented in the operating system. This is resolved on a case-by-case basis with careful engineering work based on an analysis of the trade-offs of functionality versus its performance. The *art* of operating system design is deeply intertwined with the study of computer performance.

EXCLUSIVE USE OF RESOURCES

Multiprogrammed computer systems support multiple processes and threads at the same time. This establishes a computational environment in which processes share resources. It also leads to the requirement for the OS to provide a mechanism by which one process does not *interfere* with others currently using the machine. A process should not be allowed to use a resource unless it is explicitly authorized to do so. A process must be able to determine that it has **exclusive control** of a resource before accessing it, or that the access occurs in an environment in which all participating processes accommodate resource sharing. Consequently, the OS must be able to manage configurations in which specific resources either are exclusively assigned to one process or are shared among a specific set of processes. At the same time, the OS must have the flexibility to change a configuration according to the changing needs and desires of the community of processes.

Protection **mechanisms** are tools that the OS provides to implement a security policy chosen by the system's administrator(s). A security **policy** defines the machine-specific strategy for managing access to resources. For example, a policy may specify that only one process at a time can have a particular file open for writing, but that many processes may open the file simultaneously for reading. A file protection mechanism to implement this policy would provide read and write locks on files.

Protection mechanisms are implemented and enforced by the OS software. This creates an interesting challenge for operating system designers: If *OS software* enforces a policy, how can *application software* be prevented from changing that policy? This is the second fundamental challenge of modern OS design (in addition to performance). However, like performance, secure operation is so important that its consideration permeates every design decision for every function in the OS.

In contemporary operating systems, a key point in the protection mechanism implementation is to differentiate software as being either trusted or untrusted software. **Trusted software** has been carefully written and debugged (sometimes even proven correct) at the time the OS is created or updated. On the other hand, **untrusted software** has not been subjected to such careful analysis, and the overall operation of the machine should not depend on the correct operation of untrusted software. The **kernel** of the OS is implemented as trusted software. All other software, including applications, system software, and OS extensions, are treated as untrusted software by the kernel, meaning that the secure operation of the computer only depends on the trusted software, and never on the untrusted software.

How can a programmer be certain that once trusted software has been created, it will not be changed by untrusted software? An essential element of the computer's protection mechanism is required to provide access barriers between trusted and untrusted software. Without such a barrier, it is generally not possible to ensure that some software is guaranteed to perform specific functions. The idea of trusted software recurs in various places in the discussion of the OS design. Processor modes provide the key hardware element for implementing trusted software.

PROCESSOR MODES

Contemporary processors incorporate a **mode bit** to define the execution capability of a program on the processor. This bit can be set to **supervisor** or **user mode**. In supervisor mode, the processor can execute every instruction in its hardware repertoire, whereas in user mode, it can execute only a subset of the instructions. Instructions that can be executed only in supervisor mode are called **supervisor**, **privileged**, or **protected** instructions to distinguish them from the user mode instructions. *The idea is that trusted OS software executes with the processor in supervisor mode, and all other software executes with the processor in user mode.* For example, I/O instructions are protected instructions, so an application program cannot perform its own I/O. Instead, it requests that the OS perform I/O in its behalf.

The mode bit allows us to enforce exclusive use of resources. Suppose resource access can only be specified using trusted software. Then any particular configuration isolates or permits sharing of resources according to the administrator's policy. For example, the processor could use a hardware register to identify an object that is only accessible to the running process (see Figure 3.5). When Process A is using the processor, the register points to A's own object, but when Process B is using the processor, the register does not point to A's object. The contents of such a register are only allowed to be changed with a privileged instruction; only a supervisor mode program can change the object access criteria.

✦ FIGURE 3.5 Exclusive Access to a Resource

Certain parts of the hardware such as the object pointer register in the figure can only be loaded using a privileged instruction. This makes it possible for the OS to implement exclusive reference and control of objects that are allocated on a process.

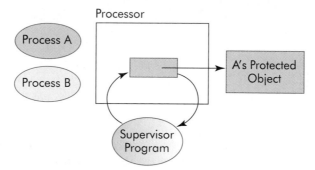

The system can also use the mode bit to define areas of memory to be used when the processor is in supervisor mode versus when it is in user mode (see Figure 3.6). If the mode bit is set to supervisor mode, the process executing on the processor can access both the supervisor and user partitions of the memory. If the processor is in user mode, the process is only allowed to access the user memory space. Operating system discussions frequently call the two classes of memory **user space** and **system** (or **supervisor**, **kernel**, or **protected**) **space**.

In general, the mode bit extends the operating system's **protection rights**. This means that when the OS is being executed in supervisor mode, it has more rights to access memory and to execute privileged instructions than when the mode bit is set to user mode.

Since the mode bit is used to distinguish between trusted and untrusted software, we need a mechanism to enable a process executing in user mode to be able to (1) switch the processor to supervisor mode and (2) begin executing OS code. It is important that *whenever* the processor switches to supervisor mode, the computer will *only* execute OS code. Also, whenever user mode software calls the OS, the processor is switched into supervisor mode. Briefly, the mode bit is set by the user mode **trap** hardware instruction (also called a **supervisor call** instruction); we will discuss this more in a few paragraphs. This instruction sets the mode bit and branches to a fixed location in the system space. It is similar to a hardware interrupt, so we will leave detailed discussion of the instruction operation until Chapter 4. The presumption is that only the OS routines will be loaded in the system space, which is explicitly protected because no user program can load its own code into it. Since only system code is loaded in the system space, only system code can be invoked via a trap. When the OS has completed the supervisor call, it resets the mode bit to user mode prior to the return.

✦ FIGURE 3.6 Supervisor and User Memory

A subset of the primary memory is treated as supervisor space. The CPU can only reference that part of the memory when the mode bit is set to supervisor.

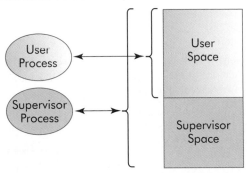

Older computers, such as the Intel 8088/8086 processor, do not include a mode bit. Hence, they do not distinguish between supervisor and user instructions. As a result, it is difficult to provide robust resource isolation in such computers. Subsequent microprocessors in the Intel chip family incorporate a mode bit, so these certain processor registers can only be changed using protected instructions. Newer Intel microprocessors are upward compatible with the 8088/8086 to accommodate software written for the older microprocessors. This compatibility is accomplished by including another processor flag that instructs, say, a 80486 or Pentium to emulate an 8086 by ignoring the mode bit, thereby effectively executing all instructions in supervisor mode.

KERNELS

The notion of trusted software and processor mode can now be combined to explain the characteristics of an OS kernel. The kernel is the part of the OS that executes as trusted software (in supervisor mode). The kernel implements the basic mechanisms that assure secure operation of the entire OS. Other software (including parts of the OS) and all application programs execute as untrusted software in user mode. So trusted software is analogous to "software that is executed with the processor mode set to supervisor."

Extensions to the OS execute in user mode. The operating system does not rely on the correctness of those parts of the system software for correct operation of the computer. Thus a fundamental design decision for any function to be incorporated into the OS is whether or not it needs to be implemented in the kernel. If it is implemented in the kernel, it will execute in supervisor space and have access to other parts of the kernel. It will also be trusted software by the other parts of the kernel. If the function is implemented to execute in user mode, it has no access to kernel data structures. While kernel-implemented functions may be easy to implement, the trap mechanism and authentication at the time of the call are usually relatively expensive. The code may run fast, but the actual system call—the trap and related code— requires a relatively long time to execute compared to a normal function call.

REQUESTING SERVICES FROM THE OPERATING SYSTEM

There are two techniques by which a program executing in user mode can request the kernel's services, both of which ultimately depend on a trap instruction:

- System call
- Message passing

Figure 3.7 summarizes the differences between the system call and message passing techniques. First, assume that a user process wishes to invoke a particular system function (represented as an annotated shaded rectangle in the figure). For the **system call** approach, the user process invokes the trap instruction. However, it would be ideal if the application programmer did not need to know the details of the trap instruction's use, particularly since the trap must use an operand that is a reference to a table (called the **trap table**) in the kernel. Therefore, the OS designer provides a library of "stub" functions with names that are exactly the same as the system call.

✦ FIGURE 3.7 Procedure Call and Message Passing Operating Systems

In the system call style interface to the OS, a user space program invokes an OS function by using a `trap` instruction to branch indirectly through the OS trap table. In the message passing approach, the process executing in user space issues a `send()` system call that transmits a message to an OS process. The OS process executes in supervisor mode, returning a message to the user space process.

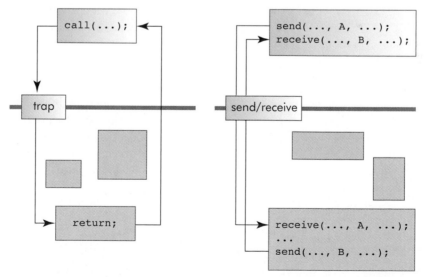

For example, the POSIX `fork()` system call has a stub function named `fork()` in the library (of course the stub function has the documented procedure signature—the right number and types of parameters). Each of these stub functions contains a trap instruction

to the OS function via the correct entry in the kernel trap table. When the application program calls the stub, all the stub does is execute the `trap` instruction with the correct operand, switching the processor to supervisor mode, and then branching indirectly through the trap table to the entry point of the function that is to be invoked (see Figure 3.8). When the OS function completes its work, it switches the processor to user mode and then returns control to the user process (thus simulating a normal procedure return). The system call then appears to the application programmer to be an ordinary function call. More details of the system call will be discussed in Chapter 4 after you have reviewed interrupts.

◆ **FIGURE 3.8** A System Call Using the `trap` Instruction

The `trap` instruction relies on the presence of a table of OS function entry point addresses. When the `trap` instruction is executed, it branches to an entry in the trap table, retrieves an entry point to an OS function, and then branches to that entry point.

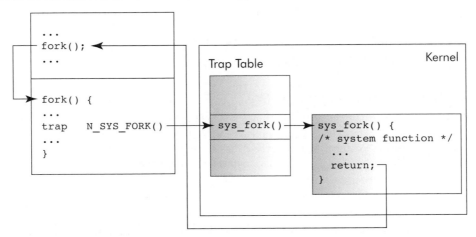

In the **message passing system call** approach, the user process constructs a message, A, that requests the desired service (see Figure 3.7). Then it uses an OS `send()` system call to pass the message to a trusted OS process. The `send()` function delivers the message to a kernel process that implements the target function. However, before the kernel process can read the mailbox, it must have been started or resumed—meaning that the mode bit was set to supervisor. In a message passing system, there are several times when the kernel process might be made active, but an obvious time is when `send()` is executed. That is, `send()` effectively executes a trap instruction. While the kernel process is executing the system function, the user process waits for the result of the service request with a message `receive` operation. When the kernel process completes the operation, it sends a message (B in the Figure 3.7) back to the user process.

The distinction between the two approaches has important consequences regarding the relative independence of the OS behavior from the application process behaviors and the resulting performance. As a rule-of-thumb, operating systems based on a system call interface are more efficient than those requiring messages to be exchanged between distinct processes. This efficiency follows from the cost of process multiplexing (with an implicit trap execution), message formation, and message copying versus the cost of just a trap instruction execution.

The system call approach has the interesting property that there is not necessarily any OS-specific thread. Instead, a thread executing in user mode changes to supervisor mode when it is executing kernel code and back to user mode when it returns from the OS call (see Figure 3.9). This notion of an OS without any threads is a reasonable model, but the OS designers usually cheat by having certain hidden OS threads. One reason this is done is so that the OS can get control of the machine in special situations, and this might be rather difficult without any special kernel threads. For example, when an interrupt occurs, the kernel begins to run without any associated user process or thread.

✦ FIGURE 3.9 A Thread Performing a System Call

When a thread performs a system call, the original user thread obtains the ability to execute privileged instructions via the `trap` instruction. It then executes the OS code with the CPU in supervisor mode. When it has completed, the OS function resets the mode bit to user mode and branches to the return address in user space.

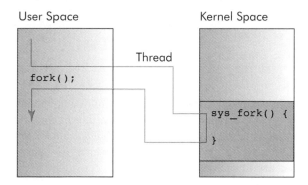

There is a second case where there are threads that look as though they might be special OS threads, even though they are normal user threads. They are called **daemons** in UNIX (a name which seems to have stuck for other operating systems as well). Daemons are created so that an administrator can set up code to execute when various external conditions are met; in a typical UNIX configuration, there is a printer daemon to keep the printer busy, a network daemon to accept incoming network packets, and so on. Daemons are user space threads that exist solely to implement OS-like functionality. The correct behavior of the OS depends on them.

SOFTWARE MODULARIZATION

In Section 3.1, four different classes of management functions were introduced, suggesting that an OS could be designed by implementing each of these management functions in its own software module. Based on this supposition, Figure 3.10 illustrates that there are a number of interactions among these modules (the lines between modules indicate interactions). The process manager creates the process definition and execution environment on top of the hardware processor. However, it also uses the abstractions produced by the other managers for implementing resource management since each of these other modules is responsible for some class of resources.

✦ FIGURE 3.10 Logical OS Organization

Logically, the OS is made up of process, memory, device, and file managers. Each of these managers often needs to read or write a data structure that is "owned" by one of the other managers. This poses a difficulty in implementing a high-performance kernel while conforming to interfaces suggested by the logical modularity.

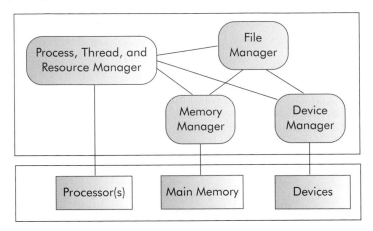

The main responsibility of the memory manager is to manage the computer's primary memory. However, if the OS supports virtual memory, then it must also interact tightly with the process manager in order to coordinate scheduling activity with memory allocation. In many contemporary file systems (for example in UNIX and Windows operating systems), files are defined in such a way that there is a considerable performance benefit by allowing the file manager to read information from a storage device prior to its being requested by a thread; this is called *buffering* (see Chapter 5 for more information about buffering). Buffering requires that the file manager and memory manager coordinate their actions for this particular type of file input/output.

Besides the interaction with the memory manager, the file manager interacts at a very high rate with the device manager, since it must read and write the storage devices. As mentioned in the previous paragraph, the interaction between the file manager and memory manager is necessary to handle buffered input/output operation.

The device manager interacts with the hardware devices. Since files are saved on storage devices, there are many interactions between the device and file managers. Conventional computers make heavy use of interrupt-driven device operation (see Chapter 4). In order to handle interrupts properly, there is a high rate of interaction between the device manager and the process manager.

The OS designer is on the horns of a dilemma: There are good reasons for modularizing software along the general lines of the four basic function classifications, since each of the four managers will have a number of data structures that should only be manipulated by "member functions" for the module. Interactions with other modules should then be implemented using an abstract data type (such as a class) interface. Since operating systems are such large pieces of software that are frequently being changed, there is a very strong argument for such modularization.

Historically, OS designers have explicitly chosen to violate normal modularization principles (along with various other software engineering principles) in order to meet performance requirements. The most obvious example of such a trade is in the implementation of the kernel of the UNIX OS: The four basic modules are combined into a single, monolithic software module—the UNIX kernel (that is, all the trusted software in UNIX is implemented in one huge module). The designers chose this approach since they knew that the OS components had a sufficiently high degree of interaction (file manager with device manager, process manager with memory manager, and so on) that they decided they would have to sacrifice modularization for performance. To avoid the cost of calls between modules, the monolithic implementation was chosen to enable functions in one logical module to directly manipulate data structures that logically belong to a different module. Such kernels are now infamous for their touchy code: Changing a line of code in the process management section of the kernel could easily break the memory manager.

Monolithic kernel organizations were the dominant approach to OS implementation from the 1970s to the 1990s, driven by the need for speed. By 1990, OS researchers had developed an alternative approach to monolithic implementations that employed modularization: the **microkernel** approach. The basis of this approach is that previous kernels (most of which were monolithic) had grown too large. Microkernel advocates decided that all kernel functionality should be revisited, and unless it was absolutely necessary for a function to be trusted, it should be implemented outside the kernel. The goal was to make the essential, trusted code be as small as possible. For example, a microkernel implements thread scheduling, hardware device management, fundamental protection mechanisms, and a few other basic functions. The remainder of the process, memory, file, and device management tasks are implemented in user space code that makes system calls into the microkernel.

Since microkernels tend to implement "small functions," in order for the overall OS to function properly, a user space OS function would generally have to make many system calls into the trusted microkernel. Each such call is as expensive in performance cost as a function call into a conventional kernel. So an important cost of a microkernel approach is the extra performance cost. The fiery issue among OS researchers in the 1990s was whether or not microkernels could be made to be fast enough so that the extra performance cost was insignificant. In this time period, every research paper that advocated a microkernel focused on the cost of using microkernels rather than on the value of its functionality (see [Liedtke,1995; Ford, et al., 1996]).

There are many more detailed aspects of OS design and implementation. A discussion of these detailed aspects would not make sense until you understand other details of the basic OS functions. Much of your study of operating systems will relate to these basic implementation considerations. In Chapter 19, after you have studied all the OS details, our discussion will return to implementation and software organization.

3.3 • CONTEMPORARY OS KERNELS

Today, the dominant commercial operating systems are versions of UNIX and Microsoft Windows operating systems. This book uses many examples from these two families of operating systems to illustrate the underlying general concepts. This section describes the general organization of UNIX kernels, and of the Windows NT kernel (used in Windows NT, Windows 2000, and Windows XP).

UNIX was designed as a timesharing OS, and its evolutionary systems, the BSD and AT&T versions, continue to basically be timesharing systems. UNIX's commercial acceptance in multiprogramming environments, such as those provided by minicomputers and workstations, is generally attributed to the fact that it is a portable timesharing OS. By contrast, personal computer software environments have been dominated first by Microsoft DOS and now by Microsoft Windows, probably because of its designers' relationship with the dominant personal computer hardware, the Intel microprocessors and the IBM PC. Although UNIX was the first to support multiprogramming and networking, Windows operating systems are more widely used. As of this writing, programmers and users generally choose between Windows 98/Me and Windows NT/2000/XP, or a variant of UNIX. Ultimately, commercial operating systems could converge on a single approach, although it is more likely that the marketplace will continue to support two or more alternatives. In either case, marketing and other commercial concerns, instead of technology, will almost certainly be the dominant factors.

The success of the UNIX and Windows OS interfaces has resulted in severe constraints on continued growth of OS technology. For a new OS to be successful, it must have language processors (compilers, linkers, and loaders), text editors, and a runtime library. The existing environments provide all of those tools and applications so new OS implementations can contain as much innovation as desired, provided they can be used by other application and system software as if they were a UNIX or Windows implementation. Today, research operating systems still follow the general trend of implementing some variant of a UNIX interface. On the commercial side of technology, abstract machines such as Java Virtual Machine and the Microsoft Common Language Runtime system are beginning to define OS-independent system call interfaces (see Chapter 19).

UNIX KERNELS

The UNIX kernel was developed in the early 1970s as a minicomputer OS in a Bell Laboratories research group [Ritchie and Thompson, 1974]. Later, UNIX was popularized as an interactive, timesharing OS for the 16-bit Digital Equipment Corporation PDP–11 (then later the VAX) minicomputer family. The UNIX designers had participated in the Multics project, so their design decisions were made with a full awareness of robust OS support and its requirement for special purpose hardware to implement segmentation and protection (as was done in Multics—see Chapter 12). UNIX takes a modest approach to design compared to Multics. It recognizes the limitations of inexpensive, slow hardware, resulting in an OS with minimal functionality. For example, Version 6 UNIX and its predecessors used swapping rather than virtual memory. When UNIX was introduced to the public in 1973, it was recognized as a departure from the extant trend in operating systems. It was unique in its simple file system, pipes, clean user interface—the shell—and extensible design.

The UNIX philosophy was to implement process, memory, file, and device management in the kernel, but only to implement the minimum functionality necessary to support a broad range of policies for each of these modules. The OS could then be tailored to various application domains by adding specialized system and application (user space) software to solve problems in any specific domain. For example, the kernel implements only byte stream files, although most applications ultimately require that information be stored in files as structured records. The rationale was that the kernel would provide the bare mechanisms to read and write byte streams, and library software (such as the `stdio` library) could be used to structure the byte stream as required. The three "layers" of the file system are then the byte stream level implemented in the kernel, the intermediate layer for formatted I/O in libraries, and the specific records to be used for an application.

A traditional UNIX kernel such as Linux is implemented as a monolithic software module (see Figure 3.11). The kernel provides minimal resource (process, memory, file and device) management. These minimal management facilities are designed so that they can be extended to create a specific computational environment. For example, in Chapter 2, you saw how a shell application can be created to provide a customized system console interface to the OS. The context for this design decision was that the UNIX developers were also the application programmers, so extending the OS would not be a big deal. However, each extension would be user space (untrusted) software, with the kernel being the carefully constructed trusted software. The developers worked hard to make a correct, secure, minimal kernel. Then they could dash off user space applications such as a shell with minimal effort.

✦ FIGURE 3.11 The UNIX Architecture

UNIX is a monolithic kernel, meaning that the process, memory, device, and file managers are all implemented in a single software module. The device driver part of device management is implemented in separate modules, but all other managers are one big program.

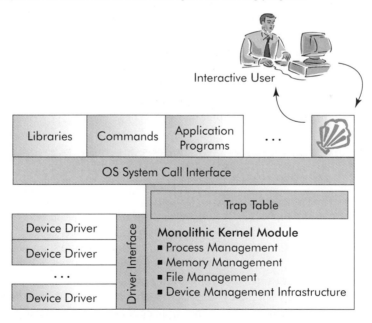

As a practical matter, the UNIX designers worked in an experimental environment where they would often add or remove devices from their computers. At that time, the OS had to be modified slightly, then rebuilt whenever a device was added. This inspired the designers to separate the device drivers from the rest of the kernel. UNIX kernels export an API that is only used by device driver programmers (we will discuss this in detail in

Chapter 5). Briefly, the driver-kernel interface relies on device drivers' having entry points with standard names, but whose locations can be determined from information in special files in the /dev directory. The kernel uses device numbers to search /dev and then to bind addresses (obtained from the corresponding special files) to the fixed entry point names. This allows any part of the device driver to be called using a standard, dynamically bound name. Today, this **reconfigurable device driver** idea is used in almost every OS.

The UNIX developers worked in a research environment in which they had computers from more than one manufacturer. Their goal was to create a new OS that could be ported to any hardware that they happened to have in their lab. This was an important motivation for the small kernel idea. It also had another interesting effect: Because they wanted the kernel to be as small and efficient as possible, they decided to implement the OS as a single, monolithic software module rather than as a collection of modules with well-specified interfaces. The original UNIX kernel was small and efficient.

UNIX is widely used today, often for relatively large systems. Over the years, the kernel has expanded to address evolving technology. For example, by 1990, almost all UNIX implementations had evolved from swapping systems to paging systems. Process management has been upgraded to address multiprocessor and distributed hardware configurations. The kernel now supports graphic devices and network protocols. The original kernel has been expanded, ported, and reimplemented many times since its inception, always retaining the monolithic structure. Today's commercial UNIX kernel is huge and complex. Most implementations are difficult to modify due to the close coupling of various parts of the kernel. Many of the reasons for using a modular approach rather than a monolithic approach now exist in UNIX environments.

However, the UNIX application program interface has become well entrenched, to the point of becoming the basis of the IEEE POSIX.1 open systems standard. There are two alternative paths taken to support the traditional UNIX system call interface: the monolithic kernel approach and a complete redesign of the kernel, such as the Mach 2 extensible kernel and the newer Mach 3 microkernel approach.

Linux

Linux is a contemporary, open source implementation of UNIX, available at no cost on the Internet. Besides its availability, the universality of Linux has made it significant: Linux is a timesharing OS, a personal computer and workstation OS, an embedded systems OS, an SCC OS, and a network OS. Although Linux is free, you can also buy an industrial-strength, supported version from various companies. Since its introduction in 1991, Linux has grown to be a highly respected, robust implementation of UNIX. It has had great success as a platform for studying contemporary operating systems, especially the internal behavior of a kernel.

In 1991, Linus Torvalds began creating the first version of Linux. (The comp.os.minix newsgroup had a few postings from Torvalds in early 1991, in which he announced to the world that he was working on a public implementation of POSIX.) Apparently he was inspired by the success of Tanenbaum's MINIX [Tanenbaum, 1987], but he intended for his OS to be more robust and useful than MINIX. Torvalds released his Linux source code to anyone who wanted to use it (by making it freely available over the Internet under the GNU Public License). It quickly caught on as a significant implementation of the POSIX system call interface. Soon, people all over the world began to contribute their own modifications and enhancements to Torvalds' original code. Today, the Linux distribution includes the OS and a spectrum of supplementary tools, written by many different contributors. Besides the original Intel 80386/80486/80586 (also called the "x86" or "i386") implementation, there are now implementations for the DEC/Compaq/HP Alpha, Sun Sparc, Motorola 68K, MIPS, and PowerPC. By 1996—five years after it was created—Linux had become a significant OS. By 1997, it had become an important part of the commercial OS scene, while continuing its first role as an open source implementation of the UNIX interface.

Linux is designed as a monolithic kernel (see Figure 3.11), but with a new twist for expanding OS functionality: Linux supports dynamically installable **modules**. A module can be compiled and installed on a running version of the kernel. This is accomplished by providing system calls to install/remove modules. Modules are most often used to implement device drivers, although a programmer can use them to implement any desired functionality (as long as they follow the kernel's specification for registering their functions).

THE WINDOWS NT EXECUTIVE AND KERNEL

The Windows NT Executive and Kernel were developed as a proprietary OS that would provide a modern computational environment for personal computers and workstations. The kernel technology was originally used for the Windows NT OS product, then Windows 2000, and now Windows XP. The Windows NT developers were experienced OS developers from various companies, universities, and research laboratories.

The product goals for the Windows NT kernel were that it should be an *extensible*, *portable*, *reliable*, and *secure* OS for contemporary computers, including symmetric multiprocessors [Solomon and Russinovich, 2000]. These terms can mean many things, so they warrant some discussion to see how they influenced the original kernel design.

EXTENSIBILITY. There are at least two dimensions to the extensibility aspect. The first relates to OS configurations. A Windows NT/2000/XP machine can be configured for a workstation or a server. In either configuration, the OS uses the same source code, but different components are incorporated into each at compile time. This allows Windows NT/2000/XP to be optimized to perform best according to the way the machine will be used—as a workstation or as a server—without building two different operating systems.

The second, and perhaps more significant, aspect of extensibility is in the way the OS software is structured. Windows NT/2000/XP is designed using the extensible nucleus software model. In this approach, only the most essential OS functions are implemented in a small nucleus of code (analogous to a microkernel). Additional mechanisms are then implemented on top of the nucleus to define policy as needed. This approach has the advantage that key mechanisms (such as protection mechanisms) can be designed carefully and tested as one trusted subassembly that can then be used to implement many different policies. This is a basic approach to support the goals of good security and reliable operation.

The **NT Kernel** provides these essential low-level mechanisms as a layer of abstraction from the hardware (see Figure 3.12). The **NT Executive** is designed as a layer of abstraction of the NT Kernel. It provides specific mechanisms (and many policies) for general object and memory management, process management, file management, and device management. Together, the NT Kernel and the NT Executive provide the essential elements of an OS, although this nucleus is extended yet again by the subsystems (as explained later).

✦ FIGURE 3.12   Windows NT/2000/XP Organization

The Windows NT OS architecture is logically layered with a hardware abstraction layer (HAL), NT Kernel, NT Executive, and various subsystems on top of the NT Executive. The system call interface is the Win32 API that is exported by the Win32 subsystem. The I/O subsystem is separate from the rest of the OS kernel, and contains the device drivers.

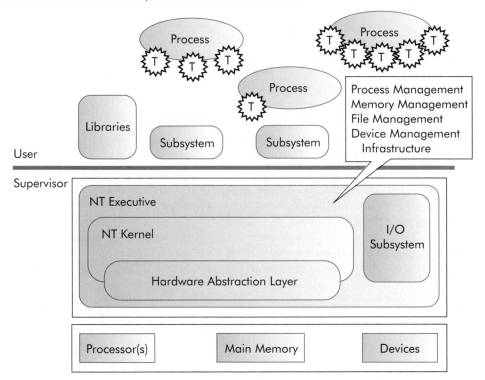

Although the NT Kernel and the NT Executive are designed and implemented as distinct software modules, they are combined into a single executable image when they are translated into machine code [Solomon and Russinovich, 2000]. This image also invokes additional dynamically linked libraries (DLLs) whenever they are needed. Thus the logical view of Windows NT/2000/XP—that of a modular nucleus—is quite different from the way the OS code actually appears in memory—as a monolithic block of code.

The next layer of abstraction of Windows NT/2000/XP is the subsystem layer. Subsystems provide application *portability* for Windows software. A **Windows subsys-**

tem is a software module that uses the services (mechanisms) implemented in the NT Kernel and the NT Executive to implement more abstract *services*, especially the services offered by some target OS. For example, Windows NT Version 4.0 has a POSIX subsystem that executes on top of the Kernel and the Executive, which makes it look like POSIX. Such subsystems are called *environment subsystems*, or *personality modules*. Other subsystems implement specialized services such as the security subsystem. All subsystems (and all application programs that use the subsystems) execute when the processor is in user mode. Subsystems are the key component in allowing Microsoft to support various computational models, such as the MS-DOS and Win16 program models. Application programs written to run on MS-DOS use the MS-DOS subsystem interface. This subsystem provides the same API to the application as does MS-DOS, thereby allowing old MS-DOS programs to run on a Windows 2000 system.

PORTABILITY. The portability aspect of the Windows NT overlaps its extensibility. Subsystems allow the base OS to be extended to meet various application support requirements, and they are also a cornerstone of portability (since a subsystem allows application programs written for other operating systems to be easily ported to Windows NT). As mentioned above, Microsoft has built various subsystems to implement OS personalities of interest to their customers. In general, it is possible for software developers to implement any subsystem to satisfy their general requirements for OS service. Even so, the Win32 subsystem takes a special role in Windows NT because it implements various extensions of the NT Executive that are needed by all other subsystems. Every subsystem relies on the presence of the Win32 subsystem. Although it is possible to add new environment subsystems to Windows NT and to omit most of them, the Win32 subsystem must always be present.

Another aspect of portability that has driven the design of Windows NT/2000/XP is the ability to port the OS itself across different hardware platforms. Microsoft's goal was to be able to reuse the NT Kernel, NT Executive, and subsystems on new microprocessors as they became available without having to rewrite the Kernel (or Executive, and so on). The goal was for Windows NT/2000/XP itself to be written to be portable. Windows NT's designers carefully identified the things that were common and the things that were different across a wide set of microprocessors. This allowed them to create a **hardware abstraction layer** (**HAL**) software module to isolate the NT Kernel (and the rest of the OS) from hardware differences. The HAL is responsible for mapping various low-level, processor-specific operations into a fixed interface that is used by the NT Kernel and Executive. The HAL also executes with the processor in supervisor mode.

The HAL, NT Kernel, and NT Executive are supervisor-mode software that collectively export an API that is used by subsystem designers (but not by application programmers). Environment subsystem designers choose a target API (such as the Win16, POSIX, or OS/2 API) and then build a subsystem to implement the API using the supervisor portion of Windows 2000. The Win32 subsystem exports the Win32 API, which is normally thought of as the system call interface to Windows. Windows NT/2000/XP application programs are written to work on the Win32 API rather than on the interface to the kernel.

RELIABILITY AND SECURITY. Both the reliability and security requirements for Windows NT/2000/XP are reflected in the details of how the NT Kernel and Executive are designed and implemented (rather than in their overall organization). Reliability is supported by separating the HAL, Kernel, Executive, and subsystem functionality from one another, thus eliminating unnecessary interactions. It is further supported through the software design techniques used in implementing Windows NT.

Windows NT/2000/XP is designed to meet modern requirements for trusted operating systems. Much of the security mechanism is implemented in a security subsystem, which depends on the Security Reference Manager in the NT Executive. Note that even though the presence of these mechanisms makes it possible to create very secure systems, if the application software does not use the security mechanisms, the overall system will not be especially secure (most production software does not use the protection mechanism).

3.4 ● SUMMARY

Operating systems define a computational environment to support applications. The environment implements processes, resources, and facilities to manage the use of resources by processes. Resources include processors, memory, and various abstractions of hardware and software facilities. In addition to these fundamental requirements on the OS, several other more detailed requirements must be satisfied. All facilities implemented in the software introduce performance overhead to the basic computation, so the value of the facility must justify the performance cost. All facility designs and implementations must be scrutinized carefully to ensure high performance. The facilities must provide a safe sharing environment in which one process cannot interfere with another process or its resources.

Modern operating systems incorporate managers for processes and resources, including specialized managers for memory, files, and devices. This modularization of basic functions has come from historical perspective rather than sound software modularization principles. It is well-entrenched, so it is not likely that the basic modules will change much in operating systems for some time.

Implementation techniques for modern operating systems rely on a few fundamental technologies. Contemporary processors incorporate a mode bit to allow the processor to execute in supervisor or user mode. If the processor is in user mode and wishes to set the mode bit to supervisor mode, it must execute a special trap instruction to set the bit and then branch to OS code. If the processor is in supervisor mode, the bit can be set to user mode with no special action. The part of the OS that executes in supervisor mode is called the kernel. Some modern operating systems use system call interfaces so that the application process executes OS software in supervisor mode. Others are designed as separate processes that interact with application processes by using message-passing mechanisms.

3.5 ● EXERCISES

1. When the trap instruction was introduced, it was suggested that it might not be good for the user program to be able to reference the trap table index for a particular system function. Give some reasons why it might not be good for this information to be specified directly by the application.

2. Speculate about some factors that differentiate between the time to do a normal procedure call from an application program to one of its own procedures, com-

pared to the time it takes to perform a system call to an OS procedure. (Several of these factors are discussed in the chapters that follow.)

3. Assume the OS for a set of workstations provides a message-passing mechanism. Explain how one might implement a shared memory environment on top of the mechanism. Think of arguments explaining why this implementation might be a good idea.

4. The original IBM PC and its clones employed the Intel 8088/8086 microprocessor. This machine did not incorporate a mode bit for supervisor and user modes. Hence, any application program (written in assembly language) could load the segment registers any time it wanted to. Suppose an assembly language procedure is called from a C program and the procedure writes a new value into the stack segment register. What will happen when the procedure returns to the C program? Suppose a procedure writes a new value into the code segment register. What will be the effect?

5. The Linux Documentation Project is a web site (http://www.ibiblio.org/mdw/index.html) that provides a comprehensive description of Linux internals. Find the Linux Kernel Module Programming Guide, or its replacement if it has been removed by the time you read this. Implement a module that prints a "Hello, world" greeting. You will have to have administrative permission to install your module on a Linux machine.

6. Consult the online documentation for your Windows NT/2000/XP machine for the *task manager*. Start the task manager running, then inspect the Applications tab. What applications are currently running? How many processes are currently running? How many threads are currently running? Where did you find the numbers of processes and threads?

Observing OS Behavior

> This exercise can be solved on Solaris and Linux systems.

The OS is a program that uses various data structures. Like all programs in execution, you can determine the performance and other behavior of the OS by inspecting its state—the values stored in its data structures. The goal of this exercise is to study some aspects of the organization and behavior of a Linux system by observing values in kernel data structures.

Write a program to report the behavior of the Linux kernel. Your program should have three different options. The default version should print the following values on stdout:

- Processor type
- Kernel version
- Amount of time since the system was last booted

A second version of the program should print the same information as the first version plus:

- The amount of time the processor has spent in user mode, system mode, and the amount of time the system was idle
- The number of disk read/write requests made on the system
- The number of context switches the kernel has performed
- The time at which the system was last booted
- The number of processes that have been created since the system was booted

The last version of the program should print the same information as the second version, plus (be sure to look at the relevant man pages for /proc to get more context for the requested information):

- The amount of memory configured into this computer
- The amount of memory currently available
- A list of load averages (each averaged over the last minute). This information would allow another program to plot these values against time so that a user could see how the load average varied over some time interval. For this version of the program, you will need to provide two additional parameters to indicate (1) how often the load average should be read from the kernel and (2) the time interval over which the load average should be read.

For example, the first version of your program might be called by ksamp, the second version with ksamp -s, and the third version with ksamp -l 2 60 (which would cause the load average observation to run for 60 seconds, sampling the kernel table about once every 2 seconds). In solving this part of the exercise, you will probably find it useful to read about the sleep() system call.

●   **BACKGROUND**   ●

In general, much of process and resource management is implemented in a UNIX kernel. Almost all of memory, file, and device management is implemented in the kernel. In this lab exercise, your goal is to determine the state of various aspects of these different managers.

The Linux kernel is implemented as a monolithic block of code loaded in supervisor space. Because it is monolithic, the data structures may be manipulated by widely disparate parts of the kernel. As a consequence, it is sometimes difficult to locate specific data structures, and hence, to determine the OS state. Linux, Solaris, and some other versions of UNIX provide the `/proc` file system, a very useful mechanism for inspecting the kernel state. This will be the key mechanism you can use to solve this lab exercise.

THE `/proc` FILE SYSTEM

McKusick et al. [1996, p. 113] mentions that the `/proc` file system comes from UNIX Eighth Edition and that it has been used with 4.4 BSD: "In the `/proc` system, the address space of another process can be accessed with `read` and `write` system calls, which allows a debugger to access a process being debugged with much greater efficiency. The page (or pages) of interest in the child process is mapped into the kernel address space. The requested data can then be copied directly from the kernel to the parent address space." They also mention (p. 239) that `/proc` can be used to collect information about processes in the system.

Linux uses the `/proc` file system to collect information from kernel data structures. The `/proc` implementation provided with Linux can read many different kernel data structures. If you `cd` to `/proc` on your local Linux system, and then list the files and directories at that location, you will see several directories and several files. The files in this directory subtree each read some kernel tables. The subdirectories with numeric names contain pseudo files to read information about the process whose process ID is the same as the directory name. The directory named `self` contains process-specific information for the process that is using `/proc`.

Files in `/proc` are read just like ordinary ASCII files. That is, you must open the file, and then you can use `stdio` library routines such as `fgets()` or `fscanf()` to read the file. The exact files (and tables) read depend on the specific version of Linux that you are using. You must read the `proc  (5)` manual page on the system before you will know exactly which file interfaces are available to you through `/proc`. For example, the Redhat Linux 2.0.36 distribution provides a file named `/proc/sys/kernel/osrelease`. If you open this file and read it, you will see the ASCII string "`2.0.36`". You can also simply use the shell `cat` command to experiment with the files in `/proc` and its subdirectories.

Before you begin using the `/proc` file system, note that the various read functions may behave differently. For example, some of the routines may read the kernel tables only when the pseudo file is opened, and others may read the tables each time the file is read.

●   **ATTACKING THE PROBLEM**   ●

Your program is required to have three different options, so you will need to parse the command line with which it is called to determine the shell parameters being passed to it via the `argv` array. Identify a file—say, `/proc/sys/kernel/foo`—that contains the information you want.

Open the file with a call such as

```
fid = fopen("/proc/sys/kernel/foo", "r");
fscanf(fid, " ...", ...);
```

After you have read the data from the appropriate pseudo file, parse the string to extract the information you need, and then print your report on stdout using stdio functions.

Computer Organization

An OS provides an abstraction to simplify the use of the hardware. Most people who study operating systems have already taken a course on computer organization, so our discussion focuses on the parts of the hardware (such as traps and interrupts) that especially concern OS designers.

Single-threaded processes are an abstraction of the operation of von Neumann computers. You can understand the intuition behind processes if you understand how a von Neumann computer executes a program. A deep understanding of operating systems depends on this basic knowledge about how computer hardware is organized, especially the control unit and device operation. Device management is introduced in this chapter and refined in Chapter 5. The information in Chapters 4 and 5 provides the classic example of the interaction between software and hardware. This interaction also introduces the recurring situation in which the OS must manage two or more distinct mechanisms at the same time. Although the focus in this chapter is on the hardware, we continue to study the computer from the system programmer's perspective.

4.1 • THE VON NEUMANN ARCHITECTURE

Operating system software is built on top of the computer hardware. The architecture of a computer refers to the nature of the subassemblies that are used to build the computer—the processor, memory, and devices—and the manner in which these subassemblies are interconnected. Although you may find it somewhat surprising, more than 95% of all modern computers use an architecture that was defined during World War II—well over half a century ago. This architecture, in turn, uses essential design elements that were invented in the early 1800s.

EVOLVING TO THE VON NEUMANN ARCHITECTURE

Charles Babbage began to work on his Difference Engine in 1822, sporadically continuing to develop the idea—later called the Analytical Engine—until 1857 [Randell, 1973]. The Difference Engine used the notion of the **stored program computer**—*implemented entirely as mechanical parts with no electronic components!* In the early nineteenth century, Jacquard weaving looms incorporated a mechanism for storing a representation of the pattern to be woven into a fabric, allowing the weaver to "program" the pattern into the loom. Babbage recognized the power of the approach and used it in his Difference Engine to store a computational pattern—the first known stored program computing machine. Babbage discovered that he could "weave a large computation" by repeatedly combining patterns of computation; he used the pattern storage of the Jacquard loom to store computational patterns (like the computation in the range of a for-loop). He described the basic elements of the revolutionary idea for stored program computational engines in a paper in 1836 [Babbage, 1836].

Babbage's ideas were reinvented, extended, and implemented using electronic elements by Zuse [1936], Atanasoff [1940], researchers at Bell Laboratories in 1945 [Alt, 1948], Aiken and Hopper [1946] and others during the 1930s and 1940s. The U.S. government commissioned a group of researchers to build the EDVAC computer in the early 1940s [von Neumann, 1945]:

> *It is evident that the machine must be capable of storing in some manner not only the digital information needed in a given computation ..., but also the instructions which govern the actual routines to be performed on the numerical data.*

The EDVAC architecture for stored program computers—now called the **von Neumann computer architecture**—came from this research group's work; it is the documented architecture of contemporary computers.

THE BASIC IDEA

Before computers, the design of an electronic device determined its functionality. For example, if the device was to meter fluid flow, then it could not be used for some other purpose. von Neumann computers are based on the idea that the machine has a fixed set of electronic parts whose actions are determined by a variable program (see Figure 4.1). Different programs can perform different sequences of operations that implement different functions using the same hardware; this idea is now trivial to programmers, but it was revolutionary in Babbage's time. As a result, the von Neumann computer can be used to solve many types of problems. This characteristic is the crucial difference between these stored program computers and other electronic devices. It is also a key property that motivates the use of embedded computers (see Section 1.2) to construct electronic subassemblies in rocket ships, hydroelectric controllers, and so on. That is, the normal electronic hardware to implement a control function contains a stored program computer—an embedded computer. The software part of the solution can then be flexible and be easily updated while the basic computer and devices are unchanged.

Stored program computers that are used for solving general problems are configured with a general set of devices. Many problems require that the computer have input devices (such as keyboard, display, and mouse), a printer, a network interface, a disk drive. Computers configured in this manner are referred to as "general-purpose computers,"

✦ FIGURE 4.1   Stored Program Computers and Electronic Devices

Stored program computers use the idea of a stored pattern from the Jacquard loom of the nineteenth century. This means that you can use one loom to "automatically" create fabrics with many different patterns. In the computer case, the fixed electronics can be programmed to do the work of different configurations of hardwired electronics.

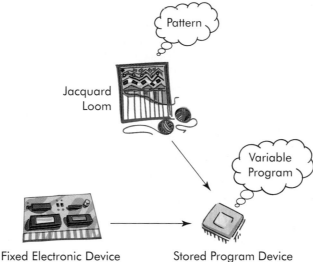

since they can be adapted to do many types of computational and information storage tasks. Personal computers, workstations, and network servers are all general-purpose stored program computers.

The von Neumann computer architecture forms the basis for almost all contemporary computer systems, particularly general-purpose computers, but also most special-purpose computers. Computers designed for very highly specialized processing tasks (like signal processing) sometimes diverge from the von Neumann architecture, although most of them evolve from the basic von Neumann idea. Section 4.8 describes some variations from the basic von Neumann architecture that were motivated by the need for high performance computation.

The hardware in a von Neumann computer has the following components (see Figure 4.2):

■ A central processing unit (CPU) made up of an arithmetical-logical unit (ALU) and a control unit

■ A primary (or executable) memory unit

■ A collection of I/O devices

■ Buses to interconnect the other components

Programs and data are brought into the computer from the external world (outside the machine) using I/O devices. An **input device** such as a keyboard is used to enter information from the external world into the computer. An **output device** such as a printer is used to copy information from inside the computer to the external world. **Storage devices**

✦ **FIGURE 4.2** The von Neumann Architecture

A von Neumann computer contains a CPU, which contains an ALU and control unit. The control unit decodes stored instructions and the ALU executes them. The primary (executable) memory is used to store the program and data that are operated on by the CPU. The devices are used for input, output, communications, and storage. The bus interconnects the CPU, primary memory, and devices.

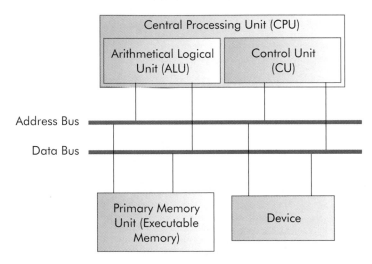

can be used to save information inside the computer. After information has been computed or read from the external world, it can then be stored in a storage device. The information can be retrieved from the storage device and placed in the primary memory for subsequent computation. Files are stored on storage devices. **Communication devices** are a combination of input and output devices. A device that services a modem, such as a serial port, is a communication device.

Before a program and data can be used, they are prepared for execution and saved on a storage device. When the program and data are ready to be used, they are copied into the primary memory unit from an input device or storage device. Once the program and data have been loaded into the primary memory, the **central processing unit** (**CPU**) performs computation on the data, producing new data that is stored in the primary memory. As shown in the figure, the CPU is made up of a control unit and an arithmetical logical unit. The **control unit** (**CU**) reads each instruction in the program, decodes the instruction, and causes it to be executed by the component responsible for executing that particular instruction. The **arithmetical logical unit** (**ALU**) performs all arithmetic operations such as adding, subtracting, multiplying, and dividing numbers. It also performs logical operations such as comparing two numbers, detecting if a number is zero, and so on.

All units are connected using a **bus** to carry electronic signals between units. In Figure 4.2, the bus is divided into an **address bus** to transmit addresses, and a **data bus** to transmit data. In some computers, this pair of buses is implemented as a single time-multiplexed bus. In others, it is replicated to provide more bandwidth for transferring addresses and data among the various units in the computer. For example, an input/output bus (consisting of an address part and a data part) might be attached only to devices and memory, but not be used by the processor. Each bus consists of many individual signal carriers ("wires"). Some of the wires are used to arbitrate access to the bus (for example, to allocate the bus to a device when it wants to transfer data between itself and memory). Others are used to carry information—addresses or data. Still others are used for control functions. It is common for a bus incorporating 16 individual wires for moving data from one unit to another to have twice as many control lines. Thus a bus can be an expensive and complex part of the computer.

All von Neumann computers have a CPU with an ALU and control unit, a primary memory unit, and a set of devices. Some of the devices are for input, some for output, some for communicating with other machines, and some for storage. (Non-von Neumann computers often diverge from the basic architecture—for example, by using alternative units in the machine, coalescing two or more of the units into a single unit, or having a single control unit and multiple ALUs.) The hardware is controlled by loading software into the primary memory and then executing it. We will discuss the units in a von Neumann computer in more detail in the next section.

4.2 ● THE CENTRAL PROCESSING UNIT

The CPU is the "brain" of the computer: It decides which instructions should be executed, and then decodes and executes them. It is the design of the CPU that distinguishes stored program computers from other electronic devices—this is the idea that Babbage began to formulate in 1822, which the von Neumann committee applied in 1945, and which is the basis of a modern Pentium or SPARC microprocessor.

The CPU is made up of an ALU and a control unit (see Figure 4.2). The ALU is the part of the CPU that actually performs the computations. The control unit is the part that decides the sequence in which instructions should be executed, and then decodes each instruction so that the ALU can execute it.

THE ARITHMETICAL-LOGICAL UNIT

The ALU can be thought of as a very fast calculator: It has a **function unit** that can perform the arithmetic (addition, subtraction, multiplication, and division) and logical (comparison, logical AND, OR, and NOT) operations. Like a calculator, the function unit performs these operations on operands. Most operations are binary, meaning that they work on two operands. For example, we specify an addition operation such as "x + y" by specifying a left operand, "x"; a right operand, "y"; and the addition operation, "+". The ALU also contains a set of general registers to hold operands that will be used by the function unit (see Figure 4.3). These registers are loaded from a primary memory location by executing a `load` machine instruction. Register contents can also be saved into a primary memory location using a `store` instruction. Contemporary CPUs have 32 to 64 registers, each typically able to hold a 32-bit value. (The number of registers and their size continue to grow with each generation of new CPUs—some new machines have 64-bit values.)

The ALU status registers are used by various parts of the CPU to capture the status of the ALU (and sometimes control unit) operations. Throughout this book, all new uses for status registers are explained as the need for them is justified. For now, think of a status register as a place where the CPU stores information regarding the computations currently being carried out in the unit, such as "the result of the last function unit operation was equal to 0."

✦ FIGURE 4.3   A General Arithmetical-Logical Unit

The ALU performs a spectrum of binary arithmetic and logical operations, such as add, subtract, and logical AND. The functional unit performs the operations, and the registers hold the operands and results. Register are loaded and stored from/to the primary memory. The status registers reflect the results from CPU operations.

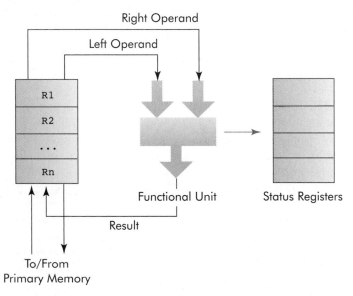

In all electronic technologies that have been used to implement computers, information is stored internally using binary representations. For numbers, this means than an integer is stored in the computer using the base 2 number system instead of the familiar base 10 number system. This means that the function unit is intended to operate only on binary representations of information instead of decimal representations. Section 4.3 has more discussion on binary representations.

Computations are accomplished by loading binary values into general registers, performing operations on the registers using the function unit (which stores the result back into a general register), and then saving the results back into memory. For example, if a C source program contains the code segment

```
a = b + c;
d = a - 100;
```

then the following symbolic representation of machine language instructions (called an *assembly language* representation) will be executed by the CPU to accomplish these two statements:

```
// Assembly language code for a = b + c;
load    R3,b    // Copy the value of b from memory to R3
load    R4,c    // Copy the value of c from memory to R4
add     R3,R4   // Sum placed in R3
store   R3, a   // Store the sum into memory cell a
```

```
// Assembly language code for d = a - 100
load       R4,=100    // Load the value 100 into R4
subtract   R3,R4      // Difference placed in R3
store      R3,d       // Store the difference in memory cell d
```

The first three machine instructions compute "b + c" by loading the value of the variable "b" from the primary memory into general register R3, loading the value of the variable "c" from the primary memory into register R4, and then having the function unit use the contents of R3 and R4 as operands for an addition operation. In this hypothetical computer, the function unit writes the result of the addition operation into general register R3, so the fourth instruction stores the contents of R3, which is the sum of "b" and "c," into the primary memory location that holds the value of the "a" variable. The last 3 instructions evaluate and save a new value for "d."

The function unit is the actual computing engine for the computer. The function unit can be simple or complex. Floating-point operations are more complex than are integer operations, so some function units do not incorporate the extra hardware logic required to perform floating-point arithmetic. Instead, either an auxiliary processor performs floating point operations or those operations are implemented using a software library routine.

THE CONTROL UNIT

The control unit causes a sequence of instructions stored in the executable memory to be retrieved and executed. As shown in Figure 4.4, the control unit includes one component to fetch an instruction from memory, one to decode the instruction, and one to signal the other parts of the computer—mainly the ALU—to execute the instruction. The **program counter (PC)** register contains the memory address of the next instruction the control unit is to load. The **instruction register (IR)** contains a copy of the current instruction once it has been fetched from the primary memory. In Figure 4.4, the IR contains the image of the load instruction from location 3050 and the PC contains 3054 (the address of the next instruction to be fetched for execution).

The operation of the control unit hardware is better understood by looking at its logical **fetch-execute algorithm** (see Figure 4.5). When the machine is initially started, the PC is loaded with the address of the first instruction to be executed. This is normally done by a hardware boot sequence. That is, the machine executes its first instruction from a primary memory address hardwired into the machine. The control unit fetches the first instruction, loads the instruction from the primary memory that is stored at the designated location, and then begins normal operation. In the algorithm description, a haltFlag is tested each time through the loop to determine when the control unit is to be stopped (there are many variants as to how this part of the algorithm is defined for any particular von Neumann computer). When the control unit is halted, the computer is halted. When the system software wishes to execute a program—this system software is being executed by the control unit—it loads the program into the primary memory and then stores the program's entry point in the PC.

The fetch-execute cycle defines the operation of a computer at a primitive level—a level below software control. When the computer is powered up, the control unit begins to execute the fetch-execute cycle, and will continue to do so until the computer is powered down. We use the term **hardware process** to refer to this basic activity: When the com-

✦ FIGURE 4.4 The PC, IR, and Memory

The control unit fetches the next instruction to be executed from the primary memory address that is stored in the PC. The contents of that primary memory location are loaded into the IR. When a new instruction is loaded into the IR, the decode unit parses the instruction to decide what action should be taken to execute it. The execution unit then causes the appropriate parts of the CPU to execute the instruction.

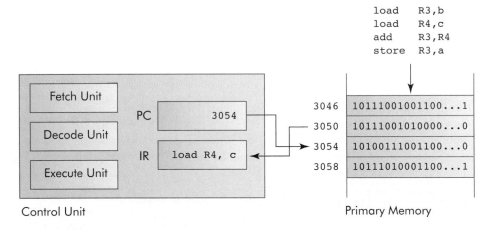

```
load    R3,b
load    R4,c
add     R3,R4
store   R3,a
```

Control Unit

Primary Memory

✦ FIGURE 4.5 The Hardware Fetch-Execute Cycle

The fetch-execute algorithm is implemented in the control unit hardware. The steps in the range of the `while` loop are those required to execute a single machine instruction.

```
PC = <machine start address>;
IR = memory[PC];
haltFlag = CLEAR;
while (haltFlag not SET during execution) {
  PC = PC + 1;
  execute(IR);
  IR = memory[PC];
};
```

puter is powered up, we say that the hardware process begins to run. It is important for you to observe that the hardware process is not an OS process at all: It is used to execute the OS and all the abstract machines that it creates. It does this by executing instructions from one program for a while, and then it switches to another program to execute instructions. The OS is just one of those programs. We will consider the behavior of the hardware process in more detail in Sections 4.6 and 6.2.

IMPLEMENTING THE PROCESSOR

The original implementations of the CPU (in the 1940s) were huge machines that used vacuum tube technology (today, vacuum tubes have just about disappeared except for their use in high-end guitar amplifiers). A vacuum tube was about the size of a household light bulb. It contained electronic circuitry that would perform a single logical function, the equivalent of a transistor. A computer built from vacuum tubes had to be physically quite large, and it consumed a lot of power. The EDVAC and other such machines filled large rooms, and even required specialized electricity service for their operation. It would not be possible to put a machine like the EDVAC in your basement (unless you have a huge house and your own power substation).

By the 1960s, vacuum tubes had been replaced by transistors, and then integrated circuits containing multiple transistors—causing a great reduction in the size and power consumption of CPUs. Not only did this enable computers to be much smaller and to consume less power, but also it encouraged computer designers to add new functionality to the hardware. The super computers that came from this era were the IBM 7090 Stretch computers, followed a few years later by the IBM System/360 Model 91 and CDC 6600. These machines had multiple functional units, and various other design tricks to make them as fast as possible. ([Thornton 1970] describes the extraordinary lengths to which the CDC designers went to make the world's fastest computer at that time.)

Integrated circuit technology continued to develop at a rapid pace, so that by the late 1970s it was possible to use large-scale integrated circuits to implement an entire CPU on a single integrated circuit chip. The trend has continued: As of this writing, a contemporary microprocessor such as the Intel Pentium 4 has almost 100,000,000 transistors.

Microprocessors use synchronous digital logic, meaning that there is a basic **clock cycle** that defines when operations are performed in the transistor-level circuitry. The microprocessor has a basic time cycle during which transistor assemblies can perform a function such as moving data from one register to another register, comparing the value of a register to zero, and so on. Thus a computer's clock cycle frequency is one factor in determining how fast the ALU can perform computations. Of course, the amount of work done in each cycle is equally important. For contemporary machines, simple machine instructions can be executed in a single clock cycle, although even memory access instructions require multiple clock cycles.

In the IBM PC AT, introduced in the early 1980s, the hardware had a basic clock cycle time of 6 MHz (6,000,000 cycles per second) [Messmer, 1995]. Thus, a lower bound on instruction execution time on this machine was the amount of elapsed time in one basic cycle, or 0.167×10^{-6} seconds. This can also be written as 0.167 microseconds (abbreviated μs, one millionth of a second) or 167 nanoseconds (abbreviated ns, a billionth of a second). By contrast, an Intel Pentium 4 processor can have a basic cycle time of more than 2GHz (2 billion cycles per second), meaning that the fastest instructions can be executed in 0.0004 μs, or 0.4 ns.

Contemporary microprocessors also attempt to increase their operating speed by employing designs that allow different parts of the CPU to run simultaneously. The first parallel operation incorporated into most microprocessors is to overlap the fetch and execute phases of operation in the control unit: A machine can be made to run almost twice as fast as normal by overlapping the fetch of the next instruction with the execution of the current instruction. For example, by overlapping the fetch and execute work, the fetch component of the control unit could be obtaining a copy of the instruction in location 3054, while the other parts of the control unit were decoding and executing the instruction in 3050.

4.3 ● THE PRIMARY (EXECUTABLE) MEMORY

The primary memory unit stores both programs and data while they are being operated on by the CPU. As shown in Figure 4.6, the memory has an interface composed of three relevant registers: the **memory address register (MAR)**, the **memory data register (MDR)**, and the **command register (Cmd)**. For information to be written into the memory, a datum is placed in the MDR, the desired memory address is placed in the MAR, and a `write` command is placed in the command register. Figure 4.6 illustrates the register and memory contents after a `write` command is placed in the command register. The memory unit stored the contents of the MDR (98765) into the memory location loaded in the MAR (1234). A `read` operation is accomplished by placing an address in the MAR and placing a `read` command into the command register. After a **memory cycle**, the memory unit copies the contents of the designated memory cell into the MDR.

✦ **FIGURE 4.6** The Memory Organization

Read operation: (1) load the MAR with the address. (2) Load the command register with read. (3) Data will then appear in the MDR after the memory has completed the command.

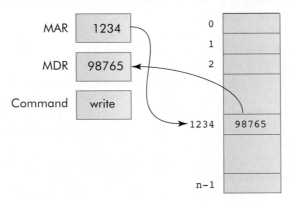

The number of cells and the width of each cell in the primary memory is determined by both the technology used to construct the memory and hardware design considerations. For example, if the memory were based on decimal technology, then a word (cell) might be capable of representing any three-digit number between 000 and 999. Each of the three digits could take on a value between 0 and 9. Since there are 10 such values, the numbers would be referred to as decimal (base 10) numbers.

With decimal technology, numbers would be stored internally using base 10 arithmetic. In contemporary computers, binary technology (base 2 arithmetic) is used to represent information. Binary technology is used because it is much easier to represent an individual subcell within a cell by an electronic component that is either off (equivalent to the value 0) or on (equivalent to the value 1) than it is to represent decimal numbers. A subcell within a word can store a single binary integer, or **bit**. Again, each cell contains a fixed number of subcells, so an 8-bit cell, a **byte**, is composed of 8 binary values. A byte can contain any binary number between 00000000 and 11111111. (In the decimal system, 00000000 base 2 = 0 base 10 and 11111111 base 2 = 255 base 10.)

Suppose the memory contains n words, each with K bits (see again Figure 4.6). The addresses of the n cells are the integers 0 through $n - 1$. The $i + 1$st memory cell has address i. In the figure, the memory cell with address 1234 contains the value of 98765 (stored in a binary memory as a 32-bit binary number 0 ... 011000010110110101). Notice that the addresses themselves can also be represented in base 2 notation, so 1234_{10} is represented by the 12-bit number 010011010010_2. If n is an integer power of 2, say $n = 4,294,967,296 = 2^{32}$, then a 32-bit cell can be used to store addresses. Now, if the memory word width K is greater than or equal to 32, one memory cell can be used to store addresses of other memory cells (these addresses can be used, for example, as indirect addresses). If K is less than 32, it is still possible, but more complex, to store an address in the memory by breaking the address into parts and storing the parts in consecutive cells.

In modern computers, a memory cell is 8 bits wide. Even in cases in which each memory cell is an 8-bit byte, groups of 2 or 4 bytes may be operated on as one unit in the CPU called a **word**; different computers define the word size according to the design of their CPU and machine instructions. Even though the CPU often operates on words, the computer hardware is usually organized so that the memory is byte-addressable—that is, each cell is a byte. The CPU can then be designed to perform numeric operations on words and character operations on bytes. This will be so even though the data bus connecting the CPU and the memory transfers words, so memory is read/written using 8-bit byte operations or 32-bit word operations.

As late as 1975, computer memories were implemented using ferrite cores (that look like a Cheerio) to store a bit. The technology severely limited the amount of primary memory (called "core memory" in those days) that could be configured into a machine. A large timeshared computer would have less than 1 MB of primary memory. In the 1970s, memory technology switched to solid state chip implementations. At about the same time, people began to refer to readable/writable primary memory chips as **random access memory**, or **RAM**. Since that time, memory manufacturers have vigorously refined their technology, designs, and chip fabrication procedures so that contemporary chips contain 512 Mb or more of memory—meaning that a bank of 8 of these chips implements 512 MB of memory.

4.4 • I/O Devices

I/O devices are attached to the computer bus. An input device transfers data from a mechanism such as a keyboard, mouse, touch sensitive screen, or microphone into a CPU register. The CPU can then store the data into the primary memory. It fetches information from the primary memory into its registers, and then writes the information over the bus to an output device such as a computer screen, a speaker, or printer. Communication devices are input and output devices that transmit information to another location. For example, serial and parallel ports, infrared transmitter/receivers, wireless network cards, and network interface cards are all communication devices. Storage devices can also be used for input and output: The input operation causes data to be moved from the storage device (such as a magnetic or optical disk) to the CPU registers, and then into the primary memory. The output operation moves data from the primary memory to the storage device.

Each I/O device consists of a controller subassembly to control the detailed operation of the device and the physical device itself. The specifics of the device operation depend on whether it is an input, output, communication, or storage device, and also on the way the specific device works (for example, capturing input information from a mouse is different from capturing a keystroke from a keyboard device). There are many types of devices of each of the four classes, ranging from slow and inexpensive ones to fast and expensive ones. As a result, there is a wide range of interfaces to the device controllers that the OS must be able to manipulate properly in order to correctly operate the device.

The device **controller** connects the device to the computer's address and data bus. The controller provides a set of components that CPU instructions can manipulate to cause the device to operate. While the details of the interface differ across controllers, each controller provides the same basic interface. As part of the goal of resource abstraction, the OS hides differences among controllers behind an interface common to all types of devices. Then, even though the speeds, capacities, and operation details differ among controllers, the programmer does not need to know the details about each device in order to use it. Commonality is achieved by abstracting the operational characteristics of device controllers into a single high-level definition in the OS (see Figure 4.7 and the earlier disk drive abstraction example in Section 1.1). Programmers use the abstract I/O paradigm implemented by the high-level definition to write I/O code for a broad spectrum of devices without knowing the details for any of the devices.

✦ FIGURE 4.7 The Device-Controller-Software Relationship

The OS device driver software manages the device hardware by interacting with the device's controller. Device drivers hide the details of controller management by exporting a common interface to the application software. The device-controller interface is a hardware-hardware interface. Its details are device-specific, and beyond the scope of operating systems.

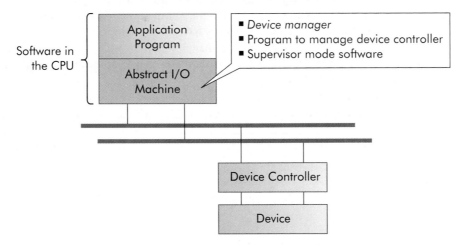

DEVICE CONTROLLERS

A device may require constant attention during its operation. If software were to control the device directly, it would need to continuously monitor the device's detailed operating status during the operation. This attention may simply be to observe status, provide detailed commands, and correct for minor errors. It is easy to design hardware algorithms to manage much of this mundane housekeeping. This is a second job of the device controller (adapting the device to the bus was the first).

The interface between devices and controllers is important to the industry that manufactures devices, but not to software designers. This device-controller interface is concerned with the means by which devices manufactured by one vendor can be connected to a controller manufactured by another. The SCSI (small computer serial interface) is an example of such an interface.

The interface between the bus and the controller is important to anyone wishing to attach a device to a computer so that the device can interoperate with other facilities in the machine. However, like the device-controller interface, this interface is transparent to software.

Figure 4.8 shows a conceptual software interface to a hardware controller. The exact interface differs from controller to controller. The goal of the interface design is to enable the software to operate the device (via the controller), and for the software to synchronize its behavior with the device operation. Controllers effectively incorporate two flags as part of their status register interface: busy and done.

- If both flags are set to 0 (or FALSE), the software can place a command in the command register to activate the device. After software has put data in one or more of the data registers for an output operation, the device is available for use.

- The presence of a new I/O command causes the controller to set the busy flag to TRUE and to begin the operation. An output operation causes the data in the data register to be written to the device, and an input operation causes a read operation to be sent to the device. The process can detect the status of the operation by checking the status register.

- When the I/O operation has completed (successfully or unsuccessfully), the controller clears the busy flag and sets the done flag. On completion of the read operation, data will have been copied into the data register from the device. On completion of a write operation, data will have been copied from the controller data register to the device.

- If the device flags have both been set to FALSE after a write operation, it is safe to write new data to the controller data register. When the software reads the data from the controller, the controller clears the done register to indicate the device is again ready for use.

If the controller encountered an unrecoverable error, then when it terminated, it would set the error code field in the status register.

Controllers incorporate a small amount of memory to hold data after it is read from the device but before it is retrieved by the program in the CPU. Conversely, the memory holds data waiting to be written to the device. This memory is called a (hardware) **buffer** and is sometimes used to increase the chances of overlapping the operation of the device and the CPU (see Chapter 5).

The normal operation of the CPU is independent of the operation of all of the devices. On the positive side of things, this means that devices can be in operation at the same time as the CPU. However, if software wants to control the operation of the devices, it is necessary for the software to determine when a device is busy, when it has finished work pre-

✦ FIGURE 4.8　The Conceptual Device Controller Interface

The driver-controller interface contains various registers which will include the done and busy flags as well as a field to report error status. The driver and controller interact by using these fields to coordinate their behavior.

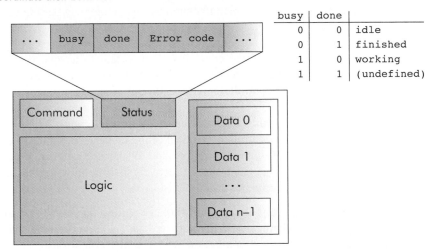

busy	done	
0	0	idle
0	1	finished
1	0	working
1	1	(undefined)

viously assigned to it, when it has encountered an error that the controller cannot recover, and so on. The busy and done flags are the essential elements in this coordination: They are used by the device to signal event occurrences to the software, and vice versa.

DIRECT MEMORY ACCESS

In I/O devices we have discussed so far, the CPU transfers data between the controller data registers and the primary memory (see Figure 4.9a). That is, the device driver copies the data from the application process's address space to the controller for each output operation and the reverse for input operations. The CPU executes a code segment such as the following when it wants to transfer a block of data from primary memory to the controller's data registers:

```
        load   R2, =LENGTH_OF_BLOCK   // R2 is index reg
loop:   load   R1, [data_area, R2]    // Load the block[i]
        store  R1, 0xFFFF0124         // Put in ctlr data reg
        incr   R2                     // Increment index
        bge    loop                   // Test for loop termination
```

In most cases, when data is read from the device, the programmer wants to copy it into memory. Similarly, when data is written to a device, it will come from memory. The CPU's only involvement is to physically copy the information between the memory and the device.

Direct memory access (DMA) controllers are able to read and write information directly from/to primary memory with no CPU intervention (see Figure 4.9b). The DMA controller hardware is designed to perform the same algorithm that the CPU software uses to transfer data between the memory and the controller *without using the CPU at all.*

(However, the controller and the CPU will compete for the bus if the CPU happens to need the bus at the same time that a device is performing a direct memory transfer.) Conceptually, a DMA controller need not even contain data registers, since it can read and write directly between the device and memory.

✦ FIGURE 4.9 Direct Memory Access

(a) Conventional devices use the CPU to move data between the device controller and the primary memory. (b) DMA controllers read and write the machine's primary memory without using the CPU.

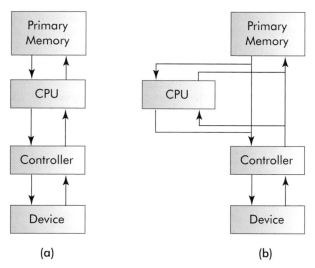

The device driver software manages the DMA controller much as it would a conventional controller. The driver uses the busy and done flags to synchronize its operation with the controller, just as with a conventional controller. Since the DMA controller will read/write a block of memory, the device driver will provide a primary memory address to the controller prior to starting the device. This address is a pointer to the relevant primary memory block.

DMA can increase the machine's I/O performance significantly, since the CPU no longer needs to be concerned with transferring data between the controller and the primary memory. The CPU can start a DMA block transfer, and then perform other work in parallel with the DMA operation. Similarly, the controller does not have to wait for the CPU to transfer data to/from the memory, so it will also run faster without these synchronization delays.

MEMORY-MAPPED I/O

An I/O device is managed by having software read/write information from/to the controller's registers. The computer designer must decide what instructions will be included in the machine repertoire to manipulate each controller's registers.

Traditionally, the machine instruction set includes special I/O instructions to accomplish this task. For example, to perform the I/O operations, an instruction set might include the following:

```
input       device_address
output      device_address
copy_in     CPU_register, device_address, controller_register
copy_out    CPU_register, device_address, controller_register
test        CPU_register, device_address
```

Here, each I/O instruction refers to the device's address by a unique hardware identifier for a particular controller board. The `input` instruction causes the read operation to be placed in the command register of the designated device. The `output` instruction places the write operation in the command register. (The controller will likely ignore an attempt to execute an `input` or `output` instruction if the device is busy. The exact effect will depend on the controller design.) The `copy_in` and `copy_out` instructions copy information into or out of a CPU register from/to the designated controller's data register. The `test` instruction copies the contents of the designated status register to a CPU register.

Figure 4.10 describes the memory-mapped I/O approach, contrasted with the traditional approach. With separate device addresses the jth component in device i has a two-component address such as (i, j), where i is the device address and j is the address of the command, status, or data registers within device i. For example, an assembly language statement such as

```
copy_in     R3, 0x012, 4
```

will cause the machine to copy the contents of data register 4 in the controller with device address `0x012` into CPU register `R3`.

✦ **FIGURE 4.10** Addressing Devices

Part (a) represents a conventional approach for referencing registers in devices. Memory-mapped I/O devices (part b) reduce the need for specialized I/O instructions by binding each device register into the computer's hardware memory address space. When software references the corresponding logical memory address, it is actually referencing the controller's registers.

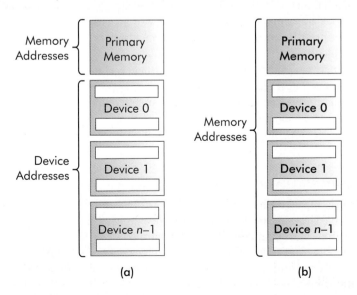

In the memory-mapped approach shown in Figure 4.10(b), devices are associated with logical primary memory addresses (**memory-mapped I/O**) rather than having a specialized device address. Each component of the device that is referenced using software is assigned a normal memory address. For example, device 0x0012 might have a block of addresses from 0xFFFF0120 to 0xFFFF012F to reference the device's command, status, and 14 data registers. A memory-mapped I/O instruction to accomplish the same task as the `copy_in` instruction might be

```
load      R3, 0xFFFF0124
```

Memory-mapped I/O reduces the number of instruction types in the processor. This happens because memory load/store instructions can be used to interact with the device's registers in a memory-mapped I/O system. In the traditional approach, the computer must incorporate additional I/O instructions to read and write the device's registers.

4.5 ● INTERRUPTS

Once a device has been started by the device driver, the application program cannot normally proceed until the I/O operation has completed. For example, if you write

```
read(devID, myData, dataLength);
x = f(myData, dataLength, ...);
```

the statement that assigns a value to x cannot be executed until the read operation has actually placed information into myData. This means that the device driver software will need to start the device, and then wait until the device has completed its operation (see Figure 4.11). The problem with this approach is that the driver software must continuously check the busy-done flags in order to determine when the device has completed its read operation. When the controller is idle, it also continuously tests these flags, but it has nothing else to do while it waits for a command. However, when the device driver is waiting by repeatedly testing the flags, it could be doing other work in a multiprogramming environment. This approach is called **polling** I/O. It introduces a **busy-wait** situation, since the CPU is busy (performing the test), but it is effectively waiting. A busy-wait wastes processor cycles that might be better used by other applications.

If the process/thread that requested an I/O operation does not use the processor to check the controller status continually, there will be a time period after which the device has completed operation but before the process checks and detects the completion. This period adds to the time the process is blocked waiting for the I/O operation to conclude.

The most efficient overlap between the device and the CPU could be obtained if the *device* would explicitly signal the processor at the instant it has completed the I/O operation. This would eliminate the need for busy-waits and minimize the idle time. The von Neumann architecture can be modified to implement this approach by incorporating a device **interrupt** that notifies the processor when it has completed an I/O operation. This requires more complex control units and device controllers: An **interrupt request** flag, `InterruptRequest`, is incorporated into the CPU and the control unit is modified so that it checks the flag during each instruction fetch-execute cycle (see Figure 4.12). Conceptually, the hardware connects all device done flags to the interrupt request flag using inclusive-OR logic, as shown in Figure 4.13. Whenever the done flag is set on any

✦ FIGURE 4.11   Polling I/O

Polling I/O requires that the software test the device's `busy-done` flags to determine when a device has completed an I/O operation. This introduces a `busy-wait` condition into driver software.

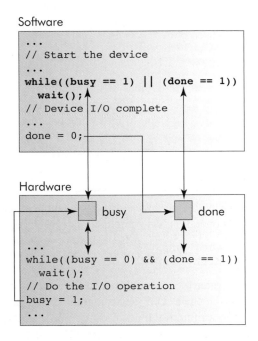

✦ FIGURE 4.12   The Fetch-Execute Cycle with an Interrupt

The control unit is modified so that it checks the `InterruptRequest` flag after it finishes executing an instruction.

```
while (haltFlag not set during execution) {
  IR = memory[PC];
  PC = PC + 1;
  execute(IR);
  if (InterruptRequest) {/* Interrupt the current process */
    memory[0] = PC;        /* Save the current PC in address 0 */
    PC = memory[1];        /* Branch indirect through address 1 */
  }
}
```

controller, `InterruptRequest` is set. The control unit will then become aware of a device completion when it finishes execution of the current instruction.

As indicated in the modified control unit algorithm (Figure 4.12), the interrupt causes the processor to cease executing the "current" sequence of instructions, and to branch to a new instruction sequence whose address is stored in memory location 1 (denoted `memory[1]`). When the interrupt branch occurs, the hardware saves the old PC location

✦ FIGURE 4.13 Detecting an Interrupt

(1) CPU incorporates the `InterruptRequest` flag. (2) When any device's busy flag changes to 0, `InterruptRequest` is set to 1. (3) The control unit detects that the interrupt occurred by checking `InterruptRequest`. (4) The PC is loaded with the address of software to handle the interrupt.

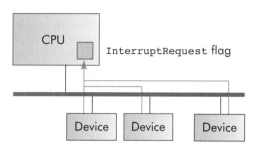

(address of the next instruction that would have been executed if the interrupt had not occurred) in `memory[0]`. In order for this to work properly, when the OS is initialized, it places the address of the interrupt handler entry point in `memory[1]`. This will cause the interrupt handler to be called whenever any device completes its operation and "raises" an interrupt. Since the interrupt handler runs whenever a device completes its operation, there is no need to poll the device to detect when it has completed.

When the interrupt handler begins to execute, the CPU registers will contain values being used by the interrupted process (excluding the PC). The interrupt handler must immediately perform a **context switch** to save all the CPU general and status registers of the interrupted process and to install its own values for every CPU register so that it can handle the completion of the I/O operation. As shown in Figure 4.14, the interrupt handler then inspects the various device done flags to determine which device caused the interrupt.

✦ FIGURE 4.14 The Interrupt Handler

The CPU incorporates an `InterruptRequest` register. When any device completes an I/O operation, it sets the `InterruptRequest` register to 1. As shown in Figure 4.11, the control unit will detect that the interrupt occurred by checking the `InterruptRequest` register, and then invoke the interrupt handler.

```
Interrupt_Handler{
  saveProcessorState();
  for (i=0; i<Number_of_devices; i++)
    if (device[i].done == 1) goto device_handler(i);
/* Something wrong if we get here */
}
```

The `InterruptRequest` flag (Figure 4.13) and the interrupt handler code schema (Figure 4.14) provide a means for a device to interrupt the CPU and to promptly begin to handle the device I/O completion. Modern computers extend the mechanism so that the source of the interrupt can be detected more rapidly than suggested by this simple mechanism. The idea is for the hardware to incorporate an **interrupt vector** rather than just a single flag. The single `InterruptRequest` flag in Figure 4.13 is replaced by an array of interrupt request flags. If the system contains N devices and the vector has K coordinates, then N/K device `done` flags are connected to each vector coordinate. Further, a table containing the entry point for K different interrupt handlers is kept in memory. If coordinate i in the interrupt vector is set to TRUE, the normal instruction sequence is interrupted, as shown in Figure 4.12, and the ith interrupt handler from the table of interrupt handlers is started.

If two or more devices finish during the same instruction cycle, then the code schema shown in Figure 4.14 will detect only the first one that finished. Once the cause of the interrupt has been determined, the interrupt handler branches to the **device handler** code for the chosen device. This action will cause the `done` flag to be cleared and the I/O operation to be completed. Completion of the processing includes signaling and subsequent resumption of the process that was blocked waiting for the I/O to complete.

Another problem must be dealt with if an interrupt occurs *while the interrupt handler is in the midst of execution.* That is, there is a **race condition** where a second interrupt *could* occur before the processor can finish handling the first interrupt. Depending on exactly which part of the interrupt or device handler is being executed for the first interrupt, the processor state may be lost or the completion processing for a device operation may never be finished. Of course, other parts of the device handler can be interrupted and then resumed later without harm.

For example, when the interrupt handler begins to execute, it begins saving the context (state) of the interrupted process and determining the cause of the interrupt. If another interrupt occurs while the interrupt handler is performing these operations, it is difficult to ensure that the proper values will be saved for the originally interrupted process and that the cause of the original interrupt will be detected. If the second interrupt causes an error in the interrupt handler, one of the two I/O operations may fail. This race condition between the execution of the interrupt handler code and the occurrence of another interrupt must be avoided if the machine is to perform I/O operations reliably.

How can we avoid these kinds of race conditions? We can add another mechanism that prevents interrupts from interrupting the handler. Suppose the CPU includes an interrupt-enabled flag, `InterruptEnabled`, a `disableInterrupt` instruction to set the flag to FALSE, and an `enableInterrupt` instruction to set the flag to TRUE. These instructions are implemented by modifying the control unit so that the part of its operation that checks for an interrupt occurrence behaves as described in Figure 4.15. If `disableInterrupt` has been executed prior to the interrupt occurrence, thereby causing the `InterruptRequest` flag to be set to TRUE, then the `InterruptEnabled` flag is FALSE and the control unit ignores the interrupt occurrence. After the interrupt handler has completed its critical code sequences, it executes the `enableInterrupt` instruction so that interrupts can once again cause I/O completion to be handled.

Once the enable instruction has been executed, the `InterruptEnabled` flag is set to TRUE. Any pending interrupt is then "caught" by the interrupt handler and dispatched to the appropriate device handler as before. The first interrupt occurring after the interrupts have been disabled will be saved by virtue of the corresponding `done` flag, which remains TRUE until the device handler executes. If two or more interrupts occur while the interrupt handler is handling an interrupt, the hardware may not save subsequent interrupts for processing—that is, the later interrupts may be lost.

✦ FIGURE 4.15 Disabling Interrupts

The `InterruptEnabled` flag is used to override interrupts. If the flag is `FALSE`, then interrupts are not allowed to change the existing sequence of instruction executions. Otherwise, interrupts can occur as described above.

```
if(InterruptRequest && InterruptEnabled) {
/* Interrupt current process */
  disableInterrupts();
  memory[0] = PC;
  PC = memory[1];
}
```

Although one or more interrupts may temporarily suspend a thread's execution, they do not alter the program control flow once the process resumes execution. After all pending interrupts have been handled, the interrupted thread will be resumed at the next instruction it would have executed had it not been interrupted.

THE TRAP INSTRUCTION REVISITED

Section 3.2 introduced the CPU mode bit for differentiating between privileged and user instructions. If a process is running in user mode and it wishes to perform an operation that requires privileged instructions, it invokes the `trap` instruction. The `trap` switches the CPU mode to supervisor and begins running trusted kernel code. Suppose the assembly language representation for a trap is

`trap argument`

Figure 4.16 (an alternative to Figure 3.8) pictorially represents the behavior of a `trap` instruction. The idea is that the `trap` should accomplish a function call operation (the effect of the grey line branch). The `trap` switches the CPU to supervisor mode and then branches indirectly through the OS `trap` table. That is, a `trap` performs exactly the same action as a vectored interrupt, where the `trap` table corresponds to the device handler entry points. This simple mechanism provides a safe way for a user-mode process to execute only predefined software when the mode bit is transitioned to supervisor mode. Because of this strong similarity to interrupts, traps are often called "software (generated) interrupts."

✦ FIGURE 4.16 The `Trap` Instruction Operation

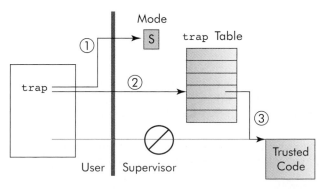

4.6 ● CONVENTIONAL CONTEMPORARY COMPUTERS

Let's reconsider the block diagram of the von Neumann computer that we used to begin our discussion of computer organization (Figure 4.2, refined in Figure 4.17). We have seen that the CPU is composed of an ALU and a control unit. This part of the architecture is responsible for fetching and executing programs that are stored in the primary (or executable) memory. I/O devices are added to the architecture by attaching them to the system bus. The software executing on the CPU can control the devices by reading and writing registers in the device's controller. On input, data flows from the device to a CPU register, and then into primary memory. On output, data flows from the primary memory to a CPU register, and then to the device controller.

✦ **FIGURE 4.17** Summary of the von Neumann Architecture

This figure is a refinement of Figure 4.2. In the refinement, we have added silhouettes of the registers and functional units of the hardware. The complex icon on the right side of the figure will be used to represent a von Neumann computer in subsequent figures.

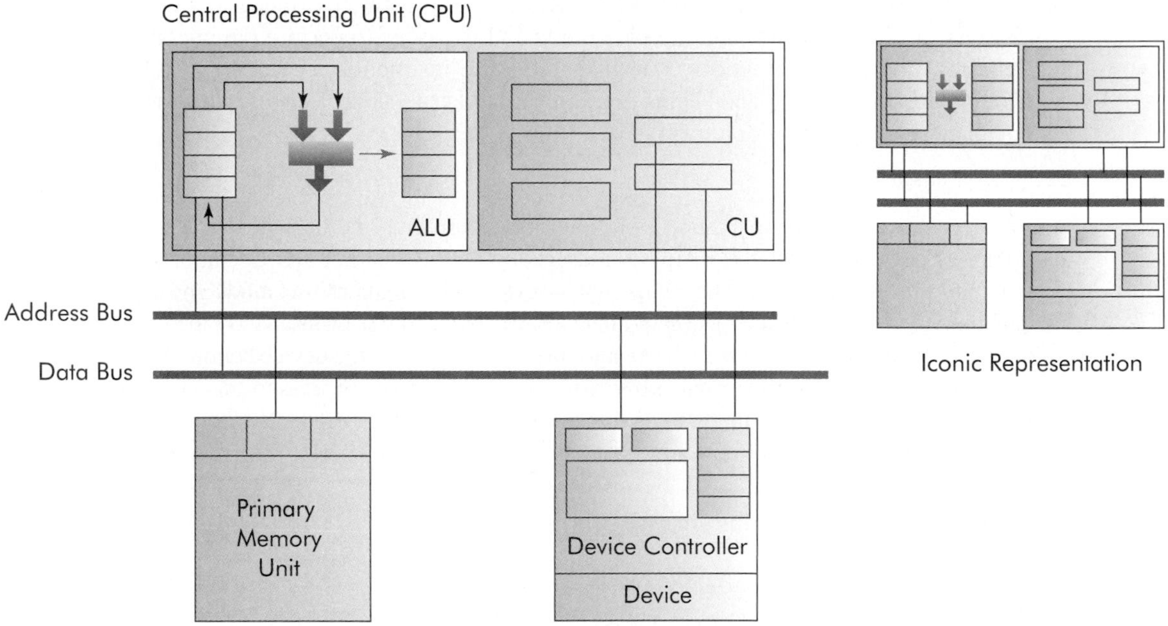

Central Processing Unit (CPU)

ALU

CU

Address Bus

Data Bus

Iconic Representation

Primary Memory Unit

Device Controller

Device

Today we think of conventional computers as servers, desktop machines, and notebook/laptop computers. We also think of *specialized* computers for mobile computing, scientific number crunching, and so on; these machines will be discussed separately below.

We all use desktop and notebook machines to solve programming assignments, read e-mail, browse the Internet, prepare typeset documents, and many other things. These machines are single-user von Neumann computers with a multiprogramming OS. They are built around a 32-bit microprocessor that contains the CPU on a single chip. At the time of this writing, clock cycle times exceed 2GHz. Most of these machines incorporate a bus capable of transmitting 32-bit words at cycle times up to 400 MHz—the CPU speed is much faster than bus speed. The primary memory can be configured to be as large as 4GB with access times near 50 ns. Notebook computers differ from desktop computers in both their physical packaging and their slower speeds.

Desktop computers are capable of working with an extraordinary collection of devices; almost any kind of computer device can be connected to a desktop computer. Besides connecting devices to the bus, these machines typically support various other internal buses, including USB and Firewire. These supplementary buses accommodate various consumer devices (such as digital cameras and MPEG players).

Your academic department may have one or more "server machines" in a back room where you never see them. These machines are used to store and process the department's global information. In some cases, you may use them to solve homework assignments or to receive your e-mail. Server machines are large, multiprogramming machines that are generally accessed via a network or interactive terminal. Almost all organizations have one or more such machines. Virtually all server machines are von Neumann computers with a timesharing-style OS. Strangely, server machine hardware is not much different from desktop hardware. Server machines are also built around microprocessor chips that are similar to (but a little faster than) desktop computer microprocessors. The early 64-bit CPUs are being used in some server machines, allowing those machines to accommodate more than 4 GB of primary memory. Finally, the server machines usually have a faster bus (and faster devices) than are incorporated into a desktop.

BOOTSTRAPPING THE MACHINE

In a contemporary Intel microprocessor, the hardware process (see Section 4.2) begins executing at a hardwired ROM location when the computer is powered up. The computer manufacturer stores a customized "power on self test" (**POST**) program in ROM at the hardwired start location (see Figure 4.18). The POST is a set of diagnostic programs that tests that particular manufacturer's hardware before any other software is installed. The POST program can be used with any OS that is installed on the system.

On an Intel microprocessor (which is typical of other microprocessors), the IBM Basic Input/Output System (**BIOS**) program is also stored in the ROM. After the POST has completed, the configuration code reads basic boot parameters from the machine's **CMOS memory** (see the data flow arrow in Figure 4.18). The boot parameters include the identification of the boot device for the computer, the location of the boot record on the device, and the number of bytes in the boot record. The CMOS memory was originally built using CMOS chip technology because of its low power requirements (although contemporary computers may use any kind of chip technology). This allowed information to be stored in the memory, which was powered by a miniature battery such as a watch battery. The CMOS memory contents would be remembered when the machine was powered down. For example, the CMOS memory contains information to identify which device contains the initial bootstrap code. Figure 4.19 shows an alternative view of the bootstrap process in which the PC contains address 0x100, referencing the entry point of the "POST & BIOS" programs stored in the ROM.

✦ **FIGURE 4.18** Intel System Initialization

When the system is started, the PC is loaded with the entry point of the POST. After the POST completes, the BIOS code reads the CMOS memory to obtain various boot parameters, such as the identity of the boot device. The bootstrap program then ultimately loads the OS into the primary memory.

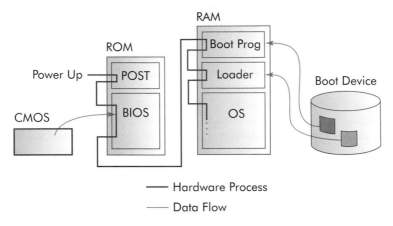

✦ **FIGURE 4.19** Bootstrapping the Machine

In this view of the bootstrap procedure, we see that the bootstrap process starts executing at a fixed location (in the ROM part of primary memory), (1) loads a bootstrap loader, (2) loads a full-function loader, then (3) loads the OS.

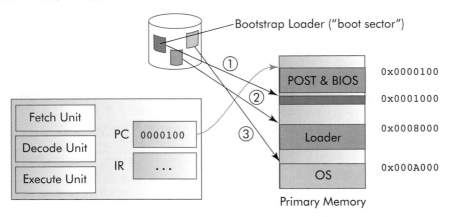

The last part of the BIOS program—the first step in loading the OS—is to run a simple *bootstrap loader* of the form shown in step (1) in Figure 4.20 (discussed in the following paragraphs). Each OS and computer uses its own version of the bootstrap procedure, but as shown by step (2) the bootstrap loader copies another loader from a fixed boot area on the computer's boot disk. This new loader contains the details needed to load other software from the particular disk device. After the sophisticated loader has been loaded, the control unit jumps to that loader, which then loads the OS (step (3) in the figure).

Figure 4.20 is a hypothetical ROM bootstrap loader. The power-up sequence causes the hardware to execute an instruction corresponding to

```
Load    PC, FIXED_LOC
```

where `FIXED_LOC` is the ROM address at which the bootstrap loader is stored. This example bootstrap loader is stored in ROM so that it is always present whenever the computer is powered on. This bootstrap loader will read `LENGTH_OF_TARGET` words from a fixed disk location, `FIXED_DISK_ADDRESS`, and store them consecutively in `FIXED_DEST`. In this symbolic representation of the machine language, you can assume that an address and register enclosed in square brackets causes the machine to compute a new address by adding the address in the instruction to the contents of the corresponding register. The bootstrap process loads the program from the fixed location on the disk and then unconditionally branches to it to begin executing.

✦ **FIGURE 4.20** A Bootstrap Loader Program

The bootstrap loader program is a special purpose loader that copies a fixed amount of information from a fixed device address into a fixed primary memory address.

```
FIXED_LOC: // Bootstrap loader entry point
      load   R1, =0
      load   R2, =LENGTH_OF_TARGET
// The next instruction is really more like
// a procedure call than a machine instruction
// It copies a block from BOOT_DISK
// to BUFFER_ADDRESS
      read   BOOT_DISK, BUFFER_ADDRESS
loop: load   R3, [BUFFER_ADDRESS, R1]
      store  R3, [FIXED_DEST, R1]
      incr   R1
      bleq   R1, R2, loop
      br     FIXED_DEST
```

Once the machine has completed the bootstrap phase and is operating normally under software control, this operating system can set the PC to start any program executing that has been loaded into memory (by setting the PC to the address of the entry point of the desired program).

4.7 • Mobile Computers

Mobile computers have emerged as an important commercial product, first as handheld personal digital assistants (PDAs). In the move toward miniaturization and portability, the notebook computer had a significant impact on personal computer sales. At the same time, calculator companies began to market calculator-sized devices that contained telephone lists. Next, a calendar was added to the device, and so on. The Palm Pilot device firmly established the market for a device that included a spectrum of functions (calendar, contact list, notes, and so on), but which was implemented as a very small computer. As various other companies began to manufacture competitive products, it quickly became obvious to everyone that these little devices were computers and could be used for much more general functions than keeping calendars and contact lists.

Today, the market expectations for a PDA are that it can communicate with other computers—in the degenerate case, with at least one other "home" computer using the desktop-PDA synchronization facility. Increasingly, the PDA is expected to have a wireless network capability that allows it to be a host machine on the Internet. An interesting trade-off in PDA performance is the relative ability to communicate on the network versus the amount of memory in the PDA. If the communication link is reliable, persistent, and fast, there may be little justification for incorporating very much memory into the PDA since its storage can be in a server that is accessed using the link. As communication links become increasingly fast and reliable, the PDA can behave more and more like a conventional personal computer.

Mobile computer hardware is rapidly evolving so that these computers can be used in an application domain in which the computer will have (access to) enough memory to store a book, collections of music, and/or an MPEG video file or a movie. The expectations are for the mobile computer to be able to deliver streaming audio and video files to the user—whether from a local storage device or over a wireless communication link.

Today's mobile computer is a von Neumann computer: It has a CPU, memory, and devices. However it is specialized along some dimensions:

- It is physically very small and has little weight.
- It is severely constrained in the rate at which it can consume power, since its power supply is a small battery.
- Size constraints prevent the machine from having large amounts of primary memory.
- The PDA usually does not incorporate a keyboard; instead, it uses a touch-sensitive screen (with a stylus) and possibly a microphone.
- Its output devices are a very small screen and possibly an audio speaker.
- It usually does not contain any storage device.
- It may use removable devices such as compact flash memory, a wireless network card, or other unusual devices such as a global positioning system device or video camera.

Because of these specialized configurations, computer designers have reconsidered ways to implement the normal von Neumann computer concepts so that they work well under all these constraints.

SYSTEM-ON-A-CHIP TECHNOLOGY

PDA hardware implementation benefits from the ever-increasing level of chip integration that is used on conventional microprocessors. In the late 1990s, chip manufacturers began to build **system-on-a-chip** (**SOC**) integrated circuits as contrasted with a CPU on a chip. The basic idea behind an SOC is to consider a set of memory and device functions that will be needed by the onboard microprocessor, and then to implement some of that functionality on the chip. For example, an SOC for a PDA could be designed to incorporate a graphics accelerator or character recognition units on the same chip as the CPU. It could also incorporate substantial amounts of primary memory that could be accessed by the CPU without it having to send a request over a bus to a separate memory unit. (Leading edge microprocessors also incorporate this approach; it is called *cache memory*, and will be discussed more in Chapter 11.) A network interface is another function that could be incorporated into the SOC, although the PDA would still have to include the transmitter and receiver for wireless communication. Streaming media support is another area where functionality can be implemented on the SOC rather than on distinct devices: In this case, the SOC can incorporate functions that are normally implemented in a device or controller such as an MPEG compression/decompression function.

Leading edge microprocessors use most of the transistors to implement faster CPUs. An SOC incorporates a microprocessor, but it is one that sacrifices some performance in exchange for using far fewer transistors. The excess transistors are then used to implement the other on-chip functions.

SOC technology is still in steep evolution. There are several challenges in SOC design, although an essential element of the design is the choice of which functions should be added to the SOC; after all, if the SOC contains functions that are not used in a PDA, then it is not likely to be chosen as the basis of the system. Correspondingly, OS technology must also evolve so that it is well-suited to the new hardware environment presented by SOCs and other mobile computer hardware implementations.

POWER MANAGEMENT

Power consumption first became an issue in computer design with notebook computers. Notebook computers contain a large display and a rotating disk, both of which consume a significant fraction of the power when the notebook is operational. Since the display and disk are distinct devices, OS designers learned that they could incorporate functions that would measure the amount of time since the display or disk was last used. If the time surpassed a threshold value, then the device could be powered down until it was next needed. This approach is crucial to preserving battery power in a contemporary notebook computer.

Mobile computers usually do not include a disk, so disk power management is not an issue. However, mobile computer displays can use significant amounts of power. PDAs (and many modern notebook computers) incorporate a variable power consumption option: If the display is bright, then it uses maximum power, but if the display is dimmed, it uses proportionally less power. For these displays, mobile computer system software can dim the screen to one level when the time since it was last written to surpasses a threshold value. The display will consume proportionally less power than if it were to continue displaying an image at maximum brightness. If the time since the display was last used passes an additional threshold, the screen can be dimmed even more, or even turned off, further reducing the rate of power consumption. This is an important and effective behavior of display devices for mobile computers.

Many of the CPUs used in mobile computers have another unique characteristic: These CPUs can operate at different clock speeds, with the power consumption proportional to the clock speed. This means that if the CPU operates at maximum speed, it will use maximum power. However, it may only use 75% of maximum power if it operates at 60% of the maximum speed. The Intel StrongARM microprocessor chip family is one example of

The Itsy Mobile Computer

Today there is a broad spectrum of commercial PDAs, including the Palm handheld computers, the Compaq iPAQ, and HP Jornada machines. The Itsy mobile computer was an experimental mobile computer that was more practical than most research prototypes, yet more elaborate than most commercial systems. It was developed in 1997 at Compaq's Western Research Laboratory to study the design of mobile computers, and "to explore the possibilities, demands, and limitations of mobile computing." [Hamburgen, et al., 2001]. The iPAQ commercial PDA evolved from the Itsy research prototype, although there are notable differences between the two machines.

The Itsy V2 is not a system-on-a-chip, but rather is a custom board computer built around the Intel StrongARM SA-1100 microprocessor. The Itsy V2 contains 32 MB of RAM plus an additional 32 MB of flash memory— all directly accessible from the CPU (so the 64 MB is all primary memory). The output devices are a 320×200 pixel backlit liquid crystal display screen with 15 gray levels and a speaker. The input devices are touch sensors on the screen (so that users can write and point on the screen using a plastic stylus), a few function buttons, and a microphone. There is a docking interface through which the Itsy interacts with a host computer (such as a workstation); communication with the host is over an infrared link, a USB connection, and a serial communication port. The Itsy also contains a two-axis accelerometer that is intended to measure movement of the entire machine (for using gestures as input). Other devices can be attached to the Itsy through a "daughterboard adaptor" that incorporates industry-standard PCMCIA card slots. This port can be used to add memory, wireless cards, and other devices.

The StrongARM SA-1100 microprocessor is a low-power 32-bit CPU. Rather than having blinding speed, raw performance is traded off against power consumption. Additionally, the CPU can operate at different clock cycle times, ranging from 59 MHz to 206 MHz. Depending on exactly what the mobile computer is being used to do, there can be up to an order of magnitude difference in the power consumption, much of which is related directly to CPU power consumption. For example, in system idle state, the CPU operates at 59 MHz and consumes 69.6 mW of power, but if a user is dictating voice to the machine, it consumes 757 mW. To see the difference in power consumption by the CPU, the researchers report that if the Itsy is playing an audio file at 59 MHz, the system uses 278 mW, but if the CPU is operating at 206 MHz, it consumes 310 mW.

The Itsy project was an experiment to push mobile computer hardware technology to its limit in the 1997–98 timeframe. The idea was to build a machine in which hardware researchers could experiment with power management and maximum compactness of the system. Software researchers used the Itsy to explore other important areas, including operating systems for mobile computers (the Itsy used a version of Linux), human-computer interaction mechanisms for a mobile computer (the Itsy had no keyboard, and encouraged voice I/O and gesture input), and support of streaming media applications (the Itsy was designed to play back MPEG audio/video files). Research continues on the descendants of the Itsy, but the iPAQ PDA is a direct commercial result from the work.

such processors [Hamburgen, et al., 2001]. This opens up an entirely new set of possibilities for economical power consumption: If the OS determines that the CPU workload is low, it can reduce the clock cycle time at which the CPU is executing. This means that the CPU performance will be lower, but so will the rate of power consumption.

4.8 • MULTIPROCESSORS AND PARALLEL COMPUTERS

In the 1960s, computer scientists began to be concerned about the limits on the ultimate speed of computation based on the speed at which electronic signals could be propagated through the computer. They realized that as the clock signal increased, the physical size of the CPU could become a barrier to the time it would take to transmit a signal from one part of the CPU to another part. Indeed, large-scale integrated circuit implementations of microprocessors push many of these limits.

They began to consider alternatives to the barriers imposed by this signal delay. This led to the idea that the computer could be made faster by implementing it as N different physical parts, all of which could be executing simultaneously. (These machines all depart from the conventional von Neumann architecture by introducing parallelism.) In a perfect world, if a problem could be decomposed into N different subproblems of exactly the same size, and if each of the subproblems could be solved by one of the N different physical parts of the computer, then a problem that would take K units of time to solve on a conventional von Neumann computer would require only K/N units of time on the machine with the N different physical parts. Defining these "parts" is the first challenge to parallel computing; ensuring that software can execute the parts simultaneously is the second challenge.

PARALLEL INSTRUCTION EXECUTION

Early approaches to parallel computing were to build multiple function units inside the ALU. Suppose the ALU was designed so that it had several specialized function units that could execute at the same time. Then it would be possible for the individual function units to execute simultaneously while ensuring the same result as if the instructions had been executed sequentially on a single function unit. For example, suppose a program called for the evaluation of the expression

```
a + (b * c) + (d * e) + f
```

By executing this on an ALU with a single function unit, the computation would take five execution cycles of the function unit:

1. $Tmp_1 = b * c$
2. $Tmp_2 = d * e$
3. $Tmp_3 = a + Tmp_1$
4. $Tmp_4 = Tmp_2 + f$
5. $Result = Tmp_3 + Tmp_4$

Now suppose that the ALU has two adder units and two multiplier units. The machine could then execute several things in parallel, enabling the computation to be completed in only 3 execution cycles:

1. $Tmp_1 = b * c$ $Tmp_2 = d * e$
2. $Tmp_3 = a + Tmp_1$ $Tmp_4 = Tmp_2 + f$
3. $Result = Tmp_3 + Tmp_4$

The two products are computed in parallel, and then the two sums are computed in parallel in the second execution phase, which is then finished by taking the sum of the two intermediate results. An ALU that contains multiple function units, some of which can perform floating point operations, will be much more complex than an ALU with a single function unit that performs only integer arithmetic and logical operations, but that can perform computations at a higher rate.

Pipelined CPUs are a twist on multiple function units. In a pipelined approach, a function unit is partitioned into N smaller units, each called a **pipeline stage** of the unit, so that for an operation to be executed, it must be processed by each of the smaller units (see Figure 4.21). Since the stages are independent units of hardware, each stage can execute at the same time. The trick is to provide a new operation to the first stage of the pipelined function unit as soon as it becomes idle. When the first stage finishes its work, it passes the operation and operands to the second stage, and accepts the next operation. Each stage accepts a partially executed instruction from its predecessor stage, and passes its completed work to its successor stage.

✦ **FIGURE 4.21** A Pipelined Function Unit

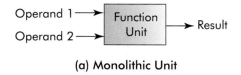

(a) Monolithic Unit

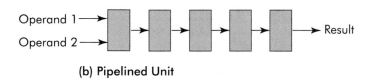

(b) Pipelined Unit

In an N-stage pipeline, an operation is complete after it has been processed by each stage. The parallelism arises because each of the stages can execute in parallel, meaning that an N-stage function unit can be working on parts of N different operations at the same time. For example, in the pipeline in Figure 4.21, the time to execute a sequential function unit might take 100 units. In the five-stage pipe shown in the figure, each stage might take only 20 units. This means that a new instruction could be started into the pipeline every

20 time units. Any particular computation would take 100 time units, but two could be done in 120 time units, three in 140 time units, and so on.

Overlapping the fetch and execute cycles can be thought of as a two-stage pipeline—fetching an instruction is the first stage and executing the instruction is the second. Pipelined machines proved to be especially effective at computations in which the data types are vectors. The technique first became widely used in supercomputers such as the Cray Research machines of the 1980s, and is widely used in contemporary high-performance microprocessors.

ARRAY PROCESSORS

Array processors have a larger grain specification of the parts of the machine that can be replicated for parallel operation. The **single-instruction, multiple-data** (**SIMD**) parallel machines are designed to execute a single program as if it were a single-threaded process. A SIMD machine CPU is composed of a single control unit and N different ALUs (see Figure 4.22). The control unit operates in the same way as one in a conventional von Neumann computer: It fetches an instruction from the primary memory, decodes it, and then transmits the execution signals to the ALU. However, instead of transmitting execution signals to one ALU, it transmits the signal to the N different ALUs. In this case, each individual instruction managed by the control unit is simultaneously *executed* on N different data streams by the N different ALUs. This kind of machine is especially effective with vector and matrix computations. However, when it must work on scalar data in which there can only be one computation in execution at a time, the SIMD machine leaves $N-1$ of the ALUs inactive while one of the ALUs performs the serial computation.

✦ **FIGURE 4.22** A SIMD Machine

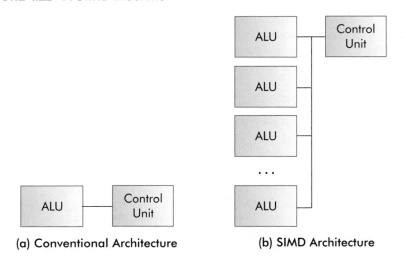

(a) Conventional Architecture   (b) SIMD Architecture

The Illiac IV and the Connection Machine CM–2 are examples of this class of machines. Operating systems have not evolved as rapidly as the hardware technology for these machines. Consequently, the SIMD machines incorporate a conventional von

Neumann front-end machine that uses a conventional sequential OS and computing environment to control the SIMD machine. The SIMD machine itself is treated as a device by the front-end machine. For example, a typical machine of this type might incorporate 2,000 processing elements in the SIMD architecture, but be controlled by a workstation.

SHARED MEMORY MULTIPROCESSORS

Shared memory multiprocessors (also called shared memory processors, SMPs, or CPU clusters) employ a collection of off-the-shelf processors such as an Intel Pentium, Compaq Alpha, or Sun SPARC— "killer micros." The processors are interconnected with one another and/or with primary memory using specialized hardware. In the 1980s, the first wave of such processors used a conventional bus as the interconnection network. This interconnection required that the processors incorporate various buffering techniques to reduce the contention for the common interconnection bus. Even so, no manufacturer was able to construct a viable machine with more than about 20 state-of-the-art processors. If the number exceeded 20, then the contention on the bus became a severe performance bottleneck, thus eliminating the possibility of adding more processors. Such machines are said "to not be scalable."

Shared memory machines quickly became popular with programmers because the software tools used to develop software for a single process could easily be used with the shared memory architecture. Doing this required the application to be partitioned into two or more sequentially executed units (each implemented by a process) that could communicate with one another using common memory locations. It has been said that these machines are scalable in the software but not in the hardware: In this machine environment, it is easy to write software that grows with the size of the problem, but difficult to build components that allow the machine to do the same.

Shared memory systems are fundamentally distinct from von Neumann machines since they execute multiple program sequences at one time. Even so, they tend to rely on the von Neumann bus mechanism to interconnect the CPUs, primary memory, and devices. This means that the bus—or other more sophisticated interconnection mechanism—introduces "the von Neumann bottleneck" to multiprocessor performance.

DISTRIBUTED MEMORY MULTIPROCESSORS

Distributed memory multiprocessors are composed of a collection of CPUs with their memory interconnected using a high-speed network. In some cases, the network is specialized and implemented internally to one physical multicomputer. In others, it is a relatively standard local area network or high-speed fiber optic network. Processes on different computers communicate with one another exclusively through messages, since there is no common memory.

Distributed memory machines do not ordinarily support sequential programming languages "transparently," like shared memory machines do. The software is based on a paradigm that calls for processes to interact with one another by exchanging messages rather than by sharing a common memory area. While it is sometimes possible to construct a compiler so that it converts shared memory references into an appropriate set of message sends and receives, this approach has been only a qualified success. In these machines, the highest levels of performance can be obtained only by writing programs with explicit message passing. Thus the software does not tend to be scalable.

NETWORK OF WORKSTATIONS

A *network of workstations* (*NOW*) is a loose federation of conventional personal computers and workstations interconnected with a network. It is distinguished from multiprocessors in that the individual computers are autonomous units executing with their own OS. A collection of workstations on a network can be coordinated to work as if they were a multiprocessor. However, this is really a software solution rather than a new hardware instance, since all the machines are conventional von Neumann computers.

4.9 • SUMMARY

Stored program computers provide a means by which fixed-function hardware can be controlled through variable software specifications. This flexibility is unique among electronic and mechanical devices, and it is the aspect of electronic devices that defines them as computers. For over half a century, the von Neumann architecture has been the dominant approach to computer design. A von Neumann computer is based on a processor that has an ALU and a control unit, a primary memory that can store the program and data, and devices to store programs and data when the computer is turned off, to introduce data into the computer, and to write the results computed by processes.

CPU design operates on a basic fetch-execute cycle in which a machine instruction is retrieved from the executable memory, decoded by the control unit, and then executed by some part of the CPU and/or devices. The ALU is the workhorse for arithmetical and logical operations. The control unit is responsible for determining the sequence of instructions to be executed. The memory is organized as a set of cells with contiguous addresses. A memory cell is used to store information for use by the processor.

Devices introduce information into the memory and record the results of computations performed by the machine. Many kinds of devices can be added to a machine, ranging from sensors for process control applications to networks capable of transferring enormous amounts of information from one machine to another in mere seconds. Communications devices are used to transmit and receive information, and storage devices are used to save information.

Each device has a controller to abstract the physical device into a higher-level interface shared by different device producers. This abstraction allows manufacturers to build a family of devices with different performance and size characteristics that provide a common hardware interface to software. It even allows competing manufacturers to provide "plug compatible" devices.

Device drivers constitute another layer of abstraction in which a standardized software interface is defined so that a programmer can interact with devices while knowing few details of the device itself. The interface is biased toward software I/O operations rather than toward device behavior.

The problem of detecting when an I/O operation has been completed has led to the development of interrupts. An interrupt enables a process that is blocked on an I/O operation to simply "sleep" until the operation has completed. It also creates situations in which race conditions can occur. If an interrupt should occur just after another interrupt has occurred and is being processed, the operating system may lose track of the correct processing and erroneously handle the I/O operation. (In Chapter 8, you will discover that the problem is actually much worse than described in this chapter!)

Almost all contemporary computers are von Neumann computers. Desktops, notebooks, and server machines all use this architecture. In recent years, mobile computing has caused a flurry of development of miniature computers and system-on-a-chip technology. Small computers often trade off raw computing power for portability.

Parallel computers and multiprocessors diverge from the von Neumann architecture by incorporating designs that support explicit simultaneous processor operation. There are many different approaches in this area, including multifunction CPUs, pipelined CPUs, SIMD machines, shared memory multiprocessors, distributed memory multiprocessors, and networks of workstations.

In the next chapter, the simplest software extension—device management—is discussed.

4.10 ● EXERCISES

1. The machine instruction

   ```
   br FIXED_DEST
   ```

   causes the computer to execute its next instruction from memory location FIXED_DEST. What are the detailed steps of the ALU and/or control unit to execute this instruction? Provide the same steps for the conditional branch instruction

   ```
   bleq R1, R2, loop
   ```

   which branches to the instruction labeled "loop" if the contents of R1 are less than or equal to the contents of R2.

2. Figure 4.5 describes the fetch-execute algorithm for a sequential control unit. The discussion of the control unit informally describes how a machine can be made to run much faster by overlapping the fetch and execute operations. List the steps necessary to accomplish this overlap by explaining any new registers that might be needed, indicating which control unit components operate at the same time, and rewriting the fetch-execute algorithm.

3. Suppose a workstation has a clock rate of 25 MHz, which means that the machine is capable of performing 25 million basic operations per second. For example, a register test instruction might take just 1 clock cycle, but an arithmetic instruction might require 10 clock cycles, while an I/O instruction might require hundreds.

   a. What is the time duration of one basic operation?

   b. Assuming the average instruction takes 2.5 clock cycles, how many instructions can be executed in 100 microseconds?

4. High-level programming languages can be thought of as abstract machines for machine language instruction sets. Given the C assignment statement

   ```
   a = b + c;
   ```

   do the following:

a. Describe an implementation of the abstract machine by using a pseudo assembly language as the machine language generated by a compiler if the statement is preceded by a declaration of the form

```
int a, b, c;
```

b. Describe an implementation of the abstract machine if the statement is preceded by a declaration of the form

```
float a, b, c;
```

Show how the machine language for this code segment differs from the code in part a.

c. Describe an implementation of the abstract machine if the statement is preceded by a declaration of the form

```
int a;
float b, c;
```

Show how the assembly language for this code segment differs from the code in parts a and b.

5. Evaluate the following expressions that have binary operands. Check your work by converting the numbers to decimal and performing the same operations.

a. 10101111 + 00101010

b. 11101011 - 10101010

c. 10111011 × 00001011

d. 01001000 / 00001100

6. Convert each number in Exercise 5 into a hexadecimal (base 16) representation, then evaluate the expressions in hexadecimal.

7. Microprocessor chips often do not include floating-point operations in their hardware instruction set. Floating-point instructions must then be implemented either by using software functions or via the inclusion of a supplementary floating-point chip to be used with the microprocessor chip.

a. Using pseudocode, describe the algorithm for summing two floating-point numbers.

b. Describe the algorithm for multiplying two floating-point numbers together.

c. What might be the performance difference between a floating-point multiplication in a microprocessor having the algorithm implemented in a floating-point chip rather than in a software algorithm? (Answer this question by indicating which method would be faster. Then estimate the difference in speeds by expressing a factor such as 3, 10, 100, and 1000.)

8. Assume it takes an average of 2.5 clock cycles to execute an instruction in a one-address machine language (that is, each individual instruction can reference at most one memory location). Estimate the number of clock cycles it would take to execute the C loop that follows if the code is compiled without optimization. Explain your answer.

```
for(i=0; i<100; i++) a[i] = 0;
```

9. Maintaining a system clock that can be read by any user program requires only that the operating system read a physical device (keeping physical time) and then write the time into a globally readable variable. Suppose the time to read the physical clock and to update the variable is 100 microseconds. What percentage of the total CPU time is spent maintaining a clock that is accurate to the millisecond resolution (that is, the clock always reflects the correct time to the closest millisecond)? The 100 microsecond resolution? The 10 microsecond resolution? Explain your rationale.

10. C++ type hierarchies could be used to define device drivers by encoding standard operations for all devices in a base class and then refining the behavior for various devices with derived classes. Describe a type hierarchy, including member functions and data, for a keyboard, display, mouse, serial line printer, floppy disk, and hard disk. Do not include details of the functions.

11. Using C-like pseudocode, describe a device driver, interrupt handler, and device status table to implement the following:

    a. `open(device)`

    b. `close(device)`

    c. `get_block(device, buffer)`

    d. `put_block(device, buffer)`

    Because this specification of the problem ignores many details of a real system, you will need to make some assumptions about the hardware and operating systems environment. You may use any system as a guideline for your assumptions. However, be sure to specify all assumptions you make in your solution.

12. Conventional high-level programming languages rely on sequential semantics for their operation. In particular, when programmers write a code segment such as

    ```
    ...
    read(io_port, &buffer, length);
    x = f(buffer[i]);
    ...
    ```

    they expect the assignment statement will not be executed until the read statement has retrieved input data and written it into memory at address buffer. Write a pseudocode description of how these semantics could be implemented with a `read()` library routine and a corresponding program to use the routine.

13. Describe a new read function, xRead(), along with other functions that could enable one to write programs in a high-level language such that the application can continue processing after the xRead() call, but can block itself before using data in the process of being read.

14. Serial asynchronous communication ports are widely used in contemporary computers to connect a terminal (keyboard and display) or a printer to the computer. The signaling protocol typically employs 1 or 2 start bits and a single stop bit to encapsulate each byte. A transmitter sends start bits to the receiver to indicate that a byte is about to be transmitted. The 8 bits in the byte are then transmitted, followed by a single stop bit. How many bytes per second can be transmitted over a 9,600-baud serial line using this protocol? What is the percentage of time spent on transmitting overhead bits?

15. Consider the performance specifications for a contemporary desktop computer given in Section 4.6. What component is likely to be the performance bottleneck in such a computer? Why?

16. The Itsy computer incorporates a two-axis accelerometer that is intended to measure movement of the entire machine. This device reports the change in orientation of the entire computer in two dimensions. The designers thought this might be useful for tracking the user's physical gestures. What parts of the OS would be effected by incorporating such a device. That is, what parts of the OS have to be changed to manage such a device?

17. Suppose a computer with a pipelined functional unit contains a 4-stage pipe, with the time for each stage to execute being 50 µs. What is the maximum number of instructions that can be executed by the machine in one second?

CHAPTER 5

Device Management

This chapter extends the discussion of devices from Chapter 4. It focuses on the software for managing devices: device drivers and the interrupt handler. The chapter begins with an overview of device management considerations: the organization of device managers, read/write semantics, polling I/O, and interrupt-driven I/O. Then we consider practical factors that influence device driver design, including buffering. The chapter concludes with a discussion about characteristics of different classes of devices.

5.1 • THE I/O SYSTEM

In an office, employees order things by giving an order request to a purchasing agent. The purchasing agent determines the best vendor to supply the item, orders it, and then delivers a purchase order to the accounting department. Imagine that you are the manager of the purchasing department, and that you have one purchasing agent who is particularly fast and accurate at processing orders. Instead of having her (the processor) pick up order requests from employees and deliver purchase orders to the accounting department, you decide to hire a person (input device) to bring orders to her, and another person (output device) to deliver the purchase orders (see Figure 5.1). This will maximize the amount of time that the purchasing agent can spend processing orders while other people handle her I/O activity. This is analogous to the job of the device manager: It should provide a subsystem that can implement I/O operations such that the devices will be able to operate in parallel with the processor.

In the earliest days of computing, the computer designers saw little reason for decoupling the CPU execution from the I/O operation. An early architect says [Alt, 1948]:

It seems that most designers of computing machines agree that the time required for the input of one number should be of the same order of magnitude as the time required for an arithmetic operation, or perhaps longer by one order of magnitude.

✦ FIGURE 5.1 Input/Output Devices

The strategy is to keep a fast processor busy by offloading input and output work to other parts of the computer.

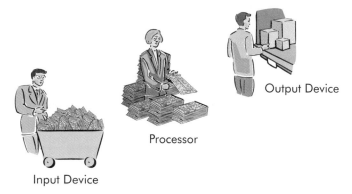

Output Device

Processor

Input Device

Within a few years, computer designers realized that I/O devices depend on mechanical motion, whereas CPU computation is pure electronic switching. Computation was soon *several* orders of magnitude faster than I/O operation. Hardware and software designers began a quest that continues today in search of techniques whereby CPU computation can continue without waiting for I/O operations. The most effective technique at this time is to create situations in which the CPU continues to perform useful computations—no busy-waiting on a device—while I/O is in progress.

Today, I/O systems are designed to:

■ Provide simple, but abstract software interfaces to manage the I/O operations needed by a computation.

■ Ensure that there is as much overlap as possible between the operation of the I/O devices and the CPU.

DEVICE MANAGER ABSTRACTION

Let's summarize the components of the I/O system. Devices have controllers that provide an interface to the software. This hardware interface can be relatively complex in the sense that there can be many parameters to set prior to starting the controller and many aspects of the status to check whenever an operation has completed. A **device driver** is a collection of functions that abstract the operation of a particular device controller (see Figure 5.2). The community of device drivers is designed to export the *same (or as similar as possible) abstraction* for all devices. For example, even though a printer device driver encapsulates the knowledge required to control a printer and a disk driver specializes in disk management, the same general driver interface invokes their services. Not every device can implement every function on the standard interface; for example, the read function for a printer is not implemented (the call is still on the interface, but there is no function to implement it).

✦ **FIGURE 5.2** The Device Driver Interface

Different devices have different controllers, and different controllers have different interfaces.
Each device driver must be written to use the unique device controller and to export a common set
of functions to be used by application programs.

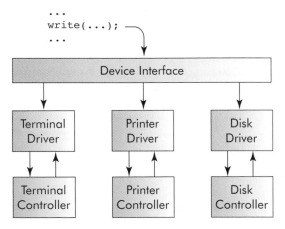

Device driver construction is a rigorous software design procedure. The designer must learn all the details of using the device controller interface. The designer then implements the abstraction by constructing functions on the standard interface in terms of the device's details. The disk drive abstraction example in Section 1.1 suggests the nature of the driver abstractions.

Over the years, OS designers have created APIs so that they look like those used to read and write files (see the file API discussion in Section 2.2). In POSIX-compliant systems, the device manager system call interface contains functions to open, close, read, write, seek, and control the device (see Table 2.1 for the file commands). The `open()` function allocates the device to the calling process and generally prepares the device manager data structures so that it can manage I/O operations. The `close()` function deallocates the device and releases the data structures. The `seek()` function sets up the device to read/write a particular address in the device; for example, a `seek()` call moves a magnetic tape record into a position where it can be read or written (with a separate command). The `control()` function is device-specific: A disk storage device can be powered up/down, while a video screen can be "reversed" so that black pixels appear white and white pixels appear black.

The device manager *infrastructure* is the part of the OS that houses the collection of device drivers. This infrastructure makes it possible for the OS to export the common device interface as system calls. Then it routes calls on the generic interface to specific device driver functions (this will be described in Section 5.3). The device manager infrastructure and the collection of device drivers constitute the **device manager**.

As illustrated in Figure 5.3, the device manager is constructed of device-dependent and device-independent parts. The infrastructure is the independent part, and the drivers are the dependent parts of the device manager. In interrupt-driven I/O situations, the device driver is partitioned into one part that initiates the operation and a matching device interrupt handler to handle the completion of the operation. The infrastructure is the device-independent part of the device manager.

◆ FIGURE 5.3 Device Management Organization

The device manager provides services to the file manager and application software. It is composed of a device-independent infrastructure and a collection of device-dependent drivers.

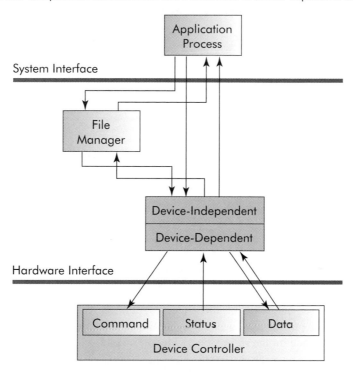

I/O-PROCESSOR OVERLAP WITHIN AN APPLICATION

Application programmers have a preconceived model of the semantics of I/O operations. They expect **serial execution semantics** for an individual thread. This means that read and write operations behave as if they were sequential operations. When programmers use a read statement in a program, they know the read instruction will complete before the next instruction is executed.

Suppose a thread executes code such as

```
...
read(dev_I, "%d", x);
y = f(x);
...
```

Figure 5.4 shows the situation while the read() system call is being executed. The read() function in the device driver has started the dev_I device, but the operation has not completed. If a process were to execute the assignment statement, y = f(x), at that moment, then the f(x) function would be executed using an *old* value of x, not the new one being read from the device. To prevent this situation, the OS blocks the process until it completes the read() call. From the process's perspective, the abstract machine environment waits for the device to complete the I/O operation before it executes the assignment statement.

✦ **FIGURE 5.4**   Overlapping the Operation of a Device and the CPU

The semantics of sequential programming languages is that statements are executed in sequence. This means that the read() statement must finish before the assignment statement begins. This ensures when the f() function is evaluated, it has the value of x that was just read.

```
...                                 ...
read(dev_I, "%d", x);               startRead(dev_I, "%d", x);
y = f(x);                           ...
...                                 while(stillReading());
                                    y = f(x);
                                    ...
```

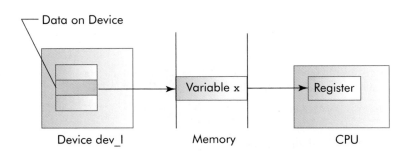

More complex semantics might allow the programmer to initiate the read() operation—that is, to *start* the device and then to continue processing without waiting for it to complete (see the code on the right side of Figure 5.4). In order to support serial execution semantics, the device driver would have to export a function to start the device, startRead(), and another one to determine when the device has completed, stillReading(). These would be alternatives to the sequential execution read() function.

Figure 5.5 shows another way for thinking about this kind of CPU and device execution (illustrated using a **Gantt chart**). The Gantt chart emphasizes overlapped operation. Suppose the application program uses the startRead() and the stillReading() functions:

■ At time t_1, the processor starts the controller with the startRead() operation, but then continues using the CPU. As long as the application does not need the result of the read operation, it can execute the program on the CPU at the same time the I/O operation is taking place. When the thread needs the result of the pending read operation, it calls stillReading(). This will cause the process to pause until the I/O has completed. If the thread can yield the CPU to other processes (as part of the stillReading() implementation), the CPU can be used on other processes while the I/O operation is in progress.

■ At time t_2, the application yields the CPU, since the device is busy and the application needs the results of the read operation before it can proceed.

■ At time t_3, the thread is reassigned the CPU and polls the device until time t_4.

■ At time t_4, the thread again yields the CPU.

- At time t_5, the thread resumes checking the device, finding it busy until t_6.
- At time t_6, the thread then begins performing work on data obtained by the read.
- At time t_7, the thread again starts the device and executes other instructions until it needs the results of the I/O at time t_8, and so on.

This overlapped CPU-device operation results in an overall reduction in the amount of time it takes to execute the program and its I/O serially. From time t_1 to t_2 and from t_7 to t_8, the CPU and controller are operating in parallel, thus reducing the overall runtime from the sum of the two time intervals to the maximum of their time intervals. From t_3 to t_4 and from t_5 to t_6, the process is in a busy-wait state, so from the viewpoint of achieving effective computation, those time periods are wasted, since there is no overlapped operation.

✦ FIGURE 5.5 Overlapping CPU-Controller Operations in a Process

By using the `startRead()` and `stillReading()` functions, the OS can allocate the CPU to other processes whenever a process is stalled on an I/O operation. This can result in an overall reduction in the time to execute a suite of programs.

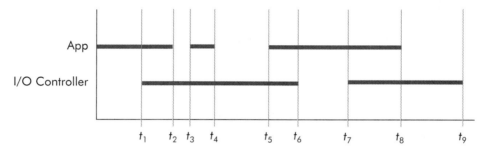

I/O-PROCESSOR OVERLAP ACROSS THREADS

There are two prerequisites for a thread to be able to overlap its CPU and I/O operation:

- The computation performed by the thread must be arranged so that while the I/O operation is taking place, the thread has other work to do.
- The programming language and OS must provide tools to allow the thread to start an I/O operation, and then to poll the device to see when the operation has completed.

If an individual thread is not able to take advantage of the overlap of CPU and I/O operation, the OS can overlap the CPU execution of one thread with the I/O operation of other threads. It does this by switching the CPU to another thread whenever one thread invokes an I/O operation. Thus, the overall system performance can be improved due to the resulting overlap, although the individual thread will still execute sequentially across the processor and the I/O device. This requirement for serialization within a thread means that the process management part of the OS must become involved in I/O operations. This ensures that an I/O call will result in the calling thread yielding control of the CPU to another application process. When the I/O completes, the original thread can be rescheduled.

The device manager enables a system to overlap device I/O operation with processor operation. This results in more effective use of computing facilities and less real time needed for a process to have its computational needs met. The Gantt chart shown in Figure 5.6 illustrates how device I/O operations can be overlapped. It features the execution of two different application programs in an interrupt-driven system.

Prior to time t_1, Application 1 is executing on the CPU.

- At time t_1, it initiates a device operation. After the controller begins the operation for Application 1, the CPU is multiplexed to Application 2.

- At time t_2, Application 2 gives up the processor. However, it begins using it again immediately because Application 1 is still waiting for the I/O operation to complete.

- At time t_3, the controller completes the operation requested by Application 1. To minimize the response time of Application 1, the application must begin executing as soon after t_3 as possible.

- In the Gantt chart, Application 2 initiates I/O activity at t_4, releasing the CPU so that Application 1 can resume operation while Application 2 waits for the I/O operation to complete.

✦ **FIGURE 5.6** Overlapping Processing and I/O

This Gantt chart shows how two different threads of execution can be managed so that one's I/O activity occurs in parallel with the other's CPU activity. The dashed line represents App 1's activity and the solid line represents App 2's activity.

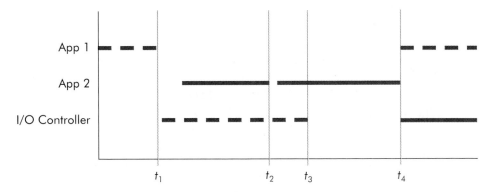

5.2 ● I/O STRATEGIES

In Chapter 4, you saw that one dimension of the I/O strategy is whether it uses direct I/O or DMA. The **direct I/O** strategy is to transfer input data from the controller to a CPU register, and then from the CPU register to a primary memory location. Similarly, the CPU copies ouput data from the primary memory cell into a register, and then from the register to the controller. The alternative to direct I/O is DMA I/O, where the data flows directly between the primary memory and the device controller. The other dimension to the I/O strategy is whether the device uses interrupts or the software has to poll the device to determine when it has completed an operation.

We can see that these two dimensions define four different I/O strategies:

- Direct I/O with polling
- DMA I/O with polling
- Direct I/O with interrupts
- DMA I/O with interrupts

DMA with polling is not ordinarily supported, because if the device is sophisticated enough to read and write the primary memory, it will also incorporate interrupts. The other three options are all used with different device controllers.

DIRECT I/O WITH POLLING

Direct I/O refers to the method of accomplishing I/O whereby the CPU is responsible for determining when the I/O operation has completed, and then for transferring the data between the machine's primary memory and the device controller data registers. Here are the specific steps required to accomplish an input operation using direct I/O with polling (see Figure 5.7):

1. The application process requests a read operation.
2. The device driver queries the status register to determine if the device is idle. If the device is busy, the driver waits for it to become idle.
3. The driver stores an input command into the controller's command register, thereby starting the device.
4. The driver repeatedly reads the status register while waiting for the device to complete its operation.
5. The driver copies the contents of the controller's data register(s) into the user process's space.

The steps to perform an output operation are as follows:

1. The application process requests a write operation.
2. The device driver queries the status register to determine if the device is idle. If the device is busy, the driver waits for it to become idle.
3. The driver copies data from user space memory to the controller's data register(s).
4. The driver stores an output command into the command register, thereby starting the device.
5. The driver repeatedly reads the status register while waiting for the device to complete its operation.

Each I/O operation requires that the software and hardware coordinate their operations to accomplish the desired effect. In direct I/O with polling, this coordination is accomplished by encapsulating the software part of the interactions with the device controller hardware wholly within the device driver. However, with this approach it is generally difficult to achieve highly effective CPU utilization, since the CPU must constantly check the controller status. As a result, CPU cycles are used to repeatedly test the controller inter-

✦ FIGURE 5.7 Polling I/O Read Operation

In polling I/O read operations, the application requests the read, and then blocks. The driver starts the device, and then continuously checks its status until the operation has completed. The driver completes the data transfer, cleans up, and then returns control to the application.

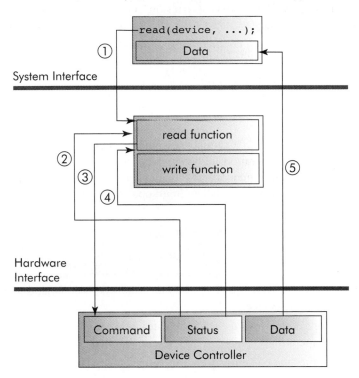

face while the device is busy. As discussed in Section 5.1, in a multiprogrammed system, these wasted CPU cycles could be used by another process. Because the CPU is used by other processes in addition to the one waiting for the I/O to complete, multiprogramming may result in sporadic detection of I/O completion. This can be addressed through the use of interrupts.

INTERRUPT-DRIVEN I/O

The motivation for incorporating interrupts into the computer hardware is to eliminate the need for the device driver software to constantly poll the controller status register. Instead, the device controller "automatically" notifies the device manager when the operation has completed. In the scenario using interrupts, the device management functionality is partitioned into four different parts:

■ "Top half" (a name coined in BSD UNIX) of the driver that initiates the operation
■ Device status table
■ Interrupt handler
■ Device handler

The following are the steps for performing an input instruction in a system by using interrupts (see Figure 5.8):

1. The application process requests a read operation.

2. The top half of the device driver queries the status register to determine if the device is idle. If the device is busy, the driver waits for the device to become idle.

3. The driver stores an input command into the controller's command register, thereby starting the device.

4. When the top half of the device driver completes its work, it saves information regarding the operation that it began in the **device status table**. This table contains an entry for each device in the system. The top half of the driver writes into the entry for the device it is using information such as the return address of the original call and any special parameters for the I/O operation. The CPU then can be used by another program, so the device manager invokes the scheduler part of the process manager. It then terminates.

✦ FIGURE 5.8 Interrupt-driven I/O Operation

In interrupt-driven I/O read operations, the application requests the read, and then blocks. The top half of the driver starts the device, and then halts. The interrupt causes the device handler to finish the I/O operation, completing the data transfer, cleaning up, and then returning control to the application.

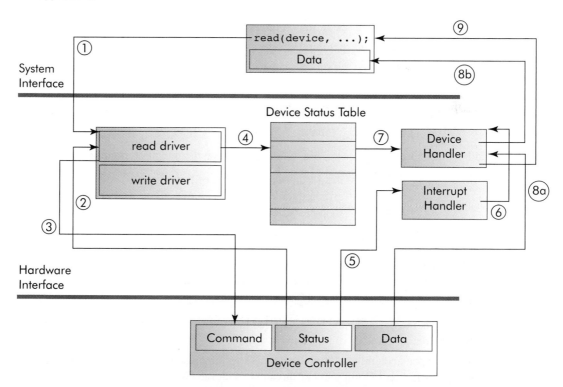

5. Eventually, the device completes the operation and interrupts the CPU, thereby causing the interrupt handler to run.

6. The interrupt handler determines which device caused the interrupt. It then branches to the device handler for that device.

7. The device handler retrieves the pending I/O status information from the device status table.

8. The device handler copies the contents of the controller's data register(s) into the user process's space.

9. The device handler—behaving as the "bottom half" of the device driver invoked by the application process—returns control to the application process.

The output operation behaves similarly. From the viewpoint of the application thread, the activity has the serial execution semantics—the same semantics as an ordinary procedure call. However, the time to execute the program may be considerably shorter than it is for a polling system, depending on the time ratio of computing, the I/O, and the timeliness with which the software processes poll the device. This added delay in a polling system stems from the accumulation of delays between the time that the device finishes the operation and the time that the executing program observes this event and continues its normal execution.

POLLING VERSUS INTERRUPT-DRIVEN I/O PERFORMANCE

In general, the time to execute a thread can be broken down into:

$time_{compute}$:   The time spent on computation

$time_{device}$:   The time spent on I/O operations

$time_{overhead}$:   The time the process spends determining when each I/O operation is complete

So the total time to execute the computation is

$$time_{total} = time_{compute} + time_{device} + time_{overhead}$$

If an I/O device manager uses polling to determine when the operation is complete, we have

$time_{overhead} = time_{polling}$ = the accumulated amount of time after a device completes an operation but before the polling loop has determined that the completion has occurred

This is generally only a few instruction execution times.

In a system with interrupts, $time_{overhead}$ is calculated as follows:

$$time_{overhead} = time_{handler} + time_{ready}$$

where

$time_{handler}$ is the accumulated time required to execute the interrupt handler and device handler routines and

$time_{ready}$ is the accumulated time the process waits to use the CPU after it has completed its I/O but another thread is using the CPU.

Polling is normally superior from the viewpoint of the individual process, since normally

$$time_{polling} < time_{handler} + time_{ready}$$

However, consider the effect of both approaches on the overall performance of the system, rather than this turnaround time for one thread. Suppose three threads are to be executed on a system. Thread 1 requires $time_{total1}$ to complete, thread 2 requires $time_{total2}$ to complete, and thread 3 requires $time_{total3}$ to complete. In a polling system, thread 1 might run to completion before thread 2 is started, and thread 2 would run to completion before thread 3 is started. The total time to execute all three threads with polling would be

$$time_{TOTAL-P} = time_{total1} + time_{total2} + time_{total3}$$

In a system with interrupts, multiprogramming can make good use of the CPU by threads 2 and 3 when thread 1 is conducting I/O. Ideally,

$$time_{device1} \leq time_{compute2}$$

$$time_{device2} \leq time_{compute3}, \text{ and}$$

$$time_{device3} \leq time_{compute1},$$

meaning the total time to execute the three threads in a system with interrupts is

$$time_{TOTAL-I} = time_{compute1} + time_{compute2} + time_{compute3} + time_{overhead}$$

where the overhead is the sum of the overhead times of the individual threads. The average time to finish a thread is $time_{TOTAL-I}$ divided by 3. Hence, the average time to execute a thread is much less with interrupts than it is with polling.

5.3 ● DEVICE MANAGER DESIGN

Device management is responsible for manipulating the hardware devices using privileged instructions (see Figure 3.10). It provides the first-level abstraction of the physical resources that will be used by both the file manager and applications to read, write, and store information.

Application programs invoke I/O operations by making system calls to request that the OS perform those functions on the devices. This means that the system call interface is configured to include the specific functions needed to operate *any* device that might be incorporated into the computer. Since devices may have very different operations, how can the system call interface possibly accomplish this task? Some devices can only be read, some can only be written, some have special commands to power up/down the device, and so on. The OS designers choose a single comprehensive set of *n* different system call functions that can be used to invoke all possible operations on all possible devices. Any particular device may not be able to respond to some of the operations—a keyboard device will probably not respond to a `write()` system call—but the function name still exists on the system call interface.

The *n* different system calls point (through the trap table) to *n* different entry points in the kernel. The trap table entry and code schema for the ith device function (for example, read()) is shown in Figure 5.9. When a user program wants to call the ith function for device number j, it issues a system call of the form func$_i$(j, ...), which traps to the dev_func_i() system function. If there is any processing that can be done which is common to all devices, it is performed in this function either before or after calling the device-specific code, devj_func_i(). Although it is not illustrated in the figure, each case in the switch statement could also have more code, for example, to package parameters correctly for the device-specific function call.

✦ **FIGURE 5.9** Device-Independent Function Call

The OS exports a common set of device functions that apply to every device. The device infrastructure uses the device ID parameter to route the request to the corresponding function in the appropriate device driver.

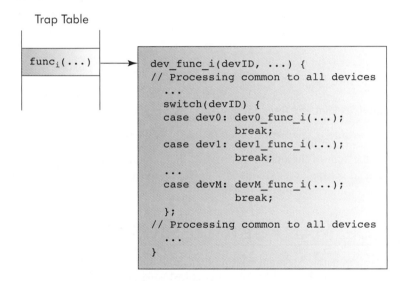

In this approach, whenever a new driver is incorporated into the system, the OS source code fragment described in Figure 5.9 is edited to call the new device driver functions, and then the OS is recompiled. Hence, the organization that installs the driver must have a copy of the OS source code and considerable prerequisite knowledge to add a driver. This scenario was acceptable when all computers and devices in the user's organization were acquired from the same vendor, since the vendor's service organization would install the driver when it installed the device. Economic pressures for open systems, however, resulted in organizations buying a device and driver from a third party and then having to modify and install the OS source code.

DEVICE-DEPENDENT DRIVER INFRASTRUCTURE FRAMEWORK

The device-independent part of the OS provides a framework that application programs use to call any of *n* different functions, {func$_i$(...) | 0 ≤ i <n}. For example, there are *n* = 6 functions in the POSIX set: {open(), close(), read(), write(),

lseek(),ioctl()}. Each device controller exports a specific hardware interface to the software: The interface details include the exact commands that can be issued to the device, the status and error reports that are returned, timing behavior, and any other requirements on how software can control the device. This interface can be complex due to the amount of detail that must be addressed for correct operation. The device driver software uses the specific device's hardware interface to implement abstract I/O operation. The device driver is partitioned into the *n* different functions that will be called via the system call interface (through the device-independent part of the manager). So each device driver implementation is constrained by two interfaces: the software interface by which the *n* functions are called via the system call interface and the hardware interface used to control the device itself.

Using the framework, device management software is added to an existing system by constructing the *n* device drivers for a new device, adding a new case clause to the switch statement (to call the functions for the new device), and then compiling the kernel and drivers so that the new function entry points in the device-independent framework are resolved.

Modern operating systems simplify this driver installation by using **reconfigurable device drivers**. Such a system allows system administrators to add a device driver to the OS without recompiling the OS (although the system will have to be reconfigured by some set of operations). This reconfiguration is accomplished by using an indirection trick so that the OS can bind its code to the driver functions at runtime. For example, the code schema shown in Figure 5.9 does this dynamic binding by transforming the switch statement into a statement that calls the jth function using an indirection table. The statement that replaces the switch statement has the form:

dev_func_i[j](...);

which calls func$_i$(j, ...) the jth entry of the dev_func_i table that contains the address of the entry point of func$_i$(j, ...). The advantage of doing this is that the address of the entry point can be written into a table at runtime. That is, the OS can be compiled to call a particular function for a device that is not known at compile time (see Figure 5.10). This is an essential element in the device-independent part of the device manager that supports reconfigurable device drivers. It implies that whenever a device driver is added to a system, there is a **device registration** procedure that makes a system call to a function to fill out the entry point table used by the dev_func_i(...) function. This is the approach used in the Linux kernel [Nutt, 2001].

Servicing Interrupts

The scenario in Section 5.2 describes how the device-dependent code is written for polling devices. For interrupt-driven devices, there are additional device-dependent parts besides the device driver: There must also be a device interrupt handler for device J and a mechanism equivalent to the device status table through which state information can be passed from the device driver to the device interrupt handler function (see Figure 5.11(a)). The system interrupt handler calls the device handler, using a mechanism similar to the one used to call the driver functions from the application domain. That is, the interrupt handler consults an interface defined by a set of functions that have been registered with the

✦ **FIGURE 5.10** Reconfigurable Device Drivers

A device manager that supports reconfigurable drivers uses an indirect table (for each system call) to reference the individual device's functions. Table entries for a particular device can be established at run time using a utility tool that registers device drivers.

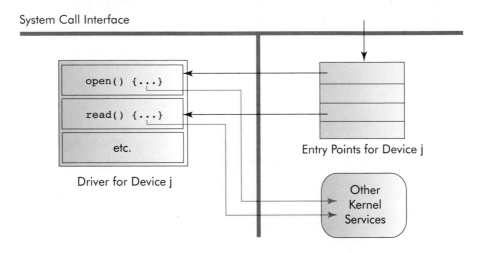

OS. With reconfigurable devices, another indirection table is used to allow the device interrupt handler entry point to be established by a special system call to install the device.

In a contemporary OS, the process manager contains at least one synchronization mechanism (explained in Chapter 8). Briefly, a synchronization mechanism can be used by two independent threads (in two different processes) so that one thread blocks itself from using the CPU until the other thread sends it a signal. The UNIX `wait()` system call (see Section 2.4) causes a thread to block until another thread sends a signal to the blocked thread. If an OS contains a synchronization function to block a process, it will always contain another function to "signal" the blocked process, unblocking it and making it ready to use the CPU again. Given a "wait" and a "signal" OS facility, the generic interrupt-driven device manager can eliminate the device status table by having the device driver contain all the state information internally (see Figure 5.11(b)). Then the device driver initiates the I/O, but instead of terminating, it uses the wait function to block itself while the device is in operation. When the device completes, the device interrupt handler will perform any cleanup operation it needs to do; then it sends a signal to the blocked driver. The device driver becomes unblocked, performs any other cleanup operations that might be needed, and returns to the application program.

✦ FIGURE 5.11 Handling Interrupts

As shown in Part (a), interrupt-driven devices logically employ two parts for the driver: The first part is called by the application program. This code starts the device, writes its status to the device status table, and then terminates. When the device raises an interrupt, the second part, the interrupt handler, dispatches the device handler. It retrieves the status, completes the I/O processing, and returns to the application program. In part (b), we see that this software configuration could be changed so that the first part just suspends itself until the device handler notifies it that the operation has completed. This means that the suspended driver keeps the state internally rather than writing it to the device status table.

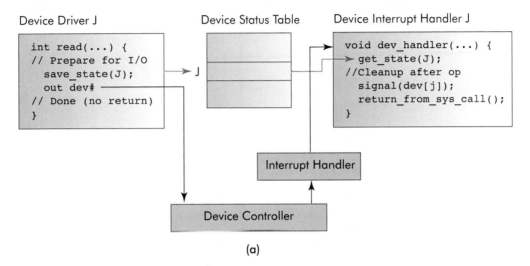

(a)

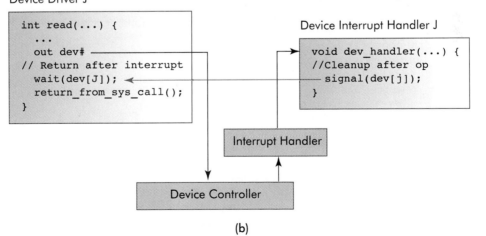

(b)

Linux Device I/O

The Linux kernel is a typical reconfigurable device driver system. It references different device drivers by a major number and minor number. The **major number** of a device normally identifies the class of devices that the driver can manage, so the same device driver can be used with different, but compatible, hard disks. The Linux community has agreed on a set of major numbers for device classes that are normally supported. For example, floppy disks have a major number of 2, IDE hard disks have a major number of 3, parallel ports have a major number of 6, and so on. The file `include/linux/major.h` file provides the full list of major numbers for each release of Linux. The **minor number** is an 8-bit number that references a specific device of a particular class (major number). Thus, two floppy disks on a machine would have a major number of 2; the first disk might have a minor number of 0, and the second a minor number of 1.

The kernel must be informed of the existence of a device. When the kernel is booted, it will normally create a special file for each device in the system. A **special file** is an entry in `/dev` for the device that will be used to identify the device driver for that device. This can be done with the `mknod` command:

```
mknod /dev/<dev_name> <type> <major_number> <minor_number>
```

The `<dev_name>` is the special file name (you can see the list of these by simply listing the files in the `/dev` directory). The `<type>` parameter is "c" for character devices and "b" for block devices. And of course the `<major_number>` and `<minor_number>` are the respective major and minor numbers for the device.

The interface to a device is intended to look the same as an interface to the file system. Each file system defines a fixed set of operations (functions) that can be applied to any of its files and directories by specifying a `struct file_operations` definition (see `include/linux/fs.h`). These same functions can be defined for any device driver:

```
struct file_operations {
  loff_t (*llseek) (struct file *, loff_t, int);
  ssize_t (*read) (struct file *, char *, size_t, loff_t *);
  ssize_t (*write) (struct file *, const char *, size_t, loff_t *);
  int (*readdir) (struct file *, void *, filldir_t);
  unsigned int (*poll) (struct file *, struct poll_table_struct *);
  int (*ioctl) (struct inode *, struct file *, unsigned int,
    unsigned long);
  int (*mmap) (struct file *, struct vm_area_struct *);
  int (*open) (struct inode *, struct file *);
  int (*flush) (struct file *);
  int (*release) (struct inode *, struct file *);
  int (*fsync) (struct file *, struct dentry *);
  int (*fasync) (int, struct file *, int);
  int (*check_media_change) (kdev_t dev);
  int (*revalidate) (kdev_t dev);
  int (*lock) (struct file *, int, struct file_lock *);
};
```

A device driver need only define functions that make sense for that particular device. For example, an input-only device probably does not have a `write()` function, and an output-only device might not have a `read()` function. The device driver designer decides which functions on the interface are required to operate the device, implements the desired functions, and then creates an instance of the `struct file_operations` with the appropriate entry points defined.

A conventional device driver for a device of type "foo" should also define an initialization function, `foo_init()`, that will be called when the kernel is booted. For example, there is a `tty_init()` function for serial ports, a `hd_init()` function for hard disks, and so on. Next, the kernel initialization code must be modified so that it calls the new `foo_init()` function. If it is a character device, then the function `chr_dev_init()` in `drivers/char/mem.c` must be modified. Similarly, block devices are initialized in `blk_dev_init()` that is stored in `drivers/block/ll_rw_bl.c`. Drivers for SCSI and network devices have their own initialization routines.

The `foo_init()` function allows the device driver to set up required data structures when the driver is installed (for example, when the machine is booted); the initialization code should also register the device driver interface—the `struct file_operations`—with the kernel using the `register_chrdev()` function for character devices or the `register_blkdev()` function for block devices. For example, if the imaginary "foo" device were a character device, its driver would contain a function:

```
foo_init()
{
    ...
    struct file_operations foo_fops = {
       NULL;             /* llseek - default */
       foo_read;         /* read */
       foo_write;        /* write */
       NULL;             /* readdir */
       NULL;             /* select */
       foo_ioctl;        /* ioctl */
       NULL;             /* mmap */
       foo_open;         /* open */
       NULL;             /* release */
    };
    ...
    register_chrdev(FOO_MAJOR, "foo", &foo_fops);
    /* Other initialization ... */
    ...
}
```

Once the driver has been initialized, the kernel will be able to route a system call such as

```
open(/dev/foo, O_RDONLY);
```

to the `foo_open()` function in the driver.

In an interrupt-style device driver, each of the entry points is the part of the driver that initiates the I/O operation. Once the device has been started, the calling process is changed to the `blocked` state and it is suspended while it awaits the interrupt from the device. Therefore, when you write an entry point function that uses an interrupt, you will also have to write a separate device handler function. Once the interrupt occurs, your device handler should be called. How does the kernel know which device handler to call? You will have to register the device handler with the kernel by associating it with a particular interrupt using the kernel function `request_irq()`.

5.4 • BUFFERING

Buffering is a technique that people use in everyday life to help them do two or more things at the same time. For example, think about a company that delivers bottled drinking water to offices (the "Pure Cycle Water Company" in Figure 5.12). The company provides an office with half a dozen full bottles of drinking water for the office workers. During the time that water is being consumed, the water company is busily cleaning and refilling empty bottles to be delivered the next week. Each water bottle is an example of a **buffer**. If the water company is willing to reserve a dozen water bottles for one customer's use, then the customer can be consuming the contents of one half dozen at the same time as the water company is filling the other half dozen bottles. You can probably think of hundreds of other examples of how buffering is used in businesses, and even in your personal life.

✦ FIGURE 5.12 The Pure Cycle Water Company

Each water bottle is a buffer. The water company delivers full bottles of water, and takes empty bottles back to the water production facility to refill. Consumers never need to wait for water, as water has been placed in buffers and delivered to the consumer prior to the consumer actually requesting a drink.

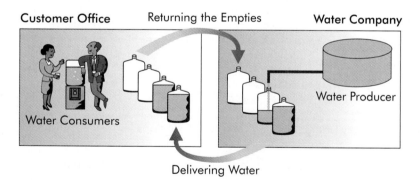

Buffering is employed by a device manager to keep I/O devices busy during times when a process is not requiring I/O operations, thus overlapping the device and CPU operation. **Input buffering** is the technique of having the input device copy information into the primary memory before the process requests it. **Output buffering** is the technique of saving information in memory and then writing it to the device while the process continues execution.

Consider a simple character device controller that reads a single byte from a modem for each input operation, as shown in Figure 5.13(a). The normal mode of operation for the controller is for the one-byte data register to contain the last character read following the driver's read operation. When an application program next calls the device driver read function, the driver passes a command to the controller. The controller, in turn, instructs the device to input the next byte and place it in the data register. The process calling for the byte waits for the I/O operation to complete and then retrieves the character from the data register.

✦ FIGURE 5.13 Hardware Buffering

Part (a) shows a shared register for sequential operation between the driver and controller. Parts (b) and (c) illustrate device controllers with two buffers. While the CPU process is processing byte i from one of the buffers, the device can be reading byte $i+1$ (or writing byte $i-1$) into the other buffer.

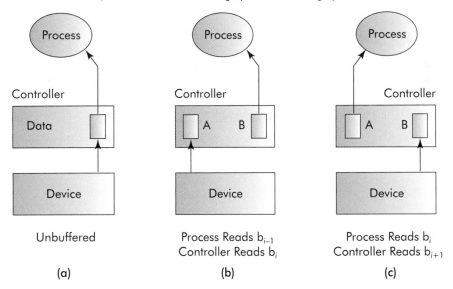

In parts (b) and (c) of Figure 5.13, a **hardware buffer** has been added to the controller. This can substantially decrease the amount of time the process has to wait for a character if the controller reads it ahead of time. In Figure 5.13(b), the next character to be read by the process has already been placed into data register B by the controller. The device is currently reading the next character from the device and placing it into data register A, even though the program has not yet called for the second read operation. In Figure 5.13(c), the process requests the character from the second read into controller data register A, so the device is started on a read operation to fill buffer B. The device read for character $i + 1$ will be overlapped with the CPU execution that uses character i. The overlap will be "well-matched" if the time to read the next character is the same as the time the process needs before it requests the next character.

The hardware buffering technique can also be applied at the controller-driver level (see Figure 5.14). This is generally called **double buffering**, since there are two software buffers. One buffer is for the driver or controller to store data while waiting for it to be retrieved by higher levels of the hierarchy. The other buffer is to store data from the lower-level module (the controller). The example in Figure 5.14 illustrates software and hardware double buffering for bytes. The technique also can be used with block-oriented devices such as magnetic tape drives. In this case, each buffer in the controller and in the driver holds an entire block rather than just a single byte.

✦ FIGURE 5.14 Double Buffering in the Driver

In this case. the double buffering technique is also used in the driver (besides being implemented in the controller hardware).

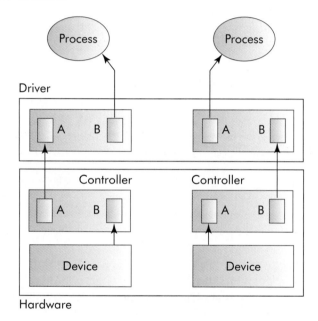

In Figure 5.15, the number of buffers is extended from 2 to n. The data "producer" (the device controller in read operations; the CPU in write operations) is writing into buffer i while the data "consumer" (the controller in write operations; the CPU in read operations) is reading from buffer j. In this configuration, buffer elements j to $n - 1$ and 0 to i $- 1$ are full. The consumer can read buffers j, j $+ 1$, j $+ 2$, ... $n - 1$, and 0, 1,... i $- 1$ while the producer is filling buffer i. Alternatively, the producer could fill buffers i, i $+ 1$, i $+ 2$,... j $- 1$ while the consumer is reading buffer j. In this **circular buffering** technique, the producer cannot "pass" the consumer because it would overwrite buffers before they had been read by the consumer. The producer can only fill up to buffer j $- 1$ while data in buffer j is waiting to be consumed. Similarly, the consumer cannot "pass" the producer because it would be reading information before it was placed into the buffer by the producer.

Can performance be increased by adding more buffers? The effect of buffering on performance depends heavily on the process's characteristics and the device type. The first prerequisite is that the device driver must know enough about the way information is read

✦ FIGURE 5.15 Using Multiple Buffers

Double buffering can be generalized so that it uses *n* buffers instead of just 2. This is called *circular buffering* because the *n* buffers are used in a circular order.

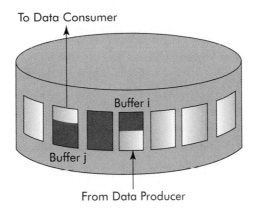

from the device that it can predict what data will be read in the near future. This is trivial with sequential devices, but essentially impossible for the device driver to do with random access devices.

The second prerequisite is that the thread behavior be conducive to buffering. Some processes are **I/O-bound**, meaning that their overall time to execute is dominated by the time to perform the cumulative I/O operations. A thread that copies one file to another is an example of an I/O-bound thread. Other threads are **compute-bound**, meaning that the time they spend in I/O operations is small compared to the amount of time spent using the CPU. A thread that computes prime numbers is compute-bound. Many threads have some phases in which they are I/O-bound and other phases in which they are compute-bound.

The device manager can use buffer management techniques to decrease the effective time to perform I/O for sequential streams of data if the application is sometimes I/O-bound and other times compute-bound. A thread that is consistently I/O-bound will tend to read every buffer as quickly as it is filled by the controller and to fill all available buffers with output before the controller has time to write them to the device. A thread that is always compute-bound will produce the opposite situation. That is, the input buffers will tend to be full and the output buffers empty. Simple threads are often purely I/O bound. More complex ones tend to have phases in which they are I/O-bound and other phases in which they are compute-bound.

Figure 5.16 illustrates the changing phases of a hypothetical program over time. Initially, the thread is I/O bound. At time t_1, it becomes compute-bound. Then it switches back to being I/O bound at time t_2, and so on. This thread profile takes good advantage of buffering, since during compute-bound phases, the controllers will be filling "input-full" buffers and emptying "output-full" buffers at a rate higher than they will be consumed. When the process becomes I/O-bound, it will have buffers available from the compute-bound phase. It will gradually use all of these buffers, ideally just when the process swings back to a compute-bound phase.

✦ FIGURE 5.16   Phases of a Program

This plot illustrates that program execution often passes through phases (and the phases are often cyclic because the code is cyclic). In this example, the thread is I/O-bound prior to t_1, then it is compute-bound from t_1 to t_2, and so on.

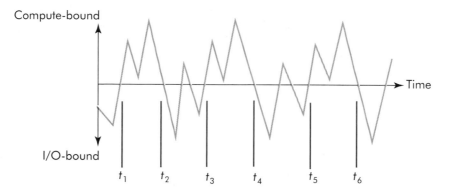

5.5 ● DEVICE CLASS CHARACTERISTICS

Until now, our device management discussion has applied to all types of devices. In this section, we will consider aspects of the most popular classes of devices. The OS distinguishes devices as being either block- or character-oriented devices. A single I/O operation on a character-oriented device reads or writes one byte. A block-oriented device reads or writes a fixed number (usually 512 or more) of bytes in one operation. Many of the character-oriented devices use serial or parallel communication ports. These devices (like modems and printers) are often connected to the device controllers with a cable. Storage devices are usually block-oriented devices, so they are usually integrated with the controller as a single hardware component. Some block-oriented devices are sequentially accessed, block $i+1$ after block i, while others can access blocks in any order (the blocks are "randomly accessed").

Communication devices transmit information between a computer and a device using a medium such as public broadcast, coaxial cable, or telephone wires. This communications technology is the predecessor of contemporary network technology. While networks dominate in large-scale computer-computer installations, simple communication devices are still heavily used for connecting terminals, printers, scanners, pointing devices, modems, and other devices to a computer.

Sequentially accessed storage devices are designed so that an operation can easily be applied to the "next" location after the last operation. For example, a magnetic tape such as a digital audio tape (DAT) is sequentially accessed, since it must be read block-by-block from the first to the last block. If the DAT is positioned in the DAT drive so that it can read block i, then the next read is expected to be block i (followed by a read of block $i + 1$). It is not necessary to provide the address of the information to be read or written in these devices, since the address is implicitly defined by the previous operation. A seek() command can be used to move the point of the next interaction with the device; thus seek() sets the address of the next block to be read or written. Sequentially accessed devices are ideally suited to buffering, because the block address of the next I/O operation is always implicitly defined.

Randomly accessed storage devices have no physical limitation to encourage reading or writing the information from/to the device in any particular order. For example, a floppy disk is a randomly accessed storage device. This is because after block i is read, the next block to be read can be any block j, since the disk read/write head can be moved directly to another block without its having to read intervening blocks. Because there is no assumption of sequential access, each read/write operation includes an address on the device to specify the point of interaction. Generally, these devices are not well-suited to buffering (unless they are accessed by a file manager as described in Chapter 13).

COMMUNICATION DEVICES

Communication devices are character devices that transfer bytes of information between a computer and a remote device (see Figure 5.17). To use the device, the driver manipulates the communications controller, which in turn manipulates the device using a controller-device protocol. The controller and device must agree on the interface as well as a **protocol** (agreement on the syntax and semantics of information) for using that interface. Thus, to connect a modem to a computer using a serial communications port, the computer must include a serial communications controller that can be attached to the modem using an external cable. Once the connection is made, the controller and the modem must exchange electronic signals according to a common protocol. (Modems can also be combined with the controller, thus eliminating the controller-device cabling. The external cabling then leads directly to a telephone jack.)

✦ FIGURE 5.17 A Generic Communication Device

Communication devices often have a controller that can be independent of the device. This requires that there be a controller-device protocol in addition to the driver-controller protocol. The RS-232 is an example of a controller-device protocol.

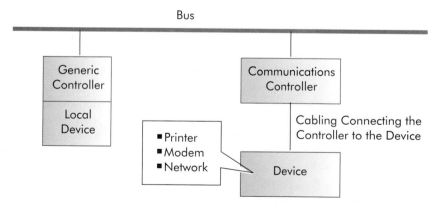

The RS-232 protocol is an example of a controller-device protocol (see the example box). This protocol specifies the connections between the controller and device as well as the way that electronic signals are exchanged between the controller and device. For example, the controller and device use the protocol to agree on the direction of data flow over the connection between them.

From a software perspective, the critical device interface is the one between the driver and the controller. This also uses a form of protocol: In this case, the protocol specifies the format and meaning of the controller's registers.

Today, serial communications controllers are implemented using a specialized microprocessor, called a Universal Asynchronous Receiver Transmitter (UART), which includes onboard ROM and RAM. It is an example of an embedded system. Because the operation has been standardized to support RS–232 controller-device interactions, the driver only needs to supply a few parameters to the UART in order to fully specify the controller-device protocol. Once the UART has been initialized (at the time the device is opened), an I/O operation is accomplished by providing a character plus a command. These drivers are among the simplest of all drivers.

Parallel communication ports are used to connect a printer to a computer; thus, the devices can be character streams, bitmaps, PostScript, or other computer-printer protocols. Although most devices connected to the parallel port are printers, these ports support two-way communication and can be used for other kinds of devices. For example, prior to the introduction of contemporary communication ports such as USB and Firewire, some external storage devices (such as a Zip drive) used the parallel port for data transfer.

Serial and parallel port technology was developed in the 1970s and came into wide use in the 1980s. By 1990, it became apparent that computers needed to have an alternative communication port that could be used for higher speed data interchange than would be possible using the older technology. At this time, devices such as video cameras, digital cameras, external CD-ROM drives, and personal digital assistants began to appear as devices that could be added to a computer without actually adding a controller card to interact with the bus. The earliest of these devices used serial and parallel ports, although these communication devices were slow. The USB and Firewire alternatives began to appear as options in personal computers by 1995. Each was influenced by a community that wanted to optimize the interconnection to suit its own purposes—streaming audio/video, block data transfer, PDA synchronization, and so on.

The **Universal Serial Bus (USB)** was developed to provide an external port that would act like a bi-directional, 1.5 to 12 Mbps internal connection to the computer's bus [USB, 2001]. (The USB 2.0 specification calls for data transmission rates as high as 480 Mbps.) The idea is to provide external sockets on a computer that support the USB protocol, yet that can be used by simply plugging in a USB-compliant device. The USB-computer port can be connected directly to a device, or to a hub that can connect multiple devices to the computer via the USB port. The device driver and USB hardware support the normal I/O operations, but, in addition, they provide functionality to handle dynamic connection and disconnection of devices via the USB socket, and to ensure that the appropriate detailed device driver is installed to manage the device over the USB port. USB also provides power to the device via the USB port; this means that the system has additional responsibility for routing power over the USB port to the device or hub.

The IEEE 1394 **Firewire** specification is a higher speed alternative to USB. Firewire was originally developed by Apple Computer in the 1980s, and then adopted as an IEEE standard in 1995 (the same time as USB) [IEEE, 2000]. The IEEE 1394a standard defines a serial bus that operates at 100, 200, or 400 Mbps, with plans to transmit data at 3.2 Gbps for devices in close proximity. Like the USB, Firewire has one or more external connectors to allow users to connect a digital camera or other devices directly onto the serial bus. The high speeds possible with Firewire make it better suited than USB for streaming media applications—Firewire can support an external DVD device.

Although contemporary computers rely on high speed networks for external communications, serial and parallel communications ports are important components on computers, particularly desktop and laptop computers. USB and Firewire are also very important for personal computers, workstations, and notebook computers, since they support modern, high speed device interconnection, and are invaluable for connecting a PDA to such a computer. Larger machines tend to use full networks (Chapter 15) in place of communication ports, although all computers seem to have at least one serial port on them.

Asynchronous Serial Devices

An asynchronous terminal is a character-oriented device that exchanges characters with the computer, using explicit signals to control the transfer of each character. Other than IBM 3270-style synchronous terminals, nearly all conventional terminals use the asynchronous technique. Data is transferred between the terminal and the computer in single-byte quantities. Each terminal is really two devices: a keyboard input device and a display output device. An input operation transfers a byte from the device's keyboard controller to a processor register or memory location. An output operation transfers a character from a register or a memory location to the display controller.

The RS–232 standard defines the interface between an asynchronous terminal (keyboard and display) and the controller for exchanging 8-bit bytes of information. The first part of the standard specifies the type of the physical connection (a 9-pin or 25-pin connector), and the second part specifies the meaning of the signal on each connected pin (only four wires are used on the RS–232 interface).

The controller accomplishes an output operation by putting a sequence of electronic signals on the wires at prescribed time intervals. The device reacts to the signals and constructs a byte based on them. The byte may be a control byte to the display (for example, to reverse the video colors—black-to-white and white-to-black) or a character to be displayed. The control bytes recognized by the display are device-dependent and typically differ among terminals. (The UNIX `termcap/terminfo` database is used to standardize and abstract these control functions.) Serial terminal devices and controllers can exchange information at speeds in the range of 110 to 57,600 signals per second. This rate of exchange is called the **baud rate** of the terminal. In the RS–232 standard, 11 signals are transmitted for each 8-bit byte transmitted. Three of the eleven signal times are used for synchronizing the operation of the device and the controller for every byte transmitted.

Asynchronous serial device controllers are typically implemented on a single chip (a UART) having the computational power of a small microprocessor. This chip is designed to provide signals to the device at one of various baud rates, with one of various parity options (odd, even, none), different numbers of overhead bits (2 or 3, depending on what the device is expecting), and so on. The chip has most of its detailed operation specified by a program stored in a ROM with the device. However, the software must choose appropriate parameters to specify the desired operations when the chip performs I/O. This selection can be done directly by either application software or a device driver. The chip itself typically costs less than a dollar, but it must be incorporated into a controller board with other logic, fasteners, and so on. The resulting serial controller still costs less than $50.

Almost every computer incorporates one or more serial device controllers as part of the basic system. The system console is usually connected to the machine via a serial device controller. The serial device's software/hardware behavior is defined by the small microprocessor and the controller's registers. When such a device is added to a system, it can be used only if software initializes the device by passing commands to the controller to select desired parameters, such as transmission speed and start/stop bits. After the controller has been initialized, it can be directed via write and read commands to transmit or receive information.

SEQUENTIALLY ACCESSED STORAGE DEVICES

Storage devices implement *persistent* storage in a computer system, meaning that information placed in a storage is preserved after the computer is turned off. Storage devices are either sequentially accessed or randomly accessed devices. Both types of storage device are usually block-oriented, which means that data are read from and written to the device as a block of bytes. The size of a block depends on the characteristics of the device and its controller.

Sequentially accessed, or sequential storage devices physically store the blocks on a recording medium in a linear sequence. Bytes may or may not be stored linearly within the block. The read/write interface to the device precludes programmers from ever really knowing exactly how bits and bytes are physically stored within a block. A read operation returns a block of bytes from the device, and a write operation copies a block of bytes to the device.

Historically, sequentially accessed storage devices were far more cost-effective than randomly accessed storage devices. Up until the 1960s, computers made heavy use of punched paper tape as an external storage medium. A typewriter-like device—a Teletype device—was used both as an online terminal to a computer and as an offline machine to store keystrokes by encoding them on a continuous stream of paper—a "tape." A programmer could prepare a program by typing it onto the paper tape offline, and then connecting the terminal to the computer and playing back the paper tape at "high speed"—approximately ten characters a second. By the 1970s, paper tape had been replaced by 7 track, and then 9 track magnetic tape (see the example box). Today, DAT is widely used to archive information stored on disks. As of 2003, DAT capacities can be as large as 40 GB. DAT is well-suited to archiving since it has enormous capacity and is relatively inexpensive; however, it is very slow to read and write blocks. It takes several hours to restore the data from a DAT to a hard disk.

Traditional Magnetic Tape

Magnetic tape is the prevalent sequential storage medium for today's systems. Traditional magnetic tape is 0.5-inch plastic tape with a ferrite coating, although smaller cassette tapes prevail today. As with DAT, information is stored on the tape by magnetizing geographical areas on the tape's surface. Tapes may be any length, although common lengths range from 600 to 2,400 feet. Special applications such as the magnetic tape on the back of a credit card may be very short—for example, 3 inches long.

Traditional 0.5-inch tapes are formatted with 9 logical tracks, each running the full length of the tape. When the tape is placed under a read/write head, the head can sense one segment—an 8-bit byte with a parity bit—crossing the 9 tracks. (The parity bit is the sum of the other 8 bits taken modulo 2. It is used as a simple way to detect if a bit is incorrectly read from or written to the medium.) A collection of bytes is packed densely on the tape to form a **physical record** containing one block of data. Physical records are separated by an inter-record gap. When the driver issues an I/O operation, the tape drive must accelerate the tape across the read/write head so that it can read or write the tracks. It is impractical to place an inter-record gap between each byte, so the block operation is the only feasible approach for reading and writing the information. The density of the bytes on a tape is a physical characteristic of the design of the read/write mechanism. The density refers to the number of bytes to be placed in some fixed length of tape. For example, 6,250-bpi tape has 6,250 bytes stored on one inch of the tape. Today's DATs are much higher density, but much slower than these classic tape drives.

The information stored on a tape is physically accessed by moving the tape forward and backward across the read/write head. Thus, data can be accessed only at reasonable rates if the process reading the tape intends to read all of the information in the order it is stored on the tape. Seeking the tape in the drive causes significant delays (seconds or minutes) in such an operation. The sequentially accessed operation prohibits the use of tapes for almost anything but sequential access.

Many of today's cartridge tape drives have a search feature that assigns an index to each physical record. A seek operation can be performed more rapidly using the index than it can if the tape drive has to read each physical record on the tape. Such drives, however, are still relatively slow compared to the access speeds possible with randomly accessed storage devices.

RANDOMLY ACCESSED STORAGE DEVICES

Randomly accessed storage devices allow a driver to access the blocks on the device in an arbitrary order. This capability exacts a small, but measurable, performance penalty for accessing blocks stored at physically distant locations on the recording surface. Rotating disks are the most prevalent form of randomly accessed storage device. These disks employ a block read/write interface between the controller and the device. The block orientation is propagated to the driver/controller interface. However, disks do not ordinarily directly support sequential access, since contiguous blocks on the device do not necessarily hold logically contiguous blocks of information. Thus, software intending to access information stored on a randomly accessed storage device is responsible for determining the order in which blocks should be read and written on the device. File abstraction fits in naturally with this assumption. The file manager (discussed in Chapter 13) implements a strategy for storing logically contiguous information (a byte stream) in noncontiguous physical blocks on the random device interface.

Magnetic Disk

Magnetic disks are organized as one or more physical disk platters, each having one or two storage **surfaces** (see Figure 5.18a). Each surface is logically divided into several **sectors**, which are defined as angular portions of the disk circle, like slices of a pie. The surface of each disk is also organized into several concentric rings, each called a **track**, that passes through each sector. Figure 5.18(b) shows one track passing through 8 sectors. If a disk has 500 tracks and 32 sectors on a surface, then each sector contains 1/32nd of each of the 500 tracks. The platters spin on a common axis (the vertical line in Figure 5.18a) past a set of ganged read/write heads. Information can be read from or written to a track by radially aligning the read/write head over the desired track, and then waiting for the target sector to rotate under the read/write head. When the head senses the beginning of the sector, it reads/writes a string of bits from/to the corresponding track as the platter rotates past the head. Thus the block of information that is read/written by a magnetic disk device is actually stored on a platter surface as a stream of bits along a circular track. In informal terminology, a track segment lying within a sector—a block of data on the disk—is called a disk sector, although technically a sector crosses all tracks.

Because of engineering economics for devices, read/write heads are ganged together by attaching them to a single arm that can be positioned over a particular track. This reduces the cost of the device by incorporating only one motor or solenoid to move the read/write heads (rather than having one motor/solenoid for each read/write head). This approach means the read/write heads for each surface are positioned over the track at the same radial distance from the center of all surfaces at the same time. The collection of tracks on the different platter surfaces is called a **cylinder** of the disk (Figure 5.18(c)).

A physical disk record is stored on one track in one sector on one surface on the rotating medium. The number of physical records (blocks) stored on the disk is determined by the number of tracks, the number of sectors, and the number of surfaces. For example, a Maxtor Model 52049U4 or a Seagate Model ST310212A disk drive has a capacity of about 10 GB stored on 16 surfaces (logically 8 platters recorded on both sides), each with 63 sectors, and 16,383 tracks (or cylinders).

The read/write head is positioned at a specified radial distance from the center of the rotating disk in order to read information on a particular track. Head movement across tracks is the most time-consuming operation in rotating media operations, since it is difficult to design physical mechanisms to accurately move the arm at high speed to fit precisely over a track. This track disk **seek time** dominates all other aspects of the time taken to access a block of information. Less expensive disk drives employ a mechanism to move

✦ FIGURE 5.18 Rotating Media

Hard disks are the most well-known randomly accessed storage device, although floppy disks and CD-ROMS are other examples. In (a) we see that hard disks can have multiple surfaces. Part (b) shows the logical organization of each disk surface. Part (c) describes a collection of tracks that are related by being the same distance from the center of the surface on all surfaces. Since the read-write heads move as a unit, information within a cylinder can be accessed without moving the heads.

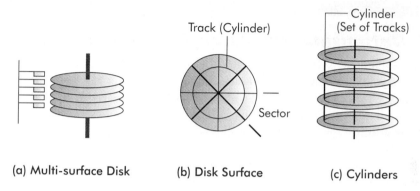

(a) Multi-surface Disk   (b) Disk Surface   (c) Cylinders

the head one track at a time. If the driver has just read a block from track 20 and next needs to read a block from track 50, it must step the head 30 times, once across each intervening track. More expensive disks can move a head directly from track 20 to track 50 with a single hardware operation. This operation is much faster than the single-track stepping mechanisms, although the time involved is still a function of the number of tracks crossed.

When the head has been positioned over the appropriate track (or in the appropriate cylinder on a multiple-surface disk), the device generally has to wait for the proper sector to rotate under the head before it can access the information. This rotational delay is called disk **latency time**, and it depends on the speed at which the disk rotates. Rotation speeds vary by at least an order of magnitude among different disk types. Floppy disks rotate at about 360 rpm, while fixed hard disks rotate as fast as 15,000 rpm or more.

Multiple-surface disks can be designed so that the controller provides an interface that makes data stored within a cylinder appear to be on a single track with many sectors. Suppose a disk has S surfaces and R sectors. The disk could provide an interface to map the block at sector r ($0 \leq r < R$) on surface s ($0 \leq s < S$), denoted (s, r), to logical sector t ($0 \leq t < RS$). The obvious mapping is to correlate the block at $(0, 0)$ with logical block 0, $(0, 1)$ with logical block 1, ... $(0, R - 1)$ to logical block $R - 1$, $(1, 0)$ with logical block R, and so on. Now, once the driver (or file system) seeks to the given cylinder, it can access any of the RS blocks in the cylinder without seek delays.

Depending on the controller design, sectors on different surfaces may be mapped so that logically contiguous sectors are on different surfaces, rather than being physically adjacent to one another. For example, logical sector 0 might be on $(0, 0)$, logical sector 1 on $(1, 1)$, and so on.

Rotating device design continues to improve. Magnetic disk technology miniaturizes the physical dimensions of the disk while decreasing seek time and increasing the transfer rate of data from the disk surface to the machine's memory. Average disk seek times depend on the number of tracks and the head movement time. One can expect contemporary magnetic disks to have an average seek time in the 5 to 25 millisecond range. Data transfer rates depend on the density at which bits are stored within a sector and the rotational speed of the disk. At the time of this writing, these rates can be expected to be on the order of 1 to 5 Mbps within a block.

Optimizing Access on Magnetic Disks

In a multiprogramming system, many different processes may attempt to access the disk at the same time. At any given moment, the disk driver may have several I/O requests it needs to service. In general, successive requests arriving at the driver will reference disk blocks physically remote from one another. As a result, the disk could spend considerable time seeking different tracks to service its requests.

For example, suppose a disk request queue receives six requests for blocks on tracks 12, 123, 50, 13, 124, and 49 in the order listed. One would expect the disk to first seek to track 12 and service the first request; seek to track 123 and service the second request; seek to track 50 and service the third request; and so on. Suppose the disk can seek to an adjacent track in X milliseconds, but it requires $X + YK$ milliseconds to seek to a track Y tracks away. If K were 3, then the disk could seek from track 12 to track 13 in $X + 3$ milliseconds but would require $X + 333$ milliseconds to seek to track 123 from track 12. For the example queue of disk requests, the driver would spend

$$(X + 3*(123 - 12))$$

$$+ (X + 3*(123 - 50))$$

$$+ (X + 3*(50 - 13))$$

$$+ (X + 3*(124 - 13))$$

$$+ (X + 3*(124 - 49))$$

or $5X + 921$ milliseconds seeking to the tracks in the order they are requested.

Since the seek time dominates the I/O time, all requests could be satisfied faster if the disk first serviced the requests for track 12, then 13, then 49, then 50, then 123, and finally for 124. The total seek time would be reduced to

$$(X + 3) + (X + 3(49 - 13)) + (X + 3) + (X + 3(123 - 50)) + (X + 3)$$

$$= (X + 3) + (X + 3 \times 108) + (X + 3) + (X + 3 \times 73) + (X + 3)$$

or $5X + 327$ milliseconds.

Obviously, the amount of savings depends on the characteristics of the seek mechanism on the disk and the mix of pending application operations. Some disks have very sophisticated seek mechanisms that allow them to seek to a track without stopping at intermediate tracks. However, even these drives will have a fixed amount of time to start a seek (the X factor) and some amount of time that is proportional to the number of tracks moved (the YK factor). The savings from optimizing the order in which requests are satisfied can have a substantial effect on all disks incurring seek time as part of the access time.

This faster approach serviced the requests according to a "scanning" algorithm in which the driver makes a sweep across the disk, servicing pending requests at the next higher-numbered track. Realistically, more requests will arrive while the driver is in the process of satisfying some set of requests in the queue. Thus, this approach could cause some requests to wait for a relatively long time. Suppose that immediately after the driver finished accessing the blocks on track 50, a request arrived for a block on track 45. Should the algorithm continue its sweep toward higher-numbered tracks, or should it return to service the request for data on track 45? In the 1970s, there was an intensive effort to study disk seek optimization algorithms, but there has been little new insight in the research since then. Here are a few of the most important strategies evolving from that research, some of which are now implemented directly in disk controller hardware rather than in the driver.

FIRST-COME-FIRST-SERVED (FCFS)

In FCFS, requests are serviced in the order in which they arrive at the driver. This approach is essentially a baseline approach in the sense that it takes no special action to minimize the overall seek time. Suppose the disk request queue contains a set of references for blocks on tracks 76, 124, 17, 269, 201, 29, 137, and 12. FCFS would begin at track 76, move 48 tracks to 124, and so on as described in Figure 5.19. The head will move across 880 tracks as it services the requests.

✦ FIGURE 5.19 FCFS Disk Optimization

The FCFS algorithm services requests in the order that they arrived. This is a simple approach, but does not give good performance.

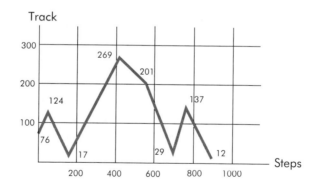

SHORTEST-SEEK-TIME-FIRST (SSTF)

Suppose the driver selected the next request as the one requiring the minimum seek time from the current position. SSTF may tend to move the head away from some requests during its local minimization. Under heavy load, SSTF can prevent distant requests from ever being serviced; this phenomenon is known as **starvation**. When the driver catches up with the load, it will ultimately have to move to the requests not serviced, thus resulting in a large performance cost for the head movement to a new part of the disk.

In contrast, SSTF responds to the disk request load used to describe the FCFS example by moving the head from track 76 to 29, 17, 12, 124, 137, 201, and 269, crossing 331 tracks, as shown in Figure 5.20.

✦ FIGURE 5.20 SSTF Disk Optimization

The SSTF algorithm inspects the set of pending requests, and then it selects the one that minimizes the amount of movement of the head from its current position. This algorithm performs well, but it is not optimal. It is also subject to starvation.

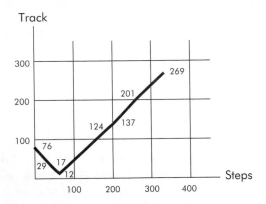

SCAN/LOOK

The Scan algorithm has the head start at track 0 and move toward the highest-numbered track, servicing all requests for a track as it passes the track. When it reaches the highest-numbered track, it reverses the direction of the scan, servicing newly arrived requests as it moves toward track 0. Look is a variant of Scan that ceases the scan in the high-numbered track direction after it has serviced the request with the highest number, and then it reverses the direction of the scan. For example, if the highest-numbered sector is 299, but the highest-numbered request is 269, Look will service the request for track 269 and then reverse the direction of its scan toward track 0, rather than continuing on to track 299 as Scan would.

Given the disk request load used in the FCFS example with the head currently at track 76 and moving toward higher-numbered tracks, Scan and Look would move the head from track 76 to 124, 137, 201, 269, 29, 17, and 12. Look would cross 450 tracks, and Scan would cross an extra 60 tracks, as shown in Figure 5.21. Both Scan and Look are guaranteed to service every request in one complete pass through the disk; thus, neither is susceptible to starvation.

CIRCULAR SCAN/LOOK

As Scan or Look move from high-to-low or low-to-high numbered tracks, new requests will continue to arrive. For example, suppose Scan has just served requests for track 15 in a scan toward the high-numbered track and a request arrives for track 13. The new request will not be serviced for almost two full scans of the disk—from 15 to the highest-numbered track and back to track 13. Circular Scan always scans the disk in the same direction—for example, from low-numbered tracks to high-numbered tracks. If the request for track 13 were to arrive right after the request for track 15 had been serviced, the request would have to wait for at most a single scan of the disk. Circular Look is related to Circular Scan in the same way Look is related to Scan. Circular Scan and Circular Look both rely on the existence of a special homing command that moves the head to track 0 in

✦ FIGURE 5.21 Scan and Look Disk Optimization

The Scan algorithm moves the head from track 0 to the highest-numbered track, servicing all requests in the queue whenever it is at the track they request. The Look algorithm variant stops the scan (up and down) when it gets to a track where there are no pending requests for tracks beyond the current track.

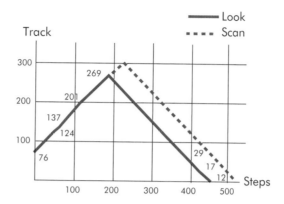

a short amount of time, relative to movement to any other track. Disks with inexpensive stepping motors (such as a floppy disk drive) do not incorporate this ability to quickly home to track 0.

Given the disk request load used in the FCFS example with the head currently at track 76 and moving toward higher-numbered tracks, Circular Scan and Circular Look would move the head from track 76 to 124, 137, 201, 269, 12, 17, and 29, as shown in Figure 5.22. In this example, assume that the drive requires the equivalent of 100 steps to move the head from 269 or 299 to 0. This is possible in some disk drives that incorporate a homing command to return the head to track 0.

✦ FIGURE 5.22 Circular Scan and Look Disk Optimizations

If the disk device includes a home command that lifts the heads and aligns them over track 0, then Circular Scan and Circular Look can be implemented. In this technique, the scan always proceeds in the same direction, for example, from low-numbered to high-numbered tracks.

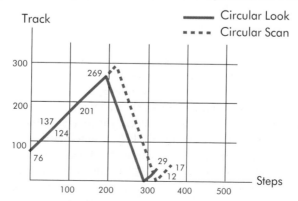

CD-ROM and DVD

Compact disks (or simply **CDs**) were originally designed in the early 1980s to contain audio information. Their target market was to replace analog vinyl recordings with a more durable, higher-quality, digital medium for distributing music (it looks like they succeeded!). CDs use a technique developed by Sony and Philips for laser video disks to record binary information on a 1.2 mm thick disk, 12 cm in diameter platter. Information is recorded by pitting the CD surface in a specified area to represent a zero or one. Each pit is tiny—0.5 micron wide, from 0.8 to 3 microns long, and 0.15 microns deep (a micron is a millionth of a meter). The recording area on a CD is organized as a helix that spirals out from the center of the CD to the edge. The spiral path is about 5,800 meters in length. This allows a CD to store enough digital information to record about 75 minutes of digitally encoded audio information.

Once a CD master has been created by pitting the surface appropriately, inexpensive copies can be reproduced from the master and distributed at low cost. CD readers can then sense the data on a copy by directing a laser beam along the helix to determine if a zero or one has been stored at locations corresponding to data addresses. For the original audio application, it is important that the CD reader deliver bits back to an amplifier at a constant bit rate. In a vinyl record or magnetic disk, the recording surface revolves at a constant angular velocity (CAV); for example, long playing vinyl records revolved at 33 rpm and magnetic disks rotate at 5,400–7,200 rpm. In CAV devices, the density of the recorded information on the outer edge of the disk is much lower than it would have to be on the inner edge of the disk. The CD standard uses an alternative approach: Information along the helical track is stored at a constant density, and the reader moves along the helical track at a constant linear velocity (CLV), meaning that the rotational speed of the disk varies with the location of the laser read head. When it is reading on the inner part of the disk, the speed is relatively fast, but when it is reading on the outer edge, the rotational speed is relatively slow.

The details of CD layout are specified in the ISO "Red Book" (ISO standard number IS 10149—available at `http://www.iso.ch/iso/en/ISOOnline.frontpage`). By the mid-1980s, people realized that the basic CD technology could be used to distribute data. The ISO "Yellow Book" updates the Red Book by specifying how graphic data can be interspersed with audio information—the new recording medium was called **Compact Disk – Read Only Memory** (**CD-ROM**) to distinguish it from the audio-only CD. The Yellow Book focused on low-level recording formats, including error detecting and correcting formats. The details of the spec are beyond the scope of this book, but the significance of the specification is that it became easy to randomly access blocks of data stored on the helical track. With a CD-ROM, data are stored in blocks with headers. A driver can search for a block by converting its address to an approximate radial location, and then beginning to search the track for the target block. This allows a CD-ROM to be read like a variable (and high) latency magnetic disk. The Yellow Book specification was again updated by the "Green Book" specification for the **Compact Disk-Interactive** (**CD-i**) device. CD-i is intended to support full multimedia data; thus, it is tailored to work with audio, video, and general data. For example, the sector header contains a type field that describes the contents of the sector.

The Yellow and Green Book specifications were driven by the entertainment industry for the distribution of audio and video content. Computer people recognized the value of adopting the technology for pure data distribution (and for entering the audio/visual arena). The High Sierra group—a consortium of interested computer manufacturers— refined the operation CD-ROMs so that they could include a directory structure that could be interpreted by a file manager. Ultimately, the High Sierra specification became an ISO standard (ISO 9660), and it is widely used today. The result of the High Sierra specification was that a CD-ROM could be mounted in an Apple or MS-DOS personal computer, and the contents could be read and played back to the user—a remarkable benefit to computer users. Today, CD-ROMs are the conventional medium for distributing software.

CD-ROM technology originated with CLV drives, delivering 75 sectors per second. The Yellow Book defines two sector types: Mode 1 and Mode 2. Mode 1 sectors carry 2,048 bytes of information and are intended for data (they are designed to exploit error detection and correction algorithms). Mode 2 sectors carry a higher payload (by eliminating error detection and correction fields), and are slightly larger—2,324 usable bytes. A CD-ROM reader reading Mode 1 sectors reads 75×2048 = 153.6 Kbps (or 174.3 Kbps for Mode 2). As CD-ROM technology has improved, it has been possible to increase the rotational speed of the drives. A 1x drive reads 153.6 Kbps, a 2x drive reads 2×153.6 = 307.2 Kbps, and so on. Another change in technology is that drive designers have moved from CLV to CAV device drives that read information at a rate higher than 12x.

It is a costly process to create a CD-ROM master. In the mid-1990s, a new innovation gave the CD-ROM market a large stimulus. By changing the physical materials used to make a CD-ROM and by building slightly higher-powered lasers into a drive, it began to be possible to have low-cost **CD-Recordable (CD-R)** devices.

The next innovation is the **CD-ReadWrite** or **Rewritable (CD-RW)** disk. This disk uses yet a different physical material for storing laser-readable information on the disk surface. With CD-RW, low-power lasers are used to read the surface, high-power laser settings are used to write the surface, and a mid-powered laser setting will remove the logical pits from the surface, erasing the data previously written to the disk.

The final step in the technology (up until this point) is the Digital Versatile Disk (DVD). Logically, DVDs differ little from CD-ROM. DVDs have higher-density information packing so that more data can be stored on the medium. A standard DVD can store up to 4.7 GB, although technologists are able to double that capacity by encoding the disk surface into two levels (8.5 GB) and by using both sides of the disk (17 GB).

The technology for CD and DVD devices is changing rapidly. If you want to know the current technology for these devices, you should consult the web. Much of the information in this section came from two or three different commercial web sites, including http://www.disctronics.co.uk/cdref/cdbasics/cdbasics2.htm for CD technology and the related site http://www.disctronics.co.uk/dvd/dvd-frame.htm for DVD technology.

5.6 ● SUMMARY

Device management is implemented across resource managers, device drivers, and device handlers. Devices vary widely in their characteristics, but device drivers are implemented to export a common API. The trend toward open systems has encouraged OS designers to make it easy for a systems administrator to add a device and driver to the system without having to change the OS source code. UNIX and Windows employ this technique by providing tools to the administrator to assist in configuring new devices as they are added.

If the execution and I/O of an individual process can be overlapped, the process will have decreased response time. If the overlap can be achieved by overlapping the I/O operation for one process with the execution of another, the system's throughput rate will be increased, meaning service to any particular process will be improved. Because many processes are I/O-bound or have large phases in which they are I/O bound, substantial effort has been invested in increasing the performance of the I/O subsystem. Buffering is a traditional technique used to increase performance through the overlap of execution. In rotating storage devices, head movement can be optimized based on the queue of I/O requests from various processes in a multiprogramming system. These optimizations increase device throughput and, on the average, reduce an individual process's waiting time for I/O.

Storage devices are a fundamental part of contemporary computer systems. As computers are applied to larger and larger information processing problems, the emphasis on processor performance is becoming more balanced with the need for performance of the storage system. Storage technology continues to rapidly improve with the development of higher-density disks, new storage media, and faster access times.

5.7 ● EXERCISES

1. Provide the detailed steps involved in performing an output operation in a system that uses interrupts. Use the explanation of the input instruction in Section 5.1 as a pattern for your answer.

2. Suppose three processes, p_1, p_2, and p_3, are attempting to use a machine with interrupt-driven I/O concurrently. Suppose p_1 has $t_{compute} = 20$ and $t_{device} = 50$, p_2 has $t_{compute} = 30$ and $t_{device} = 10$, and p_3 has $t_{compute} = 15$ and $t_{device} = 35$. Assuming that no two processes can be using any device or the CPU at the same time, what is the minimum amount of time required to execute the three processes?

3. Refer to hardware double buffering (Figure 5.13) and explain the effect of buffering on the runtime of the process if the process is I/O-bound and requests characters at a much higher rate than the device can provide them. What is the effect if the process is compute-bound and rarely requests characters from the device?

4. Should magnetic disk controllers include hardware buffers? Explain your answer.

5. System designers distinguish between the physical blocks read by the driver and the logical blocks presented to the application process. Explain how this distinction might be useful on a system that has floppy and hard disk drives.

6. Suppose that a driver is configured with 8 disk block buffers. What is the best possible read performance improvement of a program that uses this driver (compared to one that uses no buffering)? What are the conditions under which the performance is the best?

7. One of the ways magnetic disk drive manufacturers increase the capacity of a disk is by adding more surfaces. Does this change the device driver interface for the device? If not, why not?

8. Is it necessary for an operating system to have a driver-kernel interface in a system that does not use reconfigurable device drivers? Explain your answer.

9. Explain why a serial communications port that manages a terminal keyboard does not normally use the same optimization techniques as a serial communications port that manages a printer.

10. Identify some optimization techniques you would consider for a device driver for a magnetic tape drive. Justify each technique.

11. Suppose the read/write head is at track 97, moving toward track 199 (the highest-numbered track on the disk) and the disk request queue contains read/write requests for sectors on tracks 84, 155, 103, 96, and 197, respectively.

    a. What is the total number of head movements needed to satisfy the requests in the queue using the FCFS optimization strategy?

    b. What is the total number of head movements needed to satisfy the requests in the queue using the Scan optimization strategy?

    c. What is the total number of head movements needed to satisfy the requests in the queue using the Look optimization strategy?

12. Construct a scenario in which a disk optimization algorithm other than SSTF requires fewer steps to satisfy all requests for disk I/O. Use a 300-track disk with a maximum 100-track traversal time for any seek operation.

13. Overlapped execution semantics for read and write functions were defined in Section 5.2. How could you implement this in a conventional C program (using the stdio library)? *Hint*: Think about using kernel threads to solve this problem.

14. Section 5.5 describes CD-ROM devices. Notice that a CD-ROM recording track is a single helix coiling from the inside to the outside instead of a set of concentric rings like a magnetic disk. How can these devices support a seek command efficiently?

A Floppy Disk Driver

> This exercise can be solved on any Windows or any UNIX OS.

Windows and UNIX systems allow a programmer to open the floppy disk and read/write its contents as if it were a normal sequential file. In this exercise you will exploit this capability to experiment with raw I/O operations.

PART A

Write functions to determine the basic information about a diskette in logical drive A, read disk sectors, and dump the information you find in the floppy disk to the standard output stream. Here are the function prototypes:

```
Disk physicalDisk(char driveLetter);
void sectorDump(Disk theDisk, int logicalSectorNumber);
BOOL sectorRead
   Disk theDisk,
   unsigned logicalSectorNumber,
   char *buffer
);
```

The `physicalDisk()` function is called to initialize the disk for subsequent operations. The `driveLetter` parameter identifies the disk drive. The code should then use the host OS file open system call to prepare the device for use and to determine the disk geometry.

The `sectorRead()` function reads a given `logicalSectorNumber` from the designated disk (handle) into the specified buffer; the buffer size should be the same as a disk block. The read operation should return `TRUE` if it is able to read the designated block into the buffer, and `FALSE` otherwise.

The `sectorDump()` function calls `sectorRead()` and then prints the results of the call onto `stdout`. You should print an address first, and then hexadecimal representations of 16 bytes on that line. Increment the address by 16, and then print the next line, and so on. For example, your output should resemble

```
00000120 01234567 89ABCDEF ... 456789AB
```

PART B

Modify `sectorDump()` so that when it dumps logical sector numbers 0, it prints the information shown in Figure 5.23 (print the bootstrap code in the format for Part A. For sectors 1–18, format the output with an address at the beginning of the line as in part A, but group the data in 12-bit (3 hex characters) per group. Your output should resemble

```
00000004 012 345 689 ABC DEF ... 678 9AB
```

PART C

Write a driver program to illustrate that the code you wrote for Parts A and/or B works properly.

● BACKGROUND ●

The floppy disk is a widely used secondary storage device that has been configured into personal computers from the earliest days of MS-DOS to present desktop systems. The earliest systems used a 5.25-inch, 360K floppy disk, although in the 1980s, systems commonly switched to the 3.5-inch, 1.44M floppy disk. Even though software distributions increasingly use CD-ROMs (because of their larger capacity), the floppy disk drive is configured with most personal computers. It is an inexpensive, removable, universal medium for saving modest-sized files.

MS-DOS DISK FORMAT

MS-DOS defined a particular format for disks that is still used on Windows XP (and Linux). The MS-DOS BIOS provides a set of programs that can read and write blocks from a disk. BIOS also provides an additional abstraction of disk block addresses called *logical sector* addresses. Logical sector 0 corresponds to the sector at surface 0 (on a hard disk), track 0, sector 1 of the disk. (Surfaces and tracks are numbered from 0, but sectors are numbered from 1. The reasons for this have long been lost in obscurity.) Logical sector 1 is at surface 0, track 0, sector 2, and so on.

Before a disk can be used for normal I/O operations, it must be formatted to have essential information in prespecified locations on the disk. Specifically, logical sector 0 contains a *reserved area* (also called the *boot sector* or *boot record*). Personal computer boot sequences rely on the boot sector's being located at logical sector 0 and organized as shown in Figure 5.23 [Messmer, 1995]. Some of the fields may not make sense unless you see all of the pieces of a file system for an MS-DOS formatted disk.

✦ FIGURE 5.23 Boot Sector

The boot sector contains a description of the format of the disk, such as the number of sectors per track. It also contains the bootstrap program that is used to initialize the OS.

```
0x00    0x02    <A jump instruction to 0x1e>
0x03    0x0a    Computer manufacturer name
0x0b    0x0c    Bytes per sector
0x0d    0x0d    Sectors per cluster
0x0e    0x0f    Reserved sectors for the boot record
0x10    0x10    Number of FATs
0x11    0x12    Number of root directory entries
0x13    0x14    Number of logical sectors
0x15    0x15    Medium descriptor byte (used only on old versions of
                MS-DOS)
0x16    0x17    Sectors per FAT
0x18    0x19    Sectors per track
0x1a    0x1b    Number of surfaces (heads)
0x1c    0x1d    Number of hidden sectors
0x1e    ...     Bootstrap program
```

The first location in the boot sector contains a machine instruction to jump to location `0x1e`. The rationale for this is that upon booting up the system, the processor is hardwired to go to logical sector 0 of the boot disk, load it into memory, and begin executing the program loaded at the first location in the boot sector (see Section 4.6). Since there are several basic parameters that describe the *disk geometry*, and since these parameters need to be known at boot time, their values are placed at locations `0x03` to `0x1d`. Thus, when the processor begins to execute the boot sector, it immediately encounters the jump instruction to bypass the disk geometry information.

Hard disks can have an additional level of abstraction, called a *disk partition*. If a hard disk is partitioned, each resulting partition is treated like a physical disk above the abstract machine that accesses the physical disk (BIOS, in MS-DOS). In BIOS systems, a hard disk can be partitioned to have up to four different logical disks, each with its own set of logical sectors. If a disk partition is a *bootable disk partition*, then its logical sector number 0 will be a boot sector. In a partitioned disk the physical head 0, track 0, sector 1 will contain a *partition sector* rather than a boot sector. The partition sector provides information to describe how the hard disk is partitioned into logical disks. Roughly speaking, the partition sector starts off with a 446-byte program. When the hardware is powered up, it will go to head 0, track 0, sector 1 (as if the disk were not partitioned) and begin executing code. If the disk is partitioned, there will be a 446-byte bootstrap program at the first byte in the sector. If the disk is not partitioned, there will be a `jump` instruction to start the execution on the boot program stored at location `0x1e` in the sector. For partitioned disks, there is a 64-byte partition table for the disk immediately following the bootstrap program. It contains space for the four partition entries, each of which describes the portion of the physical disk that is used for its partition (the starting sector of the partition, ending sector, number of sectors in the partition, and so on). The last two bytes of the partition sector contain a "magic number," `0xaa55`, to identify the partition sector.

In Linux systems, the Linux Loader (LILO) is normally used with a partitioned disk. It replaces the boot record with a program that prompts the user to choose which disk partition to use for the bootup sequence. It is then easy to boot the computer and select the boot record to be used when the computer is started.

USING THE UNIX FLOPPY DISK API

The UNIX device interface is the same as the file manager interface. In particular, a UNIX process executing in user space can open the floppy disk by executing

```
open("/dev/fd0", O_RDONLY);
```

The process can then use the normal kernel `read()` system call to read the entire disk device as if it were a linear sequence of bytes.

```
bps = ...; //# bytes/block from 0x0b and 0x0c in the boot sector
len = read(fid, buffer, bps);
```

The byte sequence is determined by the disk layout—the first bytes in the stream are the bytes in the first logical sector on the disk, then the bytes from the second sector, and so on.

Depending on exactly how your laboratory machine is configured, the special file for your A: floppy disk drive could have a couple of different names, although it is probably

/dev/fd0. It might also be named /dev/fdnH1440, where *n* is a sequence number, probably zero.

If you wanted to write the floppy disk, you would have to run your program with super-user permission. For this exercise, you are expected to use this device interface as though it were a simplified block device interface, meaning that you are expected to open the file, then read its contents *only* as full (512 byte) disk blocks.

Since you will want to read different parts of the file—different sectors on the disk—you will need to use the lseek() function to position the disk read/write head prior to issuing a read operation.

USING THE WIN32 FLOPPY DISK API

Windows also allows you to read/write a device using the normal file functions. CreateFile() can be used to open a device such as a floppy disk. For example, if you wanted to open the floppy disk drive A and then read its contents as a linear byte stream, you could call

```
CreateFile(
    "\\\\.\\A:",
    GENERIC_READ,
    FILE_SHARE_READ,
    NULL,
    OPEN_ALWAYS,
    0,
    NULL
);
```

If there is a diskette in drive A, CreateFile() will return a handle that can be used by ReadFile() to read the entire disk contents as a byte stream. To perform efficient reads and writes, you should read and write sectors on sector boundaries. For example, with a 1.44MB floppy disk, you should read only bytes 0, 512, 1024, and so on.

Even though the floppy disk is opened as a file, you can still perform device-specific operations on it (and some of the normal I/O operations have a device-specific interpretation). Specifically, before reading or writing a floppy diskette directly, you must know the disk geometry—information stored in the boot sector. Windows returns the disk geometry using

```
BOOL DeviceIoControl(
    HANDLE hDevice, // handle to device of interest
    DWORD dwIoControlCode,
        // control code of operation to perform
    LPVOID lpInBuffer, // pointer to buffer to supply input data
    DWORD nInBufferSize, // size of input buffer
    LPVOID lpOutBuffer,
        // pointer to buffer to receive output data
    DWORD nOutBufferSize, // size of output buffer
    LPDWORD lpBytesReturned,
        // pointer to variable to receive output byte count
    LPOVERLAPPED lpOverlapped
        // ptr to overlapped structure for asynchronous operation
);
```

The hDevice handle is the result of the CreateFile() call. The dwIoControlCode parameter should be set to a value of IOCTL_DISK_GET_DRIVE_GEOMETRY. Of course, you will also have to allocate space for the result in nOutBufferSize and provide for the length of the result to be returned in lpBytesReturned. For the 1.44 MB floppy format, the values returned by DeviceIoControl() are:

- 512 bytes per sector
- 18 sectors per track
- 2 heads (double-sided)
- 80 cylinders

You could also read these directly from the boot sector. Since you will want to read different parts of the file—different sectors on the disk—you will need to use the SetFilePointer() function to position the disk read/write head prior to issuing a read operation.

● ATTACKING THE PROBLEM ●

Before you can perform disk I/O, you must create an abstraction of the details of the disk. The physicalDisk() function must detect format information about the disk and then make it available in a data structure accessible by sectorDump(). Each disk drive has a fixed geometry.

```
struct geometry {
  unsigned bytesPerSector;
  unsigned sectorsPerTrack;
  unsigned heads; /* tracks per cylinder */
  unsigned cylinders;
};
```

A disk is formatted with the geometry in its boot sector (see Figure 5.23). Primarily, you will use the bytesPerSector value from the struct, but you are also free to use the other fields as you like.

In designing your file system, use an abstraction of the physical disk to read and write logical sectors.

```
typedef struct disk *Disk;
struct disk {
  HANDLE floppyDisk;
  DISK_GEOMETRY geometry;
};
```

This defines a suggested Disk data structure. Logical sectors are numbered from 0, even though individual sectors on a track typically are numbered from 1. The logical sector L on track T, head H, sector S is located at

$$L = S - 1 + T * (\text{heads} * \text{sectorsPerTrack}) + H * \text{sectorsPerTrack}$$

You will not have to perform the translation from logical sectors to track/head/sector coordinates, as the OS will do that for you.

The first function to implement is the disk abstraction based on direct I/O to a physical disk:

```
Disk physicalDisk(char driveLetter);
```

To implement this function, you must use the kernel `open()` function for the host OS, applying it to the floppy disk drive. Be sure also to do the following:

■ Map the drive letter to an uppercase character.

■ If you are using DOS names, escape all of the backslashes in C string literals.

In Windows, use `OPEN_EXISTING` for the `dwCreationDistribution` parameter in the `CreateFile()` call. Use `FILE_FLAG_NO_BUFFERING` and `FILE_FLAG_RANDOM_ACCESS` for the `dwFlagsAndAttributes` parameter. In the `fdwShareMode` parameter, you must set the `GENERIC_READ`, `GENERIC_WRITE`, `FILE_SHARE_READ`, and `FILE_SHARE_WRITE` flags. Once you open the disk, you can get the geometry with the `DeviceIoCall()`.

The following shows the contents of the header file used for the solution.

```c
/* This interface is derived from one designed
 * by Norman Ramsey for CSci 413 at Purdue University, 1996
 */

#ifndef DISKMODULE_H
#define DISKMODULE_H

#define     BOOT  -1
#define     FAT1  -2
#define     FAT2  -3
#define     BOOT_SECTOR 0
#define     FAT1_SECTOR 1
#define     FAT2_SECTOR 10
#define     ROOT_SECTOR 19

#include <windows.h>
#include <winioctl.h>      // DISK_GEOMETRY

struct geometry {
      unsigned bytesPerSector;  // bytes in each sector
      unsigned sectorsPerTrack; // number of sectors in a track
      unsigned heads;           // number of tracks per cylinder
      unsigned cylinders; // number of cylinders on the disk
};

typedef struct disk *Disk;
struct disk {
  HANDLE floppyDisk;
  DISK_GEOMETRY geometry;
};

/* Function prototypes on the Disk interface */
```

```
// Abstraction of the NT physical disk
      Disk physicalDisk(char driveLetter);
      void sectorDump(Disk theDisk, int logSectorNumber);
      BOOL sectorRead (Disk, unsigned, char *);
#endif DISKMODULE_H
```

SOLUTION PLAN

You might consider developing your solution in the following order:

1. Write an implementation of physicalDisk().

2. Write an implementation of sectorRead() and segmentDump() that you can use to produce a hexadecimal dump of arbitrary sectors.

3. Use your segmentDump() routine to inspect a floppy diskette.

Here is a skeleton for the driver required for Part C.

```
#include      "..\???.h"    // data structures introduced above

int main(...){
  Disk theDisk;
  int firstSector, lastSector;

  firstSector = ...;      // first sector you wish to dump
  lastSector = ...; // last sector you wish to dump

  theDisk = physicalDisk(...);

// Dump some sectors
      sectorDump(theDisk, BOOT);
      sectorDump(theDisk, FAT1);
      sectorDump(theDisk, FAT2);
  if(firstSector >= 0) {
    for(i = firstSector; i <= lastSector; i++) {
      sectorDump(theDisk, i);
      printf("\n");
    }
  }
}
```

You will need to derive your solution using a real diskette. Using Windows OS, prepare a diskette with a dozen simple files. Your code should be able to open this diskette and dump arbitrary sectors from it.

CHAPTER 6

Implementing Processes, Threads, and Resources

A process, and its modern extension, the thread, are the active computational elements in a modern computer system. Processes and threads operate on passive resources such as primary memory and devices. An OS's **process manager** provides a spectrum of services to define, support, and administer the system's processes, threads, and resources. The natural place to begin a study of OS details is process management. This chapter and the next four chapters provide a complete discussion of process management. This chapter describes the general framework for the process manager, then looks at how the framework can be implemented. Subsequent chapters elaborate on the specific aspects of processor scheduling, synchronization, and deadlock.

6.1 • THE TASK AT HAND

In Chapter 1, you learned that the OS creates a collection of abstract machines, each of which can execute an application program. People have used abstract machines in many different walks of life: A company that has a single U.S. postal address can create a collection of its own postal mailboxes for its customers—an abstraction of the mailboxes at U.S. Post Offices. Older PBX telephone systems used a single public telephone number for a company, with telephones inside the company using an abstract telephone network where each subscriber had an extension number.

In Chapter 2, you saw how to *use* OS abstractions (process, thread, and file) to solve information processing problems. As a group, we called the collection of such abstractions the *OS abstract machine*. Because of technology evolution, the term "process" now has two different meanings: The notion of a **classic process** represents the concept of a program in execution on a von Neumann computer. This was an adequate abstraction for application programmers up until the late 1980s and early 1990s. At that point, new abstract machines (such as Mach C threads [Walmer and Thompson, 1989], the OSF DCE [Open Group, 1998], and Windows) began to offer new, additional support for concurrency. The idea of the new abstraction is to divide the aspects of a classic process into two parts called the *modern process* and the *thread*. The **modern process** corresponds to the part of the classic process that defines a customized computational framework in which a program executes. The **thread** is the part of the classic process that keeps track of code execution within that framework. As an analogy, the modern process is like a studio, and the thread is like a musician who uses the studio to make music. In the classic process analogy, each musician has a private studio. In the modern process, several musicians (threads) can share a single studio to work *together* on a musical piece. Extrapolating from the analogy, the value of the modern model is that it enables the programmer to design software so that various parts of the computation can work *together* as a set of threads within a single modern process framework. The two views of processes are reconciled by the fact that a classic process is the same as a modern process with one thread operating in it. Classic processes can work together to solve a problem, but they do not share a customized computational framework.

Now for a complication relating to this evolution to modern processes and threads: OS concepts that evolved prior to 1990 (such as multiprogramming, synchronization, and deadlock), were developed under the classic process model. Today all those concepts have been *generalized* so that they also apply to modern processes and threads. (It requires a surprisingly small amount of generalization.) Even so, it is often easier to first learn an OS concept as it applies to classic processes, then to generalize it for modern processes and threads.

Some contemporary operating systems (such as FreeBSD UNIX at the time of this writing in 2002) do not support the modern process model. Other operating systems such as Linux and Solaris were originally designed to support classic processes, but were subsequently refined to support modern processes and threads. This means that their basic designs were patched up to support modern processes and threads. Finally, some operating systems such as Mach and Windows were designed from the start to support modern processes and threads. Because of this history, OS designers have a tendency to refer to members of the UNIX family of operating systems as classic process systems, and to members of the Windows family as thread-based (modern process) systems. This is not quite accurate, since several versions of UNIX provide full support for modern processes and threads. Throughout the book, we will continue to make a big deal out of classic/modern processes whenever the distinction is important. When we use the term "process," the context of the discussion will specify whether we are talking about modern or classic processes. *In all other cases, we use "process" (or "process/thread" for emphasis) to refer to a computation that is either a classic process or a modern process with a single base thread.*

The purpose of this chapter is to jump right into the OS design by studying the way the process manager is designed and implemented. When you learn about a multifaceted piece of software, it is usually useful to first learn the general structure of the code, and then to look at the individual elements of the software in more detail. That is the approach taken in this chapter. This first section describes the main elements of a process manager so you can begin to see the big picture for its design. The rest of the chapter discusses design strategies for the main elements of the process manager. Some process management concepts (scheduling, synchronization, and deadlock) require more discussion than can be put into the chapter, so they have their own chapters.

THE ABSTRACT MACHINE FOR CLASSIC PROCESSES

Modern operating systems use multiprogramming to provide application programs with the illusion that they each have their own exclusive machine on which to execute the code. The idea is that the OS allocates blocks of executable memory using a space-multiplexing approach, then it allocates the processor to different classic processes using time-multiplexed sharing. With multiprogramming, if there are N processes sharing the processor, then during an interval of time equal to $K \times N$ seconds, each process will be able to use the processor approximately K seconds.

The abstract machine is a fundamental concept in multiprogramming, since it defines the logical computing environment in which a classic process executes. Ideally, the abstract machine would be a clone of the underlying physical machine. Each process could then execute binary code on an abstract machine that behaved exactly like the underlying physical machine. Figure 6.1 is a pictorial representation of this ideal abstraction. The characteristics of each abstract machine (above the OS interface line) are modeled after the behavior of the physical CPU and executable memory in a von Neumann computer. The process's abstract control unit executes the process's program according to the fetch-execute algorithm described in Figure 4.5. The abstract ALU only executes *user mode* instructions (but not privileged instructions). The program and data for the execution are stored in the abstract executable memory.

✦ **FIGURE 6.1** Implementing the Process Abstraction

The OS executes directly on top of the hardware to implement a collection of abstract machines (shown above the OS interface line). Each abstract machine is a simulation of the underlying von Neumann hardware, including a CPU and memory.

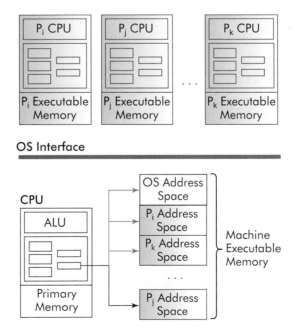

The OS implementation is shown below the "OS Interface" line in the figure. The OS program is loaded into the machine's executable memory (space-multiplexed with the application programs). When the computer is started, the OS program begins to execute. When it chooses to execute a process on an abstract machine, it causes the processor to branch to the block of executable memory that contains the code for the target abstract machine and begins to execute that code. After a timeslice has elapsed (indicated by the occurrence of a timer interrupt), the OS regains control and begins to execute its own code again. By repeating this sequence of operations, the OS causes the hardware to simulate activity for the collection of abstract machines. This simulation will not be perfect since, for example, the abstract machine cannot execute any privileged instructions. That is handled by OS services.

Application programs invoke OS services by calling functions on the OS abstract machine interface (also referred to as the system call interface and the OS API)—see Figure 6.2. The functions are implemented by different parts of the OS: The device manager, process manager, memory manager, and file manager. The process manager portion of the OS creates the process, thread, and resource abstractions, which comprise the lion's share of the abstract machine. For example, the process manager implements:

- Calls like `fork()` in UNIX and `CreateProcess()` in Windows to create classic/modern processes.
- Calls like Linux `pthread_create()`, and Windows `CreateThread()` to implement threads in the context of modern processes.
- Calls like UNIX `close()` and Windows `CloseHandle()` to request that resources be released.

The combination of the OS functions and the user mode instructions defines the abstract machine interface. The process manager is responsible for providing a seamless interface at the abstract machine interface that will allow an application program's binary representation to execute as if the abstract machine were a physical machine. The main obstacle here is to "trick" the hardware into executing only user mode instructions when they appear in the program, then to execute OS functions whenever the application wishes to execute privileged instructions. We will look at the details for doing this in Section 6.3.

SUPPORTING MODERN PROCESSES AND THREADS

Now let's consider how the abstract machine can be refined so that it implements modern processes with one or more associated threads. In the classic process case, the multiprogramming abstract machine is a model of the physical CPU and memory. Only one entity can be executing in an abstract machine—the implicit single thread (also called the **base thread**) associated with a classic process. When the abstract machine processor is running, the base thread is running. When the abstract processor is halted, the base thread is suspended.

In an OS that supports modern processes, the abstract machine allows additional threads to share the host process's resources (such as the abstract processor and memory). Conceptually, this can be done by another abstraction leap: *Suppose that each abstract machine shown in Figure 6.1 is designed to be a multiprogrammed machine!* As shown in Figure 6.3, the idea is for threads to be time-multiplexed on top of the abstract machine

✦ FIGURE 6.2 The External View of the Process Manager

Application programs view the OS as an abstract machine that is controlled by making calls on the functions on its exported API. These functions are implemented by different parts of the OS, but exported via a single interface. Different operating systems export different APIs, although they accomplish similar functions.

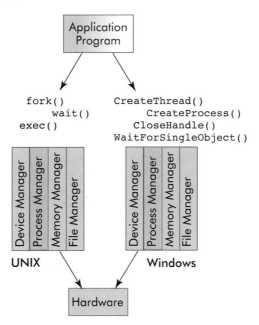

(which is, in turn, time-multiplexed on top of the physical processor). If we really implemented threads this way, it would mean that each abstract machine would include its own multiprogramming OS. This is essentially how **user space thread** packages such as the Mach C threads and POSIX threads libraries implement modern processes and threads. That is, the underlying OS implements classic processes, and the user space thread library executes on top of the OS abstract machine to multiprogram the threads within the modern process.

Modern operating systems (such as Windows) provide explicit OS support for the thread model. The essential difference between systems that support **kernel threads** and those that do not is that the OS explicitly separates the notion of process and thread by managing the two parts of a classic process as separate entities. For example, an OS that supports kernel threads time-multiplexes the execution of *threads* instead of *processes*. This means that, in contrast with user threads, when one thread in a modern process blocks, the other threads can still execute.

Classic processes and modern threads are the active element of a computation, while the process *framework* and the *resources* are the passive elements. When a process/thread needs more memory, a file, or processor time, it requests resources from the OS. Let's now look at the resource abstraction, the other cornerstone of the abstract machine.

✦ FIGURE 6.3   Modern Processes and Threads

Conceptually, threads are multiprogrammed entities that execute on a single abstract machine. User space threads are, in fact, implemented within a classic process, but kernel threads are implemented within the OS.

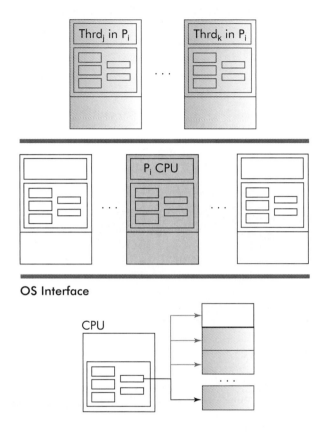

OS Interface

RESOURCES

A resource is any element of the abstract machine that a process[1] can request, and which can cause the process to be blocked if the entity is unavailable. A process requests an abstract resource by making a system call, such as UNIX `open()`. If the OS decides to allocate the abstract resource to the process, it updates data structures to reflect the allocation, then allows the process to continue execution. If the OS chooses not to allocate the resource, the process is blocked until the resource becomes available to it. Allocation of a resource results in the resource being configured into the process's abstract machine.

For example, if a device is allocated to a process, then a corresponding abstract device is configured into the abstract machine. There is no necessity for polling or interrupts in

---

[1]Here is our first use of the term "process" as a generic unit of computation. Since it is really not important if we are referring to a classic process or a modern process with a base thread, we simply refer to the unit of computation as a process.

the abstract machine, since I/O is accomplished through an OS function call. The thread executes an abstract machine instruction (implemented by `trap`) to initiate the I/O operation, and the function does not return until the I/O operation has run to completion.

Resource managers are implemented for hardware devices (as we saw in Chapter 5), the processor resource (Chapter 7), abstract synchronization resources (Chapter 8), the primary memory (Chapters 11), and files (Chapter 13). At this point, it is tempting to say, "Well, gosh, those managers account for all the hardware and important OS resources, so that must be all of the resource managers in the OS." However, all of these resource managers share some common behavior that can be described by a general model. OS designers sometimes take advantage of this common model to create new abstract machine resources (such as virtual terminals, specialized arithmetic processors, string processing mechanisms, graphics engines, and so on) that can be used by processes. We will discuss the generic resource manager model in Section 6.7.

THE PROCESS ADDRESS SPACE

The process **address space** is the collection of addresses that a thread can reference. Normally, these addresses refer to an executable memory location, but as shown in Figure 6.4, they can also be associated with other abstract machine elements. For example, some operating systems allow a programmer to read and write the contents of a file using addresses from the process address space. This is accomplished by opening the file, then binding each byte in the file to an address in the address space (this is discussed in detail in Chapter 12). There can also be other resources whose interface is presented to the application process as a collection of byte addresses (such as device registers and abstract objects). These **memory-mapped resources** can also have their interface bound to a collection of addresses in the address space, thereby allowing the components of the resource to be referenced using addresses.

The address space provides a uniform mechanism by which a process can reference bytes in all memory-mapped resources. If all resources could be memory-mapped (for example, the processor cannot), then a process could interact with all resources using the address space. The individual resource manager design determines whether the resource's interface is suitable for mapping into the address space.

Each resource manager is responsible for **binding** (or associating) addresses with addressable elements of the resource. For example, the memory resource manager associates blocks of executable memory with blocks of addresses in the address space.

For memory-mapped resources, the OS uses the address space to control which processes have access to which resources. If the OS does not bind a memory-mapped resource's interface into the address space, then the process cannot reference the resource. The address space is an important part of the OS's mechanism for protecting resources from unauthorized access.

In contemporary operating systems, each process (abstract machine) has a fixed size address space: In 32-bit computers, the address space is ordinarily 2^{32}, or 4 GB (gigabytes). Linux and Windows both provide 32-bit address spaces to processes. Future hardware and operating systems will support larger address spaces (such as 64-bit address spaces), although it appears that it might be a few years before that happens.

✦ FIGURE 6.4   The Address Space

The process address space is a large collection of contiguous addresses, usually of bytes. Any resource that can be referenced as a collection of bytes (such as the executable memory) can have each of its byte-addressable elements bound to an address in the address space. This allows a process/thread to access information by loading/storing information from/to a byte address.

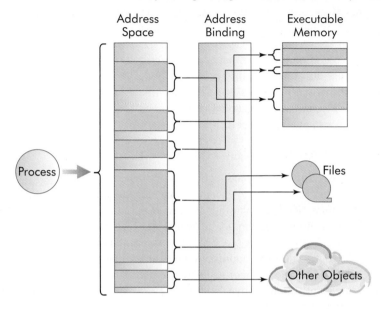

OS FAMILIES

As we have seen earlier in this section, the abstract machine's interface is determined by the host hardware's user instruction set, and by the set of functions exported by the OS. For example, the interface for Linux on a Pentium microprocessor is different from the interface for the same OS on a PowerPC microprocessor. The OS interface definition is a very important technical and business consideration: On the technical side, the interface should provide a comprehensive set of abstract machine features that make it easy to construct application programs. On the business side of the picture, the more application programs that are written to use a particular OS, the more likely it is that the OS will be used by the people that buy applications and computers to solve information problems. Today, the UNIX and Windows families of operating systems are the most widely used. Beginning with the Macintosh OS X, even Apple computers now use the UNIX API.

In 1975, the UNIX interface was well-defined. However, by 1985, many different parties had implemented their own OS to export this interface, and the details of the various interfaces began to diverge. For example, the UNIX interface defined in the Berkeley Software Distribution differed from the interface exported by the AT&T System V UNIX. By 1990, the IEEE began to address this divergence by defining the POSIX.1 OS interface. Since that time, most "UNIX-like" operating systems have been designed to export the POSIX interface.

Since there can be several different versions of software that implement the same interface, it is customary to refer to the operating systems that export a common interface as belonging to a single family. Today, Linux, OpenBSD, and FreeBSD all export similar versions of the POSIX.1 API, and are considered to be part of the UNIX family. On the other hand, each member of the family of Windows operating systems is designed to export a specific subset of the Win32 API (to address different application domains).

PROCESS MANAGER RESPONSIBILITIES

The process manager is responsible for implementing the process, thread, and resource abstractions using the underlying hardware. Specifically, the process manager must control the activity of the processor and other resources so that they provide the abstract machine functions such as:

- Process creation and termination—creating the process abstraction.
- Thread creation and termination—creating the thread abstraction.
- Process/thread synchronization.
- Resource allocation—creating the resource abstraction (except for devices, memory, and files).
- Resource protection.
- Cooperation with the device manager to implement I/O. This includes initiating an operation initiation, handling interrupts, and transferring information between the primary memory and the device controller.
- Implementation of the address space. The process manager must cooperate with the memory manager to implement the portion of address space management that corresponds to physical memory.

As we learned earlier, a modern process is a *framework* in which thread-based computations are executed. A modern process is composed of the following tangible elements:

- An **address space** through which the executing program can reference byte-addressable resources.
- A **program** to define the behavior of the process. The program is specified when the process is created, although in some operating systems it can also be changed dynamically (for example, see the UNIX `execve()` system call). The program is loaded into the address space when the process is created.
- The **data** used by the process. Some of the data are created when the process is created, and others are created and destroyed as threads execute in the process. In a classic process, only the base thread reads and writes the data, but in a modern process, all of the threads in the process share the data. In addition, each thread may have its own private data, although the default behavior is that all data in the process is accessible to all threads.
- The **resources** required for thread execution. The process will be created with some minimal set of resources as specified by the process's creating entity ("the parent process"). Once a process has been created, the process manager can allocate additional resources as required. The resources that are allocated to the child process when it is created are usually inherited resources (or inherited access to shared resources such as open files). Threads share the resources that have been allocated to the process.

■ A **process identifier** to uniquely reference a process during its existence. The process identifier is a system-wide, unique name for the process—a reference that can be used to uniquely reference the given process.

Threads (or a base thread) are the *active element* of computation that occurs within a modern process framework. Each thread has the following characteristics:

■ A host process **environment** (the process framework) in which the thread executes.

■ Thread-specific **data** accessible only to the thread that owns it. At a minimum, each thread has its own stack to represent the dynamic context in which it is executing (such as which functions it has called, which automatic variables it is using, and so on).

■ A **thread identifier** to uniquely reference a thread during its existence.

A classic process combines characteristics of a modern process and a single base thread.

Each resource is uniquely identified by a system-wide **resource identifier**. However, other characteristics of the resource depend on its specific nature. A resource manager type is defined for each resource type, and instances are created for each instance of the abstract resource according to the characteristics of the resource. For example, the file manager is a single instance of the file manager code that administers all files on the system. But there is usually a different resource manager for each disk drive in the system. The most fundamental resources are the processor and primary memory.

6.2 ● THE HARDWARE PROCESS

The OS is implemented directly on top of ("imports") the von Neumann hardware interface, and exports the abstract machine interface. The underlying hardware is capable of executing a sequence of machine instructions. The sequence can be changed by instructions that write a new address into the control unit's PC register (branch instructions). When the computer is powered up, it begins to execute the fetch-execute cycle for the program that is stored in the memory at the bootstrap entry point (see Section 4.6). In Chapter 4 we began to refer to this *single thread of execution as the* **hardware process**. Of course *hardware process* is just a name to represent the iterative activity of the control unit, as it fetches and executes instructions.

The hardware process executes the bootstrap code first, causing it to load the OS software and then to execute it. When the hardware process is executing the bootstrap code, there is no notion of "thread" or "process," since the OS has not yet been loaded in the machine's executable memory.

Once the bootstrap procedure has completed and the OS has been loaded, it begins to execute. The OS initializes itself by polling all the hardware components in the system, initializing them as necessary. Next, it initializes its data structures that are used to implement the abstract machines. Only then is the OS prepared to support processes and threads, and to administer the resources that can be requested by processes.

After the kernel has initialized itself and loaded n different processes, the process management scheduler decides which process/thread it would like the hardware process to execute. In Figure 6.5, the process manager directs the hardware process to execute a thread in process P_1 after it has finished its initialization phase. Each switch from one process/thread to another is caused by changing the PC in the control unit. Sometimes the new PC value is chosen by the scheduler's action (for example, when the hardware process branches to a new thread's code). Sometimes it happens as a result of a `trap` instruction (causing the hardware process to branch from a process's program to the kernel), and sometimes it happens as the result of an interrupt (for example, when a thread is executing in a process when an interrupt occurs). This management of the hardware process is the fundamental aspect of multiprogramming, and of the process and thread abstractions. Now we are ready to consider the details for creating a classic process.

✦ FIGURE 6.5   Tracing the Hardware Process

The hardware process represents the sequence of machine instructions executed by the CPU. This figure illustrates how that sequence can be multiplexed across different abstract machines and parts of the OS to implement multiprogramming.

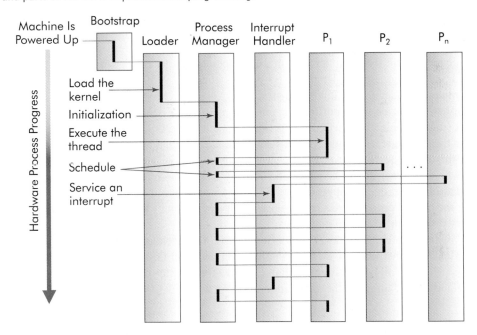

Before the OS begins normal execution, the hardware process initializes process, thread, and resource descriptors, device data structures, and any other data structures required by the OS designers. After the data structures have been initialized, the hardware process creates an **initial process** and thread (normally, this is a single-threaded process, so it is called the initial process). This is done by allocating and filling in a process and thread descriptor. The hardware process then begins to execute an idle loop of the form:

```
...
while(TRUE) {
  yield_to_other_threads(...);
}
```

This is called the **idle thread** (or **idle process**); its purpose is to execute whenever there is no other ready thread in the entire system. Even though the hardware process may begin to execute the idle loop, it will quickly be interrupted so that the initial process can continue with OS initialization. The idle thread will not run again until there is no other work to do in the system.

6.3 ● THE ABSTRACT MACHINE INTERFACE

Ideally, the abstract machine would export the same instruction set as the underlying hardware. However, some instructions (such as device I/O) are used by the OS to manage resource sharing. For example, if device I/O instructions could be executed in user mode, then any program could read or write any part of the disk device, preventing the OS from providing an adequate file sharing and protection model. The hardware distinguishes between instructions that can be used without affecting the resource sharing model (the user mode instructions) and those that are used to provide a robust sharing model (the privileged instructions). All abstract machine operations that require execution of a privileged instruction are implemented by an OS function. This means that the abstract machine interface has two kinds of instructions: User mode hardware instructions and OS functions. The trick for exporting this interface is to be sure that when a process executes an abstract machine instruction that is implemented by an OS function, the system intercepts the hardware execution and calls an OS function instead. The `trap` instruction handles this detail perfectly (see Figure 6.6)! The user mode `trap` instruction switches the CPU to supervisor mode, then branches to an OS function entry point. When a program needs to have an operation performed that involves the execution of a privileged instruction, the classic process executes the `trap` with a parameter to identify the function to be selected from the OS's trap table.

This technique allows the OS to define an abstract machine interface that contains all the user mode instructions, including `trap`, along with all OS system calls invoked using `trap` (meaning all of the system calls). Here is an example of how the abstract machine interface works: Suppose the application program contains C code such as

```
...
a = b + c;
pid = fork();
...
```

This will compile into a block of machine user instructions such as:

```
...
// a = b + c;
load        R1, b
load        R2, c
add         R1, R2
store  R1, a
// now do the system call
trap        sys_fork
...
```

✦ FIGURE 6.6   The Abstract Machine Interface

The complete abstract machine interface is defined by the set of instructions that the hardware can execute when the processor is in user mode. The `trap` instruction extends the interface so that the abstract machine instructions include all the functions on the OS system call interface.

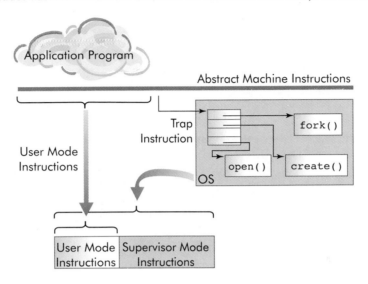

All instructions in the program are user mode instructions, and are executed directly on the hardware. Conceptually, the OS abstract machine passes user instruction through the OS layer directly to the hardware. However, the `fork()` abstract machine instruction will be executed by an OS function instead of by the hardware. The programmer specifies such abstract machine instructions as function calls. The compiler and linker will link the target function call to a system call stub that contains a `trap` instruction. For example, the `fork()` function call is linked to a system call stub that contains the `trap sys_fork` machine instruction (where `sys_fork` is an index in the trap table).

Now when the process executes on an abstract machine, it uses a machine instruction set similar to that shown in Table 6.1. The compiled code contains only machine instructions that are executed directly on the hardware. When the process needs to perform an OS task, the machine instruction is a `trap` to the appropriate OS function. The abstract machine interface supports the same kind of operations allowed on a von Neumann computer, although the privileged instruction set is embedded in the OS system calls.

OS function implementations are like any other software in the sense that they comprise a collection of algorithms and data structures. OS components are built using Parnas's abstract data type principles [Parnas, 1972] (also used in object-oriented programming): The software module exports enough information for another program to call its functions, but it does not reveal the implementation of the corresponding functions. By making the entire OS's interface public, different parties can create independent implementations of the same interface. The POSIX API is an example of a public OS interface. Linux and FreeBSD both export the POSIX API, yet the details of their internal operation are different. In general, the choice of algorithms and data structures used in an implementation depends on the characteristics of the API and the design choices made by the software designers.

TABLE 6.1   Abstract Machine Instruction Set

ALU Instructions

```
load
store
add
subtract
logical_AND
```
· · ·

Control Unit Instructions

```
branch
conditional_branch
procedure_call
```
· · ·

trap Instruction (invokes OS functions)

```
create_process()
terminate_process()
open_file()
close_file()
request_resource()
release_resource()
```
· · ·

The Linux Version 2.0.36 kernel exports 166 functions via its system call interface (meaning that its `trap` table has 166 entries). The Version 2.4.x kernel has grown to over 200 functions. By comparison, the Windows NT/2000/XP OS exports about 2,000 functions on the Win32 API. The Windows interface has more functions by the design of the interface, and also because the desktop window system is part of the OS. Since Windows NT/2000/XP supports an order of magnitude more system calls than does Linux, the Windows implementation is far larger and more complex than Linux. For example, Linux Version 2.4 is about 2.5 million lines of code, most of it C. Windows NT Version 4 is about 25 million lines of code—an order of magnitude larger than Linux. Both of these estimates include lots of code for device drivers for all kinds of devices that might be configured into a particular machine. Table 6.2 provides several examples of the Linux Version 2.0.36 system calls. You can inspect the Linux source code to see the full list of system calls.[2]

---

[2]If you want to look at the Linux source code system calls, go to the root of the source code distribution tree. Then look at the last 200 lines in the file named `arch/i386/kernel/entry.S`. This code is the declaration of the Linux `trap` table.

TABLE 6.2   Some LINUX System Calls

System Call	Kernel Function	Number
exit()	sys_exit()	1
fork()	sys_fork()	2
read()	sys_read()	3
write()	sys_write()	4
open()	sys_open()	5
close()	sys_close()	6
execve	sys_execve()	11
getuid()	sys_getuid	24
fstat()	sys_fstat()	28
ioctl()	sys_ioctl()	54
gettimeofday()	sys_gettimeofday()	78

6.4 • THE PROCESS ABSTRACTION

The process manager creates the environment in which multiple processes coexist, each with its own abstract machine. When the hardware process begins to execute OS code, it will execute an algorithm that switches the hardware process from one **context** (abstract machine) to another. These **context switches** can occur whenever the OS gets control of the processor. The OS gets control whenever a process/thread makes a system call (executes a `trap` instruction) and whenever device interrupts occur. For example, Figure 6.7 illustrates the first nine context switches from Figure 6.5:

1. The loader branches to the OS so that it can initialize.
2. The process manager switches to P_1.
3. P_1 makes a system call, which ultimately branches to the part of the process manager that performs context switches.
4. The process manager switches to P_2.
5. P_2 makes a system call.
6. The process manager switches to P_n.
7. An interrupt occurs.
8. The interrupt handler branches to the context switch algorithm.
9. The process manager switches to P_2.
10. And so on.

✦ FIGURE 6.7   Context Switching

Process/thread context refers to the status of the processor hardware whenever that particular process/thread is being executed. A context switch is the action taken by the hardware process when it suspends execution on one program and begins execution on another.

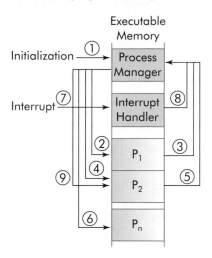

Each individual process/thread can only reference instructions that are stored in the part of the executable memory associated with the address space (physical memory/address space association is done by the memory manager). This means that a context switch can only be done with one or more privileged instructions. The process manager does all the context switching among processes/threads.

When a process is created, the process manager algorithm creates a data structure (called the process descriptor) to keep all the details it requires for managing the process. The process manager then examines the executable file (for example, an `a.out` file in UNIX or a `.exe` file in Windows) to determine what program should be loaded into the address space. It then creates the address space and binds the program addresses into the address space. The process manager can then add all other required abstract machine resources to the process. At this point, the process manager is ready to create a base thread so that the program can be executed within the process framework. In an OS that supports classic processes, the process manager does this by setting process descriptor fields that represent the execution thread. In an OS for modern processes, a separate thread descriptor is created for the base thread (see below).

The **process descriptor** (also called the *process control block*, *task control block*, *task structure*, and various other names) is the data structure where the OS will keep all information it needs to manage that process. What information should be kept in a process descriptor? Essentially, there must be enough information for the OS algorithms to uniquely identify the process (the process descriptor contains the process identifier), determine the external user that created ("owns") the process, determine the process that requests the creation of the process, and so on. Table 6.3 describes several fields that are incorporated into a classic process descriptor. The fields marked with "*" are related to thread execution, but are part of a classic process descriptor.

TABLE 6.3 Process Descriptor

Field	Description
Internal process name	An internal name of the process, such as an integer or table index, used in the operating system code.
*State	The base thread's current state.
Owner	A process has an owner (identified by the owner's internal identification such as the login name). The descriptor contains a field for storing the owner identification.
*Execution statistics	Time accumulation, start time, and so on.
Thread	A reference to a list of threads associated with this process.
List of related processes	A reference to a list of the parent/child/sibling processes of this process.
List of child processes	A reference to a list of the child processes of this process.
Address space	A description of the address space and its bindings.
Resources	A reference to a list of resources held by the process. Each resource type will describe the number and identity of the resource.
*Stack	The location of the base thread's stack in the primary memory.

The process manager also sets the fields in the descriptor to reflect which resources have been allocated to the process. For example, when a UNIX process is created, it inherits access to any files that the parent process had open at the time it created the child. On the other hand, Windows takes a more general approach: A **handle** is associated with every abstract resource allocated to a process. This means that a parent process has a collection of handles for all the resources it created. The parent process can give any subset of these handles to the child process at creation time (see the system documentation for `CreateProcess()`). For example, the parent can give the child only the handles for its open files, but not for any other resources. This would be a similar strategy to UNIX. Whenever a memory-mapped resource is allocated to the abstract machine (process), its components are also bound into the address space.

Each process descriptor is allocated when the process is created, and deallocated when the process terminates. In most operating systems, the process descriptors are allocated from a static array of process descriptor structures. This is because operating systems try to avoid using dynamic data structure allocation (to avoid running out of memory). The length of the array establishes the maximum number of processes that the OS can support at any one time.

There is one other important point about process descriptors: Even though good software engineering practice tells us that the process manager should be the only part of the OS to read/write process descriptors, operating systems rarely follow this practice. This is because the OS software is designed to favor performance over maintainability. The information hiding aspect of software modularization is often lost in the OS implementation internals. Even though the process descriptor is created and primarily managed by the process manager, various other parts of the OS query and change fields in the process's descriptor.

Linux Process Descriptor

The Linux kernel manages the execution of a collection of *tasks*. Each task is described by a `struct task_struct` kernel data structure. All Linux versions earlier than 2.2.0 associated a classic process with a kernel task. (Newer versions since 2.2.0 implement modern processes and threads.) When a process is created, an instance of the `struct task_struct` data type is instantiated to keep track of all the information about the process. Here are a few fragments of the Linux process descriptor from Version 2.2.18 (in this code fragment, "`...`" appears where fields have been omitted to simplify the discussion):

```
struct task_struct {
/* these are hardcoded - don't touch */
  volatile long state; /* -1 unrunnable, 0 runnable, >0 stopped */
  ...
  int sigpending;
  ...
  struct task_struct *next_task, *prev_task;
  struct task_struct *next_run, *prev_run;
  ...
  pid_t pid;
  pid_t pgrp;
  ...
  /*
   * pointers to (original) parent process, youngest child,
   * younger sibling, older sibling, respectively. ...
   */
  struct task_struct *p_opptr, *p_pptr, *p_cptr, *p_ysptr, *p_osptr;
  ...
/* mm fault and swap info: ...*/
  ...
/* process credentials */
  uid_t uid, ...;
  gid_t gid,...;
  ...
/* limits */
  ...
```

```
    /* file system info */
    ...
    /* open file information */
    ...
    /* memory management info */
    ...
    /* signal handlers */
    ...
    /* Thread group tracking */
    ...
};
```

The `struct task_struct` data structure has over 50 fields in it, so there are many more besides the ones shown here. The first field in the task descriptor is the `state` field, which holds an integer encoding of the current state of the process (all possible states are those shown in Figure 6.11). The `pid` and `pgrp` fields are the unique identifiers for the process and its process group membership.

UNIX processes can accept signals from the OS or from other processes. (If you are unfamiliar with UNIX signals, see the first Laboratory Exercise at the end of the chapter.) The `sigpending` field describes any signals that are queued to interrupt the normal execution of the process.

The `struct task_struct` fields (named `next_task`, `prev_task`, `next_run`, and `prev_run`) are used to place the process descriptor into a list. For example, these fields are used by the scheduler to link the task structure into a list of tasks waiting to use the processor.

The next set of pointers to task structures represents the relationships of this process to other processes: The original parent that created this process (`p-opptr`), the current parent, in case the original parent no longer exists (`p-pptr`), the task structure for the last child process created by this process (`p-cptr`), and the process that was created by this process's parent just after (`p-ysptr`) and just before (`p-osptr`) it created this process. These fields are used to keep track of process hierarchies and the resources used by members of the hierarchy.

As shown in the data structure fragment, the task structure also contains the user identification (`uid`) and group identification (`gid`). These represent the identity of the user that caused this process to be created.

Windows NT/2000/XP Process Descriptors

The Windows NT/2000/XP process manager was designed to support modern processes and threads. The process descriptor represents the modern process (but not threads). The Windows NT/2000/XP source code is not publicly available, but Solomon and Russinovich [2000] provide a detailed description of the process descriptor. As mentioned in Section 3.3, the kernel is divided into the NT Executive and the NT Kernel. When a process is created, there is a data structure instantiated in the NT Executive and a related one in the NT Kernel (the NT Executive data structure, called the EPROCESS block, contains the NT Kernel data structure, called the KPROCESS block or PCB, as a field)—see Figure 6.8.

✦ FIGURE 6.8   Windows NT Process Descriptor

The Windows NT OS is implemented in the NT Kernel and the NT Executive, which are two separate sets of software. A process descriptor is implemented in part by the NT Kernel and in part by the NT Executive. The part of the process descriptor managed by the NT Kernel relates to object management, interrupt handling, and thread scheduling. The NT Executive handles all other aspects of a process.

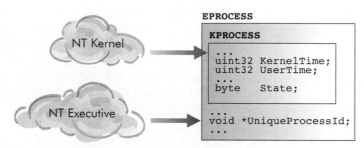

The NT Kernel provides fundamental OS services such as object management, interrupt handling, and thread scheduling. The algorithms are implemented in the NT Kernel, and the part of the process descriptor managed by the NT Kernel is declared as the struct _KPROCESS Pcb field in the struct EPROCESS. As indicated in the figure, the NT Kernel keeps track of the amount of supervisor mode time accrued by all threads in the process (in the uint32 KernelTime field) and the amount of user mode time (in the uint32 UserTime field). There is another field, void * UniqueProcessId, in the EPROCESS block. This is the unique systemwide process identifier.

The NT Kernel is designed so that groups of threads executing in a process can be controlled by manipulating the process state; as a result, there is a byte State field in the process descriptor. Like the Linux descriptor, the EPROCESS block contains fields for managing the address space, coordinating thread execution, keeping track of resources allocated to the process, and protecting and sharing the tasks resources.

The information in Chapter 6 from Solomon and Russinovich [2000] is the most complete representation of the Windows process descriptor that is not protected by software license.

6.5 ● THE THREAD ABSTRACTION

In systems that support modern processes and threads, the process manager separates the dynamic execution from the static environment aspects of the process. When a modern process is created, its base thread is also created. When all threads in a process are terminated, then the process is removed.

The thread management algorithm is the part of the process manager that creates and manages threads. Once a thread has been created, it will exist in different states (the details of states are described in the next subsection). Roughly speaking, a thread's state reflects its logical activity status in the OS. For example, the thread might be waiting for a resource or running. The major tasks in managing a thread are:

- Create/destroy a thread
- Allocate thread-specific resources
- Manage thread context switching (including scheduling)

The process manager contains algorithms to accomplish these tasks as well as a central thread descriptor data structure. The **thread descriptor** is the data structure where the OS will keep all information it needs to manage that thread.

Most resources used by a thread are allocated to the associated process instead of the thread. However, there are some resources that are specific to each thread. For example, the thread's stack must be initialized and bound into the process address space. Similarly, the thread's private storage must be bound to the address space. Table 6.4 describes a few fields that are incorporated into a generic thread descriptor. These fields also appear as part of a classic process descriptor.

TABLE 6.4 Thread Descriptor

Field	Description
State	The thread's current state.
Execution statistics	Time accumulation, start time, and so on.
Process	A reference to the process descriptor of this thread's associate process.
List of related threads	A reference to a list of the parent/child/sibling threads of this thread.
Stack	The location of the base thread's stack in the primary memory.
Other resources	A reference to the thread-specific resources.

Linux Thread Descriptor

The POSIX API defines "POSIX threads," which is a set of system calls such as:

- `pthread_create()`
- `pthread_exit()`
- `pthread_self()`
- `pthread_key_create()`

There is a user space library implementation for all the thread calls. In older versions, the thread functions were implemented by the library instead of the OS. In Linux Version 2.2.0 and newer versions, the thread interface is still implemented by the library, but the threads are implemented in the OS.

In the new kernel, each task corresponds to a thread instead of a classic process. This change required that the process manager algorithms be modified so that tasks could share resources such as devices, files, and the address space, yet be able to allocate thread-specific resources to an individual task. However, a kernel task is still described by a `struct task_struct` data type (albeit with some modifications).

In the Linux kernel, the process's *base thread process descriptor* is essentially the same as it was for the classic process descriptor. Since many application processes will be classic processes, the implementation is still efficient. However, if the `pthread` interface is used to add threads to a process, each new thread causes a new `struct task_struct` data structure to be created. The `struct task_struct` contains the same process framework-specific information as the base thread (it is just copied from the base thread).

Within the kernel, there are `sys_clone()` and `sys_fork()` system functions (called by the thread `clone()` and the classic `process fork()` system calls, respectively). The `sys_fork()` function is a single statement that calls the internal kernel function, `do_fork()` with parameters specific to the `fork()` call. The `sys_clone()` function has 4 statements, the last of which is also a call to `do_fork()`. All differences between the thread and classic processes are encapsulated in the `do_fork()` function (which is just under 200 lines of C code). The essential difference in the revised `struct task_struct` is the addition of fields to handle thread-specific resources (stack and thread-local storage).

Windows NT/2000/XP Thread Descriptors

The Windows `KPROCESS` part of the `EPROCESS` process descriptor contains a field, `struct LIST_ENTRY ThreadListHead`, which is a list of thread descriptors (called the `ETHREAD` structures)—see Figure 6.9 [Solomon and Russinovich, 2000]. The `ETHREAD` structure contains the `KTHREAD` structure as one of its fields. Just as with the process descriptor, the NT Executive manages the contents of the `ETHREAD` structure and the NT Kernel manages the contents of the `KTHREAD` structure. The `ETHREAD` contains fields such as:

- Creation time
- Associated process identification
- Entry point address

The KTHREAD contains fields such as:

- User time
- Kernel time

■ Stack details

■ Scheduling information

In Windows NT/2000/XP, the NT Kernel implements thread scheduling, so scheduling information is kept in the KTHREAD structure rather than in the ETHREAD structure.

✦ FIGURE 6.9 Windows NT Thread Descriptor

The Windows NT thread descriptor is implemented in the same manner as the process descriptor. For example, the KTHREAD structure is managed by the NT Kernel, and contains the information required by the OS when it schedules the thread for execution.

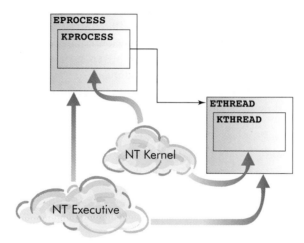

6.6 ● STATE DIAGRAMS

Now that we have seen the data structures for processes and threads, we can consider the algorithms in more detail. After a process/thread has been created, the OS has descriptors that it can use to keep track of the process/thread. Think of the process manager as being a personal assistant to the running process: For example, if a person (called the "principal") wants an assistant to arrange for transportation, the assistant will need to know where the principal is currently located. Similarly, the OS will need to know in which linked list a process is stored if it is to move the process.

In the real world, the personal assistant might keep a single-variable description that summarizes the principal's current status. For example, if the principal is asleep when the time for an appointment is approaching, the personal assistant knows that it will be necessary to wake up the principal early enough to allow time for freshening up before the appointment. Often, this summary status (such as "the principal is asleep"), can be inferred by analyzing all the fields in the descriptor. However, in process managers, it is customary to use a **state** variable as a summary status of the process/thread. The state variable summarizes the process/thread status by individual values such as "the process is blocked" or "the process is currently using the processor."

A **state diagram** represents the different states in which a thread can be at different times, along with the **transitions** from one state to another that are possible in the OS. The process manager causes the process/thread to change state by administering the process, for example, by allocating the processor to the process/thread, by blocking the process/thread until a resource is allocated to it, or by noting that the process/state is ready to use the processor.

Figure 6.10 is a simple example of a state diagram for processes/threads in a hypothetical system. (The state diagram is purposely simplified so that you can see how to use diagrams to design the process manager. The diagram will be refined later in the chapter.) In this state diagram, a process/thread may be in any one of three states—running, ready, or blocked. When the process/thread is involved in some activity, the process manager changes state, as indicated by the labels in Figure 6.10. For example, if a process/thread is in the running state and it makes a request for a resource that is not available, then the process manager suspends the process/thread until the resource is allocated, changing the process/thread state to blocked. When a process/thread, p_i, has been allocated memory and is created, the *start* transition occurs, placing p_i in the ready state. This means that p_i is waiting for the scheduler to allocate a processor to it.

✦ FIGURE 6.10   Process States

The most basic process/thread diagram has three states: running, ready, and blocked. A process in the running state is using the processor. A ready process is waiting for the processor. A blocked process was running, but requested a resource that was unavailable. It will remain blocked until it is allocated the resource.

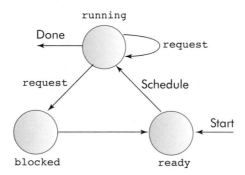

The process manager uses the state diagram to determine the type of service to provide to the process (process/thread). If the process is in the ready state, it is competing for the processor. The only transition out of the ready state is for the process to change to the running state when it is allocated the CPU. If the process is in the running state, it can complete execution, in which case the process manager will release the resources it holds and destroy the process. Alternatively, the process may request a resource when it is in the running state—for example, by requesting an I/O operation. If a running process requests and receives a resource without having to wait for it, the process is allowed to continue in the running state. Otherwise, the process manager removes the process from the processor, marks its state as blocked, and notifies the resource manager that the process is waiting for units of its resource. The OS then calls the scheduler to allocate the processor to the next selected process in the ready state. From the blocked state, the process can transition to the ready state when the resource manager allocates the requested resource. The process is then once again competing for the CPU.

UNIX State Diagram

In UNIX systems, the kernel presumes the classic process model, so it uses process state diagrams instead of thread state diagrams. A UNIX process can be in any one of 6 states: running, runnable, uninterruptible sleep, sleeping, traced *or* stopped, or zombie (see the state transition diagram in Figure 6.11). A process is created in the runnable state, meaning that after it has been created, it can be scheduled and executed on the processor. When it begins to execute, the kernel changes its state from runnable to running.

If a running process makes a system call to request a resource, it will stay in the running state only if the resource is immediately allocated to the process. Otherwise, the kernel will block the process in one of two different states—sleeping or uninterruptible sleeping. The rationale for having two different states is related to which parts of the UNIX kernel can cause a transition out of the state where the process is suspended. The kernel puts a process into the uninterruptible sleep state when the process initiates an I/O operation. Other parts of the kernel should not change the state of that process until the I/O operation has completed. In the case of interrupt-driven I/O, the device interrupt handler will change the process's state to runnable when it receives the completion interrupt. Whenever any part of the OS changes a process's state to runnable, then (1) the OS is executing a system call or interrupt handling, and (2) the scheduler will be called to give the process that just became runnable a chance to be allocated the CPU. If any other form of resource request cannot be satisfied, the kernel changes the process's state to sleeping. Any part of the kernel can change the process to the runnable state whenever it determines that this is the appropriate action (for example, it allocated the requested resource).

POSIX-compliant UNIX systems include a system call named ptrace(). This call allows a parent process to have complete control of the execution by a child process. A child that is being traced with ptrace() is stopped each time it receives a signal. This enables the parent process to inspect or audit the complete status (such as the stack) of the child process. Debuggers frequently use the ptrace() option. If a process is executing with tracing enabled and it receives a signal, it will transition from the running state to the traced or stopped state. The parent can then resume the child, causing it to transition back to the runnable state.

The zombie state is used when a process terminates. If a process calls exit(), the process manager will terminate the process. However, the process manager will not actually remove the process descriptor for the terminated process until its parent has been notified of the termination. This gives the parent process a chance to perform any cleanup that it requires when one of its children terminates. After the parent has executed a wait() system call for a terminated child, the zombie child is terminated, its process descriptor is released, and it ceases to exist in the system.

✦ FIGURE 6.11   UNIX State Transition Diagram

UNIX processes can be in any of the 6 states shown in the figure. Blocked processes can be blocked for I/O (`uninterruptible sleep`) or waiting for another resource (`sleeping`). `Traced` or `stopped` processes have made a system call and have been suspended so that their parent can inspect their state at the time of the call. A `zombie` state is a child process that terminated, but whose resources are not released until the parent notices that they terminated.

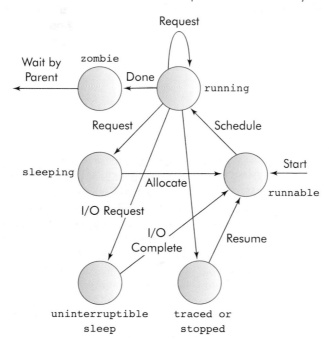

6.7 • RESOURCE MANAGERS

The idea of a resource manager is generic in that there is a basic behavioral pattern expected from each one of them, although specific managers might be implemented in diverse parts of the OS. One way to think about this is as if resource managers were implemented in an object-oriented type hierarchy. We would define a base class that would characterize all the behavior except for some details. Then, when we define a resource manager for, say, an audio speaker, we would inherit the base class behavior for the generic resource manager and define the details for the audio speaker resource in the subclass. In the OS world, we tend to describe this situation slightly differently: We say that the generic part of the resource manager is a **mechanism** for allocating resources, and the resource-specific behavior is determined by a **policy**.

Every resource manager *accepts requests* to allocate units of its resource to a process as OS functions (the `request()` function in Figure 6.12). The `request()` function will execute a resource-specific policy algorithm to determine the criteria under which it should allocate resources to processes. For example, the policy for an audio speaker resource manager might forbid sharing of the resource (otherwise multiple processes could play sound to the speaker at the same time). It might also restrict the type of process that can be allocated control of the speaker. For example, the policy may restrict use of the audio speaker to processes owned by a particular user. Another example of a policy is that the resource manager may allow certain processes to preempt the speaker from other processes, as in when a process executing an OS function might have priority to the resource over a process that is playing music from the CD-ROM device.

✦ **FIGURE 6.12**   A Generic Resource Manager

All resource managers have the general form shown in this figure. In each case, a process requests units of the resources. If the resource manager allocates the resource, then the process continues to run. Otherwise, it is placed in a pool of blocked processes to await allocation. Upon allocation, the process is removed from the pool and made ready to run.

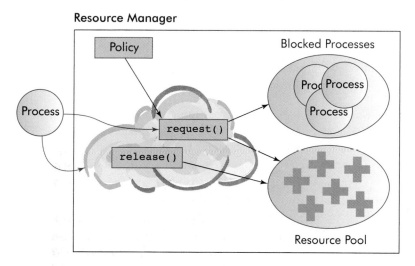

Each resource manager maintains a resource descriptor data structure for the resources it is managing. As usual, the details of the resource descriptor depend on the resource and the OS. Table 6.5 represents the kind of information you could expect to see in a resource descriptor.

In order to describe the behavior of a resource manager in more detail (without committing to any particular resource or OS), we will describe the behavior using our first formal model of an OS component. This particular model will be enhanced over the next four chapters. Here, we will only use it to describe the most general properties of resource managers. In our formal model, we want to capture these notions:

■ There are many, say m, different types of resources.

■ Each type of resource can have multiple units of the resource.

■ Processes can request variable numbers of units of the resource.

■ At any given moment, some number of units of each of the resource type are available.

TABLE 6.5   Resource Descriptors

Field	Description
Internal resource name	An internal name for the resource used by the operating system code.
Total units	The number of units of this resource type configured into the system.
Available units	The number of units currently available.
List of available units	The set of available units of this resource type that are available for use by processes.
List of blocked processes	The list of processes that have a pending request for units of this resource type.

We can write this down in set notation by writing

$$R = \{R_j \mid 0 \leq j < m\}$$

This expression can be read as follows: "The system's resources, R, are represented as a collection of individual resource types, R_j. For example, a tape drive is one resource type, a disk is another resource type, and an audio speaker is a third. There are m different resource types named $R_0, R_1, R_2, ..., R_{m-1}$." Alternatively, we could have described R as:

$$R = \{R_0, R_1, R_2, ... , R_{m-1}\}$$

Next we want to represent the number of units of each type of resource that are currently available for processes to use. To do this, let each resource type, R_j, have an associated integer count, c_j, that is the number of units of R_j that are available:

$$C = \{c_j \geq 0 \mid \text{for each resource type } R_j \in R \ (0 \leq j < m)\}.$$

Again, the set notation can be read as: "For each of the resource types, R_j, there are c_j units of that resource currently available." For example, if R_3 is the floppy disk type and the system has two floppy disk drives, then c_3 is 2. Since there are m different resource types, the OS will have m different resource managers. Each manager will have a resource descriptor that will save the count of currently available units.

Next, we will use our formal model to specify the behavior of the resource manager functions more carefully. A process, p_i, in the running state may request x units of R_j at any time (of course x must be less than or equal to c_j if R_j is a reusable resource). If the resource policy algorithm specifies that the resource should not be allocated, the process manager removes the thread from the processor (and schedules another ready thread to run). It then changes the suspended thread's state to blocked and places it into the blocked process pool for R_j (see Figure 6.12).

Once the R_j mechanism determines that it will allocate the requested resources, it:

1. Updates OS data structures (such as the process and resource descriptors) to reflect the allocation operation.

2. Allocates x units of R_j to p_i.

3. Removes p_i from R_j's blocked pool.

4. Changes the p_i's state to ready.

The resource manager for R_j accepts release commands (calls to the `release()` function in the figure) to return units of R_j to its resource pool. This may enable the R_j resource manager to then allocate these released units to a waiting process.

Recall that a resource is *anything* that can potentially block a process from executing. If a process requests a block of memory and none is available, then the memory resource manager blocks the process from execution until the memory becomes available. Given the general behavior of resource managers, the notion of a resource can be extended to abstract entities such as messages or input data. Since a process can be blocked while waiting for input data from a device, it has, in effect, *requested* data (using a read operation), and it must *suspend* execution until the data is "allocated" to the process by being read from the device.

Resources (such as memory) that can be allocated and then later returned to the system after the process has finished using them are called **reusable resources**. A more abstract resource, such as input data, that can be allocated but that is never subsequently released, is called as a **consumable resource**. The system always has a fixed, finite number of units of a reusable resource— that is, c_j is a fixed integer for a reusable resource type. However, the number of units of a consumable resource is unbounded, since there are one or more producer processes for each consumable resource. Because the number of units of a consumable resource depends on the future behavior of a program, it is not possible to know the number of units of the resource that might be produced in the future.

A process/thread *creates* a consumable resource by releasing one or more units of the resource. For example, if a message is a resource, a receiver thread will be queued on the message resource type. (If there are no pending messages of type R_j, the c_j count is 0 and the receiver thread is blocked on R_j.) When another process sends a message, the message-handling code releases a unit of R_j to the resource manager. The resource manager can then allocate the unit of resource to the receiver thread so that it can proceed.

Because the pattern of resource requests among the processes is unpredictable, there is dynamic competition for the resources. This means that a requesting process/thread could be blocked for an arbitrary time interval. The amount of time generally cannot be predicted at the time the request is made, since the resource may already be allocated to another thread, or, in the case of consumable resources, may not yet have even been produced. Generally, it is impossible to predict the amount of time such a thread may hold a reusable resource. Eventually, the thread releases resources or it terminates by executing an exit system call. Process termination causes the OS to release its resources, starting with the memory, but ultimately including all reusable resources allocated to the process. The consumable resources held by the terminating process are assumed to have been consumed by process, so they are not recovered.

6.8 • GENERALIZING PROCESS MANAGEMENT POLICIES

Process creation implicitly defines a hierarchy among the set of processes. This hierarchy allows the community of processes to agree on basic tasks such as which processes can control which other processes and how resources should be allocated to processes.

In the process creation hierarchy, a parent can have many child processes, but each child process has exactly one parent process (see Figure 6.13). The initial process is the root of the hierarchy of all processes. Whenever a process creates a child, a leaf node is added to the tree.

✦ **FIGURE 6.13**   A Process Hierarchy

Process hierarchies are a natural consequence of the creation procedure. A process can create multiple child processes, and each child has exactly one parent. If you draw a graph with an edge from each parent to its children, the graph will be a tree, rooted at the initial process.

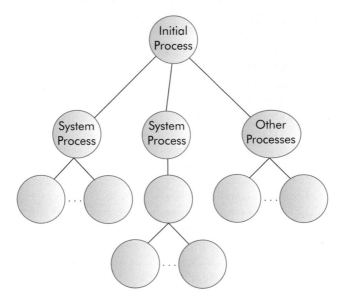

Some operating systems use this hierarchical relationship, while others simply ignore it. For example, the OS may be designed so that a parent process has the right to suspend a child process, thus preventing it from executing. The parent may also be able to activate a suspended child process, destroy a child process, or allocate resources to the child process. Suppose the OS attaches all of these semantics to the process creation relationship. Then, because all processes are created by the initial process, each child is ultimately under the full control of the initial process. The initial process can allocate resources to each child, block/activate the process, destroy each child, and so on.

REFINING THE PROCESS MANAGER

If control semantics are added to the parent-child relation, enabling, for example, a parent to control a child, process management becomes more complex. This can be illustrated by considering how the state diagram for a process becomes more complex. Figure 6.10 provided a state diagram for process management that focused only on resource management and processor multiplexing. Figure 6.14 adds more states to reflect the additional semantics. The new states show how the process is managed when a parent process is allowed to suspend and activate the child process. If a parent suspends a child, then the child is not allowed to use the processor; when a parent activates a child, the child can compete for the processor, provided it is not blocked. A parent may decide to suspend a child process for any of a number of reasons, including temporarily removing the primary memory from a process (called "swapping the process out").

This refinement was derived by refining the `blocked` state from the original diagram into `blockedActive` and `blockedSuspended` states, then showing the new transitions. Similarly, the `ready` state is divided into `readyActive` and `readySuspended` states. After an initial set of resources has been allocated to a process, the process comes into existence in the `readySuspended` state. This means that the new process is ready to use the processor when it becomes available. However, its controlling process has not yet activated it. The process can be moved to the `readyActive` state once its controlling process decides to activate it. When the process becomes `readyActive`, it is placed in the processor ready list. In this state it is blocked, waiting for the scheduler to allocate the processor to it. Based

✦ **FIGURE 6.14**   A Process State Diagram Reflecting Control

In process hierarchies, a parent may have extensive responsibilities for managing its child processes. In this state diagram example, the parent can suspend and activate any of its children.

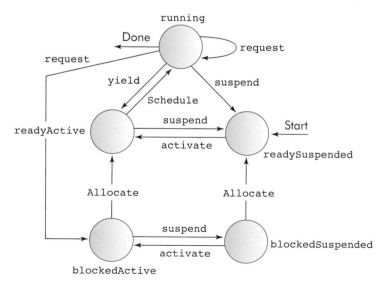

on the strategy used by the controlling process, it may choose to suspend a child process in the `readyActive` state or the scheduler may allocate the CPU to the process. If the controlling process decides to suspend the process, then it returns to the `readySuspended` state. If it is given the processor, it becomes a `running` process on the CPU.

A process in the `running` state may be *involuntarily* removed from the CPU if the scheduler chooses to do so (or if the parent, running on a different processor, chooses to block the child). The process may also *voluntarily* move itself to the `readyActive` state (by yielding the processor). It may also move to the `blockedActive` state by requesting an unavailable resource. A process is `ready` if it needs the processor in order to proceed, and it is `blocked` if it needs a different resource to proceed.

When a `blockedActive` process is allocated resources, it becomes `readyActive`. It could become `blockedSuspended` if a controlling process chose to suspend it while it had already blocked itself waiting for a resource—a double whammy of sorts. A resource allocation operation moves the process from either of the blocked states to the corresponding ready states. An `activate` operation is required to move the process from a suspended state to the corresponding active state.

SPECIALIZING RESOURCE ALLOCATION STRATEGIES

The responsibility for resource management can be delegated to each child process when it is created. This implies that the child must provide its own algorithms and data structures to manage the resources of the child processes it creates. The OS for the RC 4000 carries this approach to its extreme [Brinch Hansen, 1970]. This system was designed so that the *nucleus* provided fundamental process management mechanisms but deferred resource allocation policies to its clients and their children. Child processes were created from the nucleus process, and each of these children comprised a special-purpose OS, implementing its own resource policy in its own resource manager. This approach enabled the nucleus to support a real-time extension to the nucleus, a timesharing extension to the nucleus, and a batch extension to the nucleus, all at the same time, since the specialized resource managers were implemented in each child of the nucleus rather than in the nucleus itself. The real-time extension could allocate resources according to service priorities, the timesharing extension according to response time, and the batch extension according to turnaround time. This strategy can be propagated throughout the process hierarchy, so resources are always allocated by a process's parent rather than by the "operating system."

Obviously, this approach greatly complicates the definition of child processes when compared with other systems—UNIX, for example—since the parent program has considerably more responsibility than in systems where the OS manages resources. However, in the RC 4000 system, it is possible to design and build much more flexible process hierarchies than can be built in, say, UNIX.

6.9 ● SUMMARY

Processes are the basis of modern computational models. A process uses an application program to determine its precise behavior. In multiprogrammed operating systems, each process is provided with its own abstract machine, modeled after the underlying hardware. The OS is designed to support concurrent execution of multiple abstract machines, thereby enabling concurrent execution of multiple processes.

The process manager is the part of the OS that implements the abstract machine model. An OS that supports classic processes provides an abstract machine that behaves as much like a von Neumann computer as possible. Newer systems divide the classic process behavior into a modern process framework and one or more computational threads. The framework corresponds to the part of the classic process that defines an address space and a set of OS resources that will be needed to carry out a computation. A thread is the part of the classic process that represents the dynamic execution of the program. A modern process with a single base thread is exactly the same concept as a classic process. With the modern process model, a programmer is allowed to launch multiple, concurrent threads that operate within the process framework.

The community of processes and threads is implemented by guiding the execution of the hardware process so that it executes the OS and each of the abstract machines. The process manager creates the abstract machine environment with its own algorithms and data structures. Process and thread descriptors are fundamental elements of the abstract machine design. These descriptors are created by the process manager, although several of their fields may be manipulated by other parts of the OS. Processes obtain resources as needed by interacting with a resource manager. There is a base behavior for every resource manager, but resources such as the processor, memory, and files have specialized managers that are discussed in later chapters.

This chapter has discussed concepts, issues, and designs for process managers. This discussion provides essential information regarding how an OS works, and also creates the backdrop for subsequent discussion of the other parts of the OS. In the next chapter, we will focus on the processor resource manager, more popularly known as the scheduler.

6.10 • EXERCISES

1. Explain why all processes in a thread block when any one of them blocks in a user space thread implementation. Why is this not true in a kernel thread implementation?

2. Does the hardware process described in Section 6.2 have a process descriptor? Does the initial process have a process descriptor? Explain your answers.

3. Each process is created with an address space that defines access to every memory-mapped resource in the process. Explain how a process can refer to objects that are not in its address space (for example, a file or another process).

4. Many operating systems allocate a static array of process descriptors, meaning that there is a fixed, maximum number of processes that can exist in the OS. Provide some arguments for why the kernel does not use a dynamic data structure to allow a variable number of process descriptors to exist.

5. Below is a list of fields from a classic process descriptor. In a modern process model with threads and processes, say whether each field should be implemented in the process or thread descriptor.

   - ■ User name
   - ■ Stack bottom
   - ■ Resources blocking me

■ Primary memory allocated to me

■ Files allocated to me

■ Execution state

6. When a new process moves from the ready state to the running state (in Figure 6.10), each register in the CPU must be set either to initial values or to the values the process had when it was last interrupted. Explain why the PC register is typically the last register loaded for the new process. Show a pseudo assembly language code segment to load a new process onto a CPU (that is, to change the PC after restoring other registers) for a processor that contains arithmetic-logical registers R0–R3, processor status register PSR, condition code register CC, program counter PC, and instruction register IR.

7. Suppose an OS was designed so that processes could be in any of the following states:

■ Running: Currently using the CPU.

■ Ready: Waiting for the CPU.

■ Blocked for Interrupt: Waiting for an interrupt handler to finish, then resume running.

■ Blocked for reusable resource: Waiting for a consumable resource to be allocated, then will become ready.

■ Blocked for consumable resource: Waiting for a reusable resource to be allocated, then will become ready.

Draw a state diagram to represent a process with these states.

8. Suppose a process is defined to behave as described in Figure 6.10. Design and implement a resource manager for reusable resources. When multiple processes are blocked on a resource and one or more units become available, call a policy function to select the process to receive resources. Implement any simple policy you like. Test your resource manager by creating a testbed with N different processes (N is a testbed parameter) and M different resources (M is a testbed parameter), where R_i initially has c_i units of the resource (c_i is a testbed parameter). Only one process can be running at a time, so you will also need a simple scheduler to allocate the processor to processes in the order in which they become ready. A running process should execute for a small random amount of time and then request one of the units of resource, transitioning to the blocked state. When the resource is allocated to the process, it should be moved to the ready state. Later, the testbed should release each resource it acquired. Your testbed processes need only simulate real work by real processes. For example, your testbed might have a code schema similar to this:

```
#define N 50
...
scanf("%d", M); // Define a value for M
for(i=0; i<M; i++) { ... } // Define values for c[i]
...
```

```
for(i=0; i<N; i++) {
    waitTime = rand();
    for(j=0; j<waitTime; j++) { };    // Simulate running
                                      // process
    request(r[i%M], ...); // Ask for k < c[i%M] units
    waitTime = rand();
    for(j=0; j<waitTime; j++) { };    // Simulate running
                                      // process
    release(r[i%M], ...);             // Release resource
}
...
```

A more comprehensive test procedure would cause processes to hold more than one resource type at a time. If you have time, make your test driver check some of these more complex situations.

Experiment with various small values of $N < 8$, $M < 10$, and c_i. The random amount of time a process runs should be kept as small as possible so that your tests do not take an inordinate amount of time. Be sure your test cases cause processes to block for unavailable resources. Hand in a listing of your resource manager and testbed, along with a trace (fewer than five pages) of state transitions in a test session.

Kernel Timers

This assignment can be solved on most versions of UNIX.

Design and implement software that uses the `ITIMER_REAL`, `ITIMER_VIRTUAL` and `ITIMER_PROF` interval timers to measure the processor usage of a process. Prepare a performance report that provides real-time ("wall clock" time) of execution (using the `ITIMER_REAL` timer), processor time (the time the process is actually running in both user and kernel space), user space time, and kernel space time. You can check the accuracy of your wall clock (real) time by calling `gettimeofday()`. All times should have millisecond precision. (Your hardware may not be able to support millisecond precision. Even so, design your code as if the clock had millisecond precision.) Use the signal facility to create signal handlers to keep track of the number of seconds of real, virtual, and profile time (you should configure the three timers so that they raise a signal once per second). Demonstrate your solution by measuring the performance of a parent and two child processes, each executing the Fibonacci program included in the "Attacking the Problem" section. Experiment with Fibonacci sequence for $N = 20$, 30, and 36.

● BACKGROUND ●

Time is stated relative to some important epoch. For example, time in the United States is calculated using the Gregorian calendar, which chose a time of zero to be about 2000 years ago. When you type the `date` command to a shell, the command will read a kernel variable to determine the time, say "Mon Jun 21 09:01:28 MDT 2002", which you will probably interpret to mean that about 2,002 years have elapsed since the beginning of the epoch.

Since UNIX systems were not around before 1970, they simply avoid representing time before 1970. This is accomplished by beginning the UNIX time epoch at the beginning of the day (00:00:00 Greenwich Meridian Time) on January 1, 1970. Notice that in 30 years (or about January 1, 2000), about 946,080,000 seconds had elapsed since the beginning of the UNIX epoch, so one could represent the time to the nearest second with that integer. Commands like `date` that report in the Gregorian calendar format have to normalize the UNIX epoch to the Gregorian epoch if they want to report the time and date using the Gregorian metric.

Since about 2^{25} seconds elapse in a year, a 32-bit signed integer can keep track of the number of seconds that have elapsed for about 2^6 (64) years—or until about 2034. In UNIX kernels, two long `int` kernel variables keep track of the number of seconds and microseconds, respectively, that have passed since the beginning of the UNIX time epoch. The UNIX kernel data structure for holding a time value is

```
struct timeval {
 long tv_sec;
 long tv_usec;
};
```

How can the OS know when to update its `struct timeval` representation of the current time? Every modern computer contains a very simple programmable *timer device*. This device is not really used to do any I/O operations, but rather, to produce an interrupt at a precise time interval (for example, Linux systems set the timer device so that it produces an interrupt 100 times per second). The OS can keep accurate time using this device: When the OS is initialized, it sets the time variable to zero. The device handler increments the time variable each time the timer device interrupt occurs. That is, if the interrupt occurs once every 10 ms (milliseconds), then the timer device handler adds 10 ms to the OS time variable `tv_usec` field, carrying the overflow into the `tv_sec` field each time it occurs.

The current time maintained by a UNIX kernel is accessible to user mode programs via system calls. (`gettimeofday()` is the usual interface to the system time):

```
#include      <sys/time.h>
...
struct timeval theTime;
...
gettimeofday(&theTime, NULL);
...
```

When the code fragment completes, the `timeval` structure will have `theTime.tv_sec` set to the (`long`) integer number of seconds that have passed since the beginning of the day on January 1, 1970, and `theTime.tv_usec` is a variable of type `long` that provides the number of microseconds that have elapsed since the last second began. When the OS is initialized, the number of seconds since the beginning of the UNIX epoch is saved in a kernel variable. The `gettimeofday()` function determines the current time by adding the time that has elapsed since the system was booted to the base time.

The OS clock value that is maintained by the timer device handler is also used to determine when the currently running process should be removed from the CPU so that another process can use it, to keep track of the amount of time that each process executed in user mode or supervisor mode (using the `ITIMER` values mentioned in the problem statement), and so on.

PER PROCESS TIMERS

The kernel accumulates time and manages various timers for each process. For example, the scheduling strategy depends on each process having a record of the amount of CPU time it has accrued since it last used the CPU. The kernel also keeps track of three different intervals of time relevant to each process:

- `ITIMER_REAL`: Reflects the passage of real time, and is implemented using the `it_real_value` and `it_real_incr` fields.

- `ITIMER_VIRTUAL`: Reflects the passage of virtual time, meaning this time is incremented only when the corresponding process is executing in user mode.

- `ITIMER_PROF`: Reflects the passage of time during which the process is active (virtual time) plus the time that the kernel is doing work on behalf of the corresponding process (for example, executing a system call).

Each of these timers is actually a *countdown timer*, meaning that it is periodically initialized to some prescribed value, and then reflects the passage of time by counting down toward zero. When the timer reaches zero, it raises a signal so that another part of the system (in the OS or a user space program) will be notified that the counter has reached zero. Then it resets the period and begins counting down again.

Each timer is initialized with the `setitimer()` system call:

```
#include        <sys/time.h>
...
setitimer(
  int timerType,
  const struct timerval *value,
  struct itimerval *oldValue
);
```

The `struct itimerval` includes the fields

```
struct itimerval {
  struct timeval it_interval;
  struct timeval it_value;
};
```

You can read the details of the parameters by reading the man page for `setitimer()`. The general idea is that the `timerType` parameter is set to one of `ITIMER_REAL`, `ITIMER_VIRTUAL`, or `ITIMER_PROF` (which are constants defined in the `sys/time.h` include file). The `value` parameter is used to initialize second and microsecond fields of the given timer; the `it_value` field defines the current value for the timer, and the `it_interval` field defines the value that should be used to reset the timer whenever it reaches zero.

A timer's value can be read with the `getitimer()` system call:

```
#include        <sys/time.h>
...
getitimer(
  int timerType,
  const struct timerval *value,
);
```

In this case, the `value` parameter is used to return the value of the kernel's clock.

The following code fragment sets `ITIMER_REAL`, then reads it:

```
#include        <sys/time.h>
...
  struct itimerval v;
  ...
  v.it_interval.tv_sec = 9;
  v.it_interval.tv_usec = 999999;
  v.it_value.tv_sec = 9;
  v.it_value.tv_usec = 999999;
  setitimer(ITIMER_REAL, &v, NULL);
  ...
  getitimer(ITIMER_REAL, &v);
```

```
    printf("... %ld seconds, %ld microseconds ...",
      ...,
      v.it_value.tv_sec,
      v.it_value.tv_usec,
      ...);
...
```

When ITIMER_REAL reaches zero, it will be reset to (9, 999999) again. However, this code segment does not define any other processing that could be done when the corresponding signal is raised.

● **ATTACKING THE PROBLEM** ●

SIGNALS

Every UNIX system defines a fixed set of **signals** that can be raised by one process, interrupting another process that (optionally) catches the signal by executing previously specified code for that particular signal. Hence, signal implementations are OS system mechanisms for notifying an application process that some event has occurred. It frequently represents the occurrence of a hardware event, such as a user pressing the Delete key or the CPU detecting an attempt to divide by zero. Signals also may be used to notify a process of the existence of a software condition. For example, it can represent the fact that one of the process's three itimers reached zero.

Signals also can be used *among* application-level processes. Each signal has a type (called a "namc") associated with it. There are 31 different types built into contemporary UNIX systems (including Linux), although the signal types differ in BSD UNIX (FreeBSD), AT&T System V Release 4 (SVR4), POSIX, and ANSI C. In each version, the system include file, signal.h defines a number of symbolic names for the signal types. For example, all versions of UNIX define the SIGINT signal type, which is raised by the terminal driver when the user has pressed the terminal interrupt character, usually Delete or Control-C. Application programmers are not allowed to create new signals. But most versions of UNIX include SIGUSR1 and SIGUSR2, which can be *used* for application-to-application signaling.

A signal is raised by calling the kill() function and identifying the process to receive the signal and the signal type.[3] Essentially, a receiving application process can cause a signal to be handled in the default way, to be ignored, or to be caught by user-defined code. The signal() function is called to identify the signal number and the way the signal is to be treated. For example, to ignore the SIGALRM signal, the process must execute the system call:

```
signal(SIGALRM, SIG_IGN);
```

The default handling can be reenabled by calling signal() again with the SIG_DFL value. The application can process the alarm signal with its own code by supplying a function (that takes an integer argument and returns a void) as the second argument to signal.

---

[3]The name "kill" comes from an early use of signals so that one process could send a signal to another to request that the receiver terminate. Although the types of signals have been extended, the name of the function that transmitted the signal kill() has not changed.

The following complete program illustrates how a signal handler is registered with the signal() function call, the form of the signal handler routine itself, and how the whole mechanism operates.

```c
#include <signal.h>
static void sig_handler(int);
int main (void){
   int i, parent_pid, child_pid, status;
/* Prepare the sig_handler routine to catch SIGUSR1 and SIGUSR2 */
   if (signal(SIGUSR1, sig_handler)==SIG_ERR)
     printf("Parent: Unable to create handler for SIGUSR1\n");
   if (signal(SIGUSR2, sig_handler)==SIG_ERR)
     printf("Parent: Unable to create handler for SIGUSR2\n");
   parent_pid = getpid();
   if ((child_pid = fork())==0) {
     kill(parent_pid, SIGUSR1); /* Raise the SIGUSR1 signal */
/* Child process begins busy wait for a signal */
     for (;;) pause();
   } else {
     kill(child_pid, SIGUSR2); /* Parent raising SIGUSR2 signal */
     printf("Parent: Terminating child ...");
     kill(child_pid, SIGTERM); /* Parent raising SIGTERM signal */
     wait(&status); /* Parent waiting for the child termination */
     printf("done\n");
   }
}

static void sig_handler(int signo){
   switch (signo) {
   case SIGUSR1: /* Incoming SIGUSR1 signal */
     printf("Parent: Received SIGUSR1\n");
     break;
   case SIGUSR2: /* Incoming SIGUSR2 signal */
     printf("Child: Received SIGUSR2\n");
     break;
   default: break; /* Should never get this case */
   }
   return;
}
```

This code segment is pedagogic in that it illustrates how signals are raised and caught, but it does not implement any useful function. In the example code, we create a single signal handler, sig_handler, that is used by a parent and child process with the two calls to signal(). Next, the example code determines its own process identifier using the getpid() system call. It then creates a child so that the parent knows both the parent and child process identifiers, but the child knows only the parent's identifier. The child process sends a SIGUSR1 to the parent and then enters a wait-loop so that it will still exist when the parent sends signals to the child. The parent sends a SIGUSR2 to the child, followed by a termination signal (SIGTERM), and calls wait() to obtain the notice that the child has been terminated. The child and parent use the same signal handler definition, although the child will never see the SIGUSR1, and the parent will never see a signal for SIGUSR2.

ORGANIZING A SOLUTION

There are many different ways to organize your solution. This section provides a skeleton of one solution. In this skeleton, the parent process allocates a number of static variables that will be used by signal handlers to keep track of time for the parent process and two child processes. This program skeleton uses signals to notify the user processes about time values. You need to incorporate your own signal handler routines for this code to work properly.

```c
#include <sys/time.h>
#include <signal.h>
#include <unistd.h>
#include <stdio.h>
long unsigned int fibonacci(unsigned int n);

// These variables are used to record the accumulated times. They
// are set by the signal handlers and read by the processes when
// they report the results.
static long p_realt_secs = 0, c1_realt_secs = 0, c2_realt_secs = 0;
static long p_virtt_secs = 0, c1_virtt_secs = 0, c2_virtt_secs = 0;
static long p_proft_secs = 0, c1_proft_secs = 0, c2_proft_secs = 0;
static struct itimerval p_realt, c1_realt, c2_realt;
static struct itimerval p_virtt, c1_virtt, c2_virtt;
static struct itimerval p_proft, c1_proft, c2_proft;

main(int argc, char **argv) {
  long unsigned fib = 0;
  int pid1, pid2;
  unsigned int fibarg;
  int status;

// Get command line argument, fibarg (the value N in the problem
// statement)
  ...
// Initialize parent, child1, and child 2 timer values
  p_realt.it_interval.tv_sec = ...;
  p_realt.it_interval.tv_usec = ...;
  p_realt.it_value.tv_sec = ...;
  p_realt.it_value.tv_usec = ...;
  ...
// Enable parent's signal handlers
  signal(SIGALRM, ...);
  signal(SIGVTALRM, ...);
  signal(SIGPROF, ...);

// Set parent's itimers
  if(setitimer(ITIMER_REAL, ...) == -1)
    perror("parent real timer set error");
  if(setitimer(ITIMER_VIRTUAL, ...) == -1)
    perror("parent virtual timer set error");
```

```
if(setitimer(ITIMER_PROF, ...) == -1)
  perror("parent profile timer set error");
pid1 = fork();
if(pid1 == 0) {
// Enable child 1 signal handlers (disable parent handlers)

// Enable child 1 signal handlers

// Set child 1 itimers

// Start child 1 on the fibonacci program
  fib = fibonacci(fibarg);

// Read child 1 itimer values and report them
  getitimer(ITIMER_PROF, ...);
  getitimer(ITIMER_REAL, ...);
  getitimer(ITIMER_VIRTUAL, ...);
  printf("\n");
  printf("Child 1 fib = %ld, real time = %ld sec, %ld msec\n",
    fib, c1_realt_secs,
    elapsed_usecs(c1_realt.it_value.tv_sec,
              c1_realt.it_value.tv_usec) / 1000);
  printf("Child 1 fib = %ld, cpu time = %ld sec, %ld msec\n",
    fib, c1_proft_secs,
    elapsed_usecs(c1_proft.it_value.tv_sec,
              c1_proft.it_value.tv_usec) / 1000);
  printf("Child 1 fib = %ld, user time = %ld sec, %ld msec\n",
    fib, c1_virtt_secs,
    elapsed_usecs(c1_virtt.it_value.tv_sec,
              c1_virtt.it_value.tv_usec) / 1000);
  printf("Child 1 fib = %ld, kernel time = %ld sec, %ld msec\n",
    fib, delta_time(c1_proft, c1_virtt),
    (elapsed_usecs(c1_proft.it_value.tv_sec,
              c1_proft.it_value.tv_usec) / 1000) -
    (elapsed_usecs(c1_virtt.it_value.tv_sec,
              c1_virtt.it_value.tv_usec) / 1000));
  fflush(stdout);
  exit(0);
} else {
  pid2 = fork();
  if(pid2 == 0) {
  // Enable child 1 signal handlers
    ...
  // Set child 2 itimers
    ...
  // Start child 2 on the fibonacci program
    fib = fibonacci(fibarg);
  // Read child 2 itimer values and report them
    ...
  } else { /* this is the parent */
```

```
    // Start parent on the fibonacci program
      fib = fibonacci(fibarg);

    // Wait for children to terminate
      waitpid(0, &status, 0);
      waitpid(0, &status, 0);

    // Read parent itimer values and report them
      ...
    }
    printf("this line should never be printed\n");
}

long unsigned int fibonacci(unsigned int n) {
  if(n == 0)
    return 0;
  else if (n == 1 || n == 2)
    return 1;
  else
    return(fibonacci(n-1) + fibonacci(n-2))
}
```

Manipulating Kernel Objects

This assignment can be solved on most Windows systems.

This exercise asks you to create a set of cyclic processes with different handle inheritance attributes, to use a waitable timer to control when the main program decides that the entire community of processes should terminate, and then to terminate all the processes.

PART A

Write a program that uses a waitable timer to stop itself K seconds after it was started, where K is a command line parameter.

PART B

Modify the program from Part A so that it creates N background processes, each running a program that terminates at a random time. Make N be a command line parameter. Each process should give all of its own handles (through handle inheritance), except the thread handles, to child processes it creates. There is a skeleton for such a child process program in "Attacking the Problem".

PART C

Modify the controlling program again so that when K seconds have elapsed, it will destroy the processes that have not terminated on their own. If all background processes terminate on their own, the controlling process can run for the full K seconds.

● BACKGROUND ●

Windows NT makes broad use of objects in its implementation and through the services it provides. However, the Win32 API is not an object-oriented interface (that is, to invoke a system service, application programs call system function rather than sending messages to the system objects). Despite the Win32 API being a C interface rather than a C++ interface, when an application obtains a resource from the OS, the resource is always regarded as some form of an object. This exercise considers various facets of objects.

Windows creates an OS object whenever it allocates a resource to a process. The OS object is allocated in the OS memory and the state of the object is set to reflect the details of the resource allocation. Since the details are implemented within an object, other software cannot generally access the object's member data except through the object's public interface. Furthermore, since the OS object is allocated in the OS space, user mode programs cannot even access the memory in which the kernel object is allocated. These two levels of protection are the foundation of secure objects in Windows. The Windows NT

Executive supports a fixed set of classes (object types). Solomon and Russinovich [2000] lists the main kernel objects as:

Object directory: An object that can contain a collection of other objects. The NT Executive uses this type for various organized sets of objects.

Symbolic link: It is possible to reference another object using a symbolic name. This type is used to support that capability.

Process: The object that represents a process, specifically the process descriptor.

Thread: The object that represents a thread, specifically the thread descriptor.

Section: Used in implementing shared memory among process address spaces.

File Port: The object type that represents a file descriptor when a file is opened for use.

Access Token: The object type used by the OS to implement user authentication, and by various other parts of the system as a basic mechanism in the protection system.

Event: A class for objects that can capture the occurrence of action in the system (an "event") so that other parts of the system can perform activities when they are assured that the action has occurred. An Event object is the basis of many synchronization operations.

Semaphore: A class that implements the behavior of Dijkstra's general semaphore (explained in Chapter 8).

Mutant: Another class for synchronization mechanisms. This one is used to perform mutual exclusion for critical sections.

Timer: An object type for objects that can be used to notify a thread that a given amount of time has elapsed (see the `Sleep()` function call and `WaitableTimers` discussion later in this exercise).

Queue: A class to define objects that cause a thread to wait for I/O completions.

Key: A class used to access and manipulate information in the system Registry (a system-wide location where the computer's configuration information is kept).

Profile: An object type for objects that are used to measure the time to execute code segments in a process. Used by the measurement and program profiling tools.

Every Executive object has a standard wrapper with information that the OS object manager uses to administer the object, and type-dependent member data. The wrapper contains a header that includes fields for the object's name, description of the references to this object, and security attributes. (There are other fields in the header to implement the object model, but they are not included in this discussion.)

REFERENCING AN OBJECT

When a thread uses `CreateProcess()` and `CreateThread()` to create another process or thread, it passes a *name* to the Object Manager, then both a *handle* and a system-wide *identification* are returned. In the `CreateProcess()` case, the `PROCESS_INFORMATION` data structure is set so that there are `HANDLE`s to the new process and the new thread and `DWORD` identifications for the new process and thread. `CreateThread()` returns a HAN-DLE to the new thread and the thread identification as a `LPDWORD` (pointer to a `DWORD`) parameter. Once a user thread has obtained a HANDLE, it can pass the handle to the OS as a parameter for other requests. For example, after a thread creates another thread, it passes the HANDLE back to the OS when it closes the thread handle (see Figure 6.15):

```
ChildThreadHandle = CreateThread(...);
...
CloseHandle(childThreadHandle);
```

✦ **FIGURE 6.15**   Handles and Handle Descriptors

A handle is a user space data structure used to reference an NT Executive data structure. This can be done by assigning a table index value to the handle, and then using it as an index into a kernel process handle table. This allows the user space software to reference the appropriate NT Executive object without knowing its address.

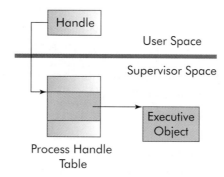

When the OS object manager processes the first call that references a particular object, it adds the object name to a set of known object names, creates an OS object with a header and body, initializes the fields in the header, and then provides the object to other OS components so they can fill in the object's type-specific body.

An OS call might find that the desired object already exists, perhaps because a different process (or different thread) already caused the object to be created. In this case, an open handle count in the object's header is incremented to indicate that there are now two handles that reference the object. Subsequent open operations on the object will continue to increment the handle count, and close operations will decrement it. If a close operation results in the handle count reaching zero (meaning that there are no more user space handles referencing the object), the OS object manager removes the name from the name space. (If any subsequent references to the object occur, the name will have to be reintroduced to the name space.)

There is one more level of complexity to object references. OS components may also reference an OS object, but they will not necessarily use a handle to do it (that is, they use the object's address directly, since they run in kernel space). The object's header also includes a reference count to keep track of the number of *all* references to the object. User space and kernel space open operations cause the reference count to be incremented, and close operations decrement it. If the reference count goes to zero, the object is not being used by any software component—in user space or kernel space—therefore, it can be deallocated when its reference count reaches zero [Solomon and Russinovich, 2000].

What is the relationship between the kernel object, a HANDLE to the object, and a DWORD identification for the object? As noted above, a kernel object is created by the OS and stored in kernel memory space, so it is not directly accessible by any user mode thread. Whenever a thread has an object created in its behalf—or otherwise begins to use an OS object—some provision must be made by which the user mode thread can ask the OS to perform operations on that object. A HANDLE is a 32-bit, user space, process-specific reference to the object. It is implemented as an offset into a process-specific handle table [Solomon and Russinovich, 2000; Richter, 1997]. When the OS provides a handle to a thread in a process, it searches the process's handle table (it knows how to find the process's handle table by referring to the process's descriptor). When an empty entry is found, the OS fills in the object's kernel space address in one field, access information in second field, and miscellaneous other information in other fields. The handle table is an extension of the process descriptor, and is stored in kernel space. The HANDLE that is returned to the user thread is the *index into the kernel space handle table* for this process. Thus, the handle that a thread uses is only accessible to threads that exist in the same process address space. Even if a thread passed the HANDLE value to a thread in another process, it would be a meaningless value.

The DWORD system-wide identification spans address spaces. In cases where an object's identity must be passed among address spaces, the identity is used rather than the HANDLE.

SECURITY ATTRIBUTES

Function calls of the form Create<Class> or Open<Class> are used to request a system resource, and hence to have a kernel object allocated and a handle returned to the calling thread. The OS object manager protection mechanism requires that the caller also indicate its desired access rights to the object. There is a set of generic rights that apply to every object (such as read and write), and there may also be type-specific rights (such as the suspend access to a newly created process). During the Create<Class> operation, the Object Manager checks the caller's rights by passing a security descriptor (of type SECURITY_DESCRIPTOR) to the security mechanism to represent the desired access rights. The security mechanisms depend on being able to authenticate the user that is running the software.

If access is permitted, the security mechanism returns the explicit set of access rights that the calling process has been granted, and the Object Manager saves those rights as part of the process's handle descriptor in the handle table. Then, when a thread in the original process uses the handle, its access rights to the given object are compared with the granted access before the kernel code uses the handle descriptor to reference the object.

In Chapter 2, CreateProcess() was used to create a new process. The part of the function prototype related to security is reproduced here:

```
BOOL CreateProcess(
    ...
    LPSECURITY_ATTRIBUTES lpProcessAttributes,
        // pointer to process security attributes
    LPSECURITY_ATTRIBUTES lpThreadAttributes,
        // pointer to thread security attributes
    ...
);
```

The `lpProcessAttributes` and `lpThreadAttributes` parameters are pointers to a `SECURITY_ATTRIBUTE` data structure (shown below):

```
typedef struct _SECURITY_ATTRIBUTES { // sa
   DWORD nLength;
   LPVOID lpSecurityDescriptor;
   BOOL bInheritHandle;
} SECURITY_ATTRIBUTES;
```

The `lpSecurityDescriptor` is a pointer to the `SECURITY_DESCRIPTOR` data structure whose details are not documented, since its fields are only to be read and set using Win32 API functions. It is the means by which the calling thread specifies the desired access rights that will be either assigned to a new object or used to authenticate access to an existing object. For example, the Win32 API functions `GetSecurityDescriptorControl()`, `SetSecurityDescriptorDacl()`, and others provide tools for setting the fields in the `SECURITY_DESCRIPTOR`.

The default value for the security attributes parameters (in the `CreateProcess()` call) is `NULL`, meaning that there is no `SECURITY_ATTRIBUTE` data structure passed on the call. The OS process manager (and the object manager) interprets the `NULL` argument to mean that the child process (or thread, if this is a security attribute for a thread) uses the existing `SECURITY_DESCRIPTOR` for an existing object, or the system default if it must create a new object.

If you wish to restrict the child's access to its own process object, it is necessary to create a `SECURITY_ATTRIBUTE`, then to perform OS calls so that the underlying data structure prevents the child from referencing the object. While it would be unusual for you to restrict the child from its own process object, the same security attributes mechanism is used for every OS object—files, memory sections, and so on.

Handle Inheritance

The entry in a process's handle table is a *secure reference* to an object. If a thread has a handle, it can reference an entry in the handle table, and hence, the corresponding object in kernel space. If it does not have a handle, then no reference is possible. If N different threads in a process execute a code segment that obtains a handle to a particular object, then the process will have N distinct handle descriptors to the object in the process table. It behooves the programmer to be very careful about how many handles are obtained with any code segment that multiple threads might execute.[4]

When a new process is created, should it be able to reference the same objects as its parent? In some cases, it is invaluable—for example, to allow a child process to be able to read a shared memory segment that the parent has already opened. In other cases, providing a reference to a parent's open objects is exactly the wrong thing to do—for example, if the parent has resources open that the child is not to use. In the `CreateProcess()` function call, the handle inheritance flag parameter, `bInheritHandles`, is used to specify if the child process should be able to reference the objects for which its parent has handles.

---

[4]A common scenario is for a child thread to obtain a handle through some common code segment, to determine that the handle is superfluous, and to close the handle, removing the redundant handle descriptor.

```
Bool CreateProcess( ...
  Bool bInheritHandles,    // handle inheritance flag
  ...
);
```

If bInheritHandles is TRUE, the new process will be given its own handles to the objects that the creating process can reference. That is, the new process will have a new handle created for its use, and each new handle will have a new handle descriptor in the new process's handle table. The handle counts to the referenced objects will be increased accordingly.

If the thread that creates an object wishes, it can explicitly mark a handle as *uninheritable*. Then even if the bInheritHandles flag is TRUE, the new process will not get a handle to the uninheritable object. If the flag is FALSE, the new process is created without any handles to the objects that the creating process contained. While you have only seen the CreateProcess() function use the inheritance flag, many other calls that create new objects incorporate an inheritance flag. This can be set to TRUE to mark the handle as inheritable or FALSE otherwise. An object is created as uninheritable if the bInheritHandles field in the SECURITY_ATTRIBUTES data structure is set to FALSE. Thus, even if you do not want to change the security access for an object from its default behavior, you will have to include a security attributes data structure in the object creation call if you want to mark the object as being uninheritable. To mark a new thread object as not being inheritable at the time a process is created, you could write a code segment such as:

```
#include            <windows.h>
#include            <stdio.h>
  ...
  SECURITY_ATTRIBUTES threadSA;
  ...
// Set threadSA parameter
  threadSA.nLength = sizeof(SECURITY_ATTRIBUTES);
  threadSA.lpSecurityDescriptor = NULL;
  threadSA.bInheritHandles = FALSE;
  if(!CreateProcess(NULL, lpCommandLine, NULL, &threadSA, FALSE,
      HIGH_PRIORITY_CLASS | CREATE_NEW_CONSOLE,
      NULL, NULL, &startInfo, &processInfo)) {
    fprintf(stderr, "CreateProcess failed on error %d\n",
    GetLastError());
    ExitProcess(1);
  };
```

PASSING HANDLES TO OTHER PROCESSES

When a thread obtains a handle, a handle descriptor is created in that process's handle table. Suppose the thread wanted to provide access to the designated object to a thread in a different process. Clearly, the handle itself would be of no use to a thread in another process since it is merely an offset into the first process's handle table. If there is a parent-child relationship between the two processes, handle inheritance can be used to share access. If there is no relationship, then either named objects will have to be used or the DuplicateHandles() function can be used to create a new handle in the receiving process's address space.

The discussion on "Referencing an Object" (above) suggested how named objects can be referenced by different processes: Some process creates the object with a name from a global system name space (these names are like file names). Another process can get a handle to the object by using an open command with the correct name. If the security attributes permit access, the second process will have its own handle descriptor inserted into its own handle table, and the thread will be given a HANDLE.

The DuplicateHandle() function is used to explicitly create a handle in another process:

```
Bool DuplicateHandle(
   HANDLE hSourceProcessHandle,
      // handle to process with handle to duplicate
   HANDLE hSourceHandle,            // handle to duplicate
   HANDLE hTargetProcessHandle,
      // handle to process to duplicate to
   LPHANDLE lpTargetHandle,         // pointer to duplicate handle
   DWORD dwDesiredAccess,           // access for duplicate handle
   BOOL bInheritHandle,             // handle inheritance flag
   DWORD dwOptions                  // optional actions
);
```

In discussing these parameters, call the process that contains a handle to be replicated the "source" process, and the process that is to receive the new handle the "target" process. The hSourceProcessHandle is a handle in the calling process for another process that has a handle that this process needs (the target's handle to the source process must have PROCESS_DUP_HANDLE permission). The hSourceHandle parameter is the offset in the source process's handle table; that is, it is a handle that has meaning only in the source process. This means that before a target process can replicate a handle into its own address space, it must have some other way of communicating with the source so it could have obtained the hSourceHandle value. The hTargetProcessHandle is a handle in the calling process and lpTargetHandle is a pointer to a variable that will be set to the off-set in the target process's handle table where the replicated handle will be placed. The hTargetProcessHandle must also have PROCESS_DUP_HANDLE permission.

WAITABLE TIMER OBJECTS

This exercise asks you to make use of a timer object to control your thread behavior. In addition to providing you with a tool for controlling execution based on asynchronous events, using a waitable timer will let you create and work with another object type besides processes and threads.

Windows NT Version 4.0 introduced a kernel object type called a waitable timer (this Win32 API function is not implemented by any of the other Microsoft operating systems). A **waitable timer** is a kernel object that will periodically signal your process that a given amount of time has elapsed. The granularity of the request is 100 ns. Not every computer can really update its clock once every 100 ns, so this is just an expression using the best clock granularity possible with contemporary computers. The waitable timer will do the best job it can to measure time in 100 ns clock ticks.

The function prototype to create a waitable timer is:

```
HANDLE CreateWaitableTimer (
  LPSECURITY_ATTRIBUTES lpTimerAttributes,
                          // pointer to security attributes
  BOOL bManualReset,      // flag for manual reset state
  LPCTSTR lpTimerName     // pointer to timer object name
);
```

The `lpTimerAttributes` is a security attribute parameter, and is used just as it would be with `CreateProcess()` or `CreateThread()` (see above). The `lpTimerName` parameter is provided to assign a name to the timer if it is being created, or to open an existing named timer (in which case `GetLastError()` will return `ERROR_ALREADY_EXISTS`). The `bManualReset` parameter controls the number of threads that will be signaled when the waitable timer sends a signal. If it is set to `TRUE`, all threads that are waiting on the timer will receive a notification, but otherwise only one thread will receive notification. The function returns a `HANDLE` to the waitable timer.

A thread can obtain a handle to an existing waitable timer using `OpenWaitableTimer()`:

```
HANDLE OpenWaitableTimer (
  DWORD dwDesiredAccess,          // access flag
  BOOL bInheritFlag,              // inherit flag
  LPCTSTR lpTimerName             // pointer to timer object name
);
```

The values to `dwDesiredAccess` describe the way the process wants to use the waitable timer with this handle. If you just want a thread to be notified when the timer sends a signal, to be able to set the time period for the timer, or to have full access to all the timer's functions, use this function (see the online reference manual).

Once a waitable timer has been created, it must be set before it will produce signals. The `SetWaitableTimer()` function does this:

```
BOOL SetWaitableTimer (
  HANDLE htimer,            // handle to a timer object
  Const LARGE_INTEGER *pDueTime,
                           // when timer will become signaled
  LONG lPeriod,            // periodic timer interval
  PTIMERAPCROUTINE pfnCompletionRoutine,
                           // pointer to the completion routine
  LPVOID lpArgToCompletionRoutine,
                           // data passed to completion routine
  BOOL fResume             // flag for resume state
);
```

The `hTimer` field is the handle returned by the create or open function. The `pDueTime` is a number in the 64-bit `FILETIME` format (see the online Win32 API reference manual)

```
typedef struct _FILETIME { // ft
  DWORD dwLowDateTime;
  DWORD dwHighDateTime;
} FILETIME;
```

where the dwLowDateTime is the low-order 32 bits of the time in the file system format, and dwHighDateTime is the high-order 32 bits. You can specify the pDueTime as an absolute time or a relative time; relative times are distinguished from absolute times by setting the 64-bit time to be a negative time (see "Attacking the Problem" below). The lPeriod parameter specifies the time in milliseconds (10^{-3} seconds, or "ms") between notifications; if it is zero, the waitable timer will only produce one notification.

Waitable timers are a Windows NT mechanism to coordinate the behavior of threads. An aspect of Windows NT that distinguishes it from many older Microsoft operating systems is its support of very general mechanisms for asynchronous coordination. The next two parameters in SetWaitableTimer (pfnCompletionRoutine and lpArgToCompletionRoutine) are used to implement a general form of asynchronous coordination between the waitable timer and user threads called Asynchronous Procedure Call (or APC). For now, it is sufficient for us to think of an APC as a form of procedure call in which a call is "scheduled" to occur at some later time, rather than at the instant it is made. This will ensure that a function is called, but only when there is sufficient time to do it.

The fResume flag is a little obscure, although it is necessary for a particular usage mode for the computer. If a waitable timer is running on a computer that is in suspended mode, then if fResume is TRUE, the time notification will resume the computer. This means that you can write code that will resume a suspended computer and perform some action (using the APC routine).

The APC parameters can be used to field a timer notification, but a simpler technique is to use another Executive facility, WaitForSingleObject(). When a thread calls this function, it is blocked until a notification is issued to this thread by the specified object. A thread can create a waitable timer, set it, then wait for it to respond with a call to WaitForSingleObject(). Here is the function prototype:

```
DWORD WaitForSingleObject(
    HANDLE hHandle;        // handle of object to wait for
    DWORD dwMilliseconds;  // time-out interval in millisec
);
```

The hHandle parameter is the handle for the waitable timer object. The dwMilliseconds specifies a maximum amount of time (in milliseconds) that the thread is willing to wait for the timer to expire. You can use GetLastError() to see if the function returned because a notification was sent by the waitable timer (WAIT_OBJECT_O), or if the maximum amount of time expired (WAIT_TIMEOUT). You can also use a value of INFINITE for dwMilliseconds, meaning that the calling thread will block until it receives a notification from the waitable timer and never timeout.

A code skeleton to use a waitable timer is:

```
HANDLE wTimer;
LARGE_INTEGER quitTime;
    ...
    wTimer = CreateWaitableTimer(NULL, FALSE, NULL);
// define quitTime
    SetWaitableTimer(wTimer, &quitTime, 0, NULL, NULL, FALSE);
    ...
    WaitForSingleObject(wTimer, INFINITE);
    ...
```

• ATTACKING THE PROBLEM •

The explanation of the mechanisms in the OS is complicated, but the organization of the controlling program is much more straightforward. The problems you will encounter with this program will be in getting the details right.

Since waitable timers are not implemented in versions of NT earlier than 4.0, and since they are not in Windows 9x or CE, you must pass a flag to the compiler to let it know you are working on Version 4.0 NT. If you are using Visual C++, add /D _WIN32_WINNT=0x400 as a compiler flag using the Project/Settings menu.

One problem you will have will be in handling the 64-bit file time values. Richter [1997] uses a code segment similar to the following one to create a parameter suitable for use with SetWaitableTimer():

```
_int64 endTime;
LARGE_INTEGER quitTime;
...
// Put the run time, K in endTime
// (the units will have to be 100 ns)
quitTime.LowPart = (DWORD) (endTime & 0xFFFFFFFF);
quitTime.HighPart = (LONG) (endTime >> 32);
```

Here is an example of a program that you can use in solving Part B of the exercise. The idea is to create a process that may or may not halt on its own, so that your modification to the controlling process must terminate the process.

```
#include      <windows.h>
#include      <stdio.h>

int main (int argc, char *argv[]) {

// Get a value for the number of this client from argv[1]
   printf("Client %s beginning to run\n", argv[1]);
   while(TRUE) {
     printf("Client[%s]: Quit (y or any other character): ",
       argv[1]);
     if(getc(stdin) == 'y') break;
       getc(stdin);        // throw away NEWLINE
   }
   return(0);
}
```

TERMINATING A PROCESS

There is a Win32 API call that allows one process to terminate another one, provided that the process that intends to terminate the other has PROCESS_TERMINATE permission on the specified handle. The function prototype is:

```
BOOL TerminateProcess (
   HANDLE hProcess,       // handle to the process
   UINT uExitCode         // exit code for the process
);
```

If `TerminateProcess()` is called with a process handle, `hProcess`, and an unsigned integer exit code, `uExitCode`, the process manager will terminate the target process. This call can be used for this exercise, but it is normally used only in extreme circumstances. The problem with the function is that it may not work with processes that are using dynamic-linked libraries (DLLs). A DLL may be loaded separately from the `.EXE` file a process uses for its main program execution; the `TerminateProcess()` function will halt the program from executing the `.EXE` file, but the interaction with the DLL may not work. In this exercise, your process does not include any DLLs, so `TerminateProcess()` will work just fine.

CHAPTER 7

Scheduling

CPU scheduling refers to the task of managing CPU sharing among a community of ready processes/threads. Conceptually, the OS scheduler is created from a mechanism used for context switching and a policy that determines the order in which ready processes will receive service. In modern operating systems, the hardware and the process manager's data structures and algorithms implement the mechanism. Ideally, the scheduling policy would be selected by each system administrator so it reflects the way that particular computer will be used. In practice, the scheduling policies are implemented as part of the OS process manager. This chapter introduces mechanisms and then considers two general classes of policies: nonpreemptive and preemptive algorithms. Nonpreemptive algorithms allow a process to run to completion once it obtains the processor. Preemptive algorithms use the interval timer and scheduler to interrupt a running process in order to reallocate the CPU to a higher-priority ready process.

7.1 • OVERVIEW

It is usually necessary to schedule the use of shared resources. For example, if a company has a conference room, then only one group can use the conference room at a time. If there are many groups competing for the use of the conference room, someone will need to act as the room scheduler: Whenever a group wants to hold a meeting in the conference room, one of its representatives contacts the room scheduler to request that it be allocated for the time of the meeting. The CPU scheduler is like a room scheduler: Whenever a process/thread wants to use the CPU, it makes a request to the CPU scheduler. If/when the CPU is available, it is allocated to the process/thread making the request.

As first mentioned in Chapter 1, a multiprogramming OS allows more than one process at a time to be loaded into the primary memory and for threads in the loaded processes to share the CPU using time-multiplexing. With multiprogramming, the behavior that a thread (or more importantly, the thread's human user) perceives is that the thread is executing at the same time as other threads. In a computer with only one physical CPU, there can only be one thread actually executing at one time. But since all abstract machines *appear* to be executing at the same time, we say that they are executing **concurrently**: There is the appearance of simultaneous operation accomplished through a high CPU multiplexing rate.

Multiprogramming is essential in contemporary computer systems. Not only does multiprogramming allow the system to support multiple window human–computer interfaces, but the fundamental operation of the system depends on it. Another reason for multiprogramming is the need for threads to perform concurrent I/O operations. Since I/O operations ordinarily require orders of magnitude more time to complete than do CPU instructions, multiprogramming systems allocate the CPU to another thread whenever a thread blocks to wait for an I/O operation to complete.

The normal state of the machine is that there are multiple ready threads waiting for the CPU to become available. When the CPU becomes available, the **scheduler** chooses one of the ready threads to use the CPU. When it is time for the running thread to be removed from the CPU (and moved to a ready or blocked state), a different thread is then selected from the set of threads that are waiting to use the CPU. The **scheduling policy** determines *when* it is time for a thread to be removed from the CPU and *which* ready thread should be allocated the CPU next. The **scheduling mechanism** determines *how* the process manager can determine that it is time to multiplex the CPU, and how a thread can be allocated to and removed from the CPU (the details of context switching). From the thread's perspective, the scheduler is the element of the system that causes the thread to transition from the ready to running state, and in some cases, from the running to ready state.

✦ FIGURE 7.1   Thread Scheduling

Threads begin life in the ready state, waiting in the ready list while the CPU is used by other threads. When the scheduler selects a thread to run, it changes to the running state and begins using the CPU. The thread may subsequently request an unavailable resource, in which case, it waits in a resource manager's pool or returns to the ready state while other threads use the CPU.

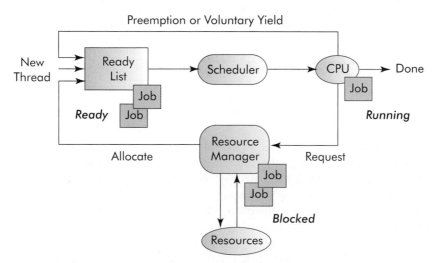

Figure 7.1 illustrates the system perspective on thread scheduling in a single CPU system. When a new thread arrives in the system, it is put in the ready state and linked into the scheduler's ready list. In a single CPU system, only one thread at a time can use the CPU: There can only be one thread in the running state at a time. The running thread may cease using the CPU for any of four reasons:

- The thread completes its execution and leaves the system.

- The thread requests a resource, but the resource manager decides that it cannot allocate the resource to the process associated with the thread. As described in Section 6.6, this thread's state is changed to blocked and the thread is enqueued on a waiting list in the resource manager. Ultimately, the resource manager will allocate the requested resource to the associated process and the thread will be changed to the ready state and placed in the ready list.

- The thread decides to *voluntarily* release the CPU and return to the ready state.

- The thread *involuntarily* releases the CPU because the system decides to *preempt* the thread by changing its state from running to ready, removing the thread from the CPU and placing it back in the ready list.

The scheduling mechanism provides the tools and environment for controlling the flow of the thread through the various states and queues shown in Figure 7.1. The scheduling policy defines which ready thread the scheduler chooses from the ready list, and when a thread should be preempted from the CPU.

7.2 • SCHEDULING MECHANISMS

In a conference room scheduler, a chart is a *mechanism* for representing room allocation. The chart can be filled in to show the times the conference room is reserved and when it is available. If executives have priority for certain conference rooms, like the corporate board room, then the scheduling *policy* might prevent engineers from using the board room for design meetings.

In an OS, the CPU scheduling mechanism depends on features in the hardware—the most important being whether or not the computer is configured with a clock device. The remainder of the scheduler is implemented in OS software, as described next.

THE PROCESS SCHEDULER ORGANIZATION

Conceptually, the scheduling mechanism is composed of several different parts: Figure 7.2 shows three logical parts incorporated into every scheduler: the enqueuer, the dispatcher, and the context switcher.

- When a process/thread is changed to the ready state, its descriptor is updated to reflect the change and the **enqueuer** component places a pointer to the descriptor into a list of processes that are waiting for the CPU (the Ready List in the figure). The enqueuer component may compute the priority for allocating the CPU to the process when it is inserted into the ready list, or the priority may be determined when the process is considered for removal from the ready list.

✦ FIGURE 7.2 The Scheduler

The scheduler changes a ready process/thread into the running state, and a running process/thread into the ready state. It uses an enqueuer mechanism to place a process into the ready list, a dispatch element to allocate the CPU to the process, and a context switch element to remove one process from the CPU and place another on it.

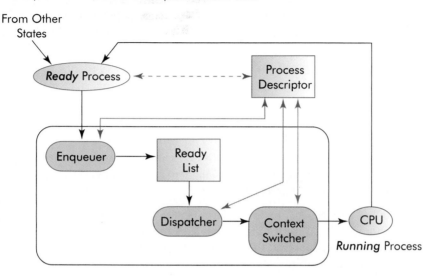

When the scheduler switches the CPU from executing one process to executing another, the **context switcher** component saves the contents of all CPU registers (PC, IR, condition status, processor status, and ALU status) for the thread being removed from the CPU in its descriptor.

The **dispatcher** is invoked after the application process has been removed from the CPU. (This requires that the dispatcher's context be loaded on the CPU in order for it to run. The CPU context is switched from the application process to the dispatcher part of the scheduler.) The dispatcher selects one of the ready threads from the ready list and then allocates the CPU to that thread by performing another context switch from itself to the selected thread.

SAVING THE CONTEXT

Whenever the CPU is multiplexed, the "old" process is removed from the CPU and a "new" process is installed to begin using the CPU. Recall from Section 4.2 that the CPU contains various registers that hold data and status relevant to the currently executing process. When a process's execution is paused, the contents of all of the CPU registers must be saved in that process's descriptor so that just before the process resumes execution, those register contents can be copied back into the physical CPU registers (see Figure 7.3). Context switching can significantly affect performance, since modern computers have a lot of general and status registers to be saved. For example, most modern CPUs incorporate 32 or more 32- or 64-bit registers, plus status registers. The context switching part of the scheduler ordinarily uses conventional load and store operations to save the register contents. This means that each context switch requires

$$(n + m)b \times K \text{ time units}$$

to save the state of a processor with n general registers and m status registers, assuming b store operations are required to save a single register and each store instruction requires K time units. To make matters worse, at least two pairs (four total) of context switches occur whenever application processes are multiplexed. In the first pair, the original running process has its context saved by the OS and the dispatcher's context is then loaded. The second pair is for the dispatcher to be removed and the selected application process to be loaded onto the CPU.

✦ FIGURE 7.3 Context Switching

The context switch is the operation that saves one process's copy of information that it has stored in the CPU's registers, and writes the corresponding information for another process into the registers. Descriptors are used to hold a copy of the CPU registers while a process is not running.

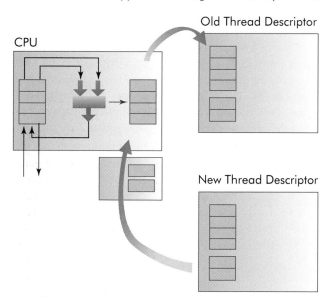

A processor might require 50 nanoseconds to store 1 unit of information in a contemporary memory (that is, $b \times K = 50$ ns). Suppose there is a 32-bit bus between the processor and the memory, and each register is 32 bits wide.

- Each register then requires 50 nanoseconds to store its contents.
- Now, if there are $n = 32$ general-purpose registers and $m = 8$ status registers, the total time to save registers is 40×50 nanoseconds, or 2 microseconds.
- Another 2 microseconds are required to restore the registers for another thread to execute (ignoring the time for the dispatcher to select another thread).

■ Of course, when the dispatcher must run between application threads, the context switch time is greater than 4 microseconds due to dispatcher context switch time and the time taken to select the next process.

A 1 GHz processor can execute a register instruction in about 2 nanoseconds. This means that during the 4 microseconds required for a context switch, the processor could have executed about 2,000 instructions doing useful work (as opposed to performing the overhead of a context switch). The cost of context switching is a significant factor in considering CPU multiplexing (scheduling) operations.

Some hardware systems incorporate two or more sets of processor registers to reduce the amount of context switching time. One set is used when the processor is in supervisor mode and the other set is for user mode threads. A context switch then can be reduced to the time to change a pointer to the current register set when moving back and forth between the OS and application code.

VOLUNTARY CPU SHARING

A key part of the scheduler's mechanism is the way the scheduler is invoked. The simplest approach is for the scheduler to assume that each process/thread will explicitly invoke the scheduler periodically, voluntarily sharing the CPU. Some hardware is designed to include a special `yield` machine instruction to allow a process to release the CPU. The `yield` instruction is similar to a procedure call instruction in that it saves the address of the next instruction to be executed and then branches to an arbitrary address. It differs from a procedure call instruction in that the address of the next instruction is not saved on the process's stack but in a designated memory location. Notice the similarity between the function of `yield` and the hardware action resulting from an interrupt (see Chapter 4).

✦ FIGURE 7.4 The `yield` Instruction

This machine instruction saves the contents of the PC in one memory location, `r`, and loads the PC from another location, `s`.

```
yield(r, s) {
  memory[r] = PC;
  PC = memory[s]
}
```

In Figure 7.4, when process p_1 executes `yield(r,s)`, the parameter `r` is an address that is determined as a function of p_1's identifier, usually an address in p_1's descriptor. Address `r` can be determined by knowing which process is currently running in the CPU, for example, by incorporating a process status register in the CPU. When a process is loaded, the content of the internal identifier field from the descriptor is placed in the process status register. The value of `r` can then be computed as a function of the register content, for example, by a table lookup operation. Hence,

r = f(p₁.identification) = f(process_status_register.identification)

Since the first parameter can be inferred from a CPU register, we will write `yield(*,s)` to represent the `yield` command.

The s parameter is similarly related to a process that will begin to run after the yield instruction has been executed. While p_1 is executing, but prior to the execution of yield, the contents of memory[r] are irrelevant. After yield has completed execution, memory[r] contains the address of the instruction following the yield and the PC has been set to resume execution of the thread p_2, where

```
s = f(p₂.identifier)
```

The CPU is switched from running the program that executes the yield to running another program whose last active PC value is stored at memory[s]. For example, suppose memory[s] contains the last PC value for p_2. When p_1 executes the yield instruction, it yields control of the CPU to p_2, which could then cooperate by executing yield(*, r) to restart p_1.

If more than two processes were ready to use the CPU, p_2 could behave as a scheduler by choosing some memory location, scheduler, that contains the entry point for p_2's program. Then it could have every thread execute yield(*, scheduler) when it releases the CPU (see Figure 7.5). When the scheduler runs as p_2, it would select some ready thread, p_i, where

```
s = f(pᵢ.identifier)
```

and then execute yield(*, s).

✦ FIGURE 7.5 Scheduling with the yield Instruction

Each application process/thread yields to a daemon process that runs the scheduler. When the scheduler begins to run (using its context from its process descriptor), it chooses the next process to receive the CPU, and then yields to that process.

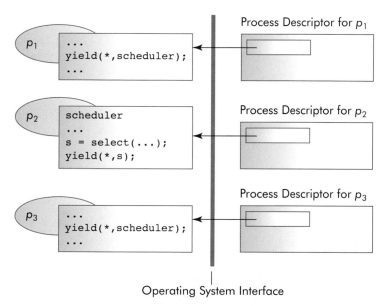

Operating System Interface

A scheduler that uses voluntary CPU sharing is called a **nonpreemptive scheduler**. In the remaining discussion, the `yield` instruction is assumed to be embedded in a system call named `yield()`. This cooperative form of multiprogramming was used in the Xerox Alto personal computer [Thacker et al., 1981]. Many of the Xerox developers went to work at Apple prior to the introduction of the Macintosh. The cooperating technique for scheduling was incorporated into earlier versions of the Macintosh operating systems.

Building a system that relies on the `yield` instruction poses a problem: Suppose the processes do not voluntarily cooperate with one another. The failure of a process to periodically execute a `yield` instruction blocks all other processes from using the processor until that process exits or requests a resource. This problem is especially serious if the running process happens to be executing an infinite loop containing no resource requests. The process will never give up the processor, so all ready processes will wait forever. This problem could be avoided entirely if the system itself could *interrupt* the running process periodically—that is, engage in involuntary sharing.

INVOLUNTARY CPU SHARING

The interrupt system can *force* periodic interruption of any process's execution; that is, it can force a thread to effectively execute a `yield` instruction. The trick is to incorporate an **interval timer** device, which produces an interrupt whenever the timer expires. An interval timer behaves like an egg timer. To use the timer, the system programmer chooses an interval of time, sets the device, and then proceeds with other processing. When the specified time interval has passed, the timer raises an interrupt.

The basic operation of the interval timer is summarized by the `IntervalTimer` procedure given in Figure 7.6. The interval timer hardware raises an interrupt each time a real-time clock ticks—for example, after T oscillations of a crystal on the interval timer device. Setting the `InterruptRequest` variable represents the timer hardware's setting the interrupt request flag. The effect is that every $K \times T$ oscillations of the crystal, the interrupt request flag will be set. The interval (K = number of ticks) is specified by the `SetInterval()` call shown in the figure, so it is called a **programmable interval timer**.

✦ **FIGURE 7.6** The Interval Timer

The `IntervalTimer()` algorithm represents the behavior of the interval timer device. It counts down K interrupts ("clock ticks"), and then it raises an interrupt. The `SetInterval()` represents a command that the driver can send to the device to "program" the interval of time between interrupts.

```
IntervalTimer(){
  InterruptCount = InterruptCount - 1;
  if(InterruptCount <= 0) {
    InterruptRequest = TRUE;
    InterruptCount = K}
  }
}

SetInterval(<programmableValue>) {
  K = <programmableValue>;
  InterruptCount = K;
}
```

An interrupt will occur every K clock ticks, thus causing the hardware clock's controller to invoke the interrupt handler. The device handler for the interrupt timer device calls the scheduler so that it can reschedule the processor without any action on the part of the running process. The scheduler is assured of being called at least once every K clock ticks.

A scheduler that uses involuntary CPU sharing is called a **preemptive scheduler**. Even if a particular process is executing an infinite loop, it cannot block other processes from running because the interrupt timer will periodically invoke the scheduler, which, in turn, will run other processes.

PERFORMANCE

The scheduler can have a dramatic effect on the performance of a multiprogrammed computer, since it determines when a process/thread is to be allocated the CPU. If the scheduler consistently selects a particular process whenever it becomes ready, the process will spend relatively little time in the ready list and tend to use the CPU whenever it needs it.

On the other hand, if the process tends to be neglected by the dispatcher, the amount of time it spends in the ready list waiting for the CPU to be allocated to it may be very large compared with the amount of CPU time it needs to complete its execution. As a result, the perceived performance will be very low, even if the hardware is very fast.

The aspect of performance related to how long a process has to wait once it becomes ready is determined by the scheduling policy and context switching time. Earlier in this section, you saw how context switching can be significant. However, policy-driven decisions tend to have even more impact on performance, because they can introduce unbounded amounts of wait time. We will see cases where this can happen when we look at a few different policies.

Analysts have studied schedulers a great deal over the last three decades for several reasons:

- Designers of multiprogramming operating systems knew the scheduler's behavior was critical to the performance from the individual thread's perspective.

- Designers also believed the scheduler's behavior might be critical to the overall behavior of the system.

- The methodologies used to study schedulers were well-entrenched in operations research.

- (Here is the cynical part ☺.) Schedulers were a nice theoretical computer science problem.

Here are several of the issues in policy design: In general, whenever a process becomes ready, there also will be other processes in the ready list. When the dispatcher selects a process to run on the processor, what criteria should it use to select from among the ready processes? If a process is continually ignored by the dispatcher, it may *never* receive the CPU time it needs to run to completion, a phenomenon called **starvation**. You have undoubtedly encountered starvation problems in many walks of life: For example, suppose you have a standby airline ticket. As long as there are premier frequent flyers who also want to fly standby, you are unlikely to get a seat on any flight.

The scheduling policy must define the criteria for choosing which process should be executed. The mechanisms described in this section are used to implement a policy chosen by the system administrator or system designer based on the way the computer is to be used. Some strategies favor predictable performance, others favor equitable sharing, and still others attempt to optimize performance for some particular class of threads. Performance determines the choice of strategy in each case. Let's now consider policies in more detail.

7.3 • STRATEGY SELECTION

The study of scheduling policies is a classic operating system research problem. During the 1980s and 1990s, it had lost some of its luster, but now it has once again become important in systems that support streaming media. This has happened because now applications need scheduling support that depends on real-time deadlines associated with, for example, video stream delivery.

SCHEDULER CHARACTERISTICS

CPU scheduling is remarkably similar to other types of scheduling that have been studied for years. The CPU can be thought of as a teller in a bank, and threads can be thought of as customers who need to interact with the teller to conduct banking business (deposits, withdrawals, loan payments, transfers, and so on). Some of the bank customers have complex transactions that take a long time, and others have short transactions that can be done in a couple of minutes. Bank administrators are interested in scheduling policy so they can determine how long a line can get before they have to add another teller, if tellers should be specialized to handle only deposits and withdrawals (but not other services), and so on.

What are the criteria for selecting a strategy?

- How can the scheduler be designed to allocate the CPU to competing processes to meet external goals?
- Should it allocate on the basis of an external priority?
- Should it attempt to allocate as equitably as possible?
- Should it attempt to give priority to threads having very short (or very long) execution times?

If the system is a real-time system, processes must be scheduled so that they meet very specific deadlines. If the OS is for a timesharing system, the criteria may focus on providing an equitable share of the processor per unit time to each user or thread or to minimize users' response times. The criteria for selecting a scheduling strategy will depend on the goals of the OS. These goals may emphasize priorities of processes, fairness, overall resource utilization, maximized throughput, average or maximum turnaround time, average or maximum response time, maximized system availability, and/or deadlines.

Scheduling algorithms for modern operating systems ultimately use internal priorities. The **internal priority** (or simply **priority**) for a process determines the rank order the dispatcher will use to select a process to execute when the CPU is available. It is possible to assign a priority to each thread so that it implements any of the general strategies mentioned in the previous paragraph. For example:

■ In an external priority scheme, each user is assigned a static priority number. When a process is created on behalf of the user, the process's threads use an internal priority that is a function of the **external priority** assigned to the user.

■ Priorities can be determined by dynamic circumstances such as the amount of time the thread has been waiting or the relative closeness of its deadline.

If the goal is to share the CPU equitably, then for every K time units in which n different processes are ready, each process should be allocated the CPU for approximately K/n time units. This can be accomplished by having a thread's priority increase the longer it waits, but decrease while it is using the CPU. Other ways to adjust the priority to reflect a strategy are discussed later in the chapter.

In systems that use involuntary CPU sharing, there is an additional degree of freedom in the strategy design. If the process manager uses an interval timer to control when multiplexing occurs, there is a known **time quantum**, or maximum—also called the **timeslice** length. The time quantum is the amount of time between interval timer interrupts (ignoring the scheduler overhead time), so it is determined by the size of the timer interval setting. A process's timeslice may be less than the maximum if the process requests a resource during its time quantum and releases the CPU. If this situation occurs, then the newly dispatched process will be allocated a full-time quantum, so it must be possible for the scheduler to reset the interrupt timer. Notice that there is no way to bound the amount of time any one process may continuously use the CPU if the hardware supports only voluntary multiplexing. Hence, these systems do not use the idea of a time quantum as part of the scheduling strategy.

Given a particular set of processes (with known amounts of processor time) in the ready queue, a preemptive scheduler, and a specific goal for scheduling, you can compute an **optimal schedule**, provided no new processes enter the ready list while those in the ready list are being served. The optimal algorithm computes the number of time quanta— the number of times the CPU will be allocated to each thread—and then enumerates all possible orders for scheduling the processor. The optimal strategy then can be selected, based on the optimality criteria, by systematically considering every ordering.

There are several unrealistic assumptions in this observation:

■ New processes *do* arrive while the current processes are being serviced, meaning the schedule has to be recomputed each time a new process becomes ready.

■ The actual running time of a process must be known before the process runs, although this is seldom possible.

■ The known algorithms for enumerating the schedule with n processes in the ready list are no better than $O(n^2)$ algorithms, meaning the scheduler might use more time computing the optimal schedule than it does for actually servicing threads.

A MODEL TO STUDY SCHEDULING

Before describing some representative scheduling algorithms, let's define a formal process model that we can use to describe scheduling policies. Let

$$P = \{p_i \mid 0 \le i < n\}$$

be a set of *modern processes*. In an implementation, each process, p_i, is represented by a descriptor that specifies a list of the threads, $\{p_{i,j}\}$, executing in the process, each of which contains a state field, $S(p_{i,j})$. The state can be running, ready, or blocked, so we say that $S(p_{i,j}) \in \{$running, ready, blocked$\}$.

Here are some commonly used performance metrics for comparing scheduling strategies:

- **Service time** $\tau(p_{i,j})$: The amount of time a thread needs to be in the running state before it is completed.

- **Wait time** $W(p_{i,j})$: The time the thread spends waiting in the ready state before its first transition to the running state.

- **Turnaround time** for thread $p_{i,j}$, $T_{TRnd}(p_{i,j})$: The amount of time between the moment a thread first enters the ready state and the moment the thread exits the running state for the last time.

In other words, the service time is the amount of time the thread will use the CPU to accomplish useful work. The wait time is the time the thread waits to receive its *first* unit of service from the processor. The turnaround time is the total time to complete a thread's execution after it has been made ready to execute.

The process model and the metrics are used to compare the performance characteristics of each algorithm. The general model must be tweaked to fit each specific class of OS environments. In a classic batch multiprogrammed system, the turnaround time is the most critical performance metric, since that time reflects the amount of time a user waits to get results from the computer. In this case, the system's average turnaround time specifies the average time to handle a single-threaded process (or job). The inverse of the average turnaround time is the system's **throughput rate** in jobs per minute. In batch systems, the *job* turnaround time is technically distinguished from the *thread* (or *classic process*) turnaround time by the time to do spooling, memory allocation, and scheduling. Since batch systems focus on jobs more than they do processes, the job turnaround time is the performance metric of most interest.

In timesharing systems, it is usually more meaningful to focus on a single phase of a thread's execution, such as the time to execute a command once a user requests that it be performed. For example, the time to execute a command can be broken down into its wait time (while the thread waits in the ready list) and its service time. An interactive user is most concerned with the amount of time required for the machine to give some kind of feedback, so the wait time—also called the **response time** in a timesharing system—is the performance metric of most interest.

Figure 7.1 indicates that an executing thread—a "job"—flows through various parts of the OS (the path of a thread from ready to running to blocked, back to ready, and so on). However, the scheduler typically ignores the details of resource management behavior, focusing only on the management of the ready list and CPU. So the model of operation that the scheduler uses is simplified as shown in Figure 7.7. This simpler model focuses only on the operations necessary to manage the thread when it is in the running or ready state. All the details of resource management are deferred to the resource managers. In this simplified model, whenever a thread first enters the ready list, it requests service from the CPU. The amount of service the thread is requesting is generally indefinite: The request is to execute until the thread explicitly yields the CPU, enters the blocked state (by virtue of a resource request), or completes execution. Analytically, the thread's entire execution sequence is partitioned into a sequence of "micro threads" that execute from the time the thread is created until it first becomes blocked, and then from each time it transitions from the blocked state into the ready state (see the boxed discussion for additional details).

✦ FIGURE 7.7 A Simpler Processor Scheduling Model

In the simplified model, resource management delays are ignored. This scheduling model focuses on the time analysis for dealing with continuous requests for CPU time.

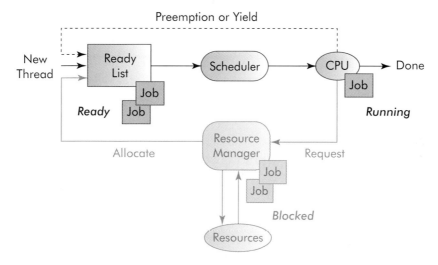

The dashed line from the CPU to the ready list in Figure 7.7 represents the case where a thread voluntarily yields the CPU, or the situation in which a thread is preempted by a timer interrupt. Preemptive algorithms are based on the notion of prioritized computation: The process with the highest priority should always be the one currently using the processor. If a process is currently using the processor and a new process with a higher priority enters the ready list, the thread using the processor should be removed and returned to the ready list until it is once again the highest-priority process in the system. Preemptive algorithms are normally associated with systems that use interrupts to force involuntary CPU sharing, while nonpreemptive algorithms are consistent with voluntary CPU sharing.

Partitioning a Process into Small Processes

Suppose a thread, $p_{i,j}$, intersperses computation and resource (including I/O) requests so that it has k different times that it needs the processor and k different times that it requests resources. Then we can think of $p_{i,j}$ as being decomposed into k smaller "micro threads," $p_{i,j,1}, p_{i,j,2}, ..., p_{i,j,k}$, where τ_{ijl} is the service time for p_{ijl}. Each p_{ijl} is intended to be executed as uninterrupted processing by the original thread $p_{i,j}$, even though a preemptive scheduler will divide each τ_{ijl} into time quanta when it schedules p_{ijl}. Now the total service time for thread $p_{i,j}$ can be written as

$$\tau(p_{i,j}) = \tau_{i,j,1} + \tau_{i,j,2} + ... + \tau_{i,j,k}$$

Recall the discussion of compute-bound and I/O-bound processes in Chapter 5. Here is a more precise discussion of that characterization: If a thread requests k different I/O operations, the result is k service time requests, $\tau_{i,j,1}$, interspersed with

$$d_{i,j,1}, d_{i,j,2}, ..., d_{i,j,k}$$

times to represent the time to accomplish device I/O. Thus, the total amount of time that the process requests CPU service plus I/O service is

$$\tau_{i,j,1} + d_{i,j,1} + \tau_{i,j,2} + d_{i,j,2}, + ... + \tau_{i,j,k} + d_{i,j,k}$$

A compute-bound process has relatively large values of $\tau_{i,j,1}$ compared to the values for the $d_{i,j,1}$, although each $\tau_{i,j,1}$ can be expected to have a different value than the other $\tau_{i,j,1}$ values. In an I/O-bound process, the $\tau_{i,j,1}$ values are small compared to the $d_{i,j,1}$ values.

7.4 • NONPREEMPTIVE STRATEGIES

Nonpreemptive scheduling algorithms allow any process/thread to run to "completion" once it has been allocated the processor. That is, in systems using a nonpreemptive scheduling algorithm, there is no preemption path from the CPU back to the ready list (the dashed line in Figure 7.7). Once a process is allocated the CPU, it uses the CPU until it has completed the logical task. It then releases the CPU to the scheduler.

Nonpreemptive algorithms are borrowed from classic operations research that studies how to schedule work in human-oriented systems. The concern in these systems is to determine how people should be scheduled for service in a bank, airport, or supermarket. Once a human begins receiving service in these systems, the full task is completed without switching to another person's task. This approach is natural to use in process management because it is intuitive. It also applies to systems that use voluntary mechanisms to invoke the scheduler. Each time a thread is allocated the CPU, it will retain it until it has completed the logical task and it decides to release the CPU to another thread.

Approximating System Load

Different scheduling algorithms use a variety of criteria for selecting a thread from the ready list, depending on the performance goals of the system. To assess the likely effects of these criteria, a designer is faced with two choices:

- Analyze a given algorithm and a hypothetical service load and predict the performance of each algorithm.

- Consider a specific real load and simply report the behavior of the algorithm under that load.

The primary goal in this book is to consider strategies for scheduling rather than to engage in an intensive study of performance prediction. Even so, performance must be considered when comparing different algorithms. You can observe the performance by looking at performance metrics such as average values and probability distributions.

The model of operation shown in Figure 7.7 can be used to *predict* one aspect of performance under a specified load. The load can be characterized by specifying the arrival rate of new threads into the ready list and the service times, $\tau(p_i)$. Let λ represent the *mean arrival rate* of new processes into the ready list (the rate in processes per time unit at which processes enter the ready list, where $1/\lambda$ is the *mean time between arrivals*). Let μ represent the *mean service rate* (where $1/\mu$ is the mean value of the $\tau(p_i)$). If we ignore context switching time and assume that the CPU has sufficient capacity to service the load, the fraction of time the CPU is busy, ρ, can be expressed by

$$\rho = \lambda \times 1/\mu = \lambda/\mu.$$

If the arrival rate, λ, is greater than the service rate, μ ($\lambda > \mu$, meaning $\rho > 1$), the CPU will be saturated (it will always have more work than it is able to do) independent of the scheduling algorithm employed in the system. In time, any finite-length ready list will overflow, since processes arrive at a higher rate than they can be serviced. Systems can reach a steady state only if $\lambda < \mu$ ($\rho < 1$). Systems operating under conditions where $\rho \rightarrow 1$ require arbitrarily large ready lists, so such conditions are also going to be a problem for long-term operation of the system.

For example, suppose threads arrive in a system at a rate of 10 threads per minute (meaning $\lambda = 10$ threads per minute) and the average service time for each thread is 3 seconds (meaning that $1/\mu = 3/60 = 1/20$ minutes per thread, or $\mu = 20$ threads per minute). The system load will be

$$\rho = \lambda / \mu$$
$$= 10 \text{ processes per minute}/20 \text{ processes per minute}$$
$$= 0.5$$
$$= 50\%.$$

FIRST-COME-FIRST-SERVED

The **first-come-first-served** (**FCFS**) scheduling strategy assigns priority to threads in the order in which they request the processor. The priority of a thread is computed by the enqueuer by timestamping all incoming processes and then having the dispatcher select the thread that has the earliest timestamp. Alternatively, the ready list can be organized as a simple FIFO data structure (where each entry points to a thread descriptor). The enqueuer adds threads to the tail of the queue, and the dispatcher removes threads from the head of the queue.

While the FCFS algorithm is easy to implement, it ignores the service time request and all other criteria that may influence the performance with respect to turnaround or waiting time. FCFS generally does not perform well under any specific set of system requirements, so it is not often used.

Let's consider a practical example of FCFS scheduling and then examine some performance metrics. Suppose there are five threads in the ready list, as shown in Table 7.1. Further assume they entered the ready list in the order p_0, p_1, p_2, p_3, and finally p_4. FCFS will schedule the threads as shown in Figure 7.8.

TABLE 7.1 An Example Load

i	$\tau(p_i)$
0	350
1	125
2	475
3	250
4	75

✦ FIGURE 7.8 FCFS Schedule

In the FCFS algorithm, processes are scheduled in the order in which they arrived. In this case, the scheduler will assign the CPU to p_0, then p_1, p_2, p_3, and then p_4.

We can determine each thread's turnaround time by observing the FCFS schedule in the Gantt chart shown in Figure 7.8:

$$T_{TRnd}(p_0) = \tau(p_0) = 350$$
$$T_{TRnd}(p_1) = (\tau(p_1) + T_{TRnd}(p_0)) = 125 + 350 = 475$$
$$T_{TRnd}(p_2) = (\tau(p_2) + T_{TRnd}(p_1)) = 475 + 475 = 950$$
$$T_{TRnd}(p_3) = (\tau(p_3) + T_{TRnd}(p_2)) = 250 + 950 = 1200$$
$$T_{TRnd}(p_4) = (\tau(p_4) + T_{TRnd}(p_3)) = 75 + 1200 = 1275$$

Therefore the average turnaround time is

$$T_{TRnd} = (350 + 475 + 950 + 1200 + 1275)/5 = 4250/5 = 850.$$

From the Gantt chart, we determine the waiting times to be

$$W(p_0) = 0$$
$$W(p_1) = T_{TRnd}(p_0) = 350$$
$$W(p_2) = T_{TRnd}(p_1) = 475$$
$$W(p_3) = T_{TRnd}(p_2) = 950$$
$$W(p_4) = T_{TRnd}(p_3) = 1200$$

So the average wait time is

$$W = (0 + 350 + 475 + 950 + 1200)/5 = 2975/5 = 595.$$

Predicting Wait Times for FCFS

You can also *predict* a thread's wait time in a system that uses FCFS scheduling. Suppose you know the service rate, μ. Let L be the length of the queue at the time thread p arrives. You can then estimate how much time that the new thread, p, will have to wait before it begins to receive service:

$$W(p) = L(1/\mu) + 1/2(1/\mu) = L/\mu + 1/(2\mu).$$

Here is the rationale for this expression: Since each of the L jobs in the queue uses an average of $1/\mu$ time units for service, $L(1/\mu)$ is the expected amount of time for all L of them to be processed. The average time for the process that is already using the CPU is half of its service time, or $1/2(1/\mu)$. According to the FCFS policy, only the load that is present when thread p arrives is relevant, since any subsequent threads will be served after thread p.

In the example, we could estimate $W(p_4)$, which is 1200 in the Gantt chart, by computing the average service time ($1/\lambda$ or average of the τ values) of the first four processes:

$$\tau = (350 + 125 + 475 + 250)/4$$
$$= 1200/4$$
$$= 300 \text{ time units.}$$

When p_4 arrives, $L = 3$; the estimated waiting time for p_4 is thus

$$W(p_4) = L/\mu + 1/(2\mu)$$
$$= 3/(1/300) + 150$$
$$= 1050.$$

SHORTEST JOB NEXT

Suppose the service time of all threads is known ahead of time—an unusual situation. The **shortest job next** (**SJN**) (also known as *shortest job first* or SJF) scheduling algorithm chooses the thread requiring minimum service time as the highest-priority job. You can see that turnaround time for p_i is the sum of all of the service times of threads in the ready list that have lower service times than does p_i, since they will all be scheduled before p_i.

SJN minimizes the average wait time because it services small threads before it services large ones. However, even though it minimizes average wait time, it may penalize threads with high service time requests. If the ready list is saturated, then threads with large service times tend to be left in the ready list while small threads receive service. In the extreme case, where the system has little idle time, threads with large service times will never be served. This starvation of large threads can be a serious liability of the scheduling algorithm.

Again suppose the ready list contains the threads shown in Table 7.1. The arrival order is irrelevant here, provided all of the threads are already in the queue at the time a job is dispatched. In this example, assume no other jobs (processes/threads) arrive during the servicing of all the jobs in the ready list. SJN will produce the schedule shown in

Figure 7.9. Since $\tau(p_4) = 75$ is the smallest service time, p_4 is scheduled first; since $\tau(p_1)$ = 125, p_1 is next to be scheduled; and so on

✦ FIGURE 7.9 SJN Schedule

In the SJN algorithm, processes are scheduled in the order of their service (execution) time. Since p_4 has the smallest service time (75), it is scheduled first. Next the SJN scheduler will assign p_1 to the CPU since its service time is the smallest of the remaining jobs.

From the Gantt chart, we compute the following:

$$T_{TRnd}(p_0) = \tau(p_0) + \tau(p_3) + \tau(p_1) + \tau(p_4) = 350 + 250 + 125 + 75 = 800$$
$$T_{TRnd}(p_1) = \tau(p_1) + \tau(p_4) = 125 + 75 = 200$$
$$T_{TRnd}(p_2) = \tau(p_2) + \tau(p_0) + \tau(p_3) + \tau(p_1) + \tau(p_4) = 475 + 350 + 250 + 125 + 75$$
$$= 1275$$
$$T_{TRnd}(p_3) = \tau(p_3) + \tau(p_1) + \tau(p_4) = 250 + 125 + 75 = 450$$
$$T_{TRnd}(p_4) = \tau(p_4) = 75$$

Therefore, the average turnaround time is

$$T_{TRnd} = (800 + 200 + 1275 + 450 + 75)/5 = 2800/5 = 560.$$

We determine the wait times to be

$$W(p_0) = 450$$
$$W(p_1) = 75$$
$$W(p_2) = 800$$
$$W(p_3) = 200$$
$$W(p_4) = 0.$$

So the average wait time is

$$W = (450 + 75 + 800 + 200 + 0)/5 = 1525/5 = 305.$$

Suppose an SJN scheduling policy controls CPU allocation, where $\rho = 1 - \varepsilon$ for some very small value ε. As new processes arrive that have service times near the mean service time, $1/\mu$, those few processes with very large service times (much larger than the mean) will be passed over for the new jobs with a lower priority. Since the CPU utilization is very high, there will tend to be multiple processes in the ready list all the time. As a result, the processes with very large service time requests will starve, even though $\rho = l/\mu < 1$.

PRIORITY SCHEDULING

In **priority scheduling**, process/threads are allocated to the CPU on the basis of an externally assigned priority. (In this explanation, lower numbers have higher priority. Some schedulers use the opposite ordering.) A process's external priority is determined from the user identification ("important people have high priorities"), the nature of the task ("a process turns on a heater when the temperature falls below a threshold value"), or any other arbitrary criteria.

Priority scheduling policies often use *static priorities*, meaning that the priority for a thread is computed once, and then never changes. A more sophisticated approach is to use a *dynamic priority* that allows the thread to become more or less important depending on how much service it has recently received.

As in SJN, static priority scheduling may cause low-priority threads to starve. This starvation can be addressed by using dynamic priorities: Suppose one parameter in the priority assignment function is the amount of time the process has been waiting. The longer a thread waits, the higher its priority (the lower its priority number) becomes. This strategy can be used to eliminate the starvation problem.

Table 7.2 describes a thread load (the same as the load in Table 7.1, but with priorities added to each process). Priority scheduling will produce the schedule shown in Figure 7.10.

TABLE 7.2 An Example Load with Static Priority

i	$\tau(p_i)$	Priority
0	350	5
1	125	2
2	475	3
3	250	1
4	075	4

✦ **FIGURE 7.10** Priority Scheduling

In the priority scheduling algorithm, processes are scheduled based on the order of their static priority . Since p_3 has priority 1 (the highest priority), it is scheduled first. Next, the scheduler will assign p_1 to the CPU since its priority is the highest of the remaining jobs.

We compute

$$T_{TRnd}(p_0) = \tau(p_0) + \tau(p_4) + \tau(p_2) + \tau(p_1) + \tau(p_3) = 350 + 75 + 475 + 125 + 250$$
$$= 1275$$

$$T_{TRnd}(p_1) = \tau(p_1) + \tau(p_3) = 125 + 250 = 375$$
$$T_{TRnd}(p_2) = \tau(p_2) + \tau(p_1) + \tau(p_3) = 475 + 125 + 250 = 850$$
$$T_{TRnd}(p_3) = \tau(p_3) = 250$$
$$T_{TRnd}(p_4) = \tau(p_4) + \tau(p_2) + \tau(p_1) + \tau(p_3) = 75 + 475 + 125 + 250 = 925$$

Therefore, the average turnaround time is

$$T_{TRnd} = (1275 + 375 + 850 + 250 + 925)/5 = 3675/5 = 735.$$

We determine the wait times to be

$$W(p_0) = 925$$
$$W(p_1) = 250$$
$$W(p_2) = 375$$
$$W(p_3) = 0$$
$$W(p_4) = 850.$$

So the average wait time is

$$W = (925 + 250 + 375 + 0 + 850)/5 = 2400/5 = 480.$$

DEADLINE SCHEDULING

Hard real-time systems are often characterized as having certain threads that *must* complete execution prior to some time deadline. The critical performance measure is whether the system will be able to meet all such threads' scheduling deadlines. Measures of turnaround and wait time are generally irrelevant. As a result, these schedulers require complete knowledge of the maximum service time for each process. In *periodic scheduling*, a thread has a recurring service time and deadline, so the deadline must be met for each period in the process's life. A process can be *admitted* to the ready list only if the scheduler can guarantee that it will be able to supply the specified service time before each deadline imposed by all processes.

For example, in streaming media systems, the deadline is required to prevent jitter (irregular delivery of information) and latency (delay) in the audio or video processing. In process control systems, the deadline may be established by the requirements for reading an external sensor.

Suppose our sample set of threads contained deadlines such as those shown in Table 7.3. There may be several different schedules satisfying the deadline. See Figure 7.11 for three such schedules. The middle schedule is an example of a strategy known as the *earliest deadline first scheduling*, an optimal algorithm for certain types of deadline scheduling.

TABLE 7.3 An Example Load with Deadlines

i	$\tau(p_i)$	Deadline
0	350	575
1	125	550
2	475	1050
3	250	(none)
4	75	200

✦ FIGURE 7.11 Possible Schedules Using Deadline Scheduling

In deadline scheduling, processes are scheduled so that each meets its deadline. Here are three different schedules that each meet every process's deadlines. The middle schedule is an example of earliest deadline first scheduling.

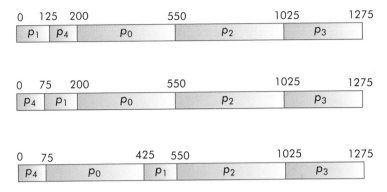

7.5 • PREEMPTIVE STRATEGIES

In **preemptive scheduling** algorithms, the highest-priority thread is allocated the CPU. All lower-priority threads are made to yield to the highest-priority thread whenever it requests the CPU. Whenever the OS changes a thread's state to ready, it can immediately interrupt the thread currently using the CPU if it has higher priority than the one using the CPU. That is, the scheduler is called by some other part of the OS each time a thread enters the ready state. It is also started each time the interval timer expires and a time quantum has elapsed.

Preemptive strategies are sometimes used to ensure quick response to high-priority threads or to ensure fair sharing of the CPU among all threads. Nonpreemptive SJN and priority scheduling have already been described. There are also preemptive versions of these algorithms. The preemptive versions differ from the nonpreemptive versions by keeping the highest-priority job in the running state at all times.

In SJN, the thread with the smallest service time request is allocated the CPU. If p_i is executing and is preempted by the arrival of another process, p_j, then SJN need only compare $\tau(p_i)$ and $\tau(p_j)$. This is because p_i is guaranteed to have the smallest service time request of any ready process when p_j arrives. For example, suppose the processor is using preemptive SJN and is operating on process p_1 (after having processed p_4) in the thread load shown in Table 7.1. If a new thread arrives with a service time of 35 and p_1 has more than 35 time units remaining on its service time request, it will be preempted and the new thread will be dispatched.

Similarly, assume a processor is operating with preemptive priority scheduling on the load shown in Table 7.2. If it is currently executing p_2 (after having executed p_3 and p_1) and a thread arrives with a priority of 2, it will cause p_2 to be returned to the ready list while the new thread uses the processor.

The discussion of nonpreemptive algorithms ignored the cost of context switching among processes, since the assumption is that a process completes a unit of work without being interrupted. In preemptive algorithms, whenever an interrupt occurs, the previously running process may be replaced by a new, higher-priority thread. This means that preemptive systems tend to have many more context switches (and more overhead) than nonpreemptive systems.

The next two sections describe a few scheduling algorithms developed especially for preemptive environments.

ROUND ROBIN

Round-robin (RR) scheduling is the most widely used of all of the scheduling algorithms. The goal of RR is equitable distribution of the processing time among all processes/threads requesting the processor. This distribution will tend to fit in with the general interactive multiprogramming philosophy in which each of n threads receives approximately $1/n$ time units of processing time for every real-time unit. (This is an approximation, since the cost of scheduling and context switching must also be factored into the real-time unit.) More precisely, suppose the CPU is idle and n arbitrary processes $\{p_i \mid 0 \le i < n\}$ are all ready to run. Also (for notational convenience) the processes appear in the ready list in the same order as their index—that is, p_i appears before p_j if $i < j$. The processor will be allocated to p_0, then p_1, then p_2, ... to p_{n-1}, then back to p_0, and so on.

There are a few options in implementing RR scheduling. If the processor finishes serving a process prior to the expiration of the time quantum, the next process receives a new time quantum (instead of just finishing the old one). When a new process arrives, it is placed in the ready list. However, its exact location in the list depends on another implementation option. If the ready list is implemented as a ring-linked list, the new process is placed in the ring immediately behind the last process to be executed so that the other $n-1$ processes receive service before the new process does. Still another option is to implement the ready list as a queue and then have the dispatcher enqueue entries in order. The new process is placed at the end of the queue independent of which process is being executed at the time it arrives. The new process will wait an average of $n/2$ timeslices before it is allocated the CPU.

Consider the effect of context switching time on RR scheduling. Let C be the time to perform a context switch between user processes (often people assume that C is small enough that it can be ignored). Each of the n processes will receive q units of time on the CPU for every $n(q+C)$ units of real time.

A system with a timer interrupt naturally fits with RR scheduling, since the interrupt interval can be set to the desired time quantum. The timer interrupt handler calls the scheduler whenever it is invoked. When a process completes, it is deleted from the ready list, and when a new process starts, it is entered into the ready list using the implementation option described in the previous paragraph.

Blocked processes can become ready processes any time a (different) executing process releases resources. When the resource manager is called with a release operation, it allocates newly available resources to one or more blocked processes, changes the state of those processes to ready, and places them in the ready list. The original process continues executing for the duration of its timeslice.

When the timer interrupt occurs, the executing process's time quantum has completed. Therefore, the scheduler removes the running process from the CPU. The scheduler then adjusts the ready list according to the implementation, resets the timer, and dispatches the process at the head of the ready list to the CPU.

Suppose the ready list contained the processes shown in Table 7.1 and the time quantum is 50, with a negligible amount of time for context switching. The Gantt chart describing the resulting schedule is shown in Figure 7.12.

✦ FIGURE 7.12 RR Schedule with a Time Quantum of 50

RR scheduling uses the programmable interval timer to periodically multiplex the CPU. In this example, the timer interrupt occurs every 50 units of time. The processes receive 50 units of time (or less if they do not need the full time quantum) at a time.

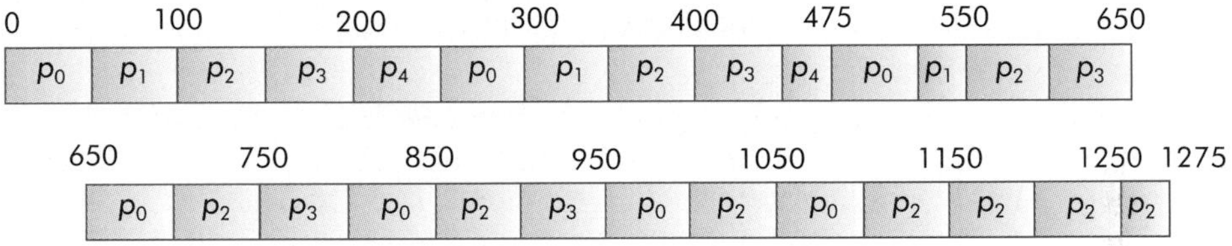

The turnaround times (derived from the Gantt chart) are

$$T_{TRnd}(p_0) = 1100$$
$$T_{TRnd}(p_1) = 550$$
$$T_{TRnd}(p_2) = 1275$$
$$T_{TRnd}(p_3) = 950$$
$$T_{TRnd}(p_4) = 475$$

Therefore, the average turnaround time is

$$T_{TRnd} = (1100 + 550 + 1275 + 950 + 475)/5 = 4350/5 = 870.$$

From the Gantt chart, we determine the wait times (the time until the thread first acquires the processor) to be

$$W(p_0) = 0$$
$$W(p_1) = 50$$
$$W(p_2) = 100$$
$$W(p_3) = 150$$
$$W(p_4) = 200.$$

So the average wait time is

$$W = (0 + 50 + 100 + 150 + 200)/5 = 500/5 = 100.$$

The wait times illustrate the obvious benefit of RR (and other algorithms based on time quanta) in terms of how quickly a thread begins to receive service. However, the average turnaround time does not differ significantly from that produced by the nonpreemptive algorithms.

Now reconsider the example in which context switching time is included. Suppose the scheduling overhead (context switches plus scheduler execution) is 10 units of time (see Figure 7.13). The turnaround times (derived from the Gantt chart) are

$$T_{TRnd}(p_0) = 1320$$
$$T_{TRnd}(p_1) = 660$$
$$T_{TRnd}(p_2) = 1535$$
$$T_{TRnd}(p_3) = 1140$$
$$T_{TRnd}(p_4) = 565.$$

Therefore, the average turnaround time is

$$T_{TRnd} = (1320 + 660 + 1535 + 1140 + 565)/5 = 5220/5 = 1044.$$

From the Gantt chart, we determine the waiting times to be

$$W(p_0) = 0$$
$$W(p_1) = 60$$
$$W(p_2) = 120$$
$$W(p_3) = 180$$
$$W(p_4) = 240.$$

So the average wait time is

$$W = (0 + 60 + 120 + 180 + 240)/5 = 600/5 = 120.$$

✦ FIGURE 7.13 RR Schedule with Scheduling Overhead

When the time for scheduling overhead is taken into account, an incremental amount of overhead time—in this case 10 units of time per scheduling operation—is inserted between adjacent time quanta . You can see that the overhead can be a serious performance barrier, depending on its size.

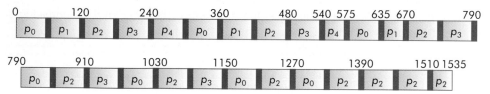

MULTIPLE-LEVEL QUEUES

Multiple-level queues are an extension of priority scheduling in which all processes of the same priority are placed in a single pool. The scheduler allocates the CPU across processes in priority pools using one strategy and allocates the CPU to threads in the same queue according to a second strategy. In the simplest case, suppose that the ready list is partitioned into J smaller ready sublists, where all processes have some priority between 1 and J. Process p_i is in ready sublist k if it has a priority of k. If we assume preemptive priority scheduling for the cross-queue strategy, then all processes in ready sublist 1 will be completed before any process is run from ready sublists 2 through J, and so on. Within sublist k, the CPU may be allocated using any strategy.

There are many variants of the strategy for distributing the CPU time across the queues. For example, you could give the fraction 2^{-j} of the time to threads in the sublist j (saving a fraction of the time for various overhead functions). In this case, during 100 seconds of real time (ignoring overhead), 50 seconds would be distributed among the processes in sublist 1, 25 seconds to the processes in sublist 2, 12.5 seconds to the processes in sublist 3, and so on.

Each of these more sophisticated scheduling algorithms increases the time to multiplex the CPU, so the most often-used scheduling algorithms for timesharing systems are simple forms of multiple-level queues, usually incorporating RR schedulers within a level.

FOREGROUND AND BACKGROUND PROCESSES Timesharing systems often support the idea of **foreground** and **background** threads. Foreground threads service an interactive user, while background threads are intended to run whenever no foreground thread requires the CPU. There is a high-priority foreground ready sublist and a low-priority background ready sublist. Any foreground job takes precedence over all background jobs.

It is easy to imagine a number of different strategies that follow the foreground/background rationale. For example, interrupt handler threads might run at priority 1, device drivers at priority 2, interactive processing jobs at priority 3, interactive editing jobs at priority 4, normal batch jobs at priority 5, and "long" batch jobs at priority 6. Of course, such a choice suggests processes might dynamically change priority levels during execution, depending on the phase of computation they are currently executing. For example, if an interactive editing process became a computation-intensive process, its priority might be dropped to a lower level, since it is attempting to use an extra share of the CPU. The dual strategy is to increase the priority to a higher level during computation-intensive phases, with the rationale that the user needs a larger share of the CPU to sustain acceptable service. A system that allows threads to change ready sublists is called a **multiple-level feedback queue**.

7.6 ● IMPLEMENTING THE SCHEDULER

The scheduler part of the process manager incorporates the logical mechanisms shown in Figure 7.2. However, the scheduler implementation will probably not reflect the structure shown in the figure because of the context in which the scheduler executes as well as the desire to make the scheduler software as efficient as possible. If you browse the source code for an OS, you will probably be able to identify the dispatcher, although it may be harder to find the code that implements the enqueuer, context switcher, and more detailed components of the overall mechanism. In order to go to a more detailed level of understanding than appears here, you will have to focus on a specific OS.

Logically speaking, the OS incorporates three functions to perform the tasks shown in Figure 7.2. The enqueuer part of the scheduler is invoked whenever a thread transitions into the ready state—a transition that is caused by either the completion of an I/O operation or the explicit action of the running thread (or one of the running threads in a multiprocessor system). In an interrupt-driven system, the I/O completion causes an interrupt; thus, the interrupt handler for each I/O device should determine which (if any) thread became ready as a consequence of the I/O completion. The I/O handler can then change the corresponding thread's state from blocked to ready (and place the thread in the ready list). Another situation that can cause a thread to become ready is that it is blocked on a pending event (such as waiting for a resource to become allocated). When the event occurs, then the OS can transition the blocked thread to the running state. After any thread has been added to the ready list, the dispatcher should be called to ensure that the highest-priority ready task will be assigned the CPU.

The OS will normally include a function that saves the internal CPU state (see Figure 6.7). This is the crucial part of the context switcher code, yet it is also an important part of the system call and interrupt handler code. That is, the CPU state save function is called whenever the OS needs to move into action, since it saves the state of the process that was running prior to the OS beginning to run. In most operating systems, this only occurs with a system call or an interrupt.

The OS dispatcher function is the heart of the scheduler, since it is called whenever a new process is to be allocated the CPU. In a voluntary scheduling mechanism, the dispatcher is called by the `yield()` system call. In a system with an involuntary scheduling mechanism, the dispatcher is invoked by the interval timer device handler. Systems that use voluntary schedulers do not normally support interrupts; if they did support interrupts, they would normally have an interval timer that would support an involuntary scheduling mechanism.

The dispatcher is also called as a side effect of various system calls. For example, if the OS decides that it must block a process after it makes a system call, for example, because it cannot fulfill a resource request, then that system call code will call the dispatcher to run a different process. In interrupt-driven schedulers, the dispatcher may be invoked after the interrupt/device handler addresses the interrupt. In our remaining discussion of the implementation, we will assume interrupt-driven schedulers, since they also incorporate all the functionality of a voluntary mechanism.

When the dispatcher runs, the CPU is switched to supervisor mode, the running process CPU state (the context) is saved, and OS code begins to run. The CPU then begins to execute the specific OS code associated with the system call or interrupt. When the OS code (either a system call or a device interrupt handler) has completed, the dispatcher is called. The dispatcher code implements the system's chosen scheduling policy to select a ready thread from the ready list. If there are no ready threads, the dispatcher will run an idle thread until an interrupt occurs. Once the user thread is selected, its state is changed to running, and the CPU context is restored from the process descriptor, thereby resuming the thread.

The Linux Scheduling Mechanism

In the Version 1.0.9 Linux scheduler (a very early version of Linux), the dispatcher is a kernel function, `schedule()`. This function gets called from other system functions, as well as after every system call and normal interrupt. Each time the dispatcher is called, it performs periodic work (such as processing pending signals), inspects the set of tasks in the TASK_RUNNING state (the ready list), chooses one to execute according to the scheduling policy, and then dispatches the task to run on the CPU until an interrupt occurs.

The policy is a variant of RR scheduling. It uses the conventional timeslicing mechanism to place an upper bound on the amount of time a task can use the CPU continuously if other tasks are waiting to use it. A dynamic priority is computed on the basis of the value assigned to the task by the nice() or setpriority() system calls, and by the amount of time that a process has been waiting for the CPU to become available. The counter field in the task descriptor becomes the key component in determining the dynamic priority of the task—it is adjusted on each timer interrupt (when the interrupt handler adjusts each timer field for the task). The dispatcher selects the ready task with the maximum counter value.

The following annotated code fragment is taken from the Linux Version 1.0.9 source code. It represents the main flow of the scheduler, although the alarm handling and debugging code have been removed. C++ style annotations have been added for this explanation and do not appear in the Linux source code.

```
/*
 * ...
 * NOTE!! Task 0 is the 'idle' task, which gets called when no
 * other tasks can run. It cannot be killed, and it cannot
 * sleep. The 'state' information in task[0] is never used.
 *
 * ...
 */
asmlinkage void schedule(void)
{
  int c;
  struct task_struct * p;  // Pointer to the process descriptor
                           // currently being inspected
  struct task_struct * next;
  unsigned long ticks;
/* check alarm, wake up any interruptible tasks that have got a
 * signal
 */
  ... // This code is elided from the description
/* this is the scheduler proper: */
#if 0
  /* give processes that go to sleep a bit higher priority.. */
  /* This depends on the values for TASK_XXX */
  /* This gives smoother scheduling for some things, but */
  /* can be very unfair under some circumstances, so.. */
  if (TASK_UNINTERRUPTIBLE >= (unsigned) current->state &&
    current->counter < current->priority*2) {
      ++current->counter;
  }
#endif
  c = -1;    // Choose the task with the highest
             // c == p->counter value
  next = p = &init_task;
  for (;;) {
```

```
      if ((p = p->next_task) == &init_task)
        goto confuse_gcc;              // This is the loop exit
    if (p->state == TASK_RUNNING && p->counter > c)
      c = p->counter, next = p;    // This task has the highest
                                   // p->count so far, but keep
                                   // looking
    }
confuse_gcc:
  if (!c) {
    for_each_task(p)
      p->counter = (p->counter >> 1) + p->priority;
  }
  if(current != next)
    kstat.context_swtch++;
  switch_to(next);                 // This is the context switch
  ... // This code is elided from the description
  };
}
```

BSD UNIX Scheduling Policy

BSD UNIX uses a multiple-level feedback queue approach, with 32 run queues [McKusick, et al., 1996]. System processes use run queues 0 through 7, and processes executing in user space are placed in run queues 8 through 31. The dispatcher selects a process from the high-priority run queue whenever it allocates the CPU. Within a queue, BSD UNIX uses RR scheduling: Only processes in the highest-priority, non-empty run queue can execute. Time quanta vary among implementations, but all are less than 100 microseconds.

Every process has an external `nice()` priority used to influence, but not solely determine, the run queue in which the process will be placed when it is ready. The `nice()` priority has a default value of 0, but it can be changed with the `nice()` system call. The `nice()` priority can vary between –20 and 20, where –20 is the highest-priority user and 20 is the lowest. Approximately once per time quantum, the scheduler recomputes each process's current priority as a function of the `nice` priority and the recent demand on the CPU by the process (more utilization means a lower priority).

The dispatcher is called by the same events in the BSD kernel as in Linux: The `sleep()` routine causes the same effect as our hypothetical `yield()` function. When a process calls `sleep()`, the scheduler is called to dispatch a new process. The scheduler is also called as a result of a trap instruction execution or the occurrence of an interrupt.

Windows NT/2000/XP Thread Scheduling

The Windows NT/2000/XP thread scheduler is also a multiple-level feedback scheduler that attempts to provide very high levels of service to threads that need very rapid response. A time quantum uses programmable interval times (for example, a time quantum might be three ticks of the host system's clock). On most Windows NT/2000/XP machines, the time quantum ranges between about 20 to 200 milliseconds (ms). Servers are configured to have time quanta that are six times longer than workstations with the same processor type because servers are assumed to have significant computation-intensive bursts as a result of client requests.

The scheduler supports 32 different scheduling levels. The 16 highest-priority queues are called *real-time level queues*, the next 15 higher-priority queues are called *variable level queues*, and the lowest-priority queue is called the *system level queue*. The scheduler attempts to limit the number of threads that are entered into the real-time queues, increasing the probability that there will be little competition among threads that execute at these high-priority levels. However, Windows NT/2000/XP is not a real-time system and cannot *guarantee* that threads running at high priority will receive the processor before any fixed deadline. The highest-level queue processing continues through the variable level queues, down to the system level queue. The system level queue contains a single "zero page thread" that corresponds to the idle thread. That is, when there are no runnable threads in the entire system, it executes the zero page thread until an interrupt occurs and another thread becomes runnable. The zero page thread is the single lowest-priority thread in the system, so it runs whenever there are no other runnable threads.

The scheduler is *fully preemptive*: Whenever a thread becomes ready to run, it is placed in a run queue at a level corresponding to its current priority. If there is another thread in execution at that time and that thread has a lower priority, then the lower-priority thread is interrupted (it is not allowed to finish its time quantum) and the new higher-priority thread is assigned the processor. In a single processor system, this would mean that a thread could cause itself to be removed from the processor by enabling a higher-priority thread. In a multiple processor system, the situation can be more subtle: Suppose that in a two-processor system, one processor is running a thread at priority 4 (it would be in queue number 32–4 = 28) and the other is running a thread at priority 10. If the priority 4 thread performs some action that causes a previously blocked thread to suddenly become runnable at priority 6, then the priority 10 thread will be halted and the newly enabled priority 6 thread will begin to use the processor that the priority 10 thread was using.

7.7 • SUMMARY

The scheduler is responsible for multiplexing the CPU among a set of ready processes/threads. It is invoked periodically by a timer interrupt, by a system call, other device interrupts, or any time that a running process voluntarily releases the CPU through a `yield()` or resource request. The scheduler selects from among a ready list of processes waiting to use the processor and then allocates the processor to the selected process.

Scheduling strategies can be divided into nonpreemptive and preemptive strategies. Nonpreemptive strategies allow a process to run to completion once it obtains the processor, while preemptive strategies use the interval timer and scheduler to periodically reallocate the CPU. FCFS, SJN, priority, and deadline algorithms are well-known nonpreemptive algorithms, while RR and multiple-level queue algorithms (along with preemptive variants of priority and SJN) are often used to implement preemptive approaches.

Scheduling algorithms have been implemented in many different ways. The more sophisticated algorithms are multiple-level feedback queue variants.

Scheduling is the heart of the CPU resource manager. It implements CPU sharing among a set of ready processes. Once the computing environment provides concurrent threads through scheduling, the process manager must add additional mechanisms to allow these concurrent threads to coordinate their operation. Thread and process coordination is discussed in the next two chapters.

7.8 • EXERCISES

1. During processor multiplexing using interrupts and the interval timer, the processor receives a timer interrupt when the interrupt request flag (`InterruptRequest`) is set to TRUE by the interval timer device. In the discussion, it is assumed that the interrupt software will reset `InterruptRequest` to FALSE when it processes the interrupt. What would happen if the interval timer interrupt software reset the flag, but another interrupt occurred before the interval timer interrupt routine and scheduler completed their work?

2. Suppose a new process in a system arrives at an average of six processes per minute and each such process requires an average of 8 seconds of service time. Estimate the fraction of time the CPU is busy in a system with a single processor.

3. Assume you have the following jobs to execute with one processor, with the jobs arriving in the order listed here:

i	$\tau(p_i)$
0	80
1	20
2	10
3	20
4	50

a. Suppose a system uses FCFS scheduling. Create a Gantt chart illustrating the execution of these processes.

b. What is the turnaround time for process p_3?

c. What is the average wait time for the processes?

4. Using the process load in the previous problem, suppose a system uses SJN scheduling.

   a. Create a Gantt chart illustrating the execution of these processes.

   b. What is the turnaround time for process p_4?

   c. What is the average wait time for the processes?

5. Suppose a system uses priority scheduling (under the following process load), where a small integer means a high priority.

i	$\tau(p_i)$	Priority
0	80	3
1	20	1
2	10	4
3	20	5
4	50	2

   a. Create a Gantt chart illustrating the execution of these processes.

   b. What is the turnaround time for process p_2 under priority scheduling?

   c. What is the average wait time for the processes?

6. Assume you have the following jobs to execute with one processor:

i	$\tau(p_i)$	Arrival Time
0	75	0
1	40	10
2	25	10
3	20	80
4	45	85

   Suppose a system uses RR scheduling with a quantum of 15.

   a. Create a Gantt chart illustrating the execution of these processes.

   b. What is the turnaround time for process p_3?

   c. What is the average wait time for the processes?

7. Assume you have the following jobs to execute with one processor:

i	$\tau(p_i)$	Arrival Time
0	75	0
1	40	10
2	25	10
3	30	55
4	45	95

Suppose a system uses preemptive SJN scheduling. Create a Gantt chart illustrating the execution of these processes.

8. Assume the context switch time is five time units with RR scheduling.

   a. Create a Gantt chart illustrating the execution of these processes.

   b. What is the turnaround time for process p_3?

   c. What is the average wait time for the processes?

9. Assume you have the following jobs to execute with one processor:

i	$\tau(p_i)$	Priority
0	80	2
1	25	4
2	15	3
3	20	4
4	45	1

   The jobs are assumed to arrive at the same time. Using priority scheduling, do the following:

   a. Create a Gantt chart illustrating the execution of these processes.

   b. What is the turnaround time for process p_1?

   c. What is the average wait time for the processes?

10. What is the effect of increasing the time quantum to an arbitrarily large number for RR scheduling?

11. Linux Version 2.2 supports kernel threads, so its scheduler operates on threads instead of processes. Do you think it would be necessary to completely redesign the Version 2.0 (or Version 1.0 scheduler described in Section 7.5) for Version 2.2? Or could the process scheduler algorithm be easily adapted to thread scheduling?

12. The BSD UNIX priority values actually range from 0 through 127, rather than from 0 through 31 (corresponding to the run queue number). Speculate why the designers decided not to incorporate 128 run queues in the scheduler.

Analyzing the
Round Robin Scheduling

This exercise can be solved on any UNIX or Windows system. Your instructor will let you know which programming language(s) you can use to solve the exercise.

In this exercise, you will study the effect of several parameters used with RR scheduling (see Section 7.5). To solve the exercise, you will need to write a *discrete simulation* to experiment with the performance of this strategy under different timeslice lengths and different dispatcher overhead times. Do this by writing a simulation program to imitate the behavior of a single-CPU system that has a preemptive RR scheduler, and then collecting performance data regarding the operation of the simulation.

Create an input file to represent process arrival and service times, where each line represents a process arriving into your simulated system. The first number is the arrival time (in integer seconds), and the second number is the amount of time the process requires to complete (in floating-point seconds). For example, the first several lines of the file might look like

```
30  0.783560
54  17.282004
97  32.814522
133 39.986730
163 42.805902
181 28.249353
204 45.561030
249 26.369485
287 48.582049
325 37.274777
365 37.144992
399 22.059136
424 47.168534
455 20.090157
488 56.053016
531 39.640908
572 0.717403
610 34.732701
637 21.593761
658 48.477451
685 21.472914
729 44.603773
```

This example file segment means that the first process arrives at time 30 and requests 0.783560 second of CPU time; the second at time 54, requesting 17.282004 seconds; and so on.

After you have implemented your simulation, run simulation experiments using the fixed input load, but change the dispatcher overhead time to be the values 0, 5, 10, 15, 20, and 25 milliseconds and time quanta of 50, 100, 250, and 500 milliseconds.

In your simulation, assume the model shown in Figure 7.7, and the RR scheduling details as suggested by Section 7.5, particularly Figure 7.13. Using at least the data given previously (or the data specified by your instructor), determine the average wait time and the average turnaround time for all processes. Plot your findings in two graphs. In the first graph, the *Y*-axis should be the average wait time and the *X*-axis should be the context switching time. You will have one curve on the graph for each time quantum you test. The second graph is the same as the first except that you should plot the average turnaround time for the processes. Report the fraction of time the processor is busy (this is just a single number) for each simulation run.

● **BACKGROUND** ●

Performance evaluation is a large discipline in computer science, with a number of books devoted to its subareas: performance measurement, analytic modeling, and simulation modeling. To help you solve this exercise, here is a brief introduction to simulation modeling.

DISCRETE EVENT SIMULATION

Computer simulation is often used to *model* the behavior of a scheduling system or other complex system, and then to *predict* the performance of the system by measuring the behavior of the *model* instead of the real system. This is the same approach that automobile designers use when they construct a clay model of a car, then put it in a wind tunnel to observe the automobile's aerodynamic behavior. A model of a complex system may itself be simple or complex, depending on the amount of effort invested in the model, and its intended use. A simple model makes many assumptions about the external stimuli, internal state, internal organization, and internal operation of the system being modeled. A simple model also produces only rough approximations of the behavior of the system. If the model becomes correspondingly more complex by addressing more and more details of (making fewer and fewer assumptions about) the operation of the target system, then its predictions of the behavior of the target system will generally be more detailed and accurate. This means that the measured behavior of the complex model will more accurately reflect measures of the real system than will a simple model. For example, a virtual reality game and an aircraft cockpit simulator try to make the model look as much like the target system as feasible.

A *discrete event simulation* program is composed of a set of software modules and an interrelationship among the modules. Each module in the simulation ordinarily represents a corresponding module in the target system, and the interrelationships in the simulation model correspond to those that exist among modules in the target system. For example, one simulation module might represent the enqueuer portion of a scheduler, another the ready list, and another the dispatcher, and so on. The enqueuer simulation module places jobs in the ready list module, the dispatcher simulation module retrieves simulated jobs from the simulated ready list, and so on. Activity in the target system is represented by activity among the corresponding simulated components in the simulation program. Thus, the level of detail in the model is reflected by both this organization mapping and the amount of detail incorporated within each simulation module.

Each simulation module is constructed as a simulation procedure—one or more programming language functions. Executing the simulation procedure represents the activation and execution of the corresponding module in the target system. Any given simulation module is activated according to the interrelationships that exist among the modules in the target system. For example, in a simulation run, when the enqueuer would enter a job into the ready list in the target system, the simulation program would call the enqueuer simulation procedure, which would then model the action of entering a job into the ready list. The simulation procedure is a model in the sense that it usually does not really manage process descriptors, although it very well may implement a ready list data structure that approaches the complexity of the ready list in the target system.

Constructing a simulation program to represent the behavior of any target system requires that you first understand the behavior of the target system. Your understanding of the system will enable you to identify critical modules in the target system—components of the target system that react according to stimuli from their environment. After you have identified target system modules, you may decide that the behavior of some of the modules is not important to the performance analysis study. (For example, an aerodynamic automobile model does not have any representation of the engine at all.) This allows you to group collections of modules in the target system into a single *logical module* that adequately represents the behavior of the collection. For example, a scheduler has modules to update various timer counts, to process signals, and so on. A logical module might simply ignore all details relating to timer maintenance and signal handling. This is the first step in model construction.

After the logical modules have been identified, determine the conditions that cause modules to interact. For example, in a scheduler simulation, there might be a module to represent when timer interrupts occur, causing the dispatcher module to be called (to multiplex the CPU). Simulation analysts often define a set of *events* that can occur in the system, where each event occurrence represents a situation that causes a simulation procedure to be called. An interrupt occurrence is an event, a resource allocation operation causes an event that should start the enqueuer, and so on. Determining the set of events is closely associated with the definition of the set of simulation modules/procedures that you will use.

For example, suppose you were going to model the behavior of a collection of bank tellers addressing the needs of customers, such as deposits, withdrawals, loan payments, and so on. On the left side of Figure 7.14, there is a picture of a bank: When a customer enters the bank to conduct a normal transaction, there is a line where they wait for a teller to become available. If there is anyone in the line, then all the tellers must be busy. Whenever a teller finishes a transaction with a customer, then the customer leaves the bank and the customer at the head of the line goes to that teller for help.

A bank might be interested in determining the average and maximum length of the line of waiting customers, given a particular customer arrival pattern. The management might also be interested in knowing how busy tellers are (on the average), or what would happen if more or fewer tellers were on duty. These and similar questions could be addressed by constructing a model of the teller operation (see the right side of Figure 7.14), and then simulating the teller and customer activity with the model.

✦ FIGURE 7.14 Bank Teller Simulation

The diagram on the left of this figure represents the physical bank lobby, with customers and tellers. On the right is the model to represent the bank behavior. The customer line is represented by a queue data structure, and each teller by a simulation function.

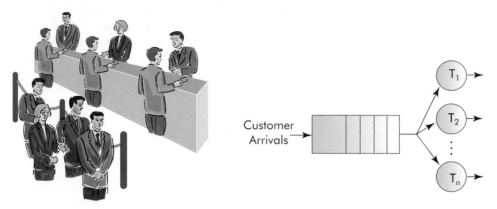

Tellers at the Bank   Model of Tellers at the Bank

A discrete event simulation model works by building the model in such a way that the entities of interest appear as data structures. The state of the entire system is represented by the values assigned to all the data structures. The model changes state by changing one or more fields in one or more data structures. In the bank model, examples of data structures (model entities) are a customer, a teller, and the line of customers. In *discrete* event simulation, the state of the model changes at discrete moments (rather than as continuous activity, as happens in the real world). The *state change* is implemented in the model by having a function corresponding to each state change execute at the right time. In the bank simulation model, if we suppose that the simulation starts with all of the tellers idle and waiting for customers, then the first state transition occurs when a customer arrives. Each situation that causes a state transition (that is, a function should be executed to change some data structures) now corresponds to our intuitive notion of an event.

Okay, now we know what the "discrete" and "event" are about in the mechanism. The simulation refers to the fact that these state transitions take place in *simulated* instead of *real* time, and that they only *model* the behavior of the system entities instead of actually doing them. For example, in the model, no one actually deposits or withdraws money—we are only modeling the time it takes to do these procedures. The events in the bank simulation could be:

■ *Event #1* (a customer arrives): This should cause something in the simulator to run an associated function that creates a new instance of a customer data structure, and then puts the instance in the data structure representing the line of waiting customers. For instrumentation purposes, fields in the customer data structure should uniquely identify the customer, save the time the customer arrived, save the time the customer began to receive service, and save the time the customer left the bank. These times would be used to determine performance behavior such as that customer's wait and turnaround times. After the customer is placed in the line, the function should check to see if there are any idle tellers; if there are, then the customer should be removed from the queue and paired with a teller. This event can also schedule the next simulated time at which Event #1 will occur (that is, when the next customer will arrive).

■ *Event #2* (a customer departs): When a customer and a teller begin a transaction, the corresponding function will adjust the data structures to remove the customer from the line and pair him or her up with the teller. Next, the function determines the time at which this transaction will be completed, and then schedules the next Event #2 occurrence at that time. When a teller finishes a transaction, then the next customer will be paired with the teller. If there are no customers waiting, then the tellers waits. This function will be able to determine enough information about the teller's activity to know the amount of time the teller is busy and idle. (The actual function would change the order of events as described here, since this event is called when a teller finishes a transaction.)

The parts of the simulation that are specific to the bank model are referred to as the *simulation application*. You should be able to model many different situations—specifically the bank or the RR scheduling algorithm behavior—using these ideas of entities with attributes, events, and functions. The *simulation kernel* is a part of the overall simulation that will manage the simulated time, calling the simulation functions associated with events when the correct simulated time occurs. The simulation kernel will be independent of all of the simulation applications, meaning that the same simulation kernel will work with many different applications. Let's take a closer look at the simulation kernel.

A FRAMEWORK FOR EVENT-ORIENTED SIMULATION

The simulation kernel is a generic framework for scheduling and executing simulation procedures according to the collection of pending events. The simulation kernel also maintains simulated time, gathers statistics about the simulation application, and produces summary reports. For this Laboratory Exercise, you will have to construct your own simulation kernel using a convention programming language (like C, C++, C#, or Java).

The major components of an event-oriented simulation kernel are facilities for defining events, representing simulation state (such as the simulated time), introducing transactions to the model, and managing the execution of events. A special-purpose simulation language allows its programmers to dynamically *register* functions and events with the simulation kernel. However, in this Laboratory Exercise, you will manually register functions and events by modifying your simulation kernel. For example, if the simulation application used a function, F, you would just modify the kernel so that it could call F.

A transaction is analogous to a customer transaction in a bank or a job in an RR scheduling model. Your simulation kernel should allow your applications to create transactions (such as jobs), and then to destroy them after they have run to completion. In an object-oriented language, an object is a natural representation of a transaction. In a conventional programming language like C, a transaction is a dynamically allocated data structure instance.

Event/function execution is the main part of the simulation kernel. Suppose that the application programmer decides that whenever `event_A` occurs, on behalf of transaction_k, the application function, F, should be called. The simulation kernel should export a function such as

```
cause(event_A, transaction_k, when_A_is_to_be_executed);
```

This cause() call is used by an application to *cause* event_A to occur on behalf of transaction_k after some amount of simulated time has elapsed. Effectively, the cause() call places a data structure (the *pending event descriptor*) into a list of *pending events*, ordered by simulated time of occurrence.

The simulation kernel has the basic schema shown in Figure 7.15. The select_next_event() call retrieves the event from the schedule of pending events that has the minimum time of occurrence, that is, the event that is to occur next. Since this event is the "next event" that occurs, the simulation kernel is able to instantaneously redefine the simulation time to be the time at which this next event is to occur. The evaluate() procedure calls (or otherwise interprets) the simulation application event declaration on the given transaction. The simulation kernel has its own queue of pending events. *Be careful not to confuse this queue with any queue in a simulation application* (like the queue of people in a bank or the ready list of jobs in a RR scheduler simulation).

✦ FIGURE 7.15 Simulation Kernel Loop

The simulation kernel loop executes as long as there are any pending events. It finds the next event to occur, advances the time, and then calls the application function associated with the event occurrence.

```
simulated_time = 0;
while (true) {
  event = select_next_event();
  if (event->time > simulated_time)
    simulated_time = event->time;
  evaluate(event->function, ...);
}
```

You can see that the fundamental tasks of the event-oriented simulator kernel are to schedule pending events, advance the simulation clock, and dispatch events.

● ATTACKING THE PROBLEM ●

There are two phases to solving this problem:

1. Design and implement the simulation kernel.
2. Design and implement the simulation application.

If you have little experience with discrete event simulation, you should consider building a draft version of your simulation kernel first. Here is a code framework for the basic loop that the simulation kernel needs to execute:

```
void runKernel(int quitTime)
{
  Event *thisEvent;
```

```
// Stop by running to elapsed time, or by causing quit execute
  if(quitTime <= 0) quitTime = 9999999;
  simTime = 0;
  while(simTime < quitTime) {
  // Get the next event
    if(eventList == NIL) {
    // No more events to process
      break;
    }
    thisEvent = eventList;
    eventList = thisEvent->next;
    simTime = thisEvent->getTime(); // Set the time
  // Execute this event
    thisEvent->fire();
    delete(thisEvent);
  };
}
```

To finish the simulator kernel, you will need to design and implement the missing functions, and define new ones such as the `cause()` function that creates an event and places it in the `eventList`. Test your simulation kernel by writing a trivial simulation application, perhaps with three procedures, A, B, and C, so that A causes B after some time delay, B causes C after some time delay, C causes A after a delay, and so on. Have each dummy simulation application print state information such as its identity, the current time, and so on.

The second task in solving this exercise is to design and implement the simulation application. This requires that you use the material in the main body of this chapter as the basis of your target system, which will define your simulation application model. Design your simulation application so that each procedure implements data structures that you need (such as the system ready list) or procedures to change the simulation's state (such as creating a new job, entering a job into the ready list, dispatching a job, simulating an interrupt, and so on).

Once you have all your simulation application modules defined, you can encode them as procedures that work with your simulation kernel. If you have never built a simulation model from scratch, you can expect that when you develop your first simulation application, you will need to refine your simulation kernel implementation.

The final touch is to *instrument* your simulation application so that it collects the data you need to measure the model's performance. You need to be able to compare the performance of the system with both different context switching times and different timeslices. Each run of your simulation model should produce performance measures for one particular configuration: context switch time and timeslice value.

You will have to run your simulation several times to get data for each configuration. When you have tried various combinations, then you can begin to plot the performance as graphs. (You need not use graphing software to plot the collective data; you can put the data in a spreadsheet and plot it with the graphing option.)

CHAPTER 8

Basic Synchronization Principles

Multiprogramming created an environment for concurrent classic processes. It also made it possible for a programmer to create a group of cooperating processes to work concurrently on a single problem. The resulting computation could even exhibit true parallelism if some of the processes were performing I/O operations while another one of the processes was using the processor. If the cooperating processes were executing on a multiprocessor, then multiple processes in the group could be executing in parallel. The threads refinement made it possible for a *single* process to take advantage of parallelism between the processor and the I/O and across CPUs on a multiprocessor. However, multiple cooperating threads introduce the potential for new **synchronization** problems in software implementations: *deadlock*, *critical sections*, and *nondeterminacy*. These synchronization problems can occur whenever two or more concurrent processes/threads use any shared resource. In this chapter, we will first see how synchronization problems arise in concurrent applications. Then, we will look at an abstract mechanism that can be used to solve synchronization problems. Finally, we will discuss ways that an OS can implement the abstract mechanisms.

8.1 • COOPERATING PROCESSES

As you have learned in your early programming courses, a program is a realization of a serial algorithm—it is a step-by-step procedure for accomplishing some information processing task. The science (and *art*) of designing serial algorithms to specify computations has dominated programming for over half a century. Consequently, computing environments have focused on supporting serial computation. A classic process and a modern thread are both sequential abstractions to execute a serial algorithm. While popular programming languages such as C and C++ have generally neglected to address concurrency, the underlying hardware technology has systematically moved toward it, using distributed and parallel computing machines. Economic pressures have driven application requirements toward the use of parallel and distributed hardware. This trend is apparent in contemporary management information systems, office computing environments, and numerical applications.

We often rely on synchronization when we meet with other people. Suppose Betty, John, and Pat decide to have a meeting in Betty's office. They must next agree on a time for the meeting. They each consult their calendars to decide when all of them wish to meet. By reaching an agreement about the time of the meeting, they are explicitly committing to **synchronize** their independent schedules so that they will all be in the same place at the same time. In an espionage movie, synchronization can be finer grained: Suppose that a team has a plan for attacking a fort in which each member of the team must be prepared to perform a specific task at exactly the same time, say 5:00, as all the others perform their own specific tasks. In this case, it is important that the team members all perform their actions at almost exactly the same time. Just before the team members start their mission, say at 1:00, they synchronize their watches by setting them to 1:00 at exactly the same moment. This provides the best assurance that 4 hours later, they will all perform their specific tasks at the same instant.

In the software context, **synchronization** refers to the act of ensuring that independent processes/threads begin to execute a designated block of code at the same logical time. Now let's see how synchronization manifests itself in concurrent software. You first saw concurrent software in the UNIX and Windows examples in Chapter 2. In the UNIX example, you saw how to use a parent process to implement a shell command line interpreter, and a child to execute each command. Here is the main loop of that code:

```
while(TRUE) {
...
// Create a process to execute the command
  if((chPID = fork()) == 0) {
  // This is the child
    execv(command.name, command.argv);
  }
// Wait for the child to terminate
  thisChPID = wait(&stat);
}
```

In the Windows example, the parent process launches the child process, but it does not wait for the child to finish before launching the next child. Here is the main loop of that code:

```
while (fgets(cmdLine, MAX_LINE_LEN, fid) != NULL) {
  // b. Create a new process to execute the command

  if (!CreateProcess(NULL, cmdLine, ...)
  { /* error handling code ... */ }
}
```

Figure 8.1 is a graph representing the code skeletons for both Laboratory Examples: Each large circle represents a block of code (such as "Execute Command"). The small circles represent places where a thread of execution can branch one way or the other (such as "Another Command?"). The arrows show the control flow among the blocks of code in the circles. Concurrency is represented by a case where multiple arrows leave a large circle (such as for the "`fork()` code" circle). The "Wait for Child to Terminate" large circle represents a case where concurrent control flow merges back into serial execution (two arrows coming into the large circle, but just one leaving it).

✦ FIGURE 8.1　Command Execution

Part (a) represents the control flow of the UNIX code segment. The parent process synchronizes with the child process activity by waiting for each child to terminate before starting the next one. Part (b) is the control flow pattern for the Windows code segment. In this case, the parent creates a child, but does not synchronize with that child again. Instead, the parent creates the next child to execute the next command.

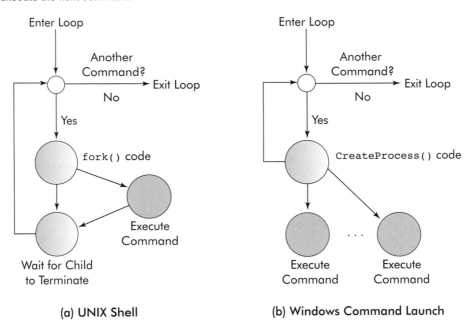

(a) UNIX Shell　　　　(b) Windows Command Launch

In Figure 8.1(a) we see that the parent program (the shaded blue circles) creates a child process to execute a command, then *waits* for the child to terminate before reading the next command. When this program processes 5 commands, the 5 processes that execute the commands will be created *sequentially*. There is concurrency between the parent and *at most one child at a time*.

In the Windows program shown in Figure 8.1(b), the parent process creates a process to execute a command, then immediately goes back to the top of the loop to create another process to execute another command. When this program processes 5 commands, the 5 processes that execute the commands will be created *to run at the same time*. There is concurrency among the parent and *all of the child processes*.

The essential difference between the two programs (other than using different operating systems) is the way the execution of the 6 processes is *coordinated*. In Figure 8.1(a), the parent and child *synchronize* when the child terminates. In Figure 8.1(b), there is *no synchronization* between the parent and child processes.

Here is another example from Chapter 2: In the Laboratory Exercise at the end of the chapter, the challenge is to write a set of concurrent programs so that a parent thread creates N child threads, then signals the child threads when they are supposed to halt. (Observe that this is synchronization among a set of threads in a process, instead of among a set of classic processes.) In this case, the child threads periodically attempt to synchronize with the parent. If the parent has not issued the signal to synchronize, then the child proceeds with its computation. Here is a much simpler version of the parent code than what appeared in the exercise (although it does almost the same thing):

```
static int runFlag = TRUE;
void main(... {
   ...
// For 1 to N
   for (i = 0; i < N; i++) {
   // Create a new thread to execute simulated work
     CreateThread(...);
   }
// runtime is the number of seconds that the children should run
// Sleep while children work ...
   Sleep(runtime*1000);
   RunFlag = FALSE;
   ...
}
```

The `Sleep(K)` call causes the thread to sleep for K milliseconds, meaning that `Sleep(1000)` would cause the thread to sleep for a second. This code skeleton uses system time to determine how long a child thread should run. While the child threads work for `runTime` seconds, the parent thread sleeps. Here is the code skeleton that each child thread executes:

```
DWORD WINAPI threadWork(LPVOID threadNo) {
   ...
   while(runFlag) {
     // Do one iteration of work, then check the runFlag
   }
// The parent just signaled me to halt
   return result;
}
```

Figure 8.2 is another graph depiction of the parent and child thread behaviors. In this graph model, there are $N+1$ threads executing concurrently. Instead of synchronizing when a child terminates, each child thread attempts to synchronize at the end of an iteration of its work. If it receives a halt signal from the parent, it terminates; otherwise, it does another iteration of work.

✦ FIGURE 8.2   Synchronizing Multiple Threads with a Shared Variable

The parent thread creates *N* child threads, each running as an iterative loop. At the end of the loop, each child checks to see if the `runFlag` has been set FALSE. If it has not, then the child iterates through the loop again. If the `runFlag` has been set FALSE, then the child terminates.

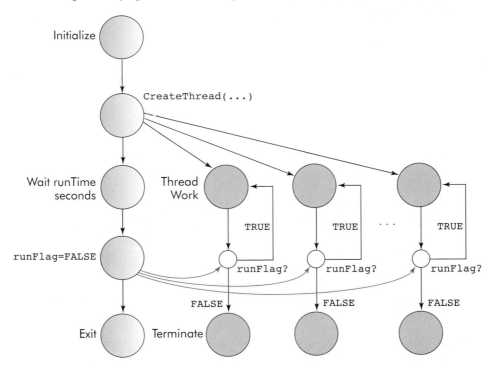

This technique works for threads that share an address space, but will generally not work for processes that do not share an address space. As you will see later in this section, this simple technique for synchronizing threads can fail. Providing robust and useful synchronization mechanisms is a fundamental problem in multiprogramming operating systems. This chapter first explains why this can be such a difficult problem, and then how this problem can be addressed by incorporating a basic mechanism—the *Dijkstra semaphore*—into the OS.

For concurrency to be useful, it must be possible to construct concurrent programs so that threads can share information, yet not interfere with one another during certain critical parts of their respective execution. The main barriers to effective use of concurrency in applications arise from the following issues:

- Software technologies have not converged on any set of generally applicable programming paradigms for concurrent programs. Each concurrent programming solution potentially requires a new approach and design. This is a primary focus of applied distributed programming.

- Synchronization is usually at the heart of any concurrent programming implementation. Operating systems classically provide only the minimum mechanism to support synchronization and concurrency, since there are so many different ways to implement concurrency and none of them dominate the area (for example, see [Jamieson et al., 1987]). This chapter and Chapter 9 explore the intricacies of synchronization.

■ Part of the difficulty with using synchronization mechanisms is in finding a good way for a high-level programming language to represent concurrency, then to fit the synchronization mechanism seamlessly into the concurrent programming language. Many widely accepted parallel programming languages do not address concurrency at all. The most modern languages such as Java and C# provide an extension for multiple active objects (a form of concurrency), but C and C++ do not support synchronization and concurrency at all.

CRITICAL SECTIONS

In automobile transportation, intersections are part of a street, but they are a unique part of the street because the intersection is a *shared* between two different streets (see Figure 8.3). In this cartoon, a bus proceeds along one street while a car moves along another. If the bus and the car get to the intersection at the same time, there will be a collision. We say that the intersection is a **critical section** of each street: It is perfectly acceptable for the bus or the car to use the intersection if the other is not currently using it. However, we can see that there will be a "transportation failure" if the bus and the car enter the intersection at the same time.

✦ **FIGURE 8.3**   Traffic Intersections

A traffic intersection is a critical section of these two streets, in the sense that only one vehicle can be in the intersection at a time. Either vehicle can use the critical section, provided that the other is not using it.

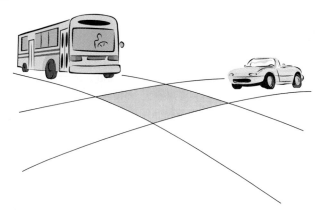

Critical sections occur in concurrent software whenever two processes/threads access a common shared variable. Like the bus and the car, there may be certain parts of the two processes that should not be executed concurrently. Such parts of the code are the software critical sections. For example, suppose that two processes, p_1 and p_2, execute concurrently to access a common integer variable, `balance`. For example, thread p_1 might handle credits to an account, while p_2 handles the debits. Both need access to the account `balance`

variable at different times (accessing `balance` is analogous to entering an intersection). This code will work exactly as expected most of the time: p_1 adds to the balance for a credit operation, and p_2 subtracts from the `balance` for a debit operation. However, disaster will strike if the two processes access the `balance` variable concurrently. The following code schema shows how the threads reference the shared `balance`:

```
shared double balance; /* shared variable */
```

Code schema for p_1

```
...
balance = balance+amount;
...
```

Code schema for p_2

```
...
balance = balance-amount;
...
```

These C language statements will be compiled into a few machine instructions, such as the following:

Code schema for p_1

```
load   R1, balance
load   R2, amount
add    R1, R2
store  R1, balance
```

Code schema for p_2

```
load   R1, balance
load   R2, amount
sub    R1, R2
store  R1, balance
```

Now suppose p_1 is executing the machine instruction

```
load   R2, amount
```

just as the interval timer expires. If the scheduler next selects thread p_2 to run and it executes its machine language code segment for the "`balance = balance-amount;`" instruction before p_1 regains control of the processor, then we will have the execution scenario shown in Figure 8.4. In this specific execution scenario (determined by *when* a timer interrupt occurred), the following sequence of actions take place:

- When p_1 is interrupted, the context switch saves its register values in its process descriptor.
- When p_2 is allocated the processor, it will read the same value of `balance` that p_1 read, compute the difference between `balance` and `amount`, and then store the difference at the memory location containing `balance`.
- p_1 will eventually resume, causing its register values to be restored from its process descriptor. It will restore the *old* value of `balance` since it had already been loaded into `R1` when p_1 was interrupted.
- p_1 will then compute the sum of `R1` (the old value of balance) and `R2` (the `amount`), and then generate a different value of `balance` from the one p_2 had written when p_1 was interrupted.
- The update of `balance` by p_2 will be lost!

The programs defining p_1 and p_2 each have a **critical section** with respect to their use of the shared variable `balance`. For p_1, the critical section is computing the sum of the `balance` and `amount`, but for p_2, the critical section is computing the difference of `balance` and `amount`. The concurrent execution of the two threads is not guaranteed to be **determinate**, *since not every execution of the two programs on the same data produces the same result.*

✦ FIGURE 8.4   A Critical Section

p_1 is interrupted as it finishes the load instruction. p_2 begins to execute, eventually entering the code block, where it subtracts the `amount` from the `balance`, storing the result back in memory. When p_1 resumes, it updates the old `balance` and overwrites `balance` with its result.

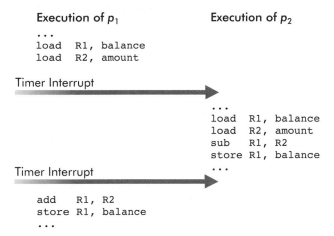

```
Execution of p₁                    Execution of p₂

...
load   R1, balance
load   R2, amount

Timer Interrupt  ───────────────────────────▶

                                   ...
                                   load   R1, balance
                                   load   R2, amount
                                   sub    R1, R2
                                   store  R1, balance
Timer Interrupt  ───────────────────────────▶   ...

add    R1, R2
store  R1, balance
...
```

We say that there is a **race condition** between p_1 and p_2, because the outcome of the computation depends on the relative times that the two processes execute their respective critical sections. If this race results in a "close finish," with the two processes executing their respective critical sections at the same time, the computation may be faulty.

It is not possible to detect a critical section problem (or race condition) by considering only p_1's program or only p_2's program. The problem occurs because of sharing, not because of any error in the sequential code. The critical section problem can be avoided by having either thread enter its corresponding critical section any time it needs to do so *except when the other thread is currently in its critical section.*

How can the two threads cooperate to enter their critical sections? In the traffic intersection case (see Figure 8.3), we can add a traffic signal so that either the bus or the car can proceed (but not both at the same time), depending on the signal. In a multiprogrammed uniprocessor, an interrupt enabled one process to be stopped and another to be started. If the programmer realized that the occurrence of an interrupt could lead to erroneous results, he or she could control interrupts to behave like traffic lights: The program would *disable interrupts* when it entered a critical section, then enable them when it finished the critical section.

Figure 8.5 illustrates how the account balance programs can be coded using the `enableInterrupt()` and `disableInterrupt()` function: This solution does not allow both threads to be in their critical sections at the same time. Interrupts are disabled on entry to the critical section and then enabled upon exit. Unfortunately, this technique may affect the behavior of the I/O system because interrupts are disabled for an arbitrarily long time (as determined by an application program). In particular, suppose a program contained an infinite loop inside its critical section. The interrupts would be permanently disabled. For this reason, user mode programs cannot invoke `enableInterrupt()` and `disableInterrupt()`.

✦ FIGURE 8.5   Disabling Interrupts to Implement the Critical Section

Interrupts are disabled while a process enters its critical section, then enabled when it leaves.

```
shared double amount, balance;    /* Shared variables */
```

Program for p_1
```
disableInterrupts();
balance = balance + amount;
enableInterrupts();
```

Program for p_2
```
disableInterrupts();
balance = balance - amount;
enableInterrupts();
```

There are alternatives to the solution in Figure 8.5 that do not require interrupts to be disabled. Such solutions avoid the problems of long/infinite compute intervals during which interrupts are disabled. The idea is to make the two threads coordinate their actions using another shared variable. (That is, the solution depends on the ability of the OS to provide shared variables.) Figure 8.6 uses a shared flag, `lock`, so that p_1 and p_2 can coordinate their accesses to `balance`. (NULL is used to emphasize the use of a null statement in the body of the `while` loop. In subsequent examples, we will omit all statements from the body of the loop.) When p_1 enters its critical section, it sets the shared `lock` variable, so p_2 will be prevented from entering its critical section. Similarly, p_2 uses the `lock` to prevent p_1 from entering its critical section at the wrong time.

✦ FIGURE 8.6   Critical Sections Using a Lock

In this solution, the `lock` variable coordinates the way the two processes enter their critical sections. On critical section entry, a process waits while `lock` is TRUE.

```
shared boolean lock = FALSE;      /* Shared variables */
shared double amount, balance;    /* Shared variables */
```

Program for p_1
```
...
/* Acquire lock */
 while(lock) {NULL;};
 lock = TRUE;
/* Execute crit section */
 balance = balance + amount;
/* Release lock */
 lock = FALSE;
 ...
```

Program for p_2
```
...
/* Acquire lock */
 while(lock) {NULL;};
 lock = TRUE;
/* Execute crit section */
  balance = balance - amount;
/* Release lock */
 lock = FALSE;
 ...
```

Figure 8.7 illustrates an execution pattern in which the two threads compete for the critical section: Suppose p_1 is interrupted during the execution of the statement

```
balance = balance + amount;
```

after having set lock to TRUE. Suppose p_2 then begins to execute. p_2 will wait to obtain the `lock` (and to enter its critical section) at its `while` statement. Eventually, the clock interrupt will interrupt p_2 and resume p_1, which can complete its critical section. Potentially p_2's entire timeslice is spent executing the `while` statement. When p_1 is running on the processor and executes

```
lock = FALSE;
```

p_1 indicates that it has completed its critical section. Eventually, p_1 will again be interrupted by the timer, and then p_2 can finally enter its critical section and continue with its work.

✦ FIGURE 8.7 The Execution Pattern

While p_1 is in its critical section, p_2 waits at its while statement. In this case, p_2 will use entire timeslices executing the wait code.

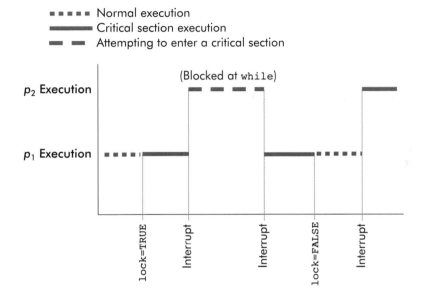

While the approach shown is conceptually sound, it introduces a new critical section related to *testing and setting the* lock *variable*. If a thread is interrupted immediately after executing the while statement, but before it sets the lock, then the solution fails: Both processes can be in their critical sections at the same time. The problem is that manipulating the lock variable is, itself, a critical section: *You have to solve a small critical section problem (manipulating* lock*) before you can solve the original critical section problem (manipulating* balance*)!*

There is an important difference between the critical section to manipulate lock, and the one to manipulate balance: The lock critical section will be exactly the same code every time a process wants to enter a critical section. But the balance critical section code is determined by the application, which means that it might take a long time to execute, or even contain an infinite loop. Using this knowledge about the lock manipulation algorithm, we recognize that it would generally be acceptable to disable interrupts while we test and set the lock variable, since it will only be 3–4 machine instructions. But since enableInterrupts() and disableInterrupts() are privileged, we can define two new OS system calls, enter() and exit(), as shown in Figure 8.8. With these routines, a process calls enter() when it wants to enter a critical section, then calls exit() when it leaves the critical section. In this case, interrupts are disabled only by the OS code (while lock is being manipulated). Even when a process is blocked, waiting to enter its critical section, the interrupts are only disabled for a few instructions at a time. This avoids the problems caused by disabling the interrupts for an extended period of time since an interrupt will never be delayed for more than the time taken to execute the `while` statement.

✦ FIGURE 8.8   Lock Manipulation as a Critical Section

The `enter()` system call uses the `while` statement to wait for a critical section to become available, but it will only disable interrupts for a few machine instructions before enabling them again. This will prevent interrupts from being delayed for more than a few instruction executions.

```
enter(lock) {                          exit(lock) {
  disableInterrupts();                   disableInterrupts();
/* Wait for lock */                      lock = FALSE;
  while(lock) {                           enableInterrupts();
    /* Let interrupt occur */          }
    enableInterrupts();
    disableInterrupts();
  }
  lock = TRUE;
  enableInterrupts();
}
```

The `enter()` and `exit()` system calls can be used to solve the general critical section problem (although we will study a more general mechanism in Section 8.3). Here is how they can be used to solve the `balance` manipulation problem:

```
shared double amount, balance;    /* Shared variables */
shared int lock = FALSE;          /* Synchronization variable */
```

Program for p_1

```
enter(lock);
balance = balance + amount;
exit(lock);
```

Program for p_2

```
enter(lock);
balance = balance - amount;
exit(lock);
```

DEADLOCK

Critical sections are fundamental to concurrent programming since they are the parts of the computation during which individual processes manipulate shared resources (such as a variable). The existence of critical sections creates an environment in which a new, subtle problem can occur: **deadlock**. In a deadlock situation, two or more processes/threads get into a state whereby each is controlling a resource that the other needs. For example, suppose two pirates have each obtained half of a treasure map (see Figure 8.9). Each pirate needs the other half of the map to obtain the treasure, but neither will give up his half of the map. This is a deadlock.

In software, deadlocks occur because one process holds a resource (such as file A) while requesting another (such as file B). At the same time, another process holds the second resource (file B) while requesting the first one (file A). Since a request operation blocks the calling process until that resource is allocated, neither process will ever have all its desired resources allocated to it and both will remain in this **deadlock state** forever.

Here is a another concrete example: Suppose there are two threads, p_1 and p_2, manipulating a common list. Each task is able to add or delete an entry, requiring that the list

✦ FIGURE 8.9 Deadlocked Pirates

Each pirate holds half of a treasure map, but needs to acquire the other half to find the treasure.

length in the list header be updated. That is, when a delete operation occurs, the length must be decremented, and when an entry is added to the list, the length must be incremented. To ensure consistency between the list and its header, we could first try the approach shown in Figure 8.10 (although this will turn out to be an incorrect solution).

If threads p_1 and p_2 are executed concurrently:

- A clock interrupt may occur after p_1 deletes an element but before it updates the length in the list descriptor.

- If p_2 adds an element to the list and updates the length before p_1 resumes, then the contents of the list and its length in the descriptor will not be consistent with one another.

In this example, a process *should update both the list and the descriptor or neither*. So we try a different solution in order to place modifications to the list and the descriptor within a more complex critical section scheme, as shown in Figure 8.11.

- When p_1 enters its critical section to manipulate the list, it sets `lock1`.

- Thus p_2 will be prevented from entering its critical section to manipulate the list when it tests `lock1`.

- The same also holds for p_2 when it enters its list manipulation critical section and for both p_1 and p_2 to update the length.

- Suppose p_1 is interrupted during the `<intermediate computation>` (after having set `lock1` to `TRUE`) and p_2 begins to execute.

- p_2 will set `lock2` and then wait for `lock1` at the while statement.

- Eventually, the clock interrupt will resume p_1, and p_1 can then complete the `<intermediate computation>` and block at its `while` statement test on `lock2` (prior to updating the descriptor).

✦ FIGURE 8.10   Multiple Shared Variables with Disabled Interrupts

This attempted solution uses `enter()` and `exit()` to encapsulate two critical sections. The problem is that p_1 could be interrupted after it deletes an element from the list but before it updates the header. If p_2 runs next, then the list and the header will be inconsistent.

```
shared boolean lock1 = FALSE;    /* Shared variables */
shared boolean lock2 = FALSE;
shared list L;
```

Program for p_1

```
   ...
/* Enter crit section to
 * delete elt from list */
  enter(lock1);
  <delete element>;
/* Exit critical section */
  exit(lock1);
  <intermediate computation>;
/* Enter crit section to
 * update length */
  enter(lock2);
  <update length>;
/* Exit critical section */
  exit(lock2);
  ...
```

Program for p_2

```
   ...
/* Enter crit section to
 * update length */
  enter(lock2);
  <update length>;
/* Exit critical section */
  exit(lock2);
  <intermediate computation>;
/* Enter crit section to
 * add elt to list */
  enter(lock1);
  <add element>;
/* Exit critical section */
  exit(lock1);
  ...
```

✦ FIGURE 8.11   Ensuring Consistency in Related Values

In this attempted solution to the list manipulation problem, the two processes may deadlock if p_1 is interrupted after it acquires `lock1`, but before it acquires `lock2`, and p_2 updates the list.

```
shared boolean lock1 = FALSE;    /* Shared variables */
shared boolean lock2 = FALSE;
shared list L;
```

Program for p_1

```
   ...
/* Enter crit section to
 * delete elt from list */
  enter(lock1);
  <delete element>;
  <intermediate computation>;
/* Enter crit section to
 * update length */
  enter(lock2);
  <update length>;
/* Exit both crit sections */
  exit(lock1);
  exit(lock2);
  ...
```

Program for p_2

```
   ...
/* Enter crit section to
 * update length */
  enter(lock2);
  <update length>;
  <intermediate computation>;
/* Enter crit section to
 * add elt to list */
  enter(lock1);
  <add element>;
/* Exit both crit sections */
  exit(lock2);
  exit(lock1);
  ...
```

However, now these two processes will deadlock: Neither thread can ever proceed, since each holds the lock that the other needs. This forms a deadlock between p_1 and p_2, where the locks are abstract resources. In our continuing exploration of synchronization approaches, we must guard against the possibility of a deadlock. Deadlock can also occur in any situation where multiple processes compete for resources (not just in the critical section case). We will study the general case in Chapter 10.

RESOURCE SHARING

The software critical section discussed earlier existed because the two processes shared the `balance` variable. The solutions synchronized the two processes so that one or the other of them had access to the shared variable at any given time. The traffic example suggested that critical sections can occur with any kind of time-multiplexed, shared resource such as the intersection of the two streets.

   The processes/threads in a concurrent application will necessarily share some resource, such as variables, but also files, buffers, and devices. For example, if an application is intended to manage a company's inventory, one process may run threads that handle the delivery of products from the inventory. A second process might handle ordering of goods whenever the inventory gets low. This means that the delivery process and the order process will need to access common information that describes the current inventory (even if it is only a file).

   Many of these resources will be time-multiplexed, reusable resources. When a process or thread gains control of the resource, its access is mutually exclusive to other processes or threads within a process, meaning that no other process or thread can use the resource while it is allocated to one process or one thread. You should think of shared variables as shared resources with mutually exclusive access. Then the critical section problem is a special case of the **mutual exclusion** problem, which is the problem of time-multiplexing a shared resource so that only one process or one thread can use the resource at a time. In the critical section variant, the abstract resource is the critical section: Processes are mutually excluded from entering their critical section at the same time.

   Our approach to synchronization solutions (and problems) has relied on the concurrent processes being executed on a single machine. In the **enter()/exit()** solution, it must be possible to prevent certain processes from executing by disabling interrupts. In all the other solutions, we rely on the presence of *shared memory*, for example, to hold a `lock` variable that can be tested and set by the concurrent processes. As we saw in Chapter 6, process address spaces prevent memory sharing. If our strategy is to synchronize using shared variables, the OS must provide some mechanism to override address space barriers so independent processes can access the shared variable.

8.2 • EVOLVING FROM THE CLASSIC SOLUTION

The need for interactions among threads (possibly in different processes) leads to the need for synchronization, and synchronization introduces the critical section and deadlock problems. Recall that in Chapter 2, FORK(), JOIN(), and QUIT() were introduced as mechanisms for creating and destroying processes. They can also be used to synchronize processes involved in a concurrent computation. In Figure 8.12(a), the schematic diagram represents how a computation can use FORK(), JOIN(), and QUIT() to achieve concurrency. The initial process (or one of its descendants) creates a process, A, by performing a FORK() operation. Process A then executes FORK() to create process B. A and B then JOIN(), leaving only one process running, say B. Next, process B executes a FORK() to create process C. Processes B and C execute concurrently and then JOIN(), leaving only one process, again say B. Finally, process B performs a QUIT() operation to complete the computation. In this example, there are three distinct processes in the application schema (ignoring the initial process).

✦ FIGURE 8.12   Synchronization using FORK(), JOIN(), and QUIT()

Part (a) represents a computation in which the concurrent tasks are executed by repeatedly creating and destroying processes. Part (b) is an alternative approach in which synchronization operators are used in lieu of some of the process creations and destructions.

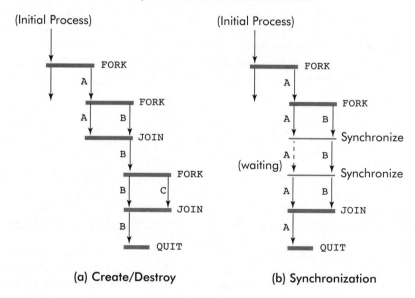

(a) Create/Destroy   **(b) Synchronization**

Figure 8.12(b) represents an alternative approach using a synchronization operator ("Synchronize" in the figure). Again, process (or thread) A is created, either directly or indirectly, by the initial process. Process A creates process B using a FORK() command. At some of the points where FORK() and JOIN() were used to create and destroy processes in Figure 8.12(a), the two processes explicitly synchronize their operation so that neither will proceed beyond a certain point in the computation until both have reached their respective synchronization points. In the analogies at the beginning of the chapter, this kind of synchronization is similar to that used in the espionage movie: Processes A and B wait until both have reached a certain point in their execution (or the clock reaches 5:00 in the espionage example). Neither process uses a JOIN() or QUIT(), so neither process terminates. Instead, the first one to reach its synchronization point suspends itself until the other has reached its synchronization points. In the figure, process A then waits while B performs sequential processing. The processes then synchronize again and continue concurrent execution. After all the work is done, the two processes JOIN( ). In Figure 8.12(b), process A is assumed to be the last to execute JOIN( ), so it continues and finally performs a QUIT( ) to finish the computation. The processes in the schematic diagram could also be threads—in one process or in different processes.

The two approaches in Figure 8.12 perform the same computation with the same amount of overlapped operation. Which approach is preferable? Since the introduction of FORK( ), JOIN( ), and QUIT( ), OS designers have observed that process creation and destruction tend to be quite costly operations because they require considerable manipulation of process descriptors, protection mechanisms, and memory management mechanisms. The synchronization operation, on the other hand, can be thought of as a resource request on a consumable resource, such as a shared Boolean variable, and can be implemented far more efficiently. Because the amount of time to create/destroy a process is three or more orders of magnitude larger than for synchronization, the trend in contemporary operating systems is to use synchronization mechanisms to complement the process/thread creation/destruction operations.

In Section 8.1, some basic ideas were discussed that showed how synchronization might be accomplished using locks on a shared variable. The example solution relied on the semantics of the particular problem. In a generalized mechanism, a thread should be able to block until some previously defined **event** has occurred in another thread (possibly in another process). Consider the example introduced in Figure 1.8 and repeated in Figure 8.13. The intent of these code segments is that proc_B should not execute its first read( ) statement until proc_A completes the write( ) for the variable x. Further, this synchronization should take place each time through the loop. When proc_B starts, it should suspend operation until the write(x) event occurs in proc_A. This is a variant of the critical section problem in that the synchronization is needed to ensure cooperation between the threads executing proc_A and proc_B, instead of to resolve competition for access to a critical section.

There are three basic approaches to implementing synchronization strategies:

- Use only user mode software algorithms and shared variables.

- Disable and enable interrupts around critical sections as indicated in Figure 8.5, although as already pointed out, such solutions potentially have a dramatic effect on the I/O system.

- Incorporate specialized mechanisms in the hardware and/or operating system to support synchronization. This approach was first proposed by Edsger Dijkstra [Dijkstra, 1968] and remains the basis of the today's solutions. It relies on the use of the *semaphore* abstract data type implemented by the operating system.

Two of the three approaches involve explicit OS support. The semaphore approach (and its extensions) is much preferred to the software and interrupt-based solutions.

✦ FIGURE 8.13 Example Concurrent Processes

These code fragments represent the activity of two different concurrent processes. `proc_A` writes a shared variable, *x*, and reads a shared variable, *y*. `proc_B` reads *x* and writes *y*.

```
shared double x, y; /* Shared variables */
proc_A() {                  proc_B() {
  while(TRUE) {               while(TRUE) {
    <compute A1>;               read(x); /* Consume x */
    write(x); /* Produce x */   <compute B1>;
    <compute A2>;               write(y); /* Produce y */
    read(y); /* Consume y */    <compute B2>;
  }                           }
}                           }
```

8.3 • SEMAPHORES: THE BASIS OF MODERN SOLUTIONS

Busy traffic intersections address the critical section problem by adding a semaphore—a traffic light—to coordinate use of the shared intersection. In software, a **semaphore** is an OS abstract data type that performs operations similar to the traffic light. The semaphore will allow one process (such as the car) to control the shared resource while the other process (such as the bus) waits for the resource to be released. Before discussing the principles of operation of semaphores, let's consider the assumptions under which semaphores operate.

An acceptable solution to the critical section problem has these requirements:

■ Only one process at a time should be allowed to be executing in its critical section (**mutual exclusion**).

■ If a critical section is free and a set of processes all want to enter the critical section, then the decision about which process should be chosen to enter the critical section should be made by the collection of processes instead of by an external agent (such as an arbiter or scheduler).

■ If a process attempts to enter its critical section and the critical section becomes available, then the waiting process cannot be blocked from entering the critical section for an indefinite period of time.

■ Once a process attempts to enter its critical section, then it cannot be forced to wait for more than a bounded number of other processes to enter the critical section before it is allowed to do so.

For purposes of discussion, this section highlights other important aspects of the problem by considering the two process skeletons shown in Figure 8.14. In this and subsequent figures, the statement

```
fork(proc, N, arg1, arg2, ..., argN)
```

means that a single-threaded process is created and begins executing `proc()` in its own address space using the *N* arguments provided. `<shared global declarations>` are intended to be the shared variables accessible in the address space of all the processes. (The order in which the procedure and shared global variables is declared is unspecified. Here the variables are declared after the procedures, but we often declare them before the procedures.)

✦ FIGURE 8.14   Cooperating Processes

This is the format for describing multiple processes or multiple threads in a process. In this example, two processes are created, one executing proc_0( ), and the other executing proc_1( ).

```
proc_0() {                        proc_1() {
   while(TRUE) {                     while(TRUE) {
      <compute section>;               <compute section>;
      <critical section>;              <critical section>;
   }                                 }
}                                 }
<shared global declarations>;
<initial processing>;
fork(proc_0, 0);
fork(proc_1, 0);
```

The following assumptions are made about the execution of the software schema in the figure:

■ Writing and reading a memory cell common to the two processes/threads is an indivisible operation. Any attempt by the two processes to execute simultaneous memory read or write operations will result in some unknown serial ordering of the two operations, but the two operations will not happen at the same time.

■ The threads are not assumed to have any priority, where one or the other would take precedence in the case of simultaneous attempts to enter a critical section.

■ The relative speeds of the threads are unknown, so one cannot rely on speed differentials (or equivalence) in arriving at a solution.

■ As indicated in Figure 8.14, the individual process executions are assumed to be sequential and cyclic.

PRINCIPLES OF OPERATION

Edsger Dijkstra was well-known as the inventor of the semaphore. It was the first software-oriented primitive to accomplish process synchronization [Dijkstra, 1968]. Over 35 years ago, Dijkstra's work on semaphores established the foundation of modern techniques for accomplishing synchronization. It is still a viable approach to managing communities of cooperating processes. Dijkstra's classic paper accomplished many things:

■ Introducing the idea of *cooperating sequential processes*

■ Illustrating the difficulty in accomplishing synchronization using only conventional (at that time) machine instructions

■ Postulating the primitives

■ Proving that they worked

■ Providing a number of examples (many of which are used in examples and exercises in this book).

At the time of Dijkstra's work, classic (single-threaded) processes were used to represent computation; threads were not invented for another twenty years. Dijkstra semaphores are described in terms of classic processes, although they apply to threads as well. In Dijkstra's original paper, the P operation was an abbreviation for the Dutch word *proberen*, meaning "to test," and the V operation was an abbreviation for *verhogen*, meaning "to increment."

A semaphore, *s*, is a nonnegative integer variable changed or tested only by one of two indivisible access routines:

```
V(s): [s = s + 1]
P(s): [while(s == 0) {wait}; s = s - 1]
```

The square braces surrounding the statements in the access routines indicate that the operations are **indivisible**, or **atomic**, operations. That is, all statements between the "[" and "]" are executed as if they were a single machine instruction. More precisely, the process executing the V routine cannot be interrupted until it has completed the routine. The P operation is more complex. If *s* is greater than 0, it is tested and decremented as an indivisible operation. However, if *s* is equal to 0, the process executing the P operation *can* be interrupted when it executes the `wait` command in the range of the `while` loop. The indivisible operation applies only to the test and control flow after the test, not to the time the process waits due to *s*'s being equal to zero.

The P operation is intended to indivisibly test an integer variable and to block the calling process if the variable is not positive. The V operation indivisibly signals a blocked process to allow it to resume operation. As our first semaphore example, let's reconsider the account balance code from Section 8.1 (see Figure 8.15). The initial value of the semaphore named `mutex` is 1 ("mutex" is a classic name from Dijkstra's original paper meaning "mutual exclusion"). When a process gets ready to enter its critical section, it applies the P operation to `mutex`. The first process to invoke P on `mutex` passes and the second blocks. When the first invokes the V operation on `mutex`, it continues to execute, thus enabling the second to proceed when it gets control of the CPU.

Next, we'll consider a series of examples that use semaphores to solve the critical section problem and to synchronize the operation of two processes or threads. We start with some simple examples using **binary semaphores**, meaning that the value of the semaphore takes on only the values 0 and 1. Usually, but not always (see the example), the semaphore is initialized to have the value 1.

✦ **FIGURE 8.15** Semaphores on the Shared Balance Problem

The semaphore solution initializes the semaphore, mutex, to be one. Each process invokes the P operation to enter the critical section, and the V operation when it leaves the critical section.

```
proc_0() {                        proc_1() {
    ...                               ...
/* Enter critical section */      /* Enter critical section */
  P(mutex);                         P(mutex);
    balance = balance + amount;       balance = balance - amount;
/* Exit critical section */       /* Exit critical section */
  V(mutex);                         V(mutex);
    ...                               ...
}                                 }
semaphore mutex = 1;
fork(proc_0, 0);
fork(proc_1, 0);
```

Using Semaphores

Various classic synchronization problems were introduced in Dijkstra's original paper, and many appeared in later papers and textbooks. This set of examples reviews several of those that illustrate recurring synchronization scenarios.

THE BASIC SYNCHRONIZING PROBLEM

You have seen how semaphores are used to solve the critical section problem in the account balance example. In Figure 8.13 you saw that there is another kind of synchronization problem where one process needs to coordinate with another by sending it a signal. The solution shown in Figure 8.16 illustrates how semaphores are used for this type of synchronization. We cannot simply substitute enable/disable calls for P and V in this example in order to return to the original solution (as we could for the account balance example) because more than one semaphore is used for the synchronization. In this case, the semaphore is used to exchange synchronization signals among processes, as opposed to solving the critical section problem.

SOFTWARE/HARDWARE DEVICE INTERACTION

In Chapter 4, you learned about the software/hardware interface between a device driver and controller. The busy and done flags in the status register can be viewed as hardware implementations of semaphores, since they are used to synchronize the operation of the software driver and the hardware controller. Figure 8.17 is a code skeleton representing the interaction.

✦ **FIGURE 8.16** Using Semaphores to Synchronize Two Processes

The proc_A and proc_B processes need to coordinate their activity so that proc_B does not attempt to read x until after proc_B has written it. Conversely, proc_A should not attempt to read y until after proc_B has written a new value to y. proc_A uses semaphore s1 to signal proc_B, and proc_B uses s2 to signal proc_A.

```
proc_A() {                         proc_B() {
  while(TRUE) {                       while(TRUE) {
    <compute A1>;                  /* Wait for proc_A signal */
    write(x); /* Produce x */          P(s1);
    V(s1); /* Signal proc_B */         read(x); /* Consume x */
    <compute A2>;                      <compute B1>;
 /* Wait for proc_B signal */          write(y); /* Produce y */
    P(s2);                             V(s2); /* Signal proc_A */
    read(y); /* Consume y */           <compute B2>;
  }                                  }
}                                  }
semaphore s1 = 0;
semaphore s2 = 0;
fork(proc_0, 0);
fork(proc_1, 0);
```

✦ **FIGURE 8.17** The Driver-Controller Interface Behavior

The busy and done hardware flags are used like signaling semaphores. The driver coordinates with the controller by setting busy, and the controller coordinates its state with the driver using the done flag.

```
/* Map the hardware flags to shared semaphores */
semaphore busy = 0, done = 0;
driver() { /* Synchronization behavior of the driver */
  <preparation for device operation>;
  V(busy); /* Start the device */
  P(done); /* Wait for the device to complete */
  <complete the operation>;
}
controller() { /* Controller's hardware loop */
  while(TRUE) {
    P(busy); /* Wait for a start signal */
    <perform the operation>;
    V(done); /* Tell driver that hardware has completed */
  }
}
```

The code fragment in this figure only models the synchronization behavior of the device driver software and the hardware controller, not all the functional behavior of the device driver and controller. (For example, if this solution were the basis of an implementation, it would cause the calling process to block—which an implementation would not do.) In the model, busy and done are initialized to 0, so when the device controller is started, it enters an endless loop in which it synchronizes its operation with the software process by testing the busy flag. If busy is 0—the initial condition—the controller blocks waiting for a signal from the driver. An application program calls the driver whenever it wants to perform an I/O operation. After preparing for the operation (for example, by setting controller registers, device status table entries, and so on), it signals the hardware process by a V operation on the busy semaphore. The V operation unblocks the controller and then blocks the driver on the done semaphore. When the device has completed the operation, it signals the driver by a V operation on the done flag.

THE BOUNDED BUFFER (PRODUCER–CONSUMER) PROBLEM

The bounded buffer problem occurs regularly in concurrent software. In Figure 5.11 we saw how "The Pure Cycle Water Company" illustrates the way buffers are used. Dijkstra used this problem to demonstrate different uses of semaphores in the same problem [Dijkstra, 1968]. Suppose a system incorporates two single-threaded (classic) processes, one of which produces information (the *producer* process) and another that uses the information (the *consumer* process). The two processes communicate by having the producer obtain an empty buffer from an empty buffer pool, fill it with information, and place it in a pool of full buffers. The consumer obtains information by picking up a buffer from the full buffer pool, copying the information from the buffer, and placing the buffer into the empty buffer pool for recycling. The producer and consumer use a fixed, finite number, N, of buffers to pass an arbitrary amount of information between them. This solution uses the buffers to keep the producer and consumer roughly synchronized.

Figure 8.18 is a program schema for the producer and consumer processes. The empty and full semaphores illustrate a new type of semaphore, called a **general** semaphore (it is also often called a **counting** semaphore). Whereas a binary semaphore takes on only the values 0 and 1, the counting semaphore takes on values from 0 to N for the N-buffer problem. In the solution, the counting semaphores serve a dual purpose. They keep a count of the number of empty and full buffers. They also are used to synchronize the process operation by blocking the producer when there are no empty buffers and blocking the consumer when there are no full buffers.

The buffers are a block of memory logically split into N parts. Each buffer must contain space for links to associate the buffer with other empty or full buffers and space for the data itself. Since the producer and consumer each manipulate these links, the code for buffer pool manipulation must be treated as a critical section. The mutex semaphore protects access to the two buffer pools so that only one process takes or puts a buffer at a time. The V() operations signal the release of a buffer to the empty or full pool of buffers.

The mutex semaphore is used to protect the critical section relating to manipulating buffers (such as list insert/delete operations). The P(empty) operation blocks the producer if there are no empty buffers. Similarly, the P(full) operation blocks the consumer if there are no full buffers.

✦ FIGURE 8.18 The Bounded Buffer Problem

This solution uses three semaphores: `mutex` is a binary semaphore, while `full` and `empty` are general semaphores (taking on values from 0 to N. The `mutex` semaphore protects the critical section related to adding/deleting buffers to/from a pool. The two general semaphores are used by the producer/consumer process to tell the other process that there are full/empty buffers available.

```
producer() {                          consumer() {
  bufType *next, *here;                 bufType *next, *here;
  while(TRUE) {                         while(TRUE) {
    produceItem(next);                  /* Claim a full buffer */
  /*Claim an empty buffer */              P(full);
    P(empty);                          /* Manipulate the pool */
    /* Manipulate the pool */            P(mutex);
    P(mutex);                              here = obtain(full);
    here = obtain(empty);                V(mutex);
    V(mutex);                            copyBuffer(here, next);
    copyBuffer(next, here);            /* Manipulate the pool */
    /* Manipulate the pool */            P(mutex);
      P(mutex);                            release(here, emptyPool);
      release(here, fullPool);           V(mutex);
      V(mutex);                         /* Signal an empty buffer */
    /* Signal a full buffer */           V(empty);
      V(full);                           consumeItem(next);
  }                                    }
}                                    }
semaphore mutex = 1;
semaphore full = 0;
semaphore empty = N;
bufType buffer[N];
fork(producer, 0);
fork(consumer, 0);
```

THE READERS–WRITERS PROBLEM

Courtois, Heymans, and Parnas [1971] posed an interesting, recurring synchronization problem called the readers-writers problem. Again, since this problem was posed using classic, single-threaded processes, the example also uses them; the solution applies to multithreaded computations as well. Suppose a resource is to be shared among a community of processes of two distinct types: readers and writers. A **reader** process can share the resource with any other reader process, but not with any writer process. A **writer** process requires exclusive access to the resource whenever it acquires any access to the resource.

This scenario is similar to one in which a file is to be shared among a set of processes (see Figure 8.19). If a process wants only to read the file, then it may share the file with any other process that also only wants to read the file. If a writer wants to modify the file, then no other process should have access to the file while the writer has access to it.

✦ FIGURE 8.19   The Readers–Writers Problem

Readers and writers compete for the shared resource (access to a book in the cartoon). Readers can share the resource, but each writer must have exclusive control of the resource.

Writers

Readers

Several different policies could be implemented for managing the shared resource. For example, as long as a reader holds the resource and there are new readers arriving, any writer must wait for the resource to become available. The algorithm shown in Figure 8.20 illustrates how this policy is implemented. In this policy, the first reader accessing the shared resource must compete with any writers, but once a reader succeeds, other readers can pass directly into the critical section, provided that at least one reader is still in the critical section. The readers keep a count of the number of readers in the critical section, with the `readCount` variable, which is updated and tested inside its own critical section. Only the first reader executes the `P(writeBlock)` operation, while every writer does so, since every writer must compete with the first reader. Similarly, the last reader to yield the critical section must perform the V operation on behalf of all readers that accessed the shared resource.

While this solution implements the first policy, it is easy to see that the policy may not produce the desired result. Readers can dominate the resource so that no writer ever gets a chance to access it. This situation is analogous to the case in which a pending update of a file must wait until all reads have completed.

In most cases, you would like the updates to take place as soon as possible. This preference leads to an alternative policy that favors writers. That is, when a writer process requests access to the shared resource, any subsequent reader process must wait for the writer to gain access to the shared resource and then release it.

✦ FIGURE 8.20   First Policy for Coordinating Readers and Writers

In this policy, readers have priority over writers. This is true since once a reader gets control of the shared resource, a stream of subsequent readers can block any writer for an indefinite period of time.

```
reader() {                              writer()( {
  while(TRUE) {                           while(TRUE) {
    <other computing>;                      <other computing>;
    P(mutex);                               P(writeBlock);
      readCount = readCount+1;           /* Critical section */
      if (readCount == 1)                   access(resource);
        P(writeBlock);                    V(writeBlock);
    V(mutex);                             }
    /* Critical section */              }
      access(resource);
    P(mutex);
      readCount = readCount-1;
      if(readCount == 0)
        V(writeBlock);
    V(mutex);
  }
}
resourceType *resource;
int readCount = 0;
semaphore mutex = 1;
semaphore writeBlock = 1;
/* Start the readers and writers */
fork(reader, 0); /* Could be many */
fork(writer, 0); /* Could be many */
```

An algorithm to implement the second policy is shown in Figure 8.21. This policy still allows a stream of readers to enter the critical section until a writer arrives. Once a writer arrives, it takes priority over all subsequent readers, except those already accessing the shared resource. When the first writer arrives, it will obtain the `readBlock` semaphore. Then it blocks on the `writeBlock` semaphore, waiting for all readers to clear the critical section. The next reader to arrive will obtain the `writePending` semaphore and then block on the `readBlock` semaphore. Suppose another writer arrives at this time. It will block on the `writeBlock` semaphore, assuming the first writer has progressed to the critical section. If a second reader arrives, it will block at the `writePending` semaphore. When the first writer leaves the critical section, any subsequent writer is required to have priority over all readers. The second and subsequent writers are blocked at `writeBlock`, and no reader is blocked on the semaphore, so the writers will dominate the resource. When all writers have completed, the readers are then allowed to use the resource.

This example highlights a new problem. Semaphores provide an abstraction of hardware-level synchronization into a software mechanism used to solve simple problems, but complex problems like the readers-writers problem are more difficult. How do we know a solution such as the second readers-writers solution is correct? We are left with two choices:

■ Create a higher-level abstraction (you will learn more about this in Chapter 9).

■ Prove that our synchronized program is correct. That is, semaphores have not eliminated the need for proofs, but they enable us to write more complex scenarios than we could without them.

✦ **FIGURE 8.21**   Second Policy for Coordinating Readers and Writers

The second readers-writers policy gives priority to writers. Even if there are readers using the shared resource, when a writer arrives, it will obtain access to the resource before any other readers are allowed access.

```
reader() {                           writer() {
  while (TRUE) {                       while(TRUE) {
    <other computing>;                   <other computing>;
    P(writePending);                     P(mutex2);
      P(readBlock);                         writeCount=writeCount+1;
        P(mutex1);                           if(writeCount==1)
          readCount = readCount+1;             P(readBlock);
          if(readCount == 1)               V(mutex2);
            P(writeBlock);                 P(writeBlock);
        V(mutex1);                           access(resource);
      V(readBlock);                        V(writeBlock);
    V(writePending);                       P(mutex2);
      access(resource);                      writeCount=writeCount-1;
    P(mutex1);                               if(writeCount==0)
      readCount = readCount-1;                  V(readBlock);
      if(readCount == 0)                   V(mutex2);
        V(writeBlock);                 }
    V(mutex1);                        }
  }
}
resourceType *resource;
int readCount = 0, writeCount = 0;
semaphore mutex1 = 1, mutex2 = 1;
semaphore readBlock = 1;
semaphore writePending = 1;
semaphore writeBlock = 1
/* Start the readers and writers */
fork(reader, 0); /* Could be many */
fork(writer, 0); /* Could be many */
```

PRACTICAL CONSIDERATIONS

There are important practical considerations related to implementing semaphores. The rest of this section deals with how to implement semaphores, avoid busy-waiting on semaphores, and view semaphores as resources. We also consider an important detail related to the implementation of the V operation: active versus passive behavior.

IMPLEMENTING SEMAPHORES   Figure 8.8 showed how interrupts can be disabled to manipulate a lock variable, but not during an entire critical section (as was done in Figure 8.5). A semaphore implementation following this model disables interrupts, but only for a short period of time, and wholly within the P and V function (see Figure 8.22). In the figure, a C++ style class is used to emphasize that the semaphore is implemented as an abstract data type with private data structures and function implementations, but exporting a public interface. Since P and V are operating system functions, the implementation code assumes that user processes can have a reference to the OS semaphore object, meaning that the P(s) semaphore function call would be called by a code segment such as

```
semaphore *s;
...
s = sys_getSemaphore();
...
s->P();
```

The interrupts are enabled most of the time that a thread is blocked on a semaphore; they are disabled only while the semaphore's value is manipulated. This has two important effects:

■ There is minimal effect on the I/O system.

■ While a process holds a semaphore, it only prevents those threads from running that are competing for a relevant critical section. All other threads are unaffected by the fact that one thread is in its critical section.

Semaphores can be implemented without disabling interrupts if the hardware incorporates a few special provisions that the OS can use. Just as in the interrupt-based design, the OS can create an abstract resource for each semaphore. Then it uses resource managers such as those described in Section 6.7 to block processes when they perform a P operation just as if they had performed a request operation on a conventional resource. The issue becomes how the semaphore resource manager can correctly implement simultaneous access to the semaphore without using interrupts.

The **test-and-set** (TS) instruction is the dominant way to accomplish the effects of P and V in modern hardware. The hardware designer can add the TS instruction repertoire with little effort. By doing so, it can make semaphore implementation simple and efficient. The test-and-set instruction

```
TS    R3, m // Test-and-set of location m
```

causes the contents of memory location m to be loaded into a register R3 (with the condition code register for R3 set to reflect the value of the data in R3) and memory location m to be rewritten with a value of TRUE. The essential aspect of TS is that it is a *single machine instruction*. Figure 8.23(a) shows the memory cell m, register R3, and the condition code for register R3 before executing the TS instruction, and Figure 8.23(b) shows the result of executing the instruction.

✦ **FIGURE 8.22**   Implementing Semaphores Using Interrupts

The P operation may cause the calling process to wait. In order to minimize the impact on the rest of the system, interrupts are enabled once per pass through the wait loop.

```
class semaphore {
  int value;
public:
  semaphore(int v = 1) {
  // allocate space for the semaphore object in the OS
    value = v
  };
  P() {
    disableInterrupts();
  // Loop until value is positive
    while (value == 0) {
      enableInterrupts(); // Let interrupts occur
      disableInterrupts(); // Disable them again
    }
    value--;
    enableInterrupts();
  };
  V() {
    disableInterrupts();
    value++;
    enableInterrupts();
  };
}
```

✦ **FIGURE 8.23**   The Test-and-Set Instruction

The "TS   R3, m" instruction loads register R3, tests its value, and writes a TRUE back to memory location *m*.

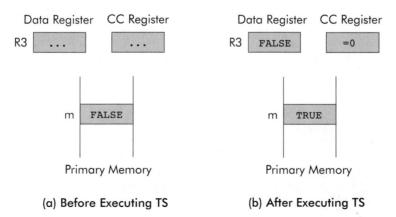

(a) Before Executing TS   (b) After Executing TS

Assume TS is in the instruction repertoire of a machine and it is implemented as an OS function named TS(m), where *m* is a memory cell. Now the critical section problem can be solved as shown in Figure 8.24(a). (Part (b) is the corresponding code using P and V, for comparison.) After the original value from location *s* has been loaded, any interrupting process will detect the value stored in *s* as being TRUE and so will block at the while loop. This occurs even if an interrupt occurs before the process actually begins processing critical section code. The assignment statement's resetting of *s* is assumed to be atomic, since it also would normally be accomplished with a single machine instruction.

✦ FIGURE 8.24 Implementing the Binary Semaphore with TS

The P operation can be implemented by embedding the TS instruction in a while loop that reads the condition code register. The V operation can be implemented by a store instruction with an immediate operand.

```
boolean s = FALSE;              semaphore s = 1;
  ...                             ...
  while(TS(s)) ;                  P(s);
    <critical section>;            <critical section>;
  s = FALSE;                      V(s);
  ...                             ...
        (a)                              (b)
```

One apparent shortcoming of TS is that it replaces only the P operation for *binary* semaphores—the ones taking on only the values of 0 and 1. The obvious question is: Can it be used to implement a general semaphore? Since a counting semaphore can take on any nonnegative value, the TRUE and FALSE values of a binary semaphore cannot represent integers larger than 1. Figure 8.25 is an algorithm that implements general semaphores.

✦ FIGURE 8.25 Implementing the General Semaphore with TS

This algorithm demonstrates that you can use the TS instruction to implement general semaphores. The idea is that you use a binary semaphore, s.mutex, to guard a critical section where integer arithmetic is used to implement a range of semaphore values.

```
struct semaphore {
  int value = <initial value>;
  boolean mutex = FALSE;
  boolean hold = TRUE;
};
shared struct semaphore s;
P(struct semaphore s) {          V(struct semaphore s) {
  while(TS(s.mutex)) ;             while(TS(s.mutex)) ;
  s.value = s.value - 1;          s.value = s.value + 1;
  if(s.value < 0) {               if(s.value <= 0) {
    s.mutex = FALSE;                while(!s.hold) ;
    while(TS(s.hold)) ;            s.hold = FALSE;
  }                               }
  else                            s.mutex = FALSE;
  s.mutex = FALSE;              }
}
```

In this figure, `s.mutex` is used to implement mutual exclusion, while a thread manipulates `s.value` to represent the general semaphore value. The `s.hold` Boolean is used to stage threads blocked by the semaphore. Thus, any thread waiting for the semaphore will be waiting at the statement

```
while (TS(s.hold));
```

in the P procedure. When `s.hold` returns a value of FALSE (the V operation will have set the value FALSE in those cases when it detected threads queued on semaphore s), the thread invoking P will block at the TS in the outer `while` loop. Also, note that a thread executing the P operation will release the critical section related to manipulating the `s.value` entry before it begins waiting on the `s.hold` variable.

One other statement in the solution merits careful consideration. In the V operation, the

```
while (!s.hold);
```

is required. This is because a race condition can occur in which a thread that is blocked in the P procedure, yet the V procedure encounters s.hold as being TRUE. This situation can occur when consecutive V operations occur before any thread executes a P operation. Without the while statement, the result of one of the V operations could be lost.

BUSY-WAITING   A **busy-wait** condition refers to a case where the code repeatedly executes a loop that tests a variable until the variable switches values—as is the case in the `while` loop in Figure 8.22. We first encountered the busy-wait condition when learning how software controls devices (see Section 4.4). Although the implementation using interrupts (Figure 8.22) or the TS instruction (Figure 8.24 and Figure 8.25) greatly reduce the amount of busy waiting compared to the technique used in Figure 8.5, it can still be quite wasteful of CPU time.

Suppose the implementation shown in Figure 8.25 were used in a multiprogrammed uniprocessor system. Then, whenever a process is scheduled to run and it blocks on a semaphore, it will repeatedly execute the

```
while(TS(s.hold));
```

instruction until the timer interrupt invokes the scheduler to multiplex the process off the processor and another process onto the processor. When the blocked process obtains its next timeslice, it will resume this busy-wait if `s.hold` is still TRUE. The result is that the blocked process is slowing down some other process that would eventually execute a V operation and allow the first to proceed. The blocked process needs to indicate to the OS that it cannot do anything useful at the moment. This can be done by executing the equivalent of the `yield` instruction (from Chapter 7). Each time the process detects it is blocked, it might yield to another process that can perform useful work. This method suggests that the busy-waiting statement should be changed to

```
while (TS(s.hold))
   yield (*, scheduler);
```

to eliminate wasting the unused portion of the timeslice by a blocked process.

ACTIVE AND PASSIVE SEMAPHORE IMPLEMENTATIONS   A semaphore value is a consumable resource. A process/thread blocks if it requests a positive semaphore value but the semaphore is zero. When a process encounters a zero-valued semaphore, it moves from the running state to the blocked state. From this perspective, the P operation is a *resource request* operation. A process moves from blocked to running when it detects a positive value of the semaphore; it decrements the semaphore at the same time it changes state. When another process *releases a resource*, by performing a V operation, the resource allocator moves the first process from blocked to ready. Being in the ready state does not mean the process is physically executing on the CPU, but it is at least on the ready list. This style of operation creates the possibility for another implementation complexity: If one process performs a V operation, should the OS "guarantee" that a waiting process will immediately perceive the action?

Figure 8.15 described the account credit and debit processes using a semaphore, `mutex`, to synchronize their access to the `balance` variable. Suppose `proc_0` obtains the semaphore and enters the critical section, while `proc_1` blocks on its `P(mutex)` operation. Suppose further that `proc_0` exits the critical section and then executes `V(mutex)`, and its own `P(mutex)`—all prior to `proc_1` actually having an opportunity to detect that the semaphore took on a positive value. Then `proc_1` could be prevented from entering its critical section even though the semaphore took on positive values while `proc_1` was waiting for the semaphore.

This scenario is most likely to occur on a multiprogrammed uniprocessor if `proc_0` does not yield the CPU immediately after incrementing the semaphore. In implementing the V operation, one is advised to add a `yield()` to the procedure definition immediately after incrementing the semaphore. This form of implementation is called the **active V** operation. This contrasts with the **passive V** operation, where the implementation increments the semaphore with no explicit context switch.

There is another aspect to semaphores that is highlighted with active and passive semaphores. Programmers sometimes treat the P operation as a "wait-for-event-occurrence" operation and the V operation as a "signal" to the waiting process (as in Figure 8.16). If the waiting process (the process blocked on a P operation) is not allowed to run at the time the signal is raised, should the event signaled by the V operation still be considered to be TRUE at the time the P operation finally sees the signal? We will revisit this issue in Chapter 9, where monitors are discussed.

8.4 ● SYNCHRONIZATION IN SHARED MEMORY MULTIPROCESSORS

Sections 8.1 and 8.3 described a technique for implementing semaphores by disabling interrupts. In a shared-memory multiprocessor, this won't work because disabling the interrupts on one CPU does not affect the interrupts on other CPUs. Therefore, commercial shared-memory multiprocessors all use specialized instructions such as TS to implement semaphores.

When a thread uses the busy-wait technique (without using `yield`), the only CPU unable to process other work is the one on which the blocked thread executes. Another thread capable of executing the V operation can be running on a different CPU. Therefore, the busy-wait is a mechanism for *very fast recognition* of the instant at which a thread becomes unblocked—the busy-wait bug becomes a busy-wait feature. In some cases, it is worth using one of N processors to *poll* the `s.hold` variable in order to detect the earliest possible moment the blocked thread becomes unblocked.

Operating systems for shared-memory multiprocessor systems typically support this scenario by including spin locks in the system call interface. A **spin lock** is a procedure that repeatedly performs the TS instruction to test a specified lock variable. To complete the abstract machine interface to the lock, there will be calls to create the lock, to lock and unlock it, and to block on the lock, and often a nonblocking call on the lock. This latter call is used so that if a thread detects it is locked out of a critical section, it can do other operations.

8.5 ● SUMMARY

Concurrent applications are made up of a group of processes/threads that share some resources used to solve the common problem. This introduces the critical section problem, which in turn makes it possible for two or more processes to become deadlocked. You saw several ways that you could address these problems: You could disable interrupts while code is in a critical section, or better, only while the OS manipulates lock variables. You could also use the classic FORK( ), JOIN( ), and QUIT( ) system calls, although those tend to be too slow to be effective. This sets the stage for Dijkstra semaphores.

Semaphores are the basic mechanism underlying all contemporary OS synchronization mechanisms. From a pragmatic viewpoint, semaphores can be implemented in the OS if the hardware supports the TS instruction. The TS instruction can be used to implement binary semaphores directly, or as a component in software to implement general semaphores. The straightforward TS implementation of a semaphore leads to busy-waiting. This waiting can be addressed by constructing the semaphore implementation so that it interacts with the scheduler. When a thread enters a phase of busy-waiting, it should yield to the scheduler. Finally, you saw that there can be active and passive implementations of semaphores. An active implementation calls the scheduler *each* time the semaphore value changes, but the passive implementation only calls the scheduler when a process blocks on the semaphore.

This chapter set the foundation of synchronization and discussed the complexity of dealing with synchronization using semaphores. The next chapter looks at synchronization abstractions.

8.6 ● EXERCISES

1. Suppose processes p_0 and p_1 share variable V_2, processes p_1 and p_2 share variable V_0, and processes p_2 and p_3 share variable V_1.

   a. Show how the processes can use enableInterrupt( ) and disableInterrupt( ) to coordinate access to V_0, V_1, and V_2 so that the critical section problem does not occur.

   b. Show how the processes can use semaphores to coordinate access to V_0, V_1, and V_2 so that the critical section problem does not occur.

2. Enabling and disabling interrupts to prevent timer interrupts from invoking the scheduler is one way to implement semaphores. This technique can influence I/O because it makes the interrupt handler wait until the interrupts become enabled

before the handler can complete an I/O operation. Explain how this could affect the accuracy of the system clock.

3. The following solution is alleged to be a solution to the critical section problem. Argue for its correctness or show a case in which it fails.

```
shared int turn;
shared boolean flag[2];
proc(int i) {
  while (TRUE) {
     compute;
   /* Attempt to enter the critical section */
 try: flag[i] = TRUE; /* An atomic operation */
     while (flag[(i+1) mod 2]){ /* An atomic operation */
         if (turn = = i) continue;
         flag[i] = FALSE;
         while (turn != i);
         goto try;
     }
   /* Okay to enter the critical section */
     <critical section>;
   /* Leaving critical section */
     turn = (i+1) mod 2;
     flag[i] = FALSE;
  }
}
turn = 0; /* Process 0 wins a tie for the first turn */
flag[0] = flag[1] = FALSE;
/* Initialize flags before starting */
fork(proc, 1, 0); /* Create a process to run proc(0) */
fork(proc, 1, 1); /* Create a process to run proc(1) */
```

4. Dijkstra posed each of the following solutions as a potential software solution to the critical section problem and then explained why they failed [Dijkstra, 1968]. Provide your explanation about why they failed.

```
a. proc(int i) {
    while (TRUE) {
       compute;
       while (turn != i);
       critical_section;
       turn = (i+1) mod 2;
    }
  }
  shared int turn;
  turn = 1;
  fork(proc, 1, 0);
  fork(proc, 1, 1);
```

b.
```
proc(int i) {
    while (TRUE) {
        compute;
        while (flag[(i+1) mod 2]);
        flag[i] = TRUE;
        critical_section;
        flag[i] = FALSE;
    }
}
shared boolean flag[2];
flag[0] = flag[1] = FALSE;
fork(proc, 1, 0);
fork(proc, 1, 1);
```

c.
```
proc(int i) {
    while (TRUE) {
        compute;
        flag[i] = TRUE;
        while (flag[(i+1) mod 2]);
        critical_section;
        flag[i] = FALSE;
    }
}
shared boolean flag[2];
flag[0] = flag[1] = FALSE;
fork(proc, 1, 0);
fork(proc, 1, 1);
```

5. In the solution to the bounded buffer problem (Figure 8.18), consider the ordering of the first two P operations in the producer and the consumer. Suppose the order of the `P(full)` and the `P(mutex)` instructions were reversed in the consumer. Would this solution still be correct?

6. Assume the `writePending` semaphore was omitted from Figure 8.21. Describe a simple sequence of reader and writer activity that causes the solution to fail for the second readers-writers policy.

7. Two processes, p_1 and p_2, have been designed so that p_2 prints a byte stream produced by p_1. Write a skeleton for the procedures executed by p_1 and p_2 to illustrate how they synchronize with one another using P and V.

8. The following is alleged to be a solution to the critical section problem. Argue for its correctness or show a case in which it fails.

```
shared int turn;        /* shared variable to synchronize
                           operation */
boolean flag[2];        /* shared variable to synchronize
                           operation */
```

```
proc(int i){
  while (TRUE) {
    <compute>;
    flag[i] = TRUE;   /* Attempt to enter the critical
                          section */
    turn = (i+1) mod 2;
    while ((flag[(i+1) mod 2]) && (turn == (i+1) mod 2));
    /* Now authorized to enter the critical section
    <critical_section>;
    /* Exiting the critical section */
    flag[i] = FALSE;
  }
}
turn = 0;
flag[0] = flag[1] = FALSE;
fork(proc, 1, 0); /* Start a process on proc(0) */
fork(proc, 1, 1); /* Start a process on proc(1) */
```

9. In Chapters 4 and 5, you learned how device driver software synchronizes its behavior with device controller hardware (using the busy and done flags in the controller's status register). In the generic schema shown in Figure 5.6, the driver starts the device in operation, writes the I/O details to the device state table, then halts. The device handler software reads the details from the device status table, completes the I/O operation, then returns from the system call (to the calling program). Some operating systems (such as Linux) use a slightly different approach, relying on the presence of a synchronization mechanism in the kernel. Instead of writing the status to a device status table and halting, the driver simply blocks until the device handler tells it to unblock and return to the caller. Write a pseudocode description for the device driver and handler that illustrates how this works.

10. *The Sleepy Barber Problem* [Dijkstra, 1968]. A barbershop is designed so that there is a private room that contains the barber chair and an adjoining waiting room with a sliding door that contains *N* chairs (see Figure 8.26). If the barber is busy, the door to the private room is closed and arriving customers sit in one of the available chairs. If a customer enters the shop and all chairs are occupied, the customer leaves the shop without a haircut. If there are no customers to be served, the barber goes to sleep in the barber chair with the door to the waiting room open. If the barber is asleep, the customer wakes the barber and obtains a haircut. Write code fragments to define synchronization schemes for the customers and the barber.

✦ FIGURE 8.26 The Sleepy Barber

Customers wait in the waiting room while the barber cuts hair in the room with the barber chair. While there are no waiting customers, the barber sleeps in the barber chair.

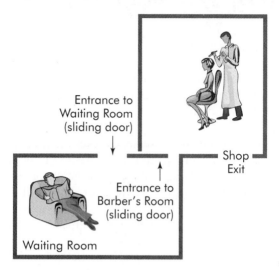

11. Provide a scenario in which a process executing the V procedure in Figure 8.25 will detect when `s.value` is less than or equal to 0 and then `s.hold` is `TRUE`.

12. Suppose a machine's instruction set includes an instruction named `swap` that operates as follows (as an indivisible instruction):

```
swap(boolean *a, boolean *b)
{
  boolean t;
  t = *a;
  *a = *b;
  *b = t;
}
```

Show how swap can be used to implement the P and V operations.

13. Semaphores are not implemented in older versions of UNIX, but processes with `stdout` of one process directed into `stdin` must synchronize their operation in a manner similar to that required in Problem 7. Write a program, `Source`, that copies a file to `stdout` and another program, `Sink`, that reads `stdin` and counts the number of bytes in the stream. Run `Source` and `Sink` with the output from `Source` piped into the input of `Sink`. How are the processes synchronized in your software?

Bounded Buffer Problem

> This assignment can be solved using any Windows or POSIX-compliant OS.

The bounded buffer (producer-consumer) problem is a classic synchronization problem introduced by Dijkstra to illustrate two different ways to use his semaphores (see Section 8.3). In this exercise, you will design two threads to execute in a single address space. A producer thread creates "widgets," and places each widget in an empty buffer for consumption by the consumer thread. The consumer retrieves the widget from the buffer, then releases the buffer to an empty buffer pool. If there are no full buffers, the consumer is blocked until new widgets are produced. If there are no empty buffers available when the producer creates a widget, the producer thread must wait until the consumer thread releases an empty buffer.

This problem asks you to design and implement a process with a producer and consumer thread using N different buffers (use a fixed size for N of 25). Base your solution on the solution to the producer-consumer problem shown in semaphore examples in Section 8.3. You will need a mutual exclusion semaphore to prevent the producer and consumer from manipulating the list of buffers at the same time, a semaphore so that the producer can signal the consumer to start processing when it creates a full buffer, and another semaphore for the consumer to signal the producer when it creates an empty buffer.

There are three subsections in the Background section for this Laboratory Exercise: The first provides general information about the problem, the second describes Windows semaphores as they are used for threads in a single process, and the third describes POSIX threads and their synchronization mechanisms. Read the first subsection and the subsection for the system you will use to solve the problem. The other subsection is optional reading.

● **BACKGROUND** ●

Threads in a single process all use the same address space and resources to solve a common problem. Since they are sharing resources, they usually need to coordinate their execution so that they do not interfere with one another. The Windows synchronization mechanisms all work with threads in a process. For UNIX, you will use the POSIX thread (or **pthread**) package. Most (but not all) UNIX systems support pthreads.

The following pseudocode is adapted from Figure 8.18 (a solution provided in an example in the chapter). As discussed in the main part of the chapter, a producer and a consumer thread are created by a parent thread (all in one modern process). The parent controls the length of time that the child threads run. Meanwhile, they continuously produce and consume widgets in buffers.

```
int runFlag = TRUE;
// pointers to semaphores (you will define the semaphore type
// These are globals and shared
semaphore empty;
semaphore full;
semaphore bufManip;
struct buffer_t {
  int buffer[N];
  unsigned int nextFull;
  unsigned int nextEmpty;
} widgets;

// The main program establishes the shared information used by
// the producer and consumer threads
main() {
// Local variables
  int runTime;                    // Amount of time to execute
  int i;

// Get a value for runTime
  ...
// Initialize synchronization objects
  empty = create_sync_object(N);
  full = create_sync_object(0);
  bufManip = create_sync_object(1);
// Initialize buffer pool
  widgets.nextEmpty = 0;
  widgets.nextFull = 0;
  for(i = 0; i < N; i++)
    widgets.buffer[i] = EMPTY;

// Create producer and consumer threads
  create_child_thread(&prod_thrd, NULL, producer, &widgets);
  create_child_thread(&cons_thrd, NULL, consumer, &widgets);
// Sleep while the children work ...
  sleep(runTime);
  runFlag = FALSE;                // Signal children to terminate

// Wait for producer & consumer to terminate
  ...

// Release the semaphores
  delete_sync_object(empty);
  delete_sync_object(full);
  delete_sync_object(bufManip);

// Now we can quit
  printf("Main thread: Terminated\n");

  exit(1);
}
```

```
... producer(void *wp) {
  struct buffer_t *widgPtr;
  widgPtr = (struct buffer_t *) wp;      // Cast buffer pointer
  srand(P_RAND_SEED);                    // Set random# seed
  itCount = 100;
  while(runFlag) {
  // Produce the buffer
    usleep(rand()%timeToProduce);// Simulate production time
  // Get an empty buffer
    P(empty);
  // Manipulate the buffer pool
    P(bufManip);
    widgPtr->buffer[widgPtr->nextEmpty] = itCount++;
    widgPtr->nextEmpty = (widgPtr->nextEmpty+1) % N;
    V(bufManip);
    V(full);
  }

// Terminate
  ...
}

... *consumer(void *wp) {
  struct buffer_t *widgPtr;

  widgPtr = (struct buffer_t *) wp;
  srand(C_RAND_SEED);                    // Set random# seed
  runFlag = TRUE;
  while(runFlag) {
  // Get a full buffer
    P(full);
  // Manipulate shared data structure
    P(bufManip);
    itCount = widgPtr->buffer[widgPtr->nextFull];
    widgPtr->nextFull = (widgPtr->nextFull+1) % N;
    V(bufManip);
  // Consume the buffer
    usleep(rand()%timeToConsume);        // Simulate consumption
    V(empty);
  }
// Terminate
  ...
}
```

Your job is to define all the italicized functions for thread management and synchroniza-tion. Feel free to use this code segment. Substitute appropriate function names for your target platform (or use these function names as wrappers if you wish). Next, we will look at the OS-specific background information (first Windows, then POSIX threads).

SYNCHRONIZING THREADS IN WINDOWS

There are several different synchronizing mechanisms in Windows, including the `Mutex` and `Semaphore`. A thread synchronizes on a `Mutex`, `Semaphore`, or other OS synchronization object using a wait function. That is, a wait function is similar to a Dijkstra P operation in that a thread calls it whenever it wants to obtain a semaphore or enter a critical section. When a thread calls a wait function, the thread is blocked until the internal state of the synchronization object determines that it is okay for the calling thread to proceed. The most commonly used wait function is `WaitForSingleObject()`:

```
DWORD WaitForSingleObject(
  HANDLE hHandle;          // handle of object to wait for
  DWORD dwMilliseconds;    // time-out interval in
                           // milliseconds
);
```

The `hHandle` parameter is the handle for the synchronization object. The `dwMilliseconds` parameter specifies a maximum amount of time (in milliseconds) that the thread is willing to wait for the object to complete the synchronization. You can use `GetLastError()` to see if the function returned because either a notification was sent by the synchronization object (`GetLastError()` returns `WAIT_OBJECT_O`) or the maximum amount of time expired (`WAIT_TIMEOUT`). You can also use a value of `INFINITE` for `dwMilliseconds`, which means that the calling thread will block until it receives a notification from the object and will never time out. `WaitForSingleObject()` can be used with `Mutex` and `Semaphore` objects. (`WaitForSingleObject()` infers the type of object it is waiting for from the object handle.)

Mutex objects are especially built to handle the critical section problem. A `Mutex` object may have an owner thread, or be unowned. Having ownership of the object means that the thread is "holding the mutex." A thread can become the owner of a `Mutex` object when the object is created, when a handle to it is opened, or by a wait function. To understand the details, consider the function prototypes:

```
HANDLE CreateMutex(
  LPSECURITY_ATTRIBUTES lpMutexAttributes,
                          // pointer to security attributes
  BOOL bInitialOwner,     // flag for initial ownership
  LPCTSTR lpName          // pointer to mutex-object name
);
```

The `bInitialOwner` attribute determines whether or not the calling thread will be the owner of the `Mutex` object. If `bInitialOwner` is set to `TRUE` (and the function call succeeds), the `Mutex` object will be created in a state that can be obtained by another thread. `CreateMutex()` can fail if it selects a name that is already in use—`GetLastError()` will return the value `ERROR_ALREADY_EXISTS`.

Once the `Mutex` object is created, any thread in the calling thread's process can use it. If threads in other processes intend to use the `Mutex` object, then they must know the name of the `Mutex` object and use `OpenMutex()` with the correct name.

If a thread wishes to hold a `Mutex` object, it uses a wait function to request control of the object. A successful call on a `Mutex` object (you must check the return code if you allow a timeout return) causes the calling thread to gain control of the `Mutex`. The `ReleaseMutex()` function call releases the `Mutex`.

`Mutex` objects can be used to solve the critical section problem. Suppose that threads X and Y share resource R—both threads perform some computation, access R, then perform more computation. Since R is a shared resource, the access is a critical section. Here is a code skeleton to handle the problem using a `Mutex` object:

```
int main(...) {
  ...
// Open resource R
  ...
// Create the Mutex objects with no owner (signaled)
  mutexR = CreateMutex(NULL, FALSE, NULL);
  ...
  CreateThread(..., workerThrd, ...) ...;      // Create thread X
  ...
  CreateThread(..., workerThrd, ...) ...;      // Create thread Y
  ...
}

DWORD WINAPI workerThrd(LPVOID) {
  ...
  while(...) {
  // Perform work
    ...
  // Obtain mutex
    while(WaitForSingleObject(mutexR) != WAIT_OBJECT_0);
  // Access the resource R
    ReleaseMutex(mutexR;)
  }
  ...
}
```

`Semaphore` objects implement Dijkstra general semaphore semantics. That is, `Semaphore` objects are able to maintain a count to represent integer values (rather than the implicit binary values of `Mutexes`). A `Semaphore` object is created with a call to:

```
HANDLE CreateSemaphore(
  LPSECURITY_ATTRIBUTES lpSemaphoreAttributes,
                    // pointer to security attributes
  LONG lInitialCount,    // initial count
  LONG lMaximmCount,     // maximum count
  LPCTSTR lpName         // pointer to semaphore-object name
);
```

A `Semaphore` object keeps an internal variable with a value between zero and `lMaximumCount` (which must be greater than zero). When the object is created, the initial value of the internal variable can be set to any value in the allowable range, and is specified by the `lInitialCount` argument. The state of the `Semaphore` object is determined by the value of the internal variable: If it is set to zero, a process that calls a wait function on the Semaphore will block. If the Semaphore has a value in the range [1:lMaximumCount], a wait call will decrement the count and return.

The internal values of the Semaphore object are manipulated indirectly using functions. The ReleaseSemaphore() function increases the internal variable count

```
BOOL ReleaseSemaphore(
    HANDLE hSemaphore,        // handle of the semaphore object
    LONG lReleaseCount,       // amount to add to the current count
    LPLONG lPreviousCount     // address of previous count
);
```

The lReleaseCount parameter specifies the amount to add to the semaphore (potentially causing a state change in the object). The lPreviousCount is a pointer to a variable that will be set to show the value of the count before ReleaseSemaphore() was called (and may be set to NULL if you do not care about the previous value).

Semaphore objects are used in situations where you need to have the synchronization mechanism count values. Suppose that threads X and Y are both using units of resource R—either may request K units, use them for some period of time, then return them. Here is a code skeleton to handle the problem using Semaphore objects:

```
#define N ...

int main(...) {
// This is a controlling thread
    ...
// Create the Semaphore object
    semaphoreR = CreateSemaphore(NULL, 0, N, NULL);
    ...
    CreateThread(..., workerThrd, ...) ...;      // Create thread X
    ...
    CreateThread(..., workerThrd, ...) ...;      // Create thread Y
    ...
}

DWORD WINAPI workerThrd(LPVOID) {
    While(...) {
// Perform some work
        ...
// Acquire K units of the resource
        for(i = 0; i < K; i++)
            while(WaitForSingleObject(semaphoreR) != WAIT_OBJECT_0);
// Perform some work
        ...
// Release the K units
        ReleaseSemaphore(semaphoreR, K, NULL);
        ...
    }
}
```

POSIX THREADS

The POSIX thread package provides a comprehensive set of functions for creating, deleting, and synchronizing threads within a modern process. Some implementations are accomplished completely in user space (meaning that the OS implements classic threads, and a library exports the thread functions). Other implementations provide thread support in the OS, then use the pthread API to export the functions to application programs. In this exercise, it will not matter whether the pthread implementation is done with user space or OS threads, since you will call the functions on the API without having to know their implementation. There are many online reference materials for the pthread package, including man pages on UNIX systems that support pthreads. You will also find it helpful to use your favorite search engine to look for "pthread reference" on the Web.

Threads are created with the pthread_create() function. Here is the function prototype:

```
int pthread_create(pthread_t *thread,
  const pthread_attr_t *attr,
  void *(*start_routine)(void *),
  void *arg
);
```

You will need to include the pthread.h header file to define various thread types (such as pthread_t and pthread_attr_t) and the function prototypes exported by the pthread package. This function creates a new thread to run in the address space of the calling thread. The thread argument is a pointer to a pthread_t, which is a reference to the pthread descriptor for the new thread. It is possible to define various attributes for the new thread (such as the stack size) using the attr argument. For this assignment you can use the default attributes, by using NULL for the attr argument. The third and fourth parameters specify the entry point for a function, start_routine, and its argument, arg. The return value is 0 on success, and nonzero on failure.

A parent thread can wait for a child thread to terminate (that is, synchronize with its termination) using this function:

```
int pthread_join(pthread_t thread, void **status);
```

The thread argument is the pthread_t of the child thread. If the child returns a value using pthread_exit(void *), it will be returned to the parent via the status argument. The child's resources (such as its thread descriptor) will not be deallocated until the parent calls pthread_join().

Suppose we wanted to create a new thread that would begin executing a function with a prototype

```
void *worker_thread(void *a_list);
```

then we could accomplish that with the following code fragment:

```
int main () {
  pthread_t my_thread;
  struct my_struct_t *my_struct;
  int *ret_val;
  ...
  my_struct = ...
```

```
   // Define the argument list for the worker thread
   if(!create(&my_thread, NULL, worker_thread, a_list)) {
     fprintf(stderr, ...);
     ...
   }
   ...
   // Wait for the child to terminate
   if(!pthread_join(my_thread, &ret_val)) { // error return}
}

void *worker_thread(void *arg) {
   int *ret_val;
   ...
   // Work is completed, terminate
   pthread_exit(ret_val);
}
```

There are various synchronization primitives in the pthread API, including mutex, condition variable, and read/write lock. The condition variable primitive combines a mutex and another synchronization primitive to export a specialized mechanism that is not quite the right tool for this exercise. Condition variables were intended to be used in a more abstract mechanism called monitors, which are described in Chapter 9. The read/write lock is intended to be used for problems like the readers-writer problems described in the examples in Section 8.3. That is, multiple readers can simultaneously obtain an rwlock, but only one write can obtain it at a time. That leaves you with the mutex as the primitive to use for solving this Laboratory Exercise.

The pthread_mutex_t type is a synchronization primitive that is created as an unowned resource, and which threads can obtain ownership through the pthread_mutex_lock() call. They relinquish ownership with the pthread_mutex_unlock() call. So pthread_mutex_lock() is used to obtain mutually exclusive control of a critical section (like the Dijkstra P operation), and pthread_mutex_unlock() is used to release that control (like the V operation). Here are the function prototypes for creating a mutex (pthread_mutex_init()), for destroying a mutex (pthread_mutex_destroy()) and the two functions for manipulating a mutex:

```
int pthread_mutex_init(pthread_mutex_t *mutex,
 const pthread_mutexattr_t *attr);
int pthread_mutex_destroy(pthread_mutex_t *mutex);
int pthread_mutex_lock(pthread_mutex_t *mutex);
int pthread_mutex_unlock(pthread_mutex_t *mutex);
```

The mutex argument in all of these functions is the reference to the pthread_mutex_t mutex descriptor. Just as you can provide attributes for a thread when you create it, you can also specify attributes for a mutex. However, the only attribute relates to performance behavior of the implementations, which we will not discuss in this book. Hence, you will use a value of NULL for the attr argument for pthread_mutex_init().

You can consult the documentation to find a few other functions to manipulate a pthread_mutex_t, although these are sufficient to solve the Laboratory Exercise.

Here is a code fragment to solve the account balance problem from Section 8.1 (also see Figure 8.15) using the `pthread_mutex_t`:

```
...
pthread_mutex_t bal_mutex; // Global, accessible to all threads
...
int main () {
   ...
   pthread_mutex_init(&bal_mutex, NULL);
   ...
// Create acct manager threads
...
}

void *acct_mgr(void *foo) { // foo is not used in this example
   ...
   amount = get_amount();
   switch(transaction) {
   case CREDIT:
     pthread_mutex_lock(bal_mutex);
     balance = balance + (double) *amount;
     pthread mutex_unlock(bal_mutex);
     break;
   case DEBIT:
     pthread_mutex_lock(bal_mutex);
     balance = balance - (double) *amount;
     pthread mutex_unlock(bal_mutex);
     break;
   ...
}
```

Notice that `pthread_mutex_t` is a binary semaphore, but you will need a general semaphore to solve the problem. Fortunately, in the main part of this chapter, you learned an algorithm for implementing a general semaphore using only the test-and-set instruction. This will be a good place for you to get started thinking about how to implement a general semaphore for your solution.

• ATTACKING THE PROBLEM •

Before you begin your solution, be sure to read the online documentation for the relevant function calls (the MSDN reference or UNIX man pages). Start with the pseudocode solution in the Background section. You may have to reformulate parts of the pseudocode, and you will certainly have to flesh out the entire implementation.

CHAPTER 9

High-level Synchronization and Interprocess Communication

Semaphores capture the essence of process synchronization, but semaphore-based solutions to complex synchronization problems like the readers-writers problem can be quite complex. Over the years, people have invented various abstractions of semaphores. While these abstractions are no more powerful than semaphores, they are often easier to use. In this chapter, we will consider a few of the most important semaphore abstractions: AND synchronization, events, and monitors. We will also study interprocess communication mechanisms—OS facilities to allow processes and threads to communicate across address spaces. You can think of interprocess communication as another level of generalization of synchronization, since many of these mechanisms have a built-in synchronization aspect. All modern operating systems provide semaphores (or one or more semaphore abstractions) and an interprocess communication mechanism.

9.1 • ALTERNATIVE SYNCHRONIZATION PRIMITIVES

In 1968, Dijkstra posed an amusing, yet difficult synchronization problem called the *dining philosophers problem* [Dijkstra, 1968]: Five philosophers are seated around a table, as shown in Figure 9.1. There are five plates of pasta and five forks on the table. While the philosophers think, they ignore the pasta and do not require a fork. When a philosopher decides to eat, he or she must obtain two forks, one from the left of the plate and one from the right of the plate. After consuming the pasta, the philosopher replaces the forks and resumes thinking. A philosopher to the left or right of a dining philosopher cannot eat while that philosopher is eating, since forks are a shared resource. (The "two fork" style of eating spaghetti comes from Dijkstra's original presentation of the problem. Sometimes the problem is described in an analogy with noodles and chopsticks.) The synchronization problem is to coordinate the behavior of the philosophers so that they are able to alternately think and eat for an indefinite period of time.

✦ FIGURE 9.1   The Dining Philosophers

Each dining philosopher alternately thinks and eats. Whenever a philosopher eats, he or she picks up the forks to the left and right of the plate. After eating, the forks are replaced so that the philosophers to the left and right can then use them .

The dining philosophers problem represents a situation that can occur in large communities of processes that share a sizeable pool of resources. Figure 9.2 is the obvious attempt to solve this problem using semaphores. There are 5 semaphores to represent the state of the 5 forks. A philosopher invokes the P operation on a fork to represent the act of picking up a fork. The problem with this solution is that the philosophers can deadlock if they all pick up their first fork at the same time. Ironically, in this case the philosophers will starve ☺.

✦ FIGURE 9.2   An Attempted Solution to the Dining Philosophers Problem

In this attempted solution, the philosophers could deadlock (and starve) if they all picked up the fork to the left of their plate at the same time.

```
semaphore fork[5];
philosopher(int i){
   while (TRUE) {
   // Think
   // Eat
     P(fork[i]);
       P(fork[(i+1) mod 5]);
         eat();
       V(fork[(i+1) mod 5]);
     V(fork[i]);
   }
}
fork[0] = fork[1] = fork[2] = fork[3] = fork[4] = 1;
fork(philosopher, 1, 0);
fork(philosopher, 1, 1);
fork(philosopher, 1, 2);
fork(philosopher, 1, 3);
fork(philosopher, 1, 4);
```

During the 1960s and 1970s, computer science researchers were highly intrigued by the problem of how to synchronize a community of sequential (single-threaded) processes. System design took a huge leap forward with the seminal work by Dijkstra, culminating in the development of the semaphore. After the discovery of the semaphore, there was a flurry of papers that used semaphores to solve more and more difficult problems (the Readers-Writers problem and the Dining Philosophers problem are examples). After understanding solutions to these difficult synchronization problems, forward thinking researchers began to grow concerned that concurrent programming might be too difficult to be widely used. Even though it was apparent that hardware and networks would evolve to support broad use of parallel computation, suppose the software that controlled the hardware was so difficult to develop that the technology would essentially fail! These forward thinkers began to ponder about abstractions that might make synchronization easier to implement. *It is important to realize that none of these new synchronization mechanisms enable solutions to problems that could not be solved using only semaphores. The goal was to make it easier to solve problems.* A number of alternatives and generalizations have been described in the literature. Next we will consider a few of the most interesting abstractions (ones that are still around today).

AND SYNCHRONIZATION

In many parallel programs, including the Dining Philosopher problem, processes need to synchronize on some *set* of conditions rather than on a single condition. For example, suppose that two shared resources, R_1 and R_2, can be accessed by a community of processes/threads, $\{p_i\}$. Some of the processes need only R_1 and others need only R_2. However, some processes require exclusive access to R_1 and R_2 at the same time. Using semaphores, we can write a code segment such as

```
P(mutexj);
  <access Rj>
V(mutexj);
```

each time a thread wants to access R_j (j is either 1 or 2).

However, suppose a thread, p_r, needs to access both resources. It is easily conceivable that p_r simply nests P operations on both semaphores, as shown in Figure 9.3(a), while p_s nests P operations on the same two semaphores in the opposite order, as shown in Figure 9.3(b). Certain execution sequences by the processes will lead to a deadlock. Suppose p_r obtains $mutex_1$ at the same time p_s obtains $mutex_2$. In this special case, p_r holds $mutex_1$ and blocks waiting for $mutex_2$, while p_s holds $mutex_2$ and blocks waiting for $mutex_1$. The problem arises because sometimes only one of the semaphores should be used, sometimes the other semaphore should be used, and sometimes both should be used. Unfortunately, different programs can be written by different programmers to obtain the semaphores in any order.

Suppose a single abstract P operation could be used to obtain all required semaphores at once or none of them at all. The operation would block the calling thread whenever any of the semaphores could not be obtained. This **simultaneous P**, or **AND synchronization**, has the form

```
Psimultaneous(S1, ..., Sn)
```

✦ FIGURE 9.3   Nesting Semaphore Operations

Different programmers may write their programs to request two semaphores in different orders: For example, p_r may attempt to obtain `mutex1` before `mutex2`, while p_s tries to obtain `mutex2` before `mutex1`. This can lead to deadlock.

p_r P Operation Order	p_s P Operation Order
``` P(mutex1); P(mutex2); <access R₁>; <access R₂>; V(mutex2); V(mutex1); ```	``` P(mutex2); P(mutex1); <access R₁>; <access R₂>; V(mutex1); V(mutex2); ```

```
P(mutex1);
  P(mutex2);
    <access R₁>;
    <access R₂>;
  V(mutex2);
V(mutex1);
```

(a)

```
P(mutex2);
  P(mutex1);
    <access R₁>;
    <access R₂>;
  V(mutex1);
V(mutex2);
```

(b)

The $P_{simultaneous}$ operation is defined as follows [Maekawa, et al., 1987]:

```
P_sim(semaphore S, int N) {
L1: if ((S[0]>=1)&& … &&(S[N-1]>=1)) {
  for(i=0; i<N; i++) S[i]--;
  } else {
    Enqueue the calling thread in the queue for the first S[i]
      where S[i]<1;
    The calling thread is blocked while it is in the queue;
    Goto L1;  // When the thread is removed from the queue
  }
}
```

The $V_{simultaneous}$ operation removes threads from queues when called:

```
V_sim(semaphore S, int N) {
  for(i=0; i<N; i++) {
    S[i]++;
    Dequeue all threads in the queue for S[i];
    All such threads are now ready to run (but may be blocked
      again in Psimultaneous);
  } else {
}
```

Implementing this operation is tricky because it requires that a "third party" enqueue the calling thread (the thread cannot enqueue itself, then release a critical section). In the discussion of monitors you will see that a thread can block itself, though it requires additional mechanisms. Figure 9.4 demonstrates the code executed by this third party for $n = 2$ threads. This solution peeks at the semaphore value (with `R.val` and `S.val`) to determine its value.

Like the other mechanisms described in this chapter, whether or not a simultaneous semaphore mechanism is considered to be "primitive" depends on how it is implemented. If it is implemented using a technique similar to the one explained in Figure 9-4, then it is an abstraction that can be implemented in a library routine. If it is implemented in the operating system—for example, by using a code segment with TS instructions—it can be thought of as a synchronization primitive.

✦ FIGURE 9.4 Simultaneous Semaphores

Simultaneous (AND-style) semaphores can be implemented using conventional semaphores that is executed by a daemon thread instead of the calling thread. A process is blocked on a P.sim operation until it can acquire both semaphores S and R.

```
int R_num = 0, S_num = 0;
Queue R_wait, S_wait;
Semaphore mutex = 1;

P_sim(PID callingThread, semaphore R, semaphore S) {
L1: P(mutex);
    if(R.val>0)&&(S.val>0)) {
       P(R); P(S);
       V(mutex);
    } else {
       if(R.val==0) {
          R_num++;
          enqueue(callingThread, R_wait);
          V(mutex);
          goto L1;
       } else {
          S_num++;
          enqueue(CallingThread, S_wait);
          V(mutex);
          goto L1;
       }
    }
}

V_sim(semaphore R, semaphore S) {
   P(mutex);
   V(R); V(S);
   if(R_num>0) {
      R_num--;
      dequeue(R_wait);   // Release a thread
   }
   if(S_num>0) {
      S_num--;
      dequeue(S_wait);   // Release a thread
   }
   V(mutex);
}
```

Using AND Synchronization to Solve the Dining Philosophers Problem

Let's reconsider the dining philosophers problem illustrated in Figure 9.1. Here we use AND synchronization (for *n*=2) to solve the problem.

```
philosopher(int i){
  while (TRUE) {
  // Think
  // Eat
    P.sim(fork[i], fork[(i+1) mod 5]);
      eat();
    V.sim(fork[I], fork[(i+1) mod 5]);
  }
}
semaphore fork[5];
fork[0] = fork[1] = fork[2] = fork[3] = fork[4] = 1;
fork(philosopher, 1, 0);
fork(philosopher, 1, 1);
fork(philosopher, 1, 2);
fork(philosopher, 1, 3);
fork(philosopher, 1, 4);
```

EVENTS

Events are an abstraction of semaphore operations. They are particularly useful for sig-naling of semaphores (as contrasted with mutex exclusion usage). An event can be used to communicate the occurrence of some condition to a set of processes. If one process needs to synchronize its operation on the occurrence of an event, it can block itself until some other element in the system raises (or posts) the event. Thus, an event is analogous to a semaphore, waiting for an event is analogous to the P operation, and posting the occur-rence of an event is analogous to the V operation.

There are a number of slightly different variants of events in different operating sys-tems, although they are all built on the same basic notion. An event is represented by a sys-tem data structure called an **event descriptor** (or *event control block* or other similar name). Processes can wait for an event, causing them to be placed in a list of processes in the corresponding event descriptor. When a process posts the event, the system call uses the event descriptor to activate one or more of the blocked processes.

The exact semantics of events vary among different systems. Here is a set of commonly used event semantics: An event name (or reference) is often defined in a global address space so that the event can be used by all threads in all modern processes. There are typi-cally three member functions for an event:

- The wait() operation blocks the calling thread until another thread performs a signal() operation.
- The signal() operation resumes exactly one waiting thread if any are suspended on the event by a wait() call. If no threads are waiting when the signal() is issued, it is ignored.
- The queue() operation returns the number of processes currently waiting for an event.

A major distinction between events and semaphores is that if no thread is waiting when a signal is raised, the result of the signal() operation is not saved and its occurrence will have no effect. The rationale for these semantics is that a signal should represent the situa-tion that an event has just occurred, not that it occurred some time in the past. If another thread detects this occurrence at an arbitrary time later (as is the case with the passive semaphore operations), the causal relationships among calls to the `signal()` and `wait()` functions are lost. These semantics are reconsidered in the discussion of monitors in Section 9.2.

Using Generic Events

Suppose an event, `topOfHour`, has been declared. Then

```
topOfHour.signal();
```

means that a process calls the `signal()` procedure for the `topOfHour` event. Another process using the `topOfHour` event can block on the event with a call such as

```
topOfHour.wait();
```

Now suppose several processes wish to suspend themselves until a certain time (say an exact hour such as 5:00:00, as in the espionage example from Chapter 8). Each process calls `topOfHour.wait()` sometime after the last time the event has occurred (after 4:00) but before the next occurrence (5:00). This causes all such processes to be enqueued on the `topOfHour` event. Meanwhile, another process, written as shown in Figure 9.5, reads the system clock to determine when the time reaches the predefined time (the top of the hour in the example). When the clock-reading process detects that the time is right, it signals *all* the enqueued processes to occur concurrently. (Of course, the scheduling strategy will influence the accuracy of this solution, although the intent is that they run as soon as possible after the event has occurred.)

✦ FIGURE 9.5 Synchronizing on an Event

The `topOfHour` event is represented here as class. A process waits for the occurrence of the event with the `wait()` call, and in this case another process polls the clock to determine when it is the top of the hour.

Windows NT/2000/XP Dispatcher Objects

Various Windows NT/2000/XP OS objects are built as subclasses of a class of NT Kernel objects called **dispatcher objects**. Each dispatcher object contains a state variable that allows the object to be in either a *signaled* or *nonsignaled* state (see the Laboratory Exercise in Chapter 8 and Figure 9.6). For example, when a thread is running, the dispatcher object portion of the thread descriptor object is in the nonsignaled state. When the thread terminates, its dispatcher object component transitions to a signaled state. Various other operations can also cause the dispatcher portion of the object state to transition; the exact nature of the operations depends on the exact nature of the OS object that uses the dispatcher object. Software can synchronize its behavior by testing the state of the object using one of the Win32 API wait functions (WaitForSingleObject() and the WaitForMultipleObjects()). The wait functions use a handle to access an OS object and to test its state. If the target object is in the signaled state, the wait function returns to the caller. If the target object is in the nonsignaled state, the wait function blocks the calling thread until the object transitions to the signaled state (or a time-out interval for the call expires). On return from the function call, the calling thread is once again in the runnable state.

What causes an object to transition from one state to the other? In some cases, the transition is a side effect of other activity by the object, and sometimes the transition is accomplished through explicit actions. Objects whose primary purpose is something other than synchronization (for example, process, thread, and file descriptor objects) have implicit state transitions. Objects intended explicitly for synchronization have a spectrum of ways to cause state changes (which is why Windows provides more than one type of synchronization object). A typical sequence for controlling a child thread is as follows:

```
childThreadHandle = CreateThread( ...);
/* The child and parent threads continue concurrently */
...
/* The parent needs to wait for the child to terminate */
WaitForSingleHandle(childThreadHandle, INFINITE);
CloseHandle(childThreadHandle);
```

The WaitForSingleHandle() call provides a parameter to identify which OS object it is waiting to become signaled (childThreadHandle), and a second (INFINITE) that indicates that the wait operation is not subject to a timeout. That is, the call blocks the calling thread for an infinite amount of time if the dispatcher object does not transition to a signaled state.

The WaitForMultipleObjects() function allows a thread to block while waiting for any one, or all, of a set of objects to return a successful synchronization result. For example, you might want to use

```
DWORD WaitForMultipleObjects(
   DWORD nCount,
      // number of handles in the object handle array
   CONST HANDLE *lpHandles,
      // point to the object-handle array
   BOOL bWaitAll,          // wait flag
   DWORD dwMilliseconds    // time-out interval in milliseconds
);
```

The first parameter, nCount, specifies the number of handles in the set of handles on which the function will block. The lpHandles parameter points to an array of the handles that are in the set. The third parameter specifies whether the function should wait for all the objects in the set to send a notification (bWaitAll = TRUE), or for just one (bWaitAll = FALSE). The dwMilliseconds parameter is the time-out value to allow the function to return in a bounded amount of time if desired (as in WaitForSingleObject()). It can have value INFINITE if no time-out is to be used. WaitForMultipleObjects() and arrays of handles can be used as illustrated by this code segment:

```
#define N    ...
...
HANDLE thrdHandle[N];
...
for(i = 0; i < N; i++) {
   thrdHandle[i] = CreateThread(...);
}
...
WaitForMultipleObjects(N, thrdHandle, TRUE, INFINITE);
```

✦ FIGURE 9.6 Windows Dispatcher Object

The Windows dispatcher object contains a variable that can contain the value signaled or not signaled. Dispatcher objects are a component of other OS objects. Each OS object determines the exact semantics of when the state changes from signaled to not signaled and vice versa. The OS object could also be defined so that it activated all threads blocked on an event.

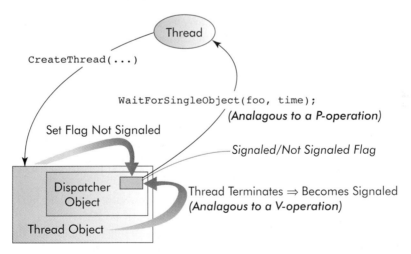

What will happen if the dwMilliseconds parameter is set to zero on a call to WaitForSingleObject() or WaitForMultipleObjects()? The synchronous behavior of the primitives is changed to act like a polling primitive since the time-out immediately expires at the time of the call. On return, the calling process can check the return value to determine the state of the queried objects.

9.2 • MONITORS

Monitors are another attempt to provide better tools for solving synchronization problems. Every synchronization problem that can be solved with monitors can also be solved with semaphores, and vice versa. Monitors just provide a simplified paradigm for some synchronization problems.

PRINCIPLES OF OPERATION

Monitors are based on abstract data types: modules that encapsulate storage, private procedures for manipulating the storage, and a public interface, including procedures and type declarations that can be used to manipulate the information in the storage. A **monitor** is an abstract data type for which only one process/thread may be executing any of its member procedures at any given time. Monitors are generally credited to Hoare [1974] and Brinch Hansen [1977].

The creation of abstract data types was motivated by programmers' desire to hide the implementation of a data structure. Like a class, the abstract data type exports a public interface with member functions and possibly some data. Other software manipulates the data type instance using the public member functions instead of directly manipulating the abstract data type's internal structures. A monitor extends this approach by forcing a process to wait if another process is currently executing one of the monitor's member functions.

Abstract data types were invented to encapsulate data manipulation inside a single software module. This prevented code in one module from directly manipulating the data in another module. The assumption was that a single thread executed the code in both of these modules. It is natural to extend this usage so that it applies to multiple processes/threads: The various processes can execute common software modules, and the abstract data type mechanism will prevent any thread executing in one module from directly manipulating data structures in a different module. The monitor extension pushes this idea one step further: Not only must a thread call a member function to manipulate the data, *member function execution is treated like a critical section!*

For example, suppose an abstract data type has been defined to manage a shared variable, `balance`, and there are interface routines to "credit" values to `balance` and to "debit" values from `balance`. For the abstract data type, its `credit(J)` function will add J to the current value of the `balance` variable inside the abstract data type and `debit(K)` will subtract K from the balance. No two threads will be able to execute `credit()` or `debit()` because they are monitor functions.

Conceptually, a monitor incorporates a critical section into a standard abstract data type template. Figure 9.7 illustrates how a monitor could be described as a standard abstract data type (syntactically the same as a C++ class in our notation) with the private `mutex` semaphore to ensure only one thread is in the monitor at a time.

Now let's look more closely at how a monitor can be used to manage the shared variable, `balance`. Some processes will increment the shared variable, and others will want to decrement it. The monitor shown in Figure 9.8 provides the `credit()` and `debit()` monitor functions to change the value, but protects the access to the shared variable as a critical section. Even though the statements in each monitor function will still be a sequence of machine code when they are compiled, a thread is guaranteed to be able to complete the full sequence of statements as a critical section, since the statements appear inside a `sharedBalance` monitor function.

✦ FIGURE 9.7 Critical Section Within a Monitor

This is a conceptual view of a monitor that illustrates how every monitor public function enforces serial execution semantics. Although monitors are not necessarily implemented this way, they will reflect the same semantics as this code fragment.

```
monitor anADT {
private:
   semaphore mutex = 1;
   <ADT data structures>
   ...
public:
   proc_i(...) {
   P(mutex);
      <processing for proc_i>
   V(mutex);
   };
   ...
};
```

✦ FIGURE 9.8 A Shared Variable Monitor

The shared variable management problem is trivial if it is solved using a monitor. The two public member functions are called to credit and debit amounts to the account. Whenever a thread is running either function, it cannot be interrupted by another thread that wants to execute one of the monitor's member functions.

```
monitor sharedBalance{
private:
   int balance;
public:
   credit(int amount) {balance = balance + amount;};
   debit(int amount) {balance = balance - amount;};
}
```

CONDITION VARIABLES

Sometimes as a process/thread is executing in a monitor, it will discover that it cannot proceed until some other process changes the state of the information protected by the monitor. For example, suppose we were to attempt to solve the second readers-writers problem using monitors, as they have been defined so far. The readers and writers have the general form shown in Figure 9.9.

The figure shows the monitor public procedures—startRead(), startWrite(), finishRead(), and finishWrite()—to be executed when a reader or a writer enters and leaves the critical section.

The solution shown in Figure 9.10 fails for this reason: Suppose that a writer is using the shared resource, meaning that it called startWrite(), which set busy to TRUE and numberOfWriters to 1. That writer then returned from the monitor and began using the shared resource. Meanwhile, a reader calls startRead() (or another writer calls startWrite()). The reader will busy-wait at the while statement until numberOfWriters becomes zero. Unfortunately, it will hold the monitor while it waits, so that when the writer does finish using the shared resource, it will not be able to enter

✦ **FIGURE 9.9** Reader and Writer Schema

Each reader calls `startRead()` before reading the resource, and `finishRead()` after it completes its use of the resource. Similarly, a writer calls `startWrite()` prior to writing the resource and `finishWrite()` after it finishes writing.

```
reader() {                         writer() {
  while(TRUE) {                      while(TRUE) {
  ...                                ...
  startRead();                       startWrite();
    <read the resource>                <write the resource>
  finishRead();                      finishWrite();
  ...                                ...
  }                                  }
}                                  }

fork(reader, 0);
...
fork(reader, 0);
fork(writer, 0);
```

✦ **FIGURE 9.10** A Failed Attempt to Solve a Readers–Writers Problem
Using a Monitor

After a writer has obtained access to the shared resource, if a reader calls `startRead()` it will block at the `while` statement. As long as it is blocked, it will hold the monitor, preventing other processes from executing a monitor member function. This prevents the writer from calling `finishWrite()` when it finishes using the shared resource. The system is deadlocked.

```
monitor readerWriter_1{
  int numberOfReaders = 0;
  int numberOfWriters = 0;
  boolean busy = FALSE;
public:
  startRead () {
    while (numberOfWriters !=0);
    numberOfReaders = numberOfReaders+1;
  };
  finishRead () {
    numberOfReaders = numberOfReaders-1;
  };
  startWrite {
    numberOfWriters = numberOfWriters+1;
    while (busy || (numberOfReaders > 0));

    busy = TRUE;
  };
  finishWrite {
    numberOfWriters = numberOfWriters-1;
    busy = FALSE;
  };
};
```

the finishWrite() monitor function. Neither process can proceed, so the system is deadlocked. The same problem will happen if another writer calls startWrite().

One way to solve this dilemma is to allow the waiting process to *temporarily* relinquish the monitor, while still maintaining its intent to detect a state change within the monitor at a later time. To accommodate this type of situation, monitors incorporate condition variables.

A **condition variable** is a data structure that can only appear within a monitor. It is global to all procedures within the monitor and may have its value manipulated by three operations:

- ■ wait(): Suspends the invoking process and releases the monitor until another process performs a signal() on the condition variable.

- ■ signal(): Resumes exactly one other process if any process is currently suspended due to a wait() operation on the condition variable. If no thread is waiting, then the signal is not saved (and will have no effect).

- ■ queue(): Returns a value of TRUE if there is at least one thread suspended on the condition variable, and FALSE otherwise.

The condition variable looks very much like the generic event that we studied in Section 9.1, and it serves the same purpose, but in the context of a monitor.

There is a variant of the behavior of the signal() operation, which is analogous to the distinction between active and passive semaphores (see Section 8.3): With Hoare's monitor semantics, if a process p_1 is waiting for the signal at the time p_0 executes it from within the monitor, p_0 is suspended while p_1 immediately begins execution within the monitor. When p_1 finishes executing in the monitor, p_0 resumes its execution in the monitor. The rationale for Hoare's approach is that a condition is true at a particular instant in time when the signal occurs, but it may not be true later—for example, when p_0 finishes with the monitor. In his original paper, Hoare uses these semantics to simplify proofs of the correct behavior of monitors.

The semantics for Brinch Hansen's monitors incorporate the "passive" approach. (These semantics are also known as *Mesa monitor semantics* because of their implementation in the Xerox Mesa programming language.) When p_0 executes a signal, the condition is saved while p_0 continues to execute. When p_0 leaves the monitor, p_1 will attempt to continue its execution in the monitor by rechecking the condition. This occurs because even though signal() indicates an event has occurred, the situation may have changed between the time p_0 performed signal and p_1 is allocated the CPU. The argument favoring Brinch Hansen semantics is that there will be fewer context switches than with the Hoare approach. Thus, overall system performance will tend to be better using the Brinch Hansen semantics.

With Hoare semantics, a situation leading to a wait operation might appear as

```
...
if(resourceNotAvailable) resourceCondition.wait();
/* Now available - continue ... */
...
```

When another process executes a resourceCondition.signal(), a context switch occurs in which the blocked thread gains control of the monitor and continues executing at the statement following the `if` statement. The signaling thread is then delayed until the waiting thread finishes with the monitor.

With Brinch Hansen semantics, the same situation would be coded as

```
...
while(resourceNotAvailable) resourceCondition.wait();
/* Now available - continue ... */
...
```

This code fragment ensures that the condition (in this case, `resource-NotAvailable`) is retested before the process executing `resourceCondition.wait()` proceeds. No context switch occurs until the signaling thread voluntarily vacates the monitor.

Using Monitors

Let's consider a few examples using monitors that have condition variables. In these examples, we write `condition.op()` to indicate that `op()` is applied to the condition variable named `condition`.

A CORRECT READERS–WRITERS SOLUTION

The readers-writers solution shown in Figure 9.10 can be modified to use condition variables so that it performs correctly, as shown in Figure 9.11. This example is taken from Hoare's paper; the strategy differs slightly from either of the Courtois-Heymans-Parnas readers-writers solutions. This solution uses the code framework shown in Figure 9.9. The `startRead()` monitor routine waits on the `okToRead` condition variable if the critical section contains a writer (indicated by `busy`'s being TRUE) or if there is a writer queued on the monitor. If the reader proceeds, it increments the number of readers in the shared resource and signals other readers to proceed. When a reader finishes, it signals the writers if there are no other readers waiting. When a writer attempts to enter the critical section, it waits if there are any readers or another writer in the critical section. When a writer finishes, it signals other writers if any are waiting or else it signals the waiting readers. (In Hoare's original paper [1974], the if test in the `finishWrite()` function is written to test the `okToRead.queue`; in compilers with lazy evaluation, this would give preference to waiting readers over waiting writers.)

SYNCHRONIZING AUTOMOBILE TRAFFIC

The exercises for Chapter 8 introduced a problem involving the synchronization of automobile traffic through a one-way tunnel. Suppose a two-way (two-lane) north-south road contains a one-lane tunnel (see Figure 9.12). A southbound (or northbound) car can use the tunnel only if there are no oncoming cars in the tunnel when it arrives at the entrance to the tunnel. When a car approaches the tunnel, a sensor notifies the controller computer by calling a function named `northboundArrival()` or `southboundArrival()` depending on the direction of travel of the car. When a car exits the tunnel, the sensor again notifies the tunnel controller computer by calling a function named `depart()` (this time with the direction of travel passed as a parameter). The traffic controller computer sets signal lights: As usual, green means proceed and red means stop. Figure 9.13 is a solution to the problem using monitors.

✦ FIGURE 9.11 Monitor for Readers–Writers Solution

This solution uses condition variables to prevent the deadlock situation. If a process is stalled, it uses a condition variable `wait()` function, and when monitor functions change the monitor's internal state, they call the `signal()` function.

```
monitor reader_writer_2{
  int numberOfReaders = 0;
  boolean busy = FALSE;
  condition okToRead, okToWrite;
public:
  startRead {
    if (busy || (okToWrite.queue)) okToRead.wait();
    numberOfReaders = numberOfReaders+1;
    okToRead.signal();
  };
  finishRead {
    numberOfReaders = numberOfReaders-1;
    if (numberOfReaders = 0) okToWrite.signal();
  };
  startWrite {
    if ((numberOfReaders != 0) || busy)
      okToWrite.wait();
    busy = TRUE;
  };
  finishWrite {
    busy = FALSE;
    if (okToWrite.queue)
      okToWrite.signal()
    else
      okToRead.signal();
  };
};
```

The monitor provides three functions: `northboundArrival()`, `southboundArrival()`, and `depart()`. When a northbound automobile arrives at the tunnel, it calls the `northboundArrival()` monitor function. The function checks to see if there are any southbound automobiles in the tunnel; if so, each northbound automobile waits on the `busy` condition. Similarly, southbound automobiles wait for northbound traffic. The `depart()` monitor function checks to see if the tunnel is clear. If there are waiting cars from the opposite direction, it signals all of them to proceed.

THE DINING PHILOSOPHERS PROBLEM

We saw a solution to the dining philosophers problem (using AND synchronization) in Section 9.1. Let's consider how we can solve this problem using monitors (see

✦ FIGURE 9.12   One-Way Tunnel

The problem is to synchronize the traffic lights so that cars need not wait when there is no traffic coming from the opposite direction.

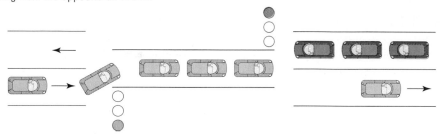

✦ FIGURE 9.13   Traffic Synchronization

The monitor functions manipulate the traffic light state as critical section code. In cases where a process can block within a monitor function, we again use condition variables so that the blocked process releases the monitor.

```
monitor tunnel{
   int northbound = 0, southbound = 0;
   traffic_signal northbound_signal = RED,
       southbound_signal = RED;
   condition busy;
public:
    northboundArrival() { // Northbound car wants to enter
                          // the tunnel
       if(southbound > 0) busy.wait; // Southbound cars in the
                                     // tunnel
       northbound = northbound+1; // OK to proceed
       northbound_signal = GREEN;
       southbound_signal = RED;
    };
    southboundArrival() { // southbound car wants to enter the
                          // tunnel
       if(northbound > 0) busy.wait; // Northbound cars in the
                                     // tunnel
       southbound = southbound+1; // OK to proceed
       southbound_signal = GREEN;
       northbound_signal = RED;
    };
    depart(Direction exit) { // A car exited the tunnel
      if(exit==north) {
        northbound = northbound-1;
        if(northbound==0) while(busy.queue) busy.signal;
      };
      else if(exit==south) {
        southbound = southbound-1;
        if(southbound==0) while(busy.queue) busy.signal;
      }
   };
};
```

Figure 9.14): All philosophers are initially thinking, represented by the state[i] being set to the value thinking. When philosopher *i* wishes to eat, the pickUpForks(i) monitor function is called. This function allows the process to proceed only if both adjacent forks are available (see the private function test() in the monitor). The philosopher moves to the eating state only if his or her two neighbors are not in the eating state. Otherwise, the philosopher waits for a signal. Suppose the philosopher had been blocked. He or she needs to be signaled when either neighbor calls putDownForks(). However, the signal should not be issued until both neighbors have left the eating state. Whenever any philosopher is hungry, he or she tests the forks of both neighbors. If both neighbors are eating and the philosopher attempts to eat, then both will have to call putDownForks() before the philosopher can move from the hungry state to the eating state. This solution allows a situation in which the philosopher never obtains both forks at once, since either the left or right neighbor might always have a fork.

◆ **FIGURE 9.14** Monitor for the Dining Philosophers

This monitor, presented by Hoare in his paper, solves the dining philosophers problem. The test() procedure is used in an attempt to pick up the forks, and again by a philosopher when the forks are released.

```
#define N
enum status {eating, hungry, thinking};
monitor diningPhilosophers{
   status state[N];
   condition self[N];
   int j;
// This procedure can only be called from within the monitor
   test(int i) {
      if ((state[i-1 mod N] !=eating) &&
          (state[i]==hungry) &&
          (state[(i+1) mod N] !=eating)) {
        state[i] = eating;
        self[i].signal;
      }
   };
public:
   pickUpForks(int i) {
     state[i] = hungry;
     test(i);
   if (state[i] !=eating) self[i].wait;
};
putDownForks(int i) {
   state[i] = thinking;
   test((i-1) mod N);
   test((i+1) mod N);
};
   diningPhilosophers() { // Monitor initialization code
      for(int i=0; i<N; i++) state[i] = thinking;
   };
}
```

SOME PRACTICAL ASPECTS OF USING MONITORS

Monitors can easily be misused. Suppose we encapsulated a monitor call within a monitor function; that is, we have *nested monitor calls*. There is a danger that one thread could hold the outer monitor while it waited for the inner monitor to become available. Of course, another thread might hold an outer monitor that is the same as the inner monitor requested by the first process, while it requests an inner monitor that is the same as the outer monitor held by the first process. The result is a deadlock.

A monitor is a powerful high-level mechanism for dealing with complex synchronization problems. In general, monitors have not been widely supported by commercial operating systems. For example, UNIX does not support general monitors (although some versions support mechanisms patterned after monitors). However, a monitor is a high-level language construct that is useful for solving many difficult problems. For example, Modula-3 and Java both incorporate monitors. We expect to see high-level tools like monitors supported in newer languages, runtime systems, and operating systems.

Perhaps the best insight into the early use of monitors comes from the implementation of a monitor in the Xerox Mesa programming language [Lampson and Redell, 1980]. The implementation experience reported in the paper highlights the difficulty of handling the myriad of details:

> *When monitors are used in real systems of any size, however, a number of problems arise which have not been adequately dealt with: the semantics of nested monitor calls; the various ways of defining the meaning of wait; priority scheduling; handling of timeouts, aborts and other exceptional conditions; interactions with process creation and destruction; monitoring large numbers of small objects.* [p. 105]

OS developers have tended to avoid the complexity of implementing monitors, leaving the programmer with tools such as locks, semaphores, events, and interprocess communication to solve synchronization problems.

9.3 ● INTERPROCESS COMMUNICATION

Monitors allow threads to share information by using shared memory within the monitor. If you are familiar with object-oriented programming, then monitors are an intuitive and natural mechanism for coordinated information sharing among threads in a process. Up to now, all the examples in which information sharing is required have assumed the existence of shared address space (or some shared memory among processes) to accomplish information sharing. In situations where the threads are in *different* processes—there is no shared address space—the OS must assist the threads in sharing information. The problem can be especially severe if the two processes are implemented on different computers; in this case, there is not even any physical primary memory that is accessible to all the processes.

This section introduces **interprocess communication (IPC)** mechanisms as a way for a thread in one process to share information with threads in other processes—even processes that exist on a different machine. (*Intraprocess* communication—communication among threads within a single process—is trivially easy, since these threads use the same address space. IPC is used for communicating across address spaces.) In IPC, the

OS explicitly copies information from a sending process's address space into a distinct receiving process's address space. If the two processes are implemented on the same machine, then the OS can perform the copy operation by overriding the memory security mechanism to read one part of the computer's primary memory that has been allocated to the sending process, and then by writing the information into the primary memory that has been allocated to the receiving process. If the sending and receiving processes are implemented on different machines, then the OS has additional work to do, although the work is not visible to the sending and receiving processes:

- The sending machine's OS will copy the information from the sender's address space to a communication device. The device will then transmit the information to a communication device on the receiver's machine.

- The OS on the receiving process's machine can then copy the information from its communication device into the address space of the receiving process.

The problem of physically transmitting information from one machine to another is discussed more in Chapter 15. This chapter focuses on the way the OS can provide the basic IPC model capable of moving information among address spaces on a single machine.

THE PIPE MODEL

UNIX introduced the notion of a kernel data structure called a pipe to support sharing across address spaces. A **pipe** is a first-in, first-out buffer implemented in the kernel. The pipe has a read end and a write end, each treated as a file reference (as returned by the file open() command). If any thread knows the file reference for the write end, it can call the normal file write() function to have the OS place data into the pipe. Similarly, if a thread knows the file reference for the read end, it uses the kernel read() function to remove the data from the pipe.

One limitation of pipes is in providing a process with a file reference. UNIX accomplishes this by treating it the same as an open file descriptor. Then, whenever a process creates a child process, the child inherits the pipe end as an open file descriptor. This effectively means that the only processes that can use pipes are a parent and the child processes it created after it created a pipe. These are called **anonymous pipes**. Soon after people began to use anonymous pipes for IPC, they recognized this limitation. As a result, UNIX systems now also provide named pipes, or pipes that have names similar to file names.

In **named pipes**, a process obtains a pipe end by using a string that is analogous to a file name, but which is bound to a pipe. This allows any set of processes to exchange information using a "public pipe" whose end names are file names. When a process uses a named pipe, the pipe is a system-wide resource, potentially accessible by any process. Just as files have to be managed so that they are not inadvertently shared among many processes at one time, named pipes must also be managed (using the file system commands).

Pipes are a very simple model for accomplishing IPC. Since they were introduced in UNIX, programmers have grown accustomed to using them. As a result, they are also provided in other operating systems such as Windows. Lab Exercise 9.1 at the end of this chapter provides details for using pipes in both UNIX and Windows.

MESSAGE PASSING MECHANISMS

People use messages to communicate with one another all the time—as email messages, instant messages, telephone messages, faxes, telegrams (at least in the last century), and so on. If you want to leave a message for another person, then you compose the message in a form you think the recipient will understand, and then you transmit it to a buffer (a "mailbox") that holds the recipient's messages.

IPC abstractions use the same idea. The sender process composes a **message** as a block of formatted information. The OS copies the message from the sending process's address space into the receiving process's address space (see Figure 9.15). The difficult thing about message transmission is that a sender is prevented from copying information into another process's address spaces by the address space isolation mechanism. Threads running in one address space have no ability to reference addresses in a separate address space, since this can only be done by supervisor mode (OS) software. Instead, the sender requests that the OS deliver a message in its address space to a receiving process or thread (using the OS identifier for the process or thread). The OS ordinarily transmits the message in a few distinct copy operations: It retrieves the message from the sender's address space, placing it into an OS buffer. It then copies the message from the buffer into the receiver's address space.

✦ FIGURE 9.15   Using Messages to Share Information

The OS copies information stored in one address space into an OS buffer. It will then copy the information from the buffer into the recipient's address space.

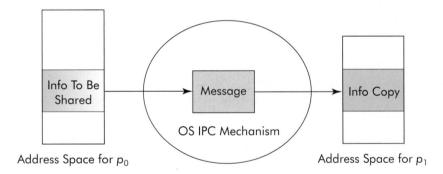

MAILBOXES

Figure 9.15 suggests that a message send operation could spontaneously change the contents of the receiving process's address space without the receiver being aware of the change. We can avoid this by not actually copying the information into the receiver's address space until the receiver explicitly asks for it with a receive operation. The OS can store incoming messages in the recipient's **mailbox** buffer prior to copying them into the receiver's address space. Figure 9.16 shows a more detailed view of message passing in which the operating system's role is explicit and the receiver's mailbox is identified.

Since the mailbox is allocated in the user space, the receive call can be a library routine instead of an OS function. That is, since the information is being copied from one part of the receiver's address space to another, it can be done without using privileged instruc-

✦ FIGURE 9.16 Message Passing with Mailboxes

A mailbox can be used to prevent information from spontaneously appearing in a recipient's address space. When the OS receives a message for a particular process, it stores the message in the address space in the mailbox area.

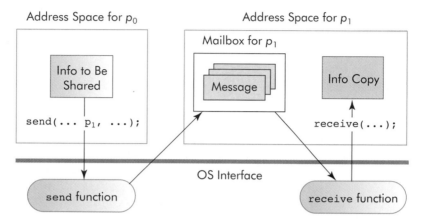

tions. However, there are a few problems with allocating space for the mailbox in the user address space: The translation system (compiler and loader) must allocate space in each process for the mailbox. Since the mailbox is in the recipient's address space, it is possible for the receiving process to inadvertently overwrite parts of the mailbox, thereby destroying links and losing messages.

One alternative is to keep each process's mailbox in the system space; this defers the copy operation until the receiver makes the receive system call (see Figure 9.17). This option places the burden of mailbox space management on the OS. It also prevents inadvertent destruction of messages or headers, since the mailbox is not directly accessible to any application process. But this option requires that the OS allocate memory space for mailboxes for each process. Thus, there is a system-wide upper bound on the number of messages awaiting delivery at any given time. In the rest of this discussion, assume that mailboxes are implemented in the operating system, since this is the more common approach.

MESSAGE PROTOCOLS

A message is a sequence of bits. For the message to have meaning to the receiving process, there must be an agreement between the sending and receiving processes regarding the format used to both store information by the sending process and interpret the information by the receiving process. That is, there must be a **protocol** between the sender and the receiver by which both agree on this message format. For example, the message may contain an instance of a C structure with the understanding that both processes have access to a common header file defining the structure.

Most message-passing facilities employ a header for the message. This header, which is understood by all processes in the system, identifies various pieces of information relating to the message, including the sending process's identification, the receiving process's identification, and the number of bytes of information being transmitted in the body of the

✦ FIGURE 9.17 Mailboxes in System Space

Modern operating systems typically keep all mailboxes in the system space. This is a conservative approach that provides better assurance that the IPC mechanism operates correctly. However, it does bound the number of pending messages in the system.

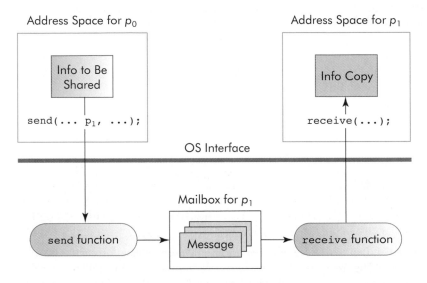

message. In robust message-passing systems, the message may even have a type, which can be used to identify messages containing specialized information such as synchronization information and error reporting. At the other end of the spectrum are IPC mechanisms (such as in UNIX pipes) in which no header or other structuring information is provided by the OS. Instead, the cooperating processes choose and implement their own protocol.

USING THE send() AND receive() OPERATIONS

There are two general options for using the send() and receive() operations:

- The send() operation may use synchronous or asynchronous semantics.
- The receive() operation may use blocking or nonblocking semantics.

THE send() OPERATION The send() call may be synchronous or asynchronous, depending on whether the sender wishes to synchronize its own operation with the receipt of the message. The **asynchronous** send() operation delivers the message to the receiver's mailbox and then allows the sending process to continue operation without waiting for the receiver to read the message. A sender that performs an asynchronous send() operation is not concerned with *when* the receiver actually received the message. In fact, the sender will not even know whether the receiver even retrieves the message from its mailbox.

The **synchronous** send() operation is intended to incorporate synchronization along with information transfer. It blocks the sending process until the message has been successfully "received" by the destination process. There is a weak form and a strong form of the synchronous send() operation: In the weak form, the sending process resumes execution after the message has been safely *delivered* to the receiver's mailbox. In the strong form, the sender remains blocked until the receiving process actually *retrieves* the message from the mailbox. The strong form of the synchronous send() operation supports the kind of semantics you would expect if you wanted to accomplish interprocess synchronization using the message system. The weak form is differentiated from the asynchronous send() in that it assures that the receiver exists and that the message has been deposited in the mailbox; it differs from the strong form in that it does not assure that the receiving process has actually retrieved the message. The weak form does not accomplish interprocess synchronization, but it does provide *reliable* message transmission (as contrasted with asynchronous send() operation, which provides neither). OS IPC mechanisms typically support the weak form of the synchronous send operation (for example, the POSIX msgsnd() system call). The Win32 subsystem provides a strong form synchronous send operation, the SendMessage() function, although it is not implemented in the Windows NT/2000/XP OS.

Strong synchronous message transmission uses the same basic cooperation paradigm as all other producer–consumer computations. The sender is a producer, and the receiver is a consumer. Think of a semaphore, messageReceived (initially 0), being used to coordinate the sender and receiver. The synchronous send operation acts as if the transmission were immediately followed by a P(messageReceived). The corresponding V(messageReceived) implicitly occurs when the receiver accepts the message.

Either the synchronous or asynchronous send() operation can fail in various situations. If the sender attempts to transmit a message to a nonexistent process, the OS will not be able to identify a mailbox in which to buffer the message. How should this situation be handled? In the case of a synchronous send() operation, an error is returned to the sender so that it synchronizes with the occurrence of the error condition rather than with the completion of message transmission. In the case of an asynchronous send() operation, the sender continues after "transmitting" the message and does not expect any return value. Without a mechanism such as UNIX signals, there is no way for the OS to inform the sending process that its operation failed. Therefore, some systems block on an asynchronous send() operation until the message is actually placed in the receiver's mailbox (they are effectively a weak form synchronous send() operation). However, there is no implied synchronization between the sending and receiving processes, since the receiver may read the mailbox at any arbitrary time after the message has been delivered.

THE receive() OPERATION A receive() operation can be blocking or nonblocking. A **blocking receive()** operation behaves like a normal file read operation in POSIX or Windows operating systems. That is, when a process calls receive(), if there is no message in the mailbox, the process suspends operation until a message is placed in the mailbox. If the mailbox contains one or more messages, the blocking receive() operation returns immediately with a message. Thus, when the mailbox is empty, the blocking receive() operation synchronizes the receiver's operation with that of the sending process. According to the synchronization paradigm, it is as if the receiver executes a P(messageTransmitted) on a semaphore with initial value of 0 before receiving the message. The synchronization is completed when the sender implicitly executes a V(messageTransmitted) when the message is sent. Notice that the receive() operation is also analogous to a resource request in the sense that it causes the calling process to suspend until the resource, an incoming message, is available.

A **nonblocking `receive()`** operation queries the mailbox and then returns control to the calling process immediately, with either a message if there is one in the mailbox or an indicator that no message is available. This method allows a receiving process to poll the mailbox, but to continue with other work if there is no pending message. The receiver can still synchronize with a message from the sender, but it is not required to do so.

Synchronized IPC

Two processes, p_1 and p_2, can copy information back and forth and synchronize their operation using the strong form of the synchronous `send()` and blocking `receive()` operations. In Figure 9.18, process p_1 sends `message`$_1$ to p_2 in an attempt to signal its intent to synchronize. If p_2 has already performed the `blockReceive()` (blocking receive) operation, it is asleep, awaiting a message. If there were other messages in the mailbox, it would have done its side of the synchronization with the senders of those messages. Assuming p_2's mailbox was empty at the time p_1 sent `message`$_1$, process p_2 will be awakened by the incoming message and p_1 will resume as a result of the message having been received. At this point, p_1 and p_2 are synchronized. After the message has been received by p_2, the two processes proceed independently. When they wish to synchronize again, they follow the protocol by which the processes have been constructed: p_2 takes the initiative to transmit the synchronizing signal by sending `message`$_2$ to p_1, and then p_1 cooperates in the synchronization by performing a `blockReceive()` operation to wait for p_2's signal.

✦ **FIGURE 9.18** Synchronizing Using Messages

Strong or weak synchronous `send()` and blocking `receive()` operations can be used to synchronize processes in cases where the receiver is waiting for a message. With the strong form of synchronous `send()`, the processes always synchronize at the operation pair.

```
Process p₁                        Process p₂
...                               ...
/* Signal p₂ for sync*/           /* Wait for p₁ signal */
syncSend(message₁, p₂);           blockReceive(msgBuffer, from)
...                               ...
/* Wait for p₂ signal */          /* Sync with p₁ */
blockReceive(msgBuffer,from);     syncSend(message₂, p₁);
...                               ...
```

DEFERRED MESSAGE COPYING

Message copying can become a major performance bottleneck, since the information must be copied from the sender's address space, first into a message buffer and then into the receiver's address space. In concurrent applications in which processes may pass messages almost as often as they call functions, the OS spends a significant fraction of its service time copying messages from user space to the message and copying the message contents into the receiver's address space.

In contemporary systems that have a single physical memory (independent of the number of CPUs), the **copy-on-write** optimization is often incorporated into the system. In many instances, information sent from one address space to another will be *read* by the receiver but never modified by either the sender or the receiver. If the OS can override the memory protection mechanism, it can use copy-on-write message semantics to reduce the number of times a message is copied. When the sender identifies a block of memory in its address space as the source of the message, rather than copying the buffered information into a message, the OS constructs a pointer from the mailbox area to the buffered information. When the message is received, the OS copies the pointer, rather than the whole message, into the receiver's address space so that it can directly reference the information in the sender's buffer area. As long as the buffered information is not changed, both processes can read the information without interfering with each other. However, if either attempts to *write* the information, the OS intervenes. It copies the information from the sender's buffer area into the private part of the receiver's address space so that each has its own copy and the effect of the write (by either process) will not be perceived by the other one.

9.4 • SUMMARY

At the highest level, the description is greatly chunked, and takes on a completely different feel, despite the fact that many of the same concepts appear on the lowest and highest levels.

—Douglas R. Hofstadter, *Gödel, Escher, Bach: An Eternal Golden Band*

As Hofstadter observed, many complex systems tend to have recursive-like solutions to problems. It can be argued that this applies to synchronization. Semaphores provide the fundamental mechanism to achieve synchronization, although they may be difficult to use to solve complex synchronization problems. Alternative primitives for semaphores include the simultaneous P operation and events. These mechanisms are abstractions of semaphores and thus invite many of the same criticisms. Monitors are a high-level language primitive for accomplishing information sharing and synchronization. They have a strong camp of followers, but do not appear in many contemporary operating systems due to implementation complexities. Even so, much of the intellectual difficulty designers encounter when using plain old Dijkstra semaphores occurs again with the higher primitives described in this chapter.

Interprocess communication abstracts synchronization to a level where the synchronization mechanism can also carry information among cooperating processes. IPC mechanisms enable processes to transmit messages among themselves. A message is a block of information copied from one process's address space indirectly into another. The sender and the receiver agree on the format of the message. Send operations may be synchronous or asynchronous, with the former enabling the sender to synchronize its operation with the receiver. Receive operations can be blocking or nonblocking. A blocking receive causes the receiver process to synchronize with a sending process in the case that the receive is executed prior to the corresponding send. Pipes in UNIX systems are the analog of mailboxes.

This chapter completes the discussion of synchronization. The next chapter looks at the fundamental aspects of deadlock, particularly at the level of abstraction used by a resource manager.

9.5 • EXERCISES

1. Suppose processes p_0 and p_1 share variable V_2, processes p_1 and p_2 share variable V_0, and processes p_2 and p_3 share variable V_1. In addition, p_0, p_1, and p_2 run concurrently. Write a code fragment (similar to those in the figures in this chapter) to illustrate how the processes can use monitors to coordinate access to V_0, V_1, and V_2 so that the critical section problem does not occur.

2. Suppose process p_0 uses variables V_0 and V_1 at the same time, process p_1 uses variables V_1 and V_2 at the same time, and process p_2 uses variables V_2 and V_0 at the same time. Further, p_0, p_1, and p_2 run concurrently. Write a code fragment using the simultaneous semaphore operations to coordinate access to V_0, V_1, and V_2 so that the critical section problem does not occur.

3. Construct a monitor that implements semaphores. This will demonstrate that a monitor can be used any place a semaphore can be used.

4. Suppose that you had created an OS facility that implemented monitors, but not condition variables. Show how to implement condition variables using Dijkstra semaphores.

5. Create a pseudocode solution for Problem 4 using POSIX semaphores.

6. Create a pseudocode solution for Problem 4 using Windows synchronization primitives.

7. *The Sleepy Barber Problem.* A barbershop is designed so that there is a private room that contains the barber chair and an adjoining waiting room with a sliding door that contains N chairs (see Figure 8.26 in Chapter 8). If the barber is busy, the door to the private room is closed and arriving customers sit in one of the available chairs. If a customer enters the barbershop and all chairs are occupied, the customer leaves the shop without a haircut. If there are no customers to be served, the barber goes to sleep in the barber chair with the door to the waiting room open. If the barber is asleep, the customer wakes the barber and obtains a haircut. Write a monitor to coordinate the barber and the customers.

8. Give an example of a concurrent application in which a sender process could use an asynchronous rather than a synchronous `send()` operation. Provide another scenario in which the sender should use a synchronous `send()` operation in order for the application to operate properly.

9. Explain why a concurrent application written using nonblocking message `receive()` operations could require less real time to execute than if it were written using blocking `receive()`operations. Also explain why the approach requiring less real time may be complex to construct.

10. Programmer-scheduled thread packages allow the programmer to control when each thread is executed and when it must wait. Calls to the thread package (executed by a thread) allow the programmer to schedule other threads. Explain how this type of control mechanism can be used to approximate the behavior of condition variables in a monitor for thread synchronization.

11. The Mach C threads and POSIX C threads libraries incorporate thread creation operations to create a new thread within a process's address space. (Example C thread code appears in Chapter 2.) Read the documentation on either package and compare the thread creation operation with the UNIX `fork()` operation. Explain how threads synchronize when a child thread exits.

12. Construct a C/C++ program for a UNIX environment to use the *trapezoidal rule* to approximate the integral of

$$f(x) = 1/(x+1)$$

for the interval [0, 2]. In quadrature (numerical integration), the value of the integral is approximated by partitioning the x-axis into n equal-sized segments. If x_i and x_{i+1} are two points on the x-axis that are the endpoints of one of these segments, then you can think of a trapezoid formed by the straight lines from $f(x_i)$ to $f(x_{i+1})$, from $f(x_{i+1})$ to x_{i+1}, from x_{i+1} to x_i, and from x_i to $f(x_i)$. The straight line from $f(x_i)$ to $f(x_{i+1})$ is an approximation of the function, so the trapezoid is an approximation of the integral for that part of the function. You can approximate the integral for [0, 2] by computing the sum of the n trapezoids in that interval. This approximation to an integral is called *numerical quadrature*. Construct your solution so that you compute the areas of the n small trapezoids by N individual worker processes. The controller process should spawn N worker processes using the `fork` and `exec()` UNIX system calls. There should be one pipe with which all N worker processes send results to the controller and N pipes the controller uses to assign a trapezoid to a worker process. Whenever a worker process is ready to compute the area for another trapezoid, it sends the controller a result on the shared "input" pipe. When the controller process receives all the sums from the worker processes, it sums them and prints the answer, along with the amount of time required to obtain the solution (and ignoring the time to set up the processes and the pipes). Experiment with various values of N between 1 and 8 for $n = 64$ trapezoids. Use a `getTime()` routine (see the exercises in Chapter 1) to instrument your program so that you can measure the amount of time spent processing your code. Include a suitably large for loop in your procedure to evaluate the area of a trapezoid so that you can measure the time to accomplish the computation. Plot the amount of time versus the value of N used in the approximation.

13. Solve the quadrature problem in the previous exercise using your local (C or POSIX) threads library. You will have to read online documentation for the thread package on your host OS, where you will find that the thread primitives are quite similar to the process primitives introduced in Section 2.3.

14. *Successive overrelaxation* (SOR) is a method used to solve linear $n \times n$ systems of equations, $Ax = b$. Given the coefficient matrix A, the right-side vector b, and an initial estimated solution vector x, the algorithm recomputes each x_i based on the x_j $(i \neq j)$, A, and b. First, write the n equations as

$$a_{11}x_1 + a_{12}x_2 + \ldots + a_{1n}x_n = b_1$$
$$a_{21}x_1 + a_{22}x_2 + \ldots + a_{2n}x_n = b_2$$
$$\ldots$$
$$a_{n1}x_1 + a_{n2}x_2 + \ldots + a_{nn}x_n = b_n$$

Arbitrarily use the ith equation to solve for x_i, yielding

$$x_i = (b_i - a_{i1}x_i - a_{i2}x_2 - \ldots - a_{in}x_n)/a_{ii}.$$

Now you can implement SOR on an n process system by having the ith process compute x_i. Implement an SOR solution using UNIX pipes calls. [*Hint: Lab Exercise11.1 solves the same problem, although that exercise requires the use of shared memory instead of pipes. Feel free to browse the notes regarding that solution in preparing your pipe solution.*]

15. Write a C/C++ program, `vt`, that will enable a user to simultaneously execute two interactive sessions. The `vt` program should support the two sessions by "filtering" all keyboard input before passing it to the subject programs and keeping a virtual screen for each program to be written to the physical screen whenever the user is interacting with a particular program. You will have to implement a time-multiplexed display of the virtual screens on the physical screen. Thus, the user will always have one or the other virtual screen visible at any given time, but never both. The visible screen represents the active program, and the invisible screen represents a dormant program. If the user types input, your keyboard routine should route the input to the active program. When the user types "ESCAPE" followed by "C," your program should make the active program dormant and the dormant program active. This toggle should change the physical screen so that it shows the virtual screen for the newly activated program. You also will need the sequence "ESCAPE followed by Q" to terminate your program. You may assume that you do not have to pass "ESCAPE sequence" to any shell. When `vt` starts executing, run a shell on each virtual terminal. If you have solved Lab Exercise 2.1, the shell from that program will be easier to use than production-level shells such as `sh`.

Using Pipes

This exercise can be solved on any UNIX or Windows system.

This problem is to write a multiple process program to manipulate information in a "pipeline" fashion. The first process, called the *source* process, is a source of information: It should use the host file interface to read information from a file, then to write the information to an anonymous pipe. The second process, called the *filter* process, reads information from the source (passed via the pipe), performs a simplified filtering step (such as converting uppercase characters to lowercase ones and vice versa), and then writes the data to a named pipe. The named pipe is used for IPC between the filter and a third process, called the *sink* process. The sink process reads the named pipe from the filter, and then writes the information to a second file. Be sure that you write the filter so that it does not block on empty input when it has output information to transmit.

✦ FIGURE 9.19 Source, Filter, and Sink Processes

For this exercise, you will use anonymous and named pipes to transmit information across address spaces.

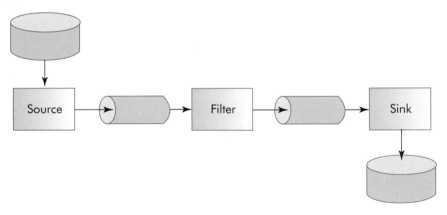

Some things that make this exercise interesting are that:

1. It uses pipes as an IPC mechanism to pass data across address spaces, and
2. The intermediate filter must read the incoming pipe asynchronously with respect to writing results to the output pipe.

● BACKGROUND ●

ANONYMOUS PIPES IN UNIX

Pipes are the main IPC mechanism in uniprocessor UNIX (complemented by sockets in multiprocessor and network BSD UNIX; see Chapter 15). By default, a pipe employs asynchronous `send()` and blocking `receive()` operations. Optionally, the blocking `receive()` operation can be changed to be a nonblocking `receive()` (see the details below). Pipes are FIFO buffers designed with an API that is as similar as possible to the file I/O interface. A pipe can contain a system-defined maximum number of bytes at any given time—usually 4KB. As indicated in Figure 9.20, a process can send information by writing it into one end of the pipe and another process can receive the information by reading the other end of the pipe.

✦ FIGURE 9.20 Information Flow Through UNIX Pipes

A pipe is a kernel buffer that can be read and written, even when there is no shared address space. The buffer interface is the same as a UNIX byte stream file interface. Once the pipe has been created, it is read and written with file I/O operations.

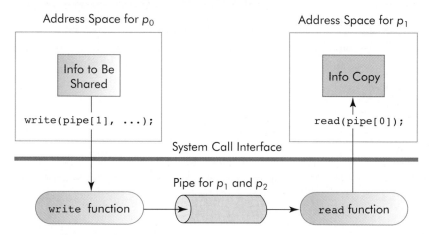

A pipe is represented in the kernel by a file descriptor. When a process wants to create a pipe, it makes a system call of the form:

```
int pipeID[2];
...
pipe(pipeID);
```

The kernel creates the pipe as a kernel FIFO data structure with two file identifiers. In this example code, `pipeID[0]` is a file pointer (an index into the process's open file table) to the read end of the pipe and `pipeID[1]` is file pointer to the write end of the pipe.

In order for two or more processes to use anonymous pipes for IPC, a common ancestor of the processes must create the pipe prior to creating the processes. Because the UNIX `fork()` command creates a child that has a copy of the parent's open file table (that is, the child has access to all files that the parent has already opened), each child inherits pipes that the parent created. To use a pipe, it need only read and write the proper file descriptors.

For example, suppose a parent creates a pipe; then it can create a child and communicate with it using a code fragment such as

```
...
pipe(pipeID);
if(fork() == 0) { /* The child process */
    ...
    read(pipeID[0], childBuf, len);
    /* process the message in childBuf */
    ...
} else { /* The parent process */
    ...
    /* Send a message to the child */
    write(pipeID[1], msgToChild, len);
    ...
}
```

The following code fragment illustrates how pipes can be used in UNIX to implement the concurrent processing example used in Figure 2.8:

```
int A_to_B[2], B_to_A[2];
main(){
  pipe(A_to_B);
  pipe(B_to_A);
  if (fork()==0) { /* This is the first child process */
    execve("prog_A.out", ...);
    exit(1); /* Error-terminate the child */
  }
  if (fork()==0) { /* This is the second child process */
    execve("prog_B.out", ...);
    exit(1); /* Error-terminate the child */
  }
/* This is the parent process code */
  wait( ...);
  wait( ...);
}

proc_A(){
  while (TRUE) {
    <compute A1>;
    write(A_to_B[1], x, sizeof(int));
      /* Use this pipe to send info */
    <compute A2>;
    read(B_to_A[0], y, sizeof(int));
      /* Use this pipe to get info */
  }
}
```

```
proc_B(){
  while (TRUE) {
    read(A_to_B[0], x, sizeof(int));
      /* Use this pipe to get info */
    <compute B1>;
    write(B_to_A[1], y, sizeof(int));
      /* Use this pipe to send info */
    <compute B2>;
  }
}
```

NONBLOCKING READ OPERATIONS IN UNIX

As with any file, the read end of a pipe, a file descriptor, or a socket can be configured to use nonblocking semantics with an `ioctl()` call in UNIX. After the call has been issued on the descriptor, a `read()` on the stream returns immediately with the error code set to EWOULDBLOCK in 4.3 BSD (or EAGAIN in POSIX). Also, the `read()` will return a value of 0, thereby indicating it did not read any information into the buffer. Alternatively, the program can check the length value to see if it is nonzero and if the read succeeded. The following code fragment illustrates the use of the `ioctl()` to switch the read end of a pipe from its default blocking behavior to nonblocking behavior:

```
#include <sys/ioctl.h>
int errno; /* For nonblocking read flag */
...
main() {
  int pipeID[2];
  ...
  pipe(pipeID);
/* Switch the read end of the pipe to the nonblocking mode */
  ioctl(pipeID[0], FIONBIO, &on);
  ...
  while(...) {
  /* Poll the read end of the pipe */
    read(pipeID[0], buffer, BUFLEN);
    if (errno !=EWOULDBLOCK){
    /* Incoming info available from the pipe-process it */
      ...
    } else {
    /* Check the pipe for input again later-do other things */
      ...
    }
  }
  ...
}
```

ANONYMOUS PIPES IN WINDOWS

Windows also supports UNIX anonymous pipes. Once a pipe has been created, `ReadFile()` and `WriteFile()` can be used to read and write the two ends of the pipe.

You can create a pipe with:

```
BOOL CreatePipe(
    PHANDLE hReadPipe,          // address of variable for read handle
    PHANDLE hWritePipe,
                               // address of variable for write handle
    LPSECURITY_ATTRIBUTES lpPipeAttributes,
                               // pointer to security attributes
    DWORD nSize                // number of bytes reserved for pipe
);
```

You must allocate space for the read and write handles (hReadPipe and hWritePipe), and then pass the resulting pointers, provide the security attributes, and supply a suggested number of bytes, nSize, to use to implement the pipe (the OS will use the value as a parameter in determining how much memory to use to implement the pipe). It is acceptable to pass zero for nSize, meaning that Windows will use a default pipe size.

If you attempt to read an empty pipe, the ReadFile() call will block the calling thread until there is data in the pipe.[1] If you attempt to write to a full pipe, the WriteFile() call will block until there is space for the characters to be written to the pipe. Since a pipe is essentially an OS memory buffer (as opposed to a real file), Windows does not support seek operations on a pipe.

The challenge in using pipes is in getting them set up so that multiple processes can use them. The first problem is that an anonymous pipe is created by one process, with read and write handles in that process's address space. How can another process get the file handles from the creating process? The standard techniques for passing a handle from one process to another are to use a global name (anonymous pipes do not have names) handle inheritance and handle duplication.

Here is a technique used in Hart [1997] that takes advantage of the processes that use the pipe being siblings where the common parent creates the pipe and passes the handles as redirected stdin and stdout:

```
int main(int argc, char *argv[]) {
    HANDLE readPipe, writePipe;
    SECURITY_ATTRIBUTES pipeSA;
    STARTUPINFO srcStartInfo, sinkStartInfo;
...
// Create the pipe
    pipeSA.nLength = sizeof(SECURITY_ATTRIBUTES);
    pipeSA.lpSecurityDescriptor = NULL;
    pipeSA.bInheritHandle = TRUE;
    if(!CreatePipe(&readPipe, &writePipe, &pipeSA, 0)) {
        fprintf(stderr, "...", GetLastError());
        ExitProcess(1);
    }
// Create process to write the process
// Make handles inheritable
    printf("Main: Creating producer process\n");
    ZeroMemory(&pStartInfo, sizeof(STARTUPINFO));
```

---

[1] Although overlapped I/O has not yet been discussed, it is worth noting here that Windows does not support overlapped I/O on anonymous pipes.

```
    srcStartInfo.cb = sizeof(STARTUPINFO);
    srcStartInfo.hStdInput = GetStdHandle(STD_INPUT_HANDLE);
    srcStartInfo.hStdOutput = pfWritePipe;
    srcStartInfo.hStdError = GetStdHandle(STD_ERROR_HANDLE);
    srcStartInfo.dwFlags = STARTF_USESTDHANDLES;
    if(!CreateProcess(..., &srcStartInfo, ...)){
       fprintf(stderr, "...", GetLastError());
       ExitProcess(1);
    }

// Create process to read the pipe
// Make handles inheritable
    ZeroMemory(&cStartInfo, sizeof(STARTUPINFO));
    sinkStartInfo.cb = sizeof(STARTUPINFO);
    sinkStartInfo.hStdInput = fcReadPipe;
    sinkStartInfo.hStdOutput = GetStdHandle(STD_OUTPUT_HANDLE);
    sinkStartInfo.hStdError = GetStdHandle(STD_ERROR_HANDLE);
    sinkStartInfo.dwFlags = STARTF_USESTDHANDLES;
    if(!CreateProcess(..., &sinkStartInfo, ...)){
       fprintf(stderr, "...", GetLastError());
       ExitProcess(1);
    }
// Close pipe handles
  CloseHandle(readPipe);
  CloseHandle(writePipe);
  ...
}
```

The created processes use any I/O functions to read and write `stdin` and `stdout`.

NAMED PIPES IN WINDOWS

Named pipes can be used to allow unrelated processes to communicate with one another in both UNIX and Windows. The following discussion explains how it works in Windows.

A **named pipe** is an IPC mechanism that can be used between address spaces. It is specifically designed to be used by a server that intends to interact with multiple clients using named pipes over a network. Named pipes differ from ordinary pipes in a few important ways:

- A named pipe can have several *instances*. All instances have the same parameters: They are intended to be copies of the same pipe. However, each instance can be used by a different pair of processes. For example, a server might use a named pipe to establish the *class* of named pipes, and then each client that connects to the server uses a new instance of the named pipe.

- Named pipes are bidirectional, so a process can read and write each end of the named pipe.

- Named pipes can extend over a network.

Since the motivation for multiple instances is a client-server scenario, one process (the server) creates the named pipe, and then clients open the named pipe using `CreateFile()` with the pipe name.

```
HANDLE CreateNamedPipe(
  LPCTSTR lpName,            // pointer to pipe name
  DWORD dwOpenMode,          // pipe open mode
  DWORD dwPipeMode,          // pipe-specific modes
  DWORD nMaxInstances,       // maximum number of instances
  DWORD nOutBufferSize,      // output buffer size, in bytes
  DWORD nInBufferSize,       // input buffer size, in bytes
  DWORD nDefaultTimeOut,     // time-out time, in millisecs
  LPSECURITY_ATTRIBUTES lpSecurityAttributes
  // pointer to security attributes structure
);
```

The lpName parameter is the name of the pipe; it must have the form \\.\pipe*pipename*. The dwOpenMode parameter specifies several aspects of the way the pipe is to behave: the access to the pipe, the overlapped mode, the write-through mode, and the security access mode of the pipe handle. Pipe access can be any of the following:

■ PIPE_ACCESS_DUPLEX. Information can be transmitted in both directions on the pipe.

■ PIPE_ACCESS_INBOUND. The data is only allowed to flow from the client to the server over the named pipe.

■ PIPE_ACCESS_OUTBOUND. The data is only allowed to flow from the server to the client over the named pipe.

If the FILE_FLAG_WRITE_THROUGH flag is set, then a write to a named pipe—even over a network—does not return until the information is placed in the buffer at the receiving machine. The FILE_FLAG_OVERLAPPED flag sets the I/O to be overlapped. The security flags are used to specify how protection settings can be changed. The dwPipeMode parameter specifies the type, read, and wait modes for the operation. If the pipe is to be used for byte stream transmission, the type value is PIPE_TYPE_BYTE; if it will be used with messages, the PIPE_TYPE_MESSAGE value is passed. The read mode can be set to accept streams or messages using PIPE_READMODE_BYTE or PIPE_READMODE_MES-SAGE. The mode flag controls whether reads are blocking (PIPE_WAIT) or nonblocking (PIPE_NOWAIT). The nMaxInstances parameter specifies the maximum number of pipe instances that can be opened for this pipe. The nOutBufferSize and nInBufferSize parameters specify the size of the pipe's output and input buffers, respectively. The nDefaultTimeOut parameter provides a default timeout that may be used by the WaitNamedPipe call.

● ATTACKING THE PROBLEM ●

This exercise will challenge your skills for organizing several processes and their components so that they work together. It will be quite difficult for you to test the asynchronous behavior of your solution without introducing some artifact to make the various processes operate at different speeds. It will be helpful if you introduce some code to simulate processes that have a lot more work to do than the actual processes you write. The idea is that you have your processes sleep (or perform a busy loop) for random amounts of time. This will allow information to build up in the pipes.

In UNIX, use the rand() function call to introduce random delay. In Windows, you can use a similar function in the C runtime library. Here is a Windows code segment using the facility that should give you the guidance you need to include the simulated work in your source, filter, and sink processes.

```
#include     <stdlib.h>                     // srand() & rand()
#define      P_RAND_SEED   1234
int main (int argc, char *argv[]) {
  const int delay = 500;
  ...
  srand(P_RAND_SEED);                        // Set random# seed
// Main loop
  while(...) {
    ...
    simulatedWork(rand()%delayFactor);  // Random delay
    ...
  }
  ...
}
```

Refining the Shell

This exercise can be solved on any UNIX system.

Starting with the shell program in the Lab Exercise 2.1, refine it to handle commands with arguments, to search the PATH variable to find a file (using the `execv()` form of the `exec()` system call), and to provide additional functionality to manage pipes and concurrency. As before, your shell program should use the same style for running programs as that used in the UNIX sh command.

When the user types a line such as

```
identifier [identifier [identifier]]
```

your shell should search the UNIX directory tree in the order identified by the PATH variable for a file with the same name as the first identifier, which may be a filename or a full path name. Then your shell should execute that file.

For this lab exercise, add the following functionality to your shell program:

PART A

Implement the "&" modifier so that if the last character on the command line is "&," the program is executed in parallel with the shell, rather than the shell's having to wait for it to complete.

PART B

Allow the standard input or output file to be redirected using the "<" and ">" symbols.

PART C

The standard output from one program may be redirected into the standard input of another program using the "|" symbol.

PART D

It is more difficult to implement the shell so that it *simultaneously* supports redirection, pipes, and putting a process in the background. This part of the exercise asks you to modify your shell so that it handles more than one of these cases on a single command line.

● BACKGROUND ●

This exercise will give you substantial insight into how UNIX systems handle file identifiers and will hone your skills in concurrent programming.

CONCURRENT PROCESSES

The normal paradigm for executing a command is for the parent process to create a child process, to start it executing the command, and then to wait until the child process terminates (see Chapter 2). If the "&" operator is used to terminate the command line, then the shell will create the child process, start it executing on the designated command, but not have the parent wait for the child to terminate. That is, the parent and the child are executing concurrently. While the child executes the command, the parent prints another prompt to `stdout` and waits for the user to enter another command line. If the user starts several commands, each terminated by "`&`," and if each of them takes a relatively long time to execute, then there can be many processes running at the same time.

When a child process is created and started executing on its own program, both the child and the parent expect their `stdin` stream to come from the user via the keyboard, and for their `stdout` stream to be written to the character terminal display. This means that the user will not know which of the child processes will receive data on its `stdin` if data is typed to the keyboard while multiple child processes are running concurrently and all expect the keyboard to define their `stdin` stream. Similarly, if any of the concurrent processes write characters to `stdout`, they will be written to the terminal display wherever the cursor happens to be positioned. The kernel makes no provision for giving each of these child processes its own keyboard or terminal (unlike the virtual terminal in Exercise 12, or a window system, both of which control the multiplexing and demultiplexing through explicit user actions).

I/O REDIRECTION

When a process is created, it has three default file identifiers: `stdin`, `stdout`, and `stderr`. If the process reads from `stdin`, then the data it receives will be directed from the keyboard to the `stdin` file descriptor. Similarly, `stdout` and `stderr` are mapped to the terminal display.

The user can redefine `stdin` or `stdout` whenever a command is entered. By providing a file name argument to the command and by preceding the file name with a "<" character, the shell will substitute the designated file for `stdin`; this is called "redirecting the input from the designated file." The output can be redirected (for the execution of a single command) by preceding a file name with the ">" character. For example, a command such as

```
wc < main.c > program.stats
```

will create a child process to execute the `wc` command, but before it launches the command, it will redirect `stdin` so that it reads the input stream from the file named `main.c`, and it will redirect `stdout` so that it writes the output stream to a file named `program.stats`.

The shell can redirect I/O by manipulating the child processes file descriptors. When a child process is created, it inherits the open file descriptors of its parent. Specifically, it inherits the same keyboard for `stdin` and the terminal display for `stdout` and `stderr` (this explains more about why concurrent processes read and write the same keyboard and display). After the child has been created, the shell can change the file descriptors used by the child so that it reads and writes streams to files rather than to the keyboard and display.

Each process has its own file descriptor table (called `fileDescriptor` in this discussion, but not in the source code) in the kernel. The file descriptor will be explained further in Laboratory Exercise 13.1. When the process is created, the first entry in this table refers by convention to the keyboard, and the second two refer to the terminal display.

Next, the C runtime environment and the kernel treat the symbol "stdin" so that it is always bound to fileDescriptor[0] in the kernel table; "stdout" is associated with fileDescriptor[1]; and "stderr" is associated with fileDescriptor[2].

The close() system call can be used to close any open file, including stdin, stdout, and stderr. By convention, the dup() and open() commands always use the earliest available entry in the file descriptor table (the one that was just closed). Therefore, a code fragment such as

```
fid = open(foo, O_WRONLY | O_CREAT);
close(1);
dup(fid);
close(fid);
```

will create a file descriptor, fid, to duplicate the entry, and place the duplicate in fileDescriptor[1] (the normal stdout entry in the process's file descriptor table). The result is that when the process writes characters to stdout, they will be written to the file named foo. This is the key to redirecting both stdin and stdout.

• ATTACKING THE PROBLEM •

The modifications to your shell program from Lab Exercise 2.1 involve considerable detail, but they use the concepts explained in the Background section of this exercise. You will have to design a way to parse the command line so that you recognize the special symbols, and then force your shell into the corresponding action. Because it is difficult to get general code where more than one of the special symbols is used in one command line, in Parts A–C, focus on solving the exercise when it uses "&," "<," ">," or "|," but do not focus on more than one of these at a time.

Deadlock

Deadlock is a significant problem that can arise in a community of cooperating or competing threads or processes. We first encountered deadlock in Chapter 8: Deadlock could subtly creep into our synchronization solutions unless we were very careful. This chapter generalizes the discussion so that it applies to overall resource management. The problem is especially interesting because its occurrence depends on the characteristics of two or more different programs and on threads executing the different programs at the same time. The programs might be executed repeatedly by several different threads without encountering deadlock and then become deadlocked because of some intricate resource usage pattern. There are three automated strategies for addressing deadlock: (1) prevention, (2) avoidance, and (3) detection and recovery, as well as manual administration. This chapter provides background for studying the problem using simple, but formal, models of processes and resources. It then considers the approach used in each of these strategies.

10.1 • BACKGROUND

Deadlock occurs in many facets of our everyday lives, although humans tend to deal with the problem by using approaches that are not easily used in software. The deadlock examples in Chapters 8 and 9 involved dining philosophers, sleeping barbers, and other situations that are analogous to software configurations. Probably the most well-known example in the real world is **gridlock** among automobiles in heavy traffic. For example, gridlock can occur when the four one-way streets around a block have heavy traffic on them and automobiles enter the intersections in an attempt to progress (see Figure 10.1). In the example, a stream of automobiles traveling along a one-way street corresponds to a thread in a process and each intersection is a shared resource. The northbound automobiles hold the intersection resource at the southwest corner of the block and require control of the northwest intersection to proceed. However, the eastbound traffic stream holds the northwest intersection and requests the northeast intersection, and the southbound traffic holds the northeast intersection and requests the southeast intersection. The westbound traffic completes the deadlock because it holds the southeast intersection and requires the southwest intersection held by the northbound stream.

✦ FIGURE 10.1 Automobile Gridlock

Deadlock can occur in all kinds of real-world situations, such as automobile gridlock in a busy metropolitan area. The problem occurs because each stream of cars holds one intersection, but needs another intersection before it can proceed.

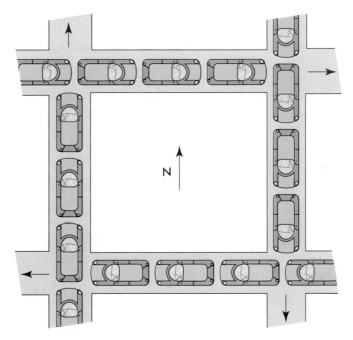

One solution to this form of deadlock is for a traffic policeman to move cars a little at a time so that one car that was blocked from entering an intersection is able to pass through, breaking the deadlock. Another solution is for one of the lines of cars to move in reverse so that an intersection will be freed, again breaking the deadlock. In computer software, there is usually no software operation that is analogous to having cars move a little, although the equivalent of having cars move in reverse can sometimes be accomplished by destroying or otherwise preempting threads and processes. Another difficulty is that in software, as in real life, it is sometimes impossible for one thread to distinguish between being temporarily blocked compared to being permanently blocked—deadlocked.

Dijkstra [1968] described a **deadly embrace** that can occur among a group of two or more processes/threads whereby each process holds at least one resource while making a request on another. (In the automobile gridlock, each intersection is a resource and a line of automobiles corresponds to a process—the line of cars holds one intersection and requests another one.) The request can never be satisfied because the requested resource is being held by another process that is blocked, waiting for the resource that the first process is holding. Figure 10.2 illustrates a deadlock among three single-threaded processes on three resources. The three processes might have put the system in the state shown in the figure by executing the following code fragments:

Process 1	Process 2	Process 3
...	...	...
request(resource1);	request(resource2);	request(resource3);
/*Holding res 1*/	/*Holding res 2*/	/*Holding res 3*/
...	...	...
request(resource2);	request(resource3);	request(resource1);

Process 1 is holding Resource 1 and requesting Resource 2; Process 2 is holding Resource 2 and requesting Resource 3; Process 3 is holding Resource 3 and requesting Resource 1. None of the single-threaded processes can proceed because all are waiting for a resource held by another blocked process. Unless one of the processes detects the situation and is able to withdraw its request for a resource and release the one resource allocated to it, none of the processes will ever be able to run.

✦ FIGURE 10.2 Three Deadlocked Processes

This figure illustrates a three-way deadlock: Process i holds Resource i but cannot progress until it acquires Resource (i+1 mod 3). Each process will wait forever for the requested resource.

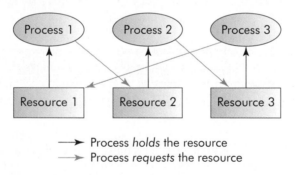

⟶ Process *holds* the resource
⟶ Process *requests* the resource

Modern operating systems support threads as the active element of computation, each running in the context of a process. This movement from the classic single-threaded processes to ones that can have several threads has improved OS designs, making it possible for an application programmer to use different threads to implement a community of distinct activities. For example, multiple threads can be activated so that an object-oriented program may have several simultaneously active objects at any given time. C programmers can create multiple threads to overlap computation with I/O: One thread creates a child thread that does a blocking I/O call while the original thread continues executing a CPU computation. Two different parts of the computation (in a process) can be active at the same time.

Deadlock becomes a little more subtle in systems that support multiple threaded processes, because in the general case like the example shown in Figure 10.2, it is threads that become deadlocked, even though system resources are allocated to processes. Let's consider two different cases where deadlock can occur:

- **Thread-thread deadlock within a process.** Suppose that a process defines two different locks, L_1 and L_2, that can be used by its threads to synchronize their access to a variable in the process (that is, the variable is global to every thread in the process, but local to the process). One block of code in the process causes a thread to obtain L_1, then to later obtain L_2, while another block of code in the same process causes a thread to first obtain L_2, and then L_1. Of course, this is a situation that can cause two threads within the process to deadlock.

- **Thread-thread deadlock across processes.** Consider a case where there are two different processes, p_1 and p_2, where a community of threads, $\{p_{1,i})$ run in p_1, and $\{p_{2,j}\}$ run in p_2. In this situation, it could be that thread $p_{1,r}$ obtains a resource, R_1 (such as a file) for p_1, and at about the same time $p_{2,s}$ obtains a resource R_2 (such as a floppy disk drive) for p_2. Later, another thread in p_1, $p_{1,u}$, requests R_2 and blocks; soon thereafter, $p_{2,v}$ requests R_1, completing the deadlock of $p_{1,u}$ and $p_{2,v}$.

In the remainder of this chapter, we will consider the simplest case so that you can focus on the concepts that are crucial to the deadlock concept. This means that the discussion will be in terms of single-threaded processes, using the classic process terminology. As you read this, remember that the same concepts apply to the case of thread-thread deadlock within a process and across processes for multithreaded situations.

Resource managers and other OS functions can be involved in a deadlock situation. Suppose a thread in a very large application process wishes to acquire a disk block, meaning that it makes a request to a disk resource allocator. When the application process was activated, suppose it was allocated almost all of the physical primary memory by the memory manager. Now suppose the disk block allocation manager is a process swapped out of the primary memory. It requires memory so that it can be loaded to satisfy the disk block request, but the application process has not left enough free memory for the disk block allocator to be loaded! As shown in Figure 10.3, the application process and the disk block allocation process are deadlocked.

◆ FIGURE 10.3 Deadlock Between an Application and the OS

Deadlock can happen between any two processes, even if one or both is executing OS code.

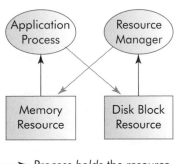

⟶ Process *holds* the resource
⟶ Process *requests* the resource

In Chapter 8, deadlock appeared as a side effect of some synchronization strategies. Because two processes wished to update a pair of shared variables in a consistent manner, they used a lock flag to ensure that when the value of one variable was changed, the other's value would be updated. Similar situations recur in communities of processes that are sharing any kind of resources. In fact, that is why a resource is defined as being anything that a process needs—consumable or reusable—in order to proceed. Memory, a tape drive, a message, a positive semaphore value, a particular tape to be mounted on a tape drive—are all resources. A process can block when it requests any of these entities; thus, any of them can contribute to a deadlock.

Like critical sections, deadlock is a *global condition* rather than a local one. As a result, if we analyzed a program for any thread involved in a deadlock, we would find no error. The problem lies not in any single thread or program, but in the collective action of the group of threads. How, then, can a programmer be expected to deal with a deadlock? An individual thread cannot generally detect a deadlock, since it is blocked and unable to use the processor to do any work. It would also have to be able to analyze all the programs for every thread with which it shared resources, which is a difficult thing to support. Because of this need to consider multiple programs and threads, deadlock management is handled by the OS instead of by the programmer or compiler.

How can operating systems be constructed to ensure that a deadlock is handled properly? There are three general approaches and one *ad hoc* approach:

- Prevention
- Avoidance
- Detection and recovery
- Manual deadlock management (the *ad hoc* approach)

PREVENTION

Suppose the following conditions hold regarding the way a process uses resources:

- **Mutual exclusion (exclusive use):** Once a process has been allocated a particular resource, the threads in the process have exclusive use of the resource. No other processes can use a resource while it is allocated to a process.

- **Hold and wait:** A process may hold a resource at the same time it requests another one.

- **Circular waiting:** A situation can arise in which process p_1 holds resource R_1 while one of its threads requests resource R_2, and process p_2 holds R_2 while one of its threads requests resource R_1. There may be more than two processes involved in the circular wait.

- **No preemption:** Resources can be released only by the explicit action in a process, rather than by the action of an external authority. This assumption includes the case in which a process places a request for a resource and the resource is not available. Then the process cannot withdraw its request.

These conditions occur in almost all resource allocation strategies in modern operating systems (but not necessarily in modern society—even though it may be illegal to drive a car backward on a busy street, some people do it anyway). A deadlock is possible only if all four of these conditions simultaneously hold in the community of processes. That is, these conditions are *necessary* for a deadlock to exist, but their presence is not *sufficient* to ensure that a deadlock does exist because even though all of the conditions may hold, there may be no deadlock in the system. Deadlock prevention strategies attack these conditions by designing the collective resource managers so that they are *guaranteed* to violate at least one of the conditions at all times. For example, Windows NT/2000 assures that there will never be a circular wait on mutex objects [Nagar, 1997]. Prevention strategies are easy to implement within certain systems or resources, such as batch systems, but essentially impossible to design for every resource in other systems. The prevention strategies are described in Section 10.3.

AVOIDANCE

Avoidance strategies rely on a resource manager's ability to predict the effect of satisfying individual allocation requests. If a request can lead to a situation in which a deadlock *could* occur, avoidance strategies will refuse the request. Since avoidance is a predictive approach, it relies on information about the resource activity that will be occurring for the process. For example, if a process announces the maximum number of resources it would ever request in advance—its maximum claim—it is possible to avoid a deadlock when specific resource requests are made. This strategy is discussed in Section 10.4. Avoidance is a conservative strategy. It tends to underutilize resources by refusing to allocate them if there is the potential for a deadlock. Consequently, it is rarely used in modern operating systems.

DETECTION AND RECOVERY

Some systems are designed to allow resource allocation to proceed with no particular intervention. Instead, the system checks to see if deadlock exists, either periodically or whenever the system seems to be a little slow or unresponsive. A difficult aspect of this approach is to determine when the detection algorithm should be executed. If it is executed too often, it wastes system resources, but if it is not run frequently enough, deadlocked processes and system resources will be tied up in a nonproductive fashion until the system is recovered. This problem occurs because the presence of deadlock results in the nonoccurrence of events rather than the occurrence of some exceptional event that might trigger the execution of the detection algorithm.

When a detection algorithm runs, there are two phases to the strategy. The first is the **detection** phase, during which the system is checked to see if a deadlock currently exists. If a deadlock is detected, the system goes through the second phase, **recovery**, by preempting resources from processes. This recovery means the nonpreemption condition has been violated and selected processes will be destroyed. Any work they may have accomplished prior to becoming deadlocked may be lost. The policeman's solution to gridlock usually involves preemption. The detection and recovery strategy is the most widely used deadlock strategy. The conditions under which detection is invoked are often determined manually; that is, the computer's operator manually invokes the detection algorithm when the system appears to be inactive. Detection and recovery are discussed in Section 10.5.

MANUAL DEADLOCK MANAGEMENT

Traditionally OS designers tended to ignore deadlock by not incorporating a strategy into their resource managers. Contemporary operating systems now include deadlock prevention and detection strategies for the resources that are most susceptible (such as semaphores). However, some of the resources still do not incorporate deadlock mechanisms because of the cost and the relative infrequence of deadlock on such resources. As deadlock becomes sufficiently costly for a given resource type, deadlock strategies are incorporated into the resource manager. Meanwhile, when a deadlock does occur in these systems, it is up to the users or operator of the system to detect it (for example, by comparing the real response time in the system with expected response time). In this case, recovery might mean something really dramatic, like rebooting the computer.

10.2 • A SYSTEM DEADLOCK MODEL

We are going to study deadlock using a formal model to represent the resource allocation status of the system's components. The model will represent which resources are allocated to each process. There are two levels of models for representing the resource allocation status: a system state-transition model, and a process-resource graph. The system state-transition model represents every state the system might be in at any given moment, with the goal of clearly identifying the states in which two or more processes are deadlocked. Although you might never actually construct the full model that contains each possible state (because there are so many different states), you can understand the situation by knowing the characteristics of the state-transition model. The idea is that it can be used to characterize particular resource allocation patterns, and then to identify deadlock states. Given the existence of such a conceptual state-transition model, one can then define the precise characteristics of the states where deadlock occurs and then use the state-transition model to determine policies for implementing avoidance, prevention, and detection strategies.

The process-resource model describes the details for an individual system state: It identifies which processes have been allocated particular resources, which processes are blocked waiting for resources, and so on. Next, we will informally describe a model of processes and resources, although the model can be formalized into a precise mathematical model. While the process-resource model is provided in sufficient detail to understand how it works, its full exposition and mathematical proofs are left to a more advanced treatment of deadlock (for example, the formal approach is used in [Nutt, 1992] or [Singhal and Shivaratri, 1994]).

We will combine the resource model introduced in Section 6.7 with the process model introduced in Section 7.3: Again, P is a set of n different processes and R is a set of m different resource types, where c_j is the number of units of resource type R_j in the system. The graph model shown in Figure 10.4 is a refinement of the representation shown in Figure 10.2. Here, a circular node represents a process, a rectangular node represents a resource, and the count of the dots inside a resource node represents the number of units of the resource, c_j. (In this example, $c_j = 1$ for every R_j—represented by there being one dot in each rectangular node.) This model is useful for analyzing the allocation and request status for every resource and every process in the system as it appears at one instant, so it is used to describe one state in the system state-transition model.

✦ FIGURE 10.4　A Simple Process-Resource Model Instance

The process-resource model represents the n processes as n circles, and the m resource types as m boxes. The "dots" inside a box R_j represent the number of units, c_j, of resource j. The edges represent requests and allocations.

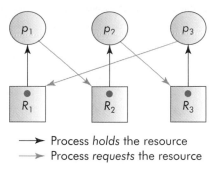

→　Process *holds* the resource
→　Process *requests* the resource

Deadlock occurs because of complex interactions among processes and resources. The process-resource model provides a snapshot of those relations, but it does not address the dynamics. The state-transition model focuses on the dynamics. As mentioned above, each instance of the process-resource model represents one state in the state-transition model. In the system, the state changes both when a process requests or releases resources and when the OS allocates resources to a process.

Let S be the set of states, $\{s_i\}$, in the model that represents the corresponding states in the system (each state is a snapshot of the process-resource relationships and is represented with an instance of the process-resource model). The **initial state** is s_0: It represents the situation in which all resources are unallocated. Each state can be analyzed by considering the corresponding process-resource model. In the remainder of this section, we are going to focus on the state-transition model. We address the details of how a specific state can be represented with the process-resource models when we examine individual deadlock strategies in the remainder of the chapter (prevention strategies do not use state definitions to deal with a deadlock).

In considering the state-transition model, the focus is on the transitions. The pattern in which resources are requested, acquired, and deallocated determines whether the system is deadlocked. This pattern corresponds to the list of transitions occurring in the state-transition model. All other activities of the process are not relevant to the study of deadlock, so they are ignored in this model.

In a set of processes, P, any process, $p_i \in P$, might cause a state transition depending on whether p_i

- ■ requests a resource (designated by a transition with the label r_i),
- ■ is allocated a resource (designated by a transition with the label a_i), or
- ■ deallocates a resource (designated by a transition with the label d_i).

Whenever the system is in state $s_j \in S$ and an event x_i (x_i is one of r_i, a_i, or d_i) occurs, then the system's state changes to a new state, $s_k \in S$, due to the occurrence of the event x_i.

Since we want to derive a model to represent system state changes, we are interested in the effect of a series of transitions that take the system from one state to another. Here is how the state-transition model can then be used: Process p_i is *blocked* in s_j if p_i cannot cause a state transition out of s_j. In other words, a blocked process is incapable of changing the state of the system, since it cannot cause any transition out of the current state. In Figure 10.5, p_2 is blocked in state s_j because all the transitions out of state s_j are caused by other processes; none are caused by p_2. Any state transition is the result of actions by p_1 or p_3, but not by p_2.

✦ FIGURE 10.5   A State in Which p_2 Is Blocked

In this state, p_1 and p_3 can cause a state transition, but p_2 cannot. So we say that p_2 is blocked in state s_j.

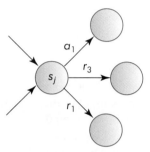

Even if p_i is blocked in s_j, some process other than p_i can change the state of the system from s_j to a new state s_k, where p_i might be able to proceed. If we can determine that there is no series of state transitions leading from the current state to one in which process p_i is unblocked, then the process can never execute again—p_i is **deadlocked** in s_j. In other words, process p_i is deadlocked in s_j if for every s_k that can be reached through some series of transitions from s_j, p_i is still blocked in s_k. If there is any process deadlocked in a state s_k, then s_k is called a **deadlock state**.

If you think about this in the context of a state-transition model, you recognize this problem as being that of checking the labels on paths in a graph model. This is a classic graph theory problem. As OS people, we love this situation: We have a model that we can use to represent deadlock, and our friends the graph theorists will give us an algorithm that can analyze the state-transition model to determine whether deadlock exists. (The bad news is that the algorithm might be very complex and require too much time to execute to be feasible.) The "Single Resource Type" example shows you how the state-transition model can be used for a trivial system, although it does not use the graph theory algorithms.

Single Resource Type

Consider a very simple system in which one process may request up to two units of a single resource type. For example, the system supports one process in a configuration with two floppy disk drives. (Of course, deadlock is not possible in a system that has only one process, although the scenario allows us to develop a simple example of the state-transition model.) Assume that the process is allowed to request only a single unit of the resource at a time (and cannot ask for a cumulative total of more than two units, since there are only two units in the system). Figure 10.6 is a state-transition model for the system. State s_0 represents the case in which the process neither holds nor requests any unit of the resource. The only possible state transition from s_0 is by a request, r, on the resource. This request will cause the system to move to state s_1, representing the case in which the process still holds no resources but now needs one unit. The system can transition to s_2 if the process acquires a unit of the resource. From s_2, two transitions are possible. Either the process may release the resource, thus changing the state to s_0 (the initial state), or the process may request a second unit of the resource, thus causing the new state to be s_3, where the process holds one unit of the resource and needs another.

✦ FIGURE 10.6 State-Transition Model for One Process

This state-transition model represents the possible actions that a process can take in a system that allows the process to request only one unit of the resource at a time.

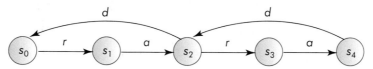

Let's extend the system so that two processes compete for the two units of the single resource type. Again, assume a process may request only one unit of the resource at a time (and cannot ask for a cumulative total of more than two units, since there are only two units in the system). In order to create our more complex diagram, we will replicate the state-transition diagram in Figure 10.6 so that it *simultaneously* represents the states for the two processes (see Figure 10.7). The states and transition events have been relabeled to distinguish between the two processes, and s_{ij} refers to the state in which p_0 is in s_i and p_1 is in s_j. Of course, several states from this "cross product" are not feasible. For example, s_{44} would represent the case in which both processes had acquired both units of the resource, which is impossible. Therefore, several states from the cross product have been eliminated from the model.

State s_{33} is a deadlock state. In s_{33}, both processes are holding one unit of the resource and requesting the other. If the system reaches this state, there is no transition out of it. Thus, both processes are blocked for all states reachable from s_{33} because there are no other states reachable from s_{33}.

If we extended this example to include more than one resource type, we would have to extend our notation for symbols to represent requests, allocations, and deallocations so that the symbol would represent the event, the process (the subscript), and the resource type (perhaps using a superscript to represent the resource type index).

✦ FIGURE 10.7 State Diagram for Two Processes

This diagram is derived by combining the states for p_0 and p_1. We have a "state explosion" since we need to represent all five states that p_1 could be in while p_0 is in s_0, then again for s_1, and so on.

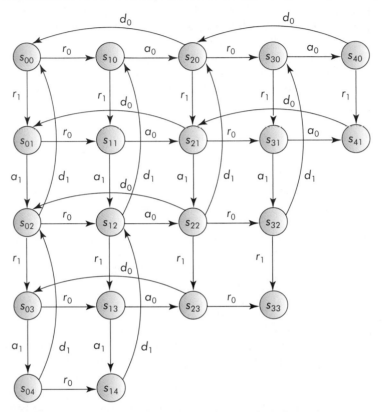

10.3 • PREVENTION

For a deadlock to occur in a system, all four of the conditions listed in Section 10.1—mutual exclusion, hold and wait, circular wait, and no preemption—must hold at the same time. Prevention strategies ensure that at least one of the conditions is always false. The mutual exclusion condition ensures that a resource can be used only by one process at a time, so it must be true all the time. For example, if an application program is being executed by a single process and it has requested that a particular tape be mounted on a tape drive, allowing another process to access the tape drive would not make sense. While it may be possible to violate the mutual exclusion condition for some resources, such as UNIX does for a terminal display, it is not possible to do so for every resource type in a conventional system. Prevention strategies focus on the other three conditions.

HOLD AND WAIT

If we want to violate the hold-and-wait condition, then we need to devise a way that prevents a process from holding some resources while requesting others. There are at least two ways we could do this: (1) we can require a process to request all of its resources when it is created, or (2) we can require the process to release all currently held resources prior to requesting any new ones. This latter approach is extreme, since it requires that a process compete for *all* the resources it wants each time it requests any incremental resource.

Batch systems operate on jobs, each of which is implemented by a single process (see Chapter 1). Since a batch job is defined by a "job file" containing all of the system commands to be applied to the job, it does not pose any real difficulty to require the job control statements to identify all resources needed to execute the job at the outset. When all the resources are available, the job/process can be placed in the ready list and executed with the knowledge that it will never request more resources during its execution. This strategy causes a job to acquire resources it may use only for a small phase in a job and to hold them for the duration of the job, thereby making them unavailable to other jobs. Batch jobs often run for hours. Hence, this technique can result in poor utilization of resources. A direct effect is that resources become more difficult to obtain, which means that throughput in the system may be dramatically reduced compared to a similar system with no prevention policy. In an extreme case, jobs may starve due to resource unavailability.

In a state-transition model for this strategy, the nature of the transitions is to have *all* requests take place before any acquisition or deallocation events (see Figure 10.8). If the system is in state s_j and p_i makes any resource requests, then p_i must request all the resources it needs. Thus, there is a single transition due to the request by p_i to some new state, s_k. From state s_k, the system may allocate the resources requested by p_i, or some other processes may cause a transition to a new state before the allocation takes place.

✦ FIGURE 10.8   Requesting All Resources Before Starting

When p_i requests resources, there is a single transition to some new state, s_k. From state s_k, the system may allocate the resources requested by p_i.

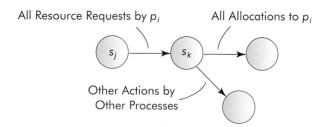

Interactive systems do not require that all commands, or even all processes, be known at the time the interaction begins. Instead, the user may create new processes, delete existing ones, execute commands requesting new processes, and so on at any time during a session. The first hold-and-wait strategy is not plausible in this type of environment. Instead, this second strategy can be used to avoid the hold-and-wait condition: Each time a new resource is required by a process, all of its currently held resources are put into a stable, persistent state and then released. For example, open files are closed, and mounted tapes are rewound and unloaded. Next, the process attempts to reacquire the resources along with any new ones it may need, thereby preventing the hold-and-wait condition from being true. This approach causes a significant amount of overhead in saving the status of held resources in preparation for acquiring new ones. It also will tend to underutilize resources and may encourage starvation.

Also in the generic state-transition model fragment for the second strategy (Figure 10.9), request transitions must occur before any acquisition or deallocation transitions. However, these state diagrams are more complex than those for the batch case, since they must have deallocation transitions leading back to the process's idle state. This is done to capture the scenarios in which a process dynamically determines it needs more resources.

✦ FIGURE 10.9 Release of All Resources Before Requesting More

In this case, the process must release all its resources before it can request additional ones.

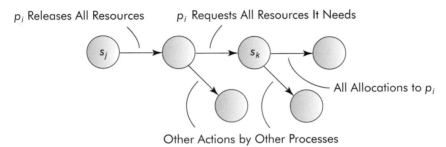

p_i Releases All Resources p_i Requests All Resources It Needs

s_j s_k All Allocations to p_i

Other Actions by Other Processes

CIRCULAR WAIT

Circular waits occur when there is a set of n processes, $\{p_i\}$, that holds units of a set of n different resources, $\{R_j\}$, such that p_i holds R_j while it requests units of a different resource in the set. In other words, each of the n resources is held by the n processes, but each process then requests unavailable units of one of the resource types held by another process. A circular wait is reflected by the process-resource relationships, so the state-transition model does not help in the study of this problem.

Suppose we use the process-resource model to get a more detailed description of the situation. We can then use this "micro model" of each state to detect a circular wait condition. As before, a square represents a resource type, a circle represent a process, an edge (p_i, R_j) denotes that p_i has a pending request for units of R_j, and an edge (R_j, p_i) means that p_i holds units of R_j. Based on this model, Figure 10.10 describes the details of a state in which the circular wait condition is true (although the model ignores the number of units of resource of each type—there are no small dots inside the resource rectangular nodes). The condition is evident by the **cycle** in the graph. The graphical representation provides the insight for how to prevent circular waits. The resource allocator must ensure that the system never achieves a state in which the internal graph contains a cycle. (The conditions are actually more complex than simple cycle detection because each resource may have multiple units of a resource. This will become evident when we consider detection algorithms. The cycle condition will actually only represent a circular wait if each resource type has only one unit of the resource.)

✦ FIGURE 10.10   A Model of a State with a Circular Wait

In a circular wait state, each of *n* processes is holding one resource and requesting another. In the graph model representation, this is reflected by a cycle in the graph. The cycle is a necessary, but not sufficient condition for deadlock.

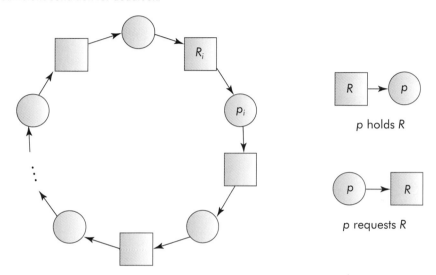

One technique for preventing the occurrence of a circular wait condition is to establish a *total order* on all resources in a system, for example, by using an index number for each of them. The resources are then $R_1, R_2, ..., R_m$, where $R_i < R_j$ if $i < j$. Suppose we only allow a process to acquire a resource, R_j, if $R_i < R_j$ for all the other resources, R_i, currently held by the process.

The total order must also establish order on all resource units as well as resource types if the units are distinguishable. It must also include consumable resources as well as reusable ones. As in the hold-and-wait situation, if a p_i requires a resource, R_j, such that $R_j < R_k$, for some R_k it currently holds, then the policy will require that p_i release all R_k, acquire R_j, and then reacquire R_k. The effect on the process performance will be negative, since this method can only increase the time that processes have to wait for resources to become available.

The deadlock that occurs in the dining philosophers solution shown in Figure 9.2 can be prevented by using this total ordering approach. Suppose we put a total order on all forks (corresponding to their indices). Now philosopher 4 must become a "left-handed philosopher" in the sense that he or she picks up the forks in a different order than the other philosophers (see Figure 10.11). By having philosopher 4 pick up the forks in the opposite order, the circular wait condition is prevented from occurring, and hence, a deadlock cannot occur.

◆ FIGURE 10.11 Dining Philosophers Revisited

In this solution to the dining philosophers problem, `philosopher4` behaves differently than the other four philosophers. He or she picks up `fork[0]` and then `fork[4]` in order to conform with the total ordering strategy.

```
philosopher(int i){
  while (TRUE) {
  // Think
  // Eat
    P(fork[i]); /* Pick up left fork */
      P(fork[i+1]); /* Pick up right fork */
        eat();
      V(fork[i+1]);
    V(fork[i]);
  }
}
philosopher4(){
  while (TRUE) {
  // Think
  // Eat
    P(fork[0]); /* Pick up right fork */
      P(fork[4]); /* Pick up left fork */
        eat();
      V(fork[4]);
    V(fork[0]);
  }
}

semaphore fork[5];
fork[0] = fork[1] = fork[2] = fork[3] = fork[4] = 1;
fork(philosopher, 1, 0);
fork(philosopher, 1, 1);
fork(philosopher, 1, 2);
fork(philosopher, 1, 3);
fork(philosopher4, 0);
```

ALLOWING PREEMPTION

Suppose the OS allowed processes to "back out of" a request for a resource if the resource was not available. For example, the system might be implemented so that whenever a process requests a resource, the system responds immediately either by allocating the resource or by indicating that there are insufficient resources to satisfy the request. In cases in which resources are unavailable, the requesting process either repeatedly polls the resource manager until the desired units become available or it does other work. (This approach implicitly assumes that the process has other useful work to do that does not require the specified resource. Use of the strategy requires the programming language and paradigm to support such an approach.)

The state-transition diagram for a system that allows a process to preempt its request—to "back out of a request"—will differ from one not allowing it. Figure 10.12 informally describes how model states change because a process is able to do this. If the system is in state s_i and process p_u makes a request, r_u, then the system transitions into a new state, s_j. Now, since p_u is informed that the resources it requested are not available, it returns the system to state s_i with a new transition, w_u (w means that the request is withdrawn by the process causing the transition). Hence, the system is now back in the state it was in prior to p_u's request. At this point, either p_u may again request the resource (transitioning the system back to s_j again) or a different process, p_v, may cause a system state change out of s_i to a new state s_k—for example, by deallocating resources. The new state s_k may be more advantageous for p_u because it allows p_u to obtain the requested resources that were unavailable in s_i. The model represents the case in which p_u continues to poll the resource manager.

✦ FIGURE 10.12 State Diagram with Preemption

If preemption is allowed, a process is never blocked on a request operation. Instead, it returns to its previous state if the resource request could not be honored.

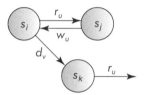

This technique cannot be characterized as "full preemption" of resources from processes (as required in a recovery procedure), yet it is sufficient to prevent a deadlock. Unfortunately, there is no guarantee that this technique will be effective, since the system may come to a set of states whereby a community of processes is polling for resources that are held by other processes within the set. While technically the system is not in a deadlock, it will not function properly due to a phenomenon called **livelock**, which means a set of processes causes transitions in the state diagram, but none of the transitions are effective in the long term.

10.4 • AVOIDANCE

Like the prevention strategy, avoidance strategies are a conservative approach to resource allocation. They control state transitions by allowing the system to make a transition only as a result of an allocation when it is *certain* that a deadlock cannot occur due to subsequent requests. The strategy is to analyze a prospective state—before entering it—to guarantee that there exists any sequence of transitions out of the state in which every process can still execute.

The avoidance strategy depends on additional information about the long-term resource needs of each process. In particular, when a process is created, it must declare its **maximum claim**—the maximum number of units it will ever request—to every resource type. The resource manager can honor the request if the resources are available, *and* if it can determine that there is some sequence of requests, allocations, and deallocations that enables every process in the system to eventually run to completion even if all of the processes use their maximum number of resources.

With the avoidance approach, the system is always kept in a **safe state**. The analysis performed at the time of a request must consider the allocation status of all resources and the pending additional resources that a process could request up to its maximum claim. It is important to note that the state analysis does not *predict* that every process will actually request its maximum claim. It merely proceeds under the assumption that *if* every process were to exercise its maximum claim, then there would still be some sequence of allocations and deallocations that would enable the system to satisfy every process's requests. A system state in which this guarantee cannot be made is an **unsafe state**.

Figure 10.13 is an intuitive description of how a community of processes might operate in a safe state and how the community could cause the system to venture into unsafe states. As indicated by the flowchart on the left side of the figure, programs normally execute with less than their maximum claim, only occasionally requiring the maximum amount of a resource. After the resource-intensive phase is completed, the process reverts to operation with a more moderate amount of a resource. Empirical evidence suggests that this is the way that programs usually are written—they only request the maximum amount of resources under exceptional conditions.

✦ FIGURE 10.13 Safe State Strategy

When a process executes a program, it usually does not require its maximum claim to all the resources: Either it may not need them all at the same time or the maximum is only necessary in an extreme case. In normal operation, all the processes are operating with fewer than their maximum of resources.

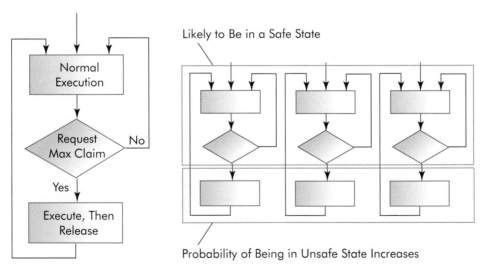

As long as the processes tend to use less than their maximum claim, the system is likely (but not guaranteed) to be in a safe state. However, if a large number of processes happen to have relatively large resource demands (at or near their maximum claim) at the same time, as indicated in the right side of the figure, the system resources will tend to be heavily used and the probability of the system state being unsafe is higher.

The avoidance strategy assumes that every process could take the "yes" branch in its respective flowchart at the same time, thus taking the system to a situation in which all processes simultaneously want to exercise their maximum claim. The strategy is to determine that if any pending request is satisfied and all programs subsequently require their maximum claim, there is a sequence of allocations and deallocations in which the requests of all processes can eventually be satisfied.

Of course, this means that the resource manager might block some processes while others use their maximum claim and then later allow the waiting processes to proceed. The strategy does not require that the system have enough resources to simultaneously meet all maximum claims, just that it can eventually service them all in some order if necessary. Even though the avoidance analysis assumes this worst case, you have probably noticed that a system could run in an unsafe state. If none of the processes request their maximum claim when the system is in the unsafe state, the system could eventually return to a safe state. This scenario can occur because the resource manager conducts its analysis under the assumption that every process *will* execute its maximum claim. The system may not be able to guarantee that all maximum claims can be met—the state is unsafe—but some processes may not execute their maximum claim until the system returns to a safe state. Clearly, conservative assumptions on the part of the resource manager can have a substantial effect on the performance of a system.

In other words, if a state is unsafe, it does not mean the system is in a deadlock or even that a deadlock is imminent (see Figure 10.14). It simply means the matter is "out of the hands" of the resource manager and will be determined solely by future actions of the processes. The state-transition diagram illustrates that the system can go into unsafe states but then return to safe states, depending on the collective actions taken by the community of processes. As long as the state is safe, the resource manager can be guaranteed to avoid a deadlock.

✦ FIGURE 10.14   Safe, Unsafe, and Deadlock States

A safe state is one in which the OS can ensure that there will be no deadlock. In an unsafe state, the system may or may not lead to a deadlock state, depending on what the community of applications does (not on the OS strategy).

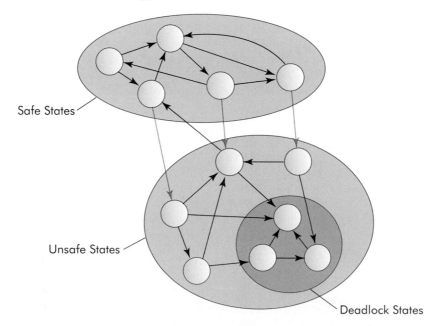

The avoidance strategy depends on the analysis of a particular system state to determine whether it is safe. This means we need a detailed model of each state in the state-transition model so that we can make judgments about safety. The classic model of a state used in the avoidance strategy comes from Dijkstra's [1968] analogy of resource allocation and the way banks work.

THE BANKER'S ALGORITHM

The banker's algorithm is the classic avoidance strategy. It is modeled after the lending policies employed in banking systems. A bank has a limited amount of funds—resources—that can be lent to different borrowers—processes. To accommodate borrowers, the bank may extend a line of credit to a customer. The line of credit is an indication by the bank that it is prepared to lend funds to the customer up to a preapproved limit. Customers agree they will not ask for more than the line of credit without first entering into a new agreement. The line of credit is a maximum claim for resources by the customer.

There is an important tacit assumption in the model. If a customer borrows some portion of the line of credit and then requests additional funds, the first amount borrowed will be paid back to the bank only if the additional funds are loaned. Hence, there is no preemption in the bank's model. The bank's strategy for distributing resources can then be guided by the total lines of credit it has extended to its customers and the total amount of loan funds controlled by the bank. At any moment, the loan department looks at the funds allocated to all customers and the maximum amount that can be requested by each customer. If there is some sequence of activity in which at least one customer's full line of credit can be met, assume that the customer can borrow up to the line of credit and then repay the entire loan. After this customer has repaid the loan, the algorithm iterates on the other accounts. If all customers can exercise their lines of credit and repay their loans, then the current state is safe.

Now let's think about bank example as a set of processes, P, using a set of resources, R. The nature of the current system state, s_k, is determined by the pattern of resources already allocated to processes. The system state can be defined by determining the number of units of each resource type held by each process. Let `alloc` be a table in which row i represents process p_i, column j represents R_j, and `alloc[i, j]` is the number of units of resource R_j held by process p_i. Let another table, `maxc`, be the maximum claim on resource R_j by process p_i. The number of available units of R_j can be computed as

```
avail[j] = c_j - Σ alloc[i, j].
              0≤i<n
```

It is possible to inspect c_j, the number of units of each resource in the system—`maxc[i, j]` and `alloc[i, j]`—and determine whether the current allocation state is safe simply by enumerating and inspecting all possible sequences of state transitions. One algorithm for doing this is shown in Figure 10.15. The algorithm computes the number of units of each resource type that are available in the current state. This gives us a vector of values where `avail[j]` is the number of units of R_j available in this state.

We then consider each process and ask: If a process were suddenly to request resources up to its maximum claim, would there be sufficient resources to satisfy the request? If there are, then this process could not be deadlocked in the state, so there is a sequence whereby this process eventually returns all its resources to the operating system. We model this by adding the units of each resource held by this process to the `avail` vector and then reconsider each process to see if any new ones could now exercise their maximum claim. If we can determine that eventually every process can execute using its maximum claim, we know the state is safe.

✦ FIGURE 10.15 The Banker's Algorithm

The banker's algorithm iteratively determines if there is any process that can have its maximum claim met. If all processes can have their claim met, the state is safe. Otherwise it is unsafe.

1. Copy the `alloc[i, j]` table to a table named `alloc'`.

2. Given C, `maxc`, and `alloc'`, compute the `avail` vector. Do this by taking the column sums for `alloc'`, `alloc'[*, j]`. Then compute

   `avail[j] = c`$_j$` - alloc'[*, j]`.

3. Find p_i such that `maxc[i, j] - alloc'[i, j]` ≤ `avail[j]` for $0 \leq j < m$ and $0 \leq i < n$. If no such p_i exists, then the state is unsafe—halt the algorithm. If `alloc'[i, j]` is 0 for all i and j, the state is safe—halt the algorithm.

4. Set `alloc'[i, j]` to 0 to indicate that p_i could exercise its maximum claim. Then deallocate all resources to represent that p_i is not permanently blocked in the state that is being analyzed. Go back to Step 2.

Using the Banker's Algorithm

Suppose a system with four resource types, $C = <8, 5, 9, 7>$, is supporting five processes that collectively have the maximum claims shown in Figure 10.16. The current system state is represented by the allocation state shown in Figure 10.17. Let's apply the banker's algorithm to determine whether the corresponding state is safe. First, we compute the column sums of the currently allocated resources:

```
alloc'.columnSum = <7, 3, 7, 5>
```

In Step 2, we determine how many units of the resource are currently available:

```
avail[0] = 8 - 7 = 1
avail[1] = 5 - 3 = 2
avail[2] = 9 - 7 = 2
avail[3] = 7 - 5 = 2
```

That is,

```
avail = <1, 2, 2, 2>
```

In Step 3, we search for a process that can have its maximum claim satisfied in the state represented by the `alloc'` table. In this search, we discover the following:

```
maxc[2, 0] - alloc'[2, 0] = 5 - 4 = 1 ≤ 1 = avail[0]
maxc[2, 1] - alloc'[2, 1] = 1 - 0 = 1 ≤ 2 = avail[1]
maxc[2, 2] - alloc'[2, 2] = 0 - 0 = 0 ≤ 2 = avail[2]
maxc[2, 3] - alloc'[2, 3] = 5 - 3 = 2 ≤ 2 = avail[3]
```

✦ FIGURE 10.16   A Maximum Claim Table

This table describes the maximum number of units of R_j that p_i will ever request.

Process	R_0	R_1	R_2	R_3
p_0	3	2	1	4
p_1	0	2	5	2
p_2	5	1	0	5
p_3	1	5	3	0
p_4	3	0	3	3

✦ FIGURE 10.17   A Safe Allocation State for a System

This table describes the number of units of R_j that p_i currently holds. In the state represented by this allocation profile, the system is in a safe state.

Process	R_0	R_1	R_2	R_3
p_0	2	0	1	1
p_1	0	1	2	1
p_2	4	0	0	3
p_3	0	2	1	0
p_4	1	0	3	0
Sum	7	3	7	5

This discovery means p_2 could exercise its maximum claim in the current state and then release all its resources, thus causing the following:

```
avail[0] = avail [0] + alloc'[2, 0] = 1 + 4 = 5
avail[1] = avail [1] + alloc'[2, 1] = 2 + 0 = 2
avail[2] = avail [2] + alloc'[2, 2] = 2 + 0 = 2
avail[3] = avail [3] + alloc'[2, 3] = 2 + 3 = 5
```

Next, we determine that p_4 could exercise its maximum claim and then release its resources, thereby resulting in avail being set to <6, 2, 5, 5>. In this hypothetical derived state, any of the other three processes could exercise its maximum claim. The state is safe.

The allocation state illustrated in Figure 10.18 is unsafe. This is determined by applying the algorithm and discovering in Step 3 that there is no process that can have its maximum claim exercised (using the maximum claim table in Figure 10.16). If p_3 happened to deallocate its single unit of R_0, it is not blocked. The state would be the same as Figure 10.17, so it would again be safe.

✦ FIGURE 10.18 An Unsafe Allocation State for a System

This allocation state is unsafe because no process can have its maximum claim met.

Process	R_0	R_1	R_2	R_3
p_0	2	0	1	1
p_1	0	1	2	1
p_2	4	0	0	3
p_3	1	2	1	0
p_4	1	0	3	0

10.5 ● DETECTION AND RECOVERY

The detection and recovery strategy allows the resource manager to be far more aggressive about allocation than does the avoidance strategy. Whereas avoidance algorithms avoid unsafe states even if the system might recover from them, detection and recovery algorithms ignore the distinction between safe and unsafe states; the resource managers are allowed to allocate units whenever they are available. If processes seem to be blocked on resources for an inordinately long time, the detection algorithm is executed to determine whether the current state is a deadlock. Detection algorithms make no predictions about states that could be reached from the current state, although they will determine if there is any sequence of transitions in which every process can become unblocked.

Resources have been defined as "anything a process needs to proceed." As pointed out before, this need could be a block of primary memory, a file, or exclusive access to a device. Such resources are called *serially reusable resources* because a process requests the OS to allocate units of the resource exclusively to the process and the process will later release the units for another process to use. Individual units of serially reusable resources focus on the time-multiplexing sharing approach.

Processes can also use *consumable resources*. For example, when a process blocks on an operation that is attempting to read the next character from a keyboard, then the character is needed by the process in order to proceed, so it is a resource. However, once the process acquires the character resource, it will never "release" it. Instances of the two resource classes are treated differently by the resource manager and processes and have different theoretical properties with respect to deadlock analysis. This section considers serially reusable and consumable resources and then explains how systems containing both classes of resources can be analyzed to detect a deadlock.

SERIALLY REUSABLE RESOURCES

Serially reusable resources represent traditional hardware resources and their abstractions. For our deadlock analysis, a **serially reusable resource**, R_j, has a finite number of identical units such that the following holds:

- ■ The number of units of the resource, c_j, is constant.
- ■ Each unit of R_j is either available or allocated to one, and only one, p_i at any time.
- ■ A unit of R_j can be released only if it was previously acquired.

Next, we the refine process-resource graph models described in Section 10.2, so that we can use them to describe each system state for systems containing only serially reusable resources. These graphs are refinements of the one given in Figure 10.4 and again in Figure 10.10.

REUSABLE RESOURCE GRAPH MODELS

A **reusable resource graph** is a micro model that describes the details of a single state in the state-transition model. It is a directed graph such that the following is true:

- ■ The $n + m$ nodes represent n processes (graphically represented as circles) and m resources (graphically represented as boxes).
- ■ Edges connect processes to resources and resources to processes.
- ■ An edge from process p_i to resource R_j is a **request edge**, which represents a request for one unit of R_j by p_i. There can be multiple edges from p_i to R_j, since each edge is a request for one unit of the resource.
- ■ An edge from resource R_j to process p_i is an **assignment edge**, which represents the allocation of one unit of R_j to p_i. There can also be multiple edges from R_j to p_i.
- ■ For each resource type, R_j, there is a count of the number of units of the type, c_j, that is graphically represented by small dots inside R_j.
- ■ The number of units of R_j allocated plus the number requested by p_i cannot exceed c_j.

Figure 10.19 is a refinement of Figure 10.10 showing a reusable resource graph (it incorporates the dots to represent units of a resource, and also has directed edges from the dots inside a resource to the processes). The refinement represents the number of units of resource configured into each resource type (by "dots" inside the resource) in addition to the processes, resources, requests, and allocations. For emphasis, we draw the edge representing allocation from a specific unit of a resource to the process.

By adding the resource count to the graphical model, additional details of the circular wait condition become obvious. In the figure, every available unit of every resource type is allocated, yet each process involved in the circular wait requests a unit of the unavailable resource. The graphical representation is also useful, since it makes it obvious that the cycle in a reusable resource graph is not a sufficient condition for a deadlock. Any resource could have more than one unit (for example, as does R_k in Figure 10.20a); hence, a single request edge could be satisfied, thus breaking the circular wait. Figure 10.10 was useful for introducing the notion of circular wait. However, it was not complete. It does not allow a detection algorithm to operate on a formal representation of the graphical depiction of the model, since it did not include the unit count.

✦ FIGURE 10.19 A Refinement of the Circular Wait Graph

This graph is a serially reusable resource graph that represents a system state. This particular graph is not complete, but if it were completed as suggested, it would be a deadlock state.

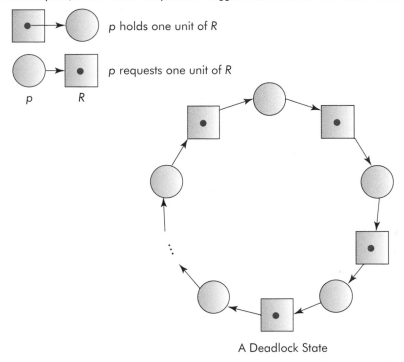

A Deadlock State

Each reusable resource graph is a detailed model of an individual state in the system state diagram. In Figure 10.20, part (a) is one system state and part (b) is a reusable resource graph for a different state that is reached from the one represented in part (a). In Figure 10.20(b), a transition has occurred in which the unallocated unit of R_k is allocated to p_i. This example gives us some insight as to how we can employ reusable resource graphs to represent states in the system model without actually constructing a state-transition model. That is, we rely on the existence of the model explained in Section 10.2, but there is no need to actually construct it.

A state transition occurs whenever one of three events occurs:

■ Any allocated resource is released through the *deallocation* event, *d*.

■ A new resource is requested via the *request* event, *r*.

■ A resource is allocated to a process with the *allocate* event, *a*.

A specific allocation policy can be represented in an OS by defining the state-transition diagram and transitions more precisely than has been done up to now. This is accomplished by describing transformations on the reusable resource graph. For example, one specific, widely used policy employs the following resource event semantics:

■ **Request:** Assume the system is in s_j. p_i is allowed to request any number, q, of units of any number of resource types R_h ($q \le c_h$), provided p_i has no outstanding requests

✦ **FIGURE 10.20** Representing a State Transition Using the Reusable
Resource Graph

This figure shows two different versions of the graph, each representing a system state. In part (a), p_i is requesting a unit of R_k. In part (b), the available unit of R_k has been allocated to p_i.

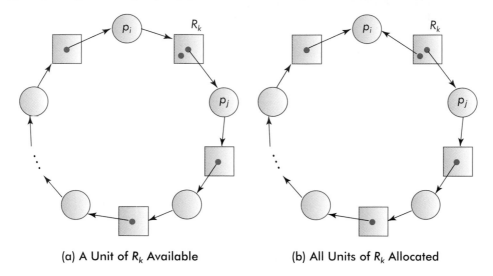

(a) A Unit of R_k Available   (b) All Units of R_k Allocated

for any resources. A request causes a state transition from s_j to s_k, where the reusable resource graph for s_k is derived from the reusable resource graph for s_j by adding q request edges from p_i to R_h (that is, one request edge for each unit requested).

■ **Acquisition:** Assume the system is in s_j. p_i is allowed to acquire units of R_h if, and only if, there is a request edge from p_i to R_h in the reusable resource graph representing s_j and all such requests can be satisfied on all resources at one time. An acquisition causes a state transition from s_j to s_k. In this case, the reusable resource graph for s_k is derived from the reusable resource graph for s_j by changing each request edge to an assignment edge from R_h to p_i.

■ **Release:** Assume the system is in s_j. p_i can release units of R_h if, and only if, there is an allocation edge from R_h to p_i and there is no request edge from p_i. A release causes a state transition from s_j to s_k. In this case, the reusable resource graph for s_k is derived from the reusable resource graph for s_j by deleting all assignment edges into p_i from R_h.

This policy, while specific, is still sufficiently generic to apply to many reasonable resource allocation strategies. It is used in the analysis of deadlock detection and recovery in the rest of the chapter.

A simple system was introduced in Section 10.2 in which two processes shared two units of a single resource type. The example implicitly assumed the resources were serially reusable. The state diagram for the system was provided in Figure 10.7. We can now consider reusable resource graph models of each state.

In Figure 10.21:

- Part (a) represents state s_{00}, where neither process holds or needs a unit of the resource.
- If p_1 requests a unit of the resource with transition r_1 (only single-unit requests were permitted in this example), the system moves to s_{01}, which has the reusable resource graph shown in (b).
- If p_0 were then to request a unit of the resource, designated by the r_0 transition, the system would change from state s_{01} to s_{11}, represented by the reusable resource graphs shown in (c).
- Part (d) represents s_{21}.
- Part (e) represents s_{22}, where both processes hold a unit of the resource. When we first considered this example, it was noted that s_{33} is a deadlock state, since there are no transitions out of it.
- Part (f) is the reusable resource graph for the state.

Again, note that there is a cycle in the reusable resource graph for s_{33} and that all the resource units are allocated.

✦ FIGURE 10.21 A Collection of Reusable Resource Graphs

This is a reusable resource graph for the single-unit resource request model shown in Figure 10.7.

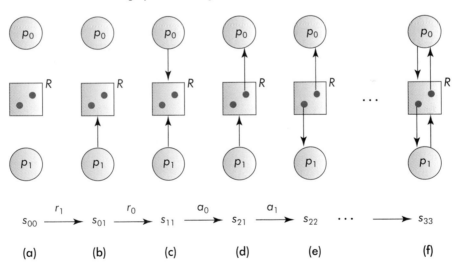

ANALYZING A REUSABLE RESOURCE GRAPH We now have a *macro* model with states and a *micro* model for representing each state in the macro model in terms of its processes and reusable resources. Using the macro model from Section 10.2, we determined that a state was a deadlock state by analyzing the state diagram in Figure 10.7. Since s_{33} contained no outgoing transitions, it had to represent deadlock. This situation would be more complex if the state diagram contained a knot; once the system entered any state in the knot, it could never transition to other states outside the knot. For example, in Figure 10.22, the system could move from state s_j or s_k into the knot, but then it would never be able to change to any of the states outside the knot. This situation complicates the algorithm for checking to see if a process can ever be involved in a transition again—that is, to see if the process is deadlocked.

✦ FIGURE 10.22   A State Diagram with a Knot

A knot in a graph is a collection of nodes in which all paths from any node in the knot lead only to other nodes in the knot.

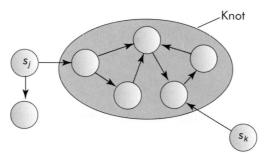

We can analyze the reusable resource graph micro model to determine whether the macro model state is a deadlock. The idea is to consider possible transitions based on the edges in the reusable resource graph. A process is deadlocked in a state if it is blocked in the current state as well as in any state reachable from the current state. According to the semantics associated with request, acquisition, and release events (under the particular policy described above), the conditions for a process to be blocked can be restated as follows: If there are p_i and R_j such that p_i's requests on R_j exceed the total number of units of R_j in state s_k, then p_i is blocked in s_k.

To detect if s_k is a deadlock state, we must be assured that there is no sequence of transitions unblocking all blocked processes. Rather than exploring the state diagram, we can consider all transformations of the reusable resource graph to determine if there is a new graph reachable by transformations corresponding to the state transitions. If we can find a series of transformations in which p_i is unblocked, the original state is not a deadlock.

A **graph reduction** is a set of transformations representing optimal action by the processes. These transformations are similar to the individual steps testing whether a state is unsafe in the banker's algorithm in the sense that they represent an analysis of a state as opposed to any prediction of future activity by the community of processes. In the banker's algorithm, the intent was to avoid unsafe states; in the detection algorithm, the intent is to decide whether the current state is a deadlock. A serially reusable resource graph can be *reduced* by p_i if the following conditions are met:

■ The process p_i is not blocked.

■ The process has no request edges.

■ There are assignment edges directed into p_i.

The reduction transforms the reusable resource graph by removing all edges into and out of p_i. A reusable resource graph is *irreducible* if it cannot be reduced by any process

p. A reusable resource graph is *completely reducible* if there is a sequence of reductions that leads to a graph's having no edges of any kind. It can be proved that given a reusable resource graph representing state s_k, state s_k is a deadlock state if, and only if, the serially reusable resource graph is not completely reducible [Nutt, 1992].

It would be satisfying if we could correlate deadlock with a static property of the reusable resource graph, such as the presence of a cycle. Unfortunately, there is no such known static property. Furthermore, the fact that graph reductions are a necessary and sufficient condition strongly suggests there is no static condition (at least in this model with this resource allocation policy). In the case of cycles, the graph of a deadlock state *must* contain a cycle; a cycle in the reusable graph is a *necessary* condition for deadlock. However, it is not a *sufficient* condition for deadlock. This was illustrated in Figure 10.20 and is again illustrated with the simple case in Figure 10.23. Process p_0 holds R_0 and requests R_1, while p_1 holds R_1 and requests R_0, as shown in the graph with a cycle and a deadlock state in part (a) of Figure 10.23. Part (b) is not a deadlock state, yet it contains the same cycle.

✦ FIGURE 10.23 The Circular Wait (Reconsidered)

Part (a) illustrates a reusable resource graph that contains a cycle and is a deadlock state (it is not possible to reduce the graph at all). However, part (b) is a similar graph with a cycle, but since we can reduce by p_0 and then p_1, the graph does not represent a deadlock state.

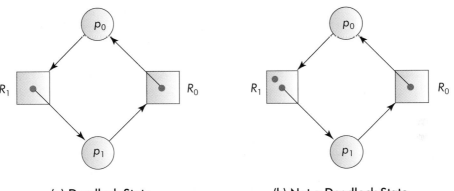

(a) Deadlock State   (b) Not a Deadlock State

Serially Reusable Resource Graphs

For example, suppose a system is in the state represented by the reusable graph shown in Figure 10.24(a).

■ Notice that p_1 and p_2 are both blocked (p_1 on R_0 and p_2 on both R_1 and R_2).

■ However, p_0 is not blocked, so we can reduce the graph by p_0 to show that there is a series of transitions possible from the current state in which p_0 acquires and releases all of its current requests.

■ After reducing by p_0, we obtain the reduced graph shown in Figure 10.24(b).

■ Now the graph can be reduced by p_1, meaning it is possible for the system to move from the state shown in part (b) into the state shown in (c).

■ Finally, we reduce by p_2, resulting in the graph shown in (d)—a completely reduced graph.

Since the analysis shows that the graph is completely reducible, it means that the original state is not a deadlock state.

✦ **FIGURE 10.24** Completely Reducible Reusable Resource Graph

This graph is reducible: Part (b) shows a reduction by p_0; part (c) shows a reduction by p_1; and part (d) is a completed reduced graph.

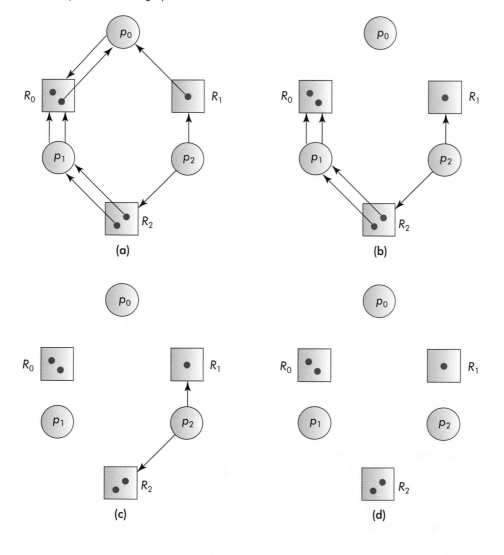

Figure 10.25 represents an irreducible state and a deadlock. Process p_0 holds one unit of R_0 and one unit of R_2, while requesting one unit of R_0; p_1 holds one unit of R_0 and requests one unit of R_2; p_2 holds both units of R_2 and requests R_1. No process can proceed.

◆ FIGURE 10.25 Deadlocked Reusable Resource Graph

This graph cannot be reduced by any process, so all processes are deadlocked in the state represented by this graph.

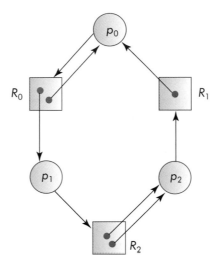

CONSUMABLE RESOURCES

Consumable resources differ from serially reusable resources in that a process may request consumable resources, but it will never release them. Conversely, a process can release units of a consumable resource without ever acquiring them. A typical consumable resource is a signal, message, or input data. The model for analyzing serially reusable resources does not apply to consumable resources because such resources may have an unbounded number of units and allocated units are not released,. However, by redefining the model for consumable resources, alternate conditions can be found to test a system state for deadlock.

A **consumable resource**, R_j, has an unbounded number of identical units such that the following holds:

- The number of units of the resource, w_j, varies. (w_j is used instead of c_j to emphasize that the number of available units for a consumable resource differs from the fixed number of units for a serially reusable resource.)

- There is one or more producer processes, p_p, that may increase w_j by releasing units of the resource.

- Consumer processes, p_c, decrease w_j for R_j by acquiring units of the resource.

Just as we used a reusable resource graph as a micro model to consider the properties of a serially reusable resource, we use a consumable resource graph to define a micro model for analyzing the properties of consumable resources.

CONSUMABLE RESOURCE GRAPH MODEL A consumable resource graph is a directed graph such that the following is true:

- The $n + m$ nodes represent n processes and m resources.
- Edges connect processes to resources and resources to processes.
- An edge from process p_i to resource R_j is a *request edge*, which represents a request for one unit of R_j by p_i.
- An edge from resource R_j to process p_i is a *producer edge*, which identifies p_i as a producer of R_j. Each resource must have at least one producer.
- The number of units of R_j is w_j, which is graphically represented by dots inside R_j.

Again, we can specify a specific resource management policy in order to study systems that have consumable resources, just as we did with serially reusable resources. This policy conforms to the usual usage of consumable resources, although we could redefine it to fit the requirements of any particular resource manager. The policy is determined by the following actions:

- **Request:** Assume the system is in state s_j. p_i is allowed to request any number of units of any number of resource types R_h, provided p_i has no outstanding requests for resources. A request causes a state transition from s_j to s_k, where the consumable resource graph for s_k is derived from the consumable resource graph for s_j by adding a request edge from p_i to R_h for each unit requested.
- **Acquisition:** Assume the system is in s_j. p_i is allowed to acquire units of R_h if, and only if, there is a request edge from p_i to R_h in the consumable resource graph representing s_j and all such requests can be satisfied at one time. An acquisition causes a state transition from s_j to s_k, where the consumable resource graph for s_k is derived from the graph for s_j by deleting each edge from p_i to R_h and by decrementing w_h once for each edge deleted.
- **Release:** Assume the system is in s_j. p_i can release units of R_h if, and only if, there is a producer edge from R_h to p_i and there is no request edge from p_i to R_g in the consumable resource graph representing s_j. A release causes a state transition from s_j to s_k, where the graph for s_k is derived from the consumable resource graph for s_j by incrementing w_h once for each unit of the resource produced.

Figure 10.26 shows a series of state transitions for a simple consumable resource system. Processes p_0 and p_1 share a single consumable resource.

- The first state in part (a) shows that p_1 is a producer of the resource, there are currently no units of the resource available, and there are no pending requests for the resource.
- The system state changes in part (b) when p_1 releases one unit of the resource.
- It changes again in part (c) when p_0 requests two units of the resource. At this point, p_0 is blocked, but p_1 continues to run.

- Part (d) shows that p_1 releases an additional three units of the resource.
- In part (e), p_0 has obtained two units of the resource, thus leaving two units available.

No process is blocked, so no process is deadlocked.

✦ FIGURE 10.26 State Transitions in a Consumable Resource Graph

This sequence of states illustrates transitions with consumable resources. p_1 produces units of R, since it is not blocked. p_0 is blocked in part (c), but eventually p_1 produces enough units to satisfy p_0's need.

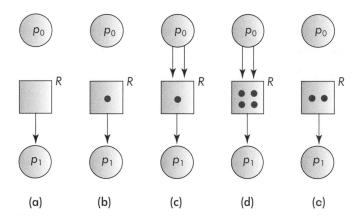

(a)   (b)   (c)   (d)   (c)

ANALYZING A CONSUMABLE RESOURCE GRAPH Consumable resource systems behave differently from serially reusable resource systems, since there are potentially an unbounded number of units of the resource available. This difference means the analyses used for reusable resource systems cannot be expected to work for consumable resource systems. We can see how this could be true by observing that if a process is blocked on a consumable resource, we can only speculate whether the process will be unblocked if the resource's producer is currently blocked. Hence, if we expect to determine whether a blocked process is deadlocked, the analysis must inspect the producers of resources that are causing other processes to be blocked.

How, exactly, can we determine if a state is a deadlock? As with all types of resources, a process is deadlocked in a state if it is blocked in the current state and in any state reachable from the current state. Thus, to detect deadlock, we again consider transformations in the consumable resource graph corresponding to state transitions. A consumable resource graph can be *reduced* by p_i if the process is not blocked. The reduction causes w_j to be decremented once for each unit of outstanding requests on R_j by p_i, and by deleting the request edges from the graph. If there are producer edges from a resource R_k to p_i, the reduction releases an unbounded number of units of R_k and deletes the producer edge, (R_k, p_i), from the graph.

As with reusable resource graphs, reduction is the basic tool for testing whether a process is permanently blocked. In Figure 10.27:

- p_0 is a producer for R_0 and p_1 is a producer for R_1.

■ In part (a), p_0 is blocked on R_1 and p_1 is blocked on R_0; because of the producer relationships, this is clearly a deadlock state.

■ However, if either R_0 or R_1 has an available unit, as in part (b), there is no deadlock.

■ Process p_0 can be allocated the unit of R_1; it then will no longer be blocked.

■ In the analysis technique, p_0 could release an arbitrary number of units of R_0, since it is not blocked.

Of course, the system may not take this sequence, but we are attempting to determine whether the state is a deadlock, so we observe that p_0 could release as many units of the resource as will be needed to unblock other processes needing units of the resource it produces.

✦ FIGURE 10.27 Deadlock in a Consumable Resource Graph

The graph in part (a) is a deadlock state since both processes are blocked. However, in part (b), p_0 is not blocked, so we can reduce by p_0. Then we can reduce by p_1. This is not a deadlock state.

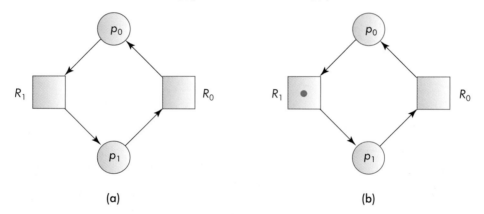

(a)   (b)

Figure 10.28 shows a consumable resource graph that represents a state in which $p_0(p_1)$ is the producer for $R_1(R_0)$. There are three requests for R_1 by p_1, and $w_1 = 2$. Since p_0, the producer of R_1, is not blocked, it may release (produce) units of R_1 to satisfy the request by p_1. Thus the state is not a deadlock.

Figure 10.29 illustrates that we cannot rely on *complete* reduction to test for absence of a deadlock when consumable resources are involved. In this figure, p_0 and p_1 each have requests for R_0 and R_1. p_0 is a producer of R_2, one unit of which is needed by p_2, which is a producer of R_1. Similarly, p_1 is a producer of R_3, one unit of which is needed by p_3, which is a producer of R_0. In the state represented by the graph, no process is deadlocked, since we can reduce by either p_0 or p_1. There is a transition to a state in which p_0 is not blocked and a transition to a state in which p_1 is not blocked. Once we reduce by one of the processes, we cannot reduce by the other.

For example, if we reduce by p_0, we can reduce by p_2. This leaves a situation in which we cannot reduce by p_1 and p_3 because the single unit of R_0 cannot be replenished by p_3, since it is blocked. Similarly, a reduction by p_1 will leave a situation in which we cannot reduce by either p_0 or p_2. The analysis will not characterize the state shown in Figure 10.29

as a deadlock state, since it is not a deadlock state. It is of no consequence that any state reachable from the state shown in the diagram happens to be a deadlock. It can be proved that in a consumable resource graph representing state s_j, process p_i is not deadlocked in s_j, if, and only if, there is a sequence of reductions that leave a state in which p_i is not blocked [Nutt, 1992].

✦ **FIGURE 10.28**   Consumable Resource Graph

This state is not deadlocked since p_0 can produce an arbitrary number of units of R_1. We can reduce by p_0, then by p_1.

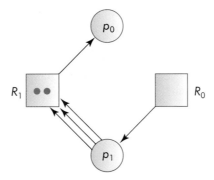

✦ **FIGURE 10.29**   A Complex Situation in a Consumable Resource Graph

This is not a deadlock state since there are different reduction sequences in which we can reduce by each process (although there is no single sequence for which this is true, and hence no complete reduction).

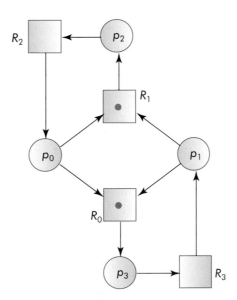

GENERAL RESOURCE SYSTEMS

Real systems incorporate a combination of reusable and consumable resources. Deadlock detection strategies need to combine the consumable and reusable resource analyses techniques. While the formal definition of **general resource graphs** and the analyses for detecting deadlock are not included here, such a system has a set of resources determined by the union of consumable and reusable resources. The necessary and sufficient conditions for a deadlock in a general resource graph are a combination of the conditions for consumable and reusable resource graphs, where the rules applying to each class are applied to the corresponding subsets of resources in a general resource graph. The detection analysis is conducted by using reusable resource graph reductions on all reusable resources and consumable resource graph reductions on consumable resources. For a state to be deadlock-free, the reusable resources must be completely isolated by reductions. However, the consumable resource graph must have a sequence in which each process can be demonstrated to not be blocked on any consumable resource.

For example, suppose we have a general resource graph as shown in Figure 10.30(a). Let R_0 and R_2 be reusable resources and R_1 be a consumable resource. p_0 and p_2 are both producers for R_1. Part (b) shows the graph after a reduction by p_3. All request and acquisition edges are removed from p_3, thus leaving all three units of R_0 available. In part (c), we have reduced by p_0, a producer of the consumable resource R_1. The request edges from p_0 are removed to indicate it could acquire and release two units of R_0. When the producer edge is removed from R_1 to p_0, the available units of R_1 are increased to an arbitrarily large number that can satisfy all future needs for R_1. Although we do not show the reductions in Figure 10.30, we could next reduce by p_1 and then finally by p_2. The state shown in Figure 10.30(a) is not a deadlock.

RECOVERY

Once deadlock has been detected in a system, the system will have to be recovered by changing it to a state in which there are no deadlocked processes. This is done by pre-empting one or more processes, releasing their resources so that the other deadlocked processes can become unblocked. In some cases, the recovery mechanism may use the general resource graph to select processes to destroy. More typically, the operator simply begins destroying processes until the system appears to be operational again. The brute force approach is to reboot the entire machine, thus destroying all processes, even though only the processes involved in the deadlock need to release their resources.

As already said, when resources are preempted from a process, the process normally is simply destroyed. However, sometimes the process can be removed without destroying all of the work it has already performed. This is accomplished by incorporating a **checkpoint/rollback** mechanism into the system by which a process periodically takes a snapshot of its current state—called a **checkpoint**. The OS saves the checkpoint for the process, and the process then continues its activity. If the OS determines that a process is involved in a deadlock, it destroys the process, thereby releasing its resources for other processes to use. Next, it reestablishes the victim process's state (including reallocating resources and rewriting files to their former state) based on the checkpoint information and then restarts the process from the last checkpoint. This method is called "rolling the process back to the checkpoint." It has been widely used in database management systems for many years, so it has become relatively sophisticated.

✦ **FIGURE 10.30** A General Resource Graph

This general resource graph has both consumable and reusable resources. It is not a deadlock state.

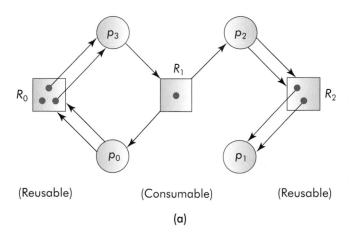

(Reusable)   (Consumable)   (Reusable)

(a)

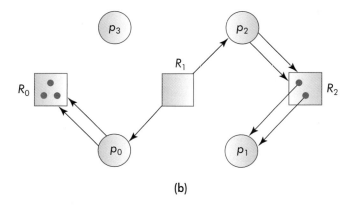

(b)

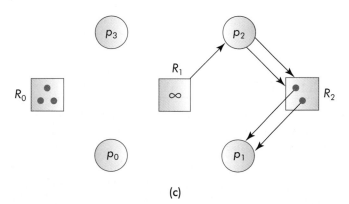

(c)

After a process is destroyed, the deadlock detection algorithm is invoked again to see if the recovery was successful. If it was, the system continues normal operation. If it was not, then another process is preempted. The recovery algorithm will eventually remove the deadlocked processes, potentially by restarting all but one of the processes involved in the deadlock. Then the system continues normal operation.

10.6 • SUMMARY

Deadlock creates a situation in which one or more processes will never run to completion without recovery. It can be prevented by designing resource managers so that they violate at least one of the four necessary conditions for deadlock: mutual exclusion, hold and wait, circular wait, and no preemption. Prevention can be effective on batch systems, but is usually not practical in timesharing or other interactive systems.

The process-resource state model provides a framework for defining deadlock independent of the strategy chosen to address deadlock. The model allows the precise definition of deadlock in terms of the state-transition diagram. It is used heavily in the subsequent discussions of avoidance and detection and recovery.

Deadlock can be avoided by using additional information, such as each process's maximum claim on each resource type, so as to not put the system into an unsafe state. The banker's algorithm is the classic avoidance algorithm. It is intuitively similar to the operation of a bank's offering lines of credit to its borrowers, even when the sum of the lines of credit exceeds the bank's total resources. Similarly, the banker's algorithm uses the maximum claim to determine if an allocation operation will lead to a state in which the resource manager cannot guarantee that deadlock will not occur. The banker's algorithm effectively performs the same operations used in a detection algorithm's graph reduction algorithm. Avoidance is overly conservative and not often used in contemporary operating systems.

Detection and recovery strategies differentiate between reusable and consumable resources in a system. Detection algorithms use graph reductions to explore state transitions that could occur from the state that is being analyzed. The details of a step in graph reduction depend on whether the reduction is applied to a consumable or reusable resource. Once a state has been determined to be a deadlock, the operating system will invoke a recovery algorithm to remove processes involved in the deadlock until the condition no longer exists.

This chapter completes the discussion of process management. The next chapter begins the discussion of memory management.

10.7 • EXERCISES

1. Draw a model like the one shown in Figure 10.2, for each of the following situations. Indicate whether or not there is deadlock in the situation. Assume that there is only one unit of each resource type.

   a. Process 1 is holding Resource 1 and requesting Resource 2; Process 2 is holding Resource 2 and requesting Resource 3; Process 3 is holding Resource 3 and requesting Resource 4; and Process 4 is holding Resource 4 and requesting Resource 1.

b. Process 1 is holding Resource 1 and requesting Resource 3; Process 2 is holding Resource 2 and requesting Resource 3; Process 3 is holding Resource 3 and requesting Resource 4; and Process 4 is holding Resource 4 and requesting Resource 2.

c. Process 1 is holding Resource 1 and requesting Resource 3; Process 2 is holding Resource 2 and requesting Resource 3; Process 3 is holding Resource 3 and requesting Resource 4; and Process 4 is holding Resource 4.

2. Provide a scenario in which two threads in different processes are deadlocked, and another scenario in which two threads in the same process are deadlocked. Try to use instances of concrete (real) resources like files.

3. Suppose three people are in a line waiting for a department store to open for "the big sale." When the door opens, all three rush the door, but the door is not big enough for all of them to pass through at once. Describe a solution for addressing this deadlock that will allow all three people to pass through the door. Which of the necessary deadlock conditions does your solution break?

4. In a music CD warehouse, sometimes orders become deadlocked because two different orders want the last two units of two different CDs. For example, two people might simultaneously order "More Themes for Young Lovers" by Percy Faith, and "Super Natural" by Carlos Santana when there is only one copy of each in stock. One order gets the Percy Faith CD and the other gets the Carlos Santana CD, then there is a deadlock. In this scenario, what strategy does the warehouse follow for addressing deadlock?

5. Reconsider the state diagram in Figure 10.7. Suppose that instead of one resource type with two units of the resource, suppose the two processes shared two resource types with one unit of each type. Draw the state diagram for this system (using the same resource management model used in the example in the chapter).

6. Identify safe, unsafe, and deadlock states in the state diagram shown in Figure 10.7.

7. Assume a system with four resource types, $C = <6, 4, 4, 2>$, and the maximum claim table shown in Figure 10.31. The resource allocator is considering allocating resources according to the table shown in Figure 10.32. Is this state safe? Why or why not?

✦ **FIGURE 10.31** Maximum Claim Table

Process	R_0	R_1	R_2	R_3
p_0	3	2	1	1
p_1	1	2	0	2
p_2	1	1	2	0
p_3	3	2	1	0
p_4	2	1	0	1

✦ **FIGURE 10.32** Current Allocation Table

Process	R_0	R_1	R_2	R_3
p_0	2	0	1	0
p_1	1	1	0	0
p_2	1	1	0	0
p_3	1	0	1	0
p_4	0	1	0	1

8. Reconsider the state-transition diagram in Figure 10.7. Describe, in words or with a diagram, a similar state-transition diagram for a system with three processes and a single resource type with two units of the resource. How many deadlock states are in the graph?

9. Based on what you studied in this chapter, explain how to change the code fragment in Figure 8.10 so that a deadlock cannot occur.

10. Using the prevention strategy for invalidating the circular wait (Section 10.3), suggest a heuristic for avoiding the nested monitor call problem explained in Section 9.2.

11. A system is composed of four processes, $\{p_1, p_2, p_3, p_4\}$, and three types of serially reusable resources, $\{R_1, R_2, R_3\}$. The number of units of the resources are $C = <3, 2, 2>$.

   ■ Process p_1 holds one unit of R_1 and requests one unit of R_2.
   ■ p_2 holds two units of R_2 and requests one unit each of R_1 and R_3.
   ■ p_3 holds one unit of R_1 and requests one unit of R_2.
   ■ p_4 holds two units of R_3 and requests one unit of R_1.

   Show the reusable resource graph to represent this system state. Show the reduced form of the graph. Which, if any, of the processes are deadlocked in this state?

12. A system is composed of four process, $\{p_1, p_2, p_3, p_4\}$, and three types of consumable resources, $\{R_1, R_2, R_3\}$. There is one unit each of R_1 and R_3 available.

   ■ p_1 requests one unit of R_1 and one unit of R_3.
   ■ p_2 produces R_1 and R_3 and requests one unit of R_2.
   ■ p_3 requests one unit each of R_1 and R_3.
   ■ p_4 produces R_2 and requests one unit of R_3.

   Show the consumable resource graph to represent this system state. Which, if any, of the processes are deadlocked in this state?

13. A system is composed of four processes, $\{p_1, p_2, p_3, p_4\}$, two types of serially reusable resources, $\{S_1, S_2\}$, and two types of consumable resources, $\{C_1, C_2\}$. S_1 has two units and S_2 has three units. C_1 and C_2 each have one available unit.

- ■ p_1 produces C_1 and is requesting two units of S_2.
- ■ p_2 holds two units of S_1 and one unit of S_2 while it requests two units of C_2.
- ■ p_3 holds one unit of S_2 and requests one unit of C_1.
- ■ p_4 produces C_2 and requests one unit each of C_1 and S_1.

Show the general resource graph to represent this system state. Which, if any, of the processes are deadlocked in this state?

CHAPTER 11

Memory Management

The memory system includes all parts of the computer that store information. It is divided into primary and secondary memory: **Primary memory** (also called the *executable memory*) holds information while it is being used by the CPU. **Secondary memory** refers to the collection of storage devices. Primary memory can be referenced one byte at a time, has relatively fast access time, and is usually volatile (it loses its contents when the computer crashes or is turned off). Secondary memory is referenced as blocks of bytes, has relatively slow access time, and is persistent (it can save contents while the computer is turned off). One modern challenge in programming is to keep programs and information in primary memory *only* while they are being used by the CPU, and to (re)store the information to secondary memory soon after it has been created or used. If the challenge is met, a process/thread makes efficient use of the primary memory, its performance is relatively high, and the danger of losing processed information due to crash or inconsistency is relatively low.

The memory manager is also the resource manager for the primary memory. This means that it allocates blocks of primary memory to processes. It also manages the OS mechanisms that implement primary memory isolation and controlled sharing. Finally, modern memory managers automatically transfer information back and forth between the primary and secondary memories using **virtual memory** technology. This chapter focuses on the basic issues in memory manager design. In the next chapter, we will see how modern memory managers extend the basic functionality to implement virtual memory.

11.1 • THE BASICS

Traditionally, offices use a **storage hierarchy** for managing their information (see Figure 11.1). An office worker's desktop is at the top of the hierarchy. Information that the worker needs to accomplish the current task is kept on the desktop. When information is not being used at the moment, but is relatively frequently used, it is kept in a file folder. When the worker wants to use information in the folder, the folder is brought to the desktop and its contents are used to do the work. If a folder is not used often, it is put in a file cabinet. Information in a file cabinet is less accessible than information in a folder on a person's desk. The file cabinet represents a lower layer in the storage hierarchy. In this office example, the lowest level of the hierarchy is the warehouse. Information is stored in the warehouse only when there is no specific plan to reference it in the immediate future, but it should not be destroyed.

✦ **FIGURE 11.1** Storage Hierarchies

Offices use a storage hierarchy for managing their information. Frequently used information is kept handy for the workers, and infrequently used information is kept in folders, file cabinets, and long-term storage.

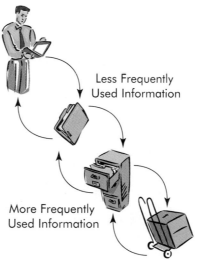

Less Frequently Used Information

More Frequently Used Information

A von Neumann computer's memory is also organized as a storage hierarchy. The memory hierarchy employs at least three levels of memory, arranged in a hierarchy (see Figure 11.2 and Chapter 4). The highest level is CPU register memory, the middle level is the primary (executable) memory, and the lowest level is secondary memory (storage devices). As in the office analogy, memory that is high in the hierarchy (such as the desktop) tends to be very fast, but limited in size. Memory near the bottom (such as the file cabinet) is relatively large, while access speed is a secondary consideration. At the bottom of the hierarchy, very large amounts of information (for example, terrabytes) are stored for long periods of time (for example, years). At this lowest level of the hierarchy, the cost of the storage medium dominates, so magnetic tape is still widely used, even though its access speed is slow and its capacity per tape is limited compared to optical and magnetic disks.

✦ FIGURE 11.2 The Basic Memory Hierarchy

von Neumann computers have three types of memory in their hierarchy. The registers in the CPU represent the highest level of the computer's memory. The primary (or executable) memory, such as RAM, is the middle layer of the hierarchy. The CPU can read and write individual bytes from/to this memory. Storage devices implement the secondary memory. Device I/O operations are used to access information in the secondary memory, so these access operations are orders of magnitude slower than primary memory operations.

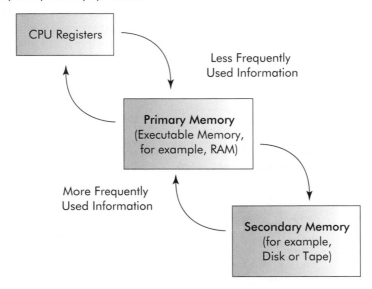

Information that is stored in a CPU register can be used (by the ALU) in one machine clock cycle. The CPU can access primary memory with a single load or store instruction within a few clock cycles. Secondary memory is implemented in the storage devices, so access involves action by a driver and a physical device. This means that secondary memory accesses take at least three orders of magnitude more time than do primary memory accesses.

Contemporary computers have many more levels in their memory hierarchy, including cache memory and various forms of secondary memory such as rotating magnetic memory, optical memory, and sequentially accessed memory (see Figure 11.3). However, each level is really just a refinement of one of the basic three levels described in Figure 11.2 (CPU registers, primary memory, and secondary memory).

The **memory manager** (see Figure 11.4) is the third major component of the OS. Memory management technology has evolved considerably over the years. In early multiprogramming systems, the memory manager's purpose was to be the resource manager for the space-multiplexed primary memory. As multiprogramming grew more popular, the memory manager was required to provide robust isolation mechanisms to prevent one process from reading or writing another process's allocated primary memory. The next generation of memory managers added the ability for processes to share parts of their allocated memory.

Contemporary memory managers continue to perform the classic functions required to manage the primary memory. In addition, they exploit storage hierarchies. Storage hierar-

◆ FIGURE 11.3 Memory Hierarchies

Storage device and cache memory technologies have introduced multilayered memory hierarchies. A contemporary microprocessor chip may contain two or more levels of cache memory. There is a large spectrum of secondary storage devices available that can implement another part of the hierarchy, ranging from hard disks to DAT tapes.

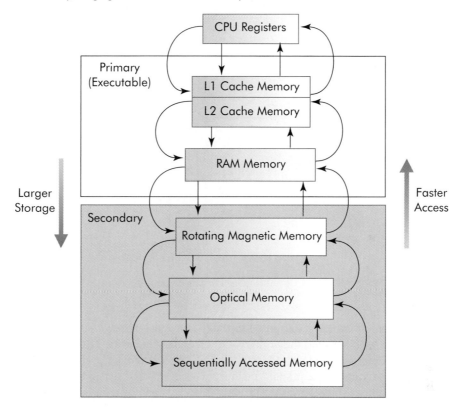

chies typically keep multiple copies of information: Roughly speaking, the "original" of the information is the copy that is stored in the computer's secondary memory. Copies are made into primary memory and CPU registers in order to reduce the time required for the CPU to access the information. The information only needs to be in the primary memory when software on the CPU is using it. For example, customer accounting information is generally kept in files on storage devices. (These files are periodically backed up to a lower-level archival storage device. This allows the files to be restored if the online storage device crashes, or if an audit of old information is required.) When the customer account is to be updated, records from the file are copied from the secondary memory to the primary memory. When the CPU actually updates a record, it copies fields for the record from the primary memory into CPU registers. After the information has been updated in the CPU, it updates the copy of the record in the primary memory. Later, the record is written back to the file in the secondary memory. Once a higher-level copy has been saved in a lower level of the hierarchy, the higher-level copy can be destroyed (since it is then redundant).

✦ **FIGURE 11.4**   The External View of the Memory Manager

The memory manager exports various system calls to manage the memory. Although both UNIX and Windows systems incorporate a memory manager, they export completely different system calls.

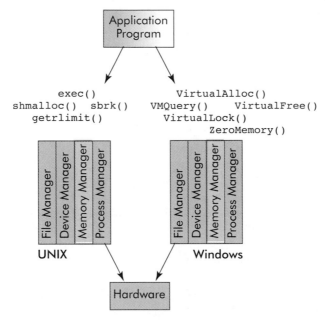

A modern memory manager (a virtual memory manager) *automatically* moves information back and forth between the primary and secondary memory. This means that the programmer need not read and write files to copy the information: The memory manager copies the information into the primary memory whenever it is needed, and then updates the secondary memory and releases the primary memory copy when it is no longer being used by the CPU.

The system call interface to the memory manager usually only includes a small number of functions: Calls are provided to request and release primary memory space, to load programs into the space, and to share blocks of memory. Modern memory managers also provide system calls to control some of the behavior of the virtual memory abstraction.

The *classic* memory manager addresses primary memory management by implementing:

■ **Abstraction.** The primary memory is abstracted so that software perceives the memory allocated to it as a large array of contiguously addressed bytes. The idea of a process address space is the main aspect of the abstraction, since it allows a process to use an abstract set of addresses to reference physical primary memory locations.

■ **Allocation.** A process may request exclusive use of a block of memory. The resource manager aspect of the memory manager allocates the primary memory as requested, and handles memory when it is released.

■ **Isolation.** When a block of contiguously addressed bytes is allocated to a process, the process is assured of exclusive use of those memory cells.

■ **Sharing.** The memory manager may permit a block of primary memory to be shared among two or more processes. In this case, it bypasses the isolation mechanism to permit shared access.

The *modern* manager supports virtual memory, which means that the memory manager is capable of automatically moving information up and down the storage hierarchy. (The file manager allocates and deallocates the secondary memory, while providing resource abstraction for the storage devices; see Chapter 13).

11.2 • THE ADDRESS SPACE ABSTRACTION

Memory managers have evolved with operating systems and hardware technology. However, the API to the primary memory is about the same as the one that was used in 1950. A process is provided with a linear address space that is used to read and write the array of bytes in the primary memory hardware. In the earliest days of operating systems, the linear address space that the programmer used was the physical primary memory address space. An executing program could directly access any primary memory address in the machine.

By the 1960s, multiprogramming operating systems had introduced an abstraction for primary memory: Each process is provided with a set of *logical* primary memory addresses that it can use to read or write locations in the *physical* primary memory. The accessible addresses are the ones that have been assigned to the process by the memory manager (see Figure 11.5). We refer to this set of logical primary memory addresses as the process **address space**: When a thread executes in the process, it can use any of the logical primary memory addresses to reference a specific block of physical primary memory. For example, if the memory manager allocated primary memory locations 0x20000 to 0x30000 to a process, then the process would reference physical primary memory location 0x20007 as logical address 0x00007. (As we discussed in Chapter 6, some of the addresses in the process's address space are bound to objects other than the primary memory locations; see also Figure 6.4.) This abstraction depends on the existence of the process address space and a system mechanism to *bind* logical primary memory addresses to physical primary memory addresses. The memory manager establishes the abstraction to support the address space and the address binding.

MANAGING THE ADDRESS SPACE

When a program is prepared for execution, it is translated into a machine executable format (see Figure 11.6). In a compiled-program environment, the source program is translated at **compile time** to produce a relocatable object module. A collection of relocatable modules is combined using a linkage editor (also called a *link editor*) at **link time** to produce an absolute (or load) module. The organization of the absolute module defines the address space that the process will use to reference the program's instructions, data, and stack.

✦ FIGURE 11.5 The Relationship Between the Address Space
and Primary Memory

When a block of primary memory is allocated to a process, the process's address space is bound
to the block of corresponding physical memory addresses.

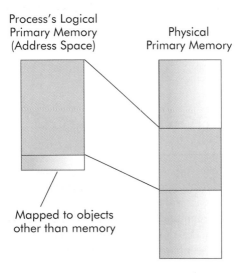

The absolute program is stored in a file (in the secondary memory) until a process is
ready to use it. After the process has obtained a block of primary memory from the memory manager, it calls the system loader to place the absolute program into that block of primary memory. The absolute program uses logical addresses, so it is constructed as if it
were to be loaded and executed at memory location 0. Every address is a *logical* rather
than a *physical* primary memory address. The loader *binds* the logical addresses to physical addresses by modifying each logical address in the load module so that it references
the corresponding physical memory address within the allocated block of memory. The
loader then copies the modified absolute program into the block of primary memory. Let's
look more closely at how addresses are managed during various phases of the translation
process.

COMPILE TIME The compiler translates a source program into a relocatable code (also
called a *relocatable object module*). In the C programming model, the relocatable object
module has the three logical blocks of addresses: A text (or code) segment, a data segment,
and a stack segment. The **code segment** is a block of machine instructions, the **data segment** is a block of static variables, and the **stack segment** represents the stack that will be
used when the program is executed.

The compiler writes all the translated machine instructions into the code segment.
Consider a procedure entry point in the relocatable object module. In general, the compiler will not be able to determine the address for the entry point, since the target procedure may be in a different relocatable module. For example, if the target is a library
routine, such as printf(), the target function will have been compiled when the system
software was built. Since this target address is unknown at compile time, it cannot be

✦ FIGURE 11.6 Multiple Segments

The source program translation system creates an *absolute program* that specifies a set of logical addresses that will be needed when the program is executed. The compiler translates source programs into *relocatable code*. The link editor combines relocatable code modules to create an absolute program. After a block of memory has been allocated to a process, the loader binds the process address space to the appropriate physical memory addresses, and then copies the program into the primary memory. The process is then ready to execute the program.

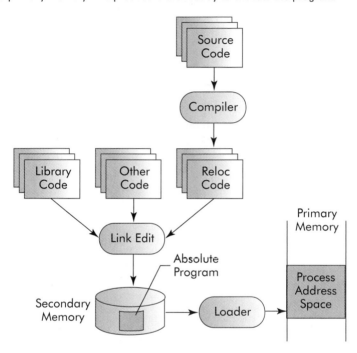

bound until the link editor combines the module that calls the function with the module that defines the function. The compiler will annotate each such reference to an external address so that the link editor can place the correct address in the code as soon as it determines where the address is in the absolute program.

Now consider how a static variable in a source program is handled. (A static variable retains the last value stored in it even when it goes out of scope.) The compiler generates code to allocate storage for the variable in the data segment and then uses the *relative address within the data segment* in instructions that reference the variable. If the variable were a C-style automatic variable, the compiler would have generated code to allocate the variable on the runtime stack. (A C-style automatic variable is defined only while the variable is in scope. If the variable goes out of scope and then comes back into scope, it will not have retained its old value.) Storage for an automatic variable is dynamically created and released as the program executes, so the compiler generates references for these variables that are *relative to the bottom of the stack* (instead of data segment addresses).

LINK TIME At link time, the code and data segments for each relocatable object module are combined to form the absolute program. To do this, the link editor combines all data segments into a single data segment, and all code segments into a single code segment. When the data segments are combined, the relative addresses of individual static variables will be changed. The linkage editor then *relocates* the addresses in the instructions so that they reference the updated addresses in the aggregated data segment. The link editor then matches entry point references to defined entry point addresses in the aggregate code segment. All the undefined address references are eventually discovered by the linkage editor as it combines relocatable modules: the resulting composition includes all the program text and data, so that every reference to data or a program entry point is resolved. The absolute module can then be stored in a file (in secondary memory) until it is to be executed.

LOAD TIME Prior to loading an absolute program, the memory manager allocates a block of primary memory to the process. Then the loader copies the absolute program and data into this newly allocated memory. Notice that the addresses in the code segment part of the absolute module must be adjusted once again (recall Figure 11.5). All addresses in the absolute program were set by the link editor as if the module were to be loaded at primary memory location 0. However, the module is now to be loaded at a particular physical address in the primary memory: the first address in the block of memory assigned by the memory manager. The loader translates each internal logical primary memory address so that it will refer to the allocated primary memory addresses (rather than an offset into the data or code segment).

The executable program is translated into its final executable form—the one expected by the hardware control unit—just before it is loaded into the primary memory at the proper location. When the PC (program counter) is set to the primary memory address of the first executable instruction—the main entry point—for the program, the hardware begins to execute the program.

As mentioned above, the procedure of associating the addresses used by a program with physical memory locations in the primary memory is called **address binding**. Traditionally, the address space is created and bound to the primary memory locations in the three-step process described here: compile time translation, link time combining of relocatable object modules, and load time adjustment of the load module when the primary memory addresses are allocated to the process. This particular form of binding is called *static* address binding: As you will see in Section 11.4, memory managers can also defer the last stage of address binding until runtime. You will almost certainly find the boxed discussion of Static Address Binding useful in gaining a full understanding of how this works. Before considering dynamic address binding, let's consider other basic functions of a classic memory manager.

Static Address Binding

The classic translation and loading process creates a relocatable logical memory address at compile time, converts it to an address in the absolute program at link time, and finally binds the logical address to a physical memory address at load time. For example, suppose we have the code segment shown in Figure 11.7.

✦ **FIGURE 11.7** A Sample Code Segment

We will use this code segment to illustrate how static address binding works.

```
...
static int gVar;
...
int proc_a(int arg){
  ...
  gVar = 7;
  put_record(gVar);
  ...
}
```

The compiler will allocate space for the variable named `gVar` in the data segment of the relocatable object module for `proc_a`. However, the procedure named `put_record()` is located in a different relocatable object module, so the compiler must leave the reference unresolved. The compiler will generate a relocatable object module similar to the example shown in Figure 11.8. The compiler reserves space for the variable named `gVar` at the relative address 0036 in the data segment and records the value in its symbol table. (Figure 11.8 shows a symbol table at relative address location 0600 in the relocatable object module.) The external references and definitions also appear in the relocatable object module.

■ The assignment statement is translated into a pair of instructions to load "7" into a register and then store it into the memory cell associated with `gVar`.

■ Relative address 0220 contains the load instruction that places the immediate operand, 7, into register R1.

■ Relative address 0224 contains the store instruction that copies the contents of R1 into data segment memory location 0036—the memory location bound to the variable `gVar` by the compiler.

■ When the compiler translates the function call, it first pushes the parameter values onto the stack with the instruction in location 0228.

■ Then, at relative address 0232, it generates an instruction to perform a function call to the externally defined entry point.

Since the compiler does not have enough information to bind the address of the entry point to the symbol `put_record`, it annotates the operand address field so that the linkage editor can complete the binding operation at link time and makes an entry in the **reference table**, or **ref table**, to be processed by the linkage editor. It also makes an entry in the **definition table**, or **def table**, for each external symbol, such as an entry point `proc_a`, that it is able to define. The example relocatable module is made up of 850 memory cells, including the code, data, and tables.

The linkage editor combines the respective segments in the relocatable object module shown in Figure 11.8 with other such modules, including the one containing the `put_record()` procedure. The result is an absolute module of the form shown in Figure 11.9. The combination is achieved by effectively concatenating all data and code segments, respectively, in relevant relocatable object modules. The relocatable addresses are

✦ FIGURE 11.8 The Relocatable Object Module

This represents the relocatable object module for the source code shown in Figure 11.7. In this representation, the gVar variable is at location 0036 in the data segment and the entry point at location 0008 in the code segment.

Code Segment
Relative

Address	Generated Code
0000	...
...	
0008	entry proc_a
...	
0220	load =7, R1
0224	store R1, 0036
0228	push 0036
0232	call 'put_record'
...	
0400	External reference table
...	
0404	'put_record' 0232
...	
0500	External definition table
...	
0540	'proc_a' 0008
...	
0600	(symbol table)
...	
0799	(last location in the code segment)

Data Segment
Relative

Address	Generated Variable Space
...	
0036	[Space for gVar variable]
...	
0049	(last location in the data segment)

also adjusted so that they reference the appropriate offsets in the generated segments. All external references and definitions will have been matched up by the link editor when it combined relocatable modules. In the figure:

■ The original code segment is relocated to location 1000 in the absolute program code segment, meaning the first location in the relocatable module compiled at location 0 is now bound to location 1000.

■ The original data segment is relocated to location 100 in the absolute program data segment, meaning that first location in the relocatable module's data is now bound to location 100.

■ This adjustment causes other relative addresses in the module to be rebound at link time. For example, the address for the gVar is changed from 0036 to 0136, so the operand reference to 0036 in the store statement must be changed to store R1 in 0136 rather than in 0036.

The linkage editor must change all relocatable addresses to reflect the new binding for the load module. By convention, the absolute module will be created so that its first address is memory location 0000.

✦ FIGURE 11.9 The Absolute Program

This figure represents the absolute program created by the link editor when it combines the relocatable program shown in Figure 11.8 with the modules that contained the externally referenced procedures.

Code Segment
Relative

Address	Generated Code
0000	(Other modules)
...	
1008	entry proc_a
...	
1220	load =7, R1
1224	store R1, 0136
1228	push 1036
1232	call 2334
...	
1399	(End of proc_a)
...	(Other modules)
2334	entry put_record
...	
2670	(optional symbol table)
...	
2999	(last location in the code segment)

Data Segment
Relative

Address	Generated variable space
...	
0136	[Space for gVar variable]
...	
1000	(last location in the data segment)

At load time, the absolute module will again have its addresses adjusted so that they reference the memory locations containing the generated images. For example, if the load module were to be placed in primary memory starting at location 4000 (see Figure 11.10):

■ The program image would have to be bound again, this time with the code and data segments combined into the primary memory address space.

■ The addresses for gVar and put_record( ) would be rebound to new physical memory locations, and the places in the program referencing those locations would be adjusted at load time.

■ Now gVar would be stored at primary memory location 0136 + 7000 = 7136, and the put_record( ) entry point would be at 2334 + 4000 = 6334.

The instruction operand addresses would be bound one final time before the program was executed.

✦ FIGURE 11.10 The Program Loaded at Location 4000

This figure represents the image of the absolute program shown in Figure 11.10 after it has been loaded at primary memory location 4000.

Physical Address	Generated Code
0000	(Other process's programs)
4000	(Other modules)
...	
5008	entry proc_a
...	
5036	[Space for gVar variable]
...	
5220	load =7, R1
5224	store R1, 7136
5228	push 5036
5232	call 6334
...	
5399	(End of proc_a)
...	(Other modules)
6334	entry put_record
...	
6670	(optional symbol table)
...	
6999	(last location in the code segment)
7000	(first location in the data segment)
...	
7136	[Space for gVar variable]
...	
8000	(Other process's programs)

DYNAMIC MEMORY FOR DATA STRUCTURES

Programming languages often define a facility to allow a program to manage part of its own address space, although the language does not define how memory allocation and binding should be handled. From the programmer's viewpoint, this facility is used to support dynamic data structures (like objects, lists, trees, strings, and so on). Since this facility is usually your first introduction to dynamic memory allocation, it is natural for you to expect that this is part of the general interface to the memory manager. However, these runtime dynamic memory allocators do not cause memory to be allocated to the process at all. Instead, they allow the programmer to manually bind parts of the process's address space to dynamic data structures. The C runtime model is representative of how this type of dynamic memory is handled by the system.

The C runtime system provides a library routine, malloc(), for requesting memory space for dynamic data structures. The programmer requests this space by writing a code sequence such as

```
struct ListNode *node;
...
node = (struct ListNode *) malloc(sizeof(struct ListNode));
...
```

When the malloc() call returns, node points to a memory block that is large enough to hold an instance of the struct ListNode data structure.

In most implementations, malloc() does not perform a system call at all. Instead, the linkage editor anticipates the use of this form of dynamic memory allocation and reserves space to accommodate such requests (see Figure 11.11). The malloc() function assigns space from a block of the process's memory called the *heap*. The maximum size of both the stack and the heap storage is determined at link time, so the translation system reserves a single block of storage to accommodate both of them. It then allows them to "grow" toward one another as the process executes. If the stack contains many temporary variables and call frames, it will use a large amount of the space. Similarly, if the program allocates a large amount of space using malloc(), the stack will be limited in its size.

What happens when this preallocated stack/heap storage is used up? When malloc() is called, or when a frame is added to the stack, this runtime code detects that the stack/heap is completely allocated, so it calls the OS memory manager (using the UNIX sbrk() system call—see [McKusick et al., 1996].) to request that the process be allocated more space. After the new space is allocated to the process, the address space may have to be rebound to the primary memory space allocated to the process so that memory references in the program will still reference the various parts of the program, stack, heap, and data areas.

MODERN MEMORY BINDING

During the 1980s, most operating systems began to incorporate memory managers that used sophisticated binding mechanisms. One result was that the address space received more attention. In the old days, the idea of an address space was implicit in the generation of the absolute program. Today, it is explicit, and defined as a standard part of the process abstraction. Each process is created with a large, empty address space: a 4 GB address

✦ FIGURE 11.11 C-Style Memory Layout

The C runtime system uses a particular memory layout for the address space. A large block of addresses is reserved for the heap and stack. When the process begins, the stack is empty and no blocks have been allocated from the heap. As allocations occur, the heap and stack grow toward one another.

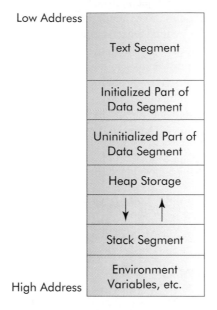

space on 32-bit microprocessors. This means that any process can run a program that uses up to 4 billion different addresses. The program is not required to use all this address space, but the memory manager is prepared to support such large address spaces.

In operating systems such as Linux and Windows, the address space is partitioned into a segment that is used by a user space program, and another segment that is used when the process is executing in supervisor mode. A typical partition allows the process to use 3 GB of the addresses when it is in user mode and 1 GB when it is in supervisor mode. By employing the idea of a fixed (but huge) size address space for every process, the static address binding strategy works as follows: Every absolute program defines the set of addresses that a process will need to execute that program. Every process is defined with a fixed size (say 4 GB) address space. The absolute program is mapped into the process's address space when the process decides to execute the program (see Figure 11.12).

This extra level of mapping is handled internally to the memory manager; it is done to simplify the design of modern memory managers and to provide extra functionality that will be needed in dynamic binding (see Section 11.4) and memory-mapped files (to be discussed in Section 12.7). Note that the programmer's view of abstract primary memory is unchanged from Figure 11.5. Now the loader binds absolute programs into the process address space instead of to physical primary memory locations. The program translation tools are not concerned with any of the primary memory details. The memory management address binding tools are only concerned with mapping a fixed-sized (but huge) process address space into the primary memory when the process runs.

✦ **FIGURE 11.12** Program and Process Address Spaces

The fixed size process address space is placed between address space generated by the program translation system and the physical memory. This is done to enable runtime binding of the address space to the primary memory.

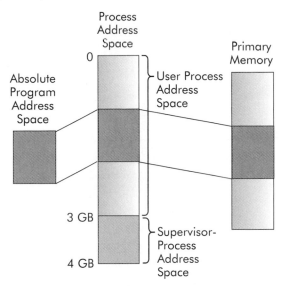

Also notice from Figure 11.12, that large parts of the process address space do not really have to be mapped into primary memory, since they are not used when a program is associated with the process address space. The idea is to not bother binding addresses from the process address space until run time. This is in preparation for our next piece of dynamic address binding. Before we look at dynamic address binding, let's consider how physical primary memory is allocated to a process.

11.3 ● MEMORY ALLOCATION

Before an address space can be bound to the primary memory, the memory manager must allocate space to the process. A multiprogramming memory manager allocates memory using space-multiplexed sharing. When a process is staged to run, it requests primary memory space from the memory manager, prepares its program (address space) for execution, and then loads it into the primary memory.

Consider early batch OS memory managers: Suppose the OS supports four-way multiprogramming. The memory manager partitions primary memory into four blocks and then allocates each block to a process. Figure 11.13 is a diagram of primary memory in which the four processes have been allocated different parts of the memory. Since the OS must have its own memory space for code and tables, there are five different memory blocks in the figure. The OS is using the memory from location 0 to A; the memory fragment between location A and B is not allocated; Process 1 has been allocated memory locations B to C; Process 3 has been allocated locations C to D; locations D to E are not allocated to a process; and so on.

✦ FIGURE 11.13 Multiprogramming Memory Support

Here is a snapshot of a machine's primary memory allocation. The OS has a block of the memory, as do processes 0-3. There are also blocks of unused memory (such as the memory block from D to E), called memory fragments.

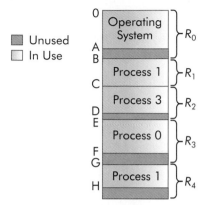

Many different strategies could be used to allocate the memory as shown in the figure. These strategies are generally separated into those that divide primary memory into a fixed number of fixed-size blocks at the time the operating system is configured and those that use dynamically determined, variable-sized blocks. The basic problem to be overcome in memory allocation is *fragmentation*—the perpetuation of small memory fragments. Ideally, the memory manager could allocate every single byte of memory to a process if any process needs memory. In practical terms, parts of the memory, called **memory fragments**, cannot be used at any given time because the memory manager is unable to allocate these parts in an efficient manner. How fragmentation occurs is covered in the discussion of the two basic strategies.

FIXED-PARTITION MEMORY STRATEGIES

Suppose the primary memory is statically divided into N fixed-size regions or partitions, where region R_i has N_i units of memory. Typically $N_i \neq N_j$ (the regions are different sizes), so processes with small address spaces use small partitions and processes with large address spaces use large partitions. Memory allocation in this kind of system requires that a process's address space be less than or equal to the size of an allocated partition. For example, if a process has an address space size of k, then it can be loaded into any R_i, where $N_i \geq k$. Upon allocation of region R_i to the process, $N_i - k$ units of the primary memory are unused during the time the process is loaded, since the space is allocated to the process but not mapped into its address space. This phenomenon is called **internal fragmentation**. This form of fragmentation is the loss of use of part of the memory due to the allocation of N_i memory locations when the process needed only k units.

If the memory diagram shown in Figure 11.13 were based on fixed partitions:

- R_0 might extend from location 0 to location B,
- R_1 from B to C,
- R_2 from C to E,

■ R_3 from E to G,

■ R_4 from G to the last address of the memory.

Thus, the memory from location A to location B is an unused internal memory fragment in R_0, the memory from location D to location E is an internal fragment in R_2, and so on. In the example shown in the figure, there is no internal fragmentation loss for R_1.

What *policy* should the memory manager use to allocate fixed-partition memories? Suppose each memory region has its own queue of processes competing for the partition. When a process requests k units of memory, the allocator places the process into the queue for some R_i, where $N_i \geq k$. Normally, the allocator would select the R_i that has the *best fit* to k, meaning it would select the R_i where $N_i - k$ is minimized. Sometimes the allocator may not use a best-fit strategy if some region's queue is becoming oversubscribed. Instead, it might choose *any* region large enough to hold the process. However, doing this would incur more internal fragmentation than the best-fit approach. Another alternative is for the allocator to keep a single queue of all processes, and then to allocate according to utilization.

Once a process has been allocated a region and it begins to run a program, the loader binds the absolute program address space to the region of memory to produce an executable program with addresses determined by the region's physical location in the primary memory.

Fixed-partition memory managers were widely used in batch multiprogramming systems, but they are generally not suitable for use in any system in which k is not known ahead of time (for example, in timesharing and other interactive systems). The memory demands of interactive users vary wildly, depending on the activity at any particular user's interactive terminal. For example, the user may be logged onto the machine but not using the terminal for an hour or two. Hence, the process effectively needs almost no memory until the user returns to the terminal and begins interacting with the system again. At other times, the user may be compiling a program, formatting a text document (or using `emacs` ☺). These programs require relatively large amounts of memory compared with the memory requirements of a text editor or mail system. Essentially, timesharing systems forced operating systems away from fixed-partition strategies and toward dynamic environments that better use memory.

VARIABLE-PARTITION MEMORY STRATEGIES

Internal fragmentation losses are aggravated by timesharing usage due to the wild variation in a process's memory needs during a login session. The obvious way to address this loss is to redesign the memory manager so that it *dynamically* defines regions according to the instantaneous space needs of a process. This approach effectively removes the possibility of internal fragmentation. (Memory managers usually allocate on multiword boundaries such as 64-byte blocks. If a process requests an amount of memory different from a multiple of the minimum size, there will be small amounts of internal fragmentation. These losses are inconsequential compared with the size of internal fragments in fixed-partition memory schemes.)

THE BASIC STRATEGY The challenge for a variable-size block memory manager is to keep track of the size of blocks of memory and to allocate them efficiently. When the system is initialized, the primary memory is configured as a single large block of N_0 units of memory (see Figure 11.14(a)). The scheduler allocates memory, n_i units to process p_i, as long as

$$\sum_{i=0}^{k} n_i \leq N_0$$

(see Figure 11.14(b)). A small amount of memory at the end of the memory space will be lost to **external fragmentation**—the part of the memory not marked as allocated to the OS or to any p_i. When no more processes can be allocated memory, the memory manager waits for one or more processes to release memory.

✦ **FIGURE 11.14** Dynamic Memory Allocation in Variable-Partition Memory

This figure illustrates several different configurations of the primary memory while it is being allocated using a variable-size block policy. In (a), only the OS is using the memory. In (b), the memory is filled by 7 processes that are adjacent in the memory. In (c), processes p_1, p_2, p_3, and p_5 have released their memory and p_7, p_8, p_9, and p_{10} have been assigned blocks of the memory. This causes external fragmentation, for example, between the memory for p_8 and p_{10}. In (d), we see that the memory blocks have been moved to eliminate the small memory fragments, producing a single large block of unallocated memory.

In Figure 11.14(c), p_5 has released its memory and p_7 has been allocated $n_7 \leq n_5$ units of memory. The memory manager selected a process "fitting" into the n_5 unit "hole" in memory that resulted from p_5 releasing its memory. Because of varying memory needs, it is possible that $n_7 < n_5$, thus resulting in the creation of a small block of unused memory between the space allocated to p_7 and p_6. This unused block is an instance of external fragmentation.

When p_6 releases its memory, n_5 units of memory are freed adjacent to the unallocated space that follows p_6. The memory manager must keep track of holes so that when two contiguous holes appear, they can be merged into one larger block of unallocated memory. In Figure 11.14(c):

- p_8 has been allocated to the block previously allocated to p_1,
- p_{10} has been allocated to the block previously occupied by p_2,
- p_9 has been allocated to the block previously allocated to p_3,
- p_7 has been allocated to p_5's block.

This new allocation has created several external fragments similar to the original external fragment at the end of memory in Figure 11.14(b).

As the system continues to run, the chances of external fragmentation increase. This situation occurs because a process can only fit into a hole that is at least as big as its memory requirements. The extra memory creates a small fragment. Furthermore, as the memory becomes increasingly fragmented, the memory manager will tend to favor processes that have smaller memory demands, thus causing the fragments, in turn, to become smaller and smaller. Eventually, the system will reach a state whereby only the smallest memory requests can be satisfied, even when there is sufficient aggregate memory to meet the requirements of larger requests. At this point, the operating system will have to compact the memory by moving all loaded processes so that they use contiguous space in the memory, thus creating one large free block (see Figure 11.14(d)).

The Cost of Moving Programs

Compaction (as shown in Figure 11.14(d)) requires that a program be moved from one block of memory to another. This in turn requires that the program in the block that is moved have its addresses relocated, since the address bindings that the loader used when the program was loaded in the first location will no longer be valid when it is loaded into a different location. Unfortunately, the loader is able to relocate only absolute images, not executable images. This happens because the absolute image (for example, as in Figure 11.9) is formatted so that the loader can easily identify addresses by flags left in the code by the compiler and the linkage editor. These flags are removed by the absolute loader when it creates an executable image, since the image is to be interpreted by the control unit as it is decoded and executed. Hence, when the program is moved, the loader must begin with the absolute image created by the linkage editor rather than using the executable image loaded in primary memory (see Figure 11.15). Any changes the process may have made to the data before the address space was moved will be lost unless they have been saved in secondary memory.

There is a better solution to the problem: Have the system change the way it binds addresses to primary memory locations. This dynamic binding approach is explained in Section 11.4.

✦ FIGURE 11.15 Moving an Executable Image

When a block of memory containing a program is to be moved, all the physical memory addresses that appear in the program's machine instructions must be adjusted because the data and entry point addresses that they referred to when the program was first loaded will change when the block is moved.

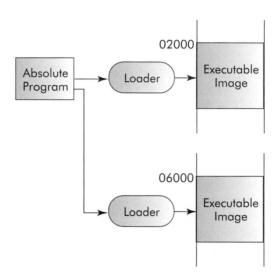

DYNAMIC ALLOCATION There is another scenario that must be considered in variable-partition memory. The system could allow a process to change the amount of memory allocated to it while it is executing, depending on its phase of computation. This scenario means that sometimes the process will request *more* memory than can fit in its current space plus any adjacent holes. For example, in Figure 11.14(c), suppose p_9 requests additional memory in an amount that exceeds its current space plus the space available in the holes above and below it. How can the request be honored? The memory manager could block p_9 until more adjacent space became available. But this strategy does not work in interactive systems, since the users might incur very long waits for service. Alternatively, the scheduler could find a larger hole in memory and move the process to the new hole, thus releasing the old space. However (as in the case of compaction suggested by Figure 11.14(d)), the system would then require some means of adjusting the program's addresses when it moves each process's address space.

In an environment that supports dynamic memory allocation, the memory manager must keep a record of the usage of each allocatable block of memory. This could be accomplished by using almost any data structure that implements linked lists. An obvious implementation is to define a *free list* of block descriptors, with each descriptor containing a pointer to the next descriptor, a pointer to the block, and the length of the block (see Figure 11.16). The memory manager keeps a free list pointer and inserts entries into the list in some order conducive to its allocation strategy; the figure simply orders the blocks in order of increasing primary memory address. Memory is ordinarily allocated in multiword blocks, with 64 or more words per block. A block of free memory is unused, meaning its contents are not used by any process. Therefore, memory allocation strategies typically use the first few words in every free block to implement the linked list shown in Figure 11.16. The free list pointer in the scheduler points to the first location of the first free block.

✦ FIGURE 11.16 Managing Free Memory Blocks

The collection of unused memory blocks can be kept in a conventional list. The memory manager maintains the list, adding blocks when they are released, removing blocks when they are allocated, and combining adjacent unused blocks.

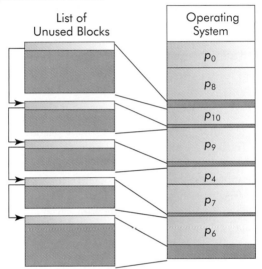

A number of different strategies can be used to allocate space to the processes that are competing for memory. Here is a brief explanation of a few of the most popular ones:

- **Best fit**: The memory manager places a process in the smallest block of unallocated memory in which it will fit. For example, suppose a process requests 12KB of memory and the memory manager currently has a list of unallocated blocks of 6KB, 14KB, 19KB, 11KB, and 13KB blocks. The best-fit strategy will allocate the 13KB block to the process.

- **Worst fit**: The memory manager places a process in the largest block of unallocated memory available. The idea is that this placement will create the largest hole after the allocations, thus increasing the possibility that, compared to best fit, another process can use the hole created as a result of external fragmentation. If the list of unallocated blocks consists of 6KB, 14KB, 19KB, 11KB, and 13KB blocks and a process requests a 12KB block, then worst fit will split the 19KB block into a 12KB block to allocate to the process, leaving a 7KB block for future use.

- **First fit**: If there are many holes in the memory, the memory manager begins traversing the list from the beginning and allocates memory from the first hole it encounters that is large enough to satisfy the request. It does this in order to reduce the amount of time it spends analyzing the free list. If the list of unallocated blocks consists of 6KB, 14KB, 19KB, 11KB, and 13KB blocks and a process requests a 12KB block, first fit will allocate the 14KB block to the process.

■ **Next fit**: The first-fit approach tends to fragment the blocks near the beginning of the list without considering blocks farther down the list. Next fit is a variant of the first fit strategy. It converts the list into a circular list, with the last block pointing to the first free one. When a process requests a block, it begins its search where the free pointer indicates. As soon as it finds a block to allocate, it assigns the space and then adjusts the free pointer to address the new fragment, or, if there is no fragment, to the block that follows the allocated block. Referring to the running example in this section, if the list of unallocated blocks consists of 6KB, 14KB, 19KB, 11KB, and 13KB blocks and the memory manager had last allocated a block from the list between the 19KB block and the 11KB block, then when a process requests a 12KB block, next fit will allocate the 13KB block to the process.

The classic exposition of these (and other) strategies appears in Knuth [1973, vol. 1].

CONTEMPORARY ALLOCATION STRATEGIES

Modern memory managers all use some form of variable partitioning. However, memory is usually allocated in fixed-sized blocks (called "pages," as you will see when virtual memory is introduced in Section 11.5), thus greatly simplifying the management of the free list (but greatly complicating the binding problem). In this case, all allocatable units are the same size, so the free list management is trivial. In older systems, such as MS-DOS and Version 7 UNIX, the memory manager deals with variable-sized blocks of memory. When a process is created, the memory manager uses a strategy such as best fit to assign an initial amount of memory. As the process executes, it requests and releases memory according to its needs for any particular phase of execution.

The part of the address space that is likely to change is that containing data because once the part of the address space that contains the program has been loaded into primary memory, it will not ordinarily change size (a change in size would mean the program had been changed). Nevertheless, suppose the part of the address space that contains the program does grow (or shrink). Then either part of the program is being unloaded from memory or the program is somehow growing. In languages like C, this is not normally possible, although it can occur in languages like Lisp. We have already determined that it is critical for the system to provide some better means than conventional static binding for changing the address space binding as the program executes. Otherwise, each time a program grows or shrinks, the loader must rebind each address in the program to the new primary memory location. (This also happens each time a program is moved—for example, by compaction or by unloading and reloading an address space from/to primary memory.)

11.4 • DYNAMIC ADDRESS SPACE BINDING

In static address binding, symbols (variables and entry points) in a source program are first bound to relative addresses in a relocatable module at compile time, then to addresses in an absolute module at link time, and finally to primary memory addresses at load time. That is, every address in the program is bound to a primary memory location prior to runtime. As described in Section 11.3, programming language runtime systems usually provide a facility to allow memory from the heap to be bound to symbols at runtime: This facility is used with dynamic heap memory allocation facilities to support dynamic data structures including objects. In this case, the programmer is responsible for binding the address to the primary memory location (using C-style pointers and type casting).

Suppose there were a more general tool for binding absolute program addresses at runtime. Then the memory manager would be able to move a program around in the memory without having to adjust the addresses in the instructions in the program. This, in turn, would enable the memory manager to use variable-partitioning strategies. The simplest mechanism that dyanamically binds addresses is called **dynamic relocation**.

Consider the algorithm the loader uses to adjust addresses in the absolute module so that they match the physical addresses. Since the absolute module is built as if it were to be loaded at memory location 0, all addresses are relative to the beginning of the module. (Programs can have "addresses" other than relative addresses compiled into operand fields. For example, an immediate operand should not change when a module is relocated. Some instruction sets include an offset address, meaning the operand is an offset from the current PC contents. This offset enables a program to branch forward or backward the number of addresses specified by the operand.) When the loader determines the actual address of the first location in the module, it can adjust any relative address by adding the value of the first location to it. In Figure 11.10, each relative address from the absolute module in Figure 11.9 had 4000 added to it because the module was loaded at location 4000.

Hardware can be designed to perform this simple relocation *each time the CPU makes a reference to memory*. Using such hardware allows the last phase of address relocation (the one done by the loader) to be deferred until runtime. Suppose the loader left all memory addresses with the value assigned by the link editor. The CPU could execute the code as if it were loaded at primary memory location 0. Each address relative to the beginning of the module would be issued to the physical primary memory (written to the MAR) as if it were a physical memory address. In the enhanced design, the relocation hardware intercepts each of these addresses and adds a *relocation value* (physical primary memory location of the first address in the module) to the relative address before sending it on to the MAR (see Figure 11.17). The **relocation register** is loaded with the first address in the primary memory block that is assigned to an address space. The relocation register is part of the process's CPU state, so it is changed each time a different process is allocated the CPU. This approach enables the executable image that is produced at load time to be used at runtime, thus avoiding the job of relocating all the addresses in a program module whenever it is moved in the primary memory. This **hardware dynamic relocation** is commonly used in contemporary processors, independent of any additional memory management strategies. It gives the OS complete freedom to choose the location at which executable images are loaded in primary memory whenever the memory manager needs to move programs in the middle of their execution.

Contemporary language translation systems exploit hardware dynamic relocation through one additional refinement. As we saw in Section 11.2, translation systems generate data and code into distinct segments within an absolute program. For example, C programs are compiled into a *text (code) segment* that contains the code, a *stack segment* that contains temporary variables, and a *data segment* that contains static variables. The UNIX

✦ FIGURE 11.17 Hardware Dynamic Address Relocation

The relocation register contains the address of the first location of the primary memory allocated to a process. Addresses that appear in the program can be relocated on-the-fly by being added to this base address. This allows the last address location that is performed by the loader in static address relocation to be performed at runtime.

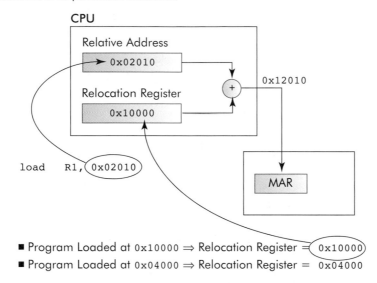

process model (revisit Chapter 2 if you need to do so) is modeled after this program modularization. To provide explicit support for such language models, the CPU is designed with three (or more) relocation registers to manage the code, stack, and data segments as separate blocks of primary memory. For example, Intel 80x86 microprocessors contain a code segment relocation register, a stack segment relocation register, and a data segment relocation register (see Figure 11.18). The code segment register relocates all addresses during the processor's fetch cycle, the stack segment register relocates addresses for stack instruction execution, and the data segment register relocates all other addresses during the execute cycle. In a machine architecture that has N relocation registers, each process can have N different blocks of the primary memory allocated to it. The code, data, and stack segments need not be contiguous in the primary memory.

Would it be possible for segment registers to be managed "automatically" by the OS (so that programmers did not even really have to know that they existed)? Suppose the compiler generates normal 16-bit addresses when it translates a source module and, as usual, leaves external references to be handled by the linkage editor. Further suppose that no individual module has a code or data segment larger than 64KB, although the resulting absolute program may be much larger than 64KB. Hence, all generated code will contain only 16-bit relative addresses into different code and data segments for the relocatable module. When any function is executed in a module, the initialization code at the entry point loads the code and data segment registers to point to the part of the absolute image corresponding to the relocatable module. The address used by this prologue can only be provided by the linkage editor. Now, when control flow moves from one module to

✦ FIGURE 11.18 Multiple Segment Relocation Registers

Many contemporary CPUs contain a bank of segment relocation registers, including one to relocate a code segment, one to relocate a stack segment, and one to relocate a data segment. This allows each process to have two distinct segments, each dynamically relocated at runtime.

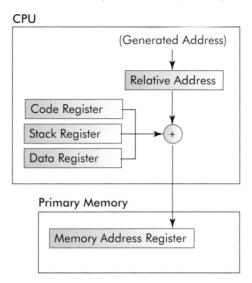

another, the calling function references an external symbol that will later be resolved by the linkage editor. The compiler recognizes that this happens so it generates code to adjust the code segment register to call the externally defined function before the instruction is executed (see Figure 11.19). Now, *every* call across modules causes the code segment register to change. Since data references outside the 64KB block must also be defined as external references in the source code, the compiler can recognize each of these references and generate code to change the data segment register. Every reference to an external variable causes the data segment register to change.

This technique is complex, and it relies on the compiler and the linkage editor to provide a large address space through manipulation of the segment register. The approach does not work for assembly language programs, for any program that inadvertently changes a segment register value, or in cases in which a source module generates a code or data segment larger than 64KB.

This technique also relies on an unusual call instruction in the machine language. What will happen if the compiler generates an instruction to set the code register in the instruction just before the call instruction? The next instruction fetched will not be the one in the location following the segment register load instruction. Rather, it will be one in a corresponding location in another 64KB segment. For this approach to work, it must be possible to load the segment register and execute the call before the segment register is updated rather than just execute the call in an instruction.

This discussion suggests that processes could make flexible use of multiple segments, even with only three relocation registers, if it were somehow possible to ensure that only trusted software changed the contents of the relocation registers. In modern computers,

✦ FIGURE 11.19   Adjusting the Code Register

The code register addresses the base of the code segment. If the code register is changed, then the control unit will fetch instructions from a new block of memory. This allows a process to branch from one segment to another.

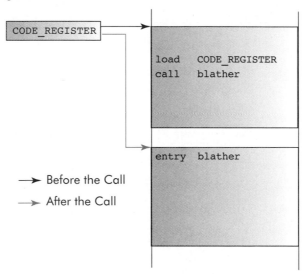

such instructions are privileged instructions. Only the OS (specifically, the memory manager) can change the relocation register contents. The compiler generates a trap instruction whenever the segment register needs to be adjusted. At runtime, the trap instruction interrupts the program execution and starts the OS. The trap is recognized as a segment trap and is passed to the memory manager. The memory manager determines the target address and then adjusts the program counter and segment register to reference the distant target address. This technique, too, requires an instruction to be able to set the program counter and the segment register before another instruction is fetched from memory.

RUNTIME BOUND CHECKING: THE ISOLATION MECHANISM

The relocation register is a fundamental addition to computer systems, since it enables dynamic address binding. Once such a mechanism has been incorporated into the hardware, it is easy to make small additions to substantially increase the ability of the system to support memory isolation. Suppose each relocation register has a companion **limit register** that is loaded with the *length* of the memory segment addressed by the relocation register. Whenever the CPU sends an address to primary memory, the relocation register is added to the address at the same time it is compared with the contents of the limit register (see Figure 11.20). If the address is less than the value in the limit register, the address refers to a location within the memory segment. If the address is larger than the limit register value, it refers to a part of primary memory not allocated to the process that is currently using the CPU. An out-of-bounds reference—also called a *segment violation*—will generate an interrupt, thus producing a fatal execution error.

✦ FIGURE 11.20 Bound Checking with a Limit Register

The limit register contains an unsigned integer value segment length. If the current address is less than the value in the limit register, then it refers to an address within the segment. But if it is greater than the length, then the address references information outside the segment.

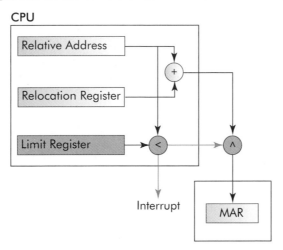

- Bound checking is inexpensive to add
- Provides excellent memory protection

11.5 • MODERN MEMORY MANAGER STRATEGIES

Virtual memory is the dominant memory management strategy in modern operating systems, followed by swapping in lower functionality operating systems and on computers with moderate mapping hardware. Swapping technology was the first to take advantage of dynamic relocation hardware, and it has influenced the way virtual memory has evolved. We will first study swapping as the basis for understanding virtual memory.

Multiple-partition memory strategies are the basis of multiprogramming. By dividing the memory into regions and allocating those regions to a set of processes, the scheduler can multiplex the CPU across the threads in the processes in the set at a high rate of speed. If one assumes that there are always threads ready to execute, then primary memory can become the bottleneck to performance. Suppose N processes are loaded into the primary memory and the threads in an additional K processes could run if they had memory allocated to them. Then whenever all of the threads in any one of the N processes are blocked on I/O, a semaphore, or other condition, the memory the process holds is not being used for any useful purpose. Neither the other $N - 1$ loaded processes nor the K waiting processes can use the memory because it is all allocated to the blocked processes. Virtual memory and swapping attack this problem by deallocating the memory from processes whose threads are blocked to enable some of the K waiting processes to use it while the other threads are blocked.

SWAPPING

Swapping memory managers are typically used in systems in which there is only a single thread per process. They attempt to optimize system performance by removing a process from primary memory when its thread is blocked, deallocating the memory, allocating to other processes, and then reacquiring and reloading the swapped-out process when its thread returns to the ready state. For example, when process p_i requests an I/O operation, it becomes blocked and will not return to the ready state for a relatively long period of time. When the process manager places p_i into a blocked state, it notifies the memory manager so that it can decide whether to swap the process's primary memory image to secondary memory (see Figure 11.21). When the process manager moves a blocked process, p_j, to the ready state, if p_j is swapped out, the process manager will inform the memory manager so that it can swap the address space back into primary memory, either immediately if primary memory is available or as soon as the space becomes available.

✦ FIGURE 11.21   Swapping

A swapping system transfers segments back and forth between the primary memory and the secondary memory. When the segment is in the primary memory, it can be used by an active process, but when it is swapped out to the secondary memory, the process that uses the address space is blocked waiting for primary memory.

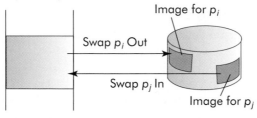

Primary Memory   Secondary Memory

When a process is swapped out, its entire executable image is copied to secondary memory. When it is swapped back into available primary memory, the executable image that was swapped out is copied into the new block allocated by the memory manager. Without relocation hardware, swapping would be very difficult to achieve due to the address binding problem. With relocation hardware, the executable image is simply copied into the newly allocated region(s) of memory and the relocation register is loaded accordingly.

Swapping is especially well-suited to timesharing systems, since such systems often have times when a user logs onto the machine (and hence is using some resources) but is inactive for relatively long time periods (and hence not using the CPU). A swapping memory manager addresses the timesharing scenario by allocating memory to a process while the user is requesting service at a relatively high rate, but deallocating memory during those times when the user makes requests for service at a low rate. That is, in a timesharing system, the memory manager may decide to swap a process out of memory even if it is ready, depending on the total load on the machine and the activity of the interactive user.

The key observation about a swapping system is that if a process is not going to use the CPU for a relatively long time, it should release its allocated primary memory. This allows other processes to use the memory and the CPU. Timesharing memory managers often turn this observation around by adopting a strategy to address the case in which there are many more requests for memory and CPU than there are memory resources available. The memory manager selects some processes that are to give up memory (and therefore the CPU) so that other processes have an opportunity to use them. The selected processes are blocked (on a memory request) by the memory manager and then their memory is deallocated. They immediately begin competing with other processes to reacquire memory. Timesharing systems (such as many older versions of UNIX) use swapping to provide equitable service to an oversubscribed system. When the number of active users surpasses a system-defined threshold, the memory manager will begin swapping processes.

Some form of swapping policy is almost always required with any multiprogramming, interactive system environment, even ones with very large amounts of physical memory. Since the overall load on the machine may be determined by continuous and unpredictable human activity, there are large periods of time when a process is holding memory but is dormant. As long as there are no other processes being blocked by the memory manager, there is no need to swap. However, once the memory request queue begins to grow, the memory manager begins swapping processes out of memory whenever they have a period of inactivity that exceeds a threshold amount. As the memory request queue grows, the threshold may decrease. The effect of swapping is easily perceived by the user, since it can result in a noticeable increase in response time.

The decision to swap out a process may depend on either the time the process is expected to be blocked or the need to swap out a process in an effort to equitably share memory and the CPU. Unfortunately, the performance increases gained through swapping are never to the process's advantage, since the process will have to compete to reacquire primary memory. The performance gain is a system-wide gain evidenced, for example, by a reduction in the average turnaround/response time for a process.

What is the cost of swapping out a process? If the process holds S units of primary memory, then we can compute the overhead time required to copy the executable image to a storage device and the time to copy it back into the primary memory when it is swapped in. If a disk block is D units of primary memory, then the memory manager will need to write at least $R = \lceil S/D \rceil$ (R is rounded to the next highest integer) disk blocks in order to save the executable image. It will need to perform the same number of read operations in order to swap the address space back into primary memory. The cost to the process is the time the process spends competing to regain primary memory after it enters the ready state while being swapped out. So wherever the memory manager arbitrarily decides to swap out a process, the delay in time—the swap time, $2R$, and the time to reacquire memory—is all overhead.

Suppose the process manager changes the state of a process holding S units of the memory to blocked and it remains blocked for T units of time. The space-time product, $S \times T$, represents the amount of resource waste due to the process's being blocked while holding memory. If S is small, then the memory manager will gain only a small amount of memory to be used by other processes if it swaps the process. If T is small, then the process will shortly begin competing for primary memory. If $T < R$, then the process will logically begin requesting memory before it has even been completely swapped out. For swapping to be effective, T must be considerably greater than $2R$ for every process the memory manager chooses to swap out, and S must be large enough that it enables other processes to execute.

The memory manager knows S for every process, but it can only predict the value of T when a process becomes blocked. If the process becomes blocked because it requests an I/O operation on a slow device, then the memory manager can estimate a lower bound on T and hence on $S \times T$. When a process becomes blocked due to an arbitrary resource request (for example, a P operation on a semaphore or a request for a serially reusable resource), the memory manager cannot estimate T. In a conservative swapping strategy, a process will not be swapped by such requests. But in an optimistic strategy, the process could be swapped on almost any request operation.

If the memory manager decides to swap out a process due to severe competition for memory, it can compute a different space-time product, $S \times T'$, where T' is the amount of time the process has held S units of memory. If $S \times T'$ is large for some p_i and other processes are waiting to be swapped in, then the process has held the memory for a relatively long time. In the interest of equitable sharing, the memory manager policy may be to swap p_i out and to swap in some other process into the space previously used by p_i.

VIRTUAL MEMORY

Virtual memory strategies allow a process to use the CPU when *only part* of its address space is loaded in the primary memory. In this approach, each process's address space is partitioned into parts that can be loaded into primary memory when they are needed and written back to secondary memory otherwise (see Figure 11.22). Programs have natural, implicit partitions. For example, the C-style translation model partitions the address space into code, data, and stack segments.

The code segment usually has a more subtle set of partitions relating to the phases of computation defined by the program. For example, almost all programs have a phase for initializing data structures, another for reading input data, one or more for the actual computation (depending on the algorithm), others for error recovery and reporting, and one for output. Similar implicit partitions usually exist in the data segment. This characteristic of programs—called **spatial locality**—is very important to the strategy used by virtual memory systems. When a program is executing in one part of its address space, its spatial locality is the set of addresses used during that phase of the computation. As the computation moves to a different phase (referencing different parts of the address space for the program and/or the data), it changes locality.

In Figure 11.22, the address space is divided into five parts. However, the program locality is such that the process is only using parts 1 and 4 at the moment. Therefore, only parts 1 and 4 are loaded in the primary memory. Different parts of the address space will be loaded at different times as the process's locality changes. *The virtual memory manager's task is to infer the process's locality and to keep the corresponding part of the address space loaded in the primary memory while the process is using it.*

In theory, the virtual memory manager allocates portions of primary memory that are the same size as the partitions in the address space and then loads the executable image for the corresponding part of the address space into the allocated primary memory. The effect is that the process uses much less primary memory, thus greatly increasing the memory available to other processes. Suppose the virtual memory manager could be designed "perfectly." That is, it always knew the exact set of addresses in the process's locality and always kept exactly those parts of the address space loaded in primary memory before they were referenced (and unloaded when they are no longer part of the local-

✦ FIGURE 11.22 Virtual and Physical Memory

The left side of the figure represents a process's address space. In this case, the address space is partitioned into five different segments. Only parts 1 and 4 are currently loaded in the primary memory (all five segments are loaded into the secondary memory), since the process is only using the information that is in these particular segments.

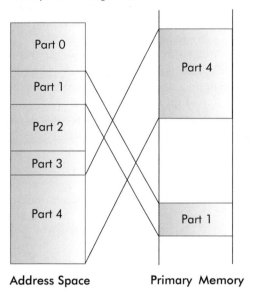

Address Space   **Primary Memory**

ity). Then, even the process could not detect that it did not have a primary memory allocation as large as its address space.

What barriers must be overcome to implement virtual memory? The memory manager must be able to partition the address space into parts that correspond to the various localities that will exist during the program's execution. The system must be able to load a part anywhere in the physical memory and dynamically bind the addresses in the part to the physical location in which they are loaded. The amount of memory allocated to the process may vary, so many parts, or only the bare minimum, may be loaded at once.

Virtual memory began to appear in high-end commercial machines in the late 1970s. At that time, primary memory costs were high, so the amount of memory on the machine limited its use. Virtual memory offered a way for processes to execute using a primary memory space that was smaller than its address space. This allowed system designers to use relatively small memory regions with higher degrees of multiprogramming. For example, a machine with 256KB of memory might support eight-way multiprogramming with virtual memory, but only four-way multiprogramming using other variable-sized regions. The motivation for virtual memory was to overcome memory size limitations with cost-effective memory configurations. Contemporary virtual memory managers also attempt to use memory hierarchies in conjunction with virtual memory techniques in order to decrease a process's execution time by reducing the memory access time delays. Whereas the original justification was motivated by memory costs, the motivation in modern operating systems is a combination of cost and performance.

Using Cache Memory

As noted earlier in the chapter, contemporary computers frequently employ a cache memory to increase a computer's performance. A cache memory is high-speed memory placed on the data path between the processor and the bus that connects the processor to the primary memory (see Figure 11.23). In part (a), when a processor references a primary memory unit, the CPU must compete with all the devices for the use of the bus. This usually causes the CPU to wait while a device finishes its access. Using the principles of virtual memory, manufacturers can design hardware to incorporate a **cache memory** between the CPU and the system bus (see part (b) of the figure). In this approach, whenever the CPU accesses the memory, a copy of the accessed information is placed in the cache memory. The next time the processor references the same memory location, the value can be found in the cache memory, so the processor need not use the bus to reference the copy kept in memory.

Just as parts are copied from secondary memory to primary memory in a virtual memory system, in a system with caching, **cache lines** are copied from primary memory into the cache. Most of the cache strategy is implemented in hardware rather than being evenly divided between the hardware and the software, as is the case with conventional virtual memory. The memory manager for an operating system makes few compensations for the presence of caching.

The use of a cache memory can affect performance profoundly, depending on the nature of the CPU's memory access patterns and the strategy used in the cache manager. In the worst case, its use brings no improvement, since the cost of the overhead dominates the access time. In the best case, the effective memory access time can be reduced by a factor of two or three.

✦ FIGURE 11.23 Cache Memory

Cache memory was invented to reduce the activity on the system bus (or other interconnection network). Part (a) shows a machine without a cache memory, and in part (b), a cache memory has been placed between the bus and the CPU. Whenever the CPU issues a read to the memory, a copy of the information that is read from the memory is deposited into the cache memory. If the CPU reads the same address again, it will use the value from the cache memory without going to the primary memory.

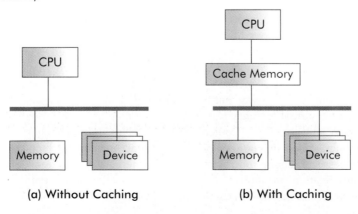

(a) Without Caching   (b) With Caching

SHARED-MEMORY MULTIPROCESSORS

Multiprocessors have been studied for several decades, but in the 1980s, they matured as viable commercial computers. A few multiprocessors depart from the von Neumann architecture in an effort to increase fundamental processing speeds, but most adapt the basic von Neumann architecture for each processor in the multiprocessor. Two general classes of multiprocessors have evolved: distributed-memory machines and shared-memory machines [Hwang and Briggs, 1984]. Naturally, computer architecture continues to evolve, with newer multiprocessors combining aspects of Hwang and Briggs characterizations. Students of computer architecture are encouraged to consult the current literature, such as the computer architecture conference proceedings [IEEE] or the IEEE/ACM annual ASPLOS conference [IEEE/ACM], to see these new and exciting developments. The discussion here is limited to distributed-memory and shared-memory organizations, since these illustrate the extensions to memory management necessary for this class of machines.

Distributed-memory machines are logically equivalent to networks in that they rely on message passing to share information across processors. Memory management in these machines, and in networks of machines, is currently a research topic in the study of operating systems. Suffice it to say that despite the fact that information can physically be moved between memories only by using some form of message passing, operating systems for these machines may go to great lengths to provide a shared-memory interface to be used by the application software.

This section focuses on shared-memory multiprocessors. A shared-memory machine takes the general form depicted in Figure 11.24. Several processors share an interconnection network (sometimes, just a bus) to access a set of shared-memory modules. The hardware-addressing mechanism allows software on any processor to access any memory location in any memory unit on the interconnection network. The trend in shared-memory multiprocessors is to employ an off-the-shelf microprocessor as the processor engine, incorporate a sophisticated interconnection network (this component is the performance bottleneck in shared memory machines) and use industry-standard memory units and devices. Most operating systems for shared-memory machines are adaptations of UNIX, where the changes provide a system call interface extension to manipulate memory addresses so that the corresponding memory locations can be shared.

✦ **FIGURE 11.24** A Shared-Memory Architecture

Shared-memory multiprocessors incorporate multiple CPUs, all sharing access to the same set of primary memory modules. Any CPU can read and write any primary memory unit.

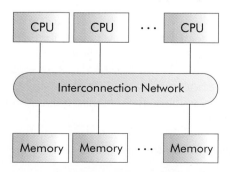

The goal of a shared-memory multiprocessor is to use classic processes or threads to implement units of computation whereby information is shared via common primary memory locations. The translation software creates a barrier by providing each process with its own isolated address space (see Figure 11.25). The address space in Process 1 has been laid out so that the last "block" in the address space is to be bound to shared primary memory. In Process 2, the first block, which is the same size as the last block in Process 1's address space, is to be bound into the same primary memory location. Now, when the programs are loaded at the same time, the parts of the two independent address spaces map to common memory locations. When Process 1 writes a variable in the memory, Process 2 can read its value. This technique results in very high performance.

✦ **FIGURE 11.25** Sharing a Portion of the Address Space

Suppose processes 1 and 2 intend to share parts of their address space with one another. This can be arranged by binding the shared part of Process 1's address space to the same primary memory locations that are bound to a part of Process 2's address space.

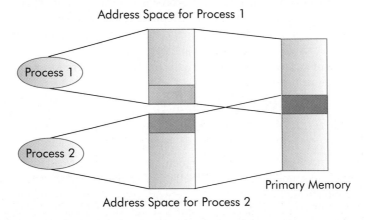

Address Space for Process 1

Process 1

Process 2

Primary Memory

Address Space for Process 2

In Figure 11.26, multiple relocation-limit register pairs are used to support block sharing. The address space is split into a private part and a shared part. One register pair points at the private part, and one pair points at the shared part. Processes 1 and 2 have their relocation-limit pair for the shared block point to the same physical memory locations. The OS extension must then incorporate a means for the program to identify a block as being shared and provide system calls, thereby causing the shared segments to be bound to a common memory location.

The interconnection network, such as a bus, is the key hardware component of a shared-memory multiprocessor. It is used by every CPU for every access of primary memory. Experience with these CPUs shows that if the network is implemented as a shared bus, the bus will saturate with as few as four CPUs. More sophisticated interconnection networks can be built, but cache memory technology is used in all shared-memory multiprocessors in order to decrease the load on the interconnection network and to increase each process's performance.

Cache memories can substantially enhance a computer's performance (even a uniprocessor's) by keeping frequently used information in the high-speed cache. This

✦ FIGURE 11.26 Sharing a Portion of the Address Space

The shared portion of an address space can be placed in a separate segment, and then a new dynamic relocation register can be used to point to the shared segment.

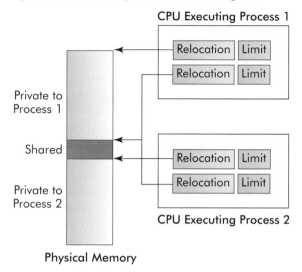

allows the processor to load the information from the cache—a much faster memory than the normal primary memory—without having to use the bus. In a multiprocessor, all CPUs may be trying to use the common bus at the same time. Thus, contention for the bus effectively limits the number of processors that can be configured into the multiprocessor.

Incorporating a cache memory for each processor has proved to be quite effective because it enables shared-memory machines to provide performance scaling almost linearly with the number of processors up to about 20 (depending on the nature of the programs executing on the machine). For shared-memory multiprocessors to scale to an even larger number of processors, caching can be combined with more complex interconnection networks.

Using caches in shared-memory multiprocessors introduces a new problem. Suppose some data structure, D, is shared by processes 1 and 2 on processors X and Y, respectively. When Process 1 reads D, it is copied from the memory into X's cache. If Process 2 were then to read D, it would be copied into Y's cache, thus resulting in three copies of D existing in the memory hierarchy: the original in the memory, one copy in X's cache, and another copy in Y's cache. Suppose Process 1 writes to the D data structure. The three copies are now said to be *incoherent*, since they represent the same data structure, D, but they contain different values.

This situation is a serious problem in a shared-memory system, since it means the programs for the two processes are written as if they have shared memory, but each process could perceive different values in the same memory cell. There are a couple of approaches to handling the problem:

■ The first is simply to not allow shared information (code or data) to be cached. The result is a performance penalty from interconnection network contention.

■ The second approach is to not guarantee memory consistency for shared memories. If there is no cache, the memory model would have strongly consistent semantics.

If a cached memory system is *strongly consistent*, the shared-memory implementation has the same semantics it would have if it were not cached. A weakly consistent memory allows each of two copies to have different values for short time periods. A weakly consistent memory incorporates a scheme for making the memory coherent "soon" after any of the copies have been changed with a write operation. Applications in a weakly consistent memory system must be written to have knowledge of the memory consistency semantics, and with explicit synchronization, in order for the programs to behave properly. Therefore, a weakly consistent memory system must guarantee that synchronization primitives can be implemented so that they behave properly independent of the memory type.

The mechanism to ensure coherency in all caches and the memory can be difficult to construct, since it must be able to detect a write to any shared memory copy the instant it happens on any processor. This ability suggests that coherency must be implemented by the interconnection network and/or caching hardware in each machine. When a shared-memory location is written, the caching mechanism must immediately inform other caching mechanisms and/or a centralized facility in all other machines that have copies of the memory contents. All copies, except the most recently written copy, are then invalidated until they can be updated with the new value. When shared memory becomes incoherent, the coherency mechanism can update both the copy and the original memory immediately by writing the new data into the memory when it writes into the cache. This approach is called a *write-through* strategy. Alternatively, the mechanism may not update the cache immediately, but defer updating memory until sometime in the near future. This strategy is called a *write-back* strategy.

11.6 ● SUMMARY

The memory manager administers the executable memory, allocating it to different processes as needed. Address binding is a fundamental barrier to data movement because the traditional program translation environment causes points in a program's address space to be bound to physical memory locations before the program begins to execute. Static binding inhibits the manager's ability to move an address space around in the memory.

The underlying mechanism for deferring binding from load time to runtime is the hardware relocation register. This mechanism allows the memory manager to easily move address spaces around because addresses are bound as an offset from the contents of the relocation register on each memory reference. The limit register complements the relocation register and, at a small cost in complexity, allows the hardware to provide a robust isolation mechanism. With relocation and limit registers, the process can reference only the part of primary memory allocated to it.

Swapping strategies allow memory to be shared among more active processes than can be loaded in the memory at once. Virtual memory extends the swapping technology by loading only parts of a process's address space at once. Contemporary memory managers have evolved (or are evolving) to virtual memory designs.

Shared-memory multiprocessors include specialized memory management software and hardware. Cache memory is included to reduce the demand on the mechanism that interconnects memory units and processors. However, once cache memories have been introduced, the system must provide a means for keeping copies of shared memory consistent.

Armed with a background in memory management provided in this chapter, you are now ready to move to the next chapter, which discusses virtual memory systems in more detail.

11.7 • EXERCISES

1. What is the distinction between a process address space and the primary memory addresses?

2. Redraw Figure 11.6 using the names of the Linux/UNIX system tools used to prepare a set of C program modules—`file1.c`, `file2.c`, and `file3.c`—for execution. Explicitly label `stdio` and the C library, `libc.a`, in the diagram. Use the default names for relocatable object modules and absolute programs.

3. In Linux/UNIX, is it possible for the link editor to combine relocatable object modules created from compilers for different programming languages? Explain why or why not.

4. A memory manager for a variable-sized region strategy has a free list of blocks of size 600, 400, 1000, 2200, 1600, and 1050 bytes.

   a. What block will be selected to honor a request for 1603 bytes using the best-fit policy?

   b. What block will be selected to honor a request for 949 bytes using the best-fit policy?

   c. What block will be selected to honor a request for 1603 bytes using the worst-fit policy?

   d. What block will be selected to honor a request for 349 bytes using the worst-fit policy?

   e. Assume the free list is ordered as the blocks are listed in the problem statement. What block will be selected to honor a request for 1603 bytes using the first-fit policy?

   f. Assume the free list is ordered as the blocks are listed in the problem statement. What block will be selected to honor a request for 1049 bytes using the first-fit policy?

5. A memory manager can sort the free list according to any criteria it chooses.

   a. How would the free list be organized for the best-fit policy?

   b. How would the free list be organized for the worst-fit policy?

   c. How would the free list be organized for the first-fit policy?

   d. How would the free list be organized for the next-fit policy?

6. A certain OS supports four different address spaces for each process, called S_a, S_b, S_c, and S_d. Suppose the memory manager loads the four address spaces into physical memory as shown:

Space	Physical Memory Location
S_a	0x00600000
S_b	0x00180000
S_c	0x01000000
S_d	0x01010000

What is the physical address of each of the following process addresses?

a. 0x00456789 in S_a.

b. 0x0000089a in S_d.

c. 0x00043210 in S_b.

d. 0x00010234 in S_c.

e. 0x000bcdef in S_a.

f. 0x01010000 in S_d.

7. Suppose a variant of UNIX provides a system call that returns a pointer to a block of memory in the system address space capable of being read from and written to by any process. Explain how a UNIX user process could use such a facility to define a block of sharable memory to be used by two or more of its children. Assume the children have already been exec-ed at the time the block is set up by the parent.

8. If the operating system kept swap images—direct images of the program as it is stored in primary memory for execution—the images would have to be relocated when they were loaded back into primary memory at a different location than the one from which they were retrieved. Explain why an analysis program could not, in general, be written to read an executable image on secondary memory and be guaranteed to find every address in the executable image, thus allowing the addresses to be relocated when the image was moved.

9. If a computer system does not have relocation hardware yet it implements swapping, then the memory manager will have to use a loader to recompute the executable image from the absolute image. Would it be possible for the swapping system to reload the data and stack segments? Explain how such a system might work, or why it would be impossible.

10. Consider the code sequence shown in Figure 11.27 for a machine with the arrangement of segment relocation registers shown in Figure 11.18. Assuming the code segment register is loaded with 0100 when the instruction in relative address 0100 is executed, from what address will the control unit fetch the next instruction?

✦ **FIGURE 11.27** A Sample Code Segment

Relative Address	Contents	
...		
0100	load	=1000, code_segment_register
0104	call	2000
...		

11. Figure 6.10 is the simplified process state diagram with running, ready, and blocked states. Modify the diagram so that it includes new states to represent when a process is swapped out. Show the transitions to represent when the process is swapped due to its becoming blocked and when the memory manager simply decides to deallocate the memory and use it for another process.

12. Suppose a system has a disk with 2KB disk blocks and the average access time on a block is 20 milliseconds. A process holding 40KB of memory changes from the running state to the blocked state due to a resource request. How long must the process remain blocked to justify swapping it out?

13. [This problem appears in Chapter 9, where the solution used pipes.] Construct a C/C++ program for a UNIX environment to use the trapezoidal rule to approximate the integral of

$$f(x) = 1/(x + 1)$$

for the interval [0, 2]. Construct your solution so that you compute the areas of n small trapezoids by N individual worker processes. The master process should spawn N worker processes using the `fork()` and `exec()` UNIX system calls. Read about using System V UNIX shared memory in Lab Exercise 11.1, and then use the facility to implement the requisite synchronization and information sharing for a concurrent solution to this problem. Whenever a worker process is ready to compute the area for another trapezoid, it synchronizes with the master using a shared variable and gets new work via shared memory. When the master process receives all the sums from the worker processes, it should sum them and print the answer, along with the amount of time required to obtain the solution. It should ignore the time to set up the shared memory. Experiment with various values of N between 1 and 8 for $n = 64$ trapezoids. Use a `getTime()` routine (see the exercises in Chapter 1) to instrument your program so that you can measure the amount of time spent processing your code. Include a suitably large `for` loop in your procedure to evaluate the area of a trapezoid so that you can measure the time required to accomplish the computation. Plot the amount of time versus the number of trapezoids used in the approximation.

If you have a shared-memory multiprocessor available to use, solve this problem using the shared-memory kernel extensions provided by the machine.

Using Shared Memory

> This exercise can be solved on any POSIX system (or UNIX system with System V shared memory).

Successive overrelaxation (SOR) is a method to solve linear $n \times n$ systems of equations,

$$Ax = b.$$

Given the $n \times n$ coefficient matrix A, the right-side vector b, and an initial estimated solution vector x, the algorithm recomputes each of the n different x_i based on the x_j $(i \neq j)$, A, and b. SOR works by rewriting equations. Notice that the original n equations are written as follows:

$$a_{11}x_1 + a_{12}x_2 + \ldots + a_{1n}x_n = b_1$$
$$a_{21}x_1 + a_{22}x_2 + \ldots + a_{2n}x_n = b_2$$
$$\ldots$$
$$a_{n1}x_1 + a_{n2}x_2 + \ldots + a_{nn}x_n = b_n$$

By rewriting the equations, we can arbitrarily use the ith equation to solve for x_i, that is:

$$x_i = (b_i - a_{i1}x_1 - a_{i2}x_2 - \ldots - a_{in}x_n) / a_{ii}.$$

Now you can implement SOR on an n-process system by defining n different processes (all running the same program) where the ith process computes x_i using the rewritten equation. Implement an SOR solution using POSIX shared memory.

● BACKGROUND ●

Shared memory refers to a common block of memory that is mapped into the address spaces of two or more processes. When a process stores information into a location in the shared memory, it can be read with a CPU register load operation in any other process that is using the shared memory. Within an individual computer—uniprocessor or multiprocessor—shared memory is normally the fastest way for two processes to share information.

The shared memory API commonly used in contemporary versions of POSIX was introduced in System V UNIX. Even though the mechanism allows multiple processes to map a common memory segment into their own address spaces—it is logically a part of the memory manager—it was designed and implemented in System V UNIX as a part of the IPC mechanism.

THE SHARED MEMORY API

Shared memory can be used to allow any process to dynamically define a new block of memory. The new block is independent of the address space created by the static program translation facilities. Every UNIX process is created with a 4 GB virtual address space, and some program-specific (usually small) portion of its address space is used to reference the compiled code, static data, stack, and heap. The remaining addresses in the virtual address space are unused. After a new block of shared memory is defined, it is bound to a block of unused virtual addresses. Once the block has been mapped into the virtual address space, the process can read and write the shared memory as if it were ordinary memory. Since more than one process can map the shared memory block into its own address space, code segments that read or write shared memory are normally considered to be critical sections.

There are four system calls that define the full system call interface to shared memory:

```
#include <sys/types.h>
#include <sys/ipc.h>
#include <sys/shm.h>

int shmget(key_t key, int size, int shmflg);
void *shmat(int shmid, char *shmaddr, int shmflg);
void *shmdt(char *shaddr);
int shmctl(int shmid, int cmd, struct shmid_ds *buf);
```

Briefly, the `shmget()` system call creates the shared memory block, `shmat()` maps an existing shared memory block into a process's address space, `shmdt()` removes ("unmaps") a shared memory block from the process's address space, and `shmctl()` is a general-purpose function (in the style of `ioctl()`) that can be used for performing all other commands to the shared memory block.

To create a new block of shared memory, the process calls `shmget()`. If `shmget()` successfully creates a new block of memory, it will return a shared memory identifier of type `int`. The shared memory identifier is a reference (or "handle") into a kernel data structure. If `shmget()` is able to create the new block of shared memory, the kernel array whose index is returned references an instance of the `struct shmid_kernel` data structure, which includes a field

```
struct shmid_kernel {
  shmid_ds u;
  ...
};
```

The arguments to `shmget()` are `key_t key`, `int size`, and `int shmflg`. The size argument is used to specify the number of bytes in the new block of memory. However, all memory allocation operations take place in terms of pages. If a process requests one byte of memory, then the memory manager will allocate a full page. (The page size is 4,096 bytes on i386 machines.) Thus, the size of the new shared memory block will be the value of the size argument rounded up to the next multiple of the page size. A size of 1 to 4,096 will result in a 4K (1 page) block; 4,097 to 8,192 will create an 8K (2-page) block; and so on.

The `key_t key` argument can be the key of an existing memory block, 0, or `IPC_PRIVATE`. If key is set to `IPC_PRIVATE`, a new block of shared memory will be created by the `shmget()` call. The `shmflg` argument can also cause a new block to be created when key is 0 if the `IPC_CREAT` flag is set in `shmflg`.[1] If a process wants to reference

---

The `shmflg` argument is a set of single-bit flags. To set multiple flags in `shmflg`, they are combined with a logical OR operator ("|") and then assigned to `shmflg`.

a shared memory block that is known to have been created by another process (such as a parent or server), it would obtain the `struct shmid_kernel` reference from the creator. However, it can also set the key argument to the key value of an existing memory block. If the value of key is set and `shmflg` is set with `IPC_CREAT | IPC_EXCL`, the `shmget()` will fail. The `shmflg` must also define the access permissions for user, group, and world access to the memory block as its lower 9 bits (using the same bit pattern as for a file).

When a shared memory region has been successfully created, the `shmget()` call returns an integer reference to its `struct shmid_ds`:

```
struct shmid_ds {
    struct ipc_perm shm_perm;       /* operation perms */
    int shm_segsz;                  /* size of segment (bytes) */
    _kernel_time_t shm_atime;       /* last attach time */
    _kernel_time_t shm_dtime;       /* last detach time */
    _kernel_time_t shm_ctime;       /* last change time */
    _kernel_ipc_pid_t shm_cpid;     /* pid of creator */
    _kernel_ipc_pid_t shm_lpid;     /* pid of last operator */
    unsigned short shm_nattch;      /* no. of current attaches */
    unsigned short shm_unused;      /* compatibility */
    void shm_unused2;               /* ditto - used by DIPC */
    void shm_unused3;               /* unused */
};
```

The struct `ipc_perm shm_perm` field defines both the owner of the shared memory block and the permissions for other processes to use the block. It contains fields that specify the owner's user and group IDs, the creator's user and group IDs, the access mode (read or write), and the key value for the memory block (the man page for `shmget()` describes the `shmid_ds` and `ipc_perm` structure fields).

The `void *shmat(int shmid, char *shmaddr, int shmflg)` system call binds the memory block to the calling process's address space.

- The `shmid` argument is the result returned by the `shmget()` that created the block.

- The `shmaddr` pointer is the abstract address to which the first location in the shared memory block should be mapped. If the calling process does not wish to choose the address to which the memory block will be mapped, it should pass a value of 0 for the `shmaddr`. The value of `shmaddr` should be aligned with a page boundary. If the `shmaddr` is specified and `SHM_RND` is asserted in `shmflg`, the address will be rounded down to a multiple of the `SHMLBA` constant.

- The `shmflg` argument is used in the same way as the corresponding flag in `shmget()`. It is used to assert a number of different 1-bit flags to the `shmat()` system call.

Besides the `SHM_RND` flag, the calling process can assert `SHM_RDONLY` to attach the memory block so that it can only be read, but not written.

When a process is through using a shared memory block, it calls `void *shmdt(char *shaddr)` where `shaddr` is the address used to attach the memory block. The kernel will update the corresponding `struct shmid_kernel` to reflect that the memory block is no longer being used by this process.

The final shared memory call is int shmctl(int shmid, int cmd, struct shmid_ds *buf), which is used to perform control operations on the shared memory block descriptor.

■ The shmid argument identifies the shared memory block, and cmd specifies the command to be applied to the descriptor.

■ If cmd is set to IPC_STAT, then the calling process must provide a buffer, buf, that is at least as large as a struct shmid_kernel. The shmctl() call fills in the current values of the shmid_ds and returns them in buf. If the cmd is set to IPC_SET, then the data structure will be updated provided that the calling process is owner or creator (or has superuser permission). A call with cmd set to IPC_RMID causes the memory segment to be destroyed (it will not otherwise be destroyed, even when there is no process attached to it). The block can be locked or unlocked by a superuser.

Here is a simple example of a parent process that creates a shared memory block and then creates a child process that can also use the block:

```
#include       <sys/types.h>
#include       <sys/ipc.h>
#include       <sys/sem.h>
#include       <sys/wait.h>

#define        SHM_SIZE       ...

void run_child(int, int);

int main() {
  int pid, shm_handle, status;
  char *my_shm_ptr;

/* Create the shared memory */
  shm_handle = shmget(IPC_PRIVATE, SHM_SIZE, IPC_CREAT | 0x1C0);
  if(shm_handle == -1) {
    printf("Shared memory creation failed\n");
    exit(0);
  }

/* Start the child */
  if((pid = fork()) == 0) {
    run_child(childNum, shm_handle);
    exit(0);
  }
/* Do work, share results with child via shared memory */
  my_shm_ptr = (char *) shmat(shm_handle, 0, 0);
  if(my_shm_ptr == (char *) -1) {
    printf("Shared memory attach failed\n");
    exit(0);
  }
  ...
```

```
/* Wait for the children to finish */
  wait(&status);
  shmctl(shm_handle, IPC_RMID, 0);   /* Remove shared memory */
  printf("Parent: Terminating\n");
}

void run_child(int me, int shm_handle) {
  char *my_shm_ptr;
  int i;
  unsigned int shm_flag = 0;

/* Attach the shared memory */
  my_shm_ptr = (char *) shmat(shm_handle, 0, 0);
  if(my_shm_ptr == (char *) -1) {
    printf("Shared memory attach failed\n");
    exit(0);
  }
  *(my_shm_ptr+64+i) = ...;        /* Write shmem location i */
  ... = my_shm_ptr+i);             /* Read shmem location i */
  ...
}
```

● ATTACKING THE PROBLEM ●

Since your job is to use *n* different processes to solve an *n* × *n* linear system using successive overrelaxation, you will need to organize your code so that a parent creates *n* different child processes, each of which will be an equation solver. First, the config.h file defines a maximum value for *n* for the solver:

#define MAX_N 4

The parent process's job is to set up the memory, launch the *n* different solvers, and then manage the termination when the solution has converged. Here is a bare skeleton of that code:

```
/* A Successive Overrelaxation (SOR) program */
#include    ...

#define     N_MEM ...

/* Shared memory */
  int shm_handle[...];
  double ...;               /* A, x, and b arrays */

main(int argc, char *argv[]) {
double epsilon;
...
  int solverPID[MAX_N];

/* Initialization */
```

```
/* Create the shared memory */
  shm_handle[N_MEM] = ...

/* Map the memory into this process's address space */
  N_ptr = ...

/* Define epsilon, N, A, b, and the initial guess of x */

/* Create N worker processes, setup IPC using pipes */
  makeWorkers(...);

/* Solve the system of equations */
  ...
  while(check(A, x, b) > epsilon) {
    ...
  }

/* System has converged */
  yield();
  cleanUp();
  printResult(x, check(A, x, b, N), N); // Print the results
  exit(0);
}
```

Finally, consider the skeleton of the solver child process:

```
void solver(int me) {
  yield();
  while(!isConverged()) {
    X_ptr[me] = solveX(A_ptr, X_ptr, B_ptr, *N_ptr, me);
    ...
  }
}
int isConverged() {
  if(...)
    return TRUE;
  else
    return FALSE;
}
```

CHAPTER 12

Virtual Memory

Virtual memory managers extend the classic memory abstraction of the computer memory, providing very large primary memory for each abstract machine. Virtual memory works by copying information from the secondary memory into the primary memory whenever it is being used, and by copying information into the secondary memory after it has been updated. The system handles this transfer of information back and forth between primary and secondary memories without programmer intervention. This chapter generalizes the dynamic relocation mechanism introduced in the last chapter and shows how it is used as the basis of *segmentation* and *paging*. We will then study paging designs, from the static paging systems that dominated in the 1980s to today's dynamic paging systems. Finally, we will see how segmented virtual memory provides a general alternative to paging.

12.1 • THE TASK AT HAND

Although virtual memory did not appear in commercial computer systems until the 1980s, it was first used in the Atlas system in about 1960 [Kilburn, et al., 1962]. By the late 1960s, people at M.I.T., IBM, and other leading research labs had demonstrated that paging virtual memory could be a commercially viable technology [Denning, 1970; Denning, 1980]. By the mid-1980s, many operating systems had upgraded their memory manager to support paged virtual memory (it had been incorporated into BSD Version 3 UNIX for the VAX by 1980 [McKusick, et al., 1996].)

As you saw earlier, the virtual memory manager copies information up and down the computer's storage hierarchy (specifically between the primary and secondary memory) so that its frequency of use determines where the CPU can find the information. In other words, information that is used regularly is copied into the primary memory. When the information is no longer being used frequently, it is restored to the secondary memory.

The virtual memory strategy avoids copying the entire address space back and forth between the two memories. Instead, only a portion of process p_i's address space is copied from the secondary memory into the primary memory when it is needed (see Figure 12.1). In paged virtual memory systems, the portion is a fixed-size **page** of the address space contents. In segmented virtual memory systems, the portion is a variable-sized **segment** of the address space contents.

✦ **FIGURE 12.1** Virtual Memory Organization

In a virtual memory system, the memory manager copies portions of process p_i's address space into the primary memory whenever the p_i is referencing the information. When p_i stops referencing the information, it is updated in the secondary memory and the copy is removed from the primary memory.

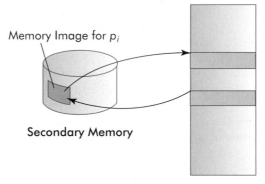

Most parts of the classic memory manager still apply to virtual memory systems (abstraction, allocation, isolation, and sharing): The memory manager is still the resource manager for the primary memory, although now it allocates memory based on virtual memory policy instead of user program requests. It will still export an abstraction for the memory, but now the abstraction is a huge "virtual memory" instead of the physical primary memory size. This is where the address space abstraction that we studied in Chapter 11 will really come into play: Programs are written to use the **virtual address space** as if it were primary memory. The memory manager can then isolate and manage sharing by binding the virtual address space into the parts of the primary memory that it assigns to processes. The trick in virtual memory is that the process is unaware of how the virtual address space is bound to the primary memory; that is solely determined by the memory manager.

We will commence our study by looking carefully at how virtual addresses are translated into primary memory addresses. This will help you understand the differences between paging and segmentation. Since paging is the dominant virtual memory approach today, we will spend most of our time examining paging. However, segmentation is ultimately the superior approach, so we will cap off the chapter by seeing how it works.

12.2 • ADDRESS TRANSLATION

Swapping systems make little distinction between the address space in the absolute module and the space in primary memory where the program will be executed, since both spaces are the same size (differing only in their relocation values). Virtual memory systems distinguish among symbolic name, virtual address, and physical address spaces. Maps (bindings) are provided from symbolic names to virtual addresses and from virtual addresses to physical addresses. There are two basic approaches to establishing the virtual-physical mapping: segmentation and paging. This section first considers how address mapping works in general and then discusses how segmentation and paging are the same and how they differ.

ADDRESS SPACE MAPPING

The components of a **source program** are represented using symbolic identifiers, labels, and variables. These entities are elements of the program's **name space**. Each symbolic name in the name space is translated into a virtual address when the program is translated into an absolute program by the compiler and link editor (see Section 11.2 and Figure 12.2). The virtual address space (which has previously been called the "address space") contains all the addresses that appear in the absolute load module. Each virtual address is converted to a physical primary memory address when the absolute program is translated into an executable image by the loader or by using dynamic address relocation hardware (see Section 11.4). In virtual memory managers, the translation from virtual to physical addresses is done at runtime using various generalizations of the basic dynamic address relocation hardware. In a few advanced virtual memory managers, some of the names in the source program are also translated at runtime; we will describe how this most general translation takes place in Section 12.6. First, let's see how virtual addresses are translated to physical addresses.

✦ **FIGURE 12.2** Names, Virtual Addresses, and Physical Addresses

Source programs are written using a set of symbolic names from a name space. When the program is translated into an absolute program, each symbolic name is translated into a virtual address (from a virtual address space). At runtime, the part of the address space that is currently being used is copied into the primary memory; thus, it has a physical primary memory address. When the information is loaded into the primary memory, the virtual addresses in that information are translated into primary memory addresses.

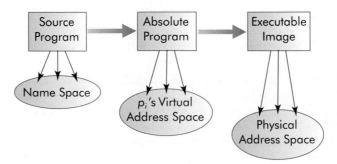

As mentioned above, the translation system creates an executable form of the program that uses virtual addresses, and then writes it into the secondary memory. When a thread in a process begins to execute the program, it only loads a portion of the program into the primary memory. Whenever the thread references a part of the virtual address space that is not currently loaded in the primary memory, the OS suspends execution and loads the missing information from the secondary memory (see Figure 12.3). After it has loaded the missing information at a particular physical address in the primary memory, it completes the execution of the instruction that causes the "missing information interruption," but using the physical address of the primary memory that contains the referenced object. In a virtual memory manager, the OS must be able to map each virtual address reference in the program image to a corresponding physical address, depending on which part of the virtual address space is loaded into the physical address space at any given time. To be precise, the **virtual address translation** map (or "binding"), B_t, is a time-varying map of a program's virtual address space to a physical address space at time t:

$$B_t: \text{virtual address space} \rightarrow \text{physical address space} \cup \{\Omega\},$$

where t is a nonnegative integer **virtual time** for the process and Ω is a distinguished symbol referring to the null address. In a particular computer, the address translation map implementation can be any technique that satisfies this mathematical definition. (That is why the problem is described as a mathematical abstraction. Any mechanism that implements the abstraction is acceptable.) Over the years, virtual memory manager implementations have used a spectrum of different implementations for the address translation map; most implementations are based on some version of a table that supports very rapid lookup functions.

When an element with virtual address i is loaded into the primary memory, $B_t(i)$ is the physical address where the contents of i are loaded. (In a table implementation, this would mean that entry i in the table contains the physical primary memory address where virtual address i is located.) If i is not loaded in the primary memory, then $B_t(i) = \Omega$. If $B_t(i) = \Omega$ at virtual time t and the process/thread tries to read or write virtual address i, the virtual memory manager copies the contents of location i from the secondary memory into the primary memory (again, see Figure 12.3). Specifically, the virtual memory manager takes the following actions:

1. The virtual memory manager interrupts the execution of the process.
2. The referenced information is retrieved from secondary memory and loaded into some primary memory location, k.
3. The manager updates the address translation by changing $B_t(i) = \Omega$ to $B_t(i) = k$.
4. The manager then enables the program to continue execution.

The referenced element from the virtual address space was determined to be missing from primary memory *after an instruction started execution*—when the memory manager attempted to translate the virtual address to a physical address. Noticing that the information was missing from the primary memory caused a series of events to load the element and to redefine the translation map. Once the element has been loaded, the instruction that was in execution when the missing element was detected can be reexecuted at the same virtual time t. Hence virtual memory systems require the CPU to be able to "back out" of

✦ FIGURE 12.3 Loading Missing Information

The contents of every process's virtual address space is kept in the secondary memory. When the information is needed by the CPU, the virtual memory manager copies a portion of the process's address space contents into the primary memory. It can then be read and written by CPU load and store instructions. Later, the virtual memory manager will restore this information back into the secondary memory.

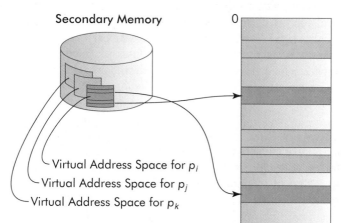

an individual instruction execution and reexecute the instruction after the address translation map has been redefined. (Again, the formal notation precisely defines how a missing page is identified and thus any mechanism that implements the abstraction is acceptable.)

In virtual memory systems, the size of the virtual address space is greater than the size of the physical address space allocated to the process. That is, the process uses more virtual than physical addresses. Recall from the discussion of classic memory management in Chapter 11 that when a process was loaded, its entire address space was loaded all at once. In a multiprogramming system, several processes could have their entire address spaces loaded at the same time. This meant that the system implicitly restricted the address space to be relatively small compared to the physical address space in the machine (the size of primary memory). If one of these classic systems was configured with 1MB of primary memory (considered to be a generous amount of memory in 1985) and if the system supported four memory partitions, each process would be allocated about 256KB. Thus, the average size of the address space used by a process would be 256K. In today's virtual memory systems, a process's address space is a few gigabytes. (Each Windows and Linux process has a 4GB virtual address space.)

SEGMENTATION AND PAGING

Segmentation is an extension of the ideas suggested by the use of relocation-limit registers for relocating and bound-checking blocks of memory. The program parts to be loaded or unloaded are defined by the programmer as variable-sized **segments**, like those described in Chapter 11. Segments may be defined explicitly by language directives or implicitly by program semantics such as the text, data, and stack segments created by C compilers. Memory contents are referenced using a two-component virtual address:

```
<segmentNumber, offset>
```

as suggested by Figure 12.4. The `segmentNumber` identifies the particular logical block of the virtual memory, and the `offset` is a linear offset from the beginning of the target segment. In pure segmentation systems, the virtual memory system transfers whole segments back and forth between the primary and secondary memories. Notice the similarity between these segments and variable-sized memory regions; like variable-sized memory allocation systems, segmentation systems are subject to external fragmentation.

✦ **FIGURE 12.4** Segment Name Space Organization

Segmentation divides the virtual address space into a set of distinct memory segments, each having a linear set of addresses for the bytes in that segment. In this kind of system, a virtual address is an ordered pair, <segmentNumber, offset>, where the segmentNumber identifies the segment, and the offset identifies the byte within the segment.

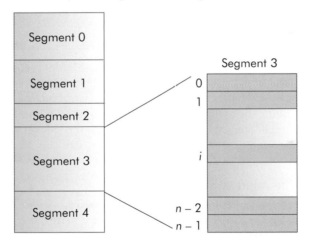

Paging uses single-component addresses, like those used to address cells within any particular segment. In paging, the entire virtual address space is a single linear sequence of virtual addresses, a format that differs from the hierarchical (2-component) address space used in segmentation (but exactly like the address space described in Figure 11.2). This single, large block of virtual addresses is divided into a collection of equal-sized **pages**, so the virtual address space size is an integer multiple of the page size. For example, if there were 1 million virtual addresses and each page was 1,000 bytes, then the first thousand addresses would be in page 0, the second thousand addresses would be in page 1, and so on. So the 1 million virtual addresses would be spread over 1,000 pages. In paging, the unit of memory that is moved back and forth between primary and secondary memory is a page.

In a paging memory manager, page boundaries are completely transparent to the programmer. The good news about this is that the virtual memory manager is completely responsible for choosing the pages to be moved back and forth between the primary and secondary memories with no concerns about external fragmentation. The programmer need not be aware of the parts of the virtual address space that are loaded into or unloaded from the physical memory. The bad news is that in paging systems, the programmer has no mechanism for informing the virtual memory system about logical units of the virtual address space. This means that the virtual memory system is operating without any *a priori* knowledge regarding the relationships that might exist among pages.

Segmentation provides explicit programmer control over the units of transfer in the memory system. This control implies that a segmentation system requires more effort to use than does a paging system, unless the segments are automatically generated, say, by the compiler. Segments can be more efficient than paging, since the programmer can specify the set of virtual address locations to be used at about the same time in the execution, such as "pass 2 of the compiler." However, the virtual memory system will have more difficulty placing segments in primary memory because they are variable-sized and cause the same kind of external fragmentation problems that variable-sized memory partition systems do. In the final analysis, segmentation is probably better suited to the behavior of a process than is paging, although it may be harder to use, and it is definitely harder to implement.

12.3 ● PAGING

The allocation strategy in a paging system is to eliminate external fragmentation by transferring a fixed-size unit of the virtual address space—a page—whenever a virtual address in it is needed to execute the program. Every process's virtual address space is logically divided into pages, with each page having the same number of locations, as shown in Figure 12.5. Only a small amount of internal fragmentation results at the end of the logical address space if it is not an exact multiple of the page size.

✦ FIGURE 12.5 The Address Space and Pages

Paging systems divide the virtual address space into a set of fixed-size pages. These page boundaries are not visible to the software. The virtual memory manager transports pages back and forth between the two levels of memory.

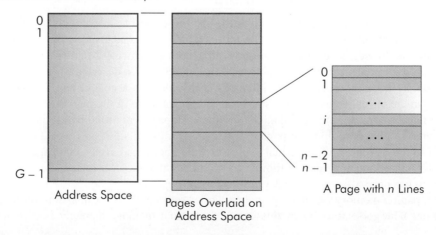

Address Space

Pages Overlaid on
Address Space

A Page with *n* Lines

The program translation facilities take no special action to prepare the absolute module for paging operation. The program translation image (say of size k bytes) is bound into the process's virtual address space. The OS and translation system determine which virtual addresses will be used to represent the program image. For simplicity, let's assume that the program image is bound to virtual addresses 0 and $k-1$. When a thread in the process executes, the process is allocated enough primary memory to store the contents of H memory locations, where H is less than the size of the process's complete virtual address space, G.

In a binary computer, the paging system maps the virtual addresses (0 to $G-1$) into a set of $n = 2^g$ pages, each of size $c = 2^h$ (examine Figure 12.5 again). For example, in Windows and Linux, $G = 2^{32}$ (about 4 billion) byte addresses. In Pentium paging hardware, a page is 2^{12} (4,096) bytes, meaning that $g = 20$ and $h = 12$. Of course the process will only use a portion, k, of the virtual addresses even though there are G virtual addresses available.

The physical address space is the portion of the primary memory allocated to the process. The unit of allocation is a **page frame**, a block of primary memory the same size as a page (a Pentium page frame is 4KB). The page frames allocated to the process need not be contiguous, since the page map, $\mathcal{B}_t$, can map each individual page in the virtual address space to any page frame in the memory (or to Ω if the page is not loaded in a page frame). More precisely, the physical address space can be thought of as a set of $m = 2^j$ page frames, each of size $c = 2^h$, so the amount of primary memory allocated to the process is $H = 2^{h+j}$. Figure 12.6 summarizes the relationship between pages and page frames.

✦ FIGURE 12.6 The Page Map

The virtual address space is composed of $n = 2^g$ pages. The process is allocated $m = 2^j$ page frames. The page translation map provides the page frame address where page i is currently loaded, or Ω if the page is not loaded.

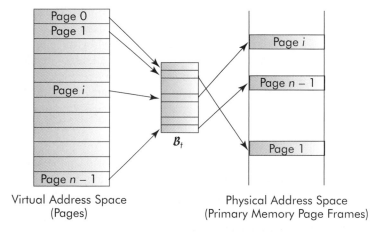

Because of the reference **locality** behavior of programs (refer to Section 11.5), the process needs to use only a subset of all the pages for execution at any given time (see Figure 12.7). That is, programs are written so that they have different phases. When the thread is in one phase, it only needs one part of the virtual address space. When it changes phases, it uses a different part of the virtual address space. Each of these "parts" defines a locality. Thread execution uses each locality for different amounts of time as determined by the length of time it executes in the corresponding phase.

✦ FIGURE 12.7 Reference Locality

This figure illustrates the fact that different parts of the address space are used during different phases of a computation. There is no correlation between the size of a part of the address space and the amount of time that a thread will execute in that locality. For example, the initialization code may be large, but the thread spends a very small fraction of its runtime in that code.

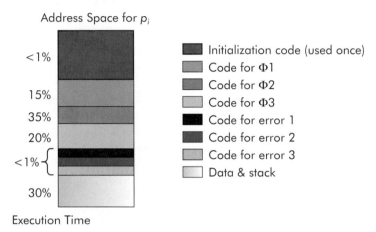

The goal of the paging system is to identify the set of pages needed for the process's current locality and then to load *only those pages* into page frames in primary memory. As the program changes phases—it leaves one locality and enters another—the pages holding the code for the old locality will be unloaded from page frames. The pages containing the code for the new locality then will be loaded into these page frames. The same phenomenon takes place for different parts of the data being used by the program.

The paging system must be able to translate each virtual address (an address between 0 and G-1) into a physical address for each primary memory reference. Furthermore, it must be able to dynamically bind pages to page frames as part of the address translation and page-loading process. This task is our first design challenge.

PAGING VIRTUAL ADDRESS TRANSLATION

In the interest of providing a precise, abstract description of virtual address translation, we continue to use mathematical descriptions of address translation. Let

$$N = \{d_0, d_1, ..., d_{n-1}\}$$

be the set of pages in the virtual address space, and let

$$M = \{b_0, b_1, ..., b_{m-1}\}$$

be the set of allocated page frames . A virtual address is a nonnegative integer, i, where

$$0 \leq i < G = 2^{g+h},$$

since there are $n = 2^g$ pages each of size 2^h words. A physical memory address, k, is,

$$k = U2^h + V \ (0 \le V < 2^h),$$

where U is a **page frame number**. In the equation, $U2^h$ is the primary memory address of the first byte in page frame number U—the page frame's offset from physical primary memory address 0. V is the offset within page frame number U.

The virtual to physical address map takes the form

$$\mathcal{B}_t : [0{:}G{-}1] \to \langle U, V \rangle \cup \{\Omega\}.$$

That is, $\mathcal{B}_t$ translates a virtual address, i (where $0 \le i < G$) into a physical address k (or into Ω if the page is not stored in the primary memory at time t). For example, if virtual address i were loaded in page frame number r at offset s, then $\mathcal{B}_t(i) = r*2^h+s$.

Next, consider how the mapping mechanism can take advantage of the assumptions about virtual addresses: Since every page has the same size, $c = 2^h$, the virtual address, i, can be converted into a *page number* and an offset within the page, also called the *line number*, as follows:

$$\text{page number} = \lfloor i/c \rfloor$$

($\lfloor i/c \rfloor$ means the integer part of the result when you divide i by c—a conventional integer divide operation) and

$$\text{line number} = i \bmod c.$$

In binary machines where numbers are represented using the base 2 numbering system, it is judicious for c to be a power of 2. In this case, a page number can be rapidly computed from the binary virtual address by shifting the virtual address right h bits and masking out the g least significant bits of the result (see Figure 12.8). This shift operation is equivalent to an integer divide operation by the page size—exactly the desired operation from the formalism above.

The offset can be obtained by masking out the h least significant bits of the virtual address before shifting—again, exactly the operation we need according to the formalism. The potentially complex divide and modulo operations can be implemented using simple (and fast) shift and mask operations.

After the mechanism has determined the page number, it needs to figure out which page frame contains the page: The page could be loaded into any page frame in the primary memory that has been allocated to the process. The page translation table—the $\mathcal{B}_t$ map—translates the page number into the page frame number where the page is loaded (again see Figure 12.8). This can be done by using the page number that was extracted from the virtual address as the entry number in a page table. The contents of the page translation table entry is the page frame base address where that page is loaded. The translation mechanism must do a table lookup operation (that implements $\mathcal{B}_t$), and then add the offset to the page frame starting address.

This type of address translation can be done entirely in hardware. Since the mid-1980s, popular microprocessor chips have a companion memory management chip (often called a **memory management unit** or **MMU**) that is used to implement the $\mathcal{B}_t$ map (the page table). Without the wide availability of such hardware, paging would not be feasible, since it must be performed for each memory reference as a part of the instruction execution.

✦ FIGURE 12.8   Address Translation with Paging

Here is a schematic diagram for hardware virtual address translation. We want to do the division and modulo functions to obtain the page number and line number for the virtual address. Since the virtual address is a binary number, we can use mask and shift operations (instead of divide operations) to extract the page number and line number.

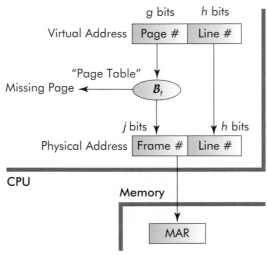

Figure 12.8 represents a simple hardware address translation mechanism implemented in an MMU (this aspect of virtual memory continues to evolve). The g most significant bits of the virtual address are passed to the page map, $\boldsymbol{B}_t$. The result of the mapping operation is a **missing page fault** if page p_i is not currently loaded, $\boldsymbol{B}_t(p_i) = \Omega$, or a page frame number, b_j, if the page is currently loaded there $(\boldsymbol{B}_t(p_i) = b_j)$. If a missing page fault occurs, the memory management chip halts the microprocessor chip so that the operating system can perform the following steps:

1. The process requesting the missing page is suspended.
2. The memory manager locates the missing page in secondary memory.
3. The page is loaded into primary memory, usually causing another page to be unloaded.
4. The page table in the memory manager is adjusted to reflect the new state of the memory ($\boldsymbol{B}_t(p_i)$ is set to b_j).
5. The process resumes at the point it was executing when it was suspended.

If the translation results in a page frame number, b_j, rather than a missing page fault, the page frame's base address is loaded into the most significant part of the physical address and the line number, V, is loaded into the least significant part of the physical address. The resulting physical address is then passed to the MAR (memory address register) for the primary memory. The sizes of the virtual and physical addresses may differ, depending on the relationship of the sizes of the page and page frame registers.

$\boldsymbol{B}_t$ maps page numbers to page frame base addresses. The map changes each time a page is loaded into primary memory. One mechanism to implement $\boldsymbol{B}_t$ is a table such as that given in Figure 12.9. Logically, the table contains n rows—one for each page number—and one column (the row number in Figure 12.9 is the same as the page number). The entry in row i is $\boldsymbol{B}_t(i)$—the base address of b_j if page i is loaded in page frame b_j—and Ω otherwise. For example, in Figure 12.9, page 0 maps to page frame 3, page 1 is not loaded, page 2 maps to page frame 7, and so on.

✦ FIGURE 12.9 The Conceptual Page Table

A table can be used to implement the $\boldsymbol{B}_t$ map, so this map is usually called "the page table." In the example table, there is one row for each page. Since page 0 is loaded in page frame 3, row 0 contains the value 3. Page 1 is not currently loaded, so row 1 contains Ω.

Page Number	Page Frame Number
0	3
1	Ω
2	7
. . .	. . .
$G - 1$	9

Consider a specific example of the address translation. Suppose 3257 is a virtual address in a system with $c = 100$. (c would normally be some power of 2 in a binary machine, but 100 is used in this example, in order to simplify the arithmetic.) The page number is computed as

$$p = \lfloor i/c \rfloor = \lfloor 3257/100 \rfloor = 32$$

and the line number is

$$\text{line number} = 3257 \bmod 100 = 57.$$

Next, the system will use $\boldsymbol{B}_t$ to bind p to a page frame b_j if p is loaded. So $\boldsymbol{B}_t(p) = b_j$ if p is loaded in page frame b_j; $\boldsymbol{B}_t(p) = \Omega$ otherwise. After the page frame containing the page has been found, the offset is added to the page frame base address to determine the physical address corresponding to x:

$$\text{physical address} = \boldsymbol{B}_t(\lfloor i/c \rfloor) + (i \bmod c).$$

In the example, loading page 32 in page frame 19 at address 1900 would produce

$$\text{physical address} = \boldsymbol{B}_t(\lfloor 3257/100 \rfloor) + (3257 \bmod 100) = \boldsymbol{B}_t(32) + 57 =$$
$$1900 + 57 = 1957.$$

If the page is not loaded, $\boldsymbol{B}_t$ will evaluate to Ω to indicate the missing page condition to the page translation system.

Contemporary Page Table Implementations

In general, a page table of the form shown in Figure 12.9 is sparse. Most of the entries map to Ω, since most pages need not be loaded at any given time (depending on the program locality). Hardware can be designed to take advantage of this situation. An **associative**, or **content-addressable**, **memory** implements the page map as an *inverted page table*. Each cell in an associative memory contains a *key* field and a *data* field. The entry is addressed by the key content rather than by cell address. As a bonus, the key search is implemented as a parallel pattern match, meaning associative memory access is very fast. Small associative memories (less than 1K entries) have been feasible since the early 1980s. The Atlas computer used a form of associative memory for its page table in the late 1950s [Kilburn et al., 1962]. In that computer, the associative memory was actually implemented as a bank of "page address registers" for the 32-page frames of the primary memory.

The page table of Figure 12.9 could be implemented with an associative memory as suggested by Figure 12.10. The resulting inverted page table has only as many entries as there are page frames allocated to the process, since unmapped pages do not appear in this type of table. If a page does not appear in the associative memory, the access will fail and cause a missing page interrupt (called a *fault* in paging systems). As in systems with page tables implemented using conventional memory technology, the page fault causes the memory manager to load the missing page.

✦ **FIGURE 12.10** An Associative Memory Page Table

An associative memory uses a key field to address data fields. If the associative memory is asked to provide the data associated with the key "2," it will return a value of 7. If there is no key equal to 2, the associative memory will ultimately raise an interrupt.

Page Number	Page Frame Number
0	3
2	7
. . .	. . .
$G-1$	9

The scheme suggested here must be modified to avoid having to save the associative memory's contents on each context switch (for example, a process might use only part of the associative memory). The associative memory could contain one entry for each page frame in primary memory (rather than just for page frames allocated to a process). Next, the key field is expanded to include some form of process identification so that a match on the key field occurs only for a particular page in a particular process's virtual address space. Unfortunately, primary memory sizes have grown more rapidly than the growth of cost-effective associative memories. Thus, this technique is fast and effective, but very expensive.

In conventional machines, yet another approach is widely used. The system includes a special cache memory called a **translation-lookaside buffer** (**TLB**) used with the address translation hardware. The full-page table is kept in primary memory. When a page is first translated to a page frame, the map is read from primary memory into the TLB. The TLB entry, then, contains the page number, the physical address of the page frame, and various protection bits. On subsequent references to the page, the map entry will be read from the TLB rather than from primary memory. Hennessey and Patterson [1990] provide more details about associative memories and TLBs.

12.4 ● STATIC PAGING ALGORITHMS

There are two basic families of paging algorithms: static allocation and dynamic allocation. With static paging algorithms, the process uses a fixed number of page frames. In dynamic paging algorithms (see Section 12.5), the number of allocated page frames changes as the process executes. In both forms of allocation algorithms, the *paging policy* defines how the page frames will be loaded and unloaded by the virtual memory system. There are three basic policies in defining any paging algorithm:

- The **fetch policy** decides *when a page should be loaded* into primary memory.
- The **replacement policy** determines *which page should be removed* from primary memory if all page frames are full.
- The **placement policy** determines *where the fetched page should be loaded* in primary memory.

As noted, with static paging algorithms, the number of page frames does not change throughout the lifetime of the process. Suppose that every page frame contains a page (which is the case at all times except right at the beginning of execution). When a page is to be removed from the primary memory, the replacement policy selects the page for removal, leaving the page frame that held the page empty. In static paging, the placement policy is simple: The new page will be loaded into the page frame that was just vacated. If we wanted to consider the spectrum of static paging algorithms, we see that they all use this simple placement policy. The fetch and replacement policies differentiate among the static paging algorithms. The placement policy will be meaningful when we study dynamic paging algorithms in the next section.

In the interest of providing the most generally applicable (yet precise) description, we can use another simple mathematical model to consider various policies. As before, suppose N is the set of pages in the virtual address space. The **page reference stream**, $\mathcal{R}$, is the sequence of page numbers from N,

$$\mathcal{R} = r_1, r_2, r_3, ..., r_i, ... \quad (r_i \in N)$$

referenced by the thread during its execution. For example, suppose that $N = \{0, 1, 2, 3, 4, 5\}$. Then an example reference stream is

$$\mathcal{R} = 2, 0, 3, 4, 3, 2, 0, 1, 1, 3, ...$$

In other words, the page reference stream is simply the list of page numbers that the process references as it executes.

In this context, the **virtual time** of a process is advanced each time the process makes a memory reference. Therefore, we can use the index of the elements of page reference stream to represent the process's virtual time. For example, if R is a page reference stream for some process, and the ith memory reference was to page 7, then r_i (the ith element in the list) would be 7.

Suppose that m page frames have been allocated to a process (and therefore shared by the threads in the process). It is also useful to refer to the identity of the pages that are loaded into those m page frames. In set notation, we will refer to the pages that are loaded into the m page frames at virtual time t (also called the **memory state** at time t) as

$$S_t(m) = \{d_{i1}, d_{i2}, ..., d_{im}\}$$

When the process begins to execute, none of its pages are loaded into the primary memory, so the initial memory state of the m page frames at time zero is, $S_0(m) = \varnothing$. If the first memory reference is to a location in page 2, then $S_1(m) = \{2\}$; if the second memory reference is to page 0 (and $m > 1$), then $S_2(m) = \{0, 2\}$; and so on. Suppose $m = 4$; then for the example reference stream given above, $S_7(4) = \{0, 2, 3, 4\}$. However, we would have to know the paging algorithm's fetch and replacement policies to determine $S_{10}(4)$'s contents, since when page 1 is loaded, one of 0, 2, 3, or 4 will have to be replaced.

We would like to think about how the memory state changes as pages are loaded and unloaded. At any given virtual time, t, we will use X_t to mean the set of pages that the memory manager decides to *fetch* (load) into the primary memory. If the memory manager loads page r_t at time t, then we know that $r_t \in X_t$. Similarly, we will refer to the set of pages that the memory manager decides to *replace* at virtual time t as Y_t. So, for example, if the paging strategy decides to unload page y_t at time t, then we say that $y_t \in Y_t$.

Now we will use $S_t(m)$, X_t, and Y_t to describe how to determine which pages are loaded into the m page frames after processing the first t references in $R = r_1, r_2, r_3, ..., r_t$. The way we can do this is to determine $S_t(m)$ in terms of $S_{t-1}(m)$ by:

$$S_t(m) = S_{t-1}(m) \cup X_t - Y_t$$

In words, "the set of pages loaded in the m page frames after processing the first t references is determined by modifying the set of pages that were loaded at time $t-1$, by adding the set of pages fetched at virtual time $t (X_t)$, and removing the set of replaced pages at virtual time $t (Y_t)$." We start by using $S_0(m)$ to compute $S_1(m)$, and $S_1(m)$ to compute $S_2(m)$, and so on. For the very first memory reference made by a thread in the process ($t=1$), we have $S_1(m) = S_0(m) \cup \{r_1\} - \varnothing = \varnothing \cup \{r_1\} - \varnothing = \{r_1\}$.

THE FETCH POLICY

The fetch policy determines when a page should be brought into primary memory. The paging mechanism will not ordinarily have prior knowledge about the page reference stream for programs executing on the machine. Thus, it is difficult to construct paging mechanisms that use an effective **prefetch policy**, where pages are fetched into the memory prior to the time they are referenced. Instead, the majority of general-purpose paging mechanisms use a **demand paging** fetch policy where a page is loaded into primary memory only when the process references it (that is, when the page reference stream calls for the page). In other words, in demand paging, one of the following conditions applies at virtual time t when page r_t appears in the reference stream:

■ If r_t was loaded at virtual time t 1, then nothing is removed from primary memory and nothing is added to it.

■ If r_t was not loaded at virtual time $t–1$ but there are empty page frames allocated to the process, then the missing page is placed into one of the empty page frames (X_t = $\{r_t\}$).

■ If r_t was not loaded at virtual time $t–1$ and all page frames contain a page, then the content of some page frame loaded with a different page, y, has its contents replaced by page r_t. That is, $Y_t = \{y\}$ with y being specified by the replacement policy.

In *static page frame allocation with demand paging*, the only variable in the overall policy is the replacement algorithm. When a process begins to run, it is allocated a fixed number of page frames. It does not change the allocation during its lifetime. A page is only fetched when it is referenced but is not loaded in the primary memory (we say that at time t the page, r_t, is not in $S_{t-1}(m)$). Since the fetch and placement policies have been established, a static demand paging policy can be described completely by specifying its replacement policy.

DEMAND PAGING ALGORITHMS

Given a page reference stream

$$R = r_1, r_2, ..., r_t, ...$$

we let y_t designate the individual page *replaced* under a given demand paging algorithm when the physical address space is in state $S_{t-1}(m)$ and the process references page r_t. Assume the m page frames allocated to the process are full, but r_t is not in $S_{t-1}(m)$. Then the memory state at time t is defined in terms of the memory state at time $t–1$ by

$$S_t(m) = S_{t-1}(m) \cup \{r_t\} - \{y_t\}.$$

Thus, by determining the identity of y_t, we will have uniquely identified the replacement strategy, since $S_{t-1}(m)$ and $\{r_t\}$ are defined at the time the page fault occurs. Let's consider some example replacement algorithms.

RANDOM REPLACEMENT In the **random-replacement** policy, the replaced page is chosen at random. That is, the memory manager randomly chooses any loaded page, y, with probability $1/m$, and then replaces page $y_t = y$. Because this policy calls for selecting the page to be replaced by choosing the page in any page frame with equal probability, it uses no knowledge of the reference stream (or the locality) when it selects the page frame to replace.

In general, random replacement does not perform well. On most reference streams, it causes more missing page faults than the other algorithms discussed in this section. After early exploration with random replacement in the 1960s, system designers quickly recognized that several other policies would produce fewer missing page faults.

Suppose a process has $m = 4$ page frames allocated (say frame 0 with page 5, frame 1 with page 7, frame 2 with page 6, and frame 3 with page 9; that is, $S_t(4) = \{5, 7, 6, 9\}$), and the process is in a phase in which it uses only two pages (say pages 7 and 9). The random-replacement strategy is equally likely to select frame 0, 1, 2, or 3 for replacement despite the fact that frame 0 (page 5) or 2 (page 6) should be selected in order to avoid unloading pages that are heavily used.

BELADY'S OPTIMAL ALGORITHM At the other extreme from random replacement is the replacement policy having "perfect knowledge" of the page reference stream. **Belady's optimal replacement** algorithm always chooses the best page to be removed from the memory. Here is how it can do that: Let the **forward distance** of a page r at time t, $FWD_t(r)$, be the distance from the current point in the reference stream to the next place in the stream where that same page is next referenced. The forward distance is always greater than 0 and is infinite if the page is never referenced again. In the optimal algorithm, the replaced page, y_t, is one that has maximal forward distance:

$$y_t = \max_{x \in S_{t-1}(m)} FWD_t(x).$$

Since more than one page is loaded at time t, there may be more than one page that never appears again in the reference stream: That means that there could be more than one loaded page with maximal forward distance. In this case, Belady's optimal algorithm chooses an arbitrary loaded page with maximal forward distance.

The optimal algorithm can be implemented only if the complete page reference stream for every thread executing in every process is known in advance. Since it is rare for the system to have such knowledge, the algorithm is not generally realizable. Instead, its theoretical behavior is used to *compare the performance* of realizable algorithms with the optimal performance.

In a few special cases (such as a program to predict the weather), large programs are used enough to merit careful analysis of their paging behavior. Although it is not possible to exactly predict the page reference stream, one can sometimes predict the next page with high probability that the prediction will be correct. For example, the conditional branch instruction at the end of a loop almost always branches back to the beginning of the loop rather than exiting it. Such predictions are based on either static analysis of the source code or observations of dynamic behavior of the program. This analysis can sometimes produce enough information to incorporate page replacement "hints" in the source code. However, the procedure is labor-intensive and only worthwhile on programs that are long running and frequently executed. The compiler and paging systems can then be designed to use these hints to predict the future behavior of the page reference stream.

As an example of Belady's optimal algorithm, suppose

$$R = 0, 1, 2, 3, 0, 1, 2, 3, 0, 1, 2, 3, 4, 5, 6, 7$$

with $m = 3$ page frames. Table 12.1 has a row for each of the three page frames and a column for each virtual time t in the page stream. A table entry at row i, column j shows the page loaded at page frame i after r_j has been referenced. The column headings are the pages in the reference stream. If the entry is marked with an *, the page shown in the entry was loaded as a result of the missing page fault. The optimal algorithm will behave as shown in Table 12.1, and will incur 10 page faults.

TABLE 12.1 Belady's Optimal Algorithm Behavior

Frame	0	1	2	3	0	1	2	3	0	1	2	3	4	5	6	7
0	0*	0	0	0	0	0	0	0	0	1*	1	1	4*	4	4	7*
1		1*	1	1	1	1	2*	2	2	2	2	2	2	5*	5	5
2			2*	3*	3	3	3	3	3	3	3	3	3	3	6*	6

LEAST RECENTLY USED The **least recently used (LRU)** algorithm is designed to take advantage of spatial locality. Programs are written to contain loops, which cause the main line of the code to execute repeatedly, with special-case code rarely being executed. This means that in the code part of the address space, the control unit will repeatedly access the set of pages containing these loops. This set of pages that contains the code is called the *program* locality of the process. If the loop or loops that are executed are stored in a small number of pages, then the program has a small program locality. In many programs, there is a similar *data* locality whereby the process tends to repeatedly read from and write to a subset of the data when it executes the program. For example, a program that is iteratively solving a system of equations will tend to repeatedly reference the part of the address space that contains the coefficient matrix for that system of equations. While almost all programs have relatively small code localities, several classes of programs have no particularly useful data locality. (For example, a transaction processing system usually has "poor data locality," meaning that there is no relationship between distinct data transactions.)

The LRU replacement algorithm is explicitly designed to take advantage of locality by assuming that if a page has been referenced recently, *it is likely to be referenced again soon*. The **backward distance** of page r at time t, $BKWD_t(r)$, is the distance (in the reference stream) from r to the most recent occurrence of the page in the preceding part of the reference stream. The backward distance is always greater than 0 and is infinite if the page has not been referenced previously (any loaded page would have been previously referenced in a demand paging system). LRU selects a page, y_t, for replacement with the maximum backward distance:

$$y_t = \max_{x \in S_{t-1}(m)}(BKWD_t(x)).$$

The assumption is that because of the characteristics of locality, the backward distance is a good estimator of the forward distance of any page. If more than one page has maximal backward distance, LRU may choose an arbitrary page with maximal backward distance for replacement.

Suppose $R = 0, 1, 2, 3, 0, 1, 2, 3, 0, 1, 2, 3, 4, 5, 6, 7$ with $m = 3$. The LRU algorithm will produce the behavior shown in Table 12.2, incurring 16 page faults.

TABLE 12.2 LRU Behavior

Frame	0	1	2	3	0	1	2	3	0	1	2	3	4	5	6	7
0	0*	0	0	3*	3	3	2*	2	2	1*	1	1	4*	4	4	7*
1		1*	1	1	0*	0	0	3*	3	3	2*	2	2	5*	5	5
2			2*	2	2	1*	1	1	0*	0	0	3*	3	3	6*	6

LEAST FREQUENTLY USED The **least frequently used (LFU)** replacement algorithm selects a page for replacement if the page has not been used often in the past. Let $FREQ_t(r_t)$ be the number of references to r_t in r_1 through r_{t-1}. Then

$$y_t = \min_{x \in S_{t-1}(m)}(FREQ_t(x)).$$

There may be more than one page that satisfies the criteria for replacement, so any of the qualifying pages can be selected for replacement.

LFU tends to react slowly to changes in locality. If a program changes the set of pages it is currently using, the frequency counts will tend to cause the pages in the new locality to be replaced even though they are currently being used. As the process proceeds, this "inertia" will eventually be overcome and the policy will select the appropriate pages.

Another problem with LFU is that it uses frequency counts from the beginning of the page reference stream. For example, initialization code can influence the replacement policy long after the process has moved into the main part of the code. A more popular variant of pure LFU uses frequency counts of a page since it was *last loaded* rather than from the beginning of the page reference stream. The frequency counter is reset each time a page is loaded rather than being allowed to monotonically increase throughout the execution of the program. The policy will still tend to load pages slowly when the program changes locality, but the effects of phases in the distant past will not influence the behavior.

Suppose we use a random rule for selecting among pages having the same frequency of use. The example reference stream results in 12 page faults, as shown in Table 12.3.

TABLE 12.3 LFU Behavior

Frame	0	1	2	3	0	1	2	3	0	1	2	3	4	5	6	7
0	0*	0	0	0	0	0	0	0	0	0	0	3*	3	3	3	3
1		1*	1	1	1	1	1	3*	3	1*	1	1	1	1	1	1
2			2*	3*	3	3	2*	2	2	2	2	2	4*	5*	6*	7*

FIRST-IN, FIRST-OUT The **first-in, first-out (FIFO) replacement** algorithm replaces the page that has been in memory longest. Let $AGE_t(r)$ be the current time less the time at which page r in $S_i(m)$ was last loaded. The replaced page is selected by

$$y_t = \max_{x \in S_{t-1}(m)}(AGE_t(x)).$$

FIFO focuses on the length of time a page has been in memory rather than how much the page is being used. FIFO's main asset is that it is simple to implement. Its behavior is not particularly well suited to the behavior of most programs (it is completely independent of the locality), so few systems use it.

This example incurs 16 page faults under FIFO, as shown in Table 12.4.

TABLE 12.4 FIFO Behavior

Frame	0	1	2	3	0	1	2	3	0	1	2	3	4	5	6	7
0	0*	0	0	3*	3	3	2*	2	2	1*	1	1	4*	4	4	7*
1		1*	1	1	0*	0	0	3*	3	3	2*	2	2	5*	5	5
2			2*	2	2	1*	1	1	0*	0	0	3*	3	3	6*	6

STACK ALGORITHMS

Certain demand algorithms are more "well behaved" than others. For example, consider the page reference stream

$$R = 0, 1, 2, 3, 0, 1, 4, 0, 1, 2, 3, 4$$

as it is processed by FIFO with $m = 3$ (see Table 12.5). There are nine page faults, each marked with an *. Now suppose we increase the physical address space to $m = 4$ page frames and process the same page reference stream with the same algorithm (see Table 12.6).

TABLE 12.5 FIFO Algorithm with Three Page Frames

Frame	0	1	2	3	0	1	4	0	1	2	3	4
0	0*	0	0	3*	3	3	4*	4	4	4	4	4
1		1*	1	1	0*	0	0	0	0	2*	2	2
2			2*	2	2	1*	1	1	1	1	3*	3

TABLE 12.6 FIFO Algorithm with Four Page Frames

Frame	0	1	2	3	0	1	4	0	1	2	3	4
0	0*	0	0	0	0	0	4*	4	4	4	3*	3
1		1*	1	1	1	1	1	0*	0	0	0	4*
2			2*	2	2	2	2	2	1*	1	1	1
3				3*	3	3	3	3	3	2*	2	2

In the allocation with four page frames there are ten page faults, one more page fault than in the allocation with three page frames! Even though the process has one more page frame, it also incurs more page faults. This is an example of **Belady's anomaly**. The paging algorithm has worse performance when the amount of primary memory allocated to the process is increased. It is natural to be concerned about the class of replacement algorithms susceptible to Belady's anomaly, since such algorithms cannot be relied on to improve performance by increasing the amount of memory allocated to the process. Is there a characterization of algorithms susceptible to Belady's anomaly?

The problem arises because the set of pages loaded with a memory allocation of 3 is not necessarily also loaded with a memory allocation of 4. For example, when page 4 is first referenced, page 0 is left in memory in the example with $m = 3$, but is chosen for replacement in the case with $m = 4$. Once this replacement occurs, the behavior over the rest of the page reference stream can diverge quickly. There is a set of paging algorithms in which the set of pages loaded with an allocation of m is always a subset of the set of pages that has a page frame allocation of $m + 1$ (this property is called the **inclusion prop-**

erty). These algorithms are also called **stack algorithms**. Algorithms that satisfy the inclusion property are not subject to Belady's anomaly [Nutt, 1992]. In the example illustrating the anomaly, notice that after page 4 is referenced (as the seventh reference), in the allocation with $m = 3$, $S_7(3) = \{4, 0, 1\}$. However, when $m = 4$, $S_7(4) = \{4, 1, 2, 3\}$, so FIFO does not satisfy the inclusion property and is not a stack algorithm. However, LRU and LFU can be shown to be stack algorithms.

Stack algorithms display behavior important to the system designer. A designer needs to be assured that if more resources are allocated to a process, performance will not degrade—that is, that the algorithm will be "well behaved." The correlation of memory use with the number of page faults holds for stack algorithms, but not for other algorithms. Stack algorithms also are more easily analyzed than many nonstack algorithms. For example, one can calculate the cost of page fetches with a single pass over the reference stream for a stack algorithm, since it is possible to predict the number of page faults by analyzing the memory state. Also, the memory state can be used to predict performance improvement obtained by increasing a process's memory allocation for stack algorithms. This performance improvement is not possible for other algorithms.

IMPLEMENTING LRU

Over time, LRU has become the most widely used of the static replacement algorithms because it is a reasonable predictor for program behavior and it produces good performance on a wide variety of page references streams. However, to implement LRU, the system has to keep track of the backward distance of every loaded page for every process. This accounting essentially requires that the page table incorporate a field to save the virtual time of the last reference. This record is costly to implement, since it introduces another page table memory write and requires virtual time maintenance. Also, the replacement algorithm must search the entire page table to find the loaded page that has the maximum backward distance. The sheer amount of information required to implement the exact behavior of LRU is difficult to implement in hardware. However, it is possible to *approximate* the behavior of the pure LRU algorithm with relatively simple hardware.

Suppose the page table incorporated a **reference bit** for each page table entry. Also assume the reference bit for each page is periodically set to 0. The address translation hardware can be designed to set the reference bit to 1 each time the corresponding page is read from or written to (this can be done much faster than updating a field with an integer time value). Now, whenever a page fault occurs, the system inspects the reference bits to see which ones were set since they were all last cleared. Pages with their reference bits set have been "recently referenced," whereas the pages with their reference bits still at 0 have not. The least recently used page is one with its reference bit cleared, so the LRU approximation arbitrarily chooses one of those pages to replace. The reference bits are then all cleared once again.

How can we extend the idea of a reference bit to keep more information about the recent usage of a page? Suppose each entry's reference bit is replaced by a shift register in which the most significant bit is treated just like the reference bit. That is, this bit is set when the corresponding page is referenced. Now, suppose the register contents are shifted to the right periodically. When a missing page fault occurs, the shift register contains more information about how recently the page was referenced. Hence, a better approximation to LRU can be obtained (see Exercise 14 at the end of this chapter). The precision of the history depends on the length of the period between shift operations and the number of bits in the shift register.

For example, the page table in part (a) in Table 12.7 illustrates the case in which the reference bits have all been cleared. Memory references in

$$R = ...4, 14, 4, 28, 5, 14, 4, 29, 6, ...$$

are processed until the reference to page 6 causes a page fault. The table in Table 12.7(b) indicates that pages 4, 5, 14, 28, and 29 have all been referenced since their reference bit was set. When the page fault occurs, one of pages 0, 9, or 19 is the least recently used page, so the mechanism will randomly select one of these pages for replacement. If all pages have been referenced since the last time the reference bit was cleared, then of course the selection of the page is purely random. Provided the latter case rarely occurs, this approach is an inexpensive approximation of LRU.

TABLE 12.7 Approximating LRU

Page	Reference	Frame	Page	Reference	Frame
0	0	103	0	0	103
4	0	78	4	1	78
5	0	99	5	1	99
9	0	24	9	0	24
14	0	65	14	1	65
19	0	40	19	0	40
28	0	42	28	1	42
29	0	33	29	1	33

| (a) Reference Bits Clear | (b) Some Reference Bits Set |

A significant part of the cost of a page fault is the task of writing a page from primary memory into secondary memory. The page table also can incorporate a **dirty bit**, to be cleared when a page is loaded and set when there is a write to the page. If the page is selected for replacement and its dirty bit is clear, the page has not been written to since it was loaded. Therefore, it is not necessary to copy the page back to secondary memory because the page frame image is the same as the page image in secondary storage. This saves one device write operation from occurring.

PAGING PERFORMANCE

Since the process/thread will be delayed when a page fault occurs, it cannot normally be expected to execute in the same amount of time in a paging system as it could in a system that allocates enough memory to load the entire address space at execution time. The paging system economizes on the amount of memory a process uses in exchange for a longer time to execute the process. The value of paging is in a favorable tradeoff between the amount of space saved versus the cost in time to execute the process. For example, it might be considered to be a good tradeoff if a process reduced its memory requirement at run-time by 50 percent, but required only a 10 percent increase in execution time. Because of the subjectivity involved in this tradeoff, performance analysis of paging algorithms is usually conducted by comparing the effect of different memory allocations, different page sizes, different page transfer rates, and different replacement strategies.

The dominant cost of paging is the I/O time for replacement. As you know, disk I/O operations are several orders of magnitude slower than primary memory reference times. Even a small difference in the number of page faults can dramatically change the execution time for a process. The simple examples given in this section demonstrate that a mismatch between the process's locality and the size of the physical address space can be disastrous because it causes the primary memory to be loaded after every few instructions. This phenomenon, called **thrashing**, can substantially increase the number of page faults and thus slow down the process's execution time by several orders of magnitude (depending on the disk I/O speed).

Each page fault will introduce considerable overhead, say R units of time. The time for page fault processing is added to the total execution time: If there are t references in a process's reference stream and it incurs f page faults, the total execution time can be written as

$$T_{exec} = t + f R$$

Normalizing the cost of page replacement across all instructions obtains the average amount of overhead per instruction:

$$\text{average overhead} = T_{exec}/t = (t + f R)/t = 1 + (f/t)\, R$$

The expression f/t, called the **fault rate**, is the fraction of page references resulting in a page fault. If the fault rate and R are small, the cost of page faults will be absorbed over the full execution without much degradation. As either grows, paging becomes ineffective, since the overhead time dominates the process's total runtime.

The value of f/t depends on the amount of memory allocated to the process, the page reference stream, and the replacement algorithm. The value of R depends on numerous factors, including the speed of the secondary storage, the page size, and the replacement policy overhead. However, the transfer time between primary and secondary storage will tend to dominate R for most implementations, since the transfer ordinarily involves mechanical movement in the storage device. Thus, the disk transfer rate is very important to the paging system's performance. Sometimes it even justifies the incorporation of a high-speed disk just to hold executable memory images for the paging system.

Over the years, considerable empirical data have been gathered concerning the performance of various paging algorithms and implementations. While these observations do not provide bounds on performance, they do provide practical insight into the performance of various replacement strategies for different processes. Investigators observed that for all page reference streams and all algorithms, thrashing will typically occur for memory allocations of less than half the virtual address space size [Coffman and Denning, 1973]. Conversely, as the memory allocation approaches the virtual address space size, the performance of all algorithms converges to Belady's optimal algorithm. The amount of memory allocated to the process has been observed to be at least as important as the replacement algorithm. Systems unable to allocate enough memory to processes will cause significant performance degradation. This observation also leads to the consideration of better ways of matching the primary memory needs of a process to the allocation than are used in static memory allocation techniques.

12.5 • DYNAMIC PAGING ALGORITHMS

Static paging algorithms assume that a process is allocated a fixed amount of primary memory when it is started and the amount does not change during the computation. These algorithms do not adjust the allocation, even if the process passes through phases in which it requires a large physical address space or its memory requirements are modest.

A program's fault rate depends on the amount of memory available to it. For stack algorithms, as the memory size increases, the fault rate will decrease. A plot of the fault rate for a particular program will usually have a small region around a point, m', where the derivative of the curve changes rapidly (this is called a *hysteresis point*). If the amount of memory allocated to the process is less than m', the process will thrash. However, memory allocation that exceeds m' does not substantially reduce the fault rate. This value, m', is the ideal memory allocation for the process with the given replacement algorithm.

The explanation for this phenomenon is that a process changes locality as it executes. When the locality changes, not only do the identities of the pages change but also the *number* of pages in the locality is likely to change (take another look at Figure 12.7). Sometimes the process needs only a few page frames to hold all the pages it is currently using, while at other times it needs many page frames. It can be argued that the value of the ideal memory allocation, m', is highly dynamic, depending on the process's behavior at each point in the execution. Therefore, as computations change phases, the locality changes and, in turn, *the number of page frames allocated to the process should change*. Dynamic paging algorithms adjust the memory allocation to match the process's needs as they change. The working set algorithm is the first well-known dynamic paging algorithm and has led to the paging algorithms used in modern operating systems.

THE WORKING SET ALGORTHM

The working set algorithm uses the current memory requirements to determine the number of page frames to allocate to the process. Suppose there are k processes sharing the primary memory. Let $m_i(t)$ be the amount of memory allocated to process i at its virtual time t. So $m_i(0) = 0$ and

$$\sum_{i=1}^{k} m_i(t) \leq |\text{primary memory}|$$

at time t.

Now, if we substitute $m_i(t)$ for m in the notation from the last section, $S_t(m_i(t))$ is the set of pages loaded in process p_i's memory at virtual time t. This notation is a bit unwieldy, and t is redundantly specified in the expression, so we just use the simplified form $S(m_i(t))$ to represent the set of pages allocated to process i at time t.

Given that $S(m_i(0)) = \varnothing$, the memory state for process i at time $t > 0$ can still be derived from the memory state at time $t-1$ using a parameter, w:

$$S(m_i(t)) = S(m_i(t-1)) \cup X_t - Y_t,$$

where X_t is the set of pages placed in primary memory at time t. Y_t is the set of pages removed (independent from the placed pages) from the memory at time t. More specifi-cally, if r_t was loaded at time $t-1$, it remains in memory; if r_t was not loaded at time $t-1$, $X_t = \{r_t\}$. Independently, page y is unloaded if the backward distance from r_t is greater than or equal to a constant value, $\boldsymbol{w}$ (that is $BKWD_t(y) \geq \boldsymbol{w}$). *Page replacement and placement are decoupled in this algorithm*; the $\boldsymbol{w}$ parameter is the size of a logical **window** on the reference stream, one that is used to bound the set of previous references used with an LRU variant. Since X_t and Y_t have been specified, the memory allocation, $m_i(t)$, is adjusted to allocate exactly the number of page frames needed to hold the pages in $S(m_i(t))$:

- ■ $X_t \neq \varnothing$ and $Y_t = \varnothing \Rightarrow m_i(t) = m_i(t-1) + 1$ (allocate a page frame)
- ■ $X_t = \varnothing$ and $Y_t = \varnothing \Rightarrow m_i(t) = m_i(t-1)$
- ■ $X_t = \varnothing$ and $Y_t \neq \varnothing \Rightarrow m_i(t) = m_i(t-1) - 1$ (deallocate a page frame)

The resulting $S(m_i(t))$ is called the **working set** for process i at time t with window size $\boldsymbol{w}$ (the window size, $\boldsymbol{w}$, determines when a page frame should be deallocated in the backward distance comparison). Notice the similarity between the working set approach and the LRU approach used with static allocation algorithms: Both rely on the backward distance computation to determine the page replacement, but the working set bounds the backward distances being considered using the window size.

Figure 12.11 is an illustration of the way the window is used to determine the working set and the page frame allocation. The segment of the reference stream shows that the current page being referenced, r_t, is to page 1, and that (including the current page) the working set window should consider the most recent $\boldsymbol{w} = 3$ page references: pages 1, 0, and 1. These three references only use two pages: pages 0 and 1. Therefore, the working set size for a window size of $\boldsymbol{w} = 3$ is two, meaning that the working set can be loaded into the primary memory if the process is allocated two page frames.

✦ FIGURE 12.11   The Working Set Window

The window size is $\boldsymbol{w} = 3$, meaning that the algorithm will look at three references to determine which pages should be loaded. This means that the working set contains two pages: 0 and 1.

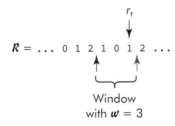

$$r_t$$
$$\downarrow$$
$$R = \ldots \; 0 \; 1 \; 2 \; 1 \; 0 \; 1 \; 2 \; \ldots$$

Window
with $\boldsymbol{w} = 3$

Working set = {0, 1} ⇒ Need 2 page frames

The working set is an approximation of the set of pages in a process's locality. For example, if a process uses only three pages at a time for 10,000 references, it should have only three page frames allocated to it. If it systematically uses 20 pages at a time in the last 10,000 references, it should have 20 page frames in its physical address space.

The original working set theory used the window size to estimate the working set [Coffman and Denning, 1973]. However, there are other measures that could be used to estimate the membership of the working set. For example, the *page fault frequency* algorithm monitors the rate at which a process incurs page faults in order to determine membership. If the rate is above a predetermined threshold value, then the page frame allocation is too small, so it is increased to accommodate the process's working set. On the other hand, if the page fault frequency falls below a different threshold, the algorithm assumes there are more page frames allocated than necessary to hold the working set, so it releases some page frames.

The **working set principle** states that a process i should be loaded and active only if it can be allocated enough page frames to hold its entire working set. Otherwise, the process should be blocked until it can obtain enough primary memory to hold its working set. Working set implementations all depend on an estimator (such as the window size or the page fault frequency threshold values) in an attempt to accurately determine the contents of the working set.

The working set algorithm defines the basis of most contemporary paging systems, although it is rarely (if ever) used in its theoretical form. While it relies on knowledge of the backward distance to determine membership in the window, it captures the idea of locality and minimum memory required to run the process. The independent variable in the working set is the window size and is determined by the characteristics of the process.

Working Set Algorithm

This example shows that the working set algorithm is susceptible to thrashing if w is too small. It is possible to measure the rate at which page faults occur and then either to adjust w so that it is larger if the page fault rate surpasses a threshold or smaller if the rate falls below a minimum threshold. Essentially, this approach attempts to adjust w for the locality based on the observed fault rate. Increases in w will tend to increase the amount of memory allocated to a process, while decreases in w will tend to have the opposite effect.

Suppose the reference stream used to illustrate static allocation algorithms was processed with the working set algorithm with $w = 3$. Then the algorithm would experience 16 page faults, as shown in Table 12.8.

Notice that the number of page frames allocated varies from 0 when the process begins to a maximum of $w = 3$ page frames. The performance of the working set algorithm could be increased considerably by adjusting the window size to $w = 4$, which is just large

TABLE 12.8 Working Set with $w = 3$

Frame	0	1	2	3	0	1	2	3	0	1	2	3	4	5	6	7
0	0*	0	0	3*	3	3	2*	2	2	1*	1	1	4*	4	4	7*
1		1*	1	1	0*	0	0	3*	3	3	2*	2	2	5*	5	5
2			2*	2	2	1*	1	1	0*	0	0	3*	3	3	6*	6
Allocation	1	2	3	3	3	3	3	3	3	3	3	3	3	3	3	3

enough to satisfy the needs of the locality for this reference stream (see Table 12.9). This window size results in eight page faults, the minimum since there are eight distinct pages in the reference stream and each must be loaded at least once.

TABLE 12.9 Working Set with $w = 4$

Frame	0	1	2	3	0	1	2	3	0	1	2	3	4	5	6	7
0	0*	0	0	0	0	0	0	0	0	0	0	0	4*	4	4	4
1		1*	1	1	1	1	1	1	1	1	1	1	1	5*	5	5
2			2*	2	2	2	2	2	2	2	2	2	2	2	6*	6
3				3*	3	3	3	3	3	3	3	3	3	3	3	7*
Allocation	1	2	3	4	4	4	4	4	4	4	4	4	4	4	4	4

In both of these examples, the maximum page frame allocation is w. For window sizes exceeding the locality sizes, the page frame allocation will be less than w. For example, suppose $w = 9$ (see Table 12.10). While this configuration uses more memory, it does not reduce the number of page faults, since it was already at the minimum.

TABLE 12.10 Working Set with $w = 9$

Frame	0	1	2	3	0	1	2	3	0	1	2	3	4	5	6	7
0	0*	0	0	0	0	0	0	0	0	0	0	0	0	0	0	0
1		1*	1	1	1	1	1	1	1	1	1	1	1	1	1	1
2			2*	2	2	2	2	2	2	2	2	2	2	2	2	2
3				3*	3	3	3	3	3	3	3	3	3	3	3	3*
4													4*	4	4	4
5														5*	5	5
6															6*	6
7																7*
Allocation	1	2	3	4	4	4	4	4	4	4	4	4	5	6	7	8

To see an example in which the page frame allocation decreases during execution, we can consider a different reference stream (in Table 12.11, assume $w = 4$):

TABLE 12.11 Another Example with $w = 4$

Frame	0	1	2	3	0	1	0	1	2	3	2	3	4	5	6	7
0	0*	0	0	0	0	0	0	0	0				4*	4	4	4
1		1*	1	1	1	1	1	1	1	1				5*	5	5
2			2*	2	2	2			2*	2	2	2	2	2	6*	6
3				3*	3	3	3			3*	3	3	3	3	3	7*
Allocation	1	2	3	4	4	4	3	2	3	4	3	2	3	4	4	4

IMPLEMENTING THE WORKING SET ALGORITHM

The working set algorithm is even more difficult to implement than the LRU algorithm (which could only be implemented cost effectively using approximate implementations). Clock algorithms were introduced as a way to approximate a pure implementation of the working set algorithm. They provide similar fault rate performance, but allow for a simpler implementation than, for example, keeping the window contents for each process. The WSClock algorithm is an early implementation of the working set based on a clock algorithm and represents the basic technique used in contemporary implementations.

In **clock algorithms**, the idea is to think of the page frames of all processes as being arranged in a single circular list, like the numerals on the face of an analog clock.

- A single pointer addresses one page frame in the list.

- When the replacement algorithm requires that a page be replaced, the pointer is advanced to the next page frame and this frame is considered for replacement.

- Each page frame contains a reference bit (as in the LRU implementation for static algorithms), which is set when the page is referenced.

- At the time a page is considered for replacement, the algorithm checks the bit.

- If the reference bit is set, then the pointer moves to the next frame.

- Otherwise, the page is replaced and all bits are cleared.

Such an interpretation causes the clock algorithm to behave like a **global LRU** algorithm for all pages held by all processes. That is, it is similar to the implementation of LRU for an individual process (discussed in Section 12.4), yet it applies to the pages held by all processes at once.

Suppose process 3 incurs a page fault, and the memory manager decides it needs to load the page. Table 12.12 represents the data structure for the clock algorithm (note the similarity between Table 12.12 and Table 12.7 for the LRU approximation). The table identifies all page frames, a reference bit, and the process to which the page frame belongs. The three columns on the left represent the data structure after the reference bits have been cleared and with the clock hand pointing at page frame 4. When it is necessary to replace a page (the right side of Table 12.12), the memory manager examines page

TABLE 12.12 Approximating Global LRU

Frame	Ref	Process	Frame	Ref	Process
10	0	3	10	0	3
⇒4	0	7	4	1	7
53	0	9	53	1	9
9	0	3	9	1	3
34	0	2	⇒34	0	2
19	0	4	19	0	4
48	0	4	48	1	4
29	0	3	29	1	3

frame 53 and determines that it has been recently referenced; then it examines page frame 9, and so on. Page frame 34 has a cleared reference bit, so it will be replaced. This means that a page frame 34 will be deallocated from process 2 and added to process 3.

The basic clock algorithm can be extended to the *WSClock algorithm* by approximating the window size using the global LRU mechanism. Suppose the clock algorithm keeps an additional variable named `lastRef` for each page frame. When the reference bit is set, `lastRef[frame]` is set to the current virtual time for the process using it, $T_{process\ i}$. When a page fault occurs, the algorithm begins inspecting records as it does in the usual clock algorithm. When it finds a page frame whose reference bit is not set, it then checks to see if the page frame should have slipped out of its process's window. It does this by comparing

$$T_{process\ i} - \texttt{lastRef[frame]} > w,$$

where $T_{process\ i}$ is the current virtual time for process i and `lastRef[frame]` is the time the page was last referenced. Although `lastRef` is the virtual time of last reference for the appropriate process rather than the actual time, it allows the global LRU clock strategy to capture the basic behavior of the working set with window size w. Variants of WSClock are used in most contemporary paging computer systems.

Here is an example using WSClock: Suppose three processes, p_0, p_1, and p_2, share 15 page frames in primary memory. Assume that p_0 has executed to virtual time 55, p_1 to virtual time 75, and p_2 to virtual time 80 so that $T_{p0} = 55$, $T_{p1} = 75$, and $T_{p2} = 80$. Table 12.13 gives the clock variable settings (where page frame 0 is considered by the algorithms after they have considered page frame 14). The clock pointer addresses page frame number 6. If a page fault has just occurred on behalf of p_0, then the basic clock algorithm would inspect the reference bit for frame 6, determine that the page had been used since the last page fault, and then move the pointer to page frame 7. The reference bit is not set here, and the page is allocated to p_0; the missing page replaces the page loaded in page frame 7.

TABLE 12.13 WSClock Behavior

Page Frame	0	1	2	3	4	5	6	7	8	9	10	11	12	13	14
Ref. Bit	0	1	0	1	1	0	1	0	1	1	0	0	0	0	0
Process #	0	0	1	2	2	1	1	0	2	0	1	2	0	1	2
lastRef	15	51	69	65	80	15	75	33	70	54	23	25	45	25	47
nextPtr							⇑								

Suppose the page fault had occurred on behalf of p_2. Again, the algorithm would have selected page frame 7 for the replacement, but it would have had to deallocate page frame 7 from p_0 and allocate it to p_2 prior to loading it with the missing page.

Now consider the behavior using WSClock with $w = 25$. If a page fault has just occurred on behalf of p_0, then WSClock will inspect the reference bit for page 6, detect that the bit was set, and move on to page frame 7 (as it would with the basic clock algorithm). $T_{p0} = 55$, so

$$T_{p0} - \texttt{lastRef[7]} = 55 - 33 = 22 < w.$$

Since the expression is less than w, the algorithm will go to page frame 8, detect that the reference bit is set, and go on to page frame 9. The reference bit for page frame 9 is also set, so WSClock will next look at page frame 10 (allocated to p_1) and compute

$$T_{p1} - \texttt{lastRef[10]} = 75 - 23 = 52 > 25 = w.$$

Page frame 10 will be deallocated from p_1, allocated to p_2, and then loaded with the missing page.

Taking Advantage of Paging with IPC

Paging systems provide an opportunity for a significant performance improvement in any situation in which information is copied from the address space of one process to another, as in message-passing IPC mechanisms. Suppose the information to be copied is loaded into a buffer that is exactly the size of a page. If the buffer is in the sender's address space, the message can be moved from the sender's to the receiver's address space. This is done by deleting the page table pointer to the page that contains the message in the sender's page table and adding it to (or replacing an existing pointer in) the receiver's page table. The information remains in the same physical page frame, but the page frame is deallocated from the sender's address space and added to the receiver's address space.

The copy-on-write semantics described in Section 9.3 also can be applied to the IPC mechanism to further increase performance (as is done in the Mach operating system). When a message is sent, its page is mapped into the receiver's space, while remaining mapped into the sender's space. As long as neither process writes to the page, it can be shared without harm to either process (provided the memory manager is instructed not to remove the page from either process's page table). If/when either process writes to the page, the copies are made and the pages are subsequently handled like any other pages in terms of selection for replacement.

Windows NT/2000/XP Virtual Memory

Every Windows NT/2000/XP process is given a fixed-size virtual address space—4 GB—which, of course, is much larger than the amount of primary memory in most contemporary computers. The process does not necessarily use all of the virtual address space—only as much as it needs. Ordinarily, the .EXE for a program is very much smaller than the address space. Part of the virtual address space, usually 2 GB, is used to allow a thread to reference user space memory objects and the remainder is used to reference addresses used by the OS (it is supervisor space).[1] Even though the supervisor space por-

---

[1] The relative sizes of the application's portion of the process address space and the kernel portion of the space is different in Windows NT/2000/XP Server than it is in Windows NT/2000/XP Professional. This is one of the configuration differences between the two OS versions. Server has a larger part of the address space for the user space, allowing applications to have large amounts of information in virtual memory.

tion of the address space exists in a process's virtual address space, the memory can be referenced only by a thread if the processor is in supervisor mode.

The OS needs some means of determining the amount of the address space that the process intends to use. The link editor builds the static execution image in an .EXE file that will generally define the address space. Dynamically linked libraries and other dynamically allocated portions of the address space can be added to the virtual address space at runtime.

✦ FIGURE 12.12 Windows NT Paging System

In step 1, the thread makes a reference to address k in page i. If the page is not loaded, it will be looked up on the disk, then loaded into page frame j. The thread can now reference the virtual memory contents.

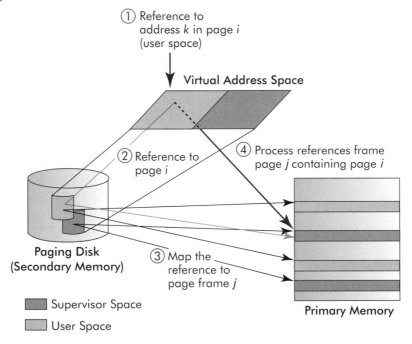

There are two phases to dynamically adding addresses to the address space (see Figure 12.12):

1. Reserving a portion of the address space called a *region*.

2. Committing a *block* of pages in a region in the address space.[2]

A thread in a process can dynamically reserve a region of virtual addresses without actually causing anything to be written to the secondary storage **page file** (also sometimes called the **paging file**). A thread in the process may also subsequently *release* a region of addresses it previously reserved.

---

[2]Just to make things complicated, the Windows documentation refers to a block of pages and an allocation region as "regions." The nomenclature here is taken from Richter [1997].

The second phase is to *commit* addresses that were previously reserved (the committed block is frequently a subset of the reserved region). Once a portion of the address space has been committed, space is allocated in the page file. If a thread in the process then references committed memory, the page containing the referenced address will be loaded from the page file into the primary memory. (Of course, the part of the address space that has been reserved and committed will not have had anything written to it when it is first referenced, so a zero-filled page will be loaded on the first reference.)

Each processor supports a particular *allocation granularity* to determine the minimum size of a block of addresses that can be reserved. On all current implementations, the allocation granularity is 64 KB. Whenever a reservation is made, the address is rounded down automatically to the next lower allocation granularity boundary before the reservation is made.

Each processor also supports its own page size (you can determine the processor's page size using `GetSystemInfo()`)—usually 4 or 8 KB. Memory is committed in units of pages, so actual reservation of addresses can be on a much smaller grain than reservation. Once virtual addresses have been committed, the thread can use the memory just like any statically allocated part of the address space.

PAGING SYSTEM INTERNALS

Address translation depends on the presence of certain elements in the hardware to detect missing pages and to map a page rapidly into a page frame. A virtual address is a 32-bit quantity generated by the processor. In contrast to conventional paging mechanisms, Windows NT/2000/XP uses a two-level address translation facility (see Figure 12.13). The page byte index is the K_1 least significant bits in the address; K_1 is 12 for Intel x86 processors with 4KB pages, and 13 for Digital Alpha processors with 8 KB pages. Conventional single-level paging mechanisms use the remainder of the address as a page number. In Windows NT/2000, the remainder is called the *virtual page number*, and it is separated into two parts called the *page table index* (K_2 bits) and the *page directory index* (the K_3 most significant bits in the address). In the x86 family of processors, K_2 and K_3 are 10, and in the Alpha processor K_2 is 11 and K_3 is 8.

Address translation uses these three fields in the address as follows:

1. The process descriptor contains a pointer, A, to the beginning of the *page directory* for the given process.

2. The page directory index, a, is an offset into the page directory where a *page descriptor entry* (*PDE*) for the specified page is located.

3. Each process can have several different *page tables*. The PDE references the particular page table to be used for this memory reference (pointer B in the figure).

4. The *page table entry* (*PTE*) is found by using the page table index, b, from the address as an index into the page table.

5. If the target page is currently loaded in primary memory at page frame j, then the PTE points to the page frame, C. If it is not loaded, the Virtual Memory Manager must locate the page in the page file, find a page frame, allocate it to the process, and then load the page into the page frame.

6. Finally, the byte index, c, is added to the page frame base address to obtain the location of the target byte in the primary memory.

✦ **FIGURE 12.13** Windows Address Translation

Windows uses a two-level page mapping mechanism: a page directory and page tables. A page table can reference a related collection of pages (such as the OS) that can be referenced from a page directory entry.

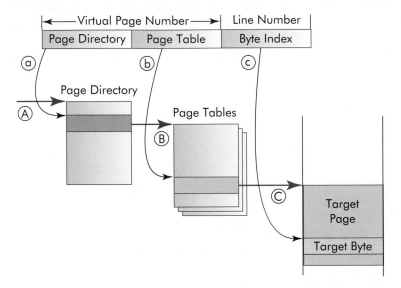

Although the page directory could be mapped to any location (pointer *A* in Figure 12.13), in practice it is located at a fixed point in the address space—0xC0300000 on x86 systems and 0xC018000 on Alpha processors. Both of these processors use a dedicated processor register to reference the page directory; the register is saved as part of the thread context whenever a new thread is dispatched to the processor.

Windows NT/2000/XP uses multiple-page tables to distinguish among different uses of the address space. The most obvious difference among pages is that some are user space pages and others are kernel space pages—they are mapped in different page tables. Notice that by putting kernel space pages in a separate page table, different processes have the PDEs for kernel space pointing to the same page tables. Further, the page tables can then make other distinctions about the physical memory used for the particular part of the address space. For example, in kernel space, some parts of the kernel memory are paged just like user space pages, but others are not allowed to be paged out—they are allocated from a special pool of nonpaged memory blocks.[3]

Each PTE references a page frame number when the corresponding page is loaded. There is also a collection of flags to describe how the page can be referenced, including whether the PTE is valid, whether the page is reserved, if it is dirty (it has had new values written into it since it was last loaded into primary memory), if it has been accessed since the last epoch, and so on.

---

[3]Nonpaged memory blocks contain information or code that needs to be in the memory because it is currently being used (such as a buffer), or it is code that must be readily available (such as the virtual memory manager or scheduling code).

A memory reference requires that the PDE be found in the page directory, and that the PTE be found in the page table. This means that an ordinary memory reference could result in several additional memory references if there were no special hardware provided in the processor. Contemporary computers, such as the Intel x86 and Digital Alpha processors, use a TLB (see the box on page table implementations in Section 12.3).

Windows NT/2000/XP uses demand paging, meaning that pages are not loaded into the primary memory until they are referenced. Further, PTEs are not even created until the corresponding page is loaded. The rationale for this approach is that a process may reserve memory addresses without ever using them. In fact, the process might even commit memory pages, and then never reference them during execution. Since the address space is so large, if PTEs were made as soon as the information were known, there is a likelihood that many might be created and then never used, resulting in considerable wasted memory for PTEs.

Because PTEs are not created until they are used, the OS must keep other data structures to maintain reservation and commitment operations. A *virtual address descriptor* (*VAD*) is created whenever a process reserves or commits virtual addresses. When a thread first references the addresses within a VAD, the PTE is created so that address translation can proceed normally.

The last aspect of paging internals considered here is primary memory allocation. Windows NT/2000/XP uses working sets with a clock algorithm. Windows NT/2000/XP distinguishes between the process working set and the system working set used by a process. The process working set grows and shrinks like a classic working set. It starts with a default minimum size—20 to 50 pages—and is not allowed to grow larger than a default maximum size—45 to 345 pages. However, the maximum working set size can be changed by the system administrator.

Linux Virtual Memory

The Linux Version 2.0.x memory manager uses a dynamic, demand-paged virtual memory strategy. Processes issue virtual addresses (that have already been mapped), and the memory manager is responsible for determining whether the corresponding page is loaded in some physical memory page frame. If it is not loaded, the page is found in the secondary memory (the disk), and then it is loaded into an unused page frame if one is available. If not, a replacement algorithm unloads a currently loaded page, as in the normal static demand paging approach. If the page is currently loaded in some page frame in the physical memory, the virtual address is translated into the appropriate physical memory address. The physical memory location can then be read or written as desired.

Linux defines an architecture-independent memory model that transcends current-day CPUs and memory management units (MMUs), so it includes components that are not used, for example, in the i386[4] implementation. In the general model, a virtual address is translated into a physical address using a three-level map. A virtual address, j, is partitioned into four parts:

---

[4]Windows uses "x86" to refer to Intel 80x86, including Pentium, processors, but Linux uses "i386."

- A *page directory* offset, j.pgd
- A *page middle directory* offset, j.pmd
- A *page table* offset, j.pte
- The offset within the page, j.offset

If a page is loaded into the physical memory, the physical address, i, for a virtual address j is determined by:

```
i = PTE(PMD(PGD(j.pgd) + j.pmd) + j.pte) + j.offset
```

where PGD represents the page directory table, PMD represents the page middle directory table, and PTE represents the page table. Conceptually (see Figure 12.14), this means that the virtual address is first divided into the four parts:

- The j.pgd part is used to locate an entry in the page directory. This page directory entry references the base of a page middle directory. This references an entry in the page middle directory.

- The j.pmd part of the address is used as an offset into the designated page middle directory. This points at the base of the page table to be used.

- The j.pte portion of the virtual address is an offset in the page table that references a page descriptor containing the physical address of the first location in the page frame that contains the target page.

- The page offset, j.offset, is added to the page frame address to determine the physical memory address, i, for the virtual address, j.

Of course, if any map is undefined, a missing page interrupt will be generated during address translation, causing the page manager to load the page and then to map the virtual address.

✦ FIGURE 12.14 Virtual Address Translation

Linux uses a three-level page mapping mechanisms: a page directory, a page middle directory, and page tables. In the Intel i386 implementation, the page middle directory is not used.

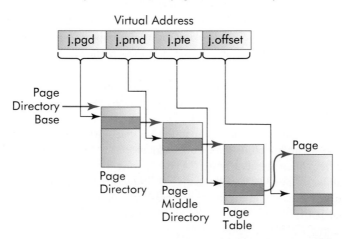

The i386 microprocessor and compatible MMUs do not have sufficient hardware to support the full three-level translation process, so in this architecture, only two of the three levels of translation are implemented. This is accomplished by reducing each page middle directory to contain only a single entry; thus, the `j.pmd` part of the address is not used since the page directory entry points directly at the single entry in the page middle table.

12.6 ● SEGMENTATION

In segmentation, programs use two-component virtual addresses of the form

`<segmentNumber, offset>`

The `segmentNumber` is an indirect reference to the base location at which the segment is loaded, and `offset` is the address of the target cell within that segment. The basic operation of segmentation was described in Chapter 11. There we saw that the "code segment" register addresses a block of compiled code, the "data segment" register points at the static data, and the "stack segment" register addresses the runtime stack.

Virtual memory segment registers use the same idea of dynamic hardware relocation through relocation registers. However, a segmentation system is designed to support a comparatively large number of segments at a given time. For example, Multics processes can have 64K different segments. The segmentation mechanism also incorporates a logical limit register for each segment. The mechanism can then check each virtual address to be sure that it is within the segment.

The rest of this section describes how addresses are translated at runtime from symbolic segments and offset addresses to runtime locations in primary memory. It also describes the Multics segmentation system, since that system is the most general segmentation system.

ADDRESS TRANSLATION

Because address translation is the fundamental concept of virtual memory, the discussion of segmentation begins by considering the nature of the mapping mechanism. The segment name space is a two-component space, so the virtual-physical address map has the form

$$\mathcal{B}_t : \text{segment space} \times \text{offset space} \to \text{primary memory space} \cup \{\Omega\}$$

Any individual name space reference has the form

$$\mathcal{B}_t(i, j) = k,$$

where i is a segment address, j is an offset within the segment, and k is the primary memory location where the segment is loaded (Ω if the information is not currently loaded in the primary memory).

Segment names are typically symbolic names, like filenames, which are translated and bound at runtime. This allows a process to use programs that contain symbolic references to other segments without needing to know their segment number (which is determined at runtime). It also prevents segments, such as those containing error codes, from being bound to the address space (and thus not loaded) unless they are needed. (This is not an issue in paging because the programmer never makes a symbolic reference to a page.) If the system postpones segment binding until runtime, then we will need another level of address translation:

$$S: \text{segment names} \rightarrow \text{segment numbers}$$

Thus, the address map has the refined form of

$$\mathbf{\mathit{B}}_t(\mathbf{\mathit{S}}(\texttt{segmentName}), j) = k,$$

where `segmentName` is a symbolic name of the target segment compiled into the executable image.

In the most general segmentation systems, the *offset* within the segment is also bound at runtime, thus requiring a third translation operation at runtime:

$$N: \texttt{offset names} \rightarrow \texttt{offset addresses}$$

Postponing the binding of the offset in a virtual address to a target offset in a destination segment means the source process need not know the offset in the destination segment at compile/link time. The destination segment offset can be symbolically defined by the compiler and linker with no concern for distributing this information to processes that might need to use the segment. The binding will be done at the first reference to the offset at runtime.

Thus, the address map could be as complex as

$$\mathbf{\mathit{B}}_t(\mathbf{\mathit{S}}(\texttt{segmentName}), \mathbf{\mathit{N}}(\texttt{offsetName})) = k,$$

where `segmentName` is a symbolic segment name and `offsetName` is the symbolic label, such as an entry point name, within the segment.

The task of designing a fully functional segmentation system to handle such general address translation is quite challenging. Each memory reference is a pair of *symbols* that have to be translated when the reference first occurs. As a further complication, the mappings are time-varying, meaning the segment could be located anywhere in primary and/or secondary memory.

An implementation can make a number of simplifying assumptions about the address translation; for example, they disallow runtime binding of segment and offset names. The most general approach is to support late-bound segment and offset names so that the full translation happens only on the first reference to the segment. Subsequent references to a previously loaded segment use the binding established on the first reference. Even though the segment may be unloaded after the first reference, the binding of the symbolic name to a segment number can be reused.

Figure 12.15 shows a design for the general segment address translation facility. The operating system maintains a **segment table** for each process. The segment table is ordinarily a segment itself. It is usually stored in primary memory as a segment that is not to be unloaded as long as the process can run. It is a collection of **segment descriptors**. Each descriptor contains base, limit, and protection register contents for the segment (as described in Chapter 11). The base field contains the segment relocation register for the target segment (if it is loaded), the limit field contains the length of the segment, and the protection field describes allowable forms of access to the segment. If the segment is not loaded, the segment descriptor contents will be marked to indicate this.

✦ FIGURE 12.15 Address Translation in Segmentation

The *S*-map and *N*-map translate the segment name and offset name, respectively. The result of the *S*-map is a segment number (offset) into the descriptor segment; the B_t map is implemented using the base register value from the segment descriptor at the specified descriptor segment offset.

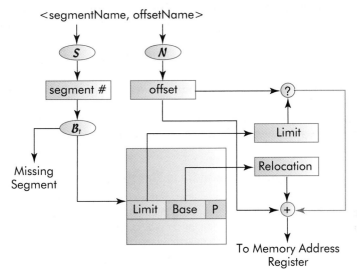

When the process makes its first reference to a particular segment, the *S*-map translates the segment name into a segment number. The result, *S*(segmentName), is an offset into the segment table that addresses the correct segment descriptor for the target segment. After the *S*-map has bound a particular reference to a segment descriptor, the system must make provision for bypassing the *S*-map operation on subsequent references to the segment. The most primitive way to do this is to rewrite the operand in the instruction so that it contains a segment number rather than a segment name. This does not require that the code segment be changed. However, it does require that an indirect reference table be used if the code is not to be changed. The next subsection gives a specific example of how this can be done.

In some systems, the offset must also be bound to a location within a loaded segment. This binding might occur if the compiler generating the segment reference did not have a load map of the target segment. Hence, it would have no way of generating the correct numeric offset. Therefore, on the first reference to the offset, the *N*-map will bind the symbolic offset to the numeric offset within the segment. Again, the system will make provisions to avoid rebinding the symbol on subsequent references.

Within the segment descriptor, the base field points to the primary memory location where the segment is loaded. The offset is added to the base to obtain the address of the specific primary memory location. Thus, the segment base and limit values are used to relocate and bound check the reference at runtime, just as the relocation and limit registers are used for hardware dynamic relocation.

IMPLEMENTATION

Most segmentation implementations make simplifying assumptions about the system, so they do not implement the full address translation model described above. For example, the hardware dynamic relocation registers are a fundamental hardware mechanism used to address segments of memory, but they do not implement any form of memory protection.

Suppose the hardware incorporates a special set of registers that, as part of the process context, are loaded when the process is loaded onto the CPU (see Figure 12.16). The **segment table register (STR)** points to the location of the segment table itself. The hardware uses three additional CPU registers to manage address translation. The code segment base value is kept in the **code base register (CBR)**, also called the **procedure base register (PBR)** in some machines. A **data base register (DBR)** is used to dynamically relocate static data references, and a **stack base register (SBR)** points to a segment containing the process's stack. The implication is that successive instruction references to the segment indirectly addressed by the CBR can be executed very rapidly because no explicit binding is required. The architecture also suggests that the successive data references are to the same segment, while successive stack references are to the same stack.

✦ **FIGURE 12.16** Segmentation Address Translation Implementation

The general translation can be speeded up considerably by adding the STR, CBR, DBR, and SBR CPU registers. The STR references the process's descriptor segment. The CBR is an offset into the descriptor segment containing the segment descriptor for the code. The DBR and SBR serve a similar purpose for the data and segment descriptors, respectively.

The figure suggests that the hardware is able to perform an indirect addressing operation on the memory when it forms the target primary memory address. So, when an instruction fetch is in progress for offset location j, the contents of the base field in the segment descriptor pointed to by the CBR are used as the base address of the target segment. A performance penalty results because each memory reference must perform two memory accesses: The first access obtains the segment base address, and the second accesses the target memory location. As long as the process references the same code, data, and stack segments for some period of virtual time, the CBR, DBR, and SBR will not change. If the hardware also incorporates dynamic relocation hardware for the code, data, and stack registers (base and limit registers), those registers can be loaded by the hardware each time the corresponding STR base register is changed. The extreme memory access time overhead is limited to cases in which the process changes the context—code, data, or stack segment—in which it is executing.

The hardware depicted in Figure 12.16 does not provide any particular assistance for dynamic binding. The **S**-map must be evaluated in software, and the result can then be stored in the appropriate base register. If the code, data, or stack segment changes, then either the **S**-map must be reevaluated (if the inter-segment reference is to a segment not previously bound into the process's physical address space) or the CBR/DBR/SBR can be adjusted to point to the segment descriptor of a previously bound segment.

The programming language and compiler must be designed to utilize the segmentation hardware. The language must provide some mechanism by which the programmer can specify symbolic segment names. In assembly language programs, this specification is typically accomplished by a pseudo operation—for example, the `using` pseudo operation. In Figure 12.17, the assembler will initially generate code for `segmentA` in its own segment. The reference to `lab1` is a simple call instruction within the current segment. The CBR will not change when the instruction is executed. However, the call to [`segmentC`, `lab20`] will assemble to include instructions to load the CBR with a value determined by the segment name. The CBR load operand will be an external symbolic reference for `segmentC`, which is bound by **S** at runtime. The call instruction will follow the CBR load instruction and is of the same form as the previous call, with an operand of `lab20`. For the current discussion, assume the value of `lab20` is resolved before runtime.

✦ FIGURE 12.17 Inter-Segment References

The `using` pseudo operation indicates the segment for which the assembler should generate code. The `call` instruction operand includes a symbolic segment name (`segmentC`) and an offset name (`lab20`).

```
        using   segmentA
        ...
        call    lab1
        ...
        call    [segmentC, lab20]
        ...
lab1:   ...
        ...
        using   segmentB
        ...
        using   segmentC
        ...
lab20:  ...
        ...
```

The `using` pseudo operation causes the assembler, linkage editor, and loader to generate separate execution images for `segmentB` and `segmentC`. It is the task of the memory manager to dynamically link the segments at runtime. When `segmentA` is to be executed, it is loaded through a standard OS command. When the process encounters the symbolic segment reference to `segmentC`, the symbolic address must be bound to an address in primary memory.

The CBR load instruction must cause a trap to the OS. The normal instruction sequence will be interrupted, and control will be given to the OS just as if an interrupt had occurred. The OS will obtain the symbolic reference and use it to search the file system for the executable image of `segmentC`. Once found, the image is loaded into primary memory and an entry is made in the segment table to record that `segmentC` is now present. The CBR load instruction is modified, possibly using indirect links to avoid actual modifications to code, to point to the newly created segment descriptor. Finally, the CBR is loaded with the segment descriptor offset, and the instruction is restarted. On the second execution, the CBR load will encounter a segment descriptor offset. This offset will be loaded into the CBR, thus enabling the rest of the address translation to occur as if `segmentC` had been present on the first execution of the instruction.

The Multics Segmentation System

The Multics operating system was designed to support a very general form of segmentation with dynamic segment and offset binding [Organick, 1972]. No contemporary machine incorporates the hardware needed to implement the most general segmentation system. Multics was several decades before its time, and the trend in memory management likely will lead back to this form of segmentation.

The hardware that supports Multics, such as the Honeywell/GE 645 computer, has three segment registers (Figure 12.18):

- The STR to point at the segment table.
- A PBR that serves the same purpose as the CBR in the general discussion.
- A linkage base register (LBR) that replaces the SBR and DBR, since Multics makes no distinction between the static and dynamic data segments.

As in the general case, the PBR points to the segment descriptor for the code currently being executed. However, to accommodate segment sharing, the compiler produces a template for another level of indirection during address formation through a **linkage segment**. Whenever the segment is "made known" (bound into the address space the first time), a unique linkage segment is constructed from a compiler-generated template for the process that is invoking the shared segment. In Figure 12.18, the shared segment is called "`main`" and the linkage segment is called "`LS/main`." The linkage segment is pointed to by the segment table, and the LBR is set to point at the segment descriptor for the current linkage segment. Since the linkage segment is created from a compile-time template, it is correlated with the segment indices that are compiled into the shared segment. For example, the references to segments 1 and 2 refer to offsets in the linkage segment, not in the segment table.

Assume the linkage segment pointers have been set. When the `load [1, i]` instruction is executed, the hardware uses the LBR to find the linkage segment and the "1" to identify an entry in the linkage segment. Entry "1" in the linkage segment, in turn, points to a segment descriptor in the segment table for the data reference. The linkage segment has provided a one-level indirect addressing mechanism for the data reference.

✦ FIGURE 12.18 Multics Segmentation Mechanism

Multics uses STR, PBR, and LBR registers to reference the descriptor segment, procedure segment, and linkage segment. In Multics, each segment name is an offset into the linkage segment: This provides flexibility for where the destination segment is placed in the descriptor segment (flexibility that is required for sharing).

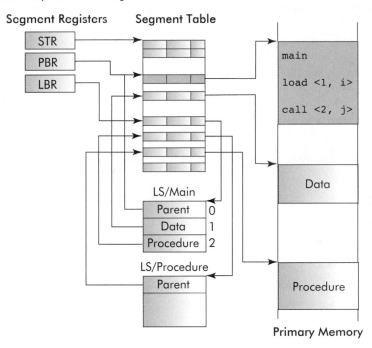

The procedure call instruction causes the PBR and the LBR to change, since the process is moving to a different segment for continued execution. The call [2, j] instruction causes the hardware to use the LBR to find the linkage segment entry and the pointer to a new segment descriptor. When the link is traversed, the system will change the LBR to point to the segment pointed to by LS/main. By convention, the first entry in the linkage segment points to the procedure segment to which it belongs. Thus, the system will follow the first pointer in the linkage segment to the segment descriptor for the called procedure segment, and the PBR will be set to address the new procedure segment descriptor, which points to the new procedure segment.

Linkage segments and procedure segments are constructed to allow runtime binding of symbolic segment names (see Figure 12.19). When the compiler encounters an intersegment call of the form

```
call [segmentName, offsetName]
```

it first creates an entry in an "out symbol table" containing the symbolic reference, segmentName. (The out symbol table is the Multics name for an external reference table that is not to be resolved by the linkage editor but rather is to contain symbols to be bound at runtime.) Next, the compiler adds an entry to the linkage segment at entry k that contains a pointer to the out symbol table entry. The entry also contains a fault flag that is ini-

✦ **FIGURE 12.19** Multics Binding Mechanism

This part of the binding mechanism binds symbolic names to segment offsets at runtime. The out symbol table keeps all the symbolic names, mapping each to a linkage segment entry. In the linkage segment, the name entry is compiled with a fault flag so that the first time the entry is referenced, it binds the name to a location. The mechanism then removes the fault flag so that subsequent references associate the bound name with the linkage address entry.

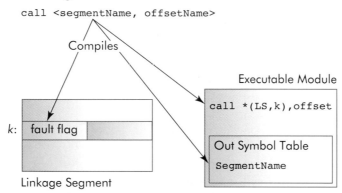

tialized to cause a fault the first time the out symbol is referenced. Finally, the compiler generates code of the form

```
call [(*linkageSegment, k), offset]
```

Now, when the call instruction is executed, it will branch indirectly to the *k*th entry in the linkage segment. On the first execution of the instruction, the fault flag will be set to cause a trap to the OS. The trap handler will follow the pointer in the linkage segment to the entry in the calling procedures out symbol table. The system can then retrieve the symbolic segment name from the out symbol table, retrieve the segment from secondary storage, enter a descriptor into the segment table, and modify the linkage segment so that it points to the appropriate segment descriptor. The fault flag is cleared to prevent subsequent missing segment faults. The symbolic offset can be handled similarly.

The Multics segmentation system is very complex, although the functionality it provides is more general than that of contemporary virtual memory systems. While it appears the complexity of the solution might severely impact performance, the hardware was designed to specifically support the segment mechanism and was very fast. Also, most of the mechanism was used only when there was an inter-segment reference.

12.7 ● MEMORY-MAPPED FILES

Some file systems provide a function to map a file's contents directly into the virtual address space so that the file can be read from or written to by referencing the corresponding virtual addresses. For one of these **memory-mapped files**, the file manager essentially forwards all `read()` and `write()` operations to the virtual memory manager. After the file has been mapped to a virtual address, X, then any reference to virtual address $X + i$ references byte b_i in the file. When parts of the file are referenced, they are copied into memory on a page-by-page basis, just as other pages are handled by the paging system. When a file is mapped into a virtual address space, that part of the virtual address space is backed up by the target file instead of the normal paging file.

For example, if process A opens a 64KB file and maps it into virtual address `0x20000000` to `0x2000FFFF`, then it can read or write the first byte in the file by reading or writing memory address `0x20000000`, or it can reference the sixteenth byte by referencing `0x2000000F`.

In Windows, the memory-mapped file mechanism provides a simple loader for executable files. After the process is created with its 4GB virtual address space, the system checks the size of the `.EXE` file, and then reserves that amount of space in the virtual address space (starting at location `0x00400000`). Finally, the system notes that the secondary storage that backs up the virtual address space is the `.EXE` file rather than in a page file. The loading process continues by determining the DLLs that are known at load time, reserving virtual addresses for each DLL, and noting that the backing store for the DLL is the DLL file rather than the page file.

There is another aspect of memory-mapped files that makes them even more useful (see Figure 12.20). Since the information is logically referenced as a filename, more than one process can map the same file into its own virtual address space at the same time. Now suppose process A mapped a 64KB file into its locations `0x2000000` to `0x2000FFFF`,

✦ FIGURE 12.20 Memory-Mapped Files

Memory-mapped files are handled much like paging files (see Figure 12.12). When a reference is made to a virtual address associated with the file, the information is loaded from the file if it is missing, or referenced in shared pages if it is loaded.

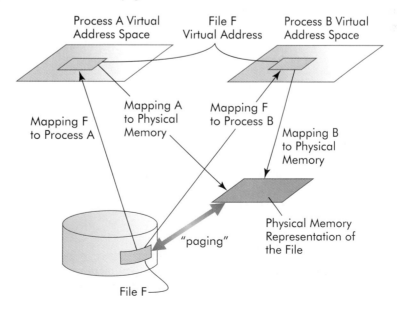

and process B opened the same file and mapped it to its virtual address 0x30000000 to 0x3000FFFF of its own address space Then process B could "transmit" information to process A by writing information at, say, location 0x30001234, and process A could read the information from its virtual address 0x20001234.

Windows assures that memory write operations are seen by both processes when they occur. If two or more processes have the file opened at the same time, the OS recognizes this and manages both processes' page table pointers so that they reference one copy of the disk block in memory. For example, suppose p_i and p_j have opened a memory-mapped file. As shown in Figure 12.21, blocks i to i + 3 have been cached into memory. p_i is using blocks $i + 2$ and $i + 3$ while p_j is using blocks i, $i + 1$, and $i + 2$. When either process changes a file block, the other process immediately sees the change, since the change is captured in the cached-in storage blocks. The memory-mapped pages could be paged out at any time. However, performance will be best if the pages being used by either process remain in memory.

✦ **FIGURE 12.21** Shared Blocks in Memory-Mapped Files

This figure illustrates how different B_t maps (page tables) reference shared blocks of information in the primary memory.

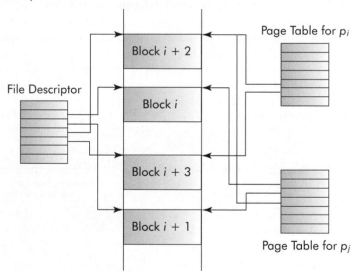

Shared memory-mapped files make no special provision for automatically managing critical sections. If a memory-mapped file is being shared by a set of threads and any of the threads is updating the file, then all of the threads will have to use a synchronization mechanism such as a semaphore to ensure that critical sections are not violated.

12.8 ● SUMMARY

Virtual memory systems are an abstraction of the primary memory in a von Neumann computer. Even in a time of decreasing physical memory costs, contemporary computers devote considerable resources to support virtual address spaces that are much larger than the physical memory allocated to a process. Contemporary software relies heavily on virtual memory to support applications such as image management with huge memory requirements.

The virtual memory abstraction is built on the idea of runtime address binding. The compiler and the linkage editor create an absolute module that the loader traditionally binds to physical addresses before the program executes. Hardware facilities enable a memory manager to automatically load portions of a virtual address space into primary memory, while the rest of the address space is left in secondary memory.

Paging systems transfer fixed-sized blocks of information between primary and secondary memories. Because of the fixed page size and page frame size, the translation from a binary virtual address to a corresponding physical address is relatively simple, provided the system has an efficient table lookup mechanism. Paging systems use associative memories to implement page translation tables.

A paging system can be characterized by specifying its fetch, placement, and replacement policies. Demand paging algorithms use a fetch policy whereby a page is loaded only when it is referenced. In contrast, a prefetch policy may load several pages when it detects any particular page missing. Most paging algorithms use the demand fetch rule.

The placement policy identifies the page frame in which to store a page when it is to be loaded. In static algorithms, the placement policy is to use the page frame of the page to be replaced if all frames are full. There are several different replacement strategies, including the random, Belady's optimal, LRU, LFU, and FIFO algorithms.

LRU and LFU are stack algorithms, while FIFO and random are not. LRU has been the dominant static demand algorithm in commercial computers, but it is difficult to implement precisely because of the need to keep an inordinately large amount of information about the reference stream. The page translation table can use reference bits to approximate the LRU strategy; the more reference bits, the better the approximation.

Dynamic allocation paging attempts to adjust the number of page frames allocated to a process according to its needs. This can be done by considering an LRU strategy on a window on the reference stream, as is done in the working set algorithm.

Segmentation is an alternative to paging. It differs from paging in that the unit of transfer between primary and secondary memories varies. The size of the segments is also explicitly known by the programmer. Translating a segment virtual address to a physical address is more complex than translating a paging virtual address. The segment and offset may both have to be translated at runtime. Multics, although over 25 years old, remains the most comprehensive segmentation system that is implemented commercially.

Segmentation makes the relationship between the primary and secondary memories depend on the existence of a file system, since segments are stored on the storage devices as files. The details of the file manager are covered in the next chapter.

12.9 • EXERCISES

1. Why are the page size, the number of pages in the virtual address space, and the number of page frames in the physical address space all a power of 2 in binary machines?

2. Suppose a paging system has 2^{g+h} virtual addresses and uses 2^{h+k} locations in primary memory for integers g, h, and k. Write an expression for the implied page size of the system. How many bits are required to store a virtual address?

3. Suppose the page size in a computing environment is 1KB. Give the page number and the offset for the following:

   a. 899 (a decimal number)

   b. 23456 (a decimal number)

   c. 0x3F244 (a hexadecimal number)

   d. 0x0017C (a hexadecimal number)

4. In a hypothetical Linux system, each virtual address is 32 bits with a 10-bit page size, 256-entry page table, 32-entry page middle directory, and 256-entry page directory. Using the Linux model described in this chapter, what is the page directory entry, page middle directory entry, page table entry, and page offset for each of the following virtual addresses?

   a. 0x12345678

   b. 0x456789ab

   c. 0xba987654

   d. 0x87654321

5. Contemporary computers often have more than 100MB of physical memory. Suppose the page size is 2KB. How many entries would an associative memory need in order to implement a page table for the memory?

6. Use an example to explain the different representations of a reference to a variable in the name space, the virtual address space, and the physical address space. Using your example, show how the virtual address is derived from the name and how the physical address is derived from the virtual address.

7. What factors could influence the size of the virtual address space in a modern computer system? In your answer, consider the memory-mapping unit, compiler technology, and instruction format.

8. What factors could influence the size of the physical address space in a modern computer system? (Consider various parts of the hardware.)

9. A researcher at Famous University invented a new static demand paging algorithm, called the future least frequently used (or FLFU) strategy in which the page chosen for replacement is the one that is currently loaded, but which will be the least frequently used in the future (the researcher did not provide an implementation for FLFU). Write the formal description for FLFU paging (in the style used in Section 12.4).

10. Professor Jabberwocky of More Famous University read about the FLFU algorithm from the previous problem, and published a paper with a proof that FLFU is optimal. Argue for or against Jabberwocky's conjecture.

11. Suppose $R = 3, 2, 4, 3, 4, 2, 2, 3, 4, 5, 6, 7, 7, 6, 5, 4, 5, 6, 7, 2, 1$ is a page reference stream.

a. Given a page frame allocation of 3 and assuming the primary memory is initially unloaded, how many page faults will the given reference stream incur under Belady's optimal algorithm?

b. Given a page frame allocation of 3 and assuming the primary memory is initially unloaded, how many page faults will the given reference stream incur under LRU?

c. Given a page frame allocation of 3 and assuming the primary memory is initially unloaded, how many page faults will the given reference stream incur under FIFO?

d. Given a window size of 6 and assuming the primary memory is initially unloaded, how many page faults will the given reference stream incur under the working-set algorithm?

e. Given a window size of 6 and assuming the primary memory is initially unloaded, what is the working-set size under the given reference stream after the entire stream has been processed?

12. Let R = 0, 3, 1, 4, 1, 5, 1, 6, 0, 5, 2, 6, 7, 5, 0, 0, 0, 6, 6, 6, 6 be a page reference stream. Answer parts a–e for Problem 11 for this reference stream.

13. Describe a program that could be expected to have the following:

a. A small code locality and a small data locality

b. A small code locality and a large data locality

c. A large code locality and a small data locality

d. A large code locality and a large data locality

14. Suppose hardware was designed to incorporate three reference bits rather than the single bit used in the LRU implementation described in Section 12.3. Explain how a better approximation to LRU could be achieved using the 3-bit field than can be achieved using the single reference bit.

15. What is the advantage of the page fault frequency algorithm over the estimation of the working set using the window size w? What is its disadvantage?

16. Construct a sample reference stream illustrating Belady's anomaly for frame allocations of 3 and 4.

17. In a paging system, page boundaries are transparent to the programmer. Explain how a loop might cause thrashing in a static allocation paging system when the memory allocation is too small.

18. Why is locality not an issue in a segmentation system?

19. Explain how it might be possible to build an OS that uses full segmentation, but has *no* file system.

20. Suppose two processes share a main program segment, but each has its own private implementation of a procedure called from the main segment and private data segments. Draw a figure similar to Figure 12.18 to illustrate how the segment registers and segments might be set up to accommodate this situation.

Memory-Mapped Files

This exercise can be solved in WindowsNT/2000/XP systems.

This Lab Exercise uses memory-mapped files to share information among pairs of processes. There are *Source* and *Sink* processes that read and write conventional disk-based files, but also two processes, *Encrypt* and *Decrypt*, that should be designed to filter the information transmitted by the Source and received by the Sink. Figure 12.22 shows the way the four processes should communicate with one another. The Sink should read a byte stream from an ordinary file and then write the output to the first memory-mapped file. Encrypt should read the memory-mapped file, encrypt each byte in the byte stream and then write it to the (named) pipe. The Decrypt process reads encrypted bytes from the pipe, decrypts them, and writes them to the second memory-mapped file. The Sink reads the data from the second memory-mapped file and then writes the data to a second ordinary file.

Your encryption algorithm can be very simple, for example, converting uppercase letters to lowercase, and vice versa. The decryption algorithm should be the inverse of the encryption algorithm. There is no real need to use a named pipe between Encrypt and Decrypt, except to practice using another IPC mechanism.

In order to see the behavior of the configuration, you should use a delay in each of the modules.

✦ FIGURE 12.22   Process Configuration

The Sink reads a byte stream from an ordinary file and then writes the output to the first memory-mapped file. Encrypt reads the memory-mapped file encrypts each byte in the byte stream and then writes it to the (named) pipe. The Decrypt process reads encrypted bytes from the pipe, decrypts them, and writes them to the second memory-mapped file. The Sink reads the data from the second memory-mapped file and then writes the data to a second ordinary file.

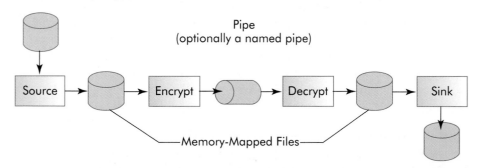

● BACKGROUND ●

Since threads within a process share the underlying process's address space, all threads implicitly share all their information with their siblings. Windows NT/2000/XP, like all modern operating systems, provides protection barriers between the address spaces for each process, meaning that a thread running in one address space is ordinarily prevented from sharing information with a thread in a different process since neither can ordinarily read or write the other's address space. Providing a mechanism to allow sharing across process address spaces is a classic problem for the OS. The IPC mechanisms described in Section 9.3 show some ways to accomplish the task. However, memory-mapped files are the preferred mechanism for sharing information among address spaces for processes on a single machine. Windows NT/2000/XP has been designed so that memory-mapped files are implemented at a low layer of the operating system—in the Virtual Memory manager—and they are made to be very efficient.

THE MEMORY-MAPPED FILE FUNCTIONS

To use a memory-mapped file you must:

- Obtain a handle to the file by creating or opening it.
- Reserve virtual addresses for the file.
- Establish a mapping between the file and your virtual address space.

A file handle is obtained using `CreateFile()` or `OpenFile()`. The `CreateFile()` function is described in Chapter 2. When it is used with memory-mapped files, the normal parameters are used to create/open the file.

After a file has been opened, a file mapping object (called a *section object* in the documentation), stores the mapping information. It is created with `CreateFileMapping()`:

```
HANDLE CreateFileMapping(
    HANDLE hfile,
    LPSECURITY_ATTRIBUTE lpFileMappingAttributes,
    DWORD flProtect,
    DWORD dwMaximumSizeHigh,
    DWORD dwMaximumSizeLow,
    LPCTSTR lpName
);
```

The `hfile` parameter is the handle returned by `CreateFile()` (or `OpenFile()`). The `lpFileMappingAttributes` parameter is the usual pointer to a `SECURITY_ATTRIBUTE` data structure, used if the handle is to be inherited. The `flProtect` parameter is one of `PAGE_READONLY`, `PAGE_READWRITE`, or `PAGE_WRITE-COPY`. The value of this parameter must be compatible with the privileges in the `hfile` handle. Read-only access means that the calling process is only requesting read access to the region holding the pages for the file, and so on. Another flag can be OR-ed with the basic protection parameter to cause virtual addresses for the mapping to be reserved or committed. The maximum size of the space to be mapped is a 64-bit value, so its two halves are passed using the next two parameters, `dwMaximumSizeHigh` and `dwMaximumSizeLow`. Finally, the mapping object may use a name, `lpName`, or use `NULL`. If `lpName` is `NULL`, the mapping object is created without a name and cannot normally be shared. If the `lpName` is defined and already exists, this request is to use the existing named mapping object. If the `lpName` is defined but does not exist, it is created.

The handle returned by the call to `CreateFileMapping()` can be used like any other handle: It can be inherited by child processes, or replicated in another address space using

DuplicateHandle(). The OpenFileMapping() function can also be used with mapping objects that have a name:

```
HANDLE OpenFileMapping(
    DWORD dwDesiredAccess,
    BOOL bInheritHandle,
    LPCTSTR lpName
);
```

Once the mapping object has been created, the address space will have been established and the mapping object created even though the file contents will not have actually been mapped to the process's address space. This is accomplished using

```
LPVOID MapViewOfFile(
    HANDLE hFileMappingObject,
    DWORD dwDesiredAccess,
    DWORD dwFileOffsetHigh,
    DWORD dwFileOffsetLow,
    DWORD dwNumberOfBytesToMap
};
```

The hFileMappingObject parameter is the handle of the file mapping object returned by the CreateFileMapping() call. The dwDesiredAccess parameter specifies the way the mapping object can be used to access data, provided it is compatible with the hlProtect parameter used with CreateFileMapping():

- FILE_MAP_WRITE. Reading and writing via the mapping object is acceptable.
- FILE_MAP_READ. Threads will only read the memory-mapped file using the mapping object.
- FILE_MAP_ALL_ACCESS. Same as FILE_MAP_WRITE.
- FILE_MAP_COPY. This value uses the copy-on-write feature of the virtual memory. If the mapping object is created with PAGE_WRITECOPY and the view with FILE_MAP_COPY, the process will have a view to file, but a write to the file will not go to the original data file.

You can map the whole file into the address space, or only a subset of it—called a **view** of the file. The 64-bit file offset—the two DWORD parameters—specifies the file pointer where the mapping should begin when mapping a view, and dwNumberOfBytesToMap specifies the number of bytes in the view. The file pointer must be a multiple of the allocation granularity. The function chooses an acceptable place in the address space to which it will map the file and then returns that value. If you want to manually choose the location, use MapViewOfFileEx(), which has a sixth parameter, LPVOID lpBaseAddress, which can be set to be the virtual address at which the file mapping starts. The lpBaseAddress must be a multiple of the allocation granularity.

File coherence refers to the situation in which every process that has the file open sees the same information in the file. The difficulty in ensuring coherence arises in a situation where there are copies of the information allocated in different parts of the system. If one copy is changed, there is a lag time until the other copies can be updated. If two processes use the same mapping object—or use mapping objects where one is derived from the other—Windows NT/2000/XP assures that both processes always see the same file content. The kernel does not make copies of the pages holding part of the file that is loaded in the primary memory. Instead, the two processes map to a single page that contains the target data.

If a memory-mapped file is being used as described above, then a third process opens the file as an ordinary file, the `ReadFile()` and `WriteFile()` operations performed by the third process will not necessarily be coherent with the memory-mapped view of the file. This situation arises because the unmapped file operations use conventional file caching and disk I/O, potentially introducing two copies of the information that should be in the file. Windows NT/2000/XP does not assure that these two copies will be the same at all times.

Finally, if you map a view of a file, then it is necessary to unmap the view when you have finished using it.

```
BOOL UnmapViewOfFile(
    LPCVOID lpBaseAddress
);
```

The `lpBaseAddress` parameter is the virtual address where the view begins: the value returned by the `MapViewOfFile` function.

● **ATTACKING THE PROBLEM** ●

This exercise involves a relatively large amount of code, so you are likely to find some challenge in getting all the code written and working together. The solution uses a fifth process to launch the four processes specified in the assignment. The skeleton for this fifth program is shown next:

```
// The main program establishes the shared information used
// by the source, encrypt, decrypt, and sink processes
int main(int argc, char *argv[]) {
// Create the pipe from encrypt to decrypt
// Create producer process
  if(!CreateProcess(...)) {
    fprintf(stderr, "...", GetLastError())
    getc(stdin);
    ExitProcess(1);
  }
  Sleep(500);       // Give producer a chance to run

// Create encryption process
  if(!CreateProcess(...)) {
    fprintf(stderr, "...", GetLastError())
    getc(stdin);
    ExitProcess(1);
  }
  Sleep(500);       // Give Encrypt a chance to run

// Create decryption process
  if(!CreateProcess(...)) {
    fprintf(stderr, "...", GetLastError())
```

```
      getc(stdin);
      ExitProcess(1);
    }
    Sleep(500);        // Give Decrypt a chance to run

// Create consumer process
    if(!CreateProcess(...)) {
      fprintf(stderr, "...", GetLastError())
      getc(stdin);
      ExitProcess(1);
    }
    Sleep(500);        // Give consumer a chance to run

// Wait for producer, encrypt, decrypt & consumer to die
  }
```

The source program has a relatively straightforward organization, as do the remaining three programs. The following code skeleton should get you started on a full solution.

```
/* The source process reads information from the source
 *file then uses a memory-mapped file to transfer
 * the information to the encrypt process.
 */
int main (int argc, char *argv[]) {
// Open the source file
  sourceFile = CreateFile (...)
  if(sourceFile == INVALID_HANDLE_VALUE) {
    fprintf(stderr, GetLastError());
    getc(stdin);
    ExitProcess(1);
  }

// Open the memory-mapped file and map it
  peMMFFile = CreateFile (...);
  if(peMMFFile == INVALID_HANDLE_VALUE) {
    fprintf(stderr, "...", GetLastError()
    getc(stdin);
    ExitProcess(1);
  }
// Create the mapping object
  peMMFMap = CreateFileMapping(...);
  if(peMMFMap == NULL) {
    fprintf(stderr, "...", GetLastError());
    getc(stdin);
    ExitProcess(1);
  }
// Create the view
  baseAddr = (PBYTE) MapViewOfFile(...);
  if(baseAddr == NULL) {
    fprintf(stderr, "...", GetLastError()
    getc(stdin);
```

```
    ExitProcess(1);
  }
  srand(P_RAND_SEED);                // Set random# seed
// Main loop to process the source file
  while(...) {
  // To exercise synch mechanisms
    Sleep(rand()%timeToProduce);
  // Write information to memory-mapped file
  // by writing to the baseAddr
  }
// Terminate
}
```

You will be sharing both memory-mapped files, with one of the threads writing each file. This means that a correct solution must incorporate a synchronization mechanism to prevent critical section violations.

CHAPTER 13

File Management

Files are the OS mechanism for saving information from one session to another. They also are used as containers for archiving information for long periods of time. The language translation system uses the file system to store relocatable, absolute, and executable programs. Segmentation virtual memory managers rely on the file system to store the segments. Programmers rely on the file system to simplify the use of storage devices to hold sets of data. An individual e-mail message is delivered as a file. An HTML web page is a file.

This chapter describes the concepts that guide file management design, including a description of the types of files the system might support and descriptions of file system implementations. Finally, the chapter discusses how the directory capability is provided to allow users to manage their files.

13.1 • THE TASK AT HAND

Files are one of the most significant OS abstractions (building on earlier device abstractions). Programmers have used files to save information on storage devices since the very early days of computing. Even into the late 1980s, the primary abstraction exported by MS-DOS was the file abstraction. Files are still the backbone of computing: They are used to transfer bulk information such as HTML web pages from one application to another (see Figure 13.1). Logically, the web page is created with an HTML editor, and read by a web browser. In reality, the web page is created, then written to a file. The file can then be written to a storage device (or copied across the network). The file consumer retrieves the file from the storage device (or from the network), and then reads its contents into its address space. The file manager creates an abstract environment in which applications are never concerned about the details of persistent storage or network transmission. The application just opens a file, writes information to it, and closes it. When another application wants to retrieve the information, it just opens the file, reads the information, and closes it.

✦ FIGURE 13.1 Transferring HTML Information

This figure illustrates the file abstraction and its implementation. In the abstraction, information is stored as structured data in a file (in the HTML case, the structure is defined by the tags). In reality, the information is converted into a stream of contiguously addressed bytes and stored on the block-oriented storage devices. When user is ready to utilize the information, it is retrieved and converted back into a byte stream by the file manager. The web browser application interprets the tags to recover the structure of the data.

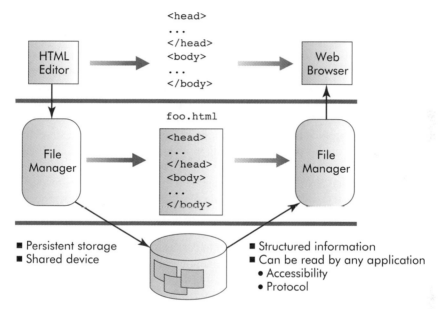

Before 1960, the motivation for having a computer was usually to perform high-speed computation. Most applications were computation-intensive procedures, designed to predict the trajectory of a missile, solve a system of equations, or perform other "scientific" computations. By 1960, a significant evolution was underway in which people realized that computers could actually be very powerful information storage and manipulation tools. Rather than just performing high-speed computations, computers could also be used to store large amounts of information, process the information to generate new forms of the information, and save the new form.

Two distinct types of computers evolved in those early years: scientific computers and commercial (or data processing) computers. The scientific computers continued to focus on high-speed computation, but the new commercial computers were designed to support I/O-intensive applications such as payroll, inventory control, billing, and decision support. Of course, this had an impact on the style of OS for the two different domains: Operating systems for the commercial computers switched their focus from factors that were important for computation-intensive applications (such as optimizing the CPU utilization) to ones that were more important in I/O-intensive applications (such as being able to overlap input and output operations with CPU computation). During the 1960s and 1970s, the two camps developed their own computers, operating systems, programming languages, and programmers. It was rare to find a programmer who was an expert in both scientific and commercial computing.

By the 1980s, the distinction between scientific and commercial computing began to grow fuzzy: People who were interested in "scientific" computing began to realize that many of their emerging applications were I/O-intensive. For example, a program to predict the weather needed to be able to read immense amounts of data describing today's weather all over the world *and* solve a large system of partial differential equations, so that it could predict the weather for the next day. At the same time, the commercial computing world began to find increasingly computation-intensive applications. For example, people began to realize that they could take all the data describing stock market behavior and use sophisticated mathematical programs to predict market behavior. By 1990, people realized that the same hardware and OS could be used to support either kind of application, so we have seen the gradual (but not complete) erosion of the distinction between the two camps. (As you have probably guessed, it is primarily the people who haven't changed. ☺)

Files are the technology base for information management in all contemporary computer systems (although databases are increasingly displacing the time-honored file abstraction). Even though commercial application domains rely on more structure in the data than do scientific application domains, both ultimately depend on fundamental behavior from the file system. From the application programmer's perspective—see Chapter 2—files are the fundamental abstraction of secondary storage devices (such as magnetic tapes or disk drives). Ultimately, each file is a named collection of data stored on a device.

File management is the part of the OS that implements the file abstraction, directories for organizing files, and file systems for organizing collections of directories (see Figure 13.2). This chapter examines the issues related to the design and implementation of all file managers (for both scientific and commercial applications domains). We first study files and their operations, then directories, and finally file systems.

13.2 • FILES

Almost every application program reads information from one or more files, processes the data, and then writes the result to one or more other files. For example, an accounts payable program reads one file containing invoices and another containing purchase orders, correlates the data, and then prints a check and writes a file to describe the expenditures. A compiler reads a source program file, translates the program into machine code, and then writes a relocatable file and an error report file. An optimization program reads a description of the space to be analyzed from a file, searches the space for global minima and/or maxima, and then writes the result to an output file.

This model of operation is so prevalent that it is built into the C programming model. For example, when a process is created in a C runtime environment (like UNIX or Windows console applications), it has default access to three files:

- `stdin` as a file abstraction of the input device
- `stdout` as an abstraction of the normal output device
- `stderr` as an error log file

✦ FIGURE 13.2 The External View of the File Manager

The file manager is the last major component of a modern OS. It makes heavy use of the device manager, since it reads and writes storage devices. Then it exports an abstraction that allows application programs to manipulate named byte streams.

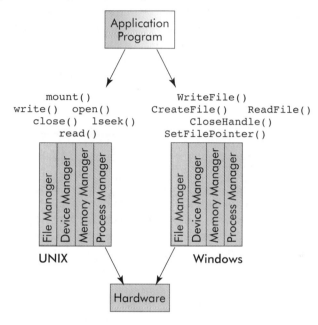

(In C runtime systems, the default is for stdin, stdout, and stderr to reference communication devices rather than storage devices, although the corresponding devices are referenced using the file interface, as explained in Chapter 5.) The extreme interpretation of this view of computing is that programs are simply a means of defining filters for reading a file, transforming the data into some other form, and then writing the result to another file. In fact, this is an early programming paradigm used to describe UNIX applications: They are just filters that translate one file's contents into information to be stored in another file [Kernighan and Pike, 1984].

In the general view, a file is a container for a collection of information. Besides providing the abstraction, the file manager provides a protection mechanism that allows users to administer how the information can be accessed by other users. File protection is a fundamental property of files because it allows different people to store their information on a shared computer, with the confidence that the information can be kept confidential.

How is the functionality provided by the file manager related to virtual memory?

■ The goals of file management and virtual memory are different. The goal of a virtual memory implementation is to support a very large address space in executable memory. A process's full address space image is created and maintained in the secondary memory, and then parts of it are loaded into primary memory as needed. The goal of file management is to provide a manual mechanism for storing/retrieving information to/from storage devices. Paging virtual memory managers provide one abstraction of secondary memory, and files provide a different one. Segmentation virtual memory coexists with file management, since segments are not logically at odds with files. In Windows NT/2000/XP, memory-mapped files straddle the notions of file and paged virtual memory (see Section 12.7), allowing broad use of both concepts.

■ The file abstraction predates virtual memory technology by several years. It had become well entrenched by the time virtual memory could be used to reference large address spaces in secondary memory. Programmers were, and still are, accustomed to using files to save information for indefinite periods of time, while virtual memory contents stored in secondary memory are temporary images (lasting as long as the related process exists).

■ The filenames of all files in secondary memory are accessible from any address space, while virtual memory contents are available only to the process associated with them. As a result, modern operating systems employ both paging and file systems as separate interfaces to secondary memory.

When applications operate on data, they rely on the presence of *structure* in the data, represented as collections of *records* that contain typed *fields* of information (see Figure 13.3). For example, an invoice is an individual record in a file. The invoice record has different fields for names, addresses, the invoice amount, and so on. There is application domain-specific structure on the data in the files to reflect numerical data, images, and audio information.

Unfortunately, as explained in Chapter 5, storage devices are capable of storing only linearly addressed blocks of bytes. The file system provides an abstraction from storage blocks to data structures suitable for use by application programs. At a minimum, the file system provides an abstraction that links blocks of the storage system together to form a logical collection of information called **stream-block translation** (or **marshalling** and **unmarshalling**) in Figure 13.3. Conceptually, such a translation allows one to store and retrieve an arbitrary stream of linearly addressed bytes on the block-oriented storage system.

When an application's data structure is written to a storage device, it will have to be "flattened" into a byte stream by a marshalling record-stream translation procedure, as shown in Figure 13.3. Then the stream can be stored as a set of blocks. Later, when the data is retrieved, it will be read block-by-block, converted into a stream of bytes, and then converted back (unmarshalled) into the application-level data structure. Should the record-stream conversion facilities be provided by the file system? Or does it make more sense for the file system to provide only a minimum structuring facility, with the expectation that programmers will impose their own structure on the data?

Traditionally, commercial systems provided extensive file facilities to support data structuring, while scientific systems left structuring to the application. Today, both UNIX and Windows operating systems follow the scientific systems approach, leaving structuring to the application. The Apple Macintosh system software provides less general facilities for structuring data than does a conventional commercial system, but more functionality than do Windows and UNIX. If an OS provides only the stream-block translation facilities, it is said to provide a **low-level file system**. If the file system provides the record-stream translation, it is a **structured** (or **high-level**) **file system**. Windows and

✦ FIGURE 13.3 Information Structure

Applications generally define their own extended data structures (the `struct` primitive in C).
Most C programmers also use the `stdio` library for formatted, buffered file I/O. In this kind of
environment, record-stream translation is accomplished by the programmer and the language runtime library. The OS is only expected to provide byte-stream files.

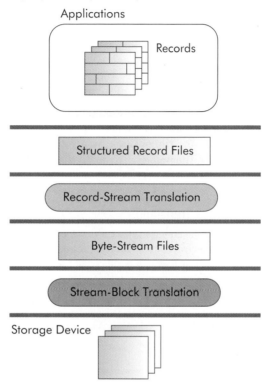

UNIX provide low-level file systems, while computers designed especially to support
commercial applications (such as the IBM MVS) provide a structured file system. Since
the Macintosh provides some record-stream translation facilities, we call it a high-level
file system.

Structured file systems must provide a specialized language (a general data structure
description language) to define data structures used by the record-stream translator. The
facility may be simple, allowing the programmer to define a record length and a key field
for identifying each record. Or it may be sophisticated enough to allow storage and
retrieval of records based on arbitrary fields. The most functional and flexible systems are
database management systems. While a database management system is a logical extension of the storage devices, the OS may provide a low-level interface used by application
programs to implement the database management system.

Storage systems that support multimedia documents are growing in importance.
Contemporary applications require the OS to be able to handle information containers that
represent, for example, numerical data, typeset textual data, graphics, images, and audio
information. Ordinary low-level file systems are not designed to accommodate these mul-

timedia documents because different media types potentially require different access and modification strategies for efficient I/O. For example, the technique for efficient access of an image differs from one for accessing a floating-point number. More and more application domains are requiring the OS to provide flexible, high-performance access methods suitable for use with multimedia data, where the methods are defined by the programmer.

LOW-LEVEL FILES

A low-level, byte-stream file manager implements the stream-block translation in Figure 13.4. A **byte-stream file** is a named sequence of bytes indexed by the nonnegative integers; you can think of a byte stream as a large array of bytes, each with an index: The first byte has index 0, the second has index 1, and so on. By convention, in byte-stream files, every process that opens a file uses a *file position* to reference a particular byte in the file. When the file is opened, the file position references the first byte in the file. Each k-byte read or write operation advances the file position by a value of k. At any given moment after the file has been opened, the file pointer references the next byte in the file to be read from or written to.

✦ FIGURE 13.4   Stream-Block Translation

Stream-block translation marshalls/unmarshalls bytes to/from the device-specific blocks. This translation mechanism uses the raw device interface to read/write blocks, and then exports the file API on the left side of the figure. Application programs can read/write byte streams without knowing the details of the device I/O.

As suggested by the specific file manipulation interfaces in Chapter 2, the following are typical operations on a byte-stream file:

■ open(fileName): The fileName is a character string that uniquely identifies a file. The operation prepares the file for reading or writing. The open() operation causes information in the file descriptor to reflect that the file is being put into use. It also may cause additional descriptors to be opened to manage the open file. (For example, if the system supports shared files, then a process-specific descriptor will be opened to keep the file position setting for this process.) The operation sets the file position to 0, and returns a file identifier used as an argument to the other file operations. If the file manager supports file modes (such as "open for reading, but not writing" or "open for reading and writing"), then the appropriate mode will also be a parameter to open().

■ close(fileID): This operation deallocates the internal descriptors created when the file was opened, along with any other resources used by the file system to manage the byte-stream I/O.

■ read(fileID, buffer, length): This operation copies a block of length (or fewer) bytes beginning at the current file position into the buffer for the specified file identifier, fileID. If the file position is L bytes from the end of the stream and $L <$ length, then only L bytes will be copied to the buffer. The operation increments the file position by the number of bytes read and returns that number. If the file is positioned at the end of the stream when read() is invoked, an end-of-file condition is returned.

■ write(fileID, buffer, length): This operation writes length bytes of the information from the buffer to the current file position and then increments the file position by length.

■ seek(fileID, filePosition): This operation changes the value of the file position to the value of the parameter, filePosition. Subsequent read/write operations reference the data whose index corresponds to the new value of the file position.

As you can see from these file manipulation commands, the programmer can read and write sequences of bytes from/to the file, according to the operation and the value of the file position. The file manager makes no provision for adding structure to the byte stream. In this kind of file manager, the interpretation of the byte stream as structured data will be done completely by the applications that read and write the byte stream.

STRUCTURED FILES

With a low-level file manager, an application that wants to treat a byte stream as a sequence of records must convert the "raw" bytes into a stream of records with application-specific data structures, as suggested by Figure 13.3. That is, they use the low-level file manipulation commands to read and write a stream of bytes, and then they implement their own record-stream translation mechanism that converts the byte stream to/from a collection of structured records. The application then operates on each structured record.

The use of character files in UNIX illustrates how a community of applications can provide this translation through both convention and the use of a library of support functions: UNIX files are byte-stream files, although various classes of UNIX applications impose additional structure on the byte stream with no explicit support from the OS. The classic example is ASCII character files. Over the years, a set of different programs has been written to process byte-stream (text) files known to contain characters. Application software makes two assumptions about these text files. First, the byte stream contains only "printable" ASCII characters, and, second, the characters are arranged into "lines," with each line terminated by the NEWLINE character.

The OS file manager does not distinguish text files from other byte streams, although several commands (including UNIX system software and library routines) *do* make the distinction. For example, the word count program, wc, reads a file, counts the number of NEWLINE characters, the number of "words" in the file as determined by the placement of punctuation and "whitespace" in the file, and the number of characters in the file as determined by the number of bytes in the file. Then it prints these counts with the name of the file. Of course, a user can apply wc to any file, such as a relocatable object file. wc will assume the file is a text file and count the number of lines, words, and characters appearing in the file—producing results that have no useful meaning. Various other programs have been written explicitly to process text files and have been added to the command library. For example, grep, diff, and vi operate on text files. These nonkernel extensions provide a substantial utility to the system, while the OS implements only the essentials of the byte stream.

The UNIX character file example highlights the fact that if the file manager does not support data structures, then the applications must provide that capability. Alternatively, the file manager might be designed so that it was able to translate storage blocks to/from application-oriented structured records (see Figure 13.5).

✦ FIGURE 13.5 Record-Block Translation

It is possible to incorporate record-block translation into the OS file manager. In this case, the application must be able to convey the target data structure definitions to the file manager; then it can translate the byte stream according to this specification.

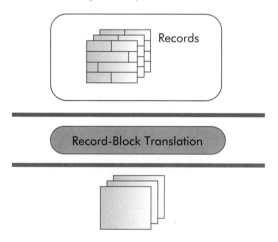

A structured file can be used to hold any kind of information, including absolute program images, relocatable object programs, libraries, numeric data organized according to the needs of some set of applications, textual data such as source programs, word processing documents, graphic images, and audio/video streams. Ultimately, structured files are represented on the storage medium as a collection of blocks. The mechanism that implements the record-block translation must be able to marshall the structure of the data when it writes it into disk blocks. Then when the information is read from disk blocks, the file manager must be able to reconstitute the structure for the application. Over the years, structured file managers have taken a spectrum of strategies for supporting structured data; the next three subsections describe the most popular approaches.

RECORD-ORIENTED SEQUENTIAL FILES Many applications need to store and access a set of records as a list. For example, an electronic mail system stores messages and folders of messages. A mail message could be processed by many different programs, such as an editor, a mail transport program, a mail receipt program, a mail posting program, and a mail browsing program. Hence, it is convenient to incorporate general information about electronic mail in well-defined parts of the file. This is done by formatting each message as a record, with the various parts of a message being fields of the record. A mail folder can then be implemented as a file containing several such records. Each mail program uses this fixed record structure in a consistent manner. This can be accomplished by building an abstract machine on top of a byte-stream file that has knowledge of a mail message structure. The programmer could also implement an alternative file system that handled collections of records directly on the device drivers (see again Figure 13.5).

A **structured sequential file** is a named sequence of logical records (as contrasted with a stream of bytes), indexed by the nonnegative integers. As with byte-stream files, access to the file is defined by a file position, but in this case the position indexes records in the file instead of bytes. Operations on the file are as follows:

- open(fileName): Performs the same function as the open() for byte-stream files on the given fileName and returns a file identifier used in the other operations.

- close(fileID): Performs the same function as the close() for byte-stream files on the given file identifier, fileID.

- getRecord(fileID, record): Returns the record addressed by file position.

- putRecord(fileID, record): Writes the designated record at the current position.

- seek(fileID, position): Moves the file position to point at the designated record.

These operations are equivalent to the operations for the byte-stream file, except the data are stored in records instead of bytes.

What is the format of a record in the file? One approach is to allocate k bytes to contain each record, with an additional H bytes for record descriptor information (see Figure 13.6). The getRecord() and putRecord() operations read and write $H + k$ bytes at a time from the storage block. The application is responsible for properly interpreting the fields in each record; for example, in C, it casts a structure pointer to an I/O buffer that contains the record.

Some applications require very large records, such as those that hold a bitmap image. Others require very small records, such as those that hold a name or address. With a file system that supports only fixed-sized record containers, either small records will waste large amounts of space when they are written to the storage system or large records will have to be fragmented before they can be written to the file. Neither constraint is acceptable in a general-purpose system. An alternative is for the file system to be enhanced to include a function to define the record size for a file. The operation, setRecordSize(fileID, size), establishes the size, in bytes, of records to be written into the file. The record size is encoded into the record or file header.

✦ FIGURE 13.6   A Logical-Physical Record Encoding

In the logical-physical record encoding, the fields of a data structure are marshaled into a list of bytes before they are stored on the device. When the record is read, the data is unmarshalled and the structure is reintroduced.

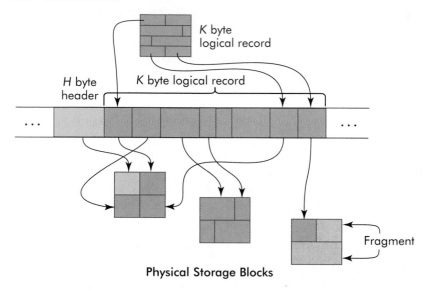

Physical Storage Blocks

Suppose records are of different sizes—perhaps some holding an address and others holding a bitmap image. Then there must be a set of record-block translation functions to be applied for the different types of records. This can be accomplished by prespecifying the set of record types or by using runtime decoding. In traditional record-oriented file structures, the record types are built into the file system itself. In these cases, the **access functions** are operations designed and implemented at the time the file manager is designed and implemented. For example, a file manager may support strings of characters, where a record is a string. Now, a putRecord() operation might write a specific number of bytes onto a stream to the storage device.

A more general file manager would support programmer-defined abstract data types. The application programmer would define the format for logical records and the access routines for reading and writing the records. The file system invokes the programmer-supplied access routines when reading from and writing to the file. As the abstract data types become more sophisticated, the file system increasingly resembles a database system.

Again using the electronic mail example, an electronic message can be defined as a structured sequential file having the form shown in Figure 13.7. A mailbox is a collection of such records as defined by the C struct message declaration. The putRecord() operation appends a mail message to the end of the mailbox file, and the getRecord() routine retrieves the message "under" the file position. Figure 13.7 also shows examples of customized access routines for the message record type. Assume the get() and put() operations can be written in terms of the read and write operations.

A structured file manager allows the programmer to export information (such as that shown in Figure 13.7) into the file manager. This can be accomplished by having the file manager rely on the existence of a fixed set of access operation names and then having the application program write definitions for each of those names. When the application instructs the file manager to read a record, the file manager uses the application-supplied access operation to define the specific format of the information to be read. The file manager provides all of the infrastructure for manipulating the file (such as interacting with the device driver), and the application writer provides the information that is specific to the record format.

◆ **FIGURE 13.7** Electronic Mail Example

In this example, data structures are defined by the application, and then the definitions are passed to the file manager. The file manager uses the definitions, along with user-provided functions, to marshall/unmarshall the byte stream.

```
struct message {
/* The mail message */
  address to;
  address from;
  line subject;
  address cc;
  string body;
};

struct message *getRecord(void) {
  struct message *msg;
  msg = allocate(sizeof(message));
  msg->to = getAddress(...);
  msg->from = getAddress(...);
  msg->cc = getAddress(...);
  msg->subject = getLine();
  msg->body = getString();
  return(msg);
}

putRecord(struct message *msg) {
  putAddress(msg->to);
  putAddress(msg->from);
  putAddress(msg->cc);
  putLine(msg->subject);
  putString(msg->body);
}
```

INDEXED SEQUENTIAL FILES Sequentially accessed information is not useful in some applications. For example, in an interactive query system, such as an automatic teller system, any particular work done by the program will be concerned only with a specific record rather than with every record in the file. The application needs to read from or write to a specific record independent of the record's location in the file. **Indexed sequential files** provide this capability, while retaining the ability to access the records sequentially when needed. Each record header includes an integer **index field**. The interface to an indexed sequential file system uses a more general read/write interface than do pure sequential files:

- ■ getRecord(fileID, index): Returns the record with an index field set to the index value.

- ■ putRecord(fileID, record): As an access operation, writes the designated record into the file at a position chosen by the file system and then returns the value of the index field as a result.

- ■ deleteRecord(fileID, index): Removes the record with the index field set to the index value.

Indexed sequential files allow the program to manage the indices so that they can access desired records. For example, suppose a customer wants to know the balance of an account. The customer can supply an account number, but not the index value. Therefore, an automatic teller machine application would keep a table to translate account numbers into record indices (see Figure 13.8).

✦ FIGURE 13.8   An Indexed Sequential File with a Lookup Table

Applications that use indexed sequential files typically contain a lookup table. The key values in the table are determined by the application, with the key mapping to an index in which the corresponding record is stored.

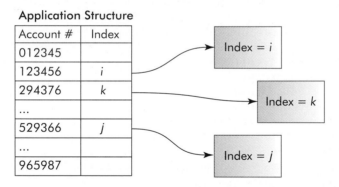

Suppose the programmer could specify the index for a record when it is written. Then the lookup table could be eliminated by using, for example, the account# field as the index field for each record. This would require the putRecord() operation to be changed to putRecord(fileID, record, index). This access operation writes the designated record into the file at a position chosen by the file system and assigns the index parameter value as the value of the index field. If there is already another record with the specified value, the operation returns a value of FALSE; otherwise, it returns TRUE.

Indexed sequential files are widely used in business-oriented computing for files that have very large numbers of records, particularly if the records are often referenced in a nonsequential manner. An indexed sequential file can also be accessed sequentially if the application intends to systematically process every record in the file.

INVERTED FILES   There are many applications in which the index field must be searched by the application before a record can be retrieved. For example, suppose the program were to allow accounts to be retrieved by using the customer's name, but a customer might have more than one account. To find the correct account, all records matching the customer's name would have to be read and then each inspected to access the desired record. In general, each record access would cause a storage I/O operation, since the records would not usually be stored in the same physical block. The number of operations could be substantially reduced by extracting the index field from each record and placing it in an **index table**. This table has the conceptual form shown in Figure 13.8, but it is maintained by the file manager, not the application. However, the application program can search the table without incurring excessive storage device I/O operations.

The case in which the application needs to search with different criteria, such as name or account number, suggests that each record might have two or more index fields. One field links the records together by names and the other by account numbers. This can be implemented by including links for each linked list in each record or by preparing one index table with names and another with account numbers. Searches take place on the appropriate table, and the record is then accessed on the storage device.

The external index table can be generalized so that an entry points to various records or fields in the file. When a record is placed in the file, keywords in the record are extracted and placed in the index table with a pointer back into the record to where the keyword appears. This is called an **inverted file**, since records are accessed based on their appearance in the table rather than their logical location or address.

Inverted files can also be generalized to support multiple index fields, each with its own index into the records. The table storage requirements are increased. The overhead to manage the indices increases, since record deletions can cause dangling pointers in an index. However, access times can be substantially reduced by using such files.

DATABASE MANAGEMENT SYSTEMS

Database management systems (DBMSs) constitute an entire area of computer science, so the remarks here are general, intended only to point out the relationship between DBMSs and operating systems. A database is a very highly structured set of information, typically stored across several low-level files and with the organization optimized to minimize access time. The DBMS enables the programmer to define complex data types in terms of data **schema** (compare this with the idea of programmers specifying the structure of data using abstract data types). These schema are then used by the database administrator to choose an internal organization for files that will allow the data to be retrieved rapidly. Once data have been stored in the database, they can be retrieved by querying the database, changed, and then written back into the database.

The data definition and manipulation languages and their processors are complex entities not considered to be part of an OS. Some DBMSs use the normal files provided by the OS for generic use. Obviously, a low-level file system will be better suited to DBMS support than will a structured file system because the low-level system does not presume any particular structure on files. It expects the application—the DBMS in this case—to do this.

While conceptually, every DBMS uses the file system to implement its functions, in many cases, it has its own storage device block organization and access routines. Hence, it completely bypasses the normal file manager in order to work directly with devices. This enables the DBMS to be more efficient in the way it accesses the storage devices. However, it precludes information stored in the database from being accessible using the file manager's interface to the storage device.

MULTIMEDIA STORAGE

Multimedia documents are highly structured files (or sets of files) designed to contain information represented as numbers, characters, formatted text, executable programs, graphics, images, audio/video streams, and so on. The storage requirements of multimedia documents (containing images) are five or more orders of magnitude higher than those for traditional alphanumeric information. For example, a page of formatted text characters might require 0.5 to 1KB to save the information, but a similar-sized color image might require 10MB of storage.

This diversity in storage requirements between components of a multimedia document naturally encourages variable-sized records. This in turn requires either of the following:

- ■ There must be considerable translation functionality in applications that use the multimedia document.

- ■ The file manager must provide a means for the application to export very comprehensive access routines (for example, specifying data transfer strategies in addition to formats) to be used by the file manager when managing the multimedia file.

Application environments have been constructed in which compound document files can be constructed as elaborate abstract data types or classes. Each abstract data type definition encodes functions able to perform "standard" operations on the information such as reading and printing along with the information. The environment is more complex than conventional file managers because it must not only store the data but also store enough of the abstract data type description for the appropriate manipulation functions to be invoked when the data is to be used.

These very large information containers also cause OS designers to rethink the mechanisms for both storing files and copying the information from the storage device to memory (and back).

13.3 • LOW-LEVEL FILE IMPLEMENTATIONS

A byte-stream file manager provides a minimal mechanism to enable a process to read from and write to information on storage devices. Popular operating systems implement only byte-stream file managers. Since byte-stream file managers implement the essential characteristics of all file managers, our discussion of implementations focuses on byte-stream file managers.

The file manager implements the file interface on a variety of storage devices; some of these devices only allow sequential access to their data (such as a magnetic tape), and others allow random access to the blocks on the device (such as a magnetic disk). In either case, as suggested by Figure 13.9, the file manager implements stream-block translation so that the application can read/write the file as a sequence of bytes. A tape realization of the low-level file abstraction requires the logical byte stream to be mapped to logical blocks, which are then mapped onto the physical records on a tape. The contiguous bytes are grouped into logical records and then are stored in physical records. Bytes 0 through $k-1$ are stored in logical record 0, which is stored in physical record 0, where k is the number of bytes in a tape physical record. The order of logical blocks on the byte stream maps to contiguous physical blocks in a magnetic tape realization of the low-level file. So, for k-byte physical blocks on the tape, bytes b_0 to b_{k-1} are stored in physical block 0 of the tape; bytes b_k to b_{2k-1} are stored in physical block 1 on the tape, and so on.

✦ FIGURE 13.9 Low-level File System Architecture

This figures illustrates how the file manager makes the details of the storage device invisible to the application programmer. The programmer reads and writes the byte stream, but the file manager handles the details of marshalling the byte stream to tape or disk blocks.

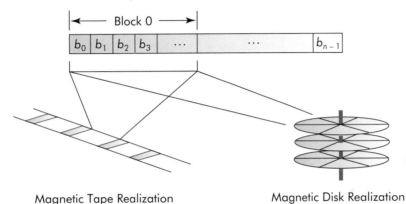

Magnetic Tape Realization   Magnetic Disk Realization

A disk realization also maps logical blocks of contiguous bytes from the byte stream, but the mapping of logical to physical blocks will *not* normally be to contiguous blocks on the disk. Instead, the disk realization provides a mechanism for managing a much more general collection of blocks to store the bytes of a particular file so that they can be accessed as if they were stored as a contiguous byte stream. We will examine issues in file manager design by considering the open() and close() operations, block management, and stream marshalling.

THE OPEN() AND CLOSE() OPERATIONS

When a file is created, the file manager creates a data structure instance called a **file descriptor**, in which it stores detailed information about the file. This file descriptor is kept on the storage device with the contents of the file. Different file managers store different information in the file descriptor, but most maintain (or are able to derive on request) the following information:

- **External name:** A character string name for the file, used at the command line or from an application program. This is the symbolic name that users associate with the file.

- **Sharable:** A field that specifies whether multiple processes can have the file open at the same time. This field identifies the file as private, read sharable, execution sharable, write sharable, and so on.

- **Owner:** The identifier associated with the user whose process created the file. In some cases, ownership may be assigned by some other policy. The file system may allow a process to pass ownership to another user.

■ **Protection settings:** The protection characterization (different operating systems have different characterizations). The minimum modes of protection are for reading and writing. The protection settings indicate whether the owner is able to read from or write to the file without overriding the protection. A second protection field specifies whether other processes can read from or write to the file.

■ **Length:** The number of bytes contained in the file.

■ **Time of creation:** The system time at which the file was created.

■ **Time of last modification:** The system time at which the file was last written to.

■ **Time of last access:** The system time at which the file was last read from or executed or had any other operation performed on it.

■ **Reference count:** The count of the number of directories in which the file appears if the directory system allows a file to appear in more than one. It is used to detect when the file is deleted from all directories so that its space can be released.

■ **Storage device details:** The field that contains the details of how the blocks in the file can be accessed. The details depend heavily on the storage device block management strategy that the file manager uses.

Before a thread can read a file, it must first open the file. This operation causes the file manager to prepare the specified file to be read or written. Locating the file in the storage device system is a directory operation, so discussion of this step is deferred until directories are covered in Section 13.5. When the file has been located on a storage device, the file manager uses the information from the external file descriptor to finish the steps in making the file ready to use.

The file manager checks to be sure that the process is authorized to access the file. This authorization involves comparing the protection flags from the external file descriptor for the file with the protection keys held by the user/process. If the process attempts to open a file for which it does not have the appropriate rights, the authorization procedure will disallow the open() operation. Independently of protection authorization, the file manager also will need to check other constraints on the open() operation. For example, it will also check the read/write locks on the file to see if access can be granted.

Once the file manager has determined that the process is authorized to access the file, it creates its own internal version of the file descriptor, called the *open file descriptor* (see Figure 13.10). The open file descriptor contains all the information that is in the external file descriptor along with any additional file-specific information that the file manager may choose to keep. For example, the internal file descriptor may contain fields such as:

■ **Locks:** Locks can be *read locks*, meaning the file is currently opened for reading. If the file is sharable, other processes can open it only for reading. A *write lock* indicates a process has opened the file for writing. Unless the file is write sharable, only one process can use the file at a time.

■ **Current state:** The state of the file; this can be *archived*, meaning that it has been written to a very low level of the storage hierarchy and cannot be opened for use without a significant delay. If the state is *closed*, the file resides in an online storage device and can be opened for use within milliseconds. The file can be *open for reading*, meaning that the file is allocated to a process reading the file; it can also be *open for writing*, meaning that the file is allocated to a process writing to the file, or *open for execution*, *open for appending*, and so on.

■ **User:** The list of processes currently having the file open. If the file is not sharable, this entry is always null or only a single process.

It is possible for multiple processes to have a file open at the same time. In this case, each process will have its own file position into the open file. Thus, when the file is opened, the file manager must create an additional data structure to represent each "session" with a file—the relationship between the process and the file I/O operations. Finally, the `open()` function will return a reference to the session-specific data structure to the application program.

✦ FIGURE 13.10 File Manager Data Structures

When a file is opened, the file manager creates various data structures to represent the current state of the file. First, the file manager copies the external file description from the secondary memory so that its information can be used to manage the file. Second, the file manager will create a process-file session data structure where it can keep the state of the I/O operations (such as the file pointer position). Finally, the file manager returns a reference to these data structures to the application that performed the `open()` operation.

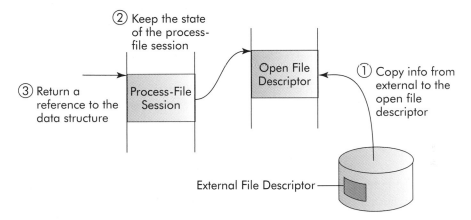

Summarizing, the `open()` operation instructs the file manager to instantiate internal data structures needed to manage the I/O. Specifically, it performs the following steps:

1. Locates the file and its external file descriptor on the storage device.

2. Extracts information regarding the file from the external file descriptor and information regarding the process from the process descriptor.

3. Authenticates that the process is permitted access to the file.

4. Creates an entry in an *open file descriptor* table to maintain basic information about any process's use of the file.

5. Creates an entry in a *process-file session* table to keep track of the state of each specific process's interaction with the file.

The open() command completes when the authentication and data structure allocation and initialization have been completed. The process's file position will address the first byte in the file, and the process can begin to read from or write to the file, depending on the way the permissions were used to open the file.

The close() operation causes the file manager to complete all pending operations (for example, to flush output buffers residing in memory), to release I/O buffers, to release locks the process may hold on the file, to update the external file descriptor, and to deallocate the file status table entry.

UNIX Open and Close

The kernel open() call for BSD UNIX is of the form

```
int open(char *path, int flags [, int mode])
```

The first parameter to the kernel call specifies the path name for the file to be opened. The flags parameter is a bitmap in which each position in the word sets a switch. For example, the O_RDONLY, O_WRONLY, and O_RDWR values set bits in the flags parameter to indicate that the file should be opened only for reading, only for writing, or for reading and writing, respectively. The man page for each system's open() describes all flag values. If the flags parameter sets O_CREAT, a file is to be created on the open() call if it does not exist. In this case, the optional mode parameter specifies the protection settings for the new file.

When a file is opened, the file manager searches the storage system for the specified path name. This can be an extended procedure, since it is necessary to open each directory in the path name (starting at the highest-named directory in the path), to search the path for the next file or directory in the path name, and to open that directory or file.

As shown in Figure 13.11, once the file manager has determined that the file can be opened, it allocates an unused entry in the process-specific *open file table*. The open() call returns the index as an integer file identifier result. This entry can then be used by each thread in the process whenever it wants to reference the file. When the process is created, stdin has an entry identifier of 0, stdout has a value of 1, and stderr has a value of 2. The next successful open() or pipe() call will create an entry in the descriptor table at location 3.

When a file is closed, its identifier becomes available; the next open() call uses the lowest-numbered available identifier. Thus, a close() immediately followed by an open() will cause an identifier to be reused. For example, in the code sequence

```
close(stdout);
...
fid = open("newOut", flags);
```

the variable, fid, will have value 1 because stdout uses identifier 1. This fact is used in implementing I/O redirection (see Lab Exercise 9.1).

The entry in the process-specific open file table points to an entry in the *system-wide* open file table called a *file structure*. In UNIX systems, the process-file session table is

✦ FIGURE 13.11 Opening a UNIX File

This figure shows the OS data structures for UNIX file management. The process-specific open file table references an entry in the system-wide file structure table. The file structure table references an inode (a copy of the external file descriptor), stored in the *inode list*. The open file table and file structure table entries together are analogous to the generic process-file session entry.

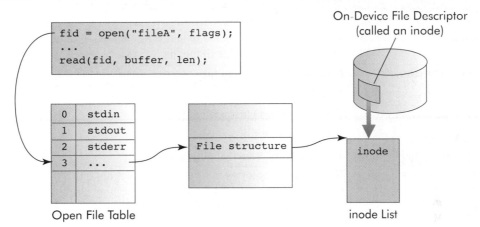

actually implemented as a combination of a descriptor table and a file structure table. The file structure entry keeps status information specific to the process that opened the file for the process. For example, the value of the file position for this process's use is in the file structure entry. If two different processes have the file open, then each will have its own copy of the file position. The file structure entry references a copy of the *inode* (the UNIX name for the open file descriptor) after it has been loaded into primary memory.

When a process/thread opens a file, new entries are created in the open file tables, but another process might have already opened the file for its own use, in which case the inode will have already been loaded into the inode list. The file manager determines if it can use an exisiting inode, or if it must load the inode from the external file descriptor. Finally, the file structure entry is set to reference the appropriate inode list entry. Table 13.1 illustrates the nature of the entries in the inode.

Changes to the in-memory version of the inode are not immediately propagated to the inode on the storage device (the external file descriptor) the moment the file manager makes the changes. Instead, the in-memory version of the inode is copied back to secondary memory periodically, when the file is closed, or when the application issues a `sync` command. If the machine halts while a file is open, the inode on the disk may differ from the one in primary memory if there have been any changes to the in-memory copy of the inode. The result will be an inconsistent file system, since the copy of the inode in secondary memory is saved, but the most recent information about the file is lost when the in-memory copy is destroyed. For example, if the block pointers in the in-memory inode have changed, with corresponding changes to disk blocks, then the disk may have an inode that is inconsistent with pointers in various storage blocks on the disk.

The `fsck` utility is designed to recover from such errors. Briefly, `fsck` reads every file in the file system, and then it reads every block on the disk and attempts to correlate the

TABLE 13.1 UNIX File Descriptor

Field	Description
Mode	Specification of access permissions for the owner and other users.
UID	ID of the user creating the file.
Group ID	ID associated with the file to identify a collection of users having group access rights to the file.
Length in bytes	Number of bytes in the file.
Length in blocks	Number of blocks used to implement the file.
Last modification	Time the file was last written to.
Last access	Time the file was last read.
Last inode modification	Time the inode was last changed.
Reference count	Number of directories in which the file appears; this field is used to detect when the file is deleted from all directories so that its space can be released.
Block references	Pointers and indirect pointers to blocks in the file.

status of each block with the file pointers. If the two views differ, `fsck` knows there is an error, although it cannot necessarily correct it.

The system tables and pointers created on opening a file are summarized in Figure 13.11. Actual implementations incorporate additional tables to handle file system buffering.

BLOCK MANAGEMENT

Block management refers to the task of keeping track of which storage device blocks are associated with which file. In the case of sequential storage devices such as tape, the task is easy, but for randomly accesses storage devices such as any kind of disk, it is a highly significant part of the file manager's work. Because storage devices have fixed-size blocks, we assume that all blocks, B_i and B_j, contain k bytes, so the ith byte, b_i, is stored in B_j, where $j = \lfloor i/k \rfloor$. Thus, a file with m bytes requires at least $\lceil m/k \rceil$ blocks on the device. There are three well-known techniques for organizing the physical storage blocks for a file:

- As a *contiguous set* of blocks on the secondary storage device.
- As a *list* of blocks interconnected with links.
- As a collection of blocks interconnected by a *file index*.

The file descriptor storage details will be designed to implement different data structures for each of the block allocation strategies.

CONTIGUOUS ALLOCATION The contiguous-allocation strategy maps the N logical blocks in the file into N contiguously addressed physical blocks. This strategy makes the randomly accessed storage device behave like a sequentially accessed device for that particular file. It allows the driver to read from or write to an entire file in a short amount of time. Now if the file system passes disk requests to the driver at a very high rate, the driver can access blocks adjacent to one another on the device without incurring seek time between block accesses. A typical file status entry for contiguously allocated blocks contains the information given in Figure 13.12.

✦ FIGURE 13.12 File Status Entry for Contiguous Blocks

The data block management can be very simple for contiguous allocation schemes, since the file manager only needs to know where the blocks start and how many of them there are.

Head Position	234
. . .	. . .
First block	2035
Number of blocks	7

Contiguous allocation does not accommodate dynamic file sizes, since it maps the logical structure directly to the physical structure. If a file is stored in some contiguous set of blocks and data is added to the end of the file, then either the next contiguous physical block on the storage device must be made available or the entire file must be copied to a larger group of unallocated contiguous blocks. Whenever the file system intends to allocate N blocks to a file, it must find N contiguous physical blocks. Presuming space is available on the storage device, it must choose some set of $r \geq N$ unallocated blocks.

Several substrategies are used in this case, the most popular being best fit, first fit, and worst fit (see Chapter 11). It is sufficient for our purposes to recognize that the best-fit algorithm chooses the set of contiguous blocks where $r - N$ is minimal. The first-fit algorithm chooses the "first" collection in a linear search of the collections where $r \geq N$. The worst-fit algorithm selects the largest collection that contains N blocks and then partitions it into two parts containing N blocks for the file and a new collection of $r - N$ unallocated blocks.

Contiguous allocation strategies will tend to externally fragment the physical disk space into small sets of contiguous blocks that are too little to contain most files (although the disk can be compacted to eliminate the fragmentation). Contiguous allocation does have the benefit of very fast access times for whole file transfers, since all blocks in the file are in close proximity on the disk (thus reducing disk head movement when the entire file is copied).

LINKED LISTS Linked lists of blocks use explicit pointers among an arbitrary set of physical blocks making up the file. Logical block $i + 1$ need not be physically located near logical block i, since i will contain a link that addresses the physical block that contains logical block $i + 1$. The file status table entry for a file will include a copy of the file position and a pointer to the first device block used in the file (see Figure 13.13). The entry may also contain other data used to manage the open file.

✦ FIGURE 13.13 File Status Entry for Linked Lists

In linked list allocation schemes, the data blocks in a file are joined together in a one-way linked list. The descriptor only needs to reflect where the list starts on the device.

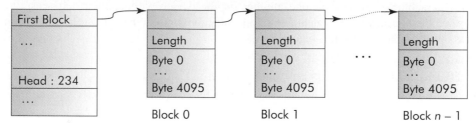

Each block in the file contains overhead information used by the file manager. In the example, two fields in a block are used to hold the next-block pointer and a count of the number of bytes actually stored in the block. The length field enables the file manager to store variable numbers of bytes in each block, thus potentially enabling the file manager to reduce the number of block allocations and deallocations in a dynamic file.

In linked-list block allocation, random access of bytes in the stream will be slow, especially as the file size grows. The `seek()` operation is the basis of random access, since it repositions the file prior to a data transfer operation. Each `seek()` will be costly in this block allocation scheme, since it requires list traversal. This in turn requires each block in the list to be read from the device so that the link field can be obtained and the next block can be referenced. Doubly linked lists (Figure 13.14) can be used to enhance performance during `seek()` operations. When a `seek()` is issued, the file manager calculates whether to move forward on the list, move backward on the list, or go to the front or back of the list to begin searching for the target block.

✦ FIGURE 13.14 Doubly Linked Blocks

Doubly linked lists can reduce the number of device read operations by enabling the file manager to seek forward or backward from the current file position.

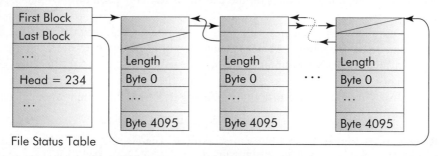

INDEXED ALLOCATION One criticism of the linked-list strategy is that seeks are read-intensive (even using the doubly linked list optimization). This criticism can be addressed by extracting the link field from each data block and putting it into a separate index block with *N* entries. Indexed allocation uses a unique block in the file as an index for all the other blocks used to store data (see Figure 13.15). The block length field is shown in the index block along with the block pointer, which simplifies file position placement because this value can be used when the file manager uses the pointers in the index block for seeking. Files may require more or fewer than the N blocks referenced from the table. If the file requires much fewer than N, the space in the index table will be wasted. If most files are less than N, then the accumulation of wasted space may be significant. This loss of space, called *table fragmentation*, can be serious if the mismatch in sizes is significant or if there are many small files.

✦ FIGURE 13.15 File Status Entry for Indexed Allocation

In indexed allocation, the file manager has an in-memory table that provides the disk address of each block in the file. Of course, this requires that the in-memory table be as large as the largest file (or at least to be expandable beyond a minimum size).

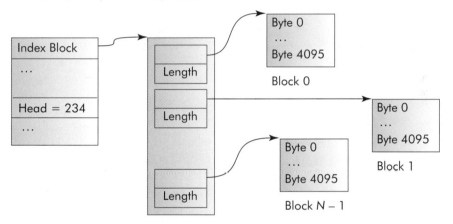

If a file requires more than N blocks, the index must be extended by adding one or more blocks to contain additional index pointers. This can be done, for example, by using a linked-list scheme for the index blocks. It also can be accomplished by using multiple levels of indirect tables, where a "super" index block points to other index blocks, which point to storage device blocks.

UNIX File Structure

The UNIX file structure uses a variant of the indexed allocation scheme. The storage device detail part of the inode contains pointers to 15 different storage blocks (see Figure 13.16). The first 12 blocks of the file are indexed directly from the first 12 of 15 pointers in the inode. The last 3 pointers are used for indirect pointers through *index blocks*. If the file manager is configured with 4KB blocks, the 12 direct pointers in the inode accommodate files up to 48KB. Experience indicates this is an efficient mechanism for addressing the blocks (see [Ousterhout et al. 1985]). If a file requires more than 12 blocks, the file system allocates an index block and links it into the *single indirect* (thirteenth) pointer of the inode. Hence, blocks 13 to k are indirectly addressed from the inode via the indirect block identified by the thirteenth pointer in the inode. Similarly, larger files use the fourteenth pointer to address a *double indirect block*, and the largest files use the fifteenth pointer to point at a *triple indirect block*.

✦ FIGURE 13.16 UNIX File Structure

The UNIX file manager uses a combination of indexed allocation and linked lists for the index table. The first 12 blocks appear in an index. Subsequent blocks are accessed by reading a single, double, or triple level indirection through other blocks containing indices.

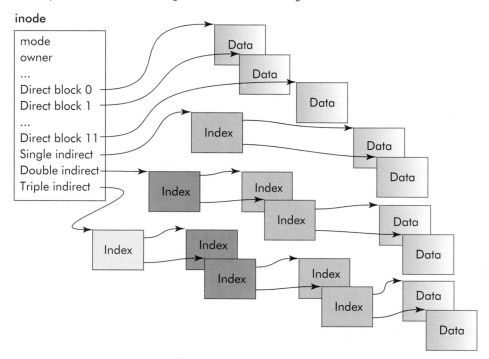

How big can UNIX files be? That depends on the size of the blocks and the size of the disk addresses used in the system. To simplify the arithmetic, suppose an indirect block can store 1,000 disk addresses. Then the single indirect block will provide pointers to an additional 1,000 disk blocks. Blocks 0 through 11 are accessed via the direct pointers in the inode, but blocks 12 through 1,011 are accessed indirectly through the single indirect block. The fourteenth block pointer in the inode is the double indirect pointer. It points to a block that contains pointers to blocks of the type referenced from the single indirect field. The double indirect pointer addresses a block pointing to 1,000 indirect blocks, so blocks 1,012 to 1,001,011 are accessed through the double indirect list. The fifteenth block pointer is the triple indirect pointer. It points to a block that contains double indirect pointers. Again, if each block can store 1,000 block addresses, then the triple indirect pointer indirectly addresses blocks 1,001,012 to the maximum-sized file (under these assumptions) of 1,001,001,011 blocks.

With this block allocation strategy, very large files are possible, even though as files grow larger, the access times are greater due to the indirection. There are other considerations that prevent a file from reaching this maximum size designed into the inode structure. For example, with the block sizes given previously, a file using the triple indirect index would require that there be a device capable of storing 4000 GB. Current versions of BSD UNIX do not use the triple indirect pointer, partly because of incompatibility of file sizes with storage device technology and partly because the 32-bit block addresses used in the file system preclude file sizes larger than 4GB.

The DOS FAT File System

The file system on an MS-DOS floppy disk is based on a **file allocation table (FAT)** file system in which the disk is divided into a *reserved area* (containing the boot program), the actual *file allocation tables*, a *root directory*, and file space; see Figure 13.17. Space allocated for files is represented by values in the allocation table, which effectively provide a linked list of all the blocks in the file. Special values designate end-of-file, unallocated, and bad blocks. The original FAT had many limitations: It had no subdirectories and was limited to very small disks, and it was very hard to recover the disk if the allocation tables were damaged.

◆ FIGURE 13.17 FAT Organization

MS-DOS disks use a file allocation table (FAT) file system in which the disk is divided into a reserved area (containing the boot program), the actual file allocation tables, a root directory, and file space.

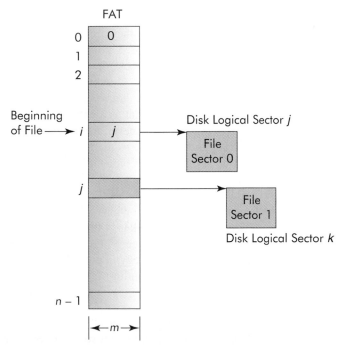

When personal computer use grew rapidly, the capacity of disk drives also increased dramatically. As capacity grew larger, different variants of FAT were derived to accommodate them. The basic FAT organization (see Figure 13.17) differs among disk types by changing the size of the entries (m in the figure can be 12, 16, or 32 in different versions of Windows), the number of actual tables, and the size of the logical sector addressed by a FAT entry.

In the simplest variant, there is one FAT entry corresponding to each block on the disk. A file is a set of disk blocks, where the FAT entry corresponding to the first entry designates the logical sector number of the second block. Similarly, the FAT entry of the second block specifies the logical sector number of the third block, and so on. The FAT entry for the last block contains an end-of-file (EOF) designator. Thus, the FAT is a linked list of disk sectors. If you know the address of the first sector, i, and therefore the index into the FAT, you can use the FAT to reference the next logical sector in the file (see the figure). The content, j, of FAT index i is a logical sector number, and it is also an index to the second FAT entry for the file.

As disk capacities grew larger than 32 MB, the FAT organization began to use the notion of a cluster of sectors. A *cluster* is a group of contiguous sectors that are treated as a virtual sector within the FAT. In contemporary implementations of the FAT file system, the FAT entry addresses a cluster rather than an individual disk sector. By using clusters, the FAT organization can address groups of, say, 4 sectors as if they were a single sector that has 4 times as many bytes in it as a single sector. This means that disk space is allocated to a file on a cluster-by-cluster basis. Today, floppy disks use 12-bit FATs and hard disks use 16-bit or 32-bit FATs.

UNALLOCATED BLOCKS When a file system is initialized, all of its blocks are unallocated; storage blocks are allocated to the files as they are created and expanded. There are different strategies for managing these unallocated blocks. At disk initialization time, the file manager creates a data structure to keep track of all the unallocated blocks (file descriptors will keep track of the allocated blocks). One obvious way to handle the collection of unused blocks is to initialize them into a dummy link-allocated or indexed file called the **free list**. The free list has the same format as a conventional file, except there is no information stored in any of the blocks. Whenever a block is needed for some real file, it is detached from the free list and allocated to the file needing the block. In the linked-list allocation, blocks can be allocated from either end of the free list file. If the free list is implemented using indexed allocation, then blocks will probably be allocated from the end of the last index block.

The free list will initially be very large, since it contains every unallocated block on the disk (in fact, it is at maximum size, since every block is in the free list). This tends to make the indexed implementation impractical for the free list because the index table would need to be quite large. Instead, the linked-list strategy is preferred to the indexed allocation strategy since the space overhead for maintaining the list comes from the unused (unallocated) blocks.

Disk drives are commonly used to support the file system. Recall from Section 5.5 that the time to move the disk read/write head—the seek time—can be very significant. This means that logically adjacent blocks in a file might be located at physically remote locations on the disk surface. In this case, if the file was being read sequentially—the normal case—then the read operation would incur a large seek time penalty when it moved from one block to the next. As a result, file managers attempt to allocate all the blocks in a file from the same physical area on the disk surface—the same or adjacent cylinders, if possible. Now we see a problem with the linked-list strategy: It is difficult to allocate disk blocks in the same physical vicinity on the disk, since the block allocator must traverse the list to search for blocks physically close to the adjacent blocks that have already been allocated to the file.

A third option is for the file manager to keep a **block status map** (also called a **disk bitmap**) of the disk blocks on the file. The ith entry in the map is set if the ith block is allocated and reset otherwise. A 1GB disk with 4KB blocks will require 256K entries in this block status map. If each entry is a single bit, then the table uses 32KB of space. Most file manager designers have decided that this is a reasonable price to pay for a mechanism that provides a quick snapshot of the unallocated blocks on the disk. As a result, the block status map can be kept in primary memory. When there is a requirement for a block to be allocated to a file, the block status map is read in order to quickly locate a storage block, hopefully one that is physically near the other blocks in the file. The file manager then assigns the block to the file by adding it to the file and sets the corresponding entry in the block status map to indicate that is allocated. When a block is released from a file, the block status map entry is reset and the file pointers are adjusted correspondingly.

Another advantage of the block status map approach is that it can be used to check a disk to see if the collective pointers in all files address exactly the set of blocks allocated, no block is allocated to more than one file, and the blocks marked as unallocated do not appear in any file's list of blocks. Briefly, this is done by traversing each file in the file system, identifying the blocks in the file, and then comparing each found block with the block status map state for that block.

ADDING BLOCKS TO THE FILE   If the application program were to perform a single-byte write with the file descriptor in the state shown in Figure 13.12 to Figure 13.15, then the contents of byte 234 would be overwritten. To accomplish this, the file system reads the block containing byte 234, overwrites the byte, and then rewrites the block to the disk. This requires two calls to the disk driver and two disk I/O operations. The file manager may delay the write-back operation under the assumption that if byte 234 was just written, then very soon subsequent bytes in the same block will be written. For example, if the next operation were an operation on any byte in the loaded block, such as byte 235 if the file were being accessed sequentially, the physical block would already be loaded into the file system's memory. In this way, a disk read operation could be avoided and the write operation could be amortized over several byte operations. If the file pointer is positioned at the end of the file when a write operation is requested, a new block must be obtained and added to the logical end of the list of blocks.

READING AND WRITING THE BYTE STREAM

Storage devices read from or write to a fixed-sized block of bytes with any individual operation. Sequential storage devices typically use removable media, such as a tape or tape cassette, so each medium ordinarily holds one file. (Of course, the file can be a composite file of other files such as a UNIX `tar` file. This enables the effective use of the medium by combining files with an external tool and then writing the resulting information onto a single byte stream.) As explained at the beginning of this section, the order of logical blocks in the file is the same as the order of physical blocks on a sequential storage device. Randomly accessed storage devices incorporate an additional mechanism to produce the equivalent of a sequentially accessed set of blocks.

In low-level file systems, then, there is a module that focuses on implementing a byte stream, $b_0, b_1, b_2,...$ on top of a set of blocks, $B_0, B_1, B_2, ...$. There are two stages to a read or write operation:

- Reading bytes into or writing bytes out of the memory copy of a block
- Reading the physical blocks into or writing them out of memory from/to storage devices

PACKING AND UNPACKING BLOCKS WITH SINGLE BYTES When a file system read operation occurs, a block of bytes is read from the storage device. The bytes are logically placed in the byte stream sequence. The corresponding string is then obtained from the point in the byte stream that is addressed by the file position for the file. When the file is opened for reading, the first block in the file is copied into memory and the file position points to the first byte in the stream (the first byte in the first block). The prescribed number of bytes is copied out of the in-memory copy of the block into the buffer for the command. If the number of bytes to be read is larger than the number remaining in the in-memory block, then the file manager reads the next block in the file. This *unpacking* (or unmarshalling) procedure is the basis of converting secondary storage blocks into a byte stream.

Write operations *pack* (marshall) strings of bytes into copies of storage device blocks that are loaded in the memory. Then they write the blocks to the device when they become full. When the file is opened for writing, the first block of the file is copied into memory so that the string will be overwritten on the existing data. When the write operations cause the file position to move from the first block into the second, the first block can be written back to the storage device and the second block is copied into memory to be altered by output operations.

File seek operations potentially cause a series of storage device block read operations. If the application calls for a seek to file position i, then the file manager must determine which logical block, j, contains position i. Assume all blocks contain the same number, k, of bytes (except the last block in the file). The simplest implementation is to determine j by computing $\lfloor i/k \rfloor$. The file manager then can read the jth block in preparation for subsequent I/O commands. Notice that "reading the jth block" only requires one device read operation if the block manager uses index tables, but can still require several reads if the block management strategy uses a linked list.

Packing and unpacking can become more complex if the file interface allows information to be inserted into a file (as opposed to overwriting information at the file position). To handle information insertion, the file manager must be able to allocate new blocks and add them to the interior of the block data structure and deallocate a block from any point in the block structure. This follows because an insert at any position other than at the end of the byte stream will require a block to be allocated just to hold the incremental information. In Figure 13.18(a), a single new byte is to be added between b_i and b_{i+1}. In this example, b_i is in a block of bytes that begins with b_k. Since there is no space in block j for the new byte, a new block, $j+1$, is added to the file and the bytes originally stored in positions $i+1$ to $k+r$ are written into the new block with new indices $i+2$ to $k+r+1$.

✦ FIGURE 13.18 Adding a Byte to a Byte-Stream File

When a byte is added to a full block, a new block must be added to the file. The information prior to the new byte is left in the old block, but the information after the new byte is written to the new block. The new byte can be written either to the beginning of the new block or at the end of the old block.

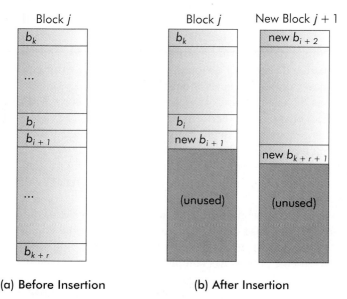

(a) Before Insertion   (b) After Insertion

If the file interface also allows the deletion of information at the file pointer, the file manager may deallocate a block and return it to the free list. With deletion, the blocks will, over time, suffer from internal fragmentation, as illustrated in Figure 13.18(b). If inserts and deletes take place at arbitrary parts of the file, the internal fragmentation will eventually cause the amount of wasted space to surpass some threshold established by the file manager, or for the file to surpass its quota of free blocks. In this case, the file can be compacted so that each block is rewritten to be dense. File compaction can also be caused by an explicit operation on the file manager interface.

Suppose the file system maintains partially full blocks. Then characters can easily be added at any point in the file by simply adding them to existing blocks. If a block must be added, it is obtained from the free list and added to the collection of blocks that constitute the file. Then the system may adjust the location of a small number of bytes between the newly allocated block and its neighbors. In indexed files, this implies the index itself must be rewritten. Because of fragmentation, the byte stream file system with insertions and deletions tends to use more physical space than does the pure byte stream file system. Whenever bytes are inserted or deleted from the interior of a file, there will be unused space in blocks.

BLOCK I/O Once the file position has been determined in a byte stream file, the file manager can read from or write to the appropriate storage device block. Recall that storage devices are read/written as needed. Modern operating systems recognize that for files of sequential information, such as a byte stream, performance can be substantially enhanced by overlapping CPU and device operation through buffering.

As discussed in Chapter 5, significant performance increases can be obtained in an OS that overlaps device I/O operation with CPU activity. File block buffering offers the main opportunity to exploit this overlap. A file is an organization of entities that are sequentially accessed by processes. This means that when a process opens a file for reading, the file manager knows there is a high probability that the process will read the information in the file from the beginning to the end. Therefore, it can read ahead on the file, depending on the amount of buffer space that it can allocate to the open file and the availability of the storage device. Similarly, files open for writing can overlap CPU and device operation by buffering information destined for a storage device, and then writing the buffered information to the storage device whenever it becomes available.

Studies such as the one by Ousterhout et al. [1985] have shown that file buffering has an enormous effect on the overall performance of the system. The cited study emphasizes another benefit of buffering that might not generally be predicted about file usage. That is, most of the references to information in a file are to a small part of the file that is read from and written to multiple times. This means that if the information is copied into a buffer on first reference, then the second and subsequent references will not even incur a disk operation.

Aside from the phenomenon of multiple accesses to a subset of the information in a file, the performance increase due to buffering is related to the number of blocks read from and written to by a process. If the total block I/O operation for a process requires $T_{\mathrm{I/O}}$ units of time and the process has computation time of T_{CPU}, then the time to execute will be no greater than $T_{\mathrm{CPU}} + T_{\mathrm{I/O}}$ and no less than a maximum $(T_{\mathrm{CPU}}, T_{\mathrm{I/O}})$. The minimum execution time occurs when the next desired storage device block has already been read whenever it is needed. Obviously, this is more difficult to achieve if the program does frequent seek operations to extremes of the byte stream when the file organization is a linked list.

13.4 • SUPPORTING HIGH-LEVEL FILE ABSTRACTIONS

The low-level file systems attempt to avoid encoding record-level functionality into the file manager. If the applications will typically use very large and very small records, a generic file manager cannot be written to take advantage of that fact. On the other hand, any strategy that is widely used by applications can usually be implemented to be more efficient if it is implemented in the operating system. The trend in modern operating systems has been toward low-level file systems. In contrast, proprietary operating systems for machines aimed at particular application domains (such as transaction processing) will usually provide a higher-layer file system. This section briefly surveys some of the classic approaches for supporting storage abstractions.

STRUCTURED SEQUENTIAL FILES

Structured sequential files contain collections of logical records. Records are referenced using an index as in byte stream files. The two types of files differ in that structured sequential files cause a full record to be read from or written to. The implementation of a structured sequential file manager is logically the same as a byte stream file manager. If the structured sequential file provides an option of inserting a record at an arbitrary point in the file, then the manager must be designed with the same issues in mind as for the `insertByte()` operation.

Generally, file managers that handle structured files must contain the same kinds of information that are kept for a low-level file, as well as additional fields to support data structure:

- **Type:** A tag describing the type of the file. For example, the type field might distinguish relocatable object files from absolute object files or PostScript files.

- **Access methods:** A composite of functions to be used to read from, write to, append to, update, or otherwise access the file. Since sophisticated structured files take on the character of an abstract data type, this part of the descriptor identifies the function interface for the abstract data type.

- **Other:** Specific structured file types may have other fields to represent the relationship of this file to related files, the minimum version number of the file manager handling this file type, and so on.

The most significant new functionality is to add access methods: either a fixed set or a mechanism for programmer-defined methods.

INDEXED SEQUENTIAL FILES

In indexed sequential files, each record contains an index field used to select it from the file. An application program provides an index value with each read or write operation. The file manager implements a mechanism to search the storage device to find the physical block that contains the record. The implementation may use the same file structure as structured sequential files. The record index ordinarily determines the order in which the records are stored in the file: Record 0 is stored as the first record in the first block, record 1 is the second record in the first block, and so on, until the first block is full. The next record is stored in the second block and so on. The first new task for the file manager is to manage the mapping of records to blocks. Record insertion and deletion may occur at any logical location in the file. Hence, internal fragmentation and compaction issues arise in indexed sequential files.

The file manager may be implemented with a mechanism for direct access of records. Rather than the records being kept in a sequentially accessed data structure, they can be placed in different blocks and then referenced from an index for the file. This requires that the file manager keep a table for each open file and map the index to the block number that contains the record. This direct access implementation can substantially reduce the access times for records in the file. The cost is primarily the space cost of the index, since the complexity of the approach is not substantial compared to the sequential approach. The read and write operations are far more complex for indexed sequential files than for stream-oriented files, since the file manager must access records according to the index value. Further, buffering is not likely to be of any particular value, since the point of having the index field is to enable the application programmer to arbitrarily select the order in which records are accessed.

DATABASE MANAGEMENT SYSTEMS

Database management systems constitute an entire area of computer science, so the discussion here only briefly mentions the part of the secondary storage management provided to the DBMS designer. DBMSs are built on a fundamental storage manager, which replaces the file manager. The storage manager interface is at a relatively low level to enable the DBMS designer to directly manipulate storage devices. This avoids performance penalties associated with generalized operation in favor of specialized strategies for databases. DBMS technology depends on the ability of the database administrator to choose the organization of records across and within files. Relational databases require that there be a means for very efficient search of records, while object-oriented databases require that the access methods be defined by application code. Conventional file system interfaces cannot support either of these functions; they require the storage manager to replace the file manager in order to accommodate them. By using a storage manager in place of a file manager, a system that supports a DBMS and a file system usually cannot allow data to be stored in a database and still be accessed via the file interface.

MULTIMEDIA DOCUMENTS

Multimedia files make demands on the storage system that are similar to those of databases. (Object-oriented databases are often justified by the need to support multimedia documents.) In particular, because multimedia documents tend to be implemented using abstract data types, it is desirable to use application-defined access methods to reference different parts of the document. This argues for a specialized storage manager interface to the secondary storage devices, the same that is used in database implementation.

The need for high-bandwidth throughput is at odds with the basic operation of contemporary file managers. If a multimedia document contains a 10MB record (with an image) and a disk block is 4KB, then a read operation will span over 2400 blocks. The block allocation strategy will have a major impact on the rate at which the image can be transferred. The contiguous allocation strategy would perform the best in terms of transfer time, although the associated fragmentation problem is a costly tradeoff. Similarly, other parts of the file manager are normally designed under the assumption that no application will request multiple blocks at a time, so the multimedia document transfers are not provided with high-performance service.

OS technology is evolving to meet the performance requirements of multimedia files and documents. As of this writing, there are no widely accepted operating systems that provide high-performance support for multimedia files.

13.5 ● DIRECTORIES

They have the directory, but the problem with the directory is even if you figure out where you are, and where you want to go, you still don't really know which way to walk because it's an upright map.

—Jerry Seinfeld, *SeinLanguage*

So far, this chapter has described files and their implementations. The second major responsibility of the file manager is to provide users with facilities to manage *collections* of files. There are overwhelming practical requirements for providing such facilities: It is not unusual for a computer to be configured with more than 50GB of secondary memory. Empirical studies indicate that most files on a 4.2 BSD UNIX system are less than 10KB in length [Ousterhout et al., 1985]. If an average length of 10KB is assumed, the system could have more than 5,000,000 files, provided the disk were filled to capacity. (As explained in Chapter 16, contemporary machines also have access to many more files via the network.) If there were 10 users for such a machine, each person might have an average of 500,000 files of his own. Even if each user accesses only 1,000 files in a system, he would need some means to organize and administer all of them. Despite Seinfeld's complaint about directories, they are a fundamental way for people to organize and find a large collection of entities like files.

A file **directory** is a set of logically associated files and other (sub)directories of files. Directories are the mechanism by which humans organize the set of files that exist in the entire system. A directory is organized as a logical container of a set of files and, possibly, nested directories. The file manager provides users with a set of commands to administer a directory, including the following:

- ■ enumerate: Returns a list of all of the files and nested directories referenced by the identified directory. Directory enumeration commands (like ls in UNIX and dir in Windows command line interpreters) are also used to return the contents of a file's descriptor to the user interface or to a program.
- ■ copy: Creates a new duplicate of an existing file.
- ■ rename: Changes the symbolic name of an existing file.
- ■ delete: Removes the identified file from the directory and then destroys it by releasing all of the blocks in the file, including the file descriptor.
- ■ traverse: The majority of directories in contemporary machines are hierarchically structured—that is, directories contain subdirectories. The traversal operation (like the cd command in UNIX and Windows) enables a user to explore the directory hierarchy by navigating from one directory to another.

Files are distinguished by their symbolic name—a set of printable characters, such as ASCII characters. Since directories are provided for the benefit of humans to organize their files, the symbolic name is used as an argument for most directory operations.

DIRECTORY STRUCTURES

The directory structure refers to the way that the collection of files and subdirectories is organized by the file manager. Generally, the structure is either a simple list of all elements or some kind of hierarchical (tree) structure. If the directory simply provides a list of all files in a particular collection, it is said to use a *flat name space* (see Figure 13.19(a)). The files in the collection may be sorted by their names, by size, by last access time, or by some other criterion, but there is generally no other structure on the collection. Directories with flat name spaces are not very useful when the collection of files surpasses some threshold (the threshold is different for every person), such as 20 files.

✦ FIGURE 13.19 Directory Structures

Here are three different ways to organize a directory of files. The flat organization keeps the files in a single, monolithic list. The strict hierarchy organizes them in a tree fashion, and the acyclic graph organization organizes them in an arbitrary graph, where no path through the graph wraps around to a filename that is already in the path.

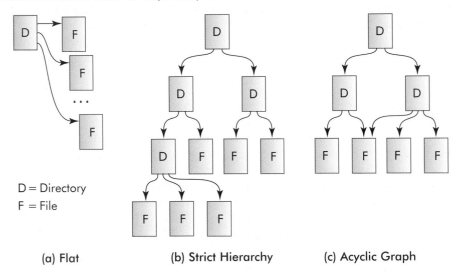

D = Directory
F = File

(a) Flat   (b) Strict Hierarchy   (c) Acyclic Graph

For larger collections of files, people like to partition the collection into smaller group-ings, and then organize those groupings. For example, if you were going to keep a collec-tion of invoices that you receive each month and the number of invoices was small, you would probably just keep a stack of invoices—a flat name space. When the number of invoices grew to 50 or so, you would probably begin to think about organizing the invoices (if you ever intended to look at them again). You might decide to put all the invoices related to home utilities (electricity, gas, water, sewer, trash removal, and so on) in one folder. Another folder might contain invoices for household purchases (clothing, house cleaning supplies, and so on). A third folder might contain invoices for entertainment, another for travel, and so on. You would end up with a stack of folders. As the collection of folders grew, you might decide to group all folders containing invoices for each year; then you could grab a collection of folders, a "folder of folders" for a particular year if you wanted to review invoices for that year because you were completing your income tax form. This approach is the basis for most physical filing systems: Information units (cor-responding to files) are grouped into collections that are kept in folders.

- Folders are then grouped into a "super folder" of folders.
- The super folders are then put into file drawers.
- The file drawers in a file cabinet are organized according to some structuring tech-nique.
- Multiple file cabinets can also be ordered, and so on.

This strategy is called a *hierarchical file organization*.

A corresponding strategy is widely used in computer file directories. Files can be collected in a **hierarchical name space** as shown in Figure 13.19b. An important concept in directories that use hierarchical name spaces is that the collection of files can also contain subdirectories—boxes labeled with a "D" in the figure. This is the concept that provides the recursive hierarchy idea: A directory can contain a (sub)directory that has the same properties as its parent. In hierarchical file systems, there is a single **root directory** that points to other directories and files. One can find any file in the hierarchical name space by starting at the root directory (the directory with no predecessor) and then by traversing from it into any of the subdirectories in the root. Once you move into a subdirectory, you can recursively traverse to its subdirectories.

In a pure hierarchical name space, the collection of files and directories forms a tree data structure (again see Figure 13.19(b)). Every directory or file is pointed to by exactly one predecessor directory (except the root directory, which has no predecessor). Tree-structured hierarchical directories are the basis of most modern directory organizations, since they allow the recursive partitioning of files into collections, and (more importantly) since they are natural to people.

Suppose two users with their own directory and subdirectories, want to *share* a file (or a subtree of files through some directory). It is then convenient to allow the directories of the two users to both point to the shared subdirectory or file. However, the resulting structure is no longer a tree; it is a graph (Figure 13.19(c)). Whenever sharing is allowed, the file system must be designed to ensure files are deallocated when all references to them have been deleted. This is commonly accomplished by including reference counts for all directories that point to a particular subdirectory or file. Graphs may be *cyclic*—they contain paths that lead from one node back to that same node—or they may be *acyclic*. Directory structures based on *directed acyclic graphs* share many properties with the more constrained tree. For example, a recursive search for a file in a subdirectory tree will terminate in an acyclic directory structure, but may not terminate in a cyclic directory structure. Because of the wide need for sharing, hierarchical organizations based on directed acyclic graphs are the dominant form of directory structure.

Some Directory Approaches

THE APPLE MACINTOSH FINDER

The *Finder* (or *Multifinder*) is the directory manager part of the Macintosh file manager. It is implemented as a user program in the Macintosh. The Finder employs a user interface that emphasizes the graphical point-and-select paradigm of the machine's overall human–computer interface. Files are organized into a tree-structured hierarchy with the "desktop" as the root. The Finder can contain several different devices (such as hard drives and floppy drives), each of which is the root of a subdirectory hierarchy. Each directory of a subdirectory is represented externally as a "folder" whose contents are viewed in a window by opening the folder. The graphical display implicitly enumerates all files in the folder by being visible, possibly after scrolling, in a window that corresponds to the directory. Files are copied and deleted by explicit commands. A file can be deleted by moving it to the "trash can" directory. A file can be copied across devices by point-and-select "drag" operations. Renaming is an editing operation in the directory window. Traversal is done by opening and closing folders. The Finder provides all the basic directory manipulation operations using a graphical user interface.

The Microsoft Windows family implements a directory system with similar syntax and semantics to the Apple Finder, although legally, the two have been shown to be distinct.

MS-DOS DIRECTORIES

The DOS directory manipulation interface is text-oriented, being invoked from the DOS shell command line interpreter. As with the Macintosh, each device on the machine has its own root directory. Thus, the list of devices can be construed as a root directory of the files (see Figure 13.20). DOS makes provisions for the user to reference a file anywhere in the storage system by using relative and absolute path names. The simplest form of a relative path name is just the filename within a directory, such as AUTOEXEC.BAT. More complex forms can be used to reference a file in a subdirectory of the directory where the name is being used. For example, if the current directory contains a subdirectory named BIN and BIN contains a file named PATCH, then a user can refer to the file using the relative path name BIN\PATCH. The path operator "\" can be used to identify any file in any part of the hierarchy below the current directory. The special filename ".." refers to the parent directory, so it is possible to reference files located at any point in the file system by using ".." in conjunction with "\". For example, if there is a directory with the same parent as the current directory and it contains a directory named PROGRAMS, which contains a program named PRIME.C, then a relative path name for the file is ..\PROGRAMS\PRIME.C.

✦ FIGURE 13.20 DOS File Directory

The DOS file directory is a hierarchy of filenames. The root of the hierarchy is "this machine." The next level is the set of storage devices for the machine, such as drive A:, C:, and so on. Each disk contains its own hierarchy.

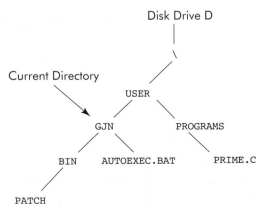

Absolute path names begin the directory traversal at a root directory. A path name of the form D:\USER\GJN\BIN\PATCH uniquely identifies a file named PATCH that appears in the directory named BIN, in the directory named GJN, in the directory named USER on the D: storage device. Similarly, the absolute path name for the PRIME.C file is D:\USER\GJN\PROGRAMS\PRIME.C.

Directory operations are invoked from the shell. For example, the DIR command lists the directory contents, the RENAME command renames a file, and the ERASE command deletes a file. The Windows Explorer user interface provides a point-and-select interface to this functionality, and the OS provides file managers consistent with the DOS logical directory structure.

UNIX DIRECTORIES

UNIX directories are directed acyclic graphs. That is, they allow a file to appear in more than one directory. UNIX also uses relative and absolute path names, although the operator for traversal is "/" rather than the "\" used in DOS. So UNIX filenames beginning with a "/" are absolute filenames describing the names of directories along a path from the root to the desired file. But UNIX does not allow the specification of device names in a filename in the sense that DOS does. (However, the machine's operator can mount other disks onto the current file hierarchy as described in Section 13.7.) An absolute filename such as /usr/gjn/books/opsys/chap13 indicates that the root directory contains an entry that describes a directory named usr, which contains a directory named gjn, and so on through the books and opsys directories to the file named chap13. If the base directory were /usr/gjn, then the same file could be referenced using the relative path name books/opsys/chap13. Or, if the current directory were /usr/gjn/books, then a file named prime.c in a sibling directory to books named programs could be referenced by the string ../programs/prime.c.

13.6 • IMPLEMENTING DIRECTORIES

Directories are intended to identify a specific collection of files and subdirectories. A directory is made up of a set of structured records, with each record describing one file or subdirectory in the collection. Each record must also provide enough information to allow the file manager to determine all known characteristics of the file, for example, the name, length, time of creation, time of last access, owner, protection state, and so on.

DIRECTORY ENTRIES

In most contemporary operating systems, a directory is implemented as a structured file in which each record contains a reference to the external file descriptor and at least enough information to be able to find the external file descriptor on the storage device. For example, the record might contain the filename and a disk address for the external file descriptor (as in Linux), or the filename, file extension (type), creation time and date, file size, and address of the first block in the file (as in the MS-DOS file system).

File management directory commands use these *directory entries* to perform their function. For example, enumeration is implemented by stepping through each directory entry record in the directory, reporting information about the corresponding file. Notice that in cases where the directory entry contains only the filename and a disk address for the external file descriptor, the enumeration command may have to read the external file descriptor before it can report information such as ownership, file length, and so on. The file manager designer considers such tradeoffs when they decide how much of the file description information should be kept in the directory entry and how much should be only in the external file descriptor.

Surprisingly, one of the difficult problems that file managers have had to solve is to be able to handle long filenames. Early versions of UNIX and Windows operating systems both limited the length of a filename to a small number of characters, usually eight. This made it easy to define the structure of a directory entry by reserving only enough space for names of eight or fewer characters. As we all know, file managers started supporting "long" names by about 1990. This forced file manager designers to innovate in order to store the extra characters in a filename. In some systems (such as MS-DOS), the file manager simply uses the space of an additional directory entry to hold the extra characters in a name. This allows the basic directory entry to remain unchanged from the old short filename format—and for all the old parts of the file manager to work without revision, provided they do not try to process a name extension block as if it were a directory entry. Another approach (used in UNIX file managers) is to create a heap in each directory, and then to allocate blocks of characters from the heap whenever a long filename is to be stored.

OPENING A FILE

When a file is opened in a hierarchical directory, the external file descriptor for the file is obtained using the directory that contains the file. In the UNIX absolute path name /usr/gjn/books/opsys/chap13 example, before chap13 could be opened for reading or writing, the system would need to find the file descriptor in /usr/gjn/books/opsys. But before the entry can be found in opsys, its directory descriptor must be found in /usr/gjn/books, and so on. Hence, when the file is opened using an absolute filename, the open() routine must first search the root directory to find the entry for the first-level directory—usr in the example. As a result, the first-level directory in the path name is opened and searched for the second-level directory, and so on.

Typical implementations of file systems allow each directory to be implemented using the same basic storage facilities as found on an ordinary file. The information stored in the directory is saved in a list of blocks managed through a file descriptor. As a result, the open procedure requires at least one disk read operation for each directory that appears in the path name. (If the open operation allocates buffers and begins filling them, the open() can cause multiple disk reads for each directory in the path name.) Opening a file requires time and effort proportional to the length of the path name, independent of whether the path is relative to a base directory or an absolute name.

File managers can avoid some of the cost of traversing the directory graph by caching directory information in the primary memory. As always, when information that exists on the storage device is cached in primary memory, the file manager must be careful to keep the two versions of the file descriptions consistent.

13.7 ● FILE SYSTEMS

Modern computer systems are usually configured with more than one storage device, and often, large disks are partitioned into logically distinct storage devices. Some storage devices also allow the computer user to replace different recording media on a fixed device (devices such as floppy disks, Zip disks, CD-ROMs, and so on). The result is that the file manager must be designed so that it can implement directory hierarchies that are stored on various devices, and combine these distinct hierarchies into a single system hierarchy.

In a hierarchical collection of files—one that is generally tree-shaped, although it may have shared files or directories wholly within the collection such as in Figure 13.19(c)—there is a single root directory for the collection. File managers can take advantage of this idea by requiring that devices that use removable media contain such a hierarchical collection of files. Then the collection of files on a floppy disk, CD-ROM, or other removable medium is organized so that there is a single root directory that leads into a directed acyclic graph of files and subdirectories. To traverse the hierarchy, one starts at the root directory and follows paths through the graph. This same idea can be extended to separate disks and disk partitions: Suppose that each disk or disk partition contains files in a single-rooted directed acyclic graph, meaning that one could start at the root directory for the disk or disk partition and traverse a path to reach any file in the disk. Each such hierarchical collection of files with a single root directory is called a **file system**. Every removable medium contains its own file system, and every disk partition contains its own file system.

A file system is an atomic collection of directories and files with a single root directory. The file system is a useful unit of system administration, since it corresponds exactly to the set of files on a removable medium. It can also be a portion of the entire secondary storage system that is archived in one operation. The MS-DOS FAT file system is described in Lab Exercise 13.1 at the end of this chapter.

The ISO 9660 File System

CD-ROMs use a file system defined by the ISO 9660 specification. Amazingly, this file specification is supported by every OS that uses CD or DVD drives. The ISO 9660 specification was derived directly from the "High Sierra" specification, which was designed by a group of industry experts in 1986. (They met at a hotel named High Sierra in Lake Tahoe; hence the name of the specification [Bechtel, 2002].) Even though there are differences between the original High Sierra and the ISO 9660 specifications, both names are frequently used to refer to the ISO 9660 standard.

Since this file system is intended to work with CD-ROMs, the focus is on reading files rather than the more general operations that include any form of writing to the medium (creation, deletion, copying, renaming, and so on). This means that, for example, block management can be greatly simplified since blocks will never be allocated to an existing file in an ISO 9660 file system. Secondly, CD-ROMs physically store information on a single helical track (see Section 5.5), so they have relatively slow seek times.

The contents of file system are called a *volume*. A volume is made up of a sequence of 2048 byte blocks (also called *sectors*). Figure 13.21 describes the organization of the file system in terms of sectors. The *system area*—the first 16 sectors—format is undefined by the standard, and can contain any information desired by the mechanism that writes the CD-ROM (for example, it could contain a boot record if the CD-ROM contained a bootable OS). The remainder of the medium is called the *data area*. The first part of the data area contains volume descriptors, and the remainder contains the directories and files.

✦ **FIGURE 13.21**　ISO 9660 File System Organization

This figure shows the overall organization of the information on an ISO 9660 file system.

Sector 0-15:	System Area (undefined by the standard)
Sector 16:	Primary volume descriptor
(subsequent	Secondary volume descriptor (optional)
sectors)	Partition descriptors (optional)
	Boot descriptors (optional)
	Volume descriptor terminator
	Path table copies (1 to 4)
	Root directory
	Subdirectories and files

The *primary volume descriptor* contains the essential information for the data area, optionally supplemented by information in the secondary volume descriptor, partition descriptor, and boot descriptor (see Figure 13.22) [ISO 9660, 1999]. Without describing each field in the descriptor, we call your attention to a few of those most relevant to implementing a file manager to handle this file system: The volume set size contains a length field that the file manager will use to determine how much of the data area is used for volume descriptors. The information in bytes 141–156 will be used by the file manager to determine the sector where the content of the file system begins. Specifically, bytes 157–190 are used to find the root directory for the file system.

✦ **FIGURE 13.22**　Primary Volume Descriptor

The primary volume descriptor contains the essential information for the data area, optionally supplemented by information in the secondary volume descriptor, partition descriptor, and boot descriptor.

Byte 1:	0x01 (this is a primary volume descriptor)
Bytes 2-6:	0xCD001 (this is an ISO 9660 volume)
Byte 7:	Version
Byte 8:	(unused)
Bytes 9–40:	System identification
Bytes 41–72:	Volume identification
Bytes 73–80:	(unused)
Bytes 81–88:	Volume space size
Bytes 89–120:	(unused)
Bytes 121–124:	Volume set size
Bytes 125–128:	Volume sequence number
Bytes 129–132:	Logical block size
Bytes 133–140:	Path table size　　(*continued next page*)

✦ **FIGURE 13.22**   Primary Volume Descriptor (*continued*)

Bytes 141–156:	Location of path tables
Bytes 157–190:	Directory record for the root directory
Bytes 191–882:	. . .
Bytes 865–882:	Volume effective date and time
Byte 883:	(reserved)
Bytes 884–1395:	Application use
Bytes 1396–2048:	(reserved for future standardization)

The file system uses a path table to address every directory. As mentioned above, the primary volume descriptor identifies the root directory; it also identifies the path table, which contains a pointer to each directory (that is, the path table is a list of each directory in the file system with a direct pointer to the sector that contains the directory).

A directory contains a variable number of directory entries. Each directory entry has the format shown in Figure 13.23. Directory operations use this information to manage the collection of files in the given directory. (The hierarchical relationships of this directory to its parent are kept in the path table.)

✦ **FIGURE 13.23**   ISO 9660 Directory Entry

A directory entry provides the detailed information for accessing a particular directory.

Byte 1:	Length of directory record
Byte 2:	Extended attribute record length
Bytes 3–10:	Location of the first block in the file
Bytes 11–18:	Number of blocks in the file
Bytes 19–25:	Recording date and time
Byte 26:	File flags
Byte 27:	File unit size
Byte 28:	Interleave gap size
Bytes 29–32:	Volume sequence number
Byte 33:	Length of file identifier
Byte 34–x:	File identifier (name)
Bytes x–y:	File identifier padding
Bytes y–end:	Reserved for system use

Finally, the subdirectories and files are written to sectors following the root directory. Every subdirectory and file is stored in an *extent*, or contiguous set of sectors. The extent contains a file descriptor and the file.

MOUNTING FILE SYSTEMS

When a computer system is booted up, part of the process is to identify the system boot disk: This is important for obtaining the master boot record; it also defines the (logical) device that will contain the root directory for the complete file system for that OS. Each time a removable medium is placed on a corresponding storage device, its file system needs to be "grafted" onto this base file hierarchy. The model used by UNIX for *mounting* and *dismounting* removable media is common to most file managers, so this description is used to represent all such operations.

The UNIX file manager incorporates a system call to allow file systems to be combined into one directory hierarchy. The `mount` command appends a file system into an existing directory hierarchy. It does this by replacing a directory in the base file system by the root of the mountable file system when the corresponding replaceable medium is placed on the system.

For example, suppose a system contains a CD-ROM disk reader. When a particular CD-ROM disk is placed in the device, the `mount` operation informs the file manager that the removable disk is to be grafted into the base file hierarchy. The root directory of the mounted file system will be treated as a subdirectory in the base file system hierarchy (see Figure 13.24). In the example, after mounting FS, the file named "bar" on the file system FS has an absolute path name of `/foo/xyz/bar` using directories "foo" and "/" on the base file system. After the temporary file system has been mounted, it can be accessed through all normal directory operations, including relative and absolute path names and directory traversal operations. When the file system is to be removed, an unmount command is sent to the file manager. This command prevents access attempts to a part of the file hierarchy that no longer exists.

✦ FIGURE 13.24   The UNIX `mount` Command

The `mount` command is used to combine a file system with the system's root file system. When a file system is mounted, the directory entry for the mount points to the root of the mounted file system.

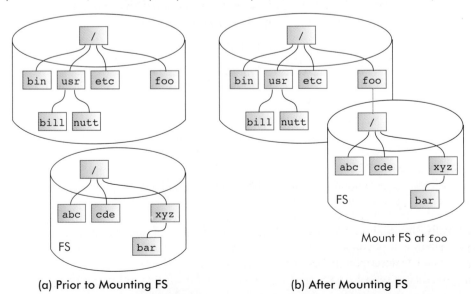

(a) Prior to Mounting FS   (b) After Mounting FS

The result of using mount is that it is possible to dynamically build a unified file hierarchy even when the different parts of the file hierarchy are implemented as distinct files systems on distinct devices or disk partitions.

HETEROGENEOUS FILE SYSTEMS

The mount capability provides a way for the file manager to seamlessly combine file systems that are implemented on diverse devices. After a file system has been mounted, software can traverse the resulting system file hierarchy without worrying about where a device, file or directory might be actually be stored. This suggests that each file system has certain basic information in it to describe its own file hierarchy and storage device details. This view that the file hierarchy can be built up by combining distinct file systems has led to the idea of **heterogeneous files systems**, a file hierarchy where the constituent file systems are not necessarily all of the same type.

Why would we care about heterogeneous file system combinations? The most obvious case is for removable media: Most CD-ROM file systems are formatted to conform with the ISO 9660 file system definition. This allows an audio CD-ROM player to read the disk, a computer CD-ROM reader to access the files, a DVD player to be able to access the files, and so on. Further, as a computer device, the medium can be accessed by a Macintosh, a Windows computer, and a UNIX computer. This is a compelling example that motivates the need for heterogeneous files systems: It is possible for a computer with any OS, with its own preferred file system format to also read ISO 9660 CD-ROMs. A more practical, but probably equally compelling reason for having heterogeneous file systems arises in UNIX systems: Over the years, the MS-DOS format for floppy disks has dominated. If you have a UNIX machine with a floppy disk drive and you would like to read or write a floppy disk, you will probably need the UNIX machine to be able to mount the floppy disk and then to read and write the MS-DOS file system that is used on the medium.

The Linux file manager handles heterogeneous file systems by incorporating a technique called a **virtual file system** (**VFS**) switch (a name that originated in an early design used in AT&T System V UNIX). The idea behind a VFS switch is that the file manager has a file system *dependent* part and a file system *independent* part. The file system dependent part of a VFS-based file manager is written for each file system type that will be used in the computer. So, for example, Linux file managers have file system dependent parts for MS-DOS file systems and ISO 9660 file systems, as well as for their own preferred file system, *ext2* (in Version 2.2 and earlier); see Figure 13.25. The purpose of the file system dependent part of the manager is to be able to read and write the file system. The purpose of the file system independent part of the manager is to implement the general algorithms for the file manager: enumeration, copying, deleting, renaming, and directory traversal.

The basic approach to designing a VFS-based file system is for the file system independent part of the manager to define its own internal file descriptor. For example, the Linux file manager defines an internal file descriptor that is based on the traditional UNIX inodes, meaning that the file system independent part of the file manager is pretty much the same as a traditional UNIX file manager [Nutt, 2001]. Each file system dependent module defines a set of functions that can be used to read the disk geometry, manipulate external file descriptors, and manipulate files and directories for its type of file

✦ **FIGURE 13.25** VFS-based File Manager

A VFS-based file manager is divided into a file system dependent part and a file system independent part. The independent part implements the file manager's general operations (such as enumerating directory contents). Each dependent part hides all the file system specific operations and formats.

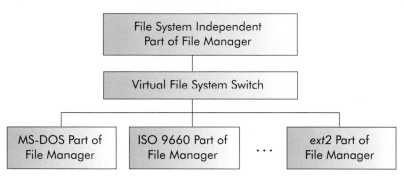

system. These functions are registered with the file system independent part of the manager, enabling it to invoke those functions whenever it needs to read the disk geometry, or to otherwise manipulate file descriptors, files, and directories on the file system.

Virtual file systems have been highly successful in modern file managers. An operating system can mount removable media that use a diversity of file system definitions, yet still be able to read and write the media. As we shall see in Chapter 16, this heterogeneous file system approach is fundamental to implementing remote file servers.

13.8 • SUMMARY

Files are the main means of managing and storing large amounts of data on a computer system. The files supported by an OS can be simple streams of bytes, streams of records, or more complex organizations of records. Byte stream files have the advantage of being a generic data structure logically used like primary memory to access the data. Their disadvantage is that most application software needs to add structure to the data for it to be suited to the application programming domain. Different operating systems take different approaches regarding the amount of support they provide for structuring the data. At one end of the spectrum are UNIX and DOS/Windows, which provide minimal support and expect system software to add data structuring mechanisms and high-level file systems at the opposite end.

File implementations translate byte streams or structured records into physical block images saved on storage devices. Sequential storage devices provide a natural mapping between the records and the physical blocks, since the sequentiality of the file is mapped to the sequentiality of the device. Mapping records to random device blocks is more challenging because the mapping can be arbitrarily complex. Block management, then, becomes a major task for the file system when it is implemented on randomly accessed storage devices.

Directories provide a road map for human users. The storage devices in a system may contain literally thousands of files. A directory provides a systematic way to name and locate those files. The directory management part of the file manager provides facilities to allow a user to navigate in the directory structure; to copy, rename, and erase files; and to administer the file organization across devices, including devices with removable media.

13.9 • EXERCISES

1. Write a program to determine how a UNIX kernel `write()` operation treats bytes that are interior to a byte stream. Does the `write()` operation insert a block of characters, overwrite a block of characters, or use some other strategy?

2. Write a program to determine how a Windows kernel `WriteFile()` operation treats bytes that are interior to a byte stream. Does the `WriteFile ()` operation insert a block of characters, over-write a block of characters, or use some other strategy?

3. Explain what the `O_APPEND` flag is used for in UNIX file I/O

4. Explain what the `O_FILE_APPEND_DATA` flag is used for as a value for the `dwFileAccess` argument in Windows file I/O.

5. Provide an example application or application domain in which sequentially accessed files are well suited to the problem. Your domain should illustrate that in some cases the information must be randomly accessed, yet at other times it must be sequentially accessed.

6. Suppose a disk free space list indicates that the following blocks of storage are available: 13 blocks, 11 blocks, 18 blocks, 9 blocks, and 20 blocks. There is a request to allocate 10 contiguous blocks to a file.

   a. Using the first-fit allocation strategy, which block would be allocated to the file?

   b. Using the best-fit allocation strategy, which block would be allocated to the file?

   c. Using the worst-fit allocation strategy, which block would be allocated to the file?

7. How many device operations (for example, disk sector `read()` and `write()` operations) are required to add a released node to a free list, where the free list is implemented with the linked-list approach? Do two-way linked lists decrease the number of device operations?

8. How many device operations are required to add a released node to a free list when the block status map approach is used to implement the free list?

9. Explain why a file system that supports indexed sequential files cannot be expected to have the same performance level as pure sequentially accessed files.

10. Suppose a file system is based on the indexed allocation strategy for managing blocks. Assume each file has a directory entry giving the filename, first index block, and the length of the file. The first index block points, in turn, to 249 file

blocks and to the next index block. If the file is currently positioned at logical block 2010 and the next operation is to access logical block 308, how many physical blocks must be read from the disk? Explain your answer.

11. Suppose a UNIX disk block will hold 2048 disk addresses. What is the maximum-sized file using only the direct pointers? Single-indirection capability? Double-indirection capability? Triple-indirection capability?

12. Early versions of the DOS file system had a limitation of 32MB of addressable space on a disk drive. Based on the description of the directory and files in the chapter, provide some conjectures for the limitation.

13. Suppose a file system is organized like the DOS file system and the device index contains 64K pointers. Explain how the file manager could be designed to use the 64K pointers to reference every 512-byte block on a 512MB disk.

14. File system checkers often take advantage of the block status map used to identify unallocated disk blocks. The basic idea is for the map to be copied into the checker's address space, with each entry in the map enlarged to capture more possibilities for the block's state (for example, allocated, not allocated, duplicate allocation, already checked, etc.). Devise an algorithm to use the block status table to check a disk to see if every block on the disk appears in one, and only one, file or on the free list.

15. Inspect the source code on your laboratory machine to see the details of the inode used in your version of UNIX. You will find the inode C structure in a header file. Its exact location will depend on the version of UNIX you are using. Write a table listing every field in the structure and its type. Also write a 25-word (or less) description of the purpose for the field.

16. Use a text editor to inspect a mail file on the computer on which you keep your electronic mail. Assuming it is similar to the Berkeley mail system, you should be able to recognize message boundaries as well as the message sender, receiver, subject line, and so on. Write an access method to read such a mail file and to print an index with one line per mail message. The line should print the sequence number of the message, the sender, the time and date the message was sent, and the first 20 characters of the subject field.

17. Read the msdn.microsoft.com. documentation for the WriteFile() function, then (in your own words) provide a description of how overlapped I/O works in Windows.

18. Implement two UNIX functions to read from and write to variable-sized records from a byte stream, where the user of the routines specifies the way information is to be formatted and unformatted when it is read. Use the following function prototypes:

```
int readRecord(int fid, char *record, char *specifier)
int writeRecord(int fid, char *record, char *specifier);
```

(This is intended to be a simple exercise using the stdio library to explore a trivial way to export application-specific record formats to the file manager.)

A Simple File Manager

This exercise can be solved using Windows 9x/Me, Windows NT, Windows 2000, or any UNIX system.

The file manager usually is the largest part of an OS, even though it does not have the most complex algorithms or data structures. Normally, the critical parts of the file manager—at least those parts described as being low-level in this chapter—are implemented in the OS. It is difficult to experiment with a real file manager, because of its size and the fact that it is supervisor mode software. This exercise is designed to give you some experience with file manager technology by having you write a simple, user-space file manager.

Because a production-level file manager is so complex, you will need to make a number of simplifying assumptions in designing and implementing your file manager:

- Your on-disk file descriptor will fit into one disk block. The on-disk file descriptor need contain only minimal information: (1) a filename of six or fewer characters and (2) at most four disk blocks per file (you can use 2-byte block addresses).

- The disk blocks will be very small—say, 50 bytes per block. (You can choose the final value after you have designed your on-disk file descriptor.)

- Directories need contain only minimal information describing the file—just enough to get your file manager working.

You will also need to remember the following:

- Do not implement file sharing—no locks.
- Do not implement file modes such as read, write, or execute.
- Do not include any protection or authentication in your file system.
- Do not implement path names, just filenames within the current directory.
- Do not implement buffering.

PART A

The file manager is required to implement the following API:

```
int fLs();
int fOpen(char *name);
int fClose(int fileID);
int fRead(int fileID, char *buffer, int length);
int fSeek(int fileID, int position);
```

Generally, fOpen(), fClose(), fRead(), and fSeek() functions should behave like the UNIX kernel functions open(), close(), read(), and lseek(), respectively (except with behavior that is simplified by the assumptions). For example, fOpen() does not have a flag parameter, so your function should operate as if O_RDWR | O_CREAT were used in the kernel function equivalent. The `fLs()` function should print all the information your system knows about the file, then return –1 if you detect an error and 0 otherwise.

Use the following disk interface:

```
#define NUM_BLOCKS   100
#define BLOCK_SIZE   50

void initDisk();
int dRead(int addr, char *buf);
```

You may also add a few more routines to the API—for example, if you wish to initialize the file manager prior to using it the first time. Although it is not necessary, you can add a `fcntl/ioctl` command if you need one.

PART B

The file manager is required to implement the following API:

```
int fMkdir(char *name);
int fCd(char *name);
int fWrite(int fileID, char *buffer, int length);
```

Generally, `fWrite()` functions should behave like the UNIX kernel `write()` function, except with behavior that is simplified by the assumptions. It returns the number of bytes actually written by the function call. The `fMkdir()` function should create the named directory, then return –1 if you detect an error and 0 otherwise. The `fCd()` function should change the current directory to the named directory if it exists, then return –1 if you detect an error and 0 otherwise.

PART C

Write a driver program that tests each function and feature (such as subdirectories).

AN EXTENSION

Note that you could solve this problem by employing the user-space floppy disk device driver from the Lab Exercise 5.1. This would require that you use the MS-DOS disk and file format. Laboratory Exercises 11 and 12 in [Nutt, 2001] describe the Linux solution, and the same exercises in [Nutt, 1999] are for Windows. (See the book's companion website for these exercises.)

● BACKGROUND ●

Much of the design of your file manager is straightforward. However, this section provides you with some useful applied information about how to organize your file system.

DISK LAYOUT

The storage device—"the disk"—provides a basic format for the way files will be stored on the disk. When a disk is formatted, it is prepared so that certain fixed locations will contain information expected by a particular file manager. Formatting a disk for one OS does not necessarily mean that it will be formatted for others. You will need to define your own format for your simulated disk.

FILE DESCRIPTORS

The file descriptor is simply a data structure: Its design is determined by the file manager designer at the time the file manager algorithms are designed. If you have Linux source code available, you can look at `struct inode` in the file named /usr/src/linux/include/linux/fs.h for the exact definition for Linux inodes. (You may also find it helpful to see Beck et al. [1998, ch. 6].)

When the file manager loads the external file descriptor into primary memory, it copies all the information from the disk representation, and then adds other information that it needs to manage the open file. For example, the external version of the file descriptor does not indicate which user and process currently has the file open or what the current location is for the file pointer; this information makes sense only for an open file.

The example in Section 13.3 describes the UNIX data structures to handle open files. To summarize: When the file is opened, the file manager looks up the file in the directory to obtain the inode. The inode is copied into a memory-resident set of inodes. The file manager then creates an entry in the file table that will contain new dynamic information needed by the process when the file is open (see the `struct file` definition in /usr/src/linux/include/linux/fs.h). The file table entry references the inode. Finally, the file manager creates an entry in the process's file descriptor table; this entry establishes the "file identification number" returned by the open command and points to the file table entry.

DIRECTORIES

Hierarchical file systems are relatively easy to support when, as is usually the case, directories are implemented using ordinary files. The part of the file manager responsible for directory manipulation just uses the normal file open, read, and write system calls. In general, the directory is treated as a file for which the internal structure and semantics are defined by the procedures that use it.

A directory entry must contain enough information to allow the file manager to match a character string filename with the entry's name and to find the external file descriptor on the disk if the names match. For example, in a UNIX system, the directory entry must have only the name and the inode number for the file. All information related to the file is kept in the inode. To list the files in a directory, the file manager would traverse the directory contents, printing the name from each entry, and then retrieving any other information to be included in the listing directly from the inode. DOS directory entries are 32-byte entries containing the filename and extension, file attributes, creation time and date, size, and the location of the first block in the file [Nutt, 1999] (on the companion website).

Windows FAT file systems use a 32-byte entry to describe a file. A directory entry contains the filename and a description of the location of the file's data. The entry also contains the file's size in bytes (in case the file size is not an exact multiple of the sector size). Since each entry is 32 bytes long, a FAT-12 (512 byte) sector contains 16 entries. The root directory has a fixed maximum number of entries (the number is stored in the boot sector), and it occupies a contiguous group of sectors at a fixed location on the disk. By contrast, subdirectories are stored in a set of sectors that are managed in the same manner as files—logically contiguous sectors are not necessarily physically contiguous on the disk, and therefore they must be accessed using the FAT.

The layout for a directory entry is shown in Figure 13.26. All multibyte integers are in *little-endian* order, meaning that the least significant byte is stored first.

✦ **FIGURE 13.26** Directory Entry

Directory entries provide enough information to describe a file: Its name, creation date and time, the address where it begins, and its size.

Offset	Length	Description
0x00	8	Filename
0x08	3	Extension
0x0B	1	Bit field for attributes
0x0C	10	Reserved
0x16	2	Time (coded as Hour*2048+Min*32+Sec/2)
0x18	2	Date (coded as (Year-1980)*512+Month*32+Day)
0x1	2	Starting cluster number A
0x1C	4	File size (in bytes)

The filename and extension are stored as uppercase ASCII characters. Invalid entries have names beginning with 0x00 (the entry has not been used before) or 0xe5 (the entry was used before, but has been released). The starting cluster number is slightly deceiving; although it references the starting cluster (sector) number, it cannot reference sectors used for the boot record, FAT copies, or root directory. If the starting cluster number is k, it actually refers to logical sector number $31+ k$.

The attribute byte stores bits for attributes, similar to UNIX attributes. The bit fields are shown in Figure 13.27. Note that bit 0 is the least significant bit. A bit set to 1 means the file has that attribute, and 0 means it does not. So for example, a file with attributes 0x20 == 00100000b has the archive bit set and all others cleared. A hidden, read-only subdirectory would be 00010011b == 0x13.

● **ATTACKING THE PROBLEM** ●

The concepts needed to solve this exercise are not especially complex, but there are a number of details that must be handled to arrive at a suitable solution. The most significant design challenge will be for you to create your disk layout and file descriptor formats. You are given a disk interface and are required to provide an API. (The extended problem would use the Windows FAT-12 format.)

DISK INTERFACE

The virtual disk used in this exercise is implemented as blocks of primary memory. It includes a statement to randomly produce disk read and write errors. You can adjust the threshold to suit your purposes. Use code similar to the following to implement your virtual disk:

✦ FIGURE 13.27 Directory Entry Attributes

The directory entry attribute bitmap describes the type of the file.

Bit	Mask	Attribute
0	0x01	Read-only
1	0x02	Hidden
2	0x04	System
3	0x08	Volume label
4	0x10	Subdirectory
5	0x20	Archive
6	0x40	Unused
7	0x80	Unused

disk.h

```
#include <stdio.h>
#define NUM_BLOCKS      100
#define BLOCK_SIZE      50

#define RELIABILITY     0.95
#define PERIOD          2147483647.0
#define ERROR           0
#define NO_ERROR        1
#define NULL            0

void initDisk();
int dRead(int addr, char *buf);
int dWrite(int addr, char *buf);
```

disk.c

```
#include <stdio.h>
#include "disk.h"

static int threshold;
static char *bList[NUM_BLOCKS];

void initDisk() {
  int i;

  for(i=0; i<NUM_BLOCKS; i++) bList[i] = NULL;
  threshold = (int) (RELIABILITY*PERIOD);
  sleep(3);
}
```

```
int dRead(int addr, char *buf) {
  int i;
  char *bufPtr;

  if(addr >= NUM_BLOCKS) return ERROR;
  if(rand() > threshold) return ERROR;
  if(bList[addr] != NULL) {
    bufPtr = bList[addr];
    for(i=0; i<BLOCK_SIZE; i++) buf[i] = *bufPtr++;
  }
  else
    for(i=0; i<BLOCK_SIZE; i++) buf[i] = 0;
  return NO_ERROR;
}

int dWrite(int addr, char *buf) {
  int i;
  char *bufPtr;

  if(addr >= NUM_BLOCKS) return ERROR;
  if(rand() > threshold) return ERROR;
  if(bList[addr] == NULL)
    bList[addr] = (char *) malloc(BLOCK_SIZE);
  bufPtr = bList[addr];
  for(i=0; i<BLOCK_SIZE; i++)
    *bufPtr++ = buf[i];
  return NO_ERROR;
}
```

This virtual disk is very simple. It statically allocates 100 blocks of 50 bytes each, then reads and writes those with the possibility of I/O failure. Use this code to implement your own virtual disk; change the block size as needed. You can also experiment with different reliability values if you like.

SOLUTION PLAN

■ The disk simulation code simply initializes a set of blocks but does not format the disk. The first step in your solution should be to design your low-level disk format (of course, you need not provide a bootstrap area, but you may need to have information regarding the disk layout, and you will certainly need information regarding the root directory). If you use a version of inodes, you will need to decide how this should be laid out on your disk.

■ The next step is to design your directories. A directory entry need not be complex— it should have just enough information to allow you to associate a name and a file descriptor. After you have designed the directory entry, you can implement the root directory. You may wish to postpone adding subdirectories until you get more of the solution working properly.

■ At this point you will almost certainly find it worthwhile to build a tool that creates a simple file system with a root directory and a few files. You will also find it worthwhile to build a tool that dumps the virtual disk contents so you can analyze it as you design and debug the rest of the system.

■ After your directory is designed and your root directory is implemented, you should implement your first version of the `fls()` command—a version that works only on the file system root directory. After you have implemented subdirectories, you can finish implementing `fls()`.

■ Now you are ready to design and implement the file descriptor and the open-file data structure(s). You may find it easiest to use either a FAT-style approach or an inode approach using only direct pointers to the data blocks.

■ You should now be ready to implement the commands on the API. It will be easier to get the whole system working if you first design and implement the directory commands—only those that read the directory but do not change it, followed by commands that write the directory (such as opening a new file).

■ After you have finished this phase, you can implement file operations—commands that open/close and read/write a file. Again, first implement commands that do not write the directory entries or file descriptors (for example, `fRead()`).

■ After you get this code working, you could implement a `fWrite()`, which would require you to do block allocation.

■ The final step is to implement subdirectories. In theory, all your previous code should work just with subdirectories, although in practice you will probably find some errors in your original code. Last, you should implement `fmkdir()` and `fCd()`.

Write your driver program as you develop the parts. When you are implementing `fLs()`, your driver program need only invoke the `fLs()` function. As you add more functions, add more tests to your program.

CHAPTER 14

Protection and Security

Files are stored on a computer's storage devices, which are space-multiplex shared among all users. This means there is the potential for a file owned by one user to be read from or written to by a different user. Sometimes this is exactly what is intended: Information stored in files is to be shared among the users. At other times, a user wants information to be private. How can the OS establish an environment in which a user can selectively either keep information private or share it with other users? That is the task of the protection and security functions in the OS. Keeping information private is even more difficult when the computer is connected to a network that is in turn connected to other computers. The information should be protected while it is being transmitted over a network as well as when it rests on a storage device.

Throughout the discussion of the OS managers, various ways to protect resources from unauthorized access have been mentioned; protection and security are pervasive in the OS. Now that you have seen all the parts of the OS (the "vertical" modularization), we will focus on the strategies and tools that cut across those functions (a "horizontal" function). Our discussion in this chapter distinguishes between external and internal security and describes relevant protection mechanisms that implement internal security policies. The classic model for studying internal protection is also discussed, followed by a consideration of how it can be implemented.

14.1 • THE PROBLEM

Protection and security are ever-increasing in importance in modern computer systems. As more and more information about our personal lives is encoded and saved on computers, our very identities potentially become accessible to any person who is able to obtain access to this information. In addition to personal information, the core of businesses and government is in information stored in computers. This information must be available so that it can be used by the organizations that own it and depend on it, yet it must not be accessible to unauthorized organizations or people. Besides protecting information, another aspect of protection and security is ensuring that computing resources that belong to a person or organization can be protected from unauthorized use by individuals or other organizations.

We can think of the problems of providing protection and security in a highly simplified model. Think of information or resources that are to be protected as "secure entities." The challenge is to protect each secure entity from all unauthorized access (see Figure 14.1). And the goal is that the computer's physical security (coupled with the internal system security) should allow access only to authorized "subjects" (such as processes and threads). Unauthorized subjects must not be allowed to access the secure entity.

✦ **FIGURE 14.1** Allowing Only Authorized Access

The OS environment can contain a number of secured entities that various subjects might attempt to access. The OS protection mechanism is intended to authenticate subjects to ensure that they have authorization to access any secure entity.

This aspect of security is generally decomposed into two parts: The task of authenticating a subject who attempts to access a secure entity, and the task of determining if the subject is authorized to have access to each specific secure entity. **Authentication** refers to the task of ensuring that a subject who attempts to access the secure entity is actually the subject that it claims to be. For example, if a subject claims to be the Sheriff of Nottingham, then the system's authentication mechanism is responsible for checking to be sure that the entity really is the Sheriff of Nottingham.

Authorization refers to the task of deciding that after a subject has been authenticated, whether it has the right to access the secure entity. Even if the subject really is the Sheriff of Nottingham, he may not have the right to inspect Robin Hood's personal calendar. A system's authorization tools only allow access to secure entities if the subject has the authorization to do so.

In the modern world of computing, a computer system is usually connected to a network, and the information that flows over the network is usually *not* protected from unauthorized access while it is in transit over the network. A third aspect of protection and security is to provide a means of ensuring that the secure entity is not copied or accessed while it is in transit. In contemporary computer systems and networks, this is accomplished using **cryptography**, or the encoding of information so that, in theory, it cannot be interpreted by a third party who happens to obtain a copy of the transmitted information while it is in transit. That is, cryptography logically encapsulates the secure entity inside a container. This provides a protection barrier for the secure entity while it is in transit in an unsafe world (see Figure 14.2), or even while it is stored in a persistent storage such as a file system. Thus, you could think of cryptography as an authorization tool, although the cryptography technology has evolved independently of other authorization work.

✦ FIGURE 14.2 Cryptographically Protected Information

Cryptography is used to protect secure entities whether they rest on a storage device or are being transferred from one machine to another.

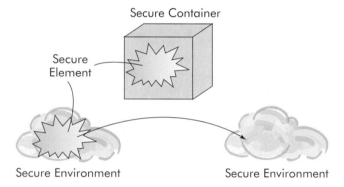

This chapter focuses on OS protection mechanisms that can enforce a broad spectrum of different security policies. The discussion addresses each aspect of current technology as an instance of authentication, authorization, or cryptography. This is an area of operating systems that is in evolution, so we will focus on the principles that are well-known and well-understood today. While each of the current technologies, issues, and problems can be characterized as pertaining to authentication, authorization, or cryptography, this could change in the next decade as research in this area continues to evolve.

THE GOAL

Modern computer systems support many users, either through sharing a single computer or many computers using a network. Organizations rely on computers to store all kinds of information, such as that describing the state of their operation and assisting them in administering their organization, as well as their proprietary and confidential information. The computers themselves also represent a significant resource of the organization, so the very use of these machines is an associated expense of operating the organization. Hence, the organization must protect both its information and computers from unauthorized use just as it needs to protect all of its other resources such as buildings, equipment, and financial funds.

The flexibility of software creates an almost impossible situation with regard to protecting against unauthorized access of resources. Within theoretical computing bounds, the functionality of software is limited only by the intellectual effort invested in that software: As long as a problem is actually solvable (the theoretical bound), programmers can eventually write software to solve just about any problem they want to solve. This means that it is probably possible to write complex software that could violate any given protection scheme incorporated in the OS. Even so, *the goal for the OS designer is to create a protection scheme that cannot be bypassed by any software that might be created in the future*. In attacking the problem, the OS designer might be able to get special assistance from hardware; the CPU mode bit is a simple example of such assistance.

Computer networks aggravate the problem because they allow many people to easily access computers without being in the same physical location as the computer. Physical protection mechanisms such as locked rooms do not present any barrier to network access of a computer. **Firewalls** are the network equivalent of physical protection. They provide one kind of barrier at the network interface that precludes certain types of access to the computer via the network.

Consider the problem of protecting a computer and its information in the context of modern system configurations. In Figure 14.3, users *A*, *B*, *C*, and *D* employ the resources in Machine *X*. User *D* accesses Machine *X* over a network from Machine *Y*. Users *A* and *B* have private resources storing private data and share other resources and information. Machine *X* also has some resources and information that are accessible to any local user, such as *C*, or remote users of Machine *Y* (such as *D*). The protection system must support this kind of environment by enforcing the desired resource access according to the organization's specific administrative policy.

POLICY AND MECHANISM

We have used the ideas of policy and mechanism throughout the book. It is particularly relevant in protection and security: Authentication, authorization, and cryptography tools are thought of as **protection mechanisms**, or tools that can be used to control access to a secure entity. A **security policy** is a specification that determines *how* the protection mechanism should be used. For example, a protection mechanism might be able to selectively allow certain subjects to access secure entities. Then a security policy will need to specify *which* of the subjects should have access to the computer's secure entities, and (at least implicitly) which subjects should not. So, an idealized protection mechanism would be capable of enforcing a broad set of different security specifications. In a computer, the operating system designer provides the protection mechanism for an entire class of computers, and the system administrator for each particular computer specifies the security policy that should be used for that computer.

Because of the need for protection mechanisms to be trusted software, they are almost always implemented as part of the OS rather than as user space software. Just as the CPU mode bit is necessary to distinguish trusted and untrusted software and the trap instruction is required to enable untrusted software to invoke trusted software in its trusted environment, general protection mechanisms can be more robust (or easier to implement) if the underlying hardware provides certain kinds of mechanisms. For example, in memory protection, the dynamic hardware relocation mechanism—particularly the limit register—provides a means by which the memory manager can almost guarantee that user space programs only read and write the memory that is mapped into their address space.

◆ FIGURE 14.3 Processes Accessing Resources

The general computing environment is designed to allow users to create processes and for the processes to use the systems resources. In systems that support remote access, the users may even create processes on a remote machine that use that machine's resources. The OS needs to protect secure entities such as resources from unauthorized use.

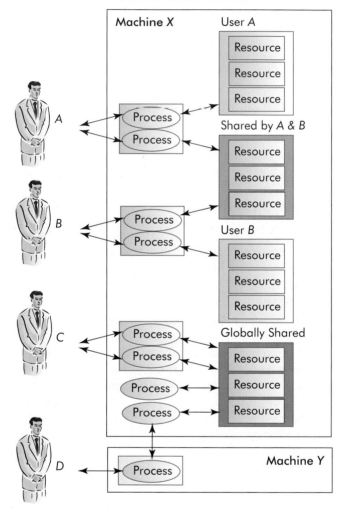

In a policy-mechanism separation for other OS functions, the approach is often to implement the mechanism as a trusted component of the system, and then to allow the policy to be defined in an untrusted world. For example, a paging mechanism could be implemented in a combination of trusted software and hardware, but the choice of a replacement policy could be rationalized as being best-chosen by the application (in user space). The rationale for this statement is that the application has the knowledge for choosing the best replacement policy, so the policy should be controlled by the application. For correctness, though, at least the mechanism needs to be implemented as a trusted mechanism. It is not clear that a security policy can always be specified in an untrusted domain. This is because the security policy may be essential to the authorization functionality: If the security policy is tainted, then the security goals for the system will be tainted. In modern systems, the security policy is sometimes specified in user space, but often it is specified in the kernel space.

There are many complex issues in designing a general protection mechanism: Given a method for specifying security policies, how comprehensive is the resulting space? How can a system administrator be assured that a particular security policy specification—set of directives—actually provides the intended type of security? What are the protection mechanisms a system might use to support a given space of policies? Given a particular set of protection mechanisms, what is the space of policies that can be supported?

CONTEXT FOR PROTECTION AND SECURITY

Computer security is more difficult to address than most of the other OS design issues. This is because security involves administrative policies, moral issues, and physical security external to the design of the OS. Because of the nature of computer security threats, the way the system is protected may be even more comprehensive than any other software and hardware of the computer system.

A protection mechanism may rely on physical isolation of the computer or on logical isolation that prevents remote users from accessing the computer with telecommunication networks. In general, this book does not address physical security issues, except to presume that unauthorized users are able to establish some kind of logical access to the computer system by interacting with a device connected directly or indirectly to the system. Note that it is difficult to solve the problem in an uncontrolled external environment. In these cases, security violators are not subject to any particular "rules of the game."

What are practical scenarios in which protection and security arise in modern computer systems? Classically, computer system designers have been concerned about intruders. An *intruder* is a subject that gains access to a computer by spoofing the authentication mechanism, or by finding a loophole in the authentication policy. An intruder might be a person or a software probe. Here are some well-known types of attacks:

- **Masquerading**: In this form of attack, the intruder is able to fool the authentication mechanism by pretending to be a different user. In the general case, the intruder approaches the authentication mechanism and provides a login identification. The authentication requires additional information to authenticate the identification, for example, a password. The intruder supplies the additional information and gains access to the machine, masquerading as an authenticated user.

- **Guessing a login and password**: An intruder may be able to fool an authentication mechanism by guessing the login and password. Suppose the human user knew the algorithm that the system administrator used for assigning logins—perhaps it is the human user's last name. Then it may be easy to guess the login. For a typical OS, the only problem then is to guess the password. Naïve users tend to choose naïve passwords. If the intruder knows the person for whom they are attempting to masquerade, then they may be able to make good guesses about the password: It might be the person's telephone number, dog's name, birthday, or other similar information. If the authentication mechanism uses simple passwords (such as 5-character strings of numbers and characters), the intruder can simply repeatedly attempt to login by writing a program that systematically provides every possible password until one works.

■ **Snooping for login and password**: More sophisticated human intruders might decide to search for passwords in unsecured locations. Notice that "About Me" and personal web page are a rich source from which an intruder can gather information about a user. As another example, suppose that a human user keeps a machine readable file with passwords to computers. If the intruder can find this file and manage to copy it, then he or she will be able to masquerade as that user. In some cases, a user's password might appear on the network in an unencrypted form. An intruder can keep a sniffer program running on the network, constantly looking for logins and passwords that might pass by on the network. When the sniffer finds a login and password, it saves it for the intruder to use at a later time.

■ **Alternate entrances**: Since computer systems are connected to networks, there is another avenue of attack that the intruder can use. Suppose the computer has a mail delivery port—a logical entrance into the computer that is used by peer email programs (or file transfer programs). A classic security bug was that a popular OS was installed with a default password used by the community of mail programs. If the system administrator did not change this password, then any intruder could masquerade as another mail program to gain access to the system. Besides mail, classic alternate entrances are the file transfer entrance and web browser entrance. Internet worm intruders (software instead of a human intruder) exploit alternate entrances to violate the authentication mechanism.

A software intruder can be more subtle than a human intruder since it silently moves into the computer and begins to violate the security policy. Here are some well-known software intruder attacks:

■ **Confinement and allocating rights**: The idea behind confinement is that any interaction between two threads in two processes results in information implicitly being learned about the communicating partner. This is true of human conversations: If you enter a conversation with a complete stranger, you may learn more about that person based on inferences than from the actual information they convey to you. In software, the goal of confinement is to prevent any intruder process from learning or inferring any unauthorized information from its interactions with a process that has a secure entity. A simple example of how confinement can be violated is in allowing an intruder to query a secure entity: Suppose an intruder wants to know if a person has a bank account. Then a balance query could result in an answer such as "you cannot access that account," meaning that the information that *the account existed was not confined*. In general, the confinement problem solution requires that a subject be guaranteed to be *memoryless*, that is, confined with respect to its ability to retain information or to leak it to other subjects. This means that the confinement problem can be fully solved only by considering the behavior of programs. If the secure entity cannot be shown to be memoryless, the confinement problem cannot be guaranteed to be solved.

■ **Trojan horse**: The Trojan horse problem describes a scenario in which an intruder provides some entity to the system, which the system accepts and incorporates into its trusted software. Viruses are the dominant example of Trojan horses: A virus is embedded in free software, a device driver update, or other unit of software that is likely to be installed without proper authentication. Once the Trojan horse has been installed, the software intruder has potentially gained entrance into the trusted domain of the computer. If it can become activated, it can operate as an authenticated process.

■ **Denial of Service**: In recent years, denial of service attacks have become popular on the Internet. The purpose of a denial of service attack is not to access a secure entity, but rather to provide so much bogus external work for a system that it is unable to perform its real work. Suppose that an Internet server normally provides content to client computers upon request. A denial of service attack can be launched by having a few client machines execute software that rapidly transmits normal content requests to the server. The server will become overwhelmed with requests for content, and will be unable to respond to normal service requests.

The protection mechanism and security policy is intended to address these types of attacks as well as others that intruders may invent. This provides a strong challenge to OS designers in which the state of the art in mechanisms and policies evolves along with the sophistication of attacks.

THE COST OF PROTECTION MECHANISMS

It is worthwhile pointing out that protection mechanisms introduce administrative overhead that can severely impact system performance. The basic protection model requires that each resource access be passed through a monitor before it can be allowed to take place. This may introduce a substantial performance cost. The OS designer must decide if the cost in performance is justified for the presence of the protection mechanism. In environments in which information must be secure (for example, information about a corporation's financial position or concerning the national defense), the performance cost may not be an issue. The information must be protected; otherwise, the computer system provides no useful benefit. Nevertheless, a challenge for OS designers is to design the most efficient mechanisms possible.

14.2 • AUTHENTICATION

Authentication is the procedure of determining if a subject is who it claims to be. In computer protection, two different techniques are typically used for internal and external authentication. External authentication is concerned with determining whether a user is the person he or she claims to be. For example, if a person logs into a system with a particular account name, then the basic external authentication mechanism will check to ensure that the person logging in is actually the person who is supposed to be using the account.

Internal authentication is intended to ensure that an executing thread (or process) cannot appear to be owned by a user other than its true owner. Generally, this means that the thread must be authenticated to be associated with a given process, and the process must be authenticated to be associated with a particular user. Without internal authentication, a user could create a thread in a process that appears to be a thread that belongs to another user. Then, even the most effective external authentication mechanism could easily be bypassed by having one user's threads behave as if they belonged to another user.

EXTERNAL USER AUTHENTICATION

The Boss: "My keyboard is broken. It only types asterisks for passwords."
Dogbert: "Try changing your password to five asterisks."
The Boss: "I hope I can remember it."
—Dilbert, *Boulder Camera*, September 6, 2001

The user's initial interaction with the computer system is with the login portion of the OS. In the login dialogue, the OS attempts to verify that users are who they claim to be. This aspect of protection is known as **external** or **user authentication**. If it were possible for a system to be unequivocally correct in its authentication of users, many aspects of protection would already be solved. However, no commercial systems are designed under this assumption since most user authentication mechanisms can be defeated. If it were possible to design an infallible user authentication mechanism, any action caused by a user would be known to be the full responsibility of that user, and not some other user masquerading as the intended user. In general, unequivocal authentication does not appear to be possible.

Consider how difficult it can be to create an infallible external authentication mechanism in a network of UNIX workstations. Originally, timesharing machines were physically located in secure computer rooms. Users logged into the machine over telecommunications lines, but had no physical contact with the machine or its operator's console. As personal computers and workstations began to incorporate UNIX, the scenario changed. Today, these types of computers are physically placed in the workspace of the user. The operator's console is a window on the physical display rather than a separate terminal in a secure area. This means that the physical security of early timesharing systems is not generally present in contemporary UNIX workstation environments.

Networks of workstations are generally administered by a central organization, with the workstation's "owner" being an ordinary user. The owner logs into the machine using the logical operator's console with no special administrative privilege. Because administrators have the root login, the system can only be administered remotely without allowing the local owner to alter any system files.

However, suppose the user turns off the power to the machine and then turns it back on. In this case, UNIX workstations were classically designed to boot up in single-user mode with the operator's console in root mode. Hence, any person wishing to have root permission could power cycle the machine to put it in single-user mode, alter permissions as desired, and then start the OS in multiuser mode. This flaw was quickly recognized and remedied by having the machine boot up in multiuser mode. However, the example illustrates how one cannot depend on simple assumptions such as "the OS has been proved to be secure, so the system is secure."

PASSWORD AUTHENTICATION The most widely used approach to user authentication mechanisms is one in which the user provides a combination of identification and password. The system inspects these two pieces of information, and then decides if the person who is attempting to access the computer is authentic. Given this approach, how difficult might it be to spoof the authentication mechanism, enabling an intruder to gain access to the computer as if he or she were some authentic user? Historically, this is a white spy versus black spy (with apologies to *Mad Magazine*) problem: Each time the computer system makes some improvement in the authentication mechanism, the intruder can exert a larger effort to fool the mechanism, leading to an improvement in the authentication mechanism, and so on. In order to get you thinking about the nature of the authentication work, consider a scenario in which a corporate computer—the *target computer*—can be accessed through conventional dialup lines or the Internet (using a telecommunications program such as telnet). An intruder intends to masquerade as some authentic user to access the target computer.

In the simplest case, the authentication mechanism keeps a file (called the *password file* in this scenario) that lists all authentic user identifications ("logins") and their corresponding passwords. For this simplest case, the system provides no particular advice or constraint on the form of the login or password. Suppose the intruder obtains a corporate directory of the employees, perhaps by finding an old list in the trash dumpster or even by finding such a list on a corporate web page (most companies do not publish this kind of information on the web, since placement firms can then easily determine the names of employees, and then begin recruiting them to work at a competitor corporation). Given that the intruder knows employee names, it will not be difficult to guess login names. For example, if there is an employee named George W. Shrub, then good candidate login names include: george, georges, georgesh, shrub, gshrub, gwshrub, gws, and so on. Think how easy it is to guess the login name of one of your friends on the university's educational computers. The intruder must also guess the password associated with the login. Suppose the authentication mechanism immediately responds to a nonexistent login name (before the password is supplied):

```
login: gshrub
There is no such user
login:
```

Then the intruder can quickly try various logins for the authentic user without being concerned about the password. Suppose the authentication mechanism were modified slightly so that it required that the user provide both the login and password before responding:

```
login: gshrub
password: ***** (The user types "texas")
Authentication failed
login:
```

Now the intruder does not know if the login or the password was unacceptable; maybe the login is authentic, but it does not match the provided password—that is (gshrub, texas) is not an acceptable pair in the password file. It might be that an authentic pair is (gshrub, dallas) or (gwshrub, texas), but the intruder will not be provided with information indicating whether it was the login or password that failed.

How could an intruder go about spoofing the user authentication mechanism? There are two well-known types of attacks: The intruder could simply try to guess the login and password; this is a simple brute force method. The second method is to try to obtain passwords through discovery, for example, by eavesdropping on a network, looking for records that contain a login and a password. Today, eavesdropping is probably more widely used than the brute force method, but both are used enough that an OS must attempt to thwart both types of attacks.

The fact that machines are not isolated from intruders introduces a major barrier to authentication. Today, many computers can be accessed using a dialup line or the Internet. This means that another computer could be the actual intruder by simulating a human who connects to the target computer. Given this situation, the brute force method can be quite effective: The human intruder can write a program that connects to the target computer, and then systematically tries (login, password) pairs. You can see that the intruder can use all kinds of external information to aid in guessing logins, for example, the knowledge of the names of people who work at the corporation.

How hard might it be to guess the password? If the intruder were to attempt a brute force enumeration of all passwords of length 1, then length 2, then 3, and so on, it might take a while. Researchers at Bell Labs were interested in knowing how hard this might be in practice, given a little additional knowledge about the employees. Morris and Thompson [1979] decided to study the passwords that were used at an internal UNIX system at Bell Laboratories. First, they analyzed a collection of 3,289 passwords gathered over a long period of time. They describe the following characterizations of passwords:

- 15 were a single character
- 72 were 2-character passwords
- 464 were 3-character strings
- 477 were strings of 4 alphanumeric characters
- 706 were strings of 5 characters that were either all upper- or lowercase
- 605 were strings of 6 all lowercase characters

The strings of 3 or fewer characters (17%) are very easily guessed strings using the brute force enumeration technique. The amount of time to search for all the criteria shown in the list is also not so great as to prohibit the brute force method. Doing so would allow the intruder to guess 71% of the passwords in the system. Next, Morris and Thompson looked for passwords that appear in online dictionaries and other lists; they found another 492 passwords. Of these, 86% of the passwords could be guessed by searching according to the string-length heuristics and the dictionary and name list searches. Even though this study was conducted several years ago, the results highlight the ease with which an intruder can guess passwords using the brute force approach with a few simple heuristics. Given the employees' names and this compiled list of the potential passwords, an intruder computer could probably break into the internal computer in a matter of minutes.

How can the system thwart a brute force attack? First, the authentication mechanism should distinguish between upper- and lowercase characters (many simple authentication mechanisms do not do this, because it is too "annoying" to the user). From Morris and Thompson's analysis, it is clear that if the authentication mechanism should encourage (perhaps even force) users to choose passwords that are difficult to guess. The mechanism may look up each potential password in its own online dictionary. If a word being proposed as a password is found, then the mechanism rejects it (requiring the user to choose a more complex password). Other tricks that the authentication mechanism typically uses are that the password has to be "long." For example, it must have more than 7 characters, some of which must be punctuation characters, some of which must be numerical, some of which must be uppercase, and some of which must be lowercase.

A second mechanism that can make the brute force method more difficult to use is for the target computer's authentication mechanism to try to detect a brute force attack. One simple technique for doing this is to count the consecutive number of failed login attempts. If this number exceeds a threshold value, the authentication mechanism can disconnect the remote user for a short amount of time (such as 5 minutes). For example, if a dialup connection gets 5 consecutive failed login attempts, then the target computer's modem disconnects the phone call. (Similarly, consecutive failed telnet connections over the Internet can terminate the telnet session and not allow another from the same source for 5 minutes.) Of course, the intruder computer can just reestablish the connection and continue, albeit at a slower enumeration rate. Notice that this may increase the time it takes to break into a specific computer, but if the intruder has 100 targets, then it is not a problem since the intruder simply tries another target computer whenever it gets disconnected by a particular target.

Windows NT/2000/XP User Authentication

Windows NT/2000/XP contains a comprehensive user authentication mechanism capable of very simple to very rigorous authentication [Solomon and Russinovich, 2000]. The default operation (the one we are used to seeing) falls on the very simple end of the scale. Logons can take place at the console or over the network. We consider the console login procedure in this example.

The basic components of the protection mechanism are the local security authority subsystem (Lsass), a user space program that manages user authentication among other duties, and the security reference monitor (SRM). The SRM is part of the OS kernel that checks access authorization for kernel objects and administers access rights to these objects. As indicated in Figure 14.4, the Lsass and SRM are assisted by the security accounts manager (SAM) server, active directory server, and the Winlogon process.

The Winlogon process is responsible for displaying the different screens, according to its internal state: In particular, when Winlogon reads the multi-keystroke "Ctr+Alt+Del," it will display the logon screen and move to a state to accept the user login and password for authentication. The logon screen is only accessible to Winlogon, meaning when the logon screen is displayed, no other process can be associated with the desktop: This is intended to prevent Trojan horse programs from handling authentication. Once Winlogon obtains the user login and password information, it attempts to authenticate the user by one of a multiple of authentication algorithms—the defaults are the Microsoft local authentication, MSV1_0, or the Kerberos authentication mechanism (discussed later in this section) for a multi-machine Windows 2000 domain. MSV1_0 determines user authenticity by searching the SAM database for the security policy. The SAM record for the user (if it exists) specifies the password, groups the user belongs to, and any access restrictions that the system administrator may have set for this user. The Lsass may also use its own policy as part of the MSV1_0 login scenario. The Kerberos-based logon procedure performs the same logical steps as the MSV1_0 logon. However, it gets the security policy information from the Active Directory instead of the SAM database.

✦ FIGURE 14.4 Windows 2000 User Authentication

The Windows NT/2000/XP user authentication uses a combination of an OS protection mechanism (the Security Reference Monitor) and various complementary user space mechanisms (implemented as Windows subsystems).

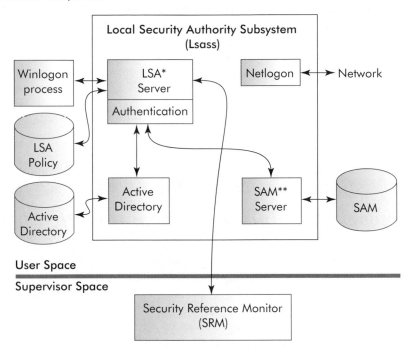

* Local Security Authority (LSA)
** Security Accounts Manager (SAM)

During user authentication, the Lsass creates a user's access token. The access token is created and managed by the kernel-level code: the SRM. The Lsass requests that the token be created for the user after the authentication procedure has completed successfully. This token effectively acts as a *key* that will be used by all threads and processes created by the user logon. Whenever a new thread or process is created, it inherits the access token.

EAVESDROPPING FOR PASSWORDS The Internet allows people to have easy and instant access to a number of different remote computers. Whenever a remote computer has valued content or resources, it will include a user authentication mechanism that must be satisfied before a person can access the remote computer. This suggests that the remote computer will start a standard authentication dialog with the person at the local computer whenever a session is initiated. For example, in a normal web browser/server dialog, the server asks the person at the web browser to provide authentication information: a login and password. In the absence of any "security paranoia," the web browser simply transmits the login and password information to the web server (probably using the popular http protocol). This means that the login and password information are placed on the Internet where any intruder could potentially see them.

Intruders write **sniffer** programs that passively inspect traffic that passes by on the network. The sniffer can be looking for any kind of information, including a login and password. How can the sniffer identify a login and password when it sees it? The intruder can conduct a few simple experiments in which he or she acts as a normal web browser user to request service. Their sniffer looks at the traffic between the browser and the client, determining the format of the login and password. For example, the information sent by the web browser might actually contain a text string such as:

```
...;login:gshrub;password:1600Penn-Ave.NW;...
```

After the intruder determines the format in which this information appears, the sniffer program begins to search for (login, password) pairs.

How can the authentication mechanism defend itself from eavesdropping? Haller published a paper describing the S/KEY™ **one-time password** system that provides an effective defense against the use of passwords that were obtained by eavesdropping [Haller, 1994]. The goal of the one-time password approach is to prevent a reusable password from ever appearing on the network; instead, a synchronized set of one-time passwords is exchanged between the user's machine and the authentication mechanism. That is, when a session is begun, the target computer issues a challenge to the user that requests the login and ith one-time password in a sequence of pass phrases. An eavesdropper might be able to copy both the challenge and the one-time password; however, once it has been supplied to the target computer, that computer will not use the one-time password again. The intruder can only copy one-time passwords that are used once, and then thrown away. The main idea in this approach is for the target computer and user to agree on an ordered list of one-time passwords. The authentication mechanism challenges the user for a one-time password from the list, and then never uses the password again.

In a naïve approach, this merely shifts the problem into how the target computer authentication mechanisms can generate a list of one-time passwords and then *securely* distribute that list to the user. The innovation in one-time password systems is that the secure list need never be distributed. The technique depends on the existence of a **one-way function**—a function, f, that is easy to evaluate (that is, $y = f(x)$ is easy to evaluate), but whose inverse is difficult to determine (that is, it is difficult to figure out what $x = f^{-1}(y)$ when you know the value of y). These kinds of functions are also very important to various protection mechanisms, and as we shall see, they are heavily used in cryptography (see Section 14.4). The target machine generates an ordered list of N different one-time passwords using the one-way function: In a secure session, the target machine authentication mechanism obtains the user's secure password. The password is combined with a *seed* value (also chosen by the user) to create a new password string, x. The first password in the sequence, y_0, is then computed by applying the one-way function N different times to x, that is,

$$y_0 = f^N(x) = f(f(f(\ldots(f(x)\ldots))$$

The second password, y_1, is generated by applying the function to the password string $N-1$ times:

$$y_1 = f^{N-1}(x)$$

and so on. This means that an eavesdropper intruder would have to be able to figure out f^{-1} in order to predict one-time password y_i, given that they had detected password y_{i-1}—and f was chosen so that determining f^{-1} is computationally infeasible. This follows because

$$y_i = f^{N-i}(x)$$

and so

$$y_{i+1} = f^{N-(i+1)}(x) = f^{N-i-1}(x) = f^{-1}(f^{N-i}(x)) = i\text{th one-time password}$$

The target computer authentication mechanism challenges the user to provide a login and the correct one-time password by giving the user the sequence number, i, and seed for the one-time password sequence. The user is expected to respond with y_i, the ith password from the list of one-time passwords.

Now, the user can use the system in one of two ways: When the target computer's authentication mechanism generates the N one-time passwords, the user can get a copy of it using a secure connection. In order to be secure, the copy is usually created as a printed copy that must be protected by the human user. Each time the user accesses the target system, the list is used to provide the correct one-time password. That copy must be carefully protected, since if the list is misplaced or publicly disclosed, the sequence of one-time passwords is useless. The second way to produce the correct one-time password is to allow the user's local computer to run a program that implements the one-way function. Then, when the authentication mechanism challenges the user to provide a one-time password, the user simply runs a program that employs the seed and the private password in the one-way function: The program responds with the correct one-time password, which is then sent to the target computer.

After S/KEY was introduced, it quickly gained in popularity as an implementation of one-time passwords. There are a number of S/KEY generator programs available for UNIX and Windows machines, and even some available for personal digital assistants (PDAs). This has made S/KEY an effective mechanism for implementing one-time passwords.

EXTENDED MECHANISMS For practical purposes, it is convenient to have software that is able to generate your own one-time password to access a remote target computer. Suppose this program were implemented on a small card for a computer—perhaps a PCMCIA card, Compact Flash (CF) card for a PDA, or any other form of "smart card" with its own physical form factor. Then it would not even be necessary to have software to generate the one-time password.

In modern computer systems, this idea of using a physical extension to the computer is increasingly being employed as an important part of authentication. Imagine a corporation that has a physical security policy that requires every employee or visitor to wear a badge with a picture of the person and machine-readable information (such as the magnetic strip on the back of a credit card, or a bar code as is used to identify commercial products). Then each computer within this environment could incorporate an authentication mechanism that read the information on the badge, using the information as part of the authentication procedure.

Extending this idea of a badge reader, the computer could take arbitrary additional measures to ensure itself that the human user is the person he or she claimed to be. Such authentication might involve techniques similar to those used by a bank to allow a person to transfer funds by telephone. The user may be asked to provide additional information besides the password, depending on the policy for authenticating a user. Contemporary protection systems may even resort to methods such as fingerprint or eye scan identification as a form of authentication.

INTERNAL THREAD/PROCESS AUTHENTICATION

Contemporary internal authentication mechanisms generally depend on the correctness of the OS process manager. Each thread and process has its own descriptor, maintained by the process manager. Normally, the contents of the thread and process descriptors are inaccessible to user space programs, although many OS implementations allow other parts of the OS to read and write the descriptor.

Internal authentication depends on trusted software to manage descriptors so that whenever a thread or process attempts to access internal information or resources, the process manager provides an **unforgeable identification** as a part of the process or thread. Any internal authentication mechanism uses the thread or process identifier to directly access the descriptor, where it can obtain all information that the OS knows about that thread or process.

As an aid to authentications, most contemporary CPUs are designed with a **process status register** that is changed on each context switch. In thread-based operating systems, the process status register provides a unique and unforgeable thread identification; in classic single-threaded process systems, the register contains the process identification.

AUTHENTICATION IN THE NETWORK

The emergence of the Internet has drawn attention to protection and security. Most of the technology focuses on cryptography, although there are some aspects of the problem that are centralized on authentication issues. As the Internet began to be heavily used, various classic applications were quickly revealed as gaping security holes. In the late 1980s, a graduate student at Cornell made worldwide headlines by exploiting one of these authentication weaknesses in a classic application.

A **worm** is a program that is designed to search for places on the network where it can live and propagate. The worm may enter the machine as a file, but then it will begin execution on its own. Once a file containing a worm has been placed in a computer's file system, the worm finds a loophole in the process manager in order to execute itself. Morris's worm was constructed to penetrate UNIX systems by taking advantage of the `finger` command (see the special section on the Internet worm in *Communications of the ACM* [1989] and Stoll [1988]).

In UNIX systems, the `finger name@host` command prints a standard set of information about a user identified by the argument. The name part of the argument can be any part of the user name found in the password file, so if one has the user's real name, it is easy to find a user's login name. The `host` part of the argument allows `finger` to connect to remote machines to execute `finger` in search of information about a user. The `finger` command also prints other information found in standard files, such as the `.plan` file. Users commonly put personalized information in the `.plan` file as a courtesy to other users, but the file might also be used as the basis from which to guess passwords.

While the `finger` command is an invaluable tool for locating login names to use with electronic mail programs, it is also an example of a tool that is used to gather information to penetrate another system.

Morris's worm executed `finger` on a remote host machine with a name too large for the string array in the `finger` program. This destroyed the runtime stack of the `finger` daemon so that when the daemon completed the command, it did not return to the program it was executing before servicing the incoming `finger` call. Instead, the daemon branched to a small block of code invoking a remote shell for the worm. The worm then had control of a process on the penetrated machine, thus enabling it to cause considerable damage by using various resources to debilitate the penetrated machine. In the case of Morris's worm, it was allegedly designed as an experiment for discovering unused computer cycles on a LAN— the worm was designed to find an unused machine, and then to begin running an innocuous program at the same time it continued to look for other unused machines. However, the worm was not constrained to a LAN, but instead, began to run all over the Internet, including on machines that were crucial to corporations and the government. Further, the worm was so successful at propagating, that it usurped most of the resources on any computer it penetrated. Finally, it was persistent, so that even if a machine that contained the worm was rebooted, the worm would continue to invade the machine.

File transfer mechanisms such as those used to transport electronic mail connections have also been used to penetrate a machine. File transfer requires one computer to be able to transfer information into another system's file space. The transmitting computer must be able to gain access to the receiving computer before it can cause the file to be stored, and the receiving machine must be prepared to accept an arbitrary file to be placed in its file system. The file transfer input port normally incorporates an authentication mechanism to verify that the transmitting computer has the right to store the file. However, in many systems this authentication mechanism is not very sophisticated, since extensive authentication increases the overhead involved in file transfer. An early loophole that was widely exploited in file transfer programs was that the authentication mechanism contained a default password. System administrators rarely changed the default password after they installed the file transfer code, thus enabling any intruder who masqueraded as a cooperating remote file transfer process to penetrate the machine.

SECURE WEB TRAFFIC Much of the traffic on today's Internet is generated by web browsers interacting with web servers. The web servers are providing content, conducting some form of electronic commerce, and so on. Consumers are pleased to have this expansive marketplace in which they can browse for information, products, and services. As the World Wide Web evolved, entrepreneurs quickly recognized the benefit of market size in hawking their wares. However, authentication also quickly became a critical technology since whenever an entrepreneur established a web server with valued content—information or a place where money was exchanged for products—it was necessary to be able to exchange critical information (for example, credit card information) with no danger that the information would be copied by an eavesdropper and then reused later.

Today, the secure sockets layer (SSL) and its successor transport layer security (TSL) are the critical network components to support web-based authentication. The secure http web protocol, https, uses SSL as the mechanism for moving information across the network (rather than conventional mechanisms such as TCP). SSL and TSL use cryptography so that when information is transported over the Internet, it is in an encrypted form rather than ordinary clear text.

THE KERBEROS NETWORK AUTHENTICATION MECHANISM   Kerberos is a set of network protocols that can be used to authenticate access to one computer by a user at a different computer over an unsecure network. Kerberos assumes that information flowing over the network could be tampered with during transmission, and it does not assume that the operating systems on the two machines are necessarily secure. The technique was developed at M.I.T. in the 1980s and is widely used today. The Internet Draft recommendation for Kerberos provides the most recent details of the authentication system [Kohl and Neuman, 1992].

In Kerberos, it is assumed that a process on one computer (the client) wishes to employ the services of a process on another computer (the server) using the network for communication. Kerberos provides an **authentication server** and protocol to allow the client and server to transmit authenticated messages to the companion process in a specific session. The following steps are observed in the protocol (diagrammed in Figure 14.5):

1. The client asks the authentication server for the *credentials* of the server process.

2. The authentication server returns the credentials as a *ticket* and a *session key* with the latter encrypted using the client's key. Section 14.4 explains more details of encryption, but for now, observe that the (composite) ticket and session key can be read only by the client. The ticket has fields containing the client's identification and a copy of the session key encrypted using the server's key. This means that the only process that can interpret the ticket's fields is the server.

3. After the client obtains the credentials, it decrypts the ticket and session key, keeping a copy of the session key so that it can authenticate information from the server.

4. The client then sends a copy of the ticket with the encrypted fields intact to the server.

5. The server decrypts the copy of the ticket so that it can obtain a secure copy of both the client's identification and the session key.

The authentication server must be trusted in this protocol, because:

■ It has a secure copy of the client's identification

■ It knows how to encrypt information that only the client can decrypt

■ It knows how to encrypt information that only the server can decrypt

■ It can create a unique session key to represent a logical conversation between the client and the server.

Since the authentication server can encrypt information for the client and the server, it can give the client a "container"—the ticket—that contains information that the client cannot read but that it can pass on to the server. This is analogous to having a credit card with an account number encoded on a magnetic strip on the back of it. You (the client) cannot actually read what is on the strip, but when you present the card to an automatic teller

✦ FIGURE 14.5 Kerberos Session Key Distribution

Kerberos generates secure session keys that can be used by a client and a server to conduct a transaction over an IPC mechanism that is not necessarily secure. The authentication server is able to encrypt information that only the client and the server can decrypt. It uses this ability to provide tickets and session keys to the two parties.

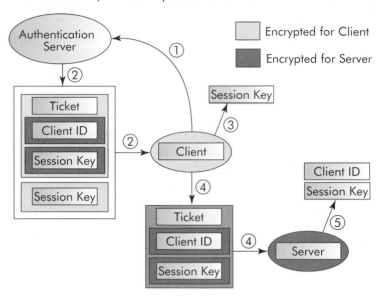

machine (the server), that machine reads your account number from the strip. The credit card is a "ticket" with an encrypted account number (although it has no session number).

After Steps 1 through 5 have been completed, the client and server processes both have a copy of the session key that they received as information encrypted by the trusted authentication server. An intruder on the network could not read the encrypted information without knowing how to decrypt it. Nor could it change the information to produce meaningful fraudulent certification. In addition, the server has a trusted copy of the client's identification so that when the client sends a message to the server, the server can authenticate the client ID and session key.

SOFTWARE AUTHENTICATION

Software authentication is concerned with the task of verifying that a software module was created by a trusted source and that the software can be expected to perform only the actions that are publicly attributed to it. Software authentication addresses the problem of preventing code that may contain a virus from being loaded into a protected computer domain. In the section on network authentication, we discussed worms and viruses: Although there is not complete agreement about terms, the Carnegie Mellon University CERT Internet security center (see http://www.cert.org/nav/index_main.html) uses the term "worm" to refer to software that actively attempts to penetrate a computer system by somehow fooling the authentication mechanism. The popular press often refers to these active intruder processes as "viruses," as in the "Code Red virus" that was designed to find web sites that used a particular version of Microsoft software and then to exploit a vulnerability in that software, causing it to overflow a buffer and penetrate the target machine (remember that Morris's worm also used the buffer overflow approach with the UNIX finger command). CERT refers to the Code Red software as a worm.

CERT uses the term **virus** to refer to a software module hidden inside another module. The virus attempts to become established in a file system by replacing some existing module as a bug fix, as an upgrade, or as some form of software that the user is inspired to install without authenticating its source. The file containing the virus will perform the task it was advertised to do, but it also will perform some unobserved function, such as leaving undetected loopholes for the intruder to use at a later time or planting a program to destroy system resources. In recent years, viruses have become a significant part of the software industry, particularly because of the evolution of two aspects of computing. First, floppy disks are widely circulated among personal computer users. A floppy disk is an ideal carrier for a virus, particularly since the recipient mounts the disk and runs its programs. Second, the Internet is a prolific breeding ground for viruses, because it offers a broad variety of mail, newsgroups, Web pages, and free software and other downloads. Today, there are various products explicitly intended to detect the presence of viruses and (if possible) to remove them.

There is a third class of software that has become popular with the wide use of web browsers: mobile code. **Mobile code** refers to software that is dynamically downloaded from a network source when it is needed, and then presumably destroyed after it has served its purpose. The most popular example of mobile code is probably Java applets that execute in a web browser. When a user requests content from a network site, the network site may download mobile code along with information content. The idea is that by downloading the mobile code, subsequent interactions between the user's web browser and the network machine can be far more efficient. In the context of security, the obvious questions regarding mobile code are:

- How is the code authenticated prior to downloading?
- Are there any "barriers" that prevent the mobile code from clandestine operation in the user's machine?

Today, software authentication has grown into a "showstopper" function in the use of the Internet for commercial purposes. People and organizations wish to connect their computer to the Internet so they can have access to the wealth of information and services available there. However, they do not want this connection to be an open door into their computer systems for intruders. Normal user authentication mechanisms can be used if the target computer is intended to support external access; many of the machines on the Internet are not intended to be remotely accessed, so there is no login mechanism and no user authentication. The lack of a login mechanism precludes the kind of penetration attempts discussed earlier in this section. Instead, the authentication problem is specifically focused on preventing worms and viruses from penetrating the target computer, and for ensuring that mobile code is authenticated prior to being loaded into the machine.

Certificates are a basic mechanism for software authentication. A **certificate** is a digital signature that is associated with mobile code (or other code that is to be downloaded over the Internet). The network host that supplies the mobile code and the user's computer exchange encrypted authentication information regarding the mobile code. The mechanism will ultimately tell the target computer's user that mobile code from a particular (authenticated) source is to be downloaded. The user can then either explicitly accept or reject the download based on knowing the identity of the source of the mobile code. If the users chooses to download mobile code that comes from an unauthenticated source or that comes from an authenticated but untrusted source, then they have explicitly bypassed the software authentication mechanism (and deserve what they get ☺).

Hartel and Moreau [2001] published a paper focusing on the safety of Java (and Java Card hardware) in mobile code situations. Java was developed explicitly to be a safe programming environment; it was inspired by the success—and fallibilities—of C++. The language was defined so that programs could not have unconstrained access to the environment in which they run. For example, Java programs use references to objects rather than the usual C-style pointers and pointer arithmetic that are the basis of buffer overruns. The runtime system was also designed to operate as a close partner of the compiled environment, enabling the compiler to generate code that the Java Virtual Machine would interpret according to the language definition. Finally, there are tools in the Java Virtual Machine to address security flaws, including a mechanism to analyze the byte codes to be executed, for example, to ensure that they neither underflow nor overflow the stack.

Microsoft has also created an environment to extend Java-like facilities for software authentication—the .NET initiative. This initiative depends on the Common Language Runtime (CLR) software in the target computer. The CLR exploits the compiler-runtime cooperation that proved to be successful in Java and also incorporates a new digital certificate facility to authenticate the mobile code. The essential technology that is leveraged in CLR is annotated byte code, which allows the compiler to pass additional information to the runtime system that the execution environment never sees. This idea is used in Java, but extended in CLR.

14.3 ● AUTHORIZATION

Authorization mechanisms are intended to ensure that users, processes, or threads are allowed to use secure entities in the computer only if the protection policy permits such use. Once a user has been authenticated to use a machine, the machine's OS will assign a process to perform actions on behalf of the user (in UNIX, this is the user's login process). After the login authentication is complete, the user is free to direct the command line interpreter (shell) process to attempt access to arbitrary information and resources. For example, a user could attempt to edit the system's password file. As suggested by Figure 14.6, each access to a secured entity must be authorized by that entity's authorization mechanism.

Authorization is part of the task of managing resources, particularly resource sharing. The goal is to protect one process's resources from the actions of other processes. Suppose process *A* has resources *W, X, Y,* and *Z,* as shown in Figure 14.6. Some of these resources are to be shared with other processes. For example:

■ Process *B* has read access rights to *W,* while process *C* has write access rights to *W.*

■ Process *B* has read/write access to *X,* while *C* has no access to *X.*

■ Process *C* has read/write access to *Y,* while *B* has no access to *Y.*

■ Process *A* has private access to *Z.*

✦ FIGURE 14.6 Controlled Resource Sharing

When a process attempts to access a secure entity, the authorization mechanism checks the system's current permissions to determine whether or not the access should be permitted. Process *A* controls Resources *W*, *X*, *Y*, and *Z*. Process *B* has read access to Resource *W*, but it can read and write Resource *X*; it cannot access Resources *Y* and *Z* at all. Process *C* has remote read access to Resource *W*, read and write access to Resource *Y*, and no access to Resources *X* and *Z*.

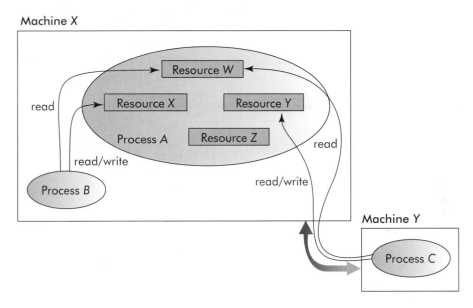

The need for authorization mechanisms has been present since the early times in which processes operating in behalf of different users were able to share the same computer, and hence the same files. This predates the usage of multiprogramming, since even uniprogrammed machines supported files. This meant that one user could create a file and save it, and then have its job finish. A subsequent job running in behalf of another user should be prevented from accessing a file that was private to the first user: The system would need to provide an authorization mechanism to handle this situation.

Although authorization has been an OS requirement since the early days of operating systems, traditionally it is only added to the OS design as an afterthought. Sometimes this occurred because the OS was originally built for one purpose, and then adapted to another (as in the case of UNIX). In other cases, the cost of implementing an authorization mechanism was deemed to be too expensive (in time to develop and in runtime cycles), so it was ignored. OS designers demonstrated how to develop reasonable effective authorization mechanisms in the Multics OS [Organick, 1972], even though the implementation and runtime costs were high.

How have OS designers addressed security concerns since 1970? Much of the effort has been on the authentication mechanisms described in Section 14.2. In cases where authorization mechanisms were needed—particularly for file and memory protection—there are a few widely used, but *ad hoc*, approaches.

AD HOC AUTHORIZATION MECHANISMS

OS designers have always recognized the threat related to protection and security, and have traditionally added some form of authorization mechanism to various OS components, almost as an afterthought. Two such examples of this *ad hoc* approach to authorization are file protection and memory locks.

FILE PROTECTION The UNIX file protection mechanism is a well-known, albeit simple, authorization mechanism. Every UNIX user is identified by a user identification, called a UID. Each user also can belong to various groups of users, noted by the group identification, or GID. The UID and GID for a process are part of the process's descriptor, which means they are easily checked by any system program when the process attempts to access a file.

Figure 14.7 is the result of executing

```
ls -lg
```

in a directory containing two subdirectories (`Tools` and `bin`) and three files (`Makefile`, `bangfix`, and `cover.tex`). The directory listing shows that each file is owned by the user with login `gjn`. `Makefile` and `bin` have a group ID of `rtsg`, `Tools` is in `ctrg`, and the others are in `faculty`. The first 10 characters in each line describe the permissions required to access the corresponding file or directory.

- ■ The `d` in the first character position means the entry is a directory and the "–" means the entry is a file.
- ■ The next 9 characters are interpreted in 3-character groups.
  - ● The first group describes the permissions that the file owner, `gjn`, has to the file or subdirectory.
  - ● The second group describes the permissions that members of the named group have to the file or subdirectory (the groups are named `rtsg`, `ctrg`, and `faculty`.
  - ● The third 3-character group of letters describes the permissions that all other users have—called *world* permission bits.

If a triplet has an `r` in the first position, the corresponding user community (owner, group, or world) has read permission on the file or directory; a "–" means the user does not have read permission. The second position in the triplet represents write permission, `w`, and the third position represents execute permission, `x`. File `Makefile` is set so that `gjn` and any member of `rtsg` have read permission to the file. Any user process can read the `cover.tex` file, but only members of `faculty` and `gjn` can write to the file.

The file manager implements the authorization mechanism. Whenever a process attempts to open a file (a prerequisite to reading, writing, or executing it), the file manager's `open()` function first determines the identity of the process that is attempting the `open()` function; from this, the file manager will know if this process is the owner, a member of any given group, or a process operating in behalf of any other user (the world collection of users). Suppose that a process, p_i, attempts to open the file named `cover.tex` in Figure 14.7 in order to write it: If the process executing the `open()` is owned by the same user that owns the file, then the file manager authorizes the access. Similarly, if the process is owned by some user that is a member of the `faculty` group,

✦ FIGURE 14.7   UNIX File Protection Mask

UNIX file protection masks specify the kinds of access that the owner, members of an explicit group, and all other processes have to the file. In the 10-character mask on the left side of the display, the most significant character is d if the file is a directory, and—otherwise. The next 3 characters specify read (r), write (w), and execute (x) permissions for the file owner. The next 3 characters are the same permissions for group members, and the 3 characters on the right end of the string are the permissions for all other processes.

```
-r--r-----   1 gjn      rtsg         2335 Apr 11   1996 Makefile

drwxr-xr-x   2 gjn      ctrg          512 Feb  5 10:27 Tools

---x--x---   1 gjn      faculty     37846 Feb  4 12:42 bangfix

drwxr-xr-x   3 gjn      rtsg          512 Feb  5 11:36 bin

-rw-rw-r--   1 gjn      faculty       853 Jan  6   1996 cover.tex
```

the file manager will authorize the access and complete the open() operation. However, if the process is owned by a user that is neither the owner nor a member of the faculty group, the file manager will deny access by refusing to complete the open() operation.

As an added feature in UNIX, each file also has a setUID flag bit that can be used to temporarily increase a process's rights when the process is *executing* a software module. When a process owned by any user executes the program that is loaded in a file with its setUID bit enabled, the process temporarily assumes the UID of the process that owns the file as long as it is executing the program stored in the file. This provision allows a program to be written to perform specific operations on data that belongs to a particular user, such that potentially any process could update the data (but only using the functions in the file with the setUID bit enabled).

MEMORY LOCKS AND KEYS Since the 1970s, considerable effort has gone into incorporating specialized authorization mechanisms for memory objects. An allocatable unit of memory may be a word, a partition, a page, or a segment. In the 1960s, machines sometimes used memory locks on each allocatable block of h bytes. Suppose each such block can be assigned a k-bit *lock* value and each process descriptor includes a k-bit *key* setting (see Figure 14.8). When a block of memory is allocated to a process, the lock is set to be the same as the process's key. Process key and memory locks can only be set with privileged instructions. The access is checked by hardware on each memory access by keeping the key value in a CPU register and by incorporating a lock register on the memory. The lock register is loaded with the lock whenever a word in its block is referenced. If the lock and key are the same, the access is allowed. Otherwise, the access attempt results in a trap to the operating system. In computers of the 1960s, $h = 16$ and $k = 4$. This meant either the degree of multiprogramming was limited to 16, or locks and keys were reused so that one process's key might coincidentally open a lock on memory held by another process.

This approach is simple to implement and is also efficient at runtime, particularly in systems that used dynamic memory relocation. However, it does not discriminate among different types of access, and it disallows sharing with the OS or among user processes,

✦ FIGURE 14.8 Memory Locks

Memory locks are binary bit patterns assigned to allocatable memory blocks. A process provides a key with the same number of bit positions as a memory lock. If the key bit pattern is the same as the memory lock pattern, the process has access to the block.

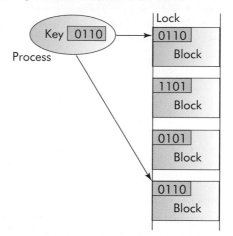

since the key and lock must match exactly. The sharing problem can be remedied by reserving patterns for special usage; for example, one key pattern might be a "master key" for any subject that has supervisor rights. The corresponding lock pattern may mean "unprotected" memory accessible by any subject. Supervisor access and sharing can then be implemented, although the sharing mechanism is weak.

A GENERAL MODEL FOR AUTHORIZATION

Even though there are not many general security mechanisms, Graham and Denning described a very general model for designing and implementing authorization mechanisms and policies [Graham and Denning, 1972]. (Others, including Lampson, had made substantial contributions to the model, but Graham and Denning provided a widely accessible description of the model.) In this subsection, we shall examine how this model unifies the aspects of a good protection mechanism for authorization and see how it relates to authorization security policies.

In the general model, a system has *active* parts and *passive* parts. Its active parts, such as processes or threads, act on behalf of users. Its passive parts, corresponding to resources and other secure entities, are called *objects* in the protection literature. (The **protection objects** described here are different from "object-oriented programming objects." The term "object" is used because it is prevalent in the protection literature.) In the protection model described next, processes access objects according to the **rights** that the process has to do so.

The authorization mechanism ought to be able to determine the particular rights—called the **access rights**—that any process has to any object at any given instant. Thus, the access rights that are in effect at any given moment reflect the security policy for the system and provide the specific directives to the authorization mechanism. Of course, these access rights also must be protected from general access—especially rewriting. They should only be revised in accordance with the security policy. Notice that even though a process may be authorized with read access of an object, it does not necessarily have write access. That is, authorization is concerned with the specific type of access that should be permitted at any given instant.

In modern operating systems, a process may have a different set of access rights to an object at different times, depending on what task it is currently doing. For example, when a process is executing a normal user mode application program, it has the access rights associated with the user who owns the process. However, when the process makes a system call, it begins to execute a system function, and then possesses the access rights of an OS (including using the CPU while it is in supervisor mode). As another example of varying access rights (from UNIX), recall that if a process executes a program from a file that has the `setUID` bit enabled, then the executing process temporarily assumes the rights of the owner of the file—this could even be the superuser.

The particular set of rights a process has at any given moment is referred to as its **protection domain**. Thus, any decision about the access a process should have to objects must include consideration of the protection domain in which the process is executing. To capture this idea succinctly, a **subject** is defined to be a process executing in a specific protection domain. For example, Subject X might be process P executing as an application, Subject Y might be the same process P executing a system call, and Subject Z might be the process executing a file that has the `setUID` bit enabled.

The notion of *access type* can also be generalized from file-like access operations to include access types that describe how one process controls another. As a result, it is convenient for us to note that subjects are also objects (but of course, not every object is a subject). This means that the set of objects includes all the passive elements of the system (non-subject objects) plus all the active elements of the system (subjects). Now the generalized protection model can be described in terms of the system, subjects, objects, and mechanisms to specify the dynamic relationship among the subjects and objects.

A **protection system** is composed of a set of objects, a set of subjects, and a set of rules specifying the protection policy. It represents the accessibility of objects by subjects as defined by the system's **protection state**. The system guarantees that the protection state is checked for each access of an object, X, by a subject, S (Figure 14.9). The internal protection state can be changed only according to a set of rules that implement an external security policy.

The protection state can be envisioned as an **access matrix**; that is, an access matrix is one realization of a way to implement the protection state. The access matrix, A, has one row for each subject and one column for each object. Every subject is also an object, since processes need to be able to exercise control over other processes. Each entry, $A[S, X]$, is a set that describes the access rights held by subject S to object X.

Each access involves the following steps (see Figure 14.10):

1. Subject S initiates type α access to object X.

2. The protection system authenticates S and generates (S, α, X) on behalf of S. A subject cannot forge a subject identity, since the authentication mechanism supplies the identity.

3. The monitor for the object X interrogates $A[S, X]$. If $\alpha \in A[S, X]$, the access is valid. If $\alpha \notin A[S, X]$, the access is not valid.

✦ FIGURE 14.9   A Protection System

The generic model for a protection system uses the protection state to determine if any subject's attempted access to an object should be permitted. The protection state changes according to a fixed set of state transitions, and the allowable state transitions are defined by the rules. The desired security policy is encoded as a set of rules.

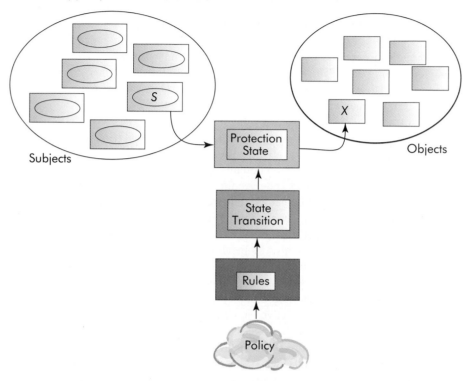

✦ FIGURE 14.10   Representing the Protection State with an Access Matrix

An access matrix is an intuitive way for describing the purpose and behavior of a protection state. The access matrix represents every type of access that each subject has to each object.

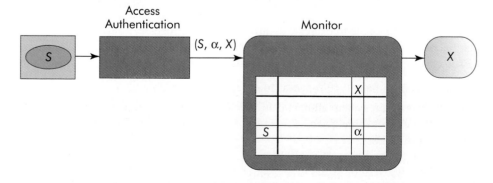

Using access matrices to represent the protection state, it is possible to implement many different security policies. For example, suppose a simple system is composed as follows:

$$\text{subjects} = \{S_1, S_2, S_3\}$$
$$\text{objects} = \text{subjects} \cup \{F_1, F_2, D_1, D_2\}$$

where F_1 and F_2 are files and D_1 and D_2 are devices. Figure 14.11 is an access matrix that represents an example protection state for the system. Each subject has control privilege to itself. S_1 has block, wakeup, and owner privileges over S_2 and control and owner privileges to S_3. File F_1 can be accessed by S_1 with read* or write* access. S_2 is F_1's owner, and S_3 has delete access to F_1.

✦ FIGURE 14.11 An Example Protection State

This example illustrates the access rights that each subject has to each object. For example, S_2 has update access to F_2; S_3 has execute and owner access to F_2; S_1 has control access to S_3.

	S_1	S_2	S_3	F_1	F_2	D_1	D_2
S_1	control	block	control	read*		seek	owner
		wakeup	owner	write*			
		owner					
S_2		control	stop	owner	update	owner	seek*
			control	delete	execute		
S_3					owner		

Given the example protection state shown in Figure 14.11, if S_2 attempts to update F_2, then the authorization mechanism intercepts the attempt and checks to see if it is authorized. When S_2 issued the update operation, this caused S_2 to be authenticated, and then (S_2, update, F_2) to be created and passed to an access monitor for the protection state. The access monitor interrogates $A[S_2, F_2]$ to see what type of rights S_2 has to F_2. Since update$\in A[S_2, F_2]$, the access is valid and the subject is allowed to update the file object. If S_2 then attempts to execute F_2, this causes the authentication mechanism to create a record of the form (S_2, execute, F_2). The record is passed to the access monitor, which interrogates $A[S_2, F_2]$. Since execute$\notin A[S_2, F_2]$, the access is invalid and the violation is reported to the OS.

IMPLEMENTING SECURITY POLICIES

As shown in Figure 14.9, the protection state can be changed by an acceptable state transition. This will cause access types to be added to or deleted from the individual entries in an access matrix implementation, or even columns and/or rows to be added to the access matrix. The goal is that any change in the protection state should be in concordance with the security policy. In the general model, this is accomplished by specifying the security policy as a set of complete, unambiguous **policy rules**. These rules describe allowable state transitions under the given security policy; that is, a policy is specified by choosing the type of accesses appearing in the access matrix and specifying a set of rules for protection state transitions. An example set of rules from Graham and Denning [1972] is used here to illustrate how rights can be passed among subjects.

The rules shown in Figure 14.12 implement a particular protection policy. They are defined using the access types shown in Figure 14.11. In the figure, there is a set of commands that can be executed by S_0. Each of these commands—transfer, grant, and delete—changes the protection state (access matrix contents) in some way. The column in the table labeled "Authorization" describes the conditions that must hold before S_0 is allowed to execute the corresponding command. If the command is authorized, its effect is shown in the column labeled "Effect." For example, S_0 might attempt to grant read access to S_3 for D_2. The command can be executed only if owner belongs to $A[S_0, D_2]$; if this command execution were authorized, it would cause read access to be added to $A[S_3, D_2]$.

✦ FIGURE 14.12 Example Policy Rules

In this example, the transfer rule allows subjects who have authorization to transfer an access right to another subject. The grant rule allows an object owner to allocate an access right to any subject. The delete rule is used to remove access rights.

Rule	Command by S_0	Authorization	Effect
1	transfer $\{\alpha\|\alpha^*\}$ to (S, X)	$\alpha^* \in A[S_0, X]$	$A[S, X] = A[S, X] \cup \{\alpha\|\alpha^*\}$
2	grant $\{\alpha\|\alpha^*\}$ to (S, X)	owner $\in A[S_0, X]$	$A[S, X] = A[S, X] \cup \{\alpha\|\alpha^*\}$
3	delete α from (S, X)	control $\in A[S_0, S]$ or owner $\in A[S_0, X]$	$A[S, X] = A[S, X] - \{\alpha\}$

In these particular policy rules, the * is called a *copy flag*. A process, S_0, can transfer an access right, α, to object X to another process, S, if S_0 has α access to X and the copy flag is set for the α access to X (meaning that $\alpha^* \in A[S_0, X]$). In Figure 14.11, S_1 can change the protection state by transferring read or read* access to S_2 or S_3 for F_1 because S_1 has the copy flag set on the read access. According to Rule 2, a subject, S_0, can grant any access to an object X—with or without the copy flag set—provided S_0 owns the X.

The copy flag and the rules are designed to prevent indiscriminate propagation of access rights among subjects. A right can be propagated only when the owner passes the copy flag to another subject. The copy flag can be transferred from one subject to another, or the right can be transferred to a subject with the copy flag cleared. The transfer rule is a nondestructive copy rule. A different security policy might require the transfer to be destructive, meaning that when a nonowner subject transfers an access to another subject, the first subject loses its own access. Such a policy might be useful to closely guard the dissemination of rights by the owner subjects. The delete rule is used to revoke a right for an object from another subject. Before a subject can delete an object, it must either have control over the subject that loses the access or be the owner of the object. According to the policy implied by this set of rules, if a subject is the owner of another subject, it also has control over the subject.

This example illustrates the basic complexity of the problem of determining whether the mechanism is sufficient to implement a broad class of policies and if the mechanism and policy combined actually implement an acceptable solution. However, it also shows how rules can be used to build up a desired policy.

Graham and Denning [1972] show that the rules in Figure 14.12 (along with a few others) define a protection system that can be used to address several previously published protection problems:

- **Sharing parameters**: A process's resource policy may be violated if other processes can indiscriminately change parameter values within its address space. For example, suppose a process calls a procedure in some other process's address space and the callee's procedure modifies parameters passed into the procedure so that when the caller regains control, variables in its address space have been changed by the called procedure.

- **Confinement**: Confinement is a generalization of the problem of sharing parameters. Suppose a process wishes to limit the dispersion of information to some particular environment. The challenge is to contain all rights to resources so that they do not propagate outside some chosen set of processes.

- **Allocating rights**: A protection system may allow a process to provide another process with specific rights to use its resources. In some cases, the first process needs to be able to revoke those rights at any time. Rights should be only temporarily allocated by one process to another. A subtle problem may occur if a process provides rights to another process and then the receiving process passes the rights on to other processes without the knowledge or permission of the resource owner. Some protection systems disallow this rights propagation without the explicit permission of the resource owner.

- **Trojan horse**: In this view of the Trojan horse problem, it is a special case of the problem of allocating rights—a service program being used by a client process using its own rights. If the server program takes advantage of the client process's rights to access resources on its own behalf, it is called a Trojan horse.

IMPLEMENTING GENERAL AUTHORIZATION MECHANISMS

The general protection model describes a logical set of components that can be used to solve various protection problems. The model incorporates mechanisms to authenticate subjects, represent the protection state, check authorization by interrogating the protection state, and change the protection state. The protection state element of the model was described by using an access matrix implementation. There are other implementations that are only required to respond to interrogation and to allow state transition.

In operating system design, it is important to have cost-effective implementations: What implementations are cost-effective for the various components of the model? How can an access matrix be implemented efficiently? As in virtual memory systems, implementing a system that behaves exactly like the theoretical model is very costly, so implementations approximate the behavior specified by the model. This section considers various implementation strategies.

The generalized protection mechanism is based on a means to save the protection state, to query the state to validate ongoing access, and to change the state. There are several issues to consider in implementing the mechanism:

■ The access matrix is not the only possible representation of the protection state, but it is the basis of most implementations.

■ The access matrix must be represented in some secure storage medium, only to be read and written by highly trusted mechanisms.

■ The protection system should be able to authenticate the source of each request by a subject, rather than being passed the subject's identity as a parameter through a procedure call.

■ The goal of the design is to route all accesses through the protection monitor (the mechanism that interrogates the protection state). Such routing will ensure that the current protection state will be used to validate each access.

■ The protection monitor must be a protected mechanism to implement the rules. It must not be possible for other subjects to compromise the monitor and state transition mechanism—for example, by sharing its resources.

The next sections describe how processes can take on different access rights in different domains, and how protection monitor and access matrices are implemented in contemporary operating systems.

PROTECTION DOMAINS

Figure 14.13 is a visualization of a system with two protection domains, for example, in a CPU that incorporates a mode bit. The inner domain represents programs executed in the supervisor mode; in the context of protection, the process is said to execute in the **supervisor domain**. Programs operating in the supervisor domain have additional access rights compared to programs operating in the user domain, for example, rights to memory as well as the right to execute the extended instruction set. If p is a process, then subject $S_1 = (p,\ \texttt{user\_mode})$ has fewer rights than does $S_2 = (p,\ \texttt{supervisor\_mode})$. Information in each domain is ordinarily stored in files or segments, where the file descriptor describes the domain in which the contents are either executed or used.

✦ **FIGURE 14.13** A Two-level Domain Architecture

A two-level protection domain system corresponds to the familiar notion of a CPU with user and supervisor modes. In this view, the domains are represented as concentric circles with the inner-most circle representing the domain where processes have the most rights.

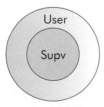

This organization of domains—as concentric rings—does not represent arbitrary domain relationships such as could be created using the UNIX `setUID` bit on executable files. However, it is the basis of a protection mechanism with a total ordering on the various domains. (This means that there is an order between any two domains, where one is "greater than" the other; supervisor domain is considered to be greater than user domain.)

The generalization of the two-level domain is a set of N concentric rings called a domain **ring architecture** for protection (see Figure 14.14). The ring architecture is described in terms of the Multics architecture in which it first appeared [Organick, 1972]. Suppose the protection system is organized as N rings of protection in which rings R_0 through R_S support the operating system domain and rings R_{S+1} through R_{N-1} are used by applications. Thus $i < j$ means that R_i has more rights than R_j because of the total order. The most critical part of the kernel (in terms of protection) executes in ring R_0. The next more secure level of the OS executes in R_1, and so on. The most secure level of user programs executes in ring R_{S+1}, with successively less secure software executing in outer rings. In this model, the hardware supervisor mode would ordinarily be used when software is executing in the lowest-numbered rings, perhaps only in R_0 (as was the case in Multics). This part of the OS is the most carefully designed and implemented and is presumably proved to be correct.

✦ FIGURE 14.14 The Ring Architecture

The ring architecture is a generalization of the two-level ring. The innermost ring represents a domain where processes have the most rights. The next outer ring has the second most rights, and so on. The outer ring represents a domain where processes have the fewest rights.

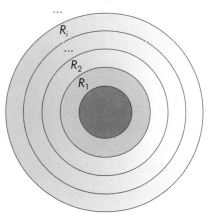

Software that executes in a ring resides in a file assigned to that ring (contrast this idea with the UNIX `setUID` idea, where there is no restriction on the domain in which a file executes). The authorization mechanism provides a means by which a process can safely change domains—that is, cross rings. If a file in R_i is being executed, then the process can call any procedure in R_j ($j \geq i$) without special permission, since that call represents a call to a domain with less protection. However, when a process calls an outer ring, the OS mechanism must ensure that the return and parameter references, which will be an inner ring reference, will be allowed.

Inner ring calls can be accomplished only by having the outer ring software enter an inner ring through a **ring gatekeeper**—a monitored procedure entry point. Each attempted crossing to an inner ring causes an authorization mechanism to validate the call, for example, by trapping to a part of R_0, which then invokes the gatekeeper for the destination ring.

Whenever a process makes a successful inward call, it changes domains; that is, it becomes a different subject. Implicitly, when a process calls a process in an inner ring, the target function is in a distinct file kept in the inner ring. An alternative view is that the OS has temporarily *amplified* the rights of the process as long as the process executes procedures in the inner ring domain. When the process returns to the outer ring, it will again change domains and resume its previous set of rights.

The generalized ring structure does not need to support inner ring data accesses, only procedure calls. Data kept in inner rings can be accessed using a corresponding inner ring access procedure, much like an abstract data type allows references to its fields only through public interfaces.

In Multics, 8 rings were implemented: 4 for the OS and 4 for application programs. Like Windows and UNIX, the kernel of the OS executes in R_0. However, administrative programs then run in rings R_1–R_3, depending on their need to change significant parts of the OS. For example, password management might run in R_1, but the administrative program that archives information to long-term storage might run in R_3. In user space, rings can be used to order communities of users; for example, an instructor might keep his or her files in R_4, and the students who interact with the instructor (by exchanging files) might operate in R_5.

Ring structures are available in contemporary computer architectures. The Intel 80386 microprocessor incorporated a four-level structure that has some similarities to the one described here. In the Intel case, there were three levels of instruction sets. Level 2 and 3 instructions were the normal application program instruction sets, although noncritical portions of the OS code were assumed to execute at level 2. Level 1 instructions included I/O instructions. Level 0 instructions manipulated segmented memory using a system global descriptor table and performed context switching. The architecture and its successors (the 80486 and Pentium microprocessors) are intended to support memory segment manipulation at level 0, while I/O operations operate at a lower security level—that is, a higher ring number. The main body of the OS operates at level 2, where its segments are protected by the ring structure.

IMPLEMENTING THE ACCESS MATRIX

As suggested by the discussion so far, an access matrix is the basis of an implementation of the protection state. However, the access matrix could be implemented in any of several ways. For most collections of subjects and objects, the matrix will be sparse, since most objects will be accessible only by a few subjects and most subjects will access only a few objects. If the access matrix were to be implemented by a rectangular array, then many entries in the array would be empty. More space-efficient implementations use lists of entries rather than storing the matrix in a rectangular array.

For example, the list can contain entries of the form $(S_i, X_j, \{\alpha\})$ if $\{\alpha\}$ is the set of strings that would logically be stored in $A[S_i, X_j]$. The tradeoff is the usual one for sparse matrices: The length of the list is proportional to the number of entries in the matrix—if the matrix is really sparse, then the space savings will be considerable. But if the matrix becomes dense, then the lists will become large, and access to the elements in the access matrix will be slow. Empirical evidence with systems reveals that the access matrix is quite sparse, so the list implementations are both space- and time-efficient. Access control lists and capability lists are further refinements on implementations of the access matrix.

ACCESS CONTROL LISTS One approach to implementing the access matrix is to partition the matrix into a collection of column vectors: Then the vector for column X_j represents the collection of rights that different subjects have to object X_j (see Figure 14.15). Now the authorization mechanism for object X_j can easily search the list whenever S_i attempts an access to the object. The column vector for X_j is called an **access control list** (**ACL**) for X_j. Of course, like the full access matrix, the ACL column vector is also likely to be sparse, so a time- and space-efficient implementation would use a variant of the sparse matrix technique. In this case, the ACL for X_j would be a list of nodes of the form $(S_i, \{\alpha\})$ so that for each subject, S_i, that has any kind of access to X_j, there is a node with the list of particular types of access, $\{\alpha\}$.

✦ FIGURE 14.15 Access Control Lists Derived from an Access Matrix

Access control lists are logical columns from an access matrix. An access control list is a list of the nonempty entries from the column for object X. The ACL is part of the resource descriptor for the resource that corresponds to the object.

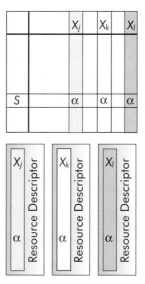

Access control lists have been used in more general forms for many years. In this approach, the resource manager incorporates an ACL for each resource. In most applications, the subject's access is authorized only when it opens (or is otherwise allocated) the resource, rather than authorizing on each access. If the subject and its access type are not in the ACL, then the allocation or open operation fails. The UNIX file protection mechanism is an application of an ACL, although it was designed more as an *ad hoc* authorization mechanism than as a simple instance of an ACL.

The lowest level of the Windows NT/2000 kernel supports secure operation by including a full ACL mechanism [Solomon and Russinovich, 2000]. The main part of the kernel checks each object's access according to a protection policy specified by user-space components. Whenever any thread makes a system call to access a kernel object, the part of the kernel that handles the access passes a description of the attempted access to the authorization mechanism. The object contains a security descriptor identifying the object's owner and an ACL of processes that are permitted access to the object. The authentication mechanism determines the thread's identity and access type, and then the authorization mechanism verifies that the thread is allowed to access the object (according to the information in the ACL).

CAPABILITIES Just as ACLs are columns from the access matrix, one could also use compressed rows (see Figure 14.16). Each such compressed row of the access matrix is associated with the subjects, so they can be stored as a collection of lists in the process descriptor. There will be one such list for each protection domain in which threads in the process may operate. Whenever the subject initiates an access, the authorization mechanism checks the appropriate list in the process descriptor to see if the subject has the right—called the **capability**—to access the designated object. If the subject does not possess a capability in its list, then it may not even know the address of the object. Thus, access rights are allocated to the subject much like tickets to an event. When the access matrix is stored as a collection of capabilities, each list associated with a subject is called a **capability list**.

✦ **FIGURE 14.16** Capability List Derived from an Access Matrix

Capability lists are logical rows from an access matrix. A capability list is a collection of the nonempty entries from the row for subject S. The capability list is part of the process descriptor for the process that corresponds to the subject.

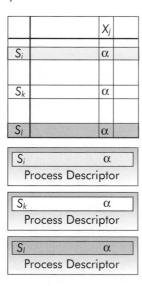

A capability is a unique, global name for an access right to an object in a system. For example, a capability might be a Kerberos ticket, as well as "read access to sector i on disk k" and "write access to virtual address i in process j's address space." Capabilities are used

in contemporary operating systems to implement a protection mechanism and to span address spaces among subjects.

By treating a capability as both a container of access rights *and* a reference to the object, the protection mechanism can be designed to be more efficient. In this case, the capability serves two purposes: First, it provides an address for a resource in a very large address space. Second, possession of the capability represents the authorization of the subject to the described object. The latter is a key aspect of capability-based systems (recall the Kerberos tickets). That is, authentication occurs only when a subject obtains a capability, and is unnecessary thereafter. In this approach, once the capability has been issued, it is not necessary for a runtime access monitor and access matrix to authenticate or authorize each access. Possession of a capability represents that authentication and authorization have already occurred, which also means that capabilities must be protected and cannot be arbitrarily passed around or copied.

Given this general model, there are certain properties that the protection mechanism must implement:

- The values taken on by a capability must be derived from a large name space because a system using capabilities will need many different instances of a capability in order to represent all accesses to all objects by all subjects.

- Capabilities must be unique and not reused once they have been assigned. This prevents a "recycled" capability from inadvertently providing a subject with access to an object left over from its original use.

- Capabilities need to be distinguishable from spurious names. For example, the system must not confuse ordinary integers or pointers with capabilities.

Capabilities must be implemented as secure, trusted entities. There are two basic approaches to implementing capabilities. Either capabilities may be wholly implemented within the operating system's address space or the hardware may incorporate specialized support for them. As a practical approach, capabilities are sometimes implemented by providing a very large space and then issuing capabilities randomly from it. This approach, however, does not guarantee absolute protection; capabilities are not guaranteed to be unique even though there is high probability that they will be.

A capability can be represented in the OS as a typed scalar value. It is conceptually a record of the form

```
struct capability{
    type tag;
    long addr;
}
```

If `c` is a capability, its tag field, `c.tag`, is set to have the value `capability`; then the address field, `c.addr`, is the global address that the capability references. A subject can access an object only if it has a capability whereby `c.addr` addresses an *entry point* to the resource that corresponds to the type of the access. If an object monitor is included at all, it need only verify that `c.tag` is set to have the `capability` value in order to be assured that the access is valid.

Each subject needs to be able to obtain and use capabilities, but none can be allowed to *generate* them. If the subject's capabilities are all maintained in the operating system's space, the subject is unable to create a data structure resembling a capability without the intervention of the OS. However, the subject can use its capabilities for accessing objects with no special handling by the OS. In the case that capabilities are exclusively managed by the OS, the tag field in the data structure can be eliminated, since the type is implied by the use of the capability. For example, in a segmented virtual-memory system, all capabilities are stored in a subject's capability segment.

Tags can be implemented in hardware by associating a tag field with each unit of memory. For example, early Burroughs computer architectures used hardware capabilities. The tag field in the word can be set to `capability` or `other` by a supervisor mode instruction. The tag field can be read only by a supervisor mode instruction in the object's protection monitor.

The Mach OS provides kernel-level capabilities. Mach is the successor of the Rochester Intelligent Gateway (RIG) and Accent operating systems. All three used capabilities in various ways. The use of capabilities in the IPC mechanism is a good illustration of how capabilities are used in many contemporary operating systems [Accetta, et al., 1986].

Mach IPC is based on messages and ports. A message is a data structure, and a port is a communication channel that is implemented in the kernel and used to receive messages from other threads. Each port accepts messages of a particular type. If one thread wishes to suspend another, it sends a suspend message to the target's thread port. Hence, if one thread knows the location and type of another thread's ports, then it has a capability with which it can control the second thread.

Ports are protected kernel objects that must be requested and allocated before they can be used. If a thread knows a port, then it has the authority to send messages to the port, and the receiver will honor those messages. The kernel must allocate a port before it can be used. Ports are equivalent to capabilities. If a thread has the capability, it can send messages to the port; if it does not, it cannot send messages to the port. Section 19.4 elaborates on this example.

14.4 ● CRYPTOGRAPHY

Cryptography is a technique by which information can be encoded into a form where its meaning is obscured until a complementary decoding operation recreates the original information. For example, suppose you wanted to encrypt the message (which has punctuation and capitalization omitted):

```
the quick sly fox jumped over the lazy brown dog
```

Then you could construct a table that mapped each character to another character. For example, if you simply added 2 (modulo 27) to each character and treated the blank character as the first character in the alphabet, then your encrypted message would be:

```
vjgbswkembun bhqzblworgffqxgtbvjgbnca bdtqynpbfqi
```

Now you could send the encrypted message to another person, knowing that if anyone made a copy of the message when it was in transit, it would appear meaningless.

Cryptography is a very old technique for sending secret messages via untrusted message carriers. In ancient times, generals would encrypt messages to their subordinates so that if the messenger was caught by the enemy, then the likelihood of the enemy under-standing the message would be decreased. During World War II, cryptography was widely used by both sides to broadcast messages via public airwaves. The essential element of cryptography is in the encoding of the message. The simple encryption used to open this discussion is no more difficult than one that might be used for a game in the weekend newspaper—even an amateur intruder could break this code with little effort. Historically, people have worked hard to find encryption algorithms that are difficult to decrypt. Today, cryptography is widely used as the basis of many protection mechanisms, particularly to protect information that is in transit on the Internet. This section describes contemporary cryptography technology.

THE BIG PICTURE

Cryptographic techniques are used to convert **clear text** (also called **plaintext**) to **cipher-text** to protect the text whenever it is exposed on an unprotected medium. An encryption function, encrypt(), and a decryption function, decrypt() (where decrypt() is an inverse function of encrypt()), are defined, where

```
decrypt(key', encrypt(key, plaintext)) = plaintext
```

That is, encrypt() with a key encodes the clear text into ciphertext. A different key, key', is used by decrypt() to translate the ciphertext back into clear text. Figure 14.17 illustrates this pictorially, and introduces notation to reflect different versions of the text. That is, M is clear text, K_e is an encryption key, E is the encryption function, K_d is the decryption key, and D is the decryption function. So, for example, when we write $E(K_e, M)$, we are referring to the ciphertext. Or if C is the ciphertext, then $D(K_d, C)$ is the clear text.

✦ FIGURE 14.17 The Basic Cryptography Model

Cryptography technology assumes that there are encryption and decryption mechanisms in the system. Clear text can be encrypted using an encryption key, K_e, and then decrypted using a decryption key, K_d. An intruder may be able to copy the encrypted clear text, and then attempt to decrypt it using side information.

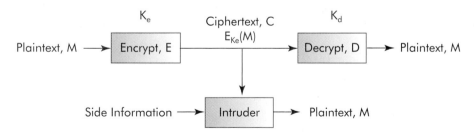

There are two strategies for constructing encryption and decryption mechanisms. One is to build a design in which details of encrypt() and decrypt() are unknown so that part of the mechanism is in the secrecy of the implementation. Another is to build a design in which the mechanism is public but the keys are secret and difficult to forge. In the first case, encrypt() and decrypt() are complex, thus making it difficult to guess how the translation is accomplished. However, if an intruder ever discovers how they work, they are useless. During World War II, the encryption mechanism used by one side was based on this approach, so Hollywood has made countless movies of high adventure and intrigue relating to capturing the encoding device.

In the second approach, the *keys* are complex, making it difficult to guess a key, so there is no need to make the mechanism design secret (and no worry about the technique failing because the design was discovered by an intruder). Contemporary cryptography implementations use the latter approach; that is, the operation of the mechanism is public but the keys are private.

In Figure 14.17, the intruder observes ciphertext. Since it is assumed that the intruder knows how the decryption mechanism works, the challenge is to guess the decryption key. In so doing, intruders may use any external information—also called *side information*— they choose. The challenge is to design the various components so that it is computationally difficult for the intruder to guess the decryption key.

PRIVATE KEY ENCRYPTION

Private key encryption corresponds to one's intuitive notion of how cryptography should work; both K_e and K_d are private to the correspondents involved in the cryptographic session. They are also often the same value ($K_e = K_d$). This is contrasted with public key encryption that is described in the next subsection. Private key encryption is used in cases where the parties exchanging information trust each other. The intruder's point of attack in private key encryption is to attempt to steal or guess the private key. After describing symmetric encryption, we discuss the most commonly used private key encryption approach, the Data Encryption Standard.

SYMMETRIC ENCRYPTION Private key encryption often uses **symmetric encryption** techniques in which the encryption key is the same as the decryption key ($K_e = K_d$). One implication of this is that the `encrypt()` function is identical to the `decrypt()` function. This form of encryption is useful if a trusted subsystem performs both the encryption and decryption of information. For example, an OS user authentication system might use this technique for saving passwords. When the user declares a password, the OS uses its private key for encrypting the data and storing it in a password object. At authentication time, the OS uses its key to decode the entry in the password object to compare it to the password supplied by the user. UNIX uses this idea as part of its approach to protect passwords.

Here is a simple example of how symmetric encryption can be implemented. Imagine that we wished to encrypt the ASCII string "`abra`". The binary representation of this string is:

`0x61627261`

Or if we write this in binary, it is:

`01100001011000100111001001100001`

Now suppose we chose a random string of bits that is the same length as the clear text (32 bits in this simple case) to use as the encryption key:

`10011101010010001111010101011100`

Next, compute the bit-wise exclusive OR of the clear text and the key:

111111000010101010000011100111101

which can be represented in hexadecimal as:

0xfc2a873d

(which has no printable interpretation as an ASCII string). This is the ciphertext. The exclusive OR is an example of a symmetric encryption function. This means that if we encrypt the ciphertext using the same key, we should get the plaintext back again—which it does (try it!). Notice how this example illustrates that the encryption algorithm itself can be made public, although the key might be difficult to guess (it is not difficult to guess with such a simple encryption algorithm).

DATA ENCRYPTION STANDARD (DES) Another critical aspect of private key encryption is in choosing the scheme for translating the clear text to ciphertext—the encryption algorithm. Today, the Data Encryption Standard, or DES [FIPS, 1993], is the most popular way to encrypt ciphertext using private keys. DES was designed so that determining a key would be a computationally difficult task. By learning how DES works, you will have a good understanding about how all private key encryption mechanisms work.

DES uses two techniques for encryption: permutation and substitution. In *permutation*, the bits in a block of text are scrambled to diffuse them. This makes it difficult to infer meaning by looking at bit patterns in the block. For example, in the ASCII example above, lowercase letters are represented by the hexadecimal numbers between 0x61 and 0x7a; the three most significant bits in ASCII bytes are always 011 for a lowercase ASCII character. By permuting the bits, such patterns are hidden. *Substitution* operations are intended to replace one block of bits by another block of bits; notice that the blocks do not necessarily have to be the same size (it is better if they are different sizes). Substitution further obscures information by transformation.

The idea in DES is to partition the clear text into a collection of 64-bit blocks, and then apply the encryption algorithm to each block. The encryption algorithm itself (summarized in Figure 14.18) first applies a bit-wise permutation operation, and then performs a complex series of substitutions. A final permutation (the inverse of the first permutation) is performed to the result to produce the ciphertext.

The original DES encryption and decryption depend on a single 64-bit pattern that contains a 56-bit key, K, and another 8-bit parity field. The parity field is used as an assurance that the 56-bit key is a correct key—the parity bits are used for parity in bytes in the actual key.

The heart of the DES algorithm is the substitution transformation. The permuted 64-bit is divided into 32-bit left and right halves. The algorithm will then perform a series of 16 iterative operations on the two halves; this is the main part of Figure 14.18. In the figure, the gray line indicates where the algorithm iterates. In each iteration, an iteration-dependent 48-bit key, K_j for the jth iteration. K_j is computed as a DES-defined function, $\varphi()$, using the overall DES key and the iteration number. From the figure you can see that

$$L_j = R_{j-1}$$
$$R_j = L_j \oplus f(R_{j-1}, K_j)$$

✦ **FIGURE 14.18** The DES Algorithm

The Data Encryption Standard uses the public method described in this figure for encrypting information. The security of the mechanism depends on the difficulty in determining the keys. Keys can range from 64 to 256 bits in different versions of DES.

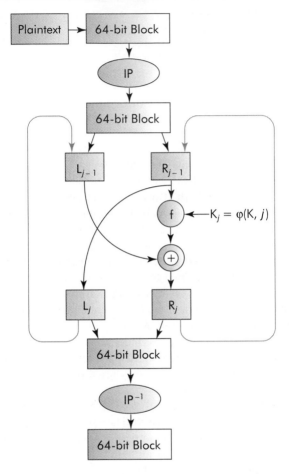

Where $\oplus$ is an exclusive OR operation and the function, f, is a publicly available substitution function (it permutes, duplicates, $\oplus$, and substitutes bits in the 32-bit domain to produce an encrypted 32-bit range value) [FIPS, 1993; Singhal and Shivaratri, 1994]. The decryption mechanism essentially runs this algorithm "backwards" to recover the clear text.

At the time DES was designed in the 1970s, the approach was generally declared to be sound (even though encryption was known to be costly in time). By 1998, there was concern that computing power had become fast enough that the 56-bit keys were no longer considered to be completely safe, and by 1999, a special-purpose machine had been built to guess a 56-bit DES key in a few hours. As a result, there are now 128-, 192-, and 256-bit key variants of DES called AES. Experts believe that the computational time and effort to search the entire key space makes them safe for several more years.

Finally, there is a private key encryption algorithm similar to DES (called SKIPJACK) that is implemented in hardware called the Clipper chip, but it is a political hotbed. The bone of contention is related to key management for each chip. The proposal is that each Clipper chip key be held in escrow by two government agencies. In an emergency situation, the key can be obtained from one of the government agencies and used to decrypt any information previously encrypted with that particular chip.

PUBLIC KEY ENCRYPTION

Public key encryption algorithms are also at the leading edge of protection technology. This approach provides a contrasting technique for cryptography, one that supports different types of interactions among correspondents. The idea is that one of the keys is private, but the other key is published to be used by anyone that wants to interact with the party that controls the keys. Let's refer to the private (secret) key as K_s and the public key as K_p. Now, if a user, U, publishes the encryption mechanism and K_p, any other party, V, that wants to send an encrypted message to U encrypts it using the mechanism and K_e—that is V sends the ciphertext, $E(K_e, M)$ to U. Since the ciphertext can only be decrypted by U (using K_s), then the ciphertext is protected when it is exposed to an intruder (unless the intruder is able to guess K_s).

Notice that public key encryption can also be used to implement the **digital signature** we used for authorization. Since $E(K_p, D(K_s, M)) = M$, the encryption algorithm can convert text that has been converted to ciphertext using the decryption mechanism. Put another way, both encryption and decryption functions convert one string to another with the property that $D(K_s, ...)$ is the inverse function of $E(K_p, ...)$. This works because the controlling user, U, digitally signs a file by concatenating an encoded signature $S = D(K_s,$ name) to the file. If the recipient can then recover the name by applying $E(K_p, S)$, then the document could only have come from U. This property of public key encryption is exactly the kind of technology needed to create software certificates to authenticate software modules.

The seminal work in this area is the Rivest-Shamir-Adelman (RSA) cryptography algorithm [Rivest, et al., 1978]. Almost all contemporary cryptography algorithms are either derived from, or use similar approaches to, the RSA algorithm. RSA-like algorithms generally depend on the use of one-way (also known as **trapdoor**) functions. The important characteristic of a one-way function, f, is that the function is easy to evaluate (that is $y = f(x)$ is easy to evaluate), but the inverse is difficult to determine (that is, it is difficult to figure out what $x = f^{-1}(y)$ when you know the value of y). Such a function was used to compute a one-time password earlier, but in the RSA approach, it is used as the basis of an encryption tool; that is, ciphertext $= f(K_p, plain\_text)$. Decryption is accomplished by computing plaintext $= f^{-1}(K_s, f(K_p, plain\_text))$.

The theoretical fact behind RSA is that the one-way function effectively uses the product of two prime numbers. To determine the inverse function, it is necessary for the intruder to figure out the two factors that were used to make a product (since they are prime numbers, there are only two numbers that fit the bill) [Maekawa, et al., 1987]. Finding prime factors is known to be a very difficult computational task, one that theoreticians have studied for many years. The RSA algorithm exploits this problem that is famous for its computational complexity as the foundation for the one-way function—a very clever application of theory to a practical problem.

Most contemporary public key encryption systems use some aspect of the RSA approach, and all depend on one-way functions. The Pretty Good Privacy (PGP) mechanism is an open mechanism that is generally available to anyone. The following box provides a brief explanation of PGP.

PGP Encryption

Pretty good privacy (**PGP**) is a popular public key cryptography system developed by Zimmerman [1994]. In PGP, public keys include the owner's electronic mail address, the time the key was created, and key characters. Secure keys include the identification and creation time, along with private key characters and a password. A key is kept in a **key certificate**, which includes the owner ID, the time the key-pair was generated, and the material defining the key. A public key certificate contains the public key material, and secure key certificates contain the secret key material. A user can keep several such public key and secure key certificates on public and secure key rings.

A **message digest** is a 128-bit "cryptographically strong one-way hash function" of a message that is to be transmitted in an unsecure network [Zimmerman, 1994]. In general, it is impossible to counterfeit a message digest. Once the message digest has been computed, a *signature* for the message is derived by encrypting the message digest using the secure key. A secret document is signed by producing a header that contains an internal 64-bit key ID, a signature, and a timestamp of when the signature was created. The recipient uses the key ID either to retrieve the sender's public key (from the receiver's own public key ring) if it is authenticating the message, or to retrieve its own secure key from its secure key ring if it is decrypting a message.

PGP is widely used for distributing information in networks, since the software is distributed without cost and (unlike Kerberos) it does not require the presence of an authentication server.

INTERNET CONTENT DELIVERY

Cryptography has become immensely popular for delivering content over the public Internet. Some web hosts contain content that is private either because it is confidential to a group or corporation or because it is only intended to be downloaded by people who paid to view it. For example, imagine that you created a web host that delivered digital videos of movies. Then you would need to pay a royalty to the studio that produced the movie each time you viewed it. If your site was intended to make a profit, then you would also want to collect revenue for yourself. If an intruder were able to obtain a clear text copy of the movie, then it could be propagated all over the Internet without gathering revenue for each viewing. The studio would not collect its royalty, and you would not collect money for your own costs and profit. Currently, cryptography is the most widely used technology to address Internet content delivery and to collect funds as part of the electronic commerce transaction.

The electronic commerce aspect of web transactions relates to how a user can make payment to the vendor over the Internet. In most cases, this means that the user authorizes payment to the vendor by providing the vendor with a credit card number. Obviously, the user would like the credit card authorization transaction to be secure, and this is most often done using cryptography.

Commercially, this has stimulated interest in a technology area called **digital rights management (DRM)**. In the DRM approach, a content owner should be able to store content on an Internet-accessible server, specify a policy that defines how users can access the content, and then deploy the system with appropriate protection mechanisms that implement the policy (see Figure 14.19)

✦ FIGURE 14.19   A Digital Rights Management System

DRM systems are general protection systems intended to allow a person to create content and then manage the access rights to that content with a flexible security policy. This figure identifies various parties that use the DRM system.

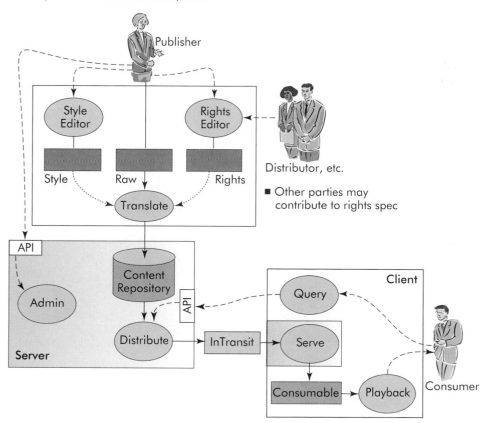

As is apparent from the figure, these are complex systems. There are several important components to the DRM system, including the cryptography approach used in the system. Contemporary commercial systems use both private and public key encryption for the cryptography element. The commercial aspect of this problem has caused DRM to be a highly complex problem that touches cryptography, data modeling languages, policy specification languages, and entire systems to implement the components. While DRM is in its early days, it could become a driving application domain for subsequent work in protection and security.

14.5 ● SUMMARY

Protection mechanisms are implemented in operating systems to support various security policies. The goal of the security system is to authenticate subjects and authorize their access to any object. If the subject is a user, the mechanism verifies that the user who he or she claims to be, with the set of predetermined rights set by the system policy maker.

Authorization is concerned with verifying that a subject, corresponding to a process executing in a protection domain, has the right to access an object according to the current protection state. The idealized protection model calls for authenticating each access operation according to the current protection state. The security policy must specify how the protection state can change. This is accomplished by specifying a set of rules that represent the policy for changing protection states.

Implementations of the idealized model make assumptions about the model so that the system can be built cost-effectively. The key components of the implementation are the subject authentication module, the resource monitor, and the representation of the protection state (using an access matrix). The innovation in protection system implementation is in the state and resource monitor designs.

Protection domains are extensions of the hardware supervisor mode ability. The ring model generalizes the domains established by the mode flag so that the operating system may support a variety of domains. The access matrix may be implemented as a list of entries in a row saved with the subject, called a capability list. It may also be implemented as an access control list—a list of entries in a column stored with the object.

Cryptography is used to protect information in cases in which it cannot always be kept in a secure medium; as Internet usage increases, the importance of cryptography increases. The information to be protected is encrypted while it is not being processed, including while it is in the file system and while it is being transmitted from one computer to another on a network.

14.6 ● EXERCISES

1. Characterize each of the following tasks as an authentication task, authorization task, cryptography task, or none.

   a. Entering your PIN number at an automatic teller machine.

   b. Allowing James Bond to enter the enemy's war room.

   c. Creating a message digest.

   d. Cashing a check at the credit union.

2. Here is a bogus "About me" description.

   George Walker Bush 43rd president of the United States (2001–). Narrowly winning the electoral college vote over Vice President Al Gore in one of the closest and most controversial elections in American history, Bush became the first per-

son since 1888 to become president despite losing the nationwide popular vote. Before assuming the presidency of the United...

[Encyclopedia Britannica, 2003]

Which of the following passwords could be guessed from the About Me?

a. Walker

b. JebBrother

c. IBeatAl

d. 1600Penn-Ave.NW

e. texas

3. Explain the value of using one-time passwords.

4. What is a one-way function?

5. How is a Java applet prevented from copying information from the client machine environment, then returning it to the server?

6. Assume that a timesharing computer provides a mechanism by which a file can be read by any user, but can be written by only one. Informally describe a security policy for administering student transcripts on the computer system (limit your description to a half of one typed page). Students should be able to read their grades, but not change them. The Registrar's office must be able to change the grade files.

7. Describe a mechanism—hardware and software—for authenticating users based on their fingerprints. This is an open-ended question in which you are to think about innovative designs based on your imagination (perhaps as it is influenced by movies, science fiction, and so on). Very high-security installations do use such mechanisms.

8. Dynamic relocation hardware is usually considered to be a basic memory protection mechanism. What is the protection state in relocation hardware? How does the operating system ensure that the protection state is not changed indiscriminately?

9. Explain the exact steps a client and server take in Kerberos to authenticate that a message is from the party it claims to be. (You may find it useful to consult the information on the Web regarding Kerberos.)

10. Given the access matrix in Figure 14.11, provide an access control list for each object.

11. Given the protection state shown in Figure 14.11 and the rules shown in Figure 14.12, do the following.

a. Explain how S_3 can cause the protection state to be changed so that it has write access to F_2.

b. Specify two different ways by which S_3 can obtain read permission to F_1.

c. Explain whether S_3 can obtain seek permission to D_1 from S_1. Why or why not?

12. Use a text editor to read a UNIX system's password file, /etc/passwd. You should be able to find a single-line entry in the ASCII file for your own login. Speculate how your password is saved in /etc/passwd. What user is the owner of /etc/passwd? Do you have write permission for /etc/passwd?

13. Consider a variant of the k-bit key and lock scheme described for memory protection whereby a process can access memory blocks for which every bit position set to 1 within the lock is also set to 1 in the process's key.

    a. How many unique locks are in the system?

    b. Characterize all keys that access a memory block with the lock 01100110 for $k = 8$.

    c. Show how this mechanism can be used to allow a process B to keep some memory blocks private, to share some with process A, and to share others with process C (but for which A and C do not share any memory blocks).

14. Suppose a UNIX system has been set up so that each student and the instructor have their own ID and all are in the same group (with no other users). The files used by the course are on a timesharing system used by other courses.

    a. What permissions should a student have on a file that contains a homework solution?

    b. What permissions should the instructor have on a file that contains course grades?

    c. What permissions should be assigned to a file (owned by the instructor) that is readable and writable by the instructor, executable by a student in the course, and inaccessible to any other student?

    d. Suppose the instructor wants a directory in which each student can write a solution file, but only the instructor can read the files. What permission should the directory have?

15. Explain how the UNIX file protection mechanism could be used to allow any process to read and modify a system file by using special commands named getSpecial and putSpecial.

16. Argue for conditions under which the access control method is superior to the capability list approach for implementing the access matrix.

Networks

Networks are a combination of computers and communications mechanisms. Within the computer, the network functionality is implemented by a combination of devices, system software, and application software. A network device connects the machine to a communication subnetwork that is shared with other machines, allowing processes/threads on all the machines to exchange information. There are many ways the information can be shared: as files that are copied back and forth among machines, as messages handled by the OS IPC mechanisms, as parameters in remote procedure calls and remote object references, and more. Although networks have been an important part of computing for more that 25 years, there is still significant innovation in this area.

Today, popular networks are based on the *ISO Open Systems Interconnection* architecture model, which defines a way to partition communication functionality into a layered model. This encourages network designers to organize the functions in their network using a common architecture, even though the physical networks may be quite different. An important benefit of the common architecture is that it may then be possible to interconnect different networks so that they work together to form a larger network, called an *internet*.

In this chapter, we focus on how today's networks have evolved from traditional computer telecommunication applications to specialized networks with elaborate software support. After discussing the general ISO OSI model, we will summarize the characteristics of network hardware, and then focus on the parts of the network that are implemented in the OS. We conclude by describing how user space software can exploit the OS network services to implement distributed computation.

15.1 • FROM COMPUTER COMMUNICATIONS TO NETWORKS

One of the landmark changes in computing has been the development of data networks interconnecting computers. This revolution began in 1980 with the introduction of the IEEE 802 (ISO/IEC 8802) Ethernet and Token Ring **local area network (LAN)** standard. Xerox designers had built several experimental versions of the Ethernet in their labs, while at the same time, IBM developers had created and begun deploying the Token Ring as part of their product line. The standard embraced both approaches. Prior to 1980, data networks existed as expensive, specialized systems used by only a few research and government organizations. LANs grew rapidly in popularity, because application programmers quickly recognized that they now had an OS abstraction that would enable them to interconnect multiple computers to work in concert on a common problem—**distributed computation**.

In the last decade or so, the ubiquity of LAN technology and the evolution of the World Wide Web caused a revolution in one area of distributed computing: People had already learned to leverage personal computers to enhance their personal productivity (with word processing, spreadsheets, and other such tools). Now network technology enabled them to connect their home computer to the Internet, which in turn enabled them to use the **World Wide Web (WWW)** protocols for obtaining information (referred to as "content" in this application domain) from diverse sources all over the world. The WWW encouraged content providers to create web sites and to make content available; in addition, electronic commerce began to emerge as a new model for conducting business. Suddenly, there was an immense collection of organizations providing content on the Internet and an even larger set of people copying the content into their own machines using web browsers and the WWW.

These are exciting times for computer technology: Tremendous numbers of people are now familiar with computers and the Internet, applying dramatic commercial pressure for technology development in which the Internet is able to support full-fledged information distribution and sophisticated electronic commerce. The next ten years will see rapid change in the way operating systems and networks evolve to address the needs of literally millions of people. The next three chapters of this book look at networks and distributed computing from the OS designer's perspective. This chapter describes the underlying information transfer technology of the network and its protocols. Chapter 16 focuses on the first really large use of LANs—remote file services. Chapter 17 looks at various evolving areas in distributed computing, including remote procedure call and distributed memory.

SWITCHED NETWORKS

Contemporary networks evolved from previous telecommunications technology. A serial port (see Chapter 5) can be used to transmit and receive bytes to/from an external device. Computer-to-computer communications take advantage of the serial port technology by connecting a **modem** (*MO*dulator-*DEM*odulator) to the serial port (see Figure 15.1). Each modem is also connected to the public switched telephone network. The modem converts digital signals sent from a serial port device into analog signals that can be transmitted over the switched telephone network. The digital signals can tell the modem to place a telephone call, answer a telephone call, and transmit binary data. Another modem attached to a remote computer receives the analog signals produced by the local computer's modem and then converts them back into the digital signals sent by the local computer. The receiving modem passes the digital signals to its serial device. Then the data can be received by the driver software on the remote computer.

✦ FIGURE 15.1 Connecting Computers Using the Telephone Network

The voice telephone network can be used to transmit and receive digital information. Before the computers communicate, a conventional call is placed from the sending modem to the receiving computer's modem. The sending computer device driver writes the information to a serial device, causing it to be written to a modem. The modem translates the digital signal to an equivalent analog signal and sends it over the telephone network to the receiver's modem. The receiver's modem translates the analog signal back to a digital signal and copies it to the serial device. The device driver reads the information from the serial device.

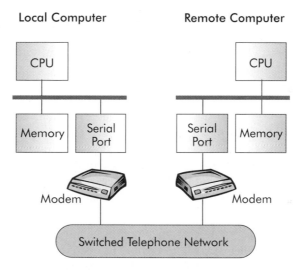

This **point-to-point,** character-oriented communications technology is the basis of modern networks. Any computer with a modem and telephone connection can be programmed to establish a connection with another computer having a modem and a telephone connection. Once the telephone connection has been established, the two computers can exchange information using a previously agreed upon **network communication protocol** (or simply **protocol**) to establish the syntax and semantics of the exchange.

Contemporary **network interface controllers** (**NIC**s) are devices that connect a computer to a specialized **data communication subnetwork** (such as an Ethernet LAN). As shown in Figure 15.2, the NIC and data communication subnetwork replace the modem, telephone connection, and telephone switching system. Most NICs contain their own means for allowing a sender to transmit a *block of bytes* to any other machine on the communication subnetwork. Part of the NIC's responsibility is to incorporate a protocol to marshall/unmarshall the stream of characters written to or read from the NIC (just like a disk driver and controller marshall/unmarshall byte stream file contents).

✦ **FIGURE 15.2** Data Communication Subnetworks

A communication subnetwork is specialized to support digital data transmission (as opposed to voice transmission). LANs like the Ethernet are communication subnetworks.

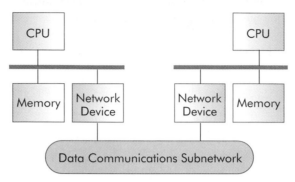

Like the other devices described in Chapter 5, the hardware/software interface to the NIC is implemented between the device driver and the NIC hardware. However, the NIC is attached to a data communication subnetwork rather than to a local device such as a storage device or terminal.

There is a need for additional protocols to coordinate the behavior of the sender and the receiver: This need covers a broad spectrum of functions, from determining how one machine detects a signal from another machine to agreement about the format of a floating-point number. Just as some of the functions in file management can be implemented as part of the applications software, so also can some of the network protocol functions. In addition, just as the basic part of the file system must be implemented in the storage devices and OS, so also must part of the network be implemented in the NIC and OS.

NETWORK HARDWARE REQUIREMENTS

A data communication subnetwork is a specialized interconnection medium by which one host computer can transmit a block of bytes, called a **packet**, to any other host computer attached to the subnetwork. The network is called a **multidrop packet network** if the sending host can select the receiving host at the time it transmits the packet. A process/thread on a host system transmits information by preparing a block of data for transmission and then calling an OS function to write the packet to the data communication subnetwork.

In a multidrop packet network, the hardware goal is to develop the most cost-effective means to deliver packets. This NIC and the data subcommunication network are designed to work together to provide functions to:

- ■ Encode a packet and then transmit the corresponding information over the physical data communication subnetwork to a destination host machine,
- ■ Deliver the packet contents to a specified destination host, and
- ■ Decode the transmitted information to form a packet at the destination NIC.

The Xerox Ethernet network is a widely used multidrop packet network in which bits are transmitted serially over a shared communications medium. When the Ethernet was first implemented in 1980, the physical medium was required to be a coaxial cable, similar to the kind of cable used for cable TV and CB radio antennae. Now the Ethernet can also use twisted pairs of wires, similar to the kind used by a telephone or modem. Software uses the Ethernet by reading and writing variable-sized packets from/to the Ethernet device controller. In a write operation, the network controller receives a copy of the packet to hold in a buffer while the network device transmits the contents bit-by-bit. In Section 15.3 you will learn how the Ethernet works. As mentioned in the introduction, techniques such as those used in the Ethernet were so economical that they created a breakthrough for the use of data networks in the early 1980s. Today's Ethernet can transmit up to 1 Gbps among a set of hosts connected by a cable up to 1 kilometer in length.

NETWORK SOFTWARE REQUIREMENTS

In the late 1960s, researchers and developers began to experiment with data networks. It soon became apparent that different applications needed to use the basic capabilities of the communication subnetwork, but by adding their own specialized functionality. For example, these additional functions would allow the network to do the following:

- Control information delivery rates.
- Provide a means for a host on one network to communicate with a host on a different network.
- Allow a stream of packets to contain a stream of bytes analogous to a byte stream file (or UNIX pipe).
- Ensure reliable transmission in cases in which information might occasionally be lost in the network.
- Provide security features.
- Provide a standard pattern of behavior for processes involved in IPC across the network.
- Be used to transfer files.
- Be used to allow a user on one machine to log in to a different machine.
- Simulate a procedure call from a process on one machine to a procedure on another.
- Translate information among machine-dependent representations (since different machines often use different representations for multibyte words).

In short, the requirements are diverse (and overwhelming). Early network designers realized that the first problem to be addressed was to organize the requirements so that different application domains could choose the requirements that mattered to them. This led to a model for defining requirements, organized as a *layered architecture*. For example, the functions implemented by network hardware are all defined at the lower layers of the architecture, since every application domain requires these functions. However, an IPC mechanism will use the basic signaling mechanisms differently than a file transfer mechanism does; the IPC mechanism would probably be designed to minimize communication delay, while the file transfer mechanism attempts to maximize bandwidth.

In the layered architecture approach, functions are divided into sets. Functions in a more abstract set (layer) can use any of the functions in its supporting layer(s). In networks, the functionality implemented in any particular layer defines a communication protocol by which the software written to *use* that layer can communicate with other software designed to use the same layer. For example, if two machines have Ethernet NICs (connected to a common data communication subnetwork), then device drivers on the two machines can exchange packets. This basic idea is called **peer-to-peer** communication.[1] Two applications can be built to use the same components at layer i of the network architecture to communicate with one another in terms of the layer i abstraction. For example, the FTP (file transfer protocol) defines a set of functions that allows two peer processes to exchange files. Because of the layered approach, neither of the two processes needs to know any of the details of the underlying NICs and data communication subnetwork. Instead, they use functions such as `get` and `put` to transfer files.

You can see that the layered architecture creates a set of layered protocols for communication. Protocols in lower layers contain simple abstractions of the network hardware operation, and protocols at higher layers are more complex abstractions of hardware operation. This idea of protocols is not unique to networks. Programmers routinely use protocols to allow one part of their program to communicate with other parts. For example, a function call protocol specifies that the calling part of the program will identify another part of the program it wishes to communicate with by using a function name. In ANSI C, the function prototype explicitly specifies the protocol for how parameters will be passed—the number and type of each argument.

As we have seen, protocols are also used in reading from and writing to files. When a thread writes to a structured file, it follows a protocol for formatting the information so that any other thread can use the same protocol to interpret the information from the file.

All network communication depends on two autonomous processes existing at the same time and on their *agreeing* to communicate. Cooperative communication can succeed only if the two processes agree on the precise syntax and semantics of the information to be exchanged. For example, if thread p_1 intends to send a file to thread p_2, both threads must first synchronize according to the mechanisms described in Chapter 8. Hence, p_2 should be prepared to read the network to accept the file when p_1 transmits it. What should the units of data transfer be? Is there a useful common model for the data? Should there be more than one model? If the machines have different representations for floating-point numbers, how should the processes ensure conversion is done appropriately? To address these and a myriad of other questions, the programs for the two processes must agree on a protocol that defines all the syntactic and semantic aspects of the communication.

File transfer is only one kind of communication. The processes may wish to exchange messages, request remote services, or download web pages. There are many different network protocols used to address the range of communications applications. This has all led to an evolutionary path in network development that is guided by an international standard, called the ISO Open Systems Interconnection architecture. The model specifies general aspects of protocols, and in some cases includes highly specific details. The ISO OSI architecture is described next.

---

[1]In the commercial world, "peer-to-peer" has taken on a broader meaning, based on this original use of the term. There, it refers to commercial software approaches in which systems can cooperatively solve various problems (for example, see http://www.peer-to-peerwg.org/whatis/index.html).

15.2 • THE ISO OSI NETWORK ARCHITECTURE MODEL

The **ISO Open Systems Interconnect** (**ISO OSI**) architecture model is the dominant model for defining network protocols in contemporary networks. The model is a standard architecture that has been adopted by almost all developers (although details within the different architecture *instances* may vary). It is helpful to consider the evolution of the model to understand why it has the form it does.

THE EVOLUTION OF NETWORK PROTOCOLS

In the late 1960s, network technology evolved to the point that distributed computing began to be cost-effective for a few application domains. By 1975, the Department of Defense *ARPAnet* had been established as a working long-haul (wide area) network to support a broad spectrum of research and defense applications in the United States. Meanwhile, in Europe, the X.25 network had become a viable technology for commercial applications.

In the late 1970s, the ISO was circulating its first draft documents on the OSI architecture model for network communication. The drafts reflected a strong influence by the X.25 network. Zimmerman [1980] wrote one of the first technical papers describing the ISO OSI model in detail. However, in the United States, the ARPAnet had already become the dominant force in network research and development.

By 1980, the Ethernet had irrefutably demonstrated the viability of the local area network (LAN) in a commercial domain [Metcalfe and Boggs, 1976]. Whereas X.25 and the ARPAnet were both directed at communications over distances measured in miles or hundreds of miles, the Ethernet was used to connect a set of machines located within a few hundred feet of one another (technically, up to 1 kilometer apart). X.25 and the ARPAnet transmitted information at variable rates of speed (in the range of 1Kbps to 1Mbps), depending on the part of the network being used. The research Ethernet transmitted information at a rate of 3 Mbps throughout its local area. The first standardized Ethernet operates at 10 Mbps.

The IBM *System Network Architecture* (SNA) also had a major impact on commercial computing installations during the 1970s. Whereas ARPAnet, X.25, and Ethernet protocols were openly available to anyone, the SNA protocols were developed as an integral part of IBM's products, so it was a proprietary (but widely used) protocol. SNA was significant in establishing data networks as a viable commercial technology. By 1980, SNA had introduced the Token Ring LAN as a publicly available alternative to the Ethernet.

In 1980, DEC, Xerox, and Intel jointly announced the commercial Ethernet LAN. They adapted the midlayer ARPAnet protocols for use with their low-layer LAN. At roughly the same time, IBM announced its Token Ring LAN, using their SNA midlayer protocols. An IEEE standards committee studied the Ethernet and the Token Ring in an attempt to arrive at a commercially viable standard LAN that complied with the spirit (if not the details) of the ISO OSI model. A draft standard, IEEE 802, was published and used as the basis of LANs in the 1980s. In the IEEE 802 standard, both the Ethernet and Token Ring were accepted as alternatives, although it is not possible to directly connect an Ethernet and a Token Ring. This is an example of how the standard architecture model (IEEE 802 in this case) can be used for two different actual implementations. An IEEE 802 network can be built with an Ethernet implementation and another with a Token Ring implementation, yet the two cannot be directly connected. In the early 1990s, the IEEE 802 draft became the ISO/IEC 8802 standard for LAN communication.

Thus, there were three major thrusts in network technology in the 1980s (see Figure 15.3).

■ The ISO OSI model established the basis of standardized network protocols. They essentially came from the X.25 networks, but were certainly influenced by the ARPAnet. Today, this model is the dominant general protocol architecture in networks.

■ The ARPAnet contributed mid-layer protocols that have been in use for over thirty years (specifically, TCP, UDP, and IP).

■ The IEEE 802 LANs created a cost-effective communication environment. When Ethernet was introduced as an IEEE draft standard, the Token Ring was its main competitor (along with another approach called the Token Bus). After considerable debate, the IEEE 802 committee adopted the Ethernet approach (IEEE 802.3), the Token Bus approach (IEEE 802.4), and the Token Ring approach (IEEE 802.5) within a single draft standard. The ISO/IEC 8802 is the international version of IEEE 802.

✦ FIGURE 15.3 Network Evolution

Modern networks almost all comply with the ISO OSI model. The ARPAnet and IEEE 802 protocols were not developed as integral parts of the ISO OSI model, even though they match its general architecture.

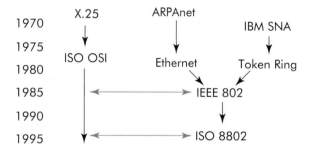

The gray lines in Figure 15.3 indicate that the developers attempted to make the ISO OSI and ARPAnet efforts converge. Today, the ISO OSI architecture is the dominant framework under which all networks are built. Even though TCP/UDP/IP do not strictly conform to ISO OSI, they are the dominant mid-layer protocols. We continue to see innovation at all levels, even the lower levels (for example, with wireless technology).

THE ISO OSI MODEL

The ISO OSI architecture model defines a general set of function types found to be useful for all network communications. It then organizes those function types into a layered architecture. Any specific use of the network, such as a file transfer capability, uses a specific subset of protocols, called a **protocol stack**, to specify the network protocol to be used for a particular application, such as file transfer. The ISO OSI model divides functionality into seven layers, as follows:

- **Physical layer:** The lowest layer in the model. A specific protocol complying with the ISO OSI physical layer defines how information is to be encoded and transmitted to another machine. The RS-232 asynchronous serial communication protocol used to connect terminals, modems, and printers to computers resembles a physical layer protocol, although it is not normally considered to be a network protocol. The Ethernet carrier sensing and collision detection protocol is a good example of a physical layer network protocol (see Section 15.3).

- **Data link layer:** Built on top of the physical layer and, in the case of Ethernet and Token Ring networks, implemented in hardware in conjunction with the physical layer. (However, in the case of SLIP and PPP, the data link layer is a software implementation using an RS–232 physical layer; see Stevens [1994, Ch. 2].) The data link layer defines a protocol that establishes the *frame*—the data link name for a packet. Frames of information incorporate a header, a block of data, and a trailer. A user of the data link layer can exchange frames with another host machine on a network. The data link layer is also discussed in Section 15.3.

- **Network layer:** Creates a very large address space of networks and hosts called an **internet address space**. This facility encouraged the development of networks of networks, called **internets**, in which each node in the internet is itself a network. Information is transmitted across the internet as packets. The network layer is usually implemented as a part of the OS. It is discussed in Section 15.4.

- **Transport layer:** Creates an extension of the network layer address space by adding multiple communication *endpoints* to each host. Provides various application interfaces to services including block, byte stream, and record stream communication. It is usually implemented, at least in part, by the OS (with the rest of the implementation being system software). It is discussed in detail in Section 15.5.

- **Session layer:** Extends the transport layer functionality by applying specific interprocess communication strategies. For example, a network message protocol or a remote procedure protocol would be implemented at the session layer. The session layer is typically implemented as application libraries. It is introduced in Chapter 17.

- **Presentation layer:** Defines data abstraction and representation protocols and is also implemented as library code. It is summarized in Chapter 17.

- **Application layer:** This layer is for application software for the distributed computation. There are no standards for the application layer, since it is intended to apply to any domain. It exists in the model to illustrate where application programs fit into the layered architecture.

The layers in the ISO OSI model define a family of layered abstractions of communications functions. Each thread uses a particular protocol stack, with selected components from different layers to implement its own network. Figure 15.4 illustrates the peer relationship between the abstractions for two communications threads in terms of the ISO OSI model. The physical layer of the sending thread is the only layer that actually transmits information to the physical layer of the receiving thread. The data link layer of the sending thread *logically* transmits a frame to the data link layer of the receiver. It does this by *physically* translating the frame into the form used by the physical layer and then passing the information to the physical layer so that it can transmit the information. The physical layer transmits the information that makes up the data link frame to the physical layer on the receiving machine, where it is abstracted into a frame in the receiver's data link layer. Thus, there is a peer-to-peer communication between the two data link layers. In Figure 15.4, the heavy, solid line is used to emphasize that information between two machines is only physically transmitted at the physical layer, yet (as indicated by the lighter lines with different patterns) there is logical communication between the peers at each corresponding level of the network.

✦ FIGURE 15.4 Peer-to-Peer Communication

An entity (such as a process) can use the network at any layer of the ISO OSI model to communicate with a peer entity at another machine. For example, a process that is executing transport layer functions can communicate with a peer that is using transport layer functions on a different machine.

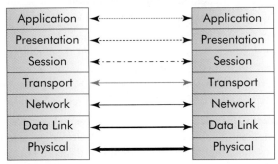

At the network layer, packets are exchanged between peers by translating a network packet into a data link frame and then into the physical layer format. The physical layer transmits the information to the receiving machine, where the information is translated into a data link frame and then into a network packet. The same technique is used for peer-to-peer communication at the transport, session, presentation, and application layers. The application layer uses a highly abstracted communications mechanism provided by the presentation layer interface, such as a remote file server interface, a remote print server interface, or a remote procedure call interface.

The ISO OSI architecture model is a general model that reflects the agreement among various manufacturers that produce networks and host machines using the networks. While the general form of the model has been accepted for several years, the detailed protocols are still evolving. For example, the ARPAnet IP protocol is the dominant implementation used with the ISO OSI network layer (even though it is not part of the standard). With the *de facto* adaptation of TCP (and UDP) at the transport layer and IP at the network layer, the interfaces at the transport layer and below are relatively stable.

Any contemporary OS provides driver support for various data link and physical layer NICs, as well as implementations of the network and transport layers. The next section summarizes the trends in data link and physical layer implementations. Then we can talk about the mid-layer protocols. Since the high-layer protocols are not well formed in modern systems, only the factors influencing the designers at these levels are described in Chapters 16 and 17. There are several excellent books describing the ISO OSI model in detail; for example, see Piscitello and Chapin [1993], Stevens [1994], and Stevens and Wright [1995].

We have said that the ARPAnet protocols can be used with an ISO OSI protocol stack. TCP and UDP are equivalent to transport layer protocols (a process would use either TCP or UDP, but not both at the same time), and IP is equivalent to a network layer protocol. The ISO OSI Transport Layer Interface (TLI) provides many of the same functions as TCP (*Transmission Control Protocol*). Thus, the pure ISO OSI protocol stack shown in Figure 15.5(a) can be implemented to use an ISO OSI session layer protocol, implemented on top of TCP, implemented on top of IP, which is implemented on top of Ethernet (see Figure 15.5(b)). A user of the ISO OSI session layer in either implementation will receive the same service, independent of the protocol stack implementation. Of course, an implementation on an Ethernet data link layer cannot communicate directly with an X.25 data link layer implementation, but the network layer software written to use the Ethernet version can be used with no change on the pure protocol stack.

✦ FIGURE 15.5 Using TCP/IP in an ISO OSI Protocol Stack

Here are two examples of ISO OSI compliant protocol stacks. The example shown in part (a) complies with the ISO OSI specification at each level, but in part (b), only the session layer is an ISO OSI protocol. However, the Ethernet and ARPAnet implementations generally comply with the ISO OSI model and are able to support session layer protocols that are in complete compliance.

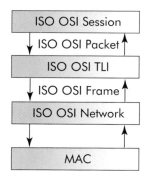
(a) Pure ISO OSI Protocol Stack

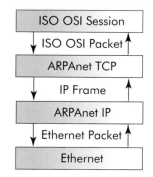
(b) ISO OSI Compliant Stack

15.3 • MEDIA ACCESS CONTROL (MAC) PROTOCOLS

The physical and data link layer protocols are often called the **media access control (MAC) protocols**. They describe NICs and data communication subnetworks. Since networks have so much functionality (compared to storage devices), they create a challenging, new hardware resource for the OS to manage. But as we have seen in the discussion of the ISO OSI model, much of the behavior of the network will be defined by user space software. As networks emerged, it became clear that the support for them would overflow the traditional device management part of the OS. We will study this overflow for file management in Chapter 16 and other parts of the OS in Chapter 17. Networks are now impacting the design of both memory and process managers.

The emergence of the 10 Mbps commercial LANs enabled organizations to interconnect computers with a relatively high-speed shared medium. Organizations began to replace serial lines that operated at speeds lower than 10 Kbps with LANs that were a thousand times faster. Since those early days of networks, LAN bandwidth has increased by another three orders of magnitude, first jumping up to the 100 Mbps range by the mid-1990s, and now into the gigabit (1 billion bits) per second range. Besides the substantially increased speed of operation of these LANs, their physical range has also gradually increased to the point that LAN technology is sometimes difficult to distinguish from wide-area network (WAN) technology.

At the time of this writing, it is still too early to characterize the full impact on operating systems of these new high-speed networks. However, we can see that this kind of raw speed for the network allows processes to have address spaces that span machines, as well as create an environment in which the scheduler can dispatch processes to a set of different computers rather than just to the local CPU. This situation requires a fundamental rethinking of the design of process and memory managers.

The change in operating systems and networks is also prompting the development of a new breed of applications in which larger amounts of data are transmitted among machines as files, continuous streams (usually of audio and video information), or typed information such as images or audio. For example, emerging networks have sufficient bandwidth to distribute multimedia information among machines on a network. This bandwidth requires that the OS be able to manage high-speed data transfers between the network device and the application program.

This rapid growth in the total technology is led by changes at the physical and data link layers of the network. While it is beyond the scope of this book to focus on these technologies, this section describes their basic behavior so that you can better understand the influence they have on the evolution of operating systems.

THE PHYSICAL LAYER

The multidrop requirement was a barrier to networking technology until it was broken in the early 1980s by the Ethernet and Token Ring networks. The difficulty arose due to the need for the network to be *scalable*. A multidrop network must allow every host node in the network to be able to send and receive information to/from all other nodes in the network. This requirement means there must be a logical transmission path between every pair of nodes in the network. If this full connectivity is implemented by directly mapping logical connections to physical connections, each computer will have a point-to-point connection to all other computers. This means that if there are n host machines, then each one of them must have $n - 1$ communication ports (see Figure 15.6). Worse, there will be

$$n(n - 1)/2$$

(which is $O(n^2)$) connections in the resulting network. Such fully connected networks do not scale, because the number of connections in the network increases as the square of the number of hosts. For large networks to be built, different topologies need to be employed at the physical layer.

✦ FIGURE 15.6 Fully Connected Network Topology

The goal of a multidrop network is to be fully connected, as shown in this figure. This topology allows any host to communicate with any other host. Unfortunately, if the physical network is implemented as suggested by the diagram, there will be $O(n^2)$ lines in the network, which will not scale.

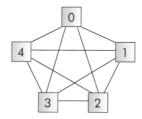

Multiaccess bus physical layer topologies, such as that used in the Ethernet, broke the cost barrier for communications networks (see Figure 15.7). Multiaccess buses employ a common signaling medium, allocating the data transmission capability of the bus to different senders using time-multiplexed sharing. Information is transmitted from one host to another by placing it on the shared medium, along with an address designator. Each receiver scans the shared medium and retrieves information addressed to it. (While this is wonderful for cost-effective networking, it is a famous security loophole: Every host computer on the network can inspect every piece of information transmitted on the network.) In this topology, much of the physical layer protocol addresses issues such as synchronous versus asynchronous operation and centralized versus decentralized allocation of the shared medium. Reliability and contention are the major issues for the multiaccess bus topology. Reliability is handled at a higher level of the architecture model, while contention is handled by the controller.

✦ FIGURE 15.7 Multiaccess Bus Network Topology

Multiaccess bus networks rely on time-multiplexed sharing. When a host is able to use the shared bus, it writes information, along with a destination host address, to the bus. All hosts read the bus, looking for packets with their address.

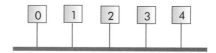

Today, wireless physical layers are having a huge impact on networks and computers. The IEEE 802.11b protocol (also called "WiFi") provides 10 Mbps Ethernet-compatible networks using the 2.4 gigahertz bandwidth space to transmit and receive information. The wireless access points act as a logical extension of an Ethernet (see Figure 15.8). By attaching such an access point to an Ethernet LAN, hosts can connect to the network with conventional wires, or by wireless communication.

✦ FIGURE 15.8 Wireless Networks Interconnected with Wired Networks

Networks such as the IEEE 802.11b (WiFi) protocol extend an Ethernet allowing hosts to transmit information over a wireless physical layer.

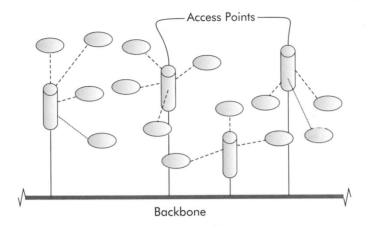

There are other wireless LAN protocols (for example, the IEEE 802.11a protocol uses a different bandwidth space and is much faster than the 802.11b protocol). The IEEE 802.15.1 protocol specification resembles the bluetooth wireless specification for personal area networks. This area of technology is very active. Consult your web browser search engine to find the latest technology in the area.

Fast Physical Layers

The signaling technique used in an Ethernet transmits information 1 bit at a time in a manner similar to the way an RS-232 serial port transfers information (see Chapter 5). The speed at which electric signals can traverse physical wires is limited to roughly 77 percent the speed of light. However, even though signals can be transmitted at that rate, contemporary electronics cannot distinguish different voltage levels at this rate. The 10 Mbps signaling rate for the Ethernet is bounded by the rate at which the voltage level can be recognized by a receiver. How can a physical layer network be made to be faster than an Ethernet? There are three techniques: (1) make a better voltage sensing mechanism, (2) transmit multiple bits at a time, or (3) use a different signaling medium. The 100 Mbps Ethernet improves on the performance of the 10 Mbps Ethernet by using a better mechanism to sense voltage levels.

In bit-parallel communications, multiple bits (such as a byte) are transmitted at a single time. For example, a parallel communication port transmits all 8 bits of a byte at the same time, while a serial communication port transmits the 8 bits one after another. Networks can be designed with multiple physical paths; for example, the fastest Ethernets actually use multiple physical wires [Schulzrinne, 1999]. The network can also employ another technique to achieve the same effect as transmitting bits in parallel. Rather than using only 3 voltage levels (no signal, transmitting 0, and transmitting 1), they can use $N = 2^k + 1$ voltage levels. For example, if 5 levels are used, the voltage levels could represent no signal, 00, 01, 10, or 11. This technique is used in the 1000BaseT (1 Gbps Ethernet) network [Schulzrinne, 1999].

Fiber optic media might be assumed to be faster than copper wire media. However, the signal propagation rate in fiber optic media is about 65 percent the speed of light (compared with 77 percent the speed of light in copper wire) [Schulzrinne, 1999]. When digital information is to be transmitted on a fiber optic medium, it is converted to a distinguishable light signal and transmitted over a fiber optic cable. Fiber optic cable can potentially provide higher effective transmission rates by using more cost-effective signal level transmitters and receivers than can be used with copper wire. Fiber optic cable can currently achieve gigabit per second transmission rates when used in contemporary high-speed physical layers.

THE DATA LINK LAYER

Data link layer protocols partition a stream of bytes at the physical layer into groups of bytes called *frames*. A frame has a header and a trailer that specify various information about the frame, such as the destination of the frame, the transmitter of the frame, the type of the frame, the number of data bytes, and a checksum.

Above the data link layer, the network allows Host *i* to send a typed frame to Host *j*. The data link network also supports flow control and error control. Flow control is used to determine the rate at which packets flow between any pair of host machines. The data link layer supports the idea of frames flowing from one host to another. Therefore, by implication, a receiver host must be able to accept frames when they are transmitted. There are several reasons why a host may not be able to accept incoming frames:

■ The frame may have been sent to a nonexistent host or to one that is currently powered down.

■ The receiving host network device driver may be interrupt-driven. If the interrupts are disabled, incoming frames will be lost.

■ The network device driver accepts frames ultimately intended for a process located at the host. Accepting a frame requires the driver to contain its own buffer space to hold incoming frames until the receiver process requests them from the local OS. If the buffer space is full, the receiver machine will be unable to accept a frame without overwriting frame buffer storage.

The receiver needs to be able to control the rate at which frames are transmitted to it, particularly from some single transmitter. The simplest protocol for accomplishing flow control is the *stop-and-wait* protocol, summarized in Figure 15.9. The *stop-and-wait* protocol corresponds to a synchronous send IPC operation. The synchronization is accomplished with the special type of packet, ACK, that has no data field. The timeout is used to prevent the sender from waiting forever if the outgoing data frame or the incoming ACK frame is lost. If the sender does not receive an ACK before the time-out expires, the sender assumes that the transmission has failed. The data link layer does not assume that frames can be transmitted reliably.

✦ FIGURE 15.9 Stop-and-Wait Flow Control

Flow control is used to adjust the rate at which frames flow from a source to a destination. If a source were allowed to send packets at an arbitrarily high rate, the destination might not be able to keep up with the incoming frames (it might be too slow, or not have enough memory). The stop-and-wait protocol controls the rate by having the destination respond to each frame before the source sends another one.

```
Sender transmits a frame;
Sender sets a time-out on the transmission;
Sender waits for an ACKnowledgment;
...
if (Sender receives ACKnowledgment) continue;
if (frame times-out)
  Retransmit timed-out frame;
```

(a) Transmitter

```
Receiver accepts the frame;
Receiver transmits the ACKnowledgment;
```

(b) Receiver

The **sliding-window protocol** is a generalization of the stop-and-wait protocol that allows a transmitter to have up to N frames in transit before it receives an ACK. Whenever the data link layer intends to transmit some number, N, of frames to another machine, it may be slowed down by the physical layer or by a slow receiver. There is no way for the transmitter to distinguish between the two. If the transmitter advances N frames beyond ACKs from the receiver, it will quit transmitting until it either times out on old transmissions or until acknowledgments are received. When frames are rejected on the receiver end, the transmission will eventually time out, thus causing frame retransmission.

Error control is intended to ensure that the contents of a frame are delivered in the same state as they were transmitted. This checking is accomplished by taking a **checksum** of the header and data and writing it in the trailer of the frame. The receiver computes the corresponding checksum upon receipt of the frame. If the computed checksum value differs from the transmitted checksum, the frame is assumed to have not been received properly. The frame is rejected by treating it as if it were never transmitted at all. This error detection and frame rejection is one of the sources of unreliability in the communication subnetwork.

CONTEMPORARY NETWORKS

A small number of low-level network technologies dominate contemporary computer systems in the United States: They include the Ethernet, the Token Ring, wireless, and various fiber optic technologies such as FDDI and ATM. This section touches on the highlights of Ethernet, Token Ring, and ATM networks.

THE ETHERNET   The Ethernet implements physical and data link layer (MAC) protocols for a LAN. Information is delivered in packets (equivalent to data link frames) with a sustained signaling rate of 10 Mbps. Newer versions of the standard transmit information at up to 1 Gbps.

As mentioned earlier in the chapter, the physical topology is a multiaccess bus. Packets are placed on the bus by the sender. One or more receivers can retrieve the packets by reading the bus. The Ethernet is logically a broadcast medium, similar to the radio broadcast used in the predecessor Aloha net [Abramson, 1970].

The unique aspect of the Ethernet is that it uses a clever technique for distributed control of the shared bus. The technique is called **carrier sense**, **multiple access with collision detection (CSMA/CD)**. The LAN is not guaranteed to be reliable, meaning the MAC layer protocols may drop packets—for example, because of congestion on the network. The Ethernet makes a "best effort" to deliver information, but the delivery may fail if successive attempts to transmit, perhaps a dozen, fail.

Whenever a host wishes to transmit a packet, it first reads the multiaccess bus. If another host is currently transmitting, the sender will see this information and wait until no other host is transmitting (this is called "sensing the carrier"). When the bus is idle, the sender begins to transmit the packet, reading the shared medium as it writes it.

There is a race condition among senders. Suppose senders at physical extremes of the shared bus each sense the carrier and begin to send at about the same time. Eventually, the signals will interfere with one another, causing a *collision* among the signals. Each sender will eventually detect this collision, since each is reading each bit as it places it on the cable. This means that contention on the network is determined by every node that is using the network at the time that the collision occurs (rather than by a single centralized arbiter).

The time frame in which the race can occur (called the *slot time*) is the amount of time required for a signal to propagate from one end of the shared medium to the other end and back again. If a sender attempts to transmit a packet, it must monitor the transmission for at least the slot time in order to guarantee that the race condition does not occur and the packet will not experience a collision.

At this point, the individual sender recognizes if the shared medium has been inadvertently allocated to two senders, and at least one of the senders needs to defer to the other. The idea is to resolve this competition for the shared medium using a decentralized algorithm. Each sender will *back off* for some interval of time and attempt to obtain the shared medium again later. To prevent the reoccurrence of the collision after the backoff time has passed, each sender chooses a random amount of time for its own backoff period. Hence, if two senders collide, one will back off for X time units and the other will back off for Y time units, where X and Y are likely to be different, since they were chosen randomly. The time units are integer multiples of the slot time, since these are the lowest time units in which one can detect collisions.

As contention for the shared medium increases, the chances of collisions increase. Furthermore, the longer the net remains in a saturated condition, the higher the chance that two or more senders will choose the same backoff time. Ethernet uses a *binary exponential backoff* algorithm to address this problem. On the first collision, a sender backs off 0 or 1 slots. On its second collision, it backs off 0, 1, 2, or 3 slots. And on the ith successive collision, it backs off between 0 and $2^i - 1$ slots. The more often a sender fails due to collision, the longer the time it likely will defer before attempting to retransmit.

THE TOKEN RING The Token Ring LAN evolved from an IBM SNA variant. At the physical layer, this LAN operates at signaling rates of up to 16 Mbps. At the data link layer, each host is assigned a logical address from a set of N nonnegative numbers. Host i

can receive packets from Host $i - 1$ (modulo N) and send packets to Host $i + 1$ (modulo N). The placement of the host on the physical layer medium is independent of this logical address assigned to a host. Thus, the data link layer implements a logical ring topology on a somewhat arbitrary medium.

The logical network contains a single, specialized packet called the token. When the token packet arrives at Host i, if the token is "available," Host i can attach information for Host j to the packet and send the token packet on to Host $i + 1$. If the token packet already contains information, Host i must wait for the token to return as an empty packet. When the token packet arrives at Host j, that host receives the information from Host i and marks the token packet as "in transit" from Host i. At Host i, the packet is again marked "available" and sent to Host $i + 1$.

The Token Ring also employs decentralized control, although in a more regimented manner than in the Ethernet. While the Ethernet allows any host to obtain the shared medium as often as it likes, the Token Ring enforces fairness by passing the token around the ring. When the Ethernet detects a collision, it must recover from the situation. Collisions do not occur in Token Rings.

However, the Token Ring depends on each host's behaving properly. If Host i crashes, the ring must be reconfigured so that Host $i - 1$ will send tokens directly to Host $i + 1$, and Host $i + 1$ must accept such packets.

ATM NETWORKS   *Asynchronous transfer mode* (*ATM*) technology has evolved from a combination of the telecommunications and computer industries rather than just the computer industry, as with the Ethernet and Token Ring. Two results of this heritage are the incorporation of reliable transmission at the low layers of the network abstraction and the potential of the network to cover relatively large geographical areas.

An ATM network employs a fiber optic physical layer that transmits data in 53-byte packets called *cells*. The lower layers of an ATM network ensure that cells will be delivered reliably. Furthermore, the network can guarantee various levels of service quality with respect to communication bandwidth and variation. This guarantee is invaluable for communications tasks that support continuous streams of data, such as an audio or video stream, particularly when the streams must be synchronized, as in multimedia applications.

The rapidly evolving ATM technology of today relies on relatively expensive switches, which are currently incapable of operating at the speeds planned for ATMs in the next few years. Today, ATMs transmit signals at less than 500 Mbps, but it is expected they will operate in the gigabit per second range soon.

15.4 ● THE NETWORK LAYER

The network layer implements a network of networks, usually called an internet. In an internet, a host computer on one network, such as Host X on Network A in Figure 15.10, can send a packet to a host located on a different network, such as Host Y on Network C. This is done by **routing** packets from Host X to Host R over Network A, then from Host R to Host S on Network B, and finally from Host S to Host Y on Network C. The network layer implements an internet by providing software to route packets across interconnected networks by having certain intermediary machines take on the responsibility of keeping track of the global internet topology and of forwarding packets as needed.

✦ **FIGURE 15.10** Routing in an Internet

Packets can be routed across networks, provided there is a computer that is connected to two or more networks. The intermediate hosts have the responsibility of maintaining information regarding the network topology and forwarding packets when necessary.

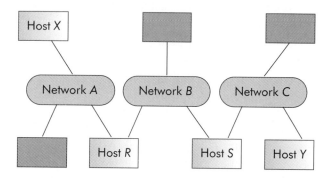

The network layer identifies host machines on the internet using a network and host address. You can think of a network layer address as an ordered pair, (net#, host#). The net# is an integer that identifies the net (within the internet) and the host# is an integer that identifies the host computer on the given network. We will explain more details of addressing below, but for now, observe that the network layer uses an entirely different address space than does the data link layer.

The network layer defines its own packet format, distinct from the data link layer frame format. The packet header contains a (net#, host#) address for the source and another (net#, host#) for the destination. In our example, Host X on Network A, (A, X), addresses the network packet to Host Y on Network C, (C, Y). In network layer designs, the Host X software would not normally know the data link layer frame address for (C, Y) since it is not even connected to Network C. Instead, Host X places the network packet *inside* a data link layer frame and then sends the frame to Host R on the same network as Host X (Network A). Now Host R will route the network packet to (B, S) inside a Network B frame with S's frame address, and so on.

Normally, one thinks of a network as being like a graph: It has a set of nodes interconnected by edges. For example, in a LAN, the nodes in the network are host machines and the edges are the communication subnetwork. In an internet, the "nodes" are *complete networks* and the "edges" are host *machines* that are connected to two or more networks. For example, Host R is connected to both Networks A and B, so Host R is logically an edge between the A and B nodes. Similarly, Host S is an edge between Networks B and C. Provided that Hosts R and S are configured with network layer software to route packets, they move information from one internet node (network) to another, where Networks A, B, and C are the nodes in the internet. A machine that connects two or more networks (and that is able to route packets) is called a **gateway** machine.

A specific network layer transmission may consist of several **hops** across individual networks (there are 3 hops in the example). Each hop is a data link layer frame transmission between a normal host and a gateway, or between gateways. The beauty of the network layer is that the details of the data link layer transmission—for example, the number of hops involved—are not visible above the network layer interface. Network layer client software is able to send packets to a set of diverse hosts on a set of diverse networks using the (net#, host#) addresses.

Let's look more closely at routing: Suppose that a process on Host X on Network A transmits information to a process on Host Y on Network C. It does so by:

- Creating a network packet with a destination address of (Network_C, Host_Y) and then making a system call to a network layer send function in the local OS.
- The local host copies the network packet into a data link layer frame and then sends it to Host R on the attached network.
- When Host R receives the data link layer frame from Host X on Network A, it removes the packet from the data link layer frame, determines the destination of the next hop by looking at the network packet header and its routing table, and then loads the packet into a frame to be transmitted to Host S on Network B.
- When Host S receives the frame from Host R, it follows the same algorithm. However, because the destination is on the network to which it is attached, it performs a normal data link layer delivery to Host Y using the data link layer frame for Network C.

Now you can see that the network layer packet is encapsulated inside of a different data link layer frame for each hop through the internet (see Figure 15.11). Network packet addresses are completely invisible to the data link layer, since they appear only in the packet header in the data field of the data link layer frame. When a gateway removes the network packet from inside a frame, it uses the internet address to determine the next hop through the internet.

✦ FIGURE 15.11 Example Network Layer Packet

Network layer packets are encapsulated inside data link layer frames when they are transmitted from one host to another on a given network. The gateway's network layer software interprets the network packet to determine where the packet should be routed, and then encapsulates it in the data link layer frame of the network it uses to forward the packet.

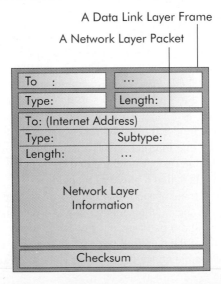

INTERNET ADDRESSES

As described above, the network layer introduces a new name space for network packets, where each host has an address such as (net#, host#). The prevalent network layer address model is the ARPAnet **Internet Protocol** (**IP**) model. The dominant current version of IP (Version 4, or IPv4) uses 32-bit addresses to specify a host and network. IPv4 is gradually being replaced by IPv6 (IP Version 6), which uses 128-bit addresses. In IPv4, an address may have any of four different formats, depending on how system administrators have configured their portion of an internet. Class A IP addresses are used in an internet that has a small number of networks, each with a large number of host machines. In most university environments, the network layer uses Class C addresses, which have a large number of networks, each with a small number of host machines.

The type of an IP address is determined by the setting of the two most significant bits in the address. Class A addresses have these bits set to 00; Class B addresses use 01; Class C addresses use 10; and Class D addresses (plus experimental addresses) have the tag field set to 11 [Stevens and Wright, 1995]. For example, suppose we had a 32-bit IP address 0x807BEA0C. When we are thinking about IP addresses, we usually write the 32-bit address using the *dotted decimal notation*: We convert the hexadecimal representation to dotted decimal notation by first separating the 32 bits into 4 bytes: 0x 80 7B EA 0C. Next, we convert each of the four bytes into a decimal number, so $80_{16} = 128_{10}$, $7B_{16} = 123_{10}$, $EA_{16} = 234_{10}$, and $0C_{16} = 12_{10}$. Finally, we write these four decimal numbers to represent the 32-bit number as 128.123.234.12. When we see a dotted decimal IP address where the first number is in the range 128–191, we have a Class C address: The 2 most significant bits are the tag, the next 22 most significant bits are the net number and the 8 least significant bits are the host number. So, after stripping out the tag field from the two most significant bits, we see that the net number for this IP address is 0.123.234 in dotted decimal notation (0x007BEA in hexadecimal notation), or 31978_{10}. The host number is the least significant byte, or 12_{10}.

Figure 15.12 shows information being delivered to a computer connected to a network. The NIC hardware recognizes the 48-bit data link layer frame address 0x80C31A80837E. The data link layer on any other machine connected to the same network will send a frame to 0x80C31A80837E if it wants to deliver information to that computer. The data link layer frame's payload data is a network packet. It is addressed to the 32-bit network layer address (0.123.234, 12), which we write as a Class C IP address as 128.123.234.12. Software at the network layer uses the IP address. Incoming information is read by the computer NIC if it is sent to address 0x80C31A80837E. Like any other input device, the NIC buffers the information until the device driver copies it into primary memory. Once it has been copied, the network layer software removes the network packet from the data link layer frame and reads its destination address (128.123.234.12). Since that is this machine's IP address, the network layer buffers the packet until its client software requests it.

All software above the network layer uses an IP address to reference other machines on its own network and on its internet. (As you will see later, the transport layer extends the IP address space, but it still uses the (net#, host#) that is defined at the network layer.) The network layer software enables the application software to address host machines on its own LAN and on an internet in exactly the same way. Additionally, the routing part of the network layer software forwards network packets if they are "just passing through" the computer (because it is a gateway computer).

✦ FIGURE 15.12   Using Data Link and Network Layer Addresses

Network information is initially delivered to the machine as a data link layer frame. If the sender were using a network layer protocol, then the frame would contain a network packet that can be interpreted by the receiving machine's network layer software.

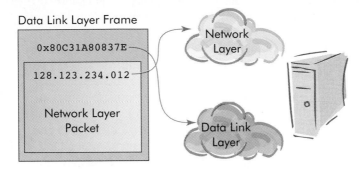

ROUTING

Routing technology has evolved directly from the original ARPAnet. Figure 15.13(a) illustrates the configuration style of the ARPAnet circa 1968. It was a set of large host machines, each with a special interface message processor (*IMP*) network frontend machine. The IMP performed routing without intervention from the host machine. At the time the ARPAnet was built, an IMP was the equivalent of a high-end I/O processor. Today, it is possible to implement its function in a device controller or, more commonly, in a device controller and network software that is executing as part of the OS. In Figure 15.13(a), the IMPs are interconnected using point-to-point communication lines. As LAN technology evolved, ARPAnet host machines began to be replaced by a LAN that interconnected a set of smaller host machines with the IMP. This evolution has led to contemporary internet configurations (see Figure 15.13(b)). The routing technology used in the original WAN-based ARPAnet evolved into the version of IP used in contemporary internets. In this configuration, IMP-gateways performed the routing function of the original ARPAnet IMPs.

Figure 15.14 represents a contemporary internet with gateway machines. Since the function of the original IMP is now packaged as a device with supplementary network layer software, the idea of an IMP has disappeared, being replaced by the idea of a gateway machine that we discussed above. Since many of the individual networks are separated by great distances (measured in miles or even hundreds of miles), an internet often contains pairs of half-gateways. A *half-gateway* machine is connected to a network on one side and a long-haul, point-to-point communication line on the other. A pair of half-gateways interconnected with a point-to-point line provides the functionality of a full gateway, where information moves between the two halves across the communication line.

Network layer software is responsible for handling routing, even in the non-gateway host machines. The particular style of routing depends on the style of the internet, but the basic tasks remain the same:

■ The sending host uses a local routing table to select a destination for the first hop in the route to the ultimate receiver. This table does not need many entries, but it does

✦ FIGURE 15.13 Routing in the ARPAnet

The ARPAnet was a leading edge research network. As shown in part (a), the nodes in the original ARPAnet were large mainframe computers with IMP frontends. As the large mainframes were replaced by LANs with many hosts, the IMPs evolved to be gateway machines, capable of routing network packets through an internet.

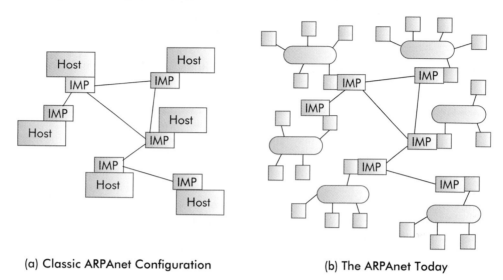

(a) Classic ARPAnet Configuration   (b) The ARPAnet Today

✦ FIGURE 15.14 A LAN-based Internet

Contemporary internets have evolved from the ARPAnet, although there are no longer IMPs or mainframes. In cases where a gateway is used to interconnect to networks that are geographical-ly separated, the gateway can be split into two half-gateways. The two halves are connected with a traditional point-to-point communication line.

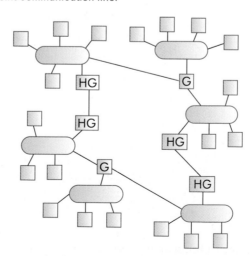

need to include the address of at least one local gateway. If the destination is on the same network as the source, the packet will be sent directly to the destination.

■ The sender software encapsulates the packet into a frame and then transmits it to the gateway or a destination host.

■ The receiver decapsulates the packet and determines whether the packet is addressed to this machine or if it should be routed to another machine. If the packet is to be routed, it uses the information in its routing table to choose the machine for the next hop.

■ The gateway encapsulates the packet into the frame for the outgoing network or local host and forwards the frame.

An internet can become quite large, which suggests that routing tables can also become quite large. If each host keeps a routing table to indicate how to reach all other hosts on the internet, the size requirement may make it impossible for a host to be part of the internet. Of course, any one host is not likely to need to communicate with all other hosts on a very large network. (The internationally shared, public Internet has thousands of networks and host machines throughout the world; see the next subsection.) In IP implementations, the host only keeps a subset of the destination hosts in its routing tables. Because the public Internet changes topology all the time, a host's routing table must be updated periodically. One of the local gateway machines can do this.

Can the same strategy be applied to a gateway machine to allow it to have a partial routing table, and to have it be updated periodically? Is it possible for a gateway machine to perform internet routing when it has only an incomplete routing table? The answer to both questions is yes, provided all the topology of the network appears in some collection of gateways reachable from any host (see Stevens [1994, Ch. 3]). In the IP approach, the gateways have their own separate protocol for updating routing tables.

USING THE NETWORK LAYER

The LAN-based internet topology common in the commercial world stimulated the creation of one large, globally accessible, public internet, commonly referred to as the *Internet*. (Internet is capitalized to distinguish the global internet from others that use the same technology.) Using the Internet, a process running on a host machine in Boulder, Colorado, can exchange packets with a process on another machine located in Paris, France via the same programs it uses to exchange packets with a process on a machine that is located down the hallway.

Network layer technology also allows users to interconnect different types of data link layer LANs, for example, an Ethernet and a Token Ring. Since each gateway acts as a host for two or more LANs, it must include physical and data link layer protocols for the respective LANs. By receiving a data link layer frame with an IP packet on one network device and then copying the contents into the frame for a different (outgoing) network, the gateway will have effectively translated the media used to carry the packet; this is called **media translation**. When a packet from one LAN is passed to another LAN by the gateway, the packet may have to be reformatted or otherwise converted to match the destination LAN protocols. Such gateway machines are said to perform **protocol translation** in addition to the normal media translation. Media translation is common in gateways, but protocol translation can become much trickier, so it is not used very often.

In theory, it is possible to use the features and functions of the network layer as the basis of application programs. In practice, IP is usually accessible only to programs with supervisor permission, since the implementation interface contains many protection loopholes. The transport layer UDP protocol (described in the next section) provides an API similar to IP, although its API is better suited for use by application programs.

Applications implemented on the network layer view the network as an *unreliable* packet network making its best effort to deliver packets. Users of this unreliable packet network must compensate for situations in which packets might be lost at some lower layer, for example, due to checksum failure in the data link layer or collisions in the physical layer. The application programs must also compensate for the possibility that a stream of packets will be delivered out of order because they might have been individually routed on different paths through the internet. The transport layer provides functions to address reliability using standardized facilities.

Latency in the Internet

As the WWW has evolved in popularity, there has been a growing demand for streaming content: content that is delivered as a stream of information rather than as a complete file. The idea is that the machine that requests the streaming content will receive portions of the content at a predefined delivery rate. When it receives a portion of the content, it renders the content to its human user (for example, as an audio/video presentation) and then discards the portion once it has been rendered. This means that the "playback" computer need never have the entire content at any given time—just the part that is currently being played back (rendered). This capability would allow a movie server to deliver a movie as streaming content to a home computer without the home computer ever storing the movie on its own file system.

Streaming video depends on a fixed rate of delivery of parts of the video stream. If the stream is delivered too fast, then the playback computer will have no place to store it. If the stream is delivered too slowly, then the contents of the stream will not be rendered correctly. For example, if the stream were an audio stream, then the playback machine would hesitate in the middle of playing back music.

While streaming content is an important commercial product for WWW, it is essentially incompatible with conventional IP network delivery (which the WWW uses as its underlying delivery protocol). IP is not able to guarantee a delivery rate since the time to deliver an IP packet—the packet latency—is not bounded. IP is explicitly designed to allow flexible routing of information through an internet; in exchange, it is unable to bound the latency on delivery.

Of course, commercial companies recognize the importance of this application, so IPV6 makes provisions by which a web site can bound delivery latency, and hence support streaming video. This is an example of a current, evolving network technology.

15.5 • THE TRANSPORT LAYER

The transport layer can provide a *reliable* mechanism for transmitting information from one host to another. Programmers using the transport layer need not be concerned with packets or internet details. The transport layer creates a new abstraction of network communication that includes a spectrum of services:

- The address space is extended beyond internet addresses so that the transmitting process can reference a specific *port* on a remote host on a remote network. The port might be an application process mailbox, a UNIX pipe end, or other OS-specific entity used to provide a means by which a process can communicate with other processes.

- The transport layer provides various data types to the application program, including datagrams, network messages, and byte streams. The ARPAnet *User Datagram Protocol* (*UDP*) and the *Transmission Control Protocol* (*TCP*) are the dominant transport layer protocols. Although technically, the ARPAnet protocols do not comply with the ISO OSI transport layer standard, they provide the same functions as compliant transport layer protocols. They can be made consistent with the ISO OSI model by adapting TCP and UDP to work with an ISO-compliant network layer.

- Reliable communication (in the face of unreliable network layer operation) is provided at the transport layer.

COMMUNICATION PORTS

The network layer enables machines to exchange information, but their address space does not specify processes or threads within machines. We would like to extend the network layer address space so that a process could have a specific place for processes on other machines to deliver messages. This is like a street address, a post office box, a telephone number, or a voice mailbox. Multiuser and multiprocess machines might need a number of these individual communication addresses within each machine, so the transport layer provides communication ports to extend the internet address.

Figure 15.15 shows host machine X with its unique (net#, host#) address used at the network layer and with a number of communication ports within the machine. Ports are managed by the transport layer, usually as an OS resource. If a process wants to use a port, it must request the use of a port just as it would any other serially reusable resource. Once a port has been allocated, it can be used to send and receive network packets via the transport layer.

Suppose a process in a host with IP address (net#, host#) uses port number *port#* as its delivery point. Then other processes on the internet can send information to that particular process by using the transport layer address (net#, host#, port#). This means that a receiver's port number must somehow be made known to any process that should send information to that receiver. Section 15.6 explains the general technique for supporting this requirement. For now, observe that before a process can receive information from the network, it must (1) have a port allocated for this purpose and (2) the port number must be known by processes that will send information. In general, port *creation* and *binding* to an internet address are separate operations. (As is traditional in transport layer protocols, we say that a process requests that a port be "created" instead of being "allocated" to the process because the OS might dynamically create ports or assign them out of a static pool.) Lab Exercise 15.1 at the end of this chapter explains how Berkeley UNIX sockets are used to create a socket and bind it to an internet address.

✦ FIGURE 15.15 Extending the Address Space with Ports

A communication port ("P" in the figure) is a network delivery point within a particular (net#, host#) machine. This allows processes and threads to have their own delivery points that will be supported by transport layer software.

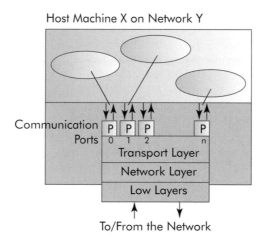

DATA TYPES

The ARPAnet transport layer protocols support two main data types: datagrams and byte streams. **Datagrams** are the same as network layer packets, except that they use the three-component transport layer addresses. Byte streams allow processes on two different machines to exchange information by transmitting and receiving contiguous bytes of information, similar to UNIX and Windows pipes. Because of the wide use of message-passing for interprocess communication, the transport layer can also implement a protocol that supports messages, similar to the message-passing extension to byte streams on a UNIX file or pipe (see Chapter 9).

UDP DATAGRAMS The *User Datagram Protocol* (*UDP*) delivers blocks of information at the transport level. A datagram is a block of information that is transmitted in a network packet (which implies that datagrams are encapsulated within network layer packets). In UDP, a datagram may be larger than a network layer packet; to accommodate this, the protocol will fragment large datagrams so that they can be transmitted as a set of network layer packets and then rebuild the datagram at the receiving machine's transport layer. The network layer delivers individual datagrams to arbitrary hosts on the internet without ensuring reliable delivery; that is, UDP does not guarantee that a packet will be delivered to its destination. However, it does guarantee that if any part of the datagram is delivered, then all of the datagram will be delivered—datagram fragmentation and rebuilding are reliable.

Datagram services provide a level of abstraction of the network similar to the block I/O abstraction for storage devices. If the programmer decides that the underlying implementations of the network and lower layers are sufficiently reliable for the application, then the application software can be written to use datagrams with a protocol such as UDP. It is rare that data would be lost when reading/writing a local storage device operation. However, it is not so rare for network layer communication to lose information. For example, the network may lose a frame at the data link layer or a packet may be lost at the network level. Even so, UDP makes no provision to notify or correct for the loss. Reliability is the full responsibility of the application program. As a result, UDP is generally not used for applications where reliable transmission is required, as in the case of most applications. It can, however, be used for transmitting audio or video information, since the application program would normally interpolate the information it received prior to using it.

The incremental OS support (beyond network layer functions) of datagram service is small—namely, the management of the port component of the address—since most of the functionality is logically part of the underlying network layer.

BYTE STREAMS The *Transmission Control Protocol* (*TCP*) implements reliable byte streams among processes on different hosts on an internet. (These byte streams are sometimes called **connections** and sometimes **virtual circuits**.) Before two threads can establish a byte stream between them, both must be willing to communicate. The two threads take on different roles in establishing the byte stream. The *active* thread requests that a byte stream be established with a passive receiver thread prior to exchanging information. If the passive receiver accepts the request, a connection (or virtual circuit) is established between the two processes that host the threads. Once the connection has been established, the sender can write variable-sized blocks to the byte stream and the receiver reads variable-sized blocks from the connection to obtain the information. In TCP, the size of the blocks read does not have to correspond to the size of the blocks that are written. Since the byte stream is created between a pair of processes, it is unnecessary to include the destination of each piece of information transmitted over the connection.

RELIABLE COMMUNICATION

Datagrams are analogous to telegrams in the sense that each is separately addressed and sent to the receiver. Byte streams implicitly assume reliable packet delivery. Reliability can be achieved by using a communication model that bears more resemblance to telephony than to telegraphy. The telephone system uses the notion of a connection (or circuit) for communication. A caller establishes a connection by placing a call to the callee prior to exchanging information. Once the connection has been established, the caller need not include addressing information, since the connection already specifies the communication ports for both the caller and the callee.

The telephone analogy is used by the TCP to implement the virtual circuits introduced in the previous subsection. If two threads agree to establish a virtual circuit between them, then either can transmit a byte stream across the virtual circuit without being concerned about packet boundaries. Furthermore, TCP *guarantees* that all packets used to hold the byte stream will be delivered in the order they were sent. This is accomplished by attaching sequence numbers to each packet used by the byte stream. The transport layer then uses a peer-to-peer protocol to generate and test sequence numbers to ensure that no packet is lost or delivered out of order.

Opening a virtual circuit requires that the sender and the receiver agree to exchange information. As described previously, any thread intending to communicate with other threads must create a port so that other threads have a delivery point, (net#, host#, port#), on which to connect the virtual circuit. After both threads have created a port, one of them—the active one—requests that the virtual circuit be established. The passive thread can then accept (or reject) the request to connect the virtual circuit to the specified communication port on behalf of the receiver.

Transport layer connections use handshaking protocols (such as those described in Section 15.3) for flow control on the byte stream. Such protocols help ensure that packets do not get lost, since lost packets will cause retransmission. When a flow control protocol such as the sliding-window protocol is used at the transport layer, it manages a stream of packets between ports, rather than the flow of frames between host machines, as is done at the data link layer. Thus, a sliding-window protocol could conceivably be used at the data link level and again at the transport level. When a pair of threads have completed their use of the virtual circuit, they must "tear it down," since network resources are required to keep the virtual circuit intact.

TCP is the prevailing transport layer implementation in contemporary networks. It provides virtual circuit capabilities that enable a sending process to establish a virtual circuit to a remote machine and to exchange information bidirectionally over the connection. Communication using TCP is reliable, so TCP has become the workhorse protocol for contemporary network applications. It is used in window systems (including the X windows system), WWW, remote file systems, and mail systems.

Datagrams and Virtual Circuits Performance

Because TCP provides reliable delivery of information and implements a byte stream, why would a programmer ever choose to use UDP? The answer to this question is: better performance.

When a block of information is sent using TCP, the block must be marshalled into a byte stream, then fragmented to fit into network layer packets with sequence numbers, and finally transmitted over the network layer. The sequence numbers are used to acknowledge the receipt of each packet and to ensure that they arrive in order. As a result, each packet that is sent must (nominally) have an acknowledgment packet transmitted back to the sender (the sliding-window protocol can eliminate some of these acknowledgments).

The overhead for ensuring reliable delivery of information is very significant. In Stevens [1990, Ch. 17], the various studies cited show that when using a 10 Mbps Ethernet that has only a sending and a receiving host using the internet, 4.2BSD TCP had a maximum throughput of about 90 Kbps, while UDP had a maximum throughput of about 185 Kbps. However, Stevens also reports that various optimizations of the software can increase the throughput of TCP to 890 Kbps using a Sun 3/60 on a 10 Mbps Ethernet. (With the normal overhead in an Ethernet, the theoretical maximum throughput for TCP for 1K packets is 1192 packets per second, or 1,203,920 bytes per second.) Stevens does not provide corresponding speed-up figures for UDP. This data suggests that TCP can be made almost as fast as UDP. Unfortunately, not all implementations incorporate the optimizations, so the trade-off between UDP and TCP remains clearly one of performance versus reliability.

15.6 ● USING THE TRANSPORT LAYER

Section 15.5 described the fundamentals that must be implemented by the OS. How applications use the transport layer is considered more fully next.

NAMING AND ADDRESSES

The transport layer address space is a shared, global address space that any process can use to send information to another process. It uses the underlying network layer internet address, (net#, host#), to identify the machine, adding the port number to create a transport layer address, (net#, host#, port#). Once a process begins to use a port number, k, in a machine, j, on a network, i, then any process in that internet can send information to (i, j, k). Since i, j, and k are just nonnegative integers, any process can construct a transport layer address; the trick is to be able to use the *right* address for sending information to a specific process. This is analogous to the situation in which it is easy to make up any telephone number; the trick is to know the number of a person that you want to call.

Let's now consider how a process can use the addresses in its private address space to transmit and receive information using the transport layer. First, recall how memory-mapped resources are bound to a process's address space: A thread in the process requests/creates a process with a system call, causing the OS to provide a reference to the relevant resource. For example, in C programming, you can create a pipe with code such as

```
...
int pipeEnds[2];
...
pipe(pipeEnds);
...
```

The `pipeEnds[0]` address is a reference used to read information from the pipe, and the `pipeEnds[1]` address is used to write information into the pipe. In order to use the transport layer facilities, the process obtains a port, and then binds that port with an address in its address space.

Now let's use what we know about process address spaces and transport layer addresses to see how a process on one machine can send information to a process on another machine. In Figure 15.16, we show that port 1234 has been *bound* to address `0x001a4772` in process A's address space (in this figure, an address is represented as a small box inside a process ellipse). Process B uses a (net#, host#, port#) address from the shared global address space to send information to a port that A is using. This means that whenever a thread in A's address space reads or writes address `0x001a4772`, it reads/writes the host OS's port #1234. Therefore, the particular (net#, host#, port#) that process B must use is (31978, 12, 1234). It does this by calling the transport layer transmit facilities (TCP connection and send, or UDP datagram send) using (31978, 12, 1234). The transport layer on

B's host machine uses its network layer to send a packet to (31978, 12). The network layer uses the internet to route the frame containing the IP packet to (31978, 12) as described in Section 15.4. The OS for (31978, 12) ultimately receives the data link layer frame, say on its NIC address `0x80C31A80837E`. The network layer removes the IP packet for (31978, 12) and passes it to the transport layer. The transport layer delivers the information to port #1234. Process A can then read the information using address `0x001a4772`.

✦ FIGURE 15.16 Sharing Names

The transport layer global address space is the set of all triples (i, j, k). Process A can request the use of one of the OS ports, #1234 in this figure, and then bind that port number to an address in its address space. Now, when process B sends information to this port number on this machine, that is, to (31798, 12, 1234), process A can read it using the address that it bound to the port.

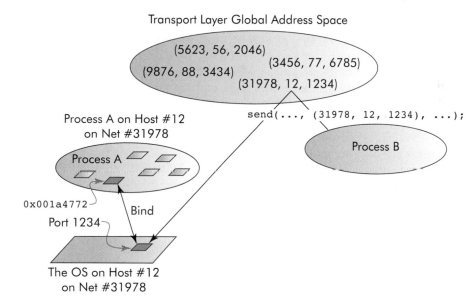

How can process B know that (31978, 12)—`128.123.234.12`—is the address of a particular host machine, and that process A is using port #1234? This is analogous to determining a corporation's telephone number (the IP address) and a person's extension (the port number) in a telephone system. Taking the telephone system as a model, you can call the local phone company's directory services to get the corporate telephone number, and then call the corporation's directory services to get the extension number for the person you want to talk to.

For a process/thread to use a global name, a **name registry** must be available to it. The name registry allows a process to use key names to look up global addresses in a directory. For example, the name registry might allow a thread to obtain the address (31798, 44, 21) using the keyword FTP@cs.colorado.edu. A name registry is a database accessed by these key names.

The name registry is usually a network service, so it has its own reserved transport layer address. This is an example of a *well-known global name*, since its address will usually not change and it can be hardcoded into applications (telephone directory services also have a reserved address, 555-1212). Subscribers remember this number, since they call it to get other numbers.

There are a number of different name registries, or directory services, used in contemporary networks. The X.500 directory service is the official ISO OSI directory service. (For a discussion of the OSI directory service, see Piscitello and Chapin [1993, Ch. 7]). A lightweight version of the X.500 service, LDAP, is now used much more widely than is the full X.500 service. The Domain Name System (DNS) is a specialized directory service for use with network layer public Internet names.

The Domain Name Service

The **Domain Name Service** (**DNS**) is widely used with the public Internet to map text strings into internet addresses (see Stevens [1994, Ch. 14]). The DNS presumes that there is only one name hierarchy for all names used in the public Internet. The hierarchy has an unnamed root with top-level names of arpa, com, edu, gov, int, mil, net, org, and so on (as specified by ISO 3166). No single organization manages the entire name space, but there is an entity to manage each top-level name by registering any children of that name. Each of the top-level names can have a large number of second-level names. For example, the top-level name edu has a second-level name of colorado. The colorado domain is managed by an entity interested in establishing names within the domain of internet names of educational institutions at the University of Colorado at Boulder. The full name of the domain is colorado.edu. Within the colorado domain is another domain called cs, which is managed by the Computer Science Department at the University of Colorado. This domain's name is cs.colorado.edu. Similarly, other names in the DNS domain have the same form; for example, cs.arizona.edu, yahoo.com, nsf.note.gov, and inf.enst.fr.

A *resolver* in each user machine keeps a copy of part of the hierarchy for reference and has the ability to contact a DNS name server for help with DNS names for which it does not know the Internet address. The gethostbyname() call in the BSD socket library invokes the resolver to determine the Internet address of the machine whose DNS name is passed as an argument. The client port of the resolver is implemented as library code, so it is linked into the calling process's address space. The server port of the resolver is a network service that is contacted by the resolver library code.

THE CLIENT–SERVER MODEL

We have informally used the terms "client" and "server" throughout this book. This terminology arose from the network **client–server model** of computation. It is a general distributed computation paradigm that relies on the transport layer facilities, including the name service. We will describe the paradigm in terms of single-threaded processes. According to the model, one process, the server, is a passive process that provides a specified service to any active process, a client, desiring the service.

Several contemporary products employ the client–server model, including file servers, print servers, database servers, and window servers. As suggested by the name, the client–server model has asymmetric behavior. The server always exists in the network, passively waiting for requests for service, while autonomous client processes decide when to utilize the server. A server is a worker process soliciting work, while a client is a supervisory process requiring services.

The server is initiated as an autonomous process in a network of machines. The schematic structure of a server process is shown in Figure 15.17. The structure suggests a datagram interface, since the server is able to accept requests from any particular client, service the request, and then accept a request from a different client.

✦ FIGURE 15.17 Server Structure

This code skeleton illustrates the structure of a passive server process.

```
int serverSkt; /* The socket used to receive requests */
struct request_type *request; /* Details of a request */

serverSkt = initialize(); /* Create a socket and bind it
                           * Register server with the registry
                           * Initialize data structures, etc
                           */
while(TRUE) { /* Service requests until the process dies */
  request = waitForRequest(); /* Get a request */
  serviceTheRequest(request); /* Then service it */
};
```

Suppose a client requests a server to send it a copy of a file. The client might want to obtain a service for a relatively long time, since the server could incur substantial I/O time to read the file from its local disk before transmitting it over the network. In this case, a client might monopolize a server's time even though it is not using all of the service potential of the server. Often the machine implementing the server would be able to support more than one request for service at a time through multiprogramming, provided the services did not interfere with one another. The client–server model can be expanded to allow this multiprogramming. Suppose the server is initiated with a special *listener* process whose only job is to accept service requests and to delegate them to other processes, which perform the actual service. Now the server processes takes the form shown in Figure 15.18.

The listener process is a persistent process (or thread) at the server's transport layer address. It accepts the initial service request from each client, authenticates it if necessary, and then creates a server process (or thread) for each request for service. Each client can exchange information with its copy of the server without blocking other clients from using the service. In this model, a machine is likely to have several processes executing identical procedures on a shared data structure that describes the state of the shared service. Context switches among the server processes can become the dominant processing task on the server machine. Thus, this application is a natural fit for thread-based processing.

Figure 15.19 is a code fragment (using BSD socket software) to illustrate server behavior for a concurrent server. The client requests service by sending a message to the address of the service—a port on the server machine. (The client program must know the server's

✦ FIGURE 15.18 A Concurrent Server

Concurrent servers use multiprogramming to support multiple simultaneous client–server sessions. The listener process accepts work requests, and then creates a server child to provide service to each client.

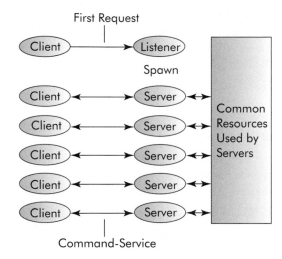

address in order to initiate a service request.) This address could be well-known, or could have been obtained from a directory service that is located at a well-known location. The initialization code queries the host OS to determine the (net#, host#) for the machine. Next it requests a port, called a **socket** in the BSD package, and then it binds the resulting (net#, host#, port#) to an address. The server then waits for a client to request service with the accept() call. The newSkt value is a new socket to be used for communication between the server process/thread and the client. After the accept() call completes, the server calls fork() to create a child server process that will provide service to the requesting client.

The client–server model is the most widely used paradigm for organizing distributed computations. OS designers use the model heavily in implementing the OS. For example, the remote file systems described in the next chapter are all designed around the client–server model. The model also highlights the need for efficient process management and encourages OS support of the thread model.

15.7 • NETWORK SECURITY

Chapter 14 focused on protection mechanisms and security policies, even though you had not yet learned the details of networks. Much of the authorization mechanisms used in contemporary network systems are built around the ISO OSI protocol family. This section discusses the primary authentication mechanisms that are in use with modern operating systems for networks.

✦ FIGURE 15.19 Refined Server Structure

This code skeleton describes how the UNIX BSD socket package can be used to implement the concurrent server shown in Figure 15.18. See the text for the details.

```
/* The Listener/Server Processes */
int main(int argc, char *argv[]) {
  void runServer(int);
  char serverHostName[HOSTNAMELEN];
  int on = 1, port, clientLen, newSkt, skt, run = TRUE;
  struct sockaddr *client, listener;
  struct hostent *host;

  initialize(); /* Determine the server's host name and port# */
              * Set up a socket for listening
              * Fill-in the internet info
              * Bind the listener's address
              */
/* Wait for client requests */
  clientLen = sizeof(client);
  while(TRUE) {
  /* wait for a service request() */
    newSkt = accept(skt, &client, &clientLen);
  /* Start a server to serve the request */
    if (fork() == 0) {
    /* Only the server child executes this code */
      close(skt); /* Server doesn't need the listener skt */
      runServerCommand(newSkt);
  /* Server done ... terminate */
      exit(0);
    }
    close(newSkt); /* Listener doesn't need the server skt */
  }
}
```

TRANSPORT LAYER SECURITY: FIREWALLS

Computers are typically connected to the public Internet using the IP protocol, meaning that most network applications interact using a transport layer protocol (such as TCP) or a layer higher in the protocol stack. A set of computers owned by a particular organization will have some form of physical security: The computers are in locked buildings, rooms, or private offices. However, since each computer can be accessed from the Internet at the transport layer, the default situation is that any computer on the Internet might have access to the organization's computers. Like other security scenarios, an organization would generally like to control the types of access that external subjects might have to the organization's objects (computers and information).

The most obvious protection mechanism to add to such an organization is a firewall computer. A **firewall** is a machine that is placed between the public Internet and every computer in the organization (see Figure 15.20). The organization's intranet is its own internal network that is used for the internal host machines to interact with one another using any protocol they like. The job of the firewall is to only allow authorized access requests from anyone on the Internet.

✦ FIGURE 15.20   A Firewall

A firewall machine is placed between a company's intranet and the public Internet. The firewall inspects each transport layer request (TCP connection request or UDP datagram delivery) before it delivers the information to a host on the intranet.

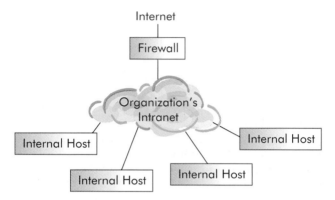

There are several different implementations of firewalls, ranging from kernel network software that can run on any machine that is positioned as a gateway to the intranet, to specialized hardware boxes that interpret a security policy provided by the network administrator. Each of these firewall implementations generally provides transport layer filtering: The security policy can be specified by providing a set of rules to the firewall that can say things like:

- Block all access except for requests from any process on the machine at (net#, host#, *) (the "*" means that the request could come from any port on the designated machine)
- Allow α access to the internet only from (net#, host#, port#)
- Allow an α access to my port 80 from any Internet host

The job of the firewall is then to check the authorization for each request based on these rules. The firewall machine may operate as a transport layer firewall (applying the rules to TCP and UDP using net, host, and port), or it could operate at a different layer in the protocol stack, say the network layer. Generally, contemporary firewalls are layer 4 firewalls. You can see that these rule-based, layer 4 firewall machines can be quite effective, yet very easy to implement.

Is a firewall machine infallible? No, of course not. The basic idea for a firewall is that it creates an impenetrable barrier that disallows any incoming traffic; then the rules allow the network administrator to "punch a hole in the firewall" that can be used by other hosts on the Internet. Web servers need to use port 80 so web browsers can communicate with them. Similarly, there can be other holes in the firewall to accommodate https (secure http), SMNP (mail), FTP, and so on. Once the firewall allows access into the intranet, it is the responsibility of other software to ensure that no damage is done by the external subject.

Firewalls are an essential element of modern network systems. Without them, intranets would be at the mercy of any subject operating on any host machine on the Internet. They are very widely used in contemporary installations.

NETWORK LAYER SECURITY: IPSEC

As networks have evolved, many people recognized the need for security mechanisms that operate at the network layer. As a result, a family of security protocols called **IPsec protocol suite** have been derived for the network layer (see [IETF, 1998]). IPsec mechanisms are "designed to provide interoperable, high quality, cryptographically-based security for IPv4 and IPv6." Different specifications in the family address authorization mechanisms, authentication of the source of information transferred over IP, protection against replay attacks, cryptography, and concealment of traffic flow patterns.

The protocol suite would ordinarily be implemented in an IP gateway machine (a network layer firewall) called the *security gateway*. The protocol suite behavior is guided by a Security Policy Database to define the particular policy, algorithms, and cryptographic keys to be applied to traffic. Like the transport layer firewall, this network layer will filter IP packets, either allowing them to pass or not. Those that are allowed to pass inward can be decrypted by the security gateway.

The basis of the protocol suite is an Authentication Header protocol that can be used to determine the source of each unit of information, and the Encapsulating Security Payload protocol that is concerned with the secure delivery of content using cryptography. Together, these two protocols implement the basic authentication and cryptography functions for transmitting information from one host to another.

The IPsec protocol suite is commonly used to implement **tunnels**, or logical connections between two hosts on an internet. An IPsec tunnel differs from an ordinary TCP connection in that it also incorporates authentication (using the Authentication Header protocol) and encryption (using the Encapsulating Security Payload protocol). The resulting IPsec tunnel, also called *virtual private network* (*VPN*), is widely used in contemporary systems.

Virtual private networks allow corporations to create an intranet (protected by firewalls) in which it keeps its corporate information and other resources. Employees can use the virtual private network to establish a secure connection through the firewall into the protected intranet. Once employees have created an IPsec tunnel into the intranet, then they can perform operations on the internal information as if they were using a machine inside the firewall.

15.8 • SUMMARY

Modern computer systems use the ISO OSI architectural model extensively as the framework for defining network protocols. The model is a layered architecture composed of these layers: physical, data link, network, transport, session, presentation, and application. This chapter described the MAC protocols, since they are hardware resources to be managed by the OS, and the network and transport layers, since they are usually implemented in the OS.

The low-level protocols define the physical signaling protocol and the structuring of byte streams into data link frames. The network layer implements the internet—a network of networks because it uses gateways to connect independent networks. Most network-level implementations are based on the ARPAnet Internet Protocol, IP.

The transport layer implements multiple data structure types and, most important, reliable network communication over the unreliable lower layers of the ISO OSI model. Addresses at the transport level differ from those at the network level through the use of the port specification to distinguish among communication endpoints on a specific (net#, host#) location. Transport layer addresses have the form (net#, host#, port#).

TCP is the dominant protocol at the OSI transport layer. It provides a virtual circuit function that enables programmers to open a virtual circuit, and to read and write bidirectional byte streams over the virtual circuit.

As networks are used more widely, security issues have become increasingly important. Today, individual networks in an internet ordinarily use a firewall to authorize access to the network's resources from remote machines on the Internet. Because of the need for firewalls, VPNs are now commonly used in the Internet so that a remote machine can have authenticated access to a network's resources.

How do applications use the network protocols to support distributed computation? Remote files are the most widely used application of the transport layer network. The next chapter explains how remote files use the transport layer to allow a process on one machine to use the files loaded on another machine.

15.9 • EXERCISES

1. Suppose a 10 Mbps network transmits 1024-byte packets containing a 128-byte header and a 4-byte checksum. If a workstation on the LAN is guaranteed to be able to transmit at least one packet every X time units (since the network is shared with other workstations), what maximum amount of time, as a function of X, should be required (based only on these factors) to transfer a 3MB file from a server to a workstation? What is the effective transfer rate from the server to the workstation?

2. A 10 Mbps Ethernet has a minimum gap between packets of 12 bytes, a 22-byte header, and a 4-byte trailer. Assume a user data field of 1464 bytes in a frame, with a minimum gap between each frame.

   a. What is the maximum theoretical rate at which user data can be transmitted on the Ethernet?

   b. IP packet headers are 20 bytes, and UDP packet headers are 8 bytes. What is the maximum theoretical rate at which user data can be transmitted using UDP on the Ethernet?

   c. IP packet headers are 20 bytes, and TCP packet headers are 20 bytes. What is the maximum theoretical rate at which user data can be transmitted using TCP on the Ethernet? (Ignore the cost of ACKs.)

3. Rewrite the stop-and-wait algorithm shown in Figure 15.9 using Windows synchronization primitives. You can use pseudocode for your solution, but use Windows function names for the synchronization calls.

4. Write a pseudocode description that generalizes the stop-and-wait algorithm in Figure 15.9 so that it implements the sliding-window protocol. In the data link layer protocol described in Section 15.3, there is a header and a trailer for a frame.

5. Many implementations put the checksum in the trailer, but all the other information describing the frame in the header. Why do network designers do this (instead of just putting the checksum as another field in the header so they could dispense with the trailer)?

6. Given an IP address of $(199_{10}, 126_{10})$:

   a. What is Class A address in dotted decimal notation?

   b. What is Class C address in dotted decimal notation?

7. What is the Class of each of the following addresses? Convert each Class C address into an IP address of the form (net#, host#):

   a. 68.38.129.63.

   b. 217.167.115.12.

   c. 130.34.153.91.

   d. 63.148.99.227.

   e. 80.109.69.127.

   f. 164.145.224.190.

8. Suppose an internet has the organization shown in Figure 15.21, with software using the given transport layer addresses and machines using the given data link layer addresses.

   a. List the network layer address for each machine.

   b. Describe the frames used to send a UDP packet from <20, 40, 1333> to <30, 40, 1888>.

✦ **FIGURE 15.21** An Internet Configuration

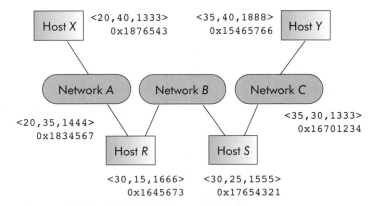

9. Consider the scheme for employing only partially complete routing tables in each node and gateway of the ARPAnet. If the union of all the information in the partial routing tables is complete, consistent, and stable, explain why routing will operate correctly. There are many details in the actual ARPAnet that constrain their solution—details not covered in this text—so you will need to state all assumptions you make about gateway behavior.

10. The Berkeley UNIX connect system call has a time-out interval of about 1 minute, but the accept call has no time-out interval. Explain why these functions might have been designed in this manner.

11. Write a pseudo C code definition of the `waitForRequest` function referenced in Figure 15.17. (*Hint*: You may find it useful to look at Figures 15.22 and 15.23 in Lab Exercise 15.1.)

Using TCP/IP

This exercise can be solved using Windows 9x/Me, Windows NT, Windows 2000, or any UNIX system with BSD sockets (for example, FreeBSD and Linux).

UNIX systems provide a shell command called `talk` that enables two different users logged into the same computer to have a real-time dialogue. One user invokes `talk` with another user's login name to request a `talk` session, and the connection between the two is completed when the second user accepts the request. This lab exercise asks you to implement a skeletal `talk` facility between two different processes on two different machines. As a simplification, assume that the facility is asymmetric in the sense that one of the processes acts as an *initiator* and the other as a *receiver*. The initiator begins the `talk` session by requesting a virtual circuit with the receiver. Use the BSD socket communication mechanism with the internet address domain as the IPC mechanism. Each process should provide a single console window for both sending and receiving (UNIX `talk` splits the screen into two windows). Precede outgoing messages with a > symbol and incoming messages with a < symbol. It is acceptable for your solution to allow an incoming line from the remote user to interrupt the local user if he or she is currently typing a line.

● BACKGROUND ●

The BSD socket mechanism implements transport layer services; it is used in many contemporary UNIX systems and in the Windows WinSock package. Earlier in the chapter, you learned how the transport layer protocol can use datagrams or virtual circuits, and that both require that a communication endpoint be established within a process's address space before that process can use the transport layer mechanism. In the BSD socket package, a **socket** is that endpoint. A socket is an OS resource that is allocated to the process through a system call having a prototype of the form:

```
int socket(int addressFamily, int socketType, int protocolNo);
```

The `addressFamily` parameter specifies a name domain and protocol family that will be used with the socket. The supported domains depend on the particular OS (for example, the Sun UNIX Release 4.1 supports a UNIX internal domain, the ARPA internet protocols, and the ARPA IMP domain [Sun, 1990]). The `socketType` parameter defines the data type that will be used on the socket. In the Sun Release 4.1, the data types are byte streams, datagrams, raw internet packets, and sequenced packets; later releases also support other protocols. The `protocolNo` parameter identifies a protocol to be used on the given data type with the given address family.

The `addressFamily` parameter indicates which name space will be used by the socket if it is mapped to an external name space. Internet addresses will be used with the socket if `addressFamily` is set to `AF_INET`. In most implementations, TCP is used with the virtual circuit type and UDP is used with the datagram data type. This means that if the socket is created with a `socketType` of `SOCK_DGRAM`, then the default `protocolNo` refers to UDP. Similarly, if the `socketType` is `SOCK_STREAM`, the default `protocolNo` will be the TCP protocol. (The default protocol will be chosen if the `socketType` is defined and `protocolNo` is passed as zero.) For example, to specify that the socket is to use internet addresses and datagrams, the call would have the form

```
int socket(AF_INET, SOCK_DGRAM, 0);
```

Even though it is necessary to specify the address family for a socket, a socket can be used to *send* information over an internet without ever being associated with an internet address. However, before information can be *received* at any specific location on the internet, the receiving socket must have been bound to an internet address (net#, host#, port#). That is, in the BSD socket package, a socket is an OS resource that can be referenced by an address in the receiving process's address space as shown in Figure 15.16. The rationale for the `socket()` system call design is that the system must know how a socket will be used—the kind of addresses and the protocol to use when sending or receiving information. However, there is no requirement that it have an associated internet address just to transmit outgoing information through the socket.

The WinSock Package

The Windows WinSocket package is closely modeled after BSD UNIX Socket package (in fact, it uses much of the same code). It allows the programmer to use UDP and TCP with IP, as well as other protocols. The WinSock package requires that you call `WSAStartup()` before you use any parts of the package, and that you use `WSACleanup()` after you have finished with them.

```
int WSAStartup(
  WORD wVersionRequested,
  LPWSADATA lpWSAData
);
```

The `wVersionRequested` parameter tells the startup package the latest version of the WinSock package that this code will use. The `lpWSAData` parameter is used to return a `WSAData` structure with the details of the version of WinSock you will be using. The `WSAData` has the form

```
typedef struct WSAData {
        WORD wVersion;
        WORD wHighVersion;
        char szDescription[WSADESCRIPTION_LEN+1];
        char szSystemStatus[WSASYS_STATUS_LEN+1];
        unsigned short iMaxSockets;
        unsigned short iMaxUdpDg;
        char FAR * lpVendorInfo;
} WSADATA, FAR * LPWSADATA;
```

See the online MSDN documentation for more details. The cleanup routine,

```
int WSACleanup (void)
```

unregisters the process from making further use of the package (and frees resources it has allocated to support the process).

In sockets that use internet addresses (those where `addressFamily` is set to `AF_INET`), a global (internet) name of the form (net#, host#, port#) can be associated with a socket. In this case, we say that the internet address is *bound* to the socket (using an explicit system call). If a local process wants to use the socket to transmit information over the internet to a remote site, then the local process references the socket in the remote process using the internet address that was bound to that remote socket. Therefore, if a process wants other processes to be able to send information, it must create a socket in its own address space, and then bind the socket to an internet address.

In BSD UNIX, port numbers 0 to 1023 are reserved for well-known services (for example, port number 21 is used by the FTP application). BSD UNIX will select a port number automatically, or the programmer can specify a specific port number (assuming it is not already bound at the time of the binding call). The `bind()` system call has the form

```
int bind(int skt, struct sockaddr *addr, int addrLen);
```

The `skt` parameter is the socket identifier returned by the socket call. `addr` is a structure holding the internet address (for sockets using the `AF_INET` name domain). The `sockaddr` type is used for any domain, but the `sockaddr_in` type refers to the `AF_INET` domain. The `addrLen` parameter is the length of the `addr` data structure.

The code segment shown in Figure 15.22 creates a socket in the UNIX process's address space and then binds it to an internet address at port 1234, where `netNo` and `hostNo` are the internet addresses of the machine executing the code, and 1234 is the port number chosen by the programmer.

✦ FIGURE 15.22 Binding a Socket to an Internet Address

This code segment shows how you can create a TCP socket and then bind it to an IP address. The `gethostbyname()` call translates a DNS name into a (net#, host#). The `addr` fields are then filled in with net#, host#, and port# (after it is converted to "network format" with the `htons()` call).

```
  . . .
  skt = socket(AF_INET, SOCK_STREAM, 0); /* Create the socket */
  host = gethostbyname(serverHostName); /* Get <host, net> */
/* Create a structure containing my internet address */
  bzero(&addr, sizeof(addr));
  addr.sin_family = host->h_addrtype;
  addr.sin_port = htons(1234);
  bcopy(host->h_addr, &addr.sin_addr, host->h_length);
/* Bind the internet address to my socket */
  if(bind(skt, &addr, sizeof(addr))) {
    printf("Bind error ... restart\n");
  . . .
```

OPENING A CONNECTION

For two processes to create a connection successfully, one of them must play the role of an active process and the other a passive process. In a telephone analogy, the active process is the entity that requests the connection ("places the call") and the passive process accepts it ("answers"). Figure 15.23 is a code skeleton representing the behavior of an active process for opening a TCP connection; here is a code skeleton representing the passive process.

✦ FIGURE 15.23 The Active Process in Opening a Connection

The active participant initiates connection establishment. It determines the passive participant's (net#, host#, port#), and then issues a `connect()` request. The `connect()` call does not return until the connection has been explicitly accepted or rejected. After the process is through using the connection, it deletes the socket with a `close()` system call, which releases the connection.

```
#include <sys/types.h>
#include <sys/socket.h>
#include <netinet/in.h>
#include <netdb.h>
/* The active (client) process */
int main (int argc, char *argv[]) {
  int skt, port;
  char serverHostName[HOSTNAMELEN];
  struct hostent *host;
  struct sockaddr passive;
  struct protoent *protocol;

#ifdef WINDOWS
/* Begin WinSock only */
  WORD versionRequested;
  WSADATA wsaData;
  versionRequested = MAKEWORD(..., ...);
  WSAStartup(versionRequested, &wsaData);
/* End WinSock only */
#endif /*WINDOWS*/
/* Get server name, serverHostName */
/* Get the port number, port */
  ...
/* Set up a socket & address to talk to the server */
  protocol = getprotobyname("tcp");
  skt = socket(AF_UNIX, SOCK_STREAM, protocol->p_proto);
  host = gethostbyname(serverHostName);
  bzero(&passive, sizeof(passive));
  passive.sin_family = host->h_addrtype;
  passive.sin_port = htons(port);
  bcopy(host->h_addr, &passive.sin_addr, host->h_length);
  if(connect(skt, &passive, sizeof(passive))) {
          printf("Connect error ... restart\n");
          printf("(Must start Server end first)\n");
          exit(1);
  };
/* The connection is ready for use ... */
  ...
/* All done - tear down the circuit */
  close(skt);
#ifdef WINDOWS
  WSACleanup();      // WinSock only
#endif /*WINDOWS*/
}
```

✦ FIGURE 15.24 The Passive Process in Opening a Connection

The passive participant waits for a connection request. It creates a socket on which it will listen for connection requests and then blocks on the accept() call. When the active side makes a connect() call, the accept() call synchronizes with the remote end to establish the connection. (This is the same code sequence as in Figure 15.19.) After the process is through using the connection, it deletes the socket with a close() system call, which releases the connection.

```c
/* The passive (server) process */
int main(int argc, char *argv[]) {
  char serverHostName[HOSTNAMELEN];
  int port, activeLen, newSkt, skt;
  struct sockaddr *active, passive;
  struct hostent *host;

#ifdef WINDOWS
/* Begin WinSock only */
WORD versionRequested;
WSADATA wsaData;
  versionRequested = MAKEWORD(..., ...);
  WSAStartup(versionRequested, &wsaData);
/* End WinSock only */
#endif /*WINDOWS*/
/* Get the server host name, serverHostName */
/* Get the port number, port */
  ...
/* Set up a socket for listening */
  skt = socket(AF_INET, SOCK_STREAM, 0);
  host = gethostbyname(serverHostName);
  bzero(&passive, sizeof(passive));
  passive.sin_family = host->h_addrtype;
  passive.sin_port = htons(port);
  bcopy(host->h_addr, &passive.sin_addr, host->h_length);
/* Bind the listener's name */
  if(bind(skt, &passive, sizeof(passive))) {
    printf("Bind error ... restart\n");
    exit(1);
  }
/* Now begin waiting for a request */
  listen(skt, BACKLOG);
/* Wait for client requests */
  activeLen = sizeof(active);
  newSkt = accept(skt, &active, &activeLen);
  close(skt); /* Release extra socket */
/* Use newSkt for the connection */
...
/* Disconnect */
  close(newSkt);
#ifdef WINDOWS
  WSACleanup();      // WinSock only
#endif /*WINDOWS*/
}
```

Both code skeletons create a socket using the internet domain and TCP. The active process then creates a data structure with the internet address of the passive process in `struct sockaddr passive` so that it can initiate the connection operation. The `connect()` call specifies the socket of the active process and the (net#, host#, port#) of the passive process. The active process blocks on calling `connect()` until either the passive process accepts the connection request or the OS for the active process decides the call has failed and thus returns with an error code. The error return can result from various conditions, including a timer expiration (that is, the passive process does not accept the connection request in some preestablished time interval—for example, one minute).

The passive process creates a socket to use to accept a connection request from an active process. Since it will receive information on this socket, it must bind the socket before the active process attempts to connect to it. The `listen()` call passes information to the OS to tell it the maximum number of connection requests it should queue up for the passive process, in this case, a constant of `BACKLOG` requests. The `accept()` call is passed the connection request on `skt`, but it creates another socket, `newSkt`, and then causes the connection to be established on the `newSkt`. The passive process blocks on the `accept()` call until either the process is killed or a connection request arrives on the socket (there is no time-out period for an `accept()` operation). After the connection has been completed, the original socket, `skt`, is no longer needed, since the connection is established on `newSkt`. Both processes use a normal `close()` operation to release the connection and the sockets.

READING MULTIPLE INPUT STREAMS IN UNIX

The `talk` program will need to be able to receive input from both `stdin` (the keyboard) and the socket. However, if it performs a conventional synchronous read on `stdin` and input arrives on the socket, the `talk` process will not see the network data until after the user enters data at `stdin`. Conversely, if the process blocks on a socket `read()` and if the user types information at the keyboard, that input will be ignored until after information arrives on the socket. This situation can be addressed in three different ways: (1) by using a nonblocking (asynchronous) read instead of the default blocking `read()` in the stdio library, (2) by using the `select()` command, or (3) by using multiple threads. The nonblocking `read()` option is described in Lab Exercise 9.1.

The `select()` command allows a process to poll all its open input streams to determine which of them have data. After calling the `select()`, a process can determine which input streams have data. It can then execute a normal blocking `read()` operation on any stream that contains data. Use the `man` page to find out more about `select()` if you decide to use this approach in your solution.

READING MULTIPLE INPUT STREAMS IN WINDOWS

The same general principle applies for a Windows solution as it does for the UNIX solution. The difference is that the console is treated differently in Windows than is `stdin` in UNIX. Solving this problem in Windows requires some ingenuity on your part and some reading of the online documentation. (*Hint*: `CreateFile()` can be used with the console. You may also find it helpful to see the routines in the console I/O package, under "Console and Port I/O" in the online MSDN documentation.)

• ATTACKING THE PROBLEM •

Your solution framework should be based on a client and a server process, where the client will initiate the talk session using a connect() system call and the server will accept() it. Thus, the server process should be started so that it will be in a state where it can accept a connection request when the client issues it.

The client and server roles are important at the time the talk session is started, but once the session has been established, then either process can temporarily assume the role of client (that sends information to the other process). If you have used talk on a single machine, then you are aware that the UNIX talk program makes no distinction about which process is the client: If the two users begin to type at the same time, the order in which information is transmitted is arbitrary. You do not need to be concerned about solving such "unorderly" communication between two people, as that part of their protocol is not addressed by talk.

Your solution will thus require that you employ a client–server architecture for establishing the talk session, but you must then have peer processes communicating with one another using byte streams over a network after the connection has been established.

Here are some suggestions for how you might go about constructing your solution:

- Write only one talk application program that can be used by your client and your server after a connection has been established.

- Focus on getting a TCP connection working first. Start by making the connection work between two processes on one machine. Let the server's system choose a port number, and then specify the port number for the client at runtime. After you get that to work, be sure your code works across an internet between two machines.

- In this phase of the work, let your connection client also be the process that sends a few bytes to the connection server. That is, you will temporarily let your connection client be the data source, and have your connection server block on a read on the socket after the connection has been established.

- Add code so that the talk program reads stdin (using a blocking read()) then transmits the information to the other program). That is, design and debug so that each process alternately reads one line of code from stdin and then from the socket.

- Generalize your talk program so that it uses nonblocking read() operations or the select() system call so that it never blocks on an input stream.

Remote Files

Network technology is the principal enabling technology for distributed computation. In a network of computers, processes can communicate with one another at bandwidths three or more orders of magnitude higher than with traditional serial communication devices. The fastest networks may eventually approach the speeds of communication across the bus within an individual machine. How can software take advantage of the additional bandwidth?

As a first approach to distributed computing, OS designers combined networks with the file abstraction to create the idea of *remote files*. With remote files, applications can read and write information from remote machines as if the file were stored on local storage devices. Today, remote files continue to be an important part of how we implement coarse-grained distribution. In this chapter, you will learn how the OS can be designed to distribute a file system across machines on the network. There are three general strategies: In the first strategy, the file manager interacts with storage devices located on remote machines. In the second strategy, the file manager functionality is distributed between the local and the remote machines. The third strategy is for the OS to automatically copy files from remote machines, keep multiple copies consistent, and restore the copy to its original machine when the file is closed.

16.1 • SHARING INFORMATION ACROSS THE NETWORK

When LAN technology became feasible in 1980, OS designers were issued a new challenge: How should the OS be redesigned so that it could take the best advantage of LAN technology? Computers could suddenly exchange information ten thousand times faster than they could with existing serial communications (10^7 bps on an Ethernet instead of 10^4 bps on a switched telephone network). Designers considered two basic extensions to the existing abstract model:

- New applications could be designed as a community of *cooperating sequential processes*, requiring that the OS abstract the network so that it would be useful for synchronization and IPC. One camp of OS designers pursued this goal (we will consider their work in Chapter 17).

- The *memory* components of the abstract machine could be partitioned and then distributed across the network. As shown in Figure 16.1, the primary or secondary memory might be placed on a remote machine. Even though the LANs of the time were relatively fast, they were not fast enough to allow primary memory to be removed from the local machine and placed at a remote server. (However, the idea of remote primary memory became feasible in the 1990s, as we will also see in Chapter 17.) The second camp of OS designers began to focus on operating systems based on the idea of remote secondary memory. We will study their work in this chapter.

✦ FIGURE 16.1 Remote Memory

One approach to exploit the network would be to place primary or secondary memory on a remote machine. A remote memory could then be large and shared. The additional cost of the memory would be amortized over all the client machines.

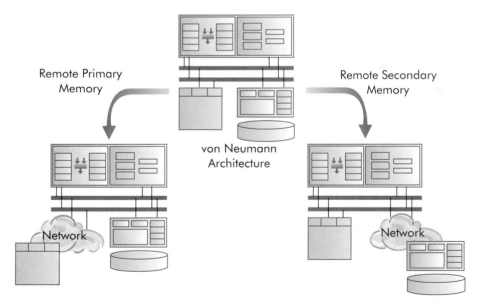

Let's start the discussion by considering all of the memory interfaces in a von Neumann computer: Primary and secondary memories provide different interfaces to the underlying storage mechanisms (see Figure 16.2). The **primary memory interface** is used to access executable memory on a byte-by-byte basis (see Chapter 4). Over time, OS designers have embraced this model through the process address space behavior described in Chapter 11. It is interesting to note that virtual memory systems use the primary memory interface to provide access to secondary memory storage devices. The secondary memory is implemented on a collection of storage devices. In a multiprogramming system, the OS forbids processes from using the device driver interface to read/write storage devices, so that it can manage sharing and isolation of the secondary memory. Instead, the **file system interface** is used by applications to read and write the secondary memory as a set of named byte streams (files).

✦ FIGURE 16.2 Traditional Memory Interfaces

The von Neumann computer architecture defines one interface to the primary (executable) memory and another to the secondary memory (storage devices). We discussed the primary memory interface in Chapters 2, 11, and 12. Chapter 5 dealt with the device driver interface to secondary memory and Chapter 13 covered the file system interface to secondary memory. Remote files use the file system interface.

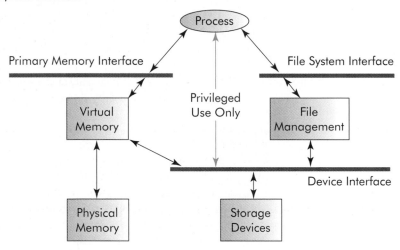

The goal of a remote file system is for the client code on one machine to be able to read and write the secondary memory on another machine by using the file system interface. Figure 16.3 illustrates how the programmer might use remote files to exchange information. The computation is divided into Parts 1 and 2; Part 1 executes a portion of the distributed computation and then writes intermediate results into the "toPart2" file. Once Part 1 has completed the initial phase of computation, Part 2 can begin to execute. First, it reads the toPart2 file so that it can retrieve the intermediate results from Part 1. After it finishes its portion of the computation, it writes new intermediate results into the "toPart1" file. Part 1 then resumes, using the information created by Part 2 that was stored in the "toPart1" file. This approach is awkward and slow; worse yet, it does not allow Parts 1 and 2 to execute simultaneously, meaning that it would have essentially no speedup.

Before we dive into remote file system designs, let's look at the way remote file technology evolved from the days of point-to-point networks to the contemporary approaches.

✦ FIGURE 16.3 Distributed Computation Using Files

Files can be used as a coarse-grained IPC mechanism. Here, Part 1 of a distributed computation computes an intermediate result then sends it to Part 2 as a file. Later, Part 2 returns a result file to Part 1.

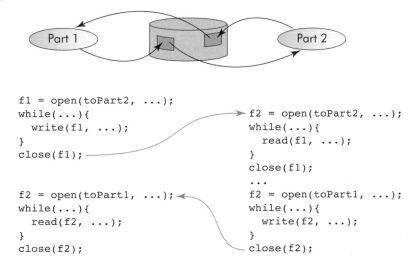

```
f1 = open(toPart2, ...);
while(...){
  write(f1, ...);
}
close(f1);
```

```
f2 = open(toPart2, ...);
while(...){
  read(f1, ...);
}
close(f1);
...
```

```
f2 = open(toPart1, ...);
while(...){
  read(f2, ...);
}
close(f2);
```

```
f2 = open(toPart1, ...);
while(...){
  write(f2, ...);
}
close(f2);
```

EXPLICIT FILE COPYING SYSTEMS

Files are the classic unit of sharing among processes. Information can be created by one process, written to a file, and then used by another process. Information can then be distributed among different machines by copying files from one machine to another. In classic communications systems, such as the ARPAnet, explicit file copy operations were the most common mechanism available to accomplish sharing across machines. When a process on a local machine intended to distribute information to other processes on remote machines, the process wrote the information to a file and then the remote users manually copied the file to their machine.

In this approach, shell commands are used to copy files from one location to another. There are two major problems (and a million smaller ones) in implementing these commands:

■ The process that executes the command on the local machine must have a peer process on the remote machine. This is a *cooperative distributed computing* problem.

■ It must be possible for the local program to uniquely reference a file located on another machine. This is a *global name space* problem.

Because of our knowledge of networks (from Chapter 15), it is easy for us to see that the cooperative distributed computing part of the problem can be solved with a client–server distributed computing model (see Figure 16.4):

1. The client process executes a local shell command, such as `get <file_name>`. The program that implements the command opens a TCP connection to the server and then transmits the file copy command to the server process.

2. The server process unpacks the command, opens `FILE_A`, and copies it back to the client.

✦ FIGURE 16.4 Client–Server Manual File Copy

Cooperating client and server processes can copy a file from the server to the client. The client requests a particular file, and the server responds by copying the file back to the client.

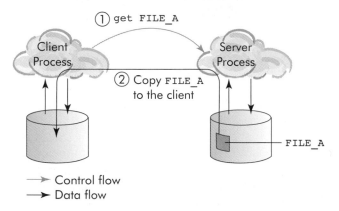

OS designers were able to reach a satisfactory solution to the cooperative distributed computing problem quickly; in fact, there is a reasonable argument that this application created the environment in which the client–server model was invented! However, the naming problem took more design iterations. Two examples of solutions from the 1970s are the UNIX `uucp` and ARPAnet `ftp` commands (described in more detail below). Although `uucp` is no longer used, `ftp` is still in wide use today.

There are other manual file transfer packages used across heterogeneous networks. (A heterogeneous network has different kinds of host machines.) The ISO OSI File Transfer, Access and Management (FTAM) protocol is the official ISO OSI mechanism for manual file transfer; although `telnet` and `ftp` (and now HTTP) are more widely used for file transfer.

THE UNIX UUCP COMMAND UUCP (*UNIX* to *UNIX* *CoPy*) is a UNIX program that exchanges files using serial communication devices and dial-up modems. The user interface program for UUCP is `uucp`. UUCP uses a routing table defined by the machine's system administrator to call up a UUCP program on another computer so they can copy files back and forth.

The UNIX `uucp` command is intended to look as much like the local `cp` command as possible. The big difference is in the format of the filenames. A remote filename has the form

```
system_name_1!system_name_2!... system_name_N!N_pathname
```

where each `system_name` is the name of a UNIX machine stored in the UUCP routing table. If there is more than one `system_name` in the remote filename, they define a path from `system_name_1` to `system_name_2` and so on to `system_name_N`. The `N_pathname` is a pathname in the file system for machine `system_name_N`.

Authentication can optionally be applied to UUCP operations at each system. Thus, UUCP is normally used to read a file from a remote host (rather than writing the file to a remote host). If the intent is to write a file to a remote host, then the protection settings may allow the user only to log in to the remote machine and to perform a uucp back to the original local machine.

UUCP has been supplanted by newer commands that operate in more modern network environments, including ftp, rcp, and rdist. In these commands, the file is referenced by providing a DNS host name to reference the remote host and an absolute pathname on that host.

THE ARPANET FILE TRANSFER PROTOCOL The File Transfer Protocol (FTP) can be invoked from a user interface—for example, the ftp program in UNIX and Windows systems—to explicitly copy files between host machines on a network using TCP/IP. As in the general solution described above, each host that supports FTP maintains a server process daemon to accept service requests. When an application process intends to use FTP, it executes ftp client code on the local machine. The client code interacts with the remote server daemon to accomplish the file transfer operation.

FTP uses a control connection and a data connection for file transfer. The server expects the initial service request to arrive on well-known port 21, so when a client wishes to use FTP, its TCP connection request is directed at (net#, host#, 21). This requires that firewall machines that protect the two hosts allow network traffic through port 21.

Data is transferred between the client and server when a file is copied (either way) and when the client obtains a listing of the files in a directory. Each time the client issues a command causing this kind of data transfer, a data connection is opened to accommodate the transfer. During an FTP session, the data connection may be opened and closed more than once, depending on the nature of the commands.

FTP is a relatively straightforward client–server program and is well documented in a number of places, including in Stevens [1994, Ch. 27]. Notice that the FTP solution to the naming problem uses IP addresses and DNS to implicitly create a shared global name space: Files are transferred to/from remote machine X by having the FTP user explicitly specify X's DNS name or IP (net#, host#). This allows the ftp client to begin interacting with the ftp server at the designated remote location.

A SEAMLESS FILE SYSTEM INTERFACE

Modern remote file systems are intended to make manual remote file copy operations unnecessary. Instead, the OS exports functions that perform the customary operations on a file, even though the file is stored on a remote machine. The dominant approach used today is suggested by Figure 16.5: The idea is that a program uses the *normal* file system API to perform operations on remote files, but with filenames reflecting whether a file is local or remote.

For normal operations to apply, remote files need to have some level of compatibility with other low-level file formats (see Section 2.2). To be compatible with UNIX and Windows files, a remote file is viewed as a named byte stream accessed by a logical read/write head. The file organization and properties must be maintained in that file's external descriptor. As described in Chapters 2 and 13, the essential operations on low-level files are open(), close(), read(), write(), and seek(). The file manager must

✦ FIGURE 16.5 Using the File System Interface for Remote Secondary Memory

The file manager is refined so that it distinguishes between local and remote files. Local file accesses are handled as usual, but remote file system calls are forwarded to a remote file server by the local client interface.

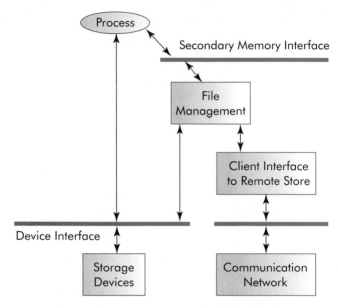

implement each of these functions using network protocols and cooperative computing with the remote file server software.

For example, if there is a file on a remote machine at IP address 128.138.148.158, then the application program should be able to perform a POSIX-style system call such as

```
open("128.138.148.158:/usr/local/foo/bar",O_RDONLY);
```

Although we made up a syntax for the filename in this example, the point is that the `open()` function for the remote file is the same as the `open()` function for a local file, where the *filename* string distinguishes the target file as being remote.

We can take advantage of a network version of the UNIX-style mount operation (see Section 16.5) to make remote filenames syntactically identical to local filenames. In this case, the file location is completely transparent to the programmer and user, although the system will have to be configured with appropriate `mount` commands.

How can we go about implementing this idea? In Section 13.7, you learned how the Linux file manager is designed as a collection of file system dependent and independent parts (see Figure 16.6, a modified version of Figure 13.25). Modern remote file managers use the same design (in fact, the Linux file manager supports remote file functions). The file system independent parts of the manager implement the system call interface and all other actions that do not have anything to do with the details of a particular file system. The file system dependent parts implement the functionality that is specific to the file system details, such as reading and writing the external file descriptor, byte stream marshalling/unmarshalling, block management, and so on.

✦ FIGURE 16.6 VFS-based File Manager

A VFS-based file manager is divided into a file system dependent part and a file system independent part. The independent part implements the general operations (such as enumerating directory contents). Like the other file system dependent components, the remote file client handles the specifics of interacting with its external file system (which just happens to be on a different machine).

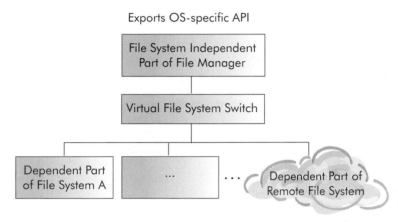

The VFS-like architecture is the predominant model for constructing a remote file system (it was first used in Sun NFS and System V UNIX). The twist for remote file service is that the file system dependent part (the cloud in the figure) will be *distributed software*, one part of which executes on the client and the other on the remote file server machine. From the file system independent core, the remote file system looks just like any other file system dependent component, since it exports the same family of functions exported by all the other dependent components. However, each of these functions is implemented through cooperative, distributed computation between the remote file service client and the server.

DISTRIBUTING THE WORK

Figure 16.7 is an elaboration of the ideas in Figure 16.5 and Figure 16.6. As mentioned above, the file system dependent component is divided into a client part and a server part. The **remote file client** executes on the client machine and is called by the file system independent part of the file manager. The **remote file server** executes on the remote machine that contains the relevant secondary memory. The remote file client and server are network peers that work together to provide the desired file system services. The key question in designing the remote file manager is to decide exactly *what* functionality should be implemented in the remote file client, and what part in the server.

On the remote file client side, we know that it has to include code to interact with the independent part of the file manager. We also know that the remote file client and server will need to agree on a protocol for exchanging commands and data. On the server side, we know the remote file server performs the operation on the server's storage devices and then returns results to the remote file client. Now we have an engineering design problem: The distribution of all the remaining remote file system dependent functionality is deter-

✦ **FIGURE 16.7** The Remote File Client and Server

The file management work is distributed between the client and server machines. The remote file client translates file system independent requests into appropriate work to the remote file server, and then translates results from the server back to the core file manager.

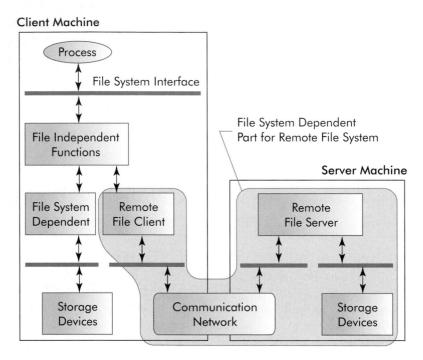

mined by trading off cost and performance in order to satisfy an overall goal. Examples of goals are to minimize file access time, network traffic, mean time between failures, and other criteria.

Once the goal criteria are chosen, then a partition can be determined on the basis of cost and performance. This will lead to more detailed questions such as: What network protocols are best suited to this distributed file manager? Can a distributed file manager provide an acceptable level of performance? How can network and server reliability be assured in such a configuration?

In the last 15 years, three basic strategies for partitioning the file system functionality have been widely used:

■ The server implements a **remote disk** functionality, meaning the client–server interface is similar to the interface that a local file system has with a local disk driver. In this case, the remote file client reads and writes disk blocks from and to the server. Almost none of the file system functionality is implemented in the server. This approach minimizes design/implementation cost and is very reliable. However, it has relatively poor network performance. Remote disks are described in Section 16.2.

■ A larger portion of functionality can be distributed to the server so that, for example, the remote file server can service file requests on the basis of information in a file's descriptor. The client–server interface is an internal interface that differs from any interface used in a normal local file system. This difference results because a conventional file manager essentially is split into two modules, with one module being implemented in the client and the other in the server. This approach is called the **remote file server** approach. It has better response and network performance than remote disks, but is usually more difficult to recover when it crashes. Remote file servers are described in Section 16.3.

■ Cooperating file managers in the client and server are replicated so that files are implicitly copied. A remote access operation obtains a local copy of the file from the remote storage when the file is opened. In this **file caching** approach, the file server is a complete file system that provides service at the level of full file operations, such as copying and deleting a file. File caching systems explicitly keep track of the location of various copies that are made for clients and manage the copies so that their contents are always consistent with one another. The idea of information caching and the consistency problem was introduced in Section 11.5. This is an equivalent problem, although consistency must be ensured for an entire file rather than a variable or a block of information. Because of this dramatic difference in information container characteristics, the techniques used to ensure consistency in file caching are different from those used for block caching. This approach is described in Section 16.4.

16.2 • REMOTE DISK SYSTEMS

In the 1980s, the cost of disk drives was a significant portion of the total cost of the hardware in a workstation. Today, disk drive costs have decreased so that they are no longer an issue in constructing cost-effective personal computers and workstations. Disk drives of the 1980s also produced considerable heat and noise, sometimes making them infeasible for computers in an office environment. Both rationales encouraged the development of OS support for remote disks. In this approach, workstations were configured with a network connection but with *no* local disk. Within the network (but not in anyone's office), one or more server machines were configured with one or more large, fast disk drives. The diskless workstations used the disks on the server machine as their sole secondary storage.

The diskless workstation is no longer as compelling of a solution, having been replaced first by diskless X terminals interacting with a server using the X protocol, and then by machines with inexpensive, quiet, low-power disks. However the approach provided an important step in the evolution of distributed computation technology. Even though it is not too expensive or intrusive to incorporate a disk drive in modern computers, there is a another trend leading back to diskless client technology. Computer and terminal manufacturers offer network computers with only a Web browser and virtual machine interpreter installed on them. There is no real need for a local disk, since the software that runs on the machines can be loaded in ROM. Their real purpose is to retrieve data over the network, not to store and process local data.

Today, mobile computers represent another opportunity for diskless client machines. A small, communicating mobile computer such as a PDA or cell phone is designed with a limited amount of persistent primary memory, allowing the mobile computer to store a small repertoire of programs, but very little data. These mobile computers are diskless workstations. Like the previous generation of X terminals and network computers, they do not keep much information locally at any given time, relying instead on remote disk services to provide information when it is needed.

REMOTE DISK OPERATION

In the remote disk approach, the client is responsible for almost all of the file manager functionality, with the server focusing on device management (see Figure 16.8). The remote file client is configured to contain all file system specific algorithms and a **virtual disk driver** (**VDD**). The file manager distinguishes between local and remote disk accesses on the basis of file system identity (remote files are handled by the appropriate file system dependent module as determined by the VFS). While references to the local devices use local disk addresses, references to remote file blocks use **virtual disk addresses**. Hence, the VDD API serves the same purpose as a local disk driver API in that it allows the file system to reference a storage device. It differs from the local disk driver in that instead of using driver function calls, it uses the network to transmit and receive commands and data to/from the **remote disk application** (**RDA**) on the server. The RDA receives low-level commands from the VDD, passes them to the server's disk driver, and then returns the result to the client VDD. Although the abstract remote disk can be read from or written to as if it were a local disk, other low-level disk operations such as powering the disk up or down cannot be done from the client machine.

✦ FIGURE 16.8   A Shared Remote Disk Server

The remote disk server is designed to process a disk-level request that it receives from client machines via the network. Conceptually, the interface between the VDD and the RDA is the same as the device driver interface for a storage device. In practice, the local disk interface supports additional functions such as disk partitioning commands.

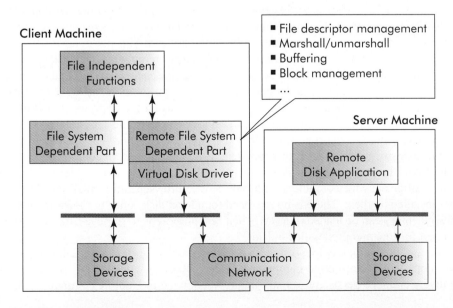

Just as a physical disk has a device address and a set of block addresses, the remote disk has a transport layer address, (net#, host#, port#), and a set of virtual disk block addresses. Hence, the VDD references the server using the transport layer naming facilities (see Section 15.6) instead of a device identification. When the remote disk server is initialized, it registers its name and transport layer address with a name server. The first reference to the remote disk requires that the client use the name server to find the remote server's address. It saves that address to avoid name lookups on subsequent accesses.

The VDD encapsulates each disk command into a network packet and then transmits it to the RDA on the disk server machine (see Figure 16.9). The RDA unmarshalls the disk command and data from the packet(s) and generates the appropriate request to its local disk (based on the command it received). For example, a read() command includes the command and a virtual disk address. The RDA translates the virtual disk address to a local disk address and issues a local disk read() operation. Similarly, a write() command packet includes the command, a virtual disk block, and the virtual disk address. When the disk server's local disk operation completes, the RDA marshalls the result of the operation—a write() completion notification, or, in the case of a read(), a disk block—and sends it to the VDD on the client machine. The client VDD unmarshalls the result and returns it to the client's file manager.

✦ FIGURE 16.9 Client–Server Machine Interaction for Remote Disks

These code fragments represent the behavior of the client VDD and the server RDA. Conceptually, the communication protocol is quite simple, with the client issuing a request and waiting until it is complete before continuing. The server waits for a request, processes it, returns the result, and then resumes waiting for requests.

Client System	Server System
...	(waiting for a request)
file_mgr: diskRequest(details);	...
VDD: Pack parameters;	...
VDD: Send request;	(waiting for a request);
(waiting for a reply)	RDA: Unpack parameters;
...	RDA: Generate local disk op;
...	(Local disk op in progress)
...	RDA: Disk op complete;
...	RDA: Generate reply;
(waiting for a reply)	RDA: Send reply;
VDD: Receive reply;	(waiting for a request);
VDD: Unpack reply parameters;	...
VDD: Return to file_mgr;	...
...	

Recall the nature of the interface to a disk driver described in Chapter 5. Since disks are block-oriented devices, units of transfer are disk sectors. Suppose a sector fits wholly within a single network packet, with a small amount of extra space for the command and address. Then it would be possible to transmit a disk sector between the client machine and the server machine by using a single packet. This observation supports the use of a datagram level service, especially since the service delivers a higher level of performance than do connection-based protocols.

With the separation of function between the client and the server, all knowledge of the file structure is kept in the server. Specifically, when a file is opened, the remote file client uses the VDD to fetch the external disk descriptor from the storage device and stores it in the client's memory. For example, in a UNIX system, the cached inodes would be kept in the client. The server would not keep a copy of the file descriptor. This means that all file descriptor manipulation, buffering, marshalling, and block management are done in the client machine.

Whenever a user runs a program on a client, the program is loaded from the remote machine's disk (block by block). When the compiler translates a program, the source program is read from the remote machine's disk and the relocatable modules are written to the remote machine's disk. The remote disk location is determined by the system administrator, so the remote access is logically invisible to the user. The primary place where remote disk access can be perceived by the user is in the time required to access a file implemented on a remote disk (although this also may be transparent depending on the relative speeds of a local disk versus the remote disk and network).

The remote disk architecture is simple, but it potentially suffers from performance and reliability problems. Is this approach fast enough? Assuming that LANs have considerably lower reliability than do computer buses (which, historically, they do), are they sufficiently reliable to carry disk access requests and responses, especially using network-level protocols? Is a client machine permanently blocked, or does it lose data stored on a disk if the disk server crashes while being used by the client? These issues are discussed next.

PERFORMANCE CONSIDERATIONS

For a remote disk server to be competitive, the client must be able to transmit a command to the server, have it perform an I/O operation on its disk drive, and return a result in approximately the same amount of time as a local disk access time.

When is a remote disk server sufficiently fast? In a remote disk server of the late 1970s, local disk operations required about 60 milliseconds to transfer a block, while a fast disk required about 25 milliseconds. In an experiment reported in the literature at that time, a client machine connected to a server machine configured with a high-speed disk of the era required about 48 milliseconds per block transfer, provided that only a single client was using the server [Swinehart et al., 1979]. (In these experiments, the client and server were connected with a prototype Ethernet operating at 3 Mbps.) However, when two clients were using the server, the access time increased to 76 milliseconds, and when three clients shared the disk server, it increased to 100 milliseconds.

If we were to compare transfer rates of a floppy disk and those of a high-speed hard disk on a server, remote disk access is much faster than the local disk access. The rotational delay and seek times in a floppy disk are so slow compared to hard disk technology that the network overhead is easily overcome in comparison.

Today's mobile computers rely on wireless networks for client–server communication. Interestingly, contemporary wireless networks offer bandwidth at rates similar to those that were prevalent in LANs at the time that these early studies were conducted. Today, the IBM 1GB Microdrive is packaged in a Compact Flash form factor, meaning that it is suitable as a tiny disk drive for a mobile computer. It has a rotational speed of 3600 RPM and an average access time of about 15 ms. The average access time for a conventional 10,000 RPM disk drive with a fast interface has an access time of 5–10 ms. This suggests that the old 1979 measurements that demonstrate the feasibility of remote disks are still roughly applicable for this situation. A mobile computer with a good wireless network connection might be able to access information on a remote disk server faster than it could access information on a local disk.

TCP provides reliable communication at the expense of explicit packet acknowledgments transmitted at the network level. UDP is faster than TCP because it does not incorporate any mechanism to ensure reliable delivery. For performance reasons, remote disk servers are designed to use datagrams or, in some cases, raw network layer packets. This approach explicitly relies on the ability of the client and server to handle reliability through their higher-level interactions.

In a remote disk environment, a network transmission cannot be permitted to wander around in the internet due to routing. Therefore, remote disk systems require the disk server and client to be attached to a common LAN. This means the network need not use the routing functionality at all. Instead, a highly specialized protocol for client–server interaction can be implemented directly on the data link layer. Hence, the datagram/packet/frame performance can begin to approach the threshold of performance possible in the physical network.

In local file systems, block caching is used to overlap the disk I/O time with the CPU time. In a remote disk server, the client can cache blocks by reading ahead, but the server cannot do this because it has no knowledge of the file organization. Client-side caching is widely used as a performance enhancement in remote disk systems.

RELIABILITY

Suppose a virtual disk sector, ordinarily the same size as a physical disk sector on the server, fits wholly within a packet. Then the overall reliability of remote disk service is related to two issues. The first is ensuring that a disk command eventually gets executed by the server. The second is synchronizing the operations of the client and the server should one or the other crash while a disk request is in process.

The network layer guarantees reliable delivery of the contents of a maximum-sized packet. This guarantee is independent of the underlying data link layer frame size. This means the network packet may be fragmented and reconstituted within the sender and receiver network layers. However, the entire packet may be lost. (In an internet configuration, packets could be delivered in a different order than they were transmitted if they were to pass through a series of gateways. For performance reasons, the configuration has already been restricted so that the client and server must be on the same LAN.) The focus for reliability is ensuring that the system works properly even if a packet is lost.

RELIABLE COMMAND EXECUTION
Local disk commands are restricted to a small number of operations: block read and write, track seek, status commands, and a few more obscure disk commands—for example, to start or stop the drive motor. The very low-level commands, such as drive motor control, are not implemented across the remote disk interface, since only the server should have this level of control over the physical disk. Similarly, support of most other obscure disk commands is not needed. Thus, the VDD is really required only to transmit read and write, but probably not seek commands. (The

argument against letting the client seek the server's disk is that two or more clients could easily cause the disk head to thrash.)

In normal operation, the client issues a read or write command and then waits for the server to respond, either with an acknowledgment of completion of a write or with the return of a disk block to complete a read. Suppose a client issued a read command and either the packet containing the command was lost before it was delivered to the server or the result was lost after the server had completed the read operation. From the client's perspective, the command was unsuccessful in both cases. What should the client do? The customary protocol is for the VDD to start a countdown timer running when it issues the command. If the result is returned before the timer expires, the timer is disabled. If the timer expires before the result is returned, the VDD assumes the read command failed and reissues it to the server.

There are three cases to consider when the timer expires:

■ If the first command never reached the server, reissuing the command is the correct thing to do.

■ Suppose the operation reached the server and was processed, but the result was lost in the network. A second read operation would not affect the correct operation of the server, but it allows the client to recover from the lost packet. In this case, the read operation is said to be **idempotent**. This means the command can be executed repeatedly, producing the same result as if it had been applied only one time (provided we do not consider higher-level problems such as a different client writing the block between the first read and the second read).

■ Suppose the server was oversubscribed so that after the client timed out and reissued the command, the server responded to the first read operation and then sometime later to the second operation. In this case, the second read did no logical harm (other than contributing to the load of an already overworked server). The client end of the protocol must be prepared to throw away such late-arriving results from a command.

There are two key points in these cases. First, idempotent operations can be issued repeatedly without causing any harm to the client or the server. Second, only the client might be harmed if it cannot handle multiple responses to repeated requests. (However, it can count how many times it repeated a command and thus be prepared to handle a bounded number of responses.) *The conclusion is that the client should always reissue the read command if it times out.* If it encounters N successive failures, it may decide to fail the read operation, assuming that the server is down or too busy to respond.

A disk write command is also idempotent. If the command packet is lost before it is delivered to the server, the VDD will time out and reissue the command. If the command was delivered to the server and the information was written to the disk but the acknowledgment was lost, a second write command will cause the RDA to overwrite the disk sector with the same information. Multiple writes will cause multiple acknowledgments to be issued to the client. These acknowledgments are easy to handle.

Are there any commands that are not idempotent? Yes, a command to step the read/write head to the next higher-numbered track is not idempotent. Suppose the head is at track 50. Then, on execution, the head will move to track 51, while a second execution will move it to track 52. This is another good reason not to allow the client to issue seek (or step) commands to the server.

Suppose the client–server interface is designed so that *all* commands issued by the client are idempotent commands and all have acknowledgments. Then, assuming the network will eventually deliver a matching pair of command and acknowledgment packets, the system can ensure that commands will be executed. The key issue in achieving this level of reliability is the idempotent nature of the commands. If any command is not idempotent, then the approach will not work.

With respect to acknowledgments, certain heuristics can be applied to reduce the number of explicit communications for them. In the case of a write command, the acknowledgment must be explicit. But in the case of a read, the acknowledgment is implied by the client's receiving the result of the read.

RECOVERING THE DISK AFTER A SERVER CRASH Suppose the server crashes during some session of read and write operations on the disk, for example, after the remote file client opened a file. If the server never recovers from the crash, the client machine will be unable to complete its work. Modern servers are designed to recover as quickly as possible, and to attempt to respond to any requests it had not serviced prior to its recovery. Because of the timeout strategy employed in the client, the client will continue to reissue commands to the server after it crashes. (Some designs count the number of consecutive failed commands and abandon the command after the number reaches some threshold. In principle, the client can continue to reissue commands for an indefinite period of time—until the server recovers from its crash.) How will the server know what commands it had received prior to crashing but had not serviced? How will the server know how to recover from the command it was executing when it crashed? What will happen to files opened by the client but stored on the server? Will their contents be destroyed by inconsistent file descriptors or disk block pointers?

With remote disk servers, most of these difficult questions can be ignored. The approach is based on the idea of a **stateless server**. A remote disk server need not keep any state related to any file, just as a physical disk need not keep any state related to the files stored on it. The disk server simply reads and writes blocks with no knowledge of any links encoded into blocks. The file descriptor is interpreted entirely by the client file manager. Hence, when a file is opened, its file descriptor is read from the disk server through one or more block read operations. The server does not need to know that the client has retrieved a file descriptor. When the file system traverses the block list for the file, it issues block read/write operations according to the client software interpretation of the file descriptor.

When blocks are added to or deleted from the file, the file system in the client reads the appropriate blocks from the disk server and then manipulates them. Later, the client writes the blocks back to the disk server according to its caching strategy. As a result, if the server crashes while a file is open, then when it recovers, there is no state for it to recover in order to be consistent with operations pending prior to its recovery. The server does not need to know what commands were issued prior to its recovery, since the respective clients will eventually timeout and reissue the commands after the recovery.

The main server side issue regarding recovery relates to the operation it was processing when it crashed. If the disk sector involved in the operation was to be written, then if the server started the physical write operation to the disk, it must complete it before crashing. Otherwise, the disk sector would contain some old and some new information. Of course, this is a requirement for local disk operations as well. If the local disk fails during a write operation, then, in general, the information in that sector is lost for either a local or a remote disk write. If the server had not started the actual disk write operation, then the server command can be repeated by the client with no harm. In order for the client to know whether the operation completed, the server must acknowledge each operation. If no acknowledgment is received by the client within a prespecified time interval, the client simply reissues the command.

THE FUTURE OF REMOTE DISKS

Remote disk servers are attractive because it is easy to design a server to recover from network and server crashes. However, such servers have performance penalties due to the nature of the work partition. Consider an operation such as file positioning in a system in which the blocks are combined using a linked list. As noted in Chapter 13, even in a local disk system, this can be a time-consuming operation, since it requires the file manager to read every disk block from the head of the file (or current position) to the disk block containing the destination. In a remote disk system, each block read also causes a network transfer from the server to the client. If the server were to be designed so that it had knowledge of the file descriptor, then substantial network traffic—and delay—could be eliminated by issuing the seek command to the server to have it locate the block that contains the target. This would be done without its interacting with the client. However, this approach changes the character of the disk server to be that of a file server.

In the first and second editions of this book (written in about 1996 and 1998, respectively), I wrote that disk technology has essentially eliminated remote disks as a viable commercial product. The rationale for the statement was that disks had become so inexpensive and were so friendly to the office environment that there was no longer any cost/environmental justification for eliminating them from a workstation. We did point out that there was considerable advantage in keeping a single copy of files on a shared server for different clients to use. However, this advantage can be addressed with remote file server technology.

Things have changed. Mobile computing in conjunction with wireless networks has now created a market demand for very small computers with only a small amount of secondary storage. PDAs and cell phones were mentioned earlier as examples of such systems. Wired internet appliances are also candidates for remote disk usage. The part of the picture that is not yet clear is whether mobile computers will settle into a remote secondary storage that uses file-level access (like HTTP), or if system designers will decide to return to broad use of remote disk technology.

16.3 • REMOTE FILE SYSTEMS

Remote file systems are an alternative to the remote disk technology. Like remote disks, remote file systems provide the same interface to the application program as local file systems. Also like remote disk servers, the remote access is implemented by distributing functionality between the client machine running the application program and the server machine where the file contents are stored. The goal in remote file systems is to reduce the amount of network traffic between the client and the server. Generally speaking, this is done by giving the server more responsibility in file management. As you will see in this section, that means that some of the work done on the client side (in a remote disk approach) is done on the server side in a remote file approach. The cost is that the client and server must each contain part of the state of the file system operation and, therefore, they must then coordinate their activities correspondingly.

THE GENERAL ARCHITECTURE

A local file is implemented on a disk device as a collection of related disk blocks. As discussed in Chapter 13, the relation may be implemented as a linked list, an index table, or some other data structure. The file descriptor provides the "road map" to the disk blocks by pointing to the first block in the list for linked lists, by addressing blocks for indexed allocation, or by indirectly addressing blocks—for example, in UNIX inodes. The goal in file server design is to increase performance over a disk server by having it take advantage of knowledge of the file structure in implementing file manipulation commands.

The remote file system general organization is the same as for the remote disk server (see Figure 16.7). However, the remote file server implements more functionality in a remote file system than it does in a remote disk system. In the remote disk server case, when a file is opened, the internal file description is kept in the client. In a remote file server, it can be kept in the server. This means that the server could then perform operations such as a traversing a file (for example, executing a seek( ) operation) without coordinating with the client software. The potential for reducing network traffic and for increasing overall performance is very high compared to remote disk behavior.

Now we have encountered a classic distributed computing problem: We want the file system dependent part of the file manager to be distributed between the remote file client and server. How can we choose a partition that will optimize according to some external goal (such as minimizing average file read time)? For example, the server might use the file descriptor to implement block management and buffering. The client would handle read/write head management, marshalling and unmarshalling the byte stream, and additional buffering (see Figure 16.10). This approach is appealing because it causes most of the details of block list management to be encapsulated in the server, while the details of block-to-stream translation are encapsulated in the client. This eliminates much of the network traffic between the client and the server, compared to the remote disk design (where every block read or write causes a network transfer). However, the client must still maintain a current copy of the file descriptor so that it can perform authentication, maintain the part of the current state related to reading and writing the byte stream, and manage locks. Conversely, the server also needs to know where the file position references the byte stream so that it can read/write blocks as required. It also must know where the file's blocks are located. The client and the server both need a copy of the internal file descriptor.

An alternative approach might be to keep block management on the client side, but to have the server implement block buffering. Unfortunately, this approach also requires that the state of an open file be kept in both the client and the server. *Every partitioning technique that has been tried (beyond the remote disk approach) requires that the client and server share information kept in the file descriptor.* This follows because the different parts of file system dependent functions use various parts of the file descriptor. When the functionality is distributed, the file descriptor must also be replicated in the client and the server.

✦ FIGURE 16.10 One Partition of the File Manager Functionality

The challenge in designing a remote file server is in deciding how to assign different functions of the file system dependent module to the client and the server. In this example, the client side of the system marshalls/unmarshalls byte streams and block buffering. The server side of the system handles device management, buffering, and block management.

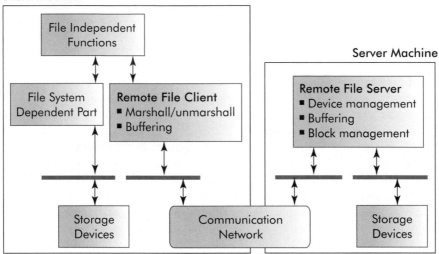

In all of the remote file server approaches, when an open() command is passed to the server, it retrieves the file descriptor, keeping a copy of it and transmitting another copy to the client side of the file system. (As described in Section 13.7, the client side translates its internal format into the format used by the file independent part of the client file manager.) Thus, redundant copies of the file descriptor exist on the remote storage device, in the remote server, and in the client.

Independent of the specific function partitioning and the inherent maintenance of two or more copies of the file descriptor, there are two other major issues to decide in designing the remote file system:

■ Since both the client and the server may buffer disk blocks, what is the most effective buffering strategy to incorporate into the system? Is there an advantage to buffering on one side or the other, or should buffering be used on both sides?

■ Idempotent operations and stateless servers can be used to implement a simple crash recovery policy but at a cost of increased network traffic. Since the file descriptor must be maintained on both the client and the server, how can this strategy be applied to file servers? What is the effect on performance if it is used?

BLOCK CACHING

Logically, when a remote file read() operation is issued by the application to the client part of the file manager, it will be packaged and sent to the server. The server decodes the message, reads the block from its disk, and then returns the block to the client file manager. Recall from the discussion of local file systems that the sequential nature of files strongly encourages buffering so that the operation of the device and the CPU can be overlapped. This can result in substantial performance gains (a reduction in runtime for the process). In a remote file server, buffering can also be used to overlap the operation of the network transmission as well as the disk access on the server by buffering in both the client and the server (see Figure 16.11). On a read() operation, the server reads ahead on the disk and buffers blocks for the client to request. When the client is able, it requests buffers from the server and enqueues them in anticipation of the client application requesting them. Buffered write information travels in the opposite direction.

♦ FIGURE 16.11   Buffering in a Remote File System

Remote file systems can buffer blocks on both the client and server machines. This allows the system to overlap CPU, device, and network operations, substantially speeding up file reads and writes.

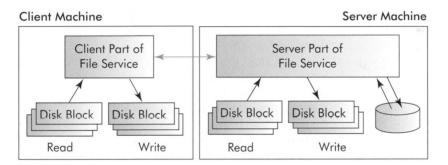

The strict read-ahead, write-behind buffering policy can be made more effective by adding one layer of sophistication to the technique. Data references to a file tend to follow a locality pattern, as was observed in virtual memory studies; when one item in a block is referenced, then the sequential file semantics suggest that the next byte will also be referenced. In many applications, however, data within a block may be referenced repeatedly without following pure sequential patterns; that is, the data references have a locality.

The existence of the locality means that when a block is copied into a memory buffer, it may be referenced repeatedly, just as a page is referenced repeatedly in a virtual memory system. Thus, it is easy to add a replacement policy to the buffering scheme so that it does not remove a buffer once it has been read from or written to by the client unless the replacement policy, such as LRU, specifies that it should be removed. Such a policy replaces the natural read-ahead, write-behind buffer semantics. Once the buffering technique takes a replacement strategy into account, it can also vary the amount of information copied into the client by applying the policy to large or small blocks of the file. Large blocks tend to capture the data locality because they keep a large number of bytes in the client buffers. However, when a new block must be loaded, the time to load it also will be high. This technique is distinguished from simple buffering by calling it **block caching**.

Remote file systems allow multiple clients to access the same files, potentially at the same time. In a local file system, if two or more processes open a file for writing at the same time, then each of their individual write() operations will be written back to the disk shortly after the logical write() has occurred. In caching, a block may be retained in the client for some time before it is written back to the server's disk. Suppose two processes have opened a single file for writing and each has cached the same block into its client machine. Now, when one writes the block in the client, the result of the write will not be perceived by the other client for an arbitrary amount of time. This is known as the *block cache consistency problem*. It is analogous to the cache consistency problem in shared-memory multiprocessors.

How can the OS address the block cache consistency problem? Some file servers support only **sequential write sharing**. In this approach, multiple clients are precluded from having any file open in which any one of the clients has write permission. If a file is written to as if it were a local disk and then closed, the caches are flushed and any subsequent open will operate on the data created by the write. Sequential write sharing ensures that tardy cache blocks from a previously opened file do not interfere with a new open command on the file. The more difficult problem of handling pending write-back blocks from some other client is addressed by forcing the tardy writer to update the server's disk image if an open arrives before the write-back has completed.

Concurrent write sharing is a more flexible approach in which several clients may have the same file open for reading or writing. In this case, newly written data must be propagated to the reader clients in a timely fashion. Concurrent write sharing is handled by simply disabling caching if any client has a shared file open for writing.

The Sprite Network File System—a UNIX-compatible file server implemented at the University of California at Berkeley—uses a more aggressive strategy for caching to achieve high performance. It was designed to take advantage of two empirical observations about UNIX files. First, high-performance local file systems make extensive use of buffering between the user-level process and the disk. Second, the amount of physical memory used for buffering has a large effect on the performance.

Sprite is carefully designed to enhance performance through caching techniques:

- Since it exploits client caching techniques, it must go to extra effort to ensure coherency among the cached copies of the file.

- It employs dynamic space allocation for each cache, in which the cache allocation strategy is intertwined with the virtual-memory mechanism.

Sprite uses a **delayed write-back policy** whenever a client writes into its cache. Instead of the clients immediately flushing the cached information to the server and through the server cache onto the disk, writes are accommodated when there is "idle" time at the server or after a suitable time interval (about a minute) has elapsed. This allows the client write() operations to complete without waiting for the server disk write() to complete. It sometimes economizes in write() operations when data is deleted shortly after it is written. For example, a compiler may create an intermediate file between passes 1 and 2 and then destroy the file when the compilation has completed. Text editors also tend to keep temporary files around for short periods of time. In the delayed write-back approach, the cached information may not yet have been written to the disk. Sprite uses a 30-second delay on write-back operations and then has another 30 seconds in which to actually accomplish the action.

Sprite researchers reported that their experiments with the file system resulted in attractive performance comparisons. Clients using caching had a 10 to 40 percent speedup over clients not using caching. Also, by using caching, diskless clients were less than 12 percent slower than workstations with a similar disk for their benchmark set. Based on the utilizations observed in the experiments, the developers conjectured that for a typical configuration of clients running "average" programs, a server ought to be able to handle up to 50 client machines.

CRASH RECOVERY

In local file systems, buffering carries another danger: If the disk or machine crashes while information is buffered, especially the file descriptor, then information may be lost. The danger is higher in a remote file system, since not only can the disk and machine crash but also information may be lost due to an unreliable network. If the server crashes and then recovers, the developer must be able to determine the full state of each session that was in effect at the time of the crash. Crash recovery is an important consideration in the design.

Some file server designs are oriented more toward reliable operation at the cost of performance, while others are more performance-oriented, thus requiring the incorporation of complex crash recovery algorithms. Both designs attempt to have high reliability and high performance, but the tradeoffs are balanced differently.

RECOVERY-ORIENTED FILE SERVERS The strategy of designing a server so that it is stateless (to simplify recovery after it crashes) can be extended from the technique used in a disk server for a remote file server. In a *stateless file server*, the file descriptor is always kept on the client machine and the client always sends a copy of the relevant parts of the descriptor to the server when requesting an operation. As a further hedge, on the execution of an open( ) command, the server retrieves the file descriptor and makes a copy of it before passing it to the client. The information in the server's file descriptor is correct at the time the open( ) command is executed. Now assume the server uses only the contents of the file descriptor as a "hint" for all subsequent operations. The copy of the file descriptor in the client keeps the actual state of the file. This means the server can use the file descriptor to perform any operation to enhance performance, such as buffering. However, the server is not allowed to perform any operation in which the correctness of the operation depends on the correctness of its copy of the file descriptor. If the server needs to know the file descriptor state before it performs an operation, such as block management, it must obtain a current copy of the appropriate part of the file descriptor with the request. The client will always cause the server to perform such operations by virtue of a request. Each such request includes the correct values of the file descriptor with the request. The server is never allowed to perform operations whose correctness depends on the file descriptor state without being instructed to do so by the client or without first obtaining permission from the client to perform the operation.

Next, the operations invoked by the client must all be idempotent. For low-level file systems, this is not difficult to ensure, since these operations are close( ), open( ), read( ), write( ), and file seek( ). The read( ) and write( ) semantics are the same as the disk read( ) and write( ) semantics and can be made to be idempotent. open( ) is idempotent because it can be repeated without the file descriptor changing. Similarly, close( ) is idempotent because it causes buffers to be flushed to the disk and the file descriptor to be written back to the disk. The `seek()` function can be made to be idempotent by restricting its argument to be an absolute position rather than relative position.

This file server design allows the system to use faster network protocols than those that require reliable communication. For example, this style of remote file server could use UDP or a raw packet interface to the data link layer of the network.

The Sun Network File System (NFS) is the most well-known crash recovery oriented file system. NFS has enjoyed tremendous popularity since its introduction in the early 1980s [Sandberg et al., 1985]. Sun's goal was to support heterogeneous file systems, even within the client machine, that were capable of reasonable performance and industrial-strength reliability through a simple crash recovery mechanism. NFS became so popular that its basic behavior became a network protocol, also called NFS. Fifteen years after its introduction, it is in Version 3 and is still the dominant commercial remote file service.

NFS has the same general organization as other remote file servers, modified as shown in Figure 16.12. The basic UNIX file system interface is replaced by a virtual file system (VFS) interface in the client and server kernels. The VFS implements the standard local UNIX file interface that can be passed through to a conventional UNIX local file manager. Using the file system dependent/independent approach, it can include a file system dependent module to translate the UNIX file operations into file operations for a different file manager on the client machine, so VFS could, for example, use a file manager from a different OS. Operations to be applied to remote files are passed to the client part of NFS.

✦ FIGURE 16.12 Sun NFS Organization

The Sun NFS (network file system) is a remote file system. It uses a virtual file system switch so that it can accommodate local and remote files.

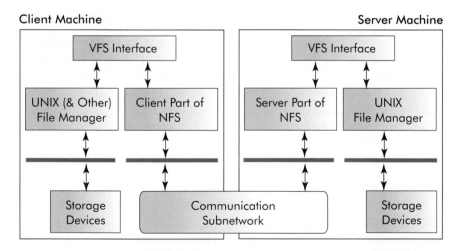

An NFS file hierarchy can be heterogeneous, so different parts of the hierarchy are implemented by different operating systems' file managers. The system is then designed to use the proper file manager for each subtree in the hierarchy. To accomplish this, any local system file interface, such as the UNIX file interface, can be implemented on top of

VFS. The VFS module can be used to match file manager interfaces to file manager implementations. But more important, it can also route a standard set of commands to a remote server. These commands use an abstract file descriptor called a **vnode** and establish a peer-to-peer protocol, called the *NFS protocol*, between the client and server. The vnode captures the correspondence between the file manager and the type of a subtree in the file hierarchy.

An NFS server manages a subtree in the network file hierarchy. If a client needs to use files in the subtree, it mounts the subtree into its own hierarchy (see Section 16.5). Then the client and server parts of NFS use the protocol to coordinate the actions at the client's VFS interface with the actions of the NFS server. In the extreme case, a diskless client can mount a server's root file system by using NFS as a remote disk server. Part of the NFS protocol is designed to implement and coordinate file system mounting.

The NFS protocol is intended to allow the server to be stateless, thus greatly simplifying crash recovery. Each server command is atomic and will either run to completion or have no effect on the server's data. This is accomplished by keeping the full file descriptor in the client and a copy of the descriptor in the server. The NFS protocol uses a `lookup()` command rather than an `open()` command to do this. Whenever the client issues a command that requires the state to be correct, it copies the relevant portion of the descriptor into the command message and transmits it to the server along with the command. Consequently, NFS can use datagrams rather than requiring a connected protocol, and either the client or the server can crash without affecting the operation of the other.

The NFS protocol is used between the NFS client and server modules, both implemented in the kernel. The first version of NFS used UDP, although versions 2 and 3 use either UDP or TCP over IP (NFS works across an internet). Additional details about the protocol can be found in Stevens [1994, Ch. 29]. Sun Microsystems' documentation describes the implementation.

PERFORMANCE-ORIENTED FILE SERVERS The recovery-oriented approach can be criticized for its need to pass a copy of the file descriptor for many operations. The alternative is to allow the client and server to distribute the file descriptor and then to use other means to ensure that the distributed file state is always consistent and can be reconstructed if either the client or server crashes. The client's and server's tasks can be simplified considerably if the network connecting the two is reliable. Therefore, this approach ordinarily uses a transport layer protocol such as TCP.

The client executes file I/O commands as byte stream operations, with the server handling the translation between the byte stream and disk blocks. Hence, the server maintains the file position for the byte stream. For example, the client issues a `write()` operation with a block of bytes to be written to the file. The command is not required to fit into a packet, since the block of bytes may be arbitrarily large. Because the client maintains part of the file descriptor and the server the rest, when the client issues the `write()` operation, it will do one of the following:

■ It will assume that the server received the command and the data and completed the `write()` operation, or

■ It will not put any part of the block onto the byte stream and the command will subsequently fail.

Both the client and the server contain part of the file descriptor, including file and record locks if they are used. Thus, if the server crashes while a client has a file open, the server is required to recover the state of each open file descriptor. Otherwise, for instance, the client might believe a file was locked while the server recovers the descriptor that indicates the file is unlocked. The client must detect when the server crashes. Virtual circuit mechanisms such as TCP will signal the client machine if the server machine crashes. When the client detects a server crash, it saves the state of the file descriptors currently distributed between itself and the server. When the server indicates that it has recovered, the suspended open files are reinstated and the remote file operations continue. Application programs can be notified by the client file manager and can be allowed to do other things, although by default, they will simply block, waiting for the server to recover.

The server memory is assumed to be volatile, so it is designed with special care to assist in recovery. First, every open file descriptor is saved in **stable storage** so that it can be retrieved if the server crashes while the file is open. When a client requests the server to perform an operation, the state of both the file and the descriptor are saved prior to the server's beginning to execute the operation. If the server crashes during the operation, the original state of the file descriptor and file are used in the recovery. When the server completes an operation, it updates the file descriptor in the stable storage and saves the changes to the file.

Stable storage is difficult to implement so that it never fails [Lampson and Sturgis, 1979]. Most implementations of stable storage are "almost always correct," but they can sometimes fail. The general idea is to create hardware-level critical sections—blocks of physical activity that run to completion even if the machine's power fails—to guarantee that information gets written to a storage device. Next, two copies of the stable storage contents are kept on different devices in order to prevent a device failure from destroying the stable storage. When a stable storage write operation occurs, the critical section encapsulates writes to both copies of the stable storage. If the machine fails during the critical section, a recovery process must be able to detect that the machine failed during the critical section. It then compares the two copies. If the first was being written, then it is discarded and the second is used. This corresponds to the case in which the machine failed before the write occurred. If the second was being written, the first is used as the stable storage content. If the crash occurred between writes, the first copy is used.

Few commercial operating systems implement stable storage. They rely instead on power backup systems to allow the machine to run for several milliseconds after a power failure. An interrupt is generated when the power fails. The system then uses battery backup to execute the power failure interrupt. Pending code completes any existing write operations so that the machine does not fail on a write. Such an approach is still susceptible to disk device failure, however, since a disk head crash will destroy the single copy of the stable storage, thereby making recovery impossible.

16.4 ● FILE-LEVEL CACHING

File caching is a logical extreme of caching in file servers. Its strategy is to automatically copy entire files from the server to the client when they are opened, and then to return the file to the server after the client closes it. For file-level caching, client machines are ordinarily expected to include at least a small disk. This approach improves overall performance by eliminating individual disk block or file block updates across the network. All changes are made to the local copy before it is rewritten to the server. File-level caching does not prevent the consistency problem, although the problem now occurs on a file-by-file basis.

There are two popular approaches to file-level caching: The *coherence* approach has the various parts of the file system coordinate with one another so that whenever one copy of a file changes, other copies are either updated or invalidated. A *versioning* approach takes a more radical approach in which a file is never modified once it has been created. Instead, a new version of the file is created to reflect the modification.

We will inspect these two approaches by discussing a coherence-based system, the Locus File System, and a version-based system, the Andrew File System.

THE ANDREW FILE SYSTEM

The Andrew File System (AFS) project is a distributed computing environment at Carnegie Mellon University [Satyanarayanan 1990]. It was the root of the remote file system technology that is incorporated into the Open Systems Foundation Distributed Computing Environment (see Chapter 18). Vice is the name for the collective servers that implement it. The file system's high-level goal is to incorporate acceptable performance in conjunction with scalability. The *Vice* file system works on the principle of file-level caching, whereby each client machine stores a copy of the file on its local disk whenever it opens the file. The motivation for file-level caching is to minimize network traffic and disk head contention at the server.

In considering these files and their inevitable updates, you can take the view that a file is either immutable or mutable. An *immutable* file cannot be changed by the client after it has been copied to the client's machine. *Mutable* files may be changed, meaning that the server is required to manage those changes.

In AFS, every file is assumed to be immutable. If a client retrieves a file and then changes it, the client creates a new version of the file with the necessary changes included. The updated file can then be written back to the server when it is closed. If no other client has retrieved a copy of the file between the time the first client retrieved its copy, then the new version becomes the default version of the original file.

On the other hand, suppose two clients obtained the same version of a file, updated it, and then wrote it back to the server. The server would assign each a unique version number. "Inconsistent" files are allowed to exist on the server as different versions of the same file. Now the server uses different versions for different operations. Note that "operations" has a different meaning in this type of file service than it does in conventional file systems. For example, a file removal operation eliminates the oldest version of a file, while an open operation uses the newest version of the file.

The consistency mechanism requires that the client and the server each maintain state about the file system. This forces the server to use a callback each time the file is written at the server location and to incorporate a crash recovery scheme.

Early versions of AFS cached only files into the client. Later versions also cache directories and symbolic links. Each client machine employs BSD UNIX, so open files are cached onto the client's disk and into the client's memory (at the block level). File changes are sent back to the server only when the file is closed. Directory changes are written through to the server when they occur.

Because the client contains a disk, a closed file may be resident on the disk when it is needed. When the client opens the file, it assumes the local copy is consistent. The server is responsible for notifying the client of inconsistencies for all files cached onto the client's disk by using a callback mechanism. When the server detects a change in a file, it notifies all clients having a copy of the file, regardless of whether the file is currently open. As a result, the server need not receive open validation requests of locally cached files. If the client machine crashes, the server assumes all its local files are inconsistent. So it generates a cache validation request for each file on its disk.

THE LOCUS FILE SYSTEM

The LOCUS file system is based on managing file coherence. Developed by Popek and his colleagues at UCLA in the late 1970s [Walker et al., 1983], LOCUS is an OS that operates on a network of local memory machines. In an effort to provide efficient sharing, LOCUS uses automatic file replication (without requiring immutability), with the OS guaranteeing file coherency. File replication is also used to increase a file's availability whenever the network fails, whereupon it partitions a single network into two or more smaller networks. As long as there is a copy of the file in each partition, the system can continue to operate until the network repairs itself, at which time the various versions of the files are made consistent.

LOCUS extends the UNIX file system model by providing a remote mount facility similar to the one described in Section 16.5. A remote directory is called a *filegroup*. Filegroups can be added to a local directory using remote mounting at local mount points. Once a filegroup has been added to the local directory, the OS has enough information to open the corresponding remote subtree root. The actual location of the remote-mounted filegroup is completely transparent to all applications and users for normal UNIX file operations.

The *using site* contains the information needed by the file manager to reference remote filegroups. When a client opens a file in a remote filegroup, the using site portion of the file manager sets up an open file interaction with a server (see Figure 16.13). Once the file has been opened, the using site will read and write pages cached from a separate *storage site*. The storage site supplies pages to the using site according to the read/write operations supplied by the application software. When a file is opened, the using site software contacts the *current synchronization site* (*CSS*) for the filegroup. The using site determines this CSS location from information in its file descriptions. The CSS may choose to replicate the file at a new storage site, or it may use a copy of the file at some existing storage site, depending on the type of access requested when the file is opened and the relative locations of the using site and the storage site. For example, files opened for reading can be copied with little penalty. LOCUS may also replicate a file to increase its availability, depending on the nature of the file path. For example, since directories are generally accessed in read mode, replicating directories throughout the network is natural, particularly directories located close to the root, since those tend to be updated less often than directories located close to leaf nodes.

Once a file has been added to a storage site, the CSS is responsible for implementing the global synchronization policy for access to the file. For example, CSS may allow only one process to have a file open for writing or it may allow multiple writers under the assumption that they will write to separate parts of the file. The CSS maintains information that specifies which storage sites have a copy of the file and which one has the most

◆ FIGURE 16.13 LOCUS Using Site, Storage Site, and Current Synchronization Site

The LOCUS file system insures coherent files by synchronizing file access whenever multiple copies are cached to clients. This requires that when a using site obtains a copy of a file for writing, it must coordinate its activity with the file's current synchronization site.

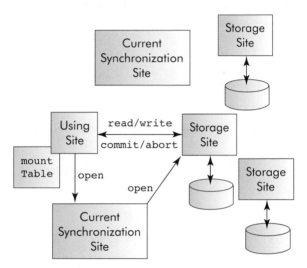

current version of the file. It passes version information to a storage site when an open is processed so that the storage site may update to a newer version if necessary. Finally, the CSS notifies the using site where its storage site is located. Subsequent read and write operations will use the storage site directly.

A process at the using site reads and writes pages from the file at its storage site the same as it would a local file. On file read operations, the LOCUS file manager at the using site caches pages from the storage site using the same algorithms as those for caching pages from a local disk. On write operations, the using site writes pages through to the storage site when they are written at the using site. If there are multiple writers for various copies of a file, transactions are used to serialize the updates to the file at all sites. The file system includes `commit()` and `abort()` commands in addition to the usual `read()`, `write()`, and others. The transaction commands —`commit()` and `abort()`—are issued by the LOCUS file manager at the using site without the application program's having to know about transactions. When a file is opened for writing, the storage server starts a pending version of the file in shadow pages for each set of writes from a using site. When a using site commits a set of write operations or closes the file, the pending version becomes the actual version of the file. If the using site aborts the transaction, the pending version is discarded.

The availability philosophy is illustrated in Figure 16.14. The CSS for a filegroup decides when to create more storage sites (SS in the figure) based on the topology of the network. If it can determine places in the network that will enable it to continue service through single-point failures in the network, it will create replicated copies of files. In the figure, the three partitions could result if the thick network connections were to fail. Files opened prior to a failure of either link could continue to be used, although the CSS would not be available to perform new open commands.

✦ **FIGURE 16.14**   File Availability in an Unreliable Network

The LOCUS file system is designed to continue operation when the network incurs single-point failures. Failure can be handled if every network partition contains a storage site (which contains copies of relevant files).

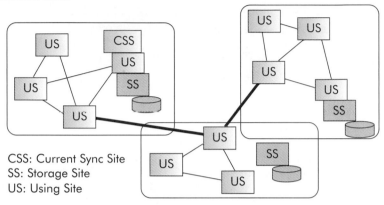

CSS: Current Sync Site
SS: Storage Site
US: Using Site

16.5 • DIRECTORY SYSTEMS AND THEIR IMPLEMENTATIONS

Directory systems typically employ a hierarchical structure because this approach naturally fits with the structuring techniques used by humans in manual filing systems. Remote file systems extend any individual host's hierarchical file organization to fit into a network of hosts. Networks themselves also use hierarchical organizations. For example, a network layer internet address is a three-layer tree with an unnamed root—presumably the name of the particular internet. The children of the root are the networks in the internet, and the children of a network are the host machines attached to the network (see the discussion of the Domain Name Service in Chapter 15). Remote file systems extend each host's hierarchical filename structure for identifying files located at various machines in the network.

FILENAMES

Files may be referenced on remote servers in two general ways: superpath names and remote mounting. While superpath names (such as the names used with uucp) were the first to be used in network file servers, most systems have evolved to the remote mounting technique, since it provides name and location transparency.

SUPERPATH NAMES **Superpath names** expand the normal hierarchical pathnames to include a "level above the root." Names in the super level are machine names taken from a flat space of names. For example, one set of remote file servers identifies files by a superpath name of the form

```
goober:/usr/gjn/book/chap16
```

The machine name is goober and the absolute pathname of the file on goober is

```
/usr/gjn/book/chap16
```

An alternative scheme selects names based on this algorithm: "Start at this machine's root, go up one level, and then follow the path from there." Files in this naming scheme have the form

```
/../goober/usr/gjn/book/chap16
```

Superpath naming causes the application software to distinguish between local files and remote files, since remote filenames have the superpath notation. A remote file system that supports this form of naming will use the machine name and parse it from the absolute pathname according to the syntax used on the machine in order to identify the host. It will then use the machine name—for example, `goober`—to look up the network location of the machine that is using a name server. The part of the file server implemented on the client machine will then collaborate with the server process on the remote machine to access the target file.

REMOTE MOUNTING   The remote mounting approach is more widely used because it supports name and location transparency. It evolved from the UNIX `mount` operation for removable media disk drives (see Chapter 13). The local mount operation allows an administrator to attach a file system—for example, one on a removable disk—to the file system on the machine. The mounted file system replaces a node in the local file system. Then pathnames can extend over the two file systems as long as the subtree file system remains mounted. The `remote_mount` command extends the `mount` command by allowing a subtree located at a remote host machine to be mounted on a local file system. Hence, a pathname on a local file system can extend across the network to another file system, provided the latter is currently remote mounted.

The `remote_mount` command shown in Figure 16.15 mounts directory `s_root` in Machine S at mount point `mt_pt` in Machine R. Thus

```
/usr/gjn/mt_pt/zip
```

in Machine R refers to the same file as

```
/m_sys/s_root/zip
```

when referenced in Machine S. This approach causes processes on each machine to see a different topography of the network file system, although local and remote filenames have the same form. One result of this different perspective is that absolute pathnames cannot be passed among processes on different machines without remote mount topography knowledge. For example, if a process, p_i, on Machine R passed the network-wide absolute pathname in a message to a process p_j on Machine S, then p_j would not be able to access the file without changing the absolute pathname.

For a file system to be remotely mounted or otherwise referenced from a client machine, the name needs to appear in a global name space—for example, by registering the name with a name server. Remote file systems ordinarily operate in a network configuration that includes such a name server. For example, a network domain (or portion of a larger network) includes a central name server to register advertised file systems within the domain. File servers may not support remote file operations that span domains. The client looks up a file system name in the name server and then remotely mounts the file system in the client's filename space. Upon completing the first remote mount between a client and a server, a virtual circuit is established between the two machines. Subsequent remote mounts use the existing virtual circuit by time multiplexing the connection.

✦ FIGURE 16.15   A Remotely Mounted File System

In this example, a subtree in Machine *S* (rooted at `s_root`) is mounted at the mount point, `mt_pt` in Machine *R*. This is like a conventional mount, except that the mount point spans the network.

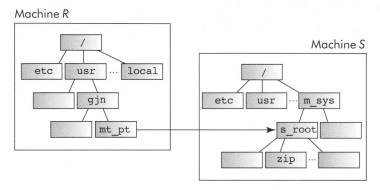

OPENING A FILE

Recall the steps for opening a file in a tree-structured directory. The pathname through the tree specifies a sequence of directories to be searched to find the file descriptor for the target file. As pointed out in Chapter 13, a path traversal can result in the file system reading a significant number of disk blocks, since each directory level will ordinarily involve at least two device read operations. When these operations are carried out over the network to a remote disk, the resulting load on the server and the delay for network transmission can become extreme.

As mentioned in the concluding remarks on disk servers in Section 16.2, this is the basic rationale for remote file systems. While remote disks are simple and relatively efficient, there are cases in which a client machine needs to do several reads with a relatively small amount of computation between each read—for example, to look up a pointer in a block. If such operations could be implemented in the server, then an overall increase in efficiency would result, caused by the elimination of network delays. A remote file system differs from a remote disk system in that some of the semantics of the file and directory system are implemented within the server as well as within the client machine. The server provides shared files, which are accessible from each client machine. As part of the file service, the server may provide concurrency control and file protection.

When a process opens a file that is located on a remote file server, this may cause a relatively complex and time-consuming set of steps. In general, the `open()` command causes a serial search of each directory in the pathname. At each level of the search, there is the possibility of encountering a remote mount point. When a remote mount point is encountered, the subsequent directory search must be handed off to the file server in the remote machine to complete the `open()` command. For example, in Figure 16.16, a network file system is organized so that directory `s_root` on Machine *S* is remotely mounted at mount point `mt_pt` on Machine *R*. Also, directory `bin` on Machine *T* is remotely mounted at mount point `zip` on Machine *S*. If a process located on Machine *R* opens a file using the pathname

```
/usr/gjn/mt_pt/zip/xpres
```

the open request is first processed in Machine *R* until the traversal encounters the remote mount point `mt_pt`. Machine *R* then passes the path search to Machine *S*, which resumes the search at directory `s_root` until it encounters the remote mount point `zip`. Machine *S* then passes the path traversal to the file system in Machine *T*, beginning at directory `bin`, which opens the file named `xpres`. Absolute pathnames in remote file systems can potentially result in a significant amount of distributed processing across the various file systems.

✦ **FIGURE 16.16** Opening Remote Files

File open operations require that the absolute pathnames be traversed in order to get to the target file. When remote mount operations are used across the networks, the open operation will cause multiple machines to be involved in resolving the operation.

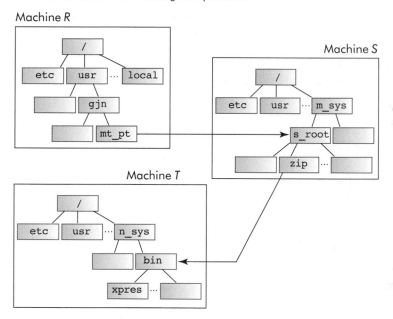

In UNIX file systems, a successful file open operation results in the file descriptor being loaded into the client's memory. This is likely also to be required in most systems, since the current state of the file is saved in the descriptor. If two different client processes open the same file, then each will have a cached version of the open file descriptor. Depending on the OS policy, both systems may be allowed to have the file open for writing at the same time. This is acceptable in many versions of UNIX. This situation illustrates the necessity for storage locks to control concurrent access to a file that has the potential for multiple open operations. Some remote file systems provide a mechanism for locking. Others—for example, early versions of Sun NFS—do not.

16.6 • SUMMARY

Files are the traditional unit of persistent storage for computers and are a natural means for exchanging information among a set of processes. The simplest form of sharing using files is via explicit file-sharing commands such as UNIX's uucp.

Network file services are a logical extension to the file abstraction. They use the normal file management interface, supported by facilities to copy or reference files located on other machines, in conjunction with a distributed file manager. Remote disk servers partition the functionality so that the device driver is implemented on the server, with the entire file manager being implemented on each client machine. Remote file servers partition the file manager so that part of it is implemented on the server and the rest on the clients.

The key issues in remote disk design are performance and recoverability. Performance concerns stem from the introduction of management overhead for implementing remote access to the disk and from the overhead incurred with network transmission. Caching is used to decrease the time to access a file, but it introduces inconsistency as a major subproblem. Recoverability can be divided into issues related to reliable command execution and crash recovery. Reliable command execution is achieved using timeouts on each client call to the server. Recoverability is most easily achieved by designing the server so that it does not contain any state. In this case, if the server crashes and then recovers, it need not recover any state in order to synchronize with its clients, since the clients contain all of the state.

Remote file servers can be characterized as either those that cache only parts of files at one time or those that cache entire files at one time. In either case, maintaining coherence among cached information is an important design issue that can be difficult to resolve. In servers that cache only part of a file, performance and recoverability are traded off against one another, although both are important. File servers that cache entire files take the position that files are immutable unless otherwise specified.

All file servers must support hierarchical filenames and directory operations. The predominant naming approach in UNIX systems is to generalize the local system `mount` command to a special `remote_mount` command in order to extend directory hierarchies across the network. Remote mounting is widely used, but it can complicate file open operations because of the need for each system's file server to resolve only the part of the pathname that passes through its part of the hierarchy.

This chapter has shown how file servers can be used to allow different machines to share their secondary memory. The next chapter reconsiders the general memory interfaces to see how the primary memory interface can be used to access information over the network.

16.7 • EXERCISES

1. Which of the following commands are idempotent? Explain your answer.

   a. A command to close a file.

   b. A command to retract the disk heads from the recording surface.

   c. A command to step the disk heads up or down one track.

   d. A command to remove a directory.

   e. A command to traverse a directory tree.

2. Suppose a remote disk server system is configured so that the disk on a server has an average block transfer time of 8 milliseconds, while a local disk for a client has an average block transfer time of 88 milliseconds (this would be a very slow disk by today's standards).

a. How fast must the throughput be on the network for the remote disk server to have an access time lower than that of a local disk?

b. What three network protocol parameters/factors would most affect this simple analysis? Why?

3. Contemporary hard disks have rotational speeds ranging from about 4,000 rpm to about 15,000 rpm. Would you expect the access time (the time to move the head over a target block and to transfer it to the disk controller buffer) for the fast disk to be almost 4 times that of the slow disk? Explain your answer.

4. In 1980, empirical studies indicated that the server was the bottleneck in a remote file system. Assume a stateless file server such as Sun NFS using a packet-level protocol such as raw IP. Hypothesize where bottlenecks would be for file read and write operations.

5. Given a file server in which the state is distributed between the client and the server, explain why the client and the server must both have copies of file locks for open files.

6. What are some arguments in favor of and against allowing the same directory to be remotely mounted from two different mount points on two different machines?

7. What is the advantage of having a file caching server allow only one client to have a file open for writing at any time?

8. Argue for or against caching files in /bin (on a UNIX system) when they are referenced by a client.

9. Describe an application domain in which immutable files might be the most effective way to handle file caching between clients and servers.

10. In the VFS-like file manager design, each file system is mounted before it can be used. Identify and explain three tasks that the independent and dependent parts of the file manager must do at mount time.

11. In the VFS-like file manager design, identify and explain three tasks that the independent and dependent parts of the file manager must do at the time a file is opened.

12. Design and implement an elementary file server that is able to save a file, copy a file to a client, and list a set of files that were previously saved in the server. (It is not necessary to implement more general directories or other file management facilities.) When the server receives a save command, it should accept a stream of *n* bytes in subsequent packets and then save the stream as a file in the local file system (using conventional UNIX file commands for the local file management). The copy command should identify a file and then cause the server to write the entire file to the client in a series of datagrams. The list command should cause the server to return a list of filenames to the client.

   The client and server should interact using UDP (rather than TCP). It is not necessary to implement reliable datagrams; that is, you may assume that datagrams are received reliably. You will have to write a simple client to exercise your server. The client should copy a few files to the server, list them, and then retrieve some of them.

CHAPTER 17

Distributed Computing

Remote file systems were the first heavily used mechanism to take advantage of high-speed networking. However, files are large-grained information containers designed to accommodate the batch processing model of computation. Using only the file manager interface constrains the form of distributed programs. Subsequent operating systems provide other ways to support computation, methods that are better suited to the network environment.

This chapter introduces the most important OS technologies that support distributed computing. In general, distributed computing is supported by creating new, specialized network protocols, so the topic could be approached as the study of high-level protocols. The chapter begins by examining characteristics of distributed primary memory systems. Next, we consider ways that the OS can allow threads on one machine to call procedures or object methods on a remote machine. Finally, we review some ideas that are used to implement process management in a distributed environment, including synchronization and IPC. The study of operating systems to support distributed computation is the topic of much OS research and the subject of OS graduate courses; it usually has the majority of a book devoted to it (for example, see Maekawa et al. [1987], Singhal and Shivaratri [1994], and Tanenbaum [1995]).

17.1 • DISTRIBUTED OS MECHANISMS

Chapters 1 through 14 described the elements of operating systems that manage a single computer. In Chapter 15, you learned how networks are added to computers to create the foundation for distributed computing. In the 1980s, LANs drew high interest in the commercial world, since they provided a fast and inexpensive way to connect computers. This was the first big step in the rapid growth of distributed computation: to harness the network so that it could immediately be used by applications that had previously been using only point-to-point communications. The immediate result was the wide use of **terminal emulators**, which allowed a person sitting at a personal computer to open a window that would behave as if it were a terminal connected to a remote timeshared computer. Even today, many people use a terminal emulator on their personal computer to establish a text-oriented session with a remote computer (I do it all the time). In this case, the network is a direct replacement for the telephone switching system and point-to-point connections.

Designers quickly recognized other ways to exploit LANs (and eventually, the public Internet). A persistent problem with using a timesharing computer is that when it becomes heavily used, the response time becomes sporadic. An alternative is to design the programs to run on a personal computer or workstation instead of on the shared computer. The data still remains on the timesharing machine, so the OS temporarily moves data from the time-sharing machine (now called a *server machine*) to the personal computer (now called a *client machine*). The client machine can run programs on the data, and then later return both the data and any results to the server.

This was the environment in which remote file server technology thrived. In Chapter 16, you learned how the remote disk approach assumed that the file manager executed wholly within the client machine, while the remote disk server was really only responsible for storing the data. The problem with remote disks was that the client had too much of the intelligence (and the server did not have enough): This caused the client to have to do too much work and also caused unnecessary network traffic. The remote file server approach addressed this by distributing the file manager software between the client and the server. By doing this, the network traffic was reduced, and there was more equitable work sharing between the client and the server. In generic distributed computation, the same evolution takes place. Application programs that run only on a client or only on a server are partitioned into two or more parts; then each of the parts is executed on different machines interconnected by a high-speed network.

Since the 1960s, there has been a camp of software developers that was concerned with achieving higher and higher performance for application programs. It is not surprising that this camp is driven by the desire to support leading edge scientific computation—the kinds of applications that are notoriously compute bound. This camp began to worry about the upper bound on application performance due to the physical bounds on the top speed of a single computer. After all, each computer ultimately depends on the speed at which electronic signals can be transferred among the computer's components. For example, in von Neumann computers, the control unit has to signal the ALU, the ALU and control unit have to signal the memory, and so on. Even 40 years ago, these developers recognized this bound and wanted to explore other ways to speed up the execution of application software. Of course, they could not possibly have guessed how single-processor architecture would progress: Today's individual computers far surpass any kinds of speeds that these early developers could imagine.

Nevertheless, there is an upper bound on the speed at which a uniprocessor machine can operate. Ultimately, software and hardware designers turn to parallelism to increase performance. As suggested by Figure 17.1(a), the general approach is to start with a sequential program that executes on a uniprocessor, then partition the computation into semi-independent parts. The rationale is that if a problem can be broken into, say five parts as shown in Figure 17.1(a), then the computation might be able to be executed on three independent processors for part of the computation. In Figure 17.1(b), Part A executes serially, followed by the parallel execution of Parts B, C, and D on the three processors, followed by the final serial execution of Part E. Given this idea of distributing the work, one could expect the distributed computation to execute in something approaching a third of the time required to do the problem on one machine. Of course, we can see by Figure 17.1(b) that we would have difficulty achieving this maximum tripled **speedup**, since Parts A and E are still serial. To achieve the maximum speedup, we would have to be able to partition the original sequential computation into N different components, all of which would have to execute at the same time in exactly $1/N$ time—an essentially impossible requirement since the computation will have initialization and cleanup phases. As a practical matter, we also know that when we partition a serial computation, we will introduce new communication and synchronization *overhead*, so that even in a perfect partition each component will require more than $1/N$ units of time.

For this application domain, distributed computing is nirvana. If the OS can provide an environment in which application programmers can partition and distribute their computation, then they can run the resulting parts on different computers interconnected by a high-speed network. Although the resulting computation would almost certainly not achieve the maximum speedup, even so, these distributed application programs might run much faster than the old sequential ones.

✦ FIGURE 17.1   Performance Through Parallelism

Classic sequential programs can be partitioned into semi-autonomous parts, called A, B, C, D, and E in part (a) of this figure. The idea is to schedule the individual parts of the computation to execute in parallel whenever that is possible. As shown in part (b), computations often have implicit serialization requirements, such as the data structured must be initialized before they are used in the computation (Part A).

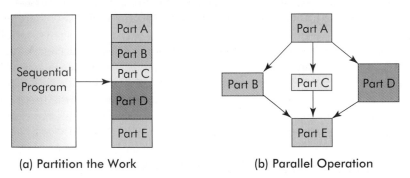

(a) Partition the Work   (b) Parallel Operation

By 1990, a hardware computing environment had emerged that the distributed application camp could use to create cost-effective solutions. Individual computers were powerful enough to execute significant computation. 10 Mbps LANs (and the extensive public Internet) were becoming ubiquitous. It was suddenly easy to interconnect many computers to work on a common task. OS developers responded by trying to create logical computing environments that took advantage of the available parallelism in the hardware. Since 1990, considerable new OS technology has been developed to support distributed computation:

- **Distributed memory** is intended to enable threads in processes on different computers to read and write common executable memory locations.

- **Remote procedure call** provides an environment in which a thread executing on one computer can call a procedure in another computer.

- **Remote objects** are an extension of remote procedure call in that this mechanism allows software on one computer to invoke member functions for objects that are located on a remote computer.

- **Process management** refers to tools provided by the OS so that it is possible to manage threads and processes on a remote computer.

- **Distributed synchronization and IPC** mechanisms allow threads to synchronize their operation, as well as transfer messages to threads that are executing in a remote computer.

The state-of-the-art in distributed programming is that operating systems now provide these important enabling mechanisms for distributed applications. However, there is still a large burden on the developer to create effective applications. Recall that the synchronization mechanisms described in Chapters 8 and 9 enable an application programmer to create multiple process, concurrent programs. But the application programmer still must decide how these mechanisms should be employed so that they can be used to solve specific problems (such as the bounded buffer and readers-writers problem).

This is also the case with distributed computation mechanisms. An OS that supports distributed computation creates an abstract environment that can support distributed applications, but ultimately the application programmer is responsible for making good use of this environment. Because of the potential complexity for distributed applications, software environments are becoming more sophisticated, with the goal of providing better support to distributed programmers. Today, system software designers commonly build middleware and runtime systems to simplify the use of underlying OS technologies; familiar examples of these extensions include I/O libraries, window systems, and dynamic memory managers. The next chapter complements the material in this chapter by describing how contemporary distributed programming runtime systems abstract the fundamental OS mechanisms. These new runtime systems are intended to reduce the amount of detail that programmers have to learn before they can make effective use of the OS distributed programming tools. In this chapter, we focus on the OS tools themselves.

17.2 ● DISTRIBUTED PRIMARY MEMORY

Figure 17.2 is an elaboration of the memory interfaces shown in Figure 16.2. It reflects the implementations of the remote disk and file servers. In distributed primary memory systems, the goal is to use the primary memory interface to reference primary memory located on remote computers. OS designers have tried several different models for handling different forms of distributed memory. The approaches that have been the most widely adopted are *remote memory* and *distributed shared memory*.

✦ FIGURE 17.2 Classic Interfaces to the Memory System

This figure summarizes the classic interfaces to primary and secondary memory, including the remote disk and file server designs. In remote memory and distributed shared memory, applications use executable memory interfaces instead of the file system interface.

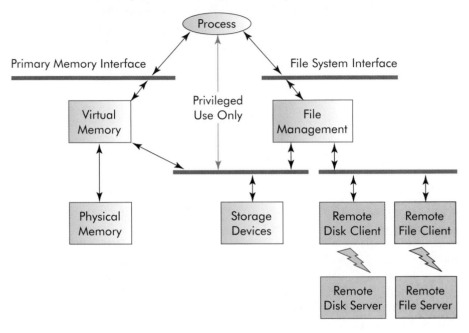

As LANs matured and became commonly available, software designers recognized the tremendous opportunity for finally being able to construct effective distributed applications. The distributed application software developers immediately recognized that it would be possible to make a huge jump in technology by exploiting LANs. At the same time, OS developers were madly trying to figure out how to manage LANs and present the best API to application programmers.

During the early 1990s, the distributed application programmers became impatient with OS evolution and began developing a number of message passing and remote memory solutions (see Figure 17.3). A **remote memory** mechanism specifies an alternative memory API that defines and shares logical memory. Further, remote memory is ordinarily implemented as middleware, for example, as a library that accomplishes the distribution of memory using the OS IPC mechanism. Perhaps the most visible of these early tools was the Linda system [Carriero and Gelernter, 1986].

While remote memory packages were being widely used by distributed application programmers, OS designers concentrated on ways to implement a better form of network memory, one that reused existing interfaces. **Distributed shared memory** systems use the general strategy shown in Figure 17.4. The general idea is to extend a local computer's paging system so that it retrieves missing pages from a remote page server.

Remote and distributed shared memory provide several alternatives for representing a remotely accessed address space. What is the best way to represent this address space to

✦ FIGURE 17.3 A New Interface to Remote Memory

Remote memory is designed with a local client that interacts with a remote memory server to read and write memory on the server as if it were local executable memory. Remote memory technology changes the fundamental von Neumann process model by adding a new interface that the processes/threads use to read and write the remote memory.

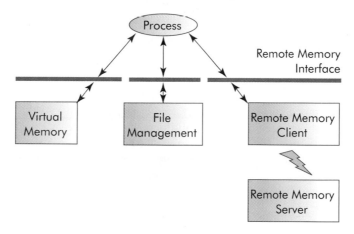

✦ FIGURE 17.4 Reusing the Primary Memory Interface in Distributed Shared Memory

Distributed shared memory ordinarily assumes the presence of paging support in the local OS. The virtual memory mechanism can then include a client that loads and unloads pages from remote paging servers.

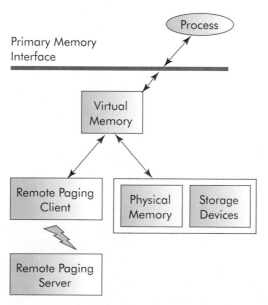

the programmer? The network memory is shared memory, since it is intended to be used by two or more threads executing on two or more machines. Hence, any design must accommodate sharing as well as provide remote access.

A network memory typically provides access to the information as a collection of blocks of memory. The block specifications could be derived from the programming language, meaning that they could have high-level semantics. For example, a block could be defined so that it corresponded to an object, a derived data structure, or a block of dynamically allocated memory (similar to that returned by the UNIX `malloc()` call).

Two classes of hardware architecture have evolved to implement distributed primary memory:

■ **Multicomputer:** Many multiprocessors are built as a "multicomputer" with several different processors having access to the entire memory of the machine. The majority of these machines are **nonuniform memory access (NUMA)** machines because access times for various memory locations are biased toward a particular processor. While these machines are interesting in their own right, their distributed memory designs are not described in this book because the solutions are primarily hardware architecture solutions. Instead, our focus is on network environments.

■ **Network of machines:** Another class of distributed-memory designs provides a logical shared-memory interface using the packet-based network to support access to the memory blocks.

Figure 17.5 illustrates two general approaches to network memory design. In Figure 17.5(a), the OS for machine S allocates a block of memory, M, to be shared by processes 1 and 2 executing on machines R and S, respectively. When process 1 references the distributed memory, the reference is translated to a server request in machine S. The communication between the distributed memory client in R and the server in S uses a suitable network protocol. This approach generally tends to be too slow to be effective since each reference to a byte of memory causes a two-way network packet exchange. It would be possible to cache blocks of memory to eliminate this high frequency traffic, as shown in part (b) of the figure.

In the second approach shown in Figure 17.5(b), machine R creates its own copy of block M in the address space of process 1. Now, each reference by process 2 to block M is local in machine S and each reference by process 1 to block M is local in machine R. The good news is that this is fast. The bad news is that, as in all other cases in which copies are created, the problem arises when process 1 writes into block M. The copies in machine R and machine S are different; we say the shared memory is *inconsistent* (or it is not *coherent*) since the two processes will see different values for the same memory cell. The network memory system must provide a mechanism to ensure memory coherence if blocks are cached.

Several other issues must be considered when designing network memory systems:

■ **Memory interface:** Should the model employ a distinct interface for referencing network memory, or can it reuse the existing primary memory interface to reference remote memory?

■ **Location transparency:** How much knowledge should the process have about the location of the remote part of the address space?

✦ FIGURE 17.5 Sharing a Block of Memory

The method of sharing a block of memory is now familiar ground to us (since we have already studied remote files). If the block of memory is shared in place, then the network traffic is excessive. If the block is shared by caching, we will have to deal with consistency.

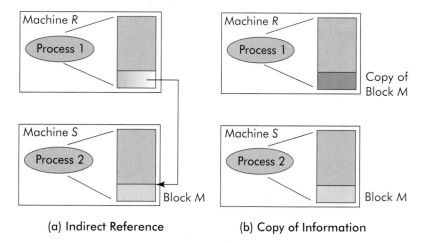

(a) Indirect Reference   (b) Copy of Information

■ **Unit of sharing:** What should the unit of sharing be in the address space? The unit could be data structures, pages, segments, or some other unit.

■ **Name management:** Information will have to be imported and exported by naming the unit to be shared. How should this be handled?

■ **Implementation efficiency:** Assume the two processes and their address spaces are on different machines. What are efficient implementations of the remotely stored shared memory?

There is no general agreement as to the best way to resolve these issues. The rest of this section considers how remote memory and distributed shared memory implement network memory.

REMOTE MEMORY

Remote memory refers to any of a broad spectrum of approaches in which the network memory is accessed using an interface that differs from both the normal primary memory interface and the file interface. The remote memory interface specifically extends the conventional programming model suggested by von Neumann machines. For example, the programmer explicitly identifies parts of the address space to be mapped to the corresponding process's shared memory, while all other parts are mapped to its private local memory. This suggests that the programming language or runtime system is extended and that the programmer must identify shared data structures at compile time—for example, by declaring a data structure and marking it as shared.

THE MEMORY INTERFACE Two critical issues are involved in designing the memory interface:

■ How is memory declared to be remote? That is, how can remote memory be mapped into a process's address space?

■ How is the memory read from and written to once it has been declared?

Memory interface design requires the development and general acceptance of a new programming paradigm for using the remote memory. There is no dominant approach in today's systems. The POSIX shared memory API described in Lab Exercise 9.1 provides one example of a shared memory interface, one that *could* be the basis of a remote memory interface. The POSIX interface could be characterized as minimal, with syntax and semantics that are intended to be as similar to other facilities (such as `malloc()`) as possible. The Linda programming language extension is on the other end of the spectrum.

The Linda Programming Language

The Linda programming language [Carriero and Gelernter, 1986] represents an extreme opposite to the POSIX-style shared memory interface. It was explicitly intended to provide a programmer's interface to remote memory by using a radical extension to conventional programming models. In Linda, data are stored remotely as *tuples*, which are referenced by associating access keys with field contents in the tuple. Rather than using conventional `load()` and `store()` operations to manipulate the memory, Linda provides a paradigm whereby tuples can be read from, added to, and removed from the tuple space. Information in the tuple space is changed by removing a tuple, updating it, and then replacing it in the space.

For example, an integer named `studentCount` with a key named `course` could be updated with a code segment of the general form

```
tmp = read(course=3753);
++tmp.studentCount;
write(tmp, course=3753);
```

While this approach may seem awkward (compared to an assignment statement), the approach provides an application programming interface that is easily compiled into memory references that can be used in conjunction with a network protocol.

In addition, coordinated reading and writing of data can be explicitly administered by managing tuple updates. It could be argued that these memory interface extensions are independent of the programming language, just as a file interface is independent of the language. However, Carriero and Gelernter take the position that Linda defines a programming language rather than an OS. In particular, Linda can be used to extend a wide class of serial programming languages into parallel programming languages.

LOCATION TRANSPARENCY AND NAME MANAGEMENT Remote memory can be placed at any network location, so some part of the system must be able to locate the remote memory referenced from within an address space. Pure location transparency implies that there is a global address space completely hiding the physical location of any address appearing in it. A process references the remote memory by using a name from its local address space that maps to a global address. The global address is statically or dynamically bound to the correct network address.

For example, if the remote memory is allocated at the transport address (net#, host#, port#), the process must be able to reference the block and offset at the given server address. Assuming the server manages more than one block, a simple address in the local name space corresponds to an address of the form

```
<(net#, host#, port#), block, offset>
```

The Linda approach addresses this problem by using associative reference operations for the shared global tuple space. A program can write a tuple to the global tuple space without knowing anything about the network location of the memory.

Alternatively, the system could be designed so that the binding takes place at compile time, load time, or runtime. Compile time binding essentially requires that the location be completely visible and "hardwired" into the software. As a consequence, few systems take this approach. With load time binding, the network location is defined by the linkage editor at the time it resolves external references. This means the user provides the remote memory's location at the time the program is linked and loaded. Few systems use this approach because runtime binding is more flexible. With runtime binding, the program is compiled with enough information to use a name server to bind the remote memory location when the memory is referenced the first time. Subsequent references reuse the first-reference binding. Runtime binding requires the system to provide a mechanism equivalent to the one used to map a segment name to a segment number, as was discussed in the Multics section in Chapter 12.

Because the implementation of the shared memory is explicit, it is possible to apply special semantics to data stored in the shared memory. Data consistency can be "defined away" by explicitly not guaranteeing that data stored in the shared memory is coherent. Coherency then becomes the responsibility of the programmer rather than the system. The programmer must add a synchronizing mechanism where it is needed. Lamport [1979] describes how these alternative memory consistency models can be used in distributed environments (as you will see, this general idea of alternative consistency models is heavily used in distributed shared memory).

It is also possible to introduce new abstract data type semantics that conform to specific application domain needs. For example, the environment can supply a specialized mechanism for computational paradigms with a single producer of data and N different consumers. The producer writes information into the shared memory, and N copies must be consumed, causing the data to be logically removed from the memory.

SUMMARY OF REMOTE MEMORY Since remote memory is generally manually defined by explicit programming directives, it is natural for the size of the units to be defined explicitly by the programmer rather than by the system. For example, the tuple is defined to be the unit of sharing in Linda and is the sharable unit size. In POSIX shared memory, blocks are variable sized, according to the command that creates the block.

The criticisms of general remote memory systems primarily concern the level of transparency at the interface. The distribution of the memory is specific, providing the programmer with maximum flexibility in tuning the access. However, as a result, the remote memory must be treated differently from local memory. Distributed shared memory addresses this concern by using the virtual memory interface to provide an interface with no special syntax and few special semantics.

DISTRIBUTED SHARED MEMORY

Shared remote memory inherently has an aspect of additional abstraction to it because threads treat it as if it were local memory even though it is physically allocated on a remote machine and accessed using network protocols. Virtual memory incorporates its own memory-mapping mechanism as an inherent part of its operation. Distributed shared memory exploits the virtual memory interface to implement network memory.

Virtual memory references differ from physical memory references because each virtual address is mapped to a physical address prior to being referenced within the physical memory module. In distributed shared memory, distributed virtual addresses are mapped into a shared virtual address space. The shared unit address identifies the location of the target memory location if it is loaded in the local machine's primary memory, or its *network location* on a global secondary memory, as indicated in Figure 17.6.

✦ FIGURE 17.6 Distributed Shared Memory

Distributed shared memory exploits the virtual address binding so that some of the virtual addresses can be mapped to network locations instead of secondary memory locations. If the virtual memory system determines that information from a network location is not loaded, then it fetches the missing page from a remote page server instead of from the local disk.

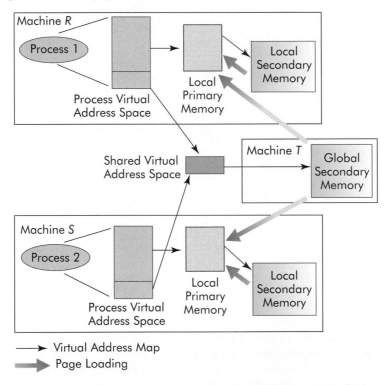

When a page from the private part of a process's address space is loaded, it is obtained from the process's local secondary memory image. When a page that is mapped to the shared part of the virtual address space is loaded, it is obtained from a shared, global secondary memory location that is accessible by more than one computer. Figure 17.6 shows the shared, global secondary memory as residing on a separate machine. However, the critical aspect is that the shared page is referenced by the cooperation of the client machine virtual memory implementation and a cooperating component in the server—on the local machine or on a remote machine.

Distributed shared memory is very attractive from the programmer's viewpoint. It can be allocated and referenced in the same manner as local virtual memory. From the memory manager's perspective, the mechanism for constructing the virtual address space needs to address the usual network naming and transparency issues.

The global secondary memory server must register its service with an appropriate name server so that clients can bind to the server at runtime. There are several ways to invoke the server name binding. The simplest is for the programmer to call an initialization routine, identifying the key name of the appropriate page server. The initialization procedure looks up the page server's transport layer address (net#, host#, port#), establishes a connection to it, and then allows the process to begin executing. When the local memory manager detects a missing page fault, it determines if the page is in the distributed memory or local virtual memory. If it is local, the fault is handled as described in Chapter 12. If it is distributed, the fault handler uses the connection to the page server to retrieve the missing page and place it in the local primary memory.

How can the various copies of pages in local primary memories be made consistent with the page image on the global pager server? Both centralized and distributed algorithms exist to do this [Li and Hudak, 1989]. A paging cache coherence solution must take the *page synchronization* and the *page ownership* strategies into account when providing a solution. Page synchronization uses an invalidation approach to ensure that when a process writes to a cached page, coherency is maintained across all other processes using the page. Each page has one "owner" processor for a writable page. The owner knows the identity of the last process to write to the page. A write fault causes all cached copies of the page to be invalidated and the processor causing the fault to change its access to the page copy to write. Now the processor "owns" the page and proceeds with the write operation.

Dynamic ownership can be implemented using a centralized or a distributed memory manager. The centralized memory manager approach relies on there being a single copy of the memory manager on a particular processor in the network. The manager keeps global information as to the current access rights, ownership, and locks existing in the network. As with other centralized approaches, this manager is relatively simple to implement; however, it tends to be a bottleneck and a crucial single point in the network.

A distributed memory manager uses a strategy whereby the set of shared pages is statically partitioned and allocated to different managers. The client machine is responsible for using the correct server to satisfy placement and replacement requests. Alternatively, rather than the client having to know the location of its server, the client can use a broadcast protocol to determine ownership.

Li and Hudak's seminal work on distributed shared memory stimulated considerable development activity for alternative designs. During much of the 1990s, researchers explored approaches in which distributed shared memory could be implemented with increasing efficiency by relaxing the memory consistency models. The basic idea is that if the shared memory is allowed to be inconsistent for small windows in time—meaning that the programmer has to take this into account when writing code—then it is possible to build a distributed shared memory that has satisfactory performance. Without relying on these weakened consistency models, many argue that distributed shared memory is not feasible. Adve and Gharachorloo [1996] wrote a tutorial paper that described the state of the art in consistency models and distributed shared memory implementations as of 1996. More recently, Steinke [2001] studied the formal relationship among known consistency models, updating the Adve and Gharachorloo survey while providing an alternative way to think about consistency models.

17.3 ● REMOTE PROCEDURE CALL

For several decades, procedures have been used to modularize computation in a sequential program. Today, professional programmers design software so that modules encapsulate data and function implementations behind public procedural interfaces. Distributed computation introduces a new level of complexity. Modularization in sequential programming hides implementation. In distributed programs, it also enables location transparency and scheduling. This suggests that programmers need to learn a new environment in which to construct application programs if they wish to take advantage of the underlying distributed hardware. However, no specific distributed programming environment has come to the forefront as the "standard" one. This can be attributed in part to the differences of opinion about the best way to partition a computation and in part to the lack of a standard distributed computing environment. Today, advocates push for a broad spectrum of different distributed environments, including the Java model, Microsoft .NET, OSF DCE, and the object-based CORBA approach. The **remote procedure call** (**RPC**) paradigm is the dominant extension to sequential programming environments that takes advantage of networks. RPC has analogs in Java, .NET, DCE, and CORBA.

HOW DOES RPC WORK?

RPC is implemented as a network protocol that allows software on one machine to call a procedure on another machine. The RPC facility will intercept a conventional procedure call, and then pass the call and parameters to the remote machine. Hence, an RPC procedure executes in a different address space from the calling procedure. Thinking about this abstractly, RPC is a specialized pattern of interprocess communication in which the initiating program performs a send operation immediately followed by a blocking read operation. The receiving program performs a blocking read until it receives the message sent by the calling process. It then provides the service and returns a result by sending it to the original process. From the calling process's point of view, the scheme behaves as if it were a procedure call from one machine to another.

This control flow/synchronization paradigm is summarized in Figure 17.7. In a conventional procedure call, the main program marshalls the arguments onto the stack and calls the procedure. The process interrupts execution of the main program and begins executing the procedure. First, the procedure obtains the parameters from the caller by popping them off the stack. Next, it executes the function. Finally, it returns, after placing any return parameters back on the stack.

The RPC crosses address spaces belonging to two different processes, called `theClient` and the `rpcServer` in Figure 17.7(b). The process for `theClient` executes the main program in its own address space, and the `rpcServer` process executes the

◆ FIGURE 17.7 Remote Procedure Call Synchronization

A conventional procedure call is shown in part (a) of the figure, and a remote procedure call is shown in part (b). The RPC calls the procedure that then executes on a server, returning the results to the calling process. This is accomplished by sending the call and arguments to the server where the call is executed, and then transmitting the results back to the client.

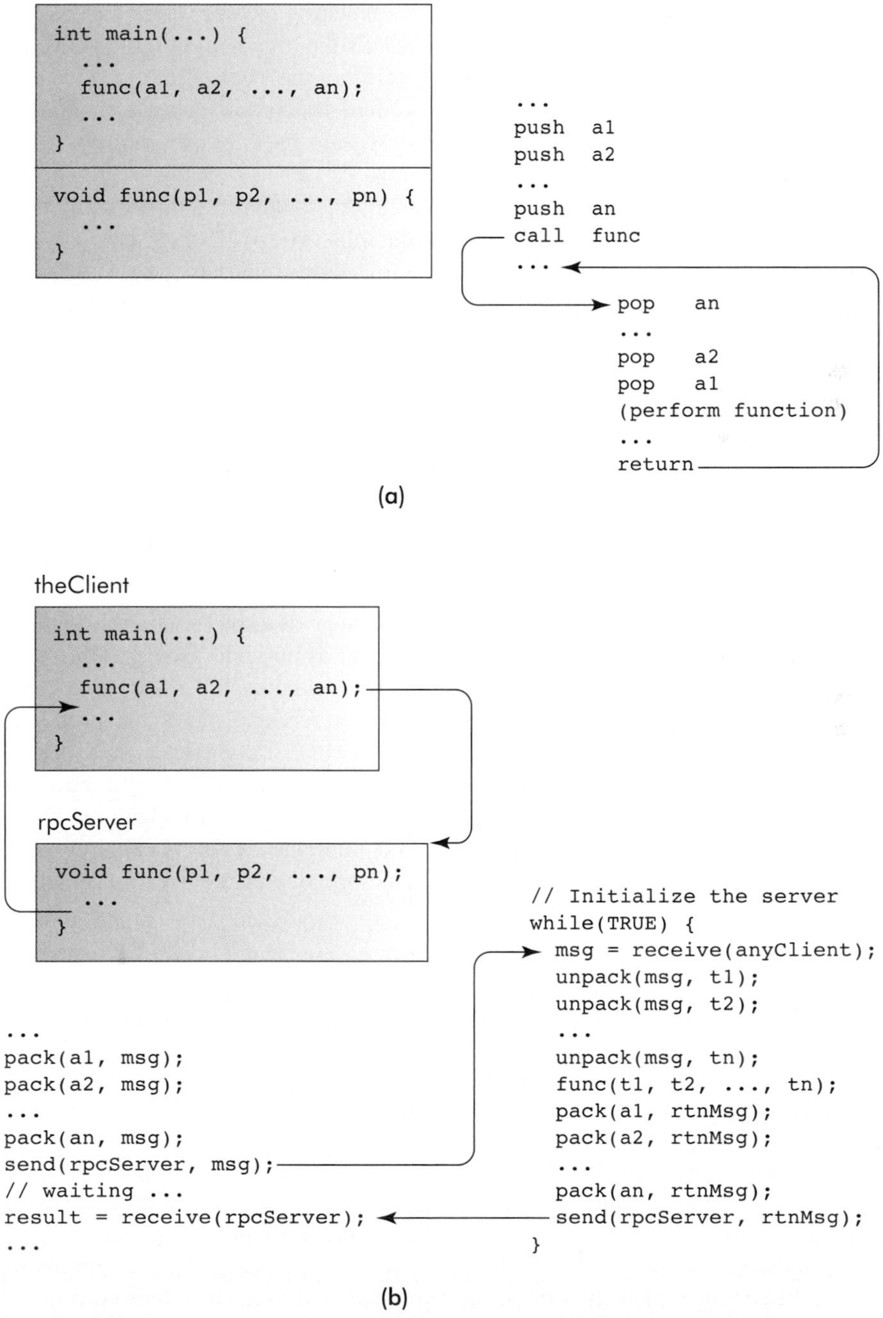

```
int main(...) {
   ...
   func(a1, a2, ..., an);
   ...
}

void func(p1, p2, ..., pn) {
   ...
}
```

```
   ...
   push   a1
   push   a2
   ...
   push   an
   call   func
   ...

         pop    an
         ...
         pop    a2
         pop    a1
         (perform function)
         ...
         return
```

(a)

theClient

```
int main(...) {
   ...
   func(a1, a2, ..., an);
   ...
}
```

rpcServer

```
void func(p1, p2, ..., pn);
   ...
}
```

```
...
pack(a1, msg);
pack(a2, msg);
...
pack(an, msg);
send(rpcServer, msg);
// waiting ...
result = receive(rpcServer);
...
```

```
// Initialize the server
while(TRUE) {
   msg = receive(anyClient);
   unpack(msg, t1);
   unpack(msg, t2);
   ...
   unpack(msg, tn);
   func(t1, t2, ..., tn);
   pack(a1, rtnMsg);
   pack(a2, rtnMsg);
   ...
   pack(an, rtnMsg);
   send(rpcServer, rtnMsg);
}
```

(b)

remote procedure in its address space. The call occurs by having the `theClient` package up (marshall) parameters in a message, appending the name of the procedure to be called, and then sending the message to the `rpcServer`. After the `theClient` sends the call message, it blocks to await the result of the RPC, thus simulating the control flow of a local procedure call. Hence, the caller is idle while the called procedure executes in both the conventional (Figure 17.7(a)) and RPC (Figure 17.7(b)) paradigms.

The `rpcServer` process will have performed a blocking receive when it is available to do work. When a call message arrives, it unmarshalls the arguments. In the conventional case, this is analogous to retrieving the parameters from the stack. It then determines the name of the procedure and calls it. Once the procedure has completed executing, it returns to the main program in `rpcServer`. The main program packages up return parameters and notifies the `theClient` of the call completion.

The RPC mechanism enables two processes to interact with one another using the control flow paradigm from conventional procedure calls. The RPC facility allows a programmer to write calling and called application procedures and then to execute the caller procedure in one process and the called procedure in a remote process on another machine without the programmer's knowing any details of messages or networks. From Figure 17.7, it is apparent that the RPC paradigm is a structured set of message sends and receives. Hence, RPC is normally thought of as a high-layer network protocol.

IMPLEMENTING RPC

There are several issues to be addressed by an RPC implementation:

■ Ideally, the *syntax* of the RPC is the same as a local procedure call in the high-level programming language.

■ While it may be difficult for the semantics of the call to be exactly the same in the remote and local cases, they should be as similar as possible. One example of when it is difficult to implement local procedure call semantics in the RPC is in the treatment of call-by-reference parameters. Call-by-reference allows the procedure to change variables in the caller's program. In the RPC case, this would require an assignment to a call-by-reference parameter to generate a send by the `rpcServer` and a receive by `theClient`, thereby resulting in `theClient` changing the value of a variable in its address space. Most RPC implementations do not support call-by-reference (since the calling and the called procedures are executing in separate address spaces).

■ The recipient of the RPC should execute in an environment similar to the one in which the call was made. In a conventional environment, a procedure can reference and change global variables. To provide the same semantic behavior, such changes would again require specialized communication between `theClient` and `rpcServer`. In general, it is usually not possible to create the caller's dynamic stack in the called procedure's address space.

GENERAL ORGANIZATION RPC implementations take the general form shown in Figure 17.8. The client machine executes the `theClient` process, which consists of the client application code, a client stub, and the transport mechanism. The server machine implements the `rpcServer` process with a transport mechanism, a server stub main program, and the server implementation of the remote procedures. The **client stub** translates local procedure calls into actions for the client side of the RPC protocol, and the **server stub** implements the server side of the RPC protocol.

✦ FIGURE 17.8 Remote Procedure Call Implementation

The RPC implementation employs client and server stubs to handle the call linkage. The client stub locates the server, then marshalls the call. It then waits for the result from the server. The server stub registers its remotely callable procedures with a name service, and then waits for RPCs. When an RPC arrives, the server stub unmarshalls the call, executes it, marshalls the results, and then returns them to the waiting client stub.

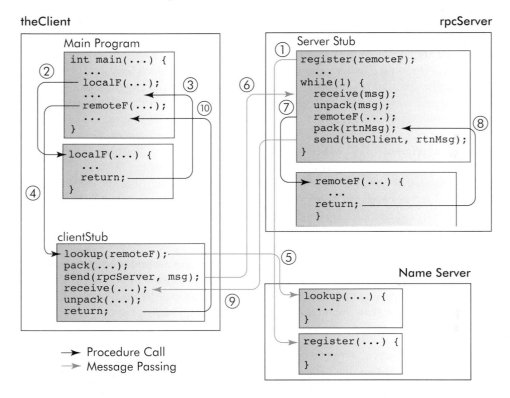

As shown in the figure, `theClient` process RPC invokes the client stub code. The client stub locates the machine executing the `rpcServer` process using a name server. (Before the name server can respond to the lookup request, the `rpcServer` process must have previously registered the global name used for the remote procedure, `remoteF()` in the example.) The lookup need only take place on the first call, after which the client and server will have established a connection. Subsequent calls use the existing connection. Next, the client stub marshalls the parameters in a message and transmits the message to the server stub in the `rpcServer` process. Since this server stub may service several different remote procedures, it will use the incoming message to select a remote procedure. The server stub performs the call and then marshalls the result parameters and returns them to the `theClient` process. Meanwhile, the `theClient` process will have been blocked waiting for the completion of the call. When it gets the return message, it unpacks the return parameters and passes them to the main program.

MODELING REMOTE CALLS AFTER LOCAL CALLS What mechanism will be used to distinguish between local and remote procedures? How and when will the remote procedure server be made known to the caller? The goal is to be able to write the client software so that the RPC has the same syntax as a local call. The first implementations of RPC were not able to accomplish this. If the procedure was to be remote, the RPC mechanism forced the programmer to distinguish between RPCs and local procedure calls at compile time. That is, the programmer had to use a different interface for an RPC than for a local procedure call. For example, a remote procedure might take the form:

```
callRemote(remoteF, a1, a2, ..., aN, ...);
```

where `callRemote()` is a local procedure that is linked into the calling program's address space. The parameters specify the name of the remote procedure, `remoteF()`, as well as the arguments for the procedure call.

However, suppose a system allows for the distinction between local and remote procedures to be deferred to link time. Then the programmer could use the same syntax for both local and remote procedure calls. The compiler would not distinguish between the two and would automatically call the client stub (see Figure 17.8) for remote procedures. The linkage editor would be required to satisfy all external references. Thus, to resolve the external reference, it would need information analogous to library linking information to specify which procedures are local and which are remote. The minimum information required by the linkage editor would be an indication that the corresponding symbol reference was to a remote procedure. The client stub will contain code to bind to a remote server at runtime. This is the dominant approach in contemporary commercial systems.

Runtime specification of remote procedures is the most general approach and effectively requires the same kind of dynamic binding support that is used for dynamic segment binding (see Section 12.6). The compiler and/or linkage editor will be unable to resolve the external reference, so the reference will be assumed to be bound at runtime. This late binding requires the static binding mechanism to leave enough information in the compiled code to enable the runtime system to resolve the external reference.

LOCATING REMOTE PROCEDURES Independent of the means by which remote procedures are identified, the calling routine must be able to locate the server that is to execute the remote procedure. Again, this information can be specified at compile time, link edit time, or runtime. Regardless of the approach used, the calling routine must generate an address in the calling process's address space mapping to the (net#, host#, RPC-port#) where the remote procedure is to be executed. If the location is determined at compile time, then the fact that it is an RPC will, of course, also be known at compile time. Hence, the RPC shown previously will have additional parameters to specify the location of the remote procedure server. One is

```
callRemote(remoteF, a1, a2, ..., aN, ..., internetLocation);
```

where `internetLocation` is a name, such as (net#, host#, RPC-port#) where the remote procedure's server process is executing.

Link time location specification is meaningful only if the identification of a remote procedure is specified at compile time or link edit time. Again, this form of static binding is conceptually the same as compile time binding. In link time specification, the remote procedure server is specified with external symbol definition information, but is static for the execution of the program.

Dynamic binding of the remote procedure network location is the most useful and most widely used approach. It is shown in Figure 17.8. The client stub is the intermediary and is statically linked into the calling program. However, as mentioned earlier in the chapter, the client stub uses runtime information to look up the RPC server's location and then establishes a connection to it. When the RPC is performed the first time, the client stub queries the naming facility to determine where the remote procedure server is located. On subsequent calls, it will already know the location.

In this dynamic binding, the client stub for a remote procedure must be generated when the procedure is compiled. Once the calling process has confirmed that the procedure is a remote procedure, it will bind itself to the client stub. For example, client stubs can easily be statically bound to the calling program at link time when local procedures are bound, but with the location determined dynamically.

STUB GENERATION How can the client stub be generated automatically? Contemporary programming languages employ procedure interface modules that define the calling sequences of all procedures. A function prototype in ANSI C or C++ is an example of an interface specification for a procedure. A module implementing a procedure is said to *export* it; a module using a procedure is said to *import* it. The interface module provides sufficient information to generate the client stub, since it identifies the symbolic procedure name and parameters. A stub compiler can use the interface module to generate calls to the local transport mechanism so as to accomplish the interchange of calls and returns and to package the parameters into appropriate network messages.

At runtime, the client stub will use a name server to locate the server and then will exchange messages with the server as required. When the remote procedure is called and the location of the server has been bound into the address space, the client stub can begin simulating the local call by using messages to call and return. It packages parameters and sends them to the server stub. The client stub, and hence the client process, waits for the RPC to complete before resuming operation.

NETWORK SUPPORT The transport mechanism supports network message passing. RPC communications must be reliable, so it would be natural to assume that they are implemented on TCP's virtual circuits. However, actual implementations tend to use a datagram protocol with a special-purpose RPC protocol. OS designers justify this approach by noting that the RPC protocol does not require the full generality of virtual circuits. A customized protocol is relatively easy to construct when the sender and receiver are always client and server stubs with known behavior.

On the server side, each module that exports a procedure must be prepared to accept remote calls. This requires the server to contain a surrogate calling process—the server stub—to accept call requests from the client stub and to make the local call. The server stub is generated by using interface modules and the export directives in the procedures implemented in its address space. In the general case, the server registers each procedure with the name server, thereby enabling the client stub to locate the procedure at call time. Registration includes adding the name to the name server and mapping internal identifiers to the procedure.

At call time, the client stub packs the calling parameters into a message and sends it to the network port specified by the name server. The transport part of the server then delivers the message to the server stub, which unpacks the parameters, identifies the procedure to be called, and calls it. When the procedure returns, the server stub packs the results and returns them to the client stub. The client stub unpacks the results and returns to the caller.

Parameters passed as call-by-value are easy to handle with this mechanism. Parameters passed by name or reference are difficult to handle. The difficulty arises because runtime references would require that the client and server stubs be able to evaluate parameters passed to the server. Various remote procedure packages use different approaches to this latter problem. However, each will require network traffic between the client stub and the server stub. The most widely used RPC mechanisms simply do not support call by name or reference.

RPCs are useful for distributing processing across different machines, but they do not encourage parallel computation. When a caller invokes a remote procedure, it blocks during the procedure's execution. Performance is always a major runtime issue when considering an RPC implementation. While RPC provides late binding, its performance penalty must be made as small as possible. Even so, remote procedures are widely used in contemporary distributed applications because they implement a traditional programming model while requiring little knowledge of distribution mechanisms and strategies.

17.4 • REMOTE OBJECTS

In recent years, object-oriented (OO) programming has become a popular programming model. In OO models, data is manipulated by an abstract data type (a class) that exports public methods. An object's method can be invoked by sending an appropriate message to the object. OO programmers have already accepted a new interface paradigm for dealing with information in objects, and have grown comfortable with the manipulating information in terms of messages (or member function calls in C++). The model's disadvantage has been the tendency of some object-oriented language semantics to undermine distributed implementations through reliance on sequential operation within a single address space. For example, C++ semantics rely heavily on single-thread, single-address space behavior in defining how parameters are passed to member functions.

Software systems have been built to extend the semantics to define an object-oriented language better suited to distributed computation (see Bennett [1988] for an early example). In these systems, each object maintains its own address space, with the union of all objects constituting the computation's address space. Hence, the object names provide the visible names for the shared name space. Provided object names can be managed across a network, the object model is a viable means for transparently representing distributed computations with inherently distributed memory. Modern OO environments such as .NET are particularly careful to preserve this idea of separate address spaces (see Chapter 5, [Nutt, 2004]).

THE EMERALD SYSTEM

Objects are difficult for an OS to manage efficiently because they can be as small as an integer or as large as a bitmap image. With distributed objects, the difficulty is in moving objects around on the network so that when an object is being heavily used by another object, the two are loaded on the same machine. Thus, object mobility is a key issue in implementing distributed objects.

Emerald is an early example of a distributed object system. It is a combination language and system to support object mobility (see Jul et al. [1988]). While the Emerald designers accepted the idea that the implementation of small and large objects differ, they believed these implementation differences should not be apparent at the object interface (see Figure 17.9). As a result, Emerald provides a single object interface for local and remote objects, as shown in part (a) of the figure, and contrasted with part (b). The compiler distinguishes between the two implementations and generates code that allows large objects to be migrated at runtime. The Emerald implementation distinguishes global objects from local objects and generates an object descriptor capable of incorporating a global name. If the object is remote, the descriptor will contain enough information for a local message to be forwarded to the object. Since objects migrate and are dynamic, the descriptor must also keep reference counts so that the descriptor space can be recovered when objects are deallocated. Global object forwarding addresses may potentially exist on several machines, depending on the system's ability to track the object's movement.

✦ FIGURE 17.9 Distributed Object Interface

Distributed object interfaces define the means by which software can invoke a method in a remote object. Ideally, there would only be one object interface, as shown in part (a). For performance reasons, some OO interfaces resort to two interfaces (part b), one for local objects and one for remote objects.

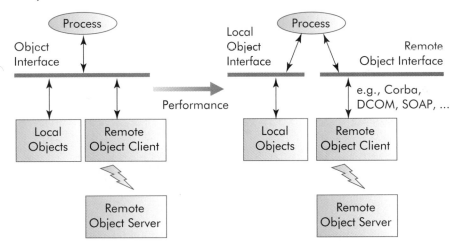

(a) Single Interface to Objects   (b) Interface to Local and Remote Objects

CORBA

The CORBA standard appeared in about 1990 as the first widely recognized specification for how distributed objects should work. **CORBA (Common Object Request Broker Architecture)** is managed by the Object Management Group, a not-for-profit organization intended to shepherd a standard for distributed objects. The goal of the CORBA specification is to define an architecture in which client software can reference remote objects, without being concerned about their implementation details (such as the language used to define the object). Further, object locations are transparent to the software that references a CORBA object.

An Object Request Broker (ORB) is the underlying system that makes remote object references work (see Figure 17.10). It is responsible for implementing the request, network, and request delivery services at the client and object server ends of a session. The ORB exports an API *ORB interface* that is used by both the client and object server for general object management functions. In addition, the ORB provides an *object adaptor* to each object in the server. Each object adaptor is responsible for converting general ORB-style requests into the object implementation requests. For example, a C++ object adaptor would convert a CORBA member function invocation into a C++ member function call at the server.

✦ FIGURE 17.10   The CORBA Approach

CORBA defines an industrial-strength remote object model, allowing software written in one language to invoke methods of objects written in a different language. Ultimately, CORBA provides an RPC-like facility, with client and server stubs, that handles the call-return behavior of the remote method invocation.

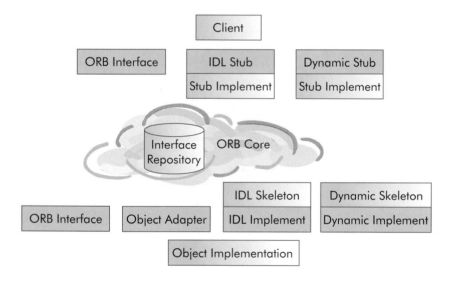

The ORB provides an *interface definition language* (*IDL*) to be used by the client software. When an object is created at a server, it exports its interface to the ORB. The ORB can then provide a CORBA-specific interface using the interface definition language (by creating a stub that can be linked into the client software). The details of the programmer-defined IDL interface are available at the object server through a matching IDL skeleton. When the client wishes to call a member function on a CORBA object, it calls a function in the interface definition language stub. The ORB then:

- ■ Translates the client request into its own format
- ■ Locates the target object server

- Transmits the request to the server
- Translates the request (using the object adaptor) so that it can be accepted by the object
- Delivers the request to the object.

Results of the call can be returned through a similar mechanism.

CORBA also provides a *dynamic* mechanism that allows a client to determine an object interface at runtime. A similar idea is also incorporated into Microsoft DCOM objects. The idea is that the ORB keeps an *interface repository* that describes the interface to all the objects it is managing. The dynamic interface binding mechanism queries the interface repository to determine the target object's CORBA interface, and then makes the call so that it complies with the interface.

Programmers using CORBA may define an IDL specification for remote objects or use the dynamic stub facility (to determine the characteristics of remote objects at runtime). Once the interface is known to the client thread, it can then invoke methods on remote objects by calling the client IDL or dynamic stub.

CORBA is significant because it was the first comprehensive remote object package that worked in a commercial environment. Further, it works well enough to allow programs written in almost any procedural language to invoke member functions on remote objects that are written in a wide variety of languages. This requires that the client and the object server both include software to translate to and from the CORBA intermediate language, and that the client and server software be able to use the network to exchange communication. CORBA provided proof that it is feasible to provide cost-effective remote object services. However, just about when CORBA began to enjoy commercial success, Java appeared, providing stiff competition for CORBA. Today, .NET extends the Java model by supporting interobject references among a set of heterogeneous languages.

JAVA REMOTE OBJECTS

The Java programming language depends on the existence of an underlying Java Virtual Machine (JVM). The JVM could, in principle, be an OS, although it is normally implemented as a runtime system extension to the OS (see Chapter 18). Java includes a mechanism called **Remote Method Invocation** (**RMI**). The idea is that JVMs implement their own network protocol that will allow one JVM to invoke a method on an object that is supported by a remote JVM (running on another computer). As usual, the operation is viewed as taking place between a client that invokes a remote method and a remote object on a server that exports the method.

An object can make itself accessible to other JVMs by being registered. That is, a Java application can decide that it wants to export some of its objects. It registers each such object with its local JVM through an appropriate JVM call. This causes these objects to be placed in a global name space within a domain. Other JVMs in this domain use the same global name space, so once an object has been registered, it can have its methods invoked by any client in the domain.

Java RMI is not nearly as complex as CORBA, since the environment is homogeneous. Communication only takes place between Java programs via cooperating JVMs. This means that the registration of an object and the identification of an object that is in the global name space are the only unusual operations required to use RMI.

17.5 • DISTRIBUTING PROCESS MANAGEMENT

Operating systems have generally evolved to support programmers who want to write distributed computation. We have seen how the evolution of networks enabled computers to communicate at relatively high speeds (compared to the older point-to-point communication). This caused the device management part of operating systems to be updated to better handle networks. Then, we discussed remote files, which caused the existing operating system to redesign and reimplement the file managers (and to further evolve device management) to support distributed computation. In this chapter, we have considered how to provide distributed computation by evolving the memory manager. We saw that there is disagreement about how to best design the next generation of technology. Some developers advocate the use of remote memory, some support distributed shared memory, some believe that there is no necessity to provide more support than the use of RPC, and a final camp believes that the way to support distributed computation is by using remote objects.

Interestingly, all these developments can (and have) been accomplished by modifying a timesharing OS such as UNIX or Windows so that its device, file, and memory managers support operation across the network. Many of the approaches used in this work have even achieved *network transparency*. This means that when applications use the devices, files, and executable memory, they use the same API to access local and remote hardware resources. Network transparency is a fundamental goal of distributed program support. Of course, a network transparent solution is only acceptable if it can be achieved without undue loss of performance.

How has process management technology evolved to support distributed computation? Some would say that this is still at the leading edge of operating system development. There is no single approach to achieving process management distribution that is widely embraced. There is a huge motivation to solve this problem though: If process managers could achieve network transparency, then the entire OS would be able to provide network transparent functions and features. This would constitute a true **distributed operating system**—one in which all operations are network transparent.

To achieve device, file, and memory management transparency, the general technique was to create client and server components of each manager at the local and remote computers. This suggests that distributed process managers could have "agents" (perhaps using the client–server protocol, but possibly using some other method of interaction) operating on each machine involved in the computation. As is to be expected, most of the early development in distributing the process manager has been experimental and *ad hoc*. As researchers and developers experiment, it is too early to have general agreement about how this should be done. Meanwhile, members of the distributed application programmer community have continued to evolve their own solutions as user space software in libraries or runtime systems (see Chapter 18). In this section, we will describe the most critical considerations in distributing the process manager.

GENERAL PROCESS MANAGEMENT

What are the general process management requirements to support distributed computation? The following major tasks have been identified in various research and development efforts:

■ **Creation/destruction:** When a computation starts, normally a single process decides at runtime what other processes should be created and used in the computation. The process manager must provide facilities to allow the process to create (and destroy) child threads and processes on other machines.

■ **Scheduling:** In some distributed environments, the location where a process executes is determined by the scheduler rather than the process. When a thread becomes ready in such an environment, the scheduler looks around the network for an appropriate place to execute the thread, attempting to automatically overlap execution.

■ **Synchronization:** The classic synchronization mechanisms described in Chapter 8 relies on the existence of shared memory to coordinate process activity. In a network, the OS generally has to provide an alternative synchronization mechanism based on messages, rather than rely on shared memory.

■ **Deadlock management:** Deadlock detection algorithms rely on the knowledge of the allocation state of the system's resources to determine whether a deadlock exists. In a network, the set of resources includes all resources on every machine. Furthermore, detecting the status of all machines at any given moment has proved to be very difficult; that is, distributed deadlock detection is a difficult issue to resolve in a network environment. The topic is not discussed further in this book, but interested readers are encouraged to see Singhal and Shivaratri [1994, Ch. 7].

PROCESS AND THREAD CREATION

Sequential operating systems provide a process creation call to invoke a new child thread or process on the same machine as the parent. This causes the process manager to create a thread/process descriptor in which it tracks all the information known about the thread/process. Further, the descriptor is linked into various lists to represent waiting for scheduling, reusable resources, synchronization events, I/O completion, and other functions. The first job in distributing the process manager is to decide how to create, share, and manage these descriptors. For example, if a thread/process is created on Machine X by a parent on Machine Y, is it necessary for a copy of the descriptor to exist on both machines? What about other machines involved in the computation? If the descriptor is cached, how can the copies be kept consistent? What should happen for crash recovery?

One way to attack the problem might be to allow threads to be distributed, but to have processes generally reside on the machine on which they were created. In this case, resource managers and threads can always find the (single) process descriptor for managing resources; then only thread context is implemented on the remote machine. Whenever the thread management mechanism needs to reference the process context, it will involve communication between the process manager for the process machine and the one for the thread machine.

The general trend in process management is to replicate the process manager in each computer on the network. Each process manager then uses a peer-to-peer protocol to achieve all the details of descriptor manipulation. By using an approach such as the example in the previous paragraph, the process manager defines a specific technique for achieving distributed management.

SCHEDULING

There are two general types of scheduling used in distributed environments:

- ■ *Explicit scheduling:* The application programmer takes responsibility for determining where the processes or threads should be executed.

- ■ *Transparent scheduling:* The application process begins to execute as a single thread in a process on one computer. Then, when new schedulable units of computation (processes or threads) are created and made ready to run, the scheduler on the local machine interacts with schedulers on other machines to determine the best place to execute a unit.

The client–server model can be used to build an explicit scheduling mechanism. The servers are started on the network at explicit locations (and registered with a name service). The clients start independently at arbitrary places in the network, using the servers. In this case, a client or server unit of computation is treated as an ordinary process within the computer in which it executes. In the default, the computer's multiprogramming scheduling policy is used to provide service to that part of the computation.

In transparent scheduling, the application can create schedulable units of computation to be executed in the distributed environment without considering which machine will actually be used to execute any particular unit. The schedulers on the machines in the network are designed to communicate with one another using their own specialized protocol. In this way, when a schedulable unit of computation is made ready to run, the unit is transferred to a selected machine and then executed in that machine. Normally, once the unit has been assigned to a particular machine, it will complete its execution on that machine. It will share the CPU with other units according to the local multiprogramming scheduler's policy. Transparency is a primary motivating factor for the OS to support network-transparent threads or objects.

MIGRATION AND LOAD BALANCING

Static scheduling strategies, such as those used with simple client–server computations, do not take dynamic behavior of computational phases into account. There is considerable ongoing research and experimental work on dynamic, adaptive techniques to attempt to maximize performance by determining situations in which a computation (or distributed system) has a load imbalance—where some processors have too much work to do and others are idle. The basic idea is to migrate work from the busy to the lightly loaded processors after work has been initially assigned, using a transparent scheduling strategy (see Figure 17.11).

The issues in process migration to achieve a balanced load across the network are primarily performance-related; that is, the impetus to use the technique is to increase performance. The goal is to overcome the implicit overhead required to achieve load balancing through global performance gain. The key performance barrier is the cost of migration. To move a process from one machine to another, it is necessary to stop the process (or thread or object), save its complete state, transfer the executable image and state to another machine, and then restart the process on its new machine. If this overhead exceeds the benefit of migrating the process, then apparent gains in performance will be lost.

✦ **FIGURE 17.11** Migration and Load Balancing

This snapshot of a distribute environment illustrates that the work allocated to different machines can vary considerably. For example, Machine A is supporting many processes, while Machine B has only one. The load can be balanced across these two machines by migrating some of the processes from A to B.

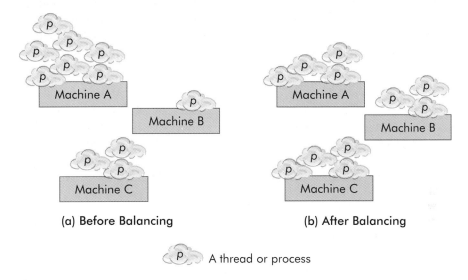

(a) Before Balancing   (b) After Balancing

p A thread or process

Researchers have followed a trend of using lighter weight units of computation in load-balancing approaches. For example, the Emerald system [Jul et al., 1988] and the follow-on PRESTO system [Bershad et al., 1988] migrate objects. This work eventually led to focusing on thread migration strategies [Bershad, 1990]. Although this research reports impressive performance gains, the effectiveness of the approach ultimately relies on the strategy by which the application programmer partitions the computation. The OS work focuses on highly efficient communication mechanisms for the environment.

DISTRIBUTED SYNCHRONIZATION

Once the schedulable units of computation have been created and are executing on different machines, the OS must provide efficient means by which the units can coordinate their execution (when that is necessary). Development in this area follows two general trends:

- **Explicit synchronization:** Units of computation use an OS mechanism to allow the programmer to synchronize the execution at desired points.
- **Transactions and concurrency control:** Critical section accesses are assumed to be handled wholly within a server, so the focus is on achieving the effect of atomic operation on the server, even when the interactions are spread out over several individual client requests.

CLASSIC SYNCHRONIZATION PRIMITIVES Semaphores and monitors implicitly assume the existence of shared memory in which a lock variable is stored. Processes synchronize by testing and setting the variable with atomic operations. An obvious solution to the dilemma is to use an underlying network memory to implement semaphores. However, this will generally not work very well because semaphore wait operations (such as the P operation) will usually have to read the network memory frequently in order to tell when the semaphore has been released. This will take thousands of times longer than the time to read/write a variable in local memory.

Another solution might be to implement a semaphore server, where a thread that intends to synchronize on a semaphore (or event occurrence) sends a message to the server announcing its desire, and then blocks waiting for a response. When the semaphore server decides that the thread can acquire the semaphore (or that the event has occurred), it responds to the client thread, enabling it to proceed. The problem with this approach is, again, the cost of interacting with the server using network protocols. This will again be orders of magnitude slower than uniprocessor semaphore implementations.

EXPLICITLY ORDERING EVENT EXECUTION Section 8.2 briefly considered using process creation/destruction as a mechanism for achieving synchronization. The technique was ignored for several years, however, because of the relatively high cost of creation/deletion compared with the use of semaphores. In the late 1970s, researchers began to note that synchronization can also be achieved by placing *precedence* on the occurrence of the set of all "important" events occurring in the collective processes. This is not as expensive as full creation/destruction, but it uses a philosophy to achieve coordination that is closer to creation/destruction than to semaphores. It has an added benefit of not requiring that synchronization be implemented using shared memory (for example, to store a semaphore, event control block, or monitor).

The basic idea behind this technique is to determine ahead of time what the synchronization points should be for the execution of the processes to map these points into recognizable events, and then to specify the order of occurrence of the events according to the desired synchronization plan. Even though we coordinate the processes' activity according to event occurrence, we do not use event control blocks to record the occurrences.

For example, if event x in p_i cannot be allowed to occur until event y has occurred in p_j, then one could require that

$$(\text{occurrence of } y \text{ in } p_j) < (\text{occurrence of } x \text{ in } p_i)$$

be a constraint on the operation of p_i and p_j (the "<" symbol means y occurs in p_j before x occurs in p_i). Notice that many processes, p_k, are unconcerned about the occurrence of x and y. Thus, proper operation of p_i could then be defined by specifying a *partial order* on all events in all the processes. This technique can be implemented using *eventcounts*—integer variables, initially with a value of 0, that take on a strictly increasing set of nonnegative values [Reed and Kanodia, 1979]. An eventcount can be manipulated only by the following functions:

- ■ advance(): The advance(evnt) function announces the occurrence of an event related to the eventcount event, thus causing it to be incremented by 1.
- ■ await(): The await(evnt, v) causes the calling process to block as long as evnt < v.

An eventcount can be thought of as a global clock ticking at each occurrence of the event through the explicit execution of an advance() call. A process synchronizes with the global clock using the `await()` call by blocking until the global clock reaches a predefined time—that is, until there have been "v" `advance()` calls.

It is interesting to note that `advance()` and `await()` are not required to be implemented as indivisible operations, as is the case with semaphore functions. If a process is interrupted during the execution of `advance()`, it is important only that the function ultimately runs to completion and increments the appropriate eventcount. Similarly, `await()` does not prescribe exactly when a calling event is to be blocked but, rather, stipulates a lower bound; interruption does not make the function fail.

Another interesting characteristic of eventcounts is that they can be implemented by replicating the eventcount in different machines on a network, thereby eliminating the need for shared memory. The exact technique to do this is an advanced OS topic inspired by theoretical work on global clocks by Lamport [1978].

Figure 17.12 demonstrates how eventcounts can be used to solve the bounded buffer problem (ignoring the critical section to manipulate buffers in the semaphore solution). The producer and consumer each maintain a private integer counter, i, used to select an eventcount value for synchronization. When the processes are initiated, the producer has N empty buffers and the consumer has no full buffers. The value $i - N$ in the producer initially takes on the value $-(N-1)$, thus causing the `await()` call in the producer to block only when out (initially 0) is less than $-(N-1)$, a nonpositive number initially. Thus, for $N \geq 1$, the producer passes through the `await()` call, produces a buffer, and then advances the eventcount. Meanwhile, the consumer will have encountered `await()` with in initially set to 0 and i initially set to 1. It will have blocked until in is advanced. Just as the processes use in to establish a total order on the events related to the manipulation of the full buffers, they use out to establish a total order on the events related to the manipulation of the empty buffers. However, there is no specific ordering on the individual events within the two sets. The producer may periodically have many full buffers waiting for the consumer and at other times be blocking the consumer.

With the eventcount primitive, many synchronization problems can be solved. However, the primitive is not complete enough to solve *all* such problems. The generalization requires a read primitive as well as a companion primitive abstract data type called a *sequencer*. The sequencer is an advanced operating systems topic derived by Reed and Kanodia [1979] in their extension of eventcounts (see their paper for an explanation of sequencers).

GLOBAL CLOCK In network-based distributed systems, synchronization can also be achieved through the use of messages to establish an order on the computation. The seminal work in this area took place in the late 1970s. For example, Lamport [1978] describes a theory by which processes executing on different computers can synchronize the operation by using an abstract **global clock** based on the order in which messages are transmitted in a network.

In this approach, messages are defined to be among the synchronizing events in each process. Each message is timestamped with the sending computer's local time. The local timestamps are then combined to determine a global order in which events associated with the messages occurred. In this abstraction, if one computer clock is behind another, an event A that occurred on the machine with the slow clock may be treated as if it occurred after an event B that occurred on a machine with a fast clock even when the actual time that A occurred was before the time that B occurred.

✦ FIGURE 17.12   Producer–Consumer Solution Using Precedence

This example illustrates how eventcounts are used for one form of synchronization. The idea is that an `advance()` call increments a "clock," and `await()` blocks a process until the related clock reaches a specific value.

```
producer() {                              consumer() {
/* i establishes local order */           /* i establishes local order */
  int i = 1;                                int i = 1;
  while(TRUE) {                             while(TRUE) {
  /* Stay N-1 ahead of consumer */         /* Stay N-1 behind producer */
    await(out, i-N);                         await(in, i);
    produce(buffer[(i-1) mod N]);            consume(buffer[(i-1) mod N];
  /* Signal a full buffer */               /* Signal an empty buffer */
    advance(in);                             advance(out);
    i = i+1;                                 i = i+1;
  }                                        }
}                                         }


eventcount in=0, out=0;
struct buffer[N];

fork(producer, 0);
fork(consumer, 0);
```

Eventcounts and global clocks are beyond the scope of this book, since they are largely experimental and relatively complex. However, they are the most promising mechanism for achieving distributed synchronization. Singhal and Shivaratri [1994] provide a comprehensive discussion of the techniques used to synchronize processes in a distributed system.

TRANSACTIONS Transactions can be used to achieve the same effect as synchronization in many cases. Interactions among distributed components can become very complex, resulting either in an exchange of related messages or in a stream of related messages being sent from one component to another. Such a stream of related messages is called a **transaction**—a sequence of commands for which the effect on associated data is as if either all of the commands are executed or none of them are. A transaction causes a specific set of micro actions and interactions between two components to achieve some macrolevel effect. For example, a computerized airplane guidance system may issue a number of microlevel operations to change the direction in which the aircraft is traveling. These operations may be changing individual engine speeds, adjusting the ailerons, and adjusting the attitude of the aircraft. The amount of adjustment depends, for example, on the aircraft's speed, perhaps on its altitude, and on the current state of the control surfaces. The macrolevel operation of changing the direction of travel requires that the individual components of the computerized system send relevant information to the guidance system, which can then change other components to produce the overall effect. In this case, it is important that either all of the course change microlevel operations take place in concert or none of them change at all.

As a software system example, suppose a server contains a set of records with N fields that can be updated by any of a set of client processes. The problem arises if two or more clients attempt to update multiple fields in a single record concurrently. Suppose process p_i changes fields 3, 6, 2, and 8 (in that order) in record k at the same time that process p_j attempts to change fields 5, 8, 4, and 6. There would be two sequences of client commands, as shown in Figure 17.13. p_i first sends a message to the server to update field 3 in record k and then sends a message to update field 6 in record k, and so on.

✦ FIGURE 17.13 Updating a Multiple Field Record

If the set of four send operations are treated as a transaction, then either p_i or p_j will execute all four of its send operations with no interleaving of the others operations, or it will execute none at all.

Process p_i	Process p_j
. . .	. . .
send(server, update, k, 3);	send(server, update, k, 5);
send(server, update, k, 6);	send(server, update, k, 8);
send(server, update, k, 2);	send(server, update, k, 4);
send(server, update, k, 8);	send(server, update, k, 6);
. . .	. . .

There is a race condition since p_i may update fields 3 and 6, and then have p_j update fields 5, 8, 4, and 6, and then have p_i update fields 2 and 8. Now the server will have the result of p_i's update in field 8, but the result of p_j's update in field 6. In some applications, this may be acceptable. But in others, it is disastrous—for example, if field 6 is a person's name and field 8 is the address.

The idea in transactions is that the sequence of operations is recognized as one that must be executed as if the commands were a single command; the transaction will behave correctly if the sequence is performed completely or not at all (until a later time). In the previous example, this would mean that either process p_i or p_j completes its entire transaction before the other begins.

Transactions are widely used in distributed databases, since this is a natural place where multiple-field records are updated in many different operations. They are also useful in systems that are susceptible to crash or in which the consequences of an unfortuitous crash are catastrophic. If the server crashes in the middle of a transaction, the record may have only some of the fields updated before the crash, thus leaving the permanent data in an inconsistent state.

The programmer identifies a transaction using markers for the beginning and the end of the sequence of instructions. The server detects the transaction-begin marker and then treats all subsequent commands from the client as part of the transaction until it receives a transaction-end marker. If the server begins processing a transaction on behalf of a particular client, then it is the responsibility of the server either to execute all commands until it receives a transaction-end marker or to leave the state of the server as if no command had been executed. When the server encounters the transaction-end marker, it *commits* the effect of the command sequence to change the server information state. If the server determines that it cannot complete the sequence due to conflicts with other transactions, then it may *abort* the transaction. In so doing, it will restore all the information that was changed by commands at the beginning of the sequence to the state they were in before the transaction was begun. A client can also abort the transaction. However, if the transaction is to be aborted, it is ordinarily aborted by the server due to command conflicts.

There are many occasions when operating systems use transactions to coordinate the operation of processes. For example, remote file systems use transactions for most forms of caching at the page level, block level, and file level, since movement of information requires the client and server state to have multiple fields updated at any given time.

Transaction implementation must in effect take a snapshot of the state of the relevant resources when a transaction is begun. The operations within the transaction are then executed on a copy of the resources or on the original resources, provided the snapshot information can be used to restore the resources to the state existing at the checkpoint. If another transaction is started when one is in progress, the state must be saved carefully so that the effect of the first transaction is preserved if it commits. If the transaction is aborted, the resource state is restored on the basis of the checkpoint information. If it is committed, the copy of the changes becomes the master version. The checkpoint information then can be released.

Transactions naturally suggest situations in which a deadlock might occur. Since a server is executing all transactions that might be involved in the deadlock, the server can execute a detection algorithm whenever transactions do not appear to be progressing. Because a server is allowed to abort any transaction due to conditions it detects, it can recover from a deadlock with only a loss in processing time on the behalf of the aborted transaction.

CONCURRENCY CONTROL Concurrency control is a technique by which the system enables a set of processes to interleave a set of transactions on a set of shared resources. This provides the same result as if each process were given exclusive control of all related resources for the duration of a transaction. Thus, concurrency control guarantees logical serializability of a set of transactions, even though the operations within the transactions may be interleaved.

Resource locks in a server are the simplest mechanism for implementing concurrency control. When a transaction changes a part of the resource, the server locks the resource for the duration of the transaction. Subsequent processes attempting to alter the locked part of the resource will be unable to do so until the first transaction completes.

The *two-phased locking protocol* ensures that a set of transactions will produce correctly serialized results without incurring a deadlock. During the first phase, the transaction acquires all the locks it needs to complete the transaction and does not release any. During the second phase, it releases locks and does not acquire any. In the degenerate case, all acquisitions take place when the transaction is initialized and all releases take place when the transaction terminates.

Two issues arising from indiscriminate use of locks are related to the size of a "part" of the resource and deadlock:

■ If the resource is a file, then should the lock apply to a disk page, a logical file block, or the entire file? Different researchers make strong arguments for each case. The arguments revolve around the trade-off of the number of locks to manage versus the amount of concurrent access supported across transactions.

■ A deadlock can occur if transactions happen to lock parts of the system's resources while requesting other parts. In cases in which the two-phased locking approach forces each transaction to acquire all of its locks when it is initiated, the concurrency control mechanism must be allowed to explicitly avoid deadlock. Otherwise, it will have to employ one of the techniques described in Chapter 10—for example, enforcing the order in which each transaction acquires locks, detection, or preemption.

Concurrency control revolves around a logically centralized lock manager. If the resources are distributed on a network, the lock manager must be able to obtain state from each of the constituent nodes. Because of the relative speed of network communication compared to that of multiprogramming environments, distributed concurrency control based on locking will encourage the use of locks that control relatively large units of resource. Recall that the earlier discussion of file caching explained how versions can be used to address concurrent file access. A similar approach can be used in concurrency control by placing a timestamp on each transaction and then maintaining copies of versions based on the timestamps. Postprocessing of the versions allows one to determine cases in which there are access conflicts and to determine the order in which the transactions occurred. While this will not resolve all conflicts, it does support many cases.

Another difficulty is the same as in general synchronization. That is, if the transactions originate on different machines, their timestamp values must have been derived from a global rather than a local clock. In general, locks are used to arbitrate conflicts at runtime, while the timestamping approach establishes an a priori order of serialization.

17.6 ● SUMMARY

This chapter introduced ways for operating systems to support distributed computation. The emerging trend is for the OS to provide some form of network memory. Network memory can be added to a computing environment by creating a new remote memory interface to be used by application programmers or by implementing distributed shared memory under the primary memory interface. While the distributed shared memory approach has the most attractive interface to the application programmer, it is the more experimental of the two. Remote memory implementations are more prevalent because they are easier to design and implement, they give the programmer more control over data placement, and they have a larger following in various application domains. In the long run, distributed virtual memory will almost certainly dominate because of its simplified programming interface.

The RPC approach has become the workhorse mechanism to support client–server computing. Contemporary remote file servers such as the Sun NFS, window systems such as X windows, and many other distributed services are implemented using RPC. Commercial systems have offered RPC programming facilities since the beginning of the decade, so there is also a rapidly emerging set of commercial applications that use RPC. Today RPC is the most widely used tool for implementing distributed software.

The OS must provide basic tools to allow process management to occur in the network environment. Synchronization must be handled as an explicit extension to local OS functionality. This has led to the use of transactions and the incorporation of mechanisms to establish an order on event occurrences across the network, rather than relying on the traditional shared-memory synchronization mechanisms.

17.7 • EXERCISES

1. In a certain program, the N elements of the A array are computed in parallel using the same program by the code fragment

```
for(i=1; i<=N; i++) {
   A[i] = A[i21] * B[i];
   <Other computation>;
}
```

Either recommend a data partitioning scheme to achieve good speedup for the computation or argue why it cannot be done.

2. These questions are associated with the ideas of data versus functional partitions of computations:

   a. Does the trapezoidal rule quadrature program in the exercises for Chapter 9 use the data or functional partitioning strategy? Explain your rationale.

   b. Does the SOR program in the Lab Exercise 11.1 use the data strategy or functional partitioning strategy? Explain your rationale.

3. Suppose that a big, sequential program requires 1,688 seconds to execute on a uniprocessor. A team of programmers partitions the computation into 15 separate computations (called C_0, C_1, ..., C_{14}). In this partition, C_0 has to run by itself to initialize the computation. C_{13} is error handling code. C_{14} prints the results, deallocates dynamic data structures, and then terminates the computation. The others all run at the same time. Using the same data set as was processed by the big, sequential program, the distributed computation was executed on a collection of 16 machines on a network. The resulting execution times are shown in the following table. What is the speedup for this computation?

Computation	Execution Time
C_0	22
C_1	161
C_2	153
C_3	99
C_4	100
C_5	133
C_6	151
C_7	164
C_8	159
C_9	196
C_{10}	142
C_{11}	131
C_{12}	163
C_{13}	0
C_{14}	36

4. Network bandwidths have increased from about 10 Mbps to 1 Gbps in the last decade. However, the latency (time for a message to be transferred from one place to another) has not increased at this rate due to signal propagation bounds. What effect has this change in bandwidth had on remote procedure call technology?

5. Given the comments about network bandwidth and latency in the previous problem, what effect has this change in bandwidth had on distributed shared memory technology?

6. Argue for or against using RPC to implement distributed shared memory.

7. Could a remote page server for a distributed virtual-memory system be designed to be faster than a conventional remote file server? Argue why or why not.

8. Compare and contrast the CORBA and Java remote object models. You might consider code mobility, method interface generality, and binding techniques in your answer.

9. Using an RPC package, implement the SOR program from Lab Exercise 11.1.

Using Remote Procedure Call

This exercise can be solved using the Sun RPC mechanism. This package is implemented in a number of operating systems, including Solaris and Linux.

This exercise uses the Sun RPC package to manipulate structured data on a server machine. First, you are to write a program that generates a stream of structured data records each of the form:

```
{
  struct timeval;
  char *;
}
```

so, for example, a record might look like this:

```
{
  {
    1016305702
    40184
  };
  "This is a string"
}
```

Using the Sun RPC package, construct three remote procedures in a common module that will execute on a remote procedure server machine:

```
int openRemote(char *file_name);
int storeRemote(int my_file, struct struct_t record);
int closeRemote(int my_file);
```

The `openRemote()` procedure opens a named file on the server. The `closeRemote()` procedure uses the return value from `openRemote()` to close a specified file. The `storeRemote()` procedure should be called once for each record that is generated, causing the record to be stored in an open file on the server machine.

Your client program should generate at least 25 records (containing random, but recognizable data), using the three remote procedures to store this in a file on a server machine. Your solution should work on a single machine, and on two machines interconnected with a network.

● BACKGROUND ●

RPC is widely supported in almost all contemporary operating systems. Sun Microcomputers was an early leader in developing a production-quality implementation. Further, Sun RPC was freely distributed, causing it to be the first widely used RPC package (particularly in UNIX systems). Meanwhile, the Open Systems Foundation defined its own RPC mechanism that ultimately became the basis of Microsoft's RPC package. There are enough differences between Sun's and Microsoft's RPC that two separate descriptions would be required to prepare you to solve this problem in either system. The discussion here is for the Sun RPC, although if you read it through, you can then read the Microsoft MSDN documentation to solve the problem in a Windows environment.

Sun RPC corresponds to the client–server model shown in Figure 17.8 (the *Remote Procedure Call Programming Guide* is available at many different URLs on the WWW; consult any copy that is easily available to you). The idea is to create a server running on a remote machine that is able to call procedures on behalf of a thread on a local machine.

The Sun software was designed to be used internally in the implementation of NFS. It was originally released with a low and an intermediate level API. The *low-level* functionality allows a programmer to be able to implement very general forms of shared computing between the client and server, although it is more complex to use than is the intermediate layer API. The *intermediate layer* is an abstraction of the low layer that enables an application programmer to implement a form of RPC without the extra features possible in the low layer API (for example, there is a signal-like facility in the low-level API that is not available in the intermediate layer). An advantage of using the intermediate layer (compared to the low layer) is that you do not have to learn any details about forming IP addresses, using sockets, and so on. The low-level API was not generally intended to be used by application programmers unless they intended to learn the details of UDP/TCP network protocols and required specialized features. If you write code using the low-level interface, then you will be explicitly managing sockets and transport layer protocols.

The intermediate layer API implements most of the concepts shown in Figure 17.8. However, an important feature it does not implement is one that makes remote procedure calls transparent to the client application. That is, all remote procedures are invoked by calling a single client stub program—`callrpc()`—explained below. A few years after the intermediate layer API had been introduced, Sun released a third layer (generally called the *rpcgen level* API rather than the "high level" API). This highest layer API implements transparency so that local and remote procedure calls have the same appearance in the calling program. The `rpcgen` level accomplishes this using a source code generation tool (the `rpcgen` program). The programmer writes a high-level language specification of remote procedures—think of it as a function prototype on steroids—that `rpcgen` uses to generate program-specific source code for both the client and the server. You will be able to provide a solution to this laboratory exercise using the `rpcgen` level, although we will consider the lower layers to see how the `rpcgen` layer is implemented.

In all levels of the API, the client machine runs an application program that uses a client stub. In the intermediate layer implementation, there is a single stub even if the application program calls more than one different remote procedure. In the high-level API, the `rpcgen` program creates a separate client stub for each remote procedure—much more like the schematic shown in Figure 17.8. The server program (or "server stub") is constructed manually in the intermediate- or low-level approaches, and it is automatically generated from the `rpcgen` specification in the high-level approach.

THE SERVER ORGANIZATION

The server program defines a persistent single-threaded process that will initialize and then run until it is halted by some external action (such as an operator terminating it). As different clients call the RPC server, it accepts a request, calls its local version of the procedure, returns the results to the client, and then waits for another request. If a client calls while the server is busy with a previous client request, the second client waits for the first to finish before it begins.

The server code first sets up a name service for the client to locate the server that can execute a particular remote procedure; this is called *remote procedure registration*. Once a remote procedure has been registered, a client can then find the remote procedure server by consulting the name service. In the simplest case, the registration is done only on the server machine, requiring the client to know the DNS name of the RPC server. After the server has registered its remotely callable procedures, it will begin waiting for RPC requests. When a request arrives, the server unmarshalls the details of the call (the procedure identification and arguments), makes the local procedure call, and then marshalls results and returns them to the client (stub).

Sun designed its RPC package to allow multiple remote procedures to be packaged together in a single RPC program. This allows the single server thread to call different remote procedures, allowing those procedures to work in the same address space on the server.

There is an additional, important consideration in providing support for RPC. Once an RPC program is deployed, it is expected to run for an indefinite period of time. Further, any number of client programs ought to be able to depend on the remote procedure once it has been made available. Suppose the procedure implementation contains a minor bug, or a programmer creates a newer version of the procedure that has additional features. Some of the clients using the existing version will not want to upgrade to the newer version, since it might require some client programming to take advantage of the newer features. Other clients may require the new version if it does, in fact, repair a minor bug. Because of these possibilities, Sun designed the RPC facility so that it supports multiple *versions* of each remote procedure. That is, there can be different remote procedures that have the same RPC program and remote procedure name, but different version numbers. This means that whenever a client looks up an implementation of its remote procedure, it has to know the remote procedure name, the RPC program name, *and* the version number. That is, the RPC server program distinguishes among implementations by (`remote_procedure`, `RPC_program`, `version`).

In implementing a particular remote procedure server, the designer first decides which remote procedures will be implemented. Suppose the server is to support n different remote procedures named RP_1, RP_2, ..., RP_n all with the same version number (`RPCPROGVERS`) in a particular RPC program (`RPCPROG`). RPC program numbers less than `0x4000000` are permanently reserved by the system. Applications (including your solution to this laboratory exercise) use a randomly selected program number that is greater than 0x4000000. Then the main program will have the form:

```
main(int argc, char *argv[]){
    register SVCXPRT *transp;

/* Register the remote procedures with the name service */
    transp = svcudp_create(RPC_ANYSOCK);
    if(!svc_register(transp,
        RPCPROG, RPCPROGVERS, RP1, IPPROT_UDP)) {
```

```
        fprintf(stderr, "%s","unable to register (X, X), udp).");
        exit(1);
    }

transp = svcudp_create(RPC_ANYSOCK);
    if(!svc_register(transp, RPCPROG, RPCPROGVERS, RP_2, IPPROT_UDP)) {
    fprintf(stderr, "%s", "unable to register (X, X), udp).");
    exit(1);
    }
    ...
transp = svcudp_create(RPC_ANYSOCK);
    if(!svc_register(transp, RPCPROG, RPCPROGVERS, RP_n, IPPROT_UDP)) {
    fprintf(stderr, "%s", "unable to register (X, X), udp).");
    exit(1);
    }

/* Turn control over to a library routine that makes the calls */
    svc_run();
    fprintf(stderr, %s", "svc_run returned");
    exit(1);    /* Should never reach this point */
};
```

Before the server can register a remote procedure, it must open a UDP socket that will be used by the client machine to address the server. This is done with the intermediate-level function call

```
svcudp_create(RPC_ANYSOCK)
```

This RPC library function creates a UDP socket at the server end that will be registered with the remote procedure name. The svc_register() procedure can then register the procedure. In this function, if the last argument specifies a protocol number (IPPROT_UDP in the skeleton), then the socket is registered for external use with the server OS port manager, called the *portmapper*. This allows clients to discover the port on which the RPC procedure is registered by using the server's portmapper as well as the more general network name server (provided the client knows the name of the machine running this server code).

If you study this code skeleton, you can see that it is made up of a collection of recurring "templates" to register each remote procedure using svc_register(). By "template," it is meant that you could copy the seven lines of code that begin with the svcudp_create() call and then paste them below to create another procedure registration (you would then have to change the remote procedure name in the new seven-line code instance). The second part of the server main program is the three-line block of code in every RPC server that calls svc_run() without ever returning from the call.

The svc_run() function is another library function that implements a canonical server loop:

```
svc_run(
    ...
while(1) {
/* Blocking read on transport socket */
    read(...);
```

```
/* Now we have a RPC request */
  switch() {
  case 0: /* issue an error */
  case RP1: /* call RP1 */
  case RP2: /* call RP2 */
  ...
  case RPi: /* call RPi */
    svc_getargs(...);      /* Unmarshall the arguments */
    rp_i_svc(...);         /* The local procedure call */
    svc_sendreply(...);    /* Marshall the args, return */
    break;
  ...
  case RPn: /* call RPn */
  default:
  }
/* Should never reach this point */
};
```

The main tasks are to wait for an RPC request from a client and then perform the call according to the number of the remote procedure being requested. We have left out all the details of how arguments are handled, although that is discussed below in the subsection about External Data Representation. In this code skeleton, you can see that after the RPC request arrives, the arguments are retrieved from the request and used to make the procedure call in the server. When the procedure returns, the results are packaged into a UDP packet and then returned to the client caller. This code—the registration and svc_run() function—define the server stub from Figure 17.8.

THE CLIENT ORGANIZATION

The client program will consist of application-specific code along with a call to the client RPC software—the client stub. Sun RPC exports interfaces to other high-level languages, but the original API and implementation were all done in C—the explanation is all based on C. The general framework again corresponds to the one shown in Figure 17.8. As mentioned above, the intermediate level RPC package does not support transparency. For example, to call RP_i at the server, the application code would have the form:

```
#include     <rpc/rpc.h>
...
main(int argc, char *argv[]) {
  int result;
  ...
/* Call RPi */
  result = callrpc(rpc_host_name, RPCPROG, RPCPROGVERS, RPi, ...);
  if(result != 0) {
    clnt_perrno(result);
    exit(1);
  }
}
```

First, the intermediate-level RPC interface presumes that the application programmer is able to determine the name of the RPC server (rpc_host_name in the code fragment) without using a name server. In a simple case, such as this laboratory exercise, the server host name can be specified to the client via command line parameter or input data (for example, read using scanf()). In a production environment, the application programmer would have to confer with a name server to determine the name of the RPC server. The remote call itself—the callrpc() library function call—also specifies the (remote_procedure, RPC_program, version) that is used by the server.

The elided arguments in the callrpc() call are the details for transmitting arguments and for receiving results passed as arguments. The server-side functions, svc_getargs() and svc_sendreply() (in the svc_run() function above) process these argument lists according to the argument number and types for the particular remote procedure. These are specified by the programmer-defined external data representation (discussed next).

We will describe how the rpcgen tool allows the application programmer to use the local procedure call interface after we consider the external data representation.

EXTERNAL DATA REPRESENTATION

In a remote procedure call, it must be possible for an application program (executing on one machine in a network) to call a procedure in another, possibly different type, machine on the network. For example, a machine that uses one representation of data must be able to pass an argument to another machine that uses another representation of the same data. This means that integers, floating point numbers, strings, structures, and so on, must be converted from the representation used in the calling machine when arguments are passed to the server. And when results are returned from the server, they must be converted into the form expected by the client software.

This is handled by adding one more piece to the RPC mechanism—the *External Data Representation* conversion mechanism (abbreviated to *XDR*). As shown in Figure 17.14, the client stub uses the XDR conversion library code to translate the data representations used in the client machine into an RPC-specific data representation (XDR). The client stub then transmits the RPC request to the server with the data in the RPC-specific format. When the request is processed by the RPC server, it converts the arguments from XDR into the internal format used by the server computer. This is a primary task of svc_getargs() shown in the svc_run() code fragment. After the procedure call has completed, svc_run() calls svc_sendreply(), which converts the results into XDR and transmits them back to the client. The client stub software uses the XDR conversion mechanism to convert the results into the client machine format before returning the results to the client application.

The Sun RPC package provides XDR specifications for various argument types. For example, if the remote procedure takes a single integer argument, the built-in XDR function, xdr_int(), provides the necessary specification used by the XDR conversion tool. Other built-in XDR specifications handle long, short, char, and their unsigned versions, as well as a few others. Now let's suppose that the remote procedure, RP_i, passes a single character argument and returns an integer result. Then the client code fragment shown above would call the remote procedure with this statement:

```
/* Call RP_i */
  result = callrpc(rpc_host_name,
              RPCPROG, RPCPROGVERS, RP_i,
              xdr_char, &arg, xdr_int, &result);
```

✦ **FIGURE 17.14** XDR Conversion

The RPC package includes a library of routines to convert data to/from a neutral representation from/to the host machine representation. This allows RPC to avoid problems such as big/little endian representations of data.

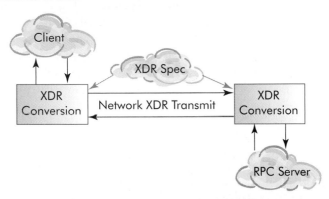

That is, the last four arguments to `callrpc()` describe the XDR conversion specifications. The general form of the call is that the fifth argument is the name of an XDR specification for the argument list (which is the sixth argument to `callrpc()`); similarly, the seventh argument specifies the XDR specification for the return value and the eighth argument is a pointer to the results.

Suppose you want to transmit multiple arguments or receive multiple results, or that your single argument is not one of the built-in types. In this case, you will need to write your own XDR specification. Here is an example from the Sun documentation. Suppose the argument is of type

```
struct simple {
    int a;
    short b;
};
```

Then you would need to define a new XDR specification by defining a C function named, say, `xdr_simple()`, as shown in this code fragment:

```
#include      <rpc/rpc.h>
...
xdr_simple(XDR *xdrsp, struct simple *simplesp) {
    if(!xdr_int(xdrsp, &simplesp->a))
        return(0);
    if(!xdr_short(xdrsp, &simplesp->b))
        return(0);
    return(1);
}
```

That is, the XDR routine should return 0 if it fails, but 1 if it succeeds. This XDR routine is used by a statement such as:

```
/* Call RP_i */
    result = callrpc(rpc_host_name,
```

```
RPCPROG, RPCPROGVERS, RP_i,
xdr_simple, &arg, ...);
```

XDR specification programs can be arbitrarily complex; for example, they can have embedded structures. Consult the online remote procedure call programming guide for more details.

THE STUB GENERATOR: rpcgen

The `callrpc()` style interface and many of the mundane details of XDR have a very regular set of tasks to handle. The Sun RPC developers recognized that they could make RPC much easier to use by creating a programming tool to generate client-side and server-side code. Further, these generated client stubs could then be given conventional function names that would look just like any local function, but when they were called, they would execute the stub code to make the remote procedure call. The programmer must write a *specification* of the remote procedures and their arguments, but once the specification is written, the rpcgen tool would create three files.

When a programmer uses rpcgen, three files will be automatically created. Figure 17.15 shows the files and their relationships to one another. The `rproc.x` is the specification file; its purpose is to provide enough information to rpcgen to allow it to generate the three C source code files. The generated files are all named using the base filename of the `.x` file; that is, if the rpcgen reads a file named `foobar.x`, it will create three files named `foobar.h`, `foobar_clnt.c`, and `foobar_svc.c`. These files contain C source statements corresponding to the "template" code in the server and as a corresponding "template" on the client side (the client stub program).

✦ FIGURE 17.15 The rpcgen Files

The rpcgen tool reads a specification file that describes a remote procedure prototype, and then creates three file skeletons to be used with the RPC library. The skeletons are the client stub, the server stub, and a header file that both stubs will need.

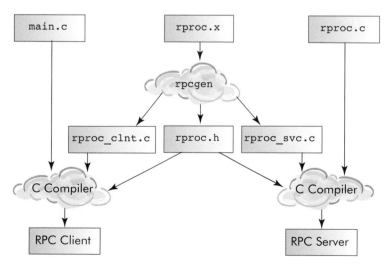

• ATTACKING THE PROBLEM •

Your solution to this problem requires that you know the details of Sun RPC programming. The Background section provides you with the minimal amount of information you will need to solve the problem. You can find more discussion and examples of RPC programming in two excellent programming guides that were originally produced by Sun, but which are now located in various places on the Web:

■ *rpcgen Programming Guide*

■ *Remote Procedure Call Programming Guide*

To find a copy of these guides, do a search on the programming guide name.

If you have solved many of the previous lab examples, you have a pretty good idea about how to go about solving this one. Here is a general set of steps to describe the way I constructed my solution:

■ Write a local version first. This will not use remote procedures at all.

■ Implement a simple remote procedure that uses a single built-in XDR type. For example, you could work on a primitive version of an `openRemote(int)` function since it takes an integer argument instead of a string. In your implementation of `openRemote(int)`, put a `switch` statement to print the integer argument. After that works, change the cases to open a few hardwired filenames (indexed by the integer argument). Then change the argument type to `string` and finish your implementation of `openRemote()`.

■ Next, implement the `closeRemote()` function; it should be easy after you get `openRemote()` working.

■ Finally, you can finish the problem by implementing `storeRemote()`. This will postpone your having to deal with XDR until this step. It will also allow you to focus only on XDR, since you will already know the rest of the Sun RPC mechanism.

CHAPTER 18

Distributed Programming Runtime Systems

Contemporary OS technology focuses on providing support for concurrent programming, particularly distributed programming where different components of the computation execute on different nodes in a network. The mechanisms provided by modern operating systems are sufficient to support distributed programming. However, distributed application programmers often want a more abstract environment with features that are easier to use than those in the OS. At the same time as OS technology continues to evolve, so too does compiler, programming language, and runtime systems technology. Today, distributed programming environments are usually defined by the runtime system that abstracts many of the OS mechanisms. This chapter considers how contemporary distributed programming runtime systems have evolved and suggests how they will influence the new development in operating systems.

18.1 • SUPPORTING DISTRIBUTED SOFTWARE WITH MIDDLEWARE

In Chapter 17, you learned that the OS provides various mechanisms to support distributed application programming. Those mechanisms are sufficient to implement distributed applications, but (as is the case for many other OS mechanisms) middleware can provide higher-level abstractions that are easier for programmers to use.

These abstractions are usually implemented as some form of library package; for example, threads were first introduced as library extensions to the language and OS. Other times, it is convenient for language designers to implement the abstraction as part of the runtime system used with the compiled form of the language. Probably the most well-known runtime system is the C runtime library (it contains functions like `malloc()`, `free()`, `exit()`, and `printf()`). In the description of "system software" in Chapter 1, these libraries and runtime systems are considered to be system software even though they are not part of the operating system.

Historically, application programming communities create or influence these middleware libraries. Over the years, functions originally implemented in this middleware have been subsequently moved into the OS; threads are a perfect example of this. And conversely, sometimes functionality is moved out of the kernel and implemented in middleware: Early support for both bitmap graphics and network protocols was implemented in the kernel, but then moved to user space libraries after the OS designers decided there was no real reason to implement these functions in the kernel. Deciding which functions should be implemented in the middleware and which should be implemented in the kernel involves subjective argument, knowledge of the nature of the hardware on which the OS is implemented, and an understanding of how the OS will be used.

This chapter diverges from the core OS topics—the topics that almost everyone agrees are OS functions—to consider distributed programming runtime systems. A **runtime system** is a library that provides a collection of specific functionality. A runtime system is sometimes distinguished from other libraries in that it complements a programming language definition. For example, all C programming systems depend on the dynamic memory allocation provided by `malloc()` and `free()`. In contemporary systems, most of the open questions about what belongs in middleware and what belongs in the OS are related to distributed programming.

Over the years, scientific problems have demanded the highest performance from the computing system. It is no surprise that this problem domain was the one that pushed the frontiers of distributed computing. Until the emergence of the Web, almost all attention in distributed computation support was for software that solved scientific problems, which demanded the highest performance possible from the hardware and was typically compute-bound.

Since the public Internet has come to be widely used to support web browsers and content servers—the World Wide Web environment—a new class of distributed software has evolved. This new class is less focused on high performance and more directed at effective content (information) distribution. People who browse the web would like to have all the content that is stored in some machine on the web be instantly available at their web browser. This includes any information that could be created as a result of a web request, for example, the response to a query such as "how many widgets did Salesman Jones sell in Detroit in July?"

These two radically different application domains use many of the same distributed programming technologies, although they have evolved as separate solutions. In this chapter, we will first take a look at the classic domain and then turn our attention to the contemporary web domain.

18.2 • CLASSIC DISTRIBUTED APPLICATION PROGRAMS

An individual computer in a network of computers can always be used with the traditional sequential process model to execute an application program. As shown in previous chapters, the challenge of operating systems is then to allow autonomous processes to execute concurrently (but not simultaneously) on a uniprocessor system. The network provides an opportunity for the computation to be partitioned into logical units and then to have the logical units executed simultaneously on different computers in the network. As noted earlier, distribution can be motivated by the desire for better performance, or by sharing information among a community of workers at their own personal computers. Many of the sharing issues are addressed by the tools described in Chapters 16 and 17: remote files, network memory, RPC, and distributed process/thread management.

In Section 17.1, the idea of speedup was introduced as a performance metric for distributed computing. Suppose a computation requires T_1 seconds to run on a uniprocessor. If it could be executed in $T_5 = T_1/5$ seconds in a network with five or more computers on it, we would say it had a speedup of 5. Because of the overhead introduced by administration, synchronization, and communication, it is rare to achieve a speedup of N in a collection of N computers, although this is a good goal toward which to work. The essence of the problem, from the application programmer's viewpoint then, is to partition a serial computation into N units that can execute simultaneously with a minimum of overhead. If this partition is "perfect" and there is no overhead from administration, synchronization, or communication, then the speedup will approach N.

How does a programmer go about partitioning a serial application so that it will have significant speedup? In general, this is a challenging intellectual exercise for which there are few fixed approaches. The application programmer must know the behavior of the algorithm used in the computation, the behavior of the system software that supports distribution, and the nature of the hardware platforms. Some years ago, people who studied this partitioning problem observed that there were two general approaches that a designer might take: Data partitioning and functional partitioning.

In some programs it is possible to use *data partitioning* to achieve parallelism and speedup. The idea is to partition the data that will be read by the original program into N different "streams." For example, suppose the sequential program is designed so that it reads records sequentially, processes each record after it reads it, and then produces output for that record. It might be possible to divide the original data set into N sub files, and then to delegate a file to each of N different clones of the original sequential program (see Figure 18.1). That is, each of the N processes operating on the N different machines is executing in its own address space. Now there can be N different processes executing simultaneously, each with the responsibility for processing only a fraction of the total data. The data for each process is loaded into that process's address space. Data partitioning can be particularly effective, provided there are no interactions among the processes executing the individual records. If a process needs to have access to data outside its own partition (in another address space) to execute the function, then data partitioning becomes much more complex than the simple case.

For example, to multiply matrix A times matrix B, the scalar value, $C[i, j]$ in row i, column j of the result matrix is computed by taking the dot product of row i in A times column j in B. If a process on Host R in a network were to compute all the values in row i of the result, then it would need to read row i in A repeatedly and to read every column in B. Similarly, if another process on Host S were to be computing all the values in row k of the result, it would need to read row k of A repeatedly and to read every column of B. This imposes an impossible constraint on any data partition (without using copies), since B must appear in the partition used at Host R and the partition used at Host S. A poor partition can cause some of the parts to be delayed for inordinate amounts of time, causing the whole computation to have poor (even negative) speedup.

✦ FIGURE 18.1 Data Partition

In data partitioning, the input data is divided into *N* different parts; then each part is given to one of *N* clones of the original sequential program.

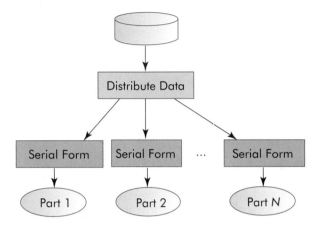

Figure 18.2 suggests another general strategy for partitioning the computation. In a *functional partition*, the program is divided into parts (instead of dividing the data into parts) and then the data are passed among the different parts. You can think of this strategy as dividing the overall function into independent stages and then passing all the data through the different stages record-by-record. If the computation has conditional control flow, then some data records may follow a different route through the computational parts than others. In either case, parallelism is achieved by having the function stages operate in parallel as an assembly line.

The philosophy behind this approach is that data management is much smaller than the function computation, so the function is partitioned into parts that can be executed simultaneously with one another. The difficulty with functional partitioning is that a sequential program must be rewritten before it can be used. Further, the resulting partition creates parts that must then have the appropriate sharing and synchronization installed.

18.3 • MIDDLEWARE SUPPORT FOR CLASSIC DISTRIBUTED PROGRAMMING

Programmers who work in classic distributed application programming want to solve diverse scientific problems, such as the SOR program in Lab Exercise 11.1. If an OS provides UDP/TCP, then the application programmers can use those IPC mechanisms as the basis for building their solution. However, this would not handle the associated process management tasks such as creating a child process on another computer. During the 1990s, the members of the scientific programming community began to develop their own middleware libraries to accomplish IPC and process management.

Basic IPC operation was discussed in Chapter 9. Briefly, messages are blocks of information sent by one process and received by another. The message serves two purposes:

✦ FIGURE 18.2 Functional Partition

In functional partitioning, the original sequential program is broken into parts; then input data is passed through each of the parts as required.

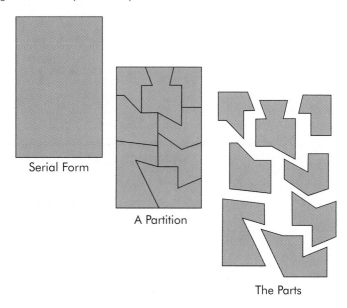

Serial Form

A Partition

The Parts

■ It is an explicit mechanism for one process to share information with another.

■ It can be used to synchronize the operation of the receiver with the operation of the sender.

A receiver process must have a mailbox to buffer messages that have been sent to, but have not yet been logically accepted by, the receiver. Send operations can be synchronous or asynchronous. In a synchronous operation, the sender waits until the message is safely delivered to the receiver's mailbox. In an asynchronous operation, the sender transmits the message and proceeds without waiting to see if the message was actually placed in a mailbox. Receive operations can be blocking or nonblocking. In the former case, when a receiver reads a mailbox, the blocking receive prevents the receiver from proceeding until a message is available. In a nonblocking receive operation, a receiver proceeds in either case.

In the remainder of this section, let's look at a few of the middleware packages that are most widely used to support scientific computing applications: PVM, Beowulf, and OSF DCE.

PVM

Probably the most widely used mechanism during the early 1990s was the *PVM* (*Parallel Virtual Machine*) software package [Geist and Sunderam, 1992]. By the late 1990s, many of the developers of PVM had joined forces with others to develop a refinement called the *Message Passing Interface* (*MPI*) [Gropp, et al., 1998]. PVM and MPI provide an API that is built on top of the OS functions, including the network message-passing facility. If a distributed application programmer implemented a program on top of PVM, then the distributed components could be executed on a wide variety of versions of UNIX as well as various other operating systems (see Figure 18.3). At the time PVM was deployed, it immediately found widespread use for high performance computing, even though the PVM package was generally user space software.

✦ FIGURE 18.3 PVM Architecture

PVM was designed to be portable so that it could be implemented on many different kinds of machines. Thus, the programmer can install PVM on a set of heterogeneous machines connected to a common network and then use the underlying TCP/UDP implementations to support interoperating PVM library routines. An application could then be written to distribute computation across machines built by different manufacturers without having to address any of the details of each machine's transport layer protocols. In cases where PVM was expected to be heavily used, the PVM implementation was implemented as part of the OS.

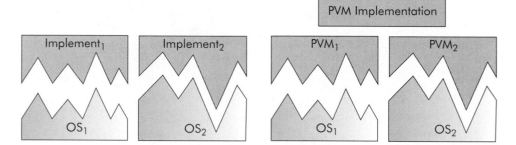

Each computer used in a PVM configuration contains applications with the PVM library for the host OS. The library functions use the local OS process management facilities to create and manage PVM processes. A PVM *task* is a schedulable unit of computation that uses a parallel virtual machine to execute. The pvm_mytid() call must be executed by each PVM task so as to associate the task with a parallel virtual machine; the call returns a task identifier. The task identifiers for other tasks using the virtual machine are obtained with the pvm_gettid() call. A task can create another task using pvm_spawn() and can destroy itself with pvm_exit(). A set of tasks can be identified as siblings by joining a logical group with the pvm_joingroup() call; a task can abandon the group using pvm_lvgroup(). So you can see that PVM exports a full set of task management functions.

PVM also contains synchronization calls, including conventional signal() (similar to the V() operation) and wait() (equivalent to P()) calls. The PVM library implements the equivalent of a semaphore using TCP/IP protocols, as if there were a shared memory with a semaphore.

PVM messages contain sets of typed data. A sending task initializes a message buffer with the pvm_initsend() call. Typed data is placed into a message buffer using packing routines. In the example below, pvm_pkint() is used to place an integer into a message. The receiver uses pvm_upkint() to retrieve the data from the message buffer. Once a sending task has filled its message buffer, it sends the buffer to another task using the task identification with the pvm_send(), pvm_multicast(), or pvm_broadcast() operations. Messages are accepted with the pvm_recv() operation, thus causing the message to be placed in a buffer where data is unmarshalled using the unpack command set, which places the values in local variables.

The examples shown in Figure 18.4 and Figure 18.5 are abstracted from an example in the PVM 3.3 documentation [Geist et al., 1994]. SPMD is a distributed computation paradigm, meaning several processes execute the same procedure ("SP") on multiple data streams ("MD"). Each host machine in a set of PVM hosts executes the code shown in the figures to pass a token from one host to another.

✦ **FIGURE 18.4** The SPMD Computation in the PVM Main Program

The PVM main program is executed by each machine that will be involved in the SPMD computation. The code determines the process PVM ID, joins a group, and then waits at a barrier synchronization point for NPROC different processes to join the group. It then calls the dowork() function (shown in Figure 18.5) to do the demonstration computation.

```
#define NPROC 4
#include <sys/types.h>
#include "pvm3.h"
main() {
   int mytid;         /* my task id */
   int tids[NPROC];   /* array of task id */
   int me;            /* my process number */
   int i;

  mytid = pvm_mytid(); /* enroll in pvm */
/* Join a group; if first in the group, create other tasks */
  me = pvm_joingroup("foo");
  if(me == 0)
    pvm_spawn("spmd", (char**)0, 0, "", NPROC-1, &tids[1]);
/* Wait for everyone to startup before proceeding. */
  pvm_barrier("foo", NPROC);
/*----------------------------*/
  dowork(me, NPROC);
/* program finished leave group and exit pvm */
  pvm_lvgroup("foo");
  pvm_exit();
  exit(1);
}
```

PVM defines an abstract "parallel virtual machine" that can be implemented on various UNIX systems that support TCP/UDP/IP. When an application uses the PVM library, the performance is likely to be lower than if the application were written directly on the OS. However, the functions provided by PVM resonated with the scientific programming community, so they were able to become productive without learning the details of OS primitives. In many cases, the scientists were very happy to be able to write parallel code at all, even though it did not squeeze all the performance out of the underlying hardware.

✦ FIGURE 18.5 The SPMD `dowork()` Function in PVM

The `dowork()` function determines which processes are its neighbors, reads the token from the neighbor with a smaller ID, and sends the token to the neighbor with a larger ID.

```
dowork(int me, int nproc) {
  int token;
  int src, dest;
  int count = 1;
  int stride = 1;
  int msgtag = 4;

  /* Determine neighbors in the ring */
  src = pvm_gettid("foo", me-1);
  dest= pvm_gettid("foo", me+1);
  if(me == 0) src = pvm_gettid("foo", NPROC-1);
  if(me == NPROC-1) dest = pvm_gettid("foo", 0);
  if(me == 0) {
    token = dest;
    pvm_initsend(PvmDataDefault);
    pvm_pkint(&token, count, stride);
    pvm_send(dest, msgtag);
    pvm_recv(src, msgtag);
    printf("token ring done\n");
} else {
    pvm_recv(src, msgtag);
    pvm_upkint(&token, count, stride);
    pvm_initsend(PvmDataDefault);
    pvm_pkint(&token, count, stride);
    pvm_send(dest, msgtag);
  }
}
```

THE BEOWULF CLUSTER COMPUTING ENVIRONMENT

In 1994, the Beowulf Project, led by Sterling and Becker, built a multiprocessor from a collection of "commodity off-the-shelf" microprocessors interconnected with Ethernet technology—a **cluster computer** [Becker, et al., 1995]. Like the PVM project, this project was driven by the need for support of high performance computing through parallelism. The system was built at the Goddard Space Flight Center by parallel programmers to solve earth and space science problems (it was *not* a systems research project); the Beowulf developers refer to themselves as "do-it-yourselfers." The Beowulf computer was so successful that other researchers in the community decided to adopt the approach and build their own "Beowulf class cluster computer." (see http://www.beowulf.org/intro.html).

Beowulf differs from the network of workstations (NOW) research systems that also use independent machines interconnected by an Ethernet [Anderson, et al., 1995]. A NOW is intended to operate on a conventional network with general purpose workstations. When a workstation is not in use by its normal user, the NOW uses its resources. This means that a significant part of the contribution of the NOW is in determining when a workstation can be used and in load balancing. In Beowulf, all the machines are dedicated to the cluster computer.

The Beowulf hardware is standard hardware, interconnected using Ethernet technology. The challenge to harnessing the hardware so that it can be used to solve high performance computing problems is in finding an appropriate set of software to support distributed application execution. Just as the Beowulf designers exhibited great initiative in building the hardware, they used the same approach in building the distributed programming environment. A Beowulf cluster uses various freely available software packages to create the environment, including Linux, PVM, MPI, and GNU software.

The first Beowulf computer was built using DX4 processors and a 10 Mbps Ethernet. The processors were much faster than the network, so the developers created a technique in which they used two Ethernets with each carrying half the transmission load. This required that they do extensive device driver development—something for which Linux was well-suited. As 100 Mbps (and 1 Gbps) Ethernets became generally available, Beowulf clusters have dropped the old "striped" Ethernet pair in favor of a single high-speed Ethernet. Network drivers are a critical part of the Beowulf approach, and these developers have contributed numerous network drivers to the Linux community.

The programmers who developed Beowulf were already quite familiar with PVM and the then emerging MPI package. They had used these mechanisms on top of other computer platforms as the basis for much of the parallel/distributed programming support. Therefore, it was natural for them to use PVM/MPI as the distributed process management approach in Beowulf.

The Beowulf Project established an avid community of people who wanted to create their own cluster of dedicated computers. By creating a simple distributed hardware platform, concentrating on network driver development, exploiting the Linux environment, and using the PVM/MPI interface, the community is able to build and use an inexpensive but very effective high performance cluster computing environment.

THE OSF DISTRIBUTED COMPUTING ENVIRONMENT

Throughout the 1980s, there was a continuing competition between the two dominant versions of UNIX: BSD UNIX and AT&T System III/V UNIX. Sun Microcomputers had adopted BSD UNIX as its OS, so the competition was primarily between Sun and AT&T. In 1988, Sun and AT&T reached an agreement in which the competition between the two versions was put to rest—essentially resulting in Sun Solaris. The Open Software Foundation (OSF) was formed in the late 1980s in response to the Sun–AT&T agreement, as a consortium of computer manufacturers that wished to support the idea of an open version of UNIX. (In 1995, OSF merged with another open software consortium named X/Open to form the Open Group.) Besides OSF's interest in versions of UNIX, it also intended to support distributed application programming.

OSF created a unified middleware package explicitly intended to support distributed computation, called the **Distributed Computing Environment (DCE)** [Open Group, 2003]. DCE can be supported by various operating systems, including OSF's own OS recommendation (called OSF/1). Whereas PVM was supported and developed primarily by the high performance scientific computing community, DCE was created by a commercial OS community. Like Beowulf, DCE was generally built by combining a collection of independently developed open technologies, rather than being derived as a new collection of functions.

The OSF DCE represents the state of the art in distributed programming runtime support for high performance computing. Like PVM, DCE was designed to support heterogeneous networks, computers, and operating systems. The goal was for programmers to be able to write distributed software using the DCE API, and then to have that software run on any of OSF/1, various forms of UNIX, and any other OS that included the DCE package. Programmers could then largely ignore the type of computer and network being used under the OS.

DCE applications are generally client programs that request services from the distributed infrastructure. Applications are implemented as a community of DCE threads that communicate with servers on remote machines using a built-in RPC protocol. The DCE middleware is implemented as a set of library routines that run on the local client machine OS—providing services if they are available at the local machine, or acting as client stubs if services are obtained from a remote machine. Remote services can be provided by the DCE, and others by application programmers. The built-in DCE services are:

- Distributed File Service
- Security Service for user authentication and resource access authorization
- Directory Service for uniformly naming and locating resources in the distributed environment
- Time Service that is able to synchronize clocks across a network

Application services are defined by the DCE programmer. Next, we will discuss the DCE mechanisms and built-in services.

THREADS Threads are the schedulable unit of computation for the DCE. The thread package is defined by the POSIX3.4 standard, which can be implemented as a library or with kernel support. (This is the dominant thread package used in various UNIX systems, including Linux and FreeBSD.) At the time that DCE was defined, most of the underlying OS platforms were single-thread per process UNIX systems. This meant that an application executed as a single classic process that multiplexed across user space threads under the control of library code. The OS kernel was unaware that a process might be multithreaded, since from the kernel point of view, thread multiplexing within the process was completely invisible to the kernel.

User space threads work fine unless one of the threads in the process happens to block. When one thread blocks, then the process is blocked, which means that all threads in the process are blocked. This is a big motivator for kernel threads—threads that are managed by the kernel instead of user space code. With kernel threads, the OS scheduler allocates the process directly to the thread instead of to the process, which means that one of the threads in a process can block without blocking the other threads in the process.

DCE implementations of threads were intended to support at least user level threads, but preferably kernel threads. Today, many implementations of the POSIX thread package use kernel threads rather than the library implementation. That, of course, was the rationale for using POSIX threads in the early days of DCE: A program could be written to work with the POSIX interface, and thus would work with both user and kernel threads without modification.

REMOTE PROCEDURE CALL DCE distributed applications use RPC for inter-process communication. The RPC model generally conforms to the discussion provided in Section 17.3, summarized in Figure 17.8. Briefly, the client is configured with a client stub for each remote procedure it calls, and the server stub is the main program for the server. The RPC server is started first. It registers the remote procedures with a name service, and then waits for a client to invoke a procedure. The address space used by the client thread has all the client stubs linked into it (as if they were normal local procedures). The RPC proceeds as follows:

- When the thread calls a remote procedure, it really calls the client stub.
- The client stub looks up the remote procedure server that implements the target procedure.
- In DCE, the global name space in which the client should search for a remote procedure is specified by an administrator-defined *cell*, or collection of host machines.
- The stub marshals the arguments and sends them to the remote procedure server.
- The client stub then blocks, waiting for a response from the server.
- The remote procedure server is normally waiting for a client call.
- When the call arrives, the remote procedure server unmarshalls the arguments and then uses them to call the target procedure.
- When the procedure returns to the server stub code, it marshalls the return results and returns them to the waiting client stub.
- The client stub unmarshalls the results and returns them to the calling code.

The DCE RPC provides a collection of tools to enable a programmer to generate client and server stubs and to specify the details of the procedures and arguments (Sun RPC also does this, as explained in Lab Exercise 17.1). It also provides flexible ways to use the mechanism, for example, so that two different clients can call the same remote procedure server at the same time, or so that a client can cancel a remote procedure call that is in process (but not yet complete).

The remote RPC server is built in the listener-server pattern (see Figure 15.19). This means that the client stub contacts the remote procedure server, which then couples the client with a listener thread on the server. In this manner, the server can support multiple concurrent calls; each call has its own listener server thread.

In a production level distributed software environment, the entire system cannot be halted to update a particular remote procedure. Although the updated procedure may fix bugs, it could also change parameter characteristics or the semantics of the original procedure. Therefore, the RPC system supports multiple versions of each remote procedure. Each remote procedure has associated *major* and *minor version numbers*; when a client calls a remote procedure, it must provide the major/minor numbers of the target procedure to assure that the correct one is called. These version numbers are also kept with the registration information in the name server.

Argument number and types are part of the definition of a procedure. The calling and called procedures must agree on the characteristics of the argument list. In ANSI C, function prototypes are used to define a procedure signature: the name of the procedure, as well as the number of arguments and the types of each argument. The DCE does not assume that all programs are written in C. It is possible for a client written in one language to call a remote procedure written in a different language. This means that the procedure interface specification is language-independent. It is generated by a tool that is part of the RPC package; the output of the tool is the header file, the client stub, and the server stub. The client stub is combined with the client application code, and the server stub is combined with the remote procedures, resulting in the running system.

DISTRIBUTED FILES The DCE DFS is a descendant of the Andrew File System—AFS (see Section 16.4). The DFS refinement of AFS was developed by HP, IBM, Locus Computing, and Transarc [Kazar, et al., 1990]. AFS/DFS uses the file caching approach, meaning that when a client opens a file, the file is copied (or cached) to the client. If the client has enough primary memory available, the file is kept in the primary memory; otherwise, it is copied to a storage device on the client machine. In the implementation of the remote file server, most of the file manager is on the server side, with a relatively small part of the functionality implemented on the client side.

Since AFS/DFS uses file caching, it must handle file consistency. Besides the immutable file versions described in Section 16.4, it provides a mechanism for file coherence. When a copy of a file is cached to more than one client and is then updated by one of them, there will be inconsistency among the versions. AFS/DFS uses tokens to manage the inconsistency: A *token* represents the right to perform certain operations on a cached (and potentially shared) file. For example, there is a token to allow a client to access file descriptor and directory information, and tokens to lock parts of a file. When a client wants to perform one of these protected operations, it must obtain the corresponding token from the server.

Client application software accesses remote files using POSIX.1 (OS) system calls. If the OS is POSIX.1 compliant, then there is no difference between DFS and local OS file manager calls; otherwise the application programmer must use the local OS system call interface for local calls and the DFS POSIX.1 calls to manipulate remote files (see Figure 18.6).

The client interacts with the server using the RPC mechanism; thus, file manager system calls are represented at the client by stubs. The other significant job on the client side is to manage cached copies of files when they are opened by application software. The *Cache Manager* is the DFS client module that handles this task. Whenever a file is opened, the Cache Manager looks in its local cache (on a local storage device) to determine if a copy of the file is already loaded at this client machine. If there is a copy, then the application uses that copy. If there is not a copy, then the Cache Manager requests one from the server.

Client side software can be implemented as middleware. The DFS server must be implemented in user and kernel space. At the file access level, AFS/DFS uses Sun vnodes and the virtual file switch (VFS)—see Section 16.3. This means that AFS/DFS has a preferred file system (called the Local File System in Figure 18.6), although it can also mount other types of file systems. The VFS+ (meaning Sun VFS plus extensions for DFS) implements the file system independent part of the server's file manager. The Local File System implements the file system dependent part of the file manager. Other types of file systems can be implemented on the server by implementing modules corresponding to the Local File System module; the VFS is explicitly designed to accommodate such implementations.

✦ FIGURE 18.6 The DCE Distributed File System

The DCE DFS client contains a cache manager to administer file copies in the client. The cache manager avoids file copies if it determines that the file is in the cache. The client can be implemented as user space code, but the file server needs supervisory permission.

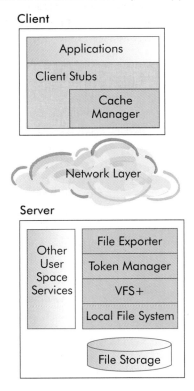

The *File Exporter* is the server stub for RPCs. Each RPC that is issued by a client is fielded by the File Exporter. It will call its own procedures (file manager system functions) to execute commands issued by the client. The File Exporter's functions make calls on the VFS+ (and thus the underlying file system modules) to cause file management operations.

Tokens are intended to enable the client and server to implement a file manager that has the same file access semantics as a UNIX file manager. This means that in cases where there is the possibility of action by clients that will introduce inconsistencies due to replication, the Token Manager must prevent that from happening. It does this by inspecting each client's request to perform actions that might break the UNIX semantics. The Token Manager can then handle these operations as critical sections to ensure consistent operation. Rather than having the Token Manager simply implement a collection of semaphores, the Token Manager allocates a token to a client that has permission to alter a file or directory. When the client has completed the operation, the Token Manager can reclaim the token and allocate it to another client if one is waiting.

There are other services provided by the DFS server. Generally, these services are related to file system administration, for example, handling file system partitions (called DFS filesets), managing the server threads, monitoring performance, and so on.

SECURITY   Considerable effort has gone into the DCE security mechanisms. The facility addresses all three aspects of security mechanisms described in Chapter 14: authentication, authorization, and cryptography. Throughout the DCE design, it is assumed that distribution is achieved by having clients interacting with servers. In providing a secure distributed environment, a Security Server is introduced to implement many of the mechanisms used in the approach. Additionally, an Administrator is assumed to be defining a protection policy at a fourth network site (see Figure 18.7).

✦ FIGURE 18.7   DCE Security Components

The DCE protection mechanism handles authentication, authorization, and cryptography. The Registry service is the administrator's mechanism for defining security policy. The Authentication service is Kerberos, with Login authentication.

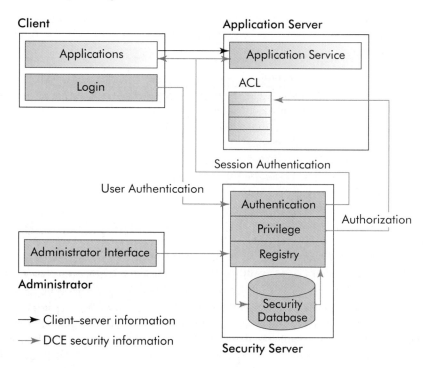

The *Registry service* in the Security Server manages the cell-wide security policy. The human administrator's interface is designed to securely interact with the Registry to create and maintain the desired policy specification. In the terminology from Chapter 14, subjects are called *principals* in DCE. The Security DB contains an entry for each principal that keeps all relevant information about that principal (for example, encryption keys and authentication information). It also maintains general security information for the cell.

The *Authentication service* is the Kerberos authentication system (see Section 14.2). Kerberos uses private key encryption to enable clients and servers to establish secure connections over an untrusted network. For example, it is possible to have a secure connection over the IP network layer where intruders can peek at all the information that crosses the network, yet not be able to interpret it. Once the client and server are able to trust one another (using Kerberos tickets), they can exchange encrypted information until their session expires.

The Authentication service relies on the client being able to authenticate its user. The Login service at the client machine is responsible for authenticating the user that launches client applications. User authentication is accomplished through login/password pairs. Once the user is authenticated, information is conveyed between the application client and server as encrypted information.

Recall that all client-server interactions use RPC. It is the RPC mechanism that invokes the authentication services, including the Kerberos session initialization. The RPC mechanism also implements encryption and decryption as part of the normal command/result transmissions.

The application service can determine which clients are authorized to use the service by checking the access using access control lists, or ACLs (see Section 14.3). The ACL service can be implemented in any server.

NETWORK DIRECTORY From its inception, DCE was intended to support large-scale distribution over large networks. In this type of environment, it can be surprisingly difficult for a thread to locate resources—machines, files, services—on the network. Developers recognized this problem several years ago: In 1988, the first version of the X.500 directory services draft standard was released (the fourth edition of the spec was released in 2001). X.500 defines an extensive set of tools. The DCE Network Directory service uses the X.500 directory service, more specifically, the LDAP subset of X.500.

The Network Directory service is based on domains—the cells mentioned in the RPC discussion. Roughly speaking, a cell is an administrative collection of network resources that can be used in a distributed computation. RPCs can be used to make procedure calls within a cell and distributed files can be accessed throughout a cell. The cell also defines the scope for security policies. The *Cell Directory Service* is the mechanism by which a client can find resources within the cell. The Global Directory Service provides a means for spanning cells if that is required, but the default operation is within a cell.

Each resource has a unique DCE name within the cell, and each cell name is unique in the space of all DCE cell names. Thus, any resource within a cell can be referenced using the intra cell name, and resources in remote cells can be referenced by using the cell name along with the intra cell name. The actual names are a bit more complicated than this, but the important idea is to note that there are names used within a cell by the Cell Directory Service, and more general names used by the Global Directory Service to reference resources in remote cells.

The *X.500 Directory Access Protocol* (*DAP*) is used to access a directory server to find a resource. DAP provides a user interface allowing users to construct their own queries of the directory server to find resources. DAP is a high-level protocol that can run on top of TCP/IP.

The *Lightweight DAP* (*LDAP*) was developed as a simplified version of DAP that required fewer client machine resources than DAP. During the 1990s, LDAP quickly caught on as a protocol for performing X.500 directory service queries without incurring the cost of supporting a full DAP client. Today, LDAP is widely used on desktops, even though the original motivation no longer holds; that is, any modern desktop has more than enough resources to support a DAP client implementation. LDAP is also important because now it is being used in mobile computers where, once again, there are limited client resources.

TIME SERVICE Distributed software components often need to synchronize according to some absolute measure such as the passage of time. For example, suppose the correct operation of the computation depended on an agreement that Event R on Machine X occurred before Event S occurs on Machine Y. The key element here is determining if the time that Event R occurred is earlier than the time at which Event S occurred. This problem would be trivial on a uniprocessor system, since one could simply observe the time that Event R occurred and the time that Event S occurred and then compare the two times. In a network of computers, there are difficulties.

When Event R occurs, it uses the time from Machine X, but when Event S occurs, it uses the time from Machine Y. What assurance can there be that the clocks for the two machines are synchronized? Even if the two machines have their time synchronized, say at the top of the hour, their clocks will drift before the top of the next hour. If the clock on Machine X loses time (counts only 59 minutes and 59 seconds in the hour) and Machine Y gains time (counts 60 minutes and 1 second in the hour), then we cannot determine if Event R actually occurred before Event S.

The DCE Time Service provides a means for the network of computers to manage time:

- There is a way for all hosts to periodically synchronize their clocks. This assures that the times at the different hosts stay within an acceptable range of one another.
- Each clock reading is given as a range of times, with the assurance that the correct time lies within the range.

Each client is configured with a *Time Clerk* that is responsible for synchronizing that machine's time with the DCE time. The Time Clerk interacts with a collection of *Timer Servers* whenever it needs to synchronize the local clock. To do this, the Time Clerk observes drift on each synchronization action. Eventually, it will determine the amount and direction of drift in the local machine's clock. Once it has determined this information, it knows that when the local clock has had time to drift too far from the DCE time, it synchronizes with the Timer Servers.

Each cell contains several Timer Servers. When a Time Clerk asks a Time Server, it returns its notion of the current time. Time Servers also query one another to determine the correct notion of time, adjusting their own clocks according to the consensus time among the Timer Servers in the cell. This will keep all machines within the cell synchronized, but it does not prevent the time within the cell from drifting away from the correct time. One of the tricky parts about synchronizing is that the time to communicate between the Time Clerk and the Time Server must be known (or at least bounded). This means that a Time Clerk is going to have a much tighter bound on the amount of time to read a new time from a Time Server on the same LAN than it can for reading a new time from a Time Server that is located on a different LAN. The packet exchange to the Time Server on the remote LAN must pass through one or more gateway machines, so it may take a while for the message carrying the time to go from the Time Server back to the Time Clerk.

In the DCE approach, each LAN should have at least three Time Servers. If the LAN only has two Time Servers, then one of them must act as a Courier Time Server that contacts a Global Time Server on a remote LAN. The Courier then injects an outside time into the time on a LAN.

Finally, some Time Servers in the cell must be able to synchronize with an External Time Provider—some external source that has an accurate representation of the correct time (perhaps a telephone connection to an atomic clock). This is the means by which the Time Servers can adjust their time to match the correct time.

18.4 • DISTRIBUTED PROGRAMMING ON THE WEB

Parallel and distributed programming has traditionally been motivated by the need for high performance solutions to scientific problems. Government funding agencies stimulated research and development in high performance computing by announcing that they would provide research support for people who were attempting to solve one or more of a set of "Grand Challenge" problems. These problems may occur in any discipline; for example, mapping the human genome is one of the Grand Challenge problems.

Prior to 1995, much of the research and development in parallel and distributed programming was motivated by high performance computing; the PVM and Beowulf projects are perfect examples of projects that evolved because of the interest in high performance computing. DCE development was strongly influenced by the need to support high performance scientific programming, although it was also intended to address other problem domains.

During the early 1990s, the World Wide Web was deployed and subsequently embraced by very large numbers of users (compared to the number of high performance computation users) [Berners-Lee, 1996]. Computers and networks went from being a laboratory curiosity to something that was used in every home. Commodity product advertisers began to provide a URL with their product advertising.

Further, a new, specific computation model emerged based on web browsers interacting with servers. In the simplest case, there is little distributed programming in web-based content retrieval: A user decides that he or she wants to look at content, which causes a request to pass through the public Internet to a server that contains the content. The server responds by transmitting a copy of a file to the web browser machine. The logical model of computation used in the simple case is file transfer: The client sends a file copy request to the server, and the server responds by sending the file to the client.

Web designers recognized that in this popular scenario, file caching would be critical to overall performance. Every web browser caches a copy of recently visited files. Many companies also began to build systems to cache files across the public Internet. The essence of this technology is that it is possible to configure a computer as a **web cache** or **web proxy**. An Internet Service Provider (ISP) would then install one of these web cache machines at its local site so that when content is first fetched by any of the ISP's clients, a copy of the file is kept on the ISP's web cache machine. Then, if another customer (or the same customer) requests the same file, it can be delivered from the ISP's web cache rather than from the content server. This eliminates the need for the file to be copied across the Internet more than once. Of course, the downside is that the web cache must be large in order to benefit from repeated file read requests, and as the file sits in the web cache, changes to the content at the content server are not reflected in the cached file. This case is particularly bad for content servers that deliver "dynamic content," such as stock market quotes.

File transfer applications tend to serialize the execution of the client and the server. The client issues a request to the server and then waits for the file to be delivered before continuing. As users and applications become more sophisticated, there will be more interaction between the web browser and the content server. For example, the web browser may request information from the server, and the server may need to respond by asking for a qualification on the type of information, for example, a catalog number. Using the simple approach, each interaction is composed of the transfer of information from the client (such as the catalog number) followed by a response from the server (such as a description of an item). That is, these more complex interactions are a set of actions that, together, make up a transaction.

Another scenario that increasingly appeared in early web applications was that the client-server traffic could be substantially reduced if a context-specific algorithm could be executed by the web browser. The Java developers demonstrated this by having a web browser download an image and then having a local algorithm animate the image. The content might be an image of a wireframe figure, and the algorithm might be to have the wireframe figure dance the Macarena.

These examples are instances of more traditional distributed computing (other than file downloading): The amount of work (and context) used by the client is greater than what can be hardwired into the web browser. System designers realized that it would be possible to provide a computational framework in the web browser that could tailor this kind of computation to the task at hand by downloading a small application program—an **applet**—from the server to the client when the transaction begins. The applet only resides in the web browser while the transaction is taking place; then it is discarded. Since the applet is downloaded from the server, it can be tailored to work well with the server once it has been downloaded. Perhaps more significantly, the server can temporarily delegate an entire computation (such as an animation sequence) to a client.

Applets were an immediate and significant success. They enabled a web browser to temporarily become a remote extension of a computation taking place on the server. Today, applets are widely used by Internet content servers. The general applet idea is referred to as **mobile code**—code that is loaded into a client machine only when it is needed.

Web-based distributed programming shares some similarities with high performance scientific programming, but it is distinctly different along other dimensions. Most of the new developments in distributed programming support are for this domain. The remainder of this chapter focuses on these new distributed programming runtime systems.

18.5 ● MIDDLEWARE SUPPORT FOR MOBILE CODE

Distributed application programmers working in the Web domain want to solve diverse information processing problems, ranging from pure content delivery to electronic commerce. While these applications are not as computationally intensive as high performance numerical computing, they can still have a nontrivial computational component. Since the web application domain is much newer than high performance computing, programmers have the advantage of using all the technology described in Section 18.3 as well as newer technology especially designed to support modern information management (such as electronic commerce). In this section, we will focus on the middleware that is designed explicitly to support these kinds of applications.

In the web environment, end users at the client machines are assumed to be using a fixed computing infrastructure in their client machine—a web browser. The web browser infrastructure can be customized for a computation by adding mobile code, plugins, or other incremental software modules. Many of these incremental modules are configured into the client machine configuration in preparation for distributed computation. Mobile code has had the most impact on middleware design because it is *dynamically* added to the client machine as needed.

There were two landmark events in the evolution of mobile code distributed computing: the launch of the web and the public launch of Java. The essence of the web is that information can be annotated with HTML tags to define its structure and then be distributed using HTTP. The resulting web comes into existence because a critical mass of people decide to use this protocol for distributing information. The popularization of web browsers, particularly the Mosaic web browser developed by researchers in NCSA at the University of Illinois in the early 1990s, was essential in making HTTP/HTML accessible to the masses.

The introduction of Java (May 1995) was a landmark event in that it made it possible to dynamically load and execute mobile code in a client's web browser. Sun Microsystems created a new, safe programming language that could execute mobile code inside the Netscape Navigator (a commercial version of Mosaic) web browser. Microsoft developers designed their web browser to execute Java mobile code, but by 2000, they began to use their .NET technology, based on the Common Language Runtime (CLR) system, as the main mobile code platform. (In December 2001, the Common Language Infrastructure (CLI) specification was adopted as the ECMA-335 standard.) The Java runtime system clearly established a new distributed programming environment first as mobile code, but then evolving into a more general distributed remote object environment. CLR/CLI technology is an evolutionary step of the Java approach, providing a more robust runtime system for mobile code distributed programming. We will next summarize the critical aspects of these two approaches, emphasizing OS and distributed system technologies.

JAVA AND THE JAVA VIRTUAL MACHINE

Java is a programming language with an associated runtime system called the Java Virtual Machine (JVM). According to the web page celebrating its third birthday (http://java.sun.com/features/1998/05/birthday.html), the Java effort began as a programming language for the Green Project, an experimental project at Sun to consider future directions in digital devices. The group built a prototype of a mobile, interactive, home-entertainment device named "*7" that could be used to control a TV, VCR, or other electronic devices. The language, initially called "Oak," was just one part of the development project.

From the beginning, Java was intended to be a language for network programming, although not necessarily for scientific programming. After its use in *7, the team realized that Java could be a useful internet programming language, particularly because it was designed explicitly with the idea of moving content across networks. Java developers embraced the idea of applets because they recognized that the underlying internet technology could easily deliver content using FTP, TCP, UDP, and other protocols. The missing element was to make it easy for an application programmer to use these protocols; this was the same motivation used for remote procedure call and remote files in the classic distributed programming domain.

The Java team built a web browser, first called Web Runner, then HotJava®, in which they could execute Java applets (see Figure 18.8). Java and the JVM were initially demonstrated by showing animation sequences in the web browser. The Java technology was also offered as free alpha software prior to its official announcement in May 1995. The demonstrations were immediately convincing to technical people, and with the free availability of Java, it caught on like wildfire. Before the end of 1995, Java was well-established as a web-based distributed programming environment—one that extended web browser functionality through mobile code.

✦ FIGURE 18.8 Mobile Java Code

A Java applet is a module of code that can be dynamically added to a JVM by a server (step (1)). Sun researchers embedded the JVM inside their web browser (Web Runner, later known as HotJava®). In step 2, the applet is used as a peer to communicate with the server.

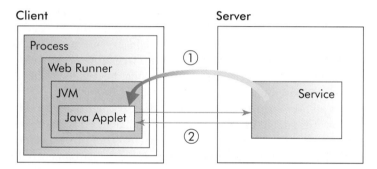

Although Java was not built to support classic distributed programming, would it be useful in that context? As you examine various aspects of Java below, you will recognize that all the proper mechanisms are in place to support high performance computing, even though they are aimed at content distribution. In February 1998, ACM sponsored a research meeting: "Workshop on Java for High Performance Network Computing" (see http://www.cs.ucsb.edu/conferences/java98/program.html). The meeting program provides an argument that Java is, indeed, appropriate for the classic distributed programming problem domain.

THE LANGUAGE Java is an object-oriented programming language evolved from the syntax used in the C and C++ programming languages. It is beyond the scope of this book to provide a comprehensive description of Java (see [Arnold and Gosling, 1996] for a complete definition). However, here are some important aspects of the language in the context of distributed programming runtime systems. Source programs are defined by declaring classes (possibly using inheritance) that can be instantiated to create an object. Following the traditional Smalltalk paradigm, an object defines its own address space containing private methods and data structures. It also exports a public interface, defining methods that can be applied to the object. Other objects communicate with a target object by sending typed messages to the object, where the type corresponds to one of the methods on the target object's exported interface.

A Java applet can be loaded into a web browser where it executes (again, see Figure 18.8). The applet would be completely unacceptable if the mobile code behaved like a Trojan horse, for example, reading or writing information outside the applet. In languages such as C/C++, the executable code is allowed to use pointers to reference data structures. Further, any code can do pointer arithmetic, enabling an applet to generate pointer references to any address in the address space in which it executes. In the web browser context, this means that a C-style applet could read or write any variable in the process that runs the web browser. Java prevents this by excluding pointer data types. When an object is instantiated, it as assigned a referent to the data structure. The language does not allow a program to perform arithmetic operations to a referent; it can only be set by type-safe operations such as the new() function used to instantiate an object. There are several other aspects of Java that prevent applets from reading or writing information outside of the applet's assigned address space. Thus, one important aspect of the authorization mechanism for Java applets is in the language definition, enforced by the compiler and JVM.

THE JVM EXECUTION MODEL The JVM defines the runtime system for executing a Java program [Lindhom and Yellin, 1997]. Each platform that is to execute a Java program must have a JVM engine. Although in principle, the JVM could actually define the OS, in conventional technology it is implemented as a user space runtime system executing on top of some native OS (such as a version of UNIX or Windows).

When Java programs are compiled, they are translated from the high level source language into an intermediate execution language called the Java **bytecode** format. Bytecodes can be thought of as a machine language for an idealized target computer, which, of course, is the JVM. In the simplest case, when a Java class is to be instantiated and executed, the JVM interprets the bytecodes for the class to execute the object's methods. This is a very powerful model, since it allows Java code to run anywhere there is a JVM. That means that Java can be enabled to run in any computing environment that supports the JVM, which is a key aspect of Java as a distributed programming system.

Interpreted execution is widely used in three different situations that are relevant to our discussion: when the program might be generated or otherwise defined on-the-fly; when programs are to be executed on a variety of different computing platforms; or when the programs are small and are executed a small number of times between changes (or downloads). All of these situations usually apply to Java applets, so the designers went with the interpretation approach for common execution.

Compiled code usually can be made to run faster than interpreted code. This means that in some cases, the Java bytecode representation will cause a performance bottleneck. In these cases, the JVM can include a "just in time" (JIT) compiler that is able to translate the Java bytecode representation into the machine language of the computer on which the JVM is executing. Then the JVM has the option of either interpreting the bytecode representation or translating bytecodes into the native machine language and executing it. In the distributed programming environment, the JIT compiler option is very important: As the amount of execution of a remote object increases, it becomes critical for the object code execution to be as efficient as possible, and this can be done by JIT compiling the object.

THE Thread CLASS Java has several essential classes that provide functionality that is normally thought of as "being in the language." Thread support is one such class, so you can think of it as a runtime/library extension to Java functionality. A Java programmer can create a new thread by defining a subclass of the Thread base class and then by instantiating an object of the subclass. The thread has all the normal properties of user space threads: It shares code, but keeps its own context. Threads are multiplexed within the OS schedulable unit of computation (thread or process), although it would be possible to implement the base Thread class so that it used a kernel thread if the underlying operating system supported them.

Creating an object whose base class is Thread starts the thread, but it does not define the work for it. The Thread class has a function named run() that does not do any work. The subclass is expected to redefine the run() method with the code that the thread is intended to execute when the thread object receives the message "new MyThread(...).start()" (see Figure 18.9). Creating the thread object will not actually start it running; that must be done by sending the created object the start() message.

✦ FIGURE 18.9 Java Thread Class

MyThread is a class that inherits behavior from the built-in Thread class. The behavior of the new thread is defined by overriding the run() method in the Thread class.

```
public class MyThread extends Thread {
   public MyThread(...) {
      // The constructor
   }
   public void run() {
      // Insert the thread code here
   }
}
```

There are other ways to define the run() method in the thread, the essential idea being that you can create a multithreaded application by instantiating an object from a class that inherits from the Thread class. You can define the code that the new thread is to execute by providing a definition for the run() method in your thread class.

When the thread is running, it makes various calls to the runtime system. Any of these functions can contain a yield() call that will cause the OS thread to multiplex to another Java thread through the action of a scheduler in the Java runtime system. This is the same way that POSIX threads are scheduled when they are implemented as user threads. The Java runtime scheduler uses priority scheduling. When a thread object is created, it inherits the priority from its parent. The priority can be altered through other calls into the runtime system, although the default is that it uses the parent's priority.

Thread synchronization uses a monitor-like approach. Any method in a thread object can be marked as synchronized, meaning that only one thread at a time can execute a synchronized method in an object. The synchronized keyword can also be used to lock every method in a particular object while an arbitrary statement is executed. Finally, synchronized methods can also use wait() and notify() (or notifyAll()) much like condition variables. If a synchronized method is in execution and the method determines that it cannot proceed until some condition becomes true, then it calls wait(), releasing the lock on the method. Thus, multiple threads could block on a particular condition, each calling `wait()`. When some other thread causes the condition to change, it can call `notify()` to unlock the thread that has been waiting the longest, or `notifyAll()` to unlock all waiting threads.

REMOTE OBJECTS AND REMOTE METHOD INVOCATION The JVM can support remote objects, meaning that it is designed to allow the programmer to dynamically define remote objects and then to cause them to execute by issuing messages to them. In the context of a web browser, mobile code (objects) can be downloaded into a remote machine and then their methods can be invoked from the local machine—**remote method invocation (RMI)**.

Once the object has been loaded, say from a server to a client machine, the server needs to be able to invoke methods on the client object. Notice that in this situation, the original client and server may change roles (see Figure 18.10). The original server is now behaving like a client, since the original server now issues a service request message to the object in the original client. The model is still client-server computing, but once the target object has been loaded into the client machine, it begins to behave like a server object.

✦ FIGURE 18.10 Remote Objects—Servers Inside Clients

This figure illustrates how a server can (1) load an object into a remote client machine, and then (2) send it a service request with an RMI. The remote object responds to the RMI (3) with the requested result.

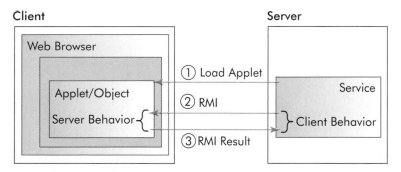

The remote object mechanism depends on the RMI mechanism, which serves many of the same purposes as conventional RPC. With RMI, the collective JVMs implement their own network protocol to enable the server JVM to invoke a method on an object in the client JVM. When an object is placed remotely, Java creates a client stub by which local objects can invoke methods on the remote objects.

Although it is not required, remote objects can behave even more like a server by advertising their existence. This is done by having the remote object register itself with a global registry (using each JVM's *rmiregistry* facility). If a remote object registers itself, then it is announcing that it is willing to act as a server for any object that wishes to send it messages.

RMI greatly simplifies many of the aspects of general remote objects and RPC by exploiting the fact that all the objects are written in the same language and they all have the same internal representation—Java bytecode. When an object is to be loaded into a client machine, there is no need to derive a correct binary representation of the object (its code and data) for the target machine, since all Java objects are represented in a standard format. Objects can simply be copied. This relies on the presence of a JVM at the remote machine to interpret the bytecode, which is part of the basic assumption for Java distribution. As a practical matter, here is where the web browser plays a critical role in implementing distributed programming: The web browser supplies the JVM in which remote objects can be executed.

SECURITY   There are two distinct aspects of security in Java: preventing applets from unauthenticated, unauthorized access of client machine resources and ensuring secure interaction between distributed Java objects (see Figure 18.11). Our study of security mechanisms (Chapter 14) addresses some components of this environment. For example, the OS prevents threads that execute in the process containing the web browser, JVM, and applet from unauthorized access of other system resources. The Java environment will provide security for the other mechanisms shown in the figure.

✦ FIGURE 18.11   Security in the Java Environment

Once an object has been authorized to be placed remotely (1), the security mechanism must prevent the object from unauthorized access of information in the host environment (2). It must also ensure that interactions between the remote object and the original server are secure (3).

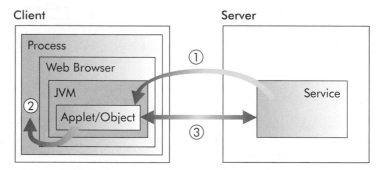

The first element of the security mechanism (number 1 in the figure) is to authenticate the source of the mobile code before it is loaded into the client machine. Considerable attention has been devoted to this problem in the commercial world. The general idea is that elements in the distributed environment are prepared to accept information from a remote location only if the information has been authenticated with a digital signature. The digital signature is an encrypted piece of information that assures the receiver that the sender is authenticated (see Section 14.4). Now, mobile code can be delivered with an associated certificate of authenticity, containing the service's digital signature. The client software can inspect the certificate and either accept or reject the mobile code based on the identity of the server that is attempting to load the mobile code.

A message digest is a refinement of the digital signature (see the discussion of Pretty Good Protection in Section 14.4). A message digest is a block of information (such as server authentication information) that has been encrypted and transformed into a relatively small, fixed sized block of information. (In PGP, the message digest is 128 bits long.) In the security context, it is common for a message digest to also be called a **hash** of the content. A message digest can be created from the applet and digitally signed, producing a robust certificate. This enables each applet to have a different digital signature—one that is dependent on the message content, yet which can be checked quickly.

Let's next consider the security mechanism that prevents the mobile code from unauthorized access of the information in the address space of the host process (access type 2 in Figure 18.11). In the discussion of language features, we observed that Java is designed as type-safe language that does not use pointers (and, thus, no pointer arithmetic). These language features are the primary mechanism for preventing a Java applet from referencing resources in its host environment when it executes as mobile code. The idea is that applets have to be written in Java (no C or assembly language allowed), meaning that the JVM/JIT compiler can always statically determine what resources an object is referencing. Popularly, this is called the "sandbox method," since it allows applets to do anything it wants to do, but they can only operate in a limited space (the sandbox).

The Java 1.2 Software Development Kit (SDK) allows distributed programmers to build more complex mechanisms, including a security manager. The security manager can define different security domains on the client machine and then use different protection policies according to the domain in which mobile code is to execute. In particular, the SDK enables code in some domains to compete for host system resources as if they were a separate process running in the host system.

Finally, consider access type 3 in Figure 18.11. This is the problem of transferring information among remote objects using an internet (even the public Internet). Here, Java uses the traditional encryption/decryption approach (with digital signatures and message digests) described in Section 14.4. There are core Java classes to support signatures, message digests, and key management.

THE ECMA-335 COMMON LANGUAGE INFRASTRUCTURE

Sun Microcomputers derived the Java approach to distributed programming. Sun intended for Java to be a portable programming environment that could convert a network of diverse workstations and servers into a logically homogeneous network of JVMs. Sun and Microsoft are commercial competitors. Microsoft decided to produce its own variant of a distributed runtime system: the Common Language Runtime system. Since CLR developers had the benefit of seeing the strengths and weaknesses of Java technology for five years prior to their design, it is natural that CLR provides new technology.

In 2000, Microsoft announced the .NET initiative. This initiative is said to focus on products that are essential to the evolution of internet-based distributed computing, ranging from support for mobile computing to support for evolving network languages and protocol (notably XML), to ways to build internet services and servers.

The CLR is a commercial product whose details are not disclosed to the public. The ECMA-335 standard defines the *Common Language Infrastructure* (*CLI*). The CLR conforms to this standard. In March 2002, Microsoft published a publicly available reference implementation of the CLI, called the *Shared Source CLI* (*SSCLI*, also known as *Rotor*) [Stutz, et al., 2004]. The SSCLI distribution includes C# and JScript compilers, as well as a base class library containing essential classes. The reference implementation runs on Windows XP, FreeBSD, and Mac OS X operating systems.

Languages that use the CLI are provided with comprehensive runtime support. Type safety is one such feature. Although the compiler handles all the static type checking, it can also generate runtime type checks, for example, to ensure that object load operations are the correct size. This will prevent the normal buffer overrun problem—the base technology used by a virus to penetrate a computing environment.

The individual languages that are supported by CLI may allow pointers and pointer arithmetic. However, pointers that extend beyond a component must refer to a symbol that is managed by the CLI when the referenced component is loaded. The environment does not allow an object in one component to point to an arbitrary location in another component. A component can only be "entered" through a designated program entry point. This provides type safety at the inter component reference level, supporting the use of components as mobile code.

The CLI assumes that all software is defined as classes (and executed as objects). The compiler translates each source program stored in a file into a *module* (contrasted with the relocatable object module output of a conventional compiler). A module contains one or more class definitions. The compiled code (called the *Common Intermediate Language—CIL*) is in a form suitable for processing by the CLI *virtual execution system* (*VES*). CIL is analogous to Java bytecode, meaning that it is not the native machine language for any specific hardware architecture, yet it is expected to be translated into native machine code prior to execution. It is assumed that CIL will always be compiled into native machine language (and never interpreted).

JVM is a runtime for a single language, so the virtual machine is built with an explicit understanding of the language semantics. There is only a limited ability for the compiler to pass the results of its static analyses to the runtime system. The CLI employs metadata to enable the compiler to pass a complete self-description of the types that are defined in the module to the runtime system. The module includes both the CIL and the metadata.

The principal advantage of using metadata is that the type checking system can combine static and dynamic techniques. When the CIL is *executed*, the VES has *all* of the type definition information available, so it can easily perform runtime type checking in the CLI.

Also by including the full type description, a module can be combined with modules written in a different source programming language, since the CLI will use the common type specifications incorporated in the metadata to implement member function invocation.

The translation environment combines modules to define an *assembly* (or a DLL that is treated much like an assembly). Within the collection of modules in an assembly, at least one of the modules must include a *manifest* to provide an overall description of the assembly (including the list of modules in the assembly). The assembly has a single main entry point in one of its modules, a set of exported type definitions (such as member functions), and a set of unbound external references to other assemblies.

An assembly is the unit of deployment managed by the CLI implementation. It defines:

■ The unit of code that will be downloaded to a machine.

■ A unit of management for security mechanisms.

■ A scope for type definitions and references (although an object in one assembly can invoke a member function in another assembly).

■ A unit of software that corresponds to a complete version of that software.

An assembly is a reusable software component that can be employed by itself or be combined with other components to implement a more complex unit of computation.

The CLI is started in an OS process when an assembly (or CLI compliant DLL) is loaded and executed. That is, a CLI compliant executable file contains information that directs the OS loader to invoke the CLI. This is accomplished by having the compiler generate code that is encountered immediately when the code in the file begins to execute; the code jumps to the entry point of the CLI, causing it to initialize itself and then to return to finish loading the file.

In all CLI implementations, an assembly is downloaded into an *application domain* abstract machine hosted by the VES. Normally, the CLI implementation expects that the external references from within an assembly will be bound into the public interface of another assembly that is to execute within the same application domain. Thus, an application domain defines a composite of assemblies that implements a particular end user functionality. Interestingly, cross assembly (intra application domain) member function calls can also be used, and they are also bound on demand as explained below. Each application domain defines an address space that is managed by the VES rather than the OS.

Application domains are loaded into CLI address spaces. Each address space provides explicit memory boundaries, usually according to the type of address space support provided by the underlying OS and hardware. For example, in Windows and UNIX implementations, the CLI address space is the same as the OS process address space.

Each address space can contain multiple application domains, each of which are assured of not interfering with other application domains. This is possible since all code that runs in an application domain is managed, type-safe code. The type safety assures that the address boundaries defined by the application domain will not be violated, so it is safe to run multiple application domains within a single address space. A CLI implementation also supports inter application domain (intra address space) communication. Of course, this requires that the CLI provide a loophole in the type checking mechanism, which is called *remoting*. Remoting can also be used to span address spaces; that is, it is used as the interface to the host OS IPC mechanism (and for RMI, as explained below).

The relationship among modules, assemblies, application domains, and address spaces is summarized in Figure 18.12. The unit created by the compiler is a module. Modules are combined to form a deployable unit called an assembly. Assemblies can operate singly or as a group within an application domain. Application domains execute in CLI address spaces (which normally execute in OS process address spaces).

VES: THE VIRTUAL EXECUTION SYSTEM When the compilation system creates an assembly, it stores it in a file. In order to deploy an assembly to a remote machine, its associated files will ultimately be copied to the target machine. An assembly can be installed using configuration directives, or when a class member in the assembly is referenced (see Figure 18.13). The installation process requires that the VES obtain a copy of the assembly from the assembly (local or remote) storage, check the authorization of the caller, confirm the validity of the assembly, and then bind the assembly into the application domain.

Once the assembly has been verified and loaded into the application domain, other executing code in the application domain can reference public members and fields in its classes. However, the elements of a class are not bound to the calling code until the cross

✦ **FIGURE 18.12**   Address Spaces, Application Domains, Assemblies, and Modules

Modules are created by the compiler. A collection of modules can be combined to form an assembly (the unit of deployment in the CLI). When an assembly is to be loaded and executed, it is bound into an application domain. Each application domain has its own address space. Multiple application domains can be executing in a single CLI address space (which normally corresponds to an OS process address space).

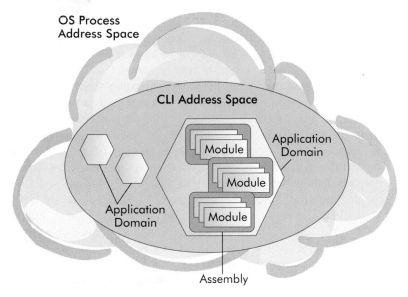

class reference is actually invoked. This causes another part of the VES to find the target class in the assemblies loaded into the application domain, verify access authorization, extract the details of the target class description from the metadata, and build an appropriate call table data structure—the "class information" in the figure.

On the first reference to a member in a class, its definition will be in the CIL form. Unlike JVM, CLI implementations always use a JIT compiler to translate the CIL into native code before it is executed (no code is interpreted in the CIL format). Subsequent references to the member will use the previously JIT compiled version of the member function rather than recompiling it.

The JIT compiler uses the metadata created by the source program compiler when it compiles the CIL. The metadata eliminates the need for function prototypes and interface description languages. Once the CIL code has been translated into native machine language by the JIT compiler, it can execute directly on the underlying OS and hardware platform. There are other features of the VES, notably a garbage collector and a structured exception handler, although our focus remains on the aspects of the CLI that relate explicitly to distributed programming.

MOBILE CODE   Assemblies can be stored locally in a specific application directory or in the machine's or user's assembly cache. Assemblies can also be stored on a server, meaning that applications executing on client machines can retrieve assemblies from the server. This means that the mobile code is "pulled" from the server by the client instead of being "pushed" into the client by the server (as is the case with applets).

✦ FIGURE 18.13 The Virtual Execution System (VES)

The VES is the heart of the CLI. It is responsible for managing the loading and binding of assemblies into application domains whenever a class in the assembly is referenced by native code execution.

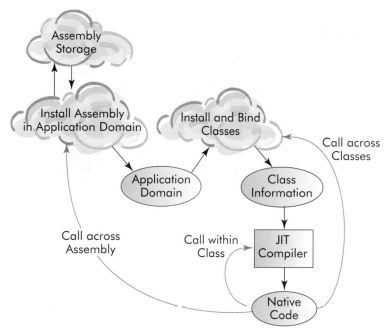

The first assembly in an application is loaded and executed when the application is started. Subsequent assemblies are not loaded until they are referenced. Upon first reference, the assembly loader invokes the downloader to locate the assembly name in the application directory, a subdirectory, a cache, or the URL of a file. The downloader then retrieves the assembly and passes it to the assembly loader so that its parts can be bound into the application domain.

REMOTE OBJECTS Remoting is the essential mechanism to support remote objects in the CLI. This facility allows an object in one CLI address space to invoke a member function in an object *in a distinct address space* (see Figure 18.14). The CLI implements remoting, with the help of the `MarshalByRefObject` base class from the class library. The idea is that a remotely accessible object is an instance of a subclass of `MarshalByRefObject` class. This creates the *Real Proxy* server stub for the remote object, registers it in a global name space, and prepares it for runtime linkage to support the RMI when a client chooses to invoke it. The `Channel` object must also be registered by the server

On the client side, the `Channel` must be registered with the CLI before it can be used. When the client references the remote object, the Transparent Proxy (client stub) is created to marshall the client side of the call. As with any form of RPC that potentially crosses machine boundaries, the client stub must serialize the RMI call so that the call itself and all its parameters (which can include call-by-value copies of objects) are translated into a network neutral format.

✦ FIGURE 18.14 Remoting

The CLI remoting mechanism allows an object to reference an object in a different application domain, so it is the fundamental mechanism to support RMI. The remoting mechanism contains a transparent proxy (equivalent to a client stub) and a real proxy (server stub). The two proxies communicate using a channel, which can be a TCP connection across machines.

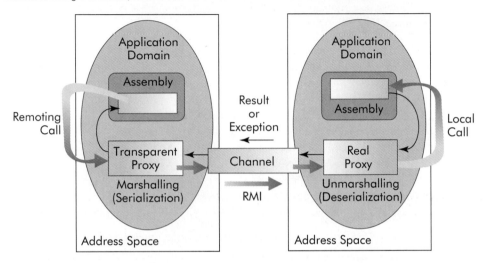

When the marshalled call arrives at the Real Proxy (server stub), it is deserialized (unmarshalled) and a local member function call is performed. If there are results or exceptions from the local call, the Real Proxy returns them to the calling object.

The CLI implements a comprehensive programming model for remoting; specifically, it supports various `Channel` protocols including TCP, HTML, and SMTP (see the online MSDN .NET Framework SDK QuickStart tutorial for Common Tasks—Remoting). This allows very general forms of interaction between the client and server, including the ability for a client object to invoke a remote object asynchronously, receiving results or exceptions with various IPC paradigms.

THREADS The CLI supports independent execution of different objects using the notion of a CLI thread (not to be confused with an OS-level thread). The CLI incorporates its own *threadpool*—a collection of objects, each of which can behave as an independent unit of computation. A CLI thread can execute according to its own synchronization paradigm, blocking and running according to conditions that exist among a set of active objects. As is the case with all thread-based systems, this allows programmers to assign asynchronous tasks to independent threads without having to explicitly poll conditions from a single thread of execution.

CLI threads are similar to JVM threads. The `System.Threading` namespace provides a `ThreadPool` class by which a programmer can instantiate a thread object as needed. The new thread inherits behavior from the `System.Threading.Thread` namespace, and is provided with application code to be executed. Once the thread object has been defined, it is started by invoking its `Start()` member function.

Threads have various public members for synchronization: `Interrupt()`, `Join()`, `Resume()`, `Sleep()`, `SpinWait()`, `Suspend()`, and `Wait()`. These members can be used to control the thread's state: `Running`, `WaitSleepJoin`, `SuspendRequested`, `Suspended`, `AbortRequested`, `Stopped`, and `Background`. CLI threads are unique in that they can be in multiple states at one time; for example, a thread could be in `Background` state and `Running`, `Suspended` and `AbortRequested`, and so on. The CLI implementation determines whether the CLI threads are mapped to kernel threads. (In the SSCLI, threads are mapped to kernel threads in Windows XP, but are mapped to POSIX user threads in FreeBSD.)

SECURITY The .NET framework provides cryptographic tools in its class library, and authentication and authorization mechanisms within the CLI. An assembly is an executable agent that must be authenticated to determine its origin, and to ensure that its execution in a given computing environment is authorized both by the assembly and computing environment "owners." The CLI uses *evidence-based* authentication and authorization, meaning the assemblies are only executed in the presence of evidence that the developer has authorized the use of the assembly and that the computing environment has the authority to use the assembly.

Assemblies can have simple names or strong names. A simple name is a text name similar to filenames used in other computing environments (for example, `autoexec.bat`, `cmd.com`, `testprogram.exe`, or `myfile`). A *strong name* is a four-component name:

- *Name.* A simple (text) name to identify the assembly to the OS file manager.
- *Version.* This is a four-part number to identify a version of the assembly. The parts are the major number, the minor number, the build number, and the revision number.
- *CultureInfo.* This part of the name identifies the spoken language and country code for the assembly. For example, "en-US" is the CultureInfo for English in the United States.
- *PublicKey.* This is either an 8-byte public key token or a 128-byte public key (message digest) that uniquely identifies the assembly developer.

There are several interesting aspects of this complex name. First, assembly names come from a huge name space. Within this name space, there is a substantial name space available to each developer. A fully qualified name is almost assuredly unique.

Second, the version field highlights the fact that assemblies may exist in a network in various versions. This is used to address a severe problem in distributed systems (and systems with many different components): Once a piece of shared software is made accessible via a dynamic binding mechanism, how can a designer be sure that it is no longer needed when a new version of the same software is released? In the Microsoft software world, this problem is known by the graphic description "DLL hell" [Richter, 2002]. RPC packages have used version numbers since their early days; each client that intends to use a remote procedure must identify it by name and version. The CLI is designed to distinguish among assembly versions and even to allow multiple versions of an assembly to be loaded into a machine at the same time (this is called *side-by-side* execution).

The third component, the CultureInfo field, is self-explanatory; it is encouraging to see internationalization/localization incorporated into CLI at such a basic level.

Fourth, the PublicKey field disambiguates the rest of the name, effectively providing each developer (or development organization) with its unique name space. Perhaps more importantly, the PublicKey is used to ensure that the assembly has not been tampered with after it was developed. When the assembly is prepared for deployment, a message digest of its contents is prepared. The message digest is a hash of all the contents of the assembly that have been encrypted with the developer's private key. If a recipient recomputes the hash, it can then use the public key to decrypt the message digest. If the decrypted value and the computed hash do not exactly match, then the assembly is different from the one that the developer deployed. This is the essential element by which a recipient can authenticate the source of the assembly.

Whenever an assembly is loaded into an execution environment, the evidence-based policy manager checks the authentication and authorization. As described in the previous paragraph, the first step is to authenticate the source of the assembly, ensuring that the assembly is the same one that the original developer created. The policy manager can then begin to extract encrypted evidence from the assembly's message digest. The message digest provides evidence relating to the source from which the assembly was obtained (the *deployment policy*), and a description of how the assembly wishes to use the computing environment's resources (the *assembly resource access*). The policy manager will next obtain the machine's *host policy* (defined by the system administrator). The policy manager can then check the authorization rights of the deployment system and host system to determine if the assembly can be executed in the given host environment.

18.6 ● Summary

The major strides in distributed programming support have traditionally been made by distributed application programmers, first as high performance distributed applications and then as content distribution applications. In the classic high performance application domain, *ad hoc* methods were first used to construct effective application code. In the 1990s, the pressure to produce adequate support for this problem domain led to the development of various kinds of middleware—libraries and runtime systems—that executed in user space (rather than being a part of the OS kernel). The PVM/MPI effort was extremely successful and still serves as an important component in Beowulf clusters. The OSF DCE provides the most comprehensive set of facilities to support high performance distributed computing.

The popularity of the public Internet, particularly the World Wide Web interface to the Internet, made distributed computing available to the public masses. The basic distribution model used in the Web is a client-server model in which web browsers use HTTP to request that files be copied from a content server to a client machine. This created the need for a distributed programming environment well-suited to content distribution. The underlying technical components for content distribution are essentially the same as for high performance computing, although implementations may be tuned better for one domain than the other. This caused a new kind of runtime environment to evolve, one especially suited for content distribution. Java defined a new model for distributed computing that relied heavily on mobile code. The CLR extends the Java mobile code functionality to provide a technology update, including secure multilanguage platforms for implementing distributed applications.

18.7 • EXERCISES

1. Does the SOR program in Section 18.2 use data or function partitioning?

2. Chaotic relaxation is a variant of SOR where the n worker processes do not bother to synchronize with one another after computing their new estimate of $x[i]$. How would the code shown in Section 18.2 change to implement chaotic relaxation?

3. Based on the description in the chapter, what are the differences between Sun RPC and DCE RPC?

4. How does the notion of a token simplify file consistency in the DCE distributed file system?

5. What is the purpose of a web proxy?

6. What prevents a Java applet from "stealing" information from the client machine?

7. What is a managed component in CLR?

8. Using PVM or DCE, implement the SOR program.

9. Using PVM or DCE, implement the quadrature program from Chapter 9.

CHAPTER 19

Design Strategies

In previous chapters, we have considered the details of individual parts of the operating system: process and resource management, device management, memory management, and file management. Chapters 15 through 18 described how processes and resources can be abstracted to work with networks of computers. The intent of this chapter is to revisit the overall system design (first introduced in Chapter 3) now that we have studied all the pieces.

An OS is a large collection of software, so designing and building the OS necessarily involves conventional software engineering methodologies. However, because of the performance constraints on OS behavior, and because of the complex input/output relationship of the OS, developers tend to design the operating system under different criteria than those used for other large software systems. Besides looking at how the OS is assembled from the individual technologies, we will explain how these other considerations have influenced generations of designers and implementers.

19.1 • DESIGN CONSIDERATIONS

Operating systems define and manage the computing environment in which application programs are executed. Part of this requirement is managing the shared resources, and the other part is providing software abstractions that are easy for application programmers to use. Throughout the previous chapters, you have learned about functionality of the OS. Designing a high performance implementation of this diverse set of functions into a single logical enterprise is usually an exercise in compromise. There are many constraints and requirements to moderate our choice of function. Let's first reconsider the critical design considerations introduced earlier in the book and that you have learned as computer programmers; then we will look at a spectrum of OS implementation strategies and case studies.

PERFORMANCE, PERFORMANCE, PERFORMANCE

There is an old story that in choosing real estate, the three most important criteria are location, location, and location. This means that location is by far the most dominating aspect in determining the value of real estate. We could adapt this saying to operating system design by saying that the three most important criteria are performance, performance, and performance. Despite the ever-increasing speed of CPUs and buses, and the declining cost of primary memory, the OS is still an overhead activity that the end user only tolerates rather than views as a desirable feature. The worse its performance, the more intrusive it becomes in trying to accomplish relevant work on the computer. We have seen various cases where OS designers have struggled to find algorithms that have modest computational complexity (for example, in scheduling). Although we have not always emphasized this fact in our previous discussion, the OS code that is chosen to implement OS functions often trades off desirable features for performance. For example, low level file systems do not support structured records, mostly because they are costly in performance.

Another place where you will see performance trade-offs is in the style used to write the code. If you read the Linux kernel source code, you will be surprised at the frequency of use of labels and `goto` statements. This was done to save every machine cycle execution possible when running the OS code. Although this results in faster executing code, it means that the source code itself is difficult to write, difficult to read, and even more difficult to modify.

In the last decade, there has been a significant evolution of programming technique. Smalltalk established the viability of object-oriented programming, and C++ popularized the idea that people could write nontrivial application programs with the technology. Java developers recognized the power of C++, but were concerned about its liberal use of pointers; thus, their language can be thought of as a version of C++ that eliminates the use of pointers wherever it is possible in order to create a programming environment in which safer code can be built.

Today's dominant operating systems are still implemented in C, but not C++, not Java, and not any other language that addresses contemporary software engineering concerns. Why is this? It is the requirement for the absolute fastest execution possible of trusted software. (Interestingly, operating systems do not typically include very much assembly language, even though it can be written to execute faster than C code. This follows because it is very difficult to write trusted assembly language code that will execute faster than code written in C. OS implementers write more than 95 percent of the kernel in C with the remaining few percent written in assembly language.)

Object-oriented languages are well accepted at the application level, partly based on arguments of reuse and maintainability. C++ programs do not necessarily execute more slowly than C programs (since after all, most C++ compilers are really C compilers with a C preprocessor). However, there is an execution inefficiency introduced by this translation; C++ functions are indirectly referenced via a function call table (necessary to implement virtual functions). This is viewed as unacceptable to most OS implementers.

At least as significant is the implicit performance cost of designing software as classes and subclasses. Since an object hides its implementation behind a public interface, even simple operations such as retrieving a value from the object involve a function call—an expensive operation compared to a memory reference. The programming value of abstraction is usually viewed as too expensive for OS implementation.

Since Java was introduced, there has been a camp of researchers interested in implementing the JVM as an OS. Although developers have implemented such operating systems, none of them have been commercially successful. This is due in part to their poor performance. Instead, the JVM is ported to run on various native operating systems.

TRUSTED SOFTWARE

In Chapter 14, we considered the broad aspects of protection and security. There, we divided the issues into ones related to authentication, authorization, and cryptography. In operating systems, a particular form of security (related to authorization) is paramount. As we have seen, the kernel is defined as the body of code that executes in supervisor mode—it is the only software capable of executing privileged instructions. The essential authorization mechanisms are intended to prevent unauthorized execution of kernel code (or the execution of nonkernel code while the CPU is in supervisor mode). The trap instruction and the interrupt mechanism are the implicit authorization mechanisms. The idea is that no thread can cause any code to execute with the supervisor mode set unless it traps into previously defined kernel code. No external event can cause the computer to execute in supervisor mode unless it causes an interrupt. Interrupts and trap design are the basic mechanisms for ensuring that the CPU only executes trusted OS code when it is in supervisor mode.

A second aspect of kernel design is to decide exactly which code should execute in the kernel and which code should not. Early UNIX kernels were built to incorporate a minimum of functionality under the premise that normal OS functionality would be added to the kernel functionality as it was needed. The kernel would have only the logical minimum of code necessary to ensure correct operation. Over the years, UNIX kernels grew at an uncontrollable rate; contemporary UNIX kernels have much more than the minimum functionality.

This has periodically led OS designers to evolve back to minimal kernels. Designers have turned to microkernel designs in an effort to implement only the essential code in the part of the OS that executes in supervisor mode (see Section 19.4). Today, there is a return to this "small is beautiful" approach, partly encouraged by the need for minimalist operating systems to operate in tiny mobile computers.

The end requirement here is simple: The core of the OS should run in supervisor mode. That core should be as small as possible, and it should implement only the functionality that is necessary to assure the correct operation of the entire OS.

MODULARIZATION

As software engineering began to emerge as a computer science discipline, software modularization was a leading issue. Parnas wrote a seminal paper on the criteria for modularizing software that essentially launched the idea of software modules [Parnas, 1972]. The fundamental arguments behind this modularization are that software should be designed using a "divide and conquer" technique. Also, each unit—a module—should be designed so that it can be reimplemented without affecting other modules. That is, the modules only interact using well-defined, fixed, public interfaces. Roughly speaking, the criteria for partitioning typically would be to encapsulate data and function in a module so that inter module references would be minimized.

The task of determining the correct internal operation of a module is related to the size of the module: Large modules are much more difficult to prove correct and to maintain, while small modules are easier to design and maintain on the basis of correctness. Since modules communicate only through the exported interfaces, the form and style of inter module communication is related to the complexity of the interface. As the number of individual interfaces on the module increases, the task of determining the correct external operation of the module increases. At the same time, the module potentially becomes more complex to use. However, a smaller number of interface components restricts the style and efficiency by which two internal parts of different modules are able to communicate. Suppose the module interface is implemented with procedure calls. When component R in module A wants to know the value of a variable X in module B, it cannot just read X as it would a local variable. Instead, R must call S on B's interface to request B to read X and return its value to R.

The job of any software designer is to consider how to design modules to implement functions so that they satisfy maintainability/correctness requirements as well as per-formance requirements. An OS is a logical collection of software modules. Each module encapsulates information that it uses to fulfill its task and exports an interface for other modules to use to obtain services from the module. In practice, an OS will be designed primarily with one of four approaches (see Figure 19.1): monolithic design (a single mod-ule), modularized design, extensible design, or a layered design. Most operating systems adopt one of these styles, although they often use elements of the other styles within the general framework. Let's look more carefully at the practical considerations in choosing a modularization approach.

Traditionally, the heart of the OS is its process and resource management functions. Devices and memory are specific instances of resources to be managed by the OS, and files are an abstraction of storage devices. OS technology has evolved around the four tasks of process and resource management, device management, memory management, and file management (see Figure 19.2). The discussion of OS topics in this book has reflected this modularization. However, the performance and security considerations for implementing the OS may not conform to this idealized functional organization.

A significant design problem for operating systems is how to implement the logical managers in comprehensive, trusted, efficient software. For example, while it is useful to discuss the theory of operation of the virtual memory system as an isolated topic, the device manager must influence the page replacement policy if it is performing I/O on a page. Similarly, the scheduler interacts with the device manager and the memory manager, the file manager depends on the device manager, and so on. Figure 19.3 summarizes the functions described in previous chapters and illustrates some of the interactions and rela-tionships among these functions. In the figure, the file, device, memory, and resource managers are explicit. Note that the process manager functionality is further subdivided into a core process manager, scheduler, IPC, and synchronization modules. Protection, deadlock, and interrupt handlers are distributed across different modules according to the system design.

The challenge in designing a modern OS (for an individual uniprocessor) is to decide how the software should be organized so as to implement these functions according to some set of external requirements. Modular design principles suggest that the functions

✦ FIGURE 19.1 Software Organization

The four software modularization approaches shown in this figure have all been used to implement different operating systems. Monolithic designs (a) use a single module. Modular designs (b) divide the OS functions and implement them in different modules. The extensible nucleus design (c) provides a skeletal nucleus that supports the implementation of the core nucleus functions. The layered design (d) is a modular design in which there is a total order among the modules.

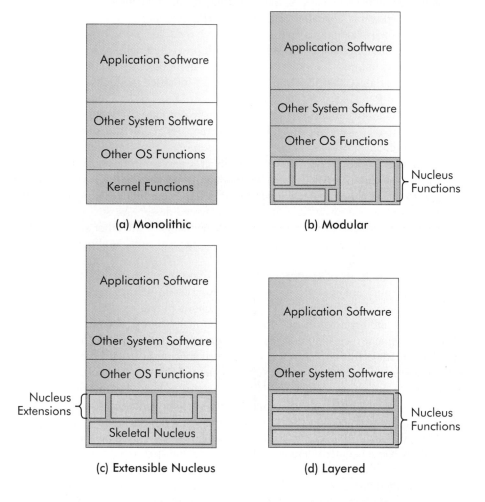

(a) Monolithic

(b) Modular

(c) Extensible Nucleus

(d) Layered

should be packaged in order to minimize interactions among the modules. Principles of correctness suggest that the overall functionality should be partitioned so that any module is not too complex. The basic problem of OS organization is to define modules that meet the principles of not only correctness but also performance, maintainability, and flexibility. Designers do not agree on how this is best achieved, since the detailed design issues may dramatically influence the modularization strategy. For example, a prevention strategy to deadlock is implemented entirely within the set of all resource managers, but a detection and recovery strategy interacts with the core process manager, memory manager, and so on.

✦ **FIGURE 19.2** OS Function Organization

This figure illustrates the logical modularization of OS function a modularization that is rarely (if ever) used in the OS software design.

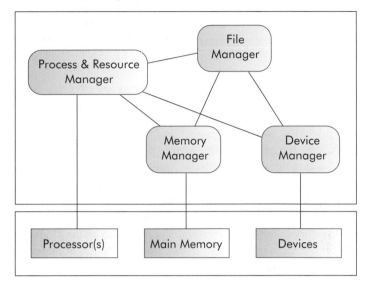

✦ **FIGURE 19.3** Function Interactions

The logical modularization is too inefficient to implement as OS modules. This figure shows several of the interactions among the logical modules from Figure 19.2.

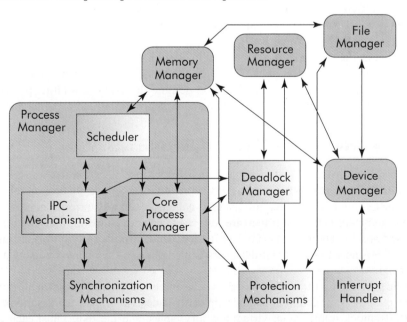

PORTABILITY

Traditionally, OS portability has not been a driving issue, although it was part of the original motivation for creating the "small is beautiful" UNIX kernel. Modern operating systems are often implemented on a variety of different computer platforms. Portability is of growing concern to OS designers. Microsoft introduced a technique in the Windows NT/2000/XP OS that is increasingly being used in other operating systems and large software packages: the **hardware abstraction layer** (**HAL**) [Solomon and Russinovich, 2000]. The HAL is a low-level software module that translates critical hardware behaviors into a standardized set of behaviors. The HAL functions are exported through a kernel-mode DLL. The OS calls functions in this DLL when it needs to determine the way the host hardware behaves. This allows the Windows NT/2000/XP code to call a HAL function (rather than just using a hardwired address) everywhere a hardware-specific address is needed. For example, device interrupts usually have addresses determined by the microprocessor architecture, and they differ from one microprocessor to another. The HAL interface allows Windows NT/2000/XP to reference the interrupt addresses via functions rather than by using the hardware addresses directly.

The HAL implementation for any specific microprocessor provides the appropriate hardware-specific information via the corresponding function on the HAL API. This means that it is possible to use the same OS source code on a Digital Equipment Alpha processor as is used on an Intel Pentium processor. It also means that it is possible to create device drivers for Windows 2000 that will also work without change in Windows 95/98.

The use of the HAL is transparent above the OS interface. Application programmers are generally unconcerned with the type of processor chip in the computer. Windows NT/2000/XP provides a fixed set of services independent of the hardware platform type.

The HAL introduces a layer of indirection between the OS and the hardware. This means that there is a clear performance penalty for using it. However, it is possible to port the OS to a different OS with much less effort than if there were no HAL. The Windows designers decided that benefits of the HAL offset the performance penalty for its use.

In Linux, this kind of portability is manually implemented through source code organization. That is, the source code is organized in directories that are architecture-dependent and architecture-independent. The Linux approach is much less structured than the Windows HAL, even though it allows the OS designer to implement larger pieces of the OS as machine-dependent (and fast) code without incorporating indirect function calls.

19.2 ● MONOLITHIC KERNELS

In a **monolithic kernel**, all software and data structures are placed in one logical module, with no explicit interfaces between any parts of the OS software (see Figure 19.1(a)). Monolithic OS organizations require the least amount of analysis prior to implementation and they can be very efficient if they are well implemented. However, they are difficult to understand and maintain and, hence, it is difficult to determine if they work as intended. Let's consider the arguments that designers contemplate as they consider using a monolithic design.

Classic program partitioning is based on data structures. The OS data structures include resource queues, process and thread descriptors, file descriptors, device descriptors, semaphores, deadlock information, virtual memory tables, and the like. Thus, each concept discussed so far requires some form of data structure to track the state of the system. The OS must keep the cumulative data structures in a safe place so that it can implement its algorithms on correct status information.

Partitioning the OS on the basis of the use of data structures can be very difficult. For example, it is tempting to encapsulate scheduling information in a module that allocates the CPU to waiting jobs. However, the scheduler will also need to know the swapping state of a process before it can make an intelligent scheduling decision. Similarly, the swapper must know about pending I/O operations involving memory buffers before it can decide to swap out a process. While a designer can find partitions that minimize the amount of inter partition communication, the minimum may be unacceptable. For example, a partitioned OS might be too inefficient for hardware with limited computing or information transfer bandwidth. The performance factor overwhelms the software engineering design aspects of the solution in this approach. The UNIX kernels are the most prominent examples of a monolithic kernel organization, possibly with the exception of MS-DOS.

MS-DOS

MS-DOS was a monolithic kernel (although it did not use supervisor mode in the CPU) that supported a single task. The basic OS kernel was wholly implemented in the read-only memory (ROM) resident Basic Input/Output System (BIOS) routines and two executable files named IO.SYS and MSDOS.SYS [Chappell, 1994]. When a computer was booted up to run MS-DOS, the CMOS memory and processor were queried to obtain various parameters for running it. Next, a 512-byte bootstrap loader was retrieved from the startup disk and then executed to begin loading IO.SYS. After loading the first few sectors in IO.SYS, the bootstrap loader jumped to IO.SYS to finish the loading process. IO.SYS subsequently loaded MSDOS.SYS and then read the user-defined CONFIG.SYS and AUTOEXEC.BAT to determine if OS extensions, called *drivers*, should be added to the kernel.

These drivers could range from loadable device drivers of the type described in Chapter 5 to memory management extensions (for example, see HIMEM.SYS). Perhaps the most interesting of these device drivers was one named EMM386.EXE: The original Intel 8086 CPU did not have a mode bit, but the 80386 did. This particular driver constructed a supervisor mode environment in which the rest of DOS executed as a single user-mode task, thus allowing supervisor mode tasks to be executed separately from the ordinary DOS task.

The UNIX Kernel

UNIX was introduced to the public by Ritchie and Thompson at the 1973 ACM SIGOPS conference, with the conference paper appearing in the Communication of the ACM the next year [1974]. The software for the version that Ritchie and Thompson introduced was not generally available to anyone outside AT&T Bell Laboratories, although the design was publicly disclosed in the paper. The OS was the hit of the conference. The other operating systems that were being discussed were very large, complex systems used to manage large mainframe computers. By contrast, UNIX was a small OS intended to manage a tiny laboratory minicomputer.

OS researchers were very excited about the revolutionary approach of UNIX, and they clamored to get a copy of the source code for their own experimentation. Over time, AT&T created a license for the software that allowed universities and research labs to buy a source license and then to use the source code as the basis for OS and other experimentation.

At the time UNIX was disclosed to the public, IBM's OS/360 operating system was the dominant commercial OS. Customers were unhappy about the number of bugs in released versions of the OS, and IBM was working hard to produce a robust version. In 1975, one of its primary architects (perhaps *the* primary architect) wrote a widely read set of essays explaining why it was so difficult to create and manage OS/360. The problem essentially came down to the complexity of OS/360 [Brooks, 1975]. Many researchers recognized the value of the small, monolithic kernel approach used in UNIX—a strong contrast to OS/360 and other dominant operating systems. The paper by Ritchie and Thompson, in conjunction with experiences such as that reported by Brooks, established the viability and acceptability of building the kernel as a small, monolithic unit of software.

The trend in the early UNIX systems was to identify the parts of the OS that were critical to its correct and efficient operation, and then to implement *only* that functionality in the kernel. The idea was that the kernel should be able to provide a platform on which other OS services could be added as user applications. For example, the kernel should implement a byte stream file system, and if user applications needed record-oriented files, then the record implementation should be executed with library code on top of the byte stream file mechanism. The kernel was to be the minimum OS functionality, with the understanding that user space code would be added to support the particular application domain in which the computer would operate. In this sense, the designers might have argued that the OS design was really a layered rather than a monolithic design, since domain-specific OS functionality would be added as layers to the kernel.

Many detailed aspects of the Linux kernel have been presented as examples throughout the book. The Linux kernel implementation is typical of a monolithic UNIX kernel. Here are some reminders of concepts that you saw as examples in earlier chapters:

■ The traditional UNIX kernel is implemented as a single logical module. The kernel exports a single system call interface that is defined in the trap table. User space software invokes one of the kernel functions by trapping via the trap table.

■ A process descriptor data structure is created whenever a process or thread is created (the thread is generally a process that uses the same address space and resources as its parent). The process descriptor fields may be read and modified by any part of the kernel. For example, the virtual memory management code updates the process descriptor fields associated with the process's address space and memory allocation.

■ The file descriptor is the inode. An inode is kept on the secondary memory device with the file. Whenever the file is opened, the file manager retrieves the inode and loads into an in-memory inode table. Since UNIX tries hard to buffer file information, the memory manager, device manager, and file manager all manipulate various aspects of the process descriptor and inode.

■ The device manager is implemented as a kernel infrastructure that passes requests to device drivers, and provides the device driver with various services (such as dynamic memory allocation and buffering).

Additional aspects of the Linux monolithic kernel are described in Chapter 20.

19.3 ● MODULAR ORGANIZATION

A **modular kernel** is one in which the functionality is partitioned among logically independent components with well-defined interfaces among the related modules. In contrast to monolithic designs, a modular OS is implemented with distinct program modules and/or processes (see Figure 19.1(b)). Here, the engineering trade-off of function encapsulation versus performance swings toward functional encapsulation. As with all such software architectures, the modular nucleus is considerably easier to maintain and modify than is the software in the monolithic approach. Data abstraction allows modules to hide implementations of data structures so they can be modified without changing the interface. The cost of modularization, compared to monolithic implementations, is potential performance degradation. Hence, the challenge is to design an organization that provides an acceptable compromise between performance and modularity requirements. A side benefit of modularization is that the system can be implemented as abstract data types or objects.

There are no leading-edge commercial operating systems that use a pure modular organization, although one could argue that the extensible nucleus is a special case of the modular organization (discussed next). An excellent example of a research OS using a pure modular approach is the object-oriented Choices operating system.

Choices: An Object-oriented OS

Choices is an experimental research OS built with an object-oriented language and design. The goals of the Choices system include being able to experiment with various approaches through rapid prototyping and to easily port the base design to new hardware. Choices demonstrates how object-oriented technology can be used in OS design and implementation. This box explains how Choices uses type hierarchies in its design environment.

FRAMEWORKS

Choices makes heavy use of object frameworks to define the basic structure of the OS. It then uses type hierarchies to specify particular characteristics for the prototyping testbed and for any particular hardware target. The framework explicitly identifies the modules in the OS as a set of base classes and then establishes generic interactions and relations among the base classes. When Choices is to be implemented on a new hardware platform, the module functions, interfaces, and interactions are already defined. The implementation of a module is inherited from the base class and then refined to define the implementation for the target hardware.

In Choices, objects model the application interface, resources, mechanisms, policies, and hardware interface. All applications are expected to be object-oriented programs that manipulate other objects and use inheritance and polymorphism to define their behavior. Computational units are *kernel objects* with a related `ObjectProxy` executing in user space. An OS "call" occurs when an object of type `ObjectProxy` sends a message to the corresponding kernel object.

The structure of the OS is captured in the framework hierarchy. A framework describes a set of subframeworks used as base classes for the parts of the OS. The base framework creates a generalized environment in which Choices' processes, address spaces, and memory objects execute as objects of type `Process`, `Domain`, and `MemoryObject`, respectively. Subframeworks describe how the memory manager, the process manager, the file manager, and the message-passing system interoperate to support processes, address spaces, and memory objects.

USING A FRAMEWORK FOR THE MEMORY MANAGER

For example, Figure 19.4, inspired by a similar figure in Campbell et al. [1993], illustrates the abstract control flow diagram for the memory manager; the numbers represent the sequence of messages. The rectangles represent the main components of the memory manager, and the arrows represent the control flow among them. Alternative diagrams represent data flow, synchronization, and other relationships that exist among the components

✦ **FIGURE 19.4** The Choices Memory Manager Subframework

This diagram illustrates the way the Choices designers used frameworks to design the OS. This (sub)framework describes the relationship among design components. Each component can then be refined for any specific implementation.

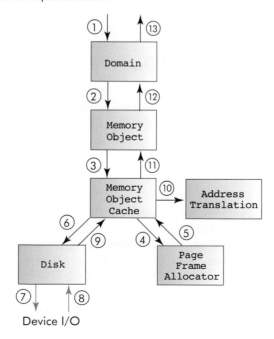

as required. The memory manager subframework inherits the `Domain` and `MemoryObject` components from the base framework. However, their behavior, in terms of control flow, is elaborated in the subframework. A `MemoryObject` is an encapsulation of pages inside an object. A process operates in a `Domain` object in the process's address space. The `Domain` translates the references into a `MemoryObject` reference, which is passed to the `Memory Object Cache`. `Memory Object Cache` then copies the relevant pages from secondary storage into primary memory. The details of the caching operation control flow are for the `Memory Object Cache` to interact with the `Page Frame Allocator` to adjust the amount of primary memory allocated to the process if required. Once the primary memory allocation has been adjusted, the `Memory Object Cache` directs the `Disk` object to read its disk. The `Disk` object is an interface to the disk hardware that encapsulates the device driver and interrupt. When the `MemoryObject` has been cached, the `Address Translation` component of the framework adjusts the page table. Hence, the `Address Translation` component is an object wrapper for the memory management hardware on the target computer.

The subframework is used as the basis of an actual implementation of the Choices memory manager in the prototyping testbed—called *Virtual Choices*—or on target hardware. The Virtual Choices facility is used to develop, modify, and test the design in a simulator environment. Figure 19.5, also inspired by a similar figure in Campbell et al. [1993], shows the Sun SparcStation implementation of the Choices memory manager. Every component in the generic subframework and in the Virtual Choices implementation

✦ **FIGURE 19.5** The Choices SparcStation Memory Manager

This figure is an instance of the subframework for the memory manager shown in Figure 19.4. It implements the memory manager on a SparcStation.

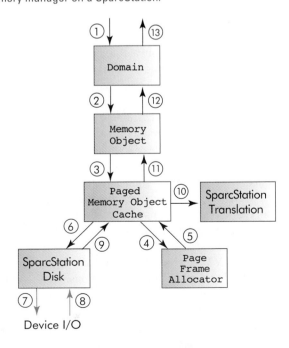

has a component in the inherited implementation. Although the SparcStation component implementations will differ from the generic implementations, the control flow will be the same. In Choices, the arrows in the control flow diagram can also represent hierarchical relationships. For example, the generic diagram can be annotated with virtual function names to be provided by the derived classes in the implementation.

CONCLUSION

Work on Choices began in 1987, and its design then evolved through several different concrete implementations. Designers are often concerned about the performance of object-oriented implementations due to the tendency for C++ implementations to proliferate small functions. In 1993, the Choices designers argued that the performance for system call, context switching, and message passing were all competitive, although still not as fast as the fastest operating systems on the same hardware.

Choices remains a research OS; it has no commercial counterpart. As object-oriented technologies continue to grow in commercial importance, the experience from Choices will help to guide operating systems designs that use the technology. For comparison, read Chapter 21 to see how Windows NT/2000/XP uses objects.

19.4 ● EXTENSIBLE NUCLEUS, OR MICROKERNEL, ORGANIZATION

The **extensible nucleus** organization is a specialized modular organization intended to implement real-time systems, timesharing systems, and the like, by using a common set of skeletal facilities (Figure 19.1(c)). The approach is to define two types of modules for any particular OS: policy-specific modules and the skeletal policy-independent modules. The policy-independent modules implement the extensible nucleus, or **microkernel**. It is not intended to provide complete OS functionality. Rather, it is supposed to create a trusted framework in which policy-specific operating systems can be defined to meet the needs of an application domain. This framework is a general-purpose foundation for policy-specific parts of the architecture.

The philosophy behind this approach is that the OS can be implemented in two parts: (1) a mechanism-dependent, hardware-dependent part and (2) a policy-dependent, hardware-independent part. The first part provides a low-level virtual machine with some form of memory and process management, usually with only the bare essentials for device management. The second part reflects the requirements of the specific OS.

This architecture supports two new directions in operating systems. It allows policy-dependent variants of an OS to be built on a single hardware platform, as shown in Figure 19.6(a). The RC 4000 nucleus was the first OS to make the architecture work in a commercial environment [Brinch Hansen, 1973]. This was followed by the tremendous commercial success of the IBM VM system. Both of these systems were driven by the requirement to support multiple OS policy implementations. Neither nucleus is capable of performing the functions expected of an OS by itself. However, both establish a virtual machine interface used to implement policy-specific extensions that complement the nucleus and form a full operating system.

✦ FIGURE 19.6 Using an Extensible Nucleus

An extensible nucleus can be used to support multiple policies (or multiple operating systems) as shown in part (a). It is also useful for supporting portable operating systems as suggested by part (b).

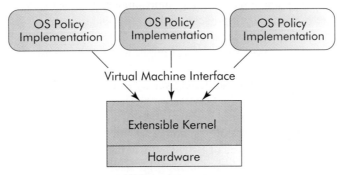

(a) Multiple-Policy Organization

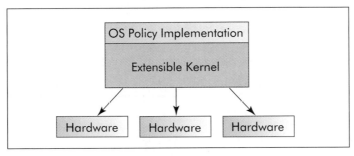

(b) Portable OS Organization

The microkernel operating systems, such as Mach (see the example in the box) and CHORUS (see Section 19.6) are logically equivalent to the extensible nucleus strategies used in the RC 4000 and VM. However, the details of the approach differ from those of these earlier systems. The microkernel provides skeletal, policy-independent functions that are extended with specialized servers to implement a policy. For example, both Mach and CHORUS have a UNIX server that works with the microkernel to implement the UNIX system call interface. In addition, this architecture allows a specific policy-dependent part of the OS to be portable (see Figure 19.6(b)). The IBM VM system was used in this way to allow any OS version to be used with any hardware platform within a broad family of products.

The Mach Operating System

A fundamental motivation for the Mach OS design was to investigate OS organizations that support efficient message-passing [Accetta et al., 1986]. The emphasis on message-passing could have substantial payoff in hardware environments that do not support shared memory, since IPC would ultimately have to use some form of messages. Thus, an explicit related motivation for Mach was to support communities of processes in a multiprocessor environment in which communication might be possible only by using messages. Other goals for Mach include investigating new virtual memory designs having large, sparse address spaces and experimenting with new computational models that are better suited to fine-grained shared-memory multiprocessors than are the classic processes. Others are to exploit capabilities to support more secure communication and network transparency, as explained above, and to explore the practical implications of implementing systems with an extensible nucleus.

Like the earlier work on UNIX at the University of California at Berkeley, Mach was selected as a research project by the Department of Defense Advanced Research Projects Agency (ARPA). ARPA was especially interested in the research and development of operating systems capable of controlling multiprocessors. Because of the common funding source and the wide acceptance of BSD UNIX in research organizations, it was natural for Mach to be designed to be binary-compatible with BSD applications. Therefore, all versions of Mach have supported the BSD 4.3 UNIX system call interface. Another factor in the success of Mach is its adaptation as the basis of the Open System Foundation standard operating system, OSF/1.

All versions of Mach have been intended to be extensible nuclei, meaning one could define certain features of the OS as user space programs. However, Version 3.0 and newer versions of Mach are explicitly designed with a microkernel to support function extensibility. Since the kernel was intended to support the BSD system call interface, versions prior to 3.0 used portions of the BSD 4.3 kernel in the kernel. Legally, this reuse required anyone acquiring the Mach source code to have a source code license for UNIX from AT&T and another for BSD 4.3 from UC-Berkeley. This encouraged the Mach design team to construct the kernel so that they could use the code independently of their possession of UNIX licenses. Interestingly, then, a primary rationale for deriving the microkernel version of Mach was driven by regulations as much as it was by technical requirements.

Today, the Mach microkernel is intended to establish a common set of critical functions used to support different operating systems that have different policies. As explained in the previous paragraph, BSD 4.3 is the default OS supported by the microkernel. Figure 19.7 illustrates other extensions of the microkernel, including the OSF/1 operating system, other UNIX variants, and RT-Mach for real-time domains.

✦ FIGURE 19.7 Mach Microkernel-based OS

The Mach microkernel supports multiple policies (multiple operating systems), including BSD UNIX, OSF/1, and others.

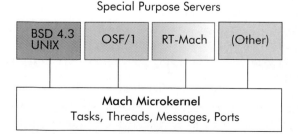

The microkernel provides *mechanisms* for process management, memory management, and device management. An OS is created by defining a server that uses the microkernel to implement the desired OS interface. The server implements the file manager and various policy modules for mechanisms implemented in the microkernel. The rest of this example describes the process and memory managers, particularly the IPC mechanism, due to its unique nature.

PROCESS MANAGEMENT

Mach supports *tasks* and *threads*, where the view of a modern process corresponds to a task. (Mach was one of the studies that popularized the modern model of processes and threads.) A task is an execution environment with its own address space, port capabilities, and a collection of associated threads. Each thread is a sequence of instruction executions within a task and shares the task's resources. A combination of one thread and a task corresponds to the classic notion of a single-threaded process. Any task may support several threads. If the task is implemented in a multiprocessor environment, the threads use inter-thread synchronization to coordinate access to resources within the task. Mach provides a set of thread-specific synchronization mechanisms to support inter-thread synchronization.

The granularity of a distributed computation partition depends in part on the speed of the communication mechanism among the individual parts of the computation. Shared-memory multiprocessors support very high-speed message passing because the transmission amounts to a memory-to-memory copy. If processes implemented the individual parts of the computation, then the limiting factor to distribution granularity changes from message transmission time to the context switching time for processes. Threads provide a lightweight model for context switching, so thread-based applications can take advantage of the fast message-passing time in a shared-memory multiprocessor.

The Mach process manager provides two levels of primitives, one for managing tasks and another for managing threads. The task-level primitives are used to create, destroy, suspend, and resume tasks. When a task is created, it may or may not inherit the parent's resources, depending on the parameters used in the create call. When a task is active, any thread in the task is schedulable, but when the task is suspended, all threads are blocked. Task suspension calls are counted so that threads in a task cannot run until there is a corresponding resume call for every suspend call.

Mach threads are kernel entities operating within a task. Thread management primitives include fork(), join(), detach(), and exit(). Since threads are defined to exist within a task, they share a common address space; hence, they have common global variables. The fork() command is patterned after the UNIX fork() command, and the join() command is similar to the join() command described in Chapter 2. The detach() command is used to break the parent-child relationship between two threads so that the parent can exit while the child continues to run.

A kernel thread also can be suspended or resumed, provided the task is active. Again, kernel thread suspension calls are counted, so the task, to be runnable, must have received at least as many resumption calls as suspension calls. Since threads may run on single processors, there is a yield() command to invoke the microkernel thread scheduler at the explicit command of the application.

The microkernel scheduler manages only threads, not tasks. In thread-based computing environments, there will tend to be many more threads than there are processes to schedule. Also, since Mach is intended to address multiprocessors, its scheduler must not assume there is only a single processor to manage. Every processor and every thread is assigned to a *processor set*. The processor set scheduler allocates runnable threads to an available processor in the processor set. The scheduler is a multilevel queue with priorities assigned according to the level of service that the thread is receiving. If the amount of service the thread has recently received is large, its priority is low. The priority is used to assign the thread to the end of one of 32 run queues. Some threads must be executed on a particular processor, for example, threads on I/O devices associated with that processor. Such threads are scheduled in a set of local run queues, while other threads can be scheduled in a global run queue for the process set. When a processor becomes idle, it selects the thread at the head of the highest-priority local run queue and dispatches it. If the local run queues are empty, the scheduler proceeds to the global run queue to select a thread. Because the global run queues are shared among the processors in the process set, locks are used to prevent more than one processor from scheduling at a time.

MESSAGE PASSING

Mach is descended from the Accent OS, which in turn is descended from the Rochester Intelligent Gateway (RIG) system. Each of these systems focuses on an efficient IPC facility to support communities of communicating processes.

MESSAGES. RIG was less concerned with the distribution of the processes across a multiprocessor or network of hardware machines than were its two successors. However, it began to focus on flexible and efficient IPC using messages. RIG used the ideas of messages and ports to support IPC, originally within a multiprogramming environment and then on a network of machines. A *message* is a header and data, while a *port* is a queue for typed message data structures associated with a process. A port can be thought of as a mailbox with a write entry point and a read entry point. A port bears a similarity to UNIX pipes by its half-duplex, typed communication, but it differs in its support of typed messages rather than byte streams. If two processes wish to exchange messages, they must each have a port so as to accomplish two-way communication.

The Accent designers found the RIG IPC mechanisms to be insufficient in several ways. First, the protection on ports was not sufficient, since there were no restrictions on which processes could write to a port. Second, the ports did not have adequate failure notification, meaning a port might allow dangling references to failed ports. Since ports were bound to both the machine and the process, it was difficult to move a process. Third, the message sizes were too small for some message-passing applications.

Accent was developed for a network of Spice workstations (also marketed by Three Rivers Computer Company as the PERQ), again using messages and ports. Messages are delivered reliably over the network using connected protocols. Recognizing the shortfalls of RIG, Accent's developers redesigned ports as protected kernel objects that are accessible with capabilities rather than with integer pointers. Thus, for a process to send a message to a port of another process, it must possess a *capability* to do so. Since the kernel manages capabilities, it knows which processes are able to send messages to any particular port. If a sender process fails, the kernel can inspect its capability list to determine which other processes depend on the failed process. Thus, the kernel knows which processes should receive failure notifications. RIG allows any sender process to know the location of the receiver port by virtue of the address. In Accent, capabilities are network location transparent, thus preventing a sender from depending on the location of a receiver port. This transparency allows Accent to easily move a process from one machine to another with no worry that senders will be unable to locate the transient process.

Part of the message size limitation in RIG can be traced to its lack of support for virtual memory as well as the small address spaces supported by the OS. Accent incorporated virtual memory and used it to address the message size limitation. An Accent message is a header followed by a collection of typed data objects. The length of the message is essentially unrestricted, although it must be less than or equal to 2^{32} bytes—the size of an address space. Accent virtual memory is built on memory objects. When one process sends a large message to another machine on the same node, Accent uses the copy-on-write strategy: The pages in the memory object are written into the receiver's page table so that both page tables reference the single memory object (see Figure 19.8). If the receiver writes to the memory object, then the pages touched by the receiver are copied and remapped prior to performing the write operation.

✦ FIGURE 19.8 Transferring Large Messages in Accent

Accent was among the first (if not the first) to use the copy-on-write technique in conjunction with paging. A message is mapped into both the sender and receiver's address spaces until either of them write to the message.

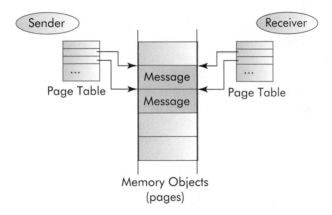

Mach reuses the basic Accent strategy for messages and ports to implement message passing. However, the goal hardware domain is extended to include shared-memory multiprocessors. These multiprocessors provide a raw IPC mechanism that supports finer-grained computation than exists on the networks of local memory machines targeted in the Accent design. As mentioned earlier in the chapter, Mach replaces the Accent notion of process by tasks and threads.

PORTS. Messages and ports are extended from process-to-process communication to be thread-to-thread communication. Ports are associated with a task and are shared by the threads associated with the task. For example, every thread in a task can read the task's ports and can write to any port for which the task has the capability. A thread uses a port to communicate with other threads within the same task or with threads in tasks on remote machines.

Although ports are kernel data structures, they are created by a thread. Any other thread in the same task has the capabilities of the creator to use the port, since the kernel does not distinguish among threads, only among tasks. If a local thread wants a remote thread (one in a different task) to communicate with it, then the kernel creates a capability in the remote task to allow its threads to send messages to the local task's port.

The communication package provides kernel calls to support all variants of synchronous/asynchronous send and blocking/nonblocking `receive()` operations. It also includes an ability to combine a `send()` operation with a blocking `receive()` to adopt the behavior of the RPC.

Since ports support typed messages, and tasks may have specialized threads executing their code, tasks usually have several different ports. This means a thread may have to use a nonblocking read to poll every port to detect incoming messages. Mach provides *port sets* to simplify reading. A blocking read on a port set returns an arbitrary message from one of the ports in the port set if any of the ports contain messages. If no port in the port set contains a message, the thread blocks on the read.

NETWORK MESSAGES. The Mach kernel does not support message transfer across the network. Instead, it provides for a user space server program to handle network-related communication. A *network message server* interacts with the kernel to address network transparency issues, including locating remote tasks and using the appropriate network protocols to transmit and receive messages. Since the network message server is not part of the kernel, it can be redefined as required by registering a new server with the kernel.

Each node in the network contains a network message server to route and receive traffic to/from the network. The abstract message network implemented by the collective network message servers creates a new name space with global *network ports* to be used by threads. When a task on a host obtains a capability to access a port on another machine, the network port is defined and the network message server maps the network port to the host location that contains the port. Now a send operation results in a series of actions in the sending and receiving machines. First, the kernel detects that the message is for a remote port, so it forwards the message to the local network message server. The local network message server uses the network port to determine the network location of the destination port. It then forwards the message to the network message server on the destination host. The remote network message server maps the network port to a local port on its own machine and then passes the message to its kernel for placement in the port queue.

Network message servers are more complex than this simple scenario suggests due to various additional tasks and complications. For example, since the network message server is a user space task, it must have an appropriate set of capabilities to various ports along the message flow path. It also must manage capabilities on behalf of the senders and receivers so that they are not compromised by either the network or the server's implementation. Besides these Mach-specific tasks, several network-oriented tasks must be performed by a server, such as supporting, naming, detecting and maintaining the location of all remote hosts, performing data type conversion when needed, and conforming to authentication requirements.

While the approach of user space servers for message management has been shown to be valuable, it also can be slow. The inefficiency comes from context switching among threads/tasks and distributing work between the kernel and the server. Mach 3.0 provides a kernel space implementation of the network message server for configurations of multicomputers with "no remote memory access," called *NORMA* multiprocessors. The presence of the kernel space implementation does not preclude the presence of a user space network message server. If both mechanisms are present, the kernel will route traffic in the NORMA multicomputer to the kernel server and all other traffic to the user space server.

MEMORY MANAGEMENT

The microkernel provides a means for the policy of managing memory objects to be implemented in a server [Rashid et al., 1988]. The basic memory manager mechanism, implemented in the microkernel, encapsulates the memory-mapping hardware much as the Choices `Address Translation` component encapsulates mapping hardware (see Figure 19.5). When the hardware detects a missing page fault, it must run another part of the memory manager to check the reference, change the protected page maps, and perform other secure housekeeping. This, too, must be microkernel code, although it is independent of the details of the memory-mapping hardware. Another part of the memory manager implements a specific, hardware-independent, secure memory management policy to keep track of disk and remote network addresses for pages as well as to identify replaced pages and other functions. As shown in Figure 19.9(a), this part of the memory manager is traditionally implemented in the kernel. However, Mach is designed to allow it to be executed in user space as an application program (Figure 19.9(b)). This requires the interface between the microkernel portion of the memory manager and the user space portion of the memory manager to have a well-defined interface so that either can use the services of the other.

A memory object is the unit of memory management in Mach. A memory object may be a page, a set of pages, a stack, or even a file. Memory objects can be associated with a region in the virtual address space used by a process—a 2^{31}-byte address space. Memory objects are loaded into the virtual address space at a particular address if desired or at an unallocated address if the application does not care where the memory object is to appear. Each memory object has a port and can react to messages.

Each task, including the kernel, has its own 2^{31}-byte paged address space managed by the kernel. When a "large" memory object is to be moved from one place in the virtual address space to another, the pages storing the memory object are logically transferred to the receiver task via its port. The microkernel copies the page table entry for the memory object from the sending process's page table to the kernel's page table while the message is queued in the port. When the destination process executes a receive for the message, the memory object's pages are mapped into the receiving process's page table. This design is exploited in *out-of-line* transfers of large amounts of data within a single node on the network.

As mentioned above, Mach uses the copy-on-write strategy so that two page tables can reference a common message body until one or the other of the two processes writes into its own logical copy. When a memory object is sent to a port on another machine, the kernel marks its pages as *copy-on-reference*, meaning the pages are not to be physically transmitted to the remote machine until that machine is referenced by the receiving process. However, the page table for the remote process will be updated to indicate that the memory object has been logically delivered. Mach can support very general policies to accom-

✦ FIGURE 19.9 Mach Memory Management

Part (a) of the figure illustrates the behavior of a conventional page manager: All parts of the manager are implemented in the hardware and in supervisor mode software. The Mach approach is shown in part (b), where the page manager is allowed to be executed as user space software.

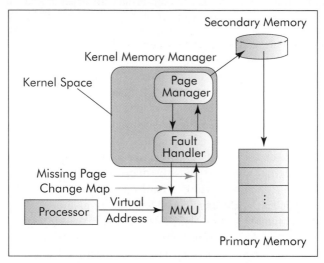

(a) Kernel-Based Memory Manager

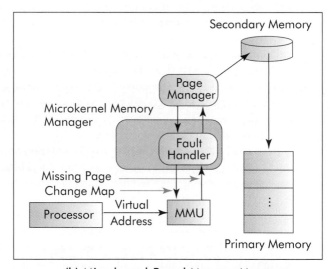

(b) Microkernel-Based Memory Manager

plish the binding. This is because the memory object is bound to a physical memory location on reference and the reference can be resolved by the memory object manager of the user space if it is "missing."

For example, in Figure 19.10, the sender's OS copies the memory object that contains the message from its kernel to the remote system kernel so that it can be mapped into the receiver's address space. However, the remote machine's Mach traps the reference and provides the sending process with the opportunity to bind information to the memory object when it is referenced, thus allowing the virtual address to be bound to an arbitrary object. This means the sending process maps virtual memory pages when they are referenced, even if they are referenced by a process on a remote machine.

✦ FIGURE 19.10 Binding Memory Objects

Memory objects can be a page, a set of pages, a stack, or other abstraction. The user space memory object manager can bind the reference to an arbitrary object.

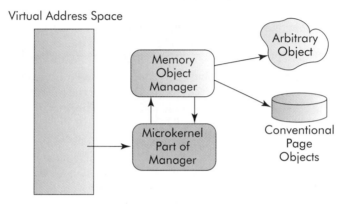

CONCLUSION

The Mach operating system is the major challenger to UNIX technology in network-oriented operating systems. The Open Systems Foundation OSF/1 OS is based on the Mach 2 technology. It also provides the basis of Mac OS X.

In the past, the prevailing criticism of Mach was its performance. Mach implementations are typically unable to achieve the performance of monolithic UNIX kernels because of the generality of the policy-mechanism separation that allows various parts of the operating system to execute in user space servers. Another limiting factor is the general message-passing mechanism. Microkernel performance in general, and Mach performance in particular, is the subject of much contemporary applied operating systems research and development.

19.5 • LAYERED ORGANIZATIONS

A **layered kernel** partitions the functionality into an abstract machine hierarchy in which the functions in layer i are implemented in terms of the functions provided by layer $i - 1$ (see Figure 19.1(d)). The layered architecture is a classic technique for dividing complex software systems into manageable parts. For example, layered architectures are the means by which ISO OSI network protocols are defined (see Chapter 15). They are used as a guiding principle in many OS architectures, but no prominent OS is pure in its use of the technique.

The intellectual challenge regarding layered architectures is in determining the order and content of the layers. How can the operating system's functions be partitioned into layers so that functions in layer i cannot use the facilities in layer $i + k$? This suggests that a designer could possibly draw a figure of the functions as an acyclic graph, with no circular dependencies among the modules. One variant to pure layering is for the kernel to use layers in which there are two types of processes: ordinary processes and system tasks. This provides the opportunity to use one form of task to implement general processes and another for applications. While this variant tends to create a lot of levels, it makes layering plausible. However, few if any contemporary operating systems are actually able to adhere to it.

The classic example of a layered OS is Dijkstra's THE system, developed in the 1960s at the Technische Hogeschool Eindhoven (THE); hence, the unusual English name [Dijkstra, 1968]. The goal of THE was to design and implement a *provably correct* OS (people still argue today whether the study met its goal). The layering approach provides a model for isolating various aspects of the OS, proving properties about a level of the system, implementing the level, and then using the level to implement more abstract levels of the system. The THE layering is summarized in Figure 19.11. Level 1 implements processes, scheduling, and the synchronization mechanism among these processes. This allows the memory management system to use processes in its implementation. However, it disallows the possibility of the scheduler's using information about memory management in making its decisions. So, for example, the scheduler could potentially dispatch processes that are swapped out of memory. The higher levels of THE had more relevance to machines in the 1960s than to contemporary machines. For example, the traditional operator console did not use the normal I/O buffering and device driver mechanisms. Instead, it provided its own. However, in the THE architecture, I/O management and the operator console can use virtual memory.

✦ FIGURE 19.11   Dijkstra's THE Layered Architecture

Layered architectures organize functionality so that it is nicely structured and much easier to manage than many other structures. Unfortunately, layering establishes a total order among functions implemented at different layers, so it is quite difficult to define a layered architecture.

Level 5	User Programs
Level 4	Input/Output Management
Level 3	Operator Console
Level 2	Memory Management
Level 1	CPU Scheduling and Semaphores
Level 0	Hardware

THE is an important OS because it illustrates how to build an OS that can be proved to be correct [Dijkstra, 1968]. As a modern OS, the layered architecture is overly restrictive. It requires the designer to establish an ordering on all of the functions, a strategy in stark contrast to the monolithic kernel or microkernel approaches. However, layering is a goal toward which most operating systems strive at one level of abstraction or another.

19.6 • OPERATING SYSTEMS FOR DISTRIBUTED SYSTEMS

The emergence of inexpensive networks of computers has stimulated a new direction in the organization of operating systems. Distributed hardware introduces a new set of requirements that encourage operating systems to be designed with a new set of modules (but still using the basic software organizations described in Figure 19.2). Network operating systems have evolved from conventional single-machine operating systems. Distributed operating systems take a revolutionary approach in an attempt to create a new abstract environment in which machine boundaries are transparent to the programmer. These two classes of operating systems are summarized next.

NETWORK OPERATING SYSTEMS

A **network operating system** is generally a single-machine operating system adapted for use in a network environment (see Figure 19.12). The modifications can be modest, providing high-speed communications facilities, such as file transfer, and terminal interconnection, such as remote login, or they can be ambitious, providing IPC, remote file systems, and RPC. Many of the more ambitious efforts could be argued to be distributed operating systems rather than network operating systems because they make several aspects of the physical distribution transparent to the application programmer.

✦ **FIGURE 19.12** Network OS Environment

A network OS operates in an environment where there are multiple host computers interconnected by a network. The OS is designed without attempting to hide the location of network resources, meaning that the application software must assume the responsibility of locating resources.

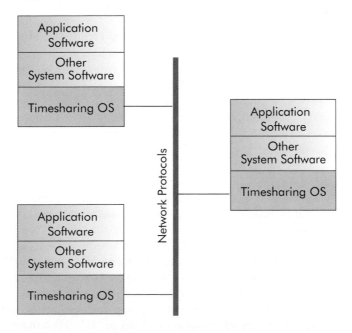

The limitations of network operating systems are generally architectural ones in which the original OS was designed specifically for a uniprocessor environment, yet it is being used to manage the resources in a multiprocessor or network environment. Because of the wide use of UNIX on individual timesharing machines and its evolution as a workstation OS, it is usually the base OS for a network extension.

Network operating systems do not necessarily attempt to make the location of a file transparent at the operating systems interface, although, as discussed in Chapter 16, the `remote mount` operation can provide application programmers with transparent access to files on a network. In older network operating systems, the lack of transparency required a user to copy a file from a remote machine to the local machine before accessing it.

Executing a program at a remote location requires overt action by the user. For example, the user may have to use a remote login facility to create a session with a shell program at the remote site and then cause the shell to execute the program.

BSD UNIX

4.4 BSD (the last official version of BSD UNIX) is an excellent example of a network OS [McKusick, et al., 1996]. It evolved from the pure timesharing UNIX OS, and was adapted to operate efficiently in a network environment. That is, the intent was that BSD UNIX should be a comprehensive OS for timesharing computers, but it should also be well-suited to workstations and servers interconnected in a TCP/IP network environment. The fundamental change to the kernel to enable it to support network computing is the socket interface (see Chapter 15). AT&T System V, Release 3, was also extended from a timesharing operating system to be a network OS. This was done through the addition of I/O streams.

BSD UNIX (and its successor open source versions, FreeBSD and OpenBSD) is a comprehensive OS. There are few features in contemporary Linux systems that do not have an equivalent mechanism in FreeBSD, and vice versa. Although they are different implementations, probably the essential difference between FreeBSD and Linux is the scope of developers contributing to the OS as it evolves.

In the 1980s, BSD UNIX was closely associated with Sun Microcomputers, primarily because a principal OS architect at UC-Berkeley (William Joy) was the OS architect at Sun. Ultimately, Sun departed from the BSD UNIX path to support Solaris. However, the influence of commercial Sun experience on the BSD kernel evolution is apparent.

As a network OS, BSD UNIX was one of the early operating systems to support TCP, UDP, and IP in the kernel. It also provided (kernel and user space) support for FTP, remote login, remote disks and files, and RPC. As the designers were confronted with this rapidly expanding set of network applications, they realized that they could support most of the transport layer protocols by distilling out the essential aspects required by the transport layer and implementing it in the kernel. It would still be necessary to provide a means by which user space programs could access these distilled kernel features. That was the motivation for the design of BSD sockets. It is an excellent piece of engineering that the BSD UNIX designers were able to recognize that all transport layer protocols could be implemented as user space code on top of the socket mechanism. It is a testament to the excellence of this design that contemporary operating systems (including Windows operating systems) use BSD sockets at the OS system call interface.

The operational aspects of sockets are described in detail in Lab Exercise 15.1. In review, here are the essential features of sockets:

- Any application program can introduce a network endpoint into its address space by creating a socket with the `socket()` system call.

- Any (or at least many) transport layer protocol can be implemented to use a socket. That is, the socket does not have any preferred transport layer protocol, and it has been designed to work with any of them.

- Once a socket has been created in a process address space, it can be exported to a global name space using the `bind()` system call. This is accomplished by defining different kinds of socket address data structures (called a `sockaddr`) that are passed to `bind()` when the address is exported. The early implementations supported an address space that corresponds to the UNIX file system address space as well as the IP extended address space where each address is a (net#, host#, port#). DNS can be added to these facilities to allow software to reference remote sockets as symbolic domain names. This ingenious invention is the essential element for allowing a thread in a process on one computer to be able to intercommunicate with a thread in a process on another computer. It is also enough to implement a broad variety of remote services, including FTP, remote login, remote disks/files, and RPC.

- But wait, there's more: The BSD UNIX kernel provides the `listen()` and `accept()` system calls to implement multithreaded servers and TCP-style virtual circuits. Although one could implement virtual circuits without these calls, they are modest additions to the system call interface that provide efficient kernel implementation of connections.

By defining the socket facility, timesharing UNIX was extended to an OS that enabled user space programmers to implement complex distributed programming runtime systems and distributed applications. Not only did BSD UNIX demonstrate the viability of the approach, but also the essential elements of most contemporary distributed software are built on the socket network facility.

Distributed Operating Systems

The state-of-the-art effort in OS research is in the design and development of **distributed operating systems**. Most contemporary OS research papers focus on one aspect or another of distributed operating systems. While several significant systems have been built, none enjoy wide commercial success. Tanenbaum and van Renesse [1985] identify five issues that distinguish distributed operating systems from network operating systems:

- **Communication primitives:** This is concerned with the need to find alternatives to shared-memory synchronization primitives such as semaphores and monitors.

- **Naming and protection:** These are related to the problem of a process on one machine identifying and communicating with processes on a remote machine.

- ■ **Network-wide resource management:** This is concerned with issues such as scheduling, load balancing, and distributed deadlock detection.
- ■ **Fault tolerance:** This is related to the robustness of the overall system in the presence of failure of individual components.
- ■ **Services to provide:** These are related to the design and use of file servers, print servers, remote execution facilities, and miscellaneous other facilities.

A distributed OS abstracts the set of distinct computer systems in a network so that an application process perceives the computing environment as a single system rather than as a collection of individual computers interconnected with a network (see Figure 19.13). Sometimes the distinction between a network OS and a distributed OS is somewhat arbitrary, since the network OS will allow some aspects of the hardware environment to be location transparent, while others will be apparent. For example, in 4.3 BSD UNIX, file services may be location transparent, although `telnet`, `ftp`, `rlogin`, `rsh`, `finger`, and other commands make the machine boundaries explicit.

✦ **FIGURE 19.13** Distributed Operating Systems

The primary goal of a distributed OS (contrasted with a network OS) is to automatically locate and manage the placement of network resources. Application programs are written without having to know the network location of resources they use.

Mach is often thought of as a distributed OS, although we have used it as an example of a microkernel OS (Section 19.4). CHORUS is another microkernel-based OS, similar in many respects to Mach, and it is an excellent example of a distributed OS.

The CHORUS Operating System

CHORUS started as a research project in distributed systems at the French national computer science research institute (INRIA) in the early 1980s. By the late 1980s, it had evolved into a commercial OS supported by Chorus Systèmes. Sun Microcomputers eventually acquired Chorus as one of its OS product offerings. The description here is based on the Chorus Systèmes description [Rozier et al., 1988].

In CHORUS-V3, the goals of the microkernel are to provide efficient support for an OS with the System V Interface Definition, real-time operating systems, and an object-oriented operating system (COOL) in an open, distributed hardware environment. Like

Mach, CHORUS evolved from earlier work on a microkernel architecture. The Version 3 microkernel, called the *nucleus*, supports heavyweight units of computation called *actors*, lightweight units called *threads*, and IPC based on messages and ports. The microkernel supports subsystems to host system servers to implement specific OS policies (see Figure 19.14).

✦ FIGURE 19.14 The CHORUS Microkernel and Servers

CHORUS was initially designed as a microkernel OS. The microkernel creates abstractions such as actors, threads, and messages. The special-purpose servers (such as System V UNIX) use the microkernel abstractions to implement distributed functionality.

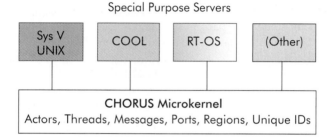

An OS is implemented as a set of system servers within a subsystem built on top of the microkernel. The microkernel itself is modularized into a machine-dependent supervisor and a machine-independent process manager, memory manager, and IPC manager. The process and memory management are local tasks, and the IPC manager is used to implement global services. These components of the microkernel implement six basic abstractions:

■ **Actors:** A unit of computation analogous to a Mach task (and to some extent, a Windows process). It has resources, ports, and a paged address space divided into regions, but it is a passive entity with respect to computation.

■ **Thread:** The active unit of serial computation. A thread executes in an actor, using its resources and address space. Threads in the same actor share the actor's resources. The thread's state is represented by a PC, registers, and a stack.

■ **Message:** A byte stream used to exchange information among address spaces. Messages are the explicit means for threads to communicate across machine boundaries.

■ **Port:** A mailbox holding messages sent to an actor. A port can be thought of as an address for a service. A port can belong to a *port group* in order to enable multicasting to several ports using the port group.

■ **Unique Identifier (UI):** A 64-bit global name intended to be unique throughout the life of the operating system, including across reboot operations.

■ **Region:** A smaller block of contiguous addresses managed by the memory manager. The actor's address space is large, for example 2^{32} addresses. Pages implement regions.

Actors in subsystems and the microkernel jointly manage three other abstractions:

- **Segment:** A unit of data encapsulation defined by the application and referenced by a capability.
- **Capability:** A 128-bit key that uniquely references resources in the distributed system. Half of the capability is a UI managed by the microkernel; the other half is defined by the subsystem.
- **Protection identifier:** An identifier appended to all messages by the microkernel and used by subsystems to authenticate the message.

A machine configuration consists of a set of *sites* interconnected by a *network*. A site may be a workstation or a CPU board in a multiprocessor, and a network may be a packet network or an internal bus. Each site has physical resources and is managed by a copy of the microkernel. An actor's address space is split into a user portion and a system portion, with all actors at the same site sharing the system portion of the address space.

The microkernel architecture is summarized in Figure 19.15. The supervisor implements the low-level handlers for external events such as interrupts and traps; hence, it is a machine-dependent module. The real-time executive implements thread-multiplexing and synchronization. It uses the supervisor for several different services, including interrupts for priority scheduling, although it is machine-independent. The VM manager implements a paged virtual memory, including page frame allocation and virtual address management. It is largely machine-independent, except for the interactions with the memory-mapping unit hardware. The VM manager is visible at the microkernel interface to allow a user space system server to participate in memory management. The supervisor, real-time executive, and VM manager provide local services. Global services are supported by the IPC manager through its message mechanism. The IPC manager implements a machine address space and location transparency and also provides higher-level mechanisms for RPCs and multicasting.

✦ FIGURE 19.15 CHORUS Microkernel Architecture

As shown in this figure, the microkernel itself is modular, containing a Supervisor, a Real-time Executive, a VM Manager, and an IPC Manager.

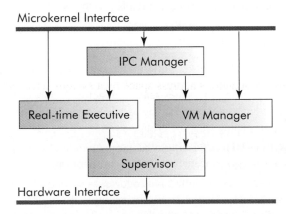

PROCESS MANAGEMENT

The process management function addresses actors and threads. An actor bears a strong resemblance to Mach tasks, and a thread resembles a Mach thread. Threads use the actor's ports to receive communications from other actors. The port is identified by a capability. An actor has a default port used by other threads to reference the actor.

Threads are scheduled by the real-time executive using preemptive priority scheduling. Priorities of each thread are adjusted by the microkernel according to fairness and response criteria. Thread synchronization is accomplished using the common memory available to all threads in an actor.

INTERPROCESS COMMUNICATION

The communication mechanism relies on the UI to implement location transparency for ports. Each port is referenced using a capability, and each capability contains a UI. Hence, when a task uses a capability to send a message to a port, it need not be concerned with the location of the actor that owns the port. Instead, the IPC manager is responsible for translating the UI into a network address, using the naming scheme in the supporting network. To avoid encoding any such scheme, such as internet addresses, into the microkernel, the IPC manager interacts with a subsystem component that is able to translate UIs to internet addresses.

In CHORUS, messages are simply byte streams rather than structured messages. The IPC manager copies the byte stream from the sender's address space into the port of the receiver's address space. Large messages use the same copy-on-write approach used in Accent.

A port group is a set of port UIs assigned to another UI. The port group UI is analogous to a multicast address in an Ethernet (and in IPv6). When a message is sent to the port group, the IPC manager delivers a copy of the message to every port in the port group. Multicasting is used by many different subsystems to implement reliability algorithms on a network. It is also useful to implement designs in which a client "broadcasts" a request to a group of servers without knowing exactly which server it should use. The correct server responds to the multicast message, while all the others ignore it. CHORUS designers refer to this use as dynamic binding to a service, since the client need not be associated with any particular server until it needs to use it.

MEMORY MANAGEMENT

A segment is a logical block of information, such as a file or swap area. Segments are mapped into a region in an actor's address space by a system actor executing in a subsystem, called a *segment server*, or *mapper*. Whereas the segment has a UI, the region has a virtual address and protection. Each region is mapped into page frames by the microkernel VM manager using demand paging. Hence, a reference to a segment is mapped to a region by a user space mapper. The region is mapped to a page frame by the nucleus and then referenced by the executing thread. A missing page fault is first handled by the supervisor and then passed to the VM manager. The VM manager informs the relevant mapper that it needs a page, and the mapper retrieves the target page from an arbitrary location according to its design principles. As in Mach, CHORUS implements the low-level paging mechanism in the microkernel and allows the page replacement policy to be implemented in the user space.

CONCLUSION

The discussion provides an overview of the organization of the CHORUS microkernel. Rozier et al. [1988] provide a complete discussion of the organization, behavior, and design rationale for CHORUS. Like Mach, CHORUS provides a commercial alternative to UNIX for network and multiprocessor environments. Just as Mach has enjoyed limited commercial success in the United States, CHORUS has enjoyed limited commercial success in the European Community.

19.7 ● SUMMARY

Operating systems include a diversity of functionality that spans process and resource management, memory management, file management, and device management. As was illustrated in Figure 19.3, the interactions among the various functions is logically complex, making it difficult to modularize the functions to minimize traffic among them. Over the last 40 years, designers have continued to experiment with software architectures to implement all of these functions in an efficient, flexible, and maintainable way. In the late 1960s and 1970s, researchers experimented with layered architectures and extensible nucleus approaches. Dijkstra's THE and Brinch Hansen's RC 4000 nucleus were important operating systems for their technology. IBM embraced the extensible nucleus machine with its VM nucleus in the 1970s. Economic considerations drove IBM to the VM approach, since the company marketed many different computers for which customers desired a single operating system interface. Conversely, some installations required that different operating systems be used on a single IBM machine. VM has proved to be a valuable component in IBM's operating system strategy. From 1975 to 1990, monolithic architectures were the dominant form of operating systems, including classic UNIX implementations.

Choices is a research OS based on the modular nucleus approach. It demonstrates the value of reuse in OS experimentation and continues to be valuable in its designer's OS and software engineering research. Objects, as opposed to full object-oriented technology, are used in many operating systems (including Windows NT/2000/XP). They allow the system to be designed to use capabilities to reference functions in distributed parts of the system, as is done in Mach, CHORUS, and others.

Today, microkernel-based operating systems are the emerging architecture of choice. This chapter described how Mach and CHORUS use this technology to implement UNIX servers as well as real-time operating systems. Both are distributed message-passing operating systems with only the critical parts of the OS implemented in the microkernel. In this class of operating systems, the file system and parts of the process manager, resource managers, and memory managers are implemented in user space.

19.8 • EXERCISES

1. Mach, CHORUS, and other operating systems use capabilities extensively. Explain how capabilities enable these systems to implement location transparency of entities in a distributed system. How do the capabilities used in CHORUS differ from the capabilities discussed in Chapter 14?

2. Can a Mach thread read a message it wrote to a task's port? Why or why not?

3. Regarding schedulable units of computation:

   a. Distinguish between a task and a thread in Mach.

   b. Distinguish between an actor and a thread in CHORUS.

   c. Distinguish between a process with two threads and two processes that each have one thread.

4. What is the distinction between a port set in Mach and a port group in CHORUS?

5. Both Mach and Chorus are implemented as groups of threads in the microkernel, yet they implement a UNIX system call interface. Speculate about how a procedure call interface can be implemented in the UNIX server, yet be implemented with threads.

6. What prevents the entire page replacement algorithm from being implemented in user space in Mach and CHORUS?

7. Choose a contemporary OS other than one discussed in this chapter and write a paper summarizing how the system addresses device management, file management, process management, and memory management. You do not need to provide a critical analysis of the papers describing the OS or of the OS itself. Part of the purpose of this exercise is for you to explore the technical literature. Do not use another textbook as the primary source of your information.

The Linux Kernel

Throughout this book, you have encountered examples from Linux. In this chapter, you will get a broad view of how all the components are implemented in the Linux kernel. Because the Linux kernel is openly available on the Internet, anyone who wants to read the source code can obtain it without a license. About a decade ago, Linux began as a graduate student's project. It rapidly caught on with OS developers, and within five years after its inception, it had become a viable commercial OS. Today, Linux is one of a handful of major commercial operating systems.

20.1 • THE LINUX KERNEL

Chapter 3 provided a general discussion of the UNIX family of operating systems. This chapter goes into more detail on how Linux implements the UNIX (POSIX.1) system call interface. In general, any kernel is responsible for abstracting and managing the machine's hardware resources, and for managing the sharing of those resources among executing programs. Since Linux implements the POSIX.1 interface, the general definition of the resource abstractions and sharing models is already defined. The OS must support processes, files, and other resources so that they can be managed with the traditional POSIX.1 system calls. Like many implementations of POSIX.1, most of the functionality is implemented in the trusted kernel code, although some of it is implemented in user-space libraries.

20.2 • KERNEL ORGANIZATION

The Linux kernel uses the same software organization as most predecessor UNIX kernels: It is designed and implemented as a monolithic kernel. In the traditional UNIX kernel, process and resource management, memory management, and file management are carefully implemented within a single executable software module. Data structures for each aspect of the kernel are generally accessible to all other aspects of the kernel. However, device management is implemented as a separate collection of device drivers and interrupt handlers (that also execute in kernel mode). The philosophy behind this design is that the main part of the kernel should never be changed. The only new kernel space software that should be added to the system should be for device management. Device drivers are relatively easy to write and add to the kernel (compared to, say, adding a feature to process management).

As technology evolved, this design assumption became a serious barrier to extending the kernel to handle new devices such as network cards and bitmapped displays. The usual interface between the kernel and the device drivers was designed to support disks, keyboards, and character displays. As hardware evolved to include these newer devices, it became increasingly difficult to provide appropriate kernel support wholly within a device driver.

Linux addressed this problem by providing a new "container" in which to implement extensions to the main part of the kernel—modules (see Figure 20.1). A Linux **module** is an independent software unit that can be designed and implemented long after the operating system has been compiled and installed, and can be installed dynamically as the system runs. The interface between a module and the kernel is more general than the one used with device drivers, providing the systems programmer with a more flexible tool with which to extend the kernel functionality than device drivers. Modules have proven to be so flexible that they are the main tool used to implement device drivers. Modules are described in Section 20.3.

◆ FIGURE 20.1   Kernel, Device Drivers, and Modules

Classic UNIX kernels are only intended to be expanded by adding device drivers. Linux provides modules as an additional mechanism for incorporating new code into the kernel.

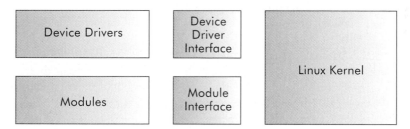

USING KERNEL SERVICES

As suggested by Figure 20.2, user programs view the kernel as a large ADT that maintains state and that has a number of functions on its public interface—the kernel system call interface. This ADT provides OS service to a user program whenever a process executing the program calls a function on its public interface. The exact nature of the service depends on the particular function that is called, its parameters, and the state of the OS when the function is called. Hence, the public interface specification for the kernel is the main description of the OS functionality interface.

✦ FIGURE 20.2   The Kernel as an ADT

The kernel has some of the properties of an ADT: It exports a public interface with a number of functions that can be called to manipulate the ADT. The implementation of the ADT functions is private.

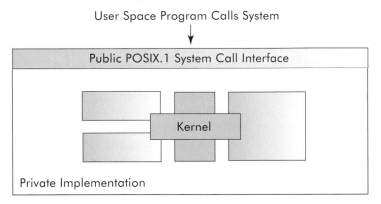

Continuing the ADT analogy, the implementation of the system call interface is private, so the implementations may differ from system to system, and even among versions of the Linux implementation. In theory, and generally in practice, the boundaries between device drivers or modules and the kernel are not discernible to the user program. These are characteristics of the internal design, not of the public interface. Thus, the POSIX.1 system call interface defines functions that normally are implemented in the kernel, device drivers, or modules. If the function is implemented in a device driver or module, when a user program invokes the function, the kernel fields the call and passes it through an internal interface to the appropriate device driver or module. In a Linux implementation of the system call interface, some functions may even be implemented as user space programs; for example, older versions of Linux rely on library code to implement the thread package [Beck et al., 1998].

If the kernel ADT were actually implemented as a C++ object, it would be a *passive* object. That is, the kernel software does not have any internal thread of execution or process; it is simply a collection of functions and data structures that maintain state. Any process that uses kernel services—the process is an *active* entity—makes a kernel request by (logically) making a procedure call on the system call interface. Thus, a process that is executing outside the kernel begins to execute the kernel code when it makes the system call. This is contrasted with the idea that the process executing user code might obtain service from a distinct kernel process. In Linux, the process executing the user program also executes the kernel programs when a system call is made.

Conceptually, then, whenever a process executing an application program desires service from the OS, it simply invokes the appropriate OS function through the POSIX.1 system call interface. Before the call, the process is executing the application program, and after the call (but before the return), the process is executing the kernel software. However, recall that the kernel is executed with the CPU in supervisor mode, but the application program is executed in user mode.

CPUs that incorporate the mode bit also typically incorporate a hardware trap instruction. A trap instruction causes the CPU to branch to a prespecified address (sometimes as a function of an instruction operand), and also to switch the CPU to supervisory mode. Of course, the details of each machine's trap instruction are unique to that machine. A trap instruction is not a privileged instruction, so any program can execute a trap. However, the destination of the branch instruction is predetermined by a set of addresses that are configured to point to kernel code and are kept in supervisory space.

Linux is a multiprogramming kernel; however, kernel functions are normally executed as if they were in a critical section. That is, once a process calls a system function, the function normally runs to completion and returns before the CPU will be allocated to a different process. However, interrupts can suspend the execution of a system call so that the interrupt can be serviced. This is called a **single-threaded kernel**, since (ignoring the interrupt service routines) only one thread of execution is allowed to execute in the kernel at a time. One thread of execution cannot start a function call and become interrupted by the scheduler to let another process run (and possibly make a kernel call). There are at least two important implications of this approach:

- A kernel function can update various kernel data structures without being concerned that another process will interrupt its execution and change related parts of the same data structures. Race conditions among processes do not occur. (However, race conditions between the process and interrupt-induced execution may occur.)

- If you are writing a new kernel function, always keep in mind that you cannot write code that will block waiting for a message or other resource that can be released only by some other process. This might produce deadlock in the kernel.

Current versions of the Linux kernel support symmetric multiprocessors (SMPs). Prior to the SMP support being incorporated into the kernel (that is, prior to Version 2.2), any potential race condition between a system call execution and an interrupt was handled by disabling the interrupts. The SMP version of the kernel introduces an elaborate set of kernel locks, since each copy of the kernel (on each of the SMPs) can have a kernel thread in execution.

DAEMONS

In a single-threaded kernel, conventional processes execute kernel code; that is, there are no special "kernel processes" that execute kernel code. Although this is accurate, there are several user-transparent processes called **daemons** that are started when a Linux machine is started, and that must exist to ensure correct operation of the operating system. For example, if the machine is connected to a network, there must be a process to respond to incoming network packets; another daemon process logs system messages and errors, and so on. The particular daemons that are running on any Linux installation varies according to the way the system administrator has set up the machine. By convention, daemon processes execute programs whose name ends with a character "d." For example, the network daemon is usually called `inetd`, the system logging daemon is called `syslogd`, and so on. You can make a good guess as to what daemons are running on your Linux machine by typing `ps aux | more` to your shell. The `ps` command reports the process status, and the `aux` parameters indicate that you want a report in user format (the `u` parameter) for all processes (the `a` parameter) including those without a controlling terminal (the `x` parameter). As you scan the list, look for commands that end with the character `d` and have a `TTY` field of `?` (no controlling terminal). You will normally see `syslogd`, `klogd`, `crond`, and `lpd` running on your system. You can find out what each of these daemons is doing by looking at the manual page (for example, use `man syslogd` to read the manual page for `syslogd`) for the program that the daemon is running.

STARTING THE KERNEL

When the machine is powered up, the hardware fetch-execute cycle begins, causing the control unit to repeatedly fetch and decode instructions, and the arithmetic-logic unit to execute them. The hardware process (see Section 6.2) is not a Linux process since it starts when the hardware starts, long before the kernel has even been loaded. After the diagnostics have completed, the boot record has been read, and the loader has placed the OS into primary memory, the booting procedure begins to run kernel code to initialize the computer's hardware. The computer is then ready to start the kernel by first setting the CPU in supervisor mode and branching to the main entry point in the kernel. This main entry point is not an ordinary C program with the conventional `main()` header line, since it is started in the boot sequence (rather than being started as a conventional main program).

Once the main entry point has been entered, the kernel initializes the trap table, the interrupt handler, the scheduler, the clock, modules, and so on. Near the end of this sequence, it initializes the process manager, meaning that it is prepared to support the normal process abstraction. Logically, the hardware process then creates the **initial process**. The initial process is allocated the first entry in the kernel's process descriptor table, so it is also referred to internally as process 0, `task[0]`, or `INIT_TASK`. The initial process then creates the first useful Linux process to run the `init` program, and then the initial process begins to execute an idle loop. That is, the initial process's only duties after the kernel is initialized are to use idle CPU time—it uses the CPU when no other process wants to use it (also referred to as the **idle process**).

The first real process continues initializing the system, but now using higher-level abstractions than were available to the hardware process. It starts various daemons and the file manager; creates the system console; runs other `init` programs from `/etc`, `/bin`, and/or `/sbin`; and runs `/etc/rc` (if necessary).

Starting the kernel is a complex procedure, and there are many opportunities for something to go wrong. There are several places in the procedure where various alternatives are checked in case the default boot algorithm fails. By the time the kernel initialization has been completed, the initial process will be enabled and several daemons will have been started. Beck, et al. [Ch. 3, 1998] provide a detailed discussion of the steps involved in starting up the kernel.

CONTROL FLOW IN THE MACHINE

Ultimately, the behavior of the computer is controlled by the action of the hardware process. Remember that there is only one hardware process and it will execute the hardware fetch-execute cycle until the computer is halted. Even though the kernel may switch from running one program—an interrupt service routine, a system call, or a user program—the hardware process operates at a level of abstraction *below* the kernel. Therefore, the hardware process has no notion of software process, interrupt handler, or other kernel abstraction; instead, it just fetches and executes instructions. At this low-level view of the behavior of the computer, even interrupts are nothing more than branch instructions.

20.3 • MODULES AND DEVICE MANAGEMENT

A Linux module is a set of functions and data types that can be compiled as an independent program (with appropriate flags to indicate that it is kernel code). It is then linked into the kernel when the module is *installed*. Linux modules can be installed when the kernel is started—called *static loading*—or dynamically while the kernel is running. Of course, if a function in a dynamic module is called before it has been installed, then the call will fail. But if the module has been installed, the kernel will field the system call and then pass it on to the corresponding function in the module.

Linux systems normally have several modules loaded during normal kernel initialization (although the kernel can be built so that modules cannot be used with it). One easy way to see which, if any, modules are running on your Linux machine is to read the file `/proc/modules`, which lists each active (static or dynamic) module.

Modules are generally used to implement device drivers, although UNIX systems have a traditional static mechanism for defining and adding these at the time the kernel is configured. One consequence of this is that the module API generally conforms to the API for a device driver. Even so, modules can be used to implement any function you desire.

MODULE ORGANIZATION

After a module is installed, it will be executed in supervisor mode in the same address space as the kernel. This means that the module can read and write kernel data structures, provided it knows their addresses. Since Linux is implemented as a monolithic kernel, it is a common problem that functions implemented in one file may need to reference data that is defined in another file. In conventional programs, this problem is handled by using external (global) variables that the link editor can resolve when it builds the program executable object file.

Because modules are compiled and linked independently from the kernel, they would not be able to reference kernel data structures by variable names, relying on static linking. Instead, the Linux kernel incorporates a mechanism by which files that implement a data structure can *export* the symbolic name of the data structure so that it can be used at run time. Debuggers rely on this kind of run time variable binding to allow users to reference data structures by symbolic name, so it was not necessary to invent it just to support modules. Recall that it is necessary to instruct the compiler to export symbols when it compiles a source file if a debugger will be used with the file; the same is true for the kernel. When the kernel is built, *kernel public* symbols are exported using the file's header file.

Modules are treated as dynamic abstract data types with an interface that can be interpreted by the static kernel. The minimum module interface must include two functions that the kernel calls when it installs and removes the module: `init_module()` and `cleanup_module()`, respectively. Since a module can implement relatively complex functions, Linux includes a mechanism for defining a new API for the module—one that has more functions than just `init_module()` and `cleanup_module()`.

For example, suppose the module was designed to allow an application program to increment an internal module value. The designer might provide, say, a function named `increment()` to do this. Since the module implementers can define any new function for the module's API, they need some way to inform the OS that these new functions exist. Then, when an application program wants to invoke the module's functions, it makes a system call. The kernel then forwards the call to the specified function in the module. Each new function that is added to the module must be *registered* with the kernel when the module is installed in the kernel. If the module is statically loaded, all its functions are registered when the kernel is booted. If the module is dynamically loaded, the functions must be dynamically registered with the kernel when the module is installed. Of course, if the module is dynamically removed, its functions must be *unregistered* so that the module functions do not get called when the module is no longer loaded. Registration is usually done in `init_module()` and unregistration is done in `cleanup_module()`.

MODULE INSTALLATION AND REMOVAL

As mentioned in the previous subsection, modules can reference kernel variables, provided the kernel code has been written so that they can be referenced from another module. Similarly, a module can export its own symbols so that other modules can use them. When you install a module by using the `insmod` program, the first step is to add the new module to the kernel address space (by a kernel function named `create_module()`). Next, the external symbol references in the module are resolved by another kernel function (named `get_kernel_syms()`), which searches the exported kernel symbols, followed by the list of other modules that have already been loaded. This means that if one module references symbols that are defined in other modules, then the module that defines the symbol must be loaded before the one that references it. After the module has been added to the kernel address space and external symbols have been resolved, `create_module()` allocates memory space for the module.

Now the module can be loaded by the `init_module()` system call. It is at this point that the symbols defined by this module are exported for use of other modules that may be loaded later. Finally, `insmod` calls the `init_module()` function for the newly loaded module.

When the module is to be removed, the `cleanup_module()` function will be called; then the space used by the module can be released and the virtual addresses can be unmapped. Notice that if a module has been installed, another module is installed after it, and the new module uses symbols from the first module, then removing the first module will cause an error in the second. Since the second module uses variables declared in the first, the first module must remain loaded as long as the second still needs to reference those variables.

20.4 ● PROCESS AND RESOURCE MANAGEMENT

The process manager is responsible for creating the process abstraction that programmers use and for providing facilities so that a process can create, destroy, synchronize, and protect other processes. Similarly, resource management involves creating appropriate abstractions to represent entities that a process might request (and block their execution if the resources are unavailable); besides abstraction, resource managers must provide an interface by which a process can request, acquire, and release resources.

✦ FIGURE 20.3 Process Abstraction

The Linux (POSIX.1) process abstraction is almost identical to the one described in Chapter 2. The process manager uses timers, interrupts, protection mechanisms, and so on, to export an address space and a virtual CPU for each process. These abstractions ultimately execute on the primary memory and physical CPU.

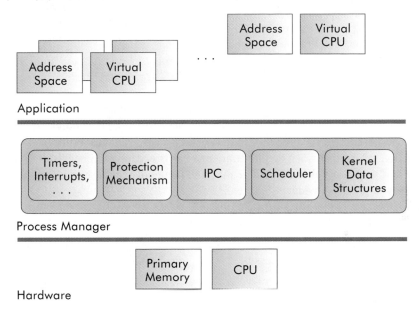

It is useful to summarize the execution of a program at various levels of abstraction to get a firm understanding of the job of the process manager (see Figure 20.3):

- **Hardware Level.** The hardware simply fetches an instruction from the memory location addressed by the PC, executes it, then fetches the next one, and so on. The hardware does not distinguish one program from another; they are all simply instructions in the primary memory. As a result, there is only the notion of the hardware process executing stored instructions, but no further abstraction such as a Linux process.

- **Process Manager Level.** The process manager creates a collection of idealized abstract machines, each of which has the characteristics of the host CPU when it is running in user mode. The process manager uses the hardware level to create a Linux process by using timers, interrupts, various protection mechanisms, interprocess communication (IPC) and synchronization mechanisms, scheduling, and a collection of data structures. Applications interact with the process manager (using the system call interface) to create instances of the virtual machine (with `fork()`), to load the address space with a particular program (using `exec()`), and to synchronize a parent and a child virtual machine (with `wait()`).

- **Application Level.** Conventional Linux processes and POSIX threads are used at the application level. The process's address space is the memory of its virtual machine (containing the text, stack, and data segments); the virtual CPU instructions are the user mode hardware instructions augmented by the system call interface functions; and the virtual resources (including devices) are manipulated via the system call interface.

The process manager manipulates the hardware process and physical resources to implement a set of virtual machines. It multiplexes the execution of the virtual machines on top of the single physical machine. (Linux supports multiprocessor CPUs, but in this section, we focus only on the single CPU implementation.) It must also provide protection and synchronization facilities to accommodate sharing.

Within the kernel code before Version 2.2, the terms *task* and *process* are used almost interchangeably. (In Version 2.2 and later, a task refers to either a classic process or a kernel thread.) In this section, generally we will use the task terminology when the execution takes place in supervisor mode and the process terminology when execution occurs in user mode. When a process is created, normally it is created with a new address space—a set of virtual addresses that the process can read or write as it executes. From the kernel perspective, this means that when the hardware process is executing in behalf of process i, it can read and write only the addressable machine components that correspond to the virtual address in process i's address space.

RUNNING THE PROCESS MANAGER

The portion of the kernel that handles process scheduling (like all other parts of the kernel) is executed only when a process begins executing in supervisor mode—due to either a system call or an interrupt (see Figure 20.4).

✦ FIGURE 20.4   Part of Task Control Flow in the Kernel

This diagram shows the relationship among different blocks of Linux kernel code. When a task is running, an interrupt request (IRQ) causes it to begin executing the interrupt service routine (ISR), which either finishes the interrupt as a slow or fast interrupt. A trap causes a system call, which has a standard epilogue to return from the system call.

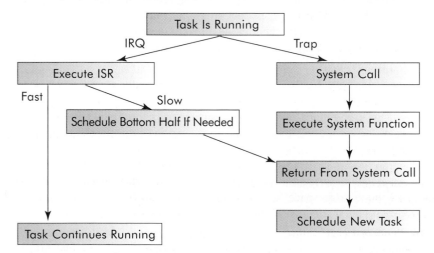

■ **System call.** Suppose a process is executing user mode software and it makes a system call. The process traps into the kernel code to the entry point for the target function. The function is executed by the kernel task corresponding to the user process that made the system call. When the function completes its work, it returns to the kernel so that it can perform a standard set of tasks in the `ret_from_sys_call` code (a block of assembly language code in the kernel). This code block dispatches any accumulated system work, such as handling signals, completing certain forms of pending interrupt process (called "executing the bottom halves of pending interrupt handlers"), or scheduling other tasks. The system call is completed with the calling process in the `TASK_RUNNING` (ready to use the CPU when it is available) state, or in the `TASK_INTERRUPTIBLE` or `TASK_UNINTERRUPTIBLE` state if the kernel cannot complete the requested work immediately. If the task is blocked (or it has used all of its timeslice), the scheduler is then called to dispatch a new task.

■ **Interrupt (IRQ).** When an IRQ occurs, the currently running process completes executing its current instruction and then the task starts executing the *ISR* (*interrupt service routine*) for the corresponding IRQ. Linux differentiates between fast and slow interrupts. A *fast interrupt* is one that takes very little time to complete, so while it is being processed, other interrupts are disabled, the interrupt is handled, the interrupts are reenabled, and the user process is continued. A *slow interrupt* involves more work: After the interrupts are disabled, the task executes the ISR. The ISR can have a bottom half, which has work that needs to be performed before the interrupt handling is completed, but which does not have to be done in the ISR itself. The pending bottom half work is scheduled in a kernel queue for the next time that bottom halves are to be processed (see the `ret_from_sys_call` processing in the system call description). Slow interrupts can, themselves, be interrupted; therefore, the queue of bottom half work can build up when nested interrupts occur. If the same ISR is invoked two or more times before the bottom halves are run, then the corresponding bottom half will be run only once even though the ISR executed multiple times. When the slow interrupt finishes the ISR, it executes the `ret_from_sys_call` block of code.

CREATING A NEW TASK

A new task/process is created when its parent process invokes the `fork()` system call (or the `clone()` system call in newer versions). When the kernel creates a new task, it must allocate a new instance of the process descriptor so that it will have a data structure to hold all the information it needs to manage the new task. In the Linux kernel, the process descriptor is an instance of the `struct task_struct` data type (see Section 6.4). The *process table* keeps the collection of process descriptors for each task/process. As described earlier, the idle task occupies the first slot in the table.

Each process descriptor may be linked into one or more lists (besides the process table), depending on the current state of the process. For example, if the process is in the `TASK_RUNNING` state, it is in a list pointed to by a static kernel variable (named `current`) indicating which processes are ready to use a CPU. If it is blocked waiting for an I/O operation to complete, then it appears in a list of processes waiting for an interrupt from the device.

The `fork()` system call creates a new process by performing the following steps:

■ Allocate a new instance of a `struct task_struct` and link it into the `task` list.

■ Create a new kernel space stack for the task to use when it is executing in the kernel.

■ Copy each field from the parent's task descriptor into the child's task descriptor.

■ Modify the fields in the child's descriptor that are specific to the child.

■ Save the new process identifier (PID).

■ Create links to this task's parent and siblings.

■ Initialize process-specific timers (including creation time, and time left in the current timeslice).

■ Copy other data structures that are referenced in the parent descriptor and that should be replicated for the child process.

■ Create a file table and a new file descriptor for each open file in the parent's file table.

■ Create a new user data segment for the child task and then copy the contents of the parent's user data segment into this new segment. (This could be very time-consuming, since the data segment could contain megabytes of information.)

■ Copy information regarding the signals and signal handlers.

■ Copy virtual memory tables.

■ Change the child's state to `TASK_RUNNING` and return from the system call.

Of course, an `execve()` system call will also greatly influence the contents of the process descriptor, since it causes the process to load and execute a different program than it was executing when it called `execve()`. Briefly, the `execve()` code causes the kernel to find the new executable file in the file system, to check access permissions, to adjust the memory requirements as necessary, and then to load the file for subsequent execution. This will require that the details of the memory references in the process descriptor be updated.

The Linux kernel also includes a system call named `clone()`, which is used to support threads in Version 2.2 and later. The `clone()` and `fork()` calls both invoke the internal kernel function named `do_fork()`, so they behave almost the same. The difference is in the way that the parent and child data segment is handled: While `fork()` copies the data segment, `clone()` shares it (and most of the rest of the parent's address space) between the parent and child tasks.

IPC AND SYNCHRONIZATION

There are two distinct synchronization mechanisms used in the kernel: One is used to coordinate concurrent kernel threads, and the other is the basis of the synchronization mechanisms for user processes. The uniprocessor kernel always executes as a single task invoked via the system call interface, or as activity caused by an interrupt. Kernel activity can never be interrupted by a system call, because when either an interrupt is being handled or a system call is being processed, no user process can issue a system call. Therefore, the primary need for synchronization within the kernel is to be sure that interrupts do not occur while the current kernel code is in a critical section. This is satisfied by disabling interrupts at the beginning of the critical section (using the `cli()`—*CL*ear *I*nterrupt kernel function) and then reenabling them (using the `sti()`—*Se*T *I*nterrupt function) when the critical section is complete. The SMP version of the kernel introduces a supplementary kernel lock mechanism.

The external synchronization mechanism is based on an event model. The kernel implements an abstract data type called a `wait_queue` to manage events. Each event has a corresponding `wait_queue`. A task can be added to a designated `wait_queue` using the `add_wait_queue()`, kernel function. Correspondingly, the `remove_wait_queue()` kernel function removes a single task from the designated wait queue. This abstract data type is the basis of any system call to perform synchronization, such as the System V semaphore system calls.

There are four different mechanisms by which a user process can perform IPC using the kernel:

- **Pipes (and named pipes).** These mechanisms export the same interface as files, so much of the implementation is like a file. A pipe uses a 4KB circular buffer to move information from one address space to another via the file `read()` and `write()` system calls. From a process management perspective, this procedure is straightforward.

- **System V IPC.** This interface allows user processes to create IPC objects (such as semaphores) in the kernel. The kernel allocates the data structure instance and then associates it with a user-space identifier that is shared among user processes. In the case of semaphores, one process creates the semaphore; then others manipulate it using the external reference and operations. The semaphore semantics are implemented using a `wait_queue` instance. System V messages generalize this approach so that structured messages can be saved/retrieved from kernel data structures.

- **System V shared memory.** The shared memory facility is the generalization of the System V IPC mechanism. In this case, a block of memory is allocated in the kernel and then an external reference is used by different processes to access the memory.

- **Sockets.** This mechanism is a special case of the general network socket functionality. A socket implementation requires that the kernel allocate and manage buffer space and socket descriptors. These kernel entities normally are used by the network code, although they can also be used in the "UNIX name domain" as a specialized form of pipe. They differ from pipes in that a socket is full duplexed, and is designed to use a protocol for reading and writing information.

THE SCHEDULER

The scheduler is responsible for multiplexing the CPU among the programs in memory (see Section 7.6), that is, among the processes that are in the `TASK_RUNNING` state. It incorporates the policy used to select the next process to be allocated the CPU. The `schedule()` kernel function can be invoked due to a trap, and it is also called as part of the `ret_from_sys_call` code block, so it always runs as a task that is associated with either a user process or an interrupt. The scheduler is responsible for determining which runnable task has the highest priority and then dispatching that task (allocating the CPU to it).

schedule() gets called from various other system call functions (for example, when a process becomes blocked), and after every system call and slow interrupt. Each time the scheduler is called, it performs periodic work (such as running device bottom halves), inspects the set of tasks in the TASK_RUNNING state, chooses one to execute according to the scheduling policy, and then dispatches the task to run on the CPU until an interrupt occurs.

After Version 2.0, the scheduler has three different scheduling strategies built into it, identified by the constants SCHED_OTHER, SCHED_FIFO, and SCHED_RR. The scheduling policy for each process can be set at runtime using the sched_setscheduler() system call (defined in kernel/sched.c). The task's current scheduling policy is saved in the policy field. Two of the policies, SCHED_FIFO and SCHED_RR, are intended to be sensitive to real-time requirements so they use scheduling priorities in the range [0:99], while SCHED_OTHER only handles the zero priority. Each process also has a priority field in its task descriptor. Conceptually, the scheduler has a multilevel queue with 100 levels (corresponding to the priorities from 0 to 99). Whenever a process with a priority that is higher than the currently running process becomes runnable, the lower-priority process is preempted and the higher-priority process begins to run. Of course, in the normal timesharing (SCHED_OTHER) policy, processes do not preempt one another since they all have a priority of zero.

Any task/process that uses the SCHED_FIFO policy must have superuser permission and have a priority of 1 to 99 (that is, it has a higher priority than all SCHED_OTHER tasks). Thus, whenever any SCHED_FIFO task becomes runnable, it takes priority over every SCHED_OTHER task. The SCHED_FIFO policy does not reschedule on a timer interrupt; once a SCHED_FIFO task gets control of the CPU, it will effectively retain control until it completes, it blocks by an I/O call, it calls sched_yield(), or until a higher-priority task becomes runnable. If it yields or is preempted by another higher-priority task, it is placed at the end of the queue of tasks at the same priority level.

The SCHED_RR policy has the same general characteristics as the SCHED_FIFO policy except that it uses the timeslicing mechanism to multiplex the CPU among tasks that are in the highest-priority queue. If a running SCHED_RR task is preempted by a higher-priority task, it is placed back on the head of its queue so that it will resume when its queue priority is again the highest in the system. The preempted process will then be allowed to complete its time quantum.

The SCHED_OTHER policy is the default timesharing policy. It uses the conventional timeslicing mechanism (rescheduling on timer interrupts) to put an upper bound on the amount of time that a task can use the CPU continuously if other tasks are waiting to use it. The priorities used to discriminate among tasks in the other two policies are ignored in this policy. Instead, a priority is computed on the basis of the value assigned to the task by the nice() or setpriority() system calls, and by the amount of time that a process has been waiting for the CPU to become available. The counter field in the task descriptor becomes the key component in determining the dynamic priority of the task: It is adjusted on each timer interrupt (when the interrupt handler adjusts the various timer fields for the task).

20.5 • MEMORY MANAGER

Linux uses a demand paged virtual memory model as the basis of its memory management design (see Section 12.5). In this model, each process is allocated its own virtual address space. Processes reference virtual addresses, and the system maps each such reference into a primary (also called physical) memory address prior to accessing the memory location. The kernel and the hardware, together, ensure that the contents of the virtual memory location are placed into the physical memory and that the corresponding virtual address is bound to the correct physical memory location when it is referenced by the process.

Like all demand paged virtual memory managers, the basic unit of memory allocation and transfer is a page. In the i386 implementation, each page contains 2^{12} (4,096) bytes. Since Linux uses a paged virtual memory approach, the general characteristics of the manager's responsibilities are that:

- Blocks are allocated and deallocated as physical memory page frames.
- The protection mechanism is on a page-by-page basis.
- The memory sharing is based on pages.
- Automatic movement through the memory hierarchy is controlled by moving pages back and forth between the secondary and primary memories.

Each process is created with its own virtual address space. In the i386 architecture, a virtual address is 32 bits wide, meaning that the space contains addresses for 4 GB. Since a page is 2^{12} bytes, this means there are 2^{20} pages in an address space.

Each virtual address space is divided into segments: a 3GB *user segment* and a 1GB *kernel segment*. A programmer can use any address in the user segment to reference all of its code and data by having the OS map information into specific virtual addresses. Unmapped virtual addresses are simply not used. The virtual addresses in the kernel segment are permanently mapped and are associated with fixed physical memory addresses used by the kernel. This means that every process's virtual address space shares the same kernel segment, since the kernel virtual addresses all map to the physical addresses used by the kernel.

Each of the kernel and user segments is further partitioned into code and data *sectors*. Each virtual address contains a sector identification and offset within the sector. When the CPU is in the instruction fetch phase, it always references a code sector (in either the user or kernel segment). Therefore, the compiler does not bother to generate the sector identification as part of the address used by an instruction (there is no need to have special object code formats for Linux).

Whenever a process is executing, its state includes a *segment selector*. If the process is executing in user space, the segment selector is set to `user`; if it is executing in the kernel segment, the selector is set to `kernel`. The memory manager forms the virtual address by using the value of the segment selector with the offset address provided by the process. Linux provides macros for setting the segment selector for each of the four segments in the virtual address space.

The mapped portions of the virtual address space are divided into 4KB pages. Pages that have been mapped can have their contents located in the secondary storage swap space (either a file or a file system). However, not all virtual address contents are defined at the time the virtual address is defined. For example, the compiler can cause space to be reserved but not initialized; the space for the stack and heap are examples of this. These mapped blocks of the virtual address space that have no initial content definition are called *anonymous memory* blocks; they are handled a little differently than those for which the content is defined in the swap space.

✦ FIGURE 20.5   Virtual Memory Components

This figure shows software (rounded boxes) and hardware (squared boxes) components. The do_mmap() function binds addresses to an internal data structure so that when a page fault occurs on the given address, the fault handler will be able to find the details of the missing information. The address translation mechanism was discussed in Section 12.5.

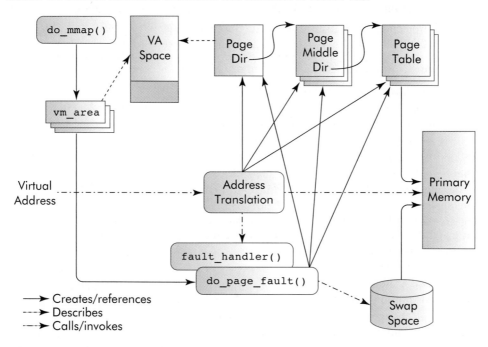

Figure 20.5 summarizes the components of the virtual memory manager. The process is ready to execute once the information that is located in the swap space has been mapped into the virtual address space (see the do_mmap() function in the figure). When the process attempts to fetch its first instruction, it references the part of the virtual address space that contains the entry point for the program. If the page address translation hardware detects that the page is not loaded, it will cause a page fault interrupt. The normal kernel interrupt processing mechanism will field the page fault interrupt, perform standard processing, and then call the page fault handler (do_page_fault()). The page fault handler is responsible for determining if the virtual address reference is within the virtual address space, and if it is, for retrieving the missing page from the swap space.

Loading the page requires that the page fault handler find a place to load the page in the primary memory, swap the page into the primary memory, and then update the Page Directory, Page Middle Directory, and Page Table (see Section 12.5). After the page is loaded—the page fault handling has been completed—the instruction that caused the interrupt is executed again, this time with the assurance that the missing page has been loaded. As the process continues to execute, it will reference different pages that contain its program as well as the data on which the program is executing. Each time a process references a virtual address that is in a page that is not currently loaded in the primary memory, a page fault will occur.

THE VIRTUAL ADDRESS SPACE

When a process is created, it inherits a 32-bit (4GB) virtual address space from its parent. Locations 0x0 to 0xBFFFFFFF can be used by the process when it is executing in user space, and locations 0xC0000000 to 0xFFFFFFFF are used when the process is executing in supervisor mode. The last 1 GB references kernel components, so this portion of the address space has the same mapping for every process. In terms of the architecture-independent model introduced in Section 12.5, every process uses the same Page Table to reference the addresses used by the kernel (meaning that the Page Middle directory entry for this part of the address space references the same Page Table in every process).

Kernel addresses are distinguished from user space addresses by the notion of segments. A full virtual address must specify a segment selector (user or kernel). Each segment is divided into segments that hold data (that can be read or written) and code (that can only be executed and read). User code has the segment selector implicitly set to user, so the code only provides offsets within the user segment. Each segment has its own page table (the collection of page tables for the process is kept in the Page Middle directory). The memory translation mechanism can then prevent the user space process from referencing locations in the kernel segment, and vice versa.

The organization of the user space segments are specific to the version of Linux and the loader format (a.out, COFF, or ELF). Figure 20.6 illustrates the layout of ELF in Version 2.0 [Beck, et al., 1998]. The heap grows in increasing address direction above the BSS area, while the stack grows toward lower addresses from the arguments and environment. Shared C libraries (each as a group of code, data, and BSS) are mapped into the address space at location 0x40000000 toward higher addresses. Whenever the loader (or any form of an exec() system call) is run, the portion of the address space between start_code and brk is (re)mapped so that the new memory image is bound to specific virtual addresses. These virtual addresses are saved in the mm field of the process descriptor by the loader:

The brk() system call can also cause addresses to be mapped. The purpose of brk() is to extend the size of the virtual address space being used by the process; this value is set at load time by the loader or exec(), and can be modified at run time by brk(). When brk() (see mm/mmap.c) is called, it does various error checking and then calls do_mmap().

THE PAGE FAULT HANDLER

The page fault handler is responsible for finding a page frame in the physical memory (possibly swapping an existing page back to the swap space), swapping the missing page

✦ FIGURE 20.6   User Space Format

This figure shows the details of a memory map (compared to the high-level view in Figure 11.11). The memory map describes the layout of a process's user space (the text, data, stack, and heap as well as space for shared libraries).

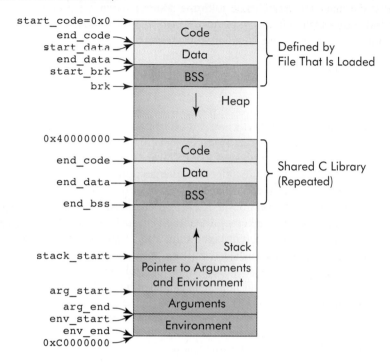

into the page frame, and adjusting the page tables. Like Mach, Linux uses the copy-on-write strategy for sharing pages among address spaces; whenever any process attempts to write to a page that is marked to be copied on a write operation (that is, it is marked as read-only), the write operation will cause a page write violation fault. The address translation mechanism raises interrupt 0x80 when it detects a missing page or other page fault (such as a protection violation). The system interrupt handler dispatches a kernel function to handle the interrupt.

Both normal page faults and copy-on-write faults are handled by the page fault handler. In the case of a copy-on-write fault, the page fault handler will simply copy an in-memory page rather than retrieve it from the secondary storage. It then resets the page descriptors in both address spaces so that no additional copy-on-write faults will cause a page fault.

The memory manager uses a dynamic page allocation strategy, meaning that the number of page frames allocated to a process varies according to the behavior of that particular process and the overall activity in the system. Here, process behavior refers to the size of the working set of the process—the number of different pages that the process is using at any given time. For example, the process might be using 10 different pages that contain code and another 15 that contain data: The size of the working set would then be 25 pages.

Another process might only be using 12 code pages and 6 data pages, or 18 total pages. When a process generates a page fault, the memory manager will ordinarily try to allocate an additional page frame in which to load the missing page. Thus, when one process needs another page frame, some other process may lose one (there are also other pools of page frames that the manager may choose to tap such as pages being used by shared library code, for memory-mapped files, or for device caching).

20.6 • FILE MANAGEMENT

The Linux file manager defines a single internal (application software) view of files that can be used to read and modify files written onto a storage device using a variety of file managers. For example, a disk that contains files written using MS-DOS (or a Windows OS with DOS compliant format) can be read or rewritten by a Linux application using the Linux file manager.

In Linux (and MS-DOS), a file is a named, linear sequence of bytes that is stored on a persistent storage device (such as a disk, a CD-ROM, or a tape). The file manager supports directory and file operations. Directory operations are used to manipulate the file hierarchy. File operations are used to manipulate the information that is stored inside a file, essentially, the functions that allow the process to read and write the file.

The system calls for performing file I/O enable a user process to open/close, read/write, and move the file position pointer (`lseek()`) in the file byte stream. As summarized in Figure 20.7, the file manager reacts to a `write()` function call by placing the information in one or more output buffers. If a buffer becomes full, the file manager will

✦ **FIGURE 20.7** Overview of File I/O

Linux file I/O coordinates activity in the file manager, memory manager (buffer management), and the device manager. An output operation causes information to be placed in a buffer, where the device driver retrieves it and writes it to a storage device. The file manager starts read operations to fill input buffers for application software.

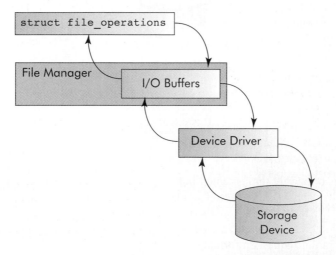

then enqueue a write request for the device driver. When the device driver detects that the storage device is idle and it decides that the buffer is the next one to write, it initiates a write operation to transfer the information from the output buffer into the storage device. A read operation causes the file manager to determine the current file position and then to issue a read operation to the device driver so that the data will be placed in an input buffer before the user process performs a read call on the `struct file-operations` interface. The following discussion describes more details of the open/close operations and the read/write operations (including block buffering).

The internal Linux view of a file is that it is a named byte stream that can be saved in the secondary storage system. The byte stream is fragmented into a set of blocks and then the blocks are stored on the secondary storage device according to a strategy chosen by a particular type of file system. The file manager fetches and puts the blocks that contain the portions of the byte stream that an application program reads or writes. That is, the file manager is responsible for determining which disk blocks should be read or written whenever any part of the byte stream is read or written.

Ordinary disk block read and write operations implicitly cause the file manager to buffer at least one input and one output sector per open file as part of serializing and packing blocks. As summarized in Figure 20.8, it is possible to exploit buffering by having a number of buffers used on input and output streams. The advantage is in performance: The file manager can "read ahead" on the input stream to avoid making the application block on a sector read. Similarly, the file manager can "write behind" so that the thread does not have to block while waiting for a sector write operation to finish.

✦ FIGURE 20.8 Buffering Sectors

The file manager ultimately controls buffer use, through read-ahead and write-behind buffering. Device I/O is asynchronous, with the control being in the file manager.

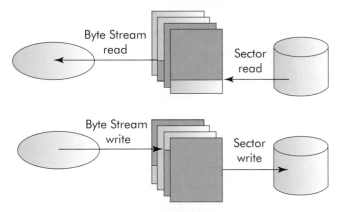

Buffering is ordinarily implemented in kernel space, although you can also implement the same mechanisms in user space. The idea is to design the file manager so that it uses asynchronous I/O to start sector reads (to read ahead N sectors on the byte stream) and writes (that write behind the current file pointer up to N sectors). When an application-level read operation requests information that has not yet been read, it must wait for the device read operation to complete before it can return a result to the application. As soon as the file manager has determined that the read operation has completed on buffer i, it can immediately start an asynchronous read on sector $i+1$. In the kernel space implementation, an interrupt notifies the software when the device has completed its operation. In a user space buffer manager, a signal (or other form of asynchronous procedure callback) can be used to notify the application that the sector read operation has completed.

The file system independent part of the file manager handles generic aspects of the work such as checking access rights, and determining when disk blocks need to be read or written. Another part of the file manager handles all file system dependent aspects of the job, such as determining where blocks are located on the disk, and directing the device driver to read or write specific blocks. The two combined parts enable Linux to provide a fixed set of operations at the API, yet to handle files on disks even if the files were written using a Windows OS, MINIX, or some other OS.

The Linux file manager API is built on an abstract file model that is exported by the Virtual File System (VFS), as explained in Sections 13.7 and 16.1. The VFS implements the file system independent operations. OS designers provide extensions to the VFS to implement all required file system dependent operations; the Version 2.x release can read and write disk files that conform to the MS-DOS format, the MINIX format, the /proc format, a Linux-specific format called *Ext2*, and others. Of course, this means that specific file system dependent components are included in Version 2.X to translate VFS operations and formats to/from each of the external formats that are supported.

The heart of VFS is the switch, which provides the canonical file management API to user space programs, and also establishes an internal interface used by the different file system translators that support MS-DOS files, MINIX files, Ext2 files, and so on (see Figure 20.9). A new file system can be supported by implementing a new file system dependent ("translator") component. Each such translator provides functions that the VFS switch can call (when it gets called by a user program), and that can translate the external file representation into the internal one. Thus, the translator is responsible for determining the strategy used to organize disk blocks on the disk device; for reading and writing disk properties; for reading and writing external file descriptor information; and for reading and writing the disk blocks that contain file data.

✦ **FIGURE 20.9** The Virtual File System Switch

The VFS allows Linux to support a variety of different file systems. The standard distribution of Linux supports MS-DOS, Ext2, ISO 9000, and other file systems.

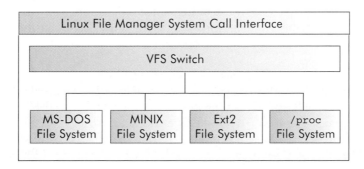

The VFS file system model is patterned after conventional UNIX file systems. A VFS file descriptor is called an *inode* (although it has its own unique format to support the multiple file system approach). Although VFS has its own format for a file descriptor, each file system dependent translator converts the contents of the external descriptor into the VFS inode format when the file is opened. VFS then operates on its own inode data structure. Conversely, when the file is closed, the contents of the internal inode are used to update the external file descriptor.

The VFS inode contains the file access rights, owner, group, size, creation time, last access time, last time the file was written, and other details about the file. The inode also reserves space for the pointer mechanism that the specific file system uses to organize the disk blocks, even though VFS does not know how these pointers will be organized. (That information is encapsulated in the file system specific translator component.) VFS also supports directories, so it presumes that the external file directories contain at least the name of each file stored in the directory and the address of its file descriptor (almost all file systems contain this minimum amount of information).

VFS assumes a minimum structure on the disk organizations:

- The first sector on the disk is a *boot block* used to store a bootstrap program. The file system does not really use the boot block, but it does presume that it is present on every file system.
- There is a **superblock**, containing disk-specific information such as the number of bytes in a disk block.
- There are external file descriptors on the disk that describe the characteristics of each file.
- There are data blocks that are linked into each file to contain the data.

Before VFS can manage a particular file system type, a translator for that type must be written and then registered with VFS. The VFS `register_filesystem()` function informs VFS of basic information it will need including the name of the file system type and the entry point of a file system's `read_super()` function that will be used when the file system is mounted.

20.7 • SUMMARY

Linux has enjoyed tremendous popularity in the last decade, due in large part to its open availability. The Linux design is similar to many other UNIX kernels, particularly tracking the BSD UNIX design. One aspect of Linux that differs from many other versions of UNIX is its module facility. Although modules are primarily used to construct device drivers, they can also be used to dynamically extend the kernel functionality in much broader terms.

The process management facilities are similar to other versions of UNIX. Alhough the process manager was originally designed to support only single-threaded processes, it has evolved to provide full kernel thread support.

The memory manager used a dynamic page allocation strategy. Each process is allocated a 4GB address space when it is created. 1GB of the address space is mapped to the kernel, and the other 3GB are used for programmer-defined entities. Whenever a process requires a new page frame, the memory manager will acquire it from the file system, another part of the OS, or another process.

The file manager is built around the virtual file system switch (VFS). This design divides the file manager design for a particular file system into file system dependent and independent parts. The file system independent part is used with all file systems, but the file system dependent part encapsulates the knowledge necessary to read and write that particular file system. This allows an administrator to mount an MS-DOS floppy disk on a Linux system and application programs to read and write the floppy as if it were a native Linux file system.

The Windows NT/2000/XP Kernel

The Windows NT/2000/XP OS is both a commercial and a technology leader. Besides the Linux examples, a number of Windows OS examples have been sprinkled throughout the book. This chapter focuses on the Windows NT/2000/XP kernel technology, which is used to implement Windows NT, 2000, and XP.

21.1 • INTRODUCTION

Microsoft began to market operating systems in about 1980 with the introduction of MS-DOS. For several years, MS-DOS was shipped with early IBM Personal computers under the name PC-DOS. During the 1980s, Microsoft refined MS-DOS, culminating in a version that supported graphic windows and multitasking. Meanwhile, development of the Windows NT operating system was well underway by 1990; it was released for public use in July, 1993 [Solomon, 1998]. In the 1995 timeframe, Microsoft also released Windows 95, so the MS-DOS windows system was replaced by two new Windows operating systems: Windows 95 and Windows NT. Windows 95 was designed to replace MS-DOS with Windows on personal computers, while Windows NT was aimed at machines that had been configured with more resources—"workstations" and servers. Windows 95 and Windows NT were developed separately, so they do not share much of the same code. However, Windows 95 implements a subset of the API supported by Windows NT. Windows NT Version 4 replaced the first release by 1997, and was the version of Windows NT that began to be embraced in the commercial world.

Windows 2000 was released in early 2000, although it had been under development as Windows NT Version 5 [Solomon, 1998]. That is, Windows 2000 is the same code as (Version 4) Windows NT but has refinements and bug fixes. The refinements addressed issues such as supporting plug-and-play device installation and power management. Considerable effort was also invested to make Windows more robust (so that it crashed less often).

Windows XP was released in 2001, soon after Windows 2000. Prior to its public release, it was known as Windows NT Version 5.1. Windows XP is intended to be a combination of Windows 2000 and Windows 98 (or the "Me" version of Windows 98). The release has a new user interface, and it also incorporates Windows 98 technology that is not subsumed by the Windows NT code base. Windows XP is also intended to be compliant with the .NET software. In the following discussion of the kernel, we will frequently refer to the Version 3, 4, and 5 NT software as the "NT kernel."

Microsoft operating systems are among the most widely used commercial systems available today. They use a modern computational model based on processes and threads. They also have a pervasive underlying object model. Even so, Windows NT carried on the early MS-DOS legacy, meaning it supports 16-bit application programs written for MS-DOS. (16-bit MS-DOS support no longer appears in current versions of Windows.)

In Section 3.3, you learned about the general organization of the Windows NT kernel. Figure 21.1 (a variant of Figure 3.12) summarizes that discussion, showing the primary components of the system. The HAL provides the first layer of the OS—the layer that is intended to make it easy to port the OS from one hardware platform to another. The NT Kernel performs many of the functions normally associated with a microkernel. It is responsible for handling interrupts, thread scheduling, and implementing objects that are used throughout the system. The NT Executive uses the NT Kernel facilities to implement the process manager, memory manager, file manager, and device manager framework. For example, a thread descriptor is an NT Executive object that contains all the information about the thread that the NT Executive knows (see Section 6.5). It also contains an embedded NT Kernel object used to synchronize parent and the child threads. In combination, the NT Executive and NT Kernel perform a similar function to the Linux kernel. However, the NT Executive and Kernel implement more system functions (about 2,000) than does the Linux kernel (about 200).

✦ FIGURE 21.1   Windows NT/2000 Organization

The Windows NT OS architecture is logically layered with a HAL, NT Kernel, NT Executive, and various subsystems on top of the NT Executive. The system call interface is the Win32 API that is exported by the Win32 subsystem. The I/O subsystem is separate from the rest of the OS kernel and contains the device drivers.

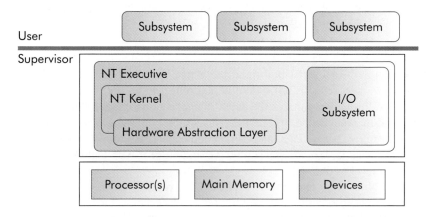

Although the NT Executive and the NT Kernel are designed and implemented as distinct software modules, they are combined into a single executable image called the NTOSKRNL.EXE before they are actually executed [Solomon and Russinovich, 2000]. The NTOSKRNL.EXE also invokes additional dynamically linked libraries (DLLs) whenever they are needed. Thus, the logical view of NT—that of a modular nucleus with a microkernel—is quite different from the way the executable image actually appears in memory. In studying Windows NT/2000/XP, it is best to use the logical view for considering different aspects of the OS, since that is the model under which it is designed. However, when writing programs that use Windows NT/2000/XP, knowing that the OS is implemented as a monolithic executable image may sometimes have an important influence on the way you use the OS.

Neither the NT Kernel nor the NT Executive is a standalone OS. An OS is created by combining the NT Kernel and NT Executive with a subsystem. The Win32 Subsystem provides a conventional OS interface. That is, the Win32 Subsystem exports the Win32 API, which is ordinarily thought of as the Windows NT/2000/XP system call interface, and constitutes the final piece of the entire Windows NT/2000/XP OS.

21.2 ● THE NT KERNEL

The NT Kernel defines the basic unit of computation—the thread—and provides the foundation for multithreading support. It does so without committing to any particular policy/strategy for process management, memory management, file management, or device management. To appreciate the level of support the NT Kernel provides, think of the NT Kernel as offering a collection of building components such as wheels, pistons, lights, and so on, that could be used to build a sports car, a sedan, a sports utility vehicle, or a truck. Similarly, the NT Kernel's clients can combine the components to build a compound component that defines a broad range of different policies for how the low-level components should be used.

The NT Kernel provides objects and threads (computational abstractions) on top of the HAL and the hardware. Software that uses the NT Kernel can be defined using objects and threads as primitives; that is, these abstractions appear to NT Kernel client software as natural parts of the hardware. To implement objects and threads, the Kernel must manage the hardware interrupts and exceptions, perform processor scheduling, and handle multiprocessor synchronization.

OBJECTS

The NT Kernel defines a set of built-in object types, usually called classes in object-oriented languages (see Section 2.5). Some kernel object types are instantiated by the NT Kernel itself to form other parts of the overall OS execution image. These objects collectively save and manipulate the NT Kernel's state. Other objects are instantiated and used by the NT Executive, subsystems, and application code as the foundation of their computational model. That is, Windows NT/2000/XP and all of its applications are managed at the NT Kernel level as objects.

NT Kernel objects are intended to be fast. They run in supervisor mode in a trusted context, so there is no security and only limited error checking for NT Kernel objects, in contrast to normal objects, which incorporate these features. However, NT Kernel objects cannot be manipulated directly by user-mode programs, only through NT kernel function calls. NT Kernel objects are characterized as being either control objects or dispatcher objects. Control objects implement mechanisms to control the hardware and other Kernel resources. Dispatcher objects are used to implement threads along with their scheduling and synchronization operations (see Section 9.1). Each dispatcher object has built-in characteristics that are used to support user-level synchronization.

THREADS

A Windows NT/2000/XP process object defines an address space in which one or more threads can execute, and each thread object represents one execution within the process. In the Windows NT/2000/XP environment, it is common to have more than one thread executing in a process. The separation of the thread concept from the rest of the process concept has been done so that it is natural to think of several different "threads of execution" within a single address space, all sharing the same resources.

The NT thread scheduler is a timesliced, priority-based, preemptive scheduler (see Section 7.6). The basic unit of processor allocation is a time quantum computed as a multiple of the number of clock interrupts. The scheduler is a multiple-level queue scheduler: As long as there are threads in the highest-priority queue, then only those threads will be allocated the processor. If there are no threads in that queue, then the scheduler will service the threads in the second highest-priority queue. If there are no threads ready to run in the second highest-priority queue, the scheduler will service the third highest-priority queue, and so on.

A thread's base priority is normally inherited from its process. It can also be set with various function calls, provided the caller has the authority to set the priority. The Win32 model defines four priority classes (REAL TIME, HIGH, NORMAL, and IDLE), and each thread also has a relative thread priority (TIME CRITICAL, HIGHEST, ABOVE NORMAL, NORMAL, BELOW NORMAL, LOWEST, and IDLE) within the class. A thread could be in the HIGH class and operating at the ABOVE NORMAL relative priority at one moment, but then be in the HIGH class and operating at the BELOW NORMAL relative priority a little later. Base priority is defined by the thread's class and the class's NORMAL relative priority. If the priority class is not REAL TIME, then the thread's priority will be for one of the variable level queues. In this case, NT may adjust priorities of threads in the variable level according to system conditions. NT does not change the priority of a thread that has been placed in the real-time levels.

As mentioned in Section 7.6, the scheduler is preemptive, so whenever a thread becomes ready to run, it is placed in a run queue at a level corresponding to its current priority. If there is another thread in execution at that time and that thread has a lower priority, then the lower-priority thread is interrupted (it is not allowed to finish its time quantum) and the new higher-priority thread is assigned the processor.

MULTIPROCESS SYNCHRONIZATION

Uniprocessor systems can support synchronization by disabling interrupts. However, Windows NT/2000/XP is designed to support multiprocessors, so the NT Kernel provides an alternative mechanism to ensure that a thread executing on one processor does not violate a critical section of a thread on another. As is traditional in multiprocessor operating systems, the NT Kernel employs spinlocks, by which a thread on one process can wait for a critical section by actively testing an NT Kernel lock variable to determine when it can enter the critical section. If the hardware supports the test-and-set instruction (or other machine instruction that is logically equivalent to test-and-set), spinlocks are implemented using the hardware. Spinlock synchronization is used only within the NT Kernel and NT Executive. User-mode programs use abstractions that are implemented by the NT Executive (see Section 9.1).

TRAPS, INTERRUPTS, AND EXCEPTIONS

In the Windows NT terminology, the Kernel *trap handler* is responsible for reacting to hardware interrupts and processor exceptions (such as system service call, execution errors, and virtual memory faults). Whenever an interrupt or processor exception is recognized by the hardware, the NT trap handler (see Figure 21.2) moves into action. It is responsible for:

1. Disabling interrupts
2. Determining the cause of the interrupt or exception
3. Saving processor state in a trap frame
4. Reenabling interrupts
5. Changing the processor to supervisor mode if required
6. Dispatching specialized code (an Interrupt Service Routine (ISR), a dynamically linked library (DLL), an exception dispatcher, or the virtual memory handler) to handle the trap.

In the case of an interrupt, the trap handler will normally run an ISR for the specific interrupt; for exceptions, the trap handler may address the cause itself or invoke the appropriate OS code to react to the exception.

✦ FIGURE 21.2 Windows NT Trap Handler

The trap handler combines the functionality of a conventional trap table and an interrupt handler. It is a single distribution point for traps and interrupts.

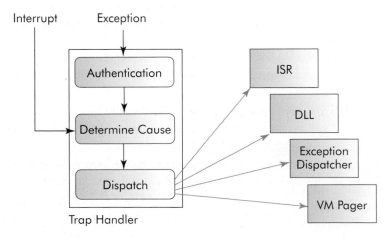

As in all system call interface OS designs, supervisor mode functions are invoked by an application program when it executes an instruction that causes an exception—the trap instruction. It is necessary to use the trap handler to call system functions since the processor mode needs to be switched from user mode to supervisor mode. Before the mode can be switched, the OS must be assured that the code to be executed (while the hardware is in supervisor mode) is trusted code. Therefore, user programs are not allowed to link and call these functions directly; instead, they can only be invoked through the trap handler. In the NT Kernel, the trap handler uses a DLL (NTDLL.DLL) to authenticate the call and start the OS code. The application links the NTDLL.DLL into its address space and then calls entry points in the DLL. They are translated into traps (using the host hardware mechanism for raising an exception) that cause the processor mode to be switched to supervisor mode and a secure call to be made on the OS code.

Interrupts are used to allow a device to notify the OS when the device completes an operation. The NT Kernel's interrupt management generally follows the same design as has been followed in other operating systems for a number of years. Each device operation is initiated by the device's driver. The thread initiating the operation may wait for the I/O call to complete (a synchronous I/O call), or continue running concurrently with the I/O operation (an asynchronous I/O call). Traditionally (for example, in standard C programs), the API does allow the application thread to use asynchronous I/O, although asynchronous I/O is fully supported in the OS. The API used with Windows NT/2000/XP extends the normal C routines so that application programs can use asynchronous I/O operations.

In either the synchronous or asynchronous case, the processor will continue to execute software concurrent with the device operation—the calling thread's code in the asynchronous case or another thread's code in the synchronous case. The device will eventually signal the processor that it has completed the I/O operation by raising an interrupt. This causes the trap handler to run and to determine which device has completed, and then to run an ISR that will finish the housekeeping related to completing the I/O operation. Each time the user moves the mouse, types a key, or receives information from a connected network, an interrupt is raised, the trap handler runs, and an ISR is called to manage the incoming information.

21.3 • THE NT EXECUTIVE

The NT Executive builds on the NT Kernel to implement the full set of Windows NT/2000/XP policies and services, including process management, memory management, file management, and device management. Since Windows NT/2000/XP uses object technology, its modularization does not strictly follow the classic separation of OS functionality. Instead, the NT Executive is designed and implemented at the source code level as a modularized set of elements [Solomon and Russinovich, 2000; Nagar, 1997].

OBJECT MANAGER

The NT Executive Object Manager implements another object model on top of the NT Kernel Object Manager (see Figure 21.3). Whereas Kernel objects operate in a trusted environment, Executive objects are used by other parts of the Executive and user mode software and must take extra measures to assure secure and reliable operation.

✦ **FIGURE 21.3** Handles, NT Executive Objects, and NT Kernel Objects

This figure repeats information from the process and thread descriptor discussion in Chapter 6. It indicates that the NT Executive and NT Kernel objects (and their handles) are managed uniformly for various OS data structures that are referenced from application code.

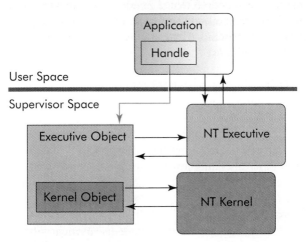

An NT Executive object exists in supervisor space, although it can be referenced by user threads. This is accomplished by having the Object Manager provide a handle for each NT Executive object. Whenever a thread needs a new NT Executive object, it calls an Object Manager function to create the object (in supervisor space), create a handle to the object (in the process's address space), and then return the handle to the calling thread. Sometimes a second thread will want to use an NT Executive object that has already been created. When the second thread attempts to create the existing object, the Object Manager notes that the object already exists, so it creates a second handle for the second thread to use to reference the existing NT Executive object. The two threads share the single object. The Object Manager keeps a reference count of all handles to an Executive object; when all outstanding handles have been closed, the Executive object is deallocated. Notice that this means that it is important for each thread to close each handle it opens, preferably as soon as it no longer needs the handle.

There is a predefined set of object types supported by the Object Manager (see Lab Exercise 6.1). When an object is created, it includes an object header (used by the Object Manager to manage the object) and a body to contain type-specific information. The header includes:

- ■ **Object name:** Allows the object to be referenced by different processes.
- ■ **Security descriptor:** Access permissions.
- ■ **Open handle information:** Details of which processes are using the object.
- ■ **Object type:** Details of the object's class definition.
- ■ **Reference count:** The number of outstanding handles that reference the object.

The information in the header is managed by the NT Executive Object Manager. For example, when a new handle is created to an object, the Executive Object Manager updates the Open handle information and reference count. The object type information defines a "standard" set of methods the object implements (by virtue of being an NT Executive object), such as open(), close(), and delete(). Some of these methods are supplied by the NT Executive Object Manager and some must be tailored to the object type. However, the interface is determined as part of the object header. The object body format is determined by the Executive component that uses the object. For example, if the Executive object is a file object, the body format and contents are managed by the File Manager part of the I/O Manager.

PROCESS AND THREAD MANAGER

The NT Executive Process Manager serves the same purpose in the NT Executive that a process manager serves in any OS. It is the part of the OS responsible for:

- Creating and destroying processes and threads.
- Overseeing resource allocation.
- Providing synchronization primitives.
- Controlling process and thread state changes.
- Keeping account of most of the information that the OS knows about each process and thread.

In short, it manages all aspects of threads and processes that are not managed by some other specialized element (such as object-specific characteristics, and the file characteristics).

The Process Manager implements the process abstraction that will be used at the subsystem and application levels. Implementing the abstraction means that the Process Manager defines a number of data structures for keeping track of the state of each process and thread (see Figure 21.4, where black lines represent pointers and gray lines represent code referencing the contents of a data structure). These components were discussed in Sections 6.4 and 6.5.

The NTOSKRNL function NtCreateProcess() is called to create a process; that is, the Win32 API CreateProcess() function calls NtCreateProcess(). When NtCreateProcess() is called (ordinarily by CreateProcess()), it performs the following work in setting up the process:

- Call the NT Kernel to have it create a kernel process object.
- Create and initialize an EPROCESS block.
- Create an address space for the process.

A process has no ability to execute code in its address space; it must have at least one thread, called the base thread, to execute the code. The NtCreateThread() NT Executive function will create a thread that can execute within the process. (The Win32 API CreateProcess() function calls both NTCreateProcess() and NtCreateThread(); the CreateThread() function calls NtCreateThread() to create additional threads within a process.) NtCreateThread() performs the following work:

- Call the NT Kernel to have it create a kernel thread object.
- Create and initialize an ETHREAD block.

- Initialize the thread for execution (set up its stack, provide it an executable start address, and so on).
- Place the thread in a scheduling queue

✦ **FIGURE 21.4** Process and Thread Descriptors

Process and thread descriptors are referenced by the EPROCESS data structure, and are handled by both the NT Kernel and the NT Executive.

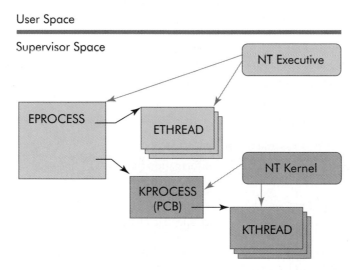

VIRTUAL MEMORY MANAGER

The Windows NT/2000 virtual memory system was introduced in Section 12.5. It is a paging virtual memory system. When a process is created, it is given 4 GB of virtual addresses, although none of the addresses are actually allocated at that time. When the process needs space, it first reserves as much of the address space as it needs at that moment. Reserved addresses do not cause any actual space to be allocated; rather, virtual addresses are reserved for later use. When the process needs to use the virtual addresses to store information, it commits the address space, meaning that some system storage space is then allocated to the process to hold information. Ordinarily, a commit operation causes space on the disk (in the process's page file) to be allocated to the process. The information is stored on the disk until it actually is referenced by a thread.

Like all demand paging virtual memory mechanisms, when an executing thread references a virtual address, the Virtual Memory Manager ensures that the page containing that virtual address is read from the page file and placed at some system-defined location in the physical executable memory. The Virtual Memory Manager *maps* the virtual address referenced by the thread into the physical memory address where the information is loaded.

The Virtual Memory Manager has been designed so that a large portion of each process's address space (usually half of it, although different configurations of Windows use different fractions) is mapped to the information used by the system when it is in supervisor mode (see Figure 21.5). There are a few important implications of this decision, as follows:

■ A process can directly reference (but not necessarily access) every location in the system space.

■ Every process shares the same view of the system's space.

■ Such a large, shared virtual address space makes memory-mapped files feasible.

In Figure 21.5, when a thread references an address in the user space, the virtual memory system loads the target location into the physical memory prior to its use so that the thread can read or write the virtual memory address by referencing a physical memory address. The same mapping takes place for OS memory references, even though these references are protected, and every process's OS addresses map to the OS memory rather than to the application-specific part of the address space.

✦ FIGURE 21.5 Virtual Memory

Virtual addresses in both the OS and user portions of the address space are mapped into a physical primary memory address. If a referenced page is not loaded when it is referenced, then the virtual address reference will cause the virtual memory system to load it from the page file.

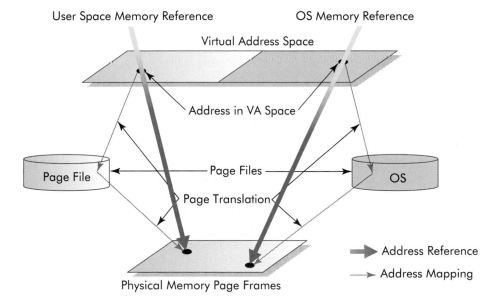

I/O MANAGER

The I/O Manager is responsible for handling all the input/output operations to every device in the system. Its operation can be quite complex [Solomon and Russinovich, 2000].

■ The I/O Manager creates an abstraction of all device I/O operations on the system so that the system's clients can perform operations on a common data structure.

■ The client can perform synchronous and asynchronous I/O.

■ The client can invoke the Security Reference Monitor whenever security is an issue.

■ The I/O Manager must accommodate device drivers written in a high-level language by third parties. Those drivers must be able to execute in supervisor mode. Installation and removal of a device driver must be dynamic.

■ The I/O Manager can accommodate alternative file systems on the system's disks. This means that some file systems might use the MS-DOS format, others might use an industry standard CD-ROM format, and yet others might use Windows 2000's own file system (NTFS).

■ I/O Manager extensions—device drivers and/or file systems—must be consistent with the memory-mapped file mechanism implemented in the Virtual Memory Manager, so extension designs are constrained by the facilities provided by the manager.

✦ FIGURE 21.6   The I/O Manager

The I/O Manager has many layers of functionality, each of which can be configured into an I/O stream as needed. Each device uses a HAL and device driver, and normally a file system driver. The other layers are used as required.

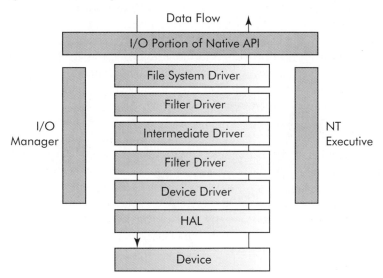

The I/O Manager is made up of the following components, as shown in Figure 21.6 [Nagar, 1997].

■ **Device drivers** are at the lowest level. They manipulate the physical I/O devices.

■ **Intermediate drivers** are software modules that work with a low-level device driver to provide enhanced service. For example, a low-level device driver might simply pass an error condition "upward" when it detects it, whereas an intermediate driver might receive the error and decide to issue a retry operation to the lower-level driver.

- **File system drivers** extend the functionality of the lower-level drivers (such as intermediate and device drivers) to implement the target file system.

- **Filter drivers** can be inserted between a device driver and an intermediate driver, between an intermediate driver and a file system driver, or between the file system driver and the I/O Manager API to perform any kind of function that might be desired. For example, a network redirector filter driver can intercept file commands intended for remote files and redirect them to remote file servers.

Drivers are the single component that can be added to the NT Executive to run in supervisor mode. The OS has not been designed to support third-party software, other than drivers, that want to add supervisor mode functionality.

The Windows NT/2000/XP I/O Manager defines the framework in which device drivers, intermediate drivers, file system drivers, and filter drivers dynamically are added to and removed from the system and are made to work together. The basic idea of a stream of modules between the API and device was first used in the AT&T System V UNIX I/O streams [Ritchie, 1984]. The dynamic stream design allows one to configure complex I/O systems easily; the System V streams were the basis of the network protocol implementations.

Also similar to System V streams, the I/O Manager directs modules by issuing *I/O request packets* (IRPs) into a stream. If the IRP is intended for a particular module, that module responds to the IRP; otherwise, it passes the IRP to the next module in the stream. Each driver in the stream has the responsibility of accepting IRPs, either reacting to the IRP if it is directed at the driver or passing it on to the next module if it is not.

All information read from or written to the device is managed as a stream of bytes called a *virtual file*. Every driver is written to read and/or write a virtual file. Low-level device drivers transform information read from the device into a stream and transform stream information into a device-dependent format before writing it.

THE CACHE MANAGER

A classic bottleneck to an application's performance is the time it has to wait for a physical device to process an I/O command. As processors become faster, the fraction of the total run time spent waiting for devices to complete their I/O operations increasingly dominates the total run time. As we have seen, the classic solution to the problem is to devise ways for the thread to execute concurrently with its own device I/O operations. This inherently means that the thread is able to predict information that it will require before it actually needs it, so it issues an I/O request in anticipation of using data and then concurrently processes data it has already read.

The Cache Manager is designed to work with the Virtual Memory Manager and the I/O Manager to perform read-ahead and write-behind on virtual files. The idea is the classic OS idea: Since files are usually accessed sequentially, whenever a thread reads byte i, it is likely to read byte $i+1$ soon thereafter. Therefore, on a read-ahead strategy, when the thread requests that byte i be read from the device, the Cache Manager asks the Virtual Memory Manager to prepare a buffer to hold $K+1$ bytes of information from the virtual file; then it instructs the I/O Manager to read byte i and the next K bytes into the buffer. Then, when the thread requests byte $i+1, i+2, ..., i+K$, they will have already been read so the thread need not wait for a device operation to complete. The write-behind strategy works similarly.

Most of the Cache Manager's operation is transparent above the NTOSKRNL API. The Win32 API has only four attributes to influence the Cache Manager's operation—essentially information to assure the Cache Manager that the thread will access the information in the file sequentially. (These attributes are set when the process calls CreateFile().) The main clients for the Cache Manager are drivers that are added to the I/O Manager; it is these modules that customize the file system and use the file caching facilities provided by this manager.

With file caching, processor-I/O overlap is achieved by having the file manager "read ahead" on an input file so that its buffers always contain the next bytes to be read by the application. Output file caching is achieved by having the file manager "write behind" the application. When the application logically writes a byte to a file, the system stores the byte in a buffer. Then, when the buffer is full and the output device is idle, the system writes the buffer to the device. There is another opportunity for fast file I/O when output is buffered: Suppose one process is writing to a file and another is concurrently reading from the file. If the data consumer is reading the file at about the same place in the file as the producer is writing data, then the consumer's read operation will just read the output buffer before it is ever written to the device. The read operation does not incur any I/O operation since the desired data is still in the system buffer.

The Cache Manager is responsible for managing the file caching strategy. By looking at the work the Cache Manager must perform, it is clear that it must interact heavily with the I/O manager to coordinate buffer management. Also, the Cache Manager must deal with multiple address spaces and buffers. This means it can be more efficient if it is well coordinated with the Virtual Memory Manager.

When the NTOSKRNL is booted, the Cache Manager reserves a region of the system virtual address space. Since this space is part of every process's address space, the Cache Manager's reserved memory is accessible (with appropriate privilege) to every process in the system. Like all virtual memory, even after the Cache Manager's space has been committed, it is not loaded until the Virtual Memory Manager allocates pages in the primary memory. If the system is lightly loaded, the Cache Manager will increase the size of its working set and will tend to be allocated more primary memory pages. Conversely, heavily loaded systems will cause the Cache Manager's working set to shrink so that the memory can be used by other processes.

File caching is built on top of the kernel memory-mapped file mechanism (see Section 12.7). A file system driver makes a function call on the Cache Manager when it begins to operate on a file byte stream. The Cache Manager responds to the call by creating a section object to map the file to its virtual address space—and hence to pages in the primary memory. The Cache Manager then performs buffering by dynamically mapping views of the file into its address space.

Nagar [Ch. 6, 1997], provides a detailed description of the steps involved in cached read and write operations (see Figure 21.7). Nagar's description of the read operation is summarized here:

1. The user space thread calls the I/O Manager with a read request, passing a buffer address for the result. The I/O Manager has different options as to how it will handle the user space buffer; for example, it may map the user buffer into system space or pass the address onto the file system driver.

✦ **FIGURE 21.7** A Cached Read Operation

The Cache Manager is designed to handle I/O buffering. The steps shown in this read operation are described in the text.

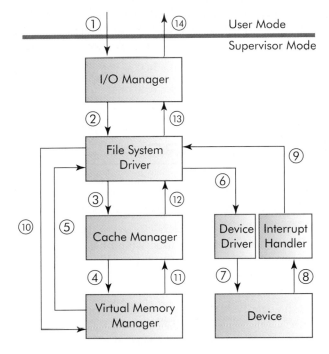

2. It then invokes the file system driver with an IRP. The file system driver detects that the read operation is for a file that was opened with a buffering option enabled. The first read operation causes the file system driver to start the Cache Manager, and the Cache Manager to create a section object to map the cached information.

3. The file system driver calls the Cache Manager with a CcCopyRead request. The Cache Manager creates a mapped view of the file if none exists and then starts a memory copy from the mapped view to the user buffer.

4. If the information to be read is still on the disk, then the attempt to reference it using a virtual address will cause a page fault. The Virtual Memory Manager will allocate physical pages to hold the information and then issue a noncached paging read to the file system driver.

5. The file system driver initiates a read operation on the device driver for the device that contains the file.

6. The device driver issues a read operation on the physical disk driver.

7. The device performs the physical page read operation.

8. The device completes and raises an interrupt that will be fielded by the interrupt handler for the device.

9. The interrupt handler returns from the page read operation to the file system driver.

10. The file system driver notifies the Virtual Memory Manager that the page is now loaded into the primary memory.

11. The instruction causing the page fault is re-executed, allowing the Cache Manager to move data from the mapped view of the file into the user buffer.

12. The Cache Manager returns the data in the user buffer to the file system driver.

13. The file system driver returns from the IRP to the I/O Manager.

14. The I/O Manager returns from the user read operation.

21.4 • KERNEL LOCAL PROCEDURE CALLS AND IPC

Threads operating in the same process use the same address space, so it is easy for them to share information among themselves. Kernel objects can be used by a thread in one process to signal a thread in another process. However, when two threads in different processes wish to exchange data, a completely new set of mechanisms must be used.

There is a specialized IPC mechanism used within the Executive (and not available through the Win32 API). The *Local Procedure Call* (LPC) mechanism is built on top of Kernel port objects. It is used for high-speed message passing by client and server processes within the NT Executive and the subsystems. For example, LPCs are used for IPC between the Local Security Authority server and the Secure Reference Monitor.

There is not much information published about LPCs, although Solomon and Russinovich [2000] report that LPC is a connection-based IPC mechanism in which processes that wish to use the LPC must create a port object to manage the communication. A client process makes a connection request to a server connection port. If the request is accepted, a server communication port and a client communication port are created and logically connected with one another. This port pair is then used as the high-speed link between the two processes.

The LPC facility provides a fast way for two threads in different address spaces to exchange information at a very high rate. The logical connection can be used to transfer a block of information from one address space to another. The "procedure call" aspect of the mechanism is that a transfer occurs using "procedure call semantics," meaning that a sender initiates the data transfer and waits until it finishes; the analogy is that when a procedure is called, the caller initiates the call and then waits until it returns.

The Win32 subsystem provides another IPC mechanism especially tailored for graphics windows based applications, but independent of the NT Executive [Richter, 1997]. A normal NT Executive thread is created without facilities to use the Windows messaging system. However, when the thread calls a User or GDI function, the system presumes that the application will operate in the full graphics windows environment, so it adds the data structures required to support Windows messaging. (In particular, this means that the threads that operate as console operations cannot use the Windows messaging system.)

The added data structures (called the THREADINFO structure) include:

■ Posted-message queue
■ Virtualized input queue

- Send-message queue
- Reply-message queue
- Other flags and state variables

Messages are directed at a window, rather than to a specific thread in the window (the thread that created the window will receive the message). When a message is received, it is appended to one of the four queues, the choice of which queue depending on the Win32 functions that sent the message. For example, the `PostMessage()` and `PostThreadMessage()` functions add a message to the posted-message queue. When a thread posts a message, it returns immediately after the message has been appended to the queue. `SendMessage()` is a fully synchronous message; when a sender calls `SendMessage()`, the function appends the message to the send-message queue, but does not return until the window thread retrieves the message. `PostMessage()` is used to send a message and continue processing asynchronously, that is, without waiting for the message to be processed by the receiver. `SendMessage()` synchronizes the activity of the sender and receiver since the sender will not continue executing until the receiver processes the message. (`SendMessageTimeout()` places a maximum amount of time the sender is willing to wait for the receiver to act on the message.) A message is placed in the reply-message queue with a `ReplyMessage()` function. This facility is used when a sender requests service that is time-consuming; the receiver may issue a `ReplyMessage()` to tell the sender that it is currently processing the request.

The Windows messaging system has a very sophisticated receipt mechanism that uses an event-driven programming model. All messages have registered types, many of which are recognized and handled by code in the Windows system. When a message arrives in one of the queues, it is likely to be delivered to and processed by the thread that created the window without the application programmer writing any particular code to do this. The Windows messaging system is a powerful application-oriented IPC mechanism, but one that is built entirely in the Win32 subsystem (it is middleware) and is logically independent of the underlying OS mechanisms.

THE NATIVE API

Although the NT Executive and Kernel are designed and programmed as separate modules, they are combined when the Windows NT/2000/XP kernel is built. The combined NT Executive and NTKernel module (with the underlying HAL) implements the full OS. The kernel exports about 240 functions [Russinovich, 1998], most of which are undocumented, meaning that only subsystem developers should base their software on the functions.

21.5 • SUBSYSTEMS

The Windows NT/2000/XP system software is constructed as a layered architecture. Layer i is constructed using the services provided by layer i–1 ("at the layer i–1 interface"), creating its own services and exporting them through its own (layer i) interface. In the Windows architecture, subsystems provide a layer of service above the Native API. There can be many different subsystems, some related, but others independent of one another, as functionality is added to the computer system. For example, a typical Windows NT2000/XP system includes the following:

- The Win32 subsystem
- The WinLogon service (to authenticate users, using the LSA server and Secure Reference Monitor described in the NT Executive section, when they begin to use the system)
- A remote procedure call service

Each subsystem uses the Native API to provide the services it implements. The *environment subsystems* behave as a traditional interior layer. In the layered architecture approach, they use the Native API, add functionality and services, and then export their own API. In the Microsoft strategy, subsystem APIs are documented APIs, meaning that a programmer can write new software at the next higher-level layer and be assured that the API will be unchanged when implementations at a lower-level layer in the architecture are changed.

Figure 21.8 shows how this layering works in Windows. The *Win32 subsystem* exports a documented interface, the Win32 API, as a set of about 2000 functions. The Win32 API is a documented interface. An application programmer can write software above the Win32 subsystem that calls the API functions to accomplish an application-specific task.

✦ FIGURE 21.8   The Win32 API

The Win32 API is an interface to the Win32 Subsystem. Microsoft encourages its use by not publishing the Native NT API (except to subsystem developers). This helps to preserve application portability among different versions of Windows.

Win32 API
Win32 Subsystem
Native NT API
NT Executive & NT Kernel

Windows XP .NET differs from Win32-based Windows NT/2000/XP in that it exports a broad range of .NET functions rather than the Win32 API. The commercial trend in the Windows operating systems is to encourage programmers to use the .NET interface instead of the Win32 API.

The Win32 subsystem also provides one other type of service: It implements a user interface management system, since the NT Executive/Kernel does not have one. This is primarily a matter of practicality: When the system begins to run, some part of the system software needs to read the keyboard and mouse and manage the display. Rather than have each environment subsystem provide its own user interface, the Win32 subsystem implements the common window manager for all subsystems. This means that there is a single human-computer interaction model implemented in a single subsystem, but used by all other subsystems.

A subsystem's design can be simple or complex. In the simplest case, each function or service that the subsystem exports is implemented wholly within the subsystem itself. For example, the subsystem might keep a data structure filled with information it extracts from information obtained through the Native API. When a program queries the subsystem, it simply reads the data structure and returns a result without ever interacting with the OS.

A slightly more complex case occurs when a subsystem function requires that the subsystem implementation interact with the OS via the Native API. For example, the Win32 API function `CreateProcess()` causes the Win32 subsystem to call the Native API functions NtCreateProcess and `NtCreateThread()`.

21.6 • SUMMARY

The Windows NT/2000/XP OS is a leading-edge operating system. It employs a layered design composed of the HAL, the NT Kernel, the NT Executive, and Subsystems (notably the Win32 Subsystem). The HAL is intended to make it easy to port the OS from one hardware platform to another. The NT Kernel implements a set of low-level functions normally associated with a microkernel: interrupt management, thread scheduling, an object store, and so on. The NT Executive uses the NT Kernel tools to implement conventional process, memory, file, and device management facilities.

Glossary

A

absolute loader. *See* **loader**.

absolute program. A form of a program derived by the linkage editor when it combines relocatable object modules with library functions. The absolute program contains a representation of all object code in the program, although it will usually be translated into a new form by the absolute loader prior to execution.

abstract data type. A module that encapsulates storage, private procedures for manipulating the storage, and a public interface, including procedures and type declarations, that can be used to manipulate the information in the storage.

abstract machine. A design concept in which the programming model is implemented by the operating system rather than by the underlying physical hardware. That is, the operating system provides a simulation of hardware for the programmer's use. Also called a **virtual machine**.

abstract resource. A system resource that is not necessarily associated with any hardware component, but which is implemented with software. A file is an abstract resource.

access control list. A list of all subjects and their access rights kept by an object in a protection system.

access functions. *See* **file access functions**.

access matrix. In a protection model, the access matrix contains one row for each protection subject and one column for each protection object. Each entry in the matrix contains the access rights that the corresponding subject has to the corresponding object. The access matrix represents the system protection state.

access rights. *See* **protection rights**.

ACL. *See* **access control list**.

address binding. The procedure of associating the addresses used by a program with physical memory locations in the primary memory.

address bus. Part of the system bus that carries addresses between system hardware components. *Also see* **bus**.

address space. The set of machine components (mainly memory addresses) that can be referenced by a thread executing in a process.

address translation. *See* **virtual address translation**.

ADT. *See* **abstract data type**.

algorithm. This is a specification of sequential instruction executions to accomplish a task. For example, a sort algorithm puts an array of numbers in ascending or descending order.

ALU (arithmetical-logic unit). The unit that performs all arithmetical and logical instructions.

AND synchronization. A synchronization operation applied to two or more semaphores in which the calling process is blocked until all of the semaphores are available. While the process is blocked in the semaphore, it does not hold any of the semaphores.

API (application programming interface). Defines a programming interface to a software module, in particular, to system software modules. Databases, window systems, and the APIs of other modules describe the data types and functions that are used to procure services from the module.

anonymous pipe. *See* **pipe**.

applet. A block of software that can be downloaded into a remote machine to perform a particular task. The term stems from the Java programming environment, where Java applets are used to extend the functionality of a web browser. *See* Section 18.4.

application domain. An information processing area that defines a particular equivalence class of application programs. For example, the accounting domain, the book publishing domain, or the nuclear reactor control domain.

application software. A program that is specific to a problem domain rather than generic across problem domains. For example, a processor scheduler is generic, but a classroom scheduler for a university is a domain-specific application.

application programming interface. *See* **API**.

arithmetical-logic unit. *See* **ALU**.

associative memory. Memory that addresses cells by using the contents of a key field on each cell rather than an explicit address. Associative memories are used to implement page tables.

asynchronous send. An IPC transmit operation in which the transmitting thread/process transmits information to a receiving thread/process (or its OS) without waiting to see if the message is deliverable.

atomic operation. *See* **indivisible operation**.

avoidance, deadlock. A strategy for addressing deadlock in which the resource allocator decides if an allocation request can be honored, while guaranteeing that there is some feasible execution sequence that honors all outstanding requests.

authentication. Refers to the task of ensuring that a subject that attempts to access the secure entity is actually the subject that it claims to be. *See* Chapter 14.

authentication server. A network service mechanism that provides authentication service. Kerberos is an authentication server.

authorization. Refers to the task of deciding that after a subject has been authenticated, whether it has the right to access the secure entity. *See* Chapter 14.

B

background. A classification of threads (contrasted with **foreground** threads) where all foreground threads have higher scheduling priority than any background threads.

backward distance. In paging algorithm, a measure of the virtual time from the current time since a designated page was last referenced.

base thread. In the modern process model, each process is created with at least one thread running in it. This thread is called the base thread for the modern process. A classic process is equivalent to a modern process with a base thread.

batch. A collection of jobs staged for execution (see **batch system**).

batch system. A batch operating system services a collection of jobs, called a *batch,* by reading the jobs into the machine and then executing the programs for each job in the batch.

baud rate. Signaling rate for a communications device, in signals per second.

Belady's anomaly. A page replacement performance anomaly in which an algorithm may perform worse if it has more page frames compared to a lesser number of page frames. *See* Section 12.4.

Belady's optimal replacement. A page replacement policy in which the page to be removed from primary memory is chosen to have maximal forward distance on the reference stream. *See* Section 12.4.

binary object program. *See* **binary program**.

binary program. The form of an algorithm/program specification that contains instructions in terms of the host computer's machine language. It is also called the **binary object program** or **executable program** form.

binary semaphore. A semaphore that only takes on the values 0 and 1.

BIOS (Basic Input/Output System). This is a collection of programs stored in an IBM Personal Computer ROM. The BIOS is a collection of independent programs that can be called by conventional software, or by the POST software when the system is being initialized. Other computers incorporate similar programs in their ROM.

bit (binary integer). A memory element capable of representing the values 0 and 1.

block caching. A technique used in file managers where information that has been copied into memory for a single file operation is retained in memory until an external policy dictates that it be removed. *See* Section 16.3.

block status map. An in-memory map describing the allocation status of each block on a disk. It is common for the map entry to use one bit to represent each block's status.

blocked. The state of a process or thread indicating that it is waiting for some resource to be allocated to it.

blocking receive. An IPC receiving operation in which the receiving thread/process blocks until information is transmitted to it.

buffer. A unit of storage that temporarily holds information. In I/O systems, a buffer holds input information that has been read from a device before an application program has requested it. An output buffer holds information that is waiting to be written when the output device is available.

bus. A hardware component used to transfer information among different computer components. For example, the bus is used to transfer data between the processor and the primary memory.

busy-wait. A situation in which a process is blocked on a resource (or semaphore) but holds the processor to constantly poll its blocked status until the status changes.

byte. A unit of memory storage composed of 8 bits. A byte can take on 256 unique bit patterns.

byte stream file. A low-level file in which information in the file is organized as a linear sequence of bytes. Byte i is accessed by first accessing byte $i - 1$.

bytecode. The intermediate language for Java.

C

c list. *See* **capability list.**

cache line. A unit information transfer into and out of a cache memory. Typically, a cache line is 16 to 128 bytes.

cache memory. A high-speed memory on the data path between the processor and the primary memory. When the processor reads a memory cell, the contents are copied to the cache, thus enabling subsequent reads to use the value in the cache.

capability. A unique, global name for an access right to an object in a system, originally used only as a right held by a subject to access an object.

capability list. A row in an access matrix in a protection mechanism. A capability list identifies the set of access rights to various objects in a system. Each access right is a capability.

carrier sense multiple access with collision detection. *See* **CSMA/CD.**

CBR. *See* **code base register.**

CD (compact disk). A removable, randomly accessible storage medium designed to store audio information.

CD-i (compact disk—interactive). A refinement of CD-ROM technology designed to support full multimedia data; thus, it is tailored to work with audio, video, and general data. *Also see* **CD-ROM.**

CD-R (CD-recordable). A compact disk whose format is similar to CD-ROM, but which has improved device characteristics. *Also see* **CD-ROM.**

CD-RW (CD ReadWrite). A compact disk whose format is similar to CD-ROM, but which can be erased and rewritten. *Also see* **CD-ROM.**

CD-ROM (compact disk—read only memory). A refinement of a CD that is able to store graphic data. *Also see* **CD.**

certificate. A certificate is a digital signature that is associated with mobile code (or other code that is to be downloaded over the Internet).

channel. *See* **I/O processor.**

checkpoint. A snapshot of a process's complete status that can be used to restart a process at the point at which the checkpoint was taken.

checksum. An object, usually an integer, that is determined as a function of the contents of some larger block of data such as a network packet or a file. A checksum is used as a simple indicator for data transmission errors.

ciphertext. In a cryptography system, this refers to encrypted information.

circular buffering. A technique in which more than 2 buffers are used to accomplish buffering. Buffers are assigned an index between 0 and $N–1$, and then they are arranged in a circular list (sorted by this index). The buffers are filled and emptied using the index. *Also see* **buffer**.

circular wait. A situation in which process p_1 holds resource R_1 while it requests resource R_2, and process p_2 holds R_2 while it requests resource R_1. There may be more than two processes involved in the circular wait.

clear text. In a cryptography system, this refers to unencrypted information.

client. *See* **client process**.

client process. A proactive process interacting with a reactive process—a server process—to obtain service.

client stub. System software residing in the client machine to prepare a remote procedure call, issue the call to the server, accept the result back from the server, and return it to the calling program.

client-server model. A distributed computation model in which one party (the client) initiates communication, and a passive party (the server) waits for client service requests. *See* Section 15.6.

clock algorithm. A technique for implementing dynamic page frame allocation algorithms (see Section 12.5).

clock cycle. The synchronous hardware cycle that defines the rate at which transistor-level operations occur in the computer's hardware. This is the basic unit to represent a CPU's speed, although instructions can actually execute during a single clock cycle.

cluster computer. A logical multiprocessor computer that may be a physical multiprocessor or a collection of tightly coupled uniprocessors with a high-speed interconnection. *See* Section 18.3.

code base register. In a segmentation virtual memory system, this is a CPU register that points at the segment descriptor containing the currently executing code segment.

Cmd (command register). The command register is any register on any memory or device that can be set by a software operation, causing the corresponding device to execute the command.

CMOS memory. Low-power consumption memory that is powered by a battery whenever a computer is not powered up. The CMOS memory is used to save information that will be needed when the computer is booted up.

code segment. In C-style relocatable and absolute program images, this is a logical block of address to represent references to machine instructions.

Common Object Request Broker Architecture. *See* **CORBA**.

command line interpreter. A program that reads operating system commands from a job stream or interactive terminal and then executes them. Also called a **shell** program.

communication device. A device used to transmit information between a computer and a device using a medium such as public broadcast, coaxial cable, or telephone wires.

communication network. A specialized network for delivering data among a set of host computers connected to the network. *See* Chapter 15.

communication subnetwork. *See* **communication network**.

compile time. The phase in program translation and loading when the source program is translated into a relocatable object module. The relocatable object module is stored on the secondary memory until link time.

compute-bound. A characteristic of a thread meaning that the time it spends in I/O operations is small compared to the amount of time spent using the CPU.

concurrency. *See* **concurrent execution**.

concurrent execution. Concurrent operation across a set of threads refers to the case in which the threads logically appear to be executing in parallel although they may be physically executing serially on a uniprocessor. Multiprogramming systems support concurrent processing in a sequential processor environment. *Also see* **parallel execution**.

concurrent write sharing. In remote file servers, this policy allows multiple clients to have a writable copy of a block at any given time. However, it precludes any block caching. *See* Section 16.3.

condition variable. A structure that may appear within a monitor, global to all procedures within the monitor, that can have its value manipulated by the wait, signal, and queue operations.

confinement. A technique to limit the dispersion of information to some particular environment. *See* Sections 14.1 and 14.3.

connection. A network abstraction in which two parties coordinate their behavior to ensure that when one sends information to the other, it will either be delivered or an appropriate error notification will be issued to the sender. *See* Section 15.5.

consistent memory. In a memory hierarchy, higher layers of the hierarchy often have copies of information that is stored lower in the hierarchy. If the copies are always kept the same when one or the other changes, then the memory is said to be consistent.

consumable resource. Any resource that is allocated to a process but is never deallocated. Instead, the process consumes it. Each consumable resource must also have at least one producer process.

consumable resource graph. A deadlock detection model that represents the allocation state of a system composed solely of consumable resources. *See* Section 10.5.

content-addressable memory. *See* **associative memory**.

context, processor. The processor context refers to the collective content of its registers as determined by the thread/process executing on the processor. The context describes the state of the abstract machine executing a thread.

context switch. A context switch is the procedure of saving all registers of one thread/process and then reloading all registers with the values for another thread/process.

context switcher. An informal name used in this book to refer to the part of the scheduler that performs context switching.

control unit. The part of the computer hardware that decodes instructions and then causes them to be executed.

controller, device. *See* **device controller**.

copy-on-write. A method in which a request to copy information from a source to a destination does not result in an actual copy operation until either the sender or the receiver writes into the shared information.

counting semaphore. *See* **general semaphore**.

CORBA (Common Object Request Broker Architecture). An open architecture for supporting multilanguage, distributed objects.

CPU (central processing unit). *See* **processor.**

critical section. A segment of code that cannot be executed while some other process is in a corresponding segment of code. For example, a critical section might be code segments in two different programs that write a shared variable.

cryptography. The practice of encoding and decoding of information so that, in theory, it cannot be interpreted by a third party who happens to obtain a copy of the encoded form of the information. *See* Chapter 14.

CSMA/CD (carrier-sense multiple access protocol with collision detection). This is the Ethernet local area network protocol.

cycle. In a graph, a cycle is a path from one node through other nodes that leads back to the original node.

cylinder, disk. In a disk drive that has multiple surfaces, the set of corresponding tracks on each surface defines a disk cylinder. All blocks stored within the cylinder can be read or written by the disk drive without moving the read/write head.

cyphertext. *See* **ciphertext.**

D

daemon. A UNIX process that operates on behalf of the operating system rather than on behalf of any particular user. For example, the line printer daemon accepts print jobs as files and prints them as the printer becomes available.

data. In the context of a process definition, data is the portion of the process that represents the static variables defined in the corresponding program.

data bus. Part of the system bus that carries the data between system hardware components. *Also see* **bus.**

data base register. In a segmentation virtual memory system, this is a CPU register that points at the segment descriptor containing the current data segment.

data communication network. *See* **communication network.**

data communication subnetwork. *See* **communication network.**

data link layer. An ISO OSI network architecture layer defining frame-based communication. This layer allows processes to send and receive frames of information across an individual network.

data segment. In C-style relocatable and absolute program images, this is a logical block of address to represent references to static variables.

datagram. A network transport level packet. Its addresses specify the sending and receiving locations using three-component addresses (net#, host#, port#). UDP is the most widely used protocol for sending and receiving datagrams.

DBMS (database management system). System software that abstracts file operations to provide an interface to the storage system where users and programs can access records by using operations such as queries. This is a major area of computer science; it has entire books devoted to it.

DBR. *See* **data base register.**

DCE (Distributed Computing Environment). A collection of middleware packages to support distributed application programming using conventional network OS platforms. *See* Chapter 18.

deadlock. A situation that can arise when two or more processes hold resources and request others. Some process holds a resource that another wants while requesting a second resource, and the other process holds the second resource while requesting the first. Hence, neither process can progress.

deadlock state. A system state in which two or more threads/processes are deadlocked.

deadly embrace. *See* **deadlock.**

def table. *See* **definition table.**

definition table. A table generated by a compiler to contain external symbols that are defined within the current relocatable module references. This is used by the link editor to combine external references and definitions.

delayed write-back policy. In a remote file server that uses block caching on the client side, block write operations are performed when there is "idle" time at the server or after a previously defined time interval has elapsed. *See* Section 16.3.

demand paging. A page is loaded only when it is referenced.

descriptor. An OS data structure used to represent the details of various OS abstractions such as processes, threads, files, and other resources.

detection and recovery. A deadlock strategy in which an algorithm is run to check the system for a deadlock. If it discovers a deadlock, then it preempts resources to remove it.

determinate. *See* **nondeterminate.**

device. A unit of a computer that can be used to store information, transmit and receive information to/from another machine, and export/import information to/from users.

device controller. This hardware unit connects the device to the computer's address and data bus. It provides a set of components that CPU instructions can manipulate to cause the device to operate.

device driver. The device dependent part of the device manager software used to administer a particular device.

device handler. The device specific part of the software to handle an interrupt occurrence.

device major number. A number that identifies the class of devices that can be handled by one particular type of device driver.

device management. The part of the operating system that creates device abstractions and provides mechanisms for manipulating and controlling them.

device minor number. A number that identifies a particular device within a class of devices. Minor numbers are normally used to locate device drivers for a device.

device registration. In a reconfigurable device driver system, the functions exported by the device driver are registered with the OS by explicit action.

digital rights management (DRM). A methodology for assigning rights to content and then for controlling the security policy for the use of the content. *See* Section 14.4.

device status table. An operating system table used to hold the pending state of a device operation that is currently in progress.

digital signature. An encrypted signature (using public key encryption) that can be used to authenticate the source of information.

direct access device. *See* **random device.**

direct I/O. An I/O operation that is managed by the processor rather than by an auxiliary I/O processor.

direct memory access. *See* **DMA.**

directory. A set of logically associated files and other directories of files.

dirty bit. A flag used in a page table to indicate if a page has been written into since it was loaded.

disk bitmap. *See* **block status map**.

disk cylinder. A set of corresponding tracks on a disk drive that incorporates multiple recording surfaces and a ganged read/write head.

disk sector. An angular portion of a track on a rotating disk that contains one block of information within a track that passes through the sector.

disk track. A circular recording area on a rotating storage medium. A disk will have several concentric rings that are divided by disk sectors to form blocks.

dispatcher. The part of the CPU scheduler that selects the next thread to schedule and then causes the associated context switching.

dispatcher object. In the Windows NT Kernel, a dispatcher object includes a mechanism to implement event-oriented synchronization. The Windows wait functions synchronize on the dispatcher object events. *See* Section 9.1.

distributed computation. A broad class of software in which two or more threads or processes work together to solve a common problem.

distributed memory. A general class of memory management schemes whereby physically separate blocks of memory are implemented on different machines, yet are accessible from the address spaces of different processes. *See* Chapter 17.

distributed memory multiprocessor. A multiprocessor architecture composed of multiple conventional von Neumann computers interconnected by a high-speed switch.

distributed operating system. One in which all operations are network transparent. *See* Section 19.6.

distributed shared memory. A network shared memory approach where the memory client uses the conventional primary memory interface to read and write the memory locations. *See* Section 17.2.

distributed synchronization. Synchronization techniques and methodologies that can be used across a network of distinct machines. *See* Section 17.5.

double buffering. A technique in which two buffers are used to accomplish buffering. Double buffering is commonly used in device controllers. *Also see* **buffer**.

DMA (direct memory access). A technique by which an I/O controller transfers information directly to/from the primary memory without intervention from the processor.

DNS (domain name service). The DNS is a name service for the public Internet. It can be used to look up the (net#, host#) for machines with symbolic names such as anchor.cs.colorado.edu. *See* Section 15.6.

domain name service. *See* **DNS**.

DRM. *See* **digital rights management**.

dynamic address space binding. *See* **dynamic relocation**.

dynamic relocation. A form of address relocation in which absolute module addresses are bound to primary memory locations at runtime.

E

embedded system. A class of computers that are incorporated as a component into a larger system. For example, a guidance computer on an airplane and a controller computer in a microwave oven are embedded systems.

entry point. The first location of a program when the program is to be executed.

enqueuer. An informal name used in this book to refer to the part of the scheduler that places a thread in the CPU ready list.

event. There are two similar uses of this term. The most informal definition refers to the occurrence of any condition, for example, a process completed a phase of execution. The stricter definition is for an OS synchronization mechanism whereby a kernel data structure (an event descriptor) captures the identity of the threads/processes waiting for an event to occur, and perhaps the state of the event occurrence.

event descriptor. An OS data structure to manage synchronization using events.

eventcounts. A synchronization mechanism that works by exploiting the known precedence among the execution of units of a computation. *See* Section 17.5.

executable memory. *See* **primary memory**.

executable program. *See* **binary program**.

exclusive control. OS resource managers must be designed so they are able to ensure that when a resource is allocated to one process, it cannot be accessed by other processes. The process that was allocated the resource is said to have exclusive control of the resource.

explicit sharing. *See* **sharing**.

extensible nucleus organization. A modular operating system organization intended to implement real-time systems, timesharing systems, and so on using a common set of underlying policy-independent modules.

external authentication. In protection mechanisms, the external authentication mechanism determines if an external user is who he or she claims to be. *See* Section 14.2.

external fragmentation. In memory management, this refers to unallocated portions of memory that are too small to meet any process's memory needs.

external priority. A number to represent the rank order of a thread when it competes for resources (usually for the CPU) that is determined by the rank order of the user.

F

FAT (file allocation table). MS-DOS file system file descriptor.

fault rate. The fraction of page references that cause a page fault.

FCFS. *See* **first-come-first-served.**

fetch policy. A paging policy that decides when a page should be loaded into primary memory.

fetch-execute algorithm. The algorithm that describes the action of the CPU's control unit. The fetch phase is to obtain an instruction from the primary memory, and the execute phase is to execute the instruction.

FIFO (first-in, first-out) replacement. A page replacement policy in which the first page in the primary memory to be loaded is chosen to be replaced. *See* Section 12.4.

file. A named abstract resource capable of storing a byte stream for later access or from which a stream of bytes can be read to obtain data.

file access functions. File manager functions used to read and write structured information from/to a file.

file caching. In general, this term refers to any technique for making copies of all or part of a file to enhance performance. In some contexts it refers to file buffering, and in the distributed OS context it refers to a remote file design strategy.

file descriptor. An OS data structure for keeping the status of a file.

file management. The part of the operating system that creates file abstractions and provides mechanisms for manipulating and controlling them.

file pointer. An index into a byte stream file addressing a particular byte in the file. When the file is opened, the file pointer references the first byte in the file.

file system. A subtree in a hierarchical collection of files that can exist as a standalone collection of files. For example, a floppy disk has its own file system.

file system interface. The file manager exports a set of system calls (the file system interface) that application programs use to read and write files. *See* Section 2.2.

firewall. A machine that is placed between the public Internet and every computer in the organization. The firewall is intended to only allow access requests from anyone on the Internet if the security policy permits it.

first-come-first-served (FCFS). A scheduling policy that assigns priority to threads in the order in which they request the processor.

Firewire. A bus controller and protocol that provides an external connector that accommodates devices such as digital cameras and MP3 audio players.

foreground. A classification of threads (contrasted with **background** threads) where all foreground threads have higher scheduling priority than any background threads.

forward distance. In paging algorithm, a measure of the virtual time from the current time until a designated page is referenced again.

free list. A linked list of unallocated blocks, usually in a file system.

frontend machine. A conventional von Neumann computer used to control an unconventional parallel machine.

function unit. A component in the arithmetical-logical unit in the CPU. Its purpose is to perform the operations on operands that are stored in the CPU's registers.

G

Gantt chart. A two-dimensional chart that plots the activity of a unit on the y-axis versus the time on the x-axis. The chart quickly represents how the activities of the units are serialized or can overlap in their occurrence.

gateway. A service that interconnects two or more different domains, thus providing some form of translation among the domains. In the network context, the gateway interconnects two or more different networks so that packets can be exchanged among hosts attached to separate networks. *See* Section 15.4.

general resource graph. A deadlock detection model that represents the allocation state of a system composed of both consumable and reusable resources. *See* Section 10.5.

general semaphore. A semaphore that may take on any nonnegative integer value.

gigabit (Gb). Approximately one billion bits. Exactly 1,073,741,824 bits.

gigabyte (GB). Approximately one billion bytes. Exactly 1,073,741,824 bytes.

global clock. Lamport's global clock is a logical clock that is used to establish a partial order on a set of events that can occur on a network. Although the clock does not actually keep time, it preserves causal relationships and is often used for network-wide synchronization. *See* Section 17.5.

global LRU. *See* **clock algorithm**.

graph reduction. In deadlock process-resource models, this is an operation to analyze the state represented by the model. *See* Section 10.5.

gridlock. Deadlock in automobile traffic. *See* the discussion at the beginning of Chapter 10.

H

HAL (hardware abstraction layer). A component of a Windows OS that abstracts various details of hardware (such as interrupt addresses) so that an OS can be written in terms of abstractions rather than with hardwired addresses.

hardware buffer. A buffer that is implemented within a device controller. *Also see* **buffer**.

hardware dynamic relocation. *See* **dynamic relocation**.

hardware process. This is a name to represent the repeated activity of the control unit, as it fetches and executes instructions. Although this is not an OS process at all, it represents the dynamic instruction execution of the hardware.

hash. In the security context, this is another name for a message digest (see Section 14.4). For example, see SHA-1 (http://www.itl.nist.gov/fipspubs/fip180-1.htm).

heterogenous file system. A file hierarchy where the constituent file systems are not necessarily all of the same type.

heterogeneous system. A parallel machine with different types of processors or a network of computers of different types.

hierarchical name space. A collection of names organized as a tree structure. Usually, this term is used with file system organizations in which there is a single root directory that contains files and other directories. The resulting organization is a tree.

high-level file system. A file system that provides support only for record streams, including mechanisms to define and manage records. *See* Chapter 13.

hold-and-wait condition. A situation in which a process/thread holds one resource at the same time that it requests another one.

homogeneous system. A parallel machine or network of machines that contains all the same type of processors.

hop. In the ISO OSI network layer, a hop refers to a forwarding operation from one machine across a data link layer network to the next machine. *See* Section 15.4.

horizontal architecture. *See* **layered organization**.

HTML (HyperText Markup Language). A language that defines a set of text formatting directives that can be embedded in a text file to specify metadata about the text in the file.

HTTP (HyperText Transfer Protocol). A session layer protocol used to transfer files containing hypertext (usually in the HTML format) across an internet.

I

idempotent operation. An operation that can be applied repeatedly, producing the same effect as if it had been applied just once. An increment operation is not idempotent, but an assignment operation is. Idempotent operations are used in stateless protocols to make interoperation more reliable.

idle process. *See* **idle thread**.

idle thread. The lowest priority thread in the system. This thread only uses the CPU when no other thread wants to do so.

inclusion property. A property of certain page replacement algorithms whereby every page loaded under a page replacement algorithm with a page allocation of m would also have been loaded for a page allocation of $m + 1$.

index block. In file managers, this is a file descriptor table that points to each block in the file.

index field. Part of a record in a structured file system that is used to identify the record.

index table. In an inverted file organization, the index table is an in-memory copy of the indices for each record in the file. *See* Section 13.2.

indexed addressing. The contents of an index register, added to the address compiled into an instruction so as to derive the target operand address.

indexed sequential file. This type of file is organized as a linear sequence of records. The file manager is able to read or write any specific record by using its index. *See* Section 13.2.

indirect addressing. The address compiled into the instruction word that references a memory cell containing the address of the target operand.

indivisible operation. An operation, such as a function, composed of more than one instruction. The collection of instructions are all guaranteed to execute as a group, or none execute at all.

infrastructure, device manager. The part of the OS designed to host device-specific device drivers. It exports the device system calls and then routes system calls to the correct device driver.

initial process. The first process created in the OS during system initialization. It is an ancestor of all other processes in the computer.

initial state. In a state-transition diagram, the initial state represents the state of a system when it is started.

initial thread. *See* **initial process**.

inode. File descriptor in a UNIX system.

input buffer. *See* **buffer**.

input device. A peripheral device for a computer that is used to enter information into the computer. Examples of input devices are a keyboard, scanner, mouse, and digital camera.

input/output processor. *See* **I/O processor.**

instruction register. *See* **IR.**

internal fragmentation. In memory management, this refers to the unused portion of an allocated block of memory. It occurs when the memory manager must allocate more memory than the process actually needs.

internal priority. *See* **priority**.

internet. A collection of individual networks configured so that some hosts on each network are connected to other networks. The resulting network of networks can be thought of as a logical graph in which nodes are an entire network and edges are the gateway machines interconnecting the networks.

internet address space. A collection of names for hosts and networks accessible using the ISO OSI network layer. *See* Section 15.2.

Internet Protocol. *See* **IP.**

interprocess communication. *See* **IPC.**

interrupt. A signal that causes the control unit to branch to a specific location, to execute code to service the occurrence of an external condition.

interrupt handler. An operating system routine that is executed whenever an interrupt occurs. It saves the processor state and then dispatches a device handler to service the device that caused the interrupt.

interrupt request. A hardware flag that is raised whenever any device completes an I/O operation. The flag is checked by the control unit once per instruction execution cycle.

interrupt vector. An array of interrupt request flags. Ideally, each device is assigned to one element of the array, although systems with more devices than array elements assign multiple devices to a single device handler.

interval timer. *See* **programmable interval timer.**

inverted file. A file for which the OS manages a table with an index that references each record in the file.

I/O-bound. A characteristic of a thread, meaning that the time it spends in I/O operations is large compared to the amount of time spent using the CPU.

I/O processor. An autonomous input/output processor capable of operating at the same time as the central processor to direct the operation of one or more I/O devices.

IP (Internet Protocol). A network layer protocol derived from the ARPAnet that provides addresses with network, host, and port components. A protocol implementation also provides routing through the corresponding internet. *See* Section 15.4.

IPC (interprocess communication). The class of mechanisms used for two processes to exchange information using messages.

IR (instruction register). A control unit register that contains a copy of the instruction currently being decoded and executed.

IRQ. Often used to mean an **interrupt request**.

ISO. International Standards Organization.

ISO OSI. A standardized architecture model that defines network protocols within a model composed of seven layers of functionality, ranging from signaling protocols to application interaction protocols. *See* Section 15.2.

ISO Open Systems Interconnect. *See* **ISO OSI.**

ISR. Often used to mean an interrupt service routine, which is also called an **interrupt handler**.

J

job. A sequence of commands, programs, and data that are combined into a single unit (the job) and then submitted to a batch OS for execution.

job control specification. The part of a job that contains the script of OS commands to be applied to the other elements of the job. In a sense, the job control specification is a program that describes the set of OS commands to be executed to complete the job.

K

kernel. The part of the operating system that is implemented to execute as trusted software. In systems where the processor has a mode bit, the kernel is the only software that runs with the mode bit set to supervisor mode.

kernel space. *See* **system space.**

kernel thread. In an OS that supports modern processes with threads, it is possible to implement the thread abstraction in a user-space library or in the OS itself. If the OS provides the support, it is said to implement kernel threads. *Also see* **user space threads**.

key certificate. *See* **certificate.**

kilobit (Kb). Approximately one thousand bits. Exactly 1,024 bits.

kilobyte (KB). Approximately one thousand bytes. Exactly 1,024 bytes.

knot. In a graph, a knot is a collection of nodes in which every path from any node in the collection only leads to nodes in the collection.

L

LAN (local area network). A communication mechanism that allows multiple computers to exchange information among themselves.

latency time. In disk technology, the rotational delay that occurs once the read/write head is aligned with the target track. In a message-passing context, it is the message transmission delay time (see Chapter 5). In networks, the latency time is the time to deliver a message from one point in the network to another (see Chapter 15).

layered kernel. *See* **layered organization**.

layered organization. An operating system organization in which the functionality is partitioned into an abstract machine hierarchy where the functions in layer i are implemented in terms of the functions provided by layer $i - 1$.

least recently used replacement. *See* **LRU replacement**.

LFU (least frequently used) replacement. A page replacement policy in which the page to be removed from primary memory is chosen based on the number of past references to that page.

lightweight process. *See* **thread**.

limit register. A CPU register that is loaded with the length of a block of memory containing a program. When the program is executed, the contents of the limit register are compared to the effective address to determine if it lies within the block. *See* Section 11.4.

link editor. A translation tool that combines relocatable object modules with library modules to produce an absolute program that is suitable for loading.

link time. The phase in program translation and loading in which the relocatable objects module from the compiler and libraries are combined to form an absolute module. The absolute module is stored on the secondary memory until load time.

linkage segment. A Multics-specific segment containing indirect addresses of segment descriptors.

livelock. A phenomenon in which a set of processes is effectively deadlocked, although each can perform operations such as polling.

loader. Also called the *absolute loader.* A tool to retrieve an absolute program module from secondary memory, translate it into a format suitable for execution, and place the resulting executable image into primary memory.

load time. The phase in program translation and loading in which the absolute module produced by the linkage editor is relocated and placed in the primary memory.

local area network. *See* **LAN.**

locality. The property of a program in execution causing it to reference pages that it has recently referenced. Locality is caused by loops in code that tend to reference arrays or other data structures by indices.

lock. A flag associated with a resource such as a file or critical section indicating that the resource is in use or available.

long-term scheduler. A device used in batch spooling systems to allocate disk space to a spooled job so that it can begin to compete for memory.

low-level file system. A file system that provides support only for byte streams, but not for higher levels of abstraction. *See* Chapter 13.

LRU (least recently used) replacement. A page replacement algorithm that selects the loaded page referenced the longest time in the past.

M

MAC (protocols). In networks, the MAC protocols are the physical and data link layer protocols. These protocols are usually implemented in hardware. *See* Section 15.3.

mailbox. An OS buffer used to hold IPC messages while they are in transit from a sender to a receiver.

main entry point. The address in an absolute program module where execution should begin. In a C program, this corresponds to the `int main (argc, argv[])` function.

major number. *See* **device major number**.

MAR (memory address register). A memory unit register that is loaded with the address of a cell for a subsequent read or write operation to the cell.

marshalling. The task of translating a language-oriented data structure into a device-specific (usually a byte stream) format. This is done by file managers and network protocols.

masquerading. In protection mechanisms, masquerading refers to the situation in which a user or process tries to bypass the authentication mechanism. *See* Section 14.1.

maximum claim. A bound on the amount of resources a process will ever request in its session. The maximum claim is used in deadlock avoidance strategies.

MDR (memory data register). A memory unit register that is loaded with the datum to be written to the memory prior to the **write** operation and which contains the result after a **read** operation.

mechanism. An operating system function that can be used to implement many different policies without commitment to any specific policy. *See also* **policy.**

media access control (protocols). *See* **MAC.**

media translation. In networks, media translation refers to the case in which a gateway receives a packet in a data link layer frame of one type and then sends the packet out in a data link layer frame of a different type. *See* Section 15.4.

medium-term scheduler. Manages primary memory allocation.

megabit (Mb). Approximately one million bits. Exactly 1,048,576 bits.

megabyte (MB). Approximately one million bytes. Exactly 1,048,576 bytes.

memory address register. *See* **MAR.**

memory cycle. The time required to read or write a computer's primary memory.

memory data register. *See* **MDR.**

memory fragment. A block of memory, usually one that is not allocated to some process.

memory hierarchy. A collection of individual memory components in which elements higher in the hierarchy tend to be faster, smaller, and more expensive than elements lower in the hierarchy.

memory management. The task of creating abstractions and providing mechanisms for manipulating and controlling the computer's memory hardware.

memory management unit. A hardware device that converts a virtual address into a physical memory address if the target is loaded in primary memory, or that raises an interrupt if the target is not currently loaded. *See* Section 12.3.

memory manager. *See* **memory management**.

memory-mapped file. In a system that supports virtual memory, a thread can map the entire contents of a file into the process virtual address space. *See* Section 12.7.

memory-mapped I/O. A device organization in which software references various parts of the controller using addresses that have the same appearance as memory addresses.

memory-mapped resource. Any abstract machine resource whose interface can be specified as a collection of byte addresses. For example, if the OS exports a device's interface as a set of byte-addressable registers, then the device can be bound into a process's address space, and is a memory-mapped resource.

memory state. This exact definition depends on the context. In the context of paging (Chapter 12), the memory state is the set of page numbers that are currently loaded in the primary memory.

message. A unit of information passed from one address space to another by an OS IPC mechanism.

message digest. A digital certificate computed by encrypting a condensed form of content and a digital signature.

message passing system call. A mechanism for requesting OS service by sending a message to an OS process or thread rather that by executing a trap-like function call.

microcomputer. The smallest class of computers available today. The processor is implemented on a single integrated circuit chip (a microprocessor).

microkernel. In some OS designs, the minimum essential functionality for trusted operation of the OS is implemented in a separate module called a microkernel. The remaining OS functionality is then implemented in the microkernel's client.

microprocessor. A complete von Neumann CPU that is implemented on a single integrated circuit chip.

microsecond. One millionth of a second.

millisecond. One thousandth of a second.

minicomputer. Early personal computers (circa 1970). The DEC PDP 11 minicomputer was one of the first computers used to implement popular versions of UNIX. Ultimately, minicomputers came to mean "medium sized" computers suitable to use to service a department of people, or to be a network server.

minor number. *See* **device minor number**.

missing page fault. *See* **page fault**.

MMU. *See* **memory management unit**.

mobile code. Mobile code refers to software that is dynamically downloaded from a network source when it is needed, and then presumably destroyed after it has served its purpose. Java applets are mobile code.

mobile computer. Any computer that can continue to operate while it is physically moved from one location to another. Examples of mobile computers include handheld computers, personal digital assistants, and emerging cellular telephones.

mode bit. A one-bit processor register that can be set to either supervisory or user mode. If the mode bit is set to **supervisor mode**, the processor can execute all instructions in its repertoire. If the mode is set to **user mode**, the processor is only allowed to execute a subset of the machine's instructions.

modem (**modulator-demodulator**). A telecommunications device that converts digital signals into analog form, and analog signals into digital form. A modem is used to connect a computer to the telephone network so that digital information can be transferred between computers that each use a modem to connect to the analog voice network.

modular kernel. *See* **modular organization**.

modular organization. A software organization in which the functionality is partitioned among logically independent components, with well-defined interfaces among the related modules.

module (**Linux**). A Linux module is an independently constructed software module that can be dynamically added to the kernel. Modules are ordinarily used to implement device drivers, but they can incorporate any desired functionality provided they meet the meta API specification exported by the kernel.

monitor. An abstract data type that can be used by multiple processes. The monitor will allow only one process or thread at a time to use the monitor.

monolithic kernel. *See* **monolithic organization**.

monolithic organization. A software organization that places all software and data structures in one logical module, with no explicit interfaces between any parts of the software.

multi queue. *See* **multiple-level queue**.

multicomputer. A multiple processor machine made up of a collection of individual uniprocessor von Neumann machines, interconnected with a high-speed network.

multidrop network. A network that can switch information between any two nodes in the network.

multidrop packet network. *See* **multidrop network** and **packet network**.

multiple-level feedback queue. A multiple-level queue where jobs change queue levels as their properties change over time.

multiple-level queue. A preemptive scheduling policy where threads are scheduled as groups, depending on their priorities. All threads with the same priority are kept in a queue; the existence of multiple priorities causes this policy to use multiple queues of waiting threads.

multiplexing, space. Sharing a resource by dividing it up into smaller units and allocating units to different processes. A process has exclusive control of its allocated units, while other processes have exclusive control of other units at any given moment.

multiplexing, time. Sharing a resource by allocating the entire resource to one process for a time segment and then to another process for another time segment. A process has exclusive control of the entire resource at any given moment.

multiprocessing. A computer architecture that incorporates two or more processors.

multiprogramming. A style of CPU management in which multiple programs are loaded into the memory simultaneously and a scheduler time-multiplexes the CPU across the threads executing the programs.

multitasking. *See* **multiprogramming**.

multithreaded computation. A computation in which multiple entities are executing the computation at one time. In modern systems, multithreading usually refers to the case where there is a modern process that has multiple threads executing in it. *See* Chapters 2 and 6.

mutual exclusion. Two or more processes cooperating so that only one of the processes has access to a shared resource (or critical section) at a time.

N

name space. The collection of symbolic names used in a source program. Each symbolic name in the name space is translated into an address where the program is translated into an absolute image by the compiler and link editor.

named pipe. *See* **pipe**.

name registry. A network service that maps names to internet addresses. *See* Section 15.6.

name server. *See* **name registry**.

nanosecond. One billionth of a second.

network communication protocol. *See* **protocol**.

network interface controller. *See* **NIC**.

network layer. An ISO OSI network architecture layer that defines facilities to address host machines on remote networks, and provides facilities for routing network packets across a collection of networks to be delivered to a host on a remote network.

network operating system. An OS designed to manage a collection of host machines on a network, where component location transparency is not a goal of the system. *See* Section 19.6.

network protocol. *See* **protocol**.

NIC (network interface controller). An NIC is a device controller used to connect a computer to a data communication subnetwork. For example, a computer will contain an Ethernet NIC if it is connected to an Ethernet. *See* Section 15.1.

nonblocking receive. An IPC receiving operation in which the receiving thread/process polls its receiver port to determine if information has been transmitted to it, but does not block on the operation.

nondeterminate. A situation in which there is no assurance that repeated execution of a parallel program will produce the same results. The differences can be explained by considering different orders in which instructions in critical sections were executed among the individual processes in the community.

nonpreemptive scheduling. A strategy for time-multiplexing the processor whereby a process does not release the processor until it has completed its work.

nonuniform memory access. *See* **NUMA.**

NT Executive. Part of the OS (executing in supervisor mode) that is implemented on top of the NT Kernel to provide conventional abstract threads, processes, and resources.

NT Kernel. Implements the essential low-level abstraction of the hardware in Windows NT/2000/XP, including interrupt handling and thread scheduling.

NT subsystem. A user space extension to the NT Executive that can be used to define different OS personalities (including Win32, Win16, OS/2, and others) as well as other critical components of the OS such as part of the protection mechanism.

NUMA (nonuniform memory access). A computer architectural style that calls for multiple memory modules. Each processor can access every memory module, although the access times vary depending on the relationship of the processor and the memory module to each other.

O

object. An instance of a class definition of an abstract data type. The object reacts to external messages. Each message causes the object to run a method that may issue other methods or execute arbitrary code from the class.

object, protection. In protection models, a protection object (or simply "object") is a passive element of the system that can be accessed by an active subject.

one-time password. A user authentication mechanism that requires a different password each time the user logs into the system. *See* Chapter 14.

one-way function. A function, f, that is easy to evaluate (that is $y = f(x)$ is easy to evaluate), but whose inverse is difficult to determine (that is, it is difficult to figure out what $x = f^{-1}(y)$ when you know the value of y). One-way functions are used in cryptography.

operating system. The part of the system software that operates with the CPU in supervisor mode.

optimal schedule. Any schedule (usually a CPU schedule) that has minimum finishing time.

OS. *See* **operating system**.

OSI. *See* **ISO OSI**.

output buffer. *See* **buffer**.

output device. A peripheral device for a computer that is used to export information from the computer. Examples of output devices are a display, a printer, and a digital projector.

P

packet. The unit of information transmitted on contemporary data subcommunication networks. A packet may contain from 8 to 8K bytes.

packet network. A subcommunication network where information is transmitted as blocks of bytes, each called a packet. Most modern digital networks are packet networks.

page. The fixed-size unit of transfer between primary and secondary memory in a paging virtual memory system.

page fault. In a paging virtual memory system, an event (usually a trap) indicating that a thread referenced a page that is not currently loaded in the primary memory.

page frame. A unit of primary memory that is allocated to hold a page while it is stored in the primary memory.

page frame number. The primary memory is divided into a collection of page frames, each addressed by a page frame number.

page reference stream. The sequence of page numbers referenced by a thread during its execution.

page table. A translation mechanism to convert page numbers into page frame addresses.

paging. A form of virtual memory in which fixed-sized blocks of the address space are transferred between the primary and secondary memories.

paging disk. *See* **paging file**.

paging file. A unit of the secondary memory that holds virtual address space contents. Pages from the page file are loaded by the virtual memory manager.

paging policy. The policy that determines when pages should be loaded and unloaded, and which page frames should be used for the operations. *See* Sections 12.4 and 12.5.

parallel execution. A situation in which the computer is able to simultaneously execute two or more processes. *Also see* **concurrency**.

password. A string of characters that users provide to the computer to authenticate their login identity.

PBR. Means **procedure base register**. *See* **code base register**.

PC. There are two widely used meanings for this abbreviation. Its classic meaning is "program counter" register, which is in the control unit that addresses the memory cell that contains the next instruction to be executed. Its more currently popular, commercial meaning is "personal computer," specifically the IBM PC.

peer-to-peer. In computer networks, peer-to-peer communication refers to cooperation between different entities using a specific protocol. For example, email peer programs can communicate with the SNMP mail protocol.

personal computer. A computer that is dedicated to the use of one person at a time. *Also see* **workstation**.

PGP. *See* **Pretty Good Privacy**.

physical layer. The lowest level of the ISO OSI network architecture model for network communications. It defines how a process on a host machine sends and receives a byte of information and how the host machines exchange bytes.

physical record. The I/O unit on a block-oriented I/O device. A physical record is a block.

PID. *See* **process identifier**.

pipe. The UNIX mechanism for passing information as a byte stream from one process to another. Pipes use the file interface. **Anonymous** pipes are shared among a group of closely related processes, but **named** pipes can be used by any process on the machine. *See* Chapter 9.

pipeline stage. A pipeline computation partitions the computation into N different parts, each called a stage. The computation is completed by passing it sequentially through all N stages. However, each stage can be working on a different computation in parallel with all the other stages.

placement policy. Paging that determines where the fetched page should be loaded in primary memory.

plaintext. *See* **clear text**.

point-to-point (communication). A communication technology in which one computer establishes a connection with another computer, for example, by creating a telephone circuit between the two computers, and then communicates over that connection.

policy. A specific scheme for managing resources, independent of the means for implementing the scheme. *See also* **mechanism**.

policy rules. In the protection model in Chapter 14, the policy rules control the transitions among different protection states.

polling. A software technique in which the code uses a loop to repeatedly test for a condition. In polling I/O, the software repeatedly tests the device status to determine when an I/O operation has completed.

POSIX. *See* **POSIX API**.

POSIX API. A standardized interface for various software packages. Specifically, the POSIX.1 specification is an OS system call interface. In common usage, "the POSIX API" refers to the POSIX.1 API.

POST (power on self test). A program loaded into ROM that is executed as soon as the computer is powered up. The POST contains diagnostic programs to test the hardware before the OS is installed.

precedence. The precedence among units of computation specifies their order of execution.

preemptive scheduling. A strategy for time-multiplexing the processor whereby a running process is removed from the processor whenever a higher-priority process becomes ready to execute.

prefetch policy. A page-fetching strategy whereby the system loads pages before they are referenced.

presentation layer. An ISO OSI network architecture layer that provides facilities to translate data from the format of one domain to another.

Pretty Good Privacy (PGP). A popular, open public key encryption methodology. PGP uses 128-bit public and private keys. *See* Section 14.4.

prevention. A deadlock strategy whereby one of the four necessary conditions for deadlock is guaranteed to be false at all times.

primary memory. Memory for which an individual byte or word can be directly addressed and accessed by the processor.

priority. A number to represent the rank order of a thread when it competes for resources (usually for the CPU). A static priority does not change as long as the thread exists, but with dynamic priorities, the priority may change according to changing conditions in the OS.

priority scheduling. A scheduling policy that depends on the external priority of a thread.

primary memory. The memory in a von Neumann computer that holds programs and data while they are being referenced by the CPU. Also called the executable memory.

primary memory interface. The hardware interface to the primary memory. *See* Chapter 4.

private key encryption. An encryption technique in which the encryption and decryption keys are secret. Contrast this with **public key encryption**.

privileged instruction. An instruction that can be executed only if the processor is in the supervisor mode. I/O instructions and instructions that affect the protection mechanisms are privileged, while all others are ordinary instructions. (*Also see* **mode bit**.)

procedure base register. *See* **code base register**.

process (classic). A serial program in execution on a von Neumann computer.

process (modern). An OS abstraction that defines an execution environment for a thread. The process is allocated resources such as an address space, files, memory, and so on; the threads then execute using the associated process's resources.

process descriptor. The data structure where the OS keeps all information it needs to manage that process.

process identifier. A unique reference to a process during its existence.

process management. The task of creating the process abstraction and providing mechanisms to manipulate processes.

process name space. A set of names for processes that any thread in any process can use to reference a different process. This could be as simple as the OS PIDs.

process status. The operating system record of the current details of a process's execution.

process status register. An abbreviated version of the processor status that is kept in a CPU register while the corresponding process is in execution.

processor. The computation unit in a computer, consisting of the control unit to fetch and decode the stored program from primary memory and the ALU to execute arithmetical-logical instructions. *See* Chapter 4.

program. A list of instructions that can be executed sequentially by a process.

program counter. *See* **PC.**

program text. The list of instructions of a program in executable format.

programmable interval timer. A hardware device that produces an interrupt after a specified amount of time has elapsed. The time period is determined by software.

protected instruction. *See* **privileged instruction.**

protected space. *See* **supervisor space.**

protection domain. An execution environment that determines the access rights a process has.

protection mechanism. A tool or environment in the OS used to enforce privacy. *Also see* **mechanism.**

protection object. *See* **object, protection.**

protection rights. The resource access rights possessed by a process in a specified protection domain.

protected space. *See* **system space.**

protection state. The collective access permissions held by all protection subjects to all protection objects.

protection system. A model of protection mechanisms and security policies that represents the fundamental aspects of all such systems. *See* Section 14.3.

protocol. An agreement among a community of threads/processes about how encoded information will be interpreted. Protocols are used in IPC mechanisms and among host machines on networks.

protocol stack. The ISO OSI architecture describes a framework for network protocols. Any instance of layer implementations is called a protocol stack.

protocol translation. In networks, protocol translation refers to the case in which a gateway receives a packet using one protocol, but forwards the packet using a different protocol. *See* Section 15.4.

public key encryption. An encryption technique that uses a private and a public key. Information encrypted with the public key can only be decrypted using the private key. Information encrypted with the private key can only be decrypted using the public key.

R

race condition. A condition in which the behavior of two or more threads depends on the relative rate at which each thread executes its programs. A race condition can cause a pair of threads to violate a critical section or to deadlock.

RAM (random access memory). The dominant memory technology used to implement executable memory.

randomly accessed storage device. *See* **random device.**

random device. A storage device in which the drive can access any block independent of the last block it accessed. Contrast with *sequential device.* An example of a random device is a magnetic disk drive.

random replacement. A page replacement policy in which the page to be removed from primary memory is chosen randomly.

RDA. *See* **remote disk application.**

read-only memory. *See* **ROM.**

read-write head. The point of access in a byte stream file; a mechanism to read from or write to a storage device.

reconfigurable device driver. A strategy for operating system design whereby a driver can be added to an operating system without recompiling or relinking the operating system code.

ref table. *See* **reference table.**

reference bit. A 1-bit flag in each entry in a page table that is cleared when any page is loaded and set when the particular page is referenced. On replacement, any page with its reference bit set has been referenced since the last page fault.

reference table. A table generated by a compiler to contain external symbols that a relocatable module references, but which are defined in some other relocatable module.

relocatable object module. A module created by a compiler or other source language translator from a single source program module.

relocation register. A CPU register that is loaded with the primary memory address of the beginning of a block of memory containing a program. When the program is executed, the contents of the relocation register are added to the effective address. *See* Section 11.4.

remote disk. A technique for enabling applications to read and write the disk storage devices on a remote machine. *See* Section 16.2.

remote disk application. This is the server software in a remote disk system. *See* Section 16.2.

remote file client. This is a file system dependent part of a client's file manager. It is the part of the file manager that interacts with the remote file server. *See* Section 16.1.

remote file server. This is the service on a remote file server that interacts with the remote file client to manage the remote server's secondary memory so that it behaves as a file system.

remote memory. A distributed-memory design whereby logical primary memory is shared through a primary memory interface extension over the normal von Neumann interface. *See* Section 17.2.

Remote Method Invocation. *See* **RMI**.

remote object. A distributed computing paradigm in which objects are instantiated on distinct machines, yet they can still interact by invoking methods on objects that are located on a remote machine. *See* Section 17.4.

remote procedure call. *See* **RPC**.

replacement policy. A paging policy that determines which page should be removed from primary memory if all page frames are full.

resource. Any abstract machine element referenced by the program and explicitly allocated to the process so that it can execute the program. If the resource is unavailable when it is requested, the process/thread that made the request is suspended until it becomes available. At the lowest level of abstraction, a machine's resources include its hardware components.

resource abstraction. The property of an OS that hides the details of underlying machinery so that application programmers can use the machinery without having to learn those details.

resource descriptor. An operating system data structure used to keep all information known about the status and characteristics of a resource.

resource identifier. A unique reference to a thread during its existence.

resource isolation. The task of the system software that ensures the execution of concurrent programs does not allow individual program executions to interfere with one another.

resource management. The task of creating resource abstractions and providing mechanisms for manipulating and controlling resources.

resource queue. An OS data structure to keep a list of threads/processes that are blocked on a particular resource.

response time. The amount of time between when a user issues a command to an interactive system and the moment that the system begins to respond to the command.

reusable resource. A resource that can be allocated to a process but which must be released back to the resource manager at some later point. A system is configured with a fixed number of reusable resources.

reusable resource graph. A deadlock detection model that represents the allocation state of a system composed solely of reusable resources. *See* Section 10.5.

rights. *See* **protection rights**.

rights amplification. The case in which a process changes its domain to one that enables it to have more access rights than it had in its original domain.

ring architecture. An OS organization in which there are a totally ordered set of protection domains. *See* Chapter 14.

ring gatekeeper. An entry point authorization monitor in a ring architecture.

RMI (Remote Method Invocation). In languages and systems that support distributed objects, the RMI facility is used to invoke a method in a remote object.

rollback. The act of restarting a process at an earlier point in its computation—the last checkpoint. The result of a rollback is as if the process did not do any computation beyond the last checkpoint.

ROM (read only memory). A type of memory that has its contents written by a special device prior to being installed in the computer. Once the ROM is installed, the computer can read the memory but not rewrite its contents. The memory contents persist even when the computer is turned off.

root directory. The base of a hierarchical collection of files. There is a path from the root directory to all other files and directories in the file system.

round robin. A preemptive scheduling policy that distributes the processing time equitably among all threads requesting the processor.

routing. In networks, routing is the procedure by which one host forwards information from a source host toward a destination host. *See* Section 15.4.

RPC. Remote procedure call is a network protocol that enables client software to call a procedure on a remote procedure server and then to use the results of the procedure call after the remote machine has complete execution. *See* Section 17.3.

RR. *See* **round robin**.

runtime. The phase of program management when the program is executed. The term is also an abbreviated term for runtime system.

runtime library. *See* **runtime system**.

runtime system. A collection of user space functions that are called by executing threads to provide system services that are not OS services. For example, the C library has a collection of runtime functions used by C programmers.

S

safe state. A system state in which the resource managers can choose a strategy that assures that the system will not enter a deadlock state. Used in deadlock avoidance approaches (see Section 10.4).

SBR. *See* **stack base register**.

SCC (small communicating computer). A computer that is implemented in a physically tiny package, and that contains a network interface. Examples of SCCs are handheld computers, personal digital assistants, and television set-top boxes.

scheduler. An OS component that manages processor allocation.

scheduling mechanism. The scheduling mechanism determines how the process manager can determine that it is time to multiplex the CPU, and how a thread can be allocated to and removed from the CPU.

scheduling policy. The scheduling policy determines *when* it is time for a process to be removed from the CPU and *which* ready thread should be allocated the CPU next.

schema. In database management systems, a specification of the data structures in the storage.

SCSI (small computer serial interface). An industry standard interface between devices and their controllers.

secondary memory. Memory that is addressed and accessed as blocks using I/O instructions. For example, disk and tape devices implement secondary memory.

sector. The angular division of a rotating medium (such as a disk) that partitions a track into blocks.

security policy. A specification statement of a desired privacy profile. *Also see* **policy**.

seek time, disk. The time needed to move the read/write heads to the target track in rotating storage devices.

segment. The unit of transfer between the primary and secondary memory systems in segmented virtual memory systems.

segment descriptor. An entry in a segment table that contains a segment base address, a segment length, and protection bits.

segment table. A table to translate symbolic segment names to segment addresses in primary memory in a segmented virtual-memory system.

segment table register. In a segmentation virtual memory system, this is a CPU register that points at a segment descriptor.

segmentation. A form of virtual memory in which variable-sized blocks of the address space are transferred between the primary and secondary memories.

semaphore. An abstract data type that contains a nonnegative integer variable with P and V operations that test and set the variable. Semaphores are the fundamental synchronization in modern operating systems (see Chapter 8).

sequential computation. Serial execution of a sequential program. This represents a single thread of computation.

sequential device. A storage device in which blocks are physically stored so that block $i + 1$ can be accessed only after block i has been accessed. Magnetic tape drives are an example of sequential devices.

sequential program. A program encoding of a serial algorithm. C and C++ programs are examples of sequential programs.

sequential write sharing. In remote file servers, a sequential write sharing policy requires that blocks can be cached to servers if they are read-only blocks. Only one client can contain a writable copy of a block at a time. *See* Section 16.3.

sequentially accessed storage device. *See* **sequential device.**

serial execution semantics. This refers to the characteristic of programming languages and systems whereby each statement in a program must be completed before its successor begins to execute.

serially reusable resource. *See* **reusable resource.**

server. *See* **server process**.

server process. A reactive process that responds to service requests from a client process.

server stub. The part of an RPC system that implements the called procedure. It accepts the RPC from the client stub, executes the procedure, and then returns the result to the client stub.

service time. The amount of time a process requires in the running state, using the CPU, before it is completed.

session layer. An ISO OSI network architecture layer providing facilities to manage virtual circuits that are implemented at the transport layer. It may also implement alternative forms of communication, such as RPC.

shared memory multiprocessor. A multiprocessor in which every processor can access every unit of memory via an interconnection network.

sharing. Resources may be used by multiple processes according to the policy and mechanism defined for the OS. **Transparent sharing** refers to resource sharing that is used to implement abstract machines, and is thus not explicitly visible to the user. **Explict sharing** refers to the case where processes use common resources according to their own policies (under the auspices of the OS mechanism).

shell. *See* **command line interpreter.**

shortest job next (**SJN**). A CPU scheduling algorithm that chooses the thread requiring minimum service time as the highest-priority thread.

short-term scheduler. *See* **scheduler.**

signal, UNIX. A mechanism by which one process can notify another of the occurrence of an event. The sender raises the signal, and the receiver catches it by providing a function associated with the signal occurrence.

single-threaded kernel. An OS kernel in which a system call executes as a thread in a passive kernel. The calling thread is normally not preempted, except by interrupts.

SIMD (single-instruction, multiple data) computer. A computer architecture in which a single control unit fetches and decodes an instruction stream, but multiple ALUs execute the single instruction at the same time.

simultaneous P. *See* **AND synchronization.**

SJN. *See* **shortest job next.**

sliding-window protocol. A network protocol in which groups of multiple packets can be in transit, yet where each will have an acknowledgement upon receipt. *See* Section 15.4.

small, communicating computer. *See* **SCC.**

SMP. *See* **shared memory multiprocessor.**

sniffer. In protection and security, this is a program that passively inspects traffic that passes by on the network.

SOC (system-on-a-chip). A class of integrated circuits that incorporates a microprocessor along with specialized functions (such as a graphics engine). These chips are intended to support SCCs.

socket. In the BSD socket package (used in UNIX and Windows), the socket is an endpoint address that is bound to a port. *See* Section 15.6.

source program. The form of a program written by a human. Source programs can be written in C, C++, Java, or other high-level languages. The computer's translation system will prepare it for execution.

space-multiplexed sharing. A shared resource is partitioned up into two or more parts; then each part can be allocated to one process at a time.

spatial locality. *See* **locality.**

spawn. An OS function that creates a new process or thread. For example, the UNIX `fork()` and Win32 `CreateProcess()`/`CreateThread()` functions are spawn functions.

special file. An entry in the `/dev` directory of a UNIX system that is used by the device manager to access drivers for devices.

speedup. The ratio of time to execute a computation on one processor compared with the time to partition and execute it on N different processors.

spinlock. A shared lock that is implemented using busy-waiting.

spooling. This is the operation of collecting executable tasks into a batch for subsequent processing. Batch operating systems spooled jobs into a batch that would be executed at roughly the same time.

stable storage. An algorithmic approach to guarantee that information committed to by an atomic write operation will either be saved or completely ignored. It is typically used in servers to assist in crash recovery (see Section 16.3).

stack. In the context of a process definition, stack is the portion of the process that represents the dynamic variables defined in the corresponding program and other information required to maintain execution (such as return addresses and parameters).

stack algorithm. A class of page replacement algorithms in which increasing the memory allocation is guaranteed not to cause more page faults.

stack base register. In a segmentation virtual memory system, this is a CPU register that points at the segment descriptor containing the current stack segment.

stack segment. In C-style relocatable and absolute program images, this is a logical block of addresses that represent references to automatic variables allocated on the runtime stack.

starvation. A phenomenon in many resource allocation strategies in which some sets of processes are perpetually ignored because their priority is not as high as that of other processes. Starvation can occur in CPU scheduling, disk arm optimization, or any other kind of resource allocation scenario.

state (thread or process). A representation of the action in which the thread or process is currently engaged. For example, the state might be "running" if the thread is using the CPU, or "blocked" if it is waiting for a resource to become available.

state (system). A representation of the particular work in which the system is currently engaged. The idle state means that the system is waiting for a process to request the CPU.

state diagram. A set of states and transitions between states. A process/thread state diagram represents the operating system's characterization of a process/thread in terms of how it is managed.

state transition. An action in a state diagram that causes the state to change. For example, the dispatcher changes a process's state from "ready" to "running."

stateless server. A remote file or disk server that does not maintain any user state. Instead, it relies on the client to maintain all states. Stateless servers can restart without having to restore a previous state (since they do not use states). *See* Section 16.2.

static address binding. A form of binding the address space defined by an absolute module to the primary memory locations in which that module is loaded. In static binding, the association is done at load time. In **dynamic address binding**, the association is done at runtime.

static variable. A variable that retains the last value stored in it even when it goes out of scope.

status. *See* **state (thread or process)**. This term is also used to refer to the information stored in the process or thread descriptor.

storage device. A peripheral device for a computer that is used to store information inside the computer. Examples of storage devices are a floppy disk, a hard disk, and a CD-ROM.

storage hierarchy. Storage mechanisms range from fast to slow, and small to big. Small, fast storage mechanisms are used to implement primary memory. Large, slow storage devices are used to implement secondary memory. The storage hierarchy is the rank order of fast to slow devices, which roughly corresponds to the rank order of small to large devices. *See* Chapter 11 for more information.

stored program computer. The von Neumann computer architecture (see Chapter 4) used in almost all contemporary computer hardware. Programs that define the operations of the computer are stored in its executable (primary) memory.

STR. *See* **segment table register**.

stream-block translation. *See* **marshalling** and **unmarshalling**.

structured file system. *See* **high-level file system.**

structured sequential file. A file format where the file is composed of indexed records that can be read and written by the OS file manager. *See* Section 13.2.

subject. In protection systems, a subject represents a process executing in a protection domain. It is the active entity that accesses passive protection objects.

superblock. A Linux name for a disk block that contains information regarding a disk drive's geometry. *See* Section 20.6.

superuser. A UNIX user mode that has full administrative authority in the machine.

supervisor call. *See* **trap instruction**.

supervisor domain. In protection mechanisms, this refers to the situation in which software is highly trusted; for example, it is executing with the CPU mode bit set. *See* **protection domain**.

supervisor instruction. *See* **privileged instruction**.

supervisor mode. *See* **mode bit.**

supervisor space. Blocks of memory that can be allocated when the mode bit is set to supervisor mode. (*Also see* **mode bit**.)

surface, disk. A division of the storage space on a hard disk, corresponding to one side of one platter on the disk drive. A surface is one side of a physical platter.

surrogate system process. The process associated with each hardware port that is configured to service interactive users.

swapping. A memory management technique where a process may periodically have its primary memory space deallocated. This forces the swapped-out process to compete for memory before it can once again compete for the processor.

swapping system. An OS that uses swapping in its memory manager.

symmetric encryption. A private key encryption technique in which the same key is used for encryption and decryption.

synchronization. The act of ensuring that independent threads of computation will begin to execute a block of code at the same logical time. Because of concurrency in computer systems, this means that all threads in a set of N threads will not proceed past a particular instruction, called the synchronization point for p_i, until all N threads have reached the their synchronization point.

synchronous send. An IPC transmit operation in which the transmitting thread/process is blocked until the receiving thread/process (or its OS) acknowledges receipt of the message.

system call. A style of invoking system functions whereby the calling process uses a trap instruction to begin running an OS function. When the function is completed, the process returns to execute the application program. The system call interface refers to the API exported by the OS.

system call interface. The set of data types and functions implemented by the operating system. These facilities are used by other system software and by application software.

system software. Software that provides an application programming environment on top of the hardware. It is provided to extend the functionality of the hardware so that it can be shared among simultaneous computer users and programmers can direct the hardware with reduced effort.

system space. *See* **supervisor space**.

T

table fragmentation. In any situation where a fixed size table is used to index units (such as in indexed allocation in files), unused table entries are wasted; this is called table fragmentation.

terminal emulator. A software package that simulates the behavior of a hardware terminal, such as a DEC VT-100 (long since dead, but the behavior lives on). The terminal emulator uses network protocols to connect to a server machine. The session simulates classic timesharing environments.

test-and-set instruction. The operation on a memory location that causes the contents of the specified memory location to be loaded into a CPU register (with condition code register contents set to reflect the value of the data) and the memory to be written with a value of TRUE.

text segment. *See* **code segment**.

thrashing. A phenomenon in paging systems whereby a process repeatedly replaces pages about to be referenced. This happens because the process has not been allocated a sufficient number of page frames.

thread. A unit of computation that contains the minimum internal state and resources. It is associated with a normal, heavyweight operating system process. An associated process is allocated resources such as an address space, files, memory, and so on; the thread then executes using the associated process's resources. *Also see* **process** (**modern**).

thread descriptor. The data structure where the OS keeps all information it needs to manage that thread.

thread identifier. A unique reference to a thread during its existence.

throughput rate. The rate at which a computer completes requests to perform processing.

time quantum. *See* **timeslice**.

time-multiplexed sharing. A shared resource is allocated exclusively to one process at a time. At a later time, it is allocated to a different process.

timesharing system. A style of multiprogramming operating system that supports interactive users.

timeslice. The amount of time that any individual process is allowed to use the CPU before a different process is scheduled to use it. A timeslice is the length of time that a process can use the CPU in a time-multiplexed sharing strategy.

time quantum. *See* **timeslice**.

TLB (translation lookaside buffer). A fast cache memory that holds a copy of the page tables used by all processes currently operating in the computer.

track. A geometric location of a recording area on a rotating medium (such as a floppy disk). The disk recording surface is organized as a set of concentric rings, each ring being called a track.

transaction. A sequence of commands for which the effect on associated data is as if either all or none of the commands are executed. *See* Section 17.5.

translation lookaside buffer. *See* **TLB**.

transparent sharing. *See* **sharing**.

transport layer. An ISO OSI network architecture layer that provides virtual circuits to implement byte streams and to ensure reliable delivery of information across an internet.

trap instruction. An instruction that causes the control unit to behave as if an interrupt had occurred. It is normally used to preempt the current process and to start the operating system at an entry point determined by the trap table.

trap table. A kernel-resident table that contains the entry points of all functions exported by the kernel. A trap instruction branches indirectly to the function entry point using the address from the trap table.

trapdoor function. *See* **one-way function**.

Trojan horse. In protection and security, the Trojan horse problem is one in which an intruder provides some entity to the system, which the system accepts and incorporates into its trusted software. The entity contains a worm or virus.

tunnel. In networks, a tunnel is a logical connection between two hosts on an internet. *See* Section 15.6.

trusted software. Software that has been carefully written and debugged, that is used to implement the parts of the OS necessary to ensure its correct operation.

turnaround time. The amount of time between the moment a process first enters the ready state and the moment the process exits the running state for the last time.

U

unforgeable identification. In protection and security, this is a unique, authenticated process of identification.

universal serial bus (USB). A bus controller and protocol that provides an external connector that accommodates devices such as digital cameras and MP3 audio players.

unmarshalling. The task of translating a linear sequence of bytes into a language-oriented data structure. This is done by file managers and network protocols.

unsafe state. *See* **safe state**.

untrusted software. Software that is not trusted software (see **trusted software**).

user mode. *See* **mode bit**.

user authentication. *See* **external authentication**.

user space. Blocks of memory that can be allocated when the mode bit is set to user mode. (*Also see* **mode bit**.)

user space thread. An implementation of threads in a modern process where the OS supports classic processes and the modern process/thread abstraction is implemented in an application library. There have been popular user space thread packages such as the Mach C threads and POSIX threads packages. *Also see* **kernel threads**.

V

VDD. *See* **virtual disk driver**.

virtual address. An address generated by the program translation system that can be bound to a physical memory location as the program executes.

virtual address space. The collection of virtual addresses that can be used by a process.

virtual address translation. A time-varying map of a program's virtual address space to a physical address space at any given time.

virtual circuit. *See* **connection**.

virtual disk address. Used in a remote disk server (see Section 16.2) to reference disk addresses on a remote server.

virtual disk driver. The client portion of a remote disk system. *See* Section 16.2.

virtual file system. A hierarchical file manager design that accommodates subtree file systems of various types. *See* Section 13.7.

virtual machine. *See* **abstract machine**.

virtual memory. An OS abstraction in which parts of a process address space are dynamically bound to primary memory addresses, then copied from secondary memory into the primary memory, and finally copied from primary memory back to secondary memory.

virtual terminal. An operating system entity that presents a programming model similar to the one used with physical terminals, except that the operations are applied to a physical terminal according to user-applied restrictions. *See also* **window system.**

virtual time. The time coordinates perceived by a thread in a process. One measure of the passage of virtual time is the number of virtual memory references that the thread has made. Another measure is the amount of CPU time the thread has accrued.

virus. A software module hidden inside another module. *See* Chapter 14.

vnode. An abstract file descriptor, analogous to a UNIX inode, used in the Sun NFS remote file server.

von Neumann architecture. The basic organization for modern computers. The architecture uses a processor composed of an arithmetical-logical and control unit, a primary memory unit, and various I/O devices.

W

wait time. The time a process spends waiting in the ready state before its first transition to the running state.

web cache. A network server especially configured to cache files it retrieves from content origin servers. *See* Section 18.4.

web proxy. *See* **web cache.**

Win32 API. A software application programming interface to Windows operating systems. The Windows NT/2000/XP OS implements the entire API. Other versions of Windows, such as Windows CE (Pocket PC) and Windows 98, implement subsets of the full API.

window. In the working set approach to virtual memory, the window is a metric used to consider the part of a reference stream that should influence the page replacement.

Windows subsystem. A user space extension to the Windows NT Executive. A subsystem may add a spectrum of different OS services, although the most well-known subsystems add OS personalities, such as the Win32 subsystem, and in earlier versions, the POSIX subsystem.

window system. System software that provides a virtualized model of a physical terminal to the application programmer. Screen operations on the window model are applied to a bounded area of the physical screen.

word. A basic unit of memory size defined by computer hardware designers. The definition arises from the size (number of bits) of operands used in the CPU.

workstation. A computer that is used by one person at a time, often connected to other computers using a network. *Also see* **personal computer**.

working set. The set of pages in a thread's locality.

working set principle. A virtual memory allocation policy that states that a process should be loaded and active only if it can be allocated enough page frames to hold its entire working set. *See* Section 12.5.

World Wide Web. A set of network protocols (primarily HTTP) operating above the ISO OSI transport layer that enables users to fetch information from diverse locations on the public Internet. *See* Chapter 15.

Worm. Software that actively attempts to penetrate a computer system by fooling the authentication mechanism. *See* Chapter 14.

write-back cache. A cache memory strategy where changing a value stored in the cache memory causes the corresponding value in the primary memory to be updated as a background activity.

write-through cache. A cache memory strategy where changing a value stored in the cache memory causes the corresponding value in the primary memory to be updated immediately.

WWW. *See* **World Wide Web**.

Bibliography

Abramson, N., "The Aloha System—Another Alternative for Computer Communications." *AFIPS Conference Proceedings 36* (1970): 295–298.

Accetta, M., R. Baron, W. Bolosky, D. Golub, R. Rashid, A. Tevanian, and M. Young. "Mach: A New Kernel Foundation for UNIX Development." *Proceedings of the 1986 Usenix Summer Conference* (1986): 93–112.

ACM. *Proceedings of the ACM Symposium on Operating Systems Principles,* ACM Publications, published biannually.

Adve, S. V., and K. Gharacholoo. "Shared Memory Consistency Models: A Tutorial." *IEEE Computer 29*, No.12 (December 1996): 66–76.

Aiken, Howard H., and Grace M. Hopper, "The Automatic Sequence Controlled Calculator." *Electrical Engineering 65* (1946): 384–391, 449–454, 522–528.

Alt, F. L. "A Bell Telephone Laboratories' Computing Machine." The American Mathematical Society, from *Mathematics of Computation*, 1948. Reprinted in [Randell, 1973].

Anderson, Thomas E., David E. Culler, David A. Patterson, and the NOW Team, "A Case for Networks of Workstations: NOW." *IEEE Micro 15*, No. 1 (February 1995): 54–64.

Arnold, Ken, and Jame Gosling, *The Java™ Programming Language*. Reading, MA: Addison Wesley, 1996.

Atanasoff, John V., "Computing Machine for Solution of Large Systems of Linear Algebraic Equations, unpublished memorandum, Iowa State College, August, 1940. Reprinted in [Randell, 1973].

Babbage, Charles, "On the Mathematical Powers of the Calculating Engine." unpublished manuscript, December, 1836. Reprinted in [Randell, 1973].

Bechtel, Brian, "The Ins And Outs Of ISO 9660 And High Sierra." *MacTech* article, http://www.mactech.com/articles/develop/issue_03/high_sierra.html, 2002.

Beck, Michael, Harald Böhme, Mirko Dziadzka, Ulrich Kunitz, Robert Magnus, and Dirk Verworner. *Linux Kernel Internals*, 2nd ed. Reading, MA: Addison-Wesley, 1998.

Becker, Donald J., Thomas Sterling, Daniel Savarese, John E. Dorband, Udaya A. Ranawak, Charles V. Packer, "BEOWULF: A Parallel Workstation for Scientific Computation." Proceedings of the International Conference on Parallel Processing, 1995.

Bennett, John K. "Distributed Smalltalk: Inheritance and Reactiveness in Distributed Systems." Ph.D. diss., University of Washington, Seattle, 1988.

Berners-Lee, Tim, "WWW: Past, Present and Future." *IEEE Computer 29*, No.10 (October 1996): 69–77.

Bershad, Brian N. "High Performance Cross-Address Space Communication." Ph.D. diss., University of Washington, Seattle, 1990.

Bershad, Brian, Edward D. Lazowska, and Henry M. Levy. "PRESTO: A System for Object-Oriented Parallel Programming." *Software Practice and Experience 18*, No. 8 (August 1988): 713–732.

Brinch Hansen, Per. *Operating System Principles*. Englewood Cliffs, NJ: Prentice Hall, 1973.

Brinch Hansen, Per. *The Architecture of Concurrent Programs*. Englewood Cliffs, NJ: Prentice Hall, 1977.

Brooks, F. P. *The Mythical Man-Month: Essays on Software Engineering*. Reading, MA: Addison-Wesley, 1975.

Campbell, Roy H., Nayeem Islam, David Raila, and Peter Madany. "Designing and Implementing Choices: An Object-Oriented System in C++." *Communications of the ACM 36*, No. 9 (September 1993): 117–126.

Carriero, Nicholas, and David Gelernter. "The S/Net's Linda Kernel." *ACM Transactions on Computer Systems 4*, No. 2 (May 1986): 110–129.

Chappell, Geoff. *DOS Internals*. Reading, MA: Addison-Wesley, 1994.

Coffman, E. G., Jr., and Peter J. Denning. *Operating Systems Theory*. Englewood Cliffs, NJ: Prentice Hall, 1973.

Conway, M. "A Multiprocessor System Design." *Proceedings of the AFIPS Fall Joint Computer Conference* (1963): 139–146.

Corbato, M., M. Daggett, and R. C. Daley. "An Experimental Time-Sharing System." *Proceedings of the Spring Joint Computer Conference 21* (1962): 334–335.

Courtois, P. J., F. Heymans, and D. L. Parnas. "Concurrent Control with 'Readers' and 'Writers'." *Communications of the ACM 14*, No. 10 (October 1971): 667–668.

Deitel, H. M. *Operating Systems,* 2nd ed. Reading, MA: Addison-Wesley, 1990.

Denning, P. J., "Virtual Memory." *ACM Computing Surveys 2*, No. 3 (September 1970):153-189.

Denning, P. J., "Working Sets Past and Present." *IEEE Transactions on Software Engineering, SE-6*, No. 1 (January 1980): 64–84.

Dennis, J. B., and E. C. Van Horne. "Programming Semantics for Multiprogrammed Computations." *Communications of the ACM 9*, No. 3 (March 1966): 117–126.

Dijkstra, E. W. "Co-operating Sequential Processes." in *Programming Languages,* edited by F. Genuys. New York: Academic Press (1968): 43–112.

Dijkstra, E. W. "The Structure of THE Multiprogramming System." *Communications of the ACM 3*, No. 9 (May 1968): 341–346.

Encyclopedia Britannica, "Bush, George W." *Encyclopædia Britannica* 2003 Encyclopædia Britannica Premium Service. 21 Mar, 2003 <http://search.britannica.com/eb/article?eu =139046>.

Ferguson, Paul, and Geoff Huston, "What Is a VPN?" white paper available at http://www.employees.org/~ferguson/vpn.pdf, April, 1998.

FIPS, "Data Encryption Standard." *Federal Information Processing Standards Publication No. 46-2,* December, 1993.

Ford, Bryan, Mike Hibler, Jay Lepreau, Patrick Tullmann, Godmar Back, and Stephen Clawson, "Microkernels Meet Recursive Virtual Machines." *Proceedings of the Conference on Operating Systems Design and Implementation* (1996): 137–151.

Geist, G. A., and V. S. Sunderam. "Experiences with Network-Based Concurrent Computing on the PVM System." *Concurrency: Practice and Experience 4*, No. 4 (June 1992): 293–311.

Geist, G. A, Adam Beguelin, Jack Dongarra, Weicheng Jiang, Robert Manchek, and Vaidy Sunderam. "PVM 3 Users' Guide and Reference Manual." Oak Ridge National Laboratories technical report (September 1994).

Gosling, James, Bill Joy, and Guy Steele, *The Java Language Specification.* Reading MA: Addison-Wesley, 1996.

Graham, G. S., and Peter J. Denning. "Protection—Principles and Practice." *Proceedings of the AFIPS Sprint Joint Computer Conference* (1972): 417–429.

Gropp, William, Steven Huss-Lederman, Andrew Lumsdaine, Ewing Lusk, Bill Nitzberg, William Saphir, and Marc Snir, *MPI—The Complete Reference, Volume 2—The MPI-2 Extensions*, 2nd ed. Cambridge, MA: MIT Press, 1998.

Haller, Neil M., "The S/KEY ™ One-time Password System." Proceedings of the Internet Society Symposium on Network and Distributed System Security, February, 1994.

Hamburgen, William R., Deborah A. Wallach, Marc A. Viredaz, Lawrence S. Brakmo, Carl A. Waldspurger, Joel F. Bartlett, Timothy Mann, and Keith I. Farkas, "Itsy: Stretching the Bounds of Mobile Computing." *IEEE Computer 34*, No. 4 (April, 2001): 28–26.

Hamilton, Graham, and Panos Kougiouris. "The Spring Nucleus: A Microkernel for Objects." *Proceedings of the 1993 USENIX Summer Conference* (1993): 147–160.

Hart, Johnson M., *Win32 System Programming.* Reading, MA, Addison Wesley, 1998.

Hartel, Pieter H., and Luc Moreau, "Formalizing the Safety of Java, the Java Virtual Machine, and Java Card." *ACM Computing Surveys 33*, No. 4 (December 2001): 517–558.

Hauser, Carl, Christian Jacobi, Marvin Thiemer, Brent Welch, and Mark Weiser. "Using Threads in Interactive Systems: A Case Study." *Proceedings of the Fourteenth ACM Symposium on Operating Systems Principles* (1993): 94–105.

Hennessy, John L., and David A. Patterson. *Computer Architecture: A Quantitative Approach.* San Mateo, CA: Morgan Kaufmann, 1990.

Hoare, C. A. R. "Monitors: An Operating System Structuring Concept." *Communications of the ACM 17*, No. 10 (October 1974): 549–557.

Hwang, K., and F. A. Briggs. *Computer Architecture and Parallel Processing.* New York: McGraw-Hill, 1984.

IEEE, "IEEE 1394: Changing the Way We Do Multimedia Communications." from IEEE Multimedia, 2000. Available at http://computer.org/multimedia/articles/firewire.htm.

IEEE. *Proceedings of the International Symposium on Computer Architecture,* IEEE Publications, published annually.

IEEE and ACM. *Proceedings of the Conference on Architectural Support for Programming Languages and Operating Systems.* IEEE Publications and ACM Publications, published annually.

IETF, "Security Architecture for the Internet Protocol." IETF RFC 2401, Network Working Group, November, 1998 (available at http://www.ietf.org/rfc/rfc2401.txt).

International Standards Organization. "Status of OSI (and Related) Standards." *ACM SIGCOMM Computer Communications Review 20*, No. 3 (July 1990): 83–99.

International Standards Organization. "Information Processing—Volume and File Structure of CD-ROM for Information Interchange." ISO/IEC 9660:1999, 1999 (see http://www.y-adagio.com/public/standards/iso_cdromr/tocont.htm).

Jamieson, L. H., D. B. Gannon, and R. J. Douglass, *The Characteristics of Parallel Algorithms.* Cambridge, MA: MIT Press, 1987.

Johnson, Michael A. *The Linux Kernel Hacker's Guide,* Alpha Version 0.6, 1992a. Available from ftp site sunsite.unc.edu.

Johnson, Michael A. "Writing Linux Device Drivers." 1992b. Available from the World Wide Web at http://www.ssc.com/ssc/Employees/johnsonm/devices.

Jul, E., H. Levy, N. Hutchinson, and A. Black. "Fine-Grained Mobility in the Emerald System." *ACM Transactions on Computer Systems 6,* No. 1 (February 1988): 109–133.

Kazar, Michael L., Bruce W. Leverett, Owen T. Anderson, Vasilis Apostolides, Beth A Bottos, Sailesh Chutani, Craig F. Everhart, W. Anthony Mason, Shu-Tsui Tu, and Edward R. Zayas, "Decorum File System Architectural Overview." *USENIX Summer Conference*, 151–163.

Kernighan, Brian W., and Rob Pike, *The UNIX Programming Environment.* Englewood Cliffs, NJ, Prentice Hall, 1984.

Khalidi, Yousef A., and Michael N. Nelson. "An Implementation of UNIX on an Object-Oriented Operating System." *Proceedings of the 1993 USENIX Summer Conference* (1993): 469–480.

Kilburn, T., D. B. G. Edwards, M. J. Lanigan, and F. H. Sumner. "One-Level Storage System." *IRE Transactions,* EC-11, No. 2 (April 1962): 223–235.

Knuth, Donald E. *The Art of Computer Programming, vol. 1, Fundamental Algorithms,* 2nd ed. Reading, MA: Addison-Wesley, 1973.

Kohl, John, and B. Clifford Neuman. "The Kerberos Network Authentication Service (V5)." Internet draft (September 1992). Available from the World Wide Web at http://mitvma.mit.edu/mit/kerberos.html.

Lamport, Leslie. "Time, Clocks and the Ordering of Events in a Distributed System." *Communications of the ACM 21,* No. 7 (July 1978): 558–565.

Lamport, Leslie. "How to Make a Multiprocessor Computer that Correctly Executes Multiprocess Programs." *IEEE Transactions on Computers,* C-28, No. 9 (September 1979): 241–248.

Lampson, Butler W., and David W. Redell "Experience with Processes and Monitors in Mesa." *Communications of the ACM 23*, No. 2 (February 1980): 105–117.

Lampson, Butler W., and Howard Sturgis. "Crash Recovery in a Distributed Data Storage System." Technical report, Xerox Palo Alto Research Center (April 1979).

Lazowska, Edward D., John Zahorjan, David R. Cheriton, and Willy Zwaenepoel. "File Access Performance of Diskless Workstations." *ACM Transactions on Computer Systems 4*, No. 3 (August 1986): 238–268.

Levy, Henry, and Richard H. Eckhouse, Jr., *Computer Programming and Architecture: The VAX.* Digital Press, 1989.

Lewin, Mark. "Windows NT: An Architectural Overview." *USENIX Winter 1994 Conference Tutorial.* 1994.

Li, Kai, and Paul Hudak. "Memory Coherence in Shared Virtual Memory Systems." *ACM Transactions on Computer Systems 7*, No. 4 (November 1989): 321–359.

Liedtke, Jochen, "On m-kernel Construction." *Proceedings of the Fifteenth ACM Symposium on Operating Systems Principles* (1995): 237–250.

Lindholm, Tim, and Frank Yellin, *The Java™ Virtual Machine Specfication.* Reading, MA: Addison Wesley, 1997.

Linton, Mark A., John M. Vlissides, and Paul R. Calder. "Composing User Interfaces with InterViews." *IEEE Computer 22*, No. 2 (February 1989): 8–22.

Maekawa, Mamoru, Arthur E. Oldehoeft, and Rodney R. Oldehoeft. *Operating Systems Advanced Concepts.* Menlo Park, CA: Benjamin/Cummings, 1987.

McKusick, Marshall Kirk, Keith Bostic, Michael J. Karels, and John S. Quarterman. *The Design and Implementation of the 4.4 BSD UNIX Operating System.* Reading, MA: Addison-Wesley, 1996.

Messmer, Hans-Peter. *The Indispensable PC Hardware Book,* 2nd ed., Reading, MA: Addison-Wesley, 1995.

Metcalfe, Robert M., and David R. Boggs. "Ethernet: Distributed Packet Switching for Local Computer Networks." *Communications of the ACM 19,* No. 7 (July 1976): 395–404.

Morris, Robert, and Ken Thompson, "Password Security: A Case History." *Communications of the ACM 22,* No.11 (November 1979), 594–597.

Murray, John, *Inside Microsoft Windows CE.* Redmond, WA, Microsoft Press, 1998.

Nagar, Rajeev. *Windows NT File System Internals: A Developer's Guide.* Sebastapol, CA: O'Reilly & Associates, 1997.

Nemeth, Evi, Garth Snyder, Scott Seebass, and Trent R. Hein. *UNIX System Administration Handbook.* Englewood Cliffs, NJ: Prentice Hall, 1995.

Nutt, Gary J. *Centralized and Distributed Operating Systems.* Englewood Cliffs, NJ: Prentice Hall, 1992.

Nutt, Gary. *Operating System Projects for Windows NT.* Reading, MA: Addison-Wesley, 1999.

Nutt, Gary. *Kernel Projects for Linux.* Reading, MA: Addison-Wesley, 2001.

Nutt, Gary, *Distributed Programming Runtime Systems: Inside Rotor.* Reading, MA: Addison-Wesley, 2004.

Open Group, "The Open Group's Distributed Computing Environment." Open Group, 2003 (available at http://www.opengroup.org/dce/).

Organick, E. I. *The Multics System: An Examination of Its Structure.* Cambridge, MA: MIT Press, 1972.

Ousterhout, John K., Hervé Da Costa, David Harrison, John A. Kunze, Mike Kupfer, and James G. Thompson. "A Trace-Driven Analysis of the UNIX 4.2 BSD File System." *Proceedings of the Tenth ACM Symposium on Operating Systems Principles* (1985): 15–24.

Parnas, D., "On the Criteria for Decomposing a System into Modules." *Communications of the ACM, 15,* No. 12 (December 1972), 1053–1058.

Peterson, G. L. "Myths About the Mutual Exclusion Problem." *Information Processing Letters 12,* No. 3 (June 1981): 115–116.

Piscitello, David M., and A. Lyman Chapin. *Open Systems Networking: TCP/IP and OSI.* Reading, MA: Addison-Wesley, 1993.

Randell, Brian, *The Origins of Digital Computers: Selected Papers.* Berlin: Springer-Verlag, 1973.

Rashid, R., A. Tevanian, M. Young, D. Golub, R. Baron, D. Black, W. Bolosky, and J. Chew. "Machine-Independent Virtual Memory Management for Paged Uniprocessor and Multiprocessor Architectures." *IEEE Transactions on Computer Systems 37,* No. 8 (August 1988): 896–907.

Reed, D. P., and K. Kanodia. "Synchronization with Eventcounts and Sequencers." *Communications of the ACM 22,* No. 2 (February 1979): 115–123.

Reeds, J. A., and P. J. Weinberger, "File Security and the UNIX Crypt Command." *AT&T Bell Laboratories Technical Journal 63,* 8 (October 1984): 1673–1683.

Richter, Jeffrey. *Advanced Windows,* 3rd ed. Redmond, WA: Microsoft Press, 1997.

Richter, Jeffrey, "Microsoft .NET Framework Delivers the Platform for an Integrated, Service-Oriented Web." *MSDN Magazine,* September, 2000 (Part 1), October, 2000 (Part 2).

Richter, Jeffrey. *Applied Microsoft .NET Framework Programming.* Redmond, WA: Microsoft Press, 2002.

Ritchie, Dennis M. "A Stream Input-Output System." *AT&T Bell Laboratories Technical Journal 63,* No. 8 (October 1984): 1897–1910.

Ritchie, Dennis, and Ken Thompson. "The UNIX Time-Sharing System." *Communications of the ACM 17,* No. 7 (July 1974): 1897–1920.

Rivest, Ronald L., Adi Shamir, and Leonard M. Adelman, "A Method for Obtaining Digital Signatures and Public-key Cryptosystems." *Communications of the ACM 21,* No. 2 (February 1978): 120–126.

Rozier, M., V. Abrossimov, F. Armand, I. Boule, M. Gien, M. Guillemont, F. Herrmann, C. Kaiser, S. Langlois, P. Léonard, and W. Neuhauser. "CHORUS Distributed Operating Systems." *Computing Systems 1,* No. 4 (Fall 1988): 304–370.

Russinovich, Mark. "Inside the Native API." Technical report (March 1998). Available at www.sysinternals.com.

Sandberg, R., D. Goldberg, S. Kleiman, D. Walsh, and B. Lyon. "Design and Implementation of the Sun Network File System." *USENIX Proceedings* (June 1985): 119–130.

Satyanarayanan, M. "Scalable, Secure, and Highly Available Distributed File Access." *IEEE Computer 23*, No. 5 (May 1990): 9–21.

Schulzrinne, Henning. Personal communication regarding physical and data link layer network characteristics. April 1999.

Singhal, Mukesh, and Niranjan G. Shivaratri. *Advanced Concepts in Operating Systems.* New York: McGraw-Hill, 1994.

Solomon, David A., *Inside Microsoft Windows 2000,* 2nd ed. Redmond, WA: Microsoft Press, 1998.

Solomon, David A., and Mark E. Russinovich, *Inside Microsoft Windows 2000,* 3rd ed. Redmond, WA: Microsoft Press, 2000.

"Special Section on the Internet Worm." *Communications of the ACM 32,* No. 6 (June 1989): 677–710.

Stallings, William. *Operating Systems,* 2nd ed. Englewood Cliffs, NJ: Prentice Hall, 1995.

Steinke, Robert Christian, *Consistency Model Transitions in Shared Memory*, Ph.D diss., University of Colorado, 2001.

Stevens, W. Richard. *UNIX Network Programming.* Englewood Cliffs, NJ: Prentice Hall Software Series, 1990.

Stevens, W. Richard. *Advanced Programming in the UNIX Environment.* Reading, MA: Addison-Wesley, 1992.

Stevens, W. Richard. *TCP/IP Illustrated,* Vol. 1. Reading, MA: Addison-Wesley, 1994.

Stevens, W. Richard, and Gary R. Wright. *TCP/IP Illustrated,* Vol. 2. Reading, MA: Addison-Wesley, 1995.

Stoll, C. "Stalking the Wily Hacker." *Communications of the ACM 31,* No. 5 (May 1988): 484–497.

Sturgis, Howard W. "*A Postmortem for a Time Sharing System.*" Ph.D. diss., University of California at Berkeley, 1973.

Stutz, David, Ted Neward, and Geoff Shilling, *Shared Source CLI Essentials.* Sebastopol, CA: O'Reilly, 2004.

Sun Microsystems. "Networking on the Sun Workstation." Sun Microsystems, Inc., Document Number 800-1345–10 (September 1986).

Sun Microsystems. "Manual Page for the socket System Call." Sun Microsystems, Inc., Release 4.1 (January, 1990).

Swinehart, Daniel, Gene McDaniel, and David Boggs. "WFS: A Simple Shared File System for a Distributed Environment." *Proceedings of the Seventh ACM Symposium on Operating Systems Principles* (1979): 9–17.

Tanenbaum, Andrew S. *Operating Systems: Design and Implementation.* Englewood Cliffs, NJ: Prentice Hall, 1987.

Tanenbaum, Andrew S. *Distributed Operating Systems.* Englewood Cliffs, NJ: Prentice Hall, 1995.

Tanenbaum, Andrew S., and R. van Renesse. "Distributed Operating Systems." *ACM Computing Surveys 17*, No. 4 (December 1985): 418–470.

Thacker, C. P., E. M. McCreight, B. W. Lampson, R. F. Sproull, and D. R. Boggs. "Alto: A Personal Computer." in *Computer Structures: Principles and Examples,* 2nd ed. New York: McGraw-Hill, 1981.

Thornton, James, *Design of a Computer: The Control Data 6600.* Glenview, IL, Scott Foresman, 1970.

USB, "A Technical Introduction to the USB." white paper available at www.usb.org, October, 2001.

Usenix. *Usenix Windows NT Workshop* (August 1997), Seattle, Washington.

von Neumann, John, "First Draft of a report on the EDVAC." University of Pennsylvania, Moore School of Engineering report, 1945.

Walker, Bruce, Gerald Popek, Robert English, Charles Kline, and Greg Thiel. "The LOCUS Distributed Operating System." *Proceedings of the Ninth ACM Symposium on Operating System Principles* (October 1983): 49–70.

Walmer, Linda R., and Mary R. Thompson, "A Programmer's Guide to the Mach User Environment." Department of Computer Science, Carnegie-Mellon University, November, 1989.

Zimmerman, H. "The ISO Model for Open Systems Interconnection." *IEEE Transactions on Communications,* Com-28, 4 (April 1980): 425–432.

Zimmerman, Philip. "Pretty Good Privacy: Public Key Encryption for the Masses, Version 2.6." 1994. Available at http://www.math.ucla.edu/pgp/PGP_Users_ Guide.html.

Zuse, Konrad, "Method for Automatic Execution of Calculations with the Aid of Computers." German patent application, 1936. Appears in [Randell, 1973].

Index